P9-CMA-036

Fodor's

NEW ZEALAND

15th Edition

Fodor's Travel Publications   New York, Toronto, London, Sydney, Auckland
www.fodors.com

Marksman Motor Inn — 40-44 Sussex
800 627 574   159.00 avail.

Be a Fodor's Correspondent

Te Aro

Your opinion matters. It matters to us. It matters to your fellow Fodor's travelers, too. And we'd like to hear it. In fact, we need to hear it.

When you share your experiences and opinions, you become an active member of the Fodor's community. That means we'll not only use your feedback to make our books better, but we'll publish your names and comments whenever possible. Throughout our guides, look for "Word of Mouth," excerpts of your unvarnished feedback.

Here's how you can help improve Fodor's for all of us.

Tell us when we're right. We rely on local writers to give you an insider's perspective. But our writers and staff editors—who are the best in the business—depend on you. Your positive feedback is a vote to renew our recommendations for the next edition.

Tell us when we're wrong. We're proud that we update most of our guides every year. But we're not perfect. Things change. Hotels cut services. Museums change hours. Charming cafés lose charm. If our writer didn't quite capture the essence of a place, tell us how you'd do it differently. If any of our descriptions are inaccurate or inadequate, we'll incorporate your changes in the next edition and will correct factual errors at fodors.com immediately.

Tell us what to include. You probably have had fantastic travel experiences that aren't yet in Fodor's. Why not share them with a community of like-minded travelers? Maybe you chanced upon a beach or bistro or B&B that you don't want to keep to yourself. Tell us why we should include it. And share your discoveries and experiences with everyone directly at fodors.com. Your input may lead us to add a new listing or highlight a place we cover with a "Highly Recommended" star or with our highest rating, "Fodor's Choice."

Give us your opinion instantly at our feedback center at www.fodors.com/feedback. You may also e-mail editors@fodors.com with the subject line "New Zealand Editor." Or send your nominations, comments, and complaints by mail to New Zealand Editor, Fodor's, 1745 Broadway, New York, NY 10019.

You and travelers like you are the heart of the Fodor's community. Make our community richer by sharing your experiences. Be a Fodor's correspondent.

Tim Jarrell, Publisher

FODOR'S NEW ZEALAND

Editors: Stephanie E. Butler (lead editor), Erica Duecy, Eric Wechter

Writers: Alia Bloom, Sue Courtney, Sue Farley, Jessica Kany, Debra A. Klein, Bob Marriott, Carrie Miller, Kathy Ombler, Richard Pamatatau, Oliver Wigmore

Production Editor: Jennifer DePrima

Maps & Illustrations: Mark Stroud and Henry Colomb, Moon Street Cartography; Ed Jacobus; David Lindroth, Inc., *cartographers;* Bob Blake, Rebecca Baer, *map editors;* William Wu, *information graphics*

Design: Fabrizio La Rocca, *creative director*; Guido Caroti, Siobhan O'Hare, *art directors*; Tina Malaney, Chie Ushio, Ann McBride, Jessica Walsh, *designers;* Melanie Marin, *senior picture editor*

Cover Photo: (Track to Mueller Hut, Mt. Cook, Aoraki National Park) Jeff Drewitz/ photonewzealand.com

Production Manager: Angela L. McLean

15th Edition

ISBN 978–1–4000–0841–4

ISSN 1531–0450

SPECIAL SALES

This book is available at special discounts for bulk purchases for sales promotions or premiums. Special editions, including personalized covers, excerpts of existing books, and corporate imprints, can be created in large quantities for special needs. For more information, write to Special Markets/Premium Sales, 1745 Broadway, MD 6-2, New York, New York 10019, or e-mail specialmarkets@randomhouse.com.

AN IMPORTANT TIP & AN INVITATION

Although all prices, opening times, and other details in this book are based on information supplied to us at press time, changes occur all the time in the travel world, and Fodor's cannot accept responsibility for facts that become outdated or for inadvertent errors or omissions. So **always confirm information when it matters,** especially if you're making a detour to visit a specific place. Your experiences—positive and negative— matter to us. If we have missed or misstated something, **please write to us.** We follow up on all suggestions. Contact the New Zealand editor at editors@fodors.com or c/o Fodor's at 1745 Broadway, New York, NY 10019.

PRINTED IN SINGAPORE

10 9 8 7 6 5 4 3 2 1

CONTENTS

6 < **Contents**

MAPS

ABOUT
THIS BOOK

Our Ratings

Sometimes you find terrific travel experiences and sometimes they just find you. But usually the burden is on you to select the right combination of experiences. That's where our ratings come in.

As travelers we've all discovered a place so wonderful that its worthiness is obvious. And sometimes that place is so experiential that superlatives don't do it justice: you just have to be there to know. These sights, properties, and experiences get our highest rating, **Fodor's Choice**, indicated by orange stars throughout this book.

Black stars highlight sights and properties we deem **Highly Recommended**, places that our writers, editors, and readers praise again and again for consistency and excellence.

By default, there's another category: any place we include in this book is by definition worth your time, unless we say otherwise. And we will.

Disagree with any of our choices? Care to nominate a place or suggest that we rate one more highly? Visit our feedback center at www.fodors.com/feedback.

Budget Well

Hotel and restaurant price categories from ¢ to $$$$ are defined in the opening pages of each chapter. For attractions, we always give standard adult admission fees; reductions are usually available for children, students, and senior citizens. Want to pay with plastic? **AE, D, DC, MC, V** following restaurant and hotel listings indicate if American Express, Discover, Diners Club, MasterCard, and Visa are accepted.

Restaurants

Unless we state otherwise, restaurants are open for lunch and dinner daily. We mention dress only when there's a specific requirement and reservations only when they're essential or not accepted—it's always best to book ahead.

Hotels

Hotels have private bath, phone, TV, and air-conditioning and operate on the European Plan (aka EP, meaning without meals), unless we specify that they use the Continental Plan (CP, with a continental breakfast), Breakfast Plan (BP, with a full breakfast), or Modified American Plan (MAP, with breakfast and dinner) or are all-inclusive (including all meals and most activities). We always list facilities but not whether you'll be charged an extra fee to use them, so when pricing accommodations, find out what's included.

Listings

★	Fodor's Choice
★	Highly recommended
⊠	Physical address
✛	Directions or Map coordinates
☞	Mailing address
☎	Telephone
🖷	Fax
⊕	On the Web
✉	E-mail
💳	Admission fee
☉	Open/closed times
Ⓜ	Metro stations
▭	Credit cards

Hotels & Restaurants

⌸	Hotel
⤵	Number of rooms
⛴	Facilities
⍩	Meal plans
✗	Restaurant
⌲	Reservations
⌂	Dress code
↘	Smoking
🍸	BYOB

Outdoors

🏌	Golf
⛺	Camping

Other

☕	Family-friendly
⇨	See also
⊠	Branch address
☞	Take note

Experience
New Zealand

NEW ZEALAND TODAY

Kia ora, or welcome, to the "Youngest Country on Earth." New Zealand's moniker may specifically reference its place as the last landmass to be discovered, but it speaks to the constant geological, social, and political shifts the country has undergone as it has tried to find its national identity. Tectonic hotbeds include three active volcanoes—Tonagariro, Ngauruhoe, and Ruapehu—on the North Island and the still-growing Southern Alps on the South Islands. In a nation of farmers with frontier ancestors, Georgina Byer, a transsexual former prostitute, won a rural seat against a conservative opponent in 1999. New Zealand's Ernest Rutherford was the first person to split the atom, but the country remains passionately anti-nuclear technology. And the All Blacks, the national rugby team, may have a historical 74% winning record, but New Zealanders still feel like underdogs. The result of all this is wild, rough-around-the-edges, utterly unique country.

A Tale of Two Islands

Together, the North and South Island make up *Aotearoa*—Land of the Long White Cloud. New Zealand is roughly the size of the United Kingdom (only with 10% of the population), but you are never more than 80 mi from the sea. New Zealand's two main islands are 995 mi long and together encompass nearly every environment on the planet: glaciers, white-sand beaches, fjords, rain forests, alpine forest and lakes, agricultural plains, and volcanic craters and cones.

The South Island is the stunner: the colorful beaches, inlets, and sunny vineyards of the north give way to the Southern Alps, a mountain range with more than 360 glaciers. Just 18 mi from the Tasman Sea, it can only be crossed in three places (Arthur's

Lewis Pass, Haast passes). On the West Coast, dense native forest, wild weather, and a sparse population provide a frontier feel. At the southern end of the West Coast is primeval Fiordland, a 1.2 million-acre park that is largely unexplored. Together, Fiordland, Mt. Cook, Westland, and Mt. Aspiring National parks have more than 620 mi of largely inaccessible coastline. On the East Coast of the South Island, sea life ranges from the giant 65-foot male sperm whale to the five-foot Hector's Dolphin.

Fourteen miles separate the North and South Island over the rough Cook Strait, but the two islands are worlds apart. Due to its volcanic origins, the North Island has fertile farmlands and rejuvenated native forest. More than three-quarters of New Zealand's 4.2 million people live on the North Island, which tends to have milder weather and a more forgiving landscape. Long beaches sweep up both coasts past small communities (many still predominantly Māori). New Zealand's largest untouched area of native forest, Te Urewera National Park, its two longest rivers (the Waikato and the Wanganui), and its largest lake (Taupo) are all found near the Central Plateau, before the landscape thins and bottle-necks around the narrow Auckland area, emerging again as the island-studded, remotely populated Northland.

A Tale of Two Cultures

New Zealand is a lonely place, 1,200 mi from the nearest landmass, and its physical distance from the world, not to mention its geographical diversity, have affected its population. On a whole, New Zealanders are genial, reserved, and friendly, but they don't suffer fools or braggarts lightly. An isolated past, when things were either unavailable or expensive, led to a nation of inventers: Kiwis invented the jet-boat,

bungy jumping, and the electric fence, to name a few, and they were the first to climb Mount Everest, the first to give women the vote, and the first to perform a prenatal blood transfusion.

Although New Zealand is a bicultural nation, New Zealanders of European descent (*pakeha*) make up 80% of the population, while Māori make up 15% (the rest is largely Pacific Islanders and Asian), and the way forward is still unclear. There are two camps: most New Zealanders want to move forward as "one New Zealand," but a significant portion still see Māoridom as culture set apart. A recent revival of Māori culture and language, as well as the 1975 establishment of the Waitangi Tribunal (created to rule on breaches of the original Waitangi Treaty, redress wrongdoings, and award compensation to local tribes) means that the topic is still a hot issue. Although many New Zealanders consider the reconciliation process to be labored and an impediment to forward progress, Māori is an oral culture, and many feel that continuing to discuss the past is a way of making certain it isn't lost in the present.

Kiwi Quality of Life

Most New Zealanders believe they have a good quality of life, and New Zealand is consistently rated as one of the best places to live. It is also one of the most active nations: most Kiwis seem to be born with a love of the outdoors, and families tramp, caravan, sail, and play rugby, cricket, and netball together. Most New Zealanders are well educated. They value travel highly, with one-third of the population traveling overseas every year, often for their post-school O.E. (overseas experience). Kiwis don't tend to be religious, with two-thirds lightly following one of the four main Christian religions (Catholic, Methodist, Presbyterian, and Anglican). New Zealand isn't a wealthy nation, either: most Kiwis prefer a good work–life balance to an overflowing bank account.

100% Pure

Despite their quality of life, many New Zealanders express concern for the country's future. The Department of Conservation now focuses on environmental issues, reflecting the national love of the outdoors and the importance of the landscape to the country's burgeoning tourism industry. Although New Zealand is making great strides in sustainability, the country aims for a "100% Pure" lifestyle. New Zealand is also facing a challenge in obesity (with 20% of adults being considered obese), a binge-drinking culture, a rise in youth gang culture and violent crime, and an increase in poverty. New Zealand is facing the same problems as the rest of the Western world—given its small size and isolation, it has just taken longer for the problems to reach its shores.

Kiwis in the World

The best thing about New Zealand is that change can happen quickly here: New Zealanders are fiercely proud and they can mobilize quickly and loudly when they want to. This is a country that thinks for itself, and more and more New Zealanders are realizing what they have in their own backyard: a multicultural population nestled in a jewel of a landscape. Young, vibrant, wild, diverse, and independent— New Zealand is like nothing else.

WHAT'S WHERE IN THE NORTH ISLAND

The following numbers refer to chapters in the book.

2 Auckland. Known as the City of Sails, Auckland has nearly one-quarter of the country's population, it is the economic (but not political) capital, and it is New Zealand's most multicultural city, home to a large number of Polynesians, Asians, and other immigrants. Dynamic, driven, and gorgeous, Auckland is the city the rest of New Zealand loves to hate.

3 Northland and the Bay of Islands. Northland has a large population of Māori, ancient kauri forests, salty harbors, and ocean inlets. The Bay of Islands is where the Treaty of Waitangi was signed in 1840. It is now known for diving, sailing, and sunning on and around the isolated beaches on its 100-plus islands.

4 Coromandel Peninsula and the Bay of Plenty. Close to Auckland but a world away, Coromandel and the Bay of Plenty have white-sand beaches, blue seas, native birds, and steep hills carpeted with forest. Coromandel has a café and board-shorts culture, while the Bay of Plenty is a Māori cultural hub. It also has the most active volcano in New Zealand (Whakaari).

5 East Coast and the Volcanic Zone. Taupo, a vibrant city next to New Zealand's largest lake, is surrounded by towering active volcanoes in the mountainous Tongariro National Park (and the Tongariro Crossing, a stunning all-day hike), and is the trout-fishing capital of the world. Te Urewera's wilderness contrasts with the mix of arty café towns like Napier, wineries, and poor but superb beach towns like Ruatoria and Tolaga Bay, where Māori community life is still present.

6 North Island's West Coast. Mt. Taranaki broods over Egmont National Park and the rural industrial area affectionately known as the 'Naki. A thin highway loops through sleepy surf towns, wet, tropical coastline, and black-sand beaches until it reaches the lower West Coast farmland. About 45 minutes outside of Wellington, sleepy beach towns border one side of the Kapiti Coast and farmland and the Tararua Ranges the other. Kapiti Island is a protected predator-free reserve where otherwise endangered birdlife thrives.

7 Wellington and the Wairarapa. Cafés, bars, restaurants, art galleries, and cinemas overflow in the capital city, giving it a vibrant quality. It's bordered by steep hillsides studded with Victorian homes and an expansive harbor and crowned by Te Papa, New Zealand's largest museum. Lyall and Houghton Bays attract surfers, while the Miramar peninsula is home to Peter Jackson's film empire.

1

Bay of Islands

Paihia
Russell

NORTHLAND

3
Whangarei

Hauraki Gulf

Pacific Ocean

Tasman Sea

Coromandel
2
Whitianga
4
Tairua
Auckland
Thames
Whangamata

Whakaari
White Island

Cape Runaway

Hamilton
Cambridge
Raglan   WAIKATO
Tokoroa

Lake
Rotorua

Tauranga

Bay of Plenty

Whakatane
Opotiki
Rotorua

East Cape

Ruatoria

5 EASTLAND

Tolaga Bay

Awakino

Lake
Taupo

Taupo

HAWKE'S
BAY

Te Urewera
Nat'l Park

Gisborne

New Plymouth

TARANAKI
Egmont
National Park   Stratford
Ohakune
Waiouru

Turangi

Tongariro
National Park

Whanganui
Nat'l Park

Waioru

Mahia Peninsula

Wairoa

Hawke Bay

Napier

South Pacific Ocean

6
Wanganui

Bulls

Palmerston North

MANAWATU

Kapiti
Island

Masterton
Martinborough
7
WAIRARAPA
WELLINGTON

Tasman Bay
Picton
Nelson
Blenheim

Cook Strait

0		50 mi
0		50 km

WHAT'S WHERE IN THE SOUTH ISLAND

8 Upper South Island and the West Coast. Across the Cook Strait from the North Island is the Marlborough Sounds, known for seafood, sauvignon blanc, sailing, and the Queen Charlotte Track. To the southeast, the wineries of Blenheim rise up into dramatic snowcapped mountains plunging to the Kaikoura coastline. To the west, the artistic town of Nelson gives way to Abel Tasman National Park. South of the park, the West Coast turns rugged with sights like the Punakaiki Pancake Rocks and the twin glaciers, Franz Josef and Fox.

9 Christchurch and Canterbury. Easygoing Christchurch, with its British gardens and meandering Avon River, is bordered in the north by the thermal resort town, Hanmer Springs. To the east is the Banks Peninsula, another volcanic remnant of green hills, hidden ocean inlets, the French-flavored town of Akaroa, and abundant marine life. To the west, the flat, vast Canterbury Plains extends to remote Arthur's Pass and the Southern Alps and 12,316-foot Aoraki (Mt. Cook), New Zealand's tallest peak.

10 The Southern Alps and Fiordland. The Southern Alps is populated by alpine towns. Queenstown is known as the Adventure Capital of the World and offers up any extreme sport you can think of. Wanaka is quieter, though no less scenic, while artsy Arrowtown displays the reminders of the area's gold-rush history. Remote Glenorchy borders the hiking tracks that lead into Fiordland. Best known for the Milford Sound and track, Fiordland is a raw, brooding forest.

11 Otago, Invercargill, and Stewart Island. The southern part of the South Island has two main towns: Invercargill and Dunedin. Dunedin is the livelier of the two, due in part to its university. The towns are bordered by the Otago Peninsula, rich in albatrosses, seals, and penguin colonies, and the Catlins, known for its bird-rich forests. To the very south lies Stewart Island, with its colonies of kiwi birds and Rakiura National Park.

N

Fi
Nat

Cape Farewell

Collingwood

Abel Tasman
Nat'l Park

Marlborough
Sounds

Kahurangi
National Park

TASMAN MTS.

Tasman Bay

Cook Strait

Karakea

Nelson

8

Picton

MARLBOROUGH

Blenheim

Mokihinui

Westport

Murchison

Paparoa
National Park

Nelson Lakes
National Park

Punakaiki

Hanmer
Springs

Kaikoura

Greymouth

Tasman Sea

Hokitika

CANTERBURY

Arthur's
Pass

Arthur's Pass
National Park

Waipara

Kaiapoi

9

Christchurch

Westland
National Park

Franz Josef

Mount
Hutt

Banks Peninsula

Fox Glacier

Mount Cook
12,316m

Akaroa

Aoraki/
Mt. Cook

Mount Cook
National Park

Rakaia

Haast

SOUTHERN ALPS

Lake
Pukaki

Ashburton

Mount Aspiring
National Park

Lake
Tekapo

Waimate

Mount
Aspiring

Lake
Hawea

Twizel

Timaru

Canterbury Bight

Omarama

Milford Sound

Lake
Wanaka

Wanaka

Waimate

Glenorchy

Arrowtown

Oamaru

Queenstown

Lake
Wakatipu

Alexandra

South Pacific Ocean

Lake
Te Anau

Palmerston

FIORDLAND

Te Anau

Otago Peninsula

Lumsden

Dunedin
Mosgiel

Clifden

Gore

Fiordland
National Park

Winton

Balclutha

Invercargill

CATLINS

Bluff

11

Foveaux Strait

Halfmoon Bay

Rakiura
National Park

STEWART
ISLAND

0   50 mi

0   50 km

NEW ZEALAND PLANNER

When to Go

New Zealand experiences winter during the American summer. Weather changes rapidly, especially in the mountains. Summer (December–March) is generally warm with long hours of sunshine. Winter (June–September) is mild at lower altitudes, but snow falls in the mountains. Rain can pour all year. It's best to visit from October to April, especially in alpine areas. Avoid the summer holiday (mid-December to February) when car rentals and accommodations are scarce.

Mark Your Calendar

New Zealand's calendar includes art, music, and wine festivals. If you miss All Blacks rugby, check out the Super 14 and Air New Zealand Cup.

Waitangi Day, New Zealand's national day, commemorates the 1840 signing of the Treaty of Waitangi between Europeans and Māori. Napier's **Art Deco Weekend** highlights wine, food, and vintage cars. At the weeklong **Queenstown Winter Festival** ski competitions end with evening entertainment. An annual calendar of events can be found at *www.newzealand.com.*

Getting Here and Around

Air New Zealand and the Australian-based Qantas are the two main carriers to New Zealand, with most international flights arriving in Auckland. Air New Zealand and Qantas are joined by Jetstar Airways and Pacific Blue as the primary domestic operators, with regular flights crisscrossing both islands to main urban areas. Flights are also available to smaller outlying towns, but expect fewer regular flights, higher prices, and smaller planes. Check the airlines' Web sites well in advance for special deals.

The best way to explore New Zealand is by car, which gives you the freedom to take in the ever-changing landscape at your own pace. New Zealanders drive on the left-hand side, and seat-belt and speeding laws are enforced. Speed cameras are often hidden in vans parked on the side of the road. New Zealand has a wide variety of multinational and independent car and camper van–rental operators to choose from, but book early if you're planning on traveling in December and January. You can use your country's driver's license; purchase insurance, as the majority of New Zealanders are uninsured. Gasoline is known as *petrol,* and can be costly—$1.53 per liter on average, with remote areas charging considerably more. If you know you're driving to a remote area, fill up in advance to avoid painful price gouging—or running out of fuel. Driving distances are the biggest road hazard in New Zealand, especially in the South Island: a straight-line distance of 18 mi may take 310 mi of driving, since the Southern Alps can only be crossed in three places.

For those who don't fancy driving, New Zealand has well-organized bus transport throughout both islands. The main companies are InterCity and Newlands, but there are a host of smaller companies to suit any budget.

Tranz Scenic offers four rail journeys with stunning scenery between Auckland and Wellington, Christchurch and Picton, Christchurch and Greymouth, and Palmerston North and Wellington.

You can ferry between islands. Interislander and Bluebridge offer services across the Cook Strait between Wellington and Picton, including car transport.

What to Pack

New Zealand's weather is as ever-changing as its landscape, so pack layers of all-weather clothing, from T-shirts to heavy sweaters. Bring a good raincoat and comfortable walking shoes. New Zealanders dress casually, so don't worry about fashion over function. The country has high-quality outdoor stores, as well as fashion boutiques, so it is easy to pick up items here. Be certain to pack your electronics, as they are expensive and elusive in New Zealand.

Customs information can be found at *www.customs.govt.nz*. The standard regulations apply: 4.5L of wine or beer, 1125mL of spirits or liquor, 250 grams of tobacco, 200 cigarettes, 50 cigars, dutiable goods up to $700, and you'll have to declare if you're leaving or entering the country with more than $10, 000. New Zealanders take biosecurity *extremely* seriously, as well they should: this is a small remote country and introduced species and bacteria can easily and quickly wreck havoc here. Clean your shoes, boots, tents, golf clubs, bicycles, and luggage before you arrive (or it could be quarantined for cleaning), and declare any plant, food, or animal products (including wood and packaged snacks). Fresh fruit should be thrown away in appropriate bins before you go through customs.

If you are planning on hiking in New Zealand, bring boots and a day pack, layers of clothing, a basic survival–injury kit, and water bottles. For hiking one of the Great Walks or camping, bring a tent, camping stove, good sleeping bag, wet-weather gear, and a comfortable pack. Be prepared for freezing conditions in the mountains, even in summer.

Lodging Options

New Zealand has a wide variety of accommodations, including international hotel chains, B&Bs, farm stays, country lodges, baches (self-contained rental cottages), backpackers (hostels), hotels, and motels.

A free accommodations guide is available at airports and tourist offices. Book in advance, especially in the summer months (December through March). Not all accommodations refund cancellations, so check policies before booking.

If you are staying in one location for a few days, consider renting a bach (⊕ *www.bookabatch.co.nz*), or home rental, an economic option.

Visitor Information

New Zealand does tourism well. Tourism New Zealand (www.new-zealand.com) is the main branch, yet almost every city and small town has an i-SITE or visitor center. These centers usually have displays on local history and flora and fauna, local weather conditions, and brochures. The staff often book activities and accommodations. Be advised, though, that i-SITES are businesses: they only promote tour operators that pay to be a part of the local tourist association.

The Department of Conservation has a good Web site (⊕ *www.doc.govt.nz*) and local offices, with in-depth hiking and weather information.

Island Hop

New Zealand is a three-hour flight from both Australia and many of the Pacific Islands, like Fiji, Tahiti, and Samoa, and it is easy to combine your New Zealand trip with one of these locations. Some major airlines offer stop-off specials, or air passes, like Air New Zealand's South Pacific Air Pass, for journeys between New Zealand, Australia, and some South Pacific Islands. Australia and each of the South Pacific islands offer their own unique cultures and experiences, which are quite different (and warmer!) than New Zealand.

NEW ZEALAND
TOP ATTRACTIONS

Abel Tasman National Park

(A) Abel Tasman National Park is New Zealand's smallest and most visited park. At the north end of the South Island, this park is an explosion of color: green waves lap orange-tinted sand fringed by green forest. Made up of limestone and marble, Abel Tasman is studded with caves and rock formations that make it an excellent hiking or kayaking destination.

Aoraki/Mt. Cook

(B) Rising 12,316 feet out of the Canterbury Plains, the South Island's Aoraki (cloud piercer) is aptly named. Aoraki (also known as Mt. Cook) is the largest mountain in New Zealand, the crown jewel of the sparkling Southern Alps. It is flanked by two glacier lakes (Lake Tekapo and Lake Pukaki) of such starling turquoise they hurt the eyes. This is where Sir Edmund Hillary cut his climbing teeth.

Bay of Islands

(C) On the north finger of the North Island is the Bay of Islands, a 100-island maze that is a stronghold of New Zealand history. Captain Cook first sailed here in 1769. In 1840, the Treaty of Waitangi was signed here. Today, New Zealanders flock to the area for the warm temperatures and pristine beaches, making it a haven for sailing, boating, and big-game fishing.

The Coromandel

(D) The Coromandel Peninsula is that local spot Kiwis don't want you to know about. Only two hours from Auckland, the Coromandel is a remote getaway of white-sand beaches, native forest, quirky cafés, and bustling marinas. Highlights include bountiful fishing, kayaking to Cathedral Cove (a huge limestone arch), and digging your own hot-tub on Hot Water Beach.

Hawke's Bay

(E) Napier, Hawke's Bay, and East Cape area on the east coast of the North Island comprise three distinct areas hemmed in by Te Urewera National Park on one side, and the curving coastline of the Pacific Ocean on the other. Napier is a quirky coastal city, an art deco phoenix risen from the ashes of a 7.9 earthquake in 1931. Hawke's Bay is known for its wine. Farther north, from Gisborne up to the East Cape, is a string of quiet coastal towns.

Otago Peninsula

(F) Tiny, rugged Otago Peninsula is north of Dunedin. Only 18 mi long and 7 mi across, it is jam-packed with wildlife, including a yellow-eyed penguin reserve and the world's only mainland royal albatross colony. Little Blue penguins, sea lions, and New Zealand Fur Seals are abundant, and Larnach Castle towers over it all at the peninsula's highest point.

Queenstown

(G) Queenstown has long been known as the Adventure Capital of the World. The city is a small and lively maze restaurants and shops, but the surrounding landscape is the real playground. The Queenstown area, including mild Wanaka and isolated Glenorchy, is a jumble of ski slopes, rivers, and alpine areas that make it a heaven for hiking, skiing, paragliding, white-water rafting, kayaking, and—after the adrenaline wears off—wine tasting.

Waitomo Caves

(H) Between Auckland and Taupo are the Waitomo Caves, a massive system of underground limestone caves. Three main caves—Glowworm Cave (named for its electric blue inhabitants), Ruakuri Cave (a *wahi tapu*, or sacred site), and Aranui Cave (known for its fantastic limestone formations)—can be rafted, hiked, or rappelled.

TOP EXPERIENCES

Overnight Cruise in the Milford Sound

The Milford Sound reaches into the 2.9 million-acre primeval forests of Fiordland National Park. Milford is an eerie place, and the best way to experience it is on an overnight cruise underneath the high rounded mountains that jut up from the inky ocean like moss-covered teeth. Spend a couple of hours kayaking the shores looking for penguins, seals, and dolphins, before retiring on deck to watch the stars wheel overhead. This is one of the few places you pray for rain and usually get it—the Milford Sound receives 22 feet of rain a year, which veins the cliff faces with rushing white waterfalls.

Hike New Zealand's Great Walks

There are nine official Great Walks, although one of them is technically a river journey, throughout some of the best scenery in the North and South Islands. These walks take travelers past glaciers, along the coasts, through volcanic areas, and deep into pristine alpine wilderness. Each walk has a well-maintained track and huts, and a booking system was created a few years ago to manage visitor pressure. The length of tracks vary—the Rakiura Track on Stewart Island is the shortest at 18 mi; the Heaphy Track the longest at 50.

Attend an All Blacks' Match

There is nothing like the intensity of an All Blacks' test match on home soil. Rugby is part of the nation's psyche: more than 135,000 New Zealanders play the winter sport, and even more are fierce supporters. With a historical 74% winning record, the All Blacks are a formidable team—except when it comes to bringing home World Cups. The 80-minute test matches are held outdoors, surrounded by a sea of supporters clad in black (rain gear, usually). From the bilingual national anthem, to the pregame performance of the haka (a dance which conveys the history, life-force, and ties to the nation), to the referee's first whistle, you know you're in for something special.

Taste the Wine

New Zealand wines are some of the best and most affordable in the world, and it's easy to loosely follow the wine trail from north to south. Auckland and Waiheke Island are known for their boutique vineyards, while the East Coast area of Hawke's Bay is one of the oldest. Some of the older estates started growing grapes in the 19th century. Martinborough, in the Wairarapa just outside of Wellington, is a small town surrounded by several local vineyards that produce excellent pinot noirs. In the South Island, Marlborough is the country's largest grape-growing area with more than 50 vineyards, producing some world-class sauvignon blancs. Nelson and Blenheim vie for the sunniest region in New Zealand, and have an excellent climate for grapes, while the Central Otago region is known for hardy reds.

Hike a Glacier

Nearly two-thirds of the glacial ice in the 140 glaciers in Westland National Park is contained in Franz Josef and Fox glaciers, only 15 mi apart and two of the most accessible glaciers in the world. Tucked in between mountains covered in subtemperate rain forest, New Zealand glaciers are unique in that they are only 12 mi from the sea, which means the glacier process of packing down layers of snow happens in fast-forward here: what usually takes about 3,000 years can happen in seven years in New Zealand. For something really special, take one of the guided heli-hiking trips on the glacier.

Mingle with Marine Life

New Zealand is surrounded by sea, and visitors have a variety of opportunities to get up close to marine life like dolphins, orca, penguins, and whales. In Kaikoura, on the east coast of the South Island, dramatic snowcapped mountains plunge 8,500 feet to the coast, and just a few miles off-shore there's another undersea plunge, allowing large mammals (like the giant sperm whale) to come close to the shore. Kaikoura used to be a whaling station, but in an environmentally friendly turn of events, whale-watching is now its biggest industry. Also on the South Island's east coast is Akaroa, where you can swim with Hector's Dolphins, New Zealand's smallest and rarest, found only in New Zealand waters.

Learn about Māori Culture

Māori is a living culture, and can be difficult to access without a proper introduction—most local communities don't want visitors turning up uninvited on their marae. Rotorua, a thermal area on the East Coast of the North Island, is famous for its Māori heritage, and even more famous for teaching visitors about that heritage. Whakarewarewa and Te Puia villages, for example, teach traditional greenstone carving and give cultural performances. The museum of Te Papa Tongarewa on the Wellington waterfront is another good place to learn about Māori traditions and history through elaborate displays and artifacts.

Tongariro Crossing

The Tongariro Crossing is known as the "greatest one-day walk in the world." This 10-mi walk is an all-day affair, going up and nearly over the 6,457 Mt. Tongariro (an active volcano), past the Red Crater and the Emerald Lakes, descending through native forest alongside rivers and waterfalls. The walk is usually done in the summer months, as ever-changing weather can be treacherous on this high-altitude hike. Bus transportation can be arranged to drop off and pick up visitors on either end of the hike; pack a picnic lunch to have alongside the gleaming Emerald Lakes, the reward for your climbing efforts.

Bird-Watch on Stewart Island

Eighteen miles off the southern tip of the South Island lies Stewart Island, a tiny piece of land with one settlement (Halfmoon Bay), 2½ mi of road, and more than 155 mi of walking tracks in Raikura National Park. Birds are king here, free from the devastation caused by the introduced predators that plague the mainland. Visitors can see any number of species here.

Visit Tane Mahuta in Waipoua Forest

Tane Mahuta (King of the Forest) is a kauri tree, one of the last massive giants that used to populate New Zealand forests. A five-minute walk into the Waipoua Forest, located 12 mi from Hokianga, Tane Mahuta lords over the surrounding rain forest, growing 168 feet tall and 45 feet in diameter. Most of the nation's kauri trees have been wiped out by logging. They aren't as tall or as old as sequoia trees, but kauri trees are massive wooden bulks of straight-grained wood that were nearly logged to extinction—less than 4% of kauri forests remain, and the Waipoua Forest contains three-quarters of all remaining kauri trees. Tane Mahuta, the last of the giants, is more than 2,000 years old and an important symbol in New Zealand history and sustainability.

IF YOU LIKE

Beaches

New Zealand has more than 15,000 km (9,300 mi) in coastline, which ripples and zigzags to create bays, coves, fjords, and countless beaches. These run the gamut from surfing hot spots to quiet sheltered lagoons to rugged, boulder-studded strands. All are open to the public, and few are crowded. The greatest hazards are sunburn—the lack of smog and a subequatorial location mean the sun is **strong**—and strong currents.

On the North Island, Coromandel's eastern shore and the Bay of Plenty—especially busy **Mount Maunganui**—are favorites during summer "time off." The black "iron sand" on the West Coast of the North Island is a result of volcanic activity. **Karekare Beach,** west of Auckland, is the striking, cliff-backed beach that made famous in Jane Campion's film *The Piano.* The dunes at **90 Mile Beach** in Northland are spectacular, and nearby **Doubtless Bay** has some of the country's loveliest caramel-colored beaches. New Zealand's most famous surf breaks are located west of Hamilton in the laid-back town of **Raglan;** you can "hang-10" here or at **Piha** near Auckland.

South Island beaches are captivating, particularly in **Abel Tasman National Park** and neighboring **Golden Bay.** The sands are golden, and the water is jade green. Westerly winds carry driftwood, buoys, entire trees, and a fascinating variety of flotsam from as far away as South America to Stewart Island's **Mason Bay,** making this dramatic sweep of sand a beachcomber's paradise. The sand is crisscrossed with the tracks of kiwis (the birds) that reside in the area by the thousands.

Birds

It is one thing to read "9.6 feet" here in ink, but it is quite another sensation to watch the magnificent royal albatross spread its wings and soar through your field of vision. You don't have to be a twitcher (bird-watching nut) to appreciate New Zealand's feathered population—this country will turn you into a bird nerd. The birds of New Zealand are extraordinary to behold: a raft of thousands of sooty shearwaters (aka muttonbirds or *titi*) move like smoke over the water; a yellow-eyed penguin pops like a cork from the bright green surf and waddles up the beach; fantails squeak and follow you through the forest; the soft cry of the *morepork* (owl) is interrupted by the otherworldly call of the kiwi. Pelagic birds such as the royal albatross will take your breath away; the Otago Peninsula colony (off Dunedin) is the only mainland breeding colony for these perfect flying machines. It may be ornithologically incorrect to say so, but many of the native birds are simply hilarious. Penguins always make people smile, and New Zealand is home to the little blue (or fairy), the extremely rare *hoiho* (or yellow-eyed), and the yellow-tweedled Fiordland-crested penguin. The kea and its cousin the kaka are wild parrots whose antics crack people up—these birds like to hang upside down from gutters and regard you with bright beady eyes. And, of course, there is the star of the bird show: the kiwi. You won't ever see another bird like this funny flightless brown bird, and to glimpse a kiwi is an unforgettable and joyful experience. Hot bird spots include Kapiti Island off the North Island and Stewart Island way down south.

Boating

There are boating and fishing options to match any mood.

If you're feeling cruisy, rent a kayak and paddle around the crystal green pools of the Abel Tasman, or the penguin-filled waters of Paterson Inlet. Take a canoe on the Whanganui River, or sail the Bay of Islands. Feeling really lazy? Just charter a boat and captain and take in the scenery of the Marlborough Sounds or busy Auckland Harbour. Fly-fish a trout from a caldera in Lake Taupo, or one of the many pristine rivers and lakes throughout the country.

If you want some fun and a bit of a rush, much of the fishing in the South is simple rod or hand lining for groper (grouper), trumpeter, and greenbone. Northerners argue their snapper is superior to the succulent Stewart Island blue cod; sample both to weigh in on this tasty debate. Go on a creaky wooden boat for the local old-school experience (some skippers will fry your catch), or opt for a sleeker vessel and a bird tour and let your heart soar with the mollymawks.

Up north ups the excitement, with big game fishing out of Russell and Paihia for big fish such as striped marlin. Tuna is always a challenging catch, and the **Hokitika Trench** off Greymouth is one of the few places in the world where the three species of bluefin tuna gather.

If you want a major adrenaline buzz, go jet-boating on the **Shotover River** near Queenstown, or raft the North Island's **Kaituna River,** near Rotorua, which has the highest commercially rafted waterfall (22 feet) in the Southern Hemisphere. Or get off the boat and go spearfishing for *moki* in the kelp forests beneath the waves.

Bushwalking

The traditional way to hike in New Zealand is freedom walking. Freedom walkers carry their own provisions, sleeping bags, food, and cooking gear and sleep in basic huts. A more refined alternative—usually on more popular trails—is the guided walk, on which you trek with just a light day pack, guides do the cooking, and you sleep in heated lodges.

The most popular walks are in the Southern Alps. The **Milford Track** is a four-day walk through breathtaking scenery to the edge of Milford Sound. The **Queen Charlotte Track** (68 km [42 mi]) winds along the jagged coast of the Marlborough Sounds region; you can see seals and sometimes orcas from the waterside cliffs.

The hard-core hiker will be challenged on remote Rakiura National Park's **North West Circuit.** The 10- to 12-day trek will sometimes feel more like mud wrestling than walking, but the scenic rewards are immeasurable, as is the pint of beer waiting at the South Sea Pub when it's over. If you would like to experience Rakiura, do the three-day **Rakiura Track,** or have a water taxi drop you along one of the many coastal trails and walk back.

The North Island has plenty of wonders of its own. The Coromandel Peninsula has forests of gigantic 1,200-year-old kauri trees, 80-foot-tall tree ferns, a gorgeous coastline, and well-marked trails. You can hike among active volcanic peaks in **Tongariro National Park.** And on a nub of the West Coast formed by volcanic activity hundreds of years ago, sits the majestic, Fuji-like **Mt. Taranaki.** If time is short, at least put aside a few hours for trekking in the **Waitakerei Ranges,** just a short drive from Auckland city.

Luxe Lodging

If you think New Zealand is provincial in its accommodations, think again—Kiwis know how to live in their landscape, and that knowledge is reflected in lodging options on offer.

Check out stunning **Blanket Bay** (⊕ *www. blanketbay.com*) on the end of Lake Wakatipu near Glenorchy, with its schist-stone chalets under shadow of the Remarkables mountain range, if you can spend more than $1,000 per night. Or try **Wharekauhau Lodge** (⊕ *www.wharekaukau.co.nz*), 5,000 acres of quiet luxury surrounded by native forest and overlooking Palliser Bay, just 90 minutes from Wellington.

Blend into the native forest at one of the environmentally friendly eco-villas at **Punakaki Resort** (⊕ *www.punakaiki-resort. co.nz*) on the wild West Coast of the South Island with views of the ocean or the rain forest in Paparoa National Park. Stay in the treetops at **Kaikoura's Hapuku Lodge & Tree Houses** (⊕ *www.hapukulodge.com*).

Kick it old-style at the granddaddy of all New Zealand lodges, **Chateau Tongariro** (⊕ *www.chateau.co.nz*), an iconic heritage building at the base of active volcano Mt. Ruapehu in Tongariro National Park.

Dream of grapes growing on the vine? Stay at one of the two cottages in Hawke's Bay's **Craggy Range Winery** (⊕ *www.craggyrange.com*) near Napier, or at **Owhanake Bay Estate** (⊕ *www.owhanake.co.nz*), a boutique accommodation and vineyard on Waiheke Island near Auckland.

Wild and rugged station life and genuine Kiwi company come with a taste of the good life at **Mt. Nicholas Lodge** (⊕ *www. mtnicholaslodge.co.nz*), a 100,000-acre working station near Queenstown.

Skiing

With all of its mountains, New Zealand is a skier's paradise, from the volcanic cones in the North Island to the massive Southern Alps on the South Island.

North Island skiing centers around **Mt. Ruapehu**, an active volcano with two skiing areas: Whakapapa (the larger of the two, with 30 groomed trails) and Turoa (20 groomed trails, including the country's longest vertical drop of 2,369 feet). Mt. Ruapehu is New Zealand's largest ski area, and no wonder: who would pass up the opportunity to ski down Mt. Doom from *Lord of the Rings*? The nearby town of Ohakune is also the Queenstown of the north in the wintertime, famous for its lively hospitality.

The South Island provides a few more major fields to choose from. Near Queenstown, the **Remarkables** is a popular area with three basins and one heckuva view. **Coronet Peak** is known for its excellent facilities, treeless slopes and night skiing, with a wide range of terrain for all levels.

Wanaka's **Treble Cone** the most challenging field in New Zealand, with intermediate and advanced downhill powder runs on a vertical drop of 2,313 feet. Nearby **Cardrona** is more suited to families, with more rolling slopes for beginners.

Mount Hutt near **Methven** (Canterbury) is New Zealand's best and highest ski slope with first-rate powder skiing; it also has the longest season.

Heli-skiing, snowboarding terrain parks and cross-country skiing are also popular, so check out the local regions to see what's available.

Surfing

New Zealand's 9,300-plus mi of coastline provide excellent surfing beaches for experts and beginners alike. The water is cold, so bring a wet suit. Since many beaches have notorious rips, be sure to talk to the locals and check the weather before heading outs.

The North Island has the highest concentration of surf beaches, with **Northland** providing ample opportunities. In **Auckland, Te Arai Point, Mangawhai, Piha,** and **Muriwai** are popular hot spots, and **Coromandel's Whangamata** is a favorite.

Find white-sand, cliff-side beaches in the **East Cape** area, including **Ruatoria, Tokomaru Bay, Tolaga Bay,** and **Gisborne.** *Whale Rider* was filmed here. The locals are fiercely protective of their land, so tread gently. Farther south are the beaches of the **Napier** and **Wairarapa** area: **Mahia, Ocean Beach, Castlepoint,** and **Cape Palliser.**

Raglan, New Zealand's most famous surf beach, is on the west coast of the North Island. Its breaks were featured in the 1964 cult-classic *The Endless Summer.* Farther south, **Taranaki's Surf Highway,** a 65-mi stretch from New Plymouth to Hawera on State Highway 45, provides inlets and remote beaches.

The South Island's coast is more difficult to get to and colder, so there are fewer surfing opportunities. **Kaikoura, Christchurch, Hokitika, Greymouth,** and **Dunedin** all have good breaks.

For a list of surf schools, events, and news, check out Surfing NZ (⊕ *www.surfingnz. co.nz*). Surf.co.nz (⊕ *www.surf.co.nz*) has surf reports.

Wine

With its cool winters and mild summers, New Zealand is fast becoming famous for fine white wines and light reds.

The largest, most well-known region is **Marlborough,** on the top of the South Island, which produces nearly half of the national crop. Marlborough produces fine sauvignon blancs, as well as unique rieslings and pinot noirs.

Hawke's Bay is the second largest region, located on the east coast of the North Island. New Zealand's premiere food and wine destination is known for chardonnays, cabernet sauvignons, syrahs, and merlots.

Auckland has about 100 vineyards and wineries. It is known for rich, bordeaux-style reds, as well as the boutique vineyards on Waiheke Island.

Gisborne, also on the east coast of the North Island, is the fourth-largest wine region, produces buttery-rich tones in its tasty chardonnays.

The **Wairarapa** features small wineries, most of which are located within walking distance of the town square. This is pinot noir country, and it produces some of New Zealand's best.

Nelson, another small, idyllic wine region in the north of South Island, is known for light reds as well as its artistic flair.

Canterbury, in the east of the South Island, is the country's newest wine region, but its rieslings and pinot noirs stand out.

Central Otago, located near Queenstown in the South Island, wins the most handsome wine region award: vineyards are hemmed in by staggering white-capped mountain ranges, producing earthy rich reds.

TALK LIKE A LOCAL

From the moment you begin your New Zealand (or *Aotearoa*, as you'll learn in the airport) adventure, you'll confront the mélange of Māori words, Briticisms, and uniquely Kiwi phrases that make the language vibrant . . . but perhaps a bit hard for American ears to navigate.

New Zealand is a bilingual nation, as reflected in its national anthem. Although Māori isn't conversational language, a basic knowledge of Māori is essential for understanding phrases, the meaning of place names, as well as the pronunciation of certain words or place names.

■ TIP➜ For a crash course in the best way to pronounce New Zealand place names, the best thing to do is watch the weather report on the news.

Talking Kiwi is not as daunting as Māori pronunciations for those with the English language under their belt. New Zealander's tend to use the Queen's English, colored up with their unique brand of abbreviated slang. Most Kiwi turns-of-phrase are easy to unravel—a *carpark* is a parking lot, for example. Others, like *dairy* (a convenience or corner store), can be confused with American terminology. Only occasionally will you find yourself at a complete loss (with words like *jandal*, for example—Kiwi for flip-flops), and even then New Zealanders will be happy to set you right. Below are common Māori and Kiwi phrases that you'll likely hear throughout the country.

Māori Pronunciation

Knowing how to pronounce Māori words can be important while traveling around New Zealand. Even if you have a natural facility for picking up languages, you'll find many Māori words to be quite baffling. The West Coast town of Punakaiki (pronounced poon-ah-*kye*-kee) is relatively straightforward, but when you get to places such as Whakatane, the going gets tricky—the opening *wh* is pronounced like an *f*, and the accent is placed on the last syllable: "fa-ca-tawn-e." Sometimes it is the mere length of words that makes them difficult, as in the case of Waitakaruru (why-ta-ka-ru-ru) or Whakarewarewa (fa-ca-*re*-wa-*re*-wa). You'll notice that the ends of both of these have repeats—of "ru" and "rewa," which is something to look out for to make longer words more manageable. In other instances, a relatively straightforward name like Taupo can sound completely different than you expected (Toe-paw). Town names like Waikanea (*why*-can-eye) you'll just have to repeat to yourself a few times before saying them without pause.

The Māori *r* is rolled so that it sounds a little like a *d*. Thus the Northland town of Whangarei is pronounced "fang-ah-day," and the word *Māori* is pronounced "mah-*aw*-dee," or sometimes "mo-dee," with the o sounding like it does in the word *mold*, and a rolled *r*. A macron indicates a lengthened vowel. In general, *a* is pronounced *ah* as in "car"; *e* is said as the *ea* in "weather." *O* is pronounced like "awe," rather than *oh*, and *u* sounds like the *u* of "June." *Ng*, meanwhile, has a soft, blunted sound, as the *ng* in "singing." All of this is a little too complicated for those who still choose not to bother with Māori pronunciations. So in some places, if you say you've just driven over from "fahng-ah-ma-*ta*," the reply might be: "You mean 'wang-ah-*ma*-tuh." You can pronounce these words either way, but more and more people these days are pronouncing Māori words correctly.

1

MĀORI GLOSSARY

Common Māori Words

Aotearoa: Land of the long white cloud (New Zealand's Māori name)

Haere mai: Welcome, come here

Haere rā: Farewell, good-bye

Haka: "dance," implies history, life-force, rhythm, words and meaning of the haka, made internationally famous by the All Blacks, who perform it before each match

Hāngi: Earth oven, food from an earth oven, also used to describe a feast

Hongi: Press noses in greeting

Hui: Gathering

Iwi: People, tribe

Ka pai: Good, excellent

Kai: Food, eat, dine

Karakia: Ritual chant, prayer, religious service

Kaumātua: Elder

Kia ora: Hello, thank you

Koha: Customary gift, donation

Kūmara: Sweet potato

Mana: Influence, prestige, power

Marae: Traditional gathering place

Moko: Tattoo

Pā: Fortified village

Pākehā: Non-Māori, European, Caucasian

Pounamu: Greenstone

Rangatira: Chief, person of rank

Reo: Language

Tāne: Man

Tangata whenua: People of the land, local people

Taonga: Treasure

Tapu: Sacred, under religious restriction, taboo

Wahine: Woman

Waiata: Sing, song

Waka: Canoe

Whakapapa: Genealogy, cultural identity

Whānau: Family

KIWI GLOSSARY

Common Kiwi Words

Across the ditch: Over the Tasman Sea in Australia (Australians are called Aussies)

Bach: Vacation house (pronounced *batch*)

Fanny: Woman's privates (considered obscene)

Footie: Rugby football

Gutted: Very upset

Kiwi: a native, brown flightless bird, the people of New Zealand, or the furry fruit

Nappie: Diaper

Pissed: Drunk

Sealed road: Paved road

Shout: Buy a round of drinks

Sticking plaster or plaster: Adhesive bandage

Stuffed up: Made a mistake

Sweet as: All good

Ta: Thanks

Torch: Flashlight

Tramping: Hiking

Whinge: To whine

When Dining Out

For most visitors, dining out is usually the cause for most lost-in-translation moments, as Kiwis tend to follow British terminology. Here are a few tips:

Aubergine: Eggplant

Capsicum: Bell pepper

Courgette: Zucchini

Cuppa: Cup of tea or coffee

Entree: Appetizer

Flat white: Coffee with milk (equivalent to a café au lait)

Lemonade: Lemon-flavored soda

Lollies: Candy

Mains: Main course

Pavlova: A meringue cake

Serviette: Napkin

Tea: Dinner (also the beverage)

NEW ZEALAND HISTORY

Aotearoa

According to Māori legend, the demigod Maui sailed from Hawaiki (believed to be one of the French Polynesian islands) in his canoe, and he caught a huge fish, which he dragged to the surface. The fish is the North Island; Maui's canoe is the South Island.

This legend describes New Zealand's history, which is one of hardship, fortitude, and discovery. This brave, isolated, and young country is still creating its history, day by day.

It began with the moa hunters, believed to have arrived in the 9th century, possibly from east Polynesia, which could make them related to present-day Māori. In 925 AD, Kupe sailed from Hawaiki and discovered New Zealand. He returned to Hawaiki, named it Aotearoa (Land of the Long White Cloud) and passed on the sailing coordinates. In 1350 AD, eight war canoes landed in New Zealand, marking the beginning of Māori culture on the landmass. Their existence was a battle of brutality and beauty. Warriors were trained at a young age, and tribal warfare and sheer survival led to a low life expectancy. At the same time, Māori became accomplished tattoo, carving, and weaving artists. (⇨ *Maori Art in Chapter 3*)

Europeans Arrive

In 1642, things changed forever: the Dutch captain Abel Tasman sighted Cape Foulwind near Westport and officially put New Zealand on the map. Captain Tasman never actually set foot in New Zealand, though—he left after his boat was attacked by Māori in Golden Bay.

In 1767, Captain James Cook visited "Nieuw Zeeland" (as it had been named) in the *Endeavour*, and he is responsible for accurately chartering the coastline. The whalers and sealers arrived in the 1790s, nearly obliterating sea-life populations in a matter of decades. Māori, also, suffered from the introduction of European diseases and firearms, which they used on each other in their brutal land wars.

The missionaries arrived in the 1800s, bringing farming and Christianity with them. The local Māori population embraced the former, but not the latter.

The Treaty of Waitangi

The date February 6, 1840, remains one of the most important dates in New Zealand history. Māori signed the Treaty of Waitangi with the British. The Treaty guaranteed Māori rights to their land, but it gave the British sovereignty. The great hope of this treaty is that it would end land wars, tame lawlessness, and put New Zealand beyond the reach of French settlement forever. The New Zealand capital was moved from Russell in the Bay of Islands to Auckland, where it remained for 25 years.

It wasn't long, however, before Māori continued to lose their land to both the government and local settlers. When pakeha outnumbered Māori for the first time in 1858, Māori tribes banded together, declaring Waikato's Te Wherowhero the first Māori king. This only galvanized the British further, and violent land wars continued well into the 1860s.

Boom Years and Social Changes

Meanwhile, on the South Island, gold was discovered, leading to a massive rush and booming period of growth in the areas around Queenstown, Arrowtown and Otago, including the establishment of New Zealand's first university in 1869 in Dunedin. The nation's capital was also moved to Wellington (1865), and Māori were given representation in parliament two years later. By 1880, the government

had established free public schooling, and railroads and roads were beginning to crisscross the country. New Zealand also became the first country to legalize unions in 1878, and it was the first country to give women the vote in 1893.

Although well-versed in land wars, New Zealand got its first taste of international war in 1899, when it backed the British in the Boer War. New Zealand's allegiance to the Crown was to make for a bloody 50 years. In World War I, New Zealanders were part of the epic battle at Gallipoli in Turkey; the country lost more than 7% of its population in that war, but it was also the forming of the strange and unique bond with Australia. New Zealand also entered the fray in World War II, once again sustaining heavy casualties that rocked the tiny country's population.

The Post WWII Years

The 1950s through the 1980s were a time of huge economic growth, then bust, populated with local tragedies. In 1952 the country's population soared to more than 2 million people, and in 1953 local boy Edmund Hillary, together with Sherpa Tenzing Norgay, became the first to summit Mt. Everest. Post-war, the economy was at an all-time high. Within the next few decades, however, disaster struck again and again, including the 1953 Mt. Ruapehu eruption that killed 151 people, the sinking of the ferry Wahine off Wellington's coast in 1968, and the plane crash in Antarctica in 1979 that killed all 257 passengers. The economy went into a slump, and mad-dash government efforts only seemed to make things worse.

The 1980s were defined by stands that started to give New Zealand her own identity. In 1981 much of the population was in an uproar about the South African

rugby team touring New Zealand. Apartheid protesters flocked to the streets and clashed with Kiwis who felt that politics had no place in rugby. In 1984, the Labour government put a ban on nuclear powered or armed ships, despite being tossed out of the Australia–New Zealand–United States defense agreement because of its antinuke stand. In 1985, the Greenpeace ship the *Rainbow Warrior* was blown up in Auckland by the French. The United States and the British, despite knowing about the eminent attack, did nothing to prevent it. In 1987, New Zealand also put its mark on the sporting world by winning the inaugural Rugby World Cup—a feat it has been unable to repeat, despite being consistent world leaders in the sport.

In the New Millennium

New Zealand continues to experience the highs and lows of a young country in constant flux. Māori culture has experienced a resurgence and greater integration, but in 2003 a new debate flared as Māori requested a legal inquiry into their precolonial customary ownership of the seabed and shore. Thousands of protesters marched on Parliament in support of Māori claims. The country beauty was on full display for the world in Peter Jackson's *Lord of the Rings* trilogy. *The Return of the King,* the final film, won 11 Academy Awards in 2004. Still, New Zealand struggles to maintain its natural beauty. Entering the Kyoto Treaty in late 2004, it bound itself to new environmental regulations. By 2007, the former Prime Minister, Helen Clarke announced the country's goals for eventual carbon neutrality. In February of 2008, the National Party defeated her Labour Party and John Key became Prime Minister.

GREAT ITINERARIES

INTRODUCTION TO NORTH ISLAND

8 to 10 days
Auckland

2 days. After a long international flight, stretch your legs and invigorate your circulation with a walk around the city center, with perhaps stops at Auckland Museum and Auckland Domain Park or Albert Park. Head to the harbor (or "harbour") and take a ferry ride round-trip between Auckland and Devonport for a great view of the city from the water. Have an early dinner and turn in to get over the worst of the jet lag.

On your second day, you'll have more wind in your sails to explore the City of Sails. Depending on your interests, head to Kelly Tarlton's Underwater World and Antarctic Encounter, the New Zealand National Maritime Museum, the Auckland Art Gallery, or the Parnell neighborhood for window-shopping. If you're feeling energetic, you can even do a bit of kayaking (or just sunbathing) at Mission Bay or Karekare Beach.

Waitomo and Rotorua

1 or 2 days. Waitomo is known for what's beneath the surface—intricate limestone caves filled with stalactites, stalagmites, and galaxies of glowworms. If this is up your alley, get an early start from Auckland to arrive here before 11 AM and sign up for a cave tour. Afterward, continue on to Rotorua, which seethes with geothermal activity. In the late afternoon you should have time for a walk around the town center, strolling through the Government Gardens, and perhaps also Kuirau Park. If you decide to skip the Waitomo worms, you can zip straight down from Auckland to Rotorua. In addition to the town proper,

visit some of the eye-popping thermal areas nearby, such as Waiotapu. At night, be a guest at a *hāngi*, a Māori feast accompanied by a cultural performance. On the next day, you can either see some of the outlying thermal areas or continue south to Taupo.

Taupo

1 day. Midway between Auckland and Wellington, the resort town of Taupo, on its giant namesake lake, is the perfect base for a day full of aquatic activities. If you're at all interested in trout fishing, this is the place to do it.

Napier

1 day. This small town is an art deco period piece; after a devastating Richter 7.9 earthquake in 1931, the center of town was rebuilt in the distinctive style, and it's been carefully preserved ever since. Take a guided or self-guided walk around the Heritage (historically significant) neighborhood. If you have a car, drive out of town and visit one of the 30-odd wineries around Hawke's Bay. In the afternoon, take a drive to the top of Te Mata Peak, or visit nearby towns Hastings or Havelock North. Otherwise, hang out at the waterfront or visit the aquarium.

Wellington

2 days. New Zealand's capital, Wellington, is a terrific walking city, and there's even a cable car to help you with the hills. The big cultural draw is Te Papa Tongarewa—the Museum of New Zealand, which, with five floors and great interactive activities for kids, can take several hours to explore. You may wish to spend the rest of your first day here along the waterfront, winding up with dinner in the area. Be sure to check out the entertainment listings, too; you could be in town during one of the many festivals or catch a cool local band. On your second day, explore more of the urban highlights, like the City Gallery and the Museum of Wellington, City & Sea, followed by a bit of browsing on the main shopping drags or a trip up into the hills to the Botanic Garden. If you'd prefer more time out in the country and have a car, drive up the Kapiti Coast and book to visit Kapiti Island Nature Reserve, or sip acclaimed pinot noir in the wine center of Martinborough.

Other Top Options

1 or 2 days. With at least one more day at your disposal, you could squeeze in one of the following destinations. The Tongariro Crossing, a challenging but spectacular daylong hike, could be added to your Taupo stay. You'll "tramp" up close to three volcanoes: Tongariro, Ngauruhoe, and Ruapehu. If you have two days and are keen on swimming with dolphins or doing some diving, loop up to Paihia, a small seaside town and gateway to the Bay of Islands, after your initial two days in Auckland. You can dip into the mellow, rural

Coromandel Peninsula, perhaps the gateway town of Thames, before going south to Rotorua. Most places on the Coromandel are within 1 to 1½ hours' drive from the Thames township.

INTRODUCTION TO SOUTH ISLAND

10 to 13 days

Picton and Blenheim

2 days. Hop or drive onto the ferry from Wellington to Picton. This small seaside township is the Marlborough region's main commercial port, and the gateway to the gorgeously jagged coastline of Marlborough Sounds. Hop on a mail boat, which makes stops at coves and islands along the Sounds; take a day walk along the famous Queen Charlotte Track for spectacular water views; or join a kayak tour (you might just see some seals and dolphins as you paddle around). Have dinner along the foreshore and turn in early.

The next morning, head out of town to the Blenheim region, where the rolling hills are covered with grapevines and filled with scores of wineries. Stop in for tastings at esteemed spots like the Seresin Estate, Cloudy Bay, and Allan Scott Wines; if you've prebooked, you might also be able to dine at Herzog or Hunter's Vineyard Restaurant. Be sure to pick up a few bottles of wine and olive oil to take with you.

Kaikoura

1 day. Get an early start and continue down the South Island's eastern coast to the seaside settlement of Kaikoura, where you can go whale-watching, reef diving, swimming with dolphins or seals, or stay on land and indulge in a big crayfish lunch ("Kaikoura" actually means "meal of crayfish" in the Māori language).

NORTH ISLAND

Christchurch

1 or 2 days. Although Christchurch, "The Garden City," is the South Island's largest city, it's still a relaxing place to be. Depending on when you get here from Kaikoura, you can stroll through the city center, visit the Arts Centre (especially fun during the weekend market), the Botanic Gardens, or one of the city's museums or galleries. For a two-day stay, fit in a couple of hours at the International Antarctic Centre after a ride on the Christchurch Gondola. You might enjoy a cruise to see the endangered Hector's dolphins. The next morning, get an early start to make the push to Queenstown.

Queenstown

2 or 3 days. Depending on your appetite for adventure, Queenstown may be the locus of your South Island trip. Take the plunge with AJ Hackett Bungy, free-fall on the Shotover Canyon Swing, try a jet-boat ride, or go rafting. As the town is set on Lake Wakatipu with the jagged peaks of the Remarkables mountains around it, you won't lack for scenic distractions. If you're interested in the area's gold-mining history, detour to nearby Arrowtown and see the Lakes District Museum. If the area looks familiar, you're not dreaming: many scenes from the *Lord of the Rings* film trilogy were shot here.

Fiordland National Park

2 days. Follow your extreme sports adventure with some extremely splendid landscapes. At Milford and Doubtful sounds in Fiordland National Park, deep green slopes fall steeply down to crystalline waters. Rare species live in the unique underwater environment here, so try to visit the Milford Deep Underwater Observatory. Drink in the views by catamaran, by kayak, or by flightseeing. Whatever

you do, don't forget your rain gear and bug repellent! If pressed, you could make a trip to Milford Sound a long day's trip from Queenstown.

Other Top Options

2 or 3 days. With more time in your schedule, build in a couple of low-key days to offset the thrills-and-chills outdoor activities. After you arrive at Picton, you can drive or take a bus to Nelson, a relaxed waterfront town that's a good base for arts and crafts shopping and wine tasting. One fun stop is the World of Wearable Art & Collectable Cars Museum. If ice is on your mind and you're willing to brave rainy conditions, push on down the rugged West Coast, stopping at the Pancake Rocks—columns of limestone resembling stacks of pancakes—on your way to the Fox or Franz Josef glaciers in Westland National Park. Their flow rates are up to 10 times the speed of most valley glaciers. (To do this, plan on three days, as it's a long drive and you'll want at least one full day at the glaciers.)

TWO-ISLAND TRIP OF A LIFETIME

14 to 15 days

New Zealand may be small, but it is one of the most geographically diverse places on the planet. This ever-changing landscape is ideal to experience from the road. While we suggest taking your time to see both islands, if you've only got two or three weeks to do it all, here's a quick-hit itinerary for both islands:

North Island

1 day. Auckland. Stop at the city's museums and galleries, but save some time to shop in the Parnell neighborhood.

1 day. Taupo. Try trout fishing, or tramp the best one-day walk in the world: the Tongariro Crossing.

1 day. Wellington. Take in Te Papa Tongarewa—the Museum of New Zealand, and then have dinner along the waterfront.

South Island

2 days. Christchurch (with a side trip to Hanmer Springs, Kaikoura or the Banks Peninsula). Visit the museums or the International Antarctic Centre after a ride on the Christchurch Gondola.

1 day. Aoraki/Mt. Cook. Experience the nearby glacier lakes. En route from Christchurch, stop for a picnic by Caribbean-colored Lake Tekapo or Lake Pukaki.

2 days. Queenstown. Bungy jump, take a jet-boat ride, or go rafting. Or, just take in stunning Lake Wakatipu and the Remarkables.

1 day. Milford Sound. Spend the morning driving through Fiordland, and then take an overnight cruise.

2 days. Wanaka. Go fishing, canyoning, kayaking, mountain biking, hiking, museum-visiting, or shopping.

1 day. Franz Josef or Fox Glaciers. See cascading waterfalls, forests, and icy blue rivers and pools before taking a glacier tour (book in advance).

1 day. Hokitika. Stroll the town shops, carve your own piece of greenstone, and have coffee on the beach. At dusk, walk to the glow-worm grotto.

1 day. Arthur's Pass. Take in remote terrain before heading back to Christchurch.

2 days. Return to Christchurch and then homeward from Auckland the next day.

TASTES OF NEW ZEALAND

The New Zealand food and wine scene had an earthy beginning. Traditional Māori staples included fish, bird, and root vegetables like *kūmara* (sweet potato) cooked slowly in an underground pit known as a *hāngi*. With the Europeans came livestock (sheep, cattle and pigs), and a meat-and-potato diet. However, the past 20 years have seen a growth spurt in the New Zealand food and wine industries. Farmers and consumers quickly developing a taste and reputation for sustainable, seasonable fare, and more and more chefs have incorporated foreign influences into local cuisine.

New Zealand food has been described as "Pacific Rim" or "Pacific Rim fusion," which is an expansive term that incorporates Asian and Pacific Island influences with traditional European-style mainstays. Breakfast includes eggs, muesli, and fruit. Sandwiches and sushi are common lunches, and Indian food, seafood, fish-and-chips, and game meats (steak, boar, and venison) are common for dinner. While vegetarian restaurants are rare most restaurants serve vegetarian options.

There isn't much cuisine that is unique to New Zealand, although it is well-known for pavlova (meringue topped with cream and fruit), hokey pokey ice cream (vanilla with golden toffee), hāngi, and Manuka honey.

New Zealand has some of the largest fishing grounds in the world, so seafood is a must-have. Greenshell mussels, often cooked with lemongrass and coconut, are large and succulent. Bluff Oysters can only be found in New Zealand and are pulled from the deep waters off the South Island in mid-April. *Paua* (abalone) are also abundant along the coast, as is crayfish (rock lobster) and hundreds of fish varieties, including Marlborough-farmed salmon, trout, and *terakihi*. A local favorite is whitebait, a small fish caught in rivers and marine estuaries from September to mid-November.

Kiwis are also known for their kiwifruits and other fresh produce, such as olives, citrus fruit, and green vegetables. The best produce is found at roadside stalls or farmers' markets, which have become hugely popular Saturday and Sunday morning haunts. Favorite markets include the Lyttelton Farmers Market, the Hawke's Bay Farmers Market, the Wellington Sunday Market, and the Farmers @ Founders in Nelson.

New Zealand's wine industry has flourished along with its cuisine. Marlborough produces award-winning sauvignon blancs, and pinots and chardonnays are also making names for themselves. Wines are reasonably priced and boutique vineyards are inviting.

But, wine isn't the only beverage on the menu. There's also a variety of quality beers, microbrews, and liquor: check out 42 Below vodka in flavors like feijoa and Manuka honey. Coffee is also becoming a serious business, alongside the burgeoning café culture. Flat whites (steamed milk over a shot of espresso) are the favorite. Kiwis take their tea British-style, with milk, so order it black if you prefer it without milk.

Kiwis love to combine quality cuisine with a good party. Hokitika Wildfoods Festival, Toast Martinborough, the Bluff Oyster & Southland Seafood Festival, Auckland's Devonport Food and Wine Festival, the Gisborne Food and Wine Festival, and Harvest Hawke's Bay are just a few local celebrations.

THE NATIONAL PARKS

Tongariro was the first national park, established in 1887, a mere 47 years after the Treaty of Waitangi was signed. Since then, a full one-third of New Zealand, more than 12 million acres, has been protected in parks and reserves. New Zealand has 14 national parks, three maritime parks, two marine reserves, three World Heritage areas, countless forest parks, and nine Great Walks—not bad for a small country.

New Zealanders love their land, which is geologically and ecologically diverse as any place on Earth. It is a love inherited from the strong relationship Māori have with the land, and visitors feel it. New Zealand's national parks are its top attraction, and anyone who stands on Tongariro and gazes down over the Emerald Lakes, or sees Mitre Peak rising fanglike from the Milford Sound, or wanders ferny trails of native forest that seems straight out of Fangorn will immediately feel the power and passion of the land.

It is a myth that New Zealand is "100% Pure." Agriculture, the leading industry, is responsible for erosion, pollution, and depletion. Although it is responsible for most of New Zealand's greenhouse gas emissions, the industry is exempt from paying carbon emissions until 2012, and it is still subsidized until 2025.

New Zealand's second leading industry, tourism, also has a huge impact on the land and this is where you can help. New Zealand can affect change quickly, and Kiwis are already making great strides toward preserving and protecting their natural resources. They have the potential to become ecotourism world leaders, and conscious travelers can help: treat the parks and landscape with respect, ask questions of tourism operators, bring your environmental knowledge here and teach what you know.

The Department of Conservation (DOC, www.doc.govt.nz) is a great resource for people looking to visit the parks. December through March is the best time to visit, but keep in mind that New Zealanders love to play in their own backyard, too, and it can get crowded. Be aware that weather conditions can change at any time, even in the summer, and some areas of New Zealand (Arthur's Pass, Tongariro, Aoraki/Mt. Cook) are virtually inaccessible in the winter. Visitors often underestimate the unpredictability of the weather or the difficulty of the terrain and search-and-rescues (and fatalities) happen. Pay attention to DOC signs and closures, even if it is a simple rope across a track—New Zealanders want to look after the safety of their visitors, but remember that this is a country of personal accountability and responsibility. Visitors to New Zealand are allowed nearly unprecedented access to the landscape, so enjoy it, but treat it with respect.

The chart on the next page indicates which outdoor sports are common in each of the parks and the best time of year to experience each activity.

NATIONAL PARKS ACTIVITIES

	Hiking	Biking	Water Sports*	Fishing	Skiing	Sailing
Tongariro National Park (Ch 5)	●	◐	○	○	●	○
	◐	○	○	○	◐	○
Te Urewera (Ch. 5)	●	○	●	●	○	●
	●	○	◐	◐	○	◐
Egmont National Park (Ch 6)	●	○	○	○	◐	○
	●	○	○	○	◐	○
Whanganui (Ch. 6)	●	○	●	●	○	○
	●	○	●	●	○	○
Abel Tasman National Park (Ch 8)	●	●	●	○	○	●
	●	●	●	○	○	●
Kahurangi (Ch. 8)	●	○	●	●	○	○
	●	○	●	●	○	○
Paparoa (Ch. 8)	●	○	●	○	○	○
	●	○	●	○	○	○
Nelson Lake National Park (Ch 8)	●	●	●	●	○	◐
	◐	◐	◐	◐	◐	◐
Westland National Park (Ch 8)	●	○	○	○	◐	○
	●	○	○	○	○	○
Arthur's Pass (Ch. 9)	●	●	○	○	◐	○
	●	◐	○	○	◐	○
Fiordland National Park (Ch 10)	●	○	◐	●	○	○
	●	○	○	●	○	○
Aoraki/Mt. Cook (Ch. 10)	●	●	○	○	◐	○
	●	◐	○	○	●	○
Mt. Aspiring (Ch. 10)	●	○	◐	○	○	○
	●	○	◐	○	○	○
Rakiura (Ch. 11)	●	○	◐	○	○	○
	●	○	◐	○	○	○

KEY

Spring/Summer ● = Frequently available ◐ = Some available ○ = Not available
Fall/Winter ● = Frequently available ◐ = Some available ○ = Not available
*Water Sports include kayaking, canoeing, diving and rafting.

TOUR OPERATORS

You can always travel without a guide, but in unfamiliar territory you'll learn more with a knowledgeable local by your side. If you're interested in a multiday excursion book it at least several weeks in advance. The companies listed here cover large regions of one or both islands. Throughout the book, more tour operators for specific locations are listed.

Fishing

Licenses and Limits: Different districts require different licenses when fishing for trout, so check at the local tackle store. Fees are approximately $60 per year, but at most tackle shops, you can purchase a daily or weekly license. No license is needed for saltwater fishing.

Season: October–June in streams and rivers; year-round in lakes and at sea.

Best Locations: Countrywide.

Cost: Big-game fishing: $275 per person, per day. Heli-fishing: from $545 per person, per day. Trolling and fly-fishing for lake trout: from $75 per hour (one to four people), on rivers and streams from $75 per hour. Charter costs vary widely.

North Island Contacts Baker Marine Charters (☎ 07/307–0015 or 0800/494–0324 ⊕ www.divenfish.co.nz). **Blue Ocean Charters** (☎ 07/578–9685 ⊕ www.blueoceancharters.co.nz). **Central Plateau Fishing** (☎ 07/378–8192 ⊕ www.cpf.net.nz).

South Island Contacts Anaru Accommodation and Charters (☎ 03/576–5260). **Dean Harrison** (☎ 021/324–229 ⊕ www.flyfishingadventures.co.nz). **Fishing & Hunting Amongst Friends** (☎ 027/535–6651 mobile ⊕ www.flyfishhunt.co.nz). **Harvey Maguire** (☎ 03/442–7061 ⊕ www.flyfishing.net.nz).

Hiking

Season: October–March for high-altitude walks, year-round for others.

Best Locations: Tongariro National Park in North Island; Aoraki, Westland, Abel Tasman, Fiordland parks in South Island.

Cost: One- to three-day guided hikes are $150 to $1,050. Prices for longer hikes vary widely.

Hike New Zealand runs 5- to 10-day group hiking tours on both islands. ☎ 0800/697–232 ⊕ www.HikingNewZealand.com.

North Island Contacts Bush & Beach (☎ 09/837–4130 ⊕ www.bushandbeach.co.nz). **Kiwi Dundee Adventures, Ltd.** (☎ 07/865–8809 ⊕ www.kiwidundee.co.nz).

South Island Contacts Alpine Guides Ltd. (☎ 03/435–1834 ⊕ www.alpineguides.co.nz). **Alpine Recreation** (☎ 03/680–6736 ⊕ www.alpinerecreation.com). **Guided Walks New Zealand Ltd.** (☎ 03/442–7126 ⊕ www.nzwalks.com). **Marlborough Sounds Adventure Company** (☎ 03/573–6078 or 0800/283–283 ⊕ www.marlboroughsounds.co.nz). **Ultimate Hikes** (☎ 0800/659–255 ⊕ www.ultimatehikes.co.nz). **Wild West Adventure Co.** (☎ 03/768–6649 ⊕ www.fun-nz.com).

Horse Trekking

Season: October–March.

Best Locations: Northland and the Coromandel Peninsula in the North Island, Nelson and Canterbury high country in the South Island.

Cost: Prices range from about $115 for two hours to $225 for a day trip, or $495 for overnight; contact outfitters for specifics on shorter or multiday trips.

Cape Farewell Horse Treks operates horse treks from Puponga in Golden Bay at the northwest tip of the South Island, taking in gorgeous beach scenery with giant limestone rocks and caves and lush

palm-studded forests. They also lead four- to five-day treks down the isolated West Coast under cliffs full of huge fossils. From $45. **South Island.** ⌖ *R.D. 1, Puponga, Collingwood 7054* ☎ *03/524–8031* ⊕ *www.horsetreksnz.com.*

Dart Stables Glenorchy, based near Queenstown, takes small groups out on trips ranging from two hours to three days; some of this South Island territory is where much of the *Lord of the Rings* was filmed. There are rides suitable for beginners and more advanced equestrians. $105 two hours, $215 full day. **South Island.** ⌖ *Box 47, Glenorchy 9350* ☎ *03/442–5688 or 0800/474–3464* ⊕ *www.dartstables.com.*

Hurunui Horse Treks has a variety of rides, including 8- and 10-day horse treks into remote backcountry, where the terrain varies from dense scrub to open meadows to alpine passes. Accommodation options include rustic huts (without electricity, showers, or flush toilets) or more comfortable farm stays; groups are generally limited to six or fewer. $150–$2,975. **South Island.** ✉ *757 The Peaks Rd.* ⌖ *R.D., Hawarden, North Canterbury 7348* ☎ *03/314–4204* ⊕ *www.hurunui.co.nz.*

Pakiri Beach Horse Rides, north of Auckland, runs trips from several hours to several days, all incorporating a ride on the namesake white-sand beach. You might ride through groves of *pohutukawa*, which are ablaze with red flowers in the summer, or across the sand dunes with inspiring views of islands on the horizon. $99 for half day, $199 full day. **North Island.** ✉ *Taurere Park, Rahuikiri Rd., Pakiri, Wellsford* ☎ *09/422–6275* ⊕ *www.horseride-nz.co.nz.*

Halfway between Whitianga and Tairua on the Coromandel Peninsula, **Rangihau Ranch** leads short rides of an hour or two; the routes follow pack-horse trails from the 1800s with wonderful views of the bush-clad Coromandel mountains, Mercury Bay, and the Pacific Ocean. They specialize in working with inexperienced riders. **North Island.** ✉ *Rangihau Rd., Coroglen* ☎ *07/866–3875.*

With **Stonehurst Farm Horse Treks,** trek through 1,000 acres of a working farm near Nelson with panoramic views over the mountains and Golden Bay. Their treks, for riders of all abilities, run from one hour to a half day. $55 per hour, $105 half day. **South Island.** ✉ *Stonehurst Farm, Clover Rd.* ⌖ *R.D. 1, Richmond, Nelson 7091* ☎ *03/542–4121 or 0800/487–357* ⊕ *www.stonehurstfarm.co.nz.*

Sailing

Season: Year-round.

Best Locations: Bay of Islands in the North Island, upper and lower South Island.

Cost: Bay of Islands from $75 for a day trip to $690 to $830; Doubtful Sound from $1,725 for five days; Fiordland National Park from $3,510 for eight days.

North Island Contacts Tauranga Sailing School and Yacht Charters (☎ *07/548–0689, 025/289–5594 mobile*).

South Island Contacts Catamaran Sailing Charters (☎ *03/547–6666* ⊕ *www.sailingcharters.co.nz*).

TRAMPING NEW ZEALAND

by Oliver Wigmore

Tramping (hiking) in the backcountry is a sacred kiwi pastime. Pristine coastal beaches, meandering rivers, glaciated peaks, steaming volcanoes, isolated lakes, cascading waterfalls, and lush native forest are often just an hour's drive from the major cities. You can "get amongst it" all with short walks, one-day tramps, or multiday hikes.

Many of New Zealand's best tramps are within the 14 national parks. The Department of Conservation (DOC) manages these parks and additional lands totalling over 80,000 km², almost 30 percent of New Zealand. DOC maintains a range of tracks, walkways, huts, and campgrounds throughout these areas.

The Great Walks are the nine most renowned hiking (though one is technically a canoeing route) tracks, which traverse the country's volcanic plateau beaches, temperate rainforest, fjords, and mountain ranges. The most famous, Milford Track, is commonly called "the finest walk in the world." Collectively the Great Walks see over 86,000 trampers annually.

However hundreds of other tracks and routes crisscross the country, ranging from gruelling week-long, self-guided adventures to mellow, half-hour strolls through native bush. Often on these tracks you'll have the scenery to yourself. The range of difficulty and variety of terrain means almost anyone can experience tramping in New Zealand.

Milford Track.

PLANNING TIPS

■ During summer book accommodations well in advance, especially for the **Milford Track**.

■ DOC lowers fees from May to September. However alpine tracks may be impassable or closed.

■ Skip popular day walks such as the **Tongariro Alpine Crossing** over long weekends to avoid crowds.

■ Many tracks require transport. Book in advance through local tour operators.

BEST ONE-DAY HIKES

You don't need to commit to a three-day trek in order to see New Zealand by foot. These one-day hikes will give you a sense of New Zealand's landscapes sans huts and tents.

Tongariro Alpine Crossing: Explore the central North Island's alpine scenery, steaming fumaroles, volcanic craters, and brilliant emerald lakes on the country's most popular day walk. In summer the hike is somewhat strenuous, though not technically difficult. In winter it requires high-alpine experience. Hikers generally walk from Mangatepopo to Ketetahi, with side trips to the summits of Ngauruhoe and Tongariro.

Abel Tasman National Park: The park's easily-accessible, golden-sand coastlines require limited fitness. Perhaps the best of the many day walks on the Abel Tasman Coast Track is from Totaranui to Separation Point, where seals are visible in winter and autumn. Water taxi from Marahau transport visitors to a number of different points along the track.

Fiordland National Park: There are a number of short walks from the roadside on the drive to Milford Sound. These range from easy to difficult and from 30 minutes to a day. Key Summit (medium) and Gertrude Saddle (difficult) take in some of New Zealand's most amazing mountain scenery. Don't miss Bowen Falls, an easy 30 minute walk along Milford Sound's foreshore.

Queenstown: A number of day walks start at Glenorchy at Lake Wakatipu's north end. You can access short sections of the Routeburn, Caples, and Greenstone tracks, where alpine scenery is the star. The walk to Routeburn Falls is particularly spectacular, well graded, and of medium difficulty.

(top left) Hollyford Track, Fiordland National Park. (right) Routeburn Falls, Mt. Aspiring National Park. (bottom left) Anchorage Hut, Abel Tasman National Park. (opposite page) Routeburn Track.

GREAT WALKS

NORTH ISLAND TRACK	DIFFICULTY	ACTIVITIES / ATTRACTIONS
❶ LAKE WAIKAREMOANA TRACK, Te Urewera National Park (Ch. 5) 46 km (28.5mi), 3-4 days	Moderate. The tougest part is the climb from lake edge to Panekiri Bluffs. Heavy rain, mosquitoes and sand-flies are common.	Much of the track runs through podocarp forest. Track condition is genearlly good. The best views are from Panekiri Bluffs. See a variety of birds: kaka, parakeets, paradise ducks, whiteheads, fantails, silvereyes, morepork (native owl), kiwi. Don't miss the short uphill side trip to Korokoro waterfall. Advance booking advised.
❷ TONGARIRO NORTHERN CIRCUIT, Tongariro National Park (Ch. 5) 49 km (30 mi), 3-4 days	Moderate. Take good gear. especially for the toughest section, the "Staircase." Do not attempt the track in rain or snow. Volcano eruptions are possbible; stay back from steam vents.	This is one of New Zealand's best walks, with wonderful alpine and volcanic vistas, warm blue-green lakes, and steam vents, but mountains are often in heavy clouds. You'll see Mt. Ngauruhoe—a.k.a Mt. Doom in *The Lord of the Rings.*
❸ WHANGANUI JOURNEY, Whanganui National Park, near Taumarunui (Ch. 8) Full Trip: 145 km (90 mi,) 5 days Short Trip: 88 km (54.5 mi,) 3 days	Moderate. Those with experience can swim, canoe, and kayak. Be prepared for rain and floods.	Although a river journey, Whanganui is a Great Walk, and there is a 3-day version from Whaka-horo to Pipiriki. The Whanganui river takes a twisting path to sea; en route, expect narrow gorges, high cliffs, waterfalls, glowworm grottos. Tieke Marae has good huts and facilities, but you'll follow Maori protocol; koha (a gift of money) will be expected. Book trip and hire kayaks in advance from operators in Turangi, Taumaruni, or Ohakune.

For mountain landscapes and alpine scenery, the South Island and stunning **Fiordland National Park** are the clear winners.

Auckland
NORTH ISLAND
Rotorua ❶
❸ ❷
Napier
WELLINGTON
❹ Nelson
❺
Christchurch
SOUTH ISLAND
❻
❼ Te Anau
❽
❾ Stewart Is.

NORTH ISLAND
Tramping on the North Island is hard to beat: rivers, beaches, and otherworldly volcanic cones are all on offer here.

SOUTH ISLAND
Abel Tasman National Park provides beautiful beaches and lazy days. Warm, more stable weather generally occurs between January and April, but they're also the busiest.

SOUTH ISLAND TRACK	DIFFICULTY	ACTIVITIES/ATTRACTIONS
❹ ABEL TASMAN COAST TRACK, Abel Tasman National Park, near Nelson (Ch. 8) 52 km (32 mi), 3–5 days	**Moderate.** In autumn and winter, walking and weather conditions are good and the track is less crowded.	Follow the coast across beautiful golden sand beaches, rocks, and regenerating rain forests (with nikau palms, ferns, and forest gians). The two estuaries are only passable around low tide. You may spot seals and penguins
❺ HEAPHY TRACK, Kahurangie National Park, near Nelson (Ch. 8) 78 km (48 mi), 4–6 days	**Moderate.** The most difficult section is between Brown and Perry Saddle huts. While normally a drier area, it does rain on the western slopes.	The track begins in dense beech and podocarp forest in north; continues up to snow tussock plateaus; and descends into palm-studded forests, rugged West Coast beaches. See bird, including kiwis and pipits, along one of the country's finest routes. This is primarily a summer route; snow can block the track in winter.
❻ ROUTEBURN TRACK , Mount Aspiring and Fiordland national parks (Ch. 10) 32 km (20 mi), 2–3 days	**Moderate.** Heavy rain, clouds, snow, and ice can be factors. On mountaintops, winter avalanches are possible.	Travel in either direction through beech forest and onto exposed mountaintops for spectacular scenery. In summer flowers, many unique to New Zealand, cover the alpine slopes. You'll need good equipment to travel this route.
❼ MILFORD TRACK, Fiordland National Park, near Te Anau (Ch. 10) 54 km (33.5 mi), 4–5 days.	**Moderate.** There are two strenuous climbs, one with a very steep descent. It frequently rains. Beware of avalanche conditions at Mackinnon Pass in winter.	You can only hike in on direction (south to north) along New Zealand's most popular track. Clinton River (often muddy) crosses Mackinnon Pass, goes through alpine meadows, and passes waterfalls, including NZ's highest, Sutherland Falls. Thick forests bookend the track, and lots of kea (mountain parrots) greet trampers. Book at least four months ahead; sandfly repellent is a must.
❽ KEPLER TRACK, Fiordland National Park, near Te Anau (Ch. 10) 60 km (37 mi), 3–4 days	**Moderate.** Day one includes a steep climb from lake to tops.	The hike goes through beech forests to sometimes snow-covered tussock tops with wonderful views in clear weather. Geology buffs will appreciate this trek, especially Mt. Luxmore. Detour to Iris Burn waterfall, 20-minute walk from Iris Burn hut.
❾ RAKIURA TRACK, Rakiura National Park, Steward Island (Ch. 11) 36 km (22 mi, including road walk), 3 days.	**Moderate.** There are two short uphill climbs. Be prepared to get muddy in the wet changeable weather. Expect mosquitoes and sandflies.	Follows the coastline through beech forest, subalpine scrub, and remote beaches. Mt. Anglem, a 3–4 hour side trip (one-way), provides wonderful views. Birdlife includes kiwi, bellbirds, tui, fantails, and parakeets. You may see seals and penguins. Hut tickets are required; there's some camping. Pack extra food and insect repellent.

WHAT TO BRING

Weather in New Zealand is unpredictable to say the least, so it is extremely important to be prepared and to carry the right equipment. In the mountains you should prepare for cold, wet weather year-round; in the north you can generally travel a little lighter, but there is nothing worse than walking for five hours shivering and wet because you forgot a decent jacket.

Tramping gear is widely available throughout New Zealand for rental or purchase, but is usually more expensive than in the United States. You must declare all used camping and hiking equipment on arrival. The Ministry of Agriculture and Fisheries (MAF) will inspect and sterilize your equipment, which is usually available for immediate collection. By not declaring your gear you risk not only a hefty fine but also the fragile New Zealand ecosystem, which is extremely susceptible to invasive foreign species.

The equipment you carry and the fitness required depends hugely on where you are heading and how long and at what time of year you're going. In general you should carry:

A good-quality three-season hiking tent (for overnighters).

Tramping clothes, i.e., polypropylene underwear, fleece, etc.

Warm sleeping bag in the winter (year-round in the South Island).

Personal first-aid kit and insect repellent.

Topographic maps (widely available throughout the country). Though not required for the majority of marked tracks, they should be carried when venturing into the back country.

Three-season Tent

Sleeping bag

Fleece jacket

Polypropylene underwear tights and top

WHAT TO WEAR

BASE LAYER: Wear lightweight thermal underwear, preferably polypropylene or other moisture wicking synthetic fabric.

MID LAYER: Fleece, wool, or synthetic jer(preferable for their lighter weight and rapid drying time) go over the base layer. This layer should keep you warm when wet (no cotton sweatshirts).

BACKPACK: Take a sturdy, comfortable pack that fits you well. Take a larger pack for longer tracks. Strong canvas fabric is best.

GAITERS: If walking through thick mud, water, or snow, tramping gaiters (covers for your shoes and pants) are a must.

The key thing to remember is layering. Wearing multiple layers of clothing allows you to rapidly adjust to changing temperatures and different exertion levels. Modern synthetic fabrics are preferable for their lightweight, quick drying times, and ability to keep you warm when wet.

HAT AND GLOVES: Bring a warm hat and gloves made from wool or synthetic.

SUN PROTECTION: Bring a sunhat and sunglasses.

OUTER LAYER: A water- and windproof outer layer, is necessary. In addition to a jacket bring overtrousers for many tracks, especially in the winter.

TROUSERS/SHORTS: Strong synthetic fabrics are best because they dry quickly when wet. No jeans!

SOCKS: Wool or synthetic hiking socks to keep your feet warm.

FOOTWEAR: The most important part, boots should be strong, sturdy, and waterproof. For longer, more rugged tramps full leather boots are best, but on shorter tramps and day walks lightweight fabric boots are often sufficient.

CHOOSING YOUR TRACK

Pick your hike based on the type of experience you're looking for and the time of year you plan on visiting. The DOC has five classifications for walks to help you decide which tracks are best suited for your experience and fitness level.

Short Walks: These easy walks last up to an hour along an even, graded surface and are suitable for all fitness levels.

Walking Tracks: These easy to moderate walks take from a few minutes to a day on reasonably well-formed but occasionally steep tracks. They are clearly signposted and suitable for people with low to moderate fitness. You may need light hiking boots in winter.

Easy Tramping Tracks: These single or multiday, signposted tracks for people of moderate fitness are well formed but may be steep and muddy. Wear light hiking boots. This category includes all the Great Walks.

Trampers crossing a bridge on the Routeburn Track, above the Hollyford Valley, Fiordland National Park

Tramping Tracks: Trampers need good fitness and moderate back country experience, including navigation and survival skills, to walk these challenging single or multiday unformed trails. Generally marked with poles or rock cairns, trails may include unbridged river crossings; appropriate equipment, sturdy hiking boots, and preparation are required.

Route: You need a lot of backcountry survival and navigational experience, a high level of fitness, sturdy hiking boots and equipment, and preparation for these treks through natural terrain. Tracks may have basic markings, but trampers should be self-sufficient.

Visit DOC's information offices, in all major towns and the national parks, for information and lists of experienced guides, and to register your intentions. Inexperienced trampers should consider guided trips, which remove some of the organizational hassle and provide additional safety. Guides are generally friendly and extremely knowledgeable, and group trips are a great way to meet other travelers.

HUTS

DOC maintains a network of over 950 backcountry huts throughout New Zealand's conservation areas that are available for a small fee. Accommodations range from basic 4-person shelters offering a roof and a mattress to 20-person buildings complete with cooking facilities, toilets, lights, and heating. It's best to book huts well in advance. Book huts on the DOC Web site or by contacting the local DOC office. During the busy months custodians check for payment; however in the off season, respect the honesty system. Fees keep these places pristine and accessible to the public.

Auckland

WORD OF MOUTH

"Before visiting Auckland I thought about staying in Ponsonby. However, I stayed in the center of Auckland and was glad I did. I took the Link bus . . . to Ponsonby for lunch or dinner. I could walk to The Viaduct, Queen Street (shopping), parks, and wine bars and restaurants. I'll stay [there] on my next visit."

—Castleblanca

WELCOME TO AUCKLAND

TOP REASONS TO GO

★ **Boating and Sailing:** Aucklanders are crazy about boating. Get on the water surrounding the "City of Sails" on a commuter ferry, a sailboat, or a racing yacht.

★ **Cuisine and Café Culture:** Auckland has some of the country's finest restaurants, as well as little bistro bars, noodle houses, and vibrant neighborhood eateries and cafés.

★ **Year-Round Golf:** Frank Nobilo's hometown has more than 20 golf courses, from informal to challenging championship level. Most have stunning scenery, and at the Muriwai Golf Club you can go surfing, too.

★ **Gorgeous Beaches:** The West Coast's black-sand beaches attract surfers from around the world; the safest swimming is on the East Coast. Takapuna Beach and Mission Bay are good places to swim. Remember to swim between the flags and slap on the sunscreen.

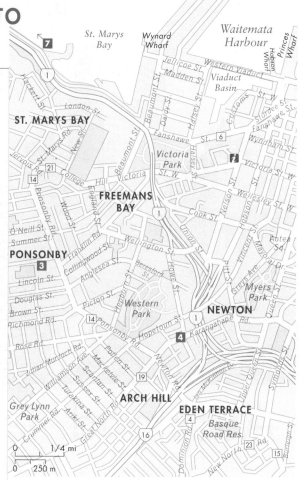

1 Central Business District. Aucklanders see the central business district as the waterfront and Queen Street.

2 Parnell. To the east of the city center this district has historic buildings, good restaurants, water views, and frequent celebrity sightings.

3 Ponsonby. Explore narrow streets lined with wooden Victorian villas and stroll along the main strip, which is lined with cafés, bars, restaurants, and local designer clothing stores.

4 Karangahape Road. K Road sits to the west of the center, with a mix of shops, cheap eateries, and clubs.

GETTING ORIENTED

The drive from the airport, once you pass some industrial parks, presents the standard image of New Zealand—clean and green with the landscape dominated by the city's 50 or so volcanic hills, many set aside as parks with their grassy flanks shorn by sheep. The Auckland region is geographically diverse, and Auckland City sits on an isthmus between the Waitemata (to the east) and Manukau Harbour (to the southwest). At its narrowest point the isthmus is only 1 km (½ mi) wide. The Orakei and Panmure basins, which are east of the city, are actually large craters that have been invaded by the sea. Like many parts of the country, there's plenty of outdoor activity on the easy rolling terrain outside the central suburban areas and in some of the city's big parks. The many islands of the Hauraki Gulf, off Auckland's east coast, give the chance to explore by sea.

5 Newmarket. One of the better areas for buying local and overseas designer goods, this neighborhood includes the Domain—a park with good walking and running trails, stunning harbor views, and sculptures.

6 Remuera. "Old money" families like to live in this tony suburb close to the Domain.

7 North Shore. The Auckland Harbour Bridge spans the Waitemata Harbour, connecting the city with the North Shore's suburbs and safe swimming beaches.

8 Hauraki Gulf Islands. Rangitoto, Waiheke, Rakino, and Motutapu islands, all have great walking and nature sites.

AUCKLAND PLANNER

Planning Your Time

Auckland is big, so plan ahead. Allow yourself three days to navigate the city.

Day 1: Go outdoors out west. The Waitakere Ranges's native forests provide easy walks. Bring walking shoes, a day pack, water, a raincoat, and a sweater. Stop at a West Coast beach, too.

Day 2: Go shopping in Newmarket or Ponsonby in the morning before ferrying to Waiheke Island to tour wineries and have dinner.

Day 3: Take in some adventure or culture. Sky Tower has high-flying city views. See Māori artifacts at Auckland War Memorial Museum or get out of town for a game of golf.

When to Go

Auckland's weather can be unpredictable, but don't let that put you off. There is always something to do whatever the weather. The warmest months are December through April and a sun hat is a good idea. Winter is between July and October. It can be humid in summer and quite chilly in winter. It often rains, so be prepared.

Getting Here

Air Travel

Auckland International Airport (AKL) lies 21 km (13 mi) southwest of the city center, about a 30-minute drive away. It has adopted a "quiet airport" policy, so it doesn't use loudspeakers to announce boarding times. Look for flight info.

A free interterminal bus links the international and domestic terminals from 6 AM to 10 PM. Otherwise, the walk between the two terminals takes about 10 minutes. Luggage for flights aboard the two major domestic airlines, Air New Zealand and Qantas Airways, can be checked at the international terminal.

Air New Zealand, Qantas and its budget airline Jetstar, and Virgin subsidiary Pacific Blue are the main domestic carriers serving Auckland. Air New Zealand connects with 25 domestic cities a day, and makes about 10 flights a day to Australia. Jetstar also connects Auckland with many cities and compliments Qantas's cross-Tasman service; Jetstar service can be unpredictable and require check-in one hour before departure. Air Tahiti Nui stops off in Auckland on its LA and New York runs.

Airport Auckland International Airport (⊠ *Fred Thomas Dr., Manukau* ☎ *09/275–0789* ⊕ *www.auckland-airport.co.nz*).

Train Travel

KiwiRail, New Zealand's train industry, has a terminal and booking office at the Britomart Transportation Centre, on the harbor end of Queen Street. Service runs between Auckland and Wellington. The service runs daily between November and April and on Friday, Saturday, and Sunday the rest of the year.

Contact Britomart Transport Centre (⊠ *Queen Elizabeth Sq., Queen and Quay Sts.* ☎ *0800/872–467* ⊕ *www.tranzscenic.co.nz*).

2

Getting Around

Bus Travel Within Auckland

The easily recognizable white Link Buses, run by Maxx, circle the inner city every 10 minutes between 6 AM and 7 PM weekdays, and then every 15 minutes until about 11:30 PM. Weekend service runs from 7 AM to 6 PM. The route includes the Britomart Centre between Customs and Quay streets, Queen Street, Parnell, Newmarket (near the Auckland War Memorial Museum), Ponsonby, and Karangahape Road. The flat-rate fare is $1.50, payable as you board the bus; use change or small notes. A free red-color bus circuits the inner city between Britomart, the university, and the Sky Tower every 10 minutes between 8 AM and 6 PM daily.

To travel farther afield, take a Stagecoach Bus, which has service as far north as Orewa on the Hibiscus Coast and south to Pukekohe. An Auckland Day Pass ($11 for unlimited travel) is the best deal for anyone planning extensive bus travel; it includes Link and Stagecoach service and is also valid on Link ferries between the city and the North Shore. The Discovery Pass ($14) also includes the local trains. You can buy the passes from the ferry office or the bus drivers. The information office at Britomart provides information, maps, and timetables.

Contacts **Information Office** (✉ *Britomart Transport Centre, Queen Elizabeth Sq., Queen and Quay Sts., City Center*). **Maxx** (☎ *09/366–6400* ⊕ *www.maxx.co.nz*).

Car Travel

Local rush hours last from 7 to 9 AM and 4:30 to 6:30 PM. The main motorways all have convenient city turnoffs, but watch the signs carefully. The main road into and out of Auckland is State Highway 1. Off-ramps are clearly marked. Most areas have meter parking, and you can pay by coin or credit card. Fines are hefty if you overstay your time.

Auckland taxi rates vary with the company. Most are around $2 per kilometer (½ mi), but some charge as much as $4. Flag-fall, when the meters start, is usually $2. The rates are listed on the driver's door. Most taxis accept major credit cards.

Taxi Companies **Alert Taxis** (☎ *09/309–2000*). **Auckland Cooperative Taxi Service** (☎ *09/300–3000*). **Corporate Cabs** (☎ *09/377–0773*). **Eastern Taxis** (☎ *09/534–4644*).

i-Help

Need some travel advice? Drop in at one of Auckland's many i-SITEs and other visitor centers. Employees will help plan trips, provide sightseeing information, and point you toward a well-priced lunch.

Contacts **Auckland International Airport Visitor Centre** (✉ *Ground fl., International Airport Terminal* ☎ *09/275–6467*). **Auckland i-SITE Visitor Centre** (✉ *Atrium, Sky City, Victoria and Federal Sts.* ☎ *09/363–7182* ⊕ *www.aucklandnz.com*). **Department of Conservation Visitor Centre** (✉ *Ferry Bldg., Quay St.* ☎ *09/379–6476* ⊕ *www.doc.govt.nz*). **New Zealand Visitor Centre** (✉ *Princes Wharf* ☎ *09/367–6009* ⊕ *www.aucklandnz.com*).

Travel Like a Kiwi

Navigating New Zealand on your own can be daunting, but some travelers find guided tours too restrictive. InterCity's TravelPass is a nice compromise. Seventeen set itineraries on comfortable buses and commentary on the passing scenery hit the most popular spots throughout the country. Hop off anytime and stay as long as you like. Passes are valid for 12 months from activation.

Contacts **InterCity FlexiPass** (☎ *0800/222–146* ⊕ *flexipass.intercity.co.nz*). **InterCity TravelPass** (☎ *0800/339–966* ⊕ *travelpass.intercity.co.nz*).

SNACKING IN AUCKLAND

New Zealand is no place to deny yourself: the freshest ingredients, simple preparations, and excellent bakeries and cafés on nearly every corner all scream "indulge!" Go for whatever catches your eye (or your nose) and enjoy the taste of unprocessed, pure, often locally sourced foods.

Many of Auckland's best sit-down dining options are in its residential neighborhoods, enclaves that are part of the city, but, with their leafy streets and tony shops, seem like a trip to the suburbs. Break away from the tourist-laden cafés on Viaduct Harbour and pull up a chair in a hidden Parnell garden, or a shaded Ponsonby sidewalk cafe for an al fresco meal enjoyed the way Kiwis do it, with good wine and friends.

English influences are everywhere but with a modern sensibility. Your afternoon tea just might be a slice of passion fruit cake and a flat white. Nearly every street with shops has a few eateries, a fish-and-chips shop, and several places for a great coffee.

PERFECT PICNICS

Auckland's parks, with impressive native trees, beckon for outdoor dining, and gourmet shops make a perfect picnic a piece of cake. Jones the Grocer on Newmarket is like the Antipodean Zabar's with everything you could want from upscale cheeses (they are known for their walk-in cheese rooms), to freshly made sandwiches, dips, and flavored oils, even hampers to carry them in.

Faster food is already wrapped and waiting at Wishbone, a unique elegant take-out chain with creative daily soups and special salads, and light sandwiches, like chicken, Brie, and cranberries.

SNACKING THE KIWI WAY

HOKEY-POKEY ICE CREAM

Yes, you've had butter brickle, the cousin of this summertime childhood favorite, but you've never had any dairy as fresh as New Zealand butter or cream. Go for the full-fat version of this vanilla ice cream dotted with toffee bits.

KŪMARA FRIES

Guilt-free snacks, *kūmara* fries—packed with potassium and fiber—are delicious, and the kūmara, or sweet potato, has a rich heritage as a Māori food staple. Red, gold, and orange varieties are plentiful in New Zealand today. Orange is the sweetest, especially fried and served Kiwi-style with sweet chili sauce and sour cream.

PAVLOVA

Like the ballerina for whom it was named, this national dessert is feather light—a meringue topped with fruit, sauce, and fresh cream. The confection is essentially hollow, but it forms the tough core of one of the many culinary Kiwi and Aussie rivalries: who invented it first and named it for visiting Anna Pavlova? So far, Kiwis have the edge: a recipe predating the Australian one by six years. Look for the treat on the menu around Christmastime.

WHITEBAIT FRITTERS

The Kiwi passion for this seafood, a smeltlike fish caught as juveniles as they head upriver to spawn, is so intense that the media reports the start of whitebait season. Find the pancake-sized fritters at markets or as a daily special in cafes. Strict controls and popularity make it a delicious delicacy, despite the main ingredient.

THE CAFFERATTI

While Auckland is known as the City of Sails, some say it is home to the cafferatti—those who live for coffee. Aucklanders happily tick off lists of go-to coffee shops and joints to avoid. The top sin is employing an inexperienced barista; decoration and food don't factor in. In fact, some follow baristas from café to café.

The big international companies are established in Auckland, but locals prefer small independent shops that often operate in tiny spots with room for little more than a coffee machine, a small food cabinet, and a few stools. Aucklanders drink on the run, so you may see people present their own cups to be filled.

To blend in with the cafferatti, order a **flat white**—thicker and less milky than a latte, with a smoother, richer flavor than cappuccino—or a **short black** (espresso). And true members of the cafferatti never order flavoring, so save your caramel craving for when you return home.

(top left) Diners enjoy outdoor seating at an Auckland café, (bottom) Homemade pavlova with pomegranate and cream, (top) Latte art adds whimsy to a caffeine fix

AUCKLAND DESIGNERS

From frilly frocks to sleek housewares to whimsical togs for kids, Auckland's designers pepper neighborhood shops with special creations combining new fabrics, colors, and design elements you will not find at your mall back home.

Auckland's streets are a far cry from the open-air runways of New York or Paris, with most residents favoring contemporary clothing and sensible wear. But the fresh ideas and unique perspectives that leading Kiwi designers weave into their clothing will definitely start conversations if you wear any back home. And since they infuse the creations with a vein of New Zealand practicality, you'll find yourself wearing them more often than you'd planned.

If there is one catchall word to describe New Zealand's hottest fashions it would be "iconoclastic," never "understated." Target great shopping neighborhoods like Ponsonby, Parnell, and Newmarket's Nuffield Precinct, where looks are easy on the eyes in a setting that's easy on your feet: small shops are interspersed with relaxing cafes when you need a break to refuel.

SAVE ON STYLE

North American shoppers enjoy a built-in climatological advantage. Since the seasons are reversed, seasonal clearance items in New Zealand will fit the bill perfectly for weather back home. Scoop up discounted woolens in November (NZ spring) to enjoy all winter, or laze away hot spring and summer days in a February (NZ summer's end) sale-priced beach wrap.

Weekend markets often attract up-and-coming designers, and you can nab one of these pieces before its maker becomes the next big thing. The inconvenience of a make-shift dressing room can mean a one-of-a-kind find for you.

DESIGNER FASHION, NZ STYLE

KAREN WALKER

Walker has long shattered the equatorial fashion ceiling and is well-known in the pages of glossy fashion magazines for clothes that are comfortable and sophisticated, made of rich fabrics and muted colors, and pulled together by playful themes. The look suggests the bad girl with good fashion sense. She draws inspiration from mold-breaking women—Amelia Earhart and Woody Allen's "Annie Hall."

KATE SYLVESTER

Another made-in-New Zealand designer gone global, Sylvester's style is eclectic and modern, with pieces made to be worn separately or mixed and matched. The colors and fabrics reflect the themes of her collections, from the tutulike skirts in the Black Swan—a riff on classic ballet—to the T-shirts and grandpa sweaters of her grunge rocker series. Sylvester's goals are to create fashion that is sustainable and that transcends trendiness.

TRELISE COOPER

New Zealand's madcap version of the Laura Ashley empire includes home, adult, and children's lines, but without the prim-and-proper boundaries. Feminine fantasy confections of ruffles, beads, and flounces define Cooper's style. Cooper celebrates individuality and her clothes reflect this philosophy. The hallmarks of her children's items are oversized ribbons and bows.

ZAMBESI

Elisabeth and Neville Findlay have been producing fresh shapes in mix-and-match fabric textures for decades and have a worldwide following. Their edgy, modern clothing has a familiar palate, but experimental shapes and materials are both functional and challenging. A skirt may have an irregular hem or a traditionally shaped dress a metallic sheen, but all pieces maintain an inherent wearability.

UP AND COMING

Turet Knuefermann is one of New Zealand's young star designers. Her work blends high-European fashion (elegant backless dresses) with a New Zealand sense for practicality (classy, everyday pieces). At her Ponsonby area boutique, tk, she aims for approachable fashion. It all begins complimentary coffee as Brazilian music plays in the background. Rather than sell visitors on "Wow" items that quickly become "Wow, I can't believe I bought that" piles in the back of the closet, Kneufermann seeks to match her designs to the customer, guiding each one to pieces that she'll wear over and over again. You'll be in good company if you do nab a few of her pieces; Kneufermann has been a styling consultant for *New Zealand Idol* contestants and has several celebrity customers. ⊠ *50 Brown St., Ponsonby* ☎ *9/361–2020* ⊕ *www.tk.net.nz.*

(top left) Trelise Cooper's runway designs, (bottom) Zambesi is known for its black-on-black wares, (top) Kate Sylvester's designs

Updated
by Richard
Pamatatau

Auckland is called the City of Sails, and visitors flying in will see why. On the East Coast is the Waitemata Harbour—a Māori word meaning sparkling waters—which is bordered by the Hauraki Gulf, an aquatic playground peppered with small islands where many Aucklanders can be found "mucking around in boats."

Not surprising, Auckland has some 70,000 boats. About one in four households in Auckland has a seacraft of some kind and there are 102 beaches within an hour's drive; during the week many are quite empty. Even the airport is by the water; it borders the Manukau Harbour, which also takes its name from the Māori language and means solitary bird.

A couple of days in the city will reveal just how developed and sophisticated Auckland is—the Mercer City Survey 2009 saw it ranked as the fourth-highest city for quality of life—though those seeking a New York in the South Pacific will be disappointed. Auckland is more get-up and go-outside than get-dressed-up and go-out. That said, most shops are open daily, central bars and a few nightclubs buzz well into the wee hours, especially Thursday through Saturday, and a mix of Māori, Pacific people, Asians, and Europeans contributes to the cultural milieu. Auckland has the world's largest single population of Pacific Islanders living outside their home countries, though many of them live outside the central parts of the city and in Manukau to the south. Most Pacific people came to New Zealand seeking a better life. When the plentiful, low-skilled work that attracted them dried up, the dream soured, and the population has suffered with poor health and education. Luckily, policies are now addressing that, and change is slowly coming. The Pacifica Festival in March is the region's biggest cultural event, attracting thousands to Western Springs. The annual Pacific Island Competition sees young Pacific Islander and Asian students compete in traditional dance, drumming, and singing. This event is open to the public.

At the geographical center of Auckland city is the 1,082-foot Sky Tower, a convenient landmark for those exploring on foot and some say a visible sign of the city's naked aspiration. It has earned nicknames like the Needle and the Big Penis—a counterpoint to a poem by acclaimed New Zealand poet James K. Baxter that refers to Rangitoto Island as a clitoris in the harbor.

The Waitemata Harbour has become better known since New Zealand staged its first defense of the America's Cup in 2000 and the successful Louis Vuitton Pacific Series in early 2009. The first regatta saw major redevelopment of the waterfront. The area, where many of the city's most popular bars, cafés, and restaurants are located, is now known as Viaduct Basin or, more commonly, the Viaduct. On New Year's Eve it becomes a sea of people getting quite kissy.

EXPLORING AUCKLAND

You can get around city center and the suburbs close to the harbor like Ponsonby, Devonport, and Parnell, on foot, by bus, and by ferry. Elsewhere, Auckland is not as easy to explore. The neighborhoods and suburbs sprawl from the Waitemata and Manukau harbors to rural areas, and complicated roads, frequent construction, and heavy traffic can make road travel a challenge. Still it's best to have a car for getting between neighborhoods and some city center sights. What might look like an easy walking distance on a map can turn out to be a 20- to 30-minute hilly trek, and stringing a few of those together can get frustrating.

If you're nervous about driving on the left, especially when you first arrive, purchase a one-day Link Bus Pass that covers the inner-city neighborhoods and Central Business District (CBD) or, for a circuit of the main sights, an Explorer Bus Pass. Take a bus to get acquainted with the city layout. Getting around Auckland by bus is easy and inexpensive. The region's bus services are coordinated through the Maxx Service, which also coordinates trains and ferries; its Web site can provide you with door-to-door information, including bus route numbers. For journeys farther afield the Maxx company runs buses to most places in the greater Auckland area. Timetables are available at most information centers.

CITY CENTER AND PARNELL

Auckland's city center includes the port area, much of it reclaimed from the sea in the latter half of the 19th century. You'll find a farmers' market close to the foot of town on weekends. Successive city administrators neglected Auckland's older buildings, so Queen Street and its surroundings are a mix of glass-tower office buildings and a dwindling number of older, some say more gracious, buildings. Tucked away in Lorne and High streets, running parallel with Queen Street, are good examples of the city's early architecture, now home to the shops of some of New Zealand's leading fashion designers. The central business district (CBD) has been energized by a residential surge since the late 1990s, boosted by apartment development and an influx of Asian students. The Auckland Domain and Parnell areas are where you'll find the city's preeminent museums as well as historic homes and shops. Parnell

TOURING THE TOWN

Several companies run city orientation tours or special-interest excursions outside town. ⇨ *City of Sails, below, for boat tours.*

BUS TOURS

The white double-decker **Explorer Bus** (☎ *0800/439–756* ⊕ *www.explorerbus.co.nz*) stops at nine city attractions; you can hop on and off anywhere along the way. Buses begin at the Ferry Building between 9 and 4 daily. Buy tickets from the driver or at the Fullers office in the Ferry Building. A day pass is $35.

Scenic Tours (☎ *09/307–7880* ⊕ *www.scenictours.co.nz*) operates a three-hour Auckland Highlights guided bus tour that leaves from Quay Street, just across from the Ferry Building, at 9:15, and tickets are $67.

MĀORI-THEMED TOURS

Potiki Adventures (☎ *0800/692–3836* ⊕ *www.potikiadventures.com*) cultivates an air of intimacy with its small groups and friendly, open tour guides. The Urban Māori Experience includes visits to a gallery, funky café, Māori village, rain forest, and black-sand beach. Seasonal kayaking and snorkeling trips are appropriate for any level. Customized private tours offer opportunities to meet Māori artists and shop with experts.

TIME Unlimited (☎ *09/446–6677* ⊕ *www.newzealandtours.travel*) integrates Māori culture with activities like kayak-fishing and trail walking. The company also offers an overnight stay at a *marae* (meeting house). TIME, through its concessions with the Department of Conservation and Māori tribes, can take visitors to places often out of reach of other tours.

WILDERNESS TOURS

Auckland Adventures (☎ *09/379–4545* or *0274/855–856* ⊕ *www.aucklandadventures.co.nz*) has one half-day ($85) and two daylong tours ($120) that go to the summit of Mt. Eden, visit at least one winery, and go to Muriwai beach to see a gannet colony. It will tailor trips and provides a mountain bike option.

Bush and Beach Ltd. (☎ *09/575–1458* ⊕ *www.bushandbeach.co.nz*) runs daily afternoon tours ($110) through the Waitakere Ranges and west coast beaches, such as Karekare Beach, where Jane Campion's *The Piano* was filmed. A daylong tour ($195) includes Auckland highlights and the ranges. Daylong, guided eco-tours to Great Barrier Island in the Hauraki Gulf ($545) include all food and the flights.

Harvey's Safaris (☎ *0800/VEG–OIL* toll-free in New Zealand, *27/383–7603* ⊕ *www.harveysafaris.com*) offers tours of Auckland with a maximum group size of 6 to West Coast beaches in a luxury, biofuel-powered coach.

WINE TOURS

Fine Wine Tours (☎ *09/849–4519* or *021/626–529* ⊕ *www.insidertouring.co.nz*), offers a four-hour West Auckland tour ($149) that takes in three wineries and includes a picnic lunch and a full-day Matakana tour ($249) with four wineries and lunch at the Ascension Winery.

NZWinePro Auckland Wine Tours (☎ *09/575–1958* ⊕ *www.nzwinepro.co.nz*) run about four hours and are based around wine-growing areas to Auckland's north and west plus Waiheke Island. The company will also organize custom tours.

was Auckland's first suburb, established in 1841, and is a good place to look for arts and crafts or sample some of Auckland's most popular cafés, bars, and restaurants.

A dozen "city ambassadors" patrol the city center on weekdays between 8:30 and 5; they can give you directions and field questions you might have. They're identified by their yellow-and-gray uniforms with "ambassador" written on their tops in red.

TOP ATTRACTIONS

4 **Albert Park.** These 15 acres of formal gardens, fountains, and statue-studded lawns are a favorite for Aucklanders, who pour out of nearby office buildings, the university, and polytechnic to eat lunch and lounge under trees on sunny days. Good cafés at the university make a range of inexpensive take-out food and coffee. The park is built on the site of a garrison from the 1840s and '50s that protected settlers from neighboring Māori tribes. There are remnants of its stone walls (with rifle slits) behind university buildings on the park's east side. It is also home to the Auckland Lantern Festival, organized by the Asian community, which celebrates Chinese New Year in late February. It runs 5 PM to 10:30 PM daily and creates a celebratory atmosphere with lantern lightings and stall selling authentic Asian food. ⊠ *Bounded by Wellesley St. W, Kitchener St., Waterloo Quad, City Center.*

3 **Auckland Art Gallery Toi o Tāmaki.** The Auckland Art Gallery has some ★ 14,000 items dating from the 12th century. The châteaulike main gallery, built in the 1880s, is closed for renovations until some time in 2011, but the **New Gallery**, directly across the street, is showing works. Historic portraits of Māori chiefs by well-known New Zealand painters C.F. Goldie and Gottfried Lindauer offer an ethnocentric view of people who some say were seen too one-sidedly as a fiercely martial people. Goldie used sitters introduced to him by friends and often used the same subject repeatedly—odd, considering he aimed to document what he considered a dying race. Look for New Zealand artists Frances Hodgkins, Doris Lusk, and Colin McCahon. There are free collection tours daily at 2 PM. ⊠ *5 Kitchener St. ✛ at Wellesley St. E, City Center* ☎ *09/307–7700* ⊕ *www.aucklandartgallery.govt.nz* ✉ *Free, except for special exhibits which vary in price* ⊙ *Daily 10–5.*

NEED A BREAK? Reflect on your gallery visit from one of the balconies, virtually suspended in the treetops, at **Reuben** (⊠ *New Gallery, Kitchener and Wellesley Sts.* ☎ *09/302-0226* ⊙ *Closed Sun.*). Bite into a fried-egg sandwich with *harissa* (Tunisian hot-chili paste) and crispy pancetta or the classic Reuben. Reasonably priced wine is available by the glass.

11 **Auckland Domain.** Saturday cricketers, Sunday picnickers, and morning runners are three types of Aucklanders you'll see enjoying the rolling, 340-acre park—not to mention loads of walkers, particularly the "Remuera Bobs," women with husbands earning fat salaries who like their wives trim and young looking. In summer watch the local paper for free weekend-evening concerts, which usually include opera and fireworks displays. Take a bottle of wine and a basket of something tasty and join in with the locals—up to 300,000 of them per show. Within the

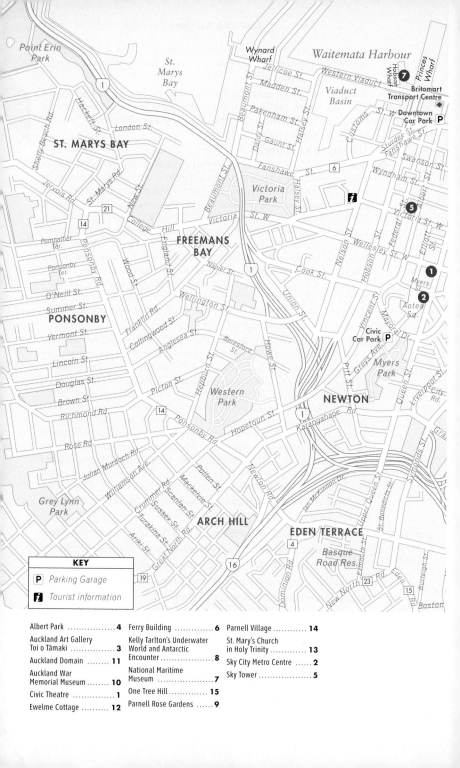

KEY

P Parking Garage

ℹ Tourist information

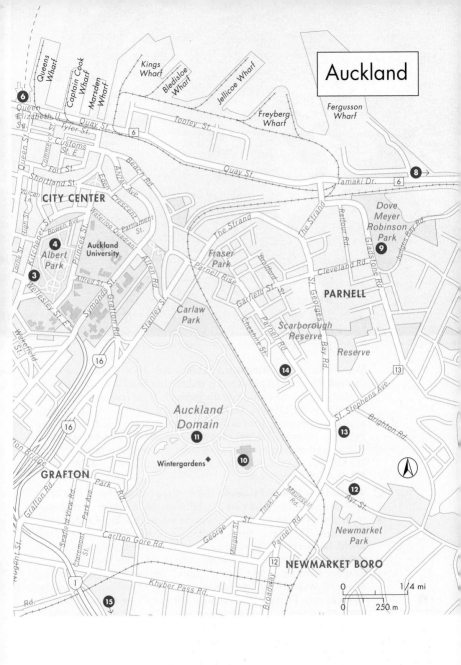

Auckland

Queens Wharf

Captain Cook Wharf

Marsden Wharf

Kings Wharf

Bledisloe Wharf

Jellicoe Wharf

Freyberg Wharf

Fergusson Wharf

Queen Elizabeth II Sq.

Quay St.

Tyler St.

Customs St. E

Commerce St.

Fort St.

Shortland St.

Tootey St.

Quay St.

Tamaki Dr.

CITY CENTER

Beach Rd.

ANZAC Ave.

Eden Crescent

Waterloo Quadrant

Parliament St.

Bowen Ave.

Kitchener St.

Princes St.

Albert Park

Auckland University

Alten Rd.

Alfred St.

Symonds St.

Grafton Rd.

Wellesley St. E

Vulcan Ln.

The Strand

Fraser Park

Parnell Rise

The Strand

Rattray Rd.

Cleveland Rd.

Gladstone Rd.

Judges Bay Rd.

Dove Meyer Robinson Park

Carlaw Park

Garfield St.

Cheshire St.

Bradford St.

St. Georges Bay Rd.

Parnell Rd.

PARNELL

Scarborough Reserve

Reserve

Stanley St.

Wakefield St.

Auckland Domain

Wintergardens

George St.

Titoki St.

Maunsell Rd.

Parnell Rd.

St. Stephens Ave.

Brighton Rd.

GRAFTON

Grafton Rd.

Seaforth Ave.

Park Ave.

Park Rd.

Carlton Gore Rd.

Morgan St.

Ayr St.

Newmarket Park

Claremont St.

St. Joseph's Rd.

Khyber Pass Rd.

Broadway

NEWMARKET BORO

Rd.

0   1/4 mi
0   250 m

Visitors go under the sea at Kelly Tarlton's Antarctic Encounter & Underwater World.

Domain, the domed **Wintergardens** (open daily 10–4) house a collection of tropical plants and palms and seasonally displayed hothouse plants— a good stop for the horticulturally inclined. There is some magnificent sculpture in the Domain. Runners can find trails that range from easy to challenging; some times of the year there are organized 10-km (6-mi) runs open to anyone. ⚠ While the Domain is perfectly safe during the day it is not a place to be at night unless there for a concert with a big crowd. ✉ *Entrances at Stanley St., Park Rd., Carlton Gore Rd., and Maunsell Rd., Parnell/Newmarket.*

❿ ☽ ★ Auckland War Memorial Museum. The museum building based on Greek Revival architecture dominates the hill it sits on and under a new director is trying to see just where it sits in the country's cultural and historic landscape. The Māori artifact collection is one of the largest in the world. Be sure to see the *pātaka*, or storehouse; these structures were a fixture in Māori villages, and this pātaka is one of the finest examples. Another must-see is "Te Toki a Tapiri," the last great Māori *waka* (canoe). It was carved from a single log, and, at 85 feet long, could carry 100 warriors. The figurehead shows off their carving abilities. To delve further into this culture, attend one of the Māori performances held at least three times daily; the show demonstrates Māori song, dance, weaponry, and the *haka* (a ceremonial dance the All Blacks rugby team has adopted as an intimidating pregame warm-up). The museum also showcases Pacific artifacts and occasional high quality visiting exhibitions. For added insight, take the deeply informed and extremely personal tour of the museum offered by the Māori tour organization Potiki Adventures. ✉ *Auckland Domain, Park Rd., Parnell* ☎ *09/309–0443*

⊕ *www.aucklandmuseum.com*
🎫 *$12.50; $25 for Māori cultural performance* ⊙ *Daily 10–5.*

NEED A BREAK?

Take in the scenery at the Pavilion on Domain (✉ *Wintergarden Pavilion, Domain Dr., Auckland Domain* ☎ *09/303–0627*). You can have brunch, a light lunch, or coffee from a table inside the pavilion or on the terrace overlooking the duck ponds. Try the smoked fish dish in a pastry, the chips with mayonnaise, or the crispy skinned duck.

■ Auckland War Memorial Museum. Get a sense of New Zealand's Māori and Pacific history in one place. The park it's in has superb harbor views.

■ Kelly Tarlton's Underwater World. See what lies beneath the ocean surface.

■ Newmarket. Get a brand-new look (for him and her) in the shops here before the next stop.

■ Devonport. A ferry ride across the water from the cruise-ship dock, you can walk through the adorable village, sip coffee, or climb a modest mountain.

① ★ **Civic Theatre.** This extravagant art nouveau movie theater was the talk of the town when it opened in 1929, but nine months later the owner, Thomas O'Brien, went bust and fled, taking the week's revenues and an usherette with him. During World War II a cabaret show in the basement was popular with Allied servicemen. One of the entertainers, Freda Stark, is said to have appeared regularly wearing nothing more than a coat of gold paint. Now the café at the front of the Civic bears her name. When you sit down to a show or movie you'll see a simulated night sky on the ceiling and giant lions with lights for eyes on stage. The theater hosts movie premiers and dance parties from time to time. ✉ *Queen and Wellesley Sts., City Center* ☎ *09/307–5075.*

⑧ ☺ **Fodor'sChoice** ★ **Kelly Tarlton's Underwater World and Antarctic Encounter.** This harborside marine park—the creation of New Zealand's most celebrated undersea explorer and treasure hunter—offers a fish's-eye view of the sea. A transparent tunnel, 120 yards long, makes a circuit past moray eels, lobsters, sharks, and stingrays. In Antarctic Encounter, you enter a reproduction of explorer Robert Falcon Scott's 1911 Antarctic hut at McMurdo Sound, then circle around a deep-freeze environment aboard a heated Sno-Cat (snowmobile) that winds through a penguin colony and an aquarium exhibiting marine life of the polar sea. You emerge at Scott Base 2000, where you can see a copy of the Antarctic Treaty and flags of all the countries involved, as well as some scientific research equipment currently used in Antarctica. You can also dive with the sharks after taking a course or feed various fish. *(See the Kelly Tarlton CloseUp box for more information on the creator.)* ✉ *Orakei Wharf, 23 Tamaki Dr.* ✛ *5 km (3 mi) east of downtown Auckland* ☎ *09/528–0603* ⊕ *www.kellytarltons.co.nz* 🎫 *$29.90 but the company offers a discount for online bookings* ⊙ *Daily 9–6, last admission at 5.*

⑦ ☺ **National Maritime Museum.** Plunge into New Zealand's rich seafaring history in this marina complex on Auckland Harbour. Experience what it was like to travel steerage class in the 1800s in a simulated rocking cabin, or check out a reproduction of a shipping office from the turn of the last century. There are detailed exhibits on early whaling and a superb collection of yachts, ship models, and Polynesian outriggers—not to mention *KZ1*, the 133-foot racing sloop built for the America's Cup challenge in 1988. A scow conducts short harbor trips twice a day on Tuesday, Thursday, and weekends, and there's a wharf-side eatery. You can also wander to the adjacent Viaduct Basin and look at the seriously rich people's yachts moored there. ⊠ *Eastern Viaduct, Quay St., City Center* ☎ *09/373–0800* ⊕ *www.nzmaritime.org* ⊠ *$16, harbor trip $8 extra* ☉ *Oct.–Easter, daily 9–6; Easter–Sept., daily 9–5.*

⑮ **One Tree Hill.** The largest of Auckland's extinct volcanoes and one of the best lookout points, One Tree Hill, or Maungakiekie, was the site of three Māori *pā* (fortifications). The hill is not as distinctive as it once was, though; its signature lone pine was attacked several times by activists who saw it as a symbol of colonialism, and in 2000 it was taken down. Sir John Logan Campbell, founding father of the city, is buried on the summit. There is fantastic walking and running in the parklands with avenues of oaks, a kauri plantation, and an old olive grove. Free electronic-barbecue sites are also on offer. Because the park is a working farm of sheep and cattle, you'll need to be wary of the cows with their calves along the paths. There's also a cricket club with old-style seating if you want to watch a game in summer and a pavilion where you can buy refreshments. ⊠ *Greenlane Rd. W.*

⑤ **Sky Tower.** This 1,082-foot beacon is the first place many Aucklanders take visiting friends to give them a view of the city. Up at the main observation level, the most outrageous thing is the glass floor panels—looking down at your feet, you see the street hundreds of yards below. Adults step gingerly onto the glass, and kids delight in jumping up and down on it. There's also an outdoor observation level. Through glass panels in the floor of the elevator you can see the counterweight of the **Sky Jump** fly up to pass you. For an adrenaline rush you can take the controlled leap off the 630-foot observation deck, for a steep $195 or saunter along the open-air **Sky Walk**, 630 feet above ground ($135). ⊠ *Victoria and Federal Sts., City Center* ☎ *09/912–6000* ⊠ *$28* ☉ *Sun.–Thurs. 8:30 AM–11 PM, last elevator 10:30 PM; Fri. and Sat. 8:30 AM–midnight, last elevator 11:30 PM.*

WORTH NOTING

⑫ **Ewelme Cottage.** Built between 1863 and 1864 by the curiously named Reverend Vicesimus Lush (*vicesimus* is Latin for "20th," his birth order) and inhabited by his descendants for more than a century, this historic cottage stands behind a picket fence. The house was constructed of kauri, a resilient timber highly prized by the Māori for their war canoes and later by Europeans for ship masts and floors. The home contains much of the original furniture and personal effects of the Lush family. You have to duck as you climb the steep, narrow stairs to the small pitched-roof bedrooms, made up as the Lushes might have left them. The drawing room, veranda, and garden appeared in Jane Campion's film *The Piano.* ⊠ *14 Ayr St., Parnell* ☎ *09/379–0202* ⊠ *$7.50* ☉ *Fri.–Sun. 10:30–noon and 1–4:30.*

CLOSE UP

Kelly Tarlton

"Diver, dreamer, explorer, inventor, instigator, worker, storyteller, father, a man who linked us all with his love of the sea." This inscription on the bust of the celebrated figure that stands in the eponymous Kelly Tarlton's Underwater World reveals something of the man whose charisma and vision knit together a team of fellow adventurers.

In 1956 Kelly Tarlton was set to join a climbing expedition to the Andes. When political unrest in Peru canceled the trip, he was left at loose ends. Bored, he went to see the Jacques Cousteau film *Silent World* and thought diving looked like more fun than climbing, with no politics to worry about. With typical Kiwi No. 8 fencing wire ingenuity (aka a do-it-yourself mentality), he built much of his own diving gear, got an underwater camera, and devised housings for the camera and flash.

In the 1960s, Tarlton focused on photographing marine life. In 1967 a trip to the Three Kings Islands to photograph and collect marine specimens whetted his appetite for treasure hunting. He and companion Wade Doak found the wreck of the *Elingamite*, which had foundered on the islands in 1902 with thousands of pounds in gold bullion on board, much of which they recovered.

One of Tarlton's most celebrated finds was the jewels of Isodore Rothschild on the *Tasmania*, which had sunk in 1897. Through his characteristic detailed research, Tarlton pinpointed the whereabouts of the wreck and succeeded in salvaging most of the jewelry in the late 1970s. The treasure was put on display in his now defunct Museum of Shipwrecks

in Paihia but was then stolen by a staff member. Though the thief was imprisoned, he has never revealed the jewelry's fate.

Tarlton's interest broadened to marine archaeology. His first major success was finding the first de Surville anchor. Jean François Marie de Surville sailed the *St. Jean Baptiste* into Doubtless Bay in Northland in 1769, where three of his anchors were lost in a storm. Tarlton plotted their whereabouts from crew accounts of the ship's dangerous proximity to a "big rock" and its position "a pistol shot" from shore, and by calculating the magnetic variations and wind directions from the original maps. The anchor is now in Wellington's Te Papa Museum.

But Tarlton is perhaps best known for the aquarium he built on Auckland's waterfront. Not having the funds to buy ready-molded acrylic to build his planned transparent viewing tunnels, Tarlton said that if he could mold his own camera housings, he could create his own tunnels, too. And do it he did, with a team of skilled and loyal friends, building an "oven" for the molding and inventing a gluing technique to form the curving tunnels.

Opened in January 1985, the aquarium was a huge success. After only seven weeks Tarlton shook the hand of the 100,000th visitor, an image captured in the last photo of him. Tragically, he died that very night, at the age of 47, of a heart complication.

—Toni Mason

2

6 **Ferry Building.** This magnificent Edwardian building continues to stand out on Auckland's waterfront. The 1912 building is still used for its original purpose, and it's here that you can catch the ferry to Devonport as well as to Waiheke and other Hauraki Gulf islands. The building also houses bars and restaurants. Nearby, and easily seen from the Ferry Building, is Marsden Wharf, where French frogmen bombed and sank the Greenpeace vessel *Rainbow Warrior* in 1985. ⊠ *Quay St., City Center.*

9 **Parnell Rose Gardens.** When you tire of boutiques and cafés, take a 10-minute stroll to gaze upon and sniff this collection of some 5,000 rosebushes. The main beds contain mostly modern hybrids, with new introductions being planted regularly. The adjacent **Nancy Steen Garden** is the place to admire the antique varieties. And don't miss the garden's incredible trees. There is a 200-year-old *pohutukawa* (puh-hoo-too-*ka*-wa) whose weighty branches touch the ground and rise up again, and a *kanuka* that is one of Auckland's oldest trees. In summer it's a popular site for wedding photographs. ⊠ *85 Gladstone Rd.,Parnell* ⧉ *Free* ☉ *Daily dawn–dusk.*

14 **Parnell Village.** The lovely Victorian timber villas along the upper slope of Parnell Road have been transformed into antique shops, designer boutiques, cafés, and restaurants. Parnell Village is the creation of Les Harvey, who saw the potential of the old, run-down shops and houses and almost single-handedly snatched them from the jaws of the developers' bulldozers in the early 1960s by buying them, renovating them, and leasing them out. Today this village of trim pink-and-white timber facades is one of the most delightful parts of the city. At night, the area's restaurants and bars attract Auckland's upmarket set. There are some good jewelry stores in Parnell including Hartfields in the center of the main strip. ⊠ *Parnell Rd. between St. Stephen's Ave. and Augustus Rd., Parnell.*

13 **St. Mary's Church in Holy Trinity.** Gothic Revival wooden churches don't get much finer than this one. Built in 1886, it was commissioned by the early Anglican missionary Bishop Selwyn. The craftsmanship inside the kauri church is remarkable, down to the hand-finished columns. One of the carpenters left his trademark, an owl, sitting in the beams to the right of the pulpit. If you stand in the pulpit and clasp the lectern, you'll feel something lumpy under your left hand—a mouse, the trademark of another of the craftsmen who made the lectern, the so-called Mouse Man of Kilburn. The story of the church's relocation is also remarkable. St. Mary's originally stood on the other side of Parnell Road, and in 1982 the entire structure was moved across the street to be next to the new church, the Cathedral of the Holy Trinity. ⊠ *Parnell Rd. and St. Stephen's Ave., Parnell* ☉ *Daily 8–6.*

2 **Sky City Metro Centre.** With design concepts that could be from a science-fiction movie (actually, some are), the Metro Centre is worth a look even if you don't intend to partake in its entertainment. Spiral staircases, bridges designed to look like film, and elevators in the shape of rockets regularly attract design and architecture students—as well as hordes of teenagers. The Metro Centre incorporates a 13-screen cineplex, an

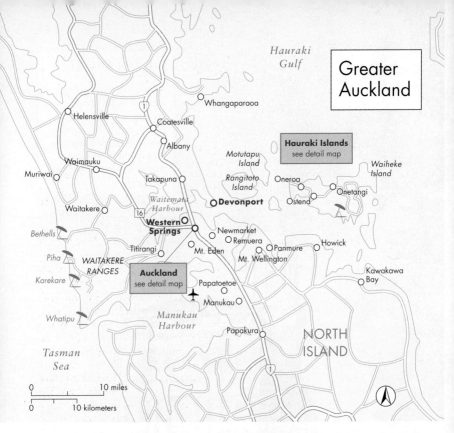

Haruaki
Gulf

Whangaparaoa

Helensville
Coatesville
Albany

Waimauku
Takapuna

Motutapu
Island
Rangitoto
Island
Oneroa
Onetangi
Waiheke
Island

Muriwai
Waitakere
Waitemata
Harbour
Devonport
Ostend

Bethells
Western
Springs
Newmarket
Remuera

Piha
WAITAKERE
RANGES
Titirangi
Mt. Eden
Panmure
Howick

Karekare
Auckland
see detail map
Mt. Wellington
Kawakawa
Bay

Whatipu
Papatoetoe
Manukau
Manukau
Harbour
Papakura
NORTH
ISLAND

Tasman
Sea

Haruaki Islands
see detail map

0   10 miles
0   10 kilometers

international food court with good food, especially Asian, and several
bars, including the **Playhouse Pub,** an English-style tavern with a Shake-
spearean theme. A video arcade, bookstore, and photo developer add to
the mix. ⊠ *291–297 Queen St., City Center* ☉ *Daily 9 AM–midnight.*

WESTERN SPRINGS

Western Springs Park is both a suburb and a park in the inner west part
of Auckland City. It takes its name from the lake there, fed by a natural
spring. Today the park, which the zoo and the Museum of Transport
and Technology, is home to Pacifica, the giant culture, food, and art
festival that takes place in summer, generally in March. The speedway
sometimes hosts rock concerts.

The lake, which is full of eels, swans, and ducks, has many surrounding
paths popular with dog walkers and joggers alike. See native plans and
wild fowl, including native Pūkeko, Teal, Australian Coot and Shovel-
ers, around the shores and wetlands.

Across the road from Western Springs is the Chamberlain Park Golf
Course, which is open to the public. Western Springs is a good place to
read a book or have a picnic.

2

☺ **Auckland Zoo.** Since the 1990s, this zoo has focused on providing its animals with the most natural habitats possible, as well as on breeding and conservation. The primates area, sea lion and penguin shores, and the Pridelands section, where lions, giraffes, zebra, springbok, rhino, and ostriches range in savannalike grasslands, best exemplify this approach. To catch a glimpse of New Zealand flora and fauna, spend time in the New Zealand Native Aviary, where you walk among the birds, and the Kiwi and Tuatara Nocturnal House, which are at opposite ends of the zoo. In 2004 an enterprising Asian elephant escaped by dropping a tree on an electric fence; she then took a walk in the neighboring park. She was coaxed home after 45 minutes, and the zoo's fences are now elephant-proof. In 2007 an otter escaped and its sightings dominated local media for weeks until it was captured. By car, take Karangahape Road (which turns into Great North Road) west out of the city, past Western Springs. Take a right onto Motions Road. Buses from the city stop opposite Motions Road. ⊠ *Motions Rd., Western Springs ✛ 6 km (4 mi) west of Auckland* ☎ *09/360–3819* ⊕ *www.aucklandzoo.co.nz* ⊠ *$19* ☉ *Sept.–May, daily 9:30–5:30; June–Aug., daily 9:30–5.*

☺ **Museum of Transport & Technology.** This is a fantastic place for anyone with a technical bent of any kind. There's a fascinating collection of vehicles, telephones, cameras, locomotives, steam engines, and farm equipment that's a tribute to Kiwi ingenuity. The aviation collection includes the only surviving Solent flying boat. One of the most intriguing exhibits is the remains of an aircraft built by Robert Pearse. There is a reproduction of another he built in which he made a successful powered flight around the time the Wright brothers first took to the skies. The flight ended inauspiciously when his plane crashed into a hedge. But Pearse, considered a wild eccentric by his farming neighbors, is recognized today as a mechanical genius. MOTAT, as the museum is called, also has the scooter that former Prime Minister Helen Clark rode to university. ⊠ *825 Great North Rd., off Northwestern Motorway, Rte. 16, Western Springs ✛ 6 km (4 mi) west of Auckland* ☎ *09/846–0199* ⊕ *www.motat.org.nz* ⊠ *$14* ☉ *Daily 10–5.*

DEVONPORT

The 20-minute ferry to Devonport across Waitemata Harbour provides a fine view of Auckland's busy harbor. Originally known as Flagstaff, after the signal station on the summit of Mt. Victoria, Devonport was the first settlement on the north side of the harbor. Later the area drew some of the city's wealthiest traders, who built their homes where they could watch their sailing ships arriving with cargo from Europe. Aucklanders have fixed up and repopulated its great old houses, laying claim to the suburb's relaxed and moneyed seaside aura.

The Esplanade Hotel is one of the first things you'll see as you leave the ferry terminal. It stands at the harbor end of Victoria Road, a pleasant street for stopping at a shop, a bookstore, or a café; we recommend picking up some fish-and-chips to eat under the giant Moreton Bay fig tree on the green across the street.

GETTING HERE AND AROUND

Various companies serve Waitemata Harbour; one of the best and least expensive is Fullers. The ferry terminal is on the harbor side of the Ferry Building on Quay Street, near the corner of Albert Street. Boats leave here for Devonport Monday–Thursday 6:15 AM–11 PM, Friday and Saturday 6:15 AM–1 AM, and Sunday 7:15 AM–10 PM at half-hour intervals, except for one 45-minute interval between the 9:15 AM and 10 AM sailings. From 8 PM Monday through Thursday and from 7 PM on Sunday they sail on the hour. The cost is $9 round-trip. However, a better deal is to buy the Auckland Day Pass for $10, which gets you a return sailing and unlimited travel on Link buses to boot.

Ferry Contacts Fullers Booking Office (⊠ *Ferry Bldg., Quay St.* ☎ *09/367–9111* ⊕ *www.fullers.co.nz*).

EXPLORING

Long before European settlement, the ancient volcano of **Mt. Victoria** was the site of a Māori *pā* (fortified village) of the local Kawerau tribe. On the northern and eastern flanks of the hill you can still see traces of the terraces once protected by palisades of sharpened stakes. Don't be put off by its name—this is more molehill than mountain. The climb is easy, but the views are outstanding. Mt. Victoria is signposted on Victoria Road, a few minutes' walk from the Esplanade Hotel. ⊠ *Kerr St. off Victoria Rd.*

New Zealand's navy is hardly a menacing global force, but the small **Navy Museum** has interesting exhibits on the early exploration of the country. Displays of firearms, swords, and memorabilia will likely grab former navy folk far more than the uninitiated. The museum is five blocks west of Victoria Wharf and next to the naval base. ⊠ *Queens Parade* ☎ *09/445–5186* ⊕ *www.navymuseum.mil.nz* ◻ *Small donation* ◷ *Daily 10–4:30.*

The position of **North Head**, an ancient Māori defense site, jutting out from Devonport into Auckland's harbor, was enough to convince the European settlers that they, too, should use the head for strategic purposes. Rumor has it that veteran aircraft are still stored in the dark, twisting tunnels under North Head, but plenty of curious explorers have not found any. You can still get into most tunnels (they're safe), climb all over the abandoned antiaircraft guns, and get great views of Auckland and the islands to the east. North Head is a 20-minute walk east of the ferry terminal on King Edward Parade, left onto Cheltenham Street, and then out Takarunga Road. The visitor information center will tell you what night the local folk-music club has events in one of the old bunkers, and it's one of the best places to watch yacht racing on the harbor. A few quiet beaches are off the coastal walk. ⊠ *Takarunga Rd.*

HAURAKI GULF ISLANDS

More than 50 islands lie in the Hauraki Gulf, forming the Hauraki Gulf Marine Park, managed by the Department of Conservation (DOC). Many of the islands are nature reserves, home to endangered plants and birds, and public access to these is restricted. Others are public reserves that can be reached by ferry, and a few are privately owned.

GETTING HERE AND AROUND

Fullers operates ferries year-round to Rangitoto daily at 9:15 and 12:15, departing the island at 12:45 and 3:30. The fare is $25 round-trip; boats leave from the Ferry Building. Fullers also arrange Volcanic Explorer tours, which include a guided ride to the summit in a covered carriage. It's $55 for the tour and ferry ride, and you must book in advance.

Fullers ferries also make the 35-minute run from the Ferry Building to Waiheke Island from 5:30 AM to 11:45 PM at a cost of $32 round-trip. Return ferries leave every hour on the hour, and every half hour at peak commuter times. However, crossings can be canceled if the seas are rough. Buses meet ferries at the Waiheke terminal and loop the island.

SeaLink runs car and passenger ferries to Waiheke, leaving from Half-moon Bay to the east of the city. The round-trip fare is $130 per car, plus $30 for each adult.

On Waiheke you can also take a shuttle to beaches or vineyards; **Waiheke Shuttles** has reliable service. The best way to get to Wha-kanewha Regional Park is by shuttle. If you're planning on going far-ther afield on the island, you can purchase an all-day bus pass from **Fullers Booking Office** at the Ferry Building on Quay Street ($8 for regular service to Oneroa, Palm Beach, Onetangi, and Rocky Bay). To use the pass, you need to take the 10 AM ferry. Return time is optional. Fullers also provides tours that include the ferry fee. After either tour, on the same day, passengers may use their ticket to travel free on regular island buses to visit additional attractions.

To get the full scoop on the various islands, or the country's entire National Conservation Park network, stop by Auckland's **Department of Conservation Visitor Centre.**

Contacts Department of Conservation Visitor Centre (✉ iSITE, Quay St. ☎ 09/379–6476 ⊕ www.doc.govt.nz). **Fullers Booking Office** (✉ Ferry Bldg., Quay St. ☎ 09/367–9111 ⊕ www.fullers.co.nz). **SeaLink** (✉ Ara-Tai Dr., Halfmoon Bay ☎ 09/300–5900 ⊕ www.sealink.co.nz). **Waiheke Shuttles** (☎ 09/372–7262).

GREAT BARRIER ISLAND

Great Barrier Island, the largest in the gulf, has a population of around 1,100, and is mostly agricultural. It's popular with surfers—particu-larly Awana Beach. Motuihe, a popular swimming spot, was a pris-oner-of-war camp during World War I and the scene of a daring escape: Count Felix Von Luckner, known as the "Sea Devil," commandeered the camp commander's boat and got as far as the Kermadec Islands before being recaptured.

TIRITIRI MATANGI

You can see rare native birds up close at **Tiritiri Matangi,** a bird sanctuary open to the public. A gentle walk on well-maintained and signposted tracks takes you to the top of the island and the oldest light-house in the gulf, still in operation. The island is free from predators,

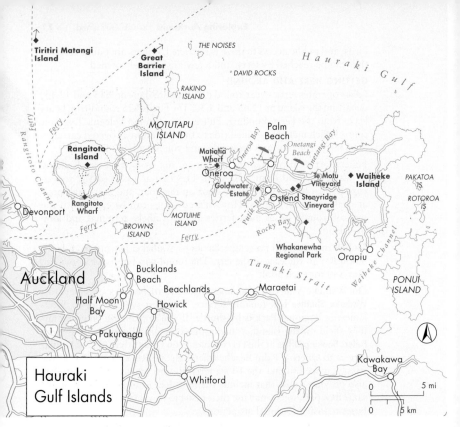

The map labels, reading roughly top to bottom and left to right:

Tiritiri Matangi Island

Great Barrier Island

THE NOISES

Hauraki Gulf

DAVID ROCKS

RAKINO ISLAND

Ferry

Ferry

Rangitoto Channel

MOTUTAPU ISLAND

Oneroa Bay

Palm Beach

Onetangi Beach

Onetangi Bay

Rangitoto Island

Matiatia Wharf

Oneroa

Te Motu Vineyard

Waiheke Island

PAKATOA IS.

ROTOROA IS.

Goldwater Estate

Ostend

Stonyridge Vineyard

Putiki Bay

Devonport

Rangitoto Wharf

BROWNS ISLAND

MOTUIHE ISLAND

Ferry

Rocky Bay

Whakanewha Regional Park

Orapiu

Waiheke Channel

Auckland

Bucklands Beach

Tamaki Strait

PONUI ISLAND

Half Moon Bay

Beachlands

Maraetai

Howick

1

Pakuranga

Whitford

Kawakawa Bay

0   5 mi

0   5 km

Hauraki Gulf Islands

and the birds are unafraid. Tiritiri is home to at least 18 *takahe,* large blue-and-green flightless birds with red beaks. You can usually spot them eating grass near the lighthouse. The grave of Mr. Blue, the hand-reared male of the first pair on the island, is marked by a plaque at his favorite spot near the lighthouse.

RANGITOTO ISLAND

When **Rangitoto Island** emerged from the sea in a series of fiery eruptions 600 years ago, it had an audience. Footprints in the ash on its close neighbor Motutapu Island prove that Māori people watched Rangitoto's birth. It is the largest and youngest of about 50 volcanic cones and craters in the Auckland volcanic field, though scientists are confident that it will not blow again. During the 1920s and '30s hundreds of prisoners built roads and trails on the island, some of which are still used as walkways. Small beach houses were also erected by families on the island in the early 20th century. Many were pulled down in the 1970s before their historical significance was recognized. Thirty-two remain, and a few are still used by leaseholders who are allowed to use them during their lifetimes. (Afterward, they'll be relinquished to the DOC.)

The most popular activity on the island is the one-hour summit walk, beginning at Rangitoto Wharf and climbing through lava fields and

CLOSE UP

Volcano Views

Auckland is built on and around 48 volcanoes, and the tops provide sweeping views of the city. **Mt. Eden,** the highest volcano on the Auckland isthmus, is probably the most popular, and several bus tours include this central site. **One Tree Hill,** the largest of Auckland's extinct volcanoes, was the site of an early Māori settlement. **Rangitoto Island** has an even better vista. This volcano emerged from the sea 600 years ago, no doubt much to the wonder of the Māori people living next door on Motutapu Island. Take a ferry to the island; then take a short ride on a covered carriage towed by a Jeep or walk an walk to the top to get a 360-degree view of the city and the Hauraki Gulf islands. It's thought that Māori settled on the volcanoes beginning in the 14th century, taking advantage of the fertile soils. There's evidence that in the 16th century the Māori used the cones as defensive *pā* (fortified villages). Evidence of complex earthworks can be seen on Mt. Eden and One Tree Hill where Māori cleared volcanic stone to develop garden plots and formed the terraces that are features of *pā*.

forest to the peak. At the top, walkers are rewarded with panoramic views of Auckland and the Hauraki Gulf. Short detours will lead to lava caves and even to the remnants of a botanical park planned in 1915. Wear stout shoes and carry water with you because parts of the walk are on exposed lava flows, which are hot in the sun. You can also swim at Islington Bay and at the Rangitoto wharf in a specially made pool.

WAIHEKE ISLAND

Waiheke Island was once a sleepy spot, summer vacation retreat, and hippie haven, with beach houses dotting its edges. Now it sports the holiday homes of affluent city dwellers and many wealthy foreigners, raising housing costs in their wake. The island is earning a reputation for its vineyards, and local cafés sometimes stock wines unavailable elsewhere. The annual Waiheke Jazz Festival at Easter attracts renowned overseas performers.

From the ferry landing at Matiatia Wharf you can walk five minutes to the small town of **Oneroa,** the island's hub, with its shops, cafés, bars, and real estate agents. Another minute's walk gets you to **Oneroa Beach,** one of the most accessible beaches. The north-facing beaches—sheltered bays with little surf—are the best for swimming. The most popular is **Palm Beach,** 10 minutes by bus from Oneroa. Around the rocks to the left is **Little Palm Beach,** one of Auckland's three nudist beaches. Another great beach on Waiheke is **Onetangi,** on the north side of the island, 20 minutes from Matiatia by bus. **Whakanewha Regional Park,** on the south side of the island, is a lovely bush reserve leading down to a half-moon bay. You can go hiking and picnic here, and the wetlands is home to rare birds such as the New Zealand dotterel. You can get to the park from Oneroa by shuttle bus. Waiheke Island is also home to 35 vineyards; some are young, so only 20-odd are producing wine.

Rangitoto Island emerged from the sea in a dramatic volcanic eruption 600 years ago.

VINEYARDS First to plant grapes on Waiheke were Kim and Jeanette Goldwater, whose eponymous wines have earned a reputation for excellence. The **Goldwater Estate** (✉ *18 Causeway Rd., Putiki Bay* ☎ *09/372–7493* ⊕ *www.goldwaterwine.com*) is open Wednesday through Sunday, noon–4, between March and November; in December and February, it's open Monday through Sunday. Call ahead for personalized tours. The estate is known for is The Goldwater Long Lunch, held on the last Friday of every month. The cost is $75 for a nine-course degustation menu, it's booked out months in advance, begins at 12:30 for a 1 PM start and you never know who you will be seated next to.

Stephen White's **Stonyridge Vineyard** (✉ *80 Onetangi Rd., Ostend* ☎ *09/372–8822* ⊕ *www.stonyridge.com*) has the island's highest profile. Its wines have followers from all over, and the Stonyridge Larose, made from the classic bordeaux varieties, is excellent. Call before you visit as he may have nothing left to taste or sell. Reservations for lunch at the Veranda Café, overlooking the vines, are essential; but if it's booked, you may be accommodated with an antipasto platter and wine on a blanket in the olive grove. The winery is open for tastings daily December through March, and Thursday through Tuesday April through November.

The friendly Dunleavy family of **Te Motu Vineyard** (✉ *76 Onetangi Rd., Onetangi* ☎ *09/372–6884* ⊕ *www.temotu.co.nz*) started planting vines in 1989. Now their Te Motu Bordeaux blend, which is made only when conditions are right, is on the wine list at many Michelin-starred restaurants in France—a great endorsement. The restaurant, the Shed, serves wonderful food in a Tuscan environment. Everything is made on-site from scratch and bookings are essential. The winery is open for tastings, but it's best to call ahead first to check for times.

WHERE TO EAT

Use the coordinate (⊕ B2) at the end of each listing to locate a site on the corresponding map.

Princes Wharf and adjoining Viaduct Quay, an easy stroll from the city's major thoroughfare, Queen Street, offer dozens of eateries in every style from cheap-and-cheerful to superposh. High Street, running parallel to Queen Street on the Albert Park side of town, is a busy café and restaurant strip. Vulcan Lane, between Queen and High streets, has some pleasant bars. Asian immigrants have created a market for a slew of cheap noodle and sushi bars throughout the inner city; the more crowded, the better.

Outside the city center, the top restaurant areas are 10-minute bus or cab ride away on Ponsonby and Parnell roads. Dominion and Mt. Eden roads in the city, as well as Hurstmere Road in the seaside suburb of Takapuna (just over the Harbour Bridge) are also worth exploring. The mix is eclectic—Indian, Chinese, Japanese, Italian, and Thai eateries sit alongside casual taverns, pizzerias, and high-end restaurants.

Peak dinnertime in Auckland is between 8 and 9, but most kitchens stay open until at least 10 PM. Many restaurants, particularly in Ponsonby and Parnell, serve food all day; some have a limited menu between 3 and 6 PM or close between services. On Sunday and Monday, check whether a place is open. Only in the most formal restaurants do men need to wear a jacket. Some restaurants have started charging a 15% surcharge on public holidays.

WHAT IT COSTS IN NEW ZEALAND DOLLARS				
	¢	$	$$	$$$	$$$$
Restaurants	under $10	$10–$15	$15–$20	$20–$30	over $30

Prices are per person for a main course at dinner, or the equivalent.

CITY CENTER

$$$–$$$$ ✕ **Dine by Peter Gordon.** New Zealand's most celebrated chef and fusion-
NEW ZEALAND   cuisine pioneer, Peter Gordon, opened this signature restaurant in 2005
Fodor's Choice   in the Sky City Grand Hotel. He oversees the restaurant from London
★   and visits regularly. As you would expect from a chef of his standing, the
refined food delights with surprises such as the wasabi-*tobiko* (flying-fish roe) spiked avocado cream served with the truffled yellowfin tuna, or the roast five-spice pork belly and rum-roast pineapple that accompanies sautéed scallops. Also in the hotel is his tapas restaurant, Bellota, which is popular with young people who work in the city. It has a good wine list and lovely little nibbley dishes. ⊠ *Sky City Grand Hotel, 90 Federal St., City Center* ☎ *09/363–7030* ▭ *AE, DC, MC, V* ⊕ *D3.*

New Zealand's own Peter Gordon represents the country's growing interest in fine, fusion cuisine.

$$$$
CONTINENTAL
Fodor's Choice
★

✕ **The French Café.** It's not really a café, and it's not strictly French—that aside it is simply one of Auckland's best and most consistent restaurants. Simon Wright is an informed chef who creates dishes inspired dishes based on the freshest available ingredients for the ever-changing menu. Dishes like the pink roasted lamb on white almond polenta with tomatoes and courgettes, olive powder, and buffalo ricotta are perfectly executed. The service is among the best in Auckland; it's efficient, friendly, and absent an attitude. The wine list is comprehensive and includes hard-to-find vintages. ✉ *210B Symonds St.* ✛ *near Kyber Pass Rd., Eden Terrace* ☎ *09/377–1911* ⊕ *www.thefrenchcafe.co.nz* ▭ *AE, DC, MC, V* ◷ *Closed Sun. and Mon.* ✛ *D6.*

$$–$$$
BRITISH

✕ **Galbraith's Ale House.** Brew lovers and Brits craving a taste of home head straight for Keith Galbraith's alehouse, which occupies the former Grafton Library with its neo-Palladian facade. You'll find a big crowd before and after rugby matches at nearby Eden Park. The English-style ales are made on the premises and served at proper cellar temperature. Keith learned the art of brewing in the United Kingdom and sticks religiously to the style. Order a pint and dig into bangers and mash (seriously good sausages made by a local butcher with meat marinated in the Grafton Porter ale atop creamy mashed potatoes). The food is well priced and tasty. People also come for the smoked fish platter—a selection of fish and seafood smoked at the Coromandel smokehouse. There's also a reasonable selection of whiskey. ✉ *2 Mt. Eden Rd., Eden Terrace* ☎ *09/379–3557* ⊕ *www.alehouse.co.nz* ▭ *AE, DC, MC, V* ✛ *D6.*

$$$$
SEAFOOD

✕ **Harbourside Seafood Bar and Grill.** Overlooking the water from the upper level of the restored Ferry Building, this pricey seafood restaurant

2

is an Auckland institution. It serves the finest New Zealand fish and shellfish, including tuna, salmon, snapper, pipi (a type of shellfish), and tuatua (a type of clam), on a menu that references a number of cuisine styles while steering clear of the latest fashion. You can also select crayfish direct from the tank. Nonfish-eaters have their choice of lamb, eye fillet (beef tenderloin), and perhaps *cervena* (farmed venison). On warm nights, reserve a table outside on the balcony where you can watch the ferries come and go. ⊠ *Ferry Bldg., Quay St., City Center* ☎ *09/307–0486* ⊕ *www.harboursiderestaurant.co.nz* ⊟ *AE, DC, MC, V* ✣ *E2.*

$$$–$$$$ ✕ **Kermadec.** The name of this restaurant and bar group comes from
SEAFOOD   the islands that lie between New Zealand and Tonga. The restaurant focuses on seafood, which is unsurprising given that it is owned by a fishing company and is close to the water. The head chef, Peter Thornley, is recognized for his thoughtful cuisine, and the service is good. The stunning roof garden literally brings the outdoors in. In the more casual brasserie, which can get awfully noisy, seek the kitchen's advice on the catch of the day. The cool Trench Bar is known for its club nights when well-known DJs spin and the crowd gets down into the wee hours. ⊠ *1st fl., Viaduct Quay Bldg., Quay and Lower Hobson Sts., City Center* ☎ *09/309–0413 brasserie, 09/309–0412 restaurant* ⊕ *www.kermadec. co.nz* ⊟ *AE, DC, MC, V* ✣ *D2.*

$$$ ✕ **La Zeppa.** *Zeppa* is Italian for "wedge," but you won't get the thin end
NEW ZEALAND   here. Tapas-style dishes are served in this generous warehouselike space that, despite its size, is always lively. It's popular with the after-work set and on a Friday and Saturday can be packed with people either on the way home from work, or on the way out to something. Mediterranean flavors come in dishes such as the good-to-share porcini-and-Parmesan risotto balls, and espresso-cured lamb loin with *machiato* dressing— served on sweet-potato salad with a New Zealand twist—but Asian influences abound. Freshly smoked salmon with a lemon glaze and added zing of wasabi caviar is delivered to your table on its individual slab of cedar, fresh from the hot plate. And the miso-cured pork on a salad of glass onion and sugar snap peas is likely to be fought over. ⊠ *33 Drake St., Victoria Park Market, City Center* ☎ *09/379–8167* ⊟ *AE, DC, MC, V* ☾ *Closed Sun. and Mon. No lunch Sat.* ✣ *C3.*

$$$ ✕ **Mecca on the Viaduct.** This restaurant in the center of the Viaduct is the
NEW ZEALAND   flagship for the Mecca Group of five restaurants. It offers New Zealand
Fodor's Choice   cuisine with a Middle Eastern twist. It's open all day and is designed to
★   cope with anything—from tables for two to larger groups—in a relaxed environment. The food is always fresh; the two signature dishes are lamb shanks slow cooked in a fragrant tomato gravy and fish baked with fresh vegetables, garlic, and chilies. People have been trying to get the shank recipe out of the owner for years. Like many of the Viaduct places it can get busy—they do take bookings, but a limited number, and the menu changes at least four times a year. The restaurant is also a popular place for blind dates. The wine list, while not adventurous, offers a good overview of the bigger New Zealand producers and the champagne bar adds extra flair. ⊠ *Viaduct Harbour, City Center* ☎ *09/358–1093* ⊟ *AE, DC, MC, V* ✣ *D2.*

$$–$$$
MEXICAN

✕ **Mexican Café.** The worn red paint on the steps leading to this lively favorite says it all. Get to this restaurant at least a half hour ahead of time and join the crowds at the bar. People go as much for the noisy, friendly vibe as they do for the food. The menu is packed with traditional choices such as nachos, tacos, and enchiladas. ⊠ *67 Victoria St. W, City Center* ☎ *09/373–2311* ▬ *AE, DC, MC, V* ✦ *D3.*

$$$–$$$$
NEW ZEALAND

✕ **Number 5 Restaurant.** The sign outside declares, "Life is too short to drink bad wine." Accordingly, the wine list here is designed to prevent such a mishap, with a vast selection by the glass and the bottle. Unlike most high-end restaurants, Number 5 is happy to serve just a small dish with a glass of wine. But you shouldn't pass up the main courses, such as individual beef Wellingtons, or venison steak with mashed kūmara, truffled mushrooms, and syrah reduction. ⊠ *5 City Rd., City Center* ☎ *09/309–9273* ▬ *AE, DC, MC, V* ☾ *Closed Sun. No lunch* ✦ *E4.*

$$$–$$$$
NEW ZEALAND
★

✕ **O'Connell Street Bistro.** The former bank vault, on one of the city's fashionable backstreets, has a cozy bar from which you can watch passersby through thin venetian blinds. Loyal diners keep coming back for the roasted pork piccata on butter-bean cassoulet, or duck two ways—roast duck breast, and duck leg confit on a pepper-and-red-onion stew with fried *haloumi* (a salty, Middle Eastern–style sheep's milk cheese)—served on tables covered in crisp white linen. On the wine list you will find varieties rarely seen elsewhere, such as Waiheke's sought-after Stonyridge Larose Cabernets. ⊠ *3 O'Connell St., City Center* ☎ *09/377–1884* ▬ *AE, DC, MC, V* ☾ *Closed Sun. No lunch Mon. and Sat.* ✦ *E3.*

$$$
NEW ZEALAND

✕ **Prime.** Diners can gaze out at the harbor over lunch in this slick, sparely designed restaurant opposite Princes Wharf. Most dishes are offered at appetizer or main course sizes, and you're welcome to simply linger over some tapas—as in small dishes, though not particularly Spanish—with a glass of wine. For something more substantial, try the perennial favorite, braised rabbit pappardelle with *rimu* wood–smoked bacon and walnut-watercress pesto. The menu suggests pairing it with the Rabbit Ranch Pinot Noir from central Otago. Tapas only are served from 3 to 6:30. ⊠ *188 Quay St.* ☎ *09/357–0188* ▬ *AE, DC, MC, V* ☾ *Closed weekends. No dinner* ✦ *D2.*

$–$$
JAPANESE

✕ **Tanuki's Cave.** A flight of dimly lighted stairs leads to a buzzing Japanese yakitori and sake bar. The oblong bar is usually jammed with film-festival types or a young arty crowd ordering cheap small plates of skewers before going out for the night. Grilled chicken, with or without cheese, and deep-fried fish are popular picks. In addition to more than 20 types of sake by the glass, you'll see large bottles of sake on the "bottle-keep" shelves—these are for people who keep their own bottle to have when they come to eat. Watch the stairs on the way out! ⊠ *319B Queen St., City Center* ☎ *09/379–5151* ▬ *AE, DC, MC, V* ☾ *No lunch. Closes at 11:30* ✦ *D4.*

$$$$
NEW ZEALAND
Fodor's Choice
★

✕ **White.** This restaurant looks like it stepped out of the pages of a 1990s design magazine. Vast windows mark the boundary between the harbor and the alabaster interior. Fittingly, New Zealand seafood dominates, with dishes such as scampi and salmon tortellini served with arugula and caper-butter sauce or *hapuka* (grouper) in a crust of hazelnut and *horopito* (an indigenous pepper) served with baby turnips and pearl onions. If you come for lunch, bring your sunglasses because the light that bounces off the walls from the water can shock the eyes. ⊠ *Hilton Auckland, Princes Wharf, 147 Quay St.* ☎ *09/978–2000* ⊟ *AE, DC, MC, V* ♺ *D1.*

2

DEVONPORT

$$–$$$ ✕ **Manuka.** Sitting on a corner on Devonport's main street makes for

NEW ZEALAND   perfect people-watching. Manuka is a relaxed spot with bare wooden tables and stacks of newspapers and magazines. Weekend brunch is hectic when the locals turn out, but tables turn over quickly. Wood-fired pizzas are available all day, with toppings ranging from classic pep-peroni to smoked chicken, Brie, and roasted cashews. You could also nibble on a delicious salad or slice into a meaty offering such as venison with blueberry-and-onion marmalade. ⊠ *49 Victoria Rd., Devonport* ☎ *09/445–7732* ⊟ *AE, DC, MC, V* ♺ *B1.*

PARNELL

$–$$ ✕ **Alphabet Bistro.** Take a table on the sidewalk for the best breakfast

NEW ZEALAND   and brunch on the strip. Classics such as eggs Benedict and boiled eggs with "toast soldiers" (strips of toasted bread for dipping) are done just right, and the coffee is great. Bigger appetites might go for the red-flannel hash, with two types of sausage (pork-and-fennel, and garlic) or panfried lamb's kidneys. Lunch is good, too, with a small but perfectly formed blackboard menu offering salads, pasta, and steak sandwiches. This is a good place for a well-priced lunch. ⊠ *193 Parnell Rd., Parnell* ☎ *09/307–2223* ⊟ *AE, MC, V* ♺ *G4.*

$$$$ ✕ **Antoine's.** Owners Tony and Beth Astle have run this renowned res-

NEW ZEALAND   taurant for more than a quarter century, and it enjoys a reputation as

Fodor's Choice   one of *the* special-occasion spots in town though it also has its reg-

★   ulars. The decoration is considered, the service immaculate, and the food delicious—and expensive. Tony is still at the stove, and his "table menu" reads as if it were designed by a chef half his age. On his "nos-talgic menu" classics such as braised duckling with orange-and-Grand-Marnier sauce remain, along with inventive dishes such as the appetizer of Bloody Mary jelly (just as it sounds: a jelly made from Bloody Mary ingredients) with prosciutto, artichokes, asparagus, and citrus-infused olive oil; or sautéed spiced watermelon, grilled scallops, and wasabi flying-fish roe topped with a lime-and-pink-peppercorn vinaigrette. The wine list is extensive. ⊠ *333 Parnell Rd., Parnell* ☎ *09/379–8756* ⊕ *www.antoinesrestaurant.co.nz* ⊟ *AE, DC, MC, V* ☉ *Closed Sun. No lunch Sat.* ♺ *G4.*

$$$–$$$$ ✕ **Cibo.** Italian for "good food," *cibo* is an apt name for this restaurant

NEW ZEALAND   with Mediterranean- and Asian-influenced dishes. The smart crowd has made this a second home, coming for the adventurous cuisine of chef Kate Fay, served by smart and relaxed staff, led by co-owner Jeremy Turner who is possibly Auckland's best maître d' and an avid cyclist. In an old chocolate factory, the restaurant opens onto a quiet courtyard where you can dine by a fishpond lined with rushes and lotus plants. Or

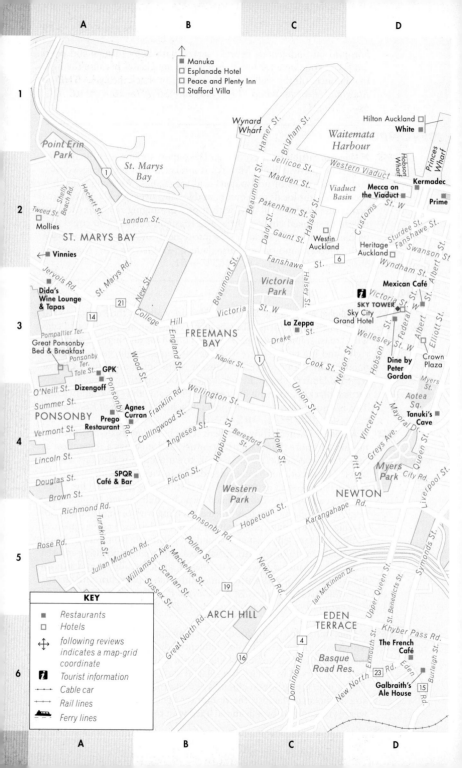

A B C D

1

↑ ■ Manuka
□ Esplanade Hotel
□ Peace and Plenty Inn
□ Stafford Villa

Wynard
Wharf

Hamer St.

Brigham St.

Hilton Auckland □

■ White

Waitemata
Harbour

Hobson Wharf

Princes Wharf

Point Erin
Park

St. Marys
Bay

1

Jellicoe St.

Western Viaduct

Madden St.

Viaduct
Basin

■ Kermadec

Beaumont St.

Pakenham St. E.

Mecca on ■
the Viaduct

St. W.

■ Prime

Shelly Beach Rd.

Hackett St.

2

Tweed St.
□
Mollies

London St.

Halsey St.

Gaunt St.

Daldy St.

Fanshawe
St.

Customs St. W.

Sturdee St.

Fanshawe St.

Swanson St.

2

Westin □
Auckland

Heritage
Auckland □

Wyndham St.

Albert St.

ST. MARYS BAY

← ■ Vinnies

Jervois Rd.

St. Marys Rd.

New St.

Victoria
Park

6

Mexican Café ■

Wellesley St. W.

SKY TOWER ◆

Albert St.

Elliott St.

Dida's
Wine Lounge
& Tapas

21

14

Hill

College

FREEMANS
BAY

Beaumont St.

Victoria

St. W.

Halsey St.

La Zeppa ■

ⓘ Victoria St. W.

SKY TOWER ◆
Sky City
Grand Hotel

Federal St.

Hobson St.

3

Pompallier Ter.

Great Ponsonby
Bed & Breakfast

Ponsonby Ter.

Tole St. ■ GPK

England St.

Wood St.

Napier St.

Drake St.

Cook St.

Nelson St.

Wellesley St.

■ Dine by
Peter
Gordon

Crown
Plaza

Myers
St.

3

O'Neill St. ■ Dizengoff

Summer St.

PONSONBY

Vermont St.

Franklin Rd.

Ponsonby Rd.

■ Agnes
Curran

■ Prego
Restaurant

Wellington St.

Collingwood St.

Anglesea St.

Hepburn St.

Beresford St.

Union St.

Aotea
Sq.

Mayoral Dr.

Tanuki's ■
Cave

Queen St.

4

Lincoln St.

Douglas St.

Brown St.

■ SPQR
Café & Bar

Picton St.

Western
Park

Howe St.

Vincent St.

Pitt St.

Greys Ave.

Myers
Park

City Rd.

NEWTON

Liverpool St.

4

Richmond Rd.

Rose Rd.

Turakina Rd.

Julian Murdoch Rd.

Williamson Ave.

Mackelvie St.

Scanlan St.

Ponsonby Rd.

Pollen St.

Hopetoun St.

Karangahape
Rd.

Symonds St.

5

Sussex St.

19

ARCH HILL

Great North Rd.

Newton Rd.

16

Ian McKinnon Dr.

Upper Queen St.

St. Benedicts St.

EDEN
TERRACE

Khyber Pass Rd.

■ The French
Café

Elmoth St.

23

Eden

Rd.

Burleigh St.

5

6

KEY

■ *Restaurants*

□ *Hotels*

✛ *following reviews*
indicates a map-grid
coordinate

ⓘ *Tourist information*

✛ *Cable car*

┿ *Rail lines*

⛴ *Ferry lines*

Dominion Rd.

4

Basque
Road Res.

New North Rd.

Galbraith's ■
Ale House

15

6

A B C D

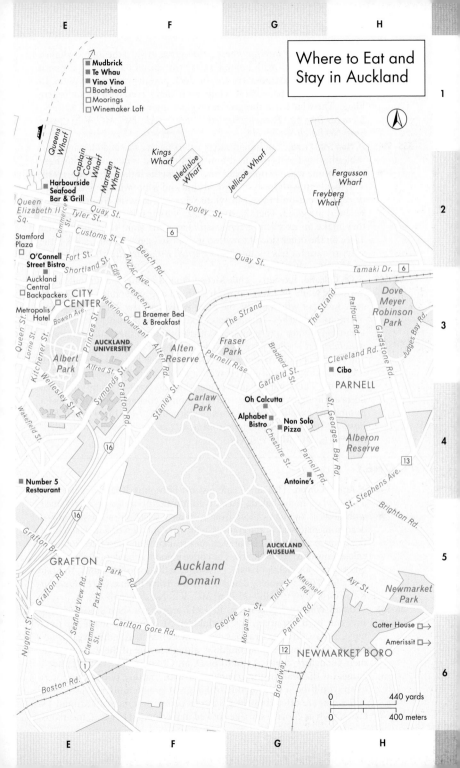

E   F   G   H

Where to Eat and Stay in Auckland

■ Mudbrick
■ Te Whau
■ Vino Vino
□ Boatshead
□ Moorings
□ Winemaker Loft

1

2

Queens Wharf
Captain Cook Wharf
Marsden Wharf

Kings Wharf
Bledisloe Wharf
Jellicoe Wharf

Fergusson Wharf
Freyberg Wharf

Harbourside Seafood Bar & Grill

Queen Elizabeth II Sq.
Commerce St.
Tyler St.
Quay St.
Customs St. E
Beach Rd.
ANZAC Ave.
Tooley St.
Quay St.
Tamaki Dr. 6

Stamford Plaza
O'Connell Street Bistro
Fort St.
Shortland St.
Auckland Central Backpackers
Metropolis Hotel
Bowen Ave.
Eden Crescent
Waterloo Quadrant
CITY CENTER
Braemer Bed & Breakfast

Dove Meyer Robinson Park
Balfour Rd.
Judges Bay Rd.
Gladstone Rd.

3

Queen St.
Lorne St.
Kitchener St.
Princes St.
AUCKLAND UNIVERSITY
Albert Park
Alfred St.
Wellesley St. E
Symonds St.
Grafton Rd.
Wakefield St.
Stanley St.
Alten Rd.
Alten Reserve
The Strand
Fraser Park
Parnell Rise
The Strand
Cleveland Rd.
■ Cibo
PARNELL

Carlaw Park
Garfield St.
Bradford St.
Oh Calcutta
Alphabet Bistro
Non Solo Pizza
Cheshire St.
St. Georges Bay Rd.
Parnell Rd.
Alberon Reserve

4

13

■ Number 5 Restaurant
16
Antoine's
St. Stephens Ave.
Brighton Rd.

Grafton Br.
Grafton Rd.
Seafield View Rd.
Park Rd.
Park Ave.
Claremont St.
16
GRAFTON
Auckland Domain
AUCKLAND MUSEUM
Ayr St.
Newmarket Park

5

Nugent St.
Carlton Gore Rd.
George St.
Morgan St.
Titoki St.
Maunsell Rd.
Parnell Rd.
Cotter House □→
Amerissit □→

1
Boston Rd.
12
Broadway
NEWMARKET BORO

6

0   440 yards
0   400 meters

E   F   G   H

take a table in the interior where palms grow toward the high skylights. They cook a steak with aplomb or try the spiced duck leg confit with arugula-and-mascarpone risotto, or duck parfait with grilled plum. In season, you can't pass up the whitebait fritter, served with lemon beurre blanc. The wine list at this grown-up place is remarkably good. ⊠ *91 St. Georges Bay Rd., Parnell* ☎ *09/303–9660* ▭ *AE, DC, MC, V* ☺ *Closed Sun. No lunch Sat.* ⊹ *H3.*

$$$–$$$$ ✕ **Non Solo Pizza.** This Italian eatery offers pasta as a single serving or in
ITALIAN table-sharing bowls that feed four or more, and is consistent. It's busy
★ at lunchtime when people head for a table in the Italian-style courtyard. The spaghetti with fresh shellfish in chili and white wine, and osso buco *di cervo* (venison braised in white wine served with creamy truffled polenta) are good. There's always pizza with traditional toppings, and they make an excellent green salad. The same team runs the popular Toto, on the other side of town, so if you can't get a seat here, ask if the sister restaurant has room. ⊠ *259 Parnell Rd., Parnell* ☎ *09/379–5358* ▭ *AE, DC, MC, V* ⊹ *G4.*

$$–$$$ ✕ **Oh Calcutta.** Executive chef Meena Anand applies traditional cook-
INDIAN ing skills while focusing on fresh seafood and vegetables. The results
★ are consistent which is why the place is always busy. You'll find plenty of traditional dishes—the butter chicken and lamb dishes are excellent —but her lighter interpretations of traditional dishes, such as prawn *malabari* (fat shelled prawns sautéed with onions, peppers, coriander, and fresh coconut cream) are a hallmark. Her fish tikka, made with deep-sea kingfish and served with a sharp mint chutney, is another standout. The wine list is average; they do have a bring-your-own license, though they charge each person a corkage fee. There are a number of excellent wine shops in Parnell. ⊠ *149–155 Parnell Rd., Parnell* ☎ *09/377–9090* ⊕ *www.ohcalcutta.co.nz* ⌕ *Reservations essential* ▭ *AE, DC, MC, V* ⊹ *G4.*

PONSONBY

¢–$ ✕ **Agnes Curran.** This small café just off Ponsonby Road tries to recall
CAFÉ a time when home baking was served for afternoon tea on plates lined
★ with doilies. You can choose from a counter selection of classic antipodean homemade cakes and cookies, which are duly served with lashings of thick cream and style. It is not ideal for breakfast but offers filled rolls and chicken mustard pie for lunch. The coffee is good. A bank of shelves holds quirky finds for sale: cookware, glassware, and assorted treasures. You can spot a local Oscar-winning designer here from time to time. ⊠ *181 Franklin Rd., Ponsonby* ☎ *09/360–1551* ▭ *MC, V* ☺ *No dinner* ⊹ *A4.*

$$–$$$ ✕ **Dida's Wine Lounge & Tapas.** In 1941 a grocer's shop stood on this
SPANISH site, run by a Croatian, Joseph Jakicevich, who also made his own wine. Today, three generations on, his descendants run this lively wine-and-tapas bar in the same building, alongside one of the wineshops in their Glengarry chain. A photo of *Dida,* Croatian for "Grandfather," hangs on the wall in the company of many family photos, and it is likely you'll be served by one of his great grandchildren. More than 100 wines are offered by the glass to accompany a menu of around 18 tapas, such as chorizo sausage cooked in merlot and bay leaf, meatballs

in sherry-tomato sauce, and salt-cod croquettes. Locals love it, so you may need to arrive early to get a table inside or outside. Thursday and Friday nights can see people spilling into the street. ⊠ *54 Jervois Rd., Ponsonby* ☎ *09/376–2813* ⌖ *Reservations not accepted* ▭ *AE, DC, MC, V* ⊕ *A3.*

¢–$ ✕ **Dizengoff.** The food is Jewish, though not kosher. The most popular
ISRAELI breakfast dish is scrambled eggs and veal sausages with homemade pesto and French bread followed by toast and an unbelievably creamy lemon-curd spread. At lunch try the beet salad (baby beets with fava beans in a balsamic dressing, topped with pesto and shaved Parmesan) or the salad made with shredded poached chicken, parsley, and lemon. The coffee is among the best around and there is an ever-changing selection of New Zealand art. This place is always busy; avoid weekends unless you get there early for breakfast (no later than 8). The lemon poppy seed muffins and coffee make an excellent take-out option. ⊠ *256 Ponsonby Rd., Ponsonby* ☎ *09/360–0108* ▭ *AE, DC, MC, V* ☽ *No dinner* ⊕ *A3.*

$$–$$$ ✕ **GPK.** The initials stand for Gourmet Pizza Kitchen or Gourmet Pizza
PIZZA Konnection—take your pick. This corner eatery was the city's pioneer posh-pizza place and soon afterward spawned a sister establishment in Takapuna at 162 Hurstmere Road and another in Albany at 198-200 Albany Road. Some of the toppings would make a traditionalist squirm (tandoori chicken with banana and yogurt), but there are plenty of more traditional toppings, and they cook a great steak. The wine and beer list is impressive. ⊠ *262 Ponsonby Rd., Ponsonby* ☎ *09/360–1113* ⌖ *Reservations not accepted* ▭ *AE, DC, MC, V* ⊕ *A3.*

$$–$$$ ✕ **Prego Restaurant.** It's no mean feat being the longest-running restau-
ITALIAN rant in Ponsonby where the locals are fussy. The broad Italian menu
Fodor's Choice includes wood-fired pizzas and good pasta. Also worth trying is the
★ fish of the day which is served in many ways. Prego is extremely noisy so don't go there for an intimate chat, though you may find the courtyard quieter. It is always full and lively; a wait is likely, but the expert staff will usher you to the bar. The wine list is comprehensive. ⊠ *226 Ponsonby Rd., Ponsonby* ☎ *09/376–3095* ⌖ *Reservations not accepted* ▭ *AE, DC, MC, V* ⊕ *A4.*

$$–$$$ ✕ **SPQR Cafe & Bar.** There's no better vantage point for people-watching
ITALIAN on Ponsonby Road than the tables outside this longtime local favorite;
★ if you want to fit in, wear black and big sunglasses. Should outdoors not be an option, you can sit in the minimalist concrete interior of what was once a motorcycle shop. You can keep your shades on there, too; with the eclectic clientele, the people-watching is just as good inside. The excellent food is largely Italian, and the place is known for its thin-crust pizzas; also frequently remarked on is the attitude of the staff who sometimes neglect customers. The food mostly makes up for service. The bar cranks up as the sun goes down, and on weekend mornings aspiring celebrities and the "love your work set" can be seen having a late breakfast in public. A lot of air-kissing goes on at SPQR, and it is decidedly popular with the gay community. ⊠ *150 Ponsonby Rd., Ponsonby* ☎ *09/360–1710* ⌖ *Reservations not accepted* ▭ *AE, MC, V* ⊕ *A4.*

Waiheke Island has fine dining, excellent wineries, and top-notch views of the Hauraki Gulf.

$$$–$$$$
NEW ZEALAND
★

✕ **Vinnies.** This shop-front restaurant has a warm intimate quality, with long filmy curtains and velvet-covered chairs. Specialty local produce prepared with elegant flair is Chef Geoff Scott's trademark. Start with savory cones filled with pork and chutney, salt cod, or delicious vegetables, or perhaps with Clevedon coast oysters chased with a lemon-and-vodka-sour shooter. Main dishes are built around seasonal produce, and the menu is ever changing. The wine list is excellent. Given this spot's lovely character, it's often busy so it pays to book ahead. ⊠ *166 Jervois Rd., Herne Bay* ☎ *09/376–5597* ⊕ *www.vinnies.co.nz* ▤ *AE, DC, MC, V* ☉ *Closed Sun. and Mon. No lunch* ✛ *A2.*

HAURAKI GULF ISLANDS

WAIHEKE ISLAND

$$$$
CONTINENTAL

✕ **Mudbrick Vineyard and Restaurant.** This is a good place to try wines that never make it to the mainland. The vineyard produces a small portfolio of whites and reds and serves them along with those of other tiny producers. Because bordeaux varieties predominate on the island, the food emphasis is on red meat; particular favorites are the rack of lamb and Black Angus eye fillet. The front terrace is the best spot to take in the harbor views. Mudbrick is open for lunch and dinner daily, year-round, and many people like to arrive by helicopter. ⊠ *Church Bay Rd., Oneroa* ☎ *09/372–9050* ⊕ *www.mudbrick.co.nz* ▤ *AE, DC, MC, V* ✛ *E1.*

$$$–$$$$
NEW ZEALAND
Fodor's Choice
★

✕ **Te Whau Vineyard and Café.** With a big wine list of the finest New Zealand and international wines, this restaurant has been described as one of the best in the world for wine lovers. Many of the vintages are only available here. Spectacularly perched atop a finger of land, the restaurant commands a nearly 360-degree view. Te Whau's own bordeaux blend is much praised; you'll be able to try their chardonnay only here. You'll always get fresh seafood like the salmon, house-smoked over oak and *manuka* (a native tea tree) wood. They also cook duck, beef, and venison to rave reviews. ⊠ *218 Te Whau Dr., Te Whau Point* ☎ *09/372–7191* ⊕ *www.tewhau. com* ▭ *AE, MC, V* ⊗ *Closed Tues. Nov.–Easter, and weekdays Easter– late Oct. No dinner* ✢ *E1.*

$$–$$$
MEDITERRANEAN

✕ **Vino Vino.** Waiheke's longest-running restaurant perches on Oneroa's main street, with a large all-weather deck overlooking the bay. The platters—Mediterranean, grilled (with Italian sausages and calamari), or seafood—are perennial favorites. Or try something with a North African spin, such as the dry-marinated chicken over a red-pepper-and-tomato salad. ⊠ *3/153 Ocean View Rd., Oneroa* ☎ *09/372–9888* ⊕ *www.vinovino.co.nz* ✍ *Reservations essential* ▭ *AE, MC, V* ✢ *E1.*

> **EAT WAY OUT**
>
> There're great eats outside of Auckland proper. To the west, near the Waitakere Ranges, the suburb of Titirangi has earned a reputation for its range of options: low-key pizza, Middle Eastern, and Southeast Asian joints; wine bars; and upscale restaurants with harbor views.
>
> Traveling east there are many inexpensive ethnic restaurants. The Panmure shopping center, about 20 minutes from central Auckland, has outstanding Malaysian and Indian restaurants. Don't be put off by the decidedly down-at-heel premises; cooks serve up super food to knowing customers.

WHERE TO STAY

Use the coordinate (✢ B2) at the end of each listing to locate a site on the corresponding map.

As New Zealand's gateway city, Auckland has most of the large international chain hotels, as well as plenty of comfortable bed-and-breakfasts, mom-and-pop motels, and other individually owned places. Many of the large flashy hotels cluster around the central business district (CBD), whereas B&Bs tend to congregate in the nearby or trendier neighborhoods. Many of the best are in suburbs close to the city center like Devonport and Ponsonby. You'll find your hosts quite chatty and keen to recommend local sights but equally happy to offer you privacy.

November to March are the busiest months for Auckland hotels, so it pays to book by August to ensure you get your first choice. Hotel rooms are usually equipped with TVs, hair dryers, ironing boards, and basic toiletries. All the major hotels have parking at a price. A number of the B&Bs offer parking, an especially useful perk since they're usually in narrow city center streets. Better yet, B&Bs generally don't charge for parking. High-speed Internet access is standard in hotels and B&Bs, and a computer is almost always available if you didn't bring a laptop. B&B owners can generally be relied on for insider knowledge on what's best close by, and many will make reservations or other arrangements for you. Only the hotels tend to have air-conditioning, but this isn't a problem when you can fling open the windows and let in the fresh air.

WHAT IT COSTS IN NEW ZEALAND DOLLARS					
	¢	$	$$	$$$	$$$$
Hotels	under $75	$75–$125	$125–$200	$200–$300	over $300

Prices are for a standard double room in high season, including 12.5% tax.

CITY CENTER, PARNELL, AND REMUERA

$$-$$$ ☷ **Amerissit.** At the end of a quiet cul-de-sac overlooking rooftops and Mt. Hobson, this architecturally modern, cedar B&B is a quiet home-away-from-home yet close to the restaurants of Parnell and shops in Newmarket. White walls and bed linen and soft charcoal carpet throughout add to the peacefulness. The two upstairs rooms have private decks, and one has a whirlpool bath. Owner Barbara McKain serves breakfast in the semicircular conservatory-style dining room, and will give you a tour of the city to help you get your bearings. **Pros:** quiet environment; well tended; gracious host. **Cons:** some may find the environment a little suburban. ⊠ *20 Buttle St., Remuera* ☎ *09/522–9297* ⊕ *www.amerissit.co.nz* ⟳ *3 rooms* ☖ *In-room: No a/c, DVD, Internet. In-hotel: Parking (free)* ▤ *AE, DC, MC, V* ❏❐*BP* ✢ *H6.*

¢-$ ☷ **Auckland Central Backpackers.** The best-equipped budget place in town, ★ this hostel is now part of the Base Backpackers group. It has air-conditioning and a security system that you would normally expect to pay much more for. Accommodation varies from a six-bed bunk room to double or en suite family rooms. Bases uses good quality linens. The lounge and Internet café area are the hostel's social hub, where you'll also find a travel center and even a New Zealand job-search service, should you be compelled to cancel your return flight. **Pros:** inexpensive; secure; in the center of town; range of rooms. **Cons:** noisy; busy; not private. ⊠ *229 Queen St., City Center* ☎ *09/358–4877* ⊕ *www.stayat-base.com* ⟳ *71 rooms, 35 with bath* ☖ *In-room: Kitchen. In-hotel: 2 restaurants, bar, laundry facilities* ▤ *MC, V* ✢ *E3.*

$$-$$$ ☷ **Braemar Bed & Breakfast.** This gorgeous B&B is in an Edwardian town ★ house in the heart of the city opposite the High Court. It's close to parks, art galleries, and the museum. The house was bought to save it from demolition, and it is a truly elegant and comfortable place to stay. The menu is mostly organic. The owners know all about close-by restaurants and local cultural events. They will make reservations for you and point you in the direction of good tours and places to visit. Braemar is extremely popular and has lots of regular clients, so book well in advance. **Pros:** lovely historic building; endearing hosts. **Cons:** no outdoor space. ⊠ *7 Parliament St., Central City* ☎ *09/377–5463* ⊕ *www.parliamentstreet.co.nz* ⟳ *3 rooms* ☖ *In-room: No a/c, DVD. In-hotel: Internet terminal* ▤ *AE, MC, V* ❏❐*BP* ✢ *E3.*

$$$$ ☷ **Cotter House.** This 1847 Regency mansion, the fifth-oldest house in **Fodor's**Choice Auckland, is the kind of place rock stars have been known to retreat ★ to after mishaps on tropical islands. The home has been refurbished in original style, with classic features such as egg-and-dart molding, recessed arches, and narrow shutters on the high windows and is extremely private with security gates. Colombian-French owner Gloria Poupard-Walbridge is a fantastic host who offers personalized service; Cotter House cannot take large numbers. Predinner drinks are served in the two lounges, and she bakes brioches and croissants herself as part of the four-course breakfast. Cotter House is elegant and a showcase for a fine art collection. The art shares the rooms with a significant collection of antiques, from writing desks, vanities, and armoires to the French scallop-shaped bath in the suite. Table d'hôte dinners are available by arrangement. **Pros:** like staying in a magical, private country house; close to upmarket Remuera and Newmarket for shopping. **Cons:** grounds are a little small. ⊠ *4 St. Vincent Ave., Remuera* ☎ *09/529–5156* ⊕ *www.cotterhouse.com* ⤳ *2 rooms, 1 suite* ♻ *In-room: No a/c, safe, DVD, Wi-Fi. In-hotel: Spa, Internet terminal* ⊟ *AE, DC, MC, V* ⊣⊚∣ *BP* ⊹ *H6.*

$$$–$$$$ ▦ **Crowne Plaza.** An escalator connects the atrium of this hotel to the "Atrium on Elliot," an average shopping complex with a remarkably good food hall that is a short walk from Queen Street. Guest rooms begin on the 16th floor; all have city views, and there is even a menu for pillow choice. The suites on the 28th floor have great views and bigger bathrooms for just a slightly higher price. **Pros:** close to town; well priced; good café. **Cons:** often frequented by conference goers; shopping center is drab. ⊠ *128 Albert St., City Center* ☎ *09/302–1111* ⊕ *www. crowneplaza.co.nz* ⤳ *352 rooms* ♻ *In-room: Internet. In-hotel: Restaurant, bar, gym, Internet terminal, Wi-Fi* ⊟ *AE, DC, MC, V* ⊹ *D3.*

$$$$ ▦ **Heritage Auckland.** This hotel mixes the historical and the contemporary; it's housed in one of Auckland's landmark buildings, the Farmers Department Store but has an additional tower wing. The main building has retained its original 1920s art deco design, including high ceilings, large jarrah-wood columns, and native timber floors. The tower wing includes New Zealand art especially commissioned for the rooms and public areas. Ask for a harbor-view room. **Pros:** close to city center; clean; good views from some rooms. **Cons:** interior is a little tired. ⊠ *35 Hobson St., City Center* ☎ *09/379–8553* ⊕ *www.heritagehotels.co.nz* ⤳ *224 rooms, 243 suites* ♻ *In-room: Safe, Internet. In-hotel: 3 restaurants, bar, tennis court, pool, gym, spa, Wi-Fi* ⊟ *AE, DC, MC, V* ⊹ *D2.*

$$$$
Fodor's Choice
★
▦ **Hilton Auckland.** Perched on the end of Princes Wharf, the Hilton resembles the cruise ships that dock alongside it. White walls and neutral furnishings in the chic, clean-lined rooms let your eyes drift to the view, best in the bow and starboard. Each room has a piece of original art—and a teddy bear. The hallways are painted chocolate on one side and white on the other, presumably to aid navigation. The hotel's restaurant, White ($$$$), is good, and the Viaduct Basin is within a five-minute walk. **Pros:** lovely views; good rooms. **Cons:** ships mooring nearby can be noisy. ⊠ *Princes Wharf, 147 Quay St., City Center* ☎ *09/978–2000* ⊕ *www.hilton.com* ⤳ *160 room, 6 suites, 35 apartments* ♻ *In-room: Safe, Internet. In-hotel: Restaurant, bar, pool, gym, Wi-Fi* ⊟ *AE, DC, MC, V* ⊹ *D1.*

SPAAAAH

Spa culture has developed slowly and against the grain of New Zealand's Calvinist roots and view that spas are an extravagance. But over the last few years a number of spas have firmly established themselves, with organic products and a strong Eastern influence. The range of spas, some in hotels, provide everything from steam treatment to pore cleanse to deep laser therapy and heated, smooth basalt pebbles and scented oils.

EAST DAY SPA. The two branches of East Day Spa provide a sophisticated, pampering environment. The spa treatments blend Eastern, particularly Indian, culture with premium treatments based on a more Western approach to beauty.

Body Treatments: Massage (shiatsu, Swedish, and Balinese), total body exfoliation, manicure, pedicure.

Beauty Treatments: Eyebrow threading, facials, hair removal, waxing.

Prices: Leg waxes from $35, manicures $95, massages from $150.

Packages: Packages include a massage and pedicure for $150 or a massage and organic facial for $250.

✉ Ground level, 123 Albert St., City Center ☎ 09/363–7050 ✉ 6 Tweed St., St Mary's Bay ☎ 09/303–4777 ⊕ www.eastdayspa.com ⊙ Weekdays 9–9, weekends 9–8.

TAMARA SPA. With two locations— one in the central city and the other at the Esplanade Hotel in Devonport—this sophisticated spa with its Indian, Ayurvedic, and holistic treatments is designed for men and women and treats couples together.

The spa offers the best in Indian rejuvenation therapies from aromatherapy massages to facial treatments using the purest ingredients. Many opt for the Chandana, a soothing treatment that leaves the skin refreshed after the application of Chandana (sandalwood) paste.

Body Treatments: Massage (Eastern, Swedish, herbal, and couples), body scrubs and wraps, waxing.

Beauty Treatments: Facials using ingredients ranging from honey to oatmeal to cleanse, exfoliate, moisturize and restore elasticity, skin polishing.

Prices: From $110 for the basic massage.

Packages: Packages with a massage and facial begin at $225 and range up to $500 for the Tamara Indulgence, which takes five hours and includes an Ayurvedic Facial, scalp massage, body exfoliation, and eye treatment.

✉ 16 Blake St., PonsonbyAuckland ☎ 09/358–2284 ⊙ Mon. 10:30–5, Wed. and Thurs. 10–6, Fri. and Sat. 10:30–5, Sun. 11–4 ✉ 1 Victoria Rd., Devonport ☎ 09/303–4777 ⊙ By appointment only ⊕ www.tamaraspa.co.nz.

Mens Works Grooming Lounge. This central city operation is aimed at the modern man of any age who wants to maximize his time while maintaining good grooming whether a wet shave before a meeting or wedding or a haircut that works without product.

Most of its services focus on those things men often neglect like eyebrows, toenails, and ears, but it also provides services such as waxing of most body parts, chest hair clipping, facials, skin toning, and what it calls a "man-i-cure."

Body Treatments: Massage (deep tissue, relaxing, skin cleansing, waxing, and herbal skin therapy).

Beauty Treatments: Wet shaves, haircuts and treatments, eyebrow coloring, hair removal.

Prices: Haircuts start at $39; facials start at $75.

Packages: All the packages are customized; the $200 two-hour executive package is built to order with what suits the customer that day.

✉ *26 Lorne St., City Center, Auckland* ☎ *09/358–4898* ⊕ *www.mensworks. co.nz* ⊙ *Mon., Wed., Thurs.–Sat 9–6, Tues. 8–6.*

Beauty on Ponsonby. This day spa and salon is loved by the trendy set who live in the comfortable suburbs of Ponsonby and Grey Lynn for its wide range of therapies. There are full body massages, some using heated stones, as well as nail care and facials.

Regulars at BOP, as it's known, often opt for the packages which combine a number of treatments: The Golden Ticket includes a massage using hot, smooth, oiled rocks and an aromatherapy-based facial.

Body Treatments: Hot Stone Massage, aromatherapy, pedicures including lower leg massage, toning skin treatment.

Beauty Treatments: Many of the facials are tailor-made after a skin-type assessment. BOP will also perform skin peels and aromatherapy.

Prices: The Golden Ticket costs $158; facials begin at $55 for a half hour.

Packages: Treatments taking more than three hours like The Alchemist which combines massage, aromatherapy, a pedicure, and nail treatments cost from $280.

✉ *334 Ponsonby Rd., Ponsonby, Auckland* ☎ *09/376–9969* ⊕ *www. beautyonponsonby.co.nz* ⊙ *Tues. and Thurs. 10–8, Wed. and Fri. 9–6, Sat. 9–4.*

CLINIC 42. Clinic 42 is a boutique specialist center offering a range of the most current international, medically based skin enhancement and rejuvenation procedures. It's recognized by New Zealand's College of Plastic Surgeons.

The clinic's team comprises three doctors, one aesthetician, and one nurse with 30 years plus of experience. They keep up-to-date with the latest techniques for men and women.

Body Treatments: Pigment reduction, skin tightening and vitamin infusions, which are "driven" into the deeper dermal layers of the skin.

Beauty Treatments: Botox-based procedures; restalin therapy for lines.

Prices: There is not single price list at this clinic; services are tailored to the client.

Packages: Packages are tailor-made and the clinic generally requires medical records.

✉ *321 Manukau Rd., Epsom, Auckland* ☎ *09/638–4242* ⊕ *www. clinic42.co.nz* ⊙ *Mon.–Thurs. 9–6, Fri. 9–5.*

Hilton Auckland

Cotter House

Mollies

2

$$–$$$ 🏨 **Metropolis Hotel.** Auckland's old Magistrate's Courthouse was trans-
★   formed into an elegant lobby with a stunning onyx ceiling for these
serviced apartment accommodations. Most rooms have decent views,
but the best sea views are higher up on the east side of the hotel. On a
clear day you can see across the harbor to the Coromandel Peninsula.
The stylish apartments are either one- or two-bedroom with sliding
doors separating the living area; most have balconies, and all come
with a kitchen, including dishwasher, and washing machine and dryer.
There is no room service or in-house dining, but there are plenty of
convenience stores close by. **Pros:** grand building; nice facilities; in the
center of town **Cons:** no restaurant or room service. ⊠ *1 Courthouse
La., City Center* ☎ *09/300–8800* ⊕ *www.the-ascott.com* ⤲ *145 suites*
⚐ *In-room: Safe, kitchen, Internet. In-hotel: Pool, gym, Internet, parking (paid)* ⊟ *AE, DC, MC, V* ✛ *E3.*

$$$$ 🏨 **Sky City Grand Hotel.** The specially commissioned works of top New
★   Zealand artists hanging in the soaring lobby of Auckland's latest
major hotel are testimony to the attention to design throughout—even
the staff uniforms were designed by local fashion leaders. Rooms are
decked in light contemporary hues, with red bed throws and iconic
New Zealand prints by late photographer Robin Morrison. On the top
floor, the Grand Suite is the size of four standard rooms, with a butler's pantry. The excellent main restaurant, Dine, is run by acclaimed
Kiwi chef Peter Gordon. **Pros:** close to the city center and casino; good
restaurant. **Cons:** average views; ugly facade. ⊠ *90 Federal St., City
Center* ☎ *09/363–7000* ⊕ *www.skycitygrand.co.nz* ⤲ *296 rooms, 20
suites* ⚐ *In-room: Internet, Wi-Fi (some). In-hotel: 2 restaurants, bar,
pool, gym, spa, laundry service, Internet terminal, Wi-Fi* ⊟ *AE, DC,
MC, V* ✛ *D3.*

$$$$ 🏨 **Stamford Plaza.** Constant upgrades, noteworthy service, and attention to detail keep this mid-city hotel at the top of its game. Standard rooms are large and furnished extensively with natural fabrics
and native woods in an updated art deco style. The best rooms are
on the harbor side—the higher the better—and while the champagne
bar is gone, Grasshoppers, the Thai restaurant, is good. **Pros:** close to
town; good service. **Cons:** work needed on refreshing the foyer and
entry court. ⊠ *Albert St. and Swanson St., City Center* ☎ *09/309–8888*
⊕ *www.stamford.com.au* ⤲ *329 rooms* ⚐ *In-room: Safe, Internet.
In-hotel: 2 restaurants, bar, pool* ⊟ *AE, DC, MC, V* ✛ *E2.*

$$$$ 🏨 **Westin Auckland Hotel.** This waterfront hotel presents the customer
with both luxury and a friendly environment. Many rooms offer views
of the ever-changing Viaduct Basin. The rooms are expertly appointed
and each has Wi-Fi Internet access. The hotel is no-smoking. The Harbour View corner rooms with their floor-to-ceiling windows are particularly in demand. The Q Restaurant and Toast Café are fine, and
travelers accustomed to the Westin style of hospitality will not be disappointed. **Pros:** new; close to the Viaduct; excellent rooms; close to
Victoria Park. **Cons:** Viaduct area can be noisy. ⊠ *21 Viaduct Harbour
Av., City Center* ☎ *09/909–9000* ⊕ *www.westin.com* ⤲ *172 suites* ⚐
*In-room: Safe, Wi-Fi. In-hotel: Restaurant, bar, pool, gym, Internet
terminal, parking (paid)* ⊟ *AE, DC, MC, V* ✛ *C2.*

PONSONBY

$$$–$$$$
★
🖼 **Great Ponsonby Bed & Breakfast.** Convivial hosts Gerry and Sally will welcome you into their Pacific-theme villa on a quiet street off Ponsonby Road. Rooms are brightened with colorful, locally made tiles and art, and the windows are sandblasted with Pacific designs. The cozy lounge is stocked with music, films, books, and magazines, and has an honor bar. Five of the rooms have kitchenettes and open off the courtyard. A few minutes' walk puts you in the thick of the Ponsonby cafés. **Pros:** friendly; relaxed; low-key. **Cons:** sophisticates may find it a bit too homely. ⊠ *30 Ponsonby Terr., Ponsonby* ☎ *09/376–5989* ⊕ *www.great-pons.co.nz* ⤴ *10 rooms, 1 suite* △ *In-room: No a/c, DVD, Internet. In-hotel: Internet terminal, parking (free)* ⊟ *AE, MC, V* ⫟⊙⫟ *BP* ✛ *A3.*

$$$$
Fodor's Choice
★
🖼 **Mollies.** Music lovers will have extra reason to admire this boutique hotel. It's run by Frances Wilson, a voice coach who taught at New York's Metropolitan Opera. Her husband, Stephen Fitzgerald, was a theater set designer and also renovated New York City apartments before transforming this two-story 1870 villa. Each individually decorated suite has a mix of antiques and stylish modern furnishings and there are nice gardens. After dinner, by request, Frances goes to the Steinway grand piano in the drawing room for a recital. Actress Tilda Swinton has stayed here and it is popular with the fashion set. The hosts are knowledgeable about the arts and also have relationships with incredibly good tour providers. **Pros:** private; sedate. **Cons:** some might find it a bit pretentious and froufrou. ⊠ *6 Tweed St., St. Mary's Bay* ☎ *09/376–3489* ⊕ *www.mollies.co.nz* ⤴ *12 suites* △ *In-room: Internet. In-hotel: Bar, spa, Internet terminal, parking (free)* ⊟ *AE, DC, MC, V* ✛ *A2.*

DEVONPORT

$$$$
🖼 **Esplanade Hotel.** Commanding the corner opposite the pier, this turn-of-the-20th-century Edwardian baroque-revival hotel is the first thing you see when approaching Devonport by ferry. Upstairs, a wide corridor hung with chandeliers leads to generous rooms with period furnishings and long drapes hanging from high windows. Harbor views come at a slightly higher rate. The elegant two-bedroom, two-bathroom "Penthouse Suite" is ideal for families (at around twice the standard rate). It also offers the Tamara Day Spa for those looking for some pampering. **Pros:** stunning views; lovely character. **Cons:** poor parking lot. ⊠ *1 Victoria Rd., Devonport* ☎ *09/445–1291* ⊕ *www.esplanadehotel.co.nz* ⤴ *15 rooms, 2 suites* △ *In-room: No a/c, Internet. In-hotel: Restaurant, bar, Internet terminal* ⊟ *AE, DC, MC, V* ⫟⊙⫟ *BP* ✛ *B1.*

$$$
★
🖼 **Peace and Plenty Inn.** Antiques brought over from England fill this lovely B&B, which is a mix of luxury and simplicity. The largest room, the Windsor, has a high antique English pine bed and a small but adorable bathroom with a Victorian clawfoot tub. Conversely, the smallest room has a brass bed and a larger bathroom with a full-size clawfoot bath. For a view of the city, ask for the upstairs Waitemata room. Children are welcome with under-five free. **Pros:** lovely environment; good

food; close to Devonport. **Cons:** some may find the antiques too fussy. ✉ *6 Flagstaff Terr., Devonport* ☎ *09/445–2925* ⊕ *www.peaceandplenty. co.nz* ⤴ *7 rooms* ⌂ *In-room: No a/c, Internet. In-hotel: Restaurant, Internet terminal* ⊟ *MC, V* ⦿ *BP* ⊹ *B1.*

$$$$ ⭐ 🛏 **Stafford Villa.** Once a missionary's home, this early-1900s building is now an elegant B&B filled with Asian antiques and other artwork. Each room has a thematic bent, such as butterfly-decorated wallpaper and China Blue's Asian inflection. The latter is a honeymoon favorite, with a four-poster bed and an antique Chinese chest. There are plenty of gracious touches, from chocolates and fresh flowers to sherry in the guest rooms and predinner drinks. The ferry to the city leaves regularly from the bottom of the road—a five-minute walk. **Pros:** quiet; warm hosts; lovely food. **Cons:** decoration is fussy; very few good restaurants close by. ✉ *2 Awanui St., Birkenhead Point, North Shore* ☎ *09/418–3022* ⊕ *www.staffordvilla.co.nz* ⤴ *3 rooms* ⌂ *In-room: No a/c, DVD. In-hotel: Internet terminal* ⊟ *AE, MC, V* ⦿ *BP* ⊹ *B1.*

HAURAKI GULF ISLANDS

WAIHEKE ISLAND

$$$$ ⭐ 🛏 **Boatshed.** An internal spiral staircase leads to the Lighthouse, a two-story suite on the top floor of a turret. The glass doors of the dayroom fold open onto a wraparound deck overlooking the golden sands of Oneroa Bay, where boats moor and the swimming is great. From the bedroom on the first floor the view is equally spectacular. A long central room, with doors onto the sail-covered deck, divides this boutique hotel and opens onto a cozy sunken lounge. In the Bridge Room, up a flight of stairs, bifold windows off the sunporch frame a view of the bay. If you go for one of the three Boatshed Rooms, leave the louvered doors to your private deck open for fresh sea air as you sleep. Owner Jonathan Scott, a former chef, prepares dinners by arrangement. **Pros:** gorgeous location; lovely rooms. **Cons:** some say the cooking is not always up to scratch. ✉ *Tawa and Huia Sts., Little Oneroa* ☎ *09/372–3242* ⊕ *www. boatshed.co.nz* ⤴ *4 rooms, 1 suite* ⌂ *In-room: DVD, Wi-Fi. In-hotel: Spa* ⊟ *AE, DC, MC, V* ⦿ *BP* ⊹ *E1.*

$$$ 🛏 **The Moorings.** From the bright guest rooms of this L-shaped Mediterranean farmhouse-style home, you can look outward or inward: out onto the bay or into a sheltered courtyard with lavender hedges and lemon trees. Each room has a king-size bed, a spacious seating area, and a small deck. Below the decks a terraced path leads to the bay. **Pros:** clean; informal; lovely location. **Cons:** the furniture appears cheap. ✉ *9 Oceanview Rd., Oneroa* ☎ *09/372–8283* ⊕ *www. themoorings.gen.nz* ⤴ *2 rooms* ⌂ *In-room: Kitchen, Internet* ⊟ *MC, V* ⦿ *CP* ⊹ *E1.*

$$$ 🛏 **Winemaker's Loft.** From the dining area of this apartment-style loft, you can look onto the vines of Cable Bay vineyard and beyond to Church Bay. Standing a short distance from the owners' home, this is a private retreat, yet it's only five minutes from the relative bustle of Oneroa. In keeping with the wine theme, all the right wineglasses are provided, and you can start with the complimentary bottle. One-night stays incur a $50 surcharge. **Pros:** friendly hosts; clean; lovely

views. **Cons:** you'll need to take a cab to town; no Internet. ✉ *20 Nick Johnston Dr., Oneroa* ☎ *09/372–9384* ⊕ *www.winemakersloft.co.nz* ↪ *1 suite* ♿ *In-room: Kitchen, DVD* ⊟ *MC, V* ⦿*CP* ✛ *E1.*

NIGHTLIFE AND THE ARTS

For the latest information on nightclubs get your hands on *What's On Auckland,* a pocket-size booklet available at all visitor information bureaus. The monthly *Metro* magazine, available at newsstands, has a guide to theater, arts, and music, and can also give you a helpful nightlife scoop. *City Mix* magazine, also published monthly and stocked at newsstands, has a complete guide to what's happening in the city, and the Friday and Saturday editions of the *New Zealand Herald* run a gig guide and full cinema and theater listings.

THE ARTS

The Auckland arts scene is busy, particularly in the area of visual arts, with some 60 dealer galleries operating. Theater is on the rise and more touring exhibitions and performing companies are coming through the city than ever before. The Auckland Philharmonia Orchestra performs regularly, including at the summer series of free concerts in the park at the Domain, when thousands of music lovers sit with picnics under the stars. The Vector Arena by the harbor attracts plenty of rock acts, too.

For tickets, **Ticketek** (☎ *09/307–5000* ⊕ *www.ticketek.com*) is the central agency for all theater, music, and dance performances, as well as for major sporting events.

ART GALLERIES AND STUDIOS

An independent contemporary gallery, **Artspace** (✉ *300 Karangahape Rd.* ☎ *09/303–4965*) shows both international artists and the best of local artists. A group of 30 artists in Waitakere, west of Auckland, have set up the **Art Out West Trail** so that visitors can view and purchase art in artists' private studios. Many require advance notice, and you'll need a car. Brochures are at the Auckland i-SITE Visitor Centre.

At the Otara Shopping Centre in Manukau City is the **Fresh Gallery** (✉ *5/46 Fairmall, Otara Town Centre, Otara* ☎ *09/274 6400* ⊕ *www. manukau.govt.nz*), an initiative of the Manukau City Council's Art Programme. This gallery space is a little off the beaten art track but worth the visit for the extraordinary work. Here emerging artists, many of whom are Pacific, test boundaries not only in materials used, but also with content and techniques.

For a one-stop sample of West Auckland art, visit **Lopdell House Gallery** (✉ *Titirangi and S. Titirangi Rds., Titirangi* ☎ *09/817–8087* ⊕ *www.lopdell.org.nz*). The gallery shows local works but also has regular exhibitions by national and international artists. In a restored villa, **Masterworks** (✉ *77 Ponsonby Rd., Ponsonby* ☎ *09/378–1256*) exhibits and sells contemporary New Zealand art, glass, ceramics, and jewelry.

MUSIC AND OPERA

The **Aotea Centre** (⊠ *Aotea Sq., Queen St., City Center* ☎ *09/309–2677* ⊕ *www.the-edge.co.nz*) is Auckland's main venue for the performing arts. The **New Zealand Opera** company performs three annual main-stage opera seasons at the Aotea Centre, accompanied by either the **Auckland Philharmonia Orchestra** or the **New Zealand Symphony Orchestra.** Both orchestras perform at the Aotea Centre on occasion, but perform more regularly at the **Auckland Town Hall** (⊠ *303 Queen St., City Center* ☎ *09/309–2677* ⊕ *www.the-edge.co.nz*).

The **Civic Theatre** (⊠ *Queen and Wellesley Sts., City Center* ☎ *09/309–2677*) is host to many of the performances by international touring companies or artists. For general inquiries about all three venues check by the information desk on Level Three of the Aotea Centre. If you haven't booked beforehand, hit the Civic and Auckland Town Hall box offices, which open one hour before performance.

THEATER

While Aucklanders endure accusations of philistinism, mostly from Wellingtonians over the lack of theater in the city, there is one shining light: the **Auckland Theatre Company (ATC)** (☎ *09/309–0390* ⊕ *www.atc. co.nz*). The ATC has a mixed repertory that includes New Zealand and international contemporary drama and the classics. The company performs at the Herald Theatre at the Aotea Centre, Sky City Theatre, and the Maidment Theatre at the university.

NIGHTLIFE

After sunset the bar action is split across four distinct areas, with the central city a common ground between the largely loyal Parnell and Ponsonby crowds. Parnell has several restaurants and bars frequented by a polished, free-spending crowd. For a more relaxed scene, head to Ponsonby Road, west of the city center, where you'll find street-side dining and packed bars—often at the same establishment. If you prefer to stay in the city center, the place to be for bars is the Viaduct, particularly in summer, or High Street and nearby O'Connell Street, with a sprinkling of bars in between. At the Queen Street end of Karangahape Road (just north of Highway 1) you'll find shops, lively bars, cafés, and nightspots. Nightclubs, meanwhile, are transient animals with names and addresses changing monthly if not weekly.

There is also a growing nightlife scene on the North Shore—particularly in the upmarket seaside suburb of Takapuna. If you make the trip over the bridge, you'll be rewarded by bars and restaurants with a particularly relaxed vibe; it's the sort of place where people spill into the streets. From Sunday to Tuesday many bars close around midnight, and nightclubs, if open, close about midnight or 1 AM. From Thursday to Saturday, most bars stay open until 2 or 3 AM. Nightclubs keep rocking until at least 4 AM and some for a couple of hours after that.

BARS AND LOUNGES

At the heart of the city center, the **Civic Tavern** (⌧ *1 Wellesley St., City Center* ☎ *09/373–3684*) houses three bars. The **London Bar** has a vast selection of beer and Scotch whiskey. The **London Underground Bar** has 8-ball pool tables and casino-style poker machines. For a glass of Irish stout, stay on the ground floor and visit **Murphy's Irish Bar.**

★ You might as well leave your inhibitions at the door when you enter **Lime** (⌧ *167 Ponsonby Rd., Ponsonby* ☎ *09/360–7167*), because everybody else does. People packed in the narrow bar inevitably end up singing their hearts out to classic tunes from the 1960s and '70s.

Vulcan Lane has long been an after-work favorite with the suit-and-tie set of downtown Auckland. The lane has been tidied up in recent years, and the **Occidental Belgian Beer Cafe** (⌧ *6 Vulcan La., City Center* ☎ *09/300–6226*) is one of the places that got a face-lift. Pair a pint of Belgian beer with a deep pot of mussels. A noble aim of the stylish **Orchid Bar** (⌧ *152B Ponsonby Rd., Ponsonby* ☎ *09/378–8186*) is to create a place where women can relax. It's not overtly feminine (men are more than welcome here), but the expertly made cocktails come garnished with an orchid. The bar has its own label of Martinborough Pinot Noir, called RGP. There's some uncertainty about what the acronym stands for, but a good guess is "really good plonk."

★ **The Whiskey** (⌧ *210 Ponsonby Rd., Ponsonby* ☎ *09/361–2666*) has cozy leather banquettes where you can talk without competing with the music. For an even more intimate tête-à-tête, you'll find a smaller room through the curtains off the main-bar area where patrons can be seen debating world issues into the night. Wines seldom available by the glass are at **the Wine Loft** (⌧ *67 Shortland St., City Center* ☎ *09/379–5070*). Jocular lawyers and other suits make up most of the after-work crowd. Quotes from the famous are scrawled on the walls—the whole world could indeed be three drinks behind after you leave here.

GAY AND LESBIAN

Not many venues are aimed at the gay and lesbian market in Auckland—that's probably because in Auckland what can be more important is the sort of car you drive rather than your sexual preference. And some joints won't let men in if they are wearing sandals or jandals—go figure. The free fortnightly *Gay and Lesbian Newspaper Express* is your best guide; some bars have women-only evenings, but this changes often. The men-only bar **Urge** (⌧ *490 Karangahape Rd., City Center* ☎ *09/307–2155*) opens Wednesday through Saturday and has theme nights from time to time. It is extremely popular with men with beards who like to dance to disco music with their shirts off.

Kamo (⌧ *386 Karangahape Rd., City Center* ☎ *09/377–2105*) is also very gay- and lesbian-friendly and can be a good place to hang out and ask where the latest joint is.

COMEDY

Classic Comedy & Bar (⌧ *321 Queen St., City Center* ☎ *09/373–4321*) is Auckland's main venue for live comedy. The caliber of the acts varies, and you'll find a mix of well-known Kiwi comedians, fresh faces, and

CLOSE UP

America's Cup

2

The uninitiated will be hard-pressed to avoid talk of Auckland's regattas and races, and inevitably, of the America's Cup. The history of this prestigious sailing race includes the longest winning streak in sports history: the United States held the prize from the race's 1851 inception until Australia successfully challenged for it in 1983. Perhaps due to the healthy rivalry New Zealand has long had with its trans-Tasman neighbor, the Kiwis developed a keen interest in the "Auld Mug" (as the silver trophy has affectionately been dubbed).

In 1995 Team New Zealand aka Black Magic (its yacht was black) challenged for the cup and won, becoming the second non-U.S. nation to ever do so. This was an enormous coup for a nation relatively small of stature and piggybank, and New Zealanders rode an ecstatic wave of national pride. Team leaders Sir Peter Blake and Russell Coutts gained hero status, and Blake's lucky red socks were elevated to icons of the Kiwi effort.

The glory continued into 2000 when New Zealand was again the victor, becoming the first non-U.S. team to successfully defend the cup. But then tragedy, infighting, equipment failure, and disappointment took the wind out

of their sails. In 2001 Sir Peter Blake was murdered by Amazonian pirates; in 2003 skipper Coutts controversially "defected" to the challenging Swiss team, which won the cup away New Zealand. Kiwi musician Dave Dobbyn's yachting anthem "Loyal" played endlessly and bitterly amid cries of *Traitor*.

The race has long been plagued by legal wrangling, and as bigger dollars and egos scrap for the mug the battleground is often more courtroom than high seas. Despite all of this unfortunate nonsense, there is still a great sailing race to behold: land-based bipeds scamper frantically over multimillion dollar super-engineered vessels, which skim over waves in an often vain but always magnificent bid to harness the forces of nature. It makes for powerful, heart-in-the-mouth display, and it's understandable that since the Kiwis have had a sip from the sailing grail, they are thirsty for more. So if you mention Black Magic, the Auld Mug, or cheap red socks to a Kiwi, you'll elicit a somewhat rueful smile: the America's Cup has been heartwarming and heartbreaking for this nation. The 33rd America's Cup will be in February 2010 in the United Arab Emirates; the defender is Switzerland's *Alinghi* (⊕ *www.33rd.americascup.com*).

—Jessica Kany

the occasional international act. The Classic is host to the International Laugh Festival every April.

LIVE MUSIC AND NIGHTCLUBS

The live music scene in Auckland is fickle—bands often perform in unexpected locations (a bowling alley isn't unheard of), so keep an eye on the entertainment guides.

Playing strictly disco and with a dance floor lighted in colored squares, **Boogie Wonderland** (⊠ *Customs and Queen Sts., City Center* ☎ *09/361–6093*) is stuck in the 1970s—*Saturday Night Fever* to be specific. You're encouraged to dress up, bust out your Travolta moves, and have a laugh. There's a $10 cover charge and the queues outside can be long. **Deschlers** (⊠ *17 High St., City Center* ☎ *09/379–6811*), a 1950s-style cocktail lounge, has live jazz on Thursday and Saturday. Park yourself at the long bar or at a paua shell–top table in one of the booths. Take three flights of stairs or the rickety elevator to **Khuja Lounge** (⊠ *Level 3, Westpac Bank Bldg., Queen St. and Karangahape Rd., City Center* ☎ *09/377–3711*), where you'll find live soul, jazz, funk, hip-hop, samba, bossa nova, or DJs. You can hit the dance floor or sink into a couch and watch the Moroccan-style lamps cast stars on the walls.

VINEYARDS

Artisan Wines. This producer of high-quality wine using grapes sourced from around New Zealand is open daily, but Saturday is best because there is a farmers' market. You can try a wide range of Artisan wines alongside local produce, much of it organic. There's a busy restaurant on-site and tasting and sales. From time to time the vineyard also provides courses in things like cheese making so check ahead. ⊠ *99 Parrs Cross Rd., Oratia Waitakere City* ☎ *09/838–7979* ⊕ *www.artisanwines. co.nz Web* ☉ *Mon.–Sun. 11–5.*

Babich Wines. The Babich family has been making wine in New Zealand for nearly 100 years beginning first in the far north where Josip Babich joined his brothers from Croatia and planted grapes near the gum fields. The Henderson cellar site has a range of tastings and snacks. The 72-acre site is unique; years ago it was amid farmland but now is almost surrounded by houses as the population in west Auckland has grown. ⊠ *Babich Rd. , Henderson, Waitakere City* ☎ *09/833–7859* ⊕ *www.babicwines.co.nz* ☉ *Weekdays 9–5, Sat. 10–5.*

Matua Valley Wines. While no longer family-owned, Matua Valley Wines is well worth a visit if you are heading to Auckland's West Coast. In addition to tasting a wide variety of wines— it's known for its sauvignon blanc—the estate offers elegant dining in its restaurant the Hunting Lodge. The wines available for tasting change about every two weeks. You can also picnic under the trees or play petanque. In summer the vineyard hosts jazz performances and in mid-winter a Christmas Dinner, which is always well received. ⊠ *Waikoukou Valley Rd., Waimauku Auckland* ☎ *09/411–8301* ⊕ *www.matua.co.nz* ☉ *Daily 10–5.*

Villa Maria Winery. This winery has grown from a small company founded by the Fistonich family to one of the country's biggest producers, with a wide range of wines using different grapes. It is recognized for its consistency, and George Fistonich, the founder, has done much for the grape industry in New Zealand. The Auckland winery is close to the airport and is a purpose-built facility; in addition to making wine and holding tastings it also hosts outdoor concerts in summer with anything from jazz to classical music. The tasting room offers selections from most of the company's vineyards. There are two tours a day, and it's a good place to stop on the way to the airport on your last day. Villa Maria can arrange shipping if you decide after tasting to buy. ⊠ *118 Montgomerie Rd., Mangere Manukau City* ☎ *09/255–0660* ⊕ *www.villamaria.co.nz* ⊙ *Weekdays 9–6, weekends 10–5.*

SPORTS AND THE OUTDOORS

BEACHES

Auckland's beaches are commonly categorized by area—east, west, or north. The eastern beaches, such as those along Tamaki Drive on the south side of the harbor, are closer to the city and don't have heavy surf. They usually have playgrounds and changing facilities. **Judge's Bay** and **Mission Bay** are recommended for their surroundings. One of Auckland's first churches, St. Stephen's Chapel, overlooks Judge's Bay, a tidal inlet. Both beaches are close to the city center and can be reached by bus.

West-coast black-sand beaches are popular in summer, but be warned: the black iron-sand can get extremely hot so you need footwear. The sea at the western beaches is often rough, and sudden rips and holes can trap the unwary. Lifeguard patrol varies among the beaches; don't be tempted in unless they are on duty.

The most visited of these beaches is **Piha,** some 40 km (25 mi) west of Auckland, which has pounding surf as well as a sheltered lagoon dominated by the reclining mass of Lion Rock. A short steep climb up the rock rewards you with a dramatic view. **Whatipu,** south of Piha, is a broad sweep of sand offering safe bathing behind the sandbar that guards Manukau Harbour. **Bethells,** to the north, often has heavy surf but is superb to walk on.

Fodor's Choice ★ In the same vicinity, **Karekare** is the beach where the dramatic opening scenes of Jane Campion's *The Piano* were shot. Steep windswept cliffs surround the beach, and the surf is rugged. A short walk from the parking lot is a 200-foot waterfall, feeding a lagoon that is good for swimming. Another beach **Muriwai** is about 40 km (25 mi) from Auckland and you have the added bonus of passing vineyards on the way home. It has spectacular cliff walks. To get to the west-coast beaches, head to Titirangi and take the winding road signposted as THE SCENIC DRIVE. Once you are on that road, the turnoffs to individual beaches are well marked. Across Waitemata Harbour from the city, a chain of magnificent beaches stretches north as far as the Whangaparoa Peninsula, 40 km (25 mi) from Auckland. Taking Highway 1 north and keeping an eye peeled for signs, for instance, you'll reach **Cheltenham,** just north of Devonport and then after that **Takapuna** and **Milford.**

Continued on page 106

CITY OF SAILS

by Debra A. Klein and Jessica Kany

Walking along the boat-lined docks of Waitemata Harbour, it's clear why they call Auckland the City of Sails. Residents revel in taking out their own boats, from dinghies to sailboats to yachts. Sailing seems to be part of the Kiwi DNA, and there are lots of opportunities for you to take part in the fun.

There are more yachts here per capita than in any other city in the world, and some of the world's fastest vessels are built on Auckland's North Shore and crewed by Kiwis. New Zealand has won two America's Cup competitions and hosted regattas of all sizes. In summer, Viaduct Harbour dazzles with some of the sleekest racing boats and splashiest yachts in the hemisphere. Aquatic innovation isn't just about racing, though. A New Zealand farmer invented the jet-boat, a high-octane contraption that thrills adrenaline junkies on shallow inland rivers.

Outside of the city, the Bay of Islands' lonely beaches, hundreds of islands, and safe inlets make for great sailing, while the South Island's dramatic geography is a cruise-taker's scenic fantasy. Inland, meandering rivers are perfect for whitewater rafting, while Abel Tasman National Park's coast is a must-kayak stretch of empty beaches and teal blue bays.

TOURING AUCKLAND'S HARBORS

There are plenty of charter companies ready to take you out for a day on the water around Auckland, and they offer a wide array of experiences, from gentle, 1½-hour trips for the sea-wary to multiday treks along the coast. Here are the top experiences for getting out on the water while in Auckland.

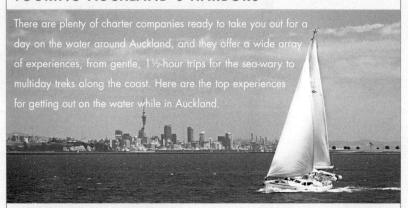

BEST FOR THE LANDLUBBER

FULLERS FERRIES

☎ 09/367-9111

🌐 www.fullers.co.nz

✉ Pier 1, Ferry Terminal, 99 Quay Street Auckland

🚢 Adult $35, Child $17.50, Senior $31.50, Family $87.50

Departure: 10:30 AM and 1:30 PM from the Downtown Ferry Terminal

ABOUT THE BOAT

Tour and commuter ferries gently ply the Waitemata Harbour between Auckland and Davenport with additional service to the islands in the Hauraki Gulf.

THE EXPERIENCE

See the Auckland skyline (and get a sense of the size of Sky Tower) on Fullers's 1½-hour **Auckland Harbour cruise**. Commentary runs while taking passengers past the Harbour Bridge, Devonport's naval base, and Bean Rock Lighthouse. There's a brief stopover on Rangitoto Island in the Harauki Gulf. Various day tours of Waiheke Island are also available.

BEST FOR THE SPEED DEMON

SAIL NZ

☎ 09/359-5987

🌐 www.sailnz.co.nz

✉ Booking Kiosk, Viaduct Harbour, Auckland

🚢 Adult $150–$195, Child $110-$175

Departure: Daily from Viaduct Harbour

ABOUT THE BOAT

Sail on America's Cup racing yachts in Viaduct or Waitemata harbours (depending on the trip).

THE EXPERIENCE

With Sail NZ's **America's Cup Sailing Experience** participate in sailing with a racing crew (or relax while they do the work). For more thrills participate in the **America's Cup Match Racing** trip. This three-hour experience includes practice drills followed by a race against other yachts with a race crew.

(above) Yacht passing Auckland, the City of Sails.

BEST FOR THE HISTORY (AND FOOD) BUFF

PRIDE OF AUCKLAND

☎ 09/373-4557

⊕ www.prideofauckland.com

✉ Auckland NZ Maritime Museum, Cnr. Quay and Hobson sts.

🎫 Adult $70–$110, child $37–$63

Departure: 1 PM, 2:45 PM, 3:45 PM, and 5:30 PM from Viaduct Harbour

ABOUT THE BOAT
Affiliated with Sail NZ, this fleet of purpose-built sailboats is based in Waitemata Harbour.

THE EXPERIENCE
Pride of Auckland trips keep customers well-fed and active as they take in the sights of Waitemata Harbour. Kermadec Restaurant & Bar provides New Zealand–style food on trips  timed for "lunch", "dinner", and "coffee breaks". Don't get too relaxed; working alongside the crew is encouraged. The fee includes entrance to the New Zealand National Maritime Museum, where you can explore the country's seafaring past.

BEST FOR THE HIGH-SEAS ADVENTURER

SOREN LARSEN

☎ 06/817-8799

⊕ www.sorenlarsen.co.nz

✉ Prince's Wharf West

🎫 Adult $125, child $59. Multiday trips start at $1,280

Departure: 10 AM (for day trips) from Prince's Wharf West

ABOUT THE BOAT
This restored square-rigger tall ship offers the opportunity to raise the sail and plunder the Hauraki Gulf.

THE EXPERIENCE
Five-hour day trips on the Soren Larsen hug the inner Hauraki Gulf and Waitemata Harbour, but for real adventure, book one of the four- or five-night trips through the Bay of  Islands or the Hauraki Gulf. Passengers on any trip are allowed to steer the vessel, raise the sail, or climb aloft and scan the seas for whales and dolphins.

BEST FOR THE WATER-SPORTS ENTHUSIAST

ROSS ADVENTURES

☎ 09/372-5550

⊕ www.kayakwaiheke.co.nz

✉ Waiheke Island

🎫 $75–$145 Multiday trips start at $435

Depature: 9 AM from the kayak shed at Matiatia

ABOUT THE BOAT
Ferry out to Waiheke (with Fullers) and join these guides on kayaking trips.

THE EXPERIENCE
Ross Adventures proves there's more to Waiheke Island than relaxed beaches and wineries. **Half-day** (appropriate for beginners), **full-day**, and **multi-day** kayaking trips take  paddlers past coastal cliffs and inlets. Explore caves, beaches, and Māori pā sites (depending on the day's route). Full-day trips include swimming and snorkeling, and you may spot blue penguins or dolphins as you kayak.

You can spend a couple of days tooling around the Hauraki Gulf, three days visiting the beaches of Abel Tasman, or three weeks exploring the sub-Antarctic Islands. Many vessels provide equipment for fishing and diving and other toys suited to the cruising area. The Bay of Islands, Hauraki Gulf, and Marlborough Sounds are maritime reserves and popular for sailing in season.

NORTH ISLAND

At the top end, you will drool over luxury vessels such as the 72-foot ketch **The Dove** (⊕ *www.charterguide.co.nz/the-dove*) which wines and dines her guests

If you'd like an independent trip, but you'd rather someone else take the actual helm, New Zealand ports offer scores of options for skippered personalized itineraries. Choices include high-speed catamarans, luxury yachts, and restored tall ships, and these vessels run the gamut from basic to swank (which, unsurprisingly, directly corresponds to cost). Skippered boats during peak season cost anywhere from $1,000 to $3,000 a day. While most have habitual cruising grounds near their home ports, many skippers are happy to discuss an itinerary that includes destinations far and wide.

LEAVE SHORE

Already a skipper? If you're planning to sail yourself around New Zealand, book your boat ahead of time for the widest selection. Charter World (⊕ *www.charterworld.com*) and New Zealand Charter Guide (⊕ *www.charterguide.co.nz*) list bareboat and crewed options by destination.

(above) Charter a yacht in Auckland and find yourself in an immense cruising ground of islands. (below) Near Harbour Bridge, Waitemata Harbour, Auckland.

around the Hauraki Gulf; the state-of-the-art **Mazarine** (⊕ *www.charterguide. co.nz/mazarine*) will let you cruise the Bay of Plenty in style. These gorgeous boats offer the trip of a lifetime.

Charter **Cool Change** (⊕ *www.sailcoolchange.co.nz*) for day-sailing around the Bay of Islands. Cost (for up to 6 people) is $1,375.

If you're more Gilligan than Thurston Howell, the no-frills **Lara Star** (⊕ *www. redquarters.co.nz*) might be for you. Budget-minded travelers can book a berth aboard this self-catering boat with shared rooms and go spear, rock, or kayak fishing around Great Barrier Island in the Hauraki Gulf.

SOUTH ISLAND

Visitors can fish for blue cod and observe penguins while exploring Stewart Island (and bird sanctuary Ulva Island), off of the South Island, with **Rakiura Charters**, which offers fully customized skippered trips (⊕ *www.rakiuracharters.co.nz*). Prices start from $1200 a day; hourly and multiday rates available.

Nelson-based **Jamarh** (⊕ *www.sailingcharters.co.nz*) has a "toy chest" that includes a hammock, kayak, scallop dredge, and fish smoker. This beautiful catamaran sails the pristine waters of Abel Tasman; rates during peak season are about $1,225 a day.

Breaksea Girl (⊕ *www.fiordland.gen.nz*) offers ecological, educational tours of Fiordland, or a visit to the Sub Antarctic Islands. Chartering the whole boat is $2,400 a day; rates are less expensive if you share a scheduled trip with other travelers.

To get an idea of what's available visit the **New Zealand Charter Guide Web site** (⊕ *www.charterguide.co.nz*) and click on Skippered-Live Aboard on the menu.

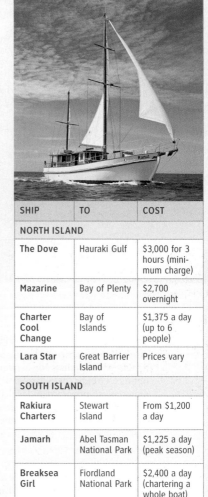

SHIP	TO	COST
NORTH ISLAND		
The Dove	Hauraki Gulf	$3,000 for 3 hours (minimum charge)
Mazarine	Bay of Plenty	$2,700 overnight
Charter Cool Change	Bay of Islands	$1,375 a day (up to 6 people)
Lara Star	Great Barrier Island	Prices vary
SOUTH ISLAND		
Rakiura Charters	Stewart Island	From $1,200 a day
Jamarh	Abel Tasman National Park	$1,225 a day (peak season)
Breaksea Girl	Fiordland National Park	$2,400 a day (chartering a whole boat)

TOP BOATING SPOTS

NORTH ISLAND
Bay of Islands: sailing
Hauraki Gulf: sailing
Bay of Plenty: fishing

SOUTH ISLAND
Abel Tasman: kayaking
Canterbury: jetboating
Marlborough Sounds: sailing

(above) Sailing on Hauraki Bay, Auckland

BIKING

Auckland can be good for cycling if you stick to certain areas, such as around the waterfront. If you are traveling with a road bike and want to join some cyclists for a "bunch ride," then there are a number of options. Groups of cyclists leave designated points around the Auckland region most mornings and welcome guests. Just call any cycle shop and they'll point you in the right direction. On weekends the bunch rides can cover up to 150 km (93 mi) and will show you parts of the countryside that most won't get to see, plus stop off for a mandatory coffee.

Adventure Cycles (✉ *9 Premier Ave.* ☎ *021/245–3868*) arms you with maps of biking routes that avoid pitfalls such as traffic. Touring bikes are $15 for a half day, $20 for a full day. Mountain bikes are $25. The rental fee includes helmets. While the company does not organize cycle tours they will provide as much information as needed and can open weekends by arrangement.

If you are staying in the central city, check out **Bike Central** (✉ *3 Britomart Pl., City Center* ☎ *09/365 1768*), which provides bikes, coffee, and showers. Charges are $10 an hour, $25 for a half day, or $40 for the full day.

BOATING, SAILING, AND KAYAKING

If you're in Auckland in February be sure to check out the Auckland Anniversary Regatta (⊕ *www.regatta.org.nz*). The Yachting New Zealand Web site has a calendar of events throughout the year (⊕ *www. yachtingnz.org.nz*). ⇨ *"City of Sails" for more on sailing.*

Whatipu Beach, on the western Auckland coast, hugs the blue waters of Wonga Wonga Bay.

KAYAKING Instead of taking the ferry to Rangitoto, you could paddle. **Ferg's**
★ **Kayaks** (✉ *12 Tamaki Dr.* ☎ *09/529–2230* ⊕ *www.fergskayaks.co.nz*),
run by four-time Olympic gold medal winner Ian Ferguson, takes guided
trips ($120) to the island twice daily, leaving at 9 and 4. The round-trip
takes about five hours—two to paddle each way and one to climb the
volcano. On the later trip you paddle back in the dark toward the city
lights. Booking is essential.

BRIDGE ADVENTURES

AJ Hackett Bungy—Auckland Harbour Bridge (✉ *Westhaven Reserve,
Curran St. Herne Bay* ☎ *09/361–2000* ⊕ *www.ajhackett.com*) is the
only bungy (New Zealand spelling for bungee) site in Auckland. The
company operates bungy jumping off the Harbour Bridge ($120) year-
round. You could also sign up for their **Harbour Bridge Experience,** a
1½-hour bridge climb ($120) with commentary on the history of the
bridge and the region. There are three trips a day and booking is recommended. Views from the bridge walk are outstanding.

GOLF

Formosa Golf Resort (✉ *110 Jack Lachland Dr., Beachlands* ☎ *09/536–
5895* ⊕ *www.formosa.co.nz*) is about 45 minutes from the city center.
The 18-hole course, designed by New Zealand golfing legend Sir Bob
Charles, has views of the Hauraki Gulf from most holes, and they have a
range of accommodations. It has quite a poor automated phone system
so be patient. Green fees are $65 and cart fees $30.

CLOSE UP

Rugby Madness

New Zealand is to host the 2011 Rugby World Cup, and Auckland is where many of the games will be played—delighting the city's tourism and business community but presenting local government with a slew of problems. Everything from the region's transport network to the condition of the stadium has become everyday conversation as power brokers discuss funding issues and who should be paying.

Rugby evolved out of soccer in 19th-century Britain. It was born at the elitist English school of Rugby, where in 1823 a schoolboy by the name of William Webb Ellis became bored with kicking a soccer ball and picked it up and ran with it. Rugby developed among the upper classes of Britain, whereas soccer remained a predominantly working-class game.

However, in colonial New Zealand, a country largely free from the rigid class structure of Britain, the game developed as the nation's number-one winter sport. One reason was the success of New Zealand teams in the late 19th and early 20th centuries. This remote outpost of the then British empire, with a population of only 750,000 in 1900, was an impressive force at rugby, and this became a source of great national pride. Today, in a country of 4 plus million, the national sport is played by 250,000 New Zealanders at club level and embraced by many with an almost religious fervor. It's not uncommon for infants to be given tiny rugby jerseys and balls as presents.

The top-class rugby season in the Southern Hemisphere kicks off in February with the Super 14, which pits professional teams from provincial franchises in New Zealand, South Africa, and Australia against one another. New Zealand's matches are generally held in main cities, and you should be able to get tickets without too much trouble. The international season runs from June to late August. This is your best chance to see the national team, the All Blacks, and the major cities are again the place to be. National provincial championship games hit towns all over the country from late August to mid-October. A winner-takes-all game decides who will attain the domestic rugby Holy Grail, the Ranfurly Shield. If you can't catch a live game, you can always count on a crowd watching the televised match at the local pubs or a sports bar.

The sport is similar to American football, except players are not allowed to pass the ball forward, and they wear no protective gear. There's a World Cup for the sport every four years since 1987, which New Zealand has won once. The New Zealand team's failure to win the trophy in 1999, despite being the favorite, sparked off a huge bout of introspection about what went wrong. More soul-searching followed during the 2002 hosting debacle, after which most of the union board members were replaced. In the end, the 2003 World Cup left the Southern Hemisphere altogether, crossing the equator for the first time with a British victory. In 2005 the All Blacks won every trophy in the cupboard but in 2007 they once again failed to win the World Cup, leaving the nation in shock.

New Zealanders worship the national rugby team, the All Blacks.

Gulf Harbour Country Club (⊠ *Gulf Harbour Dr., Rodney District* ☎ *09/424–0971* ⊕ *www.gulfharbourcountryclub.co.nz*) course was designed by Robert Trent Jones Jr., who some say is the world's finest designer of classic golf courses. It is set against the spectacular backdrop of the Hauraki Gulf and is about 40 minutes north of Auckland on the Whangaparoa Peninisula on the East Coast. Clubs can be rented; the green fee is $110 including a cart in summer. There are specials in winter, which are posted on the Web site.

Muriwai Gold Club (⊠ *Coast Rd., Muriwai Beach, Waitakere City* ☎ *09/411–8454* ⊕ *www.muriwaigolfclub.co.nz*), a 40-minute drive north of the city brings you to this links course near a bird sanctuary. The course has outstanding views of the coast. Because the links are on sandy soil it can be played even if the rest of Auckland is sodden. Clubs and golf carts can be rented; the green fee is $50. The views from the "19th hole" are outstanding.

Titirangi Golf Club (⊠ *Links Rd., Waitakere City* ☎ *09/827–5749*), a 15-minute drive south of Auckland City and with a course designed by renowned golf architect Alister MacKenzie, is one of the country's finest 18-hole courses. Nonmembers are welcome to play provided they contact the course in advance but, like Formosa, Titirangi has a really painful automated phone system. Once booked, you must show evidence of membership at an overseas club. Clubs and golf carts can be rented; the green fee is $150.

HIKING

The scenic **Waitakere Ranges** west of Auckland are a favorite walking and picnic spot for locals. The bush-clad ranges, rising sharply from the west-coast beaches, are threaded by streams and waterfalls. The 20-minute **Arataki Nature Trail** (☎ 09/817–4941) is a great introduction to kauri and other native trees. The highlight of another great trail, **Auckland City Walk,** is Cascade Falls, just off the main track of this easy hour's walk. The **Arataki Visitor Centre** displays modern Māori carvings and has information on the Waitakeres and other Auckland parks.

To get to the Waitakeres, head along the Northwestern Motorway, Route 16, from central Auckland, take the Waterview turnoff, and keep heading west to the gateway village of Titirangi. A sculpture depicting fungal growths tells you you're heading in the right direction. From here the best route to follow is Scenic Drive, with spectacular views of Auckland and its two harbors. The visitor center is 5 km (3 mi) along the drive.

For a Māori perspective on Auckland, take the **Tāmaki Hikoi** (✉ *Auckland i-SITE Visitor Centre, Princes Wharf, 137 Quay St., Viaduct* ☎ *09/307– 0612* ✉ *Atrium, Sky City, Victoria and Federal Sts.* ☎ *09/363–7182*), a walking tour with guides from the local Ngati Whatua tribe who tell ancient stories and recount their history on a trek from Mt. Eden through sacred landmarks to the harbor. The three-hour tour ($80) departs at 9 AM and 1:30 PM from the visitor centers at Princes Wharf and Sky City.

SPECTATOR SPORTS

Eden Park is the city's major stadium for big sporting events. This is the best place in winter to see New Zealand's sporting icon, the rugby team All Blacks, one of the best in the world. More frequently, it sees the Auckland Blues, a Super 12 rugby team that plays professional franchise opponents from Australia, South Africa, and other parts of New Zealand. Cricket teams arrive in summer. For information on sporting events, check out *What's On Auckland,* a monthly guide available from the Auckland i-SITE Visitor Centre. The big games sell fast and tickets can be booked through **Ticketek** (☎ *09/307–5000* ⊕ *www. ticketek.co.nz*).

SHOPPING

Ponsonby is known for its design stores and fashion boutiques. Auckland's main shopping precincts for clothes and shoes are Queen Street and Newmarket; Queen Street is particularly good for outdoor gear, duty-free goods, greenstone jewelry, and souvenirs. O'Connell and High streets also have a good smattering of designer boutiques, bookstores, and other specialty shops. There is a growing number of big malls in the suburbs, among the busiest Sylvia Park in Mount Wellington, Westfield Albany in Albany, and Botany Downs Centre in Botany Downs. These malls host a range of shopping but are more fun for people-watching than purchasing.

2

DEPARTMENT STORE

Smith and Caughey's Ltd. (✉ *253–261 Queen St., City Center* ☎ *09/377–4770*) is a good place to see plenty of local brands under one roof coupled with extremely good service. The clothing runs the gamut from homegrown favorites such as Trelise Cooper to international megabrands such as Armani. The lingerie department is known for its large, plush dressing rooms. You'll also find the largest cosmetics hall in the city and a good selection of conservative but well-made menswear and good quality china.

MALL

Dress-Smart (✉ *151 Arthur St., Onehunga* ☎ *09/622–2400*) is a whole mall of more than 70 factory outlets and is the place to go for high-quality, low-priced goods. It started as a clothing mall, but it has doubled in size and you'll also find books, records, children's toys, bags, jewelry, and housewares. Expect to pay 30%–70% less than regular retail. Take the inexpensive **shuttle service** (☎ *0800/748–885*) or, if you're driving, take the Penrose turnoff from the Southern Motorway; then follow the signs to Onehunga. This is the heart of Auckland suburbia, so a detailed road map helps. Dress-Smart is close to Onehunga Mall where you will find interesting antique shops and a good secondhand book shop.

SPECIALTY STORES

BOOKS AND MAPS

Legendary Hard to Find (but worth the effort) Quality Second-hand Books, Ltd. (✉ *171–173 The Mall, Onehunga* ☎ *09/634–4340;* **Devonport Vintage Books** ✉ *81A Victoria St., Devonport* ☎ *09/446–0300;* **Classics and Such Like Books** ✉ *201 Ponsonby Rd., City Center* ☎ *09/360–1741*) are all worth browsing in and a good place to find that book you've always wanted. **Unity Books** (✉ *19 High St., City Center* ☎ *09/307–0731*) is a general bookstore that specializes in travel, fiction, science, biography, and New Zealand–related books.

CLOTHING AND ACCESSORIES

★ Six jewelers started **Fingers** (✉ *2 Kitchener St., City Center* ☎ *09/373–3974*) in the 1970s as a place to display and sell their work. Now it showcases unique contemporary work by about 45 New Zealand artists, working with fine metals and stones. It's jewelry as art. Look out for works that combine precious metal with more mundane materials like rocks or seashells or even plastic.

Tailored women's clothing that looks like something from an old fashion magazine at **Karen Walker** (✉ *15 O'Connell St., City Center* ☎ *09/309–6299*), one of New Zealand's most recognized fashion designers. The store also stocks international labels Seven Jeans, Marjan Pejoski, and White Trash Charms accessories. Ms. Walker also now has a line of jewelry and eyewear.

Kia Kaha (✉ *1/100 Ponsonby Rd., Ponsonby* ☎ *09/360–0260* ⊕ *www. kiakaha.co.nz*), which means "Be Strong" in Māori, carries distinctive casual and sportswear with Māori designs. It makes exquisite men's shirts and has branched into particularly wearable dresses. The store also stocks the Cambo line of golf shirts, made by Kia Kaha; Michael Campbell was wearing one when he won the 2005 U.S. Open.

For bohemian glamour with a deconstructed and sometimes raggedy edge, go to **Trelise Cooper** (✉ *147 Quay St., Viaduct* ☎ *09/366–1964* ✉ *536 Parnell Rd., Parnell* ☎ *09/366–1962* ⊕ *www.trelisecooper.com*). Flamboyantly feminine designs popular with older curvy women, plush fabrics, extravagant use of colors that make the wearers look like parrots or other tropical birds, and intricate detailing are the hallmarks of this New Zealand frock designer. Ms. Cooper is also making clothes for children; these have been received to great acclaim by mothers who love to dress up their daughters. Fabulously individual **WORLD** (✉ *57 High St., City Center* ☎ *09/373–3034* ✉ *175 Ponsonby Rd., Ponsonby* ☎ *09/360–4544*) is one of New Zealand's groundbreaking fashion labels, making contemporary clothing with attitude. Find its funky street wear for men just up the street at **WORLD Man** (✉ *47 High St.* ☎ *09/377–8331*). Fashion label **Zambesi** (✉ *Vulcan La. and O'Connell St., City Center* ☎ *09/303–1701* ✉ *169 Ponsonby Rd., Ponsonby* ☎ *09/360–7391*) eschews populist trends except that global love of black-on-black and is always among the top New Zealand designers. The slim wear their garments most successfully.

SOUVENIRS AND GIFTS

Follow elephant footprints down an alley in Parnell Village to the 30-year-old **Elephant House** (✉ *237 Parnell Rd.* ☎ *09/309–8740*) for an extensive collection of souvenirs and crafts, many unavailable elsewhere, such as one-off hand-turned bowls, pottery, and glass. The sign hanging above **Pauanesia** (✉ *35 High St., City Center* ☎ *09/366–7282*) sets the tone for this gift shop—the letters are shaped from paua shell, which resembles abalone. You'll find bags, place mats, picture frames, and many other items.

SPORTS GEAR

The extensive range of gear at **Green Coast** (✉ *114 Kitchener Rd., Milford* ☎ *09/489–0242*) on the North Shore is made especially for New Zealand conditions and the shop is run by extremely knowledgeable people.

Kathmandu (✉ *151 Queen St., City Center* ☎ *09/309–4615*) stocks New Zealand–made outdoor clothing and equipment, from fleece jackets to sleeping bags to haul-everything packs.

STREET MARKETS

For many years people from all over Auckland have headed south on a Saturday morning looking for bargains to the sounds of hip-hop beats and island music at **Otara Market** (✉ *Newbury St., Otara*), which opens around 6 on Saturday morning. Vegetable stalls groan with produce such as taro, yams, and coconuts. More Asian food stalls are joining the

DID YOU KNOW?

New Zealand's rugby team is the All Blacks, but the moniker is equally appropriate to the design label Zambesi. The high-concept fashions frequently feature differently textured black pieces layered over one another.

traditional Polynesian tapa cloths, paua-shell jewelry, greenstone, and bone carvings, reflecting the city's increasingly multicultural profile, but sadly some junky stuff is creeping in. Nonetheless, look out for T-shirts bearing puns on famous brands, such as "Mikey" or "Cocolicious." The T-shirts designed by the Niuean poet Vela Manusaute are particularly sought by collectors. Stalls come down around midday. Exit the Southern Motorway at the East Tamaki off-ramp, turn left, and take the second left.

The handsome countryside of the Waitakere Ranges has attracted artists seeking an alternative lifestyle, close to a major population (and customer) base but away from the hustle and bustle. Many of their wares are on sale at the **Titirangi Village Market** (⊠ *Titirangi Memorial Hall, S. Titirangi Rd.* ☏ *09/817–3584*). It's held on the last Sunday of each month, 10–2. Auckland's main bazaar, **Victoria Park Market** (⊠ *208 Victoria St. W, City Center* ☏ *09/309–6911*), consists of 2½ acres of clothing, footwear, sportswear, furniture, souvenirs, and crafts at discount prices. Be sure to stop by **From N to Z** (☏ *09/377–2447*) for Kiwi icons such as plastic tomato-shaped ketchup dispensers and hand-carved bone and greenstone pendants. The market, housed in the city's former garbage incinerator, is open daily 9–6. On a terrace behind the market, you can recharge your batteries with a coffee at **Caffetteria Allpress** (⊠ *Adelaide and Drake Sts.* ☏ *09/369–5842*), where again sunglasses are worn with aplomb.

EMERGENCY CONTACTS

For off-hours over-the-counter needs, hit the After-Hours Pharmacy, which stays open weekdays from 6 PM to 1 AM and weekends 9 AM to 1 AM.

Emergency Services Fire, police, and ambulance (☏ *111*).

Hospitals Auckland Hospital (⊠ *Park Rd., Grafton* ☏ *09/367–0000*). MercyAscot Hospital (⊠ *90 Greenland Rd. E, Remuera* ☏ *09/623–5700*).

Late-Night Pharmacy After-Hours Pharmacy (⊠ *60 Broadway, Newmarket* ☏ *09/520–6634*).

Northland and the Bay of Islands

WORD OF MOUTH

"[The way to] Cape Reinga [had] a breathtaking walk around the lighthouse; well-documented Māori information; and gorgeous views of headlands, cliffs, and ocean. This is where the Tasman Sea and the Pacific Ocean meet. We could actually see the difference in current at the meeting point."

— Lissa2905

WELCOME TO NORTHLAND AND THE BAY OF ISLANDS

TOP REASONS TO GO

★ **Boating and Fishing:**
Take a cruise to an island, whale-watch, swim with dolphins, or fish with the Bay of Islands as the hub.

★ **Bountiful Beaches:**
Most Northland beaches are safe for swimming. On the 90 Mile Beach you can swim in both the Tasman Sea and the Pacific Ocean. Experienced surfers head to Shipwreck Bay and to the point farther south for great waves.

★ **Superb Diving:** Dive at the Poor Knights Islands, known for their huge variety of subtropical fish, or the wreck of the Greenpeace vessel *Rainbow Warrior,* sunk by French agents in 1985.

★ **Walking and Hiking:**
Superb bushwalking (hiking) provides a close look at ancient kauri trees (a local species of pine) and interesting birds, such as *tūī (too-ee), fan-tails, wood pigeons, and the occasional kiwi.

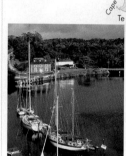

1 Northland. *Te Tai Tokerau,* or Northland, with its no-frills, tiny, friendly towns and high rates of unemployment, is extremely different from the affluent Bay of Islands. However, the scenery is just as stunning. But without the infrastructure that goes along with organized tourism you will feel a little off the beaten path. The best approach is to travel in a relaxed fashion: explore Cape Reinga, the tip of the country; take the car ferry out past the mangroves and cruise across Hokianga Harbour. The ferry is busy over summer but half the fun is people-watching —this quiet route gets its fair share of movie and music stars. Some visitors will stand in awe at the base of a giant kauri tree; others eat fish-and-chips on Opononi beach and enjoy the views of the enormous golden sand dunes across the water.

2 The Bay of Islands. This sweep of coastline is home to many islands amid a mild, subtropical climate and excellent game-fishing waters. That combination makes the Bay of Islands ideal—with a slew of things to do while visiting. You'll feel well catered to, whether your interests lie in the history of Waitangi (and New Zealand) or the sunken *Rainbow Warrior,* staying somewhere with your own private beach, or trying to catch the biggest marlin on record.

GETTING
ORIENTED

As the map indicates, Northland includes the Bay of Islands, but we've divided this chapter into two sections—Northland and the Bay of Islands. The West Coast, from Dargaville all the way up to Cape Reinga, is by far the least populated and developed; the unassuming little towns along the way and the lumbering *Kohu Ra Tuama* Hokianga Harbour ferry stand out in stark contrast to the luxurious lodges and yachts around the Bay of Islands. With the (no small!) exception of the 144 islands that make up the East Coast's Bay of Islands, the terrain is not so dissimilar; no matter where you are in the North, you're never far from the water and the combination of coast, rolling pastures, and ancient native forest is unlike any other part of the country.

NORTHLAND AND THE BAY OF ISLANDS PLANNER

Planning Your Time

Plan to spend three days in Northland. On day one take in the main town of Paihia and then catch the ferry to Russell. Drive north on the second day, stopping at beaches and Cape Reinga. Meander home via the Hokianga on day three by winding south through the forests along the West Coast to Kohukohu. Ferry south across serene Hokianga Harbour to Rawene. From Opononi, closer to the harbor's mouth, continue down the Kauri Coast to the Waipoua Forest. From there, Highway 12 runs to the arty town of Dargaville, and on to Matakohe, site of the renowned Kauri Museum. It's another half-hour to Brynderwyn, where you rejoin State Highway 1 about an hour north of Auckland.

When to Go

Snow doesn't fall in the "winterless north," but it can get cool. The best time to go is between mid-November and mid-April; peak season is December through March. During the quiet months of July and August it can be wet. For game fishing, arrive from February to June.

Getting Here and Around

Bus Travel

Taking a bus is a cheap and also easy alternative to driving. Several companies serve all but the most out-of-the way spots. InterCity (contact the Paihia branch), Newmans, and Northliner Express all run several times daily between Auckland and the Bay of Islands and connect to the other Northland centers at least once a day. Auckland to Paihia takes about 4½ hours and to Kerikeri about 5½ hours.

Contacts InterCity (☎ 09/402–7857 ⊕ www.intercity-coach.co.nz. **Newmans** (☎ 09/913–6200 ⊕ www.new-manscoach.co.nz. **Northliner Express** ☎ 09/307–5873 ⊕ www.northliner.co.nz.

Boat and Ferry Travel

Three passenger boats cross between Paihia and Russell, with departures at least once every 20 minutes in each direction from 7:20 AM to 10:30 PM from Paihia, and 7 AM to 10 PM from Russell. The one-way fare is $6. Or, join the car ferry at nearby Opua, about 5 km (3 mi) south of Paihia. It operates from 6:50 AM to 9:50 PM, with departures at approximately 10-minute intervals from either shore. The last boat leaves from Okiato on the Russell side at 9:50 PM. The one-way fare is $10 for car and driver plus $1 for each adult passenger. Buy your tickets on board (cash only). Save time by crossing the Hokianga Harbour between Rawene and Kohukohu (with or without a car) by ferry.

Car Travel

It's best to see Northland's many lovely bays, sandy beaches, and worthwhile sights by car. Northland roads are generally just two lanes wide with many one-lane bridges in remote areas. Take care on the narrow—and often unsealed—roads that thread through the region. Don't risk a drive along 90 Mile Beach; the quicksand and tides can leave you stuck, and your rental car insurance won't cover any accidents here.

From Auckland, drive up the East Coast on State Highway 1 and return down the West Coast on Highway 12 (or vice versa), but make sure to check out smaller, winding coastal roads with their stunning coastlines and dramatic island views.

Restaurants

Seafood abounds in the north with scallops and oysters farmed throughout the region, though occasional sewerage scares put them off-limits. Snapper and kingfish are available year-round, and marlin and broad-bill swordfish are abundant between January and June.

The region prides itself on its local produce, and with more skillful chefs arriving in the region, the restaurant food is improving.

People eat earlier in Northland than in the cities, with restaurants filling around 7. Dress is casual—jeans are acceptable in all but the most upscale lodges. From May through September, many restaurants close or reduce their opening hours, some to four nights a week. October sees regular hours resume.

Hotels

Northland accommodations vary from basic motels to luxury lodges. Your hosts, particularly in the bed-and-breakfasts, share their local knowledge and are great resource on less-obvious attractions.

Paihia has plenty of vacation apartments and standard motels. The larger towns, especially Russell, have a range of high-end B&Bs, and luxury lodges sometimes come with private bays. Nearly all lodgings include Internet, but high-speed access is not as common. Air-conditioning is rare but it's not really needed either.

High season runs from December through March. Some lodges have shoulder seasons in April and May, and September and October. Overall, room rates drop between May and October.

WHAT IT COSTS IN NEW ZEALAND DOLLARS

	¢	$	$$	$$$	$$$$
Restaurants	under $10	$10–$15	$15–$20	$20–$30	over $30
Hotels	under $75	$75–$125	$125–$200	$200–$300	over $300

Restaurant prices are per person for a main course at dinner, or the equivalent. Hotel prices are for a standard double room in high season, including 12.5% tax.

Top Experiences

The remnant of the once-giant Kauri Forest that covered much of Northland includes New Zealand's biggest kauri, called Tane Mahuta. It is popular, so get there early to avoid crowds and ponder what the region was like before large-scale forestry took place.

For those with a little extra time, we recommend the coastal drive to Russell. The roads are narrow and windy, but your effort will pay off when you enjoy a picnic on a solitary beach.

If you have ventured to Kaitaia—the last big and slightly scruffy town before you hit the road to Cape Reinga—take an extra hour or so and go south of 90 Mile Beach to Ahipara and Shipwrecks Bay for lovely beach views.

Visitor Information

Local visitor bureaus, many known as i-SITEs, have information on the whole region, with more extensive information on their particular environs. In addition, some helpful community Web resources include ⊕ www.russell.net.nz, ⊕ www.kerikeri.co.nz, ⊕ www.dargaville.co.nz, and ⊕ www.paihia.co.nz. Destination Northland, a regional tourism organization, maintains ⊕ www.northland.org.nz.

NORTHLAND BEACHES

No matter where you are in New Zealand, within two hours you can be at a beach from the long white-sand beaches on the East to the black-sand rugged coastline of the West Coast.

The beach experience in New Zealand is dependent on where you are. City-side beaches in Auckland are for families while the West Coast and Far North beaches attract the surfing set.

The best beaches for people staying in Auckland are Mission Bay, Kohimarama, St. Heliers, and Ladies Bay. If you take the ferry to Devonport you can walk to a number of fine beaches popular with locals.

West Coast beaches feature black sand, which gets very hot during the day. Make sure you wear sandals while you select your spot. Swim between the flags on beaches with surf patrols; the rips can be sudden and dangerous but the pounding surf is like a free massage.

The Far North beaches are glorious and often deserted but inexperienced swimmers should not venture in over waist height.

BEST TIME TO GO

New Zealanders say the best time to hit the beach is anytime they are not at work. For swimming, November through early April is best. The farther north you go the warmer the weather and water. In summer avoid the beach mid-day—the sun can be scorching—and take a hat. In winter carry a raincoat, because weather changes quickly.

FUN FACT

At 15,134 km, (9,404 mi) the New Zealand coastline is the 10th longest in the world and varies from wide sand and stone beaches to sheer cliffs and forest where the bush meets the sea.

BEST BEACHES

KAREKARE

Film buffs will recognize KareKare from the dramatic opening scenes of *The Piano*. Its size means you will never feel hemmed in, even in the peak summer months. The pounding waves make for great swimming, but again, go in only when the surf patrol is operating. Fit walkers should explore the southern end of the beach and past the point; go at low tide because getting back is difficult when the water comes in.

MISSION BAY

A warm evening at Mission Bay off Tamaki Drive—about 10 minutes drive from the central city—can see families and community groups picnicking side by side. There is a wide range of food outlets adjacent to the beach, and all have take-out options. Three extremely good ice-cream parlors and an abundance of good coffee round out the culinary options.

MURIWAI BEACH

The black sand of Muriwai Beach is a must for those exploring the west coast. Combine a trip here with a visit to Matua Valley or Babich wineries. The beach is great for surfing and swimming. Don't go out if the surf patrol is not operating, and always swim between the red and yellow flags. Or, get up-close-and-personal with the local gannet colony from the DOC viewing platforms; see the chicks in December and January.

TAKAPUNA BEACH

You'll see some of New Zealand's most expensive houses along Takapuna Beach on Auckland's North Shore. If architecture (or being nosey) isn't your thing, it's a safe swimming beach in summer. It's good for walking, and sailors, kayakers, and triathletes all use this beach. The nice cafés in Takapuna township are two minutes away from the sand.

STAY THE NIGHT

The rhythmic sound of the sea, the salty air, the breeze against the tent; this is reason enough to try camping on a beach in New Zealand. The Department of Conservation runs cost-effective beach-side campgrounds. The facilities, while basic, are generally well maintained. Go farther from city areas and you're more likely to have a beach (almost) to yourself, especially outside the peak summer period between November and March. Camping at beaches as opposed to staying in hotels offers a complete opportunity to unwind. Take some books and a towel, and spend the afternoon dipping, snoozing, and reading under the shade of a tree. If you are traveling with children it's likely others there will want to mix and mingle which always adds to a holiday. Locals will point those who like fishing to a good spot. Almost nothing beats fresh fish cooked on a beach and eaten with fresh vegetables or even just on a piece of bread and butter.

(top left) A windy day on Takapuna Beach, (bottom) Sunset on Muriwai Beach, (top) KareKare Beach

Updated
by Richard
Pamatatau

You'll be best served on a trip to Northland by taking in inspiring views from winding coastal roads or reading on a quiet beach with some fruit from owner-operated shops. This isn't the place for good coffee or fancy food—those desires are best left for the cities—but you can relax at a luxury lodge or comfortable motel.

Northland is a contradiction. The high unemployment rate, particularly among the area's Māori population, contrasts with the area's lodges, and scenery that goes from rugged to pastoral in a matter of kilometers.

You will notice the change about an hour after leaving the sometimes-confusing jumble (both charm and scourge) that makes up Auckland. Once over the hill, either by taking the free road around the coast or the toll motorway with its viaducts over streams, and with the seaside sprawl of Orewa and Waiwera behind you, the air starts to clear and you can see what some call the Northland light. The smaller Northland population means less pollution, and may account for the fact that it seems brighter the farther north you go, even on overcast days.

The Tasman Sea on the west and the Pacific Ocean on the east meet at the top of North Island at Cape Reinga. No matter what route you take you'll pass farms and forests, marvelous beaches, and great open spaces. The East Coast, up to the Bay of Islands, is Northland's most densely populated, often with refugees from bigger cities—looking for a more relaxed life—clustered around breathtaking beaches.

The first decision on the drive north comes at the foot of the Brynderwyn Hills. Turning left will take you up the West Coast through areas once covered with forests and now used for either agricultural or horticulture.

Driving over "the Brynderwyns," as they are known, takes you to Whangarei, the only city in Northland. If you're in the mood for a diversion, you can slip to the beautiful coastline and take in Waipu Cove, an area settled by Scots, and Laings Beach, where million-dollar homes sit next to small Kiwi beach houses.

An hour's drive farther north is the Bay of Islands, known all over the world for its beauty. There you will find lush forests, splendid beaches, and shimmering harbors. The Treaty of Waitangi was signed here in 1840 between Māori and the British Crown, establishing the basis for the modern New Zealand state. Every year on February 6, the extremely beautiful Waitangi Treaty Ground (the name means weeping waters) is the sight of a celebration of the treaty and protests by Māori unhappy with it.

Continuing north on the East Coast, the agricultural backbone of the region is even more evident and a series of winding loop roads off the main highway will take you to beaches that are both beautiful and isolated where you can swim, dive, picnic, or just laze.

The West Coast is even less populated, and the coastline is rugged and windswept. In the Waipoua Forest, you will find some of New Zealand's oldest and largest kauri trees; the winding road will also take you past mangrove swamps.

Crowning the region is the spiritually significant Cape Reinga, the headland at the top of the vast stretch of 90 Mile Beach, where it's believed Māori souls depart after death. Today Māori make up roughly a quarter of the area's population (compared with the national average of about 15%). The legendary Māori navigator Kupe was said to have landed on the shores of Hokianga Harbour, where the first arrivals made their home. Many different *iwi* (tribes) lived throughout Northland, including Ngapuhi (the largest), Te Roroa, Ngati Wai, Ngati Kuri, Te Aupouri, Ngaitakoto, Ngati Kahu, and Te Rarawa. Many Māori here can trace their ancestry to the earliest inhabitants.

NORTHLAND

The Bay of Islands is the target of most tourists while the rest of Northland has large stretches of green farmland separating the mostly tiny towns. Some areas, particularly in the Far North and Hokianga, have higher-than-average unemployment, and New Zealanders joke that cannabis cultivation fuels a giant hidden economy. Whatever their occupation, Northland residents are generally good-humored and hospitable, and proud of their varied lifestyles and exceptional scenery.

Northland today is also home to many wealthy people retreating from the city who may live close to people who have never left the area.

Europeans began settling in Northland in the 18th century, starting with whalers around the Bay of Islands, Scots who settled at Waipu on the East Coast, and Dalmatians who worked the West Coast's kauri-gum fields. Anglican missionaries started arriving in Northland in the early 19th century. The first mission was established at Kerikeri by the Reverend Samuel Marsden of the Church Missionary Society, who went about trying to "civilize" the Māori before conversion. He also planted the first grapevines in New Zealand.

If you're driving up the East Coast toward the Bay of Islands in December, you'll see scarlet blossoms blazing along the roadside. These are *pohutukawa* trees in flower, turning crimson in time for the Kiwi

Christmas, hence their *Pākehā* (non-Māori) name: "the New Zealand Christmas tree." To the Māori, the flowers had another meaning: the beginning of shellfish season. Along Northland roads you might also see clumps of spiky-leaf New Zealand flax (the Māori used the fibers of this plant, the raw material for linen, to weave into clothing), huge tree ferns known as *punga, and giant mangrove swamps.*

WARKWORTH

59 km (36 mi) north of Auckland.

A sleepy town on the banks of the Mahurangi River, Warkworth was established in 1853. With lime mined from the local river, it became the first cement-manufacturing site in the southern hemisphere. Today, boatbuilding and refitting are the main industries, and Warkworth also serves as a service town for the surrounding farms and market gardens. It's a convenient stopping point en route to nearby marine reserve Goat Island or the superb vineyards at Matakana.

GETTING HERE AND AROUND

There are two ways to get to Warkworth—bus or car. It's on the major bus routes north, and all you need do is let the driver know where you want to get off. InterCity, Newmans, and the Northliner Express have hop-on hop-off ticketing options, and there is frequent service. However, bus travel can be limiting because attractions are spread out. For more flexibility rent a car and rove the countryside more freely, especially if you are heading to Matakana to explore the wineries.

ESSENTIALS

Visitor Information Warkworth Visitor Information Centre (⊠ *1 Baxter St.* ☎ *09/425–9081* ⊕ *www.warkworth-information.co.nz).*

EXPLORING

Two giants stand in Warkworth, near the Warkworth Museum—two giant kauri trees, that is. The larger one, the **McKinney Kauri,** measures almost 25 feet around its base, yet this 800-year-old colossus is a mere adolescent by kauri standards. Look a few yards to the west and you'll see the Simpson Kauri. Kauri trees were highly prized by Māori canoe builders because a canoe capable of carrying 100 warriors could be made from a single trunk. These same characteristics—strength, size, and durability—made kauri timber ideal for ships, furniture, and housing, and the kauri forests were rapidly depleted by early European settlers. Today the trees are protected by law, and infant kauri are appearing in the forests of the North Island, although their growth rate is painfully slow.

☺ Head for **SheepWorld** for a taste of life on a typical New Zealand sheep farm. Twice a day there are demonstrations of working farm dogs rounding up sheep and sheep shearing. An ecotrail takes you through the bush, providing information on native trees, birds (and their calls), and boxes of *weta,* large, ugly—yet impressive—native insects. On the weekends, the farm dogs even herd ducks. Children can take pony rides, and, in August, bottle-feed lambs. ⊠ *324 State Hwy. 1* ☎ *09/425–7444* ⊕ *www.sheepworld.co.nz* ⊠ *$8, $22 including sheep-and-dog show (at 11 and 2)* ☺ *Daily 9–5.*

The **Warkworth Museum** contains a collection of Māori artifacts, plus farming and domestic implements from the pioneering days of the district, as well as implements used to dig for kauri gum. Rotating textile displays cover clothing dating to the late 1700s. There is also a display of a school dental clinic—what Kiwi children called the "murder house." Outside is a collection of old buildings, including a bushman's hut and an army hut used by Americans stationed at Warkworth in World War II. ✉ *Tudor Collins Dr.* ☎ *09/425–7093* ⊕ *www.wwmuseum.orcon.net.nz* 🗐 *$6, $12 for a family* ☉ *Oct.– Easter, daily 9–4; Easter–Sept., daily 9–3:30.*

EN ROUTE

Take a trip to the **Goat Island** marine reserve where fishing is prohibited and marine life has returned in abundance, with prominent species including blue *maomao* fish, snapper, and cod. It does get crowded here and midweek is best. You can put on a snorkel and glide safely around the island just a little ways offshore and get up-close-and-personal with a maomao. You can rent a mask, snorkel, and flippers ($14)—and a wetsuit if it's too cold for you ($15)—from **Seafriends** (☎ *09/422–6212* ⊕ *www.seafriends.org.nz*); their sign is about 1 km (½ mi) before the beach on the main drag, Goat Island Road. **Glass Bottom Boat** (☎ *09/422–6334* ⊕ *www.glassbottomboat.co.nz*) has—surprise, surprise—a glass-bottom boat that runs around the island ($25). If the weather isn't ideal, they do an inner reef trip ($20). The beach area is good for a picnic, as well.

To get to Goat Island head toward Leigh, 21 km (13 mi) northeast of Warkworth. From Leigh, take a left turn and follow the signs for a couple of miles. If you arrive by 10, you should avoid the masses especially midweek and in winter. Obtain leaflets about Goat Island from the Warkworth Visitor Information Centre.

TOURS

Great Sights, based out of Auckland, leads one-, two-, and three-day trips to the Bay of Islands. The one-day tour stops at Kaiwaka for morning tea and goes on to visit the Waitangi Treaty House and to cruise out to the Hole in the Rock. You can opt for a tour of historic Russell instead of the cruise. Taking the two-day tour allows you both to cruise and visit Russell, and the three-day itinerary adds a trip along 90 Mile Beach to Cape Reinga, where the Tasman Sea and Pacific Ocean meet. Rates start at $199 for the one-day trip. ✉ *Discover New Zealand Centre, 180 Quay St., Auckland* ☎ *09/375–4700* ⊕ *www.greatsights.co.nz.*

WHANGAREI

127 km (79 mi) north of Warkworth, 196 km (123 mi) north of Auckland.

The main center in Northland is the Whangarei (*fahng*-ar-ay) District; Whangarei Harbour was traditionally a meeting place for Māori tribes traveling south by *waka* (canoe). The full Māori name of the harbor, Whangarei Terenga Paraoa, means "swimming place of whales" but is also interpreted as "the meeting place of chiefs." Europeans started to settle in the area from the mid-1800s; now it's a town of roughly 45,000 people, rooted in the agriculture, forestry, and fishing industries.

CLOSE UP

The Treaty of Waitangi

The controversial cornerstone of New Zealand's Māori and Pākehā relations is the 1840 Treaty of Waitangi, the first formal document that bound the Māori to the British crown. This contract became the basis for Britain's claim to the entire country as its colony.

In the mid-1830s, Britain became increasingly concerned about advances by French settlers and the inroads made by the New Zealand Company, a private emigration organization. The British government had an official Resident at Waitangi, James Busby, but no actual means to protect its interests. In 1835, Busby helped orchestrate an alliance between more than 30 North Island Māori chiefs.

In 1840, Captain William Hobson arrived in Waitangi to negotiate a transfer of sovereignty. Hobson and Busby hurriedly drew up a treaty in both English and Māori, and presented it to the Māori confederation on February. On the following day, 43 chiefs signed the treaty.

But there were significant differences between the Māori and English versions. In the first article, the English version said the Māori would cede sovereignty to the Queen of England. But the Māori translation used the word *kāwanatanga* (governorship), which did not mean that the Māori were ceding the right to *mana* (self-determination).

The second article guaranteed the chiefs the "full, exclusive and undisturbed possession of their lands, estates, forests, fisheries, and other properties," but granted the right of preemption to the crown. The Māori translation did not convey the crown's exclusive right to buy Māori land, which caused friction over the decades. The third article granted the Māori protection as British citizens—and thus held them accountable to British law.

After the initial wave of signatures at Waitangi, signatures were gathered elsewhere in the North Island and on the South Island. In spring 1840 Hobson claimed all of New Zealand as a British colony. He had not, however, gotten signatures from some of the most powerful Māori chiefs, and this came back to haunt the crown during the Land Wars of 1860.

What wasn't confiscated after the Land Wars was taken by legislation. In 1877 Chief Justice Prendergast ruled that the treaty was "a simple nullity" that lacked legal validity because one could not make a treaty with "barbarians." At first European contact, 66.5 million acres of land was under Māori control, but by 1979 only 3 million remained—of mostly marginal lands.

The battle to have the treaty honored and reinterpreted is ongoing. In 1973, February 6 was proclaimed the official Waitangi Day holiday. From the get-go, the holiday sparked debate, as Māori activists protest the celebration of such a divisive document. The Waitangi Tribunal was established in 1975 to allow Māori to rule on alleged breaches of the treaty, and in 1985 the tribunal's powers were made retrospective to 1840. It has its hands full, as the claims continue to be one of New Zealand's largest sociopolitical issues. The treaty is now in the National Archives in Wellington.

Boatbuilding is a traditional business, manufacturing everything from superyachts to charter boats. The mouth of the harbor is dominated by the volcanic peaks of Whangarei Heads, atop Bream Bay. The drive from town to the Whangarei Heads takes about 20 minutes heading out on Riverside Drive, past mangrove-lined bays. At the Heads are stunning white-sand beaches and coves with safe swimming, and several hikes, including up the peaks of Mt. Manaia.

GETTING HERE AND AROUND

Whangarei is about two hours by car from Auckland on State Highway One. Bus services ($40) also travel this route but take longer as they stop at many small towns along the way.

You can fly from Auckland to Whangarei, but factoring arriving at the airport and checking in, it's often quicker to drive to Whangarei. There is no train service.

ESSENTIALS

Bus Depot (✉ *Northland Coach and Travel Bldg., 11 Rose St.* ☎ *09/438–2653*).

Hospital Whangarei Hospital (✉ *Maunu Rd., Whangarei* ☎ *09/430–4100*).

Visitor Information Whangarei Visitor Information Centre (✉ *92 Otaika Rd., Whangarei* ☎ *09/438–1079* ⊕ *www.whangareinz.com*).

EXPLORING

TOP ATTRACTIONS

Claphams Clocks—The National Clock Museum. About every conceivable method of telling time is represented here. The quirky collection of more than 1,500 clocks includes primitive water clocks, ships' chronometers, and ornate masterworks from Paris and Vienna. Some of the most intriguing examples were made by the late Mr. Clapham himself, such as his World War II air-force clock. Ironically, the one thing you won't find here is the correct time. If all the bells, chimes, gongs, and cuckoos went off together, the noise would be deafening, so the clocks are set to different times. ✉ *Dent St., Town Basin* ☎ *09/438–3993* ⊕ *www.claphamsclocks.com* 🖭 *$8* ⊙ *Daily 9–5.*

Greagh Garden. If roses are your thing then Greagh Garden is a must. The first settlers eager to farm the rich volcanic land around Whangarei found their efforts thwarted by an abundance of rock in the soil. To make use of the stuff they dug up, they built miles of walls, and these gardens cover some four acres. Gardens also contain a range of perennials, mature trees, and camellias. Greagh is the Celtic name for "land among the stone." ✉ *307 Three Mile Bush Rd.* ☎ *09/435–1980* 🖭 *$4* ⊙ *Oct.–Easter, daily 9–5; Easter–Oct. by appointment.*

Heritage Park Whangarei. Minutes out of town, this 61-acre park is home to a nocturnal kiwi house, several Heritage buildings, and the Whangarei Museum. The museum has fine examples of pre-European Māori cloaks, waka (canoes), and tools. You can also check out Glorat, an original 1886 kauri homestead, and the world's smallest consecrated chapel, built in 1859 from a single kauri tree. On the third Sunday of every month and on selected "Live Days" (call for dates), you can cruise around the park on model reproductions of steam and electric trains, as well as on a full-size diesel train. If

Scuba divers examine the notoriously friendly subtropical fish in the Poor Knights Islands Marine Reserve.

you love motorbikes then mark the first weekend in April, which the museum devotes to two-wheeled transport, with plans to add classic cars in 2010. ⊠ *State Hwy. 14, Maunu* ☎ *09/438–9630* ⊕ *www.whangareimuseum.co.nz* 🖃 *Park free, kiwi House and Whangarei Museum* *$10* ☉ *Daily 10–4.*

Historical Reyburn House. This is the oldest kauri villa in Whangarei. It contains the Northland Society of Arts exhibition gallery, which hosts exhibitions from New Zealand artists. Original works from well-known artists are available for purchase. The permanent collection focuses on the 1880s to the present. It's separated from the Town Basin by a playground. ⊠ *Reyburn House La., Town Basin* ☎ *09/438–3074* ⊕ *www.reyburnhouse.co.nz* 🖃 *Donation* ☉ *Tues.–Fri. 10–4, weekends 1–4.*

WORTH NOTING

Whangarei Falls. The falls are a lovely picnic spot, located on Ngunguru Road, 5 km (3 mi) northeast of town. Viewing platforms are atop the falls, and a short trail runs through the local bush.

Whangarei Town Basin. People often bypass Whangarei on their way to the Bay of Islands. It's easy to see why, as the town has a confusing traffic system, but if you can brave it the area known as the Whangarei Town Basin is worth a look. The marina is now a haven for traveling yachts and has cafés, restaurants, galleries, and crafts shops. There's parking behind the basin off Dent Street.

WHERE TO EAT

$$$
NEW ZEALAND
★

✕ **à Deco.** In a faithfully restored art deco house, Chef Brenton Low has managed to keep standards up and this restaurant would foot it anywhere. Its reputation is built on straightforward flavors and inventive

CLOSE UP

The Poor Knights Islands

Jacques Cousteau once placed the Poor Knights Islands among the world's top 10 dive locations. Underwater archways, tunnels, caves, and rocky cliffs provide endless opportunities for viewing many species of subtropical fish in the warm currents that sweep down from the Coral Sea. On a good day you'll see soft coral, sponge gardens, gorgonian fields, and forests of kelp.

Two large islands and many islets make up the Poor Knights, remnants of an ancient volcanic eruption 12 nautical mi off the stunning Tutukaka coast, a half-hour drive east of Whangarei. The ocean around them is a marine reserve, extending 800 meters (½ mi) from the islands. Indeed the islands themselves are a nature reserve; landing on them is prohibited.

At 7.9 million cubic feet, Rikoriko Cave, on the southern island's northwest side, is one of the world's largest sea caves. It's known for its acoustics. Ferns hang from its roof, and underwater cup coral grows toward the rear of it. (Normally found at depths of 200 meters, the cave light has tricked the coral into thinking it is deeper.) Normal visibility at the Poor Knights is between 20 and 30 meters, but in Rikoriko Cave it goes up to 35 to 45 meters.

A dense canopy of regenerated *pohutukawa* covers the islands, flowering brilliant scarlet around Christmas time. Native Poor Knights lilies cling to cliff faces, producing bright red flowers in October. Rare bellbirds (*koromikos)* and red-crowned parakeets (*kakarikis),* thrive in the predator-free environment. Between October and May, millions of seabirds come to breed, including the Buller's

shearwaters that arrive from the Arctic Circle. But possibly the most distinguished resident is the New Zealand native *tuatara,* a reptile species from the dinosaur age that survives only on offshore islands.

New Zealand fur seals bask on the rocks and feed on the abundant fish life, mostly from July to October, and year-round dolphins, whales, and bronze whaler sharks can be seen in the surrounding waters. In summer you can see minke and rare Brydes whales, too. In March stingrays stack in the hundreds in the archways for their mating season.

Conditions rarely prevent diving, which is good year-round. That said, don't expect the same experience you'll get diving in the Maldives or off Australia's Great Barrier Reef. There aren't as many colorful fish, and the water is cooler. In October, the visibility drops to about 18 to 20 meters because of a spring plankton bloom, though this attracts hungry marine life. The best places for novices are Nursery Cove and shallower parts of the South Harbour.

Dive Tutukaka (⌧ *Poor Knights Dive Centre, Marina Rd., Tutukaka* ☎ *09/434–3867* ⊕ *www.diving.co.nz)* has trips for $225 with full gear rental (plus $10 for lunch). If you're not a diver, you can see the scenery from *Cave Rider,* a 25-passenger, jet-powered inflatable boat ($90). You can also sail on *The Perfect Day,* a 70-foot luxury multilevel boat, which includes a half day of sightseeing, with the option to go kayaking, snorkeling, and diving ($130). Free transfers to and from Whangarei are provided.

—Richard Pamatatau and Toni Mason

3

twists using fresh, often organic, Northland ingredients; for instance, you might find an organic free-range sirloin served with a miso consommé and oxtail, followed by a baked chocolate tart with a smoked chocolate fondue. The tasting menu includes seven courses, each matched with local wine. The restaurant is closed for about two weeks over the Christmas break. ⊠ *70 Kamo Rd.* ☎ *09/459–4957* ▭ *AE, MC, V.*

¢–$ ✕ **Soda.** This café on the outskirts of town is good for coffee and cake, like its pear-and-ginger or apple-and-walnut. The cabinets are full of freshly made panini and sandwiches. Just off the main road north, Soda is a good place to refuel with bacon and eggs, French toast, or corn fritters before heading to the Bay of Islands or further afield. ⊠ *505 Kamo Rd.* ☎ *09/435–1910* ▭ *MC, V* ☉ *Closed Sun. No dinner.*

NEW ZEALAND

$$–$$$ ✕ **Tonic.** Owner-chef Brad O'Connell's seasonal menu may be French-inspired, but it's flavored with New Zealand; whenever possible he tries to buy local—anything from lamb to pork—and his wine list includes a big selection from the region. Seafood is a favorite and he continues to serve whatever the market has that day. ⊠ *239a Kamo Rd.* ☎ *09/437–5558* ▭ *AE, DC, MC, V* ☉ *No lunch.*

FRENCH

$$$ ✕ **Vinyl.** A stylishly funky licensed café, Vinyl serves to Whangarei's version of a hip crowd. The menu changes often and the café is on the opposite side of the marina from the Town Basin, making the alfresco tables the perfect place to enjoy a leisurely brunch of whitebait (a tiny fish) fritters served with grilled lemon and garden greens. There's live entertainment on Thursday from 6 PM. ⊠ *Vale Rd. and Riverside Dr.* ☎ *09/438–8105* ⊕ *www.vinylcafe.co.nz* ▭ *AE, DC, MC, V* ☉ *Closed Mon. No lunch Tues.*

NEW ZEALAND

WHERE TO STAY

¢ 🏠 **Bunkdown Lodge.** A popular backpackers' lodge in a large kauri villa, Bunkdown has clean, bright rooms—two four-bed dorms, one six-bed dorm, two twins, and two doubles. Linen for the dorms is available for a small fee. The lounge has videos, guitars, games, and a piano, as well as a TV; common kitchens are available along with competitively priced Internet access. This isn't a party hostel, but it's definitely popular with people who want to dive off the Tutukaka coast; dive companies pick up here at 7 am. Friendly hosts Peter and Noell know the area, and are happy to arrange visits to local attractions. **Pros:** attracts friendly guests; random open vibe; really comfortable for the price. **Cons:** can be noisy; incredibly busy; lack of privacy. ⊠ *23 Otaika Rd.* ☎ *09/438–8886* ⊕ *www.bunkdownlodge.co.nz* ⤴ *3 dorms, 2 singles, 2 doubles* ᴋ *In-room: No a/c, kitchen, no TV. In-hotel: Bar, laundry facilities* ▭ *MC, V.*

$$ 🏠 **Parua House.** From this spot on the edge of Parua Bay, you can explore the towering Whangarei Heads. The house dates from 1882 and retains its colonial character, with antiques brought over from England by the owners, Peter and Pat. You can walk through the nearby bush or even help milk their cow on the 29-acre farm. Three-course dinners with wine ($$$$) are available upon request—wholesome New Zealand fare, including vegetables from their garden and their homegrown olives. **Pros:** friendly hosts; great location; lovely food. **Cons:** interior design is a little precious; not close to town. ⊠ *Whangarei Heads Rd.,*

R.D. 4, Parua Bay ✢ 17 km (11 mi) from Whangarei ☎ *09/436–5855* ⊕ *www.paruahomestay.com* ⤳ *3 rooms* & *In-room: No a/c, no TV. In-hotel: Internet terminal* ⊟ *MC, V* ⊙❙ *BP.*

NIGHTLIFE

Killer Prawn Restaurant and Bar (✉ *28 Bank St.* ☎ *09/430–3333*) doubles as Whangarei's nightlife hub. The food is good (but not terribly chic) and it's a great place to start the evening—as the night wears on, just follow the crowd.

SHOPPING

★ Specializing in contemporary fine glass, ceramics, and jewelry, **Burning Issues Gallery** (✉ *8 Quayside, Town Basin* ☎ *09/438–3108*) is one of the best places in Northland to buy locally made arts and crafts and work from some of the country's best artisans. Look for beautifully carved *pounamu* (New Zealand greenstone) and bone pendants. A cooperative of local craftspeople, including jewelers, potters, wood turners, and weavers, runs the **Quarry Craft Co-op Shop** (✉ *Selwyn Ave.* ☎ *09/438–9884*). You will find unique crafts, including jewelry made from kauri gum. You may run into Sandy Rhynd, an ex-farmer who delights in explaining the venerable craft of stick dressing and showing you his wares, such as musterers' sticks (shepherds in New Zealand are called musterers, and their sticks are something like traditional shepherds' crooks) and walking sticks, many inlaid with stag horn, known as "New Zealand ivory."

HOKIANGA AND THE KAURI COAST

85 km (53 mi) west of Paihia.

A peaceful harbor moves inland into the Hokianga region. It's a quiet area with small towns, unspoiled scenery, and proximity to the giant kauri trees on the Kauri Coast, a 20-minute drive south on Highway 12. Here the highway winds through Waipoua State Forest, then stretches south to Kaipara Harbour. Giant golden sand dunes tower over the mouth of Hokianga Harbour, across the water from the twin settlements of Omapere and Opononi. Opononi is the place where Opo, a tame dolphin, came to play with swimmers in the mid-1950s, putting the town on the national map for the first and only time in its history. A statue in front of the pub commemorates the much-loved creature.

GETTING HERE AND AROUND

The best way to get to the Hokianga is to drive; from Auckland turn left at the bottom of the Bryderwyn Hills and follow the road. There is generally one bus service a day from Auckland, but there is no airport or train service.

ESSENTIALS

Visitor Information Hokianga Visitor Information Centre (✉ *11 State Hwy. 12, Omapere* ☎ *09/405–8869*). **Kauri Coast i-SITE Visitor Centre** (✉ *69 Normanby St., Dargaville* ☎ *09/439–8360* ⊕ *www.dargaville.co.nz*).

CLOSE UP

Twilight Encounter

The night tours to see Tane Mahuta and Te Matua Ngahere are led by **Footprints–Waipoua** (✉ *State Hwy. 12, Omapere* ☎ *09/405–8207* ⊕ *www.footprintswaipoua.com*). Tours are led by local Māori guides, experienced bushmen who enrich your experience with their knowledge of the forest and wildlife, waiata (traditional Māori song), and tales from Māori legend. The Twilight Encounter is a four-hour night walk ($75); a shortened version, Meet Tane at Night, takes 1½ hours ($50). If you're really pressed for time, but want more than your own self-guided 10-minute jaunt, there is also a 40-minute tour ($15). The same guides also run **Crossings–Hokianga** (✉ *State Hwy. 12, Omapere* ☎ *09/405–8207* ⊕ *www.crossingshokianga.com*). Centering on a guided boat cruise of the Hokianga Harbour, this day trip begins and ends in the Bay of Islands, with a focus on Hokianga history and the natural environment ($110). The cruise stops at historical spots throughout the harbor, such as Motuti, the Mangungu Mission Station, and Kohukohu. You can also take shorter harbor crossings, skipping the walk. Tours run daily November to April, and Monday, Wednesday, and Saturday, May through October.

EXPLORING

The 1838 **Mangungu Mission House** is an overlooked stop on the tourist trail. Although Waitangi is the most known site of New Zealand's founding document, this unassuming spot, which looks out over Hokianga Harbour, was the scene of the second signing of the Treaty. Here, on February 12, 1840, the largest gathering of Māori chiefs signed the Treaty of Waitangi (73 chiefs, compared with only 31 in Waitangi's signing). The house is now a museum, furnished with pre-Treaty missionary items, including portraits, photographs, and furniture. ✉ *Motukiore Rd., Hokianga Harbour* ☎ *09/401–9640* 💰 *$3* ⊙ *Dec. 26–Jan., daily noon–4; Feb.–Dec., weekends noon–4.*

Fodor's Choice
★
Waipoua State Forest contains the largest remnant of the kauri forests that once covered this region. A short path leads from the parking area on the main road through the forest to **Tane Mahuta,** "Lord of the Forest," and the largest tree in New Zealand. It stands nearly 173 feet high, measures 45 feet around its base, and is 1,200 to 2,000-odd years old. The second-largest tree, older by some 800 years, is **Te Matua Ngahere,** about a 20 walk from the road. t's If you have a few hours to spare you can visit Te Matua Ngahere and other trees of note. Head to the Kauri Walks parking lot about a mile south of the main Tane Mahuta parking lot. From there you trek past the **Four Sisters,** four kauri trees that have grown together in a circular formation, then the **Yakas Tree** (named after an old kauri-gum digger), and **Te Matua Ngahere.** The forest has a campground—check at the visitor center before you pitch a tent. Facilities include toilets, hot showers, and a communal cookhouse. When it's wet, you may spot large kauri snails in the forest. Also, the successful eradication of predators such as weasels and stoats has led to a rise in the number of kiwis in the forest. You'll need a flashlight

DID YOU KNOW?

New Zealand's oldest, biggest trees grow in Waipoua Forest. No one knows quite how old Tane Mahuta ("Lord of the Forest," in Māori), the most famous one, is, but it's been around for 1,200–2,500 years.

Bay of Islands

Rocky Point

Cape Wiwiki

Cape Brett

Purerua

Historic Kerikeri
Basin

Waipapa

Kerikeri

Kerikeri Inlet

Okahu Is

Urupukapuka
Island

Moturoa
Is

Kerikeri
Inlet

Haruru Falls Rd.

Treaty
House

Moturua Is

Motuarohia Is

Te Rawhiti Inlet

Rawhiti

Russell

Waitangi

Haruru

Puketona Rd.

Paihia

Wairoa
Bay

Russell Rd.

Orongo
Bay

Manawaora

Puketona

Seaview Rd.

Okiato

Oromahoe

Otao

Oromahoe Rd.

Opua

Ferry

Aucks Rd.

Ngaiotonga

Home Point

12

Pakaraka

Hundertwasser
Public Toilets

11

Waihaha

Whangaruru

Tūparehuia

North Head

Moerewa

Kawakawa

Karetu

1

0   4 mi

0   4 km

Oakura

to spot one, because the birds only come out at night. The Waipoua campground and Waipoua Visitor Centre is managed by Te Iwi O Te Roroa, the local Māori tribe. ⊠ *Waipoua Visitor Centre* ⊠ *Waipoua River Rd., Waipoua Forest* ☎ *09/439–6445.*

Sixty-four kilometers (40 mi) south of the Waipoua Forest along the Kaihu River, you'll come to **Dargaville**, once a thriving river port and now a good place to stock up if you're planning to camp in any of the nearby forests. It has some good craft stores, too. The surrounding region is best known for its main cash crop, the purple-skinned sweet potato known as *kūmara*. You'll see field after field dedicated to this root vegetable and shops selling it cheaper than anywhere else.

★ Continuing south of Dargaville, you reach Matakohe, a pocket-size town with an outstanding attraction: the **Matakohe Kauri Museum**. The museum's intriguing collection of artifacts, tools, photographs, documents, and memorabilia traces the story of the pioneers who settled this area in the second half of the 19th century—a story interwoven with the kauri forests. The furniture and a complete kauri house are among the superb examples of craftsmanship. One of the most fascinating displays is of kauri gum, the transparent lumps of resin that form when the sticky sap of the kauri tree hardens. This gum, which was used to make varnish, can be polished to a warm, lustrous finish that looks remarkably like amber—right down to the occasional insects trapped and preserved inside—and this collection is the biggest in the world. **Volunteers Hall** contains a huge kauri slab running from one end of the hall to the other, and there is also a reproduction of a cabinetmaker's shop, and a chainsaw exhibit. The Steam Saw Mill illustrates how the huge kauri logs were cut into timber. Perhaps the best display is the two-story replica of a late-1800s–early-1900s boardinghouse. Rooms are set up as they were over 100 years ago; you can walk down the hallways and peer in at the goings-on of the era. If you like the whirring of engines, the best day to visit is Wednesday, when much of the museum's machinery is started up. ⊠ *Church Rd., Matakohe* ☎ *09/431-7417* ⊕ *www.kaurimuseum.com* ⊴ *$15* ⊗ *Nov.–Apr., daily 8:30–5:30; May–Oct., daily 9–5.*

WHERE TO EAT

$-$$ ✕ **Boatshed Café and Crafts.** This café is on the waterfront adjacent to the
NEW ZEALAND   Rawene supermarket, craft shop, and ferry ramp. It's got a lovely outdoor deck and is a good place to take a coffee and piece of pizza while waiting for the ferry. ⊠ *Clendon Esplanade, Rawene* ☎ *09/405-7728* ⊟ *MC, V* ⊗ *No dinner.*

$-$$ ✕ **Waterline Cafe.** This café is on the waterfront next to the Kohukohu
NEW ZEALAND   Wharf. On fine days, jump off the dock for a swim before having a pizza, fish-and-chips, or a sandwich under the shade sails, or stop in for coffee and some chocolate macadamia fudge on your way out of town to the Rawene–Kohukohu ferry. ⊠ *2 Beach Rd., Kohukohu* ☎ *09/405-5552* ⊟ *MC, V* ⊗ *No dinner Sun.–Thurs.*

WHERE TO STAY

$$$ ▥ **Copthorne Hotel and Resort Hokianga.** From the deck of this charming seaside hotel you look straight out to the mouth of Hokianga Harbour, where according to legend the Polynesian navigator Kupe first arrived in New Zealand 1,000 years ago. It's safe to say that the view has not changed. The restaurant's ($$) specialty is crayfish; choose your live cray from their tank or, as some prefer, meet it for the first time on your plate. The *kaimoana* (seafood) tasting plate for two includes Pacific oysters, seared scallops and calamari, chili mussels, and creamed paua, (abalone) served with a lime and *horopito* (a traditional Māori herb) aioli. The hotel has a pleasant aura and is the base for local company Footprints–Waipoua, which takes "Twilight Encounter" tours through the Waipoua Forest to visit New Zealand's largest kauri trees. **Pros:** low key; on the beach; clean; great views. **Cons:** not what you would call a luxury resort; some patchy service reported. ⊠ *State Hwy. 12, Omapere* ☎ *09/405-8737* ⊕ *www.omapere.co.nz* ⇄ *37 rooms, 9 suites* ⚭ *In-room: No a/c, kitchen. In-hotel: Restaurant, bar, pool* ⊟ *AE, DC, MC, V.*

¢-$ ▥ **Kauri Coast Top 10 Holiday Park.** With the Trounson Kauri Park marking its northern boundary, owners Herb and Heather Iles can point you in the right direction for several outdoor activities, but perhaps the biggest draw is after-dark exploration. They give guided tours of the kauri park nightly (tours cost $20; reservations essential); guests frequently spot kiwi on the walks. The various lodging configurations—cabins with or without kitchens, and with or without bathrooms, as well as self-contained apartments—are kept spotless, and there's a camp kitchen and barbecue area. If you are traveling from the north, you need to turn left off the state highway and onto Trounson Park Road, 3 km (2 mi) before the small village of Kaihu. The holiday park is clearly signposted. **Pros:** good for families; cheap; clean. **Cons:** gets crowded; not private. ⊠ *Trounson Park Rd., 70 km (43 mi) south of Opononi* ☎ *09/439–0621* ⊕ *www.kauricoasttop10.co.nz* ⤷ *2 motel units, 3 apartments, 8 cabins, 60 campsites* ⌂ *In-room: No a/c, kitchen (some), no TV (some). In-hotel: Laundry facilities* ⊟ *MC, V.*

¢ ⊞ **The Tree House.** Amid 15 acres of subtropical jungle, native forest,
★ ponds, fruit trees, and a macadamia orchard, the Tree House is a great reason to stop in Kohukohu. It's aimed at backpackers and cycle tourists on a budget. The little wooden cabins have porches with perfect views of the bush. The two rooms in the main building are simply furnished, with wooden furniture, painted wooden floors, and adobe-painted walls. You can hike through the forest to a lookout for great views of the Hokianga Harbour. All the kitchen and bathroom facilities are in the main house. You can also rent a two-bedroom self-contained cottage in Kohukohu on the harbor for $170 a night. **Pros:** inexpensive; simple; friendly. **Cons:** basic. ⊠ *168 West Coast Rd., R.D. 1, Kohukohu* ☎ *09/405–5855* ⊕ *www.treehouse.co.nz* ⤷ *2 single-bedroom cabins, 2 2-bedroom cabin, 2 dorm rooms in main house (4 beds and 3 beds, respectively), 3 tent sites, 2-bedroom cottage* ⌂ *In-room: Kitchen (some). In-hotel: Laundry facilities* ⊟ *MC, V.*

$$$$ ⊞ **Waipoua Lodge.** Owners Nicole and Chris Donahoe have renovated
★ this 19th-century kauri farmhouse and its buildings into lovely suites that manage to be sophisticated but remain relaxing. Room decoration ranges from modern to rustic, but all come with plenty of space, natural light, and balconies or patios that look out over Waipoua Forest. After dinner, you can toast marshmallows in the central fireplace. Meals, available by arrangement ($$$$), usually focus on venison, lamb, or beef, garden vegetables, and indigenous seasonings. You can stroll through the native bush on the property, or enjoy a private hot tub by candlelight on a balcony overlooking the forest. At 2 km (1¼ mi) south of Waipoua Forest, the lodge is close to the legendary kauri Tane Mahuta and one of the few areas where you can take night walks to view kiwi. This lodge has a strong eco-friendly ethos. **Pros:** friendly and warm; peaceful, gorgeous location. **Cons:** for some, the isolation may be too much. ⊠ *State Hwy. 12, Waipoua* ☎ *09/439–0422* ⊕ *www.waipoualodge.co.nz* ⤷ *4 suites* ⌂ *In-room: No a/c, kitchen. In-hotel: Internet terminal, Wi-Fi* ⊟ *AE, MC, V* ⦿| *BP.*

THE BAY OF ISLANDS

The Bay of Islands was a large Māori settlement when Captain James Cook first anchored off Roberton Island in 1769. He noted that "the inhabitants in this bay are far more numerous than in any other part of the country that we had visited." When the English started a convict settlement in Australia a couple of decades later, many boats stayed in the South Pacific to go whaling and sealing, and the Bay of Islands became a port of call. Consequently, many of the early European arrivals were sailors and whalers, stopping to blow off steam, have a few drinks, and trade with the local Māori. A missionary, Henry Williams, wrote in 1828 that a whaling captain had told him, "all the Europeans were in a state of intoxication, except himself and two others."

It took nearly a century for the Bay of Islands to get some positive reviews. American author Zane Grey visited in the 1920s to fish for marlin and was so impressed that he wrote a book about the bay called *Tales of the Angler's Eldorado*. Game fishing remains one of the bay's many draws, with record catches of marlin and mako shark, along with diving, boating, and swimming with dolphins. Many of the 144 islands were farms, but now only one, Motoroa, is still farmed; most others are now used for vacation homes.

> ## BEST BETS FOR CRUISE PASSENGERS
>
> ■ Day Cruises. Take The Cream Trip, a boat trip in the bay that will take you through the famous hole in the rock.
>
> ■ Russell. Spend the morning in Russell across the bay from Paihia and check out Pompallier House where the first Catholic Bishop to New Zealand lived.
>
> ■ Waitangi Marae. This is the place where the Treaty of Waitangi was signed between the Māori chiefs and the British Crown.
>
> ■ Market. Enjoy local produce at the Sunday Farmer's market in nearby Kerikeri.

PAIHIA AND WAITANGI

69 km (43 mi) north of Whangarei.

As the main vacation base for the Bay of Islands, Paihia is an unremarkable stretch of motels at odds with the quiet beauty of the island-studded seascape. With its handful of hostels, plus the long and safe swimming beach, it's popular with a young backpacker crowd. Most of the boat and fishing tours leave from the central wharf, as do the passenger ferries to the historic village of Russell. The nearby suburb of Waitangi, however, is one of the country's most important historic sites. The Treaty Grounds, a lovely nearby park, was where the Treaty of Waitangi, the founding document for modern New Zealand, was signed.

The main Bay of Islands visitor bureau, in Paihia, is open daily 8 to 5 May through September; 8 to 6 October, November, March, and April; and 8 to 8 December through February. There is a really good toilet facility at the southern end of the strip.

ESSENTIALS

Bus Depot Paihia (✉ *Paihia Travel Centre, Maritime Bldg.* ☎ *09/402–7857).*

Visitor Information Bay of Islands Visitor Information Centre Paihia (✉ *Marsden Rd., Paihia* ☎ *09/402–7345* ⊕ *www.bayofislands.co.nz).*

EXPLORING

Fodor's Choice ★ **Waitangi National Trust Estate** is at the northern end of Paihia. Inside the visitor center a 23-minute video (shown from 9 to 10, noon to 1, and 3 to 6) sketches the events that led to the Treaty of Waitangi. Interspersed between the three rounds of video screenings is a half-hour *kapa haka*, a live Māori cultural performance. The center also displays Māori

The Māoris National Festival in Waitangi commemorates the signing of the Waitangi treaty.

artifacts and weapons, including a musket that belonged to Hone Heke Pokai, the first Māori chief to sign the treaty. After his initial enthusiasm for British rule, Hone Heke was quickly disillusioned, and less than five years later he attacked the British in their stronghold at Russell. From the visitor center, follow a short track (trail) through the forest to **Ngatoki Matawhaorua** (ng-ga-to-ki ma-ta-*fa*-oh-*roo*-ah), a Māori war canoe. This huge kauri canoe, capable of carrying 80 paddlers and 55 passengers, is named after the vessel in which Kupe, the Polynesian navigator, is said to have discovered New Zealand. It was built in 1940 to mark the centennial of the signing of the Treaty of Waitangi.

The **Treaty House** in Waitangi Treaty Grounds is a simple white-timber cottage. The interior is fascinating, especially the back, where exposed walls demonstrate the difficulties that early administrators faced—such as an acute shortage of bricks (since an insufficient number had been shipped from New South Wales, as Australia was known at the time) with which to finish the walls.

The Treaty House was prefabricated in New South Wales for British Resident James Busby, who arrived in New Zealand in 1832. Busby had been appointed to protect British commerce and put an end to the brutalities of the whaling captains against the Māori, but he lacked the judicial authority and the force of arms necessary to impose peace. On one occasion, unable to resolve a dispute between Māori tribes, Busby was forced to shelter the wounded of one side in his house. While tattooed warriors screamed war chants outside the windows, one of the Māori sheltered Busby's infant daughter, Sarah, in his cloak.

The real significance of the Treaty House lies in the events that took place here on February 6, 1840, the day the Treaty of Waitangi was signed by Māori chiefs and Captain William Hobson, representing the British crown (⇨ *The Treaty of Waitangi CloseUp box*). The Treaty House has not always received the care its significance merits. When Lord Bledisloe, New Zealand's governor-general between 1930 and 1935, bought the house and presented it to the nation in 1932, it was being used as a shelter for sheep.

Whare Runanga (fah-ray roo-nang-ah) is a traditional meetinghouse with elaborate Māori carvings inside. The house is on the northern boundary of Waitangi Treaty Grounds. For $10, you can take an hour-long guided tour of the Treaty Grounds. ⊠ *Waitangi Rd., Waitangi* 🕾 *09/402–7437* ⊕ *www.waitangi.net.nz* 🖃 *$12* ⊗ *Daily 9–5.*

On the National Trust Estate beyond the Treaty Grounds, **Mt. Bledisloe** showcases a splendid view across Paihia and the Bay of Islands. The handsome ceramic marker at the top showing the distances to major world cities was made by Doulton in London and presented by Lord Bledisloe in 1934 during his term as governor-general of New Zealand. The mount is 3 km (2 mi) from the Treaty House, on the other side of the Waitangi Golf Course. From a small parking area on the right of Waitangi Road, a short track rises above a pine forest to the summit.

EN ROUTE
The Hundertwasser Public Toilets. On the main street of Kawakawa, a nondescript town just off State Highway 1 south of Paihia, stand surely the most outlandish public toilets in the country—a must-go even if you don't need to. Built by Austrian artist and architect Friedensreich Hundertwasser in 1997, the toilets are fronted by brightly colored ceramic columns supporting an arched portico, which in turn supports a garden of grasses. There are no straight lines in the building, which is furnished inside with mostly white tiles, punctuated with primary colors and set in black grout (something like a Mondrian after a few drinks), and plants sprout from the roof. If you sit in one of the cafés across the road you can watch the tourist buses stop so the visitors can take pictures.

SPORTS AND THE OUTDOORS

BOATING
Carino NZ Sailing and Dolphin Adventures (⊲ *Box 286, Paihia* 🕾 *09/402–8040* ⊕ *www.sailingdolphinz.co.nz*) gets close to dolphins (primarily bottlenose) and penguins. Passengers on the 50-foot red catamaran can just relax or pitch in with sailing. This full-day trip ($105) includes a barbecue lunch at one of the islands, weather permitting, and a full bar is on board.

Fodor's Choice
★
Dolphin Discoveries (⊠ *Marsden and Williams Rds., Paihia* 🕾 *09/402–8234* ⊕ *www.dolphinz.co.nz*) provides a range of trips twice a day with an option that allows you to "Swim with the Dolphins." You might also spot Brydes whales, migrating humpback and orca whales, or groups of tiny blue penguins. Prices begin at $89 with an optional $30 if dolphins are discovered and you wish to swim with them.

★
Fullers (⊠ *Maritime Bldg., Marsden Rd., Paihia* 🕾 *09/402–7421* ⊕ *www. fboi.co.nz*) runs cruises and sea-based adventure trips departing daily from both Paihia and Russell. The most comprehensive sightseeing trip is the six-hour Best of the Bay Supercruise ($86) aboard a high-

speed catamaran. You'll follow about half of what was once called the "Cream Trip" route, but nowadays, instead of picking up cream from farms, the boat delivers mail and supplies to vacation homes. Fullers also visits Urupukapuka Island, once home to a *hapu* (subtribe) of the Ngare Raumati Māori. Little is known about their life, but there are numerous archaeological sites. It's also the only one to go to Otehei Bay, one of the island's most spectacular bays. On this particular trip, the boat stops for an hour and a half on the island, where you can go kayaking, take a short hike, or have lunch at the **Zane Grey Café**. The trip also takes in the Hole in the Rock, a natural hole at sea level in Piercy Island that boats pass through if the tide is right. A catamaran operated by **Straycat Day Sailing Charters** (☎ *09/402–6130 or 0800/101–007*) makes one-day relaxing sailing trips in the Bay of Islands from Paihia and Russell at $79 per adult and $45 per child, which includes a picnic-style lunch, sake or a kiwifruit liqueur, stops at two of the islands, bushwalks, swimming, and snorkeling.

DIVING   The Bay of Islands has some of the finest scuba diving in the country, particularly around Cape Brett, where the marine life includes moray eels, stingrays, and grouper. The wreck of the Greenpeace vessel *Rainbow Warrior,* bombed and sunk by French agents in 1985, is another underwater highlight. The wreck was transported to the Cavalli Islands in 1987 and is now covered in soft corals and jewel anemones; it's full of fish life. Water temperature at the surface varies from 16°C (62°F) in July to 22°C (71°F) in January. From September through November, underwater visibility can be affected by a plankton bloom.

Paihia Dive Compass Ltd. (⌂ *Box 210, Paihia* ☎ *09/4343–762 or 0800/107–551* ⊕ *www.divenz.com*) gives complete equipment rental and regular boat trips for accredited divers for $190 per day; they also run dive courses.

FISHING   **Marlin Fishing New Zealand** (⌂ *Box 285, Paihia* ☎ *09/402–8189 or 0274/776–604* ⊕ *www.marlinfishing.co.nz*) goes for the big ones off the Northland coast and around Three Kings Islands. The cost is $3,250 per day for a maximum of four, including all tackle and meals. A far less-expensive alternative than pricey marlin fishing is to fish for snapper and kingfish within the bay. **Spot-X** ☎ *09/402–7123* ⊕ *www.fish-spot-x. co.nz*) runs four-hour snapper-fishing trips for about $90 per person and six-hour kingfish trips for $210 per person, including bait and tackle (bring your own lunch).

WHERE TO EAT

$$–$$$ ✕ **The Saltwater Café and Bar.** If the sea air's given you an appetite, head
PIZZA   to this casual spot, known as the Salty, to grab a steaming pizza. The Salty is the restaurant's signature pizza, brimming with oysters, mussels, baby octopus, shrimp, calamari, and smoked fish, or you could try the Meat Lover's, loaded with salami, ham, bacon, and chicken. The Salty moonlights as one of Paihia's livelier nightspots, with live music and DJs. ✉ *Kings Rd., Paihia* ☎ *09/402–6080* ▭ *AE, DC, MC, V* ⊗ *No lunch.*

$$$–$$$$ ✕ **The Sugar Boat.** High and dry on the banks of the Waitangi River sits
MEDITERRANEAN   this historic kauri sailing vessel, which once carried sugar to a sugar refinery in Auckland. On deck is the Cuban-inspired **Cubar,** serving cocktails and lunch—such as blackened fish tacos and Cuban sandwiches—and

providing DJs, live music, and dancing by night; dinner is served below deck on kauri tables inset with relics that the famous New Zealand diver Kelly Tarlton salvaged from wrecks. Dishes might include ostrich fillet served with gnocchi, roasted goat cheese, char-grilled zucchini, and cherry tomatoes in a port-and-cranberry jus. ✉ *Waitangi Bridge, Paihia* ☎ *09/402–7018* ⊕ *www.sugarboat.co.nz* ▭ *AE, DC, MC, V.*

$–$$
CAFÉ
✗ **Waikokopu Café.** Set among the bush and with a view straight out to sea, this pleasant spot has a lot going for it. You can sit on the deck or the lawn and enjoy chunky sandwiches, delicious cakes, and other goodies. For something hot, the most popular dish on the menu is the Bliniville—a tribute to neighboring Dargaville and its beloved kūmara—which is a kūmara-and-garbanzo blini served with pumpkin rubbed with *ras el hanout* (an Iranian spice blend), grilled eggplant, and fig *vincotto* (a slow-cooked grape reduction). ✉ *Tau Henare Dr., Waitangi Treaty Grounds* ☎ *09/402–6275* ▭ *MC, V* ☽ *No dinner.*

WHERE TO STAY

$$$
▦ **Abri.** These freestanding studio apartments that look like tree houses take advantage of the bush setting just behind the Paihia beachfront, furnishing lovely sea views. The two units have woodwork with indigenous timber, such as *rimu* flooring and *macrocarpa* walls, and whirlpool baths; their large living-room areas open onto outside decks. The apartments have their own kitchen facilities, and even a small barbecue on the deck, but most guests take the short walk to the restaurants in town for meals. You'll find fresh cookies and flowers in your room daily. **Pros:** close to town; friendly hosts. **Cons:** entrance up a staircase. ✉ *10–12 Bayview Rd., Paihia* ☎ *09/402–8035* ⊕ *www.abri-accom.co.nz* ⇶ *2 studios, 1 suite* ☖ *In-room: Kitchen. In-hotel: No kids under 16* ▭ *MC, V.*

$$
▦ **Austria Motel.** The large, double-bed rooms are typical of motel accommodations in the area—clean and moderately comfortable but devoid of character. However, some of the rooms have sea views, and there is covered off-street parking. The shops and waterfront at Paihia are a two-minute walk away. **Pros:** friendly; clean; close to town. **Cons:** basic. ✉ *36 Selwyn Rd., Paihia* ☎ *09/402–7480* ⇶ *8 rooms* ☖ *In-room: No a/c, kitchen* ▭ *MC, V.*

$$–$$$
★
▦ **Bay Adventurer.** Accommodations range from dorm rooms ($20) to studio ($5) and one-bedroom apartments, which have kitchens, bathrooms, and TVs ($100–$195), and two-bedroom apartments (over $225). Brightly colored linen is supplied in all rooms, even the dorms (some are women-only). The apartments have two bedrooms sleeping four, a full bathroom (bubble bath supplied), kitchen, lounge, and deck. A subtropical garden surrounds the pool and hot tub, and the beach is a few minutes' walk away, although the hosts will lend you a bicycle or scooter if you feel like taking a ride. Although they serve a Continental breakfast, the hostel also has a deal going with one of the nearby restaurants, and you can have a hot breakfast delivered to your room. **Pros:** women-only dorms; fun environment; caters to budget travelers. **Cons:** noisy; mixed clientele. ✉ *28 Kings Rd., Paihia* ☎ *09/402–5162* ⊕ *www.bayadventurer.co.nz* ⇶ *14 dorm rooms, 7 doubles, 9 apartments*

Continued on page 150

CARVING

Although pre-European Māori did not have a written language, their traditional carvings served as a historical record. Every piece has a *kaupapa* (story), which can be read by those who know how. The shape of the heads, position of the body, and surface patterns work together to commemorate important events.

MĀORI ART

By
Debra A. Klein

Kiwi culture weaves together Māori and *Pakeha* (European) traditions. Māori symbols crop up in everything from the popular whale's tail pendants to a major airline's modernized koru logo. Today Māori art, likewise, melds traditional storytelling with modern concerns.

It wasn't always this way, but since the 1970s there has been a resurgence of, and interest in, Māori culture throughout New Zealand. Days begin with the Māori greeting, "kia ora," literally "be well," offered by Māoris and pakeha alike. Kiwis cheer the world-famous All Blacks rugby squad when they perform the *haka*—that fierce warrior dance that intimidates opposing teams.

There has even been a renaissance in Māori arts, crafts, and body art. Weavers gather by the hundreds to participate in the *hui* workshop. Reviving an ancient tradition they work their *harakeke* (flax) materials into baskets and skirts.

Tens of thousands of spectators attend the biannual Māori performance competition at the Te Matatini arts festival. In Rotorua, center of modern Māori life in New Zealand, there are nightly traditional chants and *hangi* feasts. Galleries all over New Zealand celebrate works of contemporary artists who express strong or glancing Māori influences in their pieces, and visitors and locals alike mimic traditional Māori *moku*, or tattoos.

Many Māori artisans see this integration as essential to preserving their culture.

Above: Whare runanga (meeting house), Waitangi

TRADITIONAL ART

Traditional Māori art is symbolic, not literal, and recurring motifs appear on meeting houses, in jewelry, and on objects. Some shapes and symbols come from nature, others represent ancestors or the geographical region of an *iwi*, or tribe.

Hei Matau—The fish hook is a popular talisman for safe journeys over water. It also represents prosperity.

Koru—The curled fern frond symbolizes beginnings or life, as well as peace and strength.

Hei Tiki—The small human figure with a tilted head depicts a fetus in the womb and symbolizes fertility.

Hiku—New Zealanders frequently wear the whale's tail, which is a sign of strength and speed.

MASKS

North Island styles of face mask include Tai Tokerau, Tai Rawhiti, and Rongowhakaata, and are distinguished by the parallel, angular lines framing the eyes. Koruru, found in the mid-North Island area, are masks characterized by rounded, bulging eyes. The point at the top of the Taranaki mask symbolizes Mount Taranaki. In the Coromandel area, look for telltale paua shell eyes in the Pare Hauraki and hollow eye sockets in the Te Whanau a Apanui. The Te Arawa Māori, who live between Rotorua and Lake Taupo, make Ruru masks with pointed ears representing a small owl.

WOOD CARVING

Whakairo (carving) holds an important place in Māori culture; it functions as both an art form and a historical record. Each line and shape has meaning, and each design connects the physical object with *mana*, or spiritual power. Intricately carved Māori meeting houses and raised storehouses, seen on both islands, demonstrate the Māori practice of designing and patterning objects to imbue them with the spirits of ancestors. For an excellent example, visit the meeting house and war canoe on the Treaty of Waitangi grounds on the North Island.

Apprentice carvers spend upwards of ten years learning their craft.

TEKOTEKO AND OTHER OBJECTS

This ancestral face on an archway greets visitors to a marae.

Tekoteko, carved human figures, adorn Māori meeting houses, homes, and, traditionally, canoe prows. These symbolic ancestors' defiant stances, protruding tongues, and weapons ward off intruders. Other carved items include ceremonial war paddles (*wahaika),* spears (*taiaha),* treasure boxes, and sticks. Look for these carvings at a marae or in museums and galleries.

PAINTINGS (KOWHAIWHAI)

Decorative patterns, called *kowhaiwhai,* are considered less sacred than wood carvings or tattoo-making and can be done by anyone. Find these temporary designs on meeting-house ridgepoles and rafters, canoe bottoms, and paddles. The standard black, white, and red paints mimic the colors produced by red ochre, white clay, and charcoal, the materials used by Māori ancestors. Designs can represent speed and swiftness or hospitality and strength.

Above: The koru symbol is common in Māori style painting.

MĀORI TA MOKO

Unlike contemporary ink tattoos, traditional Māori *moku* (tattoos) were literally carved into the body with a tool called an *uhi,* filled with soot from burnt plants or caterpillars, and covered with leaves to heal.

Only those of high rank wore facial tattoos, and they were recognized by these patterns rather than by the natural features we use to describe people today. Segments of the face were reserved for identifying features related to the social rank of the wearer's family; for example, sections on each side of the face depicted the ancestry from the mother's and father's sides.

Markings also commemorated important events in a person's life and, except for some tribes that had tattoos on their legs and buttocks, were confined to the face. Women's tattoos were, and still are, limited to an outline around the lips and thin lines from the lips down the chin. This pattern is still worn in ink tattoos today.

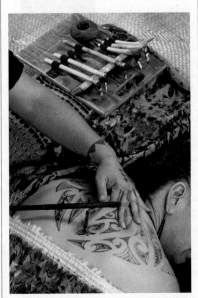

Today, talented Ta'Moko artists continue the deeply spiritual traditions of ancient Māori tattooing.

MODERN MĀORI ART

Contemporary Māori artists work in every medium, including music, weaving, crafts, film, and visual entertainment and often contain subtle cultural references or overt interpretations of historic symbols.

Museums, such as the comprehensive **Te Papa** (in Wellington), the **Auckland Art Gallery**, and tiny **Suter Art Gallery** (in Nelson), exhibit a range of art that may include portraits of Māori and their Ta Moku from the last century or modern, mixed-media art by pan-Pacific artists commenting on current events.

Contemporary artwork with traditional Māori influences

MĀORI JEWELRY AND SOUVENIRS

Māori symbols are common in contemporary pendants that are crafted of plastic and wood and hung on a braided cord. More expensive versions are made of greenstone (jade), once used for chisels and weaponry, or bone. These necklaces are popular souvenirs.

Traditional Māori pendant carved from greenstone (jade)

Many contemporary artists take the idea of these traditional pendants and reinterpret motifs in fresh ways. A modern necklace may reference a pattern from a chief's cloak or hint at the fish hook without mimicking the the pattern. While such jewelry may come in greenstone, some artists work with metals like silver or gold instead.

Modern angular and traditional rounded wooden treasure boxes, called *wakahuia*, incorporate Māori symbols.

Contemporary textile artists blend traditional materials such as flax, tree bark pigments, and feathers with nontraditional colors to craft modern purses and wall hangings.

Popular souvenirs include greenstone, ceramics, synthetic feathers, decorative flax designs, replicas of paddles and war clubs, clothing, and jewelry. The toi ho® certifies that items were produced by Māori artists (⊕ *www.toiiho.com*). Not all Māori artists participate in the program; check carefully for authenticity.

This girl wears a greenstone pendant

BUYING MĀORI ART

Woven Kete pikau (back pack)

Māori ceramics with traditional motifs

WHERE TO BUY

Those seriously interested in Māori art and culture should visit Rotorua. Creative Rotorua (⊕ *www.creativerotorua.org.nz*) is an umbrella organization that links to arts organizations, performances, various area artists, and the local Māori Arts Trail, which maps out studios you can visit. If your trip coincides with Te Matatini, a dance showcase as well as the largest Māori arts festival in the world, scour the booths for authentic crafts (⊕ *www. tematatini.org.nz*).

If Rotorua isn't on your itinerary, seek out Māori galleries in Christchurch, Queenstown, Auckland, Wellington, and Whangarei. The Te Papa Museum in Wellington has a range of Māori-influenced New Zealand artworks, jewelry and prints. Most museum shops have reproductions of pieces in the collection and rare art books.

Handcrafted necklaces start around $120; flax baskets around $120; hand-turned wooden bowls a few hundred dollars; and authentic carvings $500.

HOW TO CHOOSE

Buy what you like or choose a depiction of a place you visited. The connection you feel should motivate you more than the piece's resale value. If quality is important, seek authentication from a dealer.

CUSTOM MADE FOR YOU

New Zealand's small population and informal atmosphere allow for direct contact with artists. Visit their studios, attend a workshop, or chat with them about their pieces. Most artisans and craftspeople will happily custom-make a piece to forward to you at home. There are also dozens of online shops offering various Māori-themed wares if you regret not making a purchase after you return. By purchasing directly from the artist you'll get a one-of-a-kind piece, but don't expect a discount.

USEFUL WEB SITES

⊕ *www.Māoriart.org.nz*
⊕ *www.nzMāori.co.nz*

The Moko, or facial tattoo, on this carved figure displays ancestral and tribal messages that apply to the wearer. These messages represent the wearer's family, sub-tribal and tribal affiliations, and his place within these social structures. This carving commemorates an ancestor.

⚘ *In-room: kitchen (some). In-hotel: Pool, laundry facilities, Internet terminal* ⊟ *MC, V.*

$$$$ ⊞ **Copthorne Hotel and Resort Bay of Islands.** The biggest hotel north of Auckland and a favorite with tour groups, this complex sprawls along a peninsula within walking distance of the Treaty House. Garden and ocean-facing rooms are decorated in a French provincial style, with yellows and blues and wrought-iron light fixtures. Most rooms have a terrace or patio, giving them an airier feeling. **Pros:** big; clean; lovely location. **Cons:** sterile. ⊠ *Tau Henare Dr., Waitangi* ☎ *09/402–7411* ⊕ *www.copthornebayofislands.co.nz* ↦ *138 rooms, 7 suites* ⚘ *In-room: No a/c, refrigerator, Internet. In-hotel: Restaurant, bar, tennis courts, pool, spa, laundry facilities, Internet terminal* ⊟ *AE, DC, MC, V.*

$$$$ ⊞ **Paihia Beach Resort and Spa.** A large *pohutukawa* tree stands next to the heated saltwater pool in front of this resort overlooking the bay. All the rooms have bay views and a deck or patio plus a large whirlpool tub in the bathroom. You have free use of the sauna or steam room. The state-of-the-art day spa, which is also open to nonguests, has a full range of treatments, including Vichy showers—the mochaccino mud wrap comes highly recommended. **Pros:** close to town; stunning views. **Cons:** road noise can be disturbing. ⊠ *116 Marsden Rd., Paihia* ☎ *09/402–6140* ⊕ *www.paihiabeach.co.nz* ↦ *19 rooms, 2 suites* ⚘ *In-room: Kitchen, DVD, Internet (some). In-hotel: Restaurant, bar, pool, spa* ⊟ *AE, DC, MC, V* ⦿ *BP.*

¢–$ ⊞ **Saltwater Lodge.** This is one of the best spots in Paihia's Kings Road ★ area (the town's hostel corridor) for cleanliness and comfort. The hostel rooms start at $24 a night, and even the cheapest beds have duvets supplied. Bunk-bed dormitories have en suite bathrooms with shower, storage facilities, and reading lights over the beds. The second-floor motel units come with king beds and bunks, plus a refrigerator and a small TV. If you're lucky, you'll nab one of the rooms overlooking Paihia beach (don't worry if not; the hostel is a two-minute walk from the beach). The communal kitchen is probably the best equipped in the whole country, with everything from a wok to egg beaters. Even a small gym and bikes can be used at no extra charge. In the garden you'll find barbecues and a wood-fired brazier. **Pros:** close to beach; attracts a good crowd; modern architecture. **Cons:** can be noisy. ⊠ *14 Kings Rd., Paihia* ☎ *09/402–7075* ⊕ *www.saltwaterlodge.co.nz* ↦ *10 double rooms, 9 dorm rooms* ⚘ *In-room: No a/c, kitchen, refrigerator (some), no TV (some). In-hotel: Restaurant, gym, laundry facilities, Internet terminal* ⊟ *MC, V.*

RUSSELL

4 km (2½ mi) east of Paihia by ferry, 13 km (8 mi) by road and car ferry.

Russell is regarded as the "second" town in the Bay of Islands, but it's far more interesting, and pleasant, than Paihia. Hard as it is to believe these days, sleepy little Russell was once dubbed the "Hellhole of the Pacific." In the mid- to late 19th century (when it was still known by its Māori name, Kororareka) it was a swashbuckling frontier town, a haven for sealers and whalers who found the East Coast of New Zealand to be one of the richest whaling grounds on Earth.

Tales of debauchery were probably exaggerated, but British administrators in New South Wales were sufficiently concerned to dispatch a British resident in 1832 to impose law and order. After the Treaty of Waitangi, Russell was the national capital until 1844, when the Māori chief Hone Heke, disgruntled with newly imposed harbor dues and his loss of authority, cut down the flagstaff flying the Union Jack above the town three times before attacking the British garrison. Most of the town burned to the ground in what is known as the Sacking of Kororareka. Hone Heke was finally defeated in 1846, but Russell never recovered its former prominence, and the seat of government was shifted first to Auckland, then to Wellington.

Today Russell is a delightful town of timber houses and big trees that hang low over the seafront, framing the yachts and game-fishing boats in the harbor. The vibe can best be absorbed in a stroll along the Strand, the path along the waterfront. There are several safe swimming beaches, some in secluded bays, as well as the aptly named Long Beach, over the hill from the township.

GETTING HERE AND AROUND

The road between Russell and Paihia is long and tortuous. The best way to travel between the two is by passenger ferry, which leaves from the Russell Wharf, or by car ferry, which departs from Okiato, about 9 km (5½ mi) southwest of town.

ESSENTIALS

Visitor Information Russell Information Centre (✉ *Russell Wharf, Russell* ☎ *09/403–8020*).

EXPLORING

New Zealand's oldest industrial building, the **Pompallier Mission,** at the southern end of the Strand, was named after the first Catholic bishop of the South Pacific. Marist missionaries built the original structure out of rammed earth, because they lacked the funds to buy timber. For several years the priests and brothers operated a press here, printing Bibles in the Māori language. From December through April you can visit independently, but from May to November the mission organizes tours at set times. ✉ *The Strand* ☎ *09/403–7861* ⊕ *www.pompallier. co.nz* 🎟 *$7.50* ⊗ *Daily 10–5.*

★ **Christ Church** is the oldest church in the country. One of the donors to its erection in 1835 was Charles Darwin, at that time making his way around the globe on board the HMS *Beagle.* Behind the white picket fence that borders the churchyard, gravestones tell a fascinating and brutal story of life in the colony's early days. Several graves belong to sailors from the HMS *Hazard* who were killed in this churchyard by Hone Heke's warriors in 1845. Another headstone marks the grave of a Nantucket sailor from the whaler *Mohawk.* As you walk around the church, look for the musket holes made when Hone Heke besieged the church. The interior is simple and charming—embroidered cushions on the pews are examples of a still-vibrant folk-art tradition ✉ *Church and Robertson Sts.* ⊗ *Daily 8–5.*

OUTDOOR ACTIVITIES

FISHING   **Major Tom Charters** (☎ 09/403–8553 ⊕ *www.majortom.co.nz*) chases game fish such as marlin, kingfish, hapuka (grouper), snapper, broadbill, and tuna. A full day, with a maximum of four anglers, is $1,500, which includes lunch. **Triple B Boat Charters** (⊠ *2 Robertson Rd.* ☎ *09/403–7200 or 0274/972–177* ⊙ *Closed May–Oct.*) runs saltwater fly-fishing and light-tackle trips on a 10-meter (33-foot) boat at $600 for a minimum of four hours. The extremely affable owner Captain Dudley Smith helms the boat—all tackle is supplied along with tea and coffee but you bring your own lunch.

HIKING   There are several pleasant walks around the Russell area; the most challenging—and spectacular—is the **Cape Brett Tramping Track** out to the lighthouse. It takes about eight hours round-trip. It costs $30 to walk the track and you can stay in a hut for $12 per night. It is not for the unfit, and good shoes are a must. Check with the Russell Information Center on the wharf. For a shorter jaunt on your own (an hour each way), follow the **Whangamumu Walking Track** to the remnants of a whaling station. Many relics such as an old boiler and vats are still left at the station.

WHERE TO EAT

$$$–$$$$ ✗ **Gannets.** German chefs Fabian and René combine classic French cui-
FRENCH   sine with local flavors. You might find prawns on mashed kūmara, fla-
★   vored with lime, and served with roast peppers and mesclun greens in a mustard vinaigrette. Seafood is prevalent—try the tuna on red-and-white jasmine rice or vegetable-filled cannelloni drizzled with tama-rillo sauce. Homemade vodka infusions include a lemongrass version that is particularly refreshing at an outdoor table on a balmy evening. ⊠ *York and Chapel Sts.* ☎ *09/403–7990* ▭ *MC, V* ⊙ *No lunch.*

$$$–$$$$ ✗ **Kamakura.** The prime dining spot in Russell, this waterfront restau-
NEW ZEALAND   rant combines subtly prepared yet flavorsome cuisine with arguably the
Fodor's Choice   best restaurant view in town—especially if you nab a table up front.
★   The specialty of the house is the seven-course "Naturally Northland" *degustation* menu, which includes Orongo Bay oysters, and warm quail salad in a lavender vinaigrette. The crab, chili, and lime ravioli on a crayfish bisque with horseradish cream always sells out. If dinner sounds delicious but it's too rich for your wallet, all the lunch dishes are under $20. ⊠ *The Strand* ☎ *09/403–7771* ⊕ *www.kamakura.co.nz* ▭ *AE, DC, MC, V.*

$$$ ✗ **Sally's.** At this restaurant, overlooking Kororareka Bay from the Bay
SEAFOOD   of Islands Swordfish Club building, Sally's seafood chowder, packed
★   with fresh mussels, shrimp, and fish, is the most popular dish—despite numerous requests, the chef refuses to divulge his recipe. If you're looking for some local lamb, don't go past the char-grilled lamb rump on roasted kūmara with garlic spinach and a red currant jus. Ask for a window table, or dine outdoors when it's sunny. ⊠ *The Strand* ☎ *09/403–7652* ▭ *AE, MC, V* ⊡ *Licensed and BYOB.*

WHERE TO STAY

$$–$$$ 🏠 **Arcadia Lodge.** Rumor had it that this gay-friendly B&B, perched over Matauwhi Bay, a few minutes' walk from town, had been supported for more than 100 years by whale vertebrae. Sure enough, when brand-new owners re-piled the foundations of the turn-of-the-20th-century home in 2005, they found that that was virtually the only thing holding it up. One of the "backbones" of the house now sits in the lounge. Two spacious suites off the large guest lounge and dining area both have brass beds, sunrooms, and their own decks. Another three rooms are upstairs. The Tautoru Room has its own entrance, with a deck and a view of the bay where you can watch the boats coming and going from the Russell Boat Club (the club's bar is a good place to meet locals). Wake up with an appetite; breakfast could include fresh asparagus on Kerikeri smoked ham with focaccia and grilled cheese; or slow-roasted tomatoes on pesto bruschetta with pork-and-sweet fennel sausage; or zucchini, Parmesan, and mint fritters served with homemade chutneys. All of this comes with organic fruit from the garden, yogurt, granola, and fresh-squeezed Kerikeri orange juice, which you can eat on the deck looking over the bay. **Pros:** fantastic hosts; lovely rooms; spectacular views. **Cons:** finding the parking lot 500 meters (1,640 feet) away can be tricky. ✉ *10 Florance Ave.* ☎ *09/403–7756* ⊕ *www.arcadialodge. co.nz* ⊅ *4 rooms, 2 with bath, 2 suites* ⚹ *In-room: No TV. In-hotel: Restaurant* ▭ *MC, V* ⍾❙ *BP.*

$$$–$$$$ 🏠 **Duke of Marlborough Hotel.** This waterfront hotel with 26 rooms is a no-smoking venue, and with good reason—the previous three incarnations were burnt down (the first by the legendary Māori chief Hone Heke). It's a favorite with the yachting fraternity, for whom ready access to the harbor and the bar downstairs are the most important considerations. Antiques add character and the rooms are bright and cheerful. For more space, opt for one of the waterfront suites with large whirlpool baths, or there's a one-bedroom bungalow right on the waterfront. **Pros:** prime waterfront position; busy, lively crowd. **Cons:** can be too close to the action; quite noisy; no privacy. ✉ *The Strand* ☎ *09/403– 7829* ⊕ *www.theduke.co.nz* ⊅ *19 rooms, 6 suites, 1 cottage* ⚹ *In-room: No a/c. In-hotel: Restaurant, bar* ▭ *MC, V* ⍾❙ *CP and BP.*

$$$$ 🏠 **Flagstaff Lodge and Day Spa.** Photos of this 1912 villa, in its original state, line the central kauri hallway. Its outside appearance has changed little, but inside it has been restored with all modern conveniences. The high-ceiling rooms have Italian-tile bathrooms, super-king-size beds, and French doors onto the wraparound veranda from where you can see a peep of the bay, a minute's walk away. Two French bathtubs stand behind a screen off a small courtyard where you can soak in essential oils and rose petals. A separate room houses the spa, providing massage and beauty treatments. **Pros:** good facilities; nicely appointed. **Cons:** no views. ✉ *17 Wellington St.* ☎ *09/403–7117 or 0800/403–711* ⊕ *www.flagstafflodge.co.nz* ⊅ *4 rooms* ⚹ *In-room: No TV, Internet (some). In-hotel: Spa* ▭ *AE, DC, MC, V* ⍾❙ *BP.*

$$$$ 🏠 **The Homestead at Orongo Bay.** Tucked away in gardens off the road
★ between the car-ferry landing and Russell, this historic lodge, built in 1865, soothes with peace and quiet—which is why it's hosted people

like Jane Fonda and Jo-Anna Lumley. The two rooms in the main homestead have kauri ceilings and paneling built in a New England colonial style, with large, tiled bathrooms. A pair of bi-level barn rooms set back from the main building have angled roofs and sky-lights. Because it's set on 17 acres of native bush, it's worth bringing your binoculars. The pond hosts a number of endangered birdlife, including the New Zealand native brown teal, the fourth-rarest water-fowl in the world. Sumptuous multicourse dinners are cooked (by prior arrangement) by chef and co-owner Michael Hooper, a food critic, who grows many of his organic ingredients on the property and plucks the oysters out of the bay in front of the house. He's been known to pick the salad while the starter is being served. **Pros:** convivial host; really good food; lovely garden. **Cons:** slightly out of town; small. ⊠ *Aucks Rd.* ☎ *09/403–7527* ⊕ *www.thehomestead.co.nz* ⤵ *4 rooms* ⚬ *In-room: DVD, Wi-Fi. In-hotel: Internet terminal* ⊟ *AE, DC, MC, V* ⏐⊙⏐*BP.*

$$$$ ⊞ **Okiato Lodge.** Okiato is high up on Okiato Point, looking out on Opua, Paihia, and other Bay of Islands locales. Spacious rooms include step-down lounge areas, with high-vaulted ceilings and large windows with great views. With balconies and patios leading out onto the ter-raced grounds, each room has its own private access to the Point, and a track leads right down to the water. There is also a two-bed-room semi-detached cottage. The high-end rates include drinks and a four-course dinner, which emphasizes New Zealand favorites such as scallops, venison, and lamb. **Pros:** lovely grounds; stunning views. **Cons:** isolated. ⊠ *James Clendon Pl., Okiato Point* ☎ *09/403–7948* ⊕ *www.okiato.co.nz* ⤵ *11 rooms* ⚬ *In-room: Refrigerator, Internet (some). In-hotel: Restaurant, bar, pool* ⊟ *AE, MC, V* ⏐⊙⏐*MAP.*

¢–$ ⊞ **Sheltered Waters Backpackers.** This small hostel, a leisurely 10-minute walk from town, brings guests back for repeat visits. One dorm room can sleep 10, a double room with a bunk can take 4, and a suite also has beds and bunks. Palms circle the large garden, home to a little aviary with a bird that talks. If you're lucky, you'll stay on one of the nights the hosts cook up a pot of seafood chowder (made with local oysters and mussels), or you can always cook your own steak on the barbecue. The place is wheelchair friendly. **Pros:** affordable; clean; busy. **Cons:** dorms can be noisy; lack of privacy. ⊠ *18 Florance Ave.* ☎ *09/403–8818* ⊕ *www.russellbackpackers.co.nz* ⤵ *1 dorm room, 1 double room, 1 suite* ⚬ *In-room: Kitchen, DVD. In-hotel: Bicycles, laundry facilities, Internet terminal, some pets allowed* ⊟ *No credit cards.*

$$$–$$$$ ⊞ **Te Pa Helios.** With views across the sea and a charming host this cliff-top establishment has lots of repeat business. An old Māori *pā* (hilltop fortification) site and a small bay frame a view of islands dot-ting the clear blue sea. The property evokes Greece with its angular whitewashed buildings. All the rooms have access to kitchens and are stocked with good basic provisions. In the main villa are the Island Suite, with a balcony on the cliff edge, and the spacious Russell Room, with a small terrace also set on the cliff. The self-catering Little Villa has two bedrooms and two bathrooms. All bedrooms look out onto the ocean. Local art hangs in most of the rooms. Paths lead to the

two beaches at the base of the cliff, where there is a three-bedroom bungalow in which you can stay. There is a two-night minimum. **Pros:** relaxed; breathtaking views. **Cons:** Russell not within walking distance. ✉ *44 Du Fresne Pl., Tapeka Point* ☎ *09/403–7229* ⊕ *www.babs.co.nz/helios/index.htm* ⤶ *1 room, 1 suite, 1 villa, 1 cottage* ⚄ *In-room: No a/c* ▭ *MC, V* ☾ *Closed May–Oct.* ⦿ *CP.*

KERIKERI

★ *20 km (12 mi) north of Paihia.*

Kerikeri is often referred to as the cradle of the nation because so much of New Zealand's earliest history, especially interactions between Māori and Europeans, took place here. The main town is small but gaining a reputation for its crafts and specialty shops. A major citrus and kiwifruit growing area, it was once principally a service town for the whole mid-north region. Though newcomers have flocked to Kerikeri for its low-key lifestyle, it still feels like a small town.

The **Kerikeri Proctor Library,** open weekdays 8 to 5, and Saturday from 9:30 to 2, is the only place in Kerikeri that provides visitor information, and it's far less extensive than other bureaus.

GETTING HERE AND AROUND

Kerikeri is about four hours drive from Auckland following State Highway 1. Buses connect from Auckland directly and from the other centers. There is also a good airport with regular flights, but it is expensive to fly, particularly from Auckland. There is no train service.

ESSENTIALS

Visitor Information Kerikeri Proctor Library (✉ *6 Cobham Rd., Kerikeri* ☎ *09/407–9297*).

EXPLORING

TOP ATTRACTIONS

Bay of Islands Farmers' Market. If you're in Kerikeri on a Sunday, head to the market to sample just about everything the region has to offer, from music to fresh produce, local wines, cheeses, preserves, oils, and handmade soaps. Grab a locally roasted coffee and wander among the stalls. ✉ *Parking lot, off Hobson Ave., Kerikeri* ☾ *Sun. 9–noon.*

Historic Kerikeri Basin. Most of the interest lies just northeast of the modern town on the Kerikeri Inlet. Anglican missionaries arrived in this area in 1819; they were invited to Kerikeri by its most famous historical figure, the great Māori chief Hongi Hika. The chief visited England in 1820, where he was showered with gifts. On his way back to New Zealand, during a stop in Sydney, he traded many of these presents for muskets. Having the advantage of these prized weapons, he set in motion plans to conquer other Māori tribes, enemies of his own Ngapuhi people. The return of his raiding parties over five years, with many slaves and gruesome trophies of conquest, put considerable strain between Hongi Hika and the missionaries. Eventually his warring ways were Hongi's undoing. He was shot in 1827 and died from complications from the wound a year later.

Kerikeri Mission Station. The Kerikeri Mission Station, which includes the 1821 Mission House (**Mission House**) and the **Stone Store**, provide a fascinating—and rare—look at pre-treaty New Zealand. **Kemp House,** otherwise known as Mission House, has gone through many changes since 1821, but ironically, a major flood in 1981 inspired its "authentic" restoration. The flood washed away the garden and damaged the lower floor, and during repair much information about the original structure of the house was revealed. Its ground floor and garden have been restored to the style of missionary days, and the upper floor, which remained unharmed by the flood, retains its Victorian decoration.

Stone Store. New Zealand's oldest stone building is a striking example of early colonial architecture. Designed by Wesleyan missionary John Hobbs and built by an ex-convict stonemason from New South Wales between 1832 and 1836, the Store was meant to house New Zealand mission supplies and large quantities of wheat from the mission farm at Te Waimate. When the wheat failed, the building was mainly leased as a kauri gum-trading store. The ground floor is still a shop. The upper stories display the goods of a culture trying to establish itself in a new country, such as red Hudson Bay blankets, which were sought after by Māori from the *pā* (hilltop fortification), forged goods, steel tools, an old steel flour mill, and tools and flintlock muskets—also prized by local Māori. Guided tours are available; bookings are essential. ⊠ *Kerikeri Historic Basin, Kerikeri Rd.* ☎ 09/407-9236 ▣ *$7.50* ☻ *Daily 10–5.*

WORTH NOTING

Kororipo Pā. Across the road from the Basin's Stone Store is a path leading to the historic site of Kororipo Pā, the fortified headquarters of chief Hongi Hika. Untrained eyes may have difficulty figuring out exactly where the pā (Māori fortification) was, as no structures are left. The pā was built on a steep-sided promontory between the Kerikeri River and the Wairoa Stream. There's still a fine view over both.

Rewa's Village. This museum re-creates a *kāinga* (unfortified fishing village) where local Māori lived in peaceful times. In times of war they took refuge in nearby Kororipo Pā. In the village are good reproductions of the chief Hongi Hika's house, the weapons store, and the family enclosure, as well as two original canoes dug up from local swamps and original *hāngi* stones which were heated by fire and used to cook traditional Māori feasts, found on-site. A "discoverers garden" takes you on a winding path past indigenous herbs and other plants; information is posted describing the uses of each plant. ⊠ *Kerikeri Historic Basin, Kerikeri Rd.* ☎ 09/407-6454 ▣ *$5* ☻ *Nov.–Apr., daily 9:30–5:30; May–Oct., daily 10–4; Jan. and Feb., daily 9–5.*

OUTDOOR ACTIVITIES

FISHING John Gregory of **Primetime Charters & Gamefishing** (⊠ *Conifer La., Kerikeri* ☎ 09/407-1299 ⊕ *www.primetimecharters.co.nz*) has more than 25 years experience at sea. The company, which holds the New Zealand record for most marlin caught, goes after all sport fish, specializing in broadbill swordfish. Prices start at $3,350 per day, with most trips between January and June taking five to seven days.

GOLF **Carrington** (⌧ *Matai Bay Rd., Karikari Peninsula* ☎ 09/408–1049 ⊕ *www.heritagehotels.co.nz/Carrington-Resort*) has an 18-hole, par-72, tournament-quality course, which meanders along 100 acres of coastline. The course shares the land with the Karikari Estate winery, and **Carrington Resort**, a luxury lodge. Green fees are $85 per person, and clubs cost $40 to $65 to rent. The spectacular par-72 championship course at **Kauri Cliffs** (⌧ *Matauri Bay Rd., Matauri Bay* ☎ 09/407–0010 ⊕ *www.kauricliffs.com*) has four sets of tees to challenge every skill level. Fifteen holes have views of the Pacific, and six are played alongside the cliffs. You can rent Callaway clubs from the pro shop ($75). Green fees are $400 per person from October thru April and $300 other times. Kauri Cliffs is approximately 45 minutes' drive from Kerikeri.

3

WHERE TO EAT

$ ╳ **Birdies Cafe.** The servings at this café in Kaitaia are almost too big.
CAFÉ The omelet is loaded with your choice of toppings, then grilled with cheese before being served with pesto and relish; the stack of pancakes is enough for two. Regrettably the coffee is hit-and-miss, but friendly service makes up for that. If you sit outside in summer make sure you have a hat. ⌧ *14 Commerce St., Kaitaia* ☎ 09/408–4935 ▤ *AE, DC, MC, V* ⊘ *Mon.–Sat. 7:30 AM–7 PM, Sun. 8:30 AM–7 PM.*

¢–$ ╳ **Fishbone Café.** The coffee is good as are the sandwiches, panini, and
CAFÉ frittatas. The extensive blackboard menu grants a range of tastes including a char-grilled chicken Caesar salad with garlic aioli dressing, and a noodle salad. Follow this up with a fresh muffin or the ever-disappearing caramel slice. The service can be a bit patchy. ⌧ *88 Kerikeri Rd.* ☎ 09/407–6065 ▤ *AE, DC, MC, V* ⊘ *No dinner.*

$$$ ╳ **Marsden Estate Winery and Restaurant.** Named after the missionary
ECLECTIC Samuel Marsden, who planted New Zealand's first grapevines in Ker-
★ ikeri in 1819, this winery is a popular lunch spot and that's because it is really good. On a fine day ask for a table on the terrace. The seasonal menu is eclectic; try the black pudding (blood sausage) with blue cheese, pear, and blueberry sauce, cherry tomatoes in a pomegranate molasses jus, or sample the oxtail stew on mashed potatoes. Of the winery's small but notable output, the full-bodied Black Rocks Chardonnay has won national and international awards and the 2007 Pinot Gris is worth a try. The winery is open for tastings. ⌧ *Wiroa Rd.* ☎ 09/407–9398 ⊕ *www.marsdenestate.co.nz* ▤ *MC, V* ⊘ *No dinner Sun.–Thurs.*

WHERE TO STAY

$–$$ ☲ **Kauri Park.** This small cluster of chalets is a notch above the usual, with modern style and a magnificent setting among fruit trees adjacent to farmland. Friendly hosts Dallas and Delphine Eves display the usual Kiwi welcome with a free drink on arrival in the guest lounge. Each unit has a veranda and colorful furnishings. Kauri Park is a little out of town, with a more rural setting, but it's still only a few minutes' drive from the historic sights. **Pros:** clean; relaxed; friendly. **Cons:** not within walking distance of town; cheap, plastic outdoor furniture. ⌧ *512 Kerikeri Rd. (south end)* ☎ 09/407–7629 ⊕ *www.kauripark. co.nz* ⤳ *9 units* ⌂ *In-room: No a/c, Internet (some). In-hotel: Bar, Wi-Fi* ▤ *AE, DC, MC, V.*

$–$$ ▣ **Paheke.** An enormous cedar of Lebanon stands in front of this gracious 1864 kauri homestead; both the tree and the house are listed with the Historic Places Trust. The restored home has one modern wing, but it's designed to blend with the original building. Two rooms with private baths are in the new wing; one has a balcony overlooking the gardens. The rooms in the older wing are smaller but elegantly furnished with antiques; they share a bath. A three-course dinner and picnic lunches are available for an additional fee. Paheke is about a 15-minute drive southwest of Kerikeri and Paihia. **Pros:** well priced; relaxing; stunning grounds. **Cons:** not close to town. ⊠ *State Hwy. 1, Ohaeawai* ☎ *09/405–9623* ⊕ *www.paheke.co.nz* ⤴ *4 rooms, 2 with bath* ♿ *In-hotel: Laundry facilities, Internet terminal* ▭ *MC, V* ⑩ *BP.*

$$$–$$$$ ▣ **The Summer House.** Hosts Christine and Rod Brown come from artistic families, a background that infuses this B&B. The downstairs room, slightly detached from the house, is done in a South Pacific style. It has the most space, a kitchenette, and a higher room rate. The two upstairs rooms in the main house share a guest lounge. One room has an 1860 French bed with furniture to match, and the other has a Victorian brass bedstead. Christine's breakfasts are wonderful, including freshly squeezed juice and fresh or poached fruits—all from the 2½ acres of citrus orchards on the property—and Greek yogurt, homemade muesli, jams and marmalade, and free-range eggs cooked as requested. The landscaped subtropical garden surrounding the house attracts native birds, doves, and monarch butterflies. **Pros:** lovely environment; friendly hosts. **Cons:** interior is overstyled. ⊠ *424 Kerikeri Rd.* ☎ *09/407–4294* ⊕ *www.thesummerhouse.co.nz* ⤴ *3 rooms* ♿ *In-room: No a/c In-hotel: W-Fi* ▭ *MC, V* ⑩ *BP.*

SHOPPING

At **Makana Confections** (⊠ *Kerikeri Rd.* ☎ *09/407–6800*) favorites include the macadamia butter toffee crunch, and it's almost impossible to leave without a bagful of chocolate-coated, locally grown macadamias or liqueur truffles. **Origin Art and Craft Co-op** (⊠ *128 Kerikeri Rd.* ☎ *09/407–1133*), 450 yards south of the Kerikeri turnoff, stocks locally made arts and crafts, such as place mats made from local timber; stained-glass lamp shades and trinket boxes; silver jewelry, textiles and felt work; and artfully made calfskin and doeskin bags. Andrew and Robyn Leary of **Scopes NZ** (⊠ *265 Waipapa Rd.* ☎ *09/407–4415*) produce fabulous kaleidoscopes from kauri wood that was buried in swamps for thousands of years. They also make "bubble scopes" (their own inventions), which view colored liquid in a transparent ball. Prices start at around $45 for small kauri scopes produced with materials such as *paua* (abalone shell), shards of glass, or bits of fishing tackle.

Coromandel Peninsula and the Bay of Plenty

WORD OF MOUTH

"Be sure to check out Hot Water Beach. It's only a few miles from Cathedral Cove and if you get there with the tide is right, you can dig a hole in the sand and have your own beach-front Jacuzzi (nearby stores sell shovels or you can borrow from other tourists; don't worry, the holes are easy to dig)."

—kjost25

WELCOME TO COROMANDEL PENINSULA AND THE BAY OF PLENTY

TOP REASONS TO GO

★ **Beach Bounty:** The forest-fringed inlets, coves, and sprawling sand dunes include some of the most popular beaches in the country. The coastline is endless; you'll never feel overcrowded.

★ **Volcanoes and Vistas:** From the coastal cliffs of the Coromandel to the Bay of Plenty's signature volcanic peak, Mauao, hypnotic views abound. White Island's steaming fissures are a dramatic sight by sea, air, or at the rim of the marine volcano itself.

★ **Walking and Hiking:** Follow the "footsteps of Toi" to the secluded bay of Otarawaiwere, or take a forest walk to swim in one of the lagoons formed by the tiers of Kaiate Falls. The Coromandel is full of easy roadside walks through native forest brimming with birdlife.

★ **Watery Wonders:** Dive or snorkel in the region's marine reserves, or take a swim with dolphins. Charter a boat and go deep-sea fishing, or kayak among the glowworms by moonlight.

1 The Coromandel Peninsula. The Coromandel beckons from the Hauraki Plains like a big lizard lying in the sun—the dark forest on the central mountainous spine promising more than just pretty pictures. When you arrive at the peninsula you'll be surprised how lush the forest growth is, wonder at how the road hugs the coast literally feet above the water, and instantly see why people like living here.

2 The Bay of Plenty. People refer to the Bay of Plenty as New Zealand's food bowl—some of the most fertile land for stone fruit and vegetables is found in the region, and seafood is abundant. From the high points on the road you'll notice rolling countryside that's a rich green in winter and a golden sheen in summer as the grasses dry.

GETTING ORIENTED

The Coromandel and Bay of Plenty region is about two to three hours southeast of Auckland and west of the Waikato farming district and is a mix of rugged and forested hill country and rich plains used for agriculture. It's about a seven-hour drive from Wellington and a few hours from Hamilton and Rotorua. The area, with its strong agricultural focus, is dotted with small rural towns fanning out from Tauranga's relatively big port. Many of the Coromandel's small settlements are based on former ports that were used to transport logs from the forestry works.

4

0   10 mi

0   10 km

Motiti
Island

Bay of Plenty

Papamoa
Te Puke
Maketu

White
Island

Motuhora
Island

Matata
Thornton

Whakatane

33

2

Edgecumbe

Wainui

Mourea

Pekatahi

COROMANDEL PENINSULA AND THE BAY OF PLENTY PLANNER

When to Go

These regions are well loved for their beaches, and they are crowded between October and February when the weather is mild enough to swim in the ocean; otherwise-sleepy seaside towns are filled with citysiders, with a tourist surge during the weeks around Christmas and the New Year. Don't overlook the off-season (from March through September): the weather's usually sunny, climate is temperate, prices are lower, and locals have more time to chat. Some of them—often older ladies—swim every day whatever the weather.

Planning

Set aside three to four days and get a rental car. The Bay of Plenty and Coromandel need to be approached with flexibility. The region has much to provide in a relatively small area, so that five-minute stop at a beach may turn into a long coastal walk. Likewise, the many forest walks can be as challenging as you choose—from an hour to a whole day. You can approach the journey as a loop that begins in Thames (in the north) or Whangamata (in the south). And be patient—the curvy roads challenge many drivers, especially tourists in camper vans.

Getting Here and Around

Bus Travel

InterCity Coachlines, Go Kiwi Shuttles, and **nakedbus** link Whitianga and Thames with Auckland daily; the trip is just over two hours from Auckland to Thames and just over three hours to Whitianga. Bus travel within the region is reliable, although less frequent in winter. InterCity, Go Kiwi, and nakedbus make daily trips between Coromandel, Thames, Whitianga, and other stops throughout the peninsula.

InterCity and Go Kiwi have special Coromandel hop-on hop-off passes; the Go Kiwi pass is good for a month, and the InterCity pass is valid for three. Nakedbus is an inexpensive "no frills" option.

Contacts Go Kiwi Shuttles (☎ 07/8t66–0336 ⊕ www. go-kiwi.co.nz). **InterCity Coachlines** (☎ 07/868–7251 or 0800/222–146 ⊕ www.intercitycoach.co.nz). **nakedbus** (☎ 0900/62533 ⊕ www.nakedbus.com).

Car Travel

The best way to explore is by car. Most roads are well maintained and clearly signposted, and a car gives you the freedom to explore hot pools and waterfalls along side roads. The Pacific Coast Highway is popular with cyclists.

From Auckland take the Southern Motorway, following signs to Hamilton. Just as you get over the Bombay Hills, turn left onto State Highway 2; then take the turnoff to State Highway 25, signposted between the small towns of Maramarua and Mangatarata. Follow the signs to Thames. Allow 1½ to 2½ hours for the 118-km (73-mi) journey. State Highway 25 is the peninsula's main loop, and though winding, the road is in good condition.

To reach the Bay of Plenty from Auckland, take the Southern Motorway, following signs to Hamilton. Just past the narrowing of the motorway, turn left onto State Highway 2, and travel through Paeroa. Stay on Highway 2 all the way to Tauranga, driving through Waihi and Katikati on the way. The driving time between Auckland and Katikati is around 2 hours, 40 minutes. Between Auckland and Tauranga, it's at least 3 hours, 15 minutes.

Restaurants

There are many dining options across the Coromandel and Bay of Plenty. You can buy food from roadside seafood shacks and take-out fish-and-chips joints to cafés serving sandwiches and city-style coffee, right through to white-linen affairs. Even when restaurants are formal in appearance, diners and hosts tend toward a relaxed country-casualness. Restaurant owners make a point of using the region's abundant resources: the fish is likely to have been caught that morning from a nearby bay, and shellfish are from local mussel and oyster farms. A huge community of artists lives in the region and their work is likely to be for sale even though it adorns restaurant walls.

Dinner service begins about 6 PM in the winter and around 7 PM during the summer months, though many places have "all-day menus." In peak season most places keep serving until at least 9 PM. For many restaurants reservations are a good idea, especially in the summer and particularly in Coromandel. In winter, when it's quiet, phoning ahead means the restaurant will know to stay open.

Hotels

Like mellow places around the world, you'll find plenty of comfortable bed-and-breakfasts and mom-and-pop motels, but both the Coromandel and the Bay of Plenty also have a sprinkling of luxe boutique lodges tucked away in the forest or along coastal coves. In peak season, from October through February, advance booking is essential across the board and many of the better places have long-term customers who book as much as a year in advance. You'll rarely find air-conditioning in lodgings here, but then you'll rarely need it.

WHAT IT COSTS IN NEW ZEALAND DOLLARS

	¢	$	$$	$$$	$$$$
Restaurants	under $10	$10–$15	$15–$20	$20–$30	over $30
Hotels	under $75	$75–$125	$125–$200	$200–$300	over $300

Prices are per person for a main course at dinner, or the equivalent. Prices are for a standard double room in high season, including 12.5% tax.

Visitor Information

The Coromandel, Katikati, Mount Maunganui, Tauranga, Thames, Pauanui, Tairua, Waihi, Whakatane, Whangamata, and Whitianga visitor centers are open daily between at least 10 and 4. For tidal information, check the back page of the *New Zealand Herald* newspaper. *Tait's Fun Maps* of Coromandel, Thames, and Whitianga are not drawn to scale, but they clearly mark roads and main attractions. Pick up a copy at almost any hotel, tour-operator office, or visitor center.

On the Road

Tip: Slow down! Some of the Coromandel's best bits aren't points A or B but what's stumbled upon in between. Lopsided signs advertising local artists beckon from gateposts; green-and-yellow DOC (Department of Conservation) signs point out short walks off the road; and those bags of feijoas, avocadoes, and oranges at that roadside stand will beat their grocery store counterparts in a taste test every time.

Caution: Coromandel's meandering, winding roads mean that locals tend to measure driving distance by time, not kilometers. Listen to them when they tell you it will take an hour to get from Coromandel to Whitianga, even though it's only 60 km (37 mi)—you'll drop down to 25 km per hour (16 mph) for every other dip and curve.

Updated by
Alia Bloom

Beautiful sandy beaches, lush native forests, and some steamy geothermal activity make the Coromandel Peninsula and Bay of Plenty quite a departure from überurban Auckland. Most residents live in fishing villages or small rural towns, with the occasional artsy community or alternative-lifestyle commune thrown in, particularly in the Coromandel.

Both areas bask in more than their fair share of sun for much of the year, so avocado, citrus, kiwifruit, nuts, and even subtropical fruits flourish here, and many growers adopt organic practices. Keep an eye out for the ubiquitous unmanned fruit stands accompanied by "honesty boxes."

Follow State Highway 25—the Pacific Coast highway—as it meanders up the west coast and down the east coast of the peninsula. Traffic can build up on this road, particularly in the busy summer months or weekends. As you drive south down the Peninsula's east coast, the Pacific Highway stretches out to the coastal plains and forests of the Bay of Plenty.

From the Bay of Plenty's northern gateway of Katikati as far as Whakatane, the coastline consists of huge stretches of sand, interrupted by rivers, estuaries, and sandbars. Inland, the soil is rich and fertile; this is farming territory with sprawling canopies of kiwifruit vines, fields of corn and other produce, and pockets of dense native forest. You'll see people fishing in some of the bays, but others have strict rules; signs in the shape of a fish outline whether or not you can fish.

The Bay of Plenty was one of the country's first areas settled by Māori, and the descendants of these earliest arrivals moved north to the Coromandel Peninsula as well. Although intertribal fighting and European-introduced diseases took a heavy toll on Coromandel communities, the Bay of Plenty still has a strong Māori presence.

THE COROMANDEL PENINSULA

4

New Zealand has countless pockets of beauty that escape standard itineraries. As with so many other lands "discovered" by Europeans, the Coromandel Peninsula was looted for its valuable resources: kauri trees, then kauri gum, and finally gold in the 1870s. Relative quiet since the 1930s has allowed the region to recover its natural beauty, and has attracted many bohemian types.

In the 1960s and '70s, dairy farms and orchards sprang up, as did communes, spiritual retreats, and artists' communities. The population is a mix of artists, those who appreciate the country lifestyle (and the easy access to organic food), and a growing number of Aucklanders looking for a weekend or retirement home.

A craggy range of peaks rises sharply to almost 3,000 feet and dominates the center of the peninsula. The west coast cradles the Firth of Thames, which in places is muddy, and along the east coast the Pacific has carved out a succession of beaches and inlets separated by rearing headlands. Because of its rich soil, the peninsula has many spectacular gardens, and several are open to the public. From the town of Thames, the gateway to the region, State Highway 25 and the 309 Road circle the lower two-thirds of the peninsula—an exhilarating drive with the sea on one side and great forested peaks on the other.

ONE-LANE BRIDGES

During your travels throughout the Coromandel, you'll become familiar with a sign showing two arrows: one big, one small. This means you're about to approach a really narrow section of road—often a bridge—that only allows room for cars traveling in one direction at a time. If you're heading in the direction of the smaller arrow, you must yield to oncoming traffic and wait until the road is clear. Even if you're heading in the direction of the bigger arrow, take it easy! These narrow stretches often include a blind corner or two.

THAMES

120 km (75 mi) southeast of Auckland.

The peninsula's oldest town, Thames has evolved from a gold-mining hotbed in the 1920s to an agricultural center. Locals have a saying that when the gold ran out, "Thames went to sleep awaiting the kiss of a golden prince—and instead it awoke to the warm breath of a cow." The main street used to be lined with nearly 100 hotels (read: bars); gold mining and logging was thirsty work. Only five of these hotels still operate, but the town and environs still provide glimpses of the mining era. In 1867 two towns, Grahamstown in the north and Shortland in the south, merged to form Thames, and many locals still refer to upper Thames as Grahamstown. Thames today is also the gateway to the Kauaeranga Valley Forest Park, home to waterfalls, ancient kauri groves, and the Pinnacles, the peninsula's highest accessible point.

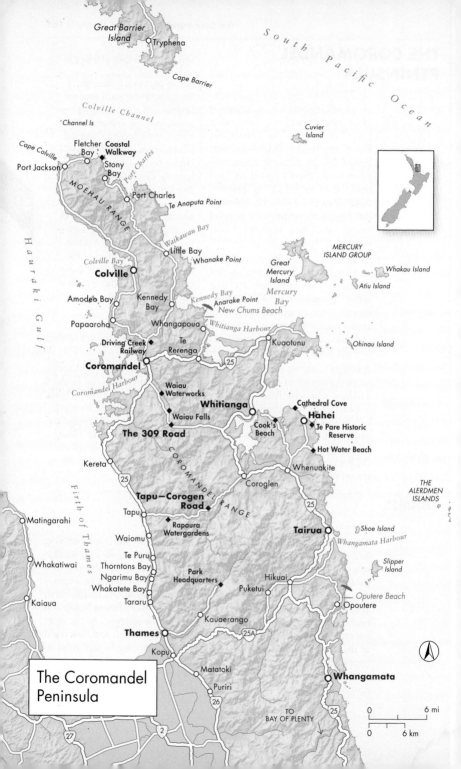

The Coromandel Peninsula

GETTING HERE AND AROUND

If you're not driving, you can take a public bus to Thames from Auckland, Hamilton, Tauranga, or any of the smaller towns on the main road en route from these cities. If you're coming from the nearest big city, such as the ones mentioned above, a bus ticket shouldn't cost you more than about $15–$25.

You can pick up a rental car at the Auckland airport and drive on down to the Coromandel, or you can take a bus and rent a car when you arrive in Thames; there are two rental car companies—Ultimate Rentals and John Davy Rentals—both of which you'll be directed to when the bus deposits you at the Thames Information Centre.

ESSENTIALS

Bus Depot (⊠ *Thames Information Centre, 206 Pollen St.* ☎ *07/868–7284).*

Car Rentals John Davy Rentals (⊠ *214 Pollen St., Thames* ☎ *07/868–6868).*
Ultimate Rentals (⊠ *400 Pollen St., Thames* ☎ *07/868–6439).*

Hospitals Thames Hospital (⊠ *Mackay St., Thames* ☎ *07/868–6550).*

Visitor Information Thames Information Centre (⊠ *206 Pollen St.* ☎ *07/868–7284* ⊕ *www.thamesinfo.co.nz).*

EXPLORING
TOP ATTRACTIONS

Goldmine Experience. If you want to learn more about early gold-mining efforts in the Coromandel, stop in at the Goldmine Experience, north on the way out of town, and take a 40-minute underground tour of the old Golden Crown Claim, which was first worked in 1868. You'll need sturdy, closed-toed footwear because it can be muddy underground. You can also pan for gold on the surface. Five hundred feet below, the Caledonia strike was one of the richest in the world. Call to book a tour. ⊠ *State Hwy. 25, north of Waiotahi Creek Rd.* ☎ *07/868–8154* ⊕ *www.goldmine-experience.co.nz* 🖱 *$10.*

Grahamstown Saturday Market. On Saturday mornings, the northern end of Thames' main street is transformed into a bustling market. Stalls line the street, with vendors selling local organic produce and cheeses, antiques, jewelry, and arts and crafts. Most, if not all, of the shops get in on the act as well. ⊠ *Upper Pollen St.* ☉ *Sat. 8–1.*

🅲 **Tropical Butterfly Garden.** A few minutes' drive north on the way out of
★ Thames, it's easy to miss this garden unless you're specifically looking for the signs. It doesn't look impressive when you get there—but don't let that put you off. Roger and Sabine Gass have brought some color to the Coromandel with a flock of butterflies from Australia. Now, up to 20 species and 400 butterflies from all over the world may be on view at any time, including large Birdwing butterflies. Birds such as finches, doves, and quails join the butterflies along with about 100 different plant species. The heliconia (or false bird-of-paradise) and orchids are particularly stunning. ⊠ *Dickson Holiday Park, Victoria St.* ☎ *07/868–8080* ⊕ *www.butterfly.co.nz* 🖱 *$9* ☉ *Late Aug.–mid-July, daily 10–4.*

WORTH NOTING

Bounty. This design store–cum–gallery is Thames' best option for buying local arts and crafts, including jewelry, pottery, weaving, and paintings. ✉ *644 Pollen St.* ☎ *07/868–8988* ⊕ *Weekdays 10–5, Sat. 9–4.*

Meonstoke. This is one of New Zealand's most unusual gardens. Since 1954, Pam Gwynne has been working every square inch of her ¼-acre lot. Numerous paths wind through a junglelike space; no lookouts or vistas distract you from the lush surroundings. Pam collects found objects and ingeniously incorporates them into surreal and often humorous tableaux with the plantings. On one path, a row of ceramic pitchers is suspended from a rod. Although the garden is small, allow yourself time to peer at the details. The entry fee goes to local charities. ✉ *305 Kuranui St.* ☎ *07/868–6560 or 07/868–6850* ⌸ *$10* ☻ *1st 2 weekends in Oct., 10–4, otherwise by appointment only (after 4).*

The Organic Co-op. This small shop in Thames sells some of the region's best organic produce. If you want to try fresh fruit and vegetables that remind you of how good things can taste, then this is worth a visit. ✉ *736 Pollen St.* ☎ *07/868–8797* ▭ *AE, DC, MC, V* ☻ *Weekdays 9–5, Sat. 9–noon.*

Pete's Collectibles. If you're interested in the retro side of New Zealand, Pete's is one of a cluster of stores in Thames selling 1950s–1970s New Zealand–made knickknacks, including old records, secondhand books, and cool kitchen crockery. The wares are too quirky to be conventionally "antique." Look out for his range of Crown Lynn—these iconic dinner sets have attained cult status in New Zealand. The maker of these kitschy cups and saucers was once the largest pottery manufacturer in the Southern Hemisphere and provided dishware to the New Zealand railways in the 1940s. Crown Lynn is probably the most popular item for ceramic collectors in the country. ✉ *756 Pollen St.* ☎ *07/868–3066* ☻ *Weekdays 9–4:30, Sat. 8–1.*

St. George's Anglican Church is worth a quick look for its gorgeous kauri-wood interior. It was opened in 1872 and the vicar allows it to be used for arts events. ✉ *Willoughby and MacKay Sts.* ☎ *07/862–6267* ☻ *Tues.–Fri. 9–2.*

Thames Historical Museum. At this tiny museum you can look into earlier ways of life in the town. The museum contains photographic displays of the gold-rush and logging industries, good re-creations of period rooms from the 1800s, and info on the original Māori inhabitants and early European settlers. The garden, with period roses and other flora that settlers commonly planted, is a nice place to rest. ✉ *Pollen and Cochrane Sts.* ☎ *07/868–8509* ⌸ *$5* ☻ *Daily 1–4.*

Thames School of Mines Mineralogical Museum. The Thames School of Mines Mineralogical Museum gives a geologic take on the area's history. The School of Mines provided practical instruction to the gold miners of the mid-1880s; the museum was established in 1900 to exhibit geological samples. The school closed decades ago, but the museum's still kicking, displaying those turn-of-the-20th-century rock specimens along with scales, models of stamper batteries, and other gold-mining paraphernalia. ✉ *Brown and Cochrane Sts.* ☎ *07/868–6227* 🖻 *$5* ⏱ *Wed.–Sun. 11–3.*

OUTDOOR ACTIVITIES

★ **Kauaeranga Valley Forest Park** has 22 walking trails that offer anything from a 15-minute stroll to an overnight trek. The most accessible starting point is the delightful Kauaeranga Valley Road, where the **Department of Conservation Visitors Center** (☎ *07/867–9080* ⊕ *www.doc. govt.nz*) provides maps and information.

The hike to the Pinnacles is the most popular walk in Kauaeranga Forest Park and indeed on the peninsula; the trek from the trailhead to the Pinnacles hut takes three hours one-way. From the hut you can continue to the peak (another hour one-way) for a view that spans both coasts. An overnight in the Pinnacles hut costs $15; you need to reserve it through the DOC center. You can hike back via the three-hour-long Webb Creek trail or come down the longer (four-hour) alternative route, the Billy Goat track.

Always read the signs at the start of the track to check their state. If you're traveling in the busy season, plan to visit midweek. To reach the Kauaeranga Valley, head south from Thames and on the outskirts of the town turn left on Banks Street, then right on Parawai Road, which becomes Kauaeranga Valley Road.

The DOC center provides information on many other walks or tramps to places such as Fantail Bay, Cathedral Cove, or Opera Point. There are numerous places to swim and the beaches are quite safe as you head out along the Coromandel Peninsula. There are not many changing rooms but it's acceptable to change car side with a towel.

WHERE TO EAT

$$–$$$ ✕ **Rocco.** Through the double gates and beyond the shell-and-stone patio
SPANISH   is a little Spanish getaway housed in a classic 1912 kauri villa. Run by an ex-winemaker and a Chilean chef, the inevitable focus is on wine and Latin cuisine made with local products. The Spanish angle is a little garbled; empanadas and tacos mingle freely with tapas and chorizo pizza, but the intentions are good and the portions generous. ✉ *109 Sealey St.* ☎ *07/868–8641* ⊕ *MC, V* ⏱ *Wed.–Sun. 5–9; lunch Wed.–Fri. and Sun.*

$ ✕ **Sola Café.** This little self-styled cafe is outstanding. Don't be fooled
VEGETARIAN   by the vegetarian menu; this is no health bar. The counter displays
★   risotto cakes, Florentines, and apple, pear, apricot, and fig shortbread; the berry friend (a small, sweet, cake made from ground almonds and egg whites, often topped or filled with fruit) are as good as any you will find. Part-owner Clare Rodley has been baking for pocket money since she was a kid. The wraps are irresistible, and the local cheeses and chutneys from the deli counter make great picnic fixings. Sola is easily the hippest place in Thames for coffee. They also support local artists and ever-changing works are for sale on the wall. The store sells local cheeses outside the door during the Grahamstown Saturday Market. ✉ *720b Pollen St.* ☎ *07/868–8781* ⊕ *www.solacafe.co.nz* 🖻 *AE, DC, MC, V* ⏱ *Closed Sun.*

WHERE TO STAY

$ ⊡ **Brookby Motel.** In this low row of units, the off-white brick rooms are small but tidy, with wooden balconies overlooking a tree-lined stream. The best deal is the studio attached to the office and owners' home, a turn-of-the-20th-century pioneer cottage. This studio has wooden floors and furnishings as well as stained-glass windows, but it costs no more than the standard rooms. The property is close to some easy to moderately challenging walks, and you can explore the road up to the old settlement of Irishtown. **Pros:** low-key; quiet; clean; close to bush-walks. **Cons:** too basic for some. ✉ *102 Redwood La.* ☎ *07/868–6663* ⊕ *www.brookbymotel.co.nz* ⮑ *4 rooms, 2 studios* ♿ *In-room: No a/c, kitchen, refrigerator, Internet (some). In-hotel: No-smoking rooms* ▭ *AE, DC, MC, V.*

$$ ⊡ **Brunton House.** Built by a local draper in the 1870s and later owned by three Thames mayors, this two-story colonial villa was built entirely from kauri wood. All bedrooms but one open out onto the upstairs wraparound veranda, and although there are only two bathrooms to share between four bedrooms, the clawfoot bathtubs make up for it. Breakfast, which is included in the price, consists of pancakes and fruit, or you can opt for a true Kiwi fry-up of bacon, eggs, sausages, and hash browns; if you have other requirements, let your hosts know the night before. **Pros:** lovely setting; endearing hosts; historic building. **Cons:** out of the way. ✉ *210 Parawai Rd.* ☎ *07/868–5160* ⊕ *www.brunton-house.co.nz* ⮑ *4 rooms with shared bath* ♿ *In-room: No a/c, no phone. In-hotel: Tennis court, pool* ▭ *AE, DC, MC, V* ⦿ *BP.*

$$ ⊡ **Coastal Motor Lodge.** Set in three acres of gardens, with native bush-walks to the rear of the property and the Thames coast just across the road, this is a good place to bed down and get your bearings as you enter the Coromandel. Rooms are certainly not upscale, but they are clean and simple. Many have views of the water. **Pros:** close to Thames; lovely views. **Cons:** basic furnishings. ✉ *608 Tararu Rd., Thames* ☎ *07/868–6843* ⊕ *www.stayatcoastal.co.nz/motorlodge.html* ⮑ *4 cottages, 10 studios, 2 bedroom unit in the lodge* ♿ *In-room: No a/c, kitchen, Wi-Fi. In-hotel: Spa, laundry facilities, parking (free)* ▭ *AE, DC, MC, V* ⦿ *EP*

NEED A BREAK?   **Waiomu Beach Cafe** sits across from Waiomu Beach, and if you've had enough of the twists and turns of the coastal road, this is the spot to stop. The café serves everything from ice cream to coffee to pizza, with local favorites like mussel sausages and the Coromandel's ubiquitous mussel chowder in between. Sit at the picnic tables to the side, or cross over to Waiomu Beach Park and have a picnic. You'll know you've hit Waiomu Bay when you see the perennial stripy deck chairs in front of the café. ✉ *622A Thames Coast Rd.* ☎ *07/868–2554* ▭ *AE, DC, MC, V* .

TAPU–COROGLEN ROAD

25 km (16 mi) north of Thames.

GETTING HERE AND AROUND

The intermittently paved **Tapu–Coroglen Road** turns off State Highway 25 in the hamlet of Tapu to wind into the mountains. It's a breathtaking route where massive tree ferns grow out of the roadside hills. But it's not for the faint-hearted as stretches of the road are quite narrow with access for only one vehicle. Signs indicate these places. About 6½ km (4 mi) from Tapu you come to the magical Rapaura Watergardens. Travel another 3½ km (2 mi) along the road and pull over to climb the 178 steps up to the huge, 1,200-year-old **Square Kauri**, so named for the shape that a cross section of its trunk would have. At 133 feet tall and 30 feet around, this is only the 15th-largest kauri in New Zealand. From a tree-side platform there is a splendid view across the valley to Mau Mau Paki, one of the peaks along the Coromandel Ranges. Continuing east across the peninsula, the road passes through forests and sheep paddocks—a shimmeringly gorgeous drive in sun or mist.

EXPLORING

Rapaura Watergardens is in a 65-acre sheltered valley in the Coromandel Ranges. Rapaura means "running water," and in the garden's various streams, waterfalls, fountains, and 14 ponds, fish and ducks swim among colorful water lilies while songbirds lilt overhead. Paths wind through collections of grasses, flaxes, gunneras, rhododendrons, and camellias. Giant tree ferns and rimu, *rata* (related to the pohutukawa, it too has bright red flowers), and kauri trees form a lush canopy overhead. You'll find hokey words of wisdom painted on signs around the garden, such as keep your values in balance and you will always find happiness. It takes 15 minutes to walk around the property, but take the time to do the half-hour return walk to the "seven stairs to heaven," a stunning, tiered waterfall, where you can take a dip into one of the lagoons. Koru, the café on the property, is worth a visit in its own right. A wood cottage and a two-story lodge are available for those who wish to stay longer ($165 and $275 per night, respectively, which includes breakfast). We suggest setting aside at least an hour to see the grounds and the waterfalls and spend some time taking in the scenery from one of the benches. ⊠ *586 Tapu–Coroglen Rd., 6 km (4 mi) east of Tapu* ☎ *07/868–4821* ⊕ *www.rapaurawatergardens.co.nz* ⊠ *$12* ☯ *Daily 9–5; café open daily 9–4, Nov.–Apr.*

COROMANDEL

60 km (38 mi) north of Thames, 29 km (18 mi) northwest of Whitianga.

Coromandel town became the site of New Zealand's first gold strike in 1852 when sawmill worker Charles Ring found gold-bearing quartz at Driving Creek, just north of town. The find was important for New Zealand, because the country's workforce had been severely depleted by the gold rushes in California and Australia. Ring hurried to Auckland to claim the reward that had been offered to anyone finding "payable" gold. The town's population soared, but the reef gold could be mined only by heavy and expensive machinery. Within a few months Coromandel resumed its former sleepy existence as a timber town—and Charles Ring was refused the reward.

Nowadays, Coromandel is extremely touristy but manages to retain a low-key charm even when SUVs and camper vans fill the streets. With 19th-century buildings lining both sides of its single main street, an active artists' collective, and the requisite fish-and-chips shops at either end, you could not find a truer example of a relaxed and slightly hippie Kiwi town. The local mussel farm means that mussels are served every which way, from smoked-mussel pies to chowder.

GETTING HERE AND AROUND

Upon arriving, head over to the Coromandel Visitor Information Centre and pick up a copy of "Coromandel's Walking Tracks." This unassuming photocopied booklet points out all the local walks in Coromandel town and the greater area.

ESSENTIALS

Bus Depot (✉ *Coromandel Visitor Information Centre, 355 Kapanga Rd.* ☎ *07/866–8598*).

Hospital Coromandel Medical Centre (✉ *80 Kapanga Rd., Coromandel* ☎ *07/866–8200*).

Visitor Information Coromandel Visitor Information Centre (✉ *355 Kapanga Rd., Coromandel* ☎ *07/866–8598* 🌐 *www.coromandeltown.co.nz*).

EXPLORING

Opened around 1900, the **Coromandel Gold Stamper Battery** was New Zealand's last functional gold-processing plant. You can take a guided tour of the old plant, do some gold panning, or stroll through the bush to a lookout. The huge working waterwheel in front of the building is said to be New Zealand's largest. The Stamper Battery is 2 km (1 mi) north of Coromandel township. The battery is only open for tours; call for the schedule. ✉ *410 Buffalo Rd.* ☎ *07/866–7933* 🎫 *$10* 🕐 *The battery is only open for tours: Apr.–Oct., Tues., Thurs., and weekends; Nov.–Mar., daily except Fri.*

Driving Creek Railway is one man's magnificent folly, and popular with New Zealanders and tourists alike. Barry Brickell, a local potter, discovered that the clay on his land was perfect for his work. The problem was that the deposit lay in a remote area at the top of a steep slope, so he hacked a path through the forest and built his own miniature railroad to haul the stuff. Visitors to his studio began asking if they could go along for a ride, and Brickell now takes passengers on daily tours aboard his toylike train. The diesel-powered, narrow-gauge locomotive's route incorporates a double-decker bridge, three tunnels, a spiral, and a switchback through native forest and sculpture gardens, all the way to Barry's "Eyeful Tower," an old-style railway refreshment room and viewing platform. On a clear day you can see all the way to Auckland. The railway also funds a reforestation program; to date, more than 20,000 native trees have been planted. You can take a walk through the some of the native bush on the property and through a sculpture garden while you're waiting for the next train. Barry has also built a protected wildlife sanctuary, which acts as a wetland refuge for endangered New Zealand birds, frogs, and reptiles. The railway's round-trip takes about an hour. The "station" is 3 km (2 mi) north of Coromandel township. ■TIP➔ Bookings are advised, and essential during the peak summer months. ✉ *380 Driving Creek Rd.* ☎ *07/866–8703* ⊕ *www.drivingcreekrailway.co.nz* ✆ *$20* ⊗ *Jan.–Apr., daily 10–evening, with trains running every 1¼ hrs; May–mid-Dec., daily 10–3:30, with trains at 10:15 and 2.*

The Source is a collectively run gallery that has an outdoor courtyard selling huge ceramic works inspired by native plants. The good thing is that the sculptures (some are over 12 feet tall) can be broken down for shipping overseas. The Source also has smaller, well-priced jewelry, paintings, other crafts, and sometimes clothing. ✉ *31 Kapanga Rd.* ☎ *07/866–7345* ⊗ *Daily 10–4.*

The **Weta Design** gallery is named after the country's largest native insect, which looks like a grasshopper with armor. This gallery has a wide range of items, from large and really lovely glass totems to small, finely made tiles, not to mention fabric art, carving, and ceramics. The gallery also has New Zealand jewelry. Keep an eye out for the silver work by Anna Hallissey. Her delicate brooches are based on the tiny branches of the manuka tree, while a wittier piece is a silver version of the plastic clip used to close bread bags. For a truly unique gift they sell a surprisingly packaged weta. ✉ *46 Kapanga Rd.* ☎ *07/866–8060* ⊕ *www. wetadesign.co.nz* ⊗ *Daily 10–4.*

OUTDOOR ACTIVITIES

FISHING **Top Catch: Bait, Tackle, Advice.** The name says it all. If you're new in town and are hankering for a spot of fishing, start here. Wayne, the shop's proprietor, can arrange fishing trips with local fishing boats to suit all levels. He also sells all the fishing gear you could need, although he doesn't hire out equipment—generally that is arranged through the fishing boats. Advice is given freely, although it may be—by Wayne's own admission—dodgy. ✉ *2 Kapanga Rd.* ☎ *07/866–7397* ⊗ *Sept.–Apr., Mon.–Thurs. 6–5; Fri. 6–7, weekends 5–5; May–Aug., Tues.–Sat. 8–5*

HIKING **Kauri Block Pa Track.** On a clear day, head up to the Kauri Block Pa Track (1½ hours return), which provides panoramic views over the town, harbor, and coast. Follow the main road to Coromandel town's western outskirts, where a signpost points out the start of the trail at 356 Wharf Road. The trail goes through native and regenerating bush to the summit, a Māori *pā* site, before winding down through the bush and emerging onto Harbour View Road, which you follow back to town. ✉ *356 Wharf Rd., Coromandel.*

★ **Long Bay Scenic Reserve and kauri Grove.** A gentle 40-minute walk (one-way) will take you to one of the lovelier beaches in the immediate area. Pack a picnic and enjoy a relaxing afternoon. The track starts at the end of Long Bay Road, at the Long Bay Motor Camp (about 3 km [1.8 mi] from Coromandel town), and slopes up through a grove of young kauri trees and down to the secluded Tucks Bay, a prime spot

to unpack a picnic lunch. Either turn back here, or head across Tucks Bay and follow the coastal track back to the motor camp. ✉ *3200 Long Bay Rd., Coromandel.*

WHERE TO EAT

¢ ✕ **Coromandel Cafe.** The menu may not be extensive or adventurous
CAFÉ and the decoration is tired, but the substantial servings of tried-and-true choices such as pancakes with maple syrup or bacon and eggs are popular with locals. You won't miss out if you sleep in, as breakfast runs right through the afternoon. ✉ *Kapanga Rd.* ☎ *07/866–8495* 🖃 *AE, MC, V* ☉ *No dinner.*

$ ✕ **Driving Creek Cafe.** Although the owners aren't old enough to have
VEGETARIAN experienced the communes that used to thrive on the peninsula, this café
☺ captures their essence while providing food that appeals to the masses. It is surrounded by fruit trees, and there is outdoor seating in a sculpture garden and on the porch. The vegetarian menu includes nachos and hand-cut fries, tofu burgers, lasagna, piles of baked goods, locally roasted coffee, and fresh juices and smoothies. The food is fresh, the portions generous, and the prices reasonable. The café also sells a small range of organic goods, local art, and pottery, and it has Internet (paid). ✉ *180 Driving Creek Rd.* ☎ *07/866–7066* ⊕ *www.drivingcreekcafe. com* 🖃 *MC, V* ☉ *Open daily Aug.–Apr.; closed Wed. May–July.*

$$$ ✕ **Pepper Tree Restaurant and Bar.** It's a good thing the only real restau-
SEAFOOD rant in town is a national beef-and-lamb multi-award winner. While the restaurant's meat dishes—such as the rack of lamb with pressed *kūmara* or the scotch fillet wrapped in honey-cured bacon with horse-radish *panna cotta*—are indeed sought after, Coromandel seafood still

A Pohutukawa tree overlooks farmland outside of Coromandel town.

takes precedence. Locally farmed oysters are served on the half shell, and Greenshell mussels are steamed open or turned into fritters. Lunch segues into dinner in the courtyard or in front of the fire, depending on the season. ⊠ *31 Kapanga Rd.* ☎ *07/866–8211* ▭ *AE, DC, MC, V.*

$$ ✕ **UMU Café.** Like many places to eat on the peninsula, this cafe does a
CAFÉ roaring trade with their mussel chowder. The pizzas are popular, and they make a delicious club sandwich with pickles, ham, mashed egg, and lettuce. Both the restaurant menu and café counter sell largely organic produce, lots of seafood, and good vegetarian options. If you're not in for lunch or dinner, grab an exquisite sorbet from their stand out front. ⊠ *22 Wharf Rd.* ☎ *07/866–8618* ▭ *AE, DC, MC, V.*

WHERE TO STAY

$–$$ ⊡ **Anchor Lodge.** At first glance, these lodgings may not appeal; the motel units flank a concrete parking lot. However, each unit also looks out onto a bank of native forest, and the views from each of the units' grapevine- and passion fruit-draped porches encompass the Coromandel Harbour. Inside, the rooms are clean and modern—tiled floors, white walls, blocky comfortable couches, and chrome-and-glass dining furniture—it's obvious that this is the newest motel in Coromandel. Extra perks include the 45-minute bushwalk to the harbor lookout next door to the property and the free loans of flashlights and gum boots to visit the nearby gold mine and glowworm cave. **Pros:** wide choice of accommodations to suit range of travelers. **Cons:** externally underwhelming. ⊠ *448 Wharf Rd.* ☎ *07/866–7992* ⊕ *www.anchorlodgecoromandel.co.nz* ⌁ *22 rooms* ⌂ *In-room: No phone, kitchen, refrigerator, DVD, Internet, Wi-Fi. In-hotel: Room service, pool, laundry facilities, parking (free).* ▭ *AE, D, DC, MC, V.*

$$$ ⊡ **Buffalo Lodge.** Perched on a hillside and surrounded by bush just
★   out of Coromandel town, this lodge looks across the Hauraki Gulf
toward Auckland. Bedrooms and bathrooms are minimalist in design,
with huge windows and balconies with spectacular views of the sur-
rounding native trees and countryside. ■**TIP→** The cottage room is a
special treat. Its giant tub set beside an enormous window makes you feel
as if you're bathing in the middle of the forest. The restaurant's prix-
fixe dinner ($95) has specialties such as king salmon, lamb, veni-
son, and locally caught fish. They also roast their own coffee beans.
Pros: splendid environment; private; multilingual host. **Cons:** some
might find the design tired; not suitable for children under 14. ⊠ *860
Buffalo Rd.* ☎ *07/866–8960* ⊕ *www.buffalolodge.co.nz* ⇩ *4 rooms
⟐ In-room: No a/c, no TV. In-hotel: Restaurant, no kids under 12* ⊟
MC, V ⊗ *Closed May–Sept.* ⦿*BP.*

$–$$ ⊡ **Coromandel Court Motel.** Tucked behind the Coromandel Information Centre, these down-to-earth units are basic and clean. Rooms are
equipped with kitchenettes and dining-room tables. All have showers;
only two have baths. **Pros:** in town; friendly; wireless Internet. **Cons:**
generic; not for those who desire a luxury lodge. ⊠ *365 Kapanga
Rd. 3506* ☎ *07/866–8402* ⊕ *www.coromandelcourtmotel.co.nz* ⇩ *10
units ⟐ In-room: No a/c, kitchen. In-hotel: Laundry facilities* ⊟*AE,
DC, MC, V.*

$$$ ⊡ **Driving Creek Villas.** Tucked away in the trees of Fraser Reserve
♺   are three two-bedroom, self-contained villas. Each house has a full
kitchen, dining and living areas, and its own secluded garden. Wood
furnishings dominate, and Māori and Pacific prints and quilts adorn
the walls and beds. The bathrooms only have showers, but there is
a private, wooden, Japanese hot tub in each garden. Wraparound
verandas overlook the creek, the bush, and many fruit trees (help
yourself). The spacious houses make this a good place to spread
out and use as a base for a few days. **There is a two-night minimum
stay policy. Pros:** close to town; secluded; lots of space; good for
families. **Cons:** can feel a little isolated after dark. ⊠ *21a Colville
Rd.* ☎ *07/866–7755* ⊕ *www.drivingcreekvillas.com* ⇩ *3 villas ⟐
In-room: Kitchen, refrigerator, DVD, Wi-Fi. In-hotel: Spa, bicycles,
laundry facilities, parking (free)* ⊟*MC, V.*

$–$$ ⊡ **Goldminers Retreat.** Built around one of the main gold mining spots
in Coromandel, and part of the growing Driving Creek community,
these small cabins are set up to resemble a more comfortable version of an old mining village. With high ceilings and views over a
creek, the one-room cabins each have a queen bed below and a bunk
above; a mini-refrigerator and tea-and-coffee facilities are tucked into
a corner. The cabins are built on low stilts over a creek; a winding
wooden walkway connects them with a shared kitchen and bathroom.
Open-plan and open-air, the fully equipped kitchen is constructed of
slabs of wood. With the water and foliage below and mining relics
scattered throughout the buildings, the place feels like part treetop
village and part miners' camp. **Pros:** affordable; unique. **Cons:** small
cabins; shared facilities may get on your nerves after more than a day.

⌂ *425 Driving Creek Rd.* ☎ *07/866–7771* ⊕ *www.goldminersretreat. co.nz* ⤳ *3 cabins* ☼ *In-room: No a/c, no phone. In-hotel: Parking (free), some pets allowed* ▭ *MC, V* ❘⦾❘ *CP.*

$$–$$$ ⊡ **Indigo Bush Studios.** From burnished clay floors, copper pipes, and old beams of timber arise two creatively designed studios. It comes as no surprise that the host is an artist; in addition to the rooms themselves, host and local artist Robyn Lewis' paintings and sculptures accent the rooms. Each self-contained studio is utterly private; French doors swing out onto the native bush, and sunken into the wooden front deck are deep outdoor baths. The interiors are spare but stylishly furnished. **Pros:** secluded; visually lovely. **Cons:** lack of mod cons; not kid-friendly; clay floor is cold on your feet in the morning! ⌂ *19 Flays Rd.* ☎ *07/866–7388* ⊕ *www.indigo-bush-studios.co.nz* ⤳ *2 studios* ☼ *In-room: No a/c, no phone, kitchen, refrigerator, DVD. In-hotel: no kids over 1* ▭ *MC, V.*

$$ ⊡ **Karamana Homestead.** It's not hard to imagine a distinguished family occupying this 1872 home, built for Jerome Cadman, a prominent Auckland contractor. From the gentlemen's smoking lounge to the huge canopy bed of English oak to the well out back, the house is a well-kept piece of Coromandel history. The adjacent 1850 kauri cottage, with its high-beamed ceilings, wrought-iron bed, and kitchenette, is wonderfully private. Breakfast, included in the price, is a silver-service affair. **Pros:** historic property; sweet hosts; close to town. **Cons:** basic facilities. ⌂ *84 Whangapoua Rd.* ☎ *07/866–7138* ⊕ *www.karamanahomestead.com* ⤳ *3 rooms, 1 cottage* ☼ *In-room: No a/c, no phone, no TV. In-hotel: No-smoking rooms* ▭ *MC, V* ❘⦾❘ *BP.*

$$ ⊡ **Te Kouma Harbour Cottages.** A little off-the-beaten-track, these single-story wooden chalets are excellent for families or groups wanting a little time away from the shops. There are plenty of activities to keep you busy: kayaking, soccer, *pétanque* (the French game similar to boccie), and swimming in the pool. Large, bright multiroom cabins have contemporary furniture and kitchen areas, and the log home has its own pool overlooking the harbor. The cabins are down a long drive that is signposted from State Highway 25 north out of Thames, and the hosts John and Rose Dean are happy to arrange activities. **Pros:** fantastic views; spacious; clean; self-contained. **Cons:** a little out of town; basic furnishings; can be busy at times. ⌂ *1159A State Hwy. 25, Te Kouma Harbour* ☎ *07/866–8747* ⊕ *www.tekouma.co.nz* ⤳ *6 cabins, 1 lodge, 1 log home* ☼ *In-room: No a/c, kitchen. In-hotel: Pool* ▭ *AE, DC, MC, V.*

EN ROUTE

Once a grassy cow pasture, **Waitati Gardens** (⌂ *485 Buffalo Rd.* ☎ *07/866–8659* ⌲ *$7* ☉ *Daily 10* AM*–dusk*) now includes a native-plants area and swarms of unusual flowers. Flower-bordered glades and shady spots make for perfect picnic settings.

THE 309 ROAD

22 km (13½ mi).

GETTING HERE AND AROUND

Although named for a journey that used to take 309 minutes, the 309 Road is now the shortest route between Coromandel and Whitianga; it cuts right across the peninsula. The mostly unpaved road is winding and narrow and takes 35–40 minutes to cross. If you are traveling in a camper van, it's best to leave early in the morning to avoid traffic. If you end up behind one, be patient. The surrounding landscape alternates between farmland, pine trees, and native forest, with numerous reasons to stop along the way.

EXPLORING

Five kilometers (3 mi) from Coromandel, the **Waiau Waterworks** is a quirky playground in a series of grassy clearings surrounded by bush, ponds, streams, and a river with a swimming hole. There are sculpture gardens, a number of water-powered artworks, and some unusual takes on playground equipment that invite the inner child to come out and play. ✉ *309 Rd.* ☎ *07/866–7191* ⊕ *www.waiauwaterworks.co.nz* ✑ *$12* ☉ *Daily 9–dusk.*

About 7½ km (4½ mi) from Coromandel, stop for a swim at **Waiau Falls,** a forest-fringed waterfall lagoon that's just a short, signposted walk from the road. Additional walking tracks lead farther into the woods. Less than 2 km (1 mi) east of Waiau Falls, a series of easy, clearly marked gravel paths and wooden walkways takes you through lush forest to a protected giant kauri grove. ■**TIP→** The full walk takes about 15 minutes, but the trees are so majestic that you may want to allow a half hour to stroll through this ancient forest. Continuing along the 309, the road winds through more forest and farmland, past the **309 Manuka Honey Shop,** and eventually comes out on State Highway 25, about 20 minutes south of Whitianga.

COLVILLE AND BEYOND

30 km (19 mi) north of Coromandel.

To reach land's end in the wilds of the Coromandel Peninsula—with rugged coastline, delightful coves, and pastures—take the 30-minute drive from Coromandel up to **Colville.** The town has a grocery store–gas station, post office, a community hall, and café, and in summer a temporary shop sells items from India and Nepal. There are also a magnificent Buddha shrine, or stupa, on the drive in and public toilets with a mosaic worthy of a picture. Colville is the gateway to some of the peninsula's most untamed landscape, as well as some long-established communes. Maps of the area are available in Coromandel at the Visitor Information Centre and in Colville at the General Store (⇨ *below*).

GETTING HERE AND AROUND

Other than driving to Colville, the only way to get here is by bus. If you're staying in Coromandel town and you don't have a car but want to explore some of the more remote bays, such as Fletcher Bay, the best option is Strongman Coachlines (⇨ *below*), which provide day trips around the area.

4

EXPLORING

Colville's classic counterculture **General Store** (☎ 07/866–6805) sells food-stuffs (there's a well-stocked organic section), wine, and gasoline. It is the northernmost supplier on the peninsula, so don't forget to fill your tank.

The **Colville Cafe** (☎ 07/866–6690), right next door to the General Store, is the only place in Colville to eat out. With a focus on locally sourced organic food and fair-trade coffee, this is a good place to pick up fixings for a picnic or a morning coffee and cake.

Beyond Colville, a twisty, gravel (but well-maintained) road will take you to **Fletcher Bay.** The road goes north, coming to a T-junction about 5 km (3 mi) out of town. It's impossible to fully circumnavigate the peninsula; at the junction, the road to your left follows the West Coast to the stunning sandy beach at Port Jackson. It continues along the cliff top to a smaller, sandy cove banked by green pasture rolling down to the beach. Fletcher Bay is the end of the road, at 60 km (38 mi) from Coromandel—a 1¼-hour drive.

From Fletcher Bay, hikers can follow the signposted **Coastal Walkway** to Stony Bay; it's about a three-hour walk each way.

WHERE TO STAY

$–$$ 🏨 **Anglers Lodge Motel and Holiday Park.** Tucked in a valley off the main road between Coromandel and Colville, these wooden motel units face the Motukawa Islands of Amodeo Bay. The rooms are small and basic but clean. If you are traveling with a tent, they have sites. You can head out into the bay for a three-hour fishing trip ($80 per person, $240 minimum). The motel is 7 km (4½ mi) south of Colville. **Pros:** friendly operators; interesting mix of guests; stunning location. **Cons:** basic; focused toward budget travelers. ⊠ *Amodeo Bay, Coromandel* ☎ 07/866–8584 ⊕ *www.anglers.co.nz* 🛏 *8 rooms* ⚐ *In-room: No a/c, no phone, kitchen, refrigerator. In-hotel: Tennis court, pool, laundry facilities, no-smoking rooms* ⊟ MC, V.

OUTDOOR ACTIVITIES

HIKING If you want to hike the Coastal Walkway but don't fancy driving your-self there, **Strongman Coachlines** (☎ 0800/668–175 or 07/866–8175 ⊕ *www.coromandeldiscoverytours.co.nz*) will pick you up either in Colville or in Coromandel and drive you to Fletcher Bay. From there you can walk to Stony Bay, where you will be driven back to your hotel. The full-day trip ($95) includes stops along the way, including one at Colville's General Store and the Colville Cafe, where you can get lunch for the hike. They also provide a range of other trips in the area.

WHITIANGA

46 km (29 mi) southeast of Coromandel.

As you descend from the hills on the Coromandel's east coast, you'll come to the long stretch of Buffalo Beach, named for the British ship that used to ferry convicts from the United Kingdom to Australia before stopping in Coromandel town en route back to the United Kingdom to load up on Kauri building supplies. It ran ashore and sank in 1840, and it still lies buried in the sandy bottom of the bay.

The beachfront is lined with motels and hostels, all within walking distance of the ferry to Flaxmill Bay and the shops of Whitianga, the main township on this side of the peninsula. Most people use the town as a base for fishing or boating trips, and others stock up for camping at nearby beaches. Over summer it hosts some great rock music and jazz shows, and people use it as a base for the region's gorgeous beaches.

The Whitianga Information Centre can help you choose an excursion.

EN ROUTE

★ If you're driving between Whitianga and Coromandel and the sun is shining, make some time to head north towards Whangapoua. Park your car and grab your bathing suit and a surfboard if you're keen, and make the 30-minute trek over to New Chums beach, a native forest-fringed bay of golden sand. It's accessible only by foot, and you have to wade through an estuary to get there, but the secluded beach—rated by the U.K. *Observer* as one of the world's top 20 beaches—is well worth the walk.

GETTING HERE AND AROUND

Unless you're driving or on a charter flight from Auckland, bus is the only way to get to Whitianga (with the exception of those stalwart few who are conquering the Coromandel by bicycle!). Bus companies stop at the Whitianga Information Centre.

A nice way to explore Flaxmill Bay or Whitianga (if you're based at either of these points) is to leave your car on the dock and take the $2 ferry across and explore the beaches and cafes on foot.

ESSENTIALS

Bus Depot Whitianga (✉ *Whitianga Visitor Information Centre, 66 Albert St.* ☎ *07/866–5555*).

Hospital Mercury Bay Medical Centre (✉ *87 Albert St., Whitianga* ☎ *07/866–5911*).

Visitor Information Whitianga Information Centre (✉ *66 Albert St., Whitianga* ☎ *07/866–5555* ⊕ *www.whitianga.co.nz*).

OUTDOOR ACTIVITIES

BOATING, FISHING, AND DIVING

DIVE HQ (✉ *7 Blacksmith La., Whitianga* ☎ *07/867–1580* ⊕ *www. divethecoromandel.co.nz*) is the place to go for diving gear, training, and trips.

You can rent both diving and fishing gear from the **Whitianga Sports Centre** (✉ *32 Albert St., Whitianga* ☎ *07/866–5295*).

The **Cave Cruzer** (☎ *07/866–2574 or 0800/427–893* ⊕ *www.cavecruzer.co.nz*) gives you an unusual spin on a boat tour to Cathedral Cove (⇨ *Around Hahei, below*). At one point, you'll head into a sea cave where the guides demonstrate the acoustics by playing a Spanish guitar and African drums.

Glass Bottom Boat Scenic Boat Cruises (☎ *07/867–1962* ⊕ *www.glassbottomboatwhitianga.co.nz*) will take you into Te Whanganui-A-Hei Marine Reserve, where you can see multitudes of marine life through the bottom of their boat. Informed guides discuss the formation and history of the land, Captain Cook's adventures, and the Ngāti Hei, the

SPAAAAAAH

★ Fodor's Choice **The Lost Spring.** After 20 years of listening to local legend, planning, and digging, owner Alan Hopping finally struck gold with this spa. In this case, it's hot mineral water that comes from 644 meters (2,113 feet) underground and fills a man-made waterway of steaming lagoons, waterfalls, and quartz-studded caves. Lie back in the water and watch native birds eating berries from the trees and ferns, and butterflies darting among the hibiscus, or focus your attention on a poolside massage, manicure, or pedicure. Water fountains along the bank ward off dehydration, and waiters at the water's edge supply snacks, fresh juices, and drinks from the bar. If you need a break from the heat, wander along the paths and over the swingbridge to the restaurant or upstairs for a massage and hot oil treatment. The only thing stopping the Lost Spring from being a truly therapeutic health spa is your thermal: cocktail ratio. ⊠ *121 A Cook Dr., Whitianga* ☎ *07/866-8456* ⊕ *www.thelostspring.co.nz* ⌨ *$20 per hr; $45 for the day* ⊗ *Daily 11–9:30.*

Māori tribe who once dominated the region. The boat goes out up to five times a day from Whitianga Wharf; trips take two hours and cost $85. When the water's warm, they'll also stop for a snorkel. Trips are subject to weather conditions.

Hahei Explorer (☎ *07/866–3910* ⊕ *www.haheiexplorer.co.nz*) heads out twice a day to Cathedral Cove in a small eight-seater to explore the ocean caves.

If you're interested in fishing, contact **Water's Edge Charters** (☎ *07/866–5760* ⊕ *www.watersedgecharters.co.nz*).

WHERE TO EAT

$–$$ ✗ **Cafe Nina.** Locals gravitate here for breakfast and lunch every day of
CAFÉ the week, and it is always busy. For breakfast, "The Classic" (bacon, sausages, eggs, fried potatoes, tomato, and toast) will set most people up for the day. At lunch you'll find simple dishes such as roasted root vegetables with dips and bread, or seafood chowder, a staple for regulars. The Hummingbird Cake—a banana, pineapple, and coconut cake, laden with cream cheese icing—goes extremely well with a bowl of latte. Jasmine vines cloak the front porch of this adorable 1890 miner's cottage. ⊠ *20 Victoria St.* ☎ *07/866–5440* ▤ *MC, V.*

$ ✗ **Monk Street Market.** By local accounts, this is the best place to prep
CAFÉ for a picnic. The owner's obsession with cheese is on display along the wall behind the counter. Stacks of cheeses from as near as down the road and as far as Holland, France, Spain, and Italy line the shelves. The market also sells local and imported salami, organic breads, dips, olives, organic fruit and juices, and an enormous array of chutneys, chocolates, and locally made macadamia nut brittle. ⊠ *1 Monk St., Whitianga* ☎ *07/866–4500* ⊗ *Dec.–Apr., daily 10–6, otherwise closed Sun.*

$$$ ✗ **Salt.** The table-studded, tiered deck reaches all the way down to the
NEW ZEALAND palm-edged marina, while jazz lilts from the restaurant. Housed in the oldest building in Whitianga, Salt serves delicious food in a casual

environment—the only rule is that patrons must have shoes and clothes on (not bathing suits). The porcini-and-portobello mushroom risotto with Parmesan and truffle oil is delicious, as is the seared market fish served with a shellfish bouillabaisse rouille and grilled sourdough. The dessert menu showcases such treats as pear tarte tatin with *manuka* honey and chest-

SCALLOPS GALORE

The **Whitianga Scallop Festival**, held during August, is one of the region's main events. Stalls serve scallops prepared every which way, and there are music performances, kids' activities, and cook-offs. ⊕ *www.scallopfestival.co.nz*

nut ice cream. The bar snacks include tuna sashimi and Coromandel mussels. The oversized leather couches in front of the fireplace are a good place to while away the afternoon on rainy days, otherwise it's all hands on deck. During the summer, we recommend making reservations. ⊠ *1 Blacksmith La., Whitianga* ☎ *07/866–5818* ⊕ *www.whitangahotel.co.nz* ⊟ *AE, DC, MC, V.*

$$–$$$
CONTINENTAL
✗ **Uncle Harry's Café and Winebar.** Housed in a refurbished 1950s art deco villa, this classy but low-key restaurant serves an unusual blend of German-inspired New Zealand food, such as a steak sandwich with caramelized onion-and-apple relish, or Flammenkuchen, bread baked with red onion and bacon and topped with nutmeg and sour cream. Take your pick between eating on the deck overlooking the marina, inside within the whitewashed walls, or out back in the garden of ferns and flowers. ⊠ *2 Mill Rd., Whitianga* ☎ *07/866–0053* ⊕ *www.uncleharrys.co.nz* ⊟ *AE, DC, MC, V* ⊗ *Closed Tues.–Thurs. May–Oct.; closed Wed. Nov.–Apr.*

WHERE TO STAY

$$–$$$
🛏 **Admiralty Lodge.** A mile from the town center, but only across the road from Buffalo Beach, this is a good spot if you're planning on a few days beachside. From private patios and balconies, each suite in this two-story, terra-cotta–tiled motel looks out over Mercury Bay, while inside comfortable leather couches sit opposite big TV screens. **Pros:** beach location; very clean and tidy. **Cons:** dated bedspreads and furnishing. ⊠ *69–71 Buffalo Beach Rd., Whitianga* ☎ *07/866–0181* ⊕ *www.admiraltylodge.co.nz* ➔ *18 rooms* ⚷ *In-room: No a/c, safe, kitchen, refrigerator, DVD, Internet, Wi-Fi. In-hotel: Golf course, pool, bicycles, laundry facilities, parking (free)* ⊟ *AE, D, DC, MC, V* ⍟ *EP.*

$$–$$$
🛏 **Beachfront Resort.** Step out of this tiny, family-run resort's garden and onto a breathtaking beach. The downstairs rooms claim the best beach access, but great views and the most sun are upstairs. Either way, seven of the eight rooms have beach views. The rooms are simple but comfortable. Sports equipment, including kayaks and bodyboards, is available at no extra charge. These are the only accommodations in Whitianga that sit right on the beach, so booking in advance during the summer months is essential. Only one room has a full bath; the rest have showers. **Pros:** stunning location; friendly hosts; good self-contained accommodations. **Cons:** not for those looking for a luxury resort. ⊠ *111–113 Buffalo Beach Rd.* ☎ *07/866–5637* ⊕ *www.beachfrontresort.co.nz* ➔ *8 rooms* ⚷ *In-room: No a/c. In-hotel: Spa* ⊟ *AE, DC, MC, V.*

Beachgoers enjoy remote Cathedral Cove's natural rock arch and deep blue waters.

$$-$$$ ⊞ **Oceanside Motel.** The views of Mercury Bay are this motel's best assets. Rooms are small and simply furnished, but each has floor-to-ceiling sliding-glass doors, with unobstructed views of the bay. Most have their own patios, or you can just cross the street to the beach. **Pros:** excellent location; friendly and down-to-earth hosts; clean and tidy. **Cons:** small rooms. ⊠ *32 Buffalo Beach Rd.* ☎ *07/866–5766* ⊕ *www.oceansidemotel.co.nz* ⇗ *12 rooms* ⚴ *In-room: No a/c, kitchen, refrigerator. In-hotel: Room service, laundry facilities* ⊟ *AE, DC, MC, V* ⊚I *BP, CP.*

AROUND HAHEI

57 km (35 mi) southeast of Coromandel, 64 km (40 mi) northeast of Thames.

The beaches, coves, and seaside villages around Hahei make for a great day of exploring—or lounging. If you're craving a true beach vacation, consider basing yourself in Hahei rather than in Whitianga. From Hahei, you can easily reach Cathedral Cove, the Purangi Estuary, and Flaxmill Bay; the famous Hot Water Beach is only minutes away.

GETTING HERE AND AROUND

If you're day-tripping from Whitianga, take the five-minute ferry ride (which leaves every hour, $4 round-trip) across to Flaxmill Bay and explore by foot. Alternatively, follow State Highway 25 south from Whitianga. The road takes you past the Wilderlands roadside stand (selling organic produce and delicious honey from a local commune) and on to Flaxmill Bay, Cook's Beach, and Hahei.

EXPLORING

Past Hahei on Pa Road, **Te Pare Historic Reserve** is the site of a Māori *pā* (fortified village), though no trace remains of the defensive terraces and wooden spikes that ringed the hill. At high tide, the blowhole at the foot of the cliffs adds a booming bass note to the sound of waves and the sighing of the wind in the grass. To reach the actual pā site, follow the red arrow down the hill from the parking area. After some 50 yards, take the right fork through a grove of giant pohutukawa trees, then through a gate and across an open, grassy hillside. The trail is steep and becomes increasingly overgrown as you climb, but persist on to the summit, and then head toward more pohutukawa to your right at the south end of the headland. There's no entry fee.

★ **Cathedral Cove** is a lovely white-sand crescent with a rock arch. The water is usually calm and clear, good for swimming and snorkeling. The beach is accessible only at low tide, however, about a 45-minute walk each way. To get there, travel along Hahei Beach Road, turn right toward town and the sea, and then, just past the shops, turn left onto Grange Road and follow the signs. ■TIP➔ Check the local paper, or call the Whitianga Information Centre (07/866–5555) for tide times.

Cook's Beach lies along Mercury Bay, so named for Captain James Cook's observation of the transit of the planet Mercury in November 1769. The beach is notable because of the captain's landfall—it was the first by a European. Because of the surrounding suburban sprawl, the beach is less appealing than its more secluded neighbors.

★ The popular **Hot Water Beach** is a delightful thermal oddity. A warm spring seeps beneath the beach, and by scooping a shallow hole in the sand, you can create a pool of warm water; the deeper you dig, the hotter the water becomes. The phenomenon occurs only at low to mid-tide, so time your trip accordingly. If you are an adventurous sort, it can be fun in winter to sit in warm water while it rains. Hot Water Beach is well signposted off Hahei Beach Road from Whenu-akite (fen-oo-ah-*kye*-tee). ⚠ Do not swim in the surf at Hot Water Beach; the spot is notorious for drownings. However, nearby, at the end of Hahei Beach Road, you'll find one of the finest-protected coves on the coast, with sands tinted pink from crushed shells; it's safe to swim here. If you need to while away some time before the tide goes out, there is a gallery and a café across the road from the beach.

OUTDOOR ACTIVITIES

BOATING
AND DIVING
You can go on a sea-kayaking tour with **Cathedral Cove Sea Kayaks** (✉ *88 Hahei Beach Rd., Hahei* ☎ *07/866–3877* ⊕ *www.seakayak-tours.co.nz*); prices start at $85 for a half-day trip, and they're happy to work with beginners. You can get a peek of what they do on their Web site video. They take groups of about eight in double kayaks and pride themselves on taking visitors to places they are unlikely to see on foot. **Cathedral Cove Dive and Snorkel Hahei** (✉ *Shop 2, Grange Ct., Hahei* ☎ *07/866–3955* ⊕ *www.hahei.co.nz/diving*) gives beginner, advanced, and dive-master courses, as well as daily dive trips.

WHERE TO EAT

$$$
NEW ZEALAND

✕ **Grange Road Café.** With its roster of seafood, burgers, and vegetarian dishes paired with New Zealand wines from small boutique vineyards, this restaurant has a big summer draw. However, the potbellied stove brewing complimentary mulled wine and the live music performances are reasons enough to visit in winter. ⊠ *7 Grange Rd., Hahei* ☎ *07/866–3502* ☐ *DC, MC, V* ⊗ *Closed June and July.*

$$–$$$
CAFÉ

✕ **Luna Café.** There's no doubt you're at the beach here: the design incorporates scallop-shell lei, woven baskets, and cowrie shells, and the walls are lime and blue. The menu sticks to tried-and-true favorites like roast rack of lamb with *kūmara* (native sweet potato) and ginger slice (shortbread with ginger frosting). You can also get muffins and sandwiches, or stop in for brunch. In winter, dinner is served only on Mondays. ⊠ *1 Grange Ct., Grange Rd., Hahei* ☎ *07/866–3016* ☐ *MC, V.*

WHERE TO STAY

$–$$

🏨 **The Church.** Originally a 1916 Methodist church, the Church is worth a visit even if you're not staying the night. The church itself, on the main road heading into Hahei, is now a gracious upmarket restaurant, although easily the most expensive in the area ($$$$). Travelers and locals mull over choices such as Black Angus Eye fillet served on a local blue cheese mash with chili jam, or the macadamia dukkha-crusted rack of lamb with roast vegetables with a red currant jus. Though it's a white-linen place, it maintains a relaxed country vibe; you don't have to pull out your Sunday best. Behind the building are wooden studios and cottages connected by winding garden paths, each decorated with stained glass and small arched windows. The rooms are small but bright, and each has a back porch overlooking the gardens. **Pros:** range of accommodations; lovely garden. **Cons:** basic furnishings. ⊠ *87 Hahei Beach Rd., Hahei* ☎ *07/866–3533* ⊕ *www.thechurch-hahei.co.nz* ⇄ *4 studios, 7 cottages* ⌂ *In-room: No a/c, no phone, kitchen (some), refrigerator, no TV (some). In-hotel: Restaurant, laundry facilities, no-smoking rooms* ☐ *MC, V* ⊗ *Jan. and Feb. daily; closed Sun. and Mon.; closed mid-June–late Aug.* ⅋⎐ *BP.*

$$–$$$

🏨 **Flaxhaven Lodge Bed & Breakfast.** Your hosts Lee and John will welcome you with a glass of wine or a cup of tea and some baked goods while you sink into one of the plush couches in their living room. The guest wing, with its own living room and bathroom, is set off to one side of the main house and looks out onto a well-kept garden and neighboring fields and trees. The self-contained, two-bedroom cottage opens out to its own private deck and gardens. **Pros:** friendly hosts; amazingly comfortable beds; lovely garden. **Cons:** rudimentary tea and coffee facilities. ⊠ *995 Purangi Rd.* ☎ *07/866–2676* ⊕ *www.flaxhavenlodge.co.nz* ⇄ *1 guest suite, 1 cottage* ⌂ *In-room: Kitchen (some), refrigerator (some). In-hotel: Laundry facilities, Wi-Fi, some pets allowed, no kids under 5* ☐ *AE, D, DC, MC, V* ⅋⎐ *BP.*

$$
Fodor's Choice
★

🏨 **Purangi Gardens Accommodation.** As you open the door to your wood cottage nestled in 100 acres of protected park on the shores of the Purangi Estuary, expect to find a loaf of still-warm home-baked bread, a bowl of fruit from the garden, homemade granola and yogurt, and some fresh-laid eggs. Hosts Rod McLaren and Susan Grierson extend homegrown hospitality here. They'll lend you a kayak and send you down the river, but you might prefer lazing on your veranda and enjoying the views. The wood-raftered rooms in the cottages are cozy and compact. If you're traveling *en masse*, or simply wish to spread out, two spacious houses sleep up to 10 and 6 people respectively, and the yurt sleeps four. Set apart from the cottages (two of them are amid orchards), they're fully furnished and have kitchens. **Pros:** private; enjoyable garden; relaxing property. **Cons:** style is plain; not for those wanting luxury. ⊠ *321 Lees Rd., Hahei* ☎ *07/866–4036* ⊕ *www.purangigarden.co.nz* ⇨ *2 cottages, 3 houses* ⚭ *In-room: No a/c, no phone, kitchen (some), refrigerator. In-hotel: Beachfront, water sports, laundry facilities, Internet terminal, no-smoking rooms* ⊟ *MC, V* ⊺⊙⊺ *CP.*

$$–$$$ ⊞ **Tatahi Lodge.** In the center of Hahei and across the street from the beach, this lodge comprises a number of low-lying wooden buildings. Surrounded by trees, accommodations range from doubles and studios to dorms (there's a wide price range, too). **Pros:** range of accommodation; good for budget travelers. **Cons:** can get crowded with younger travelers. ⊠ *Grange Rd., Hahei* ☎ *07/866–3992* ⊕ *www.dreamland. co.nz/tatahilodge* ⇨ *5 double rooms, 2 studios, 1 2-bedroom cottage, 2 6-bed dorms, 1 4-bed dorm* ⚭ *In-room: No a/c, kitchen (some). In-hotel: Wi-Fi, no-smoking rooms* ⊟ *AE, DC, MC, V.*

$$ ⊞ **Wairua Lodge.** Although only 15 minutes from Whitianga, the journey to Wairua Lodge takes you off the main drag and through the infamous 309 Road before heading down into a sunny, sheltered valley. Amid 15 acres of native forest flanked by creeks and swimming holes sit four studios—known to the hosts as "snugs" because they're so cozy—and a two-bedroom suite. There is an outdoor hot tub, but the highlight is the deep outdoor bath, on a balcony in a private room and suspended 40 feet above a ravine. At night, the ravine is lit by a spotlight; from the bath you can look out onto the trees and the creek below, while checking out the nocturnal native birdlife. Because of its proximity to both the east and west coast of the Coromandel, the lodge is a good base from which to explore the area. **Pros:** divine location; fantastic river swimming. **Cons:** unsealed road access—albeit a short distance—can make driving challenging, particularly if traveling at night. ⊠ *251 Old Coach Rd., Whitianga* ☎ *07/866–0304* ⊕ *www.wairualodge.co.nz* ⇨ *4 rooms, 1 2-bedroom suite* ⚭ *In-room: No a/c, no phone, kitchen (some), DVD, In-hotel: Spa, laundry facilities* ⊟ *MC, V* ⊺⊙⊺ *CP.*

EN
ROUTE

★ ☾ **Colenso Country Café and Shop** (⊠ *State Hwy. 25, Whenuakite* ☎ *07/866–3725*), on State Highway 25 just south of the Hahei turnoff on the way to Tairua, is a relaxed cottage café named after William Colenso, an early explorer of New Zealand. Set in a garden full of citrus and olive trees, lavender, and kitchen herbs, the café serves fresh juices, soups, focaccia sandwiches, an outstanding vegetable frittata, addictive chocolate fudge biscuits (also called slices), and Devonshire teas. In summer a pavlova stack—three meringues layered with cream and fresh fruit—is served. The open grassy space, play area, and tame donkeys make this an especially good place to stop with kids. Colenso is open from 10 to 5 daily, October through July, and 10 to 4 daily from May through September. Closed August.

TAIRUA

28 km (18 mi) south of Hahei, 37 km (23 mi) north of Whangamata.

A town that you'll actually notice when you pass through it, Tairua is one of the larger communities along the coast. Because State Highway 25 is the town's main road, it's convenient for a bite en route to the prettier seaside spots around Whitianga and Hahei. In Tairua, the twin volcanic peaks of Paku rise up beside the harbor. The short ferry ride from Tairua across the harbor to Pauanui, which is an upmarket area, takes you to the immediate area's best beach; the ferry runs continually October through April, and six times a day during the rest of the year ($4 round-trip). For activities and maps check out the Pauanui and Tairua information centers.

GETTING HERE AND AROUND

If you're based in Thames, Tairua is an easy drive across the base of the Coromandel Peninsula along State Highway 25A. Otherwise, whether you're heading up or down the eastern side of the Coromandel, you can't miss it. The information center on the main road is a good place to stop in and get your bearings.

ESSENTIALS

Visitor Information Pauanui Information Centre (⊠ *Vista Paku and Shepherd Ave.* ☎ *07/864–7101)*. Tairua Information Centre (⊠ *Main Rd., Tairua* ☎ *07/864-7575* ⊕ *www.tairua.info/index.html)*.

WHERE TO EAT

$$–$$$
ECLECTIC
✕ **Manaia Café and Bar.** This spacious, centrally located restaurant is welcoming and it shows—it can get busy. You can sit inside or out, depending on your mood and the weather. Try venison served with arugula, Parmesan, lemon, and olive oil, or the mussels in brandy-and-cream sauce. It's also open for breakfast—the smoked-salmon eggs Benedict is popular. If you arrive during the day, pop into the adjacent Manaia Gallery, which sells jewelry, art, and crafts. ⊠ *228 Main Rd., Tairua* ☎ *07/864–9050* ⊟ *MC, V.*

¢
SEAFOOD
✕ **Surf and Sand.** This is a fantastic place to get a quintessential Kiwi-style beachside lunch of kūmara chips, Coromandel mussels, and fresh fish, washed down with a bottle of Lemon & Paeroa (L&P—the iconic Kiwiana soda). The chips are crisp (they're fried in rice bran oil). Come early to get your "takeaways"; they close at 8 PM. ⊠ *Shop 7, Main Rd.* ☎ *07/864–8617.*

WHERE TO STAY

$$–$$$
▦ **Blue Water Motel.** These blue-and-white units are at the southern end of Tairua, across the street from a small sandy beach. Each unit mimics a simple beach cottage, with a deck overlooking the harbor. **Pros:** simple and basic; close to the beach; friendly hosts. **Cons:** underwhelming interior. ⊠ *213 Main Rd. Tairua* ☎ *07/864–8537* ⊕ *www.bluewatermotel.co.nz* ⇨ *6 studios, 1 1-bedroom units, 2 2-bedroom units* ⚅ *In-room: No a/c, kitchen, refrigerator, Wi-Fi. In-hotel: Spa, laundry facilities, no-smoking rooms* ⊟ *MC, V.*

$$–$$$
▦ **Pacific Harbour Lodge.** This resort-style property is on the main street in Tairua and looks like it escaped from a tropical island. With a grand Pacific-styled portico, it's a cluster of island-style chalets connected by a

white shell path. The units are spacious and quiet with the added bonus of parking outside your door. Furnishings are simple and comfortable and all the touches expected in an upmarket hotel are present. **Pros:** tropical quality; good location; well priced. **Cons:** some may find the woody decoration overbearing. ✉ *223 Main Rd., Tairua* ☎ *07/864–8581* ⊕ *www.pacificharbour.co.nz* ⤶ *48 rooms* ⚷ *In-room: No a/c. In-hotel: Wi-Fi* ⊟ *AE, DC, MC, V.*

$$$–$$$$ 🏨 **Puka Park Resort.** This stylish hillside hideaway, which attracts a largely European clientele, lies in native bushland on Pauanui Beach, at the seaward end of Tairua Harbor. Timber chalets are expertly furnished. Sliding glass doors lead to a balcony perched among the treetops. The restaurant's daily menu merits perusal; keep an eye out for the fish of the day on a roasted red onion risotto with lemon beurre blanc. The turnoff from State Highway 25 is about 6 km (4 mi) south of Tairua. **Pros:** upmarket and well appointed; attracts dressy people. **Cons:** aloof (although helpful) staff; environment too dressy for the laid-back, beachy flavor of the region. ✉ *Mount Ave., Pauanui Beach* ☎ *07/864–8088* ⊕ *www.puka-park.co.nz* ⤶ *42 rooms* ⚷ *In-room: No a/c, safe. In-hotel: Restaurant, bar, tennis court, pool, spa, bicycles* ⊟ *AE, DC, MC, V.*

EN ROUTE Stop at the dazzling, white-sand Opoutere Beach and the **Wharekawa Wildlife Refuge** for a 15-minute stroll through the forest to another great stretch of white sand. The long beach is bounded at either end by headlands, and there are stunning views of Slipper Island. An estuary near the parking lot is a breeding ground for shorebirds. A handsome bridge arches over the river to the forest walk. For information and maps about the Wharekawa (fah-ray-*ka*-wa) Wildlife Refuge, ask at the Tairua or Whangamata information centers. Another good info source is the **YHA Opoutere Hostel** (✉ *389 Opoutere Rd., Opoutere* ☎ *07/865–9072* ⊕ *www.yha.co.nz/Hostels/North+Island+Hostels/Opoutere*), an exceptional hostel set in 2 acres of native bush, fruit trees, and an herb garden, across the road from the estuary. A notice board marks a number of walking trails, including those to the wildlife refuge, the beach, and a glowworm grotto. Aside from the dormitories in an old schoolhouse, there is a self-contained cabin, and double units are throughout the grounds, which cost $72 a night. The hostel is closed May to October.

WHANGAMATA

37 km (23 mi) south of Tairua, 60 km (38 mi) east of Thames.

The Coromandel Ranges back Whangamata (fahng-a-ma-*ta*), another harborside village. This was once a town of modest houses and a population of 4,000, but it's been discovered by people wanting a holiday home reasonably close to Auckland. Its harbor, surf beaches, mangroves, and coastal islands are glorious. In summer, the population triples. It's a great spot for deep-sea fishing, and its bar break creates some of the best waves in New Zealand. For classic and muscle car enthusiasts, the Whangamata Beach Hop held each year at the end of April is a must-go. You'll see amazing classic cars and listen to some of the best rock-and-roll bands around.

GETTING HERE AND AROUND

Whangamata is the Coromandel's last port of call, as the Peninsula segues southward into the Bay of Plenty. If you're only passing through but you've got a couple of hours to spare, check out some of the short bush walks in the area, or of course, head down to the beach.

ESSENTIALS

Visitor Information Whangamata Information Centre (⊠ *616 Port Rd., Whangamata* ☎ *07/865–8340* ⊕ *www.whangamatainfo.co.nz*).

OUTDOOR ACTIVITIES

A trip to New Zealand really wouldn't be complete without a day or more with Doug Johansen and Jan Poole or one of their expert associate guides from **Kiwi Dundee Adventures** (⊠ *Box 198, Whangamata* ☎ *07/865–8809* ⊕ *www.kiwidundee.co.nz*). Their total enthusiasm for the region rubs off on anyone who takes a Kiwi Dundee tour. There are one- to five-day or longer experiences of Coromandel's majesty, or 14- to 20-day tours all of New Zealand if you'd like.

FISHING   **Go Deep Sea** (⊠ *261K Kaitemako Rd., Tauranga* ☎ *0800/118–845* ⊕ *www.godeepsea.com*) is equipped to fish the deep waters off the coast and around Mayor Island; they'll take you out for a full day of "bottom fishing" for *hapuka, terakihi,* and snapper and pick you up from Whangamata. The minimum trip is a full day, starting at $225 but they have a range of others including a four-day trip from about US$2,000, including transfers from Auckland. **Te Ra** (⊠ *120 Moana Anu Anu Ave., Whangamata* ☎ *07/865–8681* ⊕ *tera.whangamata.co.nz*) is licensed for marine-mammal watching and can incorporate it into a day's fishing or cruising around the bays. Half-day fishing trips start at $45 per person (available during the day on Wednesdays and Friday evenings), or you can charter the boat for the day for $750.

SURFING   In the center of town, the **Whangamata Surf Shop** (⊠ *634 Port Rd.* ☎ *07/865–8252*), recognized by its bright orange exterior, has surfboards and boogie boards for rent, and wet suits. If you want a surfing lesson, $50 covers surfboard rental and an instructor for an hour.

WHERE TO EAT

$$$–$$$$ ✕ **Oceana's Restaurant.** With its white-linen tablecloths, candles, and aura
NEW ZEALAND   of upscale, urban dining, Oceana's may not be what you'd expect in this small seaside town. But that hasn't stopped people from flocking to the restaurant for traditional New Zealand cuisine. The restaurant's two signature dishes—the seafood platter for two and the oven-baked lamb loin rubbed with mustard and roasted garlic—are always popular, or you could go easy and have a bowl of seafood chowder and finish up with some old-fashioned bread-and-butter pudding. ⊠ *328 Ocean Rd.* ☎ *07/865–7157* ▭ *AE, DC, MC, V* ☺ *Closed Mon. Apr.–Nov. No lunch.*

$ ✕ **Vibes Café.** This café boasts of being the friendliest place in town, and
CAFÉ   the daylong crowds support the claim. Paintings by local artists cover
★   the walls (not surprisingly, a beach theme predominates), and magazines and newspapers are on hand for a quick read over your espresso. It's the sort of place where surfers might be seated next to older people out for an afternoon coffee. Of the light meals, the vegetarian dishes are the most exciting, with choices such as kūmara stuffed with pesto and

sun-dried tomatoes, though the menu is often changing. ⊠ *638 Port Rd.* ☎ *07/865–7121* ⊟ *AE, DC, MC, V* ⊘ *Closed Tues. No dinner.*

$–$$ ✕**Whanga Bar.** Once a truck repair yard, now a café with a surfboard
CAFÉ   countertop, the Whanga Bar is not actually a bar; it's named for the locally known surf spot created by the "Whanga Bar," a sandbar out in Whangamata Bay. The biggest trade is breakfast; dishes like "The Barrel"—poached eggs, bacon, and avocado, served on an English muffin with hollandaise sauce, roast tomato, and hash browns—will last you all day. ⊠ *101 Winifred Ave., Whangamata* ☎ *07/865–6472* ⊟ *MC, V* ⊘ *May–Oct., closed Thurs., and only open Fri. and Sat. for dinner; Nov.– Apr. open daily 8* AM*–11* PM.

WHERE TO STAY

$$$$ 🛏 **Brenton Lodge.** Looking out over Whangamata and the islands in its harbor from your hillside suite, you'll have no trouble settling into a luxurious mood. Fresh flowers and a tray of fruit and handmade chocolates greet you on arrival. The lodge suites all have views of the ocean. Stroll around the garden, peep at the birds in the aviary, and in springtime breathe in the scent of orange and jasmine blossoms. **Pros:** peaceful settings; breathtaking views. **Cons:** a little too far from town to walk home in the evening. ⊠ *1 Brenton Pl., Box 216* ☎ *07/865–8400* ⊕ *www. brentonlodge.co.nz* ⤴ *4 suites* ⌂ *In-room: No a/c, no phone. In-hotel: Pool, laundry service, no-smoking rooms* ⊟ *AE, MC, V* ⍾ *BP.*

$$ 🛏 **Pipinui Motel.** Just out of town, a two-minute walk to Whangamata harbor and a 10-minute walk to the beach, this motel has simple, modern units, with plain white walls, and dark, stylishly utilitarian furniture. **Pros:** simple furnishings; good location. **Cons:** too plain for some. ⊠ *805 Martyn Rd.* ☎ *07/865–6796* ⊕ *www.pipinuimotel.co.nz* ⤴ *4 suites* ⌂ *In-room: No a/c, kitchen (some), refrigerator, Internet. In-hotel: No-smoking rooms* ⊟ *AE, DC, MC, V.*

THE BAY OF PLENTY

Explorer Captain James Cook gave the Bay of Plenty its name for the abundant sources of food he found here; these days it's best known for its plentiful supply of beaches. Places like Mount Maunganui and Whakatane overflow with sunseekers during peak summer-vacation periods, but even at the busiest times you need to travel only a few miles to find a secluded stretch of beach.

The Bay of Plenty has a strong Māori population; traditional lore (and common belief) has it that this is the first landing place of *Takitimu, Tainui, Arawa,* and *Mataatua,* four of the seven Māori *waka* (canoes) that arrived in New Zealand from Hawaiki. These first arrivals formed the ancestral base for the Māori tribes of the Tauranga region: Ngāti Ranginui, Ngāi Te Rangi, and Ngāti Pūkenga.

The gateway to the region is the small country town of Katikati, but the central base is Tauranga, which has retained its relaxed vacation-town vibe despite recent development. From here you can take day trips to beaches, the nearby bush, and offshore attractions such as volcanic White Island.

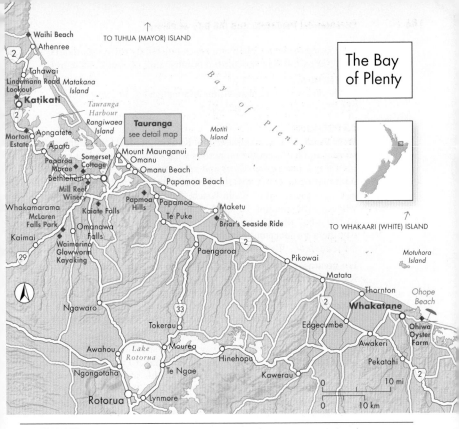

KATIKATI

62 km (39 mi) southeast of Thames, 35 km (22 mi) northwest of Tauranga.

Katikati was built on land confiscated from local Māori after the 1863 land wars and given to Irish Protestant settlers by the Central Government. But before being settled in the 1870s, Māori had long recognized the area's potential for growing food crops. These days, fruit growing—particularly kiwifruit and avocado—keeps the Katikati economy afloat, perhaps providing one (of many) explanations for Katikati's name, "to nibble" in Māori. Katikati's most noticeable features are the 42 murals around town and good antique stores. Another unusual attraction is the **Haiku Pathway,** a walking trail studded with haiku-etched boulders. The path starts at the Katikati Bus Company on Katikati's Main Street and leads down to the river. Pick up a map of the route at Katikati Visitor Information.

GETTING HERE AND AROUND

While remaining on the Pacific Coast Highway, heading south from the Coromandel toward the Bay of Plenty, State Highway 25 switches and becomes State Highway 2. The first town you'll meet along State Highway 2 is Katikati. An interesting choice for the Bay of Plenty's gateway town, Katikati is one of the few towns in the Bay of Plenty that is not built along the water. Neither a beach nor fishing town—Katikati is far better known for its agricultural bounty, and, of course, its murals.

ESSENTIALS

Visitor Information Katikati Visitor Information (✉ *36 Centre Main Rd.* ☎ *07/549–1658* ⊕ *www.katikati.org.nz*).

EXPLORING

Waihi Beach, 19 km (12 mi) north of Katikati, is ideal for swimming and surfing and has access to numerous walkways. At low tide, people dig in the sand looking for *tuatua* and *pipi*—delicious shellfish that you boil until they open. Don't miss the drive to the top of the Bowentown heads at the southern end of Waihi Beach. This is an old Māori pā (fortified village) with stunning views. A short but steep walk from here leads to Cave Bay directly below the viewing point. ⚠ Don't swim at Cave Bay; there are dangerous currents. Stop by the **Waihi Information Centre** (✉ *Seddon St., Waihi* ☎ *07/863–6718*) for maps and tide times.

For great views over the Bay of Plenty, go a couple of minutes north of Katikati on State Highway 2 to the **Lindemann Road Lookout.** The only sign to the lookout is right at the turnoff. The road is good but narrow in parts. Once at the lookout (where the road ends), you'll find a map embedded in rock to help orient you. Look for Mayor Island just to the north and Mt. Maunganui to the south.

Just south of Katikati on Highway 2, you'll spot the Cape Dutch design of the **Morton Estate** winery building. Winemaker Evan Ward has won a stack of awards over the years. He also holds some bottles back until he thinks they're at their drinking best, so you'll likely find earlier vintages than at most wineries. The Black Label Chardonnay is particularly good as is the sparkling wine. ✉ *Main Rd., Katikati* ☎ *0800/667–866* ⊕ *www.mortonestatewines.co.nz* ⊗ *Weekdays 10–5*

WHERE TO EAT

$ ✕ **Katz Pyjamas Café.** It's easy to miss this tiny main-street café, but make
CAFÉ   a point of searching it out—it easily serves the best lunch in town. Opt for the "Paw cakes," corn cakes draped with bacon, mushrooms, and chicken in a rosemary cream sauce, or choose something from the counter, such as the layered pumpkin tart or the chicken cottage pie. If you're lucky enough to arrive during feijoa season, ask for the almond, feijoa, and lime cake, served with yogurt and a berry coulis drizzled in the shape of a cat's paw. Many of the dishes are wheat- and gluten-free. ✉ *4 Main St., Katikati* ☎ *07/549–1902* ⊟ *MC, V* ⊗ *Open weekdays 8–4.*

$$–$$$ ✕ **The Landing.** You'll find this contemporary restaurant in the 1876
NEW ZEALAND   Talisman Hotel. Sit down for a bowl of seafood chowder or a pizza. For something more substantial, try the fillet steak served with scallops and prawns in a white-wine-and-cream sauce. ✉ *7–9 Main Rd., State Hwy. 2* ☎ *07/549–3218* ⊟ *AE, DC, MC, V.*

WHERE TO STAY

$$ ▣ **Crindau Lodge.** Gardens, grassy paths, ferns, and a feijoa orchard surround this renovated barn, and the views stretch all the way to Mauao. Guests are greeted with tea and freshly baked muffins in the main part of the house, before being shown to their quarters—a self-contained

two-bedroom wing. The art and furnishings reflect the owners' long-standing love of travel throughout Asia and the Pacific. A hot tub in the garden looks out over the hills to Mt. Maunganui. The property flanks the Kaimai Mamuku National Park, which includes a lovely walk along the ridgeline. **Pros:** appealing environment; thoughtfully appointed furnishings and art. **Cons:** out of the way. ⊠ *530A Lund Rd., Katikati* ☎ *07/549–4750* ⊕ *www.crindaulodge.co.nz* ⟳ *2 rooms* ⌂ *In-room: No a/c, no phone, refrigerator, Wi-Fi. In-hotel: Spa, laundry service* ⊟ *MC, V* ⊙*CP.*

$ 🏠 **Kaimai View Motel.** The rooms in these low-lying buildings are carefully furnished with original local artwork and colorful linens. The motel has panoramic views of the Kaimai Ranges. Right on Katikati's main strip, its proximity to the area's activities makes this a low-key and handy base. **Pros:** disabled access in one unit; warmly decorated. **Cons:** traffic noise. ⊠ *78 Main Rd. (State Hwy. 2)* ☎ *07/549–0398* ⊕ *www. kaimaiview.co.nz* ⟳ *7 rooms, 7 suites* ⌂ *In-room: No a/c, kitchen, refrigerator, DVD, Internet, Wi-Fi. In-hotel: Pool, laundry facilities, parking (free), no-smoking rooms* ⊟ *AE, DC, MC, V.*

$$$$ 🏠 **Matahui Lodge.** This lodge is a prime example of the boutique hotels popping up around the area. The harbor views may tempt you to stay on the patio all afternoon, even on cooler days when the outdoor stone fireplace is lit. The bedrooms are spacious and uncluttered, with simple wooden furniture, olive-and-taupe walls, and wide windows that look out onto the grounds and harbor. Consider staying for dinner—they've stockpiled some excellent New Zealand vintages, including those from their own vineyard. **Pros:** nice architectural design; lovely gardens; good wine list. **Cons:** a little far from town for some. ⊠ *187 Matahui Rd., 9 km (5½ mi) south of Katikati* ☎ *07/571–8121* ⊕ *www.matahui-lodge. co.nz* ⟳ *3 suites* ⌂ *In-room: No a/c, refrigerator, Internet. In-hotel: Gym, spa, laundry service* ⊟ *AE, DC, MC, V* ⊙*BP.*

$$–$$$ 🏠 **The Point.** The Point does not take bookings from people who smoke and generally is not interested in guests with children under 18, though babies under age 1 may stay if prior arrangements are made. Built from local river stones and untreated timber, the lodge looks half stone-cottage and half sprawling-barn. The guest rooms have beamed ceilings and four-poster beds; one turreted suite overlooks a small vineyard and the harbor. For an extra charge, hosts Kerry and Anne Guy prepare dinner, accompanied by wine, from their own vineyard or a picnic basket to take away. **Pros:** nice location; spectacular views. **Cons:** cheap furniture and bedspreads. ⊠ *444 Tuapiro Rd., Tuapiro Point, 8 km (5 mi) north of Katikati* ☎ *07/549–3604* ⊕ *www.thepointlodge.co.nz* ⟳ *3 suites* ⌂ *In-room: No a/c, no phone (some), kitchen (some), refrigerator (some), Internet, Wi-Fi. In-hotel: Room service, beachfront, bicycles, laundry service, Internet terminal, parking (free), no kids, no-smoking rooms* ⊟ *AE, DC, MC, V* ⊙*BP.*

TAURANGA

216 km (134 mi) southeast of Auckland.

The population center of the Bay of Plenty, Tauranga is one of New Zealand's fastest-growing cities. Along with its neighbor, Whakatane, this seaside city claims to be one of the country's sunniest towns. Unlike most local towns, Tauranga doesn't grind to a halt in the off-season, because it has one of the busiest ports in the country, and the excellent waves at the neighboring suburb of Mount Maunganui—just across Tauranga's harbor bridge—always draw surfers and holiday folk.

GETTING HERE AND AROUND

To explore the town center, start at the **Strand**, a lovely tree-lined street that separates the shops from the sea. Bars, restaurants, and cafés line the Strand and nearby side streets. If you're interested in the beachier side of Tauranga, head 8 km (5 mi) east out of the city center and over the Harbor Bridge to Mount Maunganui. Here, you'll find one of the best surf spots in the country and a sheltered swimming bay along the 20 km (12½ mi) shoreline, as well as shopping, restaurants, and the majestic Mauao.

ESSENTIALS

Bus Depot InterCity Tauranga Depot (⊠ *95 Willow St.* ☏ *07/578–8103*).

Hospitals South City Medical Centre (⊠ *454 Cameron Rd.* ☏ *07/578–6808*). Tauranga Hospital (⊠ *375 Cameron Rd.* ☏ *07/579–8000*). **Mount Medical Centre** (⊠ *257 Maunganui Rd., Mount Maunganui* ☏ *07/575–3073*).

Pharmacies John's Photo-Pharmacy (⊠ *Cameron Rd. and 2nd Ave., Tauranga* ☏ *07/578–3566*). **Dispensary First** (⊠ *Girven Rd. and Grenada St., Mount Maunganui* ☏ *07/574–8645*).

Visitor Information Mount Maunganui Visitor Information Centre (⊠ *Salisbury Ave.* ☏ *07/575–5099*). **Tauranga Visitor Information Centre** (⊠ *95 Willow St.* ☏ *07/578–8103* ⊕ *www.bayofplentynz.com*).

EXPLORING

TOP ATTRACTIONS

Kaiate Falls (Te Rerekawau). The falls are a little off-the-beaten-track but worth the trip. About 15 minutes southeast of Tauranga, just off Welcome Bay Road, the Kaiate Stream drops over bluffs in a series of waterfalls and rocky lagoons, culminating in a deep green lagoon flanked by moss- and fern-fringed cliffs. A 20- to 30-minute loop trail takes you down to the main lagoon and through lush greenery. The falls' summit (and the parking lot) affords views over Tauranga and the coast. ⊠ *Upper Papamoa Rd.* ☏ *07/578–8103.*

☾ ★ **Mauao (Mt. Maunganui).** The formerly volcanic mountain is the region's geological icon, with its conical rocky outline rising 761 feet above sea level. White-sand beaches with clear water stretch for miles from Mauao—this is one of New Zealand's best swimming and surfing areas. One of the early Māori canoes, *Takitimu,* landed at the base of the mountain. A system of trails around Mauao includes an easy walk around its base and the more strenuous Summit Road from the campground by the Pilot Bay boat ramp. The trails are clearly signposted and heavily used, so no bushwhacking is necessary. All roads lead to "the Mount," as they say; follow any road running parallel to the beach. The Mount Maunganui area gets crowded around Christmas and New Year's Eve; to see it at its best, come in November, early December, or between mid-January and late March. On the first weekend in January, you can watch the Tauranga Half Iron-man race while drinking coffee at a sidewalk café, and if keen, you can sit on the path around Mauao and cheer runners on. Find information at the Mount Maunganui Visitor Information Centre (⇨ *above*).

WORTH NOTING

Elms Mission House. Built in 1847, this was the first Christian mission-ary station in the Bay of Plenty. The lovely late-Georgian house, named for the 50 elms that grew on the property, was home to descendants of pioneer missionaries until the mid-1990s. You can explore the lush grounds, but the real appeal lies in the main house, the small wooden chapel, and the collection of furniture, crockery, and other period items. ✉ *15 Mission St.* ☎ *07/577–9772* ⊕ *www.theelms.org.nz* ✆ *$5* ⊗ *House Wed. and weekends 2–4; grounds daily 9–5.*

McLaren Falls Park. A 15-minute drive south of Tauranga off State High-way 29, the park offers a 10-minute easy bushwalk to the falls and more strenuous walks to Pine Tree Knoll or the Ridge for great vistas across the park. ✉ *State Hwy. 29* ☎ *07/578–8103.*

Mount Surf Museum. This quirky spot displays nearly 700 surfboards, some from the beginning of surfing in New Zealand, and other surf memorabilia—reportedly the largest collection in New Zealand. The museum is housed in the outlet branch of the Mount Surf Shop, Mount Maunganui's surfing specialist store. ✉ *139 Totara St., Mount Maun-ganui* ☎ *07/927–7234* ⊗ *Daily 9–5.*

Papamoa Hills Cultural Heritage Regional Park (Te Rae o Papamoa). Twenty kilometers (12½ mi) from Tauranga, the 45-minute summit walk through the 108-acre park will take you past Māori pā sites dating back to 1460, native forest, and farmland. At the top of the ridge, views take in everything between Mauao and White Island, against the silhouettes of the Coromandel Peninsula in the north and the East Cape to the south. ✉ *Poplar La., Papamoa Hills* ☎ *07/577–7000* ⊗ *Daily 7:30–6 Apr.–Oct.; daily 7:30–8:30 Nov.–Mar.*

Zohar. If you're looking for easily packaged New Zealand objet d'art, this Mount Maunganui design store is a good place to stock up. Although Zohar does not exclusively stock New Zealand-made items, the selection is still good, and goes well beyond tacky souvenirs aimed at visitors. ✉ *104 Maunganui Rd., Mt. Maunganui* ☎ *07/574–7428* ⊕ *www.zohar.co.nz* ⊗ *Weekdays 10–5, Weekends 10–4.*

OFF THE
BEATEN
PATH

Paparoa Marae. The *whānau* (family) of Paparoa Marae provides a marae (meeting house) experience that is down-to-earth. It's a working marae so, along with a traditional welcome and cultural performance, Māori elders explain the marae, Māori carvings, and other aspects of Māori history, culture, and protocol. You're invited to share in a *hāngi* (the traditional method of Māori cooking) meal. A marae visit costs around $35–$75, including the hāngi. It's about 20 minutes out of Tauranga, just off State Highway 2 in the village of Te Puna. ✉ *Paparoa Rd., Te Puna, Tauranga* ☎ *07/552–5904.*

OUTDOOR ACTIVITIES

BOATING AND
FISHING

Blue Ocean Charters operates three vessels and has half- and full-day trips, plus overnight excursions. A half day of reef fishing costs about $70, but if you want to go for a large *hapuka* (grouper), the cost goes above $100. Equipment is provided and you do need to phone ahead as they get busy. ✉ *Coronation Pier, Wharf St., Box 13–100, Tauranga* ☎ *07/578–9685* ⊕ *www.blueoceancharters.co.nz.*

HELICOPTER
TOURS

Aerius Tuhua. Teaming up with local Māori as their guides, Aerius Helicopters run trips to the volcanic island Tuhua (Mayor Island). The trip includes a guided walk through one of New Zealand's largest Pohutukawa forests all the way up to the Devil's Staircase, the island's stronghold where the reigning tribe used to defend the island in battle. Tuhua is considered particularly significant by Māori, in part because of the presence of obsidian—a volcanic glass prized for its strength and sharpness—found in great streaks throughout the island. The helicopter ride to the island is an event in itself, providing aerial views of the Tuhua's unusual landscape and colored lakes. Guides will tell you just about everything there is to know about plant and birdlife on the island, as well as legends and tales of early Māori life on Tuhua. ✉ *Jean Batten Dr., Tauranga Airport, Tauranga* ☎ *0800/864–354* ⊕ *www.aerius.co.nz* 🖃 *$495 for a half-day trip.*

KAYAKING
★

After you've had your fill of local wines, cheeses, and fresh fruit on the banks of Lake McLaren at dusk, the guides of **Waimarino Glowworm Kayaking** will help you into your kayak and take you on a gentle, two-hour, nighttime trip across the lake and through a canyon corridor, where thousands of glowworms light up everything. ✉ *36 Taniwha Pl., Wairoa River, Bethlehem, Tauranga* ☎ *07/576–4233* ⊕ *www.waimarino.com* 🖃 *$120.*

SURFING

The **New Zealand Surf School, Mount Maunganui** gives lessons mid-November through March at 10, noon, and 2 every day, starting at $50, which includes all the gear. They also rent surfboards and wet suits by the hour or day and have the experience to work with people with a range of special needs. ✉ *Marine Parade and Tay St., Mount Maunganui* ☎ *021/477–873* ⊕ *www.nzsurfschools.co.nz.*

SWIM-
MING WITH
DOLPHINS

Swimming with dolphins is a big summer activity in the Bay of Plenty, especially off Mount Maunganui. The Department of Conservation licenses and regularly inspects operators and sets limits on the number of boats allowed around any pod of dolphins. Touching, handling, and provoking the dolphins are prohibited. Locals say that the dolphins call the shots; if they don't want anyone swimming with them, they'll take off, and no boat has yet managed to catch up with an antisocial dolphin.

Graeme Butler of **Butler's Swim with Dolphins** has been running dolphin-swimming and whale-watching voyages on the *Gemini Galaxsea* since the early 1990s. Bring your bathing suit and lunch. Trips leave at 9 AM from Tauranga and 9:30 AM from Mount Maunganui, any day that weather allows. Cost is $125, which includes drinks, but you'll need to bring your own lunch. If you don't see dolphins you can take another trip for free. ☎ *07/578–3197 or 0508/288–537* ⊕ *www.swimwithdolphins.co.nz.*

Dolphin Seafaris will take you out for a dolphin encounter. Wet suits, dive gear, and towels are included in the $140 price tag for a trip leaving

Paragliders take in the Mt. Maunganui area scenery from above.

at 8 AM and back around 1 PM with breakfast and drinks included. Phone ahead for daily departure times from the Bridge Marina. ⊠ *90 Maunganui Rd., Mount Maunganui* ☎ *07/577–0105 or 0800/326-8747* ⊕ *www.nzdolphin.com.*

The South Sea Sailing Company will take you out for a full day of sailing on a 60-foot custom-built catamaran around the islands off the coast of Tauranga. With two kayaks on board, as well as snorkels and wet suits, you can jump in for a swim and paddle among the dolphins. You may also see the odd shark or whale—no swimming advised with those guys. Trips are daily (weather-dependent), cost $120, and depart at 10:30 AM (returning around 4:30 PM). Be sure to bring your own lunch, although they will provide it on request for a fee and a day's notice. ⊠ *Mirrielees Rd. (dock)* ☎ *07/579–6376* ⊕ *www.southseasailing.com.*

WINERIES

Owner–winemaker Paddy Preston of **Mills Reef Winery** used to make kiwifruit wine, but he hasn't looked back since he turned to the real thing. The lovely 20-acre complex includes pétanque courts, a fancy tasting room, and an underground wine cellar. The restaurant is also worth a visit (it's open for lunch, coffee, and dessert year-round); sautéed black tiger prawns with passion fruit, lemongrass, and pink grapefruit are fabulous with a glass of sauvignon blanc. Although open all year for brunch and lunch, the restaurant is open only occasionally for dinner; it's best to call in advance. ⊠ *143 Moffat Rd., Bethlehem* ✛ *about 5 km (3 mi) north of Tauranga* ☎ *07/576–8800* ⊕ *www.millsreef.co.nz* ☉ *Daily 10–5.*

WHERE TO EAT

Use the coordinate (✛ B2) at the end of each listing to locate a site on the corresponding map.

$$–$$$
ITALIAN

✕ **Bella Mia.** The Roman owner succeeded in re-creating a little piece of home in this cozy central eatery. The style hits classic, though some would say tacky, notes, with red-and-white checked tablecloths and grapes hanging from the ceiling. But the food is good, all of the pasta is homemade—the tortellini is prepared every afternoon—and the flavorful pizzas are thin crusted. Be sure to leave room for dessert—Bella Mia makes its own gelato, sorbets, and tiramisu. ⊠ *73A Devonport Rd.* ☎ *07/578–4996* ▭ *MC, V* ⌷ *Licensed and BYOB* ☻ *Closed Mon. for lunch* ✛ *B3.*

$$$
NEW ZEALAND

✕ **Bravo Restaurant Café.** With jazz music and tables spilling out onto the sidewalk patio, this restaurant is most popular during brunch, when you can sip a strong latte and enjoy a dish of smoked salmon with scallion, fried potatoes, poached eggs, and hollandaise sauce. The pizza's a good choice, too, with unusual toppings such as lamb shank, wood-fired vegetables, elate (a locally made cheese that tastes like feta, but has the consistency of sour cream), and rosemary jelly. A range of other dishes changes with the seasons. ⊠ *Red Sq.* ☎ *07/578–4700* ⊕ *www.cafebravo.co.nz* ▭ *AE, DC, MC, V* ☻ *No dinner Sun. or Mon.* ✛ *B3.*

$$$–$$$$
NEW ZEALAND

✕ **Mount Bistro.** The prices set this restaurant apart from other Mount Maunganui options, but then, so does the menu. The street-side restaurant looks out onto Mauao. In the open plan kitchen, locally renowned chef Stephen Barry specializes in fusing indigenous ingredients with Pacific Rim flavors. Scallops served with lemongrass-infused black sticky rice with a honey, orange, and sesame vinaigrette make a good starter, followed by rabbit casserole with chestnut dumplings and rewena loaf (a traditional Māori bread). ⊠ *6 Adams Ave., Mount Maunganui* ☎ *07/575–3872* ▭ *AE, DC, MC, V* ☻ *No lunch. Closed Mon.* ✛ *B1.*

$–$$
MEXICAN

✕ **Mundo Mexicano.** With mariachi music, murals, and colors to rival even Frida Kahlo's house, this Mexican restaurant is a surprising—and welcome—find down an alleyway off the main drag of Maunganui Road. It serves typical Mexican food, from chilequiles (a tortilla, mole, and meat dish) to tacos to fajitas, washed down with a glass of cold horchata (a milky beverage of rice and flavors like cinnamon) or, of course, a margarita. ⊠ *147 Maunganui Rd., Mount Maunganui* ☎ *07/572–5152* ⊕ *www.mundomexicano.co.nz* ▭ *AE, DC, MC, V* ☻ *Closed Mon.* ✛ *B1.*

$
CAFÉ

✕ **Sidetrack Cafe.** At the base of Mauao and across the street from the beach, this bustling café is a great place for breakfast or lunch after a climb or swim. Grab a table (there are more outside than in) for a plate of coconut toast, a salad, or a dense chocolate brownie. Or get a huge sandwich and a smoothie to go, and head off to a quiet spot on the trail that rings the Mount. ⊠ *Shop 3, Marine Parade, Mount Maunganui* ☎ *07/575–2145* ▭ *DC, MC, V* ☻ *No dinner* ✛ *B1.*

$$$$
NEW ZEALAND

✕ **Somerset Cottage.** The name says it all—Somerset is a genuine country cottage, and many locals consider it one of the region's best restaurants.

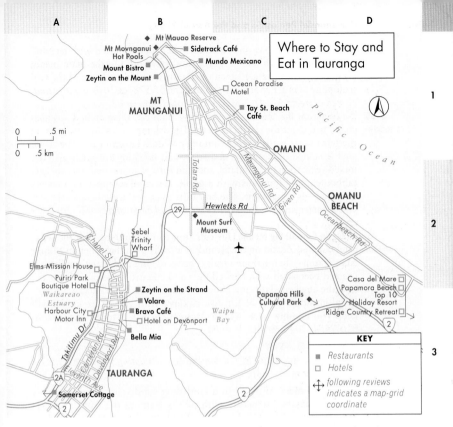

The menu is eclectic, with dishes such as panfried squid with tamarind-lime dressing, or roast duck on vanilla-coconut kūmara (native sweet potato) with orange sauce. They also sell some of the products they cook. ⊠ *30 Bethlehem Rd., 5 km (3 mi) north of Tauranga center on State Hwy. 2* ☎ *07/576–6889* ✎ *somersetcottage@xtra.co.nz* ⛖ *Reservations essential* ☰ *AE, DC, MC, V* 🍽 *Licensed and BYOB* ⊗ *No lunch Sat.–Tues.; no dinner Mon.* ✛ *A3.*

$$–$$$ ✕ **Tay Street Beach Cafe.** The tables out on the patio across the road from
CAFÉ the dunes of Maunganui Beach are the place to be when the weather's right; otherwise, head inside to the cool, grey, vinyl bench seats. Tay Street's menu serves a range of dishes, from old favorites like eggs Benedict or fish-and-chips, to seared ahi tuna with Asian salad and a ginger-soy dressing. They charge city prices for the coffee at $4 a cup, but that hasn't stopped the place from filling up every weekend for the all-day brunch. ⊠ *Tay St. and Marine Pde. , Mt. Maunganui* ☎ *07/572–0691* ☰ *AE, DC, MC, V* ⊗ *Mon.–Sat. 8 AM–10 PM; Sun. 8–4* ✛ *C1.*

$$–$$$ ✕ **Volare.** Although this restaurant is crammed in between half a dozen
ITALIAN other restaurants overlooking the marina, the Italian opera music, bare wood floors, exposed beams, and brick walls create an environment that is miles away from Tauranga. The lounge bar is at street level; head up the wrought-iron staircase to the restaurant, where you can order

from a range of tapas, such as spicy bell peppers stuffed with feta and pesto or squid with lemon, garlic, and olive oil. On the main menu, try gnocchi with pears, pistachios, walnuts, and blue cheese or the veal scaloppini. ⊠ *85 The Strand, Tauranga* ☎ *07/578–6030* ⊕ *www.eatout. co.nz/volare* ⊟ *AE, DC, MC, V* ☾ *Closed Sun.* ✚ *B3.*

$–$$ ✕ **Zeytin on the Strand.** The brightly painted, mismatched wooden
TURKISH   chairs bring out the colors from the Turkish tapestries and artifacts on the terra-cotta walls of this Tauranga Middle Eastern café. The fresh, well-seasoned food arrives in a snap, and portions are generous. The mixed vegetarian pita—falafel, zucchini fritters, marinated red cabbage, tabbouleh, and hummus with a garlic sauce, all wrapped in a chewy flatbread—is a highlight. The best time to go is during lunch—the service is faster and the food is fresher. ⊠ *83 The Strand* ☎ *07/579–0099* ⊟ *MC, V* ✚ *B3.*

$$ ✕ **Zeytin Café at the Mount.** This café (not to be confused with the sepa-
TURKISH   rately owned Zeytin on the Strand) is a really good bet when in Mount Maunganui—their haloumi (salty cheese of goat and sheep's milk) and roasted beet salad with toasted nuts and cilantro dressing is fantastic, as is the chicken, date, and almond tagine. Their superb flat white coffee alongside a plate of Kurdish baklava with vanilla ice cream will keep you coming back. ⊠ *118 Maunganui Rd., Mount Maunganui* ☎ *07/574–3040* ⊟ *MC, V* ✚ *B1.*

WHERE TO STAY

Use the coordinate (✚ B2) at the end of each listing to locate a site on the corresponding map.

$$ ⌂ **Casa Del Mare.** Situated in a confusing subdivision, the house—a huge neoclassical structure with pillars framing the front door—is not your typical beachside cottage The hosts are generous with their time and completely hospitable. The two guest bedrooms are linked by a shared living room and open onto a courtyard patio planted with climbing roses and topiary. While not local to anything except the magnificently expansive Papamoa Beach across the street, it is well placed for day trips either down the coast to Whakatane or up to Mount Maunganui and Tauranga. **Pros:** welcoming hosts; comfortable rooms. **Cons:** too far from Mount Maunganui or Tauranga to use as a base for multiple trips during the day. ⊠ *35 Monticello Key, Papamoa* ☎ *07/542–2996* ⊕ *www.casadelmare.co.nz* ⤴ *2 rooms* ♦ *In-room: Refrigerator, DVD, Wi-Fi. In-hotel: Laundry service, Wi-Fi* ⊟ *AE, D, DC, MC, V* ⊺⊙⊺ *BP* ✚ *D3.*

$–$$ ⌂ **Harbour City Motor Inn.** You certainly won't miss this two-story, bright yellow building. Inside, rooms are a little more subdued, with blue-tiled floors, and gold-and-burgundy furnishings. The motel is right in Tauranga's central district, so you're in walking distance to the wharf, restaurants, and shops. **Pros:** central location; clean and cheery. **Cons:** built around a car park; no outdoor spaces; not particularly kid friendly. ⊠ *50 Wharf St., Tauranga* ☎ *07/571–1435* ⊕ *www.taurangaharbourcity.co.nz* ⤴ *20 rooms* ♦ *In-room: Kitchen, Internet. In-hotel: Laundry facilities, parking (free)* ⊟ *AE, D, DC, MC, V* ✚ *A3.*

Continued on page 209

STAYING ON A FARM

By Alia Bloom

Farmstays are an increasingly popular choice with travelers to New Zealand, whether you're the type to roll up your sleeves and "muck in" (i.e., help out) or recline on a porch with a glass of wine and watch the sunset. Here's how to plan an unforgettable farm visit.

New Zealand's farm experiences are ideal for active vacationers and visitors interested in local Kiwi culture. Guests can arrange to participate in farm activities—from simply touring the farm's facilities to milking cows, harvesting produce, rounding up livestock, and even shearing sheep. And itineraries can easily be customized to fit a visitor's interests.

With more than half of the country's land dedicated to farming, there are numerous options available for overnight or weeklong stays. More than 1,000 farmers around the country welcome travelers to their farms, ranging from a 14-acre country manor with apple orchard near Hawke's Bay to a 4,000-acre, high-country cattle farm (with fly-fishing) in Canterbury. The accommodations range from bunk beds with shared baths to luxurious private cottages on the property and are affordable when compared to hotels with similar amenities.

Leading farmstay providers such as **Rural Tourism** and **Rural Holidays NZ** emphasize that farmstays are as much about tasting a slice of rural life, meeting locals, and experiencing a down-to-earth brand of Kiwi hospitality as they are about helping out with whatever needs to be done on the property. In their words: you can bet the farm on it.

(Above) Sheep herder at Grassmere Lodge, Arthur's Pass National Park, Southern Alps

WHICH FARM SHOULD I CHOOSE?

Four Peaks Lodge, Geraldine

Farms are as diverse as the New Zealand countryside. Some are smack in the middle of the grasslands; others stretch for miles along the coast. Note that most farms raise and harvest several types of plants and animals, even if they specialize in a single species. Here are the main types of farms you're likely to encounter, and a few property recommendations (find more suggestions on the Rural Tourism and Rural Holidays NZ sites).

BEEF/DAIRY FARMS

These farms often stretch over several hundred acres. Other than riding alongside ranchers to tend broken fences, or to offload feed in the fields, there may not be much hands-on farm work to be done. But there are ample opportunities for hiking, fishing, and riding horses on most properties. **Hiwinui Country Estate** (see review in Palmerston North section of Ch. 6) is a rare combination of a luxury lodge and a 1,100-acre working dairy and sheep farm, with an award-winning focus on environmental sustainability. Guests are as likely to enjoy a spa treatment as they are to climb aboard a four-wheeler and help round up the cattle for milking.

SHEEP STATIONS

As a guest, you might find yourself rounding up livestock, watching the shearing gang at work, or taking a turn bottle-feeding an orphaned baby lamb. You'll have plenty of photo ops with New Zealand's woolly icon, and the possibility of enjoying slow-cooked, honey-braised lamb shanks for your dinner. **Tunanui Station Cottages** (see review in Gisborne section of Ch. 5) is home to almost 10,000 cattle, lambs, and goats. Depending on the season, you might be around for lambing, rounding up stock, or shearing. Swimming holes and walking trails provide entertainment for those less keen on the grittier side of farming.

ORCHARD & GARDEN PROPERTIES

New Zealand has excellent biodiversity resulting from the country's geographic isolation. Whether your interest is in wild flora or cultivated fruit species, numerous properties around the country welcome guests. If you arrive on the orchard at harvest time, an extra hand picking fruit is always welcome. In the far north, **The Summer House** (see review in Kerikeri section of Ch. 3) is nestled among landscaped gardens and acres of citrus orchards. On the east coast of the North Island, **Goldspree Kiwi Fruit Orchard Stay** (see review in Gisborne section of Ch. 5) offers a self-contained cottage in a kiwi orchard near wineries and beaches.

WINERIES

The environment and activities here are more refined than those at most farmstays, but you could still find yourself pruning a vine or two, harvesting grapes, and, of course, helping with the terribly arduous task of sampling the wines. Wineries are often similar to B&Bs in terms of what they offer, with lodgings that are more upscale than most farms.

(Opposite bottom) Perendale sheep flock running in paddock

WHAT CAN I EXPECT?

Grape harvest in Martinborough

Hay bales in a field near Queenstown

LODGING TYPES

Accommodations listed as a "farmstay" run an enormous gamut, from cottages to backpacker-type dorms. Some farms offer upscale accommodations (hot tubs and pools, gourmet meals, and designer furnishings), while others provide simple lodgings and a hearty meal.

If you work with a farmstay provider such as **Rural Tourism** or **Rural Holidays NZ**, you can ask them for recommendations based on your interests and budget. A typical reservation includes overnight lodging, breakfast, and dinner. Check to see whether lunch is also included with your booking. Rural Tourism offers the choice of standard or deluxe options; "deluxe" ensures your own ensuite, private bathroom, whereas "standard" usually includes a shared bathroom.

Some farmstays offer accommodations without meals included. These "self-catered" accommodations may be a shared dorm, a cottage, or a suite attached to the main house. The self-catering option works best if you're staying in less remote areas, where you're close to restaurants or grocery stores.

COSTS

Farmstays cost less than most hotels. Guests can expect to pay between $100-$200 per person, per night. Unlike New Zealand's burgeoning industry of luxury lodges (and upmarket winery stays), which can charge upwards of $300 per night, farmstays tend to have more of a "down home" feel, and this is reflected in the price.

WHAT CAN I DO ON THE FARM?

A sheep-shearing marathon

Just-picked Cabernet Sauvignon grapes

Farmstay hosts are keen to share their lifestyle with international visitors. Here are a few activities you might observe or participate in:

Guided tour of the farm: Don a spare pair of galoshes and some overalls before getting into a four-wheel drive or climbing on the back of a tractor to explore the terrain. You'll have the opportunity to interact with farm animals while farming activities are viewed and explained.

Milking cows: Depending on the farm, this could be a vast, machinery-operated process in a milking shed, where you might watch hundreds of cows being milked in tandem, or perhaps you'll join your host with their resident cow and nothing more than a tin pail.

Harvesting produce: Depending on the season and the farm's particular produce, you could find yourself armed with a basket as you pick a bushel of blueberries, apricots, or cherries. But you won't be put to work if you don't

want to be, and some farms may not consider it safe for visitors to take part in the harvest, depending on the types of machinery used.

Sheep shearing: A day's shearing has been compared by more than one shearer to running a marathon, and seeing a team shear 300 sheep in a day will make you tired just watching. Shearing occurs

DINING ON THE FARM

Some farmstays offer gourmet meals with wine pairings, while others offer more humbler farm fare. Most farms provide home-grown vegetables and meat from the farm, or at least offer meals made from locally sourced ingredients.

Traditional dishes likely to make it on the menu include a classic roast dinner—lamb, chicken, or beef, depending on the farm—with home-harvested vegetables and gravy, followed by a fruit crumble or another New Zealand staple: Pavlova (an airy meringue) with fresh whipped cream and fruit. If you visit during the summer months, you're likely to eat barbecue and overdo it on smoky, grilled lamb chops and potato salad. Discuss any special dietary needs when you make your reservation.

Tending to dairy calves in Westland

FAMILIES & FARMSTAYS

Most farmstays are family friendly, offering activities designed to appeal to a range of ages, including horseback riding, feeding farm animals, sheep shearing demonstrations, forest walks, and river swims.

Farmstays offering self-contained accommodations, such as cottages, are a fantastic option if you're traveling with your children. You get the perks of being off the hotel circuit, but can still spread out and make the place your own.

Inquire ahead to make sure the farm you're staying at has animals that are friendly and comfortable being touched and hand-fed. Many smaller farms are better able to provide these experiences. The larger working farms do not always have animals that closely interact with children or adults, and you may miss out on a hands-on experience.

Huntaway Lodge (⊕ *www.huntawaylodge. co.nz*) is a good family-friendly option. It is a small, family-run farm; their main business are alpacas, but there are also a smattering of ducks, pigs, "chooks" (New Zealand slang for chickens), cows, and a very mellow horse.

about four times per year, so there's a good chance you'll get to see shearers in action. Otherwise, some farms will shear a sheep at the time of your visit, so you can see how it's done.

Feeding and interacting with farm animals: Almost every farm will provide the opportunity to feed the animals, whether throwing grain to the chickens, feeding lambs, kids, and calves, or tossing hay to sheep and cattle.

Riding tractors, trail bikes, and horses: During feeding seasons, you may be able to hitch a tractor ride with a farmer as they disperse hay among the stock. Or you could find yourself on the back of a trail bike rounding up sheep.

Lambing: The months of August to October are lambing time. Lambing tends to be a hands-off experience from a farmer's perspective, as sheep often give birth in pastures unassisted. If you time your visit with the beginning of lambing season, you'll be able to see sheep giving birth, help tag newborns (putting a plastic tag on their ears to help keep track of them), and bottle-feed lambs.

Many kids enjoy hand-feeding lambs

WHEN SHOULD I GO?

The season of your trip will help shape your farmstay experience. The warmer, drier months are the liveliest time of year on a farm, and less rain also means you're less likely to get bogged down in the mud in the "paddocks," or pastures. Winter is generally the quietest time on a farm. Rural Tourism has a chart on their Web site that describes the activities on cattle, sheep, dairy, and deer farms on a monthly basis to help you time your visit.

How far in advance should you plan your farmstay? Last-minute reservations don't allow host farmers much time out of their schedule to prepare for your stay. For best results, reserve at least a few days in advance (a few weeks is better).

A tip from Rural Tourism: Remember that the farm is a working establishment. Please be guided by your hosts with regards to safety on the property. Don't forget to shut farm gates, and keep away from any paddock or areas that the farmer asks you to avoid.

Lunch in the garden at Four Peaks Lodge

Note that farmstays booked through **Rural Tourism** and **Rural Holidays NZ** must comply with the New Zealand Government's health and safety regulations; you may not be able to take the tractor for a spin or go horseback riding. Let Rural Tourism and Rural Holidays know in advance what you're interested in, and they can advise accordingly.

USEFUL WEB SITES & RESOURCES

Rural Tourism (⊕ *www.ruraltourism.co.nz*) is New Zealand's largest database of farmstays. You can choose from a range of rural B&Bs and farms (cattle, beef, dairy, sheep, etc.), selecting by region and type of farm. The detailed descriptions make it easy to compile a shortlist. Upon choosing a farm that captures your interest, Rural Tourism staff then work with you to arrange your stay and make sure your requirements are met.

Rural Holidays NZ (⊕ *www.ruralholidays. co.nz*) is also a national database of more than 500 farmstays, country home stays, and city home stays, divided by region. Descriptions of each property are brief and frustratingly coded; however, staff are helpful and come from both a farming and tourism background. They avoid listing properties

with self-contained accommodation, preferring for guests to fully immerse themselves in rural New Zealand life.

The **New Zealand Tourism Board** (⊕ *www.newzealand.com*) provides a massive database of accommodations, sights, and activities listings, along with general information about New Zealand. The farmstay section of the database has about 100 listings, and you can contact each property directly and make your own booking.

The **New Zealand Tourism Guide** (⊕ *www.tourism.net.nz*) includes a national database of accommodations that are thematically grouped (farmstays, winery stays, eco-lodges, etc.). Similar to the New Zealand Tourism Board site, you can make your own inquiries and bookings.

MAKETU

About halfway between Tauranga and Whakatane is the small seaside village of Maketu, one of the area's least developed places and one of the first points of Māori landfall.

Briar's Seaside Ride. The most highly recommended horse trekkers in the Bay of Plenty, the guides will ask for your height, approximate weight, and level of experience before assigning you to a gentle plodder or a galloping steed. The trek will take you across paddocks, over hills, through sand dunes, and down to the beach. Treks start at 1½ hours long, or you can go all day. Riding hats, gloves, and wet weather gear all provided. Booking essential. They accept cash only, but you can pay through their Web site or pick up vouchers from the Tauranga Information Centre. ⊠ *Newdicks Beach Rd., Maketu* ☎ *07/533–2582* ⊕ *www. briarshorsetrek.co.nz* ✆ *Prices start from $70 for 1½ hrs*

Maketu Pies. You'll find maketu pies in almost every supermarket and dairy throughout the country, but this little pie shop is where it all begins. Hardly haute cuisine, the humble pie is one of New Zealand's icons—you have to at least try one. ⊠ *Corner of Little Waihi and Beach Rds., Maketu* ☎ *07/533–3458* ⊕ *www.maketupies.co.nz* ☉ *Mon.-Fri. 6:30–3; closed weekends.*

$$$ ✕ **Maketu Seaside Cafe.** With a wraparound enclosed porch overlooking the beach, and a good range of chowders, toasted sandwiches, fish-and-chips, and cakes, this is as good a place as any to take time out and enjoy the superslow pace of Maketu, particularly after a morning of horse trekking. If you're staying in Maketu overnight, come down for some slow-roasted lamb shanks for dinner. ⊠ *2 Townpoint Rd., Maketu* ☎ *07/533–2381* ⊕ *www.seasidecafe. co.nz* ▭ *No credit cards.*

$$–$$$ ⊡ **Hotel on Devonport.** At the most central hotel in Tauranga, each earth-toned room has a balcony looking over the city, the harbor, or the port. It's a groovy little place with a big-city character, especially in terms of design and attitude. In winter, you'll be greeted with a huge fire in the foyer (along with a complimentary drink). **Pros:** smart; modern; close to town. **Cons:** slightly impersonal vibe. ⊠ *72 Devonport Rd.* ☎ *07/578–2668* ⊕ *www.hotelondevonport.net.nz* ✆ *38 rooms* ⟐ *In-room: Safe, kitchen, refrigerator, Internet. In-hotel: Room service, laundry service, parking (free), no-smoking rooms* ▭ *AE, DC, MC, V* ⊙❘ *BP* ⊹ *B3.*

$$–$$$ ⊡ **Ocean Paradise Motel.** One of the few motels in Mount Maunganui, this low-lying stucco building only has four studio suites, two of which look out onto Maunganui Beach across the road. The rooms are comfortably furnished and quite inviting. But, they are compact, with the whirlpool adjacent to the bed. **Pros:** proximity to beach and Maunganui attractions. **Cons:** reserved style of hospitality. ⊠ *30 Marine Pde., Mount Maunganui* ☎ *07/574–3625 or 0800/303–160* ⊕ *www.ocean-waves.co.nz* ✆ *4 rooms* ⟐ *In-room: No phone, kitchen, Internet, Wi-Fi. In-hotel: Laundry facilities, parking (free)* ▭ *MC, V* ⊹ *B1.*

$$–$$$ ⊡ **Papamoa Beach Top 10 Holiday Resort.** This resort complex has the
★ widest range of accommodations in the area, and they're all on the beach, about five minutes down the road from the madding Mount

Maunganui crowd. If you feel like roughing it, campsites begin at $15. There are also spartan cabins, where you'll need to bring your own bed linens, and bathrooms and kitchen are shared. Or you can stretch out in one of the private rooms, or the spacious, light-filled, cedar-wood suites; the decks are built onto the sand dunes, a couple of feet from the water. This property is popular and the "seaside villas" make a fantastic base for the region. **Pros:** wide range of accommodations; cheap; on the beach. **Cons:** gets wildly busy over summer; can be noisy. ⊠ *535 Papamoa Beach Rd.* ☎ *07/572–0816* ⊕ *www.papamoabeach.co.nz* ⇨ *260 campsites, 9 cabins, 13 rooms, 13 suites* ⋄ *In-room: No a/c, no phone, kitchen, refrigerator, no TV (some). In-hotel: Tennis courts, beachfront, laundry facilities, Internet terminal, parking (free), some pets allowed, no-smoking rooms* ⊟ *MC, V* ⊹ *D3.*

$$ 🏨 **Puriri Park Boutique Hotel.** In the mass of Tauranga's central hotels, this Spanish Revival–influenced property is priced just above the nearby motels but is still less expensive than its location and facilities would suggest. The spacious rooms have private balconies and solid oak work-tables. Breakfast can be provided, and for lunch and dinner, you can walk to a selection of nearby restaurants that have a "charge-back" arrangement with the hotel. **Pros:** comfortable; clean; close to town. **Cons:** slightly tacky furnishings. ⊠ *32 Cameron Rd.* ☎ *07/577–1480 or 0800/478–7474* ⊕ *www.puriripark.co.nz* ⇨ *21 suites* ⋄ *In-room: Kitchen (some), refrigerator, Internet. In-hotel: Room service, pool, laundry service, parking (free)* ⊟ *AE, DC, MC, V* ⊹ *A2.*

$$$$ 🏨 **Ridge Country Retreat.** Set on 35 acres—a short drive from town—
Fodor's Choice the lodge overlooks a brilliant green valley, all the way to Mauao and
★ the ocean. The outdoor pool has stellar views. The in-room hot tubs and the private outdoor baths are filled with geothermal mineral water sourced on the property. Beautifully furnished suites have private balconies and heated bathroom floors, but the best room is the dining room, with its huge stone fireplace, a wall of windows, and a 22-foot-high beamed ceiling. Dinner is a five-course affair, and breakfast is whatever you want it to be; hosts Penny and Joanne pull out all the stops. Massage and beauty treatments are also available, and there are walking paths throughout the native forest on the property. Some guests like to arrive by helicopter. **Pros:** sophisticated hosts; handsome lodge without being overdone; superb location. **Cons:** pricey. ⊠ *300 Rocky Cutting Rd.* ☎ *07/542–1301* ⊕ *www.rcr.co.nz* ⇨ *11 suites* ⋄ *In-room: No a/c, refrigerator, Internet, Wi-Fi. In-hotel: Restaurant, room service, bar, pool, gym, spa, parking (free), no kids under 12, no-smoking rooms* ⊟ *AE, DC, MC, V* ⧖⊙⧗ *AI* ⊹ *D3.*

$$$ 🏨 **The Sebel Trinity Wharf.** Perched over the edge of Tauranga Harbor, this
★ is probably the most luxurious hotel in the Bay of Plenty. Three stories high and built across three piers, the best of the rooms curve around the water's edge and look out into the harbor. Rooms are spacious and simply designed; local artwork catches the red of the pohutukawa trees that flank the hotel. All of the bathrooms have bathtubs (unusual in this region) along with heated floors. The hotel's reasonably priced restaurant, Halo ($$$), is frequented by locals and guests alike for meals or cocktails. On Friday nights a pianist turns out jazz numbers

CLOSE UP

Whakaari (White) Island

With its billowing plumes of steam, the active volcano of Whakaari (White) Island makes for an awesome geothermal experience. Forty-nine kilometers (29 mi) off the coast of Whakatane, the island is New Zealand's only active marine volcano—and New Zealand's most active volcano overall. Although the last major eruption was in 2000, steam issues continuously from the many *fumeroles* (vents) and from the central crater, and the area reeks of sulfur. The island itself is eerie but exquisite, with fluorescent sulfuric crystal formations and boiling mud pools.

The least expensive way to see the island is by boat, and, as a bonus, you might see dolphins, seals, and even a whale en route. Peter and Jenny Tait, the official guardians of White Island, operate ★ **White Island Tours**

(☎ 0800/733–529 ⊕ www.whiteisland. co.nz). Upon arrival, you are issued a hard hat and gas mask and taken for a walk around the volcano and through the remains of a sulfur mine. The cost is $175 and includes lunch. Bring your bathing suit in summer. The main trip is not suitable for small children—check with the tour operators for their family-friendly tours. Alternatively, you can get a bird's-eye view of the steaming hulk. **Vulcan Helicopters** (☎ 0800/804–354 ⊕ www.vulcanheli.co.nz) has a three-seat and a four-seat helicopter; pilot–owner Mark Law is also an authority on the island. The 40-minute return flight and 1½ hour walk on the island starts at $455. **East Bay Aviation** (☎ 07/308–7760) has a four-seater aircraft that flies over the island's crater; 55-minute trips cost $199.

4

on the grand piano in the lobby. Despite the hotel's clearly "high-end" status, staff are extremely friendly and unpretentious. **Pros:** fantastic views; comfortable, spacious rooms; warm staff. **Cons:** ten-minute walk into the city center; some rooms have parking-lot views. ⊠ *51 Dive Crescent, Tauranga* ☎ *07/577–8700* ⊕ *www.mirvachotels.com/sebel-trinity-wharf-tauranga* ↻ *120 rooms* ⚒ *In-room: Safe, kitchen (some), Internet. In-hotel: Restaurant, room service, bar, pool, gym, laundry service, parking (free)* ▭ *AE, D, DC, MC, V* ⊹ *A2.*

WHAKATANE

100 km (62 mi) southeast of Tauranga.

For yet another chance to laze on the beach, Whakatane (fah-kah-*tah*-nee) claims to be the North Island's sunniest town. This was landfall on New Zealand for the first migratory Māori canoes, and the fertile hinterland was the first part of the country to be farmed.

GETTING HERE AND AROUND

Whakatane is 97 km (60 mi) south of Tauranga. It's an easy 1½ hour drive down the Pacific Highway along a spectacular stretch of coast. Don't be lulled into breaking the speed limit, an easy thing to do when you've got one eye on the ocean and one on the road.

ESSENTIALS

Bus Depot InterCity Whakatane Depot (✉ *Quay and Kakahoroa Sts.* ☎ *07/306–2030*).

Hospital Whakatane Hospital (✉ *Stewart St., Whakatane* ☎ *07/306–0999*).

Visitor Information Whakatane Visitor Information Centre (✉ *Quay and Kakahoroa Sts., on the Strand* ☎ *07/306–2030* ⊕ *www.whakatane.com*).

EXPLORING

The most popular and safest swimming beach in the area is the 11-km-long (7-mi-long) **Ohope Beach**, in Ohope, a 10-minute drive east of Whakatane. Take the well-signposted Ohope Road out of Whakatane's town center and over the hills to the beach. Pohutukawa Avenue, Ohope's main road, runs parallel to the beach, flanked by lush native forest, citrus trees, and grazing cows, as well as private residences. The beach is far less developed than others along the bay.

NEED A BREAK?

Just beyond Ohope, it's not uncommon to see locals out on the Ohiwa Harbor mudflats harvesting dinner. If you don't want to "pick your own," head for **Ohiwa Oyster Farm** (☎ *07/312–4565*). This roadside oyster shack is the place for oysters by the basket, a burger, fish-and-chips, Māori *rewena* (a traditional leavened bread), whitebait fritters, crayfish, and *kina* (akin to a sea urchin).

The native forest reserves around Whakatane provide a range of bushwalks and **hiking trails.** The 6-km (4-mi) walkway called *Nga Tapuwae o Toi* ("the footprints of Toi") is named for a descendant of Tiwakawaka, one of the first Māori to settle in New Zealand. It's divided into eight shorter walks that take you past historic pā sites, along the coastline and the Whakatane River, around Kohi Point (which separates Whakatane from Ohope), and through the Ohope and Makaroa Bush Scenic Reserves. Walks range from one to three hours. No guide is necessary, and most tourist operators and information centers in Whakatane stock free trail maps. The trailhead is on Canning Place, behind the Whakatane Hotel on the corner of George Street and the Strand. Follow the steps up the cliff and you'll be at the beginning of the trail. For an easier wander (30 minutes round-trip), start at the west end of Ohope Beach and head over to Otarawairere, a delightful secluded cove. ■TIP➔ Some trail crossings depend on the tidal schedule, so be sure to check low-tide times.

If you've a hankering to see the stars from an antipodean perspective, check out the **Whakatane Observatory.** With a claim to the clearest skies in the country, on a good night you can see some rare sights indeed, such as the "jewel box," a cluster of multi-colored stars near the Southern Cross. Nighttime presentations are informal and informative. ✉ *Hurinui Ave., Whakatane* ☎ *07/308–6495* ⊕ *www.skyofplenty.com* ☎ *$10* ☉ *Tues. and Fri., opens between 7:30 PM and 8:30 PM (depending on how late the sun sets).*

SPORTS AND THE OUTDOORS

Fishing, diving, and swimming with dolphins are popular activities in the Whakatane area. The water surrounding White Island has some extremely warm pockets, with abundant, colorful marine life.

DOLPHIN- AND WHALE-WATCH-ING

For closer aqueous encounters of the mammalian kind, **Whales and Dolphin Watch** (⊠ 96 The Strand ☎ 0800/354–7737 or 07/308–2001 ⊕ www.whalesanddolphinwatch.co.nz) runs four-hour cruises. Wet suits and snorkels for swimming with the dolphins are provided (or just watch). From November though March, cruises leave daily at 7:15 AM, 8:30 AM, and 1 PM; other times of the year cruise times are dependent on weather and demand. Costs range from $110 to $150.

FISHING AND DIVING

Diveworks provide diving and fishing trips on their 33-foot Sportfisher speedboat. They'll take you out fishing or diving around local reefs and bays, to the "Seafire" shipwreck, or to Whale Island for a swim with dolphins. ⊠ The Strand, Whakatane ☎ 07/308–5896 or 0800/308–5896 ⊕ www.diveworks-charters.com ✉ $80 for a half day fishing; $100 for a half day diving; $150 to swim with dolphins.

John Baker (⊠ 15A James St. ☎ 07/307–0015 ⊕ www.divenfish.co.nz) is one of the area's best-known dive masters. For $1,320, he'll take up to six people out to White Island and some of the smaller nearby islands for an overnight trip of fishing or diving (or both) on his 40-foot boat. Wetsuit and fishing-rod rentals are available, as are $750 half-day trips. A certified diving instructor and local character with stints as a Māori All Black and a radio announcer in his past, **Val Baker** (⊠ Matata ☎ 07/322–2340 ✉ anthea.val@clearnet.co.nz) has been diving for more than 30 years. He can take you to some of the smaller islands in the bay in his 18-foot "fizzboat." Wetsuits and snorkels are provided, and if you want to fish off the boat, he'll provide gear for that, too. ■ TIP→ Ask him to show you the shell of a giant mussel (all that's left of a good meal) he caught in the Cook Strait. Costs begin at around $100 for a half day. He also gives a four-day intensive diving course for beginners.

WHERE TO EAT

$ CAFÉ

✕ **The Bean.** Mellow jazz, and drum and bass plays in the background, local art graces the walls, and the retro couches and armchairs are a great spot to chill out and enjoy a coffee, which is freshly roasted every day in the café. When you walk in you'll see—and smell—the roasting machine. ⊠ 72 The Strand, Whakatane ☎ 07/307–0494 ☐ MC, V ☺ Weekdays 11–3; closed weekends.

$–$$ NEW ZEALAND

✕ **Peejays Coffee House.** Peejays specializes in breakfast. If you're preparing for a trip out to White Island, nab a table on the deck to get an eyeful of your destination, and then fuel up with a traditional Kiwi spread of sausages, bacon, eggs, and toast. ⊠ 15 The Strand E. ☎ 07/308–9588 or 0800/242–299 ☐ AE, MC, V ☺ Mon.–Sat. 6:30 AM –11 AM, Sun. 6:30 AM–1 PM.

$$$–$$$$ NEW ZEALAND

✕ **The Wharf Shed.** At this restaurant on the Whakatane marina, the dinner menu focuses on seafood, bought that day from the quay outside the kitchen door. However, it pays to check out the meat dishes, such as the lamb shank braised in locally brewed Mata Manuka beer;

the restaurant has received the "New Zealand Beef and Lamb Award for Excellence" multiple times. Seared scallops with cucumber salsa is also a popular choice. The marine theme continues in the interior, with models of yachts, a ship's figurehead, and tools of the fishing trade; large windows look out over the water. There are tables outside on the quay, too—a good spot for a bowl of chowder or for coffee and dessert. Try the "Berry White Island," their signature dish, a meringue-and-custard stack topped by an "eruption" of berries. The kitchen closes at 8:30, but you can linger until 10. ⊠ *Whakatane Wharf, The Strand E* ☎ *07/308–5698* ⊕ *www.wharfshed.com* ⊟ *AE, DC, MC, V.*

WHERE TO STAY

$$ ⊞ **Moanarua.** Hosts Miria and Taroi Black provide their own variety of Māori *manaakitanga* (hospitality). The doorway of the guest *whare* (house) is framed with traditional carvings representing the *kaitiaki* (caretakers) of Miria and Taroi's respective tribes, while the interior is decorated with contemporary Māori art, such as *harekeke* (woven flax). Murals, sculpture, and carvings in the garden depict the cultural history of the area. Those staying longer than two nights are invited to share a hāngi (a traditional method of cooking food). Miria and Taroi's hospitality, humor, and stories make up for the whare's humble furnishings; this is a smaller-scale, more intimate version of a Māori cultural experience provided on tours. **Pros:** welcoming, relaxed environment; close to beach. **Cons:** not luxurious; may be too far off-the-beaten-track for some. ⊠ *2 Hoterini St., Ohope Beach* ☎ *07/312–5924* ⊕ *www. moanarua.co.nz* ⤴ *1 room* ♨ *In-room: No a/c, no phone, kitchen, refrigerator, DVD, Internet. In-hotel: Spa, water sports, laundry facilities* ⊟ *No credit cards* �‖ *CP.*

$$ ⊞ **White Island Rendezvous.** Convenient if you're heading out to White Island, this motel run by the owners of White Island Tours is across the road from the marina and within walking distance of town. Rooms have a somewhat nautical cream-and-blue color scheme and fish-theme art on the walls. **Pros:** friendly hosts; clean and relaxed. **Cons:** basic. ⊠ *15 The Strand E.* ☎ *07/308–9500 or 0800/242–299* ⊕ *www.whiteisland.co.nz* ⤴ *22 studios, 2 suites* ♨ *In-room: No a/c, kitchen, refrigerator. In-hotel: Restaurant, laundry facilities* ⊟ *AE, DC, MC, V.*

East Coast and the Volcanic Zone

WORD OF MOUTH

"I think those who are disappointed in Rotorua don't realize that you have to get out of the city to see the incredible scenery. Waimangu Volcanic Park was a highlight of a trip filled with beauty. To me, it's a 'must-see.' We're returning on our next trip."

—Songdoc

WELCOME TO EAST COAST AND THE VOLCANIC ZONE

TOP REASONS TO GO

★ **Hiking and Walking:** The eastern coast of the North Island has several excellent bushwalking trails, including the Tongariro Crossing, which brings you through the alpine areas in Tongariro National Park. Some of the most rugged bush in the country is in Te Urewera National Park.

★ **Māori Ceremonial Feast:** Rotorua may be the best place in New Zealand to try the Māori feast known as a *hāngi*.

★ **Soaking:** In Rotorua and Taupo, thermal springs are on tap. You can soak in your own thermal bath in even the cheapest hotels in Rotorua or take advantage of public facilities such as Polynesian Spa.

★ **World-Class Fishing:** Central North Island is trout country. You can get out on any of the designated lakes and waterways if you have your own gear and a fishing license—but a local guide can take you to the right spots.

1 The Rotorua Area.
Home of geothermal unrest and oddities, Rotorua today is almost entirely a product of the late-19th-century fad for spa towns; its elaborate bathhouses and formal gardens date to this era. You'll find surreal wonders that include limestone caverns, volcanic wastelands, steaming geysers, and bubbling, hissing ponds.

2 Lake Taupo and Tongariro National Park.
Fishing and water sports are popular activities in Lake Taupo, the largest lake in New Zealand, and rivers running into it. The area has its share of geothermal oddities. Tongariro National Park, dominated by three volcanic peaks, has some great otherworldly hiking trails.

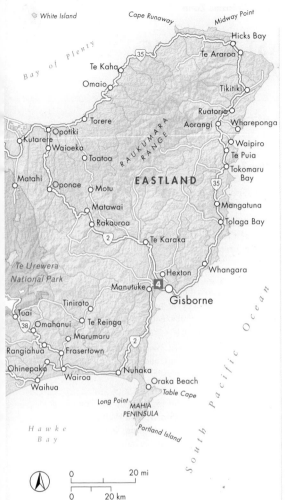

White Island
Cape Runaway
Midway Point
Hicks Bay
Te Araroa
Bay of Plenty
35
Te Kaha
Omaio
Tikitiki
Ruatoria
Aorangi
Whareponga
Torere
Opotiki
Waipiro
Kutarere
Te Puia
Waioeka
Toatoa
Tokomaru Bay
Matahi
Oponae
Motu
EASTLAND
35
Mangatuna
Matawai
Tolaga Bay
Rakauroa
Te Karaka
2
Te Urewera National Park
Hexton
Whangara
Manutuke
4
Gisborne
Tiniroto
Tuai
38
Omahanui
Te Reinga
Marumaru
Rangiahua
Frasertown
2
Ohinepaka
Nuhaka
Wairoa
Oraka Beach
Waihua
Table Cape
Long Point
MAHIA PENINSULA
Portland Island
Hawke Bay
South Pacific Ocean
RAUKUMARA RANGE

N
0   20 mi
0   20 km

GETTING ORIENTED

This region lies to the northeast of the North Island, and covers some of the most naturally splendid areas in the country. The main towns are busy despite being connected by isolated roads that wind across mountain ranges through vast areas of bush. Expect steaming thermal regions, rolling farmland, or peaceful sun-drenched vineyards.

5

3 **Napier and Hawke's Bay.** On the shores of Hawke Bay, you'll find a fabulous architectural anomaly: the town of Napier, a time capsule of colorful art deco architecture. The Hawke's Bay countryside is thick with vineyards, as this is one of the country's major wine-producing areas.

4 **Gisborne and Eastland.** Gisborne is the area's largest town. Above it juts the largely agricultural East Cape, a sparsely populated area ringed with stunning beaches, and inland lies the haunting beauty of Te Urewera National Park.

THE EAST COAST AND THE VOLCANIC ZONE PLANNER

Planning Your Time

Start in Rotorua and then head down to Taupo and the National Park region. If fishing is your game, stop over at Turangi. Napier and Hastings, with Hawke's Bay, is an area not to be missed. Prepare for a lengthy stretch to Gisborne and the East Cape, and if you have the time (allow for 2½ hours each way and don't forget to fill the tank in Wairoa), take the rugged side road to Lake Waikaremoana. It's a little piece of heaven.

North Island's East Coast and volcanic zone include some of the country's most popular attractions. Plenty of excellent tours and bus routes hit most highlights, but having your own vehicle gives you the flexibility to seek out an untrammeled scenic spot or that lesser-known-but-outstanding winery.

Information centers known as "i-SITEs" are found throughout the region. They supply free information and brochures on where to go and how to get there, available accommodations, car hire, bus services, restaurants, and tourist venues. The centers often serve as bus and tour stops.

Getting Here and Around

Air Travel

Air New Zealand runs regular flights from Wellington, Auckland, Christchurch, Dunedin, and Queenstown into Napier, Gisborne, and Rotorua. Flights from Napier to Auckland or Wellington take about an hour; to Christchurch roughly two hours.

Contact Air New Zealand (☎ 0800/737–000 ⊕ www.airnewzealand.co.nz).

Bus Travel

Inter-City, along with their subsidiary company **Newmans,** runs regular bus services for the entire region. Comfortable, reasonably priced, and efficient, they are particularly useful to backpackers and people who are in no particular hurry.

Contacts Inter-City (⊕ www.intercitycoach.co.nz). **Newmans** (⊕ www.newmanscoach.co.nz).

Car Travel

The best way to travel in this region is by car. Rotorua is about three hours from Auckland. Take Highway 1 south past Hamilton and Cambridge to Tirau, where Highway 5 breaks off to Rotorua. Roads in this region are generally in good condition.

The main route between Napier and the north is Highway 5. Driving time from Taupo is two hours, five hours if you're coming straight from Auckland. Highway 2 is the main route heading south; it connects Hastings and Napier. Driving time to Wellington is five hours.

The most direct route from the north to Gisborne is to follow State Highway 2 around the Bay of Plenty to Opotiki, Eastland's northern gateway, then continue to Gisborne through the Waioeka Gorge Scenic Reserve. The drive from Auckland to Gisborne takes seven hours. South from Gisborne, continuing on Highway 2, you pass through Wairoa, about 90 minutes away, before passing Napier, Hawke's Bay, and Wairarapa on the way to Wellington, about 7½ hours by car.

Restaurants

Rotorua has the area's most diverse dining scene. You can find anything from Indian to Japanese fare, or try a Māori *hāngi* (meal cooked in an earth oven or over a steam vent). Hawke's Bay is another hot spot; its winery restaurants emphasize sophisticated preparations and food-and-wine pairings. Around Eastland, which is so laid-back it's nearly horizontal, the choices are simpler, and you'll be treated with the area's characteristic friendliness. One thing you won't find on any menu is fresh trout. Laws prohibit selling this fish, but if you catch a trout, chefs at most lodging establishments will cook it for you.

Dressing up for dinner, or any other meal, is a rarity, expected at only the most high-end lodges and restaurants.

Hotels

Accommodations range from superexpensive lodges to multistory hotels and a great selection and price range of motels. Another excellent option are the bed-and-breakfast establishments in town centers or in the depths of the countryside where you can succumb to the silence, curl up, and read a book, or cast a fly in a quiet stream.

Rotorua has lodgings in all price ranges. If you're willing to stay out of the town center, you can find bargain rates virtually year-round. In both Rotorua and Taupo, many hotels and motels give significant discounts on their standard rates in the off-season, from June through September. For stays during the school holidays in December and January, book well in advance. Also note that peak season in Tongariro National Park and other ski areas is winter (June–September); summer visitors can usually find empty beds and good deals. Many places, even the fanciest lodges, don't have air-conditioning, as the weather doesn't call for it.

WHAT IT COSTS IN NEW ZEALAND DOLLARS					
	¢	$	$$	$$$	$$$$
Restaurants	under $10	$10–$15	$15–$20	$20–$30	over $30
Hotels	under $75	$75–$125	$125–$200	$200–$300	over $300

Prices are per person for a main course at dinner, or the equivalent. Prices are for a standard double room in high season, including 12.5% tax.

Safety

Remember that driving is on the left, and in places roads can be quite narrow and winding. Always keep the tank full, as gas stations in country areas can be hard to come by. Cameras and other valuables left in cars are magnets for thieves, so don't leave them in view. Always lock your vehicle even if only leaving it for a short time.

When to Go

Mid-November through mid-April is the best time in central and eastern North Island. The weather is balmy and everything is open. This is also the season for vineyard festivals, so keep an eye on the local calendars. Try to avoid the school holidays (from mid-December to late January), when the roads and hotels get clogged with Kiwi vacationers. To see the gannet colony at Cape Kidnappers, you need to go between October and March, when the birds are nesting and raising their young.

Hawke's Bay and Gisborne can be remarkably mild in winter, but Rotorua and Taupo can get quite cold. If you want to do some skiing, August is the month to hit the slopes of Tongariro National Park.

5

TONGARIRO NATIONAL PARK

Tongariro National Park is the oldest national park in New Zealand and the largest on the North Island. Given to the nation by the Ngati Tuwharetoa people in 1887, this stunning mountainous region provided much of the dramatic scenery for the *Lord of the Rings* films.

The park has a spectacular combination of dense forest, wild open countryside, crater lakes, barren lava fields, and rock-strewn mountain slopes. Its rugged beauty and convenient location, almost in the center of the North Island, make it the most popular and accessible of New Zealand's parks. Three volcanoes, Tongariro, Ngauruhoe, and Ruapehu, tower above its Central Plateau overlooking miles of untamed country that stretches to the West Coast on one side and to the aptly named Desert Road on the other. The volcanoes are no sleeping giants; Tongariro is the least active, but Ngauruhoe and Ruapehu have both erupted in recent years. In 1995, 1996, and again in 2007, Ruapehu spewed ash, created showers of rock, and released *lahars* (landslides of volcanic debris) that burst through the walls of the crater lake.

BEST TIME TO GO

The best chance for decent weather is November to the end of March. Keep in mind that even during the summer weather ranges from hot and sunny to cool and rainy and even snowy. Expect alpine conditions in winter. The busiest time is between Christmas and New Year. Any time of year make sure to dress for changeable weather.

FUN FACT

Anglers beware! Locals will barely keep a straight face as you drop your line into the waters of the Whangaehu River. Flowing from Ruapehu's crater lake, the river is far too acidic to support fish or any other life form.

PARK HIGHLIGHTS

VOLCANOES

Massive and downright awesome, Tongariro, Ngauruhoe, and Ruapehu dominate from whichever direction one approaches, and the views from the Desert Road are a photographer's dream. Travel from the south on State Highway 1 on a clear day, and the first glimpse of Ruapehu as the road crests will take your breath away. Farther north on the same road, as you tackle a series of hairpin bends, the enormous, almost perfectly truncated cone-shaped bulk of Ngauruhoe looms alongside.

WILD, WILD HORSES

White settlers first brought horses to New Zealand in 1814, and within a few years mobs of feral horses became common. A herd known as the Kaimanawa Wild Horses established itself on the Central Plateau, under the eastern shadow of Mount Ruapehu. For a number of years they have been confined to a protected area, and visitors along the Desert Road (State Highway 1) often see the herd while driving by.

SNOWY PEAKS

In the winter months (June to September) the slopes of Mount Ruapehu come to life with hundreds of skiing and snowboarding enthusiasts. On occasion the runs have to be cleared when the mountains' crater lake threatens to overflow, but this hasn't decreased the area's popularity. The combined fields of Turoa and Whakapapa form the largest ski slope in New Zealand and have brought a measure of prosperity to the one-time sleepy villages of National Park and Ohakune.

TOURS

BY WATER: Cruises on Lake Taupo visit local bays and modern Māori rock carvings. **The Barbary** is a 1920s wooden yacht believed to have once been the property of Errol Flynn. Departures are at 10:30 and 2, and summer evenings at 5 ($40). **Huka Falls River Cruise** runs trips to the falls on the *Maid of the Falls* leaving from Aratiatia Dam (north of Taupo) at 10:30, 12:30, and 2:30. In the summer also at 4:30 ($35).

BY LAND: Tongariro Expeditions runs trips to Tongariro National Park from the Taupo visitor information center and serves the Tongariro Alpine Crossing. Within Taupo, the **Hot Bus** is a hop-on–hop-off service that takes in all the local sights. Each attraction stop costs $15, or you can get an unlimited pass for $30–35. **Paradise Tours** also visits the local attractions in Taupo. Tours start at $85.

5

(above left) Emerald Lakes, (bottom) The crater lake of Mt. Ruhapehu, (above) Lake Taupo

BEST WAYS TO EXPLORE

ON FOOT

The one-day **Tongariro Alpine Crossing** is the park's most famous walk, but there are numerous others. The **Round the Mountain Track** and the **Tongariro Northern Circuit** both take several days. The **Ketetahi Hut Track,** an 8 mi (13 km) walk, joins up with the Tongariro Northern Circuit. Trek to, and through, the volcano craters for mind-blowing views of countryside, lakes, and mountains. For a real out-of-this-world experience, few walks compare to the ones in this park.

ON WATER

There are no navigable rivers in the park, but just outside, visitors will find excellent canoeing on the Whanganui River, the longest navigable river in New Zealand. White-water rafting, canoeing, and excellent trout fishing are available at Turangi.

ON THE LOOKOUT

Bird watchers will enjoy the Lake Rotopounamu Walking Track on the northern side, as well as the Managawhero Forest Walk and the Rimu Track on the western side. Blue duck, North Island robin, whitehead, kereru, fantail, silvereye, and chaffinch are all spotted along the trails. Take a night excursion, and with a bit of luck, see the North Island kiwi. Remember most of the birds stay in the bush, and there is no bush on the higher reaches of the park. Above the bush line it is just bare mountainside.

ECO-TIPS

While in the park, remember these few rules to be an eco-friendly visitor:

Never light fires! They can easily get out of control and spread quickly through bush with disastrous consequences.

If you have a dog keep it under control. Many kiwi birds have been killed by unleashed dogs.

Don't stray from the marked trails; precious native plants are easily crushed by unwary feet.

Anglers should clean their gear before moving to different waters.

And, finally, the golden rule is to take only photographs and leave only footprints.

ONE-DAY ITINERARY

The best one-day itinerary is undoubtedly the **Tongariro Alpine Crossing**. The 11.5 mi (18 km) walk starts and finishes in different places, so make transportation arrangements with a tour operators or your lodgings (*see the Tongariro section later in the chapter*). Good footwear and warm clothing (any time of year) is essential. Bring food and drink; there's none on the track.

The track inclines slowly up Mangatepopo Valley, past a stream and old lava flows. It's a harsh environment for growing vegetation, but moss, lichens, and occasional wetland plants do grow here. It's a steep climb to the Mangetepopo Saddle, which lies between Tongariro and Ngauruhoe, but there are spectacular views on clear days. Then head to the south crater of Tongariro to a ridge leading up Red Crater, the highest point on the track (1,886 m, or 6,120 feet). Here you may smell sulfur, a sure sign that the mountain is still active.

The track is extremely rough underfoot as it descends to three smaller water-filled craters, the Emerald Lakes. Continue across Central Crater to the Blue Lake and the North Crater. Walk downhill to the Ketetahi Hut; take a breather before hiking to the springs of the same name. (They're on private land, so enjoy the impressive steam cloud from a distance.) From here it's all downhill through tussock slopes to the bush line and through forest to your prearranged pickup. You'll delight in the knowledge that you have accomplished something to boast about for years to come.

STAY THE NIGHT

On the northern side, Discovery Lodge is the only lodging where you can get a view of all three volcanoes in one panorama. From here it's a short drive north to Turangi, a small town set on the banks of the Tongariro River, which, is world renowned for trout fishing. On various occasions during their visits to this country, members of the British Royal Family have cast a line here. Try your hand at landing the big one, with or without a guide, or go for a spot of white-water rafting or kayaking. If your limbs ache after all that hiking, the natural hot pools at close-by Tokaanu will ease the pain, and you're right by State Highway 1 ready to head north for Taupo and Rotorua.

(left) South Crater at Mt Tongariro with Mt Ngauruhoe beyond (right) Dome Ridge, Mt. Ruapehu

TE UREWERA NATIONAL PARK

Te Urewera is New Zealand's fourth largest national park, and it protects the biggest area of native forest remaining on the North Island. The ancestral home of the Tuhoe people, the park's main attraction is Lake Waikaremoana, which draws hikers, canoeists, and fishing enthusiasts from around the world.

The remote park is rugged and mountainous. Lake Waikaremoana, formed over 2,000 years ago when a massive landslide blocked the Waikaretaheke River. It's not easily accessible—the road from the north is narrow, winding, and mostly unpaved, and the road from Wairoa is still gravel in parts. However, both roads pass through spectacular countryside of high, misty ridges covered with silver and mountain beech. Waterfalls and streams abound, and on the lower levels the forest giants, rimu, rata, kamahi, totara, and tawa attract native birds like the New Zealand Falcon, Kaka, North Island brown Kiwi and the Kokako. The Lake Waikaremoana Track, one of New Zealand's great walks, is here.

BEST TIME TO GO

The best time to visit the park is in the summer months, October to March. But even then there are many misty, rainy days. Summer is also when local tourists flock to the park, so accommodations may be limited.

FUN FACT

Legend has it that many years ago a Māori chief lay by the fire and his cloak caught fire. His injury is immortalized in the park's name: Ure means penis; wera means burnt

BEST WAY TO EXPLORE

ON FOOT

For the nature lover who likes solitude, Te Urewera is paradise. Tracks by the lake reveal great fishing and bathing spots, and many follow old Māori tracks. Bird-watchers can catch glimpses of native species that are rare in other parts of the country, including the largest surviving population of Kokako. You might even spot native bats, green gecko, and skinks. The most popular walk is the Lake Waikaremoana Track, or Great Lake Walk, a three- to four-day tramp that mostly follows the Western Lake shore. The three- to four-day Manuoha–Sandy Track, takes you to the highest part of the park where on a clear day you can see the volcanoes of Tongariro National Park. Hikes are generally moderate to difficult.

ON THE WATER

Take a canoe trip along the lake shore for a picnic or a spot of fishing. In this secluded green world birdsong and the insect chirps are often the only sounds. The adventurous can kayak to the remote spots around the lake. Kayaks and canoes can be hired at the Aniwaniwa Visitor Centre. The walk to Lake Waikareti, a much smaller lake that stands a thousand feet higher and is 2½ mi to the northeast, is one of the forest's finest.

ON HORSEBACK

Horse trekking is a magnificent way to take in the park, but options are fairly limited. **Ngahere Adventures Horse Treks** (*07/304–9133 www.ngahereadventures.co.nz*) run by Ben and Sharon Hudson offer treks ranging from nine hours to overnight at about $160 to $200 per person.

ECO-TIPS

Park accommodations are quite limited, and most people camp in tents or campervans. There are a number of designated camping grounds that have facilities—usually mattresses, cold water on tap, wood fires, a wood-fired stove (some), and toilets connected to a cesspit. Overnight huts on the Great Lake walk have similar facilities. Eco-friendly tourists will use and respect these amenities, taking away their rubbish, and leaving as little evidence of their stay as possible. Never leave garbage on the tracks, around the lakes, or in the water. In the forest areas walkers should stick to the marked paths in order to avoid trampling or damaging vegetation. Birds nests must never be destroyed or eggs taken, and it is better that they are not approached at all.

5

(top left) On the Lake Waikaremoana Track, (bottom) Forested hiking trail, (top) Korokoro Falls

Updated by
Bob Marriott

When you get to Rotorua, after a trip through the rolling, sheep-speckled fields of the Waikato and the wild Mamaku Ranges, the aptly named "Sulfur City," with its mud pots, geysers, and stinky air, comes as a complete surprise. Rotorua, the mid-island's major city and Māori hub, has been a tourist magnet since the 19th century, when Europeans first heard of the healing powers of local hot springs.

South of Rotorua is the small town of Taupo, which stands alongside Australia's largest lake bearing the same name and is the geographical bull's-eye of the North Island. From the lake, you'll have a clear shot at Ruapehu, the island's tallest peak and a top ski area, and its symmetrically cone-shaped neighbor, Ngauruhoe. Ruapehu dominates Tongariro National Park, a haunting landscape of craters, volcanoes, and lava flows that ran with molten rock as recently as 1988. As part of the Pacific Ring of Fire (a zone that's earthquake- and volcanic-eruption prone), the area's thermal features remain an ever-present hazard—and a thrilling attraction.

Southeast of Lake Taupo lies Hawke's Bay and the laid-back art deco town of Napier with neighboring Hastings. Laze the days away drinking at the local vineyards or to truly get off the beaten path, head north to Gisborne, the easygoing center of isolated Eastland, the thick thumb of land that's east of Rotorua.

THE ROTORUA AREA

Rotorua sits on top of the most violent segment of the Taupo Volcanic Zone, which runs in a broad belt from White Island in the Bay of Plenty to Tongariro National Park south of Lake Taupo. In many parts of this extraordinary area, the earth bubbles, boils, spits, and oozes. Drainpipes steam, flower beds hiss, jewelry tarnishes, and cars corrode. In Rotorua the rotten-egg smell of hydrogen sulfide hangs in the air, and even the local golf course has its own thermal hot spots where a lost ball stays lost forever.

ROTORUA

One thing that many New Zealanders and visitors share is a love-hate relationship with Rotorua (ro-to-*roo*-ah), but every year thousands of local and overseas visitors either brave or ignore the vibe to enjoy what is a vacationer's haven. This unashamedly touristy town has capitalized on nature's gifts to become one of the country's most famous spots. The "Great South Seas Spa," as Rotorua was known, was among the earliest spa ventures in the country—dating as far back as the 1860s.

The city's Māori community traces its ancestry to the great Polynesian migration of the 14th century through the Arawa tribe, whose ancestral home is Mokoia Island in Lake Rotorua. The whole area is steeped in Māori history and legend—for hundreds of years, the Māori have settled by the lake and harnessed the geological phenomena, cooking and bathing in the hot pools.

For stunning scenery and idyllic picnic spots, drive around Lake Rotorua. About halfway around the lake look for Hamurana Springs, a large area of land with free public access where crystal-clear water bubbles from springs forming a river that flows into the lake. Walking through this area you will see birdlife and pass through several groves of magnificent redwood trees.

GETTING HERE AND AROUND

Rotorua Airport (airport code ROT) is 10 km (6 mi) from the city center on Highway 33. Taxi fare to the city is about $25–$32. You could also arrange for a ride ($15–$20) with Super Shuttle; call ahead for a reservation.

Rotorua is easy to get around. The streets follow a neat grid pattern, and walking from the lake to the southern end of town takes only a few minutes. Fenton Street, the wide main drag that comes into town from Taupo, starts around the thermal spot of Whakarewarewa. For about 3 km (2 mi), it's lined with motels and hotels until just before it reaches the lakefront, where it becomes more commercial, with shops, restaurants, and the **Tourism Rotorua Visitor Information Centre,** which has a tour-reservation desk, a map shop operated by the Department of Conservation, and a lost-luggage facility. Right alongside in the same building is an Internet café and a gift shop.

ESSENTIALS

Airport Transfers Rotorua Taxis (☎ *07/348–1111*). **Super Shuttle** (☎ *07/349–3444*).

Bus Depot Rotorua (✉ *Tourism Rotorua Visitor Information Centre, 1167 Fenton St.*).

Car Rentals Avis New Zealand (✉ *Rotorua Airport* ☎ *07/345–7133* ⊕ *www.avis.com/nz*).

Emergency Services Fire, police, and ambulance (☎ *111*).

Hospital Rotorua Hospital ✉ *Pukeroa St.* ☎ *07/348–1199*).

CLOSE UP

The Hinemoa Legend

One of the great Māori love stories has a special local connection, because it takes place on Mokoia Island in Lake Rotorua—and it's a true tale at that. Hinemoa, the daughter of an influential chief, lived on the lakeshore. Because of her father's status she was declared *puhi* (singled out to marry into another chief's family), and the tribal elders planned to choose a husband for her when she reached maturity. Although she had many suitors, none gained the approval of her tribe.

Tutanekai was the youngest son of a family who lived on Mokoia Island. Each of his older brothers had sought the hand of Hinemoa, but none had been accepted. Tutanekai knew that because of his lowly rank he would never win approval from her family. But he was handsome and an excellent athlete—and eventually Hinemoa noticed him and fell in love.

From the lakeshore, Hinemoa would hear Tutanekai play his flute, his longing music drifting across the water. Hinemoa's family, suspicious that their daughter would try to reach the island, beached their canoes so that she could not paddle across to Mokoia. The sound of Tutanekai's flute lured Hinemoa to try to swim to the island. After lashing gourds together to help her float, she slipped into the lake; guided by the music, she reached Mokoia. Cold and naked, she submerged herself in a hot pool, where she was discovered by Tutanekai. Enchanted, he slipped her into his home for the rest of the night. When they were discovered, Tutanekai's family feared an outbreak of war with Hinemoa's tribe, but instead the two tribes were peacefully united.

—Bob Marriott

Visitor Information Tourism Rotorua Visitor Information Centre (☎ *1167 Fenton St.* ☎ *07/348–5179* ⊕ *www.rotoruanz.com*).

EXPLORING

Heading south from the lake takes you to the **Government Gardens,** which occupy a small peninsula. The Māori call this area Whangapiro (fang-ah-*pee*-ro, "evil-smelling place"), an appropriate name for these gardens, where sulfur pits bubble and fume behind manicured rose beds and bowling lawns. The high point is the extraordinary neo-Tudor Bath House. Built as a spa at the turn of the 20th century, it is now the **Rotorua Museum of Art & History.** One room on the ground floor is devoted to the eruption of Mt. Tarawera in 1886. On display are a number of artifacts unearthed from the debris and remarkable photographs of the silica terraces of Rotomahana before the eruption. Don't miss the old bathrooms, where some equipment would be right at home in a torture chamber—one soaking tub even administered electric current to the body. ⊠ *Government Gardens, Arawa St.* ☎ *07/349–4350* ⊕ *www.rotoruamuseum.co.nz* ➲ *$11* ⊙ *Oct.–Apr., daily 9–8; May–Sept., daily 9–5.*

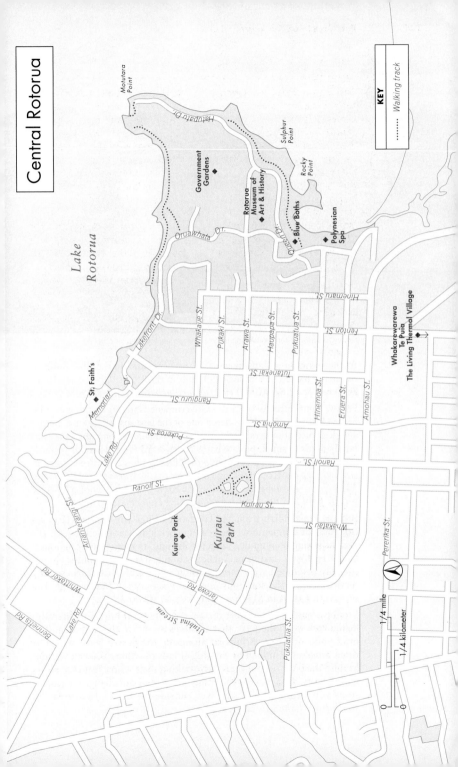

Central Rotorua

KEY
······ Walking track

Lake Rotorua

Motutara Point

Hatupatu Dr.

Government Gardens

Sulphur Point

Rotorua Museum of Art & History

Blue Baths

Rocky Point

Polynesian Spa

Oruawhata Dr.

Queens Dr.

Lakefront Dr.

St. Faith's

Memorial Dr.

Whakaue St.

Pukaki St.

Arawa St.

Haupapa St.

Pukuatua St.

Hinemaru St.

Fenton St.

Whakarewarewa Te Puia The Living Thermal Village

Rangiuru St.

Tutanekai St.

Hinemoa St.

Eruera St.

Amohau St.

Pukeroa St.

Lake Rd.

Amohia St.

Ranolf St.

Ranolf St.

Ararireangi St.

Kuirau St.

Whakatau St.

Pererika St.

Kuirau Park

Kuirau Park

Lake Rd.

Whittaker Rd.

Bennetts Rd.

Tarewa Rd.

Utuhina Stream

Pukuatua St.

1/4 mile
1/4 kilometer
0
0

Geothermal activity around Rotorua means something is always steaming, bubbling, or erupting.

At the southern end of the gardens, you can soak in the **Blue Baths**, a thermally heated swimming pool built in the 1930s. Open daily 10–6. ✉ *Arawa St.* ☎ *07/350–2119* ⊕ *www.bluebaths.co.nz* 🎫 *$9.*

Follow pumice paths from the Government Gardens to the naturally heated **Polynesian Spa**. Considered one of the best spas of its kind, there's a wide choice of mineral baths available, from large communal pools to family pools to small, private baths for two. You can also treat yourself to massage or spa treatments, and the Lake Spa has exclusive bathing in shallow rock pools overlooking Lake Rotorua. ✉ *Hinemoa St.* ☎ *07/348–1328* ⊕ *www.polynesianspa.co.nz* 🎫 *Family or adult pool $13–$20, private pool $25 per ½ hr, lake spa $40* ⊙ *Daily 8 AM–11 PM.*

A short walk north from the lakefront brings you to the Māori *pā* (fortress) of Ohinemutu, the region's original Māori settlement. It's a still-thriving community, centered around its *marae* (meetinghouse) and **St. Faith's**, the lakefront Anglican church. The interior of the church is richly decorated with carvings inset with mother-of-pearl. Sunday services feature the sonorous, melodic voices of the Māori choir. The service at 9 AM is in Māori and English. ✉ *Memorial Dr.*

From St. Faith's it's a short distance to the local hot spot (literally) **Kuirau Park**, a public park that includes an active thermal area. The mud pools and hot springs sit alongside the flower beds, which at times are almost hidden by floating clouds of steam. You can wander around the park or join the locals soaking their weary feet in shallow warm pools. This place is thermally active and can change overnight, so as you stroll around, stay well outside the fences. ✉ *Kuirau St., south from Lake Rd.* 🎫 *Free.*

Whakarewarewa (*fa*-ka-*ree*-wa-*ree*-wa). Whaka, as the locals call it, is the most accessible of the area's thermal spots. It's closest to town, but it's also the most varied, providing insight into Māori culture. The reserve is divided between two different groups; both give you some firsthand exposure to the hot pools, boiling mud, and native culture. **Te Puia** (⊠ *Hemo Rd.* ☎ *07/348–9047* ⊕ *www.tepuia.com*) has a carving school that hosts workshops and, on the grounds, the Pohutu Geyser and silica terraces. The Whaka Māori community was founded by people who moved here from Te Wairoa after the catastrophic eruption in 1886. Don't miss the Nocturnal Kiwi House, where you might spot one of the birds. Open daily October–March 8–6 and April–September 8–5. Guided tour and Māori concert costs $50, with cultural show and dinner costing $99. For another introduction to Māori traditions, visit the **The Living Thermal Village** (⊠ *Tryon St.* ☎ *07/349–3463* ⊕ *www.whakarewarewa.com*), an authentic Māori village in a landscape of geothermal wonders. On the guided tours you'll see thermal pools where villagers bathe, boiling mineral pools, and natural steam vents where residents cook. Arts and crafts are available at local shops. The village is open to visitors daily from 8:30 to 5, and entry fees are $25, or $56 with cultural show and hāngi. Whakarewarewa is at the southern end of Tryon Street, signposted on Fenton and Sala streets. If you don't have a car, sightseeing shuttle buses leave from the visitor center on Fenton Street.

WHERE TO EAT

$$–$$$ ✕ **Capers Epicurean.** The pleasing scent of spices may entice you into
NEW ZEALAND this large, open restaurant, which opens early and closes late. Look for the grilled minute steak on a toasted onion bagel with fresh slaw, Swiss cheese, sautéed mushrooms, and onion jam. Then wander to the dessert cabinet and choose from tiramisu, trifle and crumble, or lemon citron tart, and other goodies. Half of the space is a delicatessen that sells preserves and specialty foods such as chutney made from *kūmara* (a local sweet potato) and *kawa kawa* (a native herb) rub. ⊠ *1181 Eruera St., Rotorua* ☎ *07/348–8818* ⊕ *www.capers.co.nz* ▭ *AE, DC, MC, V.*

$$$ ✕ **The Fat Dog Café and Bar.** The eclectic style and fine food attracts
ECLECTIC young, old, and everyone in between. A line of paw prints trails along the maroon ceiling. Poetry of somewhat dubious merit also winds along the walls, is painted on the chair backs, and even circles the extremities of plates. On the psychedelic blackboard menu look for the sirloin steak with fries, onion rings, and mustard-tomato-mushroom sauce. ⊠ *69 Arawa St., Rotorua* ☎ *07/347–7586* ⊕ *www.fardogcafe.co.nz* ▭ *AE, DC, MC, V* 🍷 *Licensed and BYOB.*

$$$ ✕ **Lewishams.** Green matchboard walls with a classy selection of Euro-
ECLECTIC pean prints are illuminated by cartwheel chandeliers under a plum-colored ceiling at this Bavarian-style restaurant featuring international fare. The furniture is Austrian Tyrol style. Grilled fish of the day with citrus fruit garnished with a spinach flan and parsley potatoes, followed by crepes with a Black Forest filling, is exquisite dining. ⊠ *Lake end, Tutanekai St., Rotorua* ☎ *07/348–1786* ⊕ *www.lewishamsrestaurant. co.nz* ▭ *AE, D, MC, V.*

CLOSE UP

Dinner on the Rocks

Rotorua, the cultural home of the Māori, is the best place to experience a *hāngi*, a traditional Māori feast for which the meal-to-be is cooked over steaming vents. Several local organizations offer the chance to try this slow-cooked treat, paired with a concert—an evening that may remind you of a Hawaiian luau. Don't pass it up!

As a *manuhiri* (guest), you'll get the full treatment, beginning with a *powhiri*, the awe-inspiring Māori welcome that generally includes the *wero* (challenge), the *karanga* (cries of welcome), and the *hongi*, or pressing together of noses, an age-old Māori gesture that shows friendship. If you're not comfortable bouncing noses, a simple handshake will suffice.

While the food cooks, a show begins with haunting harmonious singing, foot stamping, and *poi* twirling

(rhythmic swinging of balls on strings). The performance might raise the hair on the back of your neck—but this will be assuaged with food, glorious food. The lifting of the hāngi will produce pork, sometimes lamb and chicken, kūmara (sweet potato), vegetables, and maybe fish and other seafood, followed by dessert.

Matariki Hāngi and Concert. Starting at 6:30 PM in a hall almost alongside the Royal Lakeside Novotel Hotel, the show is informative and enthusiastic, with ample and delicious food. ☒ *Tutanekai St., lake end* ☎ *0508/442–644* ⊕ *www. novotel.co.nz* ☞ *$60 for food and concert, $28 concert only.* There is a free pick-up service from all local hotels. The **Heritage Hotel** (☒ *Froude and Tryon Sts.* ☎ *07/348–1189*) also has an excellent cultural show and hāngi for $65.

$$$
NEW ZEALAND
★
✕ **Pig & Whistle.** The name winks at this 1940s city landmark's previous incarnation—a police station. This is pub fare at its absolute best: fish-and-chips are a favorite or go for twice-roasted pork belly with thyme dumplings set on oven-roasted vegetables topped with a red wine juice followed by a snooze under the enormous elm tree outside. Live music entertains Friday and Saturday nights. ☒ *1182 Tutanekai St., Rotorua* ☎ *07/347–3025* ⊕ *www.pigandwhistle.co.nz* ⊟ *AE, DC, MC, V.*

$$-$$$$
NEW ZEALAND
★
✕ **Relish.** A pizza oven fed on *manuka* wood (a kind of tea tree) is the heart of the kitchen of this busy modern café. The specialty is slow-cooked homemade food in generous portions. Try the roasted lamb shanks with mashed kūmara (sweet potato), caramelized shallots, stuffed button mushrooms, and a rosemary jus. There is a great selection of pizzas. The wine list is limited but select; the all-day breakfasts are momentous. ☒ *1149 Tutanekai St., Rotorua* ☎ *07/343–9195* ⊟ *AE, DC, MC, V* ⊙ *No dinner Sun.–Wed.*

WHERE TO STAY

$-$$
▦ **Ashleigh Court Motel.** Each well-maintained modern room has an individual hot tub, which helps distinguish this place from the many motels on Fenton Street. It's near Whakarewarewa and the golf course, and not too far to city shops and restaurants. The owner's wife speaks fluent Mandarin. **Pros:** Clean; tidy; reasonably priced; close to Whakarewarewa and the golf course. **Cons:** the owner is a rugby fanatic: fair enough—but he supports Wales! ☒ *337 Fenton St., Rotorua* ☎ *07/348–7456* ⊕ *www.ashleighcourtrotorua.co.nz* ⤵ *13 rooms* ⟳ *In-room: No a/c, kitchen. In-hotel: No-smoking rooms* ⊟ *AE, DC, MC, V.*

¢–$
▦ **Base-Rotorua.** The dorm rooms sleep anywhere from 4 to 12 people and several doubles and a pair of family rooms have private baths and balconies. If you're sore from hiking or hauling luggage, there are two indoor thermal pools and an outdoor heated pool. A youthful buzz and the on-site Lava Bar give this place a high profile. It's by Kuirau Park, a few minutes' walk from the center of town. **Pros:** great to soak in the thermal pools; it's really handy to Kuirau Park. **Cons:** the disco could keep you awake. ☒ *1286 Arawa St., Rotorua* ☎ *07/348–8636* ⊕ *www.stayatbase.com* ⤵ *13 rooms, 18 dorm rooms* ⟳ *In-room: No a/c, no phone, kitchen, no TV. In-hotel: Bars, pools, laundry facilities, Internet terminal* ⊟ *MC, V.*

$$
▦ **Cedar Lodge Motel.** These spacious, modern, two-story units, about 1 km (½ mi) from the city center, are a good value, especially for families. All have a kitchen and lounge on the lower floor, a bedroom on the mezzanine above, and at least one queen-size and one single bed; some have a queen-size bed and three singles. Every unit has its own hot tub in the private courtyard at the back. Green-flecked carpet, smoked-glass tables, and recessed lighting give a clean, contemporary look. Request a room at the back, away from Fenton Street. **Pros:** put the kids to bed in the upstairs room and get in the hot tub. **Cons:** if you get this the wrong way round you might be in trouble! ☒ *296 Fenton St., Rotorua* ☎ *07/349–0300* ⊕ *www.cedarlodgerotorua.co.nz*

5

⤸ *15 rooms* ⚭ *In-room: No a/c, kitchen. In-hotel: Laundry facilities* ▭ *AE, DC, MC, V.*

$$$ 🏨 **Heritage Hotel.** From the massive but welcoming entrance foyer with its giant stone fireplace, to the thermal and lake views from the tower wing, this up-to-the-minute hotel spells class. Next to the Whakarewarewa reserve, it runs a complimentary shuttle service to town. The superb Pohutu Cultural Theatre inside the hotel, with its carvings and giant statue of the Māori deity Maui, is home to a colorful nightly concert and hāngi feast (meal cooked in an earth oven or over a steam vent). At Chapmans Restaurant ($$$), you can indulge in the chicken breast wrapped in triple-smoked bacon with potato-basil pancakes and tomato-chorizo jus, or sample the extensive buffet. **Pros:** top-class accommodations at all levels; a Māori concert and hāngi on the premises. **Cons:** it's close enough to Whakarewarewa to get more than a whiff of the local vapor. ⊠ *Froude and Tryon Sts., Rotorua* 🕾 *07/348–1189* ⊕ *www.heritagehotels.co.nz* ⤸ *203 rooms, 3 suites* ⚭ *In-room: Internet terminal. In-hotel: Restaurant, pool, gym, spa, laundry facilities* ▭ *AE, DC, MC, V.*

¢–$ 🏨 **Kiwi Paka.** This well-maintained lodge overlooking the thermal Kuirau Park is a 10-minute walk out of town. You can take advantage of the area's natural heating by soaking in the thermal pool for free. Rooms range from shares for four or five people to single rooms for $35. Meals at the café are a steal as well. **Pros:** nice quiet location; you could snag an en suite chalet. **Cons:** it's quite a walk to town. ⊠ *60 Tarewa Rd., Rotorua* 🕾 *07/347–0931* ⊕ *www.kiwipaka-yha.co.nz* ⤸ *83 rooms* ⚭ *In-room: No a/c, no phone, no TV. In-hotel: Restaurant, bar, pool* ▭ *MC, V.*

$$$–$$$$ 🏨 **Novotel Lakeside Rotorua.** The Royal Lakeside has the handiest position of any of the large downtown hotels—it overlooks the lake and is a two-minute walk from the restaurants and shops. Guest rooms have sleek furnishings and are decently sized, though you should specify a lake view when booking. At the Atlas Brasserie ($$$–$$$$), the pork fillet with mashed potatoes, charred corn-and-apple salad, pea puree, and cider glaze may take your fancy. **Pros:** on the lake you might snag a room with a view; the Matariki Concert Hall is right alongside. **Cons:** they're a bit aloof and you won't get the same friendly service as a B&B. ⊠ *Tutanekai St., Rotorua* 🕾 *07/346–3888* ⊕ *www.novotel.co.nz* ⤸ *199 rooms* ⚭ *In-room: Internet terminal. In-hotel: Restaurant, bar, pool, spa, no-smoking rooms* ▭ *AE, DC, MC, V.*

$$–$$$$ 🏨 **Princes Gate Hotel.** This ornate timber hotel was built in 1897 on the Coromandel Peninsula; it was transported here in 1920. Guest rooms are large and wonderfully appointed, and the bathrooms have both tubs and showers. The restaurant has live shows Saturday and Sunday evenings, and there's a deck where you can pull up a chair and gaze across the street at the Government Gardens. **Pros:** it's elegant and sophisticated with an air of old-fashioned charm. **Cons:** you'll feel you have to whisper in the lounge. ⊠ *1057 Arawa St., Rotorua* 🕾 *07/348–1179* ⊕ *www.princesgate.co.nz* ⤸ *36 rooms, 2 suites, 12 apartments* ⚭ *In-room: No a/c, kitchen (some). In-hotel: Restaurant, bar, pool, no elevator* ▭ *AE, DC, MC, V.*

$$ **Regal Palms 5 Star City Resort.** Well-appointed studio, one-bedroom,
★ and two-bedroom suites are surrounded by spacious grounds. You can
also happily lounge on the patio of the outdoor pool, purify in the
sauna, or while away the evening in front of the fire in the guest lounge
bar. It's 2 km (1 mi) from downtown Rotorua. **Pros:** good facilities with-
out leaving the complex; roomy accommodations. **Cons:** you'll want
to take the car to town. ⊠ *350 Fenton St., Rotorua* ☎ *07/350–3232*
⊕ *www.regalpalms.co.nz* ⤳ *44 suites,* ⌂ *In-room: Kitchen, Wi-Fi. In-
hotel: Bar, tennis court, pool, gym, spa, laundry facilities, no-smoking
rooms* ⊟ *AE, DC, MC, V.*

SHOPPING

Te Puia (⊠ *Hemo Rd., Rotorua* ☎ *07/348–9047* ⊕ *www.tepuia.com*)
was established in 1963 to preserve Māori heritage and crafts. At the
institute you can watch wood-carvers and flax weavers at work and see
New Zealand greenstone (jade) sculpted into jewelry. The gift shop sells
fine examples of this work, plus other items, from small wood-carved
kiwis to decorative flax skirts worn in the Māori cultural shows.

TOURS

ADVENTURE   Mount Tarawera 4WD Tours has a sensational half-day, four-wheel-
TOURS   drive trip to the edge of the Mt. Tarawera crater. Departures are at
8 AM and 1 PM; the tour costs $133 or a fly-drive combination including
helicopter trip is $455.

Contacts Mount Tarawera Volcano Tours (☎ *07/349–3714*
⊕ *www.mt-tarawera.co.nz*).

BOAT TOURS   Licensed for 300 passengers, the *Lakeland Queen*, a genuine stern-wheel
paddle ship, has breakfast, luncheon, and dinner cruises. A popular trip
includes dinner on the boat and costs $55. *Kawarau Jet,* a speedboat,
takes trips on Lake Rotorua costing $64–$120 per adult.

Contacts Kawarau Jet (☎ *07/343-7600* ⊕ *www.nzjetboat.co.nz*). **Lakeland
Queen** (☎ *07/348-0265* ⊕ *www.lakelandqueen.com*).

BUS TOURS   Newmans Coach Lines (working with InterCity) runs a variety of
trips around Rotorua. A tour that includes Whakarewarewa Thermal
Reserve Te Puia, Rainbow Springs, and the Agrodome is $119, includ-
ing all entrance fees. Geyser Link runs several local tours that include
attractions such as Hells Gate and Waiotapu; prices start at $25–$85.

Contacts Geyser Link (☎ *0800/000-4321 or 027/544-8820* ⊕ *www.geyser-
link.co.nz*). **Newmans Coach Lines Rotorua** (☎ *07/348-0366* ⊕ *www.new-
manscoach.co.nz*).

HELICOPTER   Volcanic Air Safaris fly helicopters and floatplanes from their office on
TOURS   the Rotorua Lakefront. Trips include over-city flights, crater-lake flights,
and excursions to Orakei Korako and White Island. The floatplane trip
over the Mount Tarawera volcano is extremely popular. Prices run from
$70 to $825 per adult.

Contact Volcanic Air Safaris (☎ *07/348-9984* or 0800/800-848
⊕ *www.volcanicair.co.nz*).

ROTORUA ENVIRONS

The countryside near Rotorua includes magnificent untamed territory with lakes and rivers full of some of the largest rainbow and brown trout on Earth. Fishing is big business from here down through Taupo and on into Tongariro National Park. If you're dreaming of landing the "big one," this is the place to do it.

GETTING HERE AND AROUND

Most of the sights outside the city area can be reached from State Highway 30, which branches right off Fenton Street at the southern corner of town. Lake Tarawera, the Blue and Green lakes, and the Buried Village are all accessed from Highway 30; farther east, you reach the airport, lakes Rotoiti and Rotoma, and Hell's Gate. Keeping on Fenton Street will lead to Lake Road and back onto Highway 5, which goes to Paradise Valley, Fairy Springs Road, and farther out of town to Ngongotaha and the Agrodome.

EXPLORING

TOP ATTRACTIONS

Agrodome. At this working sheep-and-cattle farm you can get a guided tour through the farm and the kiwifruit orchard, but the main attraction is the farm show. Well-trained dogs run across the backs of sheep, and there are a shearing demonstration and lots of barking, noise, and farmyard smells. Heads-up to the uninitiated: what the shearer is wearing is *not* an undershirt but a shearing vest, a classic Kiwi item worn at some point by every red-blooded male and, yes, a few women, too! Expect plenty of wisecracks about pulling the wool over your eyes and about Whoopi Goldberg (here, a Lincoln sheep with dreadlock-style wool). Sure, it's corny, but it's fun. Shows are at 9:30, 11, and 2:30 daily. ⊠ *Western Rd., Ngongotaha, 6 km (4 mi) north of Rotorua* ☎ *07/357–1050* ⊕ *www.agrodome.co.nz* ✉ *Farm show $24, farm tour and show $46* ☉ *Daily 8:30–5.*

Buried Village Te Wairoa. At the end of the 19th century, Te Wairoa (tay why-*ro*-ah, "the buried village") was the starting point for expeditions to the pink-and-white terraces of Rotomahana, on the slopes of Mt. Tarawera. As mineral-rich geyser water cascaded down the mountainside, it formed a series of baths, which became progressively cooler as they neared the lake. In the latter half of the 19th century these fabulous terraces were the country's major attraction, but they were destroyed when Mt. Tarawera erupted in 1886. The explosion, heard as far away as Auckland, killed 153 people and buried the village of Te Wairoa under a sea of mud and hot ash. The village has been excavated, and of special interest is the *whare* (*fah*-ray, "hut") of the *tohunga* (priest) Tuhoto Ariki, who predicted the destruction of the village. Eleven days before the eruption, two separate tourist parties saw a Māori war canoe emerge from the mists of Lake Tarawera and disappear again—a vision the tohunga interpreted as a sign of impending disaster. Four days after the eruption, the 100-year-old tohunga was dug out of his buried whare still alive, only to die a few days later. An interesting museum contains artifacts, photographs, and models re-creating the day of the disaster, and a number of small

A visitor gets close to a kiwi chick at Kiwi Encounter.

dwellings remain basically undisturbed beneath mud and ash. A path circles the excavated village, then continues on as a delightful trail to the waterfall, the lower section of which is steep and slippery in places. Te Wairoa is 14 km (9 mi) southeast of Rotorua, a 20-minute drive. ⊠ *Tarawera Rd.* ☎ *07/362–8287* ⊕ *www.buriedvillage.co.nz* ⌫ *$27* ⊙ *Oct.–Apr., daily 9–5; May–Sept., daily 9–4:30.*

Hell's Gate. Arguably the most active thermal reserve in the Rotorua area, the 50 acres of Hell's Gate hiss and bubble with steaming fumaroles and boiling mud pools. Among the attractions here is the Kakahi Falls, reputedly the largest hot waterfall in the Southern Hemisphere, where, according to legend, Māori warriors bathed their wounds after battle. Warm mud pools are available for public bathing; at the Wai Ora Spa, you can soak in a mud bath or try a *mirimiri* (a traditional Māori massage). Spas and mud treatments cost $70–$230. ⊠ *State Hwy. 30, Tikitere, 15 km (9 mi) east of Rotorua* ☎ *07/345–6497* ⊕ *www.hellsgate.co.nz* ⌫ *$25* ⊙ *Daily 8:30–8:30.*

☼ **Kiwi Encounter.** Next to Rainbow Springs Nature Reserve this conservation center receives kiwi eggs, then hatches and rears these endangered birds before returning them to the wild. From September to April you'll see eggs or baby chicks, which have an extremely high cute factor. ⊠ *Fairy Springs Rd.* ☎ *07/350–0440* ⊕ *www.kiwiencounter. co.nz* ⌫ *$27.50* ⊙ *Daily 10–5.*

☼ **Rainbow Springs Nature Park.** Stroll through the bush and take a close-up look at native birds such as *tūī*, kea, *kereru*, and *kakariki*. You can also eyeball a tuatara (endangered lizard) and see skinks, geckos,

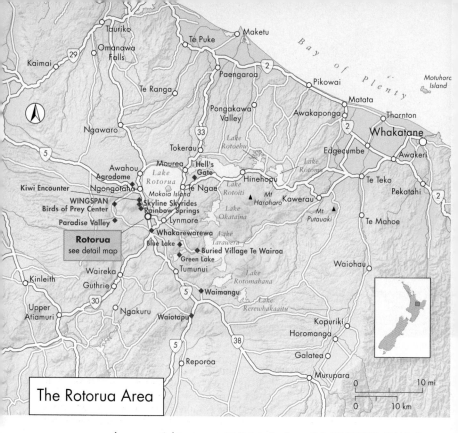

The Rotorua Area

and some mighty trout. ✉ *Fairy Springs Rd.* ☎ *07/350–0440* ⊕ *www.rainbowsprings.co.nz* 🖃 *$25* ⊙ *Daily 8–10 PM.*

Skyline Skyrides. A 2,900-foot cable-car system brings you to the summit of Mt. Ngongotaha for spectacular views over Lake Rotorua. At the summit, 1,600 feet above sea level, there's a café, a restaurant, a souvenir shop, a shooting gallery, and the Sky Swing, another Kiwi way of triggering a heart attack. Don't miss the luge track, where you can take hair-raisingly fast rides on wheeled bobsled-like luges. (You can also go slowly; a braking system gives you full control of your speed.) The track runs partway down the mountain, winding through the redwood trees; from the bottom, you can return to the summit on a separate chairlift. ✉ *Fairy Springs Rd.* ☎ *07/347–0027* ⊕ *www.skylineskyrides.co.nz* 🖃 *$24 cable car, $9 luge.*

★ **Waimangu.** When Mt. Tarawera erupted in 1886, destroying Rotomahana's terraces, not all was lost. A volcanic valley emerged from the ashes, extending southwest from Lake Rotomahana. It's consequently one of the world's newest thermal-activity areas, encompassing the boiling water of the massive Inferno Crater, plus steaming cliffs, bubbling springs, and bush-fringed terraces. A path (one–two hours) runs through the valley down to the lake, where a shuttle bus can get you back to the entrance. Or add on a lake cruise as well. Waimangu is

26 km (16 mi) southeast of Rotorua; take Highway 5 south (Taupo direction) and look for the turn after 19 km (12 mi). ✉ *Waimangu Rd.* ☎ *07/366–6137* ⊕ *www.waimangu.com* 🖂 *$34, including cruise $74* ⊗ *Daily 8:30–5; last entry at least 1 hr prior.*

★ **Waiotapu.** This is a freakish landscape of deep, sulfur-crusted pits, jade-color ponds, silica terraces, and a steaming lake edged with red algae and bubbling with tiny beads of carbon dioxide. The **Lady Knox Geyser** erupts precisely at 10:15 daily; other points of interest include the Devil's Ink Pots, a series of evil-looking, bubbling, plopping mud pools, and the spectacular, gold-edged Champagne Pool, which is 60 meters (195 feet) across and 60 meters deep. Birds nest in holes around the aptly named Birds' Nest Crater—the heat presumably allows the adult birds more time away from the eggs. Waiotapu is 30 km (19 mi) southeast of Rotorua—follow Highway 5 south (Taupo direction) and look for the signs. ✉ *State Hwy. 5* ☎ *07/366–6333* ⊕ *www.geyserland.co.nz* 🖂 *$28* ⊗ *Daily 8:30–5; last entry at 3:45.*

WORTH NOTING

Blue and Green Lakes. You'll find these vibrant lakes on the road to Te Wairoa and Lake Tarawera. The Green Lake is off-limits except for its viewing area, but the Blue Lake is popular for picnics and swimming. The best place to view the lakes' rich color is from the isthmus between the two. Take Highway 30 east (Te Ngae Road) and turn right onto Tarawera Road at the signpost for the lakes and buried village. The road loops through forests and skirts the edge of the lakes.

The Landing-Lake Tarawera. On Spencer Road, 2 km (1 mi) beyond the Buried Village, this clear, blue lake provides a number of water activities. Boats and kayaks can be hired and there are water taxis and trout fishing available. The Landing Café has a small but varied menu and a decent wine list. ✉ *Clearwater Cruises* ☎ *07/362–8590.*

WINGSPAN Birds of Prey Centre. A must-see for ornithology fans, WING-SPAN has a complex of 10 light and roomy aviaries where you can see native birds of prey. In Māori mythology, falcons, harriers, and moreporks (little owls) all acted as messengers to the gods. The aviaries, which are connected by an undercover walkway, echo with the cries of these fierce raptors, and they can be seen flying, feeding, and nesting. Open-air flying and obedience displays take place daily at 2 PM. Some of the birds are brought in to recuperate from injury before being released back into the wild. ✉ *1164 Paradise Valley Rd.* ☎ *07/357–4469* ⊕ *www.wingspan.co.nz* 🖂 *$15* ⊗ *Daily 9–3.*

SPORTS AND THE OUTDOORS

BIKING

Planet Bike (✉ *Waipa Mill Rd.* ☎ *07/346–1717* ⊕ *www.planetbike. co.nz*) runs mountain-bike adventures for everyone from first-timers to experts. You can ride for a couple of hours or several days, and some tours combine biking with rafting, kayaking, indoor climbing, or horseback riding. Prices start at $55 for a full day, or bike the lake for $99; bikes and helmets are provided.

5

The geothermal activity at Waimangu keeps the water of Inferno Crater Lake at a boil.

EXTREME ADVENTURE

The folks in Rotorua keep coming up with ever more fearsome ways to part adventurers from their money (and their wits). Try white-water sledging with **Kaitiaki Adventures** (☎ *0800/338–736* ⊕ *www.sledge-it. com*). For $149 you get a trip shooting rapids on a plastic water raft the size of a Boogie board, fish-and-chips, and a soak in a natural hot pool. They supply a wet suit, helmet, fins, and gloves. Outside town and part of the **Agrodome** complex, there's **Agrodome Adventures** (☎ *07/357–1050* [this is also the number of the shuttle service to take you there] *9–5 daily*) Try bungy jumping from a 140-foot-high crane, or **the Swoop** where one, two, or three people are put into a hang-gliding harness and raised 120 feet off the ground before a rip cord is released. That might be the ground whizzing by at 130 kph (80 mph) as the shrieking fliers swoop overhead but a donkey and a solitary emu graze on nonchalantly. If you're looking for further thrills, try **Freefall Extreme,** where a 180-kph (108-mph) wind from a giant fan lifts you 10 feet into the air . . . or then again there's the **Shweeb,** a five-car monorail racetrack using pedal power. The cost to get you screaming varies from $45 to $95, or your choice of any three for $120.

FISHING

If you want to keep the trout of a lifetime from becoming just another fish story, go with a registered guide. Prices vary but expect to pay about $90–$100 per hour for a fishing guide and a 20-foot cruiser that takes up to six passengers. The minimum charter period is two hours; fishing gear and tackle are included in the price. A one-day fishing license costs $21 per person and is available on board the boat. (You'll need a special fishing license to fish in the Rotorua area, and also in Taupo.)

For general information about local lake and river conditions, check with the Tourism Rotorua Visitor Information Centre.

In Rotorua fishing operators include **Clark Gregor** (☎ 07/347–1123 ⊕ www.troutnz.co.nz), who arranges boat fishing and fly-fishing excursions with up to 10 anglers per trip. With **Bryan Colman** (☎ 07/348–7766 ⊕ www.TroutFishingRotorua.com) you can troll Lake Rotorua or try fly-fishing on the region's many streams, including a private-land source. He takes up to five people at a time. A trip with **Gordon Randle** (☎ 07/349–2555, 0274/938–733 boat) is about $90 per hour. *See Chapter 11 for more fishing information.*

RAFTING AND KAYAKING

The Rotorua region has rivers with Grade III to Grade V rapids that make excellent white-water rafting. For scenic beauty—and best for first-timers—the Rangitaiki River (Grades III–IV) is recommended. For experienced rafters, the Wairoa River has exhilarating Grade V rapids. The climax of a rafting trip on the Kaituna River is the drop over the 21-foot Okere Falls, among the highest to be rafted by a commercial operator anywhere. The various operators run similar trips on a daily schedule, though different rivers are open at different times of year, depending on water levels. All equipment and instruction are provided, plus transportation to and from the departure points (which can be up to 80 km [50 mi] from Rotorua). Prices start around $82 for the short (one-hour) Kaituna run; a half day on the Rangitaiki costs from $108. Many operators sell combination trips. **Kaituna Cascades** (☎ 07/345–4199 or 0800/524–8862 ⊕ www.kaitunacascades.co.nz) organizes one-day or multiday expeditions. **Raftabout** (☎ 07/343–9500 ⊕ www.raftabout. co.nz) focuses on day trips, some pairing rafting with jet-boating or bungy jumping. **River Rats** (☎ 07/345–6543 or 0800/333–900 ⊕ www. riverrats.co.nz) provides day trips to the main rivers as well as adventure packages. **Wet 'n' Wild Adventure** (☎ 07/348–3191 or 0800/462–7238 ⊕ www.wetnwildrafting.co.nz) has multi-adventure and double-trip options. One-day itineraries cover the Rangitaiki, Wairoa, and Kaituna rivers. *See Chapter 11 for further rafting information.*

Gentler natures can opt for a serene paddle on one of Rotorua's lakes. **Adventure Kayaking** (☎ 274/997–402 cell ⊕ www.adventurekayaking. co.nz) has a variety of tours, from half a day spent paddling on Lake Rotorua ($80) to a full day on Lake Tarawera ($110) including a swim in a natural hot pool. Especially magical is the twilight paddle ($80) on Lake Rotoiti that incorporates a dip in the Manupirua hot pools (which you can't otherwise reach) and a BBQ dinner (extra cost).

WHERE TO STAY

$$$–$$$$ ⊡ **Cottage at Paradise.** A 20-minute drive from the city center, this cottage stands back from the road on a 12-acre block of rural land (called a "lifestyle block"). With the gin-clear Ngongotaha stream running directly behind the property, it's heaven in a basket for the ardent trout angler. The faux log cabin exterior gives way to a tastefully decorated, contemporary interior, and luxurious self-contained accommodations with gas fire and full kitchen facilities. The cottage is serviced daily and the fridge stocked with breakfast provisions. **Pros:** quiet and remote;

great trout fishing at the doorstep. **Cons:** it's a fair drive to town and a decent restaurant or pub. ✉ *801 Paradise Valley Rd.* ☎ *07/357–5006* ⊕ *www.cottagesatparadise.co.nz* ⊲ *2 bedrooms* ᧕ *In-room: DVD. In-hotel: Spa, laundry facilities, Internet terminal* ▤ *MC, V.*

$$$
Fodor'sChoice
★
🛏 **Country Villa.** Morning sunshine floods through stained-glass windows in Anneke and John Van der Maat's lovely country home, which has scenic views of the lake and Mt. Tarawera. Colored friezes run at ceiling height around every room; as befits two former professional rose growers, the design emphasizes flowers. Throughout the house are mementos of the hosts' travels—a Buddha figure here, a prayer wheel there, blue-eyed dolls from Europe. An antique chandelier is suspended over the table in the five-sided breakfast room, where the morning meal includes homemade bread. One room is self-contained, with a separate entrance and a small kitchenette. **Pros:** the hosts are welcoming and sincere; the homemade cookies are delicious. **Cons:** so, it's a drive to town! But you won't want to leave anyway. ✉ *351 Dalbeth Rd.* ☎ *07/357–5893* ⊕ *www.countryvilla.biz* ⊲ *5 rooms* ᧕ *In-room: No a/c, no phone, no TV (some). In-hotel: Internet terminal, Wi-Fi, no-smoking rooms* ▤ *MC, V* ⊙ *BP.*

$$$$
🛏 **Solitaire Lodge.** Nestled in native bush on a private peninsula, the lodge commands extensive views over Lake Tarawera and the legendary mountain. Check out the volcanoes from the telescopes in the library-bar, or settle down in a shaded garden nook and sip a drink, in surroundings perfect for hiking, boating, and fishing. **Pros:** it's quiet secluded class in superb surroundings; good fishing. **Cons:** high tariff due to exclusive location and low guest numbers. ✉ *Ronald Rd., Lake Tarawera* ☎ *07/362–8208* ⊕ *www.solitairelodge.com* ⊲ *8 suites, 1 villa* ᧕ *In-room: DVD. In-hotel: Restaurant, bar, spa* ▤ *AE, DC, MC, V* ⊙ *MAP.*

FARM STAYS

$–$$
🛏 **Arias Farm.** This modern home is set on a peaceful lifestyle farm landon the hills overlooking Rotorua, yet only a few minutes from the city center. Chris and Kerris are delightful hosts and provide excellent facilities and a warm welcome. There are areas for volleyball and petanque (lawn bowling) and children can roam among the lambs and chickens while lop-eared rabbits scurry through the grass. A delightful place to spend some time for old and young alike. **Pros:** quiet and peaceful; lovely, young welcoming hosts; on the hill above the sulfur smell. **Cons:** breakfast provisions are delivered by the host daily. ✉ *396 Clayton Rd.,, Rotorua* ☎ *07/348–0790, 021/753–691 cell* ⊕ *www.ariasfarm.com* ⊲ *1 2-bedroom cottage, 1 3-bedroom cottage, 1 double room, 1 sleep 3—both with en suite* ᧕ *In-room: No a/c kitchen (some), refrigerator (some), DVD (some), no TV (some), Internet* ▤ *MC, V* ⊙ *BP.*

$$
🛏 **Westminster Lodge and Cottage.** The views over Rotorua and the surrounding countryside are outstanding from this lovely home-away-from-home only a few minutes from the city center. The house is in immaculate gardens with the cottage and other accommodations right alongside. No meals are provided for the cottage so you will need to provide your own food. Hosts Gillian and Barry are gracious and a warm welcome is assured. Sheep and cattle roam the surrounding farm

with pigs, dogs, and a pet cockatoo that likes its neck scratched. **Pros:** magnificent views over the surrounding countryside; lovely spacious accommodations. **Cons:** it's about a ten-minute drive to nearest restaurants. ⊠ *58A Mountain Rd., Rotorua* ☎ *07/348–42 73* ⊕ *www.westminsterlodge.co.nz.* ⤷ *1 self-contained cottage, 2 adjoining self-contained units, separate from the house with all facilities* ♿ *In-room: No a/c, kitchen, refrigerator. In-hotel: Parking (free)* ⊟ *MC, V* ⏹️*BP.*

SHOPPING

See jade carvers at work at the **Jade Factory** (⊠ *1288 Fenton St.* ☎ *07/349–1828*), a bright, spacious shop where handcrafted gifts are for sale.

LAKE TAUPO AND TONGARIRO NATIONAL PARK

5

The town of Taupo on Lake Taupo's northeastern shore has blossomed into a major outdoor activities center, providing everything from rafting to skydiving. Taupo is also home to geothermal wonders.

Fishing is a major lure, both on Lake Taupo and on the rivers to the south. The lake and backcountry rivers are some of the few places where tales of the "big one" can actually be believed. The Tongariro River is particularly well known as an angler's paradise.

Southwest of Lake Taupo rise the three volcanic peaks that dominate Tongariro National Park, New Zealand's first national park. Even if you don't have much time, skirting the peaks provides a rewarding route on your way south to Wanganui or Wellington.

TAUPO

82 km (51 mi) south of Rotorua, 150 km (94 mi) northwest of Napier.

The tidy town of Taupo is the base for exploring Lake Taupo, the country's largest lake. Its placid shores are backed by volcanic mountains, and in the vicinity is more of the geothermal activity that characterizes this zone. Water sports are popular here—notably sailing, cruising, and waterskiing—but Taupo is most known for fishing. The town is the rainbow-trout capital of the universe: the average Taupo trout weighs in around 4 pounds, and the lake is open year-round. Meanwhile, the backpacker crowd converges upon Taupo for its adventure activities. The town has skydiving and bungy-jumping opportunities, and whitewater rafting and jet-boating are available on the local rivers.

GETTING HERE AND AROUND

Taupo is four hours from Auckland, taking Highway 1 the whole way. It's 70 minutes from Rotorua, also via Highway 1. The streets are laid out in a grid pattern. Lake Terrace runs along the lakefront; it turns into Tongariro Street as it heads north, crossing the Waikato River and the gates that control the flow of water from the lake. Heu Heu Street is the main shopping street and runs from the traffic lights on Tongariro Street.

InterCity Buses (☎ *09/913–6100* ⊕ *www.intercitycoach.co.nz*) run daily from Auckland to Taupo. The trip takes approximately five hours. From Rotorua to Taupo, the trip takes 1 hour and 20 minutes.

ESSENTIALS

Bus Depot Taupo (✉ *Gasgoine St.*).

Pharmacy Main Street Pharmacy (✉ *Tongariro and Heu Heu Sts., Taupo* ☎ *07/378–2636*).

Visitor Information Taupo Visitor Information Centre (✉ *30 Tongariro St., Taupo* ☎ *07/376–0027* ⊕ *www.laketauponz.com*).

EXPLORING

The Waikato River is dammed along its length; the first construction is the **Aratiatia Dam,** 10 km (6 mi) northeast of Taupo (turn right off Highway 5). The river below the dam is virtually dry most of the time, but three times a day (at 10, noon, and 2), and four times a day in summer (October–March, also at 4), the dam gates are opened and the gorge is dramatically transformed into a raging torrent. Watch the spectacle from the road bridge over the river or from one of two lookout points a 15-minute walk downriver through the bush.

The construction of the local geothermal project had an impressive—and unforeseen—effect. Boiling mud pools, steaming vents, and large craters appeared in an area now known as **Craters of the Moon.** A marked walkway snakes for 2.8 km (2 mi) through the belching, sulfurous landscape, past boiling pits and hissing crevices. Entrance (during daylight hours) costs $6. The craters are up Karapiti Road, across from the Huka Falls turnoffs on Highway 1, 3 km (2 mi) north of Taupo.

At **Huka Falls,** the Waikato River thunders through a narrow chasm and over a 35-foot rock ledge. The fast-flowing river produces almost 50% of the North Island's required power, and its force is extraordinary, with the falls dropping into a seething, milky-white pool 200 feet across. The view from the footbridge is superb, though for an even more impressive look, both the Huka Falls Jet and the Maid of the Falls (⇨ *Outdoor Activities and Taupo and Tongariro National Park Tours, below*) get close to the maelstrom. The falls are 3 km (2 mi) north of town; turn right off Highway 1 onto Huka Falls Road.

Huka Prawn Park is New Zealand's only prawn farm where you can take a tour around the property. Check out the holding tanks where prawns are bred in specially heated river water (in some, baby prawns eat out of your hand). You can also catch your own prawns using a small rod and fishing line, or just buy some on-site; either way you can have them cooked and served as you like in the adjoining café. ✉ *Huka Falls Rd., Wairakei Park Taupo* ☎ *07/374– 8474* ⊕ *www.hukaprawnpark.co.nz* 💲 *$24* ☉ *Nov.–Apr. 9–6; May–Oct. 9–3:30.*

Even if you've seen enough bubbling pools and fuming craters to last a lifetime, the thermal valley of **Orakei Korako** is still likely to captivate you. Geyser-fed streams hiss and steam as they flow into the waters of the lake, and a cream-and-pink silica terrace is believed to be the largest in the world since the volcanic destruction of the terraces of

Kayakers paddle the Waikato River, New Zealand's longest waterway.

Rotomahana. At the bottom of Aladdin's Cave, the vent of an ancient volcano, a jade-green pool was once used by Māori women as a beauty parlor, which is where the name *Orakei Korako* (a place of adorning) originated. The valley is 37 km (23 mi) north of Taupo (take Highway 1 out of town) and takes about 25 minutes to reach by car; you could always see it en route to or from Rotorua, which lies another 68 km (43 mi) northeast of the valley. ☎ 07/378–3131 ⊕ *www.orakeikorako.co.nz* ✉ *$34* ⏱ *Oct.–May, daily 8–5:30; June–Sept., daily 8–5.*

SPORTS AND THE OUTDOORS

BUNGY JUMPING
Taupo Bungy (⊠ *202 Spa Rd., off Tongariro St., 1 km [½ mi] north of town* ☎ *07/377–1135 or 0800/888–408* ⊕ *www.taupobungy.com*) provides jumps from a cantilevered platform projecting out from a cliff 150 feet above the Waikato River. You can go for the "water touch" or dry versions. Even if you have no intention of "walking the plank," go and watch the jumpers from the nearby lookout point. The jumps cost from $109 a shot and are available daily from 9 to 5.

FISHING
There is some great fishing in the Taupo area and an attendant number of guides with local expertise. Guides work the Tongariro River and the lake. The high season runs from October to April. Costs are usually $90–$100 per hour and include all equipment plus a fishing license (note that you need a special license to fish here and in Rotorua). Book at least a day in advance.

A luxury cruiser on Lake Taupo costs about $150 per hour; for more information, contact **Chris Jolly Outdoors** (☎ *07/378–0623* ⊕ *www.chris-jolly.co.nz*). *See Chapter 11 for more fishing information.* **Mark Aspinall** (☎ *07/378–4453*) leads fly-fishing trips for rainbow and brown trout.

Gus Te Moana, who runs **Te Moana Charters** (☎ 07/378–4839), also provides fishing trips on his 24-foot boat and will quote you a price from $100 per hour that includes the trip, all equipment, a license, and usually lunch and beer.

JET-BOATING For high-speed thrills on the Waikato River take a trip on the **Huka Falls Jet** (☎ 07/374–8572 ⊕ *www.hukafallsjet.com*), which spins and skips its way between the Aratiatia Dam and Huka Falls. Departures are every 30 minutes from Karetoto Road throughout the day; cost is from around $95 per person.

RAFTING The Grade 5 Wairoa and Mohaka rivers are accessible from Taupo, as are the Rangitaiki and more family-friendly Tongariro. Different rivers are open at different times of year, and operators run similarly priced trips, starting around $95 per person. Call **Rapid Sensations** (☎ 07/378–7902 or 0800/353–435 ⊕ *www.rapids.co.nz*), which provides transportation, wet suits, equipment, and much-needed hot showers at the end. *See Chapter 11 for more rafting information.*

SKYDIVING On a tandem skydive you're attached to a professional skydiver for a breathtaking leap. Depending on altitude, free fall can last from a few seconds to close to a minute. **Freefall** (☎ 07/378–4662 or 0800/373–335 ⊕ *www.freefall.net.nz*) is one local operator. **Taupo Tandem Skydiving** (☎ 07/377–0428 or 0800/275–934 ⊕ *www.tts.net.nz*) is another option. Call at least one day in advance to arrange your jump—weather permitting—and expect to pay around $219–$314 per jump.

WHERE TO EAT

$$$$
CONTEMPORARY
✕ **Brantry Restaurant.** The menu is updated seasonally at this converted 1950s town house—but if you're lucky, chef-owners Prue and Felicity Campbell may have a main dish of slow-cooked lamb shoulder set on a Mediterranean chilli couscous with a cucumber-and-yogurt dressing. For dessert try the hazlenut chocolate and coffee-layered parfait with a waffle crisp. Wines include those from emerging and boutique vineyards. ⊠ *45 Rifle Range Rd.* ☎ *07/378–0484* ⊕ *www.thebrantry.co.nz* ⌂ *Reservations essential* ▭ *MC, V* ☉ *No lunch. Closed Sun. and Mon. June–Aug.*

$$$
ITALIAN
✕ **Milano.** Natural light comes from deep skylights over polished wood floors with a resplendent brass antique coffee machine standing on the bar. A gas fire heats the soul on a cool evening. Go for the fettucine tuttomare—delicately panfried scallops, mussels, calamari, and prawn cutlets flambéed with white wine in pomodoro-and-cream sauce. Follow it up with a delicious tiramisu for a truly memorable meal! ⊠ *34 Tuwharetoa St., Taupo* ☎ *07/378–3344* ▭ *AE, DC, MC, V* ☉ *No lunch.*

$
CAFÉ
★
✕ **The Replete Food Company.** There's no wine license but the food brings the crowds and there is a breakfast and lunch menu. The panini sandwiches are especially popular at lunch; they come stuffed with various goodies, including eggplant with an Indian-spiced salsa. Good salads include a Thai beef salad with coconut-and-lime dressing or Asian chicken with crispy noodles. In the morning, try the Complete Replete Breakfast—honey-cured bacon, tomato relish, poached eggs, and roasted field mushrooms with grilled focaccia. ⊠ *45 Heu Heu St.* ☎ *07/377–3011* ▭ *AE, MC, V* ☉ *No dinner.*

WHERE TO STAY

$$–$$$ ⊡ **Cascades Motor Lodge.** Set on the shores of Lake Taupo, the pleasing brick-and-timber rooms are large, comfortable, and smartly decorated. The two-story "luxury" apartments, which sleep up to seven, have a lounge room, bedroom, kitchen, and dining room on the ground floor in an open-plan design, glass doors leading to a large patio, and a second bedroom and bathroom on the upper floor. Studios have one bedroom. All rooms are equipped with a hot tub. Room 1 is closest to the lake and a small beach. **Pros:** on the lakeside with a safe beach; heated swimming pool. **Cons:** a busy road, traffic noise could be a problem. ⊠ *Lake Terr., 3 km (2 mi) south of Taupo, just beyond State Hwy. 5 (Napier) turnoff* ☎ *07/378–3774* ⊕ *www.cascades.co.nz* ⤴ *22 rooms* ⚐ *In-room: No a/c. In-hotel: Pool, laundry facilities* ⊟ *AE, DC, MC, V.*

$$$$ ⊡ **Huka Lodge.** Set in 17 acres on the banks of the Waikato River this lodge is the standard by which New Zealand's other luxury lodges are judged. Large, lavish guest rooms have French doors that open to a view across lawns to the river. In the interest of tranquillity, they're not equipped with phones, TVs, or radios. Two separate cottages are the height of luxury. The lodge can arrange practically any activity under the sun. **Pros:** one of the world's best lodges; royalty and celebrities stay here. **Cons:** perfection does not come cheap. ⊠ *Huka Falls Rd., Box 95* ☎ *07/378–5791* ⊕ *www.hukalodge.co.nz* ⤴ *20 rooms, 1 cottage* ⚐ *In-room: No a/c, no phone, no TV. In-hotel: Restaurant, bars, tennis court, spa* ⊟ *AE, DC, MC, V* ⛾*MAP.*

$$$–$$$$ ⊡ **The Pillars.** Three of the four suites at this modern, Mediterranean-style country manor have private verandas that look out over the expansive grounds. They're individually furnished, but all have voile curtains, comfortable plush furnishings, and modern bathrooms. Guests have the use of a large sunny lounge, and breakfast can be taken in the spacious dining room with stunning views of a lake and the mountains beyond. **Pros:** top-class accommodations in extensive immaculately kept grounds. **Cons:** you need transport to see the sights. ⊠ *7 Deborah Rise, Bonshaw Park* ☎ *07/378–1512* ⊕ *www.pillarstaupo.co.nz* ⤴ *4 suites* ⚐ *In-room: Internet (some). In-hotel: Tennis court, pool* ⊟ *AE, DC, MC, V* ⛾*BP.*

$$$–$$$$ ⊡ **Richlyn Homestay.** Eponymous owners Richard and Lyn are well traveled and sociable. Their home is surrounded by well-tended gardens, and the patio is a peaceful haven, with the silence broken only by birdsong. Guest rooms are tastefully furnished and look out onto the gardens, ensuring a stay that is relaxing and restful. Two of the rooms share a bathroom. **Pros:** a homey place, but spacious and tasteful; a great cooked breakfast. **Cons:** you might prefer to be nearer the bright lights and the lake. ⊠ *1 Mark Wynd, Bonshaw Park* ⊹ *8 km (5 mi) southeast of Taupo* ☎ *07/378–8023* ⊕ *www.richlyn.co.nz* ⤴ *4 rooms, 1 with en suite, 1 with private bath.* ⚐ *In-room: No a/c, no phone. In-hotel: Spa, laundry facilities, Internet terminal, no-smoking rooms* ⊟ *MC, V* ⛾*BP.*

Continued on page 259

5

ROCK STARS & HOT SPOTS

Its strategic location at the southern end of the Pacific Ring of Fire makes New Zealand a geologic wonderland of volcanoes, earthquakes, and geothermal activity. Most travelers don't know the difference between a shield volcano and a rhyolite caldera, but it's the geology that creates the scenery—and the scenery brings the visitors. The North Island's Taupo Volcanic Zone has been active for the past 1.6 million years. Here you can explore the crater of an active volcano, soak in hot mud baths, and watch spectacular geyser eruptions. Some of the world's best hiking is found here, in one of Earth's most dramatic volcanic zones.

Pohutu Geyser at Whakarewarewa, Rotorua

BLAME IT ON PLATE TECTONICS

Volcanic eruption, White Island, Bay of Plenty, North Island

Some 20 million years ago, two massive plates of the Earth's crust under the Pacific Ocean crashed into each other at the turtle-like rate of one to two inches a year. The result: geologic mayhem. Over time, on the South Island, the collision pushed up rock that was underwater to heights over 12,000 feet. The result: Mt. Cook and the Southern Alps. And as the Pacific plate slid under the Australia plate, its rock melted, creating magma—molten rock—that runs under much of the North Island, where most of New Zealand's volcanic and geothermal activity is centered. The highly active Taupo Volcanic Zone (TVZ)—which stretches 200 miles from White Island to Ruapehu—is characterized by slow-moving and gassy rhyolitic and andesite magma, which tends to create large explosive stratovolcanoes and calderas. The Taupo eruption in 181 AD was the world's most powerful eruption over the past 5,000 years, producing about 25 cubic miles of rock and ash. Tongariro National Park is the site of three interrelated majestic stratovolcanoes, Ruapehu, Ngauruhoe, and Tongariro, each looming over the Central Plateau.

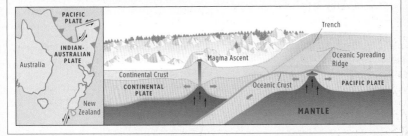

MAJOR TYPES OF VOLCANOES

STRATOVOLCANOES

Typically these powerful volcanoes (also called composite volcanoes) build over time as repetitive eruptions of ash, lava, and other debris create ever-rising layers of mountain. Stratovolcanoes tend to have steep slopes and dome- shaped summits, created by eruptions of the-slow moving andesite lava.

Mt. Ruapehu's eruptions in 1995 and 1996 were New Zealand's largest in more than a century, and it experienced a *lahar* (mudslide) in 2007. Mt. Ngauruhoe, the center of the youngest vent in the Tongariro National Park, has been the site of ash eruptions occurring, on average, every six years. But Ngauruhoe has been silent since 1975, suggesting that it may be overdue for a major eruption.

At the northern edge of the TVZ lies White Island, where New Zealand's most frequently active volcano bubbles. Though the most intense volcanic activity ended in the early 1990s, gas and ash plumes are still visible. On any given day visitors may be assaulted by gas or eruptions of fine ash.

SHIELD VOLCANOES

In contrast to stratovolcanoes, shield volcanoes tend to have faster moving, corn-syrup-like basalt lava, creating mountains that are more gently sloped as the lava travels greater distances before solidifying. Some shield volcanoes—think the Big Island in Hawaii—can be huge. But Rangitoto Island, at 260 meters (850 feet), is a smaller shield, created 600 years ago in Auckland's Waitemata Harbour. The island's scenic reserve includes seven lava caves where quickly moving lava once flowed. Rangitoto is notable because it exhibits every stage a lava field goes through, from barren land to nascent forest.

Rangitoto is the youngest and largest of among 50-odd cone volcanoes in and around Auckland that first began erupting 60,000 to 140,000 years ago. All of these volcanoes are relatively small—large hills, really—under 1,000 feet.

It is unlikely that any particular existing volcano in the area will erupt again, but Auckland lies over a relatively young hot zone. Scientists believe there will be other eruptions and new volcanoes will form around Auckland.

Left: Ngaurŭhoe Volcano. Right:, Rangitoto Island at sunset

CALDERA FORMATION

CALDERAS

These volcanic structures are created when a mammoth eruption of magma leads to a huge underground void, causing a collapse of the surrounding rock. Calderas, which can be up to 20 to 30 miles wide, rarely originate from volcanic mountains. Instead, huge deposits of magma collect below the surface and can stretch for 10 miles or more. Magma under pressure rises and erupts, spewing ash, magma, and volcanic rock. Caldera eruptions are among the most violent, causing significant local destruction, and, with ash rising high into the atmosphere, can create temporary worldwide cooling. Deep lakes often form after a caldera forms. The lake at the Taupo caldera is over 610 feet deep and almost 30 miles wide. The Rotorua caldera, created 220,000 years ago from a series of eruptions, is almost 12 miles wide. Rotorua city is one of the few to be built in an active caldera. Although the volcano has been quiet for eons, residents live over hot magma and superhot water that produce hot springs and steam vents, and occasionally cause cold tap water to run hot and boil. Other calderas are Okataina, Reporoa, and Maroa.

❶ Magma collects in a massive chamber within a few miles of the surface. Some magma rises, fueling smaller volcanic eruptions.

❷ More explosive eruptions partially empty the chamber, leaving a void in the upper level of the magma chamber.

❸ Without support, the summit collapses into the partially emptied magma chamber. The remaining magma may lead to smaller volcanic eruptions.

❹ The caldera gradually fills with water, often creating deep lakes like those found at Taupo and Rotorua.

Above: aerial view of Lake Rotorua

5

IN FOCUS ROCK STARS & HOT SPOTS

HOW DO GEYSERS WORK?

A geologic rarity, geysers need a lot of water, a plumbing system, and rock hard enough to withstand some serious pressure. Frequently, plumbing systems are lined with rhyolite, which forms a particularly water- and pressure-tight seal. The layout of any one geyser's underground plumbing may vary, but we know that below each vent is a system of fissures and chambers, with constrictions that prevent hot water from rising to the surface. As the underground water heats up, the constrictions and the cooler surface water "cap" the system, keeping it from boiling over and ratcheting up the underground pressure. When a few steam bubbles fight through the constrictions, the result is like uncapping a shaken-up soda bottle, when released pressure causes the soda to spray.

Some scientists do not believe that escaping steam bubbles, which displace water from the throat of the geyser and lower the pressure at constriction, cause the eruption. Instead, they argue that the water inside the plumbing system turns to steam as superhot water raises the temperature past boiling. Sadly, New Zealand's geyser activity has diminished as development depletes hot water sources. Geyser fields at Orakeikorako amd Wairakei have been destroyed by human activity.

BEST PLACES TO SEE THEM

- Pohutu Geyser, Whakarewarewa thermal area

- Lady Knox Geyser, Waiotapu Scenic Reserve

- Te Puia, Roturua

Whakarewarewa Thermal Area, Rotorua

❶ RECHARGE STAGE

Groundwater accumulates in plumbing and is heated by the volcano. Some hot water flashes to steam and bubbles try to rise toward surface.

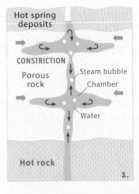

❷ PRELIMINARY ERUPTION STAGE

Pressure builds as steam bubbles clog at constriction. High pressure raises the boiling point, preventing superheated water from becoming steam.

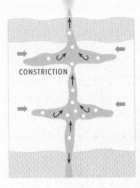

❸ ERUPTION STAGE

Bubbles squeeze through constriction, displacing surface water and relieving pressure. Trapped water flashes to steam, forcing water out of chambers and causing chain reaction.

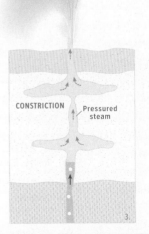

❹ RECOVERY STAGE

Eruption ends when chambers are emptied or temperature falls below boiling. Chambers begin to refill with ground water, and the process begins again.

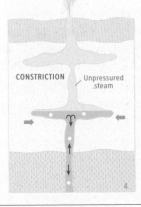

5

IN FOCUS ROCK STARS & HOT SPOTS

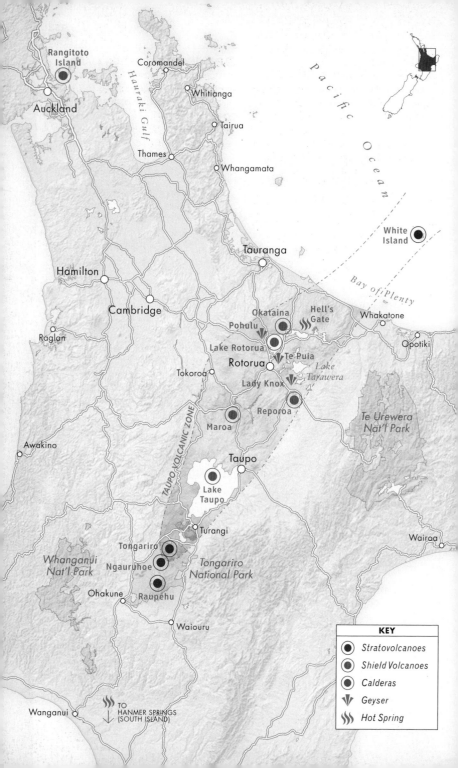

Rangitoto
Island

Coromandel

Whitianga

Auckland

Hauraki Gulf

Tairua

Thames

Whangamata

Pacific Ocean

White
Island

Tauranga

Bay of Plenty

Whakatone

Hamilton

Opotiki

Cambridge

Raglan

Okataina

Hell's
Gate

Pohulu

Lake Rotorua

Te Puia

Rotorua

Lake Tarawera

Tokoroa

Lady Knox

Te Urewera
Nat'l Park

Reporoa

Maroa

Awakino

TAUPO VOLCANIC ZONE

Taupo

Lake
Taupo

Turangi

Wairoa

Whanganui
Nat'l Park

Tongariro

Tongariro
National Park

Ngauruhoe

Ohakune

Raupehu

Waiouru

Wanganui

TO
HANMER SPRINGS
(SOUTH ISLAND)

KEY	
⊚	*Stratovolcanoes*
⊙	*Shield Volcanoes*
⊙	*Calderas*
▼	*Geyser*
⌇⌇	*Hot Spring*

HOW DO HOT SPRINGS WORK?

Essentially, what keeps a hot spring from becoming a geyser is a lack of constriction in its underground plumbing. Like their more explosive cousins, hot springs consist of water that seeps into the earth, only to simmer its way back up through fissures after it's heated by hot volcanic rock. Unlike in constricted geysers, water in a hot spring can circulate by convection. Rising hot water displaces cooling surface water, which then sinks underground to be heated by the magma chamber and eventually rise

again. Thus the whole mixture keeps itself at a gurgly equilibrium. As it rises, superheated water dissolves some subterranean minerals, depositing them at the surface to form the sculptural terraces that surround many hot springs.

BEST PLACES TO SEE THEM

- Hell's Gate, Rotorua
- Hanmer Springs, Canterbury (South Island)
- Waiotapu, Rotorua.

The famous colored boiling steaming hot spring "Champagne Pool," Waiotapu, Rotorua.

WHAT'S THAT SMELL?

Sulphur gases escaping from the volcano produce distinctive smells. Other gases are reduced to the stinky chemical hydrogen sulfide, which bubbles up to the surface.

THE INNER WORKINGS OF HOT SPRINGS

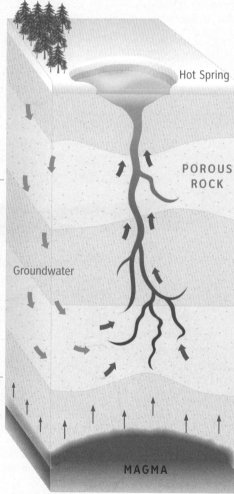

4 The water carries up dissolved minerals, which get deposited at the edges of the pool.

Hot Spring **3**

3 Heated water pools on the surface—it can be churning or quite calm.

POROUS ROCK

1

1 Water draining from the earth's surface filters down through rock.

Groundwater

2

2 Water rises back up as it gets heated geothermally.

A hot spring's inner plumbing isn't constricted, as in a geyser, so pressure doesn't reach an explosive point.

MAGMA

OTHER GEOTHERMAL PHENOMENONS

FUMAROLES

Take away the water from a hot spring and you're left with steam and other gas, forming a fumarole. Often called steam vents, these noisy thermals occur when available water becomes trapped near the surface and boils away. All that escapes the vent is heat, vapor, and the whisper-roar of a giant, menacing teakettle. Fumaroles are often found on high ground. The gases expelled from fumaroles might include carbon dioxide, sulfur dioxide, and hydrogen sulfide. In an active volcano, the steam from a fumarole may exceed 200°C, but in a geothermal field, it may be a relatively balmy 100°C.

BEST PLACES TO SEE THEM

■ Within the crater at White Island, where you can see vivid yellow sulfur crystals around the vents.

■ You can also see fumaroles around any of the thermal parks in Rotorua including Whakareearewa, Hell's Gate, and Waimangu.

MUD POOLS

Might as well say it up front: mud pools are great because their thick, bursting bubbles can sound like a chorus of rude noises or "greetings from the interior." A mud pool is basically just a hot spring where the water table results in a bubbling broth of water and clay. The acid gases react with the surface rocks, breaking them down into silica and clay. As gas escapes from below, bubbles swell and pop, flinging mud chunks onto the banks to form gloppy clay mounds. The mud's thickness varies with rainfall through the seasons.

BEST PLACES TO SEE THEM

■ At Hell's Gate you can soak in a mud bath.

■ Te Whakarewarewa, Te Puia, Rotorua, has mudpools as well as silica terraces and unusual geothermal vegetation.

Left: Tongariro crossing walk. Tongariro National Park. Right: Boiling mud, Rotorua

GETTING UP CLOSE

Left: Hot Springs: Tongariro Crossing. Right: Late winter hikers on Mount Ngauruhoe

Bruce Houghton, the Gordon Macdonald Professor of Volcanology at the University of Hawaii and a New Zealander by birth, recommends three top experiences for those who want to get up close and personal with active volcanoes.

THE TONGARIRO ALPINE CROSSING. This full-day 16-km (10-mile) hike passes through lava flows, emerald-colored lakes, steam vents, and hot springs. The seven- to nine-hour walk, which starts at Mangatepopo carpark and ends Ketetahi Car Park, passes between the summits of Tongariro and Ngauruhoe. It's free, but it can get crowded, especially in the summer. It is considered the best day hike in New Zealand, but be forewarned: the first 45 minutes consists of a steep ascent and the weather can be fickle.

A TOUR OF THE ACTIVE VOLCANO OF WHITE ISLAND. From Whakatane, you can take an 80-minute boat ride to White Island, where **White Island Tours** will escort you on a walking tour of hot thermal streams, mud pools, fumoroles, yellow sulphur crystals, and a pale-green crater lake. It's an active volcano so the crew will issue you a gas mask and hardhat. ⊠ *15 The Strand East Whakatane* ⊕ *www.whiteisland.co.nz.* ⊙ *Tours run year-round.* ⊠ *$175.*

A CHAIRLIFT RIDE AND HIKE TO THE TOP OF MT. RUAPEHU. During the summer, hikers can take a ski lift from the Whakapapa Ski Area to the Knoll Ridge Chalet. From there you take a five- to six-hour guided walk up to Dome Shelter overlooking Crater Lake at an altitude of almost 9,000 feet.

Tour group admiring sulphur fumarole on White Island.

SHOPPING

K F L. The letters stand for knitwear, fur, and leather, and that's just what you'll find at Louis Pogoni's exclusive store. Their top-quality clothes and accessories are manufactured in New Zealand. ⊠ *20 Heu Heu St.* 📞 *07/377–4676* ✎ *knitfurleather@ihug.co.nz* 🕒 *Daily 9–5.*

TONGARIRO NATIONAL PARK

110 km (69 mi) southwest of Taupo.

GETTING HERE AND AROUND

The approach from the north is along Highway 4 on the park's western side; turn off at National Park for Whakapapa and the northern ski slopes. Coming from the south turn off State Highway 1 at Waiouru for Ohakune. From Taupo to the park, follow State Highway 1 south and turn off at Turangi onto State Highway 47. The roads are generally good. Around the national park, snow and ice can be a problem in the winter.

It's difficult to reach Tongariro National Park by public transportation, though there is a daily summer InterCity–Newmans bus service (mid-October–April) between Taupo, Whakapapa Village, and the village of National Park; the trip takes around 1½ hours.

The Tranz Scenic *Overlander,* which connects Auckland and Wellington, stops at National Park village and Ohakune Friday, Saturday, and Sunday from May to December and daily from December to April. Note: These times can vary and need to be checked locally. The journey from Wellington passes over five high viaducts. The train from Auckland goes around the remarkable Raurimu Spiral, where the track rises 660 feet in a stretch only 6 km (3½ mi) long.

ESSENTIALS

Train Contact Tranz Scenic Overlander 📞 *0800/872–467* ⊕ *www.tranzscenic. co.nz).*

Tour Information Barbary (📞 *07/378–3444* ⊕ *www.barbary.co.nz).* **Huka Falls River Cruise** (⊠ *Aratiatia Dam Rd.* 📞 *0800/278–336* ⊕ *hukafallscruise. co.nz).* **Hot Bus** (📞 *0508/468–287).* **Paradise Tours** (📞 *07/378–9955* ⊕ *www. paradisetours.co.nz).* **Tongariro Expeditions** (📞 *07/377–0435* ⊕ *www.theton-garirocrossing.co.nz).*

Visitor Information Department of Conservation ⊕ *www.doc.govt.nz).* **Ruapehu Promotion Site** ⊕ *www.ruapehu.co.nz).* **Whakapapa Visitor Centre** (⊠ *Hwy. 48, Mt. Ruapehu* 📞 *07/892–3729* ⊕ *www.doc.govt.nz* 🕒 *Oct.–Apr. 8–6 daily; May–Sept. 8–5 daily).*

For helpful hiking and skiing advice, stop off at the **Whakapapa Visitor Centre.** This is the best place to buy maps and guides, including the Department of Conservation park map—essential for hikers—and individual local-walk leaflets. Check the seismograph in the office that records the seismic activity from the mountain. If it starts trembling, at least you'll have a head start. Whakapapa Village, on the north side of Ruapehu, is the only settlement within the park with services and is the jump-off point for the Whakapapa ski slopes. The second ski area is Turoa, and its closest town is **Ohakune,** which is just beyond the southern boundary of the park—take Highway 49, which runs between Highways 1 and 4. Although ski season is the busiest time of year, these towns keep their doors open for hikers and other travelers when the snow melts.

The Department of Conservation's Web site includes a good rundown on Tongariro National Park. There's also a Ruapehu promotion site, with events listings, snow conditions, and more.

SPORTS AND THE OUTDOORS

HIKING

Fodor's Choice
★

The **Tongariro Alpine Crossing** trail grabs the hiking limelight. A one-way track starting at Mangatepopo, the crossing is a spectacular six- to seven-hour hike that follows an 18½-km (11-mi) trail up and over the name-sake mountain, passing craters, the evocatively named Emerald Lakes, old lava flows, and hot springs. Although children and school groups commonly do the hike, it is not to be taken lightly. Be prepared for rapidly changing weather conditions with warm and waterproof clothing. Wear sturdy footwear, and take food, plenty of water, sunblock, and sunglasses—and don't forget a hat! Also, be careful not to get too close to steam vents; the area around them can be dangerously hot. From late November to May, you'll be sharing the trail with many other hikers. In the colder months, it's really only for experienced winter hikers who can deal with snow and ice; some transport companies will take you only if you have an ice axe and crampons. It is recommended that you get up-to-date track and weather conditions from the Department of Conservation (DOC) Whakapapa Visitor Centre before starting out. A number of track transport operators provide shuttles to and from the Tongariro Alpine Crossing picking up from a number of locations in Whakapapa Village usually around 6, 7, 8, or 9 AM. Bookings can be made at accommodations providers in the area.

Mountain Shuttle (☎ 0800/117–686 ⊕ www.tongarirocrossing.com ✉ mountainman989@hotmail.com) provides transport to the trailhead from Turangi for $30–$35. For an extra charge they will supply boots, clothing, day packs, and more. In addition, many of the motels and lodges in National Park village can arrange transport to the track for about $15. You usually need to make a reservation; they pick you up at the end of the track. The longest hikes in the park are the three-day **Northern Circuit,** which goes over Tongariro and around Ngauruhoe, and the four-day **Round-the-Mountain Track,** which circles Ruapehu. There are trailside huts throughout the park to use on overnight trips. You'll need to buy a hut pass at the visitor center; it costs $20 from October 1 to the first weekend in June and $10 the rest of the year. Reservations cannot be made. Gas cookers are available in the huts. You can also tackle short half-hour to two-hour walks if all you want is a flavor of the region. A 1½-hour round-trip trek to the Tawhai Falls via the **Whakapapanui Track** takes you through the forest, and a two-hour round-trip to Taranaki Falls is in sub-alpine surroundings.

SKIING

The **Mt. Ruapehu ski slopes** (⊕ www.mtruapehu.com) add up to New Zealand's most extensive skiing and snowboarding terrain. The **Whakapapa** ski area, on the mountain's north side, has more than 30 groomed trails,

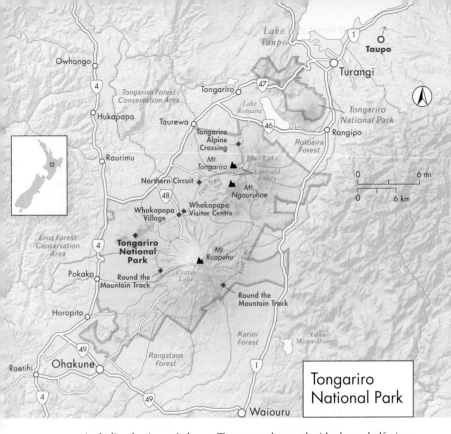

Tongariro National Park

including beginners' slopes. **Turoa,** on the south side, has a half-pipe. Ski season generally runs from June through October. Both areas can provide lessons and rental equipment. Lift passes cost around $60–$80 for access to the whole mountain, but a variety of combination tickets are available. The area's Web site includes snow reports, trail maps, and other information.

WHERE TO EAT AND STAY

$$$ ✕ **Eivins Café, Wine Bar, and Restaurant.** This modern diner's trump card
NEW ZEALAND   is the panoramic mountain views from its front veranda. The pesto-encrusted, oven-baked lamb served with savory tomatoes, vegetable sauce, and apricot-and-parsley couscous might take your fancy. Don't let it go cold while you're gazing at the mountains. ⊠ *State Hwy. 4, National Park Village* ☎ *07/892–2844* ☰ *MC, V* ☾ *No lunch.*

$$$ ✕ **The Station Cafe.** Paintings by local artists alight the dusky pink and
NEW ZEALAND   wood-paneled walls of this café-cum-bar where the tracks of the north–south railway are right outside the door. Coffee comes in all shades, and at lunch, the food runs from nachos to ploughman's sarnies (thick sandwiches with meat, cheese, and onion). In the evening the Denver leg venison cloaked with a rich Belgian chocolate and black plum sauce is served on a mashed kūmara (sweet potato) with green beans. Finish off with an apple-and-passion fruit parcel with

vanilla-and-pineapple Anglaise. ⊠ *Findlay St., National Park Village* ☎ *07/892–2881* ⊟ *AE, DC, MC, V.*

$$$$ 🛏 **Bayview Chateau Tongariro.** Built in 1929, this French neo-Georgian style property stands out in Whakapapa Village. Most rooms have views of the surrounding National Park. Meals are taken in the Ruapehu Restaurant ($$$–$$$$)—serving traditional New Zealand cuisine with a modern slant—or there's a less formal café. The hotel can arrange guided hikes on all the best-known routes in the park. **Pros:** classy restful place; the enormous lounge area has a welcoming open fire and a full-size billiard table. **Cons:** when the mist comes down you won't get a view from even the most expensive suite. ⊠ *Hwy. 48, Private Bag 71901, Mt. Ruapehu* ☎ *07/892–3809 or 0800/242–832* ⊕ *www.chateau.co.nz* ⏎ *106 rooms, includes 7 suites and 9 motel units* ♿ *In-room: No a/c (some). In-hotel: 2 restaurants, bar, golf course, tennis court, pool, gym* ⊟ *AE, DC, MC, V.*

$$ 🛏 **Discovery Lodge.** The only tourist accommodations in the park to give a panoramic view of three active volcanoes is this friendly complex, only minutes from the ski slopes. Most accommodations are in self-contained motel units and chalets. One-bedroom units sleep up to six people. There are also some doubles priced for backpackers, and powered campsites. The restaurant serves breakfast and dinner, and you can request a packed lunch. There is a fully licensed bar and a guest lounge with sundeck. The lodge runs its own shuttle to the Tongariro Track, arriving just before 6 AM. **Pros:** handy to the village; close to the start of the Tongariro Alpine Crossing and their shuttle gets you there quite early. **Cons:** bleak in winter. ⊠ *State Hwy. 47, Whakapapa Village* ☎ *07/892–2744 or 0800/122–122* ⊕ *www. discovery.net.nz* ⏎ *22 rooms* ♿ *In-room: No a/c, no phone, no TV (some). In-hotel: Restaurant, bar, laundry facilities, Internet terminal, no-smoking rooms* ⊟ *AE, DC, MC, V.*

> ### BEST BETS FOR CRUISE PASSENGERS
>
> Many tours can be prebooked by the **Napier Visitor Centre** (*www. portofnapier.co.nz*) before your ship docks. Art deco guided walks, bus, or vintage car tours are all popular. Or try a wine-tasting tour, which will include visits to vineyards in lovely countryside as far as Te Mata Peak. The **Gannet Safari** (*www.gannetsafaris.com*) is wonderful for up-close inspection of one of the largest gannet colonies in the world, and you could pull in a visit to the World of Wool which is almost alongside. Walk along the promenade to the **National Aquarium** then don a wetsuit and swim with the sharks.

EN ROUTE Straddling State Highway 1 between National Park and Taupo sits the small town of **Turangi.** A regular stopover for motorists on the main north-south route, its number-one attraction is trout fishing on some of the world's most productive rivers, but there is also great local walking, kayaking, and white-water rafting. Hot pools are also close by. The Turangi i-Site Centre,is located on Ngawhaka Place, Turangi. ☎ *07/386–8999.*

$ ▦ **Riverstone Back-Packers.** Riverstone is handy to State Highway 1 and the Tongariro River. A large comfortable lounge with an open fire and a sheltered outdoor area make this tidy place with modern facilities a good stopover for fishing or other outdoor activities. They will also organize transport for the Tongariro Crossing ✉ *222 Tautahanga Rd., Turangi* ☎ *07/386–7004* ⊕ *www.riverstonebackpackers.com* ↩ *5 double rooms (2 with en suite), 1 bunk room sleeps 6* ⌂ *In-room: No a/c, kitchen. In-hotel: Bicycles, laundry facilities* ⊟ *MC, V.*

NAPIER AND HAWKE'S BAY

New Zealand prides itself on natural wonders. But Napier (population 50,000) is best known for its architecture. After an earthquake devastated this coastal city in 1931, residents rebuilt it in the art deco style of the day. Its well-kept uniformity of style makes it an exceptional period piece. There's a similar aspect to Napier's less-visited twin city, Hastings, just to the south, which was also remodeled after the earthquake. After stretching your legs in either place, go on a brief wine-tasting tour—the region produces some of New Zealand's best wines. The mild climate and beaches of Hawke Bay make this a popular vacation area. (*Hawke* Bay is the body of water; *Hawke's* Bay is the region.) Make a point of visiting the gannet colony at Cape Kidnappers, which is best seen between October and March.

NAPIER

150 km (94 mi) southeast of Taupo, 345 km (215 mi) northeast of Wellington.

The earthquake that struck Napier at 10:46 AM on February 3, 1931, was—at 7.8 on the Richter scale—the largest quake ever recorded in New Zealand. The coastline was wrenched upward several feet. Almost all the town's brick buildings collapsed; many people were killed on the footpaths as they rushed outside. The quake triggered fires throughout town, and with water mains shattered, little could be done to stop the blazes that devoured the remaining wooden structures. Only a few buildings survived (the Public Service Building with its neoclassical pillars is one), and the death toll was well over 100.

The surviving townspeople set up tents and cookhouses in Nelson Park, and then tackled the city's reconstruction at a remarkable pace. In the rush to rebuild, Napier went mad for art deco, the bold, geometric style that had burst on the global design scene in 1925. Now a walk through the art deco district, concentrated between Emerson, Herschell, Dalton, and Browning streets, is a stylistic immersion. The decorative elements are often above the ground floors, so keep your eyes up.

GETTING HERE AND AROUND

Driving is more relaxed around this region and does not have the traffic problems often found in the larger cities. Daily flights by Air New Zealand from Wellington, Auckland, and the South Island arrive at Hawke's Bay Airport in Napier. Avis Car Rentals are located at the airport.

Camper vans are also available. Taxis are on call. GoBay—Hawke's Bay regional transport—runs a limited public bus service covering Hawke's Bay and Napier on weekdays approximately 7 AM–6 PM.

ESSENTIALS

Airline Contacts Air New Zealand (☎ *06/835–1130* ⊕ *www.airnz.co.nz*). **GoBay** (☎ *06/878–9250* ⊕ *www.hrc.govt.nz*). **Hawke's Bay Airport** (☎ *06/835–3427* ⊕ *www.hawkesbay-airport.co.nz*).

Pharmacy Radius Care Pharmacy (✉ *32 Munroe St.,* ☎ *06/834–0884*).

Taxi Contacts Napier Taxis (☎ *06/835–7777* ⊕ *www.napiertaxis.net.nz*).

Tour Information Art Deco Trust (✉ *Art Deco Shop, 163 Tennyson St.* ☎ *06/835–0022* ⊕ *www.artdeconapier.com*). **Deco Affair Tours** (✉ *Box 190, Napier* ☎ *025/241–5279* ✐ *decoaffair@yahoo.co.nz*).

Visitor Information Napier Visitor Information Centre (✉ *100 Marine Parade* ☎ *06/834–1911www.portofnapier.co.nz*).

EXPLORING
TOP ATTRACTIONS

❽ **Hawke's Bay Museum.** Newspaper reports, photographs, and audiovisuals re-create the suffering caused by the earthquake. The museum also houses a unique display of artifacts of the Ngati Kahungunu Māori people of the East Coast—including vessels, decorative work, and statues. ✉ *65 Marine Parade and 9 Herschell St.* ☎ *06/835–7781* ⊕ *www.hawkesbaymuseum.co.nz* 🎫 *$10* 🕐 *Daily 10–6.*

❿ **National Aquarium.** Stand on a moving conveyor that takes you through
☺ the world of sharks, rays, and fish. Environmental and ecological dis-
★ plays showcase a saltwater crocodile, tropical fish, sea horses, tuatara, and other creatures. For $50—all gear provided—you can swim with the sharks. There is also a kiwi enclosure where these birds can be seen in ideal viewing conditions. ✉ *Marine Parade* ☎ *06/834–1404* ⊕ *www.nationalaquarium.co.nz* 🎫 *$15.50* 🕐 *Daily 9–5.*

WORTH NOTING

❶ **ASB Bank.** One of Napier's more notable buildings is at the corner of Hastings and Emerson streets. The Māori theme on the lintels is probably the country's finest example of *kowhaiwhai* (rafter) patterns decorating a European building. The traditional red, white, and black pattern is also continued inside around a coffered ceiling. ✉ *100 Hastings St.*

❷ **Criterion Hotel.** This is typical of the Spanish Mission style, which Napier took on because of its success in Santa Barbara, California, where an earthquake had similarly wreaked havoc just a few years before the New Zealand catastrophe. It has smooth plastered concrete walls (in imitation of adobe construction) and tiled parapets. The small square windows and larger round-arched glass doors also reflect features of mud-brick construction. ✉ *48 Emerson St.*

❺ **Daily Telegraph Building.** This is another Napier classic, now a real-estate office. It has almost all the deco style elements, incorporating zigzags, fountain shapes, ziggurats, and a sunburst. ✉ *Tennyson St.*

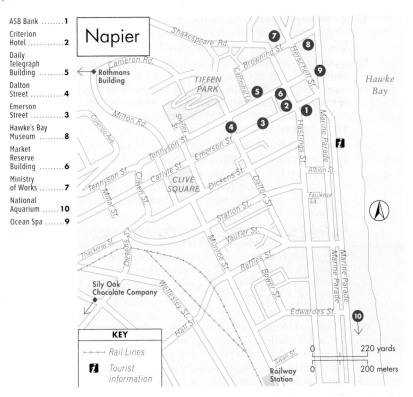

Napier

KEY

⊦—⊦ Rail Lines

🛈 Tourist
information

---

❹ **Dalton Street.** South of the intersection with Emerson Street, the pink **Countrywide Bank Building,** with its balcony, is one of Napier's masterpieces. **Hildebrand's,** at Tennyson Street, has an excellent frieze, which is best viewed from across Dalton. Hildebrand was a German who migrated to New Zealand—hence the German flag at one end, the New Zealand at the other; the wavy lines in the middle symbolize the sea passage between the two countries.

❸ **Emerson Street.** Here you can stroll the pedestrian mall and view some of the city's finest art deco buildings such as **Hannahs** and the **Hawke's Bay Chambers. Bowmans Building** is a Louis Hay design in brick veneer with the characteristic eyebrow (brick or tiles, often curved, set over a window). Some of Hay's work was influenced by Chicago's Louis Sullivan; his best-known design is the National Tobacco Building in Ahuhiri.

❻ **Market Reserve Building.** On Tennyson and Hastings Streets, this was the first building to rise after the earthquake. Its steel metal frame was riveted, not welded, so that the construction noise would give residents the message that the city was being rebuilt. The bronze storefronts with their "crown of thorns" patterned leaded glass are still original.

➐ The Ministry of Works. A decorative lighthouse pillar at the front takes on the almost-Gothic menace that art deco architecture sometimes has (like New York's Chrysler Building). ✉ *Browning St.*

➒ Ocean Spa. In a place where the beaches are not really suitable for bathing, this spa complex is a delight for the sun- and water-seeking tourist, its open-air pools being right alongside the beach. Sun beds, spa treatments, and massage are also available. ✉ *42 Marine Parade, Napier* ☎ *06/835–8553* 💰 *$6.50; treatments run $15–$90* ⊙ *Mon.–Sat. 6–10, Sun. 8–10.*

Rothmans Building. A little over a kilometer (½ mi) north of the central area stands one of the finest deco buildings. The magnificent 1932 structure has been totally renovated and its original name reinstated: the National Tobacco Company Building. It has a rose theme on the stained-glass windows and on a magnificent glass dome over the entrance hall. ✉ *Bridge St.*

Silky Oak Chocolate Company. This complex comprising factory, museum, shop, and café is a chocoholic's fantasyland. The museum details the story of chocolate through the ages, and the café has a nice selection of goodies. ✉ *1131 Links Rd., Napier* ☎ *06/845–0908* ⊕ *www.silkyoakchocs.co.nz* 💰 *Museum-tasting tours $14–$57* ⊙ *Mon.–Thurs. 9–5, Fri. 9–4, weekends 10–4.*

WHERE TO EAT

$$$
NEW ZEALAND
✕ **Caution.** Massive wood-frame mirrors reflect the candles behind the bar in this northern Napier spot overlooking the boat masts in the basin. Try the whole flat fish roasted in the wood-fired oven with limes and rosemary. The red-berry curd with caramelized crème brûlée and licorice ice cream may have you begging for more. Caution shares ownership and the same kitchen with the attached Shed 2, a casual restaurant and bar open for lunch and dinner. ✉ *West Quay, Ahuhiri* ☎ *06/835–2202* 💳 *AE, DC.*

$$$$
NEW ZEALAND
✕ **The Old Church Restaurant & Bar.** From the high-vaulted ceiling to the overly ornate fittings, this restaurant (a converted church) is a stunner. Sit on red velvet upholstered chairs by an open fire and gaze at the massive chandelier while waiting for your meal of spiced roast venison with herb mashed potatoes, almond butter-glazed vegetables, parsnip puree, truffle oil, and chocolate juice. Sweet and sinful temptations include classic vanilla bean crème brûlée with balsamic mixed berries. Hallelujah! ✉ *199 Meanee Rd., Hawkes Bay* ☎ *06/844–8866* ⊕ *www.theoldchurch.co.nz* 💳 *MC, V* ⊙ *No lunch Tues.*

$$$$
NEW ZEALAND
✕ **Pacifica Restaurant.** Watch Jeremy Remeka at work producing your panfried blue cod fillet, spicy coconut baby paua (shellfish), and saffron fumet, from a menu that changes nightly. Follow this with steamed Valrhona chocolate fondant and truffle-scented ice cream before sipping a nightcap in the small bar area overlooking the tree-lined Marine Parade. It's got to be good for you! ✉ *209 Marine Parade, Napier* ☎ *06/833–6335* 💳 *AE, MC, DC, V* ⊙ *Closed weekends.*

WHERE TO STAY

$$$$ ☆ The County Hotel. Built in 1909 as the Hawke's Bay County Council headquarters, this is one of the few Napier buildings that survived the 1931 earthquake. Wood paneling, chandeliers, and clawfoot bathtubs conjure up a more gracious era. At the Chambers Restaurant ($$$–$$$$) highlights include the herb-encrusted rack of lamb, cumin-scented field mushrooms, fondant potato, and the vanilla bean crème brûlée with a poached pear, steeped in cranberry sauce. Churchill's Bar is decorated with quotes from the great man's speeches, and a cellar room is used for evening wine tastings. **Pros:** you'll sleep in a room with a bit of history and dine well without leaving the building. **Cons:** wood paneling is not everyone's choice of decor. ☒ *12 Browning St.* ☎ *06/835–7800* ⊕ *www.countyhotel.co.nz* ⤳ *18 rooms* ⚠ *In-room: Internet (some). In-hotel: Restaurant, bar, spa, laundry facilities, no-smoking rooms* ▭ *AE, DC, MC, V.*

¢ ☐ Criterion Art Deco Backpackers. On the top floor of the old Criterion Hotel, one of Napier's central art deco buildings, this hostel rents well-maintained rooms and secure storage. All rooms have washbasins; a few have bunks, but most have regular beds. Prices include continental breakfast. There's a roomy lounge and a separate TV room. **Pros:** bang in the center of town; great value; café on the premises. **Cons:** basic beds; sometimes bunks. ☒ *48 Emerson St.* ☎ *06/835–2059* ⊕ *www. criterionartdeco.co.nz* ⤳ *27 rooms* ⚠ *In-room: No a/c, no phone, no TV (some). In-hotel: Restaurant, bars, laundry facilities, Internet terminal, no-smoking rooms* ▭ *MC, V.*

$$–$$$ ☐ Esk Valley Lodge. Eileen and Jes Roddy are the welcoming owners of this lovely homestead in peaceful surroundings with superb expansive views over their own acres of vines. The accommodations are roomy and well appointed and feature a large guest lounge with comfortable furnishings, books, and a large plasma screen television. The suite has its own attached sitting room and a full breakfast is served. **Pros:** quiet surroundings yet handily situated for both the Taupo and Gisborne roads out of Napier. **Cons:** 10-minute drive to restaurants and the town center. ☒ *362, Hill Rd., RD 2 Napier* ☎ *06/836–7904* ⊕ *www.eskvalleylodge.co.nz* ⤳ *2 bedrooms, both en suite* ⚠ *No a/c (some), refrigerator (some), DVD, Internet. In-hotel: Laundry facilities* ▭ *MC, V* ⦿ *BP.*

$$$$ ☐ The Masters Lodge. New Yorkers Joan and Larry Blume fell in love with this art deco masterpiece and are now its gracious hosts. Stunning views from an elevated veranda stretch seaward to Cape Kidnappers, but it's the lovely interior and magnificent stained-glass windows in every room that will keep you entranced. **Pros:** incredible views; fabulous coffee; welcoming hosts. **Cons:** limited parking, but it's a reasonable stroll to shops or restaurants. ☒ *10 Elizabeth Rd.,* ☎ *06/834–1946* ⊕ *www.masterslodge.co.nz* ⤳ *2 rooms* ⚠ *In-hotel: Internet terminal, no-smoking rooms* ▭ *AE MC, V.*

$$$$ ☐ McHardy House. The gardens at this colonial mansion, high on Napier Hill, have panoramic views of the Pacific Ocean and the splendid Kaweka Ranges. John and June McEnallay are the hosts at this

Napier classic. The rooms have native timber floors, American king-size beds, and elaborate bathrooms. Large verandas open onto land-scaped grounds, where you can lounge by the heated swimming pool; there's also a lovely fireplace in the lounge. Dinners must be booked in advance. **Pros:** a warm welcome from friendly hosts; fabulous views; most of the vegetables are homegrown. **Cons:** it could be hard to find on a dark night. ✉ *11 Bracken St.* ☎ *06/835–0605* ⌨ *2 rooms, 4 suites* ☖ *In-room: No a/c, no TV. In-hotel: Bar, pool, laundry facilities, no-smoking rooms* ▭ *MC, V* ⍗ *MAP.*

$$$ ⌂ **Mon Logis.** Built in the 1860s and one of the few houses that escaped destruction in the 1931 earthquake, this splendid mansion–cum–bou-tique hotel feels like a little piece of France. Its front windows over-look the ocean and distant Cape Kidnappers; in the guest rooms, white matchboard ceilings hover above white bedspreads and lace-trimmed pillowcases. Gallic host Gerard Averous is passionate in his desire to ensure his guests are comfortable and enjoy their stay. Breakfast can include freshly baked croissants and a French omelet. **Pros:** a superb breakfast with a genial Gallic host; sea views. **Cons:** his rugby team knocked the All-Blacks out of the world cup, twice! ✉ *415 Marine Parade* ☎ *06/835–2125* ⊕ *www.babs.co.nz/monlogis* ⌨ *4 rooms* ☖ *In-room: Internet. In-hotel: Laundry facilities* ▭ *AE, DC, MC, V* ⍗ *BP.*

$$–$$$ ⌂ **Pebble Beach Motor Inn.** All the units have balconies facing Marine Parade, overlooking the sea with superb views of the Bay and Cape Kidnappers. It's just a short walk to many of the town's sights, res-taurants, and cafés. The plush rooms are spacious and finished in soft tones of beige and gray, and all have whirlpool baths. **Pros:** every suite has an ocean view and balcony; step out of bed into a whirlpool bath; air-conditioning throughout. **Cons:** apartment-style living. ✉ *445 Marine Parade* ☎ *06/835–7496* ⊕ *www.pebblebeach.co.nz* ⌨ *25 suites* ☖ *In-room: Internet. In-hotel: Spa, laundry facilities, no-smoking rooms* ▭ *AE, DC, MC, V.*

SHOPPING

Napier's Art Deco Trust maintains an **Art Deco Shop.** This perfectly laid-out shop sells everything from table lamps to tiles to ceramics, as well as hats, jewelry, rugs, and wineglasses. You can also pick up booklets outlining self-guided walks through town. ✉ *163 Tennyson St.* ☎ *06/835–0022* ⊕ *www.artdeconapier.com.*

Opossum World pairs a shop selling opossum fur products with a mini-museum about the opossum's effects on New Zealand's environment. Products made with opossum fur include hats, gloves, and rugs; a soft blend of merino wool and opossum fur is made into sweaters, scarves, and socks. ✉ *157 Marine Parade* ☎ *06/835–7697* ⊕ *www.opossumworld.co.nz* ☽ *9–5 daily.*

A gannet comes in for a landing on the rocks of Cape Kidnappers in Hawke's Bay.

HAWKE'S BAY

Not for nothing is Hawke's Bay, bounded by the Kaweka and Ruahine ranges, known as the fruit basket of New Zealand. You can't travel far without seeing a vineyard or an orchard, and the region produces some of the country's finest wines. Roughly 20 years ago, a dry, barren area known as the **Gimblett Gravels** was about to be mined for gravel. Then an enterprising vine grower took a gamble and purchased the land. The stony soil turned out to be a boon for grapevines because it retains heat, and now several wineries benefit from its toasty conditions. Chardonnay is the most important white variety here; you'll also find sauvignon blanc, Bordeaux varieties, and syrah.

On the coast east of Hawke's Bay is Cape Kidnappers and its colony of gannets, a fascinating area that is home to as many as 15,000 of these large seabirds. To the south, the architecturally notable town of Hastings sits near the adorable town of Havelock North, known locally as "the Village," with the Te Mata Peak rising dramatically beyond.

Farther south, a hill near Porangahau is the place with **the longest name in the world.** Take a deep breath and say, "Taumatawhakatangihangakoauauotamateaturipukakapikimaungahoronukupokaiwhehuakitanatahu." Now, that wasn't too hard, was it? Just remember it as "the place where Tamatea, the man with the big knees who slid, climbed, and swallowed mountains, known as land-eater, played his flute to his loved one," and it should be no problem at all!

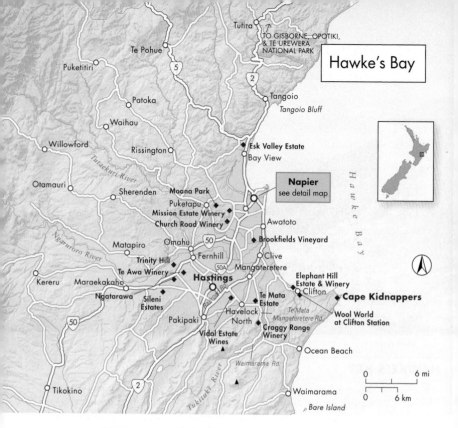

Hawke's Bay

TO GISBORNE, OPOTIKI, & TE UREWERA NATIONAL PARK

Tutira

Te Pohue

Puketitiri

Patoka

Waihau

Tangoio

Tangoio Bluff

Willowford

Rissington

Otamauri

Sherenden

Esk Valley Estate

Bay View

Napier
see detail map

Moana Park

Puketapu

Mission Estate Winery

Church Road Winery

Awatoto

Omahu

Matapiro

Brookfields Vineyard

Trinity Hill

Fernhill

Clive

Te Awa Winery

Mangateretere

Hastings

Kereru

Maraekakaho

Elephant Hill
Estate & Winery

Ngatarawa

Sileni
Estates

Te Mata
Estate

Clifton

Cape Kidnappers

Pakipaki

Havelock
North

Te Mata
Mangateretere Rd.

Wool World
at Clifton Station

Vidal Estate
Wines

Craggy Range
Winery

Ocean Beach

Waimarama Rd.

Tikokino

Waimarama

Bare Island

Tutaekuri River

Ngaruroro River

Tukituki River

0   6 mi

0   6 km

GETTING HERE AND AROUND

Hawke's Bay Tourism, a regional organization, puts up the ⊕ *www. hawkesbaynz.com* Web site for area information. The small Hawke's Bay Airport (NPE) is 5 km (3 mi) north of Napier. Shuttle taxis run into town. Daily flights by Air New Zealand from Wellington, Auckland, and the South Island arrive at Hawke's Bay Airport. Avis Car Rentals are located at the airport. Camper vans are also available. GoBay—Hawke's Bay regional transport—runs a limited public bus service covering Hawke's Bay and Napier on weekdays approximately 7 AM–6 PM.

ESSENTIALS

Air Contacts Air New Zealand (☎ 06/835–1130 ⊕ www.airnz.co.nz). **GoBay** (☎ 06/878–9250 ⊕ www.hrc.govt.nz). **Hawke's Bay Airport** (☎ 06/835–3427 ⊕ www.hawkesbay-airport.co.nz).

Taxi Contacts Hastings Taxis (☎ 06/878–5055).

EXPLORING

Fodor's Choice
★

Cape Kidnappers. This outstanding geological feature was named by Captain James Cook after local Māori tried to kidnap the servant of Cook's Tahitian interpreter. The cape is the site of a large **gannet colony.** The gannet is a large white seabird with black-tipped flight feathers, a golden crown, and a wingspan that can reach 6 feet. When the birds find a shoal of fish, they fold their wings and plunge straight into the sea at tremendous speed. Their migratory pattern ranges from western Australia to the Chatham Islands, about 800 km (500 mi) east of Christchurch, but they generally nest only on remote islands. The colony at Cape Kidnappers is believed to be the only mainland gannet sanctuary in existence. Between October and March, about 15,000 gannets build their nests here, hatch their young, and prepare them for their long migratory flight.

You can walk to the sanctuary along the beach from Clifton, which is about 24 km (15 mi) south of Napier, but not at high tide. The 8-km (5-mi) walk must begin no earlier than three hours after the high-tide mark, and the return journey must begin no later than four hours before the next high tide. Tidal information is available at Clifton and at Napier Visitor Information Centre. A rest hut with refreshments is near the colony.

Gannet Beach Adventures. One easy way to get to the colony is to take a tractor-trailer, which is pulled along the beach starting from Clifton Reserve, Clifton Beach. Tractors depart approximately two hours before low tide, and the trip ($33–$50)—with pick-ups from Napier, Hastings, and Havelock North—takes 4–4½ hours Tours run daily October–late April (☎ 06/875–0898 ⊕ *www.gannets.com*).

Gannet Safaris. If tides prevent the trip along the beach the only other access is across private farmland. A four-wheel-drive bus runs to Cape Kidnappers from Summerlee Station, just past Te Awanga. A four-person minimum is required for this three-hour tour ($50 each). Advance booking is essential for all gannet colony tours. Both pick up by shuttle at an additional cost. Tours operate September to April (☎ 06/875–0888).

Hastings. Napier's twin city in Hawke's Bay is 18 km (11 mi) south of Napier, down Highway 2. The town doesn't have the same concentrated interest of Napier, but buildings in the center exhibit similar art deco flourishes—the 1931 earthquake did a great deal of damage here, too. Where Hastings stands out is in its Spanish Mission buildings, a style borrowed from California, which produced such beauties as the **Hawke's Bay Opera House.** (⊠ *Hastings St. and Heretaunga St. E*).

The Westermans Building. (⊠ *Russell St. and Heretaunga St. E*) is also a shining example of art deco architecture. For picnic supplies, visit the **Hawke's Bay Farmers' Market** (⊠ *Kenilworth Rd.*). The market is held at A&P Showgrounds on Sunday from 8:30 to 12:30. Local products include handmade cheese, breads, ice cream, and fruit. The **Hastings Visitor Information Centre** (⊠ *Russell St. N, Hastings* ☎ *06/873–5526*) is open from 8:30 to 5 on weekdays, and from 10 to 4 on weekends.

Te Mata Peak. Just out of town, a short drive 3 km (2 mi) to the southeast of the village of Havelock North provides access to this famed local viewpoint where it's possible to gaze across the plains to Napier and the rumpled hills beyond. The summit is a 15-minute (signposted) drive along Te Mata Peak Road from Havelock North.

CLOSE UP

The Elusive Te Kooti

Of all the Māori leaders who opposed the early Pākehā settlers in New Zealand, Te Kooti was the most elusive and most awe inspiring. He was born at Matawhero, near Gisborne, in the early 19th century. As a young man he fought with government troops in a local uprising, but he was accused of treachery and deported without trial to the remote Chatham Islands in 1866. While detained on the island, he experienced visions and initiated a creed he called Ringatu ("raised hand," for the practice of raising the right hand after prayer). Ringatu is still practiced by several thousand people in New Zealand.

With his charismatic personality, Te Kooti became the de facto leader of the island's more than 200 prisoners. After two years he engineered their escape by capturing a ship and

forcing the crew to sail them back to Poverty Bay. With arms seized from the ship, Te Kooti led his followers to the Urewera Mountains, fighting off government troops as they went. In the years that followed, he was relentlessly hunted but continued to carry out vicious raids on coastal settlements. His last stand (and the last major engagement of the New Zealand wars) was at a fortified position at Te Porere, which you can still see near the road between Turangi and Te Urewera National Park. Te Kooti was defeated but escaped yet again. He eluded capture and spent the late 1870s in Te Kuiti, near Waitomo, under the protection of the Māori king. The government formally pardoned him in 1883; he died a decade later.

—Bob Marriott

Wool World at Clifton Station. Capture the rustic aura of life on the farm in an original 1890s woolshed. View century-old equipment, learn the history of wool in Hawke's Bay, and watch sheep being shorn daily at 2 PM by hand and machine. The small shop has a nice range of mainly New Zealand-made quality articles. This is the real McCoy! ⊠ *459 Clifton Rd., Hawkes Bay* 🕾 *06/875–0611* ⊕ *www.cliftonstation.co.nz* 🔖 *$5 museum; $20 show* 🕙 *Daily 10–4.*

WINERIES

Brookfields Vineyard. One of the most handsome wineries in the area, Brookfields features rose gardens and a tasting room that overlooks the vines. The gewürztraminer and pinot grigio are usually outstanding, but the showpiece is the reserve cabernet sauvignon–merlot, a powerful red that ages well. Syrah grapes are proving spectacular as is the Brookfields Hillside Syrah. From Napier take Marine Parade toward Hastings and turn right on Awatoto Road. Follow it to Brookfields Road and turn left. Signs will point to the winery. ⊠ *376 Brookfields Rd., Meeanee* 🕾 *06/834–4615* ⊕ *www.brookfieldsvineyards.co.nz* 🕙 *Daily 10:30–4:30.*

Church Road Winery. Owned by Pernod-Ricard, this winery operates pretty much as a separate entity. The wines are labeled Church Road; their chardonnay is a nationwide restaurant staple, and the many variations on the cabernet sauvignon and merlot themes are all worth sampling. A cuvée series features limited-release wines with styles and varieties unique to this winery. A wine tour of the unique wine museum and expertly restored cellars (a tasting is included, too) costs $12; bookings are essential. Dining can be enjoyed in the indoor-outdoor restaurant. ✉ *150 Church Rd., Taradale* ☎ *06/845–9137* ⊕ *www.churchroad.co.nz* ⊗ *Daily 9–5; tours at 10, 11, 2, and 3.*

★ **Craggy Range Winery.** Situated by a small lake with the towering heights of Te Mata Peak beyond, this vineyard has a stunning backdrop for wine making and tasting. The wines include single-varietal chardonnay, merlot, and syrah; a predominantly merlot blend called Sophia; and a cabernet sauvignon blend known as the Quarry. You can sample wines at the cellar, tour the facility by appointment, or enjoy a meal at the Terroir restaurant overlooking the lake. ✉ *253 Waimarama Rd., Havelock North* ☎ *06/873–0141* ⊕ *www.craggyrange.com* ⊗ *Daily 10–6.*

Elephant Hill Estate & Winery. Blending contemporary architecture with the traditional aspect of wine making, this stunning estate overlooks jagged rows of vines with expansive views from the terrace taking in the ocean and Cape Kidnappers. Sip a wine in the sunken lounge or enjoy lunch or dinner in the high-ceilinged ultramodern dining room—it's an unforgettable experience. ✉ *86 Clifton Rd., Te Awanga, Hawkes Bay* ☎ *06/873–0400 winery; 06/872–6060 restaurant* ⊕ *www.elephanthill.co.nz* ⊗ *Daily. Cellar door 11–5, restaurant 11* AM*–10* PM.

Esk Valley Estate Winery. Winemaker Gordon Russell produces merlot, syrah, and blends with cabernet sauvignon, merlot, cabernet franc, and malbec in various combinations, including a rare and expensive red simply called The Terraces. White varieties include chardonnay, sauvignon blanc, riesling, verdelho, chenin blanc, and pinot grigio. Look for the reserve versions of chardonnay, syrah, and merlot-malbec blend to find out what he has done with the best grapes from given years. The winery stands on a north-facing hillside, ensuring it captures full sun; it's 12 km (8 mi) north of Napier, just north of the town of Bay View before Highways 2 and 5 split. ✉ *745 Main Rd., Bay View* ☎ *06/872–7430* ⊕ *www.eskvalley.co.nz* ⊗ *Daily 10–5, tours by appointment.*

★ **Mission Estate Winery.** Surrounded by gardens this classic winery stands in the Taradale hills overlooking Napier. As the country's oldest winery, dating back to 1851, it should be added to your "must-see" list. Award-winning wines, including the Mission Jewelstone range, can be bought or tasted at the cellar door. Join one of the tours for a look at the underground cellar and a discussion of the mission's history. A gallery sells local handmade pottery and crafts. If you stay for a meal, get a seat on the terrace for a terrific view of the vineyard and Napier. To reach the vineyard, leave Napier by Kennedy Road, heading southwest from the city center toward Taradale. Just past Anderson Park, turn right into Avenue Road and continue to its end at Church Road. ✉ *198 Church Rd., Taradale* ☎ *06/845–9353* ⊕ *www.missionestate. co.nz* ⊗ *Mon.–Sat. 9–5, Sun. 10–4:30.*

Moana Park. Specific wine styles are selected and handcrafted from each vintage at this small boutique producer, based on its Gimblett Gravels and Dartmoor Valley vineyards. All grapes are grown on either organic or sustainable sites and are vegetarian approved. ✉ *530 Puketapu Rd.* 🚗 *Taradale* 📞 *06/844–8269* 🌐 *www.moanapark.co.nz* ⊙ *Year-round. Nov.–Apr. 10–6; May–Oct. 11–5.*

Ngatarawa. Set among superb countryside, this former racing stable has become a medium-size boutique family winery. Producing premium wines in the Alwyn, Glazebrook, Silks, and Stables ranges and drawing grapes from around the region, their wines are often referred to in the classic style. ✉ *305 Ngatarawa Rd., Bridge Pa* 🚗 *Hastings, RD 5* 📞 *06/879–7603* 🌐 *www.ngatarawa.co.nz* ⊙ *Daily Nov.–Apr. 10–5; May–Oct. 11–4.*

Te Mata Estate. This is one of New Zealand's top wineries, and Coleraine, a rich but elegant cabernet–merlot blend named after the much-photographed home of the owner, John Buck, is considered the archetypal Hawke's Bay red. Bullnose Syrah-Elston Chardonnay and Cape Crest Sauvignon Blanc show similar restraint and balance. If there's any viognier open (it's made only in tiny quantities), try it—it's excellent. From Napier head south on Marine Parade through Clive and turn left at the Mangateretere School. Signs will then lead you to Te Mata Road and the estate. ✉ *349 Te Mata Rd.* 🚗 *Box 8335, Havelock North* 📞 *06/877–4399* 🌐 *www.temata.co.nz* ⊙ *Weekdays 9–5, Sat. 10–5, Sun. 11–4; tours mid-Dec. and Jan., daily at 10:30.*

Trinity Hill. Situated in the Gimblett Gravels region, this winery produces distinctive wines reflecting the character of the vineyard sites. A diverse range includes chardonnay, viognier, pinot grigio, and many others. Wines with the Hawkes Bay White label are suited for early drinking. Have a glass of wine with a cheese or antipasto platter in the landscaped grounds. The winery holds periodic art exhibitions. ✉ *2396 State Hwy. 50, Hastings* 📞 *06/879–7778* 🌐 *www.trinityhill.com* ⊙ *Oct.–Easter, daily 10–5; Easter–Oct., daily 11–4.*

Vidal Wines. Founded in 1905, this is one of Hawke's Bay's oldest boutique wineries and a producer of premium quality wines. Its restaurant is a popular spot to laze away the afternoon with a glass of sauvignon blanc, chardonnay, or syrah. ✉ *913 St. Aubyn St. E, Hastings* 📞 *06/872–7440* 🌐 *www.vidal.co.nz* ⊙ *Year-round 10–5.*

WHERE TO EAT

$$$
CONTEMPORARY
★

✕ **Corn Exchange.** On sunny days, you can sit outside on the patio. In the rustic interior a large fireplace warms you in winter. Either way, the service is swift and friendly. Try the beef Scotch fillet grilled to your liking with dauphine potato and Yorkshire pudding with a choice of garlic or mushroom sauce. The pizzas are heaven on a plate and the lemon-and-lime tart, homemade with a confit of citrus fruits, is delicious. ✉ *118 Maraekakoho Rd., Hastings* 📞 *06/870–8333* ▭ *AE, DC, MC, V.*

$$
IRISH

✕ **Rose & Shamrock.** This lovely old-world pub in the heart of Havelock North village has the largest selection of tap beer in Hawke's Bay. The pints mix with pub fare like grilled beef sirloin and a generous platter of seafood or hearty beef-and-Guinness pie. It's all extremely reasonably priced. ✉ *Napier Rd., Havelock North* 📞 *06/877–2999* ▭ *AE, DC, MC, V.*

Bikers tour Gimblett Gravels Vineyard in Hawke's Bay.

$$–$$$
CONTEMPORARY

✕ **Sileni Estates.** More than a simple winery, this property houses a restaurant, gourmet cellar store, Wine Discovery Centre, Culinary Arts Centre, and the Village Press Olive Oil press house. Sileni Estates restaurant, specializing in the finest wines and freshest local produce matched with Sileni's extensive range of wines, is open seven days for lunch. ✉ *2016 Maraekakaho Rd., Bridge Pa, Hastings* ☎ *06/879–8768* ▭ *AE, DC, MC, V.*

$$$
CONTEMPORARY

✕ **Te Awa Winery.** Profiting from the Gimblett Gravels terrain, this winery produces single-estate wines, which are carefully matched with the restaurant's menu. You might find you like the seven spice South Island salmon with ramen noodles, shredded fennel, and seaweed salad with tofu and red miso dressing paired with a Leftfield Chardonnay 2007 or a Te Awa Pinotage 2005. ✉ *2375 State Hwy. 50, Hastings* ☎ *06/879–7602* ▭ *AE, DC, MC, V* ⊘ *No dinner.*

$$$$
FRENCH
★

✕ **Terroir Restaurant.** The massive cedar doors and high circular roof give this well-regarded restaurant at Craggy Range Winery a rustic character. Although the menu is loosely country French, "rustic" here is far from unsophisticated. The open wood fire turns out dishes such as confit-stuffed rabbit leg with pancetta, pearl barley risotto, sautéed liver, and chestnuts. From the eclectic dessert menu, pressed apple terrine with French toast and burnt-butter ice cream is an appealing choice. On a warm evening, you can dine on the terrace with views of Te Mata Peak. ✉ *253 Waimarama Rd., Havelock North* ☎ *06/873–0413* ▭ *AE, DC, MC, V* ⊘ *Closed Mon. and Easter–Labor weekend. No dinner Sun.*

$$$$
CONTEMPORARY

✕ **Vidal Wines Restaurant.** Open seven days for lunch and dinner, Vidals is acknowledged as one of Hawke's Bay's finest eating places. A good choice is the fillet of corn-fed free-range chicken with truffled herb gnocchi, confit carrot, and chanterelle mushroom sauce. ⊠ *913 St. Aubyn St. E, Hastings* ☎ *06/876–8105* ⊕ *www.vidal.co.nz* ⊟ *AE, DC, MC, V.*

WHERE TO STAY

$$–$$$ 🚇 **Harvest Lodge.** Close to the center of Havelock North, this up-to-the-minute motel has spacious studios with original artwork and comfortable king-size beds. All units have bifold windows that open wide onto the lovely courtyard and whirlpool baths. **Pros:** it's just a short stagger from the Rose & Shamrock pub. **Cons:** very close to main road, don't stagger off the sidewalk! ⊠ *23 Havelock Rd., Havelock North* ☎ *06/877–9500* ⊕ *www.harvestlodge.co.nz* ↘ *19 rooms* ⚫ *In-room: Internet (some). In-hotel: Spa, laundry facilities, no-smoking rooms* ⊟ *AE, DC, MC, V.*

$$$$ 🚇 **Mangapapa Petit Hotel.** This restored luxury residence, built in 1885,
★   stands in 20 acres of working orchards. A dozen guest suites are luxuriously furnished and the manicured gardens include a grass tennis court, a heated swimming pool, and a sauna. Local produce features on the five-course dinner menu, with dishes such as fresh whole baby Aoraki salmon in a creamy champagne-and-mushroom sauce, and the wine list includes superb Hawke's Bay wines. **Pros:** a private, quiet place; luxury to lighten your heart. **Cons:** it will also lighten your wallet. ⊠ *466 Napier Rd., Havelock North* ☎ *06/878–3234* ⊕ *www.mangapapa.co.nz* ↘ *12 suites* ⚫ *In-room: Internet (some). In-hotel: Restaurant, bar, tennis court, pool, spa, bicycles* ⊟ *AE, DC, MC, V* ⫶❑⫶ *BP, MAP.*

$–$$ 🚇 **Portmans Motor Lodge.** These 20 units surround a spacious courtyard; they're also conveniently near the center of town. Ten rooms have whirlpool baths; the outdoor swimming pool is not heated in winter. **Pros:** reasonably priced accommodations; really handy to town. **Cons:** some parking a little cramped. ⊠ *401 Railway Rd., Hastings* ☎ *06/878–8332* ⊕ *www.portmans.co.nz* ↘ *20 rooms* ⚫ *In-room: No a/c, kitchen. In-hotel: Pool, spa, laundry facilities, no-smoking rooms* ⊟ *AE, DC, MC, V.*

GISBORNE AND EASTLAND

Traveling to Eastland takes you well away from the tourist track in the North Island. Once here, you will find rugged coastline, beaches, dense forests, gentle nature trails, and small, predominantly Māori communities. Eastland provides one of the closest links with the nation's earliest past. Kaiti Beach, near the city of Gisborne, is where the *Horouta* landed, and nearby Titirangi was named by the first Māori settlers in remembrance of their mountain in Hawaiki, their Polynesian island of origin. Kaiti Beach is also where Captain Cook set foot in 1769—the first European landing in New Zealand. Cook's initial landing was unsuccessful, for even though the natives were friendly, several were killed because of misunderstandings. When Cook left, he named the place Poverty Bay—"as it afforded us no one thing we wanted." Although Cook's name stuck to the body of water that hugs the eastern shore, the region is now generally known as Eastland.

Gisborne's warm climate and fertile soil produce some of New Zealand's top wines. Often overshadowed by Hawke's Bay (and its PR machine), Gisborne has about 7,000 acres under vine, and it is the country's largest supplier of chardonnay grapes.

The region has some of the finest and often almost deserted surfing beaches in the country; it's also ideal for walking, fishing, horse trekking, and camping. The international spotlight focused briefly on Eastland when scenes for the film *Whale Rider* were shot at Whangara, north of Gisborne, but there have been few changes to what is mainly a quiet, rural place.

GISBORNE

210 km (130 mi) northeast of Napier, 500 km (310 mi) southeast of Auckland.

The Māori name for the Gisborne district is Tairawhiti (tye-ra-*fee*-tee), "the coast upon which the sun shines across the water," and Gisborne is indeed the first city in New Zealand to see sunrise. Although the city (population 30,000) is hardly large, you need a day or so to get around town properly. The landmark Town Clock stands in the middle of Gladstone Road; nearby, in a house on Grey Street, Kiri Te Kanawa, New Zealand's world-famous opera diva, was born in 1944 (the house is no longer there).

Europeans settled the Gisborne area early in the 19th century. A plaque on the waterfront commemorates the first official sale—of an acre of land—on June 30, 1831. On that site, the first European house and store was reportedly erected (it's long gone, too).

GETTING HERE AND AROUND

Air New Zealand Link flies daily to Gisborne from Auckland and Wellington. Flights last about an hour. The small Gisborne Airport (GIS) is about 5 km (3 mi) from town. You can catch a taxi to the city center for $20. Gisborne is a long way from almost anywhere, though the coastal and bush scenery along the way makes the drive wholly worthwhile. Most of the town's historical sights and other attractions are too spread out to explore them by foot, and a car is needed for the spectacular countryside. The main driving approach is by SH 2, which becomes Gladstone Street as it enters the town.

ESSENTIALS

Airport Gisborne Airport (✉ *Aerodrome Rd.* ☎ *06/867–1608*).

Bus Depot Gisborne (✉ *Gisborne–Eastland Visitor Information Centre, Grey St.*).

Visitor Information Gisborne–Eastland Visitor Information Centre ✉ *209 Grey St., Gisborne* ☎ *06/868–6139* ⊕ *www.gisbornenz.com*).

EXPLORING

The **Tairawhiti Museum.** With its Māori and Pākehā (non-native) artifacts and an extensive photographic collection, this small but interesting museum provides a good introduction to the region's history. A maritime gallery covers seafaring matters, and there are changing exhibits of local and national artists' work. The Exhibit Café serves excellent light refreshments and the Art Bear Gallery Shop sells locally made artifacts.

Te Poho o Rawiri Meeting House. This is one of the largest Māori marae (meeting houses) in New Zealand, and the interior has excellent, complex traditional carving. One example is the *tekoteko*, a kneeling human figure with the right hand raised to challenge those who enter the marae. There are also unusual interior alcoves and a stage framed by carvings; it's essentially a meetinghouse within a meetinghouse. Photography is not allowed inside. On the side of the hill stands the 1930s Toko Toro Tapu Church. You'll need permission to explore either site; contact the Gisborne-Eastland Visitor Information Centre *(see above)*, and donations are requested.

The **Titirangi Domain.** Titirangi was the site of an extensive *pā* (fortified village), which can be traced back at least 24 Māori generations. It has excellent views of Gisborne, Poverty Bay, and the surrounding rural areas. **Titirangi Recreational Reserve** is a part of the Domain, and a great place for a picnic or a walk. The Domain is south of Turanganui River. Pass the harbor and turn right onto Esplanade, then left onto Crawford Road, then right onto Queens Drive, and follow it to several lookout points in the Domain where the views are extraordinary.

Wyllie Cottage. Standing outside, but part of the museum, this colonial-style cottage, built in 1872, is the oldest house in town. ⊠ *10 Stout St.* ☎ *06/867–3832* ⊕ *www.tairawhitimuseum.org.nz* 🖃 *$5* ⊘ *Mon.–Sat. 10–4, Sun. 1:30–4.*

OFF THE
BEATEN
PATH

Eastwoodhill Arboretum. Inspired by the gardens seen on a trip to England in 1910, William Douglas Cook returned home and began planting 160 acres. His brainchild became a stunning collection of more than 600 genera of trees from around the world. In spring and summer daffodils mass yellow, magnolias bloom in clouds of pink and white, and cherries, crab apples, wisteria, and azalea add to the spectacle. The main tracks in the park can be walked in about 45 minutes. Maps and self-guided tour booklets are available. Drive west from Gisborne center on Highway 2 toward Napier, cross the bridge, and turn at the rotary onto the Ngatapa–Rere Road. Follow it 35 km (22 mi) to the arboretum. ⊠ *Ngatapa–Rere Rd.* ☎ *06/863–9003* ⊕ *www.eastwoodhill.org. nz* 🖃 *$10* ⊘ *Daily 9–5.*

Morere Hot Springs. Set in 1,000 acres of native bush, this unique place provides modern bathing facilities in an unusual natural environment. A cold outdoor pool is alongside a warm indoor pool, and in the forest a few minutes' walk away are smaller hot or warm pools with a cold plunge pool. Two private hot pools are also available. Following the walking trails through the forest can take 20 minutes or stretch to two to three hours. Morere is roughly halfway between Wairoa and Gisborne, north of the Mahia turnoff. ⊠ *State Hwy. 2, Morere, Gisborne* ☎ *06/837–8856* ✉ *morere@xtra.co.nz* 🖃 *$6, private pools $9* ⊘ *June–Oct., daily 10–6; Nov.–May, daily 10–9.*

SPORTS AND THE OUTDOORS

FISHING Albacore, yellowfin tuna, mako shark, and marlin along with the yellow-tail kingfish are prized catches off the East Cape from January to April (no fishing licenses needed). There are various fishing operators.

Dive Tatapouri (☎ *06/868–5153* ⊕ *www.divetatapouri.com*) is 14 km (9 mi) north of the city off State Highway 35. Dean and Chrissie of Dive Tatapouri cater for all types of fishing and diving; you can even do the shark encounter from a cage at the back of the boat. If you get to the dive shop at the right time, (tides allowing), you might be lucky enough to hand-feed stringrays that swim close in to the nearby rocks.

Surfit Boat Charters. (☎ *06/867–2970 or 027/230–7016* ⊕ *www.surfit. co.nz*) Their fishing trips start at $140 per person. If you fancy being lowered in a shark cage to come face-to-face with a white pointer shark, aka a "great white," you can take the plunge for $250.

GOLF The **Poverty Bay Golf Course** (⊠ *Lytton and Awapuni Rds., Gisborne* ☎ *06/867–4402*), an 18-hole championship course, ranks among the top-five courses in the country. The green fee is $35 if affiliated otherwise $40.

SURFING Gisborne has three good surfing beaches close to town. Waikanae Beach, a short walk from the visitor information center on Grey Street, usually has good learners' surf, and the Pipe and the Island are for the more experienced. The Pipe is just south of Waikanae; the Island fronts the Titirangi Domain. You can arrange for lessons at the **Gisborne Surf School** (☎ *06/868–3484, 027/482–7873 cell* ⊕ *www.gisbornesurfschool. co.nz*). Rates start at $45 per person for two hours, group session; a private two-hour session costs $60. Surfboard rentals are $25 for a half day or $40 for a full day.

WINERIES

Bushmere Estate. In the Central Valley region of Gisborne and only a few minutes drive from the city center, this small estate grows mainly chardonnay grapes along with some gewürztraminer, viognier, pinot grigio and merlot. In the summer, along with the tasting, light food is available. ⊠ *166 Main Rd. SH2, Gisborne* ☎ *06/868–9317* ⊕ *www. bushmere.com* ⊙ *Oct.–Dec. and Mar.– Easter, weekends 11–6; Jan. and Feb., Tues.–Sun. 11–6.*

Kirkpatrick Estate Winery. One of Gisborne's unique boutique wineries, Kirkpatrick Estate Winery is located on the Patutahi Plateau in a lovely environment with fabulous views out to the hills. Their range includes chardonnay, merlot, malbec, gewürztraminer, and viognier. Antipasto plates are available during the summer. ⊠ *569 Wharekopae Rd. RD2, Gisborne* ☎ *06/862–7722* ⊕ *www.kew.co.nz* ⊙ *Summer, daily 11–4; fall/spring, Fri.–Mon. noon–4.*

Millton Vineyard. This lovely vineyard has a garden area, where you can sit with a picnic lunch and sip barrel-fermented chardonnay. The Te Arai Vineyard Chenin Blanc and Malbec are wonderful wines, and the award-winning Opou Riesling is also recommended. James and Annie Millton grow their grapes organically and biodynamically, following the precepts of philosopher Rudolf Steiner. The vineyard is signposted off State Highway 2, about 11 km (7 mi) south of Gisborne. ⊠ *Papatu*

Rd., Manutuke ☎ *06/862–8680* ⊕ *www.millton.co.nz* ☽ *Nov.–Mar., Mon.–Sat. 10–5; Apr.–Oct., by appointment.*

WHERE TO EAT

$$$$
FRENCH

✗ **The Marina Restaurant & Bar.** In the high-ceiling dining room, light filters through stained glass, and floor-length cappuccino-colored silk drapes grace the windows that look out towards the river. Crisp white table linen and sparkling glassware enhance the interior of this former ballroom of a local stately home. Seafood is the specialty; look for the seafood risotto of sauté fish, prawns, and calamari in a creamy butternut risotto rice with steamed green beans. ⊠ *Marina Park* ☎ *06/868–5919* ⊟ *AE, MC, V* ☽ *Closed Aug. Closed Sun. and Mon. No lunch.*

$–$$
NEW ZEALAND

✗ **Muirs Bookshop Cafe.** Situated over a stellar bookshop, this redbrick walled café, with its bookshelves, high-vaulted ceiling, and comfortable furniture, is a book-lovers paradise—with great food as an added bonus. Choose from the cabinet goodies then sit in the sunshine on the wrought-iron verandah overlooking the main street and enjoy excellent coffee. ⊠ *62 Gladstone Rd., Gisborne* ☎ *06/867–9742* ⊕ *www.muirsbookshop.co.nz* ⊟ *MC, V* ☽ *Closed Sun.*

$$
IRISH

✗ **The Rivers.** A casual place to hoist a few while nibbling hearty pub fare, this is the popular spot for Gisborne locals. Stained-glass partitions separate the dining alcoves, which have brass chandeliers, dark woodwork, and green leather upholstery. A good choice is the fresh snapper with scalloped potato, washed down with a glass of real ale. ⊠ *At Reads Quay and Gladstone St.* ☎ *06/863–3733* ⊟ *MC, V.*

$$$$
NEW ZEALAND

✗ **The Wharf Café Bar Restaurant.** At a former storage shed overlooking the Gisborne Wharf, find a seat at a sunny outdoor table for breakfast or go for a lively evening. The fresh market fish of the day comes with a kūmara croquette, seasonal vegetables, and smoked tomato Romesco sauce. It's matched with a TW Black Label Chardonnay or a Clearview Semillon. If you have room, try the sticky date pudding with butterscotch sauce and vanilla ice cream. The wine list leans to local and other New Zealand producers. ⊠ *60 The Esplanade, Gisborne* ☎ *06/868–4876* ⊕ *www.wharfbar.co.nz* ⊟ *AE, DC, MC, V.*

$$$$
NEW ZEALAND
★

✗ **The Works Café & Winery.** In a building that was once the Gisborne Freezing Works, this restaurant harks back to the industrial past, with a large drive shaft and pulleys on the brick walls. The menu builds on local products, from cheeses to fruit, scallops to calamari. A fillet of salmon poached in a vodka liqueur and lime juice, served on a potato with parsnip puree drizzled with coriander pesto, is excellent. The Works sampler is a tasting of six desserts, and is great to share. Wrought-iron gates at the back lead to a boutique winery. ⊠ *Kaiti Beach Rd.* ☎ *06/863–1285* ⊟ *AE, DC, MC, V.*

WHERE TO STAY

$–$$

▦ **Captain Cook Motor Lodge.** A stone's throw from Waikanae Beach, all the units are roomy, with clean, modern lines and comfortable furnishings, including king-size beds and kitchen facilities. Three of the rooms have whirlpool tubs. There is a restaurant and bar for in-house guests and a children's play area. **Pros:** spacious well-furnished units; convenient to the beach and town facilities. **Cons:** you might get

Chef Charles Royal forages for Māori herbs and plants used in many New Zealand restaurants.

some early morning traffic noise. ✉ *31 Awapuni Rd., Waikanae Beach* ☎ *06/867–7002* ⊕ *www.captaincook.co.nz* 🛏 *21 rooms* ⚐ *In-room: Kitchen, Wi-Fi. In-hotel: Restaurant, bar, no-smoking rooms* 🟰 *AE, DC, MC, V.*

$$ 🏨 **Cedar House Bed & Breakfast.** Bay windows overlook the garden at this gracious Edwardian villa with its huge paneled entrance hall, period furniture, and massive rooms. Crisp linen and a guest lounge with outdoor deck and shared kitchen facilities ensure a comfortable stay. **Pros:** nothing has been overlooked for a cozy stay. **Cons:** you have to be keen on that English stately home look. ✉ *4 Clifford St., Gisborne* ☎ *06/868–8583* ⊕ *www.cedarhouse.co.nz* 🛏 *4 rooms, 2 with bath, 1 self-contained unit* ⚐ *In-room: No a/c. In-hotel: Pool, spa, no-smoking rooms* 🟰 *AE, MC, V* 🍽 *CP.*

$$$–$$$$ 🏨 **Portside Hotel.** This modern hotel is a sparkling addition to the local accommodations. Overlooking an outdoor pool, the lofty open foyer is inviting, the contemporary look complimented by dark wood furniture on a tiled floor, and quality local paintings. All rooms and suites—one, two, or three bedrooms—are spacious with comfortable furnishings and full kitchen facilities. You pay more for an estuary or sea view. **Pros:** quiet, comfortable, well-appointed suites; well situated for a quiet stroll by the river, yet handy to all facilities. **Cons:** the pool is not heated. ✉ *2 Read Quay,* ☎ *06/869–1000* ⊕ *www.portsidegisborne.co.nz* 🛏 *64 suites* ⚐ *In-room: DVD, Internet (some). In-hotel: Gym, no-smoking rooms* 🟰 *AE, DC, MC, V.*

$$$$ 🏨 **Repongaere Estate.** Situated for privacy, these three modern villas stand on separate elevated positions. Each villa has a spacious ultramodern living area with huge ranch-sliders taking in mind-blowing rural views

that extend over the vineyard to Young Nicks Head and Gisborne City. The facilities include two large double bedrooms each with private bathroom and laundry, and full kitchen facilities. Basic breakfast provisions are provided, and with notice, meals can be arranged. Olive oil and white wines are produced on the estate and tasting is available on request. **Pros:** the silence is golden and the views outstanding; you can do wine tasting without worrying about driving afterward. **Cons:** it's a 15-minute drive to town. ⊠ *30 Repongaere Rd., RD 2, Gisborne* ☎ *06/862–7515* ⊕ *www.repongaere.co.nz* ⊗ *In-room: No a/c, Wi-Fi. In-hotel: No-smoking rooms* ⊟ *AE, MC, V.*

FARM STAYS

$ ⊞ **Goldspree Kiwi Fruit Orchard Stay.** This large self-contained cottage, with windows overlooking 25 acres of grapevines and kiwifruit orchards, is ideal for a quiet family holiday. There are two bedrooms, a roomy sitting area, a modern bathroom, and a fully equipped kitchen. Yummy breakfast supplies are brought to the door every day, and meals and picnic lunches can be supplied. Gisborne Centre and beaches are also close by. **Pros:** good homey accommodation; quiet setting. **Cons:** far from town. ⊠ *37 Bond Rd. Ormond, Gisborne* ☎ *06/862–5688* ⊕ *www.kiwifruitorchardstay.co.nz* ⇗ *1 cottage* ⊗ *In-room: kitchen. In-hotel: pool, no-smoking rooms* ⊟ *MC, V.*

$$ ⊞ **Tunanui Station Cottages.** For a taste of the real New Zealand, relax on the 5,000-acre sheep-and-cattle station of Leslie and Ray Thompson. Among the trees is a fully restored 90-year-old cottage with original rimu flooring, kauri doors, and open fireplace; or, you may prefer the modern, spacious, comfortably furnished four-bedroom farmhouse. From here views over the Mahia peninsula to the ocean are spectacular. Both houses have great self-catering facilities, ideal for longer stays (bring your own supplies). City dwellers beware: the silence at night has been known to keep folks awake. **Pros:** these cottages are full-size houses with excellent facilities; ideal for families and people who want to stay in one place after traveling a while. **Cons:** a fair distance from the main road and beaches, but only the owls give a hoot! ⊠ *1001 Tunanui Rd., Opoutama, Mahia* ☎ *06/837–5790* ⊕ *www.tunanui.co.nz* ⇗ *1 cottage, 1 farmhouse* ⊗ *In-room: No a/c, kitchen. In-hotel: Laundry facilities* ⊟ *No credit cards.*

GISBORNE–OPOTIKI LOOP

Soak in the beauty and remoteness of Eastland driving the Provincial Highway 35 loop between Gisborne and Opotiki, the northwest anchor of the East Cape. Rolling green hills drop into wide crescent beaches or rock-strewn coves. Small towns appear along the route, only to fade into the surrounding landscape. It is one of the country's ultimate roads-less-traveled. Some scenic highlights are **Anaura Bay,** with rocky headlands, a long beach favored by surfers, and nearby islands; it is between **Tolaga Bay** and **Tokomaru Bay,** two former shipping towns. Tolaga Bay has an incredibly long wharf stretching over a white sand beach into the sea, and Cooks Cove Walkway is a pleasant amble (two-hour round-trip) through the countryside past a rock arch. In **Tikitiki,** farther up the coast, an Anglican church is full of carved Māori panels and beams. Tikitiki has a gas station.

East of the small town of **Te Araroa,** which has the oldest *pohutukawa* (po-hoo-too-*ka*-wa) tree in the country, the coast is about as remote as you could imagine. At the tip of the cape (21 km [13 mi] from Te Araroa), the East Cape Lighthouse and fantastic views are a long steep climb from the beach. **Hicks Bay** has another long beach. Back toward Opotiki, **Whanarua** (fahn-ah-*roo*-ah) **Bay** is one of the most gorgeous on the East Cape, with isolated beaches ideal for a picnic and a swim. Farther on, there is an intricately carved Māori marae (meetinghouse) called Tukaki in **Te Kaha.**

If you plan to take your time along the way, inquire at the **Gisborne–Eastland Visitor Information Centre** (✉ *209 Grey St., Gisborne* ☎ *06/868–6139* ⊕ *www.gisbornenz.com*) about lodging. There are motels at various points on the cape and some superbly sited motor camps and backpackers' lodges, though you'll need to be well stocked with foodstuffs before you set off. Driving time on the loop—about 330 km (205 mi)—is about five hours without stops. You can, obviously, drive the loop the other way—from Opotiki around the cape to Gisborne: to get to Opotiki from the north, take Highway 2 from Tauranga and the Bay of Plenty.

TE UREWERA NATIONAL PARK

163 km (101 mi) west of Gisborne.

GETTING HERE AND AROUND
There is an extremely limited local bus service, so the best way to get around is to hire a car. Camper vans are also popular as there is plenty of space for the outdoor style of living.

ESSENTIALS
Tour Information Paradise Leisure Tours (☎ *027/223–9440, 06/868–6139 Gisborne-Eastland Information Centre booking* ⊕ *www.gisbornenz. com*). **Tipuna Tours** (☎ *06/867–6558 or 027/240–4493*).

EXPLORING
Fodor'sChoice **Te Urewera National Park** is a vast, remote region of forests and lakes
★ straddling the Huiarau Range. The park's outstanding feature is the glorious **Lake Waikaremoana** *("sea of rippling waters")*, a forest-girded lake with good swimming, boating, and fishing. The lake is encircled by a 50-km (31-mi) walking track; the three- to four-day walk is popular, and in the summer months the lakeside hiking huts are heavily used. For information about this route, contact the **Department of Conservation Visitor Centre** (☎ *06/837–3803* ⊕ *www.doc. govt.nz*) at Aniwaniwa, on the eastern arm of Lake Waikaremoana. You can pick up walking leaflets and maps and ask advice about the walks in the park, such as the one to the **Aniwaniwa Falls** (30 minutes round-trip) or to **Lake Waikareiti** (five to six hours round-trip). The motor camp on the lakeshore, not far from the visitor center, has cabins, chalets, and motel units. In summer a launch operates sightseeing and fishing trips from the motor camp. There are areas

of private Māori land within the park, so be sure to stay on marked paths. Access to the park is from Wairoa, 100 km (62 mi) southwest of Gisborne down Highway 2. It's then another 63 km (39 mi) from Wairoa along Highway 38 to Lake Waikaremoana. Parts of this road are unsealed and have been for years.

North Island's West Coast

WORD OF MOUTH

"The drive to Waitomo was spectacular—windy roads through huge rolling green hills with sheep. We were still so sore and tired from the Tongariro Crossing we switched to do a less intense trip that was just blackwater rafting. We walked through caves. We had to jump backwards off waterfalls—it was fun!"

—AngelaS

WELCOME TO NORTH ISLAND'S WEST COAST

TOP REASONS TO GO

★ **Caving:** Waitomo's underground landscape encompasses miles of passageways, streams, limestone formations, fossils, and glowworms. Explore with underground walks, boat rides, or "black-water" rafting and rappelling tours.

★ **Hiking and Walking:** Explore the wetlands, alpine fields, and dense lowland rain forest of Egmont National Park. Multiday and short walks provide impressive views.

★ **Kayaking and Canoeing:** Whanganui River is the longest navigable waterway in the country; it's also an ideal beginner's river. Pass amazing scenery and historic Māori settlements on a multiday journey by kayak or canoe.

★ **Surfing:** The black-sand surfing beaches along the North Island West Coast rival the world's best. Near Raglan find Whale Bay and Manu Bay, famous for its consistent, left-hand break. In Taranaki, "Surf Highway 45" accesses premier surfing coastline.

1 **Waikato and Waitomo.** Waikato's landscape is a mosaic of dairy farms, stud-horse farm and rural service towns. In the west, forest-covered ranges form a buffer between the farms and famed West Coast surfing beaches of Raglan. To the south, the Waitomo Caves region is surrounded by steep country, a mix of forest reserve and sheep-and-cattle farms.

2 **New Plymouth and Taranaki.** Taranaki juts away west from the North Island landmass. Dominating the landscape is Mt. Taranaki (Egmont is its English name) the nearly perfectly symmetrical volcano that forms the basis of Egmont National Park. The mountain's lower, forested slopes give way to farmland, interspersed by outstanding public gardens. Along the coastline are popular surf beaches. Think, then, of this region for climbing, hiking, surfing, fishing, cultural museums, and "event city," New Plymouth.

3 **Wanganui, the Whanganui River, and Palmerston North.** The Whanganui River, flowing through a vast, forest-covered wilderness from the central North Island mountains, is the focus of this region. At its mouth, Wanganui City was established when river travel was the main form of transport. Today, kayakers and jet-boaters enjoy the scenic, historic, and wilderness experiences of Whanganui National Park. Close by is the university city and farming center, Palmerston North.

GETTING ORIENTED

The region's landscape includes the majestic volcano, Mt. Taranaki; the gorges and wilderness of the Whanganui River; the underground wonders of the Waitomo Caves; world-renowned surfing beaches; two national parks; and a host of forest-covered conservation areas, along with highly productive farmland.

In the north, Cambridge is close to Hamilton and about a 90-minute drive from Auckland, on the main State Highway 1. Surfing town Raglan is in a sparsely populated area of the West Coast, yet an easy hour's drive from Hamilton. Continuing south, Waitomo sits on a popular North Island tourist trail linking Rotorua and Tongariro National Park. It's also on the westward route to New Plymouth city and the Taranaki region. While State Highway 1 traverses the center of the North Island, State Highway 3 travels the west coast through the Taranaki bight to Wanganui, then meets again with State Highway 1 close to Palmerston North.

6

NORTH ISLAND'S WEST COAST PLANNER

Planning Your Time

Whether surfing or just enjoying the harbor, spare at least a couple of days for Raglan, another day or two for exploring the Waitomo Caves. Cambridge warrants a day, perhaps en route to Rotorua. From Waitomo travel southwest to Taranaki, where two to three days would allow exploration of the gardens, museums, a beach trip, and short walk in Egmont National Park—allow longer for more serious hiking, climbing, or surfing adventures. Wanganui City is worth a day or two; a river trip can be a quick jet-boat glimpse or five-day kayak journey, then take a good day or two to absorb the rural life of Feilding and university town Palmerston North before heading on south to Wellington.

When to Go

Although the most popular time is from December through mid-April, most attractions can be enjoyed any time. Summer is obviously warmer—great for swimming or surfing. However, the weather is often more settled during winter, there are fewer people and, unlike some South Island regions, generally no harsh snow or ice conditions to thwart travel.

Getting Here and Around

Air Travel

Airports serve the main centers but driving or taking a bus is best for other areas. **Air New Zealand** operates flights daily from Auckland and Wellington to Hamilton, New Plymouth, Wanganui and Palmerston North. And from Christchurch to New Plymouth and Palmerston North.

Contacts Air New Zealand (☎ 0800/737–000 ⊕ www. airnewzealand.co.nz).

Bus Travel

InterCity links cities and towns in the region with regular daily service. Flexible travel passes let travellers stop off along the way as they like. Shuttles to major sites are available. **Newmans Coach Lines** provides daily direct links with Waitomo from both Auckland and Rotorua. The **Waitomo Wanderer** links Rotorua and Waitomo once daily each way. From Otorohanga, the **Waitomo Shuttle** (book in advance) connects with bus and train arrivals. **White Star** provides daily service among New Plymouth, Wanganui, Palmerston North, and Wellington.

Contacts Intercity (☎ 09/913–6100 ⊕ www.intercity-coach.co.nz). **Newmans** (☎ 09/913–6200 ⊕ www.new-manscoach.co.nz). **Waitomo Shuttle** (☎ 0800/808–279). **Waitomo Wanderer** (☎ 07/349–2509 or 0508/926–337 ⊕ www.waitomotours.co.nz). **White Star** (☎ 0800/465–622 ⊕ www.yellow.co.nz/site/whitestar/index.html).

Car Travel

Driving is the most flexible way to travel through this region. Roads are nearly all clearly signposted, and drivers pass through diverse and scenic landscapes of farmland, forest-covered ranges, and rugged coastline.

Train Travel

The *Overlander,* the 12-hour Auckland–Wellington train, stops at Hamilton, Otorahanga (near Waitomo), Te Kuiti (near Waitomo), and Palmerston North. It travels daily from September to May and during July school holidays, and Friday to Sunday from May to September. **Contacts The Overlander** (☎ 0800/872–467 ⊕ www.tranzscenic.co.nz).

Restaurants

Throughout western North Island, city restaurants and small, tourist-town cafés alike feature an overall sophistication you might not expect away from major cities: think wholesome and hearty food, good espresso and loose-leaf teas, and wine lists with high-quality local wines. Counter food will generally be fresh salads, paninis, focaccia, filled rolls, quiche, pies, and homemade winter soups.

Dinner menus in the higher-end restaurants will likely be the chef's latest creations using high-quality New Zealand eye fillet of beef (beef tenderloin), fish, salmon, lamb racks, pork fillets, and chicken. The best focus on fresh regional and seasonal ingredients. You will also find Indian, Thai, Malaysian, Japanese, Mexican, and Italian restaurants, even in smaller provincial centers. "Smart-casual" is about as formal as attire gets. A legacy of the more basic cafés and hotel restaurants lives on, particularly in some smaller towns; check the guidebook to avoid anything less-than-professional.

Hotels

Bed-and-breakfasts are often stylishly converted country homesteads; sometimes they're custom built. Find luxury lodges and a wonderful range of self-catering villas and cottages (some on working farms, others with spectacular coastal locations, and a few deep in the forest-covered hinterland). National parks have mountain lodges, river lodges, and basic backcountry huts and camping spots managed by the Department of Conservation.

In tourist towns and larger cities, there's the full range of options: boutique hotels, standard hotels with basic rooms, motels with full kitchens, holiday parks with RV sites and sometimes motels and apartments, and backpacker hostels. Although hostels are generally budget options, many with shared facilities, an increasing number are modern and with private en suite rooms.

Visitor Information

Tourism Waikato (⊕ www.waikatonz.co.nz), online only, is a helpful regional resource. The regional tourism organization in Taranaki maintains a Web site, ⊕ www.taranakinz.org, with local listings and event information. The site ⊕ www.windwand.co.nz also has good regional listings.

Detouring

If you are making just one trip to New Zealand and, as many visitors do, you're starting from Auckland and working your way south to catch some top spots, consider making some "dog leg" detours across the North Island.

For example, between Cambridge and the Waitomo Caves head east to catch the geothermal action of Rotorua. Or, from the Waitomo Caves, before turning west to Taranaki head south an hour or so to Whakapapa, the northern gateway to Tongariro National Park. From the south, turn inland from Wanganui to reach the park before heading to Palmerston North.

For an adventure go south from surfing spot Raglan, keeping close to the west coast, inland to the Waitomo Caves and head back to the coast and follow the Marakopa Road to Taranaki.

WHAT IT COSTS IN NEW ZEALAND DOLLARS					
	¢	$	$$	$$$	$$$$
Restaurants	under $10	$10–$15	$15–$20	$20–$30	over $30
Hotels	under $75	$75–$125	$125–$200	$200–$300	over $300

Prices are per person for a main course at dinner, or the equivalent. Prices are for a standard double room in high season, including 12.5% tax.

EGMONT NATIONAL PARK

BEST TIME TO GO

Summer is the best time for walking, hiking, and viewing alpine flowers (best in December and January). Snow-climb in winter.

FUN FACT

Although often described as dormant, few believe that Taranaki's volatile volcanic life has ended. Both scientists and Maori elders hold the view that, one day, the mountain will again erupt in volcanic upheaval.

The volcanic mountain Taranaki, also known as Mt. Egmont, dominates the landscape, the weather, and the history of the region. New Zealand's second oldest national park, Egmont was created in 1900 to protect the mountain, the forests of its lower slopes, and the great outdoor playground these provide.

From a distance the landscape of this national park looks simple; a perfect, cone-shaped mountain draped white with snow in winter and flanked by a near-perfect circle of forest. Look closer, or try walking on the park trails, and a different picture emerges. Thousands of years of volcanic buildup and erosion have crafted a steep gullies and rivers, immense lava bluffs, unstable slips, and forests of everything from moss-covered "goblin" trees to tall, ancient forest giants. It makes a fascinating place to explore and, thankfully, there are many ways of doing this no matter what your level of fitness.

BEST WAY TO EXPLORE

CLIMB THE MOUNTAIN
The steep climb is a serious undertaking, especially with frequent bad weather. The summit itself is regarded as sacred and local Maori ask climbers to avoid the very top rocks. The main summer route (7–8 hours return) follows the northeast ridge. When there's no snow it's all rock underfoot—slippery shingle or big tangled boulders. In winter, climbing the mountain requires snow- and ice-climbing gear and expertise. Mountain guides can be hired in both winter and summer.

MULTIDAY HIKES
The two- to three-day Pouakai Circuit explores all the park's landscapes: subalpine terrain, lava cliffs and gorges, the vast Ahukawakawa wetland, the broad tussock tops of the Pouakai Range, and lichen-covered montane goblin forest. Hiking around the mountain (4–5 days) is another option, if you're keen to climb in and out of steep gullies and through a lot of mud. A second mountain loop above the tree line (3–4 days) can be stunning in summer, but icy in winter and exposed to extreme weather at any time.

TAKE A SCENIC DRIVE
Three main access roads lead into the park, climbing quickly (allow 10 to 20 minutes) up the mountain's steep slopes before opening up stunning views. Short walks along these roads enable you to appreciate the plants, trees, waterfalls, and streams. The interesting displays and photos at the main North Egmont Visitor Centre will enhance your experience—as will the taste temptations in the café!

TAKE A SHORT WALK
Several gentle, well-signposted, short walking trails leave from the three main park entrances. Some top examples are Wilkies Pools (mountain stream, sculpted rocks, goblin forest, 1½ hour return), Patea Loop (mountain cedar forest, stony riverbeds, 2 hours), and Potaema (giant rimu and rata forest and a vast wetland, 20 minutes).

ECO-STAYS

If you stay in the park, rather than driving in and out from your city accommodations, you'll give yourself a better chance of being at one with this magnificent natural place. Check out the sunset or sunrise. Watch the light change across the summit snows, and hear the birds waking in the forest. The Camphouse, at North Egmont, offers self-catering, backpacker-style accommodations in a grand vantage spot, just above the tree line. At East Egmont, you can absorb the forest freshness with host Berta at Anderson's Alpine Lodge, or even cooler air at the Mountain House, 850 meters (2,625 feet) up the mountain.

6

(top left) View from the peak of Mt. Egmont, (bottom) Hikers at the bottom of the mountain, (top) Dawson Falls

WHANGANUI NATIONAL PARK

BEST TIME TO GO

The Whanganui, New Zealand's longest navigable river, cuts its way through a vast remote wilderness, the single largest tract of lowland forest remaining in the North Island.

Anytime! Guided river trips generally operate during summer, however the climate is mild and a winter journey, while a little cooler and possibly wetter, will be equally rewarding—and less crowded. The same applies for the two hiking trips through the park, and the historic Whanganui River Road is open all year-round.

While the river itself is technically not within the national park, the two are integrally linked. The Whanganui's special characteristics—its often muddy appearance, fearsome floods, deep-cut gorges, bluffs, and waterfalls—all affect the easily eroded sandstones and volcanic soils in which the lowland forest thrives.

For centuries, Māori people have lived beside the river, its gentle rapids and deep gorges providing transport long before roads and rail were built. Māori still live along the lower reaches, some farming, some welcoming visitors into their villages or on river tours.

In the early 1900s riverboats carried thousands of admiring passengers through the river's gorges and forests. Now protected as national park, this wild landscape remains intact and today's tourists admire from canoe, kayak, or speedy jet-boat or drive themselves on a journey through history, culture, and a most scenic piece of backcountry New Zealand.

FUN FACT

Don't let the rain put you off. The waterfalls will be even more stunning and, if you're traveling by canoe or kayak, they'll make your paddling easier, with a faster flowing river carrying you along.

BEST WAY TO EXPLORE

CANOE THE RIVER

The Whanganui is New Zealand's most canoed river, popular both for the wilderness it transects and its suitability for beginners. While the river flows through long gorges and forested wilderness, its gradient is gentle and most of its 239 named rapids have little more than a meter fall. The river is suitable for all kinds of craft, from kayak to open-style Canadian canoes. Department of Conservation huts and campsites provide basic (but very scenic) riverside accommodations. Most people take a three- or five-day trip through the heart of the wilderness to Pipiriki, though paddling the lower reaches past historic Maori settlements is also rewarding.

DRIVE THE WHANGANUI RIVER ROAD

Drive slow—there's a heap of history, culture, wild river scenery, and a perhaps a little excitement here. The narrow winding road follows the river's lower reaches, climbing around bluffs and steep gullies and passing through historic Māori settlements that were established before the road was built, when the river was the only access. Heritage stops include an old flour mill, mission settlement, village churches, and traditional Māori *marae* (village)—check with a local before venturing into these. You can drive yourself, or take the daily mail delivery tour from Wanganui.

TAKE A JET-BOAT RIDE

New Zealand ingenuity pioneered the planing jet-boat, enabling fast, safe travel into the most remote, rapid-filled rivers. If your time is limited or the challenge of kayaking too great, take a scenic jet-boat trip into the heart of the national park. (You can also charter one to take you to the river end of one of the isolated three-day walking tracks that traverse the park.) Tours, mostly run by family operators who have long associations with the river people, depart from settlements in the upper, middle, and lower reaches, and last anything from one hour to one day.

ECO-STAYS

Along the river's lower reaches, hosts Annette and John have built a piece of paradise to share with visitors. Their Flying Fox lodge is named for the cage-on-a-wire access across the river (you can take a boat if you prefer). Individual cottages are built from recycled timbers. The home is a certified organic property, with vegetable gardens and heritage fruit trees. Annette's amazing meals include this home-grown produce, baked bread, and preserves; she is also the driving force behind Wanganui River traders' market.

Bridge to Nowhere Lodge has come a long way since the former owner, a fur trapper and tourist jet-boat driver, extended what was then his family home. River access is the only way to reach the lodge, nestled on a small riverside patch of farmland. There's no electric power, but diesel generators, wood-fueled stoves, and hosts Jo and Mandy provide all the comforts of home. Jo also runs jet-boat tours from Pipiriki to the abandoned "Bridge to Nowhere."

6

(top left) Canoeing Whanganui River, (bottom) Waterfall in the park, (top) Whanganui River is a popular canoeing destination

Updated by
Kathy Ombler

The North Island's West Coast encompasses a diversity of landscapes: top surfing beaches; world-renowned limestone caves; and two national parks, one centered on a volcanic mountain, the other on a wilderness river.

The land is generally rural, ranging from tidy thoroughbred horse-stud farms to sheep-and-cattle farms located on remote, rolling hill country and a jumble of forest-covered mountain ranges. Small cities and rural towns throughout the region provide a high level of sophistication, for their size, accommodations, food service, and tourism ventures.

The Taranaki region sprang from the ocean floor in a series of volcanic blasts, forming that distinctive curve along the West Coast of the North Island. The symmetrically shaped cone of Mt. Taranaki is the province's dramatic symbol and the backdrop for climbing routes and hiking tracks (trails). Agriculture thrives in the area's fertile volcanic soil, and the gardens around Taranaki and New Plymouth city are some of the country's most spectacular. The mythology and historical sites relating to the local people are an integral part of Taranaki.

THE WAIKATO AND WAITOMO

Many think of the Waikato region—a fertile, temperate, agricultural district south of Auckland—as the heartland of the North Island. It's home to New Zealand's largest inland city (Hamilton) and some of the most important pre-European sites. Polynesian sailors first landed on the region's West Coast as early as the mid-14th century; by way of contrast, Europeans didn't settle here until the 1830s. In the 1860s, the Waikato's many tribes united to elect a king in an attempt to resist white encroachment. This "King Movement," as it is known, is still a significant cultural and political force within Waikato Māoridom.

Hamilton is a city you can miss if time is tight. Instead, explore and enjoy three nearby attractions: the surfing hot spot and magnificent harbor of Raglan on the West Coast; delightful Cambridge, an agricultural town renowned as a horse-breeding center; and the extraordinary cave formations at Waitomo.

RAGLAN

176 km (110 mi) south of Auckland, 44 km (27 mi) west of Hamilton.

It's hard to think of a more laid-back, welcoming town than Raglan. ■ **TIP→** On the drive out, tune in to radio station Raglan FM 98.1 to catch the local news and grooves. On sheltered Raglan Harbour, and in the lee of Mt. Karioi, the tiny town owes its easygoing ways to the legions of young surfers drawn to the legendary breaks at nearby Manu Bay and Whale Bay, both 8 km (5 mi) southwest of town. The Raglan surf is featured in movies and regularly plays host to international surfing competitions. When the surf's up, drive out to the parking areas above the sweeping bays to see scores of surfers tackling what's reputed to be world's longest, most consistent left-hand break.

While surfers have made this seaside village cool, and along the main drag, Bow Street, barefoot dudes in designer shades pad in and out of the hip café–bars or hang in the smattering of crafts and surf-wear shops, there's much more to Raglan. The huge harbor, with its long Māori history, sandy beaches, and opportunities for kayaking, fishing, and relaxation draws vacationers throughout the year.

GETTING HERE AND AROUND

The main driving route to Raglan is from Hamilton, a pleasant 45 km (28 mi) through rural and forest landscape. Travelers from Auckland can turn off State Highway 1 at Ngaruawahia (10 minutes north of Hamilton) and follow State Highway 39 to Whatawhata to join the road from Hamilton. Turn right to Raglan. Buses to Raglan ($7.30) run from Hamilton three times daily.

ESSENTIALS

Bus Depot Raglan Library (✉ *Bow St.*).

Visitor Information Raglan Information Centre (✉ *2 Wainui Rd.* ☎ *07/825–0556*).

OFF THE BEATEN PATH

Kawhia. With time on your hands, explore the road from Raglan to this isolated, coastal harbor settlement 55 km (34 mi) to the south. It's a fine route, skirting the eastern flank of Mt. Karioi and passing the turnoff for Bridal Veil Falls, but much of the road is gravel. The region is steeped in history and little developed. In 1350 Kawhia was where the Tainui people, the region's earliest Polynesian settlers, first landed after their long sea voyage from Polynesia. Beside Kawhia Wharf the Kawhia Regional Museum and Visitor Information Centre interprets this long history. Volunteers run the museum; it's easy to find since it's the only building on the "street." What those in the know come for, however, are the Te Puia hot springs at Ocean Beach, east of town. There's road access to the beach (or it's a two-hour walk from Kawhia). You can find the springs only by digging into the sand a couple of hours either side of low tide, so check the tide tables in Raglan before you set off.

Visitor Information Kawhia Regional Museum and Visitor Centre (✉ *1 Kaora St.* ☉ *Wed.–Sun. 11–4 (3 in winter)*).

SPORTS AND THE OUTDOORS

BOATING Local boatman Ian Hardie of **Raglan Harbour Cruises** (☎ 07/825–0300) welcomes you aboard the *Harmony* for a 1½-hour cruise around the tidal inlets and bays of huge Raglan Harbour. See forest reserves, historic habitation sites, isolated beaches, the "pancakes" limestone outcrops, seabirds, and, if your timing is lucky, the pod of orca that occasionally visits the harbor. Ians has been operating these cruises for 15 years, so he knows his way around the harbor. Dinner cruises are available, and there's a barbecue on board. Sailings are weather permitting. It's $20 for adults and $10 for children. Advance phone reservations are essential as cruise times change with the tide. Bookings can be made directly with Raglan Harbour Cruises or with the **Raglan Information Centre** (☎ 07/825–0556).

SURFING If you're itching to hit the waves, stop by **Raglan Surf Co.** (✉ *3 Wainui Rd.* ☎ *07/825–8988*), a top surfing store. It stocks equipment by all the leading brands and rents surfboards, wet suits, and boogie boards. It's open daily, and the staffers pass along helpful, local surf tips.

Raglan Surfing School (✉ *Summer: Whaanga Rd., Whale Bay; winter: Karioi Lodge* ☎ *07/825–7873* ⊕ *www.raglansurfingschool.co.nz*) has a variety of options for learning to ride the waves. Several present or past national surfing champions work as instructors. A three-hour session (which includes board and wet suit) is around $89, and ends with a free sauna! Surf Adventure Packages run two to five days and include transport, daily surfing lessons, and accommodation, as well as other adventures such as rappelling, paragliding, and jet-boating. There's also a choice of "surf dames," women's and luxury surfing retreats on offer throughout the year. The school (and surf beaches) is a little way out of town; however, transport is provided throughout Raglan. The school also rents boards at the main Ocean Beach (Ngarunui) daily (9:30–5 November–April). Rental boards are available from the surf school in winter.

Fodor's Choice There's no better way to explore huge Raglan Harbour than on nature's
★ terms, with Steve and Candide Reid and their company **Raglan Kayak** (☎ *07/825–8862* ⊕ *www.raglaneco.co.nz*). Like surfer Tim Duff, local boy Steve searched the world for the perfect place to work on water, then realized it was back home. People of any age and ability are welcome on his shorter kayak trips, where the focus is on paddling with the tide and wind, swimming on secluded beaches, great scenery, espresso, and home-baked goodies. The main trip runs for three hours ($70). Kayaks are also available for rent ($20 single, $30 tandem per hour; $40–$60 per half day; $50–$80 per day). Closed in winter (Easter to end of October).

SWIMMING Although the surf looks inviting at most of the West Coast beaches, there can be dangerous rips and undertows, so be careful where you take a dip. The safest spots around Raglan are Te Aro Bay (Wallis and Puriri streets), Te Kopua, and at Cox and Lorenzen bays at high tide. Call Raglan Information Centre (☎ 07/825–0556) for tide times. In summer, lifeguards patrol the beach at Ngarunui; to avoid the strong rips, swim between the flags.

Surfers enjoy the Raglan Beach waves.

WALKING AND HIKING From Raglan, a number of walks and hikes give you wonderful views of the coastline and take you through splendid native bush. The closest and easiest is from the township itself, through Wainui Reserve to gorgeous Ngarunui Beach. You can climb above coastal bluffs to a lookout point and enjoy the drama of the kite surfers at play at Ocean (Ngarunui) Beach, or follow the beach (except at high spring tides) all the way (6 km). Ask for a brochure at the Raglan Information Centre. ⚠ Don't leave valuables in your vehicle while you're away walking.

The spectacular **Bridal Veil Falls** make an appealing destination. A 10-minute shaded hike through tall native forest from the parking lot leads to two viewing platforms near the top of the 150-foot drop. This section of track is wheelchair accessible. Another extremely steep track continues to a midway-viewing platform; from there a 10-minute trail descends to a bridge and viewing platform at the base of the falls. The tall native trees and the sight of the falls cascading over the hard basalt cliff are worth the effort required to climb back to your car. The falls are 20 km (12 mi) south of Raglan; take the Kawhia road from town.

A great walk, although somewhat more difficult than the Bridal Veil Falls trail, is up **Mt. Karioi**. Some sections are quite steep, so good walking gear and attitude is required. It's worth the challenge for the fantastic views of the coast. The Te Toto Gorge Track takes about 2½ hours (one-way) to a lookout. Wairake Track, from Whaanga Road, is a shorter option to the summit (2 to 3 hours one-way).

WHERE TO EAT

$$–$$$
ECLECTIC

✕ **Blacksand Cafe.** Live music is an occasional treat at this favorite spot for surfers and locals. The cafe supports local organic suppliers and carries one of the country's top espresso brands, Havana. The food is made in-house; there's a comprehensive breakfast menu, fresh baked goods, and a lunchtime salad bar. Dishes include herb-and-corn fritters with spicy tomato relish, organic salad, and minted yogurt; Moroccan chicken, and the Catch of the Day. It's open from 8 to 3 and occasional evenings in summer. ⊠ *17 Bow St.* ☎ *07/825–8588* ⊟ *AE, DC, MC, V* ☾ *No dinner Feb.–Oct.; evening hrs vary Nov.–Feb.*

$$–$$$
NEW ZEALAND

✕ **Orca Restaurant and Bar.** Nestled harborside, its big windows make this the restaurant with the best views in Raglan. When orca come into the harbor, as they do from time to time, it's possible to see them from your table. Brunch is served all day and light meals, including fish soup and burgers, are available at 5. The evening menu brings out the chef's creativity, with dishes such as roasted pork belly with parsnip and apple-and-walnut salad, and braised beef cheek. Classy New Zealand wines join an international selection on the wine list. Orca also offers a casual bar; watch the sunset over the harbor, play a game of pool, or chill listening to the live music on weekends. ⊠ *2 Wallis St., Raglan* ☎ *07/825–6543* ⊕ *www.orcarestaurant.co.nz* ⊟ *DC, MC, V.*

$–$$
CAFÉ

✕ **Tongue & Groove.** This grungy corner café's comfy couches and Formica tables are popular with the locals and the surfer set. The walls are lined with surfboards and decorated with Raglan beach scenes—there's even a surfboard table. The menu is huge and the meals are hearty, starting at 9 with breakfast. Try the stewed fruit and organic yogurt with toasted almonds, or the "hell fry-up in chunky pots, mushies, bacon, sausie, eggs, toast, and caramelized onions." All-day meals come from around the globe: tofu burgers, chicken kebabs, and miso noodles, for example. A local favorite of this eclectic mix is chicken roti, with potato, bacon, cheese aioli, and the café's own chutney. There's a great selection of beers, wines, espresso, loose-leaf teas, smoothies, and juices. ⊠ *19 Bow St.* ☎ *07/825–0027* ⊟ *AE, DC, MC, V* ☾ *Closed evenings Sun.– Wed. end of Mar.–end of Oct.*

WHERE TO STAY

¢

☷ **Karioi Lodge.** Nestled into the hills above Raglan, this backpackers' lodge and outdoor adventure center is the ultimate off-the-beaten-path place to kick back and unwind—or not. American proprietor Charlie Young and his partner, Erin, may have you "sucking back the fresh air of the native bush" and amped up to ride the waves before you know it. Or, if you'd rather do yoga, meditate in the sun, doze in a hammock, chill out in the sauna, play pool, or take a *gentle* bushwalk, they'll arrange that, too. Dorm rooms, most with four beds (two bunk beds) per room, are clean and comfy, but they share baths and there are no extras (don't expect plugs for hair dryers, for instance). There's a regular transport service to town, which is 8 km (5 mi) away. **Pros:** laid-back; you can learn to surf! **Cons:** out of town; you might be sharing with a school group. ⊠ *Whaanga Rd., Whale Bay* ☎ *07/825–7873 or 0800/867–873* ⤴ *5 double rooms with shared bath, 15 dorm rooms (58 beds) with shared bath* ⚴ *In-room: No a/c. In-hotel: Laundry facilities, Internet terminal* ⊟ *MC, V.*

$$ ⊡ **Waters Edge.** Leaving will be the hardest part of a stay in one of Therese
★ and Edi's holiday villas. They will happily leave you alone to enjoy the
harbor outlook and the subtropical gardens and bushy dell. But they'll
be just as keen to take you kayaking to their hidden waterfall; take you
to the Raglan Club to meet the locals and share a Thursday night roast
special ($8); or send you for a beach walk to the fishing wharf where you
can buy the day's catch to barbecue back at your villa. The villas have
lots of special touches, quirky artifacts, and modern comforts; a break-
fast of generous, home-cooked treats is included by arrangement. **Pros:**
welcoming hosts; gorgeous over-water outlook; quiet, relaxing environ-
ment; friendly cat (optional). **Cons:** three minute's drive from town; your
visit might not coincide with when the orcas swim past your cottage.
⊠ *100 E. Greenslade Rd., Raglan* ☎ *07/825-0567* ⊕ *www.watersedge.
co.nz* ⤵ *3 self-contained villas* ⚬ *In-room: No a/c, kitchen, refrigera-
tor, DVD, Wi-Fi. In-hotel: Beachfront, water sports, laundry facilities,
parking (free), no-smoking rooms* ⊟ *AE, D, DC, MC, V.*

CAMBRIDGE

53 km (33 mi) east of Raglan.

Because it's on State Highway 1, Cambridge provides a good lunch
break on your way elsewhere. But this cute town, with its galleries,
cafés, historic buildings, and rural English character, is worth a closer
look. The tree-lined Village Square provides plenty of entertainment:
watch summer cricket matches, or explore the Farmers' Market (Satur-
day 8–noon) or the Lions Trash and Treasure Market (second Sunday
each month). Cambridge is known for its English trees, which provide
an elegant canopy over the town's specialty designer shops, art galleries,
and cafés. It's also home to the country's thoroughbred industry.

GETTING HERE AND AROUND

Travel on either State Highway 1 or State Highway 1B (which avoids
Hamilton city and is clearly signposted from Taupiri); Cambridge is
an easy 2-hour drive from Auckland and 20 minutes from Hamilton.
Continuing south, Rotorua is a 1-hour drive and Taupo is 1½ hours
away. InterCity coach services connect daily from these cities and towns.
By air, you'll arrive at Hamilton Airport, 14 km (9 mi) northwest of
Cambridge; shuttle and taxi services connect you to town.

ESSENTIALS

Bus Depot Cambridge Bus Stop (⊠ *Lake St., Cambridge*).

Visitor Information Cambridge i-SITE Visitor Centre (⊠ *Queen and Victoria
Sts* ☎ *07/823–3456*).

EXPLORING

Visit the **Cambridge Country Store**, housed in an old pink church, a his-
toric building not least because this writer was christened here. In its
current retail form, the store offers a good selection of New Zealand–
made jewelry, possum/merino fur/wool blend clothing, accessories,
and wine. Upstairs, the Toccata Café sells muffins, pies, quiche, salads,
and sandwiches. With its café, quality New Zealand products, Internet

access, and clean toilets the store makes a good one-stop shop. ✉ 92 *Victoria St.* ☎ 07/827–8715 ⊕ *www.cambridgecountrystore.co.nz.*

Cambridge Thoroughbred Experience offers a close-up look at all facets of the Cambridge horse industry. Maree Thomas, herself a trainer, provides professional insight along with access to famous studs not normally on view. Most tours last about three hours, but Maree will personalize her tours to suit your time and level of interest. Take your pick from an early morning at the town's main training track, a look at Maree's own farm and training facility (including a ride on a quiet steed), a visit to the specialist Equine Hospital, or a private visit to the internationally renowned Cambridge Stud, home of Sir Tristram, Zabeel, and other greats. What you'll see there depends on the time of year. Book through the Cambridge i-SITE Information Centre. ✉ *$60 per couple, $50 minimum.*

Walk among some of the most ancient forests in the region at the small "mountain" called **Maungatautari,** where the Maungatautari Ecological Island Trust, in conjunction with the Department of Conservation, is carrying out one of New Zealand's many successful conservation stories. The trust has built a $14 million, 50-km (31-mi) pest-proof fence around 8,400 acres of native forest on Maungatautari, creating a refuge for some of New Zealand's rarest native species. Several endangered birds, including the kaka bush parrot, have been reintroduced here. Interpretive signs at the entrances to the forest describe the conservation project. The closest walk, 14 km (9 mi) from Cambridge, is Te Ara Tirohia Loop Track, but this involves a 20-minute climb through farmland just to reach the enclosure. There is more to see on the more-accessible southern side of the mountain, at the end of Tari Road, Pukeatua (32 km [20 mi] from Cambridge). From the parking lot at the end of the road there is a double-gate entrance into the enclosure. Five km (3 mi) of high-quality tracks lead you through forests, and to an aviary (kaka feeding around 10:30 daily), and to a 16-meter viewing tower, where you can climb into the treetops and be at one with the birds. Experience forest nightlife on an after-dark tour, which can be arranged through the trust ($90 per person, minimum of four people). ✉ *Tari Rd., Pukeatua* ☎ 07/823–7455 ⊕ *www.maungatrust.org* ✉ *By donation* ☿ *Daily dawn–dusk.*

At **New Zealand Horse Magic** at Cambridge Thoroughbred Lodge, experienced ringmasters tailor shows for each audience, easily moving from expert-level information to antics for kids. There is no set schedule for shows. Generally they run for tour groups at which time individual tourists are also welcome. You'll need to call or email ahead for times and a reservation, but it can be difficult to get ahold of someone at this working stud farm. Different breeds of horses, including a Lippizaner, are part of the show. Kids can go for a short ride on more placid horses, with the guidance of instructors, while you have a cup of coffee and a muffin. ✉ *State Hwy. 1, 6 km (4 mi) south of Cambridge* ☎ 07/827–8118 ⊕ *www.cambridgethoroughbredlodge.co.nz* ✉ *Show $12, stud tours $8* ☿ *Tues.–Sun. 10–3 (reserve ahead).*

Near the center of the town, the 100-year-old **St. Andrew's Anglican Church** has excellent stained-glass windows.

WHERE TO EAT

¢–$ ECLECTIC **Fran's Café.** Snag a table in the main room, the comfy lounge, or the sunny courtyard garden, and enjoy your choice of amazing homemade sandwiches, pasta, frittatas, and salads. Chose from decadent chocolate fudge or the dairy- and sugar-free loaf. The menu changes regularly and reflects the owners' interest in a variety of foods and styles. Artwork by locals is on display (and for sale), and Fran's is the only place in New Zealand that sells the famous Granny Dunn's Preserves. And if all that's not enough to interest you, take a look at the incredible, international teapot collection. *62 Victoria St. 07/827–3946 www.franscafe.co.nz AE, MC, V BYOB.*

$$$–$$$$ NEW ZEALAND **GPO Bar & Brasserie.** "Mum used to bring me here to post letters and bank my savings, now I bring my Mum to take her out to dinner." What was the town's post office and savings bank is now one of its most popular eateries, serving contemporary New Zealand dishes with strong Mediterranean, Pacific Rim, and Asian flavors. There's a choice of char-grilled steaks and the sauces to go with them. Pork ribs are perennially popular and the large helping of seared Denver venison leg on hazelnut spaetzle is also well worthwhile. Choose among a semiformal dining restaurant, a cozy bar serving top local and New Zealand beers, alfresco street dining, and a covered rear courtyard. The aura is in keeping with this 1908 Victorian era building, complete with its 53-foot-high clock tower. *Victoria St., Cambridge 07/827–5595 AE, DC, MC, V Weekdays 10:30–late, weekends 9:30–2 and 5:30–late.*

$–$$ CAFÉ Fodor's Choice ★ **Rata Café.** Rata Café is a daytime café, with wood floors, redbrick walls, local artwork, and comfy sofas that serves, arguably, the best coffee in town. Food is made on the premises. The basic-but-wholesome breakfast menu (try the organic Greek yogurt-and-berry compote) is available all day, as are tempting premade salads and pastas, muffins, and bagels. There are dairy- and gluten-free options. Drinks include fresh-squeezed juices and berry smoothies. *64C Victoria St. 07/823–0999 AE, DC, MC, V.*

$$$–$$$$ NEW ZEALAND **Stables Bar and Grill.** This Speights beer-branded establishment aims to please everyone, with a cozy stone fireplace, three casual bars, a garden bar, and gaming room. The gastropub fare is both of good quality and good value and ranges from platters (seafood, Asian, antipasto) and light lunches (Thai chicken curry, burgers, fish-and-chips), to hearty dinners (steaks from the grill, traditional roast pork, and The Stables Sticky Ribs). There's a good community vibe here; Stables sponsors local sports teams, and live bands perform some weekends. *72 Alpha St., Cambridge 07/827–6699 AE, DC, MC, V.*

WHERE TO STAY

$$–$$$ **Cambridge Mews.** Self-contained units have modern amenities and whirlpool baths. Each unit is configured differently, so you can choose the arrangement that best suits your party. With a DVD library and guest barbeque area, it's obvious that owners Jocelyn and Ian Hughes care for their guests, even before seeing the Cambridge Chamber of Commerce "Best Customer Service Award" (2008) hanging in reception. Tucked among the trees just off the main road from Hamilton

6

and a two-minute drive from downtown Cambridge, the Mews is handily located and easy to find. Continental and cooked breakfasts are available. **Pros:** modern; whirlpool bath; well equipped; caring hosts **Cons:** some traffic noise. ✉ *20 Hamilton Rd. , Cambridge* ☎ *07/827–7166* ⊕ *www.cambridgemews.co.nz* 🔄 *4 1-bedroom units, 2 2-story, 2-bedroom apartments, 6 studios* ♿ *In-room: Safe, kitchen, refrigerator, DVD (some), Internet, Wi-Fi. In-hotel: Laundry facilities, parking (free), no-smoking rooms* ⊟ *AE, MC, V.*

$$$$ 🏠 **Maungatautari Lodge.** In an idyllic country locale overlooking Lake Karapiro, and a 10-minute drive from Cambridge, is one of New Zealand's fine luxury lodges. The suites and villa are luxuriously appointed with private balconies, double whirlpool baths, radio-clock-CD players, Sky television, and in-room wireless broadband. The lodge has a spacious lounge, sitting room, formal dining room, and sunny conservatory, where breakfast is served. Outside are grass terraces, formal rose and lavender gardens, and an infinity pool. Rates include breakfast, and dinner can be arranged. The dining room also serves as a public restaurant in summer. Host Donna is a keen advocate of the Maungatautari Ecological Island Trust, just up the road. **Pros:** great outlook; infinity pool; restful aura. **Cons:** 10 minutes from town. ✉ *844 Maungatautari Rd., Lake Karapiro* ☎ *07/827–2220* ⊕ *www.malodge.com* 🔄 *5 suites, 1 villa* ♿ *In-room: Wi-Fi. In-hotel: Restaurant, bar* ⊟ *AE, DC, MC, V* ⏐⊙⏐ *MAP.*

$–$$ 🏠 **Out in the Styx Cafe and Guesthouse.** As the name suggests, this place
Fodor's Choice is in the country, a 25-minute drive from Cambridge. The delight-
★ ful rural environment includes a view of Maungatautari, and some of the North Island's most pristine native forest are a two-minute drive from the guesthouse. Guest rooms are spacious, six with king beds and four with queen beds; three have tribal themes. Smart, tidy, shared bunk rooms (five bunks to a room) are a budget option. Listen to native birdsong while soaking in one of the two hot tubs in the garden, catch a quiet moment in one of the two small guest lounges (with tea-and-coffee facilities), or join the conviviality in the restaurant and bar, where hosts Mary and Lance Hodgson (former local farmers) ply you with wholesome country food and enthuse about the conservation story of Maungatautari. Lance is a Trustee of the Maungatautiri Ecological Island Trust, kaka-feeding volunteer, and the "Maungatautiri After Dark" tour guide; his enthusiasm is infectious. Amazing-value prices include a cooked breakfast and a four-course dinner. Airport transfers from Hamilton Airport (40 minutes) can be arranged. **Pros:** four-course dinner and breakfast included in price; environmental focus; hot tubs. **Cons:** country isolation; Lance might convince you to join the Maungatautari Trust. ✉ *2117 Arapuni Rd., Pukeatua* ☎ *0800/461–559* ⊕ *www.styx.co.nz* 🔄 *3 bunkrooms each with 5 bunks and shared bathrooms; 10 en suite rooms* ♿ *In-hotel: Wi-Fi* ⊟ *AE, MC, V.*

WAITOMO

80 km (50 mi) southwest of Hamilton, 65 km (41 mi) southwest of Cambridge, 150 km (95 mi) west of Rotorua.

A short drive from the main highway, Waitomo is a small but busy rural village catering to tourists visiting the region's famous cave systems. There's a small but good selection of cafés and a tavern in town. To explore the caves there's a dizzying range of options: some 20 different tours include experiences ranging from gentle walking on well-lighted pathways to rapelling, tubing, and climbing underground waterfalls. Above ground, the surrounding hills are a mix of native bush and verdant farmland, and everything is within walking distance of the village center.

The Waitomo Caves are part of an ancient seabed that was lifted and then spectacularly eroded into a surreal underground landscape of limestone formations, gushing rivers, and contorted caverns. Many of these amazing subterranean passages are still unexplored, but four major cave systems are open for guided tours: Ruakuri, Spellbound, Aranui, and Waitomo Glowworm Cave. Each has its own special characteristics, and you won't be disappointed by any. Your guides are likely to be descendants of local chief Tane Tinorau (who discovered Waitomo Glowworm Cave) or local caving experts who have spent years exploring the amazing network of shafts and passageways around Waitomo.

Bookings for all cave tours and activities can be made with the individual tour operators, or at the Waitomo i-SITE Visitor Centre.

GETTING HERE AND AROUND

Although in the countryside Waitomo is handily located close to State Highway 3, one of the major highways, that link Waikato and Rotorua with Taranaki and Tongariro, the Waitomo Wanderer offers a daily return trip from Rotorua, arriving at 10 and departing at 3.45. The Overlander Auckland–Wellington train runs daily through summer and Friday–Sunday in winter. The Waitomo Shuttle ($10 per person) can be booked to meet the train at Otorahanga, 16 km from Waitomo (contact the Waitomo i-SITE Visitor Centre for bookings). For day-trippers, Newmans offers a number of bus-tour package options to the Waitomo Caves originating in Auckland or Rotorua.

ESSENTIALS

Bus Depot Waitomo depot (✉ *Waitomo i-SITE Visitor Centre, Waitomo Caves Rd., Waitomo Caves Village* ☎ *07/878–7640*).

Bus and Tour Information Newmans Coach Lines (☎ *09/623–1504* ⊕ *www. newmanscoach.co.nz*). **Waitomo Wanderer** (⊕ *www.waitomotours.co.nz*).

Train Information Overlander Auckland-Wellington (⊕ *www.tranzscenic.co.nz*).

Visitor Information Waitomo i-SITE Visitor Centre (✉ *Waitomo Caves Rd., Waitomo Caves Village* ☎ *07/878–7640* ⊕ *www.waitomodiscovery.org*).

EXPLORING
TOP ATTRACTIONS

Fodor's Choice
★

Ruakuri Cave. Discovered several hundred years ago by a Māori hunting party, Ruakuri takes its name from the pack of wild dogs that used to inhabit the cave entrance—*rua* means "den" or "pit," and *kuri* means "dog." The cave's original

entrance, an *urupa* (burial site) for Māori, has been closed. Visitors now enter through a dramatic, man-made spiral "drum passage," then proceed through narrow passages (breathe in!). Surrounded by magical limestone formations, you'll hear the roar of hidden waterfalls, pass beneath ancient rock falls, and follow a dark, underground river that twinkles with glowworm reflections. The two-hour tours are limited to 15 people. This is the longest cave-walking tour at Waitomo, but it's easily managed by people of reasonable fitness. All pathways are wheelchair accessible. ⊠ *Tour groups meet at the Waitomo Glowworm Cave Visitor Centre (see above) or Long Black Cafe, 585 Waitomo Caves Rd.* ☎ *0800/228–464* ⊕ *www.waitomo.com* ✉ *Tours $58, for combo options see Waitomo Glowworm Cave* ☉ *Tours daily at 9, 10, 11:30, 12:30, 1:30, 2:30, and 3:30; book in advance.*

Spellbound and Te Ana o Te Atua Caves. With Glowworm & Cave Tours you'll explore Spellbound and Te Ana o te Atua caves, two different underground experiences, and take a short, scenic walk in the countryside. At Spellbound, a gentle raft floats you through a glowworm chamber that has been filmed by Sir David Attenborough for the BBC. Te Ana o te Atua (Cave of the Spirit) has been known to the Ngati Kinohaku people for centuries, and features limestone formations, fossils, and bones. The 3½-hour tour includes tea and coffee and is limited to 12 people. Tours leave from the distinctive Spellbound Tower, at the entrance to Waitomo Village. ⊠ *Waitomo Caves Road, Waitomo Village* ☎ *0800/773–552* ⊕ *www.glowworm.co.nz* ✉ *Tours $60 adult, $22 child* ☉ *Tours are 10, 11, 2, and 3; book in advance.*

★ **Waitomo Glowworm Cave.** This is the most "genteel" option of all the cave tours at Waitomo. The cave takes the first part of its name from the words *wai* (water) and *tomo* (cave), since the Waitomo River vanishes into the hillside here. Glowworm refers to the larvae of *Arachnocampa luminosa*, measuring between 1 and 2 inches, that live on cave ceilings. They snare prey by dangling sticky filaments, which trap insects attracted to the light the worm emits. A single glowworm produces far less light than any firefly, but when they are massed in great numbers in the dark, their effect can be like looking at the night sky in miniature. The Waitomo Glowworm Cave was first officially explored in 1887 by local Chief Tane Tinorau, accompanied by the English surveyor Fred Mace. They built a raft of flax stems and, with candles as their light source, floated into the cave where the stream goes underground. Today's cave explorers walk into the cave on high-quality pathways, to explore features such as the limestone cathedral (and, like famous opera diva Kiri Te Kanawa, are invited to sing

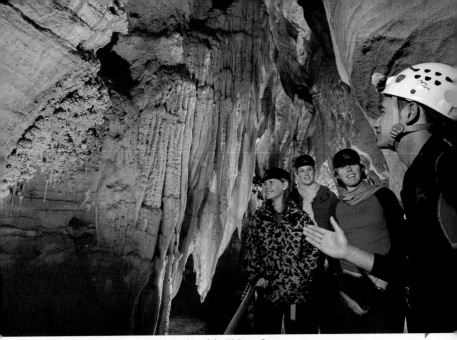
Novice spelunkers learn about the natural wonders of the Waitomo Caves.

to make best use of the amazing acoustics here), then board a boat for a magical cruise beneath the "starry" glowworm-lit cave ceiling, floating out of the cave on the Waitomo River. Tours are 45 minutes and groups meet at the brand-new Waitomo Glowworm Cave Visitor Centre, about 100 meters (300 feet) beyond Waitomo Caves i-SITE Visitor Centre. ✉ *39 Waitomo Caves Rd., Waitomo Caves Village* ☎ *0800/456–922* ⊕ *www.waitomo.com* ✉ *Tours $38, $58 combo ticket with Aranui Cave, $78 combo with Ruakuri Cave, $98 for "three of the best" Waitomo, Aranui, and Ruakuri* ⊙ *Tours daily every half hr 9–5; bookings not required.*

WORTH NOTING

Aranui Cave. At Aranui Cave, eons of dripping water have sculpted a delicate garden of pink-and-white limestone. Keep an eye out for the resident native insects, cave *weta*! The cave is named after Te Rutuku Aranui, who discovered the cave in 1910 when his dog disappeared inside in pursuit of a wild pig. Tours (45 minutes) lead along boardwalks into tall, narrow chambers. Tickets must be purchased from the Waitomo Glowworm Cave Visitor Centre before meeting at Aranui. ✉ *Cave entrance at Ruakuri Reserve, on Tumutumu Rd., 3 km (2 mi) beyond Waitomo Caves Village* ☎ *0800/456–922* ⊕ *www.waitomo. com* ✉ *Tours $38, $58 combo ticket with Waitomo Glowworm Cave* ⊙ *Several tours daily; book in advance.*

SPORTS AND THE OUTDOORS

Several companies provide an initially confusing range of adventures. Each company has its own booking office and base, but activities can also be booked through the **Waitomo i-SITE Visitor Information Centre**

(⊠ *Waitomo Caves Rd., Waitomo Village* ☎ *07/878–7640* ⊕ *www. waitomodiscovery.org*). This free service gives unbiased advice and information to help you decide which tour is most suitable.

CAVE ADVENTURES Most of Waitomo's subterranean adventure tours involve black-water rafting—that is, floating through the underground caverns on inflated inner tubes, dressed in wet suits and equipped with cavers' helmets. Be prepared for the pitch-black darkness and freezing cold water. Your reward is an exhilarating trip gliding through vast glowworm-lighted caverns, clambering across rocks, and jumping over waterfalls. There are also dry options. Some tours involve steep rappelling and tight underground squeezes. Each company runs several trips daily.

★ Most adventurous types will handle the basic trip, "Black Labyrinth," offered by **the Legendary Black Water Rafting Company** (⊠ *585 Waitomo Caves Rd.* ☎ *07/878–6219 or 0800/228–464* ⊕ *www.waitomo.com*). Trips finish with welcome hot showers and a mug of soup back at base. The cost is $105 per person for three hours, or $205 per person for the slightly more challenging "Black Abyss" (five hours). Departure times vary, depending on demand. It's a physical and emotional challenge, with great guides and underground scenery. It can also be scary. Thrill seekers can venture out with **Rap, Raft 'n' Rock** (⊠ *95 Waitomo Cave Rd.* ☎ *0800/228–372* ⊕ *www.caveraft.com*), which has a five-hour combo adventure that includes rappelling, black-water rafting, rock climbing, caving, and checking out the glowworms. The trips cost $135 per person. **Waitomo Adventures** (⊠ *Waitomo Adventure Centre, Waitomo Cave Road* ☎ *0800/924–866* ⊕ *www.waitomo.co.nz*) present a challenging 100-meter (328-foot) rappel into the famous Lost World cave system and tours with enticing names such as TumuTumu Toobing (climbing, swimming, rubber tubing, and rafting), Haggas Honking Holes (abseiling, rock climbing, and crawling) and the seven-hour Lost World Epic (abseiling, wading, swimming, and climbing).

WHERE TO EAT AND STAY

$$$–$$$$ NEW ZEALAND ✕ **HUHU Cafe.** Locals know a good thing and smile quietly when visitors inevitably express surprise that such a classy café exists "way out here in the country." The café brings a touch of urban chic to the town, and its big windows display great views of the countryside. Local produce and organic beef from neighboring Te Anga, feature on the contemporary New Zealand–style menu. Small, tapa-style plates include ostrich, spinach ravioli, steamed pork belly, and rewena, a traditional Māori bread and the café's signature dish. Throughout the day hungry cavers can stock up on a fresh supply of muffins, scones, soups, and bagels. Top New Zealand wines are available. Downstairs, HUHU Gallery showcases classy New Zealand giftware, ceramics, and jewelry. ⊠ *10 Waitomo Caves Rd., Waitomo Village* ☎ *07/878–6674* ▭ *MC, V.*

$$ Fodor's Choice ★ ⛺ **Abseil Breakfast Inn.** "Approach with enthusiasm": the sign at the bottom of the awfully steep driveway aptly summarizes this inn. When hosts John and Helen say they treat you better than family, they aren't joking (though beware their quirky senses of humor). This delightful B&B property overlooks the green Waitomo countryside and resounds with birdsong on the outside and conviviality within. Four rooms, each

DID YOU KNOW?

Underground streams slowly
dissolved limestone to form
the Waitomo Caves over
thousands of years. The
water picked up lime and as
it moved left deposits that
eventually formed intricate,
beautiful stalactites and
stalagmites.

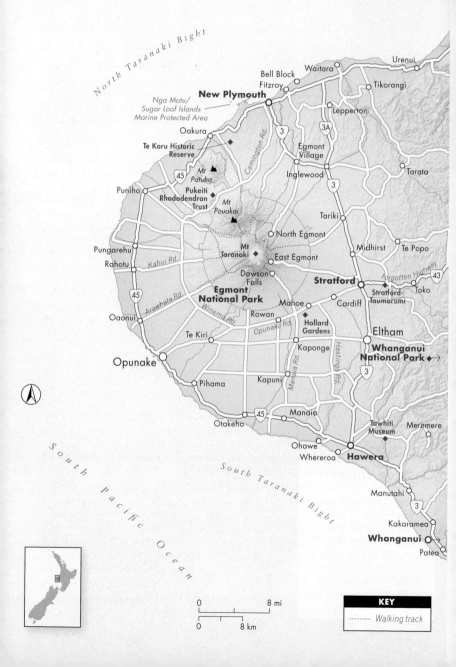

Taranaki

North Taranaki Bight

Urenui

Waitara

Bell Block
Fitzroy

New Plymouth

Tikorangi

Nga Motu/
Sugar Loaf Islands
Marine Protected Area

Oakura

Lepperton

3A

**Te Koru Historic
Reserve**

Carrington Rd.

3

Egmont
Village

Tarata

Mt
Patuha

45

Inglewood

Puniho

**Pukeiti
Rhododendron
Trust**

3

Mt
Pouakai

Tariki

Pungarehu

North Egmont

Midhirst

Te Popo

Kahui Rd.

Mt
Taranaki

East Egmont

Rahotu

45

Dawson
Falls

Stratford

Forgotten Highway

43

Stratford-
Taumarunui

Toko

Arawhata Rd.

**Egmont
National Park**

Mahoe

Cardiff

Oaonui

Winemu Rd.

Rowan

Opunake Rd.

**Hollard
Gardens**

Eltham

Te Kiri

Kaponge

**Whanganui
National Park**

Opunake

Kapuni

Mania Rd.

Hastings Rd.

3

Pihama

45

Manaia

Otakeho

Kapuni

**Tawhiti
Museum**

Meremere

Ohawe
Whereroa

Hawera

South Pacific Ocean

South Taranaki Bight

Manutahi

3

Kakaramea

Whanganui

Patea

KEY
------- Walking track

0   8 mi

0   8 km

tastefully decorated with a local theme (Farm, Cave Room, Bush, and Swamp), have super-queen beds and an entrance from the deck; one has a two-person bathtub. The comfy guest lounge features recycled native timbers, books, wide-screen TV, DVD, and great views. Some excellent New Zealand wines are available at reasonable prices in a trusting self-service, pay-later system. The breakfasts—including free-range eggs and local honey—are seriously good. The story goes that John bought the inn as a present for Helen. Now he says it was really an excuse for him to augment his beloved wine cellar. A complimentary bottle of wine comes with Internet bookings or a stay of more than two days. **Pros:** quirky, helpful hosts; John's big breakfasts; comfy rooms. **Cons:** steep driveway; not for those who like big impersonal hotels. ⊠ *Waitomo Caves Rd.* ☏ *07/878–7815* ⊕ *www.abseilinn.co.nz* ⤳ *4 rooms* ♨ *In-room: No TV. In-hotel: Wi-Fi, parking (free), no kids under 7* ▤ *MC, V* ☉ *Closed June* ⊺◎⊺ *BP.*

¢–$ ⬚ **Waitomo Top 10 Holiday Park.** Modern and clean, this hotel is in the ☾ delightful heart of Waitomo Village. The park offers tents, powered camper-van sites, cabins, en suite units, and a self-contained motel. Some cabins have breakfast-making facilities, but there's also a well-equipped communal kitchen, guest lounge with TV (free movies available), guest laundry, and bathrooms. All guests are welcome to enjoy the free gas barbecue, swimming pool, hot tub, children's playground, and Internet room. Wireless Internet is also available throughout the park, and there are great views of the surrounding forest. **Pros:** central location; spacious bush and rural environment; friendly hosts. **Cons:** likely to be busy in summer; kid-friendly environment may not suit some. ⊠ *Waitomo Caves Rd., Waitomo Caves Village* ☏ *07/878–7639* ⤳ *50 tent sites, 26 powered sites, 8 cabins, 2 en suite, 8 motel rooms* ♨ *In-room: No phone (some), kitchen, refrigerator, Wi-Fi. In-hotel: Laundry facilities, Internet terminal, Wi-Fi, parking (free)* ▤ *MC, V.*

NEW PLYMOUTH AND TARANAKI

On a clear day, sometimes with a cover of snow, Mt. Taranaki (also known as Mt. Egmont) towers above green flanks of forest and farmland. The solitary volcano peak, symmetrical in shape like Japan's Mt. Fuji, sits at the heart of the Taranaki region, and the province has shaped itself around the mountain. Northeast of Taranaki, the provincial city of New Plymouth hugs the coast, and smaller rural towns dot the roads that circle the mountain's base.

Mt. Taranaki and Egmont National Park are tucked away, but they reward those who discover them with mountain climbing (a serious challenge in winter, requiring expertise), hiking, and short forest walks to streams and waterfalls. Heading seaward, there's some 200 km (124 mi) of coastline, top surf breaks, beach walks, shipwrecks, seal colonies, small estuaries, and fishing spots along the Taranaki coast.

Taranaki is a particularly productive agricultural region; layers of volcanic ash have created superb free-draining topsoil and the western, coastal location ensures abundant rainfall. What serves farmers also serves gardeners. Some of the country's most magnificent gardens grow in the rich local soil, and the annual Rhododendron Festival, held late in the year, celebrates the area's green-fingered excellence.

This and other festivals, such as the biannual Taranaki International Arts Festival and annual World of Music, Art, and Dance (WOMAD), Parihaka Peace Festival (a cultural celebration with great Kiwi music), World Cup Triathlon, and regular appearances by top international performers at the Bowl of Brooklands in Pukekura Park, add immensely to the area's attractions.

> ### THE FICKLE SKIES
>
> The weather here is constantly in flux—dictated by the peak of Mt. Taranaki, said to be brooding over lost love when hidden by cloud. Day in and day out, this meteorological mix makes for stunning contrasts of sun and clouds on and around the mountain.

Taranaki has other delights. By the water's edge—along Surf Highway (Highway 45) that follows the coast around the Taranaki bight—you can surf, swim, and fish. Several museums delve into Taranaki history, which is particularly rich on the subject of the Māori. Taranaki is also people-friendly: In November 2008 North and South magazine declared it the best place to live, work, and play, and in the same month it won an international Livable Communities best small city award.

NEW PLYMOUTH

375 km (235 mi) south of Auckland, 190 km (120 mi) southwest of Waitomo, 163 km (102 mi) northwest of Wanganui.

New Plymouth serves one of New Zealand's most productive dairy regions as well as the gas and oil industries. This natural wealth translates into an optimistic outlook that is reflected in New Plymouth's healthy arts scene, the abundance of cafés and restaurants, and a lifestyle that maximizes the great outdoors—from Egmont National Park, with Mt. Taranaki at its heart, to the extensive gardens and parklands, and the first-class surf beaches.

Taranaki has a strong Māori history and a strong history of Māori–European interaction, not all of it friendly. Before the arrival of Europeans in 1841, *kainga* (villages) and *pā* (fortified villages) spread along the coast. In the mid-1800s, European land disputes racked Taranaki. An uneasy formal peace was made between the government and local Māori tribes in 1881, and New Plymouth began to play its current role as a trading port. On the edge of the Tasman Sea, today's city is second to its surroundings, but its few surviving colonial buildings, cafés, stores, galleries, museums in the city center, and extensive parklands, merit a half-day's exploration.

GETTING HERE AND AROUND

Air New Zealand flies daily to New Plymouth from Auckland, Wellington, and Christchurch. **New Plymouth Airport** (NPL) is about 12 km (7½ mi) from the city center.

Travel by private car is the best option for getting around New Plymouth and Taranaki. The roads in are generally paved and in good condition. From the north, State Highway 3 passes through Te Kuiti, near Waitomo, and then heads west to New Plymouth. The highway continues south through Taranaki to Wanganui and onto Bulls, where it connects with State Highway 1. New Plymouth is 6 to 7 hour's drive from Auckland, and 5 hour's drive from Wellington. If you're traveling west on a sunny afternoon, watch out for strong glare from the setting sun.

You can take in most of Taranaki in a couple of days, using New Plymouth as a base, but that would keep you on the run. Ideally, treat yourself to a leisurely week, choosing accommodations from fine lodges, B&Bs, motels, backpacker hostels, or holiday parks spread throughout the region, to rest.

ESSENTIALS

Airport Contacts New Plymouth Airport (NPL) (✉ *192 Airport Dr.* ☎ *06/755–1040*).

Airport Transfers Airport Shuttle (☎ *06/769–5974 or 0800/373–001* ⊕ *www.npairportshuttle.co.nz*).

Bus Depots Ariki Street Bus Station (✉ *19 Ariki St., City Center*).

Bus Information CityLink (⊕ *www.taranakibus.info*). **Taranaki Bus** (☎ *0800/872–287 CityLink, 0800/111–323 SouthLink* ⊕ *www.taranakibus.info*).

Hospital Taranaki Base Hospital (✉ *David St., New Plymouth* ☎ *06/753–6139*).

Visitor Information New Plymouth i-SITE Visitor Information Centre (✉ *Puke Ariki, 1 Ariki St.* ☎ *06/759–6060 or 06/759–6072* ⊕ *www.newplymouthnz.com*).

EXPLORING
TOP ATTRACTIONS

Gardens of International and National Significance. There are 38 Gardens of National Significance in New Zealand, of which five are in Taranaki. Many more are deemed regionally significant according to the New Zealand Gardens Trust. Te Kainga Marire, a native plants garden in New Plymouth, is deemed one of only four New Zealand gardens of international significance. The rainfall and fertile volcanic-ash soils provide excellent growing conditions, in particular for rhododendrons and azaleas, which are celebrated each spring (October and November) during the Taranaki Rhododendron and Garden Festival. During the festival, these splendid gardens and their colorful profusions are open to the public. Some are open throughout the year, such as Pukerua Park, Pukeiti Rhododendron Trust, and **Hollard Gardens**. Others are open by appointment outside festival time. Most of these gardens are the labors of love of their private owners, whereas the Taranaki Regional Council supports the development of publicly owned gardens. A brochure listing these gardens is available from i-SITE visitor centers in New Plymouth, Stratford, and Hawera. Or, contact the **Taranaki Regional Council** (☎ *06/765–7127* ✎ *regional.gardens@tre.govt.nz*).

Govett-Brewster Art Gallery. This is one of New Zealand's leading modern art museums. The gallery has a strong collection of New Zealand conceptual abstract and contemporary art from the 1970s to today. The gallery first opened in 1970, and has a prolific publishing and events program revolving around contemporary art from New Zealand and the Pacific. It is also the home of the internationally acclaimed Len Lye collection and hosts regular visiting exhibitions from abroad. ⊠ *42 Queen St.,* 🕾 *06/759–6060* ⊕ *www.govettbrewster.com* 🖃 *Free* ⊙ *Daily 10:30–5; café daily 8–4.*

Fodor's Choice **Puke Ariki.** Across the road from the *Wind Wand* is the region's heri-
★ tage, research, and information center. Though not as large as Wellington's Museum of New Zealand, Te Papa Tongarewa, Puke Ariki displays tell compelling stories of the region, from its volcanic inception, to the Land Wars, to the discovery of natural oil and gas in 1959, to today's surfing culture. Interactive science exhibits for children are on the lower level. The café is worth a stop, too, as the presence of many locals will tell you. ⊠ *Puke Ariki Landing, St. Aubyn St.* 🕾 *06/759–6060* ⊕ *www.pukeariki.com* 🖃 *Free* ⊙ *Mon., Tues., Thurs., and Fri. 9–6, Wed. 9–9, weekends 9–5.*

★ **Pukeiti Rhododendron Trust.** The Pukeiti Rhododendron Trust spreads over 900 acres of lush, native rain forest, surrounded by rich Taranaki farmland. The Pukeiti (poo-ke-*ee*-tee) collection of 2,500 varieties of rhododendrons is the largest in New Zealand. Many of the varieties were first grown here, such as the giant winter-blooming *R. protistum var. giganteum*, collected from seed in 1953 and now standing 15 feet tall— or the delightful Lemon Lodge and Spring Honey hybrids that bloom in spring. *Kyawi,* a large red "rhodo" is the last to bloom, in April (autumn). Rhododendrons aside, there are many other rare and special plants to enjoy at Pukeiti. All winter long the Himalayan daphnes fragrance the pathways. Spring-to-summer-growing candelabra primroses reach up to 4 feet, and for a month around Christmas, spectacular 8-foot Himalayan *cardiocrinum* lilies bear heavenly scented, 12-inch, white trumpet flowers. This is also a wonderful bird habitat. Pukeiti is 20 km (12½ mi) southwest of New Plymouth's center. ⊠ *2290 Carrington Rd.* 🕾 *06/752–4141* ⊕ *www.pukeiti.org.nz* 🖃 *$14–$16 (depending on season)* ⊙ *Sept.–Mar., daily 9–5; Apr.–Aug., daily 10–3.*

☉ **Pukekura Park and Brooklands Park.** The jewels of New Plymouth are most definitely Pukekura and Brooklands parks. Together the valley lawns, lakes, groves, and woodlands of these connected parks make up a tranquil, 121-acre heart of the city. From December through mid-February, and in March during the WOMAD Festival, **Pukekura Park** comes to life at night with the stunning summer Festival of Lights. Special lighting effects transform the gardens and giant trees into a children's (and big children's) delight, and there's free entertainment most evenings. Pukekura has water running throughout; hire a rowboat (from near the lakeside café) and explore the small islands and nooks and crannies of the main lake. The park also has a fernery— caverns carved out of the hillside that connect through fern-cloaked tunnels—and botanical display houses.

CLOSE UP

Nga Motu and the Sugar Loaf Islands

About 17,000 seabirds nest in the Nga Motu–Sugar Loaf Islands Marine Protected Area. Shearwaters, petrels, terns, penguins, shags, and herons, some of them threatened species (the reef heron is one), nest and feed on and around these little islands. The islands are also a breeding colony and hauling grounds for New Zealand fur seals; in winter more than 400 seals congregate here. Dolphins and orca and pilot whales frequent the waters around the islands, and humpback whales migrate past in August and September.

Beneath the water's surface, caves, crevices, boulder fields, and sand flats, together with the merging of warm and cool sea currents, support a wealth of marine life. More than 80 species of fish have been recorded here, along with jewel and striped anemones, sponges, and rock lobsters. The diving is fabulous; visibility is best in summer and autumn (up to 20 meters [65 feet]). Contact **Taranaki Dive Shop** (⌧ *35A Ocean View Parade* ☎ *06/758–3348).* On land, more than 80 different native plant species survive on the islands. Cook's scurvy grass, almost extinct on the mainland, grows on two of the islands. The palatable species is rich in vitamin C and was sought by early sailors to treat scurvy.

The best way to appreciate these islands is by boat. Landing is restricted, but kayaking and chartered launch trips leave regularly from New Plymouth. Nga Motu–Sugar Loaf Islands are managed by the **Department of Conservation** (☎ *06/759–0350).* Contact the New Plymouth i-SITE Visitors Information Centre for information.

On Brooklands Road, **Brooklands Park** was once a great estate, laid out in 1843 around the house of Captain Henry King, New Plymouth's first magistrate. Today, Brooklands is best known for its amazing variety of trees, mostly planted in the second half of the 19th century. Giant copper beeches, pines, walnuts, and oaks, and the Monterey pine, magnolia *soulangeana*, ginkgo, and native *karaka* and *kohekohe* are all the largest of their kind in New Zealand. Take a walk along the outskirts of the park on tracks leading through native subtropical bush. This area has been relatively untouched for the last few thousand years, and 1,500-year-old trees are not uncommon. A *puriri* tree near the Somerset Street entrance—one of 20 in the park—is believed to be more than 2,000 years old.

For a reminder of colonial days, visit Brooklands former hospital, the **Gables,** built in 1847, which now serves as an art gallery. Brooklands has a rhododendron dell and the extremely popular Bowl of Brooklands, a stage and natural amphitheater used for a variety of concerts and events. ⌧ *Park entrances on Brooklands Park Dr. and Liardet, Somerset, and Rogan Sts.* ☎ *06/758–9311* 🖼 *Free* ☉ *Daily dawn–dusk; restaurant Wed.–Mon. dawn–dusk; display houses daily 8:30–4.*

New Plymouth Coastal Walkway. To get a feel for the city, take a stroll or rent a bike and ride along the New Plymouth Coastal Walkway, judged by the United Nations in 2008 as the world's top environmentally sustainable project. This path runs alongside the city for 7 km

(4 mi) from Port Taranaki to Lake Rotomanu and leads past four of the city's beaches, three rivers, four playgrounds, the Aquatic Centre, a golf course, a skating park, and numerous food vendors. You also pass under the *Wind Wand,* a sculpture almost as iconic to New Plymouth residents as the *Statue of Liberty* is to New Yorkers. Created by the late New Zealand artist Len Lye, the red carbon-fiber tube stands 45 meters (147 feet) high and, like a conductor's baton, dances in the wind as Lye's tribute to what he called "tangible motion."

Te Kainga Marire, Valda Poletti and Dave Clarkson's creation, transformed what was a clay wasteland in 1972 into one of New Zealand's four Gardens of International Significance. It was featured in the BBC documentary, *Around the World in 80 Gardens.* With everything from alpine to forest plants, the garden resembles a piece of native New Zealand bush. There's even a hunter's camp and bushman's hut, legacies of Dave's earlier days as a professional deer hunter. Though within the city limits, the garden is in a green oasis beside Pukatea Dell Reserve and the Ti Henui Walkway and Stream. ✉ *15 Spencer Pl., New Plymouth* ☎ *06/758–8693* ⊕ *www.tekaingamarire.co.nz* ▣ *$10* ⊙ *Sept.–Apr. 9–5, other times by appointment.*

WORTH NOTING

Te Koru Historic Reserve. To get a sense of the turbulent history in Taranaki, drive through the countryside inland from Oakura to Te Koru Historic Reserve. A Department of Conservation track leads ½ km (about ¼ mi) to the site of the pā (fortified village), a former stronghold of the Nga Mahanga a Tairi *hapū* (subtribe). Regenerating native forest has covered part of the site, but still visible are the main defensive ditch and stonewall terraces that drop a considerable way from the highest part of the pā to the Oakura River. No facilities are at the reserve. Take Highway 45 southwest out of New Plymouth to the beach suburb of Oakura, 17 km (10 mi) away. Just past Oakura turn left onto Wairau Road and follow the signs to the parking lot, which is 3.7 km (2½ mi) from the turnoff. ☎ *06/759–0350 Department of Conservation* ▣ *Free* ⊙ *Daily dawn–dusk.*

OFF THE BEATEN PATH

Taranaki–Waitomo. Mt. Taranaki is an ever-receding presence in your rearview mirror as you head northeast up the Taranaki coast from New Plymouth on Highway 3. The highway provides the most direct route to Waitomo Caves and Hamilton, turning inland at Awakino, 90 km (56 mi) from New Plymouth. The Awakino Gorge, between Mahoenui and the coast, is particularly appealing. Forest-filled scenic reserves are interspersed with stark, limestone outcrops and verdant farmland, where sheep have worn trails that hang on the sides of precipitous green hills. At the mouth of the Awakino River, little whitebaiting shacks dot the river's edge. **Awakino** is worth a stop, either at the family-oriented country hotel or for a rest at the river mouth. Turn off the main road by the hotel for a lovely, sheltered picnic spot beneath the summer flowering *pohutukawa* trees. A little farther along is **Mokau,** with a couple of little cafés where, if the whitebait are running, delicious whitebait fritters can be on the menu September to November.

From Awakino, you could be in Waitomo within the hour if you stick to the main highway, but if time is not your master, a far more adventurous route is to follow the minor road north, at the turnoff just beyond Awakino. This runs for 58 km (36 mi) to Marokopa. It's a gravel road for the most part, but a reasonable trip, provided you take care and remember to keep left—especially on blind corners. The drive is through superb sheep country, passing through the Manganui Gorge, and with a possible 4-km (2½-mi) detour down the Waikawau Road to the stunningly isolated Waikawau Beach. The sweep of black sand here, backed by high cliffs, is reached through a hand-dug drover's tunnel. Total driving time from Awakino to Marokopa, including a picnic stop, is about three hours, plus another hour from Marokopa to Waitomo.

OUTDOOR ACTIVITIES

BEACHES Coastal waters can be quite wild, so it's wise to swim at patrolled beaches. The beaches have black sand and rocky outcrops, which make for interesting rock-pool exploring. In summer, *pohutakawa* trees provide shade in some spots; otherwise bring plenty of sunblock. **Fitzroy Beach** has lifeguards in summer and is easily accessible from New Plymouth, just 1½ km (¾ mi) from the city center. Adjoining Fitzroy Beach is **East End Beach**, which also has lifeguards. **Ngamotu Beach**, along Ocean View Parade, is calm and suitable for young children.

BICYCLING Line up a rental bike with **Cycle Inn** (⊠ *133 Devon St.* ☎ *06/758–7418*) to ride the New Plymouth Coastal Walkway. They've got touring bikes (as in road, not mountain, bikes) with helmets at $10 for three hours, $15 for a full day.

BOATING AND KAYAKING A launch with **Happy Chaddy's Charters** (⊠ *Ocean View Parade* ☎ *06/758–9133* ⊕ *www.windwand.co.nz/chaddiescharters*) starts with the guide announcing, "Hold on to your knickers, because we're about to take off." Then the old English lifeboat rocks back and forth in its shed (with you on board), slides down its rails, and hits the sea with a spray of water. If your time in town is limited, do try to spare an hour for this trip ($30 adults, $10 under 12), during which you'll see seals, get a close-up view of the Nga Motu–Sugar Loaf Islands just offshore from New Plymouth, and be thoroughly entertained by skipper, former fisherman, and definite character Happy Chaddy. You can also hire kayaks here ($10 per hour, singles and doubles available) and charter a boat for a fishing trip ($60 per person, minimum six people); these start at 7 AM to avoid choppy water. **Canoe & Kayak Taranaki** (⊠ *631 Devon Rd., Waikwakiho* ☎ *06/769–5506* ⊕ *www.canoeandkayak.co.nz/Taranaki*) has a range of guided trips, lasting from a couple of hours to a couple of days. Two popular options include the Sugar Loaf Islands Marine Park, just offshore of New Plymouth ($60 per person [minimum two people], three hours) and the scenic Mokau River (one day $75 per person minimum four, multiday trips also available).

SURFING Not for nothing is the coastal road between New Plymouth and Hawera known as the **Surf Highway. Oakura**, a village 17 km (10 mi) southwest of New Plymouth, teems with cafés and crafts shops, but the main draw is the good surf. Oakura's environmental effortsy have been recognized by the Blue Flag program, an international organization dedicated to developing sustainable beaches and marinas. Closer to New Plymouth than Oakura, Fitzroy and East End are both popular with surfers, as are **Back Beach** and **Bell Block Beach.** At **Opunake,** in South Taranaki, there is an artificial surf reef.

Beach Street Surf Shop (⊠ *39 Beach Rd., Fitzroy Beach.* ☎ *06/758–0400* ⊕ *www.taranakisurf.com*) is run by local legend Wayne Arthur, who'll give you the lowdown on the hot surf spots in Taranaki. The shop rents equipment and organizes lessons for beginners and advanced surfers.

Taranaki Tours (☎ *06/757–9888 or 0800/886–877* ⊕ *www.taranakitours. com*) takes experienced surfers on half-day trips to the best breaks of the day (and offers various other tours with cultural, scenic, heritage, or garden focus). Prearrangement required.

Vertigo Ltd and Sirroco Surf is the spot at Oakura surfing village to find the latest in surfing gear and advice on local conditions. ⊠ *605 Surf Hwy. 45, Oakura* ☎ *06/752–7363.*

WHERE TO EAT

¢–$
CAFÉ

✕ **Empire.** This sedate café serves excellent espressos but is best known for its huge range of loose-leaf teas, a heady selection that includes jasmine, rose, sunflowers, and calendula flowers, and mixes such as "Cooletta," a refreshing and fruity blend of rose hip, hibiscus, papaya, blackberry leaves, and mango. Food includes a full breakfast menu, bagels served all day, filled rolls, crepes, and salads, and the Empire's signature two-in-a-bowl soup, its flavors changing according to the weather. Vegetarian and gluten-free options are available. ⊠ *112 Devon St. W* ☎ *06/758–1148* ▱ *AE, MC, V* ☺ *Closed Sun. No dinner.*

$$$–$$$$
CONTINENTAL

✕ **L'Escargot Restaurant and Bar.** New Plymouth's oldest commercial building houses what many consider the town's finest restaurant. The menu updates classic southern French cuisine like French burgundy snails stuffed in button mushrooms with herb butter or blue-cheese sauce; half-cured beef Provençal; or classic salade niçoise. White linens contrast pleasingly with dark-wood furnishings. The intimate dining room seats 50, and the mezzanine area 20. Top French, New Zealand, and Australian wines are available. ⊠ *37–41 Brougham St.* ☎ *06/758–4812* ⊕ *www.andres.co.nz* ▱ *AE, DC, MC, V* ☺ *Closed Sun.*

$$–$$$
NEW ZEALAND
Fodor's Choice
★

✕ **Macfarlanes Cafe.** This lively place energizes the café scene in Inglewood, a town midway between New Plymouth and Stratford. It's the original outlet of the Macfarlanes Group, which operates several espresso bars, Arborio Cafe at Puke Ariki, and the Ozone coffee roastery in New Plymouth. The famous eggs Benedict, on crispy homemade hash browns (calorie-counters might want to request the hollandaise sauce on the side) draws people from far and wide to the all-day breakfast (from 9 AM). Lunches highlight fresh salads and pastas. The evening dinner menu is seasonal, New Zealand–inflected international cuisine. Unusual main courses such as Trio of Wild Boar and Cornish and Kranskey sausages, sit alongside a standard menu of steaks, curries, salads, fish-and-chips, and more. ⊠ *1 Kelly St., Inglewood* ✛ *20 km (12½ mi) east of New Plymouth* ☎ *06/756–6665* ⊕ *www.macfarlanes. co.nz* ▱ *AE, DC, MC, V* ☺ *No dinner Sun.–Wed. (closes at 5 PM).*

WHERE TO STAY

$$$ **Ahu Ahu Beach Villas.** A magical place to stay, on coastal farmland just
Fodor's Choice above the beach, this property, with five rustic villas (each sleeps four),
★ has magnificent sea views: you can catch the moon rise over the ocean
horizon. The villas are made of recycled materials, including 100-year-old
French clay tiles and hardwood wharf piles. There's also the spectacu-
lar "underground" villa that's built against the bank and has a grassed
roof and dramatic view. Inside there are two queen-size double beds and
enough space to host a small party. Wi-Fi is shared between villas. The
owners can provide breakfast supplies, or you can drive five minutes to
Oakura Village, which has a renowned surf beach. The villas are about a
15-minute drive south of New Plymouth. **Pros:** dramatic coastal outlook;
recycled, zany design. **Cons:** a drive to town. ⊠ *321 Ahu Ahu Rd., Oakura*
☎ *06/752–7370* ⊕ *www.ahu.co.nz* ⟿ *5 villas* ⟁ *In-room: No a/c, kitchen,
Internet, Wi-Fi. In-hotel: Laundry facilities, Internet terminal* ⊟ *MC, V.*

$$$ **Nice Hotel & Table.** Local entrepreneur and now attentive host Terry
Fodor's Choice Parkes transformed this 19th-century hospital into an opulent city-center
★ retreat. Modern art, including works by leading Taranaki artists Don
Driver, Tom Kriesler, and Michael Smither, lines the walls. The chic guest
rooms and opulent suites come complete with traditional armchairs, good
work desks, DVD players, broadband Internet, and double whirlpool
baths or massage showers. The bistro, Table ($$$–$$$$), is regarded as
one of the city's best, and has been the recipient of many local restau-
rant awards. The menu (main course prices are fixed at $35) changes
seasonally to emphasize fresh local fare but is likely to showcase deli-
cious presentations of salmon, duck, organic Angus beef fillet, or twice-
cooked confit of pork belly. Individual tastes are catered to: vegetarian,
gluten free, dairy free, and so on; current menus are on the hotel's Web
site. The wine list features New Zealand's best varieties. But before you
drink, Terry might let you take a hotel bike for a spin to drink in the city's
shoreline. **Pros:** small, intimate character; artwork; the house restaurant.
Cons: bookings a must for the hotel and the restaurant. ⊠ *71 Brougham
St.* ☎ *06/758–6423* ⊕ *www.nicehotel.co.nz* ⟿ *7 rooms, 2 suites* ⟁ *In-
room: Internet. In-hotel: Restaurant* ⊟ *AE, DC, MC, V.*

¢ **Shoestring Backpackers.** Within walking distance of New Plymouth's
shops, cafés, and Pukekura Park, this lovely old home has spacious
rooms and a welcoming staff. Two dorms each sleep four; rooms come
with one double bed, two single beds, or one single bed. All rooms
share bathrooms, but there are plenty to go around. There's an outdoor
veranda, a communal kitchen, sun porch, and two lounges—one really
sunny with spacious couches, the other with a cozy log fire in winter. A
small private lawn out the back is suitable for tents. **Pros:** comfortable
lounge; lots of books to read; friendly hosts. **Cons:** shared bathrooms.
⊠ *48 Lemon St.* ☎ *06/758–0404* ⊕ *www.shoestring.co.nz* ⟿ *13 rooms,
2 dorms (8 beds) with shared bath* ⟁ *In-room: No a/c, no phone, no TV.
In-hotel: Laundry facilities, Internet terminal* ⊟ *AE, MC, V.*

$$ **Villa Heights B&B.** Country serenity is just a 15-minute drive from
the city. Retired farmers John and Rosemary will sit you down with
a cup of tea and make you feel welcome when you arrive at their
restored Victorian villa. The house is in lovely gardens with great

6

views of Mt. Taranaki, the countryside, and the sea. There are three spacious queen-sized en suite bedrooms, an elegant, wood-paneled guest lounge with Sky TV and open fire in winter, a dining room, and a sunny conservatory. Your stay includes a magnificent breakfast, and dinner can be arranged. Old world charm still comes with mod cons like free Wi-Fi and a GPS to direct you to town. **Pros:** welcoming hosts; country serenity; great views; home away from home. **Cons:** might be too far out of town for some. ⌧ *333 Upland Rd., New Plymouth* ☎ *06/755–2273* ⊕ *www.villaheights.co.nz* ⤴ *3 rooms* ⧖ *In-room: Refrigerator. In-hotel: Laundry facilities, Wi-Fi, parking (free), no-smoking rooms* ▭ *MC, V.*

$$ �〒 **The Waterfront.** Stylish and modern, this is New Plymouth's only waterfront lodging. And it's handily placed next to the Puke Ariki Museum and the information center. Each room has sea or city views. Configurations range from studios with showers (no tubs), to elite studios with individual whirlpool baths, to the Penthouse Suites with separate bedroom, double whirlpool bath, shower, full laundry and kitchen facilities, and other options in between. All rooms have super-king or queen beds. Salt ($$$), the restaurant and bar, feels almost minimalist, all the better to appreciate the beach vista, the walkway, and the 45-meter (148-foot) flexible statue *Wind Wand* by Len Lye across the road. Have a traditional Kiwi breakfast as you read the morning paper. Dinner ranges from Angus beef fillet, braised-and-roasted pork hock, and the catch of the day, to a small-but-delectable offering of salads and lighter, vegetarian meals. **Pros:** the beach; Puke Ariki Museum; city right next door; good restaurant. **Cons:** port traffic rumbles past. ⌧ *1 Egmont St.* ☎ *06/769–5301* ⊕ *www. waterfront.co.nz* ⤴ *42 rooms, 2 suites* ⧖ *In-room: No a/c (some), refrigerator, Internet. In-hotel: Restaurant, bar, room service* ▭ *AE, DC, MC, V.*

SHOPPING

Devon Street, which runs from Fitzroy in the east to Blagdon in the west, is New Plymouth's main shopping street.

Boutique destination store **Et Vous** (⌧ *40 Powderham St.* ☎ *06/759–1360*) has the best selection of designer clothing in town, carrying leading New Zealand labels such as Stitch Ministry, Sable and Minx, and Moss (for the larger form), plus exclusively imported European shoes and vintage French furniture. For magnificent locally made arts and crafts with an edge, visit **Kina** (⌧ *101 Devon St. W* ☎ *06/759–1201*), which exhibits the works of Taranaki artists and stocks contemporary design pieces, from jewelry to sculpture. If you're after some serious outdoor gear, check out **Taranaki Hardcore Surf Shop** (⌧ *454 Devon St. E* ☎ *06/758–1757*), which stocks designer surf-and-snow wear and gear.

EGMONT NATIONAL PARK

Fodor's Choice
★

North Egmont Visitor Centre is 26 km (16 mi) south of New Plymouth; Dawson Falls Visitor Centre is 68 km (42 mi) southwest of New Plymouth.

GETTING HERE AND AROUND

Three well-marked main roads provide access up the mountain, and to walking tracks, lodgings, and visitor centers. The first mountain turnoff, as you drive south from New Plymouth on State Highway 3, is Egmont Road and leads to the start of many walking trails and the **North Egmont Visitor Centre**. Drop in to peruse the excellent displays and grab a bite at the café. The second road up the mountain from State Highway 3, Pembroke Road, takes you to the Mountain House Motor Lodge, a few walking tracks and, a little farther on, to **Stratford Plateau,** where there are stunning views and an access track to the mountain's small, club ski slope. A third turnoff (Manaia Road), turns right off Opunake Road, heading from Stratford, and leads up the south side of the mountain to the **Dawson Falls Visitor Centre.**

Book a local transport operator from New Plymouth through the New Plymouth i-SITE Visitor Information Centre.

ESSENTIALS

Tour Information Air New Plymouth (⊠ *New Plymouth Airport* ☎ *06/755–0500* ⊕ *www.airnewplymouth.co.nz).* **Heliview Taranaki** (⊠ *Ocean View Parade, Port Taranaki* ☎ *0508/435–484 toll-free* ⊕ *www.heliview.co.nz).* **Taranaki Tours** (☎ *06/757-9888 or 0800/886-877* ⊕ *www.taranakitours.com).*

Visitor Information Dawson Falls Visitor Centre (⊠ *Manaia Rd. RD29, Kaponga, Hawera* ☎ *027/443-0248* ⊙ *Open Thurs.–Sun. 8:30-4 and public and school holidays).* **North Egmont Visitor Centre** (⊠ *Egmont Rd.* ☎ *06/756-0990* ⊙ *Daily 8-4:30).*

EXPLORING

Mt. Taranaki dominates the landscape and is the focal point of **Egmont National Park.** The mountain rises steeply, 8,320 feet above sea level; it's difficult not to be drawn toward it. The lower reaches are cloaked in dense and mossy rain forests; above the tree line, lower-growing tussocks and subalpine shrubs cling to spectacularly steep slopes. The English name for the mountain is Egmont; James Cook named it in 1770 after the Earl of Egmont, who supported his exploration. Both names are officially acceptable today. The mountain and its forest covered lower slopes form Egmont National Park, and as such are protected in perpetuity.

Mt. Taranaki is notorious for its ever-changing weather conditions, and many climbers and hikers are caught with insufficient gear. On a clear day, from even the mountain's lower slopes you can see the three mountains of Tongariro National Park in the central North Island—and sometimes even as far as the South Island.

6

OUTDOOR ACTIVITIES

MOUNTAINEERING Mt. Taranaki is a potentially perilous mountain to climb; unpredictable weather and the upper slopes, with their sheer bluffs and winter ice, are an extremely dangerous combination. For summit climbs, when there is snow on the mountain, use a local guide. To the local Māori people, the mountain is sacred, regarded as an ancestor. They ask that climbers respect the spirituality and not clamber over the summit rocks.

Don Paterson brings a wealth of outdoor instruction and guiding experience from Britain, North America, India, and New Zealand to his operation, **Adventure Dynamics**, on Mt. Taranaki. He offers winter and summer summit climbing, rock climbing, and ski guiding. ☎ *027/248–7858* 🌐 *www.adventuredynamics.co.nz.*

Ian MacAlpine of **MacAlpine Guides** (☎ *06/751–3542 or 0274/417–042* 🌐 *www.macalpineguides.com*) has made more than 1,500 ascents of Mt. Taranaki and climbed in Nepal, India, and Antarctica. He guides individual and group climbs, and leads other outdoor pursuits ranging from bushwalking to rappelling to bridge swinging. Summit-climb daily rates are $250.

Ross Eden, who has been mountaineering since the 1980s throughout New Zealand and the Himalayas, is the head guide for **Top Guides** (☎ *0800/448–433* 🌐 *www.topguides.co.nz*). His organization guides adventurers in summit climbs, and instructs and guides in everything from rappelling to avalanche awareness, rock climbing, and bushwalking. Daily climbing rates start at $250 for one person with one guide (a summit climb can be made in a day trip).

SKIING **Manganui** is the only ski slope on Mt. Taranaki. It is a small club-owned and -operated facility and, depending on snow conditions, only operates for 10 to 30 days each winter (June–October). Nonmembers can buy tow passes for a day. Facilities are limited, and the terrain is for intermediate and advanced skiers.

WHERE TO STAY

$$ **Anderson's Alpine Lodge.** In 5 acres of native forest beside the national park entrance is Berta Anderson's modern, purpose-built Swiss alpine-style B&B. The trio of rooms includes a deluxe Top Room, with glorious mountain views from a separate lounge area. Cooked or continental breakfast is included. The lodge has a log staircase, wood-burning fire, and wooden deck; the walls are decorated with paintings of Taranaki, talented works by Berta's late husband, Keith Anderson. **Pros:** mountain view; Swiss-style lodge character; proximity to national park walks; hear kiwi calls at night. **Cons:** not for nature-haters. ✉ *922 Pembroke Rd., Stratford* ☎ *06/765–6620* 🌐 *www.andersonsalpinelodge.co.nz* *3 rooms* *In-room: No a/c. In-hotel: No kids under 10, no-smoking rooms* *MC, V* *BP.*

$$ **Mountain House.** High on Mt. Taranaki, this hotel, motel, and restaurant has a long-standing reputation for its dramatic environment and European-style restaurant. Trails from the lodge traverse the lower reaches of the mountain, through a mix of subalpine shrublands and dense forest, and the small ski club is a 10-minute drive and 20-minute walk away. There are seven stylish double and two twin rooms all featuring high thread-count sheets, flat-screen TVs, whirlpool baths, and complimentary minibars. In-house guests also have use of a small gym, sauna, spa, and massage service. In the kitchen chef–manager Rolf Becker has introduced influences from his work in hotels around the world and the menu features his home-made breads, preserves, and baked goods. Dining options ($$–$$$) include elegant dining in the Egmont Room and wholesome lunches and breakfasts in the conservatory-style Summit Room. There's a hearty German beer selection available along with excellent New Zealand and European wines. Accommodation and dining packages are available. There are regular dinners of food and wine pairings, and casual diners can pop in for a meal after a day of skiing or hiking. Try the braised, German-style beef roulade or the Swiss fondue. **Pros:** dramatic mountain views; fine food. **Cons:** bush obscures views; it can rain often; need your own laptop for Internet access. ⊠ *Pembroke Rd., E. Egmont, Stratford* ☎ *06/765–6100* ⊕ *www. mountainhouse.co.nz* ⤴ *11 rooms (9 double, 2 twin)* ⚒ *In-room: Internet, no a/c. In-hotel: 2 restaurants, bar, gym, laundry facilities, Internet, parking (free)* ⊟ *AE, DC, MC, V.*

STRATFORD

41 km (27 mi) southeast of New Plymouth.

The town of Stratford sits under the eastern side of Mt. Taranaki, and is a service town for surrounding farms. Its streets are named after characters from Shakespeare's works, and it has the first glockenspiel in New Zealand, which chimes four times a day. Because the town is at the junction of Highways 3 and 43, you'll likely pass through at some stage if you're exploring Taranaki. Some of the country's most interesting private gardens, including Te Popo and Hollard, are found in the rich volcanic soil here.

GETTING HERE AND AROUND

Stratford is in central Taranaki, at the junction of State Highway 3, which passes through the region along the eastern side of Mt. Taranaki, and State Highway 43 "The Forgotten Highway." Traveling by car, Stratford is just more than a 30-minute drive from New Plymouth. Daily bus services through Stratford, linking New Plymouth and Wanganui are available with InterCity and White Star. Timetables vary throughout the week. Bookings can be made through i-SITE Visitor Centres in the region.

ESSENTIALS

Bus Information InterCity (⊕ www.intercitycoach.co.nz). **White Star** (⊕ www.yellow.co.nz/site/whitestar).

Visitor Information Stratford i-SITE Visitor Information Centre (⊠ *Prospero Pl., Miranda St.* ☎ *06/765–6708 or 0800/765–6708* ⊕ www.stratfordnz.co.nz).

EXPLORING

Fodor'sChoice ★

Surrounded by dairy farms, the **Hollard Gardens** were created by dairy farmer Bernard Hollard, who, in 1927, fenced a 14-acre patch of native bush on his farm and started what is now a Garden of National Significance. There are two distinct sections, one an old woodland garden of mature native and exotic trees, with closely underplanted rhododendrons, azaleas, camellias, and perennials, the other a more recent creation. Broad lawns, paths with mixed borders, and vistas of Mt. Taranaki are features of the garden, established in 1982. Further upgrades to the paths and visitor facilities were made in 2008. The gardens are particularly colorful during the rhododendron flowering season from September to late November. ⊠ *Upper Manaia Rd., off Opunake Rd., Kaponga* ✛ *8 km (5 mi) south of Dawson Falls* ☎ *0800/736–222* ⊕ *www.hollardgardens.info* ⊠ *Free* ☉ *Daily 9–5.*

OFF THE
BEATEN
PATH

Stratford–Taumarunui. Known as the Forgotten World Highway, Highway 43, heading northeast from Stratford, takes travelers on an intriguing, history-rich tour of Māori and colonial heritage as it winds through rolling farmland and pristine subtropical rain forests to Taumarunui (the northern access point for the Whanganui River region). Highlights on the way include Mt. Damper Falls, the spectacular view from Tahora Saddle, the dramatic Tangarakau Gorge, two road tunnels, and riverboat-landing sites. The only place to stop for refreshment along this road is the over-100-year-old **Whangamomona Hotel** (⊠ *6018 Ohura Rd.* ☎ *06/762–5823*). The 155-km (96-mi) highway is sealed for all but 11 km (7 mi). Allow three hours and fill your tank before leaving Stratford. For information contact the **Stratford i-SITE Visitor Centre** (☎ *06/765–6708 or 0800/765–6708* ⊕ *www.stratfordnz.co.nz*).

6

WHERE TO STAY

$$

Te Popo. On a back road northeast of Stratford, this peaceful homestead is magnificently set in one of Taranaki's Gardens of National Significance. The 34 acres of sprawling woodland and park features a fine collection of exotic trees, open lawns, perennial borders, and native forest. Native birdlife is prolific, and glowworms shine at dusk. The spacious guest rooms have wood-burning fireplaces and private garden views. Breakfast is served in a sunny conservatory. A kitchen adjacent to the conservatory is for guest use. Te Popo is a 15-minute drive from Stratford on good country roads, if rather winding in places. You can visit the gardens separately by appointment ($8). **Pros:** magnificent garden; huge guest library; organic fruit and vegetables from the home garden; conservatory. **Cons:** it helps to like gardens; out in the country. ⊠ *636 Stanley Rd., Stratford* ⬦ *R.D. 24, Stratford* ☎ *06/762–8775* ⊕ *www.tepopo.co.nz* ⬗ *3 rooms, 1 apartment* ⬙ *In-room: No a/c, Internet. In-hotel: Laundry facilities* ⬛ *AE, DC, MC, V* ⭑⭑ *BP.*

SHOPPING

Environmental Products (⊠ *1103 Opunake Rd., Mahoe* ☎ *06/764–6133* ⊕ *www.envirofur.co.nz*), a small but thriving business near Stratford, is turning possum, a local environmental pest into excellent products, using all-natural tanning processes (no chemicals) to produce high-quality, designer possum fur and leather products such as hats, rugs, coats, and scarves. Deerskin products are also available. It's open weekdays 9–5 and weekends 10–4.

HAWERA

29 km (18 mi) south of Stratford.

This quiet country town, a hub for the farming community, can give you a close look at the local history and way of life. For the more adventurous there is the opportunity to "dam-drop" on the Waingongoro River.

GETTING HERE AND AROUND

Hawera is in southern Taranaki on State Highway 3, which passes through the region along the eastern side of Mt. Taranaki. Traveling by car, the town is one hour south of New Plymouth and just more than an hour drive north of Wanganui. Two daily bus services (InterCity and White Star) link Hawera with New Plymouth and Wanganui. Timetables vary throughout the week. Bookings can be made through i-SITE Visitor Centres in the region.

ESSENTIALS

Visitor Information South Taranaki i-SITE Visitor Centre (✉ *55 High St., Hawera* ☎ *06/278-8599*).

EXPLORING

An unlikely find in Hawera is the **Kevin Wasley Elvis Presley Memorial Room,** a private museum devoted to "The King." The unique collection includes more than 2,000 records and impressive memorabilia. The museum does not keep regular hours; phone ahead for an appointment with Kevin. ✉ *51 Argyle St.* ☎ *06/278-7624 or 0274/982-942* ⊕ *www.digitalus.co.nz/elvis* ✉ *By donation.*

Fodor's Choice
★

The **Tawhiti Museum** is a labor of love for Nigel Ogle, and an outstanding presentation of regional history. The former schoolteacher-cum-historian bought an old cheese factory in 1975 and proceeded to fill it up with life-size figures from Taranaki's past. He creates the fiberglass figures from molds of local people and sets them in scenes depicting the pioneering days. Nigel is continually adding "stories"; dioramas depict the huge intertribal wars of the 1830s and European–Māori land wars of the 1860s. More than 800 model warriors, none of them the same, have been created. The latest attraction, which opened in 2009, "Traders and Whalers" is separate from the main museum and regarded as a first of its kind in the country. Full size fiberglass models help depict the colorful stories of the traders and whalers who plied the coastline and were the first Europeans to interact with the Maori people. On the first Sunday of each month, the museum's Tawhiti Bush Railway springs to life, rattling through a variety of outdoor displays that highlight the historical logging operations in Taranaki. In the museum is **Mr. Badger's Café,** with its delightful *Wind in the Willows* theme, quite simply one of the best cafés in southern Taranaki. To get to the museum, take Tawhiti Road northeast out of Hawera and continue 4 km (2½ mi). ✉ *401 Ohangai*

Rd. ☎ 06/278–6837 ⊕ www.tawhitimuseum.co.nz ☎ $10 to Tawhiti Museum; $10 to Traders and Whalers ☉ Sept.–May, Fri.–Mon. 10–4; June–Aug., Sun. 10–4; Dec. 26–Jan. 31, daily 10–4.

OUTDOOR ACTIVITIES

White-water sledging (like sledding, but on water) has become one of New Zealand's many zany adventure sports, and Taranaki is where it all started. You'll have your nose to the water as you maneuver your sledge headfirst over a short steep dam on the Waingongoro River. **Kaitiaki Adventures** (☎ 06/752–8242 or 0274/706–899 ⊕ www.dam-drop.com) runs daily trips, leaving from the Powerco Aquatic Centre on Waihi Road in Hawera. Bring a swimsuit and towel; you'll be out-fitted with a padded wet suit, booties, life jacket, helmet, fins, and a sledge (which resembles a small surfboard). The trips take about three hours and include a journey around Okahutiti Pā, an old fortification. The cost is from $100; advance reservations are required. Kaitiaki Adventures also organizes surfing and mountain-biking tours.

WHERE TO STAY

$$ 🖼 **Tairoa Lodge.** The translation for *tairoa* is "linger, stay longer," and that's what you'll want to do at this relaxing B&B. In this renovated kauri villa, built in 1875, the two spacious guest rooms look out over the woodland garden and swimming pool. Both rooms have ornamental fireplaces with carved wooden mantels; one room is done in deep reds, the other in cheery yellows-and-blues. Breakfast is included. A separate two-bedroom cottage ($195 double) can accommodate families; it has a full kitchen as well as a home-theater system and veranda overlooking a spacious lawn. To keep busy, you can peruse piles of the latest maga-zines, play chess or *pétanque* (the French version of boccie), or take a dip in the pool. **Pros:** private; spacious; quiet, rural location; swim-ming pool. **Cons:** not for those who prefer larger hotels. ⊠ *3 Puawai St. ☎ 06/278–8603 ⊕ www.tairoa-lodge.co.nz ✍ 2 rooms (1 queen, 1 queen and single), 1 cottage (with 2 rooms, 1 queen and 2 king singles) ⚓ In-room: DVD In-hotel: Restaurant, pool, laundry facilities, Wi-Fi, parking (free) ⊟ AE, DC, MC, V ⛐ BP.*

WANGANUI

163 km (102 mi) southeast of New Plymouth, 193 km (121 mi) north of Wellington, 225 km (141 mi) southwest of Taupo.

Wanganui is a river city and the Whanganui River its raison d'être. It began as a small port settlement and a transport junction between the sea and the river, which is navigable for miles into the forested interior. With trains, roads, and now planes stealing the transportation lime-light, Wanganui city sat quietly for some years while other North Island towns flourished. Today there has been a considerable resurgence; Wan-ganui's compact city center has lively streets with shops and galleries and restored heritage buildings that hark back to colonial times and busy trading days. Locals gather at the River Traders riverside market on Saturday mornings for fresh produce and crafts, and then disperse to the city's cafés and restaurants for a leisurely brunch.

For hundreds of years, the Māori people have lived along the banks of the Whanganui River, a major access route between the coast and interior. In the 1800s, Wanganui township became established as one of New Zealand's most prosperous early European settlements. Local Māori people trace their occupation of the land around the Whanganui River back as far as the 10th century. European settlers started moving to the area in the 1840s. Subsequent appropriation of land caused conflict with local Māori, and a British garrison was temporarily established in the town. From the 1880s the port and riverboat transport that provided a link to the North Island interior led to a prosperous time for trade and tourism, until completion of the main trunk railway line meant that Wanganui was essentially bypassed. Today, Wanganui has evolved into a small-but-appealing provincial city, serving local industry, tourism, and the region's farming community.

GETTING HERE AND AROUND

Wanganui is a three-hour drive from Wellington; take State Highway 1 north to Sanson and Highway 3 west from there. From New Plymouth drive south on State Highway 3 and allow about 1½ hours for the journey. Access to the lower and middle reaches of the Whanganui River from the city is via the Whanganui River Road, a minor winding route—expect it to take two hours to drive from Wanganui to Pipiriki. Remember to keep left on the narrow corners. For a scenic backcountry day trip, drive north up the Whanganui River Road, cut east along the minor road connecting Pipirike to Raetihi, and then return down Highway 4, a paved though winding road through steep farmland and forest, to Wanganui. To reach the kayak starting points, take Highway 4 north from Wanganui; it's a three-hour drive to Taumarunui, via Raetihi.

ESSENTIALS

Bus Depot Wanganui Travel Centre (✉ *156 Ridgeway St.*).

Hospital Wanganui Hospital (✉ *155 Heads Rd.* ☎ *06/348–1234*).

Visitor Information Wanganui i-SITE Visitor Centre (✉ *101 Guyton St.* ☎ *06/349–0508* ⊕ *www.wanganui.com*).

EXPLORING

Fodor's Choice
★

For an overview of the region's history and one of the best collections of Māori treasures in the country, drop into the **Whanganui Regional Museum,** by Queens Park. The museum contains *taonga* (Māori ancestral treasures) of the River people. There are some wonderful *waka* (canoes), as well as carvings, jewelry, ornaments, kiwi-feather cloaks, greenstone clubs, tools, bone flutes, and ceremonial portraits. The museum also re-creates 19th-century pioneer-town Wanganui in a series of traditional shop windows filled with relics and curios. Another treasure in this museum is Te Pataka Whakaahua (the Lindauer Gallery), with 19th-century paintings of Māori leaders by respected artist Gottfried Lindauer. ✉ *Watt St.* ☎ *06/349–1110* ⊕ *www.wanganui-museum.org.nz* ✉ *$5* ⊙ *Daily 10–4:30.*

On a small hill overlooking the town is the domed **Sarjeant Gallery,** one of New Zealand's finest art galleries and most handsome heritage buildings, renowned for its neoclassical architecture, natural lighting, and magnificent display spaces. The gallery is highly regarded for the quality of its collection and regularly changing exhibitions from local, national, and international artists. With 6,000 works of art in its care, including 19th- and 20th-century international and New Zealand art, photography, and a dynamic collection of contemporary New Zealand art to draw from, visitors are assured of a stimulating art experience. The gallery's shop stocks a quality selection of glasswork and jewelry, much of it crafted by local artists. ⊠ *Queens Park* ☎ *06/349–0506* ⊕ *www.sarjeant.org.nz* 🔖 *Entry by donation* ⊙ *Daily 10:30–4:30, Anzac Day 1–4:30* PM.

For a taste of the old days on the river, catch a ride on the restored paddle steamer, the **Waimarie**, built in 1899 by Yarrow and Company at Poplar London. Two-hour cruises, which include a Devonshire tea or coffee, take you up the Whanganui River from Wanganui. The *Waimarie* worked the river for 50 years before sinking in 1952. Critics said it couldn't even be salvaged, let alone restored to working order, but a dedicated volunteer team proved them wrong and have since continued restoration on two more formerly derelict riverboats. A museum at the River Boat Centre houses a collection of photographs from the days when riverboats were commonplace. Also on view are images of the salvage of the *Waimarie*, a great engineering feat. Another, smaller, salvaged river vessel, MV *Waiua*, can be chartered. ⊠ *Whanganui River Boat Centre, 1A Taupo Quay* ☎ *06/347–1863* ⊕ *www.riverboats.co.nz* 🔖 *Cruise $45, museum by gold coin donation* ⊙ *Cruises Oct. 22 (approximately)–May 1, daily at 2; May 2–Oct. 21, weekends; school and public holidays at 1. No cruises in Aug. Museum daily 9–5 (9–4 winter).*

Wanganui is home to a thriving glass community, with more than 30 glass artists who exhibit internationally. At **Chronicle Glass Studio** two such artisans, Katie Brown and Lyndsay Patterson, can be watched at their glassblowing work in their very own studio. A mezzanine retail gallery offers stunning glass pieces for sale. This is also a teaching studio; the masters provide individual instruction and in a one-hour class; absolute beginners get to work with hot molten glass and create their own paper- weight. Just give the studio a call to arrange a time. ⊠ *2 Rutland St., Wanganui* ☎ *06/347–1921* ⊕ *www.chronicleglass.co.nz* 🔖 *Free entry; $100 for paperweight class* ⊙ *Weekdays 9–5; weekends 10–3 (closed Sun. Easter–end of Oct.).*

By day, the formal gardens of **Virginia Lake** are a delight, and at night, the trees and lake fountain are softly illuminated. A gentle 25-min- ute stroll leads around the lake through woodlands and gardens and past rose-and-wisteria pergolas. There's a pleasant café here, too, with indoor and outdoor dining. The lake is just north of Wanganui, off State Highway 3.

WHERE TO EAT

$$–$$$ ✕ **The Orange Café and Ceramic Lounge.** Mingle with the many locals who
CAFÉ   gather here, be it for their first coffee of the day, a social weekend brunch, lunch or dinner, or late night wine in the laid-back lounge. The dual format café–wine bar caters to every meal or mood. By day there are homemade cakes, *friands,* and small pies in the café cabinet and a full breakfast menu (we recommend the baked Spanish eggs with chorizo and veg). A tapas menu offers tastes to match your evening wine, and

veal osso bucco is a signature, evening menu dish. Dine alfresco on the Victoria Avenue pavement, or snuggle into a leather banquette in the comfy lounge. Wireless Internet is also available. ⊠ *51 Victoria Ave, Wanganui* ☎ *06/348-4449* ▭ *AE, MC, V.*

$$–$$$ ✕ **Stellar.** This relaxed restaurant specializes in giant gourmet pizzas (with
PIZZA ominous names like "Silence of the Lambs" and "Foul Play") and generic New Zealand food. The space, which includes a bar and music venue, retains the brick-and-stone interior of an 1850s former hotel. There's a strong Kiwi vibe throughout with stained-and-polished wool presses for bar stands and giant plasma television screens for engaging in that favorite Kiwi pastime, watching sports. More features are the spacious veranda, free wireless Internet for diners, and totally stylish bathrooms. There's live music some nights. ⊠ *2 Victoria Ave.* ☎ *06/345–7278* ▭ *AE, MC, V.*

$$$ ✕ **Vega.** This restored former warehouse is a stylish spot to sample New
NEW ZEALAND Zealand dishes such as roast rack of lamb and premium eye fillet with roast mushrooms. In winter, dining inside by the open fire is cozy; come summer the alfresco riverside tables out back are the place to be. ⊠ *49 Taupo Quay* ☎ *06/345–1082* ▭ *AE, MC, V.*

$$$ ✕ **Vincent's Yellow House Café and Art Gallery.** Spread throughout the
CAFÉ veranda, garden, and several cozy, intimate rooms of this old yellow villa is a café showing local art (for sale). Open daily from 7:30 to late, serving breakfast, lunch and dinner, the menu changes weekly, but expect something nourishing such as seafood chowder chock-full of kingfish, bluenose (sea bass), mussels, and salmon. The café is across the road from the river and a two-minute drive from the city center. ⊠ *Pitt St. at Dublin St.* ☎ *06/347–9321* ▭ *MC, V.*

WHERE TO STAY

$–$$ 🛏 **151 on London.** In a quiet spot close to the city center and main highways, this apartment complex incorporates rustic barnlike iron cladding and farming memorabilia into amenities- and service-packed units. There's a flexible mix of en suite studios and one-bedroom suites with whirlpool baths, tea-and-coffee facilities, refrigerators, and microwaves. There are also two-level, two-bedroom family units with full kitchens, two fully accessible units, and a luxury honeymoon suite with double whirlpool baths. All units have 26-inch flat-screen televisions, lock-up safes, Internet, and king beds that can be separated to singles. Continuing the farming theme, a barn-style building houses a café and conference room, and a small gym is handily equipped with fitness equipment and a tempting massage chair. The location is close to supermarkets, fast food outlets, the city's Splash Aquatic Centre, and a major sports stadium. **Pros:** modern; quality amenities; handy location **Cons:** close to busy roads; industrial location lacks charm. ⊠ *151 London St., Wanganui* ☎ *06/345–8668* ⊕ *www.151onlondon.co.nz* ↵ *26 units (mix of studio, 1-bedroom and 2-bedroom units with full kitchen and luxury 1 bedroom spa-bath units)* ☖ *In-room: No a/c, safe, kitchen (some), refrigerator, Internet. In-hotel: Restaurant, gym, laundry facilities, parking (free)* ▭ *AE, DC, MC, V.*

$$–$$$ 🛏 **Aotea Motor Lodge.** Modern, luxury (Qualmark 5-star), self-contained serviced apartments include studio, one-bedroom, two-bedroom, and interconnected rooms. Though very much an inner-city business accommodation, it's spacious and comfortable. Locally owned by a Whanganui River

The Waimarie Paddle Steamer plies the Wanganui River.

family, all apartments are soundproofed. Cooked breakfasts are available. **Pros:** double whirlpool baths; close to supermarkets and fast-food restaurants. **Cons:** beside busy road. ✉ *390 Victoria Ave., Wanganui* ☎ *06/345–0303* ⊕ *www.aoteamotorlodge.co.nz* ⌖ *38 apartments* ⌂ *In-room: DVD, Internet. In-hotel: Laundry facilities, parking (free)* ⊟ *AE, DC, MC, V.*

$–$$
Fodor's Choice
★
🏨 **Anndion Lodge and Apartment.** With its blend of upmarket backpacker rooms and stylish apartments, along with fantastic facilities and personal attention to match, Anndion is one of New Zealand's market leaders. Owners Ann and Dion (get it?) sold their Harley bikes to afford the standard they want to provide. The range of accommodations includes bunk rooms ($35 per person), singles (bed for one), twins (two single beds), and doubles with shared bathrooms—though soaps and shampoos are provided. The fully equipped and modern shared kitchen has a sandwich press, rice cooker, electric knives, and a cappuccino maker. Outside is an inviting, covered barbecue area beside a saltwater pool, hot tub, and infrared sauna; inside a TV lounge with an extensive DVD library, pool table, and free Internet access provide plenty of entertainment. The lodge sits across the road from the Whanganui River, and a free shuttle takes you on the five-minute drive to and from town. **Pros:** free extras; lots of bathrooms; thoughtful hosts. **Cons:** a few minute's drive from downtown. ✉ *143 Anzac Parade, Wanganui* ☎ *06/343–3593 or 0800/343–056* ⊕ *www.anndion-lodge.co.nz* ⌂ *In-room: No a/c, no phone. In-hotel: Restaurant, bar, pool, laundry facilities, Internet terminal, Wi-Fi* ⊟ *AE, D, MC, V.*

$–$$
🏨 **Bushy Park Forest Reserve.** This B&B is in a grand old Edwardian homestead, surrounded by ancient forest and prolific native birdlife. There are six spacious bedrooms, a formal dining room, several lounges, and a television lounge. The homestead's Category One Heritage status restricts

significant changes; the rooms are grand but large and extremely hard to heat in winter (panel heaters and open fires do their best). Rates include breakfast; dinner can be prearranged. The daytime café is known for its Devonshire teas. Backpackers can share a bunkhouse ($25 per person) that sleeps 11; you'll bring your own bedding cook your own meals. Bathrooms are in the adjoining stables. **Pros:** outstanding forest reserve location; varied accommodation options. **Cons:** hard to heat in winter. ⊠ *Rangitautau East Rd., 24 km (15 mi) northwest of Wanganui* ☎ *06/342–9879* ⊕ *www.bushypark.co.nz* ✈ *6 rooms, 1 bunkhouse; all with shared bath* ⚹ *In-room: No phone, no TV. In-hotel: 2 restaurants, bars, Wi-Fi* ⊟ *MC, V* ⦿ *BP.*

$$ — NEW ZEALAND

⚏ **Rutland Arms.** This renovated Edwardian inn in the center of Wanganui is a top choice in town. The guest rooms have Posturepedic queen beds, reproduction Victorian period furniture, and lots of mahogany throughout. Four rooms have whirlpool baths, including the luxury special occasion Captain Laye Suite, which has a double whirlpool bath. Downstairs, the restaurant–bar ($$–$$$) has traditional English character with a Kiwi twist: cozy, a roaring fire (in winter), lots of delightful old Wanganui pictures on the walls, a wide choice of imported beers, and more than 50 single malt whiskies. You can eat here or in the sunny quiet courtyard. Food is generous, contemporary New Zealand–style cuisine, and while the menu changes regularly, lamb shanks, liver-and-bacon, and fish-and-chips remain perennial favorites. **Pros:** CBD location, cozy, English pub vibe. **Cons:** no elevator. ⊠ *Ridgeway St.* ☎ *06/347–7677* ⊕ *www.rutland-arms.co.nz* ✈ *8 en suite rooms* ⚹ *In-room: Wi-Fi. In-hotel: Restaurant, bar* ⊟ *AE, DC, MC, V* ⦿ *CP.*

THE WHANGANUI RIVER AND WHANGANUI NATIONAL PARK

GETTING HERE AND AROUND

The Whanganui River and Whanganui National Park, through which the river flows for most of its journey, is located in the hinterland of the central North Island. The closest centers and access points are the township of Taumarunui, to the north, and Wanganui city in the south.

Taumarunui sits on State Highway 4. There are daily Intercity bus services from Auckland and Wellington. The Overlander Auckland–Wellington train runs daily through Taumarunui in summer and Friday–Sunday in winter (Easter to end of September).

Traditional entry points for a Whanganui River journey are Taumarunui and the small settlements of Whakahoro and Pipiriki. To reach Whakahoro turn off State Highway 4 at Owhango, just south of Taumarunui. Pipiriki is 27 km from Raetihi (also on State Highway 4) or 79 km from Wanganui, via the Whanganui River Road. Shuttle services for kayakers, hikers and jet-boat travelers are operated by tourism operators based in the Whanganui/Ruapehu region, including from the towns of Ohakune, National Park, and Taumarunui. In the lower reaches, the Whanganui River Road turns off State Highway 4, 14 km north of Wanganui City, and follows the river through a mix of national park and farmland and past small settlements to Pipiriki.

ESSENTIALS

Visitor Information **Wanganui i-SITE Visitor Centre** (✉ *101 Guyton St.* ☎ *06/349–0508* ⊕ *www.wanganui.com*). **Taumarunui i-SITE Visitor Centre** (✉ *Hakiaha St.* ☎ *07/895–7494* ⊙ *Daily 9–4:30*).

EXPLORING

The city of Wanganui sits near the mouth of the Whanganui River, which flows through the heart of **Whanganui National Park** and is one of New Zealand's most historic and scenic waterways. The Whanganui begins its journey high on the mountains of Tongariro National Park and flows 329-km (204-mi) through steep gorges, forested wilderness, and isolated pockets of farmland. For several hundred years the *Te Atihau nui a paparangi* tribe of Māori has lived along the riverbanks, and they still regard the river as their spiritual ancestor.

The river's wilderness, its rich culture and history, and its relatively easy navigability are its main features. Guided trips generally operate in summer, the most popular time for kayakers; however, a river trip is feasible any time of the year.

For those without the time or inclination to travel by kayak is to explore the river's lower reaches by following the **Whanganui River Road** from the city of Wanganui. Built in the 1930s to provide access to communities otherwise reliant on the then-less-frequent riverboat services, the road runs for 79 km (49 mi) north, as far as Pipiriki. It's a narrow backcountry road, unpaved in stretches, although current upgrades that include paving the entire length are due for completion by 2011. Paved or not, be sure to keep left and take it slowly.

★ Many choose to take the early-morning **Whanganui River Road Mail Tour** (☎ *06/347–7534*), which gets you to Pipiriki and back in a day and includes sightseeing stops and optional extra tours. The tour is $55, given weekdays only, departs Wanganui between 7:15 and 7:30 AM, and returns mid-afternoon: times vary depending on how much mail the postman has to deliver, or whether he waits while you enjoy a jet-boat trip on the river. Weekend trips ($60 per person, minimum of two) are also an option, although there's no mail to deliver. Pickups are from city accommodations. You'll see the remains of giant, fossilized oyster shells at **Oyster Cliffs** (28 km [17 mi] from Wanganui). You'll call at the *marae* (village) of **Koriniti** (47 km [29 mi]), with its historic (and still much-used) ceremonial buildings and small Anglican church. You're welcome to look around. If there's anything happening just ask the people there whether it's appropriate to visit—unless it's a private funeral you're likely to be made completely welcome. The restored **Kawana Flour Mill** (56 km [35 mi]) and colonial miller's cottage are always open, if you'd like a glimpse of bygone pioneer life. At the farming settlement of **Ranana** (60 km [37 mi]), a Roman Catholic church from the 1890s is still used today. And there is the larger St. Joseph's Church and Catholic Mission, established by Home of Compassion founder Mother Aubert, at superb **Hiruharama** (66 km [41 mi]), better known locally as Jerusalem. Drive up the track to see the carved altar inside the church.

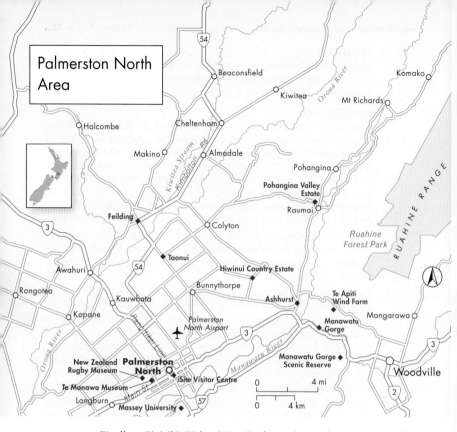

Palmerston North Area

Komako
Beaconsfield
Kiwitea
Oroua River
Mt Richards
Halcombe
Cheltenham
Makino
Almadale
Kimbolton Rd
Pohangina
Kiwitea Stream
Pohangina Valley Estate
Raumai
Feilding
Colyton
Ruahine Forest Park
RUAHINE RANGE
Awahuri
Taonui
Hiwinui Country Estate
Rongotea
Kauwhata
Bunnythorpe
Ashhurst
Te Apiti Wind Farm
Mangarawa
Kopane
Palmerston North Airport
Manawatu Gorge
Oroua River
New Zealand Rugby Museum
Palmerston North
iSITE Visitor Centre
Manawatu Gorge Scenic Reserve
Woodville
Te Manawa Museum
Manawatu River
Longburn
Main St
Massey University

0   4 mi
0   4 km

Finally at **Pipiriki** (79 km [49 mi]), the turnaround point, it's possible to arrange a jet-boat tour to the magnificent river gorges farther upriver. A popular trip continues to the Mangapurua Landing, where a short walk leads to the Bridge to Nowhere, a huge concrete bridge in remote forested country that is a remnant of the pioneering Mangapurua farming settlement, abandoned in 1942.

OUTDOOR ACTIVITIES

For information about canoe and jet-boat trips, contact the Wanganui i-SITE Visitor Information Centre.

CANOEING AND KAYAKING

The main season for Whanganui River trips is between October and Easter; the busiest period is during the summer holidays (Christmas–January). Winter trips are doable; the weather will be slightly colder, but you'll probably have the river to yourself. In summer, although there can be several hundred travelers on the river at any one time, they are all moving in one direction and so a group can travel long periods without seeing another soul. The time they do come together is in the evenings, at the huts and campsites.

Transport on the river is generally in open, two-seater, Canadian-style canoes or in kayaks. Tour options range from one-day picnic trips to five-day camping expeditions. Operators can supply all equipment, transfers, and the necessary hut and campsite passes, and trips can either be guided and catered, or independently undertaken (you supply your own food).

Your first call should be to one of the licensed commercial operators or the **Department of Conservation** (☎ 06/348–8475 ⊕ www.doc.govt.nz) to discuss itineraries. No experience is necessary; the Whanganui is considered a beginner's river—however, while it's definitely not "white-water" adventure, the river should be respected and one or two rapids can play nasty tricks on paddlers. Prices vary considerably according to the length and style of the trip, but you can expect to pay from about $55 for a simple one-day trip and in the $500–$600 range for a fully inclusive three-day excursion.

The **Whanganui Journey,** a canoe journey down the Whanganui River, is regarded as one of nine "Great Walks" in New Zealand's national parks and can be paddled independently or with tour operators. Park huts and campsites are along the river. Most tours go from Taumarunui to Pipiriki, a four- to five-day trip, or from Whakahoro to Pipiriki (three to four days). Whakahoro to Pipiriki is a true wilderness experience; there is no road access. A lower river trip, from Pipiriki to Wanganui, passes through a mix of native forest, farmland, and several small communities. Tour operators give anything from five-day wilderness experiences to one-day or overnight trips on the lower reaches.

Canoe Safaris (☎ 06/385–9237 ⊕ www.canoesafaris.co.nz) leads two- to five-day trips on the Whanganui; their "big boats," six-person open canoes, are built on the lines of the Canadian fur-trapper boats. The price, which starts at $320 for a two-day safari, covers all equipment, including a waterproof gear bag.

Yeti Tours offers two-, three-, four-, and six-day guided tours, plus the only 10-day guided tour all the way from Taumarunui to Wanganui, with camping accommodations. Tours include meals, kayaks, and Department of Conservation (DOC) pass. You provide (or rent) your own camping gear. ✉ 1 Rata St., ☎ 06/385–8197 or 0800/322–388 ⊕ www.canoe.co.nz.

Bridge to Nowhere Jet-boat Tours (☎ 0800/480–308 ⊕ www.bridgetono-wheretours.co.nz) runs jet-boat trips from Pipiriki to the Bridge to Nowhere (a four-hour trip) and other natural and historic sights.

Brent Firmin is a direct descendant of the early Māori of the river and grew up on his family farm close to Pungarehu Marae. His **Spirit of the River Jet** tours incorporate a visit to eco-lodge Flying Fox, canoe and jet-boat combos, longer tours upriver to the Bridge to Nowhere, and hunting safaris. ✉ Whanganui River Road, Pungarehu ☎ 06/342–5572 or 0800/538–8687 ⊕ www.spiritoftheriverjet.co.nz.

Ken and Josephine Haworth grew up on the river, now their company **Whanganui River Adventures** (✉ R.D. 6, Pipiriki ☎ 06/385–3246 ⊕ www.whanganuiriveradventures.co.nz) has a range of tours from Pipiriki to the Bridge to Nowhere, and shorter tours to scenic delights such as the Drop Scene, and Manganui o te ao River.

Owner and operator Mark Wickham's **Whanganui Scenic Experience Jet** tours are flexible and range from 1½ to 8 hours. They can include morning or afternoon tea stops at the Jerusalem Convent and Flying

Fox eco-lodge. Tours generally start from Pungarehu, a 20-minute scenic drive from Wanganui city, though city trips can be arranged. Other options include a one-hour jet-boat and two-hour canoe combo ($95). ✉ *Whanganui River Rd., Pungarehu* ☎ *06/342–5599 or 0800/945–335* ⊕ *www.whanganuiscenicjet.com.*

WHERE TO STAY

$$–$$$ 🏠 **Bridge to Nowhere Lodge.** In a private enclave deep in Whanganui National Park, 21 km (31 mi) upriver from Pipiriki, this lodge can only be reached by jet-boat (arranged by the lodge). The payoff for the remote location is magnificent forest vistas, birdsong at dawn, and the chance to bathe under the stars (there's an outdoor tub). Accommodations range from doubles in the amazingly comfortable lodge, with bush and river views to self-catering family and bunk rooms, to "The Paddlers Rest," a six-berth dorm-style cabin, also self-catering. There's also a camping area (bring your own tent). In the lodge rooms, you can choose between self-catering, or bed, breakfast, and dinner; packages are available that include a trip farther upriver to the Bridge to Nowhere. Lodge owner Jo also runs jet-boat tours to the Bridge to Nowhere, canoe trips, canoe rental, and jet-boat access to hiking trips in the National Park. **Pros:** wilderness; birdsong at dawn. **Cons:** river access only. ✉ *Whanganui River, Box 4203, Wanganui* ☎ *06/385–4622 or 0800/480–308* ⊕ *www.bridgetonowhere-lodge. co.nz* ⤳ *6 rooms* △ *In-room: No a/c, no phone, no TV. In-hotel: bar* ⊟ *MC, V* ⦿ *MAP.*

$–$$ 🏠 **The Flying Fox.** Even the arrival is exceptional at this truly unique ★ lodging. You'll arrive by river (jet-boat or kayak) or reach it by its namesake Flying Fox—a simple, aerial cable car—which deposits you high above the west bank of the Whanganui River. There you'll find a pair of cottages, each accommodating two to four people, plus the romantic "Glory Cart" gypsy caravan hideaway. They're distinctly eco-friendly, from their construction (by host John) using recycled materials to their facilities, such as the wood- and gas-fired showers, solar lighting, and outdoor clawfoot tub. Inside, they're warmly comfortable, with rug-covered brick floors, tie-dye throws, carved screens, and wood-burning stoves. Meals by host Annette (arrange in advance; $110–$120 per day) are really generous, country-style, and hinge on mostly organic and homegrown ingredients: avocadoes from the owner's trees; smoked eel from the river; seasonal produce; homemade ice cream, kūmara bread (a top seller at the River Traders Whanganui Market, which Annette helped to set up), and muffins. Or you can bring your own groceries. Camping in a bush clearing is another "lodging" option ($15 per person). You can get here from Wanganui on the Whanganui River Road Mail Tour; for those who are driving, there's secure parking on the road side of the river. **Pros:** river wilderness; eco-friendly and organic; Annette's home cooking; getting there. **Cons:** no cell phone reception. ✉ *Whanganui River Rd., Koriniti* ☎ *06/342–8160* ⊕ *www.theflyingfox.co.nz* ⤳ *2 cottages* △ *In-room: No a/c, no phone, kitchen, no TV* ⊟ *MC, V* ⦿ *MAP.*

PALMERSTON NORTH

145 km (87 mi) northeast of Wellington, 72 km (45 mi) southeast of Wanganui.

Palmerston North—or "Palmy" as the locals call it—is home to several major educational and research institutes. Thanks to these, young students make up one-third of Palmerston North's population. The biggest influence on the city is Massey University, one of the country's leading universities. The Massey campus has two Palmerston North locations: Turitea, set among huge trees and lovely gardens, and Hokowhitu, on the city side of the Manawatu River, with modern buildings near the lagoon. Campus also includes the Sport and Rugby Institute, where the All Blacks and other national and international elite sports people come to train.

The city also provides services for the thriving, surrounding farming industry. Rolling, rural sheep and cattle farms, stunning gardens and rural homestay retreats are all in close vicinity, nestling at the foot of the steep, snow-covered in winter, Ruahine Ranges.

A six-hour drive south from Auckland and two hours north of Wellington, Palmerston North is one of New Zealand's largest regional cities, with a population of 79,000.

GETTING HERE AND AROUND

The Palmerston North International Airport (PMR) is a 10-minute drive from the city center. The taxi stand is outside the terminal, and shuttle services are available for roughly $15. The airport also has an Internet kiosk. Activity in Palmerston North is centered on the Square. From there, you can easily explore on foot most of the city's cafés, restaurants, shops, art galleries, and museums.

ESSENTIALS

Airport Contact Palmerston North International Airport (✉ Airport Dr., Palmerston North ☎ 06/351–4415 ⊕ www.pnairport.co.nz.

Bus Depot Palmerston North Travel Centre (✉ Main and Pitt Sts.).

Hospital Palmerston North Hospital (✉ 50 Ruahine St. ☎ 06/356–9169).

Visitor Information i-SITE Palmerston North Visitor Centre (✉ The Square ☎ 06/350–1922 ⊕ www.manawatunz.co.nz ⊙ Weekdays 9–5; weekends 10–4).

EXPLORING

The distinctive **Te Manawa** complex is divided into three sections that weave together the region's history, art, and science. There are artworks and natural history displays, and the history of Rangitane, the local Māori people. If traveling with young ones, the Mind Science Centre, with its quirky interactive science exhibits, is entertaining and educational. ✉ 396 Main St. ☎ 06/355–5000 ⊕ *www.temanawa.co.nz* ✉ *Life and Art galleries free; Mind Science Centre starts from $5 depending on current exhibitions* ⊙ *Daily 10–5.*

The only one of its kind in New Zealand, the small **New Zealand Rugby Museum** is worth a visit whether or not you're a fan of the sport, for an insight into the tradition surrounding a game that many in New Zealand treat like a religion. The collection of rugby memorabilia dates back to the start of this national game in 1870. Look for the historic whistle that is used to open the World Cup every four years. The museum plans to relocate to Te Manawa in 2011. As of this writing, it will be open until August of 2010, at which point a temporary display until the museum reopens. ⊠ *87 Cuba St.* ☎ *06/358–6947* ⊕ *www.rugbymuseum.co.nz* ⊠ *$5* ⊗ *Mon.–Sat. 10–4, Sun. 1:30–4.*

Take yourself into the countryside, 30 minutes from Palmerston North, for a sip of an acclaimed vintage at **Pohangina Valley Estate**. This young winery (first vintage 2004), established on a working farm nestled beneath the Ruahine Ranges, is the only vineyard in the delightful Pohangina Valley. Unpretentious, even though the wines have already collected coveted Bragato awards, you can mingle with the chooks and dogs as you sip, and chat with the owners, sisters Fiona and Bronwyn, about the hands-on work of setting up in the wine business. ⊠ *1034 Valley Rd.,* ☎ *06/354–7948* ⊕ *www.pohanginavalleyestate.co.nz* ⊠ *Free* ⊗ *Jan.–Apr., weekends 11–4:30, Oct.–Dec., Sun. 11–4:30.*

Few rivers cut right through a mountain range, as does the Manawatu where it scythes a deep forest-lined gorge through the North Island divide, separating the Ruahine and Tararua Ranges. **Manawatu Gorge Experience** offers jet-boat trips into the gorge that climb narrow chutes, skim past huge boulders, and reveal scenery road travelers can't see. Manawatu Experience boats run 25-minute rides departing from the eastern side of the gorge, a 25-minute drive from the city. ☎ *0800/945–335* ✉ *tours@manawatugorgejet.com* ⊕ *www.manawatugorgejet.com* ⊠ *$65 per person, bookings essential.*

WHERE TO EAT

$$–$$$
ECLECTIC
Fodor's Choice
★

✕ **Bella's Café.** Serving a mix of Italian, Thai, and Pacific Rim dishes, Bella's has been a city favorite for more than a decade. It's right on the Square, smart and cheerful. Try the Bella's classic Thai chicken curry, or steamed mussels with riesling and sweet chili–cream reduction. ⊠ *2 The Square* ☎ *06/357–8616* ⊟ *MC, V.*

$$$
NEW ZEALAND

✕ **Brewer's Apprentice.** Just off the Square, Brewer's Apprentice features New Zealand crafted Monteiths beer and has plenty of character with lots of brick, stone and timber, open fires, flat-screen televisions, a spacious bar, street-front garden bar, and quiet dining alcove. Meals range from tasting platters (a local legend) to brunch of black pudding (blood sausage) on potato rosti; lunches of soups, pizzas, roast meats, and Monteith's (a popular Kiwi beer) battered fish-and-chips; dinners with upscale grill selections; and slow braised lamb rump on kūmara rosti. Live music entertains some evenings. Open 11 AM (10 weekends) until late. ⊠ *334 Church St.* ☎ *06/358–8888* ⊕ *www.brewersapprentice. co.nz* ⊟ *AE, DC, MC, V.*

$$–$$$
ECLECTIC

✕ **Café Cuba.** Just off the Square, this café is a funky and popular local haunt for breakfast, brunch, lunch, dinner, and after shows. Laid-back music plays in the background, and there are plenty of magazines to peruse while you enjoy the Cuba Breakfast—a hearty plate of eggs, bacon, mushrooms, and tomatoes—or later in the day perhaps a Cajun chicken "sarnie" (sandwich) with fried banana, salad greens, and *tzatziki* (tangy cucumber–yogurt sauce). Pastas and salads fill the lunch cabinet. Chocolate Silk Cake is highly recommended—one serving will satisfy two! ✉ *Cuba and George Sts.* ☎ *06/356–5750* 🖃 *AE, MC, V.*

$$$–$$$$ ✕ **Déjeuner.** This well-regarded restaurant in an old character bungalow
ECLECTIC draws on influences from French to Asian and Pacific. Try the signature Déjeuner lamb shank (slow-cooked lamb atop garlic mashed potatoes) or the Jack Daniels whiskey-barrel house-smoked venison on mashed kūmara (a native sweet potato) and port-and-rhubarb coulis. When you phone for your reservation, inquire about the tasting menu, offered occasionally. ✉ *159 Broadway Ave.* ☎ *06/952–5581* ⊕ *www.dejeuner. co.nz* 🖃 *AE, DC, MC, V* 🍽 *Licensed and BYOB.*

$$–$$$ ✕ **The Herb Cafe.** A worthy lunch stop if you're out exploring the country-
CAFÉ side or returning from a round-trip to the wind farm is the Herb Café at The Herb Farm, 10 minutes from the city. Wholesome homemade fare includes a Ploughman's Platter, chicken curry on jasmine rice, or sirloin steak on mashed pumpkin with salad, plus soups, phyllo pies, and more. There's also opportunity to calm the spirit with a wander through the 2 acres of herb gardens ($3.50 self-guided). The herbs from these gardens are used in the healing products made here, and available for sale in the shop by the café. ✉ *Grove Rd., Palmerston North* ☎ *06/326-7479* ⊕ *www.herbfarm.co.nz* 🖃 *MC, V* ⊙ *Café open Wed.–Sun. 10–4.*

$$–$$$ ✕ **Mao Bar.** Based on the philosophy that cuisine evolves as popula-
ECLECTIC tions change, the goal here is to fuse Eastern and Western cultures. It works, with a menu divided into four legs, two legs, and no legs (meat, poultry, and seafood). Try the Gobi rack of lamb in black pepper sauce, Hunan Chicken (with hot chili and aniseed flavors), or a choice of hot or mild curries. Platters are also a social option for a couple or group. ✉ *64 George St., Palmerston North* ☎ *06/354–8410* ⊕ *www.maobar.co.nz* ⊙ *Daily for brunch (from 7 AM, lunch, and dinner* 🖃 *AE, DC, MC, V.*

WHERE TO STAY

$$$$ 🏨 **Hiwinui Country Estate.** For a luxurious farm stay and a beauty and day spa, do the short (18-km [11-mi]) drive from Palmerston North to this 1,100-acre working sheep-and-dairy farm, hosted by the family that has farmed this land for five generations. Photos and artifacts relate their history. The homestead looks across lawns and gardens, beyond farm paddocks to the forest-covered Ruahine Ranges. Relax by the roaring stone fireplaces; in the private garden with hot tub and fireplace, have breakfast delivered to your room, or indulge yourself with Hiwinui's resident massage therapist in the beauty and day spa. You can also choose a delightful dinner of fresh local produce, complemented by New Zealand wine (by advance arrangement only). The two rooms open out to gardens, lawns, and rural views; all have under-floor heating and high-quality linens. One room has a whirlpool bath, and one has a double shower. Packages including beauty treatments are available. **Pros:** luxury on a working farm; interesting artwork; beauty and day spa. **Cons:** you might not want luxury on a working farm; no kids. ✉ *465 Ashhurst–Bunnythorpe Rd.* ☎ *06/329–2838* ⊕ *www.hiwinui. co.nz* ⇝ *2 rooms* ⚑ *In-room: DVD, Wi-Fi. In-hotel: no kids under 10* 🖃 *DC, MC, V* 🍽 *BP.*

6

$$ **Plum Trees Lodge.** An adorable inner-city retreat, this lodge was built
Fodor's Choice   in 1999 as a coach house in keeping with the style of the 1920s house,
★   the home of hosts Robyn and Robert Anderson. The apartment is spa-
cious but best suited to couples or solo travelers, because it has only
one room. It's full of character, with its stained-glass windows and
use of aged native timbers; it also has a private balcony. The lounge
area centers on a fireplace, and the room is sunny and light all year-
round. The breakfast basket is stocked with tasty local nibbles and
treats. Dial-up Internet is available for those with laptops. **Pros:** pri-
vacy; garden; Robyn's cookies. **Cons:** stairway access only. ⊠ *97 Russell
St.* ☎ *06/358–7813* ⊕ *www.plumtreeslodge.com* ⇥ *1 studio apartment*
⌂ *In-room: Kitchen, Wi-Fi* ⊟ *MC, V* ⦿*BP.*

$–$$ **Travelodge Palmerston North.** In a 1927 Heritage building (check out
the cage-style lift, one of the country's oldest), this city hotel is minutes
by foot from shops, theaters, and cafés. The city's only international
hotel has a restaurant (serving New Zealand cuisine with Mediterranean influence), small house bar, and larger bar with big-screen television for sports watching. There's also major conference and function
facilities here, so your stay might be shared with wedding guests or
meeting delegates. Rooms in this Qualmark 4-star hotel have queen
beds. **Pros:** in the city, good facilities; off-street parking. **Cons:** comfortable but guest rooms lack character; traffic noise. ⊠ *175 Cuba
St.* ☎ *06/355–5895* ⊕ *www.travelodge.co.nz* ⇥ *85 rooms* ⌂ *In-room:
Safe, refrigerator, Wi-Fi. In-hotel: restaurant, bar, Internet terminal,
Wi-Fi, parking (free), no-smoking rooms* ⊟ *DC, MC, V.*

THE ARTS

Several theaters in the city center host local and visiting productions.
Centrepoint (⊠ *Pitt and Church Sts.* ☎ *06/354–5740* ⊕ *www.centrepoint.
co.nz*) is the only professional theater company outside New Zealand's
main cities and has performances Tuesday through Sunday. Ballet,
traveling musical productions, opera, and rock groups take the stage
at the opulent **Regent on Broadway** (⊠ *63 Broadway* ☎ *06/350–2100*
⊕ *www.regent.co.nz*), which was built in 1930.

SHOPPING

Palmerston North's shopping is concentrated around the Square;
Broadway Avenue and the Plaza shopping centers are within easy
walking distance. George Street, which is also just off the Square, has
a number of specialty shops, galleries, and cafés.

If you're looking for a good read, **Bruce McKenzie Booksellers** (⊠ *51
George St.* ☎ *06/356–9922*) is considered among New Zealand's leading independent bookstores. **IHI Aotearoa** (⊠ *71 George St.* ☎ *06/354–
0375*) sells high-quality, contemporary art and crafts, jewelry, and
street wear, much of it made by local artists. Check out **Taylor Jensen
Fine Arts** (⊠ *39 George St.* ☎ *06/355–4278*) for contemporary and
traditional New Zealand and international art, sculpture, jewelry,
crafts, and furniture.

Wellington and the Wairarapa

WORD OF MOUTH

"We enjoyed wandering funky Cuba Street . . . and walking along the waterfront. The Te Papa museum had a special exhibition that was wonderful. But the big surprise came when we drove out to Lower Hutt and Porirua . . . I had no idea that there was such a beautiful coastline so close to the city."

—Songdoc

WELCOME TO WELLINGTON AND THE WAIRARAPA

TOP REASONS TO GO

★ **Arts and Culture:**
The national symphony, ballet, and opera are headquartered here. And the biennial New Zealand International Arts Festival celebrates an extensive program of drama, music, dance, and other arts events.

★ **A Wealth of Wineries:**
Spend a day or two (or three) wine tasting your way through the Wairarapa, home to more than 30 vineyards.

★ **Eclectic Cuisine:**
The great variety of Wellington's restaurants allows you to sample foods from dozens of cuisines, while also serving plenty of down-to-earth Kiwi fare.

★ **The Waterfront:**
Wandering along the Wellington waterfront is one of the most pleasurable ways to spend a day. You can visit (for free!) Te Papa Tongarewa, one of the country's best museums, and the Museum of City and Sea. Or you can walk to Oriental Bay, where you can join the local residents jogging, swimming, riding a bike, or people-watching.

1 Wellington. People are never far from the water; surfers can be happy on beaches that are virtually in the city, and families can take a meal overlooking the harbor. Wellington's also gained a reputation for fostering the arts, and it's easily explored on foot.

GETTING ORIENTED

All main roads from Wellington and the adjacent Wairarapa head north, as the two regions are at the North Island's southern point where the sometimes-stormy waters of Cook Strait divide the country's two main islands. Separated by mountain ranges that virtually tumble into the Strait, road travel between the two regions is via the Hutt Valley and the winding Rimutaka Hill road. Expect peaceful river scenery, a green and pleasant outlook and spectacular views.

7

2 **Wairarapa.** In the eastern Wairarapa, rugged windswept cliffs form a boundary against the vast Pacific; on the western side the rugged Rimutaka and Tararua ranges outline a massive division from the capital city and coastal region beyond. Spreading north from the cold deep waters of Palliser Bay, a rural panorama of fields and quiet vineyards stretches north as far as the eye can see.

WELLINGTON AND THE WAIRARAPA PLANNER

Planning Your Time

In Wellington make time to enjoy a relaxing day on the waterfront; it's a stone's throw from the city center. This area is mainly flat easy walking with interesting shopping and numerous cafés and restaurants. You don't need a car in the city, but to explore the Wairarapa, and its vineyard-rich countryside, it's best to make a day trip of it and drive. You also need to drive to go north to the long sweeping beaches of the Kapiti Coast.

When to Go

November to mid-April is the best time weather-wise in the Wellington area. Most establishments are open (apart from Christmas Day, New Year's Day, and Good Friday). Book well ahead if you're traveling during summer school holidays from mid-December to the end of January. From February to April, you can expect fewer crowds and many brilliant, warm days. Winters bring more rain, but they're rarely bitterly cold. Be prepared for unpredictable weather; rain and southerly gales are possible even during the summer.

Getting Here and Around

Air Travel

Wellington International Airport (WLG) lies about 8 km (5 mi) from the city. Domestic carriers serving Wellington are **Air New Zealand, Qantas**, and **Sounds Air**. A taxi from the airport to central Wellington costs about $25.
Airport Wellington Airport (✉ Stewart Duff Dr., Rongotai ☎ 04/385–5100 ⊕ www.wellingtonairport.co.nz).
Airport Transfers Co-operative Shuttle (☎ 04/387–8787). **Stagecoach Flyer** (☎ 04/801–7000).

Boat and Ferry Travel

The **Interislander** runs a ferry service between Wellington and Picton; the Interislander boats take three hours, and fares vary by time of year and range from $52 to $72 one-way per person; for a car and driver, fares are $165–$255. You can book up to six months in advance. A free bus leaves Platform 9 at the Wellington Railway Station for the ferry terminal 40 minutes before sailings. **Bluebridge Cook Strait Ferry** vessels, Santa Regina and Monte Stello, sail up to four times per day between Wellington and Picton. Fares are $55 one-way per person, $185 for a driver with car up to 20 feet long. Most car-rental agencies offer North Island–South Island transfer programs.
Contacts Bluebridge Cook Straight Ferry (☎ 0800/844–844 ⊕ www.bluebridge.co.nz). **Interislander** (☎ 0800/802–802 ⊕ www.interislander.co.nz).

Car Travel

The main access to the city is via the Wellington Urban Motorway, which starts just after Highways 1 and 2 merge, a few miles north of the city center. The motorway links the city center with all towns and cities to the north. Avis, Budget, and Hertz have offices at Wellington airport.

Train Travel

TranzMetro operates trains to Wellington Railway Station from the Hutt Valley, Palmerston North, and Masterton.
Contacts TranzMetro (⊕ www.tranzmetro.co.nz).
Wellington Railway Station (✉ Bunny St. and Waterloo Quay ☎ 04/498–3000).

Restaurants

In Wellington, restaurants, cafés, and sports bars have been springing up overnight like mushrooms. Although we'll never be without the classic meal of steak, fries, and ale, Wellington restaurants have embraced more adventurous fare. Chinese, Thai, Japanese, Malaysian, Mexican, and Italian cuisines are increasingly common. Indigenous food, too, is appearing in restaurants around the city—native plants might be paired with traditional seafood or made into sauces to accompany meat or sweet-potato dishes.

In rural areas outside Wellington, the wine industry has revolutionized local tables, with excellent dining and wine-tasting spots. In the Wairarapa, restaurants are winning a reputation for creative cuisine.

Generally, lunch runs from noon until 2, and most restaurants close for a few hours before opening for dinner around 6. On Monday, many restaurants are shuttered. Dress codes are still really relaxed; jeans would be frowned upon only in the top restaurants.

Hotels

Accommodations in Wellington range from no-frills backpacker hostels and motel units, to classic bed-and-breakfasts in colonial-era villas, to sleek central hotels.

As more people move into the city, apartments moonlighting as "serviced-apartment" hotels are gaining steam. Rates are significantly more expensive than those of the average motel, but the apartments, such as City Life Wellington, are a good option if you're planning to stay a while. Most of these apartment-hotel hybrids have weekend or long-term specials.

Lodgings generally do not have air-conditioning, but the temperate weather in Wellington rarely warrants it.

WHAT IT COSTS IN NEW ZEALAND DOLLARS

	¢	$	$$	$$$	$$$$
Restaurants	under $10	$10–$15	$15–$20	$20–$30	over $30
Hotels	under $75	$75–$125	$125–$200	$200–$300	over $300

Prices are per person for a main course at dinner, or the equivalent. Prices are for a standard double room in high season, including 12.5% tax.

Visitor Information

There is a comprehensive information service for Wellington and surrounding districts. **Positively Wellington Tourism** (☎ 04/916–1205 ⊕ www.WellingtonNZ.com) is a comprehensive site that will tell you everything you need to know about Wellington from shopping to restaurants.

Wellington i-SITE Visitor Centre (✉ *Victoria and Wakefield Sts.,* ☎ 04/802–4860) is sited in Civic Square, providing brochures, booking tours, theater tickets, and more. They also have a number of computers available for Internet access plus a decent café and souvenir shop.

Wellington Walking

Because Wellington is such a great walking city you'll likely find yourself strolling along a beach, a bushwalk, or around the vineyards. Be sure to pack some comfortable walking shoes or boots. For those cooler evenings a sweater and beanie can prevent a few shivers. For any serious walking a small backpack is useful for things such as bottled water, sun block, sunglasses, and a sun hat; all essential in the summer. Dress is quite casual, even in the city. Jeans, a sweater, and walking shoes won't warrant a second glance from the locals.

7

Updated by
Bob Marriott

People are finding their way to Wellington, and not merely because it's the sailing point for ferries heading south. From the windswept green heights overlooking New Zealand's capital, a crystal-clear winter morning reveals stunning views over the deceptively quiet waters of Cook Strait stretching to the snowcapped mountains of the South Island; and it's sheer heaven on a mild summer night when a silver medallion of moon tops mysterious misty hillsides.

Wellington has developed a lively, friendly, and infectious spirit of a city coming into its own. Pleasant and compact enough to be a good walking city, you might find yourself content to laze around the harbor, perhaps sipping a chilled glass of chardonnay from a nearby vineyard. The burgeoning film industry—thanks to the *Lord of the Rings (LOTR)* extravaganzas—has injected life into the local arts scene. Ardent film fans can still visit the many *LOTR* sites around the region, but everyone benefits from the lively cafés and the rapidly expanding restaurant culture. On the waterfront the first-class Te Papa Tongarewa–Museum of New Zealand has many hands-on exhibits equally fascinating for children and adults, and the Museum of City and Sea is dedicated to the history of Wellington.

Wellington and the adjacent Hutt Valley are the southern gateway to the Wairarapa, a region whose name has become synonymous with wine. Journey over the hills and meander along quiet byways from vineyard to vineyard for a day—or two, or three—of wine tasting. If wine isn't your thing, the Wairarapa is still worth an excursion for its gardens, fishing, walks, and even hot-air ballooning. Head for the coast, too, where waves crash against craggy, windswept beaches, and the dramatic sunsets intoxicate you with their beauty.

WELLINGTON

Wellington, the seat of government since 1865, is between the sea and towering hillsides that form a natural arena with the harbor as the stage. The ferries carve patterns on the green water while preening seabirds survey the scene. Houses cascade down the steep hillsides and create a vibrant collage of colorful rooftops against a spectacular green backdrop. An old brick monastery peers down on the marina—a jigsaw of masts and sails bobbing alongside the impressive Te Papa museum. Modern high-rises gaze over Port Nicholson, one of the finest natural anchorages in the world. Known to local Māori as the Great Harbor of Tara, its two massive arms form the "jaws of the fish of Maui" (Maui is the name of a god from Māori legend).

GETTING HERE AND AROUND

Wellington is a great **walking** city. The compact area around Lambton Quay and on Cuba Street is flat. A stroll along the waterfront around Oriental Bay provides outstanding sea views. If you head for the hills, take the cable car, and see the sights with a walk down.

For **cyclists**, designated bike lanes in and around Wellington are marked with a continuous white line and a white bike image on the pavement. More details about urban cycling are on the city's Web site, ⊕ *www.wcc.govt.nz*. **Penny Farthing Cycles** (✉ *89 Courtenay Pl.* ☎ *04/385–2279* ⊕ *www.pennyfarthing.co.nz*) rents bikes for $50 per day (includes helmets) for around-town riding, mountain biking, and off-road use.

Buses are a great way to navigate the city, though service outside the city center is sporadic. In Wellington, buses are operated by several companies; for information on all routes and fares contact Metlink. The main terminals are at the railway station and from Courtenay Place. For all inner-city trips, pay when you board the bus. Bus stops are marked with red-and-white signs. STARpass tickets ($12) allow a day's unlimited travel on all area buses; a $5 ticket gives you a day's bus travel within the city center.

A **car** is unnecessary to get around central Wellington, which is compact; its many one-way streets can frustrate drivers. However, a car is convenient for outlying places such as Akatarawa and the coastal region around Paraparaumu and essential for exploring the Wairarapa.

Taxi ride rates are $3 on entry, then $2.50 per 1 km (½ mi). Taxis idle outside the railway station, on Dixon Street, and along Courtenay Place and Lambton Quay.

ESSENTIALS

Bus Depot Wellington Railway Station (✉ *Bunny St. and Waterloo Quay* ☎ *04/498–3000*).

Bus and Train Services Met link (☎ *04/801–7000* ⊕ *www.metlink.org.nz*). **TranzScenic** (☎ *0800/872–467 or 04/495–0775* ⊕ *www.tranzscenic.co.nz*).

Emergencies Fire, police, and ambulance (☎ *111*).

Hospitals After-Hours Medical Centre (✉ *17 Adelaide Rd., Newtown* ☎ *04/384–4944*), open 24 hours. **Wellington Hospital** (✉ *Riddiford St., Newtown* ☎ *04/385–5999*).

Rental Cars Avis (☎ *04/801–8108*). **Budget** (☎ *04/802–4548*). **Hertz** (☎ *04/384–3809*).

Visitor Information Wellington Visitor Information Centre (✉ *Civic Administration Bldg., Victoria and Wakefield Sts.* ☎ *04/802–4860* ⊕ *www.wellingtonnz.com*).

EXPLORING

Civic Square represents the heart of town and forms a busy shopping area with Willis and Cuba streets. The entertainment district is centered on Courtenay Place, south of Civic Square. Thorndon, the oldest part of the city, is notable for its many historic wooden houses just north of the Parliamentary district, which includes the distinctive (some might say bizarre), "Beehive" government building.

At the northern end of the waterfront, the Westpac Trust Stadium, home to rugby matches, soccer games, and rock concerts, dominates the skyline, and Lambton Quay is part of a seafront constructed on reclaimed land. At the southern end of the harbor, Norfolk pines line the broad sweep of Oriental Bay, a suburb with a small beach and a wide promenade, backed by art deco buildings and Wellington's most expensive real estate.

TOP ATTRACTIONS

1 **Kelburn Cable Car.** The Swiss-built funicular railway makes a short-but-sharp climb to Kelburn Terminal, from which there are great views across parks and city buildings to Port Nicholson. Sit on the left side during the six-minute journey for the best scenery. A small Cable Car Museum is at the top in the old winding house with a display of restored, former cable cars (entry is free). ✉ *280 Lambton Quay, at Grey St. and Upland Rd.* ☎ *04/472–2199* ⊕ *www.wellingtonnz.com/cablecar* 🖃 *$ 2.50 each way; $4.50 round-trip* ☉ *Departures about every 10 min, weekdays 7 AM–10 PM, weekends 9 AM–10 PM.*

NEED A BREAK? Sip your coffee at the character-filled **Smith the grocer** . Ornaments range from old radios and beer crates to an ancient set of golf clubs. They serve great coffee and the soup of the day or a chicken wrap hot or cold is delicious. It's open daily. (✉ *The Old Bank Arcade, 233–237, Lambton Quay* ☎ *04/473–8591*)

3 ★ **Lady Norwood Rose Garden.** On a fine summer day you couldn't find a better place to go to enjoy the fragrance of magnificent flowers. The rose garden is the most popular part of the **Wellington Botanic Garden.** Situated on a plateau, the formal circular layout consists of 106 beds, each planted with a single variety of modern and traditional shrubs. Climbing roses cover a brick-and-timber colonnade on the perimeter. Adjacent to the rose beds, the Begonia House conservatory is filled with delicate plants and has a teahouse. ✉ *North end of Wellington Botanic Garden, Tinakori Rd. for parking lot*

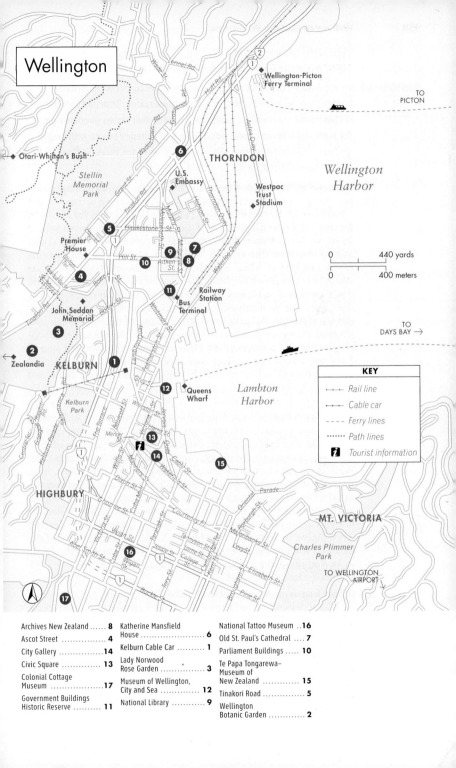

Wellington

Otari-Whiton's Bush

Stellin Memorial Park

THORNDON

Wellington-Picton Ferry Terminal

TO PICTON

U.S. Embassy

Wellington Harbor

Westpac Trust Stadium

Premier House

5

6

9 **7**

8

10

4

11

Railway Station

Bus Terminal

John Seddon Memorial

3

2

Zealandia

KELBURN

1

Kelburn Park

12

Queens Wharf

Lambton Harbor

TO DAYS BAY →

13

14

Mercer St.

15

HIGHBURY

Charles Plimmer Park

MT. VICTORIA

TO WELLINGTON AIRPORT

16

Colonial Cottage Museum

17

0 — 440 yards
0 — 400 meters

KEY	
⊢⊢⊢	Rail line
⊢⊢⊢	Cable car
- - -	Ferry lines
.....	Path lines
𝐢	Tourist information

☎ *04/801–3071* ✉ *Donation appreciated* ☉ *Begonia House daily 10–4, main gardens daily dawn–dusk.*

NEED A BREAK? **Picnic Botanic Garden Café.** In a sun-drenched corner of the Botanic Gardens this delightful café is in a large conservatory attached to the Orchid House. You can't go wrong with a menu that serves goodies from the lamb and kūmara (sweet-potato) pie to the crepes served with maple syrup and bacon. Sit outside, sip a latte, and smell the roses. ⊠ *Tinakori Rd.* ☎ *04/472–6002* ☉ *8:30–5.*

⓬ **Museum of Wellington, City & Sea.** You can smell the hessian (burlap) sacks,
★ hear the gulls, and see the (mechanical) rats scuttling around in this refurbished 1892 bond store, now a museum that portrays the history of the original Māori tribes and the European settlers who arrived around 1840. Spread over three floors, the displays cover work, leisure, crime, and education in 19th-century Wellington. Holographic effects bring to startling life two Māori legends, and in the Wahine Gallery, exhibits and a short film depict the 1968 *Wahine* ferry sinking that cost 52 lives. The Plimmer's Ark Gallery tells the story of John Plimmer, known as the "Father of Wellington" for his work in developing the city. You can see **Plimmer's Ark,** the excavated remains of the ship *Inconstant,* wrecked in 1849 on Pencarrow Head, in the Old Bank Arcade, a shopping center on Lambton Quay. Plimmer bought the damaged ship in 1850 and used it as a loading dock. Eventually it became landlocked and later demolished, except that the remains of its hull were discovered in 1997. ⊠ *The Bond Store, Queens Wharf* ☎ *04/472–8904* ⊕ *www.museumofwellington.co.nz* ✉ *Free* ☉ *Daily 10–5.*

★ **Otari-Wilton's Bush.** Devoted to gathering and preserving indigenous plants, Otari's collection is the largest of its kind. With clearly marked bushwalks and landscape demonstration gardens, it aims to educate the public and ensure the survival of New Zealand's unique plant life. While in the garden, you'll learn to identify plant life in the forest, from the various *blechnum* ferns underfoot to the tallest trees overhead. An aerial walkway crosses high above the bush, giving an unusual vantage point over the gardens. Look and listen for the native birds that flock to this haven: the bellbird (*korimako*), gray duck (*parera*), New Zealand wood pigeon (*kereru*), silver eye (*tauhou*), and *tūī,* among others. Take the No. 14 Wilton bus from downtown (20 minutes) and ask the driver to let you off at the gardens. ⊠ *Wilton Rd., Wilton* ☎ *04/475–3245* ✉ *Free* ☉ *Daily dawn–dusk.*

⓯ **Te Papa Tongarewa–Museum of New Zealand.** This museum remains one of
☾ New Zealand's major attractions. It provides an essential introduction
Fodor's Choice to the country's people, cultures, landforms, flora, and fauna. Unusual
★ exhibits include a simulated earthquake and a visit to a *marae* (Māori meetinghouse), where a *pōwhiri* (Māori greeting involving song and speeches) welcomes you. You can explore an outdoor forest area with moa (the extinct, ostrichlike native bird), bones, and glowworms or delve into the stories of New Zealand's early European migrants. In the Time Warp area, a sort of theme park where most activities have additional fees, you can simulate a bungy jump or leap three generations ahead

Performers welcome visitors to the marae at Te Papa Tongarewa–Museum of New Zealand.

to Wellington, 2055. Four discovery centers allow children to weave, hear storytelling, and learn a bit of Māori through song. ✉ *Cable St.* ☎ *04/381–7000* ⊕ *www.tepapa.govt.nz* ✉ *Free; some exhibitions cost up to $12* ☉ *Daily 10–6, Thurs. 10–9.*

② ★ **Wellington Botanic Garden.** In the hills overlooking downtown is a concentration of splendidly varied terrain. Woodland gardens under native and exotic trees fill the valleys, water-loving plants line a pond and mountain streams, and lawns spread over flatter sections with beds of bright seasonal bulbs and annuals. The lovely **Lady Norwood Rose Garden** is in the northeast part of the garden. If you don't want to walk the hill up to the garden, the **Kelburn Cable Car** *(see above)* can take you. Or take the No. 12 bus (direction: Karori) from Lambton Quay to the main (Glenmore Street) entrance. ✉ *Tinakori Rd. for parking lot; main entrances on Upland Rd. (for cable car) and Glenmore St.* ☎ *04/801–3071 gardens, 04/472–8167* ✉ *Free* ☉ *Main gardens daily sunrise–sunset.*

Zealandia: The Karori Sanctuary Experience. Just minutes from downtown Wellington, 623 acres of regenerating forest and wetland have been turned into a unique safe haven for some of New Zealand's most-endangered native animals. A specially designed fence keeps out introduced mammals, creating a cage-free sanctuary for species that had disappeared from the mainland: tuatara, New Zealand's unique "living fossil"; saddleback and hihi, back from the brink of extinction; and, at night, little spotted kiwi. Pick up a map and explore at your leisure, or take a guided tour. The night tour is particularly popular. A major exhibition centered on New Zealand's natural history and world-famous conservation movement opens in April 2010. ✉ *31 Waiapu Rd., Karori* ☎ *04/920–9213*

⊕ *www.sanctuary.org.nz* ✉ *Self-guided walk $14, tours from $28, 2-hr night tours $60* ☉ *Daily 10–5. Closed Christmas wk.*

WORTH NOTING

8 **Archives New Zealand.** History buffs should make a beeline here, as these national archives are a gold mine of documents, photographs, and maps. One highlight, displayed in the Constitution Room, is *Te Tiriti o Waitangi,* the Treaty of Waitangi. This controversial 1840 agreement between the British crown and more than 500 Māori chiefs is considered the founding document of modern New Zealand. *(See the Close-Up box The Treaty of Waitangi in Chapter 3.)* Outside the Constitution Room is a bowl of water called a *wai whakanoa.* Because documents in the Constitution Room are associated with the dead and regarded as *tapu* (taboo), visitors are invited to sprinkle a little of the water over themselves after leaving the room to lift the tapu and return to the land of the living. The oldest document on display is the Declaration of Independence of the Northern Chiefs, signed by 34 northern Māori chiefs on October 28, 1835, a confederation agreement that led up to the Waitangi treaty. Also on view is the 1893 Women's Suffrage Petition, which led to New Zealand becoming the world's first nation to grant women the vote. ✉ *10 Mulgrave St., Thorndon* ☎ *04/499–5595* ⊕ *www.archives.govt.nz* ✉ *Free* ☉ *Weekdays 9–5, Sat. 9–1 for exhibitions only.*

4 **Ascot Street.** Built in the 1870s, the tiny, doll-like cottages along Ascot remain the finest example of a 19th-century streetscape in Wellington. A bench at the top has been thoughtfully provided in the shady courtyard should you need to catch your breath. ✉ *Off Glenmore St. and Tinakori Rd. northeast of Wellington Botanic Garden, Thorndon.*

14 **City Gallery Wellington.** At this writing, City Gallery, in the heart of the capital at Civic Square, is undergoing major building works, improving what was already a first-class facility for the Capital. This stunning contemporary art gallery, renowned for its groundbreaking New Zealand and international exhibitions, now has three additional smaller galleries within it. The Deane Gallery for Māori and Pacific art; the Michael Hirschfeld Gallery dedicated to Wellington artists and designers, and the Hancock Gallery for the civic art collection. ✉ *Civic Sq., Wakefield St.* ☎ *04/801–3021* ⊕ *www.city-gallery.org.nz* ✉ *Most exhibitions free; charges for special exhibits vary* ☉ *Daily 10–5.*

13 **Civic Square.** Wellington's Civic Square is reminiscent of an Italian piazza; its outdoor cafés, benches, lawns, and harbor viewpoints make both a social hub and a delightful sanctuary from the traffic. The **City Gallery** *(see above),* perhaps the nation's finest art space, the library, and the Town Hall concert venue are just steps apart. Architect Ian Athfield's steel sculptures of *nikau* palms are a marvel, and Māori artist Para Matchitt contributed the impressionistic sculptures flanking the wide wooden bridge that connects the square to the harbor. With its sweeping water views, this bridge is a popular spot for picnics or as a place to sit and dream. ✉ *Wakefield, Victoria, and Harris Sts.*

17 **The Colonial Cottage Museum.** Built in 1858 as a family home by immigrant carpenter William Wallis, this cottage is Wellington's oldest remaining building. With its steep shingled roof and matchboard ceilings, kauri wood paneling and somber Victorian wallpapers, the house has been kept almost completely in its original state. The spinning wheel, smoke-blackened cooking pot, hand-pegged rugs, and oil lamps re-create the feeling of those pioneer days. Outside, there's a handmade butter churn, and a garden of flowers and herbs blooms in a riot of color and perfume in summer. ⊠ *68 Nairn St.* ☎ *04/384–9122* ⊕ *www.colonialcottagemuseum.co.nz* ⊒ *$5* ⊙ *Late Dec.–end of Feb., daily 10-4. Rest of year weekends only noon–4.*

⓫ **Government Buildings Historic Reserve.** This second-largest wooden structure in the world is now home to Victoria University's law faculty. After the earthquakes of 1848 and 1855 it was found that wooden buildings suffered less damage than brick. The building was constructed in 1876 and designed to look like stone, though it was actually entirely fashioned from kauri timber. Inside are historic exhibits about the building and an information center, though it's the exterior that most captivates. ⊠ *15 Lambton Quay* ☎ *04/384–7770, Department of Conservation Visitors Centre administers the building* ⊒ *Free* ⊙ *Weekdays 9–4:30.*

❻ **Katherine Mansfield House.** Here the writer, née Kathleen Beauchamp, came into the world (1888) and lived the first five years of her life. Mansfield left to pursue her career in Europe when she was 20, but many of her short stories take place in Wellington. A year before her death in 1923, she wrote, "New Zealand is in my very bones. What wouldn't I give to have a look at it!" The house, which has been restored as a typical Victorian family home, contains furnishings, photographs, and videos that elucidate Mansfield's life and times. ⊠ *25 Tinakori Rd., Thorndon* ☎ *04/473–7268* ⊒ *$5.50* ⊙ *Tues.–Sun. 10–4.*

❾ **National Library.** Opposite the Parliament Buildings is the country's national library. The Alexander Turnbull Library, a "library within a library," specializes in documentary materials about New Zealand and the Pacific. Its books, manuscripts, photographs, newspapers, maps, and oral history tapes are open for research. Exhibitions are regularly held in the National Library Gallery. The Gallery has a lively public events program. ⊠ *Molesworth St. at Aitken St., Thorndon* ☎ *04/474–3000* ⊕ *www.natlib.govt.nz* ⊒ *Free* ⊙ *Weekdays 9–5, Sat. 9–1.*

⓰ **National Tattoo Museum of New Zealand.** This small museum gives a fascinating glimpse of body art, from biceps to buttocks. Tattooing is an important part of Māori culture; like a coat of arms, a traditional *moko* (tattoo) demonstrates a person's heritage. The volunteer-run collection introduces the art with carvings, pictures, and plenty of literature. One video shows a 74-year-old Māori woman having her chin moko renewed the traditional way: her skin is carved with a bone chisel . . . and she doesn't utter a word of complaint. If you're inspired, you can get tattooed. ⊠ *29 Wigan St. (Underground Arts Bldg.)* ☎ *04/385–2185* ⊕ *www.tat2.co.nz* ⊒ *$5* ⊙ *Tues.–Sun. noon–5:30.*

❼ **Old St. Paul's Cathedral.** Consecrated in 1866, the church is a splendid example of the English Gothic Revival style executed entirely in native timbers. Even the trusses supporting the roof transcend their mundane function with splendid craftsmanship. ⊠ *Mulgrave St., Thorndon* ☎ *04/473–6722* ⊒ *Free* ⊙ *Daily 10–5.*

10 **The Parliament Buildings** consist of **Parliament House** with its **Debating Chamber**, a copy of the one in the British House of Commons in Westminster right down to the Speakers Mace. Here legislation is presented, debated, and voted on. There is fine Māori artwork in the Māori **Affairs Select Committee Room**. The adjoining building is the **Parliamentary Library**. The neighboring **Executive Wing** is known for architectural reasons as **The Beehive**. Here the Prime Minister and Cabinet Ministers of the elected Government have their offices and Cabinet meetings and press conferences are held. Across the road at the corner of Bowen Street and Lambton Quay, **Bowen House** is also part of the complex. Tours start in The Beehive, and a guide explains the Parliamentary process in detail. ⊠ *Molesworth St.* ☎ *04/471–9999, 04/471–9503 tour desk* ⊕ *www.ps.parliament.govt.nz* ▣ *Free* ⊙ *Tours depart on the hr weekdays 10–4, Sat. 10–3, Sun. 11–3.*

Premier House. The official residence of New Zealand's prime minister was a simple cottage when first erected in 1843. It has increased in size and grandeur somewhat since then. Prime ministers remained in residence until 1935, when the labor government, caught up in its reforming zeal, turned it into a dental clinic. The house had fallen into disrepair by the early 1990s. Since then it has been restored—and the prime minister has moved back in. The house isn't open to the public. ⊠ *260 Tinakori Rd., Thorndon.*

5 **Tinakori Road.** The lack of suitable local stone combined with the collapse of most of Wellington's brick buildings in the earthquake of 1848 ensured the almost-exclusive use of timber for building here in the second half of the 19th century. Most carpenters of the period had learned their skills as cabinetmakers and shipwrights in Europe, and the sturdy houses in this street are a tribute to their craftsmanship. Two notables are the tall and narrow No. 306 and **Premier House** *(see above).*

AROUND WELLINGTON
TOP ATTRACTIONS

★ **Māori Treasures.** A visit to this exceptional Māori enterprise gives you a wonderful, firsthand look at Māori arts and culture. Based on the Waiwhetu marae (meetinghouse) about 21 km (13 mi) from Wellington, the complex showcases artisans at work carving, weaving, and fashioning instruments. On the tour you might even hear someone playing the nose flute or get your hands on a woven cloak. A traditionally carved *waka* (war canoe) is on display; other examples of carving and artwork produced in the studio are sold in the gift shop. Guided tours can be arranged through Flat Earth New Zealand Experiences *(⇨ Tours, below).* ⊠ *58 Guthrie St., Hutt City* ☎ *04/939–9630* ⊙ *Daily 9–4; tours as arranged.*

★ **Southward Car Museum.** The largest collection of vintage cars in the Southern Hemisphere has more than 300 vehicles on display. A Davis three-wheeler, one of only 17 ever made, was used in the inaugural parade of U.S. President Harry Truman. It stands among Cadillacs, Bugattis, and gleaming Rolls-Royces. The motorcycle section is a must for two-wheeler buffs. The museum is just off Highway 1, a 45-minute drive north of Wellington. ⊠ *Otaihanga Rd., Paraparaumu* ☎ *04/297–1221* ⊕ *www.thecarmuseum. co.nz* ▣ *$10* ⊙ *Daily 9–4:30.*

CLOSE UP

Akatarawa Valley

Winding through the steep bush-clad hills north of Wellington, the narrow road to the Akatarawa Valley (in the Māori language, Akatarawa means "place of tangled vines") requires a degree of driving care, but it leads to a number of hidden gems. About 35 minutes out of Wellington on State Highway 2, turn left at the clearly marked Brown Owl turnoff north of Upper Hutt. About two minutes after the turnoff, look for **Harcourt Park**, where a number of scenes in the *Lord of the Rings* movies were filmed. Nearby, **Harcourt Holiday Park** (☎ 04/526-7400) has 21 motel-type units and tourist cabins, with tent sites in lovely bush surroundings. It's right alongside Harcourt Park. Half a mile farther on, a bridge at the junction of the Hutt and Akatarawa rivers leads into the Akatarawa Valley proper. Drive over the bridge, go past the cemetery, and then on the left, look for the **Blueberry Farm** (☎ 04/526-6788), where you can pick your own blueberries (January) or go for a swim in the river. Nearby **Bluebank Blueberry and Emu Farm** (☎ 04/526-9540) also grows delicious blueberries and raises the large flightless emus.

Continue on to **Efil Doog Garden of Art** (☎ 04/526-7924 ⊕ www.efildoog-nz.com), where Shirley and Ernest Cosgrove tend a stunning 11-acre garden and sculpture display. They also have an art gallery exhibiting some fine early–New Zealand paintings. The grounds are magnificent at rhododendron time, October–early December. The garden's open October through March, Wednesday–Sunday; entry is $14. The winding road crosses some wonderful old trestle bridges over the Akatarawa River before reaching **Staglands Wildlife Reserve** (☎ 04/526-7529 ⊕ www.staglands. co.nz), filled with friendly animals and birds that will eat out of your hand. As you wander through these peaceful 25 acres, meet the kea, kune-kune pigs (a native variety), deer, peacocks and feed trout in the pools. Stop by the falcon aviary before picnicking by the river or enjoy some refreshment at the log-cabin café. The reserve is open daily and costs $16.

Look on the right for the tiny wooden Church of St. Andrews, then turn right almost immediately for the **Reikorangi Potteries** (☎ 04/293-5146). Here, Wilf and Jan Wright display local handicrafts and paintings, plus their own pottery. Wander around the small animal park to view rabbits, llamas, wallabies, and a host of different birds, or stroll along the riverbank and take a swim. If you haven't eaten yet, the café is a delightful stop. The potteries are open November through March, Tuesday–Sunday, and April through October, Wednesday–Sunday. Admission is $5. The road continues for about 3 km (2 mi to join State Highway 1 at the Waikanae traffic lights, where you can head back to Wellington; from here, you're about 45 minutes north of the city. You can get more information on the Akatarawa Valley from the **Upper Hutt Information Centre** (✉ 84–90 Main St., Upper Hutt ☎ 04/527-2141 ⊕ www.upperhuttcity.com).

★ **Stansborough.** Step back to the 1890s to a working mill where wool from an ancient breed of gray sheep, together with alpaca, is woven on 100-year-old looms. Fabric produced here was used for costumes in *The Lord of the Rings, The Lion, the Witch and the Wardrobe*, and other films—and you have the opportunity to buy the type of cloak worn by Frodo or Sam. Contact info@stansborough.co.nz for guided tour bookings. ⊠ *100 Hutt Park Rd., Seaview, Hutt City* ☎ *04/566–5591* ☞ *$22* ☉ *Weekdays and Sat. 9:30–4. Closed Sun.*

Weta Cave. Take a fascinating "behind the scenes look" around this compact but comprehensive display detailing the characters and equipment used in special effects for *The Lord of the Rings, The Chronicles of Narnia, King Kong*, and other Academy Award–winning movies. A wonderfully furnished theater shows continuous clips from these spectacular shows. Models, limited edition sculptures, books, DVDs, posters, and T-shirts can be purchased. ⊠ *Corner of Weka St. and Camperdown Rd., Miramar, Wellington* ☎ *04/380–9361* ⊕ *www.wetaNZ.co.* ☞ *Free* ☉ *Daily 9–5:30.*

WORTH NOTING

The Hutt Valley. A 10-minute drive north of Wellington on State Highway 2—with magnificent harbor views all the way—leads you to the Hutt Valley and its namesake river. Attractions in the bustling Hutt City include the **New Dowse** (⊠ *45 Laings Rd., Hutt City* ☎ *04/570–6500*), where you will find a changing array of exhibitions showcasing a range of creativity from New Zealand's extraordinary jewelry to fashion, photography, and ceramics to youth culture. Sites such as Māori treasures and Stansborough are adding a fresh dimension to tourism in the area and the tempting shops and cafés around Jackson Street in Petone make for an interesting morning. Don't miss the small-but-interesting **Petone Settlers Museum** (⊠ *The Esplanade, Hutt City* ☎ *04/568–8373*), on the waterfront of Wellington Harbour near the landing site of the first organized European settlement in New Zealand. The Petone Esplanade on the eastern side of the harbor, overlooked by houses clinging to steep bush-clad hills, winds about 8 km (5 mi) through the suburb of **Eastbourne.** Stop in the tiny shopping area for an alfresco bite before driving on to where the road eventually transforms into a 4-km (2½-mi) walking track, following the coast to **Pencarrow Head** and its lighthouse, with views across the strait. (There's a kiosk where you can rent a bike if you wish.)

Back in Hutt City, the **Hutt River Trail** starts at Hikoikoi Reserve on Petone Marine Parade near the Hutt River mouth. Specifically for walkers and cyclists, this scenic trail follows the river for more than 32 km (20 mi) between Hutt City and Upper Hutt.

Back on State Highway 2 heading north, enjoy the views of the distant Tararua Ranges, snow covered in winter. If you're a *Lord of the Rings* fan, stop by the **Dry Creek Quarry,** where the scenes of Helms Deep and Minas Tirith were filmed; it's at the bottom of Haywards Hill Road—look for the traffic lights for the turnoff from State Highway 2.

From Upper Hutt, continuing north on State Highway 2 leads to the Wairarapa region, but just beyond Upper Hutt, look for **Kaitoke Regional Park** (⊠ *Waterworks Rd., off State Hwy. 2* ☎ *04/526–7322 for rangers*), a great camping and picnic spot with pleasant walks by the river. In the park, *LOTR* fans can check out the bridge, which stood in for Rivendell, the rallying place for elves. Pause by the crystal-clear river, flanked by towering trees and native bush, and listen to the birdsong.

OFF THE BEATEN PATH

The Rimutaka Incline. The Rimutaka Incline Railway operated from 1878 until 1955, connecting Wellington and the Wairarapa. Special locomotives known as Fell engines were needed to haul trains up the steepest grade in the country. In 1955, a tunnel superseded the Rimutaka Incline, the tracks were torn up, and the former railway route was converted into a path for walking and cycling. The track runs for about 16 km (10 mi) from Kaitoke, just north of Upper Hutt, to a parking area just beyond Cross Creek near Featherston on the Wairarapa side. It takes about five hours to walk the length. The track passes through two old tunnels, several bridges, and some wild countryside. The track is mostly compacted gravel, but it can get muddy in bad weather. Beware of high winds on the Wairarapa side; a train was once blown off the tracks here!

To arrange transport at both ends of the track, contact Fred Roberts of **Valley Shuttles** (☎ *04/973–8150, 027/248–1745 cell*). The only remaining Fell engine is now on display at the Fell Locomotive Museum in the Wairarapa (⇨ *Around Masterton in the Wairarapa, below*).

AKATARAWA TREK

Liz and Keith Budd lead two-day walks through the Akatarawa Valley for active groups of up to six. The walks, which take five–six hours, operate from October to April 30 and include all transport, luggage transfer, and comfortable accommodations. Gardens and wildlife park admissions and meals are also included in the cost of $275. Bookings are essential. ☎ *04/526–4867* ⊕ *www.akatrack.co.nz.*

WHERE TO EAT

Use the coordinate (✛ B2) at the end of each listing to locate a site on the corresponding map.

$$$
NEW ZEALAND
★

✕ **Back-Bencher Pub & Café.** Right across the way from the Parliament buildings sits "the house that has no peers," a landmark watering hole where politicians grab a cold beer after a hot debate. The walls have become a gallery of political cartoons and puppets tweaking government characters and well-known sports figures. Don't labor over the prices; it'll be a national disaster if you miss this one. Elect for Bombay lamb sausages, potato–marsala gravy and yogurt–mint drizzle. There's a bit of bite in this one—you'll be ready to tackle the opposition. ✉ *34 Molesworth St.* ☎ *04/472–3065* ⊟ *AE, DC, MC, V* ✛ *B3.*

$$$$
ECLECTIC

✕ **Boulcott Street Bistro.** A well-respected institution on the Wellington dining scene, this old colonial-style house conveys tradition. Dishes such as the braised lamb shank, mashed potatoes, lentil sauce, and mint peas satisfy the discerning clientele. On the dessert list, keep an eye out for the profiteroles with Baileys ice cream and chocolate sauce. ✉ *99 Boulcott St.* ☎ *04/499–4199* ⊟ *AE, DC, MC, V* ☻ *No lunch weekends* ✛ *B4.*

Visitors dine alfresco in Courtenay Place, Wellington's entertainment center.

$$
AMERICAN
★

✕ **Dixon Street Gourmet Deli.** The owner's grandfather opened this establishment in 1920; the friendly staff and excellent pickings have kept it a local favorite ever since. You could snag provisions for a picnic lunch or get a table inside for a grilled chicken salad or an antipasto platter. The chocolate Danish pastries along with a great variety of cakes and confectionary are mouthwatering. ✉ *45–47 Dixon St.* ☎ *04/384–2436* ▭ *AE, MC, V* ✛ *B5.*

$$$$
NEW ZEALAND

✕ **Dockside Restaurant & Bar.** A wooden-beam roof and oiled floorboards give this former warehouse on the wharf a nautical vibe. You can get close to the water, too, outside on the large harbor-front deck. Inside or out, it's a lively spot, particularly on Friday nights, when a DJ spins to a packed house. The menu changes daily but has a seafood bias, including whole flounder oven baked with tomato Provencale, basil, and Chilean olives. Phone first as this place gets crowded and noisy on weekends. ✉ *Shed 3, Queens Wharf, Jervois Quay* ☎ *04/499–9900* ✎ *Reservations essential* ▭ *AE, DC, MC, V* ✛ *B4.*

$$$–$$$$
NEW ZEALAND
★

✕ **The Green Parrot.** Talk about character: this stalwart steak-and-seafood joint, which has been serving meals continuously since 1926, has a grill made from melted-down gun barrels. Kosta Sakoufakis, the welcoming chef and co-owner, makes people feel at home and can talk about American Marines visiting the place during World War II. Politicians and celebrities like Peter Jackson gravitate here, and a mural depicts notable clients ranging from famous writers to two former prime ministers. You definitely won't walk out feeling hungry! ✉ *16 Taranaki St.* ☎ *04/384–6080* ▭ *AE, DC, MC, V* ⊗ *No lunch* ✛ *B5.*

$$$
CONTEMPORARY

✕ **Juniper.** In this narrow space, red leather couch-style seating blends with plum-colored walls under subdued lighting. An upstairs dining area is more open. The beef tournedos fillet comes wrapped with streaky bacon, served with bok choy–garlic confit, mushroom ravioli, potato cake, and merlot jus. The desserts, such as ginger crème caramel served with ginger-and-pineapple confit and a matching wine are sensational. ⊠ *Corner of Featherston and Johnston Sts., Wellington Central* ☎ *04/499–3668* ⊕ *www.juniperrestaurant.co.nz* ⊟ *AE, DC, MC, V* ☉ *Closed Sun.* ⊹ *B3.*

$$　　× **La Bella Italia.** Within sight of Petone Wharf, this old warehouse has
ITALIAN　 been turned into a vital restaurant and delicatessen, the walls alive with in-your-face murals, photographs, and posters with an Italian theme. There is also a wood-fired pizza oven. Savor the vibe and fresh food and exotic wines. Enjoy baked fish fillets of the day with broccoli, cauliflower, sun-dried tomatoes, and black olives; warm salad; and a matching pinot grigio from an ever-changing menu of authentic Italian cuisine. It's food for the gods! ⊠ *10 Nevis St., Petone* ☎ *04/566–9303* ⊕ *www. labellaitalia.co.nz* ⚒ *Reservations essential* ⊟ *AE, MC, V* ⊹ *D1.*

$$$$　　× **Logan Brown.** Partners and TV personalities Steve Logan and Al Brown
NEW ZEALAND have created a winner in this stylishly renovated 1920s bank building.
Fodor's Choice An aquarium tank is set into the bar top, so that fish swim by under your
★ cocktail. The merino short loin with pea gnocchi, Parmesan sweetbreads, and tomato ragout followed by rhubarb tarte tatin with cranberry–and–black-pepper parfait makes for a memorable meal. ⊠ *Cuba St. at Vivian St.* ☎ *04/801–5114* ⊟ *AE, DC, MC, V* ☉ *No lunch weekends* ⊹ *B5.*

$$$　　× **Maria Pia's Trattoria.** Patrons relax and laugh often in this homey Italian
ITALIAN　 gem. Large potted plants sprawl across window ledges and dark, polished wood tables reflect candlelight through glasses of red wine. From the delicious aromas pervading the interior, the pasta parcels filled with organic Zany Zeus ricotta and spinach served with sage-infused butter and freshly grated Parmesan cheese might tickle your palate. Poached pear with vino cotta sauce and vanilla bean ice cream should complete a lovely meal. Wines by the bottle or glass are matched with the menu. ⊠ *55 Mulgrave St.* ☎ *04/499–5590* ⊟ *AE, DC, MC, V* ☉ *Closed Sun.* ⊹ *B2.*

$$$　　× **Matterhorn.** A long passage from the street leads you to this hidden
NEW ZEALAND treasure where the bar stretches nearly as far. A large wood-burner lends warmth to rather plain walls and basic furniture. For warm days there is a covered outside area with its own bar. The Northland snapper with a warm salad of roast artichoke, saffron-poached fennel, confit tomato, Gordal olives, and preserved lemon-and-fennel cream is a good choice. Then a cheese selection or baked rhubarb tart with honeycomb-and-almond mascarpone and ginger-wine reduction should satisfy the most discerning palate. ⊠ *106 Cuba St., Te Aro, Wellington* ☎ *04/384–8918* ⊕ *www.matterhorn.co.nz* ⊟ *MC, V* ⊹ *B5.*

$$$　　× **The Potters Kiln Café.** If you've got wanderlust and an appetite, drive
NEW ZEALAND out to this tiny cottage in the Reikorangi Potteries, 48 km (30 mi) from town. The menu serves mouthwatering creations such as roasted rack of lamb in a spiced plum sauce, and sticky date pudding topped with hot caramel sauce. Pottery and paintings fill the walls, as do interesting curios—an old wooden butter churn stands next to a small accordion. To get here from Wellington, take State Highway 1 north to Waikanae and turn right at the second traffic light. Cross the train tracks,

and in about 4½ km (2¾ mi) turn left into the Reikorangi Potteries. Reservations are a good idea. ⊠ *27 Ngatiawa Rd., Reikorangi* ☎ *04/293–5146* ⊟ *MC, V* ⊙ *Closed Mon. and Tues.* ✛ *D1.*

$$$$ ✕ **Pravda.** Three king-size chandeliers dominate the high ceilings in this
EUROPEAN classic, old Wellington building. The café area has half-paneled walls and a matching bar that gives a touch of understated class. The lamb shank on Parmesan grits with kūmara chips and tapenade jus is a wise choice; the chocolate bread-and-butter pudding with prune and balsamic ice cream are irresistible. ⊠ *107 Custom House Quay, Wellington Central* ☎ *04/801–8858* ⊕ *www.pravdacafe.co.nz* ⊟ *AE, DC, MC, V* ✛ *B4.* ⊙ *Closed Sun.*

$$$ ✕ **Shed 5.** Huge windows facing the harbor belie the fact that this historic
SEAFOOD building on the wharf was once a woolshed. Crisp white tablecloths and sparkling tableware gleam under the dark-wood beams in the spacious dining room. On the broad-ranging, comfort food menu, seafood stands out, especially the Akaroa salmon with pepper, roasted on sauteed spinach with lemon vinaigrette. Rich desserts include pineapple lasagna with piña colada sorbet and spicy caramel. ⊠ *Shed 5, Queens Wharf, Jervois Quay* ☎ *04/499–9069* ⊕ *www.shed5.co.nz* ⊟ *AE, DC, MC, V* ✛ *B4.*

$$$ ✕ **SOI Café & Bar.** With floor-to-ceiling windows providing sweeping
ECLECTIC views of Evans Bay, this restaurant feels a bit like being on a cruise ship. The menu is varied, and the helpings are generous and not too expensive. The fresh salmon, served on a potato rosti (potato pancake) with avocado and dressed watercress finished with crème fraîche makes a great main. While watching the white horses (whitecaps) gallop across the bay, finish with the apple-ginger crumble served with runny cream. ⊠ *301 Evans Bay Parade* ☎ *04/386–3830* ⊟ *DC, MC, V* ✛ *D4.*

$$–$$$ ✕ **Vista.** For a breezy meal and some morning sunshine, grab an out-
CAFÉ door table at this busy café with views across Oriental Parade to the bustling harbor. Breakfast is available until 4 PM; try the twice-baked goat cheese soufflé with arugula salad or the crumbed veal tenderloin on garlic mashed potatoes with wilted spinach and Madeira jus; it's all delicious. ⊠ *106 Oriental Parade* ☎ *04/385–7724* ⊟ *AE, DC, MC, V* ⊙ *No dinner Sun.–Tues.* ✛ *D5.*

$$$$ ✕ **White House.** A Wellington icon that has been serving exceptional food
NEW ZEALAND for over 16 years, the menu is driven by seasonal produce and leans
Fodor's Choice to organic wherever possible. *Sous vide* (vacuum cooking) breast and
★ leg of duck, mashed orange kūmara, and mandarin puree followed by pineapple tarte tatin with coconut ice cream should please the most avowed foodie. Windows on both floors of the namesake house, an early-20th-century beach cottage, give stunning views across Oriental Bay and the harbor. ⊠ *232 Oriental Parade* ☎ *04/385–8555* ⊟ *AE, DC, MC, V* ⊙ *No lunch Sat.–Thurs.* ✛ *D4.*

$$$ ✕ **Zibibbo Restaurant & Bar.** From the cozy bar, walk upstairs to the restaurant
ECLECTIC where a large access hatch provides a panoramic view of a spotless white-tiled kitchen with a wood-fired pizza oven. Start with a Zibibbo tapas platter, then go for lemon- and rosemary-rubbed rotisserie chicken with salsa rosso before working your way through to the Zibibbo dessert platters. Wow! ⊠ *25–29 Taranaki St.* ☎ *04/385–6650* ⊕ *www.zibibbo.co.nz* ⊟ *AE, DC, MC, V* ⊙ *No lunch weekends* ✛ *B5.*

WHERE TO STAY

Use the coordinate (✛ B2) at the end of each listing to locate a site on the corresponding map.

¢–$ 🏨 **Base Backpackers.** This handsome Heritage building in a great location draws a varied crowd of budget travelers. Rooms are spacious, bedding is provided, and all except the double rooms share bathrooms. The whole establishment is decked out in burgundy and white, with the exception of the Sanctuary floor, a women-only dorm section where, surprise, rooms are pink and white. Sanctuary guests also get some girly perks (full-length mirrors, hair dryers, free Aveda hair products, and feather pillows). The place is kept remarkably clean and the staff are friendly. There is an in-house travel desk and bike rental is available. **Pros:** handy to the city; women-only section. **Cons:** there might be some traffic noise. ✉ *21–23 Cambridge Terr.* ☎ *04/801–5666* ⊕ *www.stayatbase.com* ↘ *11 rooms, 10 dorms* ⅖ *In-room: No a/c, no phone. In-hotel: Restaurant, bar, laundry facilities, Internet terminal, no-smoking rooms* ⊟ *AE, DC, MC, V* ✛ *C5.*

$$ 🏨 **Booklovers B&B.** Residents of the Mount Victoria neighborhood claim
★   to live in the sunniest part of town, and the lovely wooden Victorians and views of the city and harbor make Mount Victoria one of the most-painted city landscapes. Wellington author Jane Tolerton has set up house in this villa and, true to her passion, lined the hallways and all the rooms with books. Some books are free to take away with you (Jane doesn't believe in leaving a good book unfinished). In addition to books, the big bright rooms are furnished with a hodgepodge of antiques, comfortable sofas, and armchairs. Jane provides a steady supply of homemade oatmeal chocolate-chip cookies. **Pros:** comfortable and close by the city; a hostess who really cares; guest lounge with free Internet access. **Cons:** parts of this district are a little well worn. ✉ *123 Pirie St.* ☎ *04/384–2714* ⊕ *www.booklovers.co.nz* ↘ *4 rooms, 3 with bath* ⅖ *In-room: Internet, no a/c (some). In-hotel: restaurant, bar* ⊟ *MC, V* ❍❙ *BP* ✛ *C6.*

$$$ 🏨 **CityLife Wellington.** This all-suites hotel is smack-dab in the middle of the city—and if you can snag a suite at a weekend or special summer rate, you've got one of the best-value lodgings in town. You have a wide selection of studios and spacious one-, two-, and three-bedroom suites with comfortable lounge furniture. Facilities are similar in all suites and include kitchens, washers, dryers, and dishwashers (the rooms are also serviced). Despite the location, you don't get street noise in the rooms. **Pros:** in the heart of the city; just an elevator ride to Lambton Quay. **Cons:** more suited to a longer stay. ✉ *300 Lambton Quay* ☎ *04/922–2800 or 0800/368–888* ⊕ *www.heritagehotels.co.nz/citylife-wellington* ↘ *70 suites* ⅖ *In-room: Kitchen, Internet. In-hotel: Gym* ⊟ *AE, DC, MC, V* ❍❙ *BP* ✛ *B4.*

¢–$ 🏨 **Downtown Backpackers.** Opposite the train station, this hostel stands out by virtue of its amenities and its landmark art deco building. The rooms are clean (if small) and range from singles to six-person shares. Some private rooms have TVs. The extensive communal areas include a travel desk, a café (serving big-and-cheap breakfasts), kitchen, bar, and pool room; computers are at the ready. Check out the old Māori carved fireplace in the bar; you won't see anything better in the national museum. **Pros:** right by the city and the railway; across the road from

CLOSE UP

Kapiti Coast and Kapiti Island

A drive up the West Coast from Wellington is not to be missed. State Highway 1 takes you north, and about a half hour out of the city you hit the coast at Paremata. From here you can follow South Highway 1 straight up the Kapiti Coast, so called for the view of Kapiti Island. Alternatively, you can take the longer—but infinitely more scenic—drive around the Pauatahanui Inlet and Bird Sanctuary, following the road along the ridge of the rugged, winding, and windy Paetariki Hill where stunning views of the coastline and Kapiti Island await you. Both routes lead to **Paekakariki** (pie-*kahk*-a-reeky), a small, artsy beach town.

Paekakariki's draw is the shore, but it's also the main entry point of **Queen Elizabeth Park** (✉ *Entrance on Wellington Rd.* ☎ *04/292–8625*), more than 1,000 acres of fields and sand dunes along the coast. The park has a walking trail, horseback riding, mountain biking, and a playground. A little farther up the coast on State Highway 1 is **Lindale Farm** (☎ *04/297–0916*), which is home to **Kapiti Cheeses and Ice Cream**. Along with terrific locally made cheeses, you can try decadent ice cream with Kiwi flavors, such as feijoa, fig, or *manuka* honey (manuka is a kind of tea tree). The farm is just past Paekakariki's neighboring town, Paraparaumu. Paraparaumu is the departure point for one of Wellington's best-kept secrets: **Kapiti Island** ☎ *04/298–8195*). The island has been a protected reserve since 1897 and is a fantastic place to hike. All pests have been eliminated from the island, and birdlife flourishes, including saddlebacks, stitchbirds, and colonies of little spotted and South Island brown kiwi. Don't be surprised if a curious and fearless weka bird investigates your daypack or unties your shoelaces. Climb to the more than 1,700-feet-high Tuteremoana lookout point.

The island's most famous inhabitant was the Ngati Toa chief Te Rauparaha, who took the island by ruse in 1822. From this stronghold, he launched bloodthirsty raids before he was captured in 1846. He died in 1849, but his burial place is a mystery. Old tri-pots (used for melting down whale blubber) on the island bear testimony to the fact that Kapiti was also used as a whaling station in the late 19th century.

The **Department of Conservation** (*DOC* ✉ *18 Manners St.* ☎ *04/384 7770* ⊕ *www.doc.govt.nz*) oversees the island and restricts visitors to 50 a day. You'll need a permit ($11). Book in advance. Two tour companies provide transportation to the island: **Kapiti Marine Charter** (☎ *0800/433–779 or 04/297–2585* ⊕ *www. kapitimarinecharter.co.nz*) and **Kapiti Island Tours** (☎ *0800/527–484 or 04/237–7965* ⊕ *www.kapititours. co.nz*). Boats leave from the beach at Paraparaumu; both companies charge $55 round-trip. Once on the island, you're taken to the DOC headquarters, where you can get trail maps. For more information about Kapiti Island, contact the Wellington Visitor Information Centre (⇨ *Visitor Information in Wellington Essentials, above*) or the **Paraparaumu Visitor Information Center** (☎ *04/298–8195* ⊕ *www.naturecoast.co.nz*).

7

DID YOU KNOW?

Matiu Island in Wellington Harbour was a human and livestock quarantine station until 1980 and served as an internment camp during both World Wars. Today it is a tranquil wildlife preserve with native birds, reptiles, and plants.

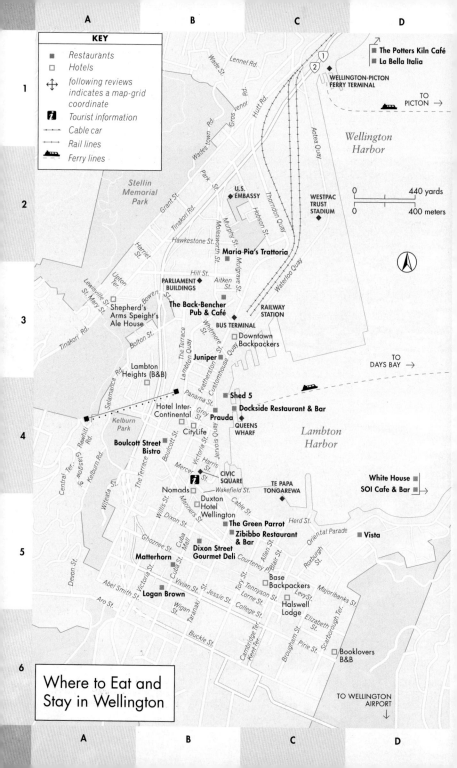

KEY

■ Restaurants

□ Hotels

⟺ following reviews indicates a map-grid coordinate

ℹ Tourist information

⋯ Cable car

━ Rail lines

⛴ Ferry lines

1 **2** WELLINGTON-PICTON FERRY TERMINAL

■ The Potters Kiln Café
■ La Bella Italia

TO PICTON →

Wellington Harbor

Stellin Memorial Park

440 yards

400 meters

Lennel Rd.

Wade St.

venar Rd.

Hutt Rd.

Park St.

Wades town Rd.

Gros venor

Grant St.

Tinakori Rd.

Harriet St.

Upton Ter.

Lewisville St.

St. Mary St.

Bowen St.

Hawkestone St.

Hill St.

Aitken St.

Murphy St.

Molesworth St.

Mulgrave St.

Hobson St.

Thorndon Quay

Aotea Quay

Waterloo Quay

Westpac Quay

U.S. EMBASSY ◆

WESTPAC TRUST STADIUM

■ Maria Pia's Trattoria

PARLIAMENT BUILDINGS ◆

■ The Back-Bencher Pub & Café

RAILWAY STATION

BUS TERMINAL

□ Downtown Backpackers

Shepherd's Arms Speight's Ale House

Tinakori Rd.

Bolton St.

The Terrace

Lambton Quay

Whitmore St.

Featherston St.

Customhouse Quay

■ Juniper

Lambton Heights (B&B) □

TO DAYS BAY →

Salamanca Rd.

Kelburn Park

Rawhiti Rd.

Glasgow St.

Central Ter.

Kelburn Rd.

Witeata St.

The Terrace

Bowen St.

Panama St.

Grey St.

Hotel Inter-Continental □

□ CityLife

■ Shed 5

■ Dockside Restaurant & Bar

■ Prauda

QUEENS WHARF

Lambton Harbor

■ Boulcott Street Bistro

Boulcott St.

Victoria St.

Jervois Quay

Harris St.

Mercer St.

Willis St.

ℹ CIVIC SQUARE

□ Nomads

Wakefield St.

TE PAPA TONGAREWA ◆

Cable St.

■ White House
■ SOI Cafe & Bar →

Ghuznee St.

Dixon St.

Cuba Mall

Manners St.

□ Duxton Hotel Wellington

■ The Green Parrot

■ Zibibbo Restaurant & Bar

Herd St.

Oriental Parade

■ Vista

Devon St.

Aro St.

Abel Smith St.

Victoria St.

Cuba St.

C.Vivian St.

Wigan St.

Taranaki St.

Jessie St.

Lorne St.

College St.

Tory St.

Tennyson St.

Blair St.

Allen St.

Courtenay Pl.

Roxburgh St.

Levy St.

Majoribanks St.

Elizabeth St.

Scarborough Ter.

■ Matterhorn

■ Dixon Street Gourmet Deli

■ Logan Brown

□ Base Backpackers

□ Halswell Lodge

Buckle St.

Cambridge Ter.

Kent Ter.

Brougham St.

Pirie St.

□ Booklovers B&B

TO WELLINGTON AIRPORT ↓

Where to Eat and Stay in Wellington

the ferries. **Cons:** some of the rooms are looking a little worn. ⊠ *Bunny St. and Waterloo Quay* ☎ *04/473–8482* ⊕ *www.downtownbackpackers. co.nz* ⟿ *60 rooms, 54 with bath* ⚹ *In-room: No a/c, no phone, kitchen, no TV (some). In-hotel: Restaurant, bar, laundry facilities, Internet terminal* ☰ *AE, DC, MC, V* ⏐⚬⏐ *EP* ⟐ *B4.*

\$\$–\$\$\$ 🏨 **Duxton Hotel Wellington.** Near the waterfront and Te Papa Tongarewa–Museum of New Zealand, this hotel is also close to the central business district and shopping, with the vibrant entertainment area of Courtenay Place at the back door. Rooms are decorated in pastel shades, and furnishings include writing desks, coffeemakers (that also brew tea), and marble bathrooms with separate bath and shower. All but four of the rooms have stunning views over the harbor or the city. Valet parking is provided, and the hotel is minutes from the airport. **Pros:** right by the action; extremely convenient parking; an excellent restaurant. **Cons:** some rooms are dated. ⊠ *170 Wakefield St.* ☎ *04/473–3900 or 0800/655–555* ⊕ *www.duxton. com* ⟿ *192 rooms* ⚹ *In-room: Internet. In-hotel: Restaurant, bar, gym, laundry facilities* ☰ *AE, DC, MC, V* ⟐ *B5.*

\$–\$\$ 🏨 **Halswell Lodge.** For restaurant, theater, and cinema going, you can't beat this hotel's location, right by the eastern end of Courtenay Place. And you'll find it hard to beat the prices. Standard hotel rooms at the front of the building are small and functional. Motel units are set farther back, each with a kitchenette (two have whirlpool baths). Finally, a restored 1920s villa is at the rear of the property. Six superior rooms (four with whirlpool baths,) have cane chairs, burnished wood furnishings, antique wardrobes, and restored fireplaces. You can use the villa kitchen to prepare light meals. **Pros:** reasonably priced accommodation; close by all the action. **Cons:** traffic noise might be a problem. ⊠ *21 Kent Terr.* ☎ *04/385–0196* ⊕ *www.halswell.co.nz* ⟿ *25 rooms, 11 motel units* ⚹ *In-room: No a/c, kitchen (some). In-hotel: Laundry facilities* ☰ *AE, DC, MC, V* ⏐⚬⏐ *EP* ⟐ *C5.*

\$\$–\$\$\$\$ 🏨 **InterContinental Wellington.** In the heart of the business district, and
Fodor's Choice a stone's throw from the waterfront, this landmark high-rise gets the
★ details right. The spacious art deco–inspired foyer is complemented by ferns, orchids, and fruit bowls (help yourself). New Zealand paintings and prints line the hallways and the guest rooms, which also have a faintly deco style. The standard rooms have one or two queen beds and plasma-screen TV, with quality embossed wallpaper. The top-end "club rooms" are more modern; snowy white duvets on the king-size beds stand out against the dark-wood furnishings. There's even a 24-hour car service. **Pros:** comfortable; affordable; on the doorstep of the city happenings. **Cons:** large and rather soulless. ⊠ *Featherston and Grey Sts.* ☎ *04/472–2722* ⊕ *www.intercontinental.com* ⟿ *231 rooms* ⚹ *In-room: Internet. In-hotel: Restaurant, bars, pool, gym, laundry service, no-smoking rooms* ☰ *AE, DC, MC, V* ⏐⚬⏐ *EP* ⟐ *B4.*

\$\$–\$\$\$ 🏨 **Lambton Heights.** John and Cushla Owens are the welcoming owners of this large character-filled heritage home. There is some interesting original interior woodwork dating from 1905, varnished floors, and huge mirrors. From two of the guest rooms leaded-light windows give a view over the city, and there is a guest lounge with good tea and coffeemakers overlooking the garden with its whirlpool bath. **Pros:** quiet;

7

classy; close to city center. **Cons:** parking is restricted. ✉ *20 Talavera Terr., Kelburn, Wellington* ☎ *04/976–6336* ⊕ *www.lambtonheights. co.nz* ⮡ *2 king and 1 double, all with modern en suite.* ♿ *In-hotel: Internet* ▭ *MC, V* ⑩ *CP* ✣ *A4.*

¢–$ 🛏 **Nomads.** This well-kept backpackers place has a prime position in central Wellington across the street from the Michael Fowler Centre and Information Centre. Adjoining and with Internet access is Blend, an excellent bar and café. Private en suite rooms supply towels. There are a good number of computers for Internet access and a free evening meal. **Pros:** good location. **Cons:** you have to like the backpacker thing. ✉ *118–120 Wakefield St.* ☎ *04/978–7800* ⊕ *www.nomadshostels.com* ⮡ *48 private rooms with bunk rooms making a total of 198 beds* ♿ *In-room: No a/c* ▭ *AE, MC, V* ✣ *B4.*

$–$$ 🛏 **Shepherd's Arms Speight's Ale House.** New Zealand's oldest hotel, the Shepherd's Arms, has been refurbished to approximate its original 19th-century state. Two rooms have four-poster beds, all have deep-blue carpets and burgundy curtains, and all are fairly small, especially the three single rooms, which share a bathroom. You can head to the bar and mix with the local after-work crowd; old photos on the wall show Wellington in the hotel's early days. **Pros:** reasonably priced; fairly close to the city; a short walk to the Botanic Gardens. **Cons:** there can be some noise from the bar crowd. ✉ *285 Tinakori Rd., Thorndon* ☎ *04/472–1320* ⊕ *www.shepherds.co.nz* ⮡ *12 rooms, 9 with bath* ♿ *In-hotel: Restaurant, bar, no-smoking rooms* ▭ *AE, DC, MC, V* ⑩ *EP* ✣ *B3.*

NIGHTLIFE AND THE ARTS

For current event listings in Wellington, check the entertainment section in the *Dominion Post,* Wellington's daily newspaper, or the free weekly entertainment newspaper, *Capital Times.* The free booklet *Wellington What's On,* available from the Wellington i-SITE Visitor Centre, has seasonal listings of cultural events. The Wellington City Council lists events, exhibits, lectures, and workshops. The Web site for the **Wellington i-SITE Visitor Centre** (⊕ *www.wellingtonnz.com*) also has up-to-date listings, from movies to theater and music. **Ticketek** (☎ *04/384–3840*), between the Michael Fowler Center and the Town Hall, sells tickets for local performances.

THE ARTS

FESTIVALS   The major arts event is the **New Zealand International Arts Festival,** held in March on even-numbered years at venues across the city. A huge array of international talent in music, drama, dance, the visual arts, and media descends upon Wellington. Advance information and a festival program are at the **Festival Office** (☎ *04/473–0149* ⊕ *www.nzfestival.telecom. co.nz*). Events fill up quickly; book a month in advance if you can.

Wellingtonians turn out in droves for the many free festivals that occur from November to April. One of the largest summer fests is the six-week **Summer City,** which includes more than 70 events throughout the city. At the **Cuba Street Carnival,** which runs on alternate years to the Arts Festival for two days in March, food-and-crafts stalls, and music-and-dance performances sweep the length of Cuba Street, culminating in a nighttime parade (a family-friendly show, not a rowdy Mardi Gras–style blowout).

One of the key Māori occasions in Wellington is **Matariki,** the North Island Māori New Year in late May–early June, beginning with the first new moon after the appearance of Matariki (Pleiades). Te Papa Tongarewa–Museum of New Zealand hosts nearly a month of musical, storytelling, and dance performances; the events begin with a ceremony at dawn. Pick up a brochure and calendar of events at the museum. For a unique gift or souvenir, Te Papa Press also publishes a superbly illustrated Matariki calendar, which runs from June until May and is based on traditional Māori lore of the seasons.

PERFORMING ARTS Wellington is the home of the **Royal New Zealand Ballet,** known as much for contemporary works by New Zealand and international choreographers as for its perennial *Nutcracker* and *Swan Lake* performances. The **NBR New Zealand Opera** and the **New Zealand Symphony Orchestra** mix equal parts "old favorites" with contemporary works. The glass, concrete, and steel Michael Fowler Center and the adjacent, older **Wellington Convention Centre** (⊠ *111 Wakefield St.* ☎ *04/801–4231*) jointly operate as the main venue for the symphony and other classical music performances.

The ornate, turn-of-the-20th-century **St. James Theatre** (⊠ *77–83 Courtenay Pl.* ☎ *04/802–4060* ⊕ *www.stjames.co.nz*) has dance performances, musicals, and opera. The equally well-preserved **Opera House** (⊠ *111–113 Manners St.* ☎ *04/384–3840*), with its plush carpets and tiered seating, has a similar lineup. Because the Opera House and the St. James Theatre are under the same ownership, the NBR New Zealand Opera and the Royal New Zealand Ballet use either venue as schedules allow.

Bats Theatre is Wellington's long-standing source for experimental, sometimes off-the-wall theater. Bats hosts the Fringe Festival during the International Arts Festival, and a range of performances throughout the year. ⊠ *1 Kent Terr.* ☎ *04/802–4175* ⊕ *www.bats.co.nz.*

Circa Theatre is a good bet for catching contemporary New Zealand pieces along with established masterworks from Harold Pinter to Oscar Wilde. It's on the wharf next to the Te Papa museum. ⊠ *1 Taranaki St.* ☎ *04/801–7992* ⊕ *www.circa.co.nz.*

Downstage Theatre holds performances of stage classics, contemporary drama, comedy, and dance. ⊠ *Hannah Playhouse, Courtenay Pl. and Cambridge Terr.* ☎ *04/801–6946* ⊕ *www.downstage.co.nz.*

NIGHTLIFE

Wellington's after-dark scene splits between several main areas. The "alternative" set spends its time at **Cuba Street**'s funky cafés, bars, and clubs, which stay open until around 1 AM during the week and about 3 AM on weekends; cocktails are innovative, and the music is not top-20 radio.

Courtenay Place is home to the traditional drinking action with a selection of brash Irish pubs, sports bars, and a few upscale establishments. It's packed on Friday and Saturday nights, especially when a rugby game is on, and the streets fill with beery couples in their late teens and early twenties (New Zealand's legal drinking age is 18) lining up to get plastered.

In the downtown business district—between Lambton Quay and Manners Street—a couple of brewpubs and a few taverns cater to the after-work mob. Down by the harbor, a flashy corporate crowd hangs out in several warehouse-style bars, sipping martinis on weeknights and filling the dance floor on weekends.

BARS If beer is your thing, head downtown and make an early start at the **Arizona Bar** (✉ *Grey and Featherston Sts.* ☎ *04/495–7867*), a Western-theme bar on the ground floor of the Hotel InterContinental. Modern with polished wood and plate glass aplenty, **Malthouse's** (✉ *48 Courtenay Pl.* ☎ *04/802–5484*) long bar with illuminated lettering is a point of interest. Of Courtenay Place's Irish spots, try **Molly Malone's** (✉ *Taranaki St. and Courtenay Pl.* ☎ *04/384–2896*), a large traditional bar with regular live music and a rowdy crowd, particularly on weekends. You can also check out the crowd from **Kitty O'Shea's** (✉ *28 Courtenay Pl.* ☎ *04/384–7392*) outside veranda; traditional live music is regularly played. The well-lived-in **Shooters Bar** (✉ *69–71 Courtenay Pl.* ☎ *04/801–7800*), once a brewery and then a distillery, has exposed brick walls, timber floors, and four levels with everything from a 400-person main bar to a garden bar to a 10-table poolroom.

Wellington's hipsters gravitate toward **Motel** (✉ *45 Tory St.* ☎ *04/384–9084*), with its dimly lighted booths and the DJ playing funky, downtempo hip-hop. As an added bonus, you can order food at the bar from the adjacent **Chow**, a Pan-Asian eatery. Although it's not formal, you'll want to leave the jeans and sneakers behind. Centrally located **Matterhorn** (✉ *106 Cuba St.* ☎ *04/384–3359*), which also has a good restaurant, draws a refreshing mix of urban hipsters and after-work corporate crowds with its indoor-and-outdoor fireplaces, a laid-back DJ, and a list of inventive cocktails.

Although it's right on bustling Cuba Street, **Good Luck** (✉ *126 Cuba St.* ☎ *04/801–9950*) is a little hard to find. Stairs take you below street level to a club done in the style of a Shanghai opium den, glowing with candles in Chinese teapots. On the waterfront, the two big draws are restaurant bars. **Shed Five** (✉ *Shed 5, Queens Wharf, Jervois Quay* ☎ *04/499–9069*) is an airy, high-beamed space, decked out with lilies, stained-glass windows, and gilded mirrors. **Dockside** (✉ *Shed 3, Queens Wharf, Jervois Quay* ☎ *04/499–9900*), a restaurant and bar with a nautical theme, has antique boats hanging from the ceiling. In good weather, everyone spills outside for the best close-up harbor views in Wellington. Later on, move across to **Chicago** Sports Café. (✉ *Jervois Quay* ☎ *04/473–4900*) on Queens Wharf, a spacious sports bar that sees boisterous postgame parties.

LIVE MUSIC **Valve** (✉ *154 Vivian St.* ☎ *04/385–1630*) is one of the best places to catch
AND DANCE live, local rock music. It's a classic hole-in-the-wall: small, dark, and a
CLUBS little seedy, with concrete floors. Another good bet for local bands is **Bodega** (✉ *101 Ghuznee St.* ☎ *04/384–8212*), which pulls in a slightly more wholesome crowd than Valve. It's larger, with couches in the front

and a dance floor by the stage. Both spots attract a predominantly university student crowd; the nights with cheap drink specials are packed.

Bigger international stars play at **Westpac Stadium** (✉ *1 Waterloo Quay* ☎ *04/471–0333*). The **TSB Bank Arena** (✉ *Queen's Wharf, Jervois Quay* ☎ *04/801–4231 or 04/499–4444* ⊕ *www.tsbbankarena.com*) also gets its share of the headlining tours. At the bottom end of Courtney Place, **Sandwiches** (✉ *Majoribanks St. and Kent Terr.* ☎ *04/385–7698*) has a stylish bar filled with long, black vinyl couches on one side and a dance floor on the other, where international DJs play soul, funk, disco, and jazz. Live jazz is played on Wednesday and on the last Sunday of every month.

SHOPPING

The main downtown shopping area, for department stores, clothes, shoes, books, outdoor gear, and souvenirs, is the so-called **Golden Mile**—from Lambton Quay, up Willis, Victoria, and Manners streets. For smaller, funkier boutiques, visit **Cuba Street**.

DEPARTMENT STORE AND MALLS

★ **Kirkcaldie & Stains** (✉ *165–177 Lambton Quay* ☎ *04/472–5899*) is Wellington's version of Harrod's. If you appreciate having the door opened by a top-hatted, liveried doorman as you enter a lovely early-19th-century facade, then this is the place for you. The extensive perfume department is a delight to the nose, and you can relax in the modern café and listen to live piano music between browsing.

A couple of indoor malls are on upper Lambton Quay: **Harbour City** and **Capital on the Quay** have a decent range of jewelry, lingerie, housewares, and clothing boutiques. A better mall is the **Old Bank Arcade** (✉ *233–237 Lambton Quay, at Customhouse Quay and Willis St.* ☎ *04/922–0600*) in the old-fashioned former Bank of New Zealand building, which is becoming something of a fashion enclave. The Arcade contains a slew of well-known boutiques, including New Zealand designer Andrea Moore and the tempting Minnie Cooper shoe store. Napoleon Cosmetics does wonderful makeovers, and for both guys and dolls Rixon Groove are shirt- and tie-makers par excellence.

MARKETS

For a look at the weekly market of a close-knit ethnic community, catch an early train or take a drive north of Wellington on State Highway 1 to Porirua and hit the morning-only **Porirua Market** (✉ *Cobham Ct.*). The stalls sell everything from eggplants and pineapples to colorful clothing to woven basketry and beadwork. Entertainers and hoarse-voiced evangelists play to the crowd. If you get hungry, there are food stalls galore selling curry and roti, chop suey, banana pancakes, and nearly every other treat you can imagine. The stalls open at 5:30 AM but close at 10 AM sharp.

Two **outdoor markets** (✉ *Chaffers St. opposite New World supermarket* ✉ *Willis St. between Vivian and Ghuznee Sts.*) set up every Sunday between dawn and noon in parking lots at either end of the city. These fruit-and-vegetable markets are among the most culturally diverse

7

gathering points in the city. If you're looking to picnic, you can pick up supplies.

SPECIALTY STORES

BOOKS AND MAPS

Arty Bee's Books (⊠ *Oaks, Manners St.* ☎ *04/384 9724* ⊕ *www.artybees. co.nz*) is a friendly store for secondhand books and sheet music. **Parson's Books & Music** (⊠ *126 Lambton Quay* ☎ *04/472–4587*) is not the largest bookstore in town, but it's one of the most intriguing—strong on New Zealand writing and travel, and featuring extensive classical recordings and a small upper-floor café. **Unity Books** (⊠ *57 Willis St.* ☎ *04/499–4245*) stocks a generous supply of New Zealand and Māori literature.

CLOTHING AND ACCESSORIES

The nifty (and free) Wellington **Fashion Map,** which you can pick up at the Visitor Information Centre or any number of stores, divides the city into easily navigable shopping quarters and lists a good cross section of women's and men's designer boutiques throughout the city. Slightly off-the-beaten-track streets such as Woodward Street, Customhouse Quay, Wakefield Street, and upper Willis Street are home to some uniquely New Zealand designers and are well worth exploring.

Area 51 (⊠ *Cuba and Dixon Sts.* ☎ *04/385–6590*) stocks street-savvy clothing brands like Diesel, but the real reason to come in is to check out the popular, local Huffer label. **Gold Ore Silver Mine** (⊠ *Left Bank, Cuba Mall* ☎ *04/801–7019*) has one of the city's largest selections of jewelry made from carved *pounamu* (a green stone similar to jade). Prices are reasonable, starting at around $18 for a pendant. The store also sells gold and silver jewelry, crafted on the premises.

Karen Walker (⊠ *126 Wakefield St.* ☎ *04/499–3558*) has made a name for herself overseas. Her Wellington store carries her own designs and also stocks international labels, such as Victor & Rolf. **Unity collection** (⊠ *101 Customhouse Quay* ☎ *04/471–1008*) carries clothing from a clutch of New Zealand designers, good for a one-stop view of the local talent. Long-standing New Zealand designer Elisabeth Findlay of **Zambesi** (⊠ *107 Customhouse Quay* ☎ *04/472–3638*) whips up innovative but extremely wearable clothes.

OUTDOOR EQUIPMENT

Wellington is a fine place to stock up on camping supplies before hitting the great outdoors. **Kathmandu** (⊠ *57 Willis St.* ☎ *04/472–0113*) carries its house brand of clothing and equipment. **Ski & Snowboard Centre–Gordons** (⊠ *Cuba and Wakefield Sts.* ☎ *04/499–8894*) focuses on snow-sport equipment and clothing.

SOUVENIRS

Kura Contemporary Art and Design (⊠ *19 Allen St.* ☎ *04/802–4934*) is part gallery, part gift store, with a strong Māori current running through the work. Some of the smaller, less-expensive items make unique souvenirs. On Lambton Quay, the best bet for souvenirs is **Sommerfields** (⊠ *296 Lambton Quay* ☎ *04/499–4847*). Everything in the store—from jewelry to artwork, scarves, and soaps—has been made in New Zealand.

TOURS

BOAT TOURS **East by West Ferries** runs the *Dominion Post* Ferry, a commuter service between the city and Days Bay, on the east side of Port Nicholson, and it's one of the best-value tours in the city. On the way to Days Bay you can stop at Matiu or Somes Island; this former quarantine station makes an unusual picnic spot on a warm afternoon and you might see a native tuatara. Days Bay has seaside village character, a lovely bathing beach, local craft shops, and great views of Wellington. Weekdays the catamaran departs from Queens Wharf every 25 minutes from 6:25 AM to 8:45, then at 10, noon, and 2:15 and from 4:30 every half hour until 7 PM. The return boats leave Days Bay roughly 30 minutes later. The sailing schedule is cut back on weekends and holidays but additional Harbour Explorer Tours visit Petone Wharf and Seatoun Wharf. The one-way fare to Days Bay is $10; the cost if you include a Matiu–Somes Island stop is $21 round-trip. You can pick up tickets at the ferry terminal between 8 and 5; otherwise, tickets can be bought on board. All sailings may be cancelled in stormy weather.

Contact **Dominion Post Ferry** (✉ *Queens Wharf* ☎ *04/499–1282 or 04/494–3339* ⊕ *www.eastbywest.co.nz).*

BUS TOURS **Wellington Rover** runs local tours that range from a two-hour overview ($50) to a full-day *Lord of the Rings* sites tour ($150), which includes a picnic lunch. Tours leave from the visitor information center on Wakefield Street. Reservations are essential.

Contact **Wellington Rover** (☎ *021/426–211 cell* ⊕ *www.wellingtonrover.co.nz).*

PRIVATE GUIDES **Wally Hammond,** a tour operator with a great anecdotal knowledge about Wellington, runs a 2½-hour minibus tour of the city. This can be combined with a half-day Kapiti Coast Tour, which includes a Southward Car Museum visit. The city tour costs $50, and the Kapiti Coast tour is $85. A full-day Palliser Bay and *Lord of the Rings* sites tour is $170 and that includes lunch and transfers.

Contact **Wally Hammond** (☎ *04/472–0869* ⊕ *www.wellingtonsightseeingtours. com).*

SIGHTSEEING TOURS **Flat Earth–New Zealand Experiences** runs a wide range of tours to scenic areas both locally and countrywide. They include a full-day tour to Kapiti Island and their LOTR tour at $65 is a popular option. Tours to Matiu–Somes Island at $145 also include lunch.

Contact **Flat Earth–New Zealand Experiences** (☎ *04/977–5805 or 0800/775–805* ⊕ *www.flatearth.co.nz).*

TRAVEL AGENCIES

Local Agents House of Travel (✉ *6 Margaret St., Lower Hutt* ☎ *04/569–0950).* **Lambton Quay Flight Centre** (✉ *182 Lambton Quay* ☎ *04/471–2995 or 0800/354–448).*

THE WAIRARAPA

To cross the Rimutaka Ranges, which form a natural barrier between Wellington and the Wairarapa, you climb a twisting snake of a road known locally as "The Hill." Near a small plateau at the road's peak, at a height of about 1,800 feet, a footpath leads to even higher ground and spectacular views on all sides. Heading down from the summit, the road plunges through a series of hairpin turns to reach the plain that the Māori called "Land of Glistening Water."

For some years, the rather-daunting access road gave a sense of isolation to the Wairarapa, which was essentially a farming area. But the emergence of the wine industry has triggered a tourism boom in the region. Red grape varieties flourish in the local soil (the pinot noir is particularly notable), and Wairarapa wines, produced in small quantities, are sought after in New Zealand and overseas. These days, vineyards, wine tasting, olive farms, and the twice-yearly Martinborough Fair are firmly established attractions. Hot-air ballooning, sea-and-freshwater fishing, walking, the "Golden Shears" shearing competition, and other outdoor activities have also brought visitors over "The Hill."

GETTING HERE AND AROUND

You need a car. State Highway 2 runs north–south through the region between Napier and Wellington. From Wellington you drive through Upper Hutt (the River Road bypasses the town), over the hills into the gateway town of Featherston. Highway 53 takes you to Martinborough; turn southwest here on Lake Ferry Road for Lake Ferry and Cape Palliser. Masterton is farther north along State Highway 2, roughly a half-hour drive from Martinborough. The journey from Wellington to Martinborough takes 1½ hours; Masterton is another half hour. From Napier, Masterton is about 3 hours.

MARTINBOROUGH

70 km (44 mi) north of Wellington.

The pleasant town of Martinborough embodies the changes that have taken place in the Wairarapa as a result of the burgeoning wine industry. The town gets its name from its founder, John Martin, who, in 1881, laid out the streets in a union jack pattern, radiating from the square that forms the hub. Most restaurants and shops are on or close to the square.

To tap into the Wairarapa wine world, Martinborough is the place to come. More than 20 vineyards are within a few miles of town—an easy walk or bike ride to some and a pleasant drive or horse-drawn-carriage ride to most.

GETTING HERE AND AROUND

During weekdays the roads are mostly quiet, ideal for cycling and relaxed motoring; however driving on rural roads can be deceptive. Keep a sharp eye out for livestock movement—large herds of cattle or sheep can be just around that bend.

Weekends at virtually any time during the year can bring a flood of visitors. The first Saturday in March and April, the two Martinborough

Continued on page 379

SEARCHING FOR
MIDDLE-EARTH

By Debra A. Klein

7

With the Oscar-winning *Lord of the Rings* trilogy Peter Jackson secured his place among great location directors like John Ford and Martin Scorsese. He also sealed New Zealand's reputation for otherworldly beauty, putting the country on the map by celebrating it on screen.

The sets have long been struck, but New Zealand's vistas will inspire your imagination to fill in the castles, coombs, and creatures. It seems as if half the country was involved in filming, so you can always ask a local to tell a tale of Middle-earth. Or take a tour—elf ears are optional!

The Lord of the Rings marked New Zealand scenery's star turn, but, like an aspiring actor, it has worked its way up, often as a stand-in for better-known, bigger names. Mountain peaks outside of Queenstown double for the Rockies in advertisements, and Mt. Taranaki on the North Island played Japan's Mt. Fuji alongside Tom Cruise in *The Last Samurai*.

Now, thanks to generous incentives and a favorable exchange rate, New Zealand has lured other large international productions such as *The Chronicles of Narnia*. And Tolkien followers are already buzzing about Jackson and director Guillermo del Toro's next production, *The Hobbit*.

Above: Scene from *The Lord of the Rings: The Two Towers*

MIDDLE-EARTH

TONGARIRO NATIONAL PARK

The peaks near Mt. Ruapehu, the country's largest ski slope and its largest and most active volcano, played **Emyn Muil**; its slopes starred as **Mount Doom.** Frodo and Sam tracked and caught Gollum on rocky cliffs here, and Gollum caught fish at Ohakune, a World Heritage Site.

Cape Reinga   Kerr Point

Bay of Islands

NORTHLAND

Whangarei

NORTH ISLAND

Great Barrier Island

MATAMATA, WAIKATO

Matamata stood in for **The Shire,** Bilbo Baggins's home and the starting point for Frodo's quest. The rolling hills are here, but those sod homes were struck; only the Hobbit holes are left. Tour with Hobbiton Tours for the backstory (🌐 www.hobbitontours.com).

Hauraki Gulf

Firth of Thames

Whangamata

Tauranga

Bay of Plenty

Cape Runaway

Hamilton

Matamata

WAIKATO

EASTLAND

Tasman Sea

Raglan

Rotorua

TE UREWERA NATIONAL PARK

Gisborne

North Taranaki Bight

Taupo

Lake Taupo

New Plymouth

Ohakune

Mt. Taranaki

Mt. Ruapehu

TONGARIRO NATIONAL PARK

Hawke Bay

Cape Egmont

TARANAKI

Napier

HAWKE'S BAY

WANGANUI

Wanganui

Palmerston North

MANAWATU

WAIRARAPA

Upper Hutt

Lower Hutt

⊕ WELLINGTON

Putangirua Pinnacles

Cook Strait

SOUTH ISLAND

SOUTH PACIFIC OCEAN

WELLINGTON

Wellington served as home base for the cast and crew, and digital work was done here. Scenes of **The Shire,** the **Tower of Saruman, Rivendell,** and **Dunharrow** were all shot in suburbs of Upper and Lower Hutt. Wairarapa's Putangirua Pinnacles were the movie's **Paths of the Dead.**

0   100 miles

0   100 km

NELSON

Nelson artisans created the One Ring, costumes, and props. Kahurangi National Park's peaks stood in for **Dimrill Dale** and **Eregion Hills**. **Chetwood Forest** is 90 minutes from Nelson. Helicopter tours offer the best views.

QUEENSTOWN

Milford Sound and Fiordland National Park played **Amon Hen, Nen Hithoel,** and **Fangorn Forest.** Paradise became **Lothlorien,** where Frodo looks into the Mirror of Galadriel. Tour operators have a range of trips.

CANTERBURY

The Canterbury region became Gandalf's isolated fortress city of **Edoras** and the dramatic plains of **Rohan,** where Aragorn, Gimli, and Legolas track Merry and Pippin's captors in *The Two Towers.* And Twizel (a place, not a Hobbit) was the site of the winged-beast battle of **Pelennor Fields.**

NORTH ISLAND

Cape Farewell · Farewell Spit · KAHURANGI NATIONAL PARK · Golden Bay · Tasman Bay · WELLINGTON · Nelson · Cook Strait

NELSON · MARLBOROUGH · Blenheim

Cape Foulwind · Murchison · Grey R. · Kaikoura

Greymouth

WEST COAST

Franz Josef · Fox Glacier · CANTERBURY · Christchurch · Akaroa

Lake Tekapo · Twizel · Lake Pukaki · Farlie · SOUTH ISLAND

Mt. Aspiring · Lake Wanaka · Milford Sound · Paradise · Oamaru

FIORDLAND NATIONAL PARK · Queenstown · OTAGO

Doubtful Sound · Lake Te Anau · Lake Wakatipu · Te Anau

Lake Manapouri · SOUTHLAND · Dunedin

Invercargill · Foveaux Strait · Stewart Island

Muttonbird Islands · 0 · 100 miles · 0 · 100 km

TOURS OF THE *RINGS*

If you're familiar with the concept of "second breakfast," and know the difference between a smaug and a warg, you may want to break the bank for Glenorchy Air's **Three Ring Trilogy Tour**, an all-day adventure, including flying to and touching down at three filming locations on the South Island, or try their shorter **Two Ring** option for half a day. You can drive to some locations outside major cities on your own, but without a guide it may be difficult to "see" where the films were made (⊕ *www.trilogytrail.com*).

YOUR *RINGS* CYCLE (LOTR ITINERARY)

Begin as Frodo Baggins did, in Waikato, outside Auckland, then continue your quest to Lake Taupo (Mount Doom) and Tongariro National Park. Next stop: Wellington. From here fly to Nelson on the South Island and drive to Canterbury and through the plains of Rohan to Queenstown to access Milford Sound and Fiordlands. Your quest is complete.

PRECIOUS MOMENTS

Many LOTR tours feature capes, swords, and flag replicas in the famous settings. Ogle the Weta Cave in Wellington, the museum of the movies' special-effects team (⊕ *www.wetanz.com*), or Minaret Lodge's Barliman's Room in Wanaka, featuring oversized furniture and a special Hobbit menu (⊕ *www.minaretlodge.co.nz*).

(top) The leisurely two-hour ride across the river flats at Glenorchy. (bottom) Mount Aspiring National Park

Fair Days, can see traffic jams for miles. On a good, sunny winter weekend, Wellington people regularly pop 'over the hill' to sample a vineyard meal and a glass of vino. Plan your visit if you want to avoid the crowds.

ESSENTIALS

Visitor Information Martinborough Visitor Information Centre (✉ 18 Kitchener St. ☎ 06/306–5010).

EXPLORING

The **Horse and Carriage Establishment** (✉ *The Square, Martinborough* ☎ *021/035–3855* ⊕ *www.horseandcarriage.co.nz*) runs tours around the Martinborough-area vineyards. It's $60 per person for a two-hour tour; advance booking is essential. The company has twilight carriage drives, scenic picnic tours, and horse-and-carriage rental for any specific journey.

For an overview of the area's wines, take an oenophile's shortcut and hit the **Martinborough Wine Centre** (✉ *6 Kitchener St.* ☎ *06/306–9040* ⊕ *www.martinboroughwinecentre.co.nz*). The shop stocks a thorough selection of local vintages for sipping and purchasing, plus books and wine accessories, and ships wines all over the world. It's open daily 9–5.

Olives are another local crop. For a taste-bud-tickling exercise that doesn't involve grapes, head to **Olivo** (✉ *Hinakura Rd.* ☎ *06/306–9074* ⊕ *www.olivo.co.nz*), Helen and John Meehan's olive grove, 3 km (2 mi) north of Martinborough. You can tour the grove and its 5 acres of gardens to learn how their oils are produced. Tastings (and sales) of their extra-virgin and infused olive oils are encouraged. They're open weekends and otherwise by appointment.

The **Toast Martinborough Wine, Food & Music Festival** (☎ *06/306–9183* ⊕ *www. toastmartinborough.co.nz*) occurs on the third Sunday of November; thousands of tickets are typically sold within hours. You can get tickets ($50) through the Web site.

WHERE TO EAT AND STAY

$$$$
FRENCH
✗ **The French Bistro.** Like the black-and-white photos of Parisian models that adorn the walls of this compact trendy bistro, the regional cuisine is done with style. Settle into the modern chrome-and-black room for chef–owner Wendy Campbell's similarly contemporary creations. Critics from as far flung as New York heap praise on the food. You might enjoy the roasted duck à la orange with vegetables and potatoes. The French rustic tarte with figs from Wendy's own garden is served with a crème anglaise. There is an excellent selection of local wines. ✉ *3 Kitchener St.* ☎ *06/306–8862* ⌖ *Reservations essential* ▭ *AE, DC, MC, V* ⊗ *Closed Mon. and Tues. No lunch Wed.–Fri.*

BEST BETS FOR CRUISE PASSENGERS

Explore the waterfront taking in the **Museum of City & Sea,** and **Te Papa** then walk to Lambton Quay and ride the Cable Car to the Botanic Gardens and **Lady Norwood Rose Garden.** *Lord of the Rings* fans must try the Weta Cave, and for wildlife buffs the Zeelandia Karori Wildlife Centre is a must.

7

CLOSE UP

Matiu and Somes Island

A wonderful place to spend a day walking and exploring, the Matiu Island Scientific and Historic Reserve lies in Wellington Harbour approximately 8 km (5 mi) from the city. The island has lots of walking tracks, great beaches for swimming, good picnic spots, and opportunities to see whales, dolphins, penguins, and other birds (sharp eyes may also pick out skinks, tuatara and other small lizards, and giant weta insects on the paths). Because the boats carry a limited number of passengers to the island at a time, it's never crowded.

Although the 62-acre island was opened as a DOC reserve in 1995, it has an interesting history. From the early 1880s until around 1980 it was used as a quarantine station by early European settlers for both humans and animals—including dogs, cattle, sheep, red deer, llamas, and other livestock—on their way into the country. During the world wars, it was also used as a place of internment for aliens considered a security threat.

In 1981 Matiu became a project of the Royal Forest and Bird Protection Society. Volunteers began planting trees that year to replace vegetation that had previously been cleared to allow grazing for quarantine animals. Many other native plants that flourished before the arrival of Europeans have also been replanted, and native insects such as wetas reintroduced. The island is now a breeding ground for a variety of seabirds.

The island is strictly a place to enjoy natural beauty for a few hours at a time. The few man-made structures on Matiu today include the old quarantine station, and gun emplacements from World War II—which were never used, and which remain on the southernmost summit of the island. An automated lighthouse built in 1900 to replace the original structure from 1866 also still sends out its southward beacon to ships traveling from Wellington Harbour.

The island can be reached by the Dominion Post East–West ferry service; there are nine round-trip runs made from Wellington Harbour per day. *For more information, see Tours.*

—Bob Marriott

$–$$

NEW ZEALAND

✕ **The Village Café.** At this barnlike rustic café with a sunny outdoor courtyard, all the food is made from local produce. The cooks smoke their own salmon and make their own sausages. Try the big breakfast of eggs, bacon, sausage, and potato on toast; it will keep you going all day. The café shares a building with Martinborough Wine Centre. ⊠ 6 *Kitchener St.* ☎ *06/306–8814* ▭ *MC, V* ⊙ *No dinner.*

$$

▦ **The Claremont.** In a quiet rural area just outside the village center, this motel complex has a variety of stylishly modern, self-contained accommodations to suit a range of budgets. All have decks; the apartments have whirlpool baths. The studios and one- and two-bedroom apartments are in a garden environment, and have ample parking. **Pros:** quiet location out of the town center; good modern accommodation. **Cons:** no swimming pool or activities; you need to go into town for a restaurant. ⊠ *38 Regent St.* ☎ *06/306–9162* ⊕ *www. theclaremont.co.nz* ⤴ *16 rooms, 7 apartments* ⚷ *In-room: No a/c,*

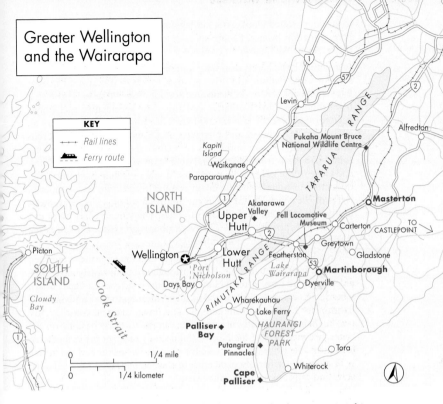

kitchen. In-hotel: Bicycles, laundry facilities, no-smoking rooms 🖃 AE, DC, MC, V.

$$$ 🏨 **Peppers Martinborough Hotel.** Sitting on a corner of the Martinborough ★ Square, this 1890s hotel has rooms that open onto either the veranda or the garden. The rooms mix antique and contemporary fittings, such as four-poster beds or writing tables, and the classic decorating styles vary from French provincial to Shaker to comfortable country. The hotel restaurant food is contemporary using classical French techniques; it has an extensive wine list. **Pros:** fine accommodations in the town center; handy to everything. **Cons:** you'll need your best manners to match the design. ✉ The Square ☎ 06/306–9350 ⊕ www.martinboroughhotel. co.nz ⇴ 16 rooms ⌖ In-room: No a/c, Wi-Fi. In-hotel: Restaurant, bar 🖃 AE, DC, MC, V ⏦ EP.

PALLISER BAY AND CAPE PALLISER

Southwest of Martinborough: 25 km (16 mi) to Lake Ferry, 40 km (25 mi) to Putangirua Pinnacles, 60 km (37 mi) to Cape Palliser.

To witness Wairarapa's most remote blustery scenery—and to see the North Island's southernmost point, Cape Palliser—drive southwest from Martinborough. It's 25 km (16 mi) through rolling sheep country to the coast at the tiny settlement of **Lake Ferry** on Palliser Bay. The lake in question, called Onoke, is a salt lagoon formed by the long sandbank here. Vacation homes, fishing spots, and remarkable sunsets bring in the weekend Wellingtonian crowd.

Just before Lake Ferry, turn left (coming from Martinborough) at the sign for Cape Palliser and drive another 15 km (9 mi) around Palliser Bay to Te Kopi, where the **Putangirua Pinnacles Scenic Reserve** is protected from the hordes by its relative isolation. The spectacular rocks have been formed over the last 120,000 years as rains have washed away an ancient gravel deposit, and pinnacles and towers now soar hundreds of feet into the air on both sides of a stony riverbank. An hour-long round-trip walk from the parking area takes you along the riverbank and close to the base of the pinnacles. If you're feeling adventurous, a three- to four-hour bushwalk involves some steep climbs and wonderful vistas of the coast—as far off as the South Island on a clear day. Stout footwear and warm clothing are essential. The Pinnacles are an hour's drive from Martinborough. The Martinborough visitor bureau is the best place to check for more information.

The road to Cape Palliser deteriorates after the Pinnacles and is unpaved in places. It's a dramatic, bleak ride, though not particularly hard, provided you take care. After 20 km (12 mi), the road ends at **Cape Palliser**, where 250 (sign says 258) wooden steps climb up to the candy-striped lighthouse. The views from here, up and down the wild coastline, are terrific. Below the lighthouse, splashing in the surf and basking on the rocks, are members of the North Island's only resident **fur seal colony.** You'll be able to get pretty close for photos, but not too close—these wild animals are fiercely protective of their young. Don't get between seals and pups, or seals and the ocean.

WHERE TO EAT AND STAY

¢–$ 🏨 **Lake Ferry Hotel.** The North Island's southernmost pub sits almost on the beach, with breathtaking views across Cape Palliser to the South Island's Kaikoura Ranges. The rooms are no-frills (in addition to the doubles, there's a 10-bunk dorm), but having a drink on the deck at sunset is an unbeatable experience. The menu ($$) focuses on fish and the fish-and-chips are supreme. The local, classic whitebait fritters are served on salad greens with tomato salsa. This place is so Kiwi, you get a chocolate fish with your cappuccino. (Chocolate fish are iconic Kiwi candy, chocolate-covered pink marshmallows.) **Pros:** if you like the feeling of being at the end of the earth, this is for you; you'll also love the food and the friendly welcome. **Cons:** don't expect the Ritz. ✉ *Lake Ferry* ☎ *06/307–7831* 🛏 *8 rooms, 1 with shower; 1 10-bunk*

PUB BOAT

An interesting bit of trivia about Lake Ferry Hotel: apparently under an old ruling written into the license, the licensee of the pub must provide a ferry service across the lake if requested. Years ago it would have been a rowboat, today an outboard motor, but the proprietor says he has only been asked for this service once, probably for a joke as there is precious little on the other side, unless you want to travel a novel way to Wharekauhau.

CLOSE UP

Wairarapa's Best Wineries

Pick up a map of the area vineyards at Martinborough's visitor center, then hit the road to sample some of the country's best up-and-coming vineyards. Here are the top local picks. (Any organized wine tour cost will include tasting.)

Ata Rangi Vineyard. This family-owned and family-managed winery makes exceptional chardonnay, sauvignon blanc, pinot noir, and Célèbre (a cabernet-merlot-shiraz blend) in small quantities. ⊠ *Puruatanga Rd.* ☎ *06/306–9570* ⊕ *www.atarangi. co.nz* ⊗ *Tastings Daily weekdays 1–3, weekends 11–5.*

Coney Wines. Have lunch here for a view over the vines that produce a terrific pinot noir and pinot grigio plus a rosé you can get only on-site. ⊠ *Dry River Rd.* ☎ *06/306-8345* ⊗ *Tastings Fri.–Sun. 11–5.*

Martinborough Vineyard. This fine regional winery was the first to convince the world of the Wairarapa's pinot noir potential. The chardonnay is also

exceptional. ⊠ *Princess St.* ☎ *06/306–9955* ⊕ *www.martinborough-vineyard. co.nz* ⊗ *Tastings daily 11–3.*

Murdoch James Vineyard. This boutique producer of a wide range of Martinborough wines is a 10-minute scenic drive out of town. Try their smooth 2007 Blue Rock Pinot Noir in the on-site Riverview Café—it goes perfectly with the Riverview tasting plate, or with the ham off the bone with aged cheddar and pear-and-date chutney. ⊠ *Dry River Rd.* ☎ *06/306–9165* ⊕ *www.murdochjames.co.nz* ⊗ *Tastings year-round, daily 11–5:30. Café Dec.-Feb., Thurs.-Mon. 11:30–3:30, rest of yr Fri.–Sun.*

Palliser Estate. Don't miss the whites here—they're some of the best locally. Of particular note is the sauvignon blanc, which is renowned for its intense ripe flavors, and the pinot noir, which is made in an elegant classic style. ⊠ *Kitchener St.* ☎ *06/306-9019* ⊕ *www.palliser.co.nz* ⊗ *Tastings daily 10–4.*

7

---

dorm ⚒ In-room: No a/c, no phone, no TV. In-hotel: Restaurant, no-smoking rooms ⊟ MC, V ⊺◉ BP.

$$$$

Fodor's Choice
★

🏨 **Wharekauhau.** This Edwardian-style lodge is set on a 5,500–acre sheep station; guest cottages scattered around the main lodge each have a king-size bed, a small patio, and an open fireplace. Walks around the gloriously remote coastline are an option plus tours to the seal colony at Palliser Bay. The dining room menu ($$$$) highlights the best of local produce—especially lamb and fish—with fine Martinborough wines. **Pros:** luxury and privacy. **Cons:** you won't want to move far from the open fire in rough weather; don't expect the nightlife to set you alight. ⊠ *Western Lake Rd., Palliser Bay ⌂R.D. 3, Featherston☎06/307-7581 ⊕www.wharekauhau.co.nz ⌁12 cottages* ⚒ In-room: No a/c, no TV, Internet. In-hotel: Restaurant, bar, tennis court, pool, gym, no-smoking rooms ⊟AE, DC, MC, V ⊺◉ MAP.

FARM STAY

$

🏨 **Kawakawa Station.** On 5,000-acres of rolling hills with sheep, cattle, horses, and dogs is a cozy, self-contained hillside cottage that welcomes guests. If you can peel your eyes from the far-reaching views of the blue

Pacific you'll find a refrigerator stacked with breakfast goodies, a warming wood burner, and comfortable furniture. For fishing folk and hardy surfers, a beach is within walking distance. Enjoy relaxing walks around the farm or try a two-night option staying a second night at a secluded hut in the hills; it's fully catered at $250 per person. **Pros:** if you want a real Kiwi farm stay, this place is unbeatable. **Cons:** not suitable for children; the silence might keep you awake at night. ⊠ *2631 Cape Palliser Rd., Cape Palliser* ⚐ *Internet.* ▭ *No credit cards* †⊙| *BP.*

AROUND MASTERTON

Masterton is 40 km (25 mi) northeast of Martinborough.

State Highway 2 strings together a handful of eye-catching small towns on its way north past the Rimutakas.

ESSENTIALS

Visitor Information Featherston Visitor Centre (⊠ *The Old Courthouse, State Hwy. 2, Featherston* ☎ *06/308–8051* ⊕ *www.wairarapanz.com*). **Masterton Visitor Centre** (⊠ *316 Queen St., Masterton* ☎ *06/370–0900* ⊕ *www.wairarapanz.com*).

EXPLORING

★ The tiny town of Featherston is worth a stop for the **Fell Locomotive Museum** (⊠ *Lyon and Fitzherbert Sts., behind Information Centre on State Hwy. 2, Featherston* ☎ *06/308–9379* ✉ *fell.loco.museum@xtra.co.nz*).

Along with photos, models, and memorabilia, it has the last remaining Fell locomotive in the world; built in 1875 and expertly restored, the engine is one of only six that clawed their way up the notorious Rimutaka Incline on the way to Wellington. The museum's open weekdays 10–4:30 and weekends 10–4; admission is $5.

Roughly 10 km (6.2 mi) farther up the arrow-straight highway is **Greytown,** where well-preserved Victorian buildings now filled with cafés and boutiques line the main street. After a few miles more you'll reach **Carterton,** another small town with a handful of tempting crafts and antiques stores—especially Paua World (⇨ *Shopping, below*).

Masterton is Wairarapa's major population center, and like Martinborough to the south, it's in a developing wine region. There's not much to do in the town, but it's a handy gateway for hiking in the nearby parks and on the coast. Popular annual events include the Hot Air Balloon Festival in the first few days of April and the Golden Shears sheep-shearing competition, usually held the first weekend in March.

★ Nearby **Pukaha Mount Bruce** (⊠ *State Hwy. 2, 30 km [19 mi] north of Masterton* ☎ *06/375–8004* ⊕ *www.mtbruce.org.nz*) makes a fine introduction to the country's wildlife, particularly its endangered bird species. An easy trail (one hour round-trip) through the bush takes you past aviaries containing rare, endangered, or vulnerable birds, including the *takahē,* a flightless bird thought to be extinct until it was rediscovered in 1948. The real highlight, though, is the nocturnal habitat containing foraging kiwis, the country's symbol, who are endearing little bundles of energy. It takes a while for your eyes to adjust to the artificial gloom, but it's worth the wait. The *kaka* (indigenous parrots) are fed daily at 3. Don't miss the eel feeding at 1:30, when the reserve's stream writhes with long-finned eels. The center is open daily 9–4:30; admission costs $15.

An hour's drive east of Masterton along Te Ore-ore Road (which turns into the Masterton–Castlepoint road), **Castlepoint** is perhaps the most spectacular site on the entire Wairarapa coast. Castle Rock rises a sheer 500 feet out of the sea; below, in **Deliverance Cove,** seals sometimes play. There's a fantastic walk to the peninsula lighthouse, and surfers flock to the beach break at Deliverance Cove.

Enjoyable bushwalks in gorgeous forests laced with streams are in **Tararua Forest Park** (☎ *06/377–0700 DOC office*), which also has picnic facilities. The Mt. Holdsworth area at the east end of the park is popular for tramping. To get there turn off State Highway 2 onto Norfolk Road, 2 km (1 mi) south of Masterton.

WHERE TO EAT

$$$
NEW ZEALAND

✕ **Gladstone Vineyard & Cafe.** Sip a pinot noir or try your hand at pétanque while you're waiting for an antipasto platter, or Cape Palliser paua fritters with pan-fried mushrooms, at this sweet little vineyard. The inside dining room has a barnlike ceiling, wine casks, and a display of local art. ⊠ *Gladstone Rd., RD2 Carterton* ☎ *06/379–8563* ▭ *AE, MC, V* ⊘ *Closed Mon.–Wed.*

$$
CUISINE TYPE

✕ **Horseshoe Café Restaurant.** The high-ceilinged room with glistening chandeliers takes its name from the horseshoe shape. Padded seating and windows follow the pattern and along with an open fireplace create an appealing and warm interior. The rich venison fillet with a pumpkin-and-pistachio nut risotto, finished with a juniper berry-and-port glaze and followed by baked rhubarb cheesecake served with apple-and-cinnamon cream sounds like a nice combination. ⊠ *Queen St. N, Masterton* ☎ *06/377–1107* ▭ *AE, DC, MC, V* ⊘ *Lunch and dinner daily.*

$
CONTEMPORARY

✕ **Salut.** A recent remodel has installed a copper-topped bar with large tangerine lampshades and seating options that include bistro tables with stools or dark-leather comfort couches in cozy corners. The tapas-style menu advocates a number of small plates. The chicken liver parfait and char-grilled Turkish bread are a favorite; or try the green olives stuffed with chorizo and crispy fried aioli. The lemon fritters with pomegranate molasses and lemon ice cream would be our pick of the desserts. In summer a large outdoor courtyard with oak trees and a fountain is the perfect place to while away the afternoon. ⊠ *83 Main St., Greytown* ☎ *06/304–9825* ▭ *AE, MC, V* ⊘ *Closed Mon. and Tues.*

$$$$
EUROPEAN

✕ **Tirohana Estate and Cellars Restaurant.** The dark-tiled floor and white tablecloths with sparkling cutlery and glassware put this classy dining area way above the usual winery restaurant. A wrought-iron door entrance, black leather chairs, and polished-brass ceiling fan add to the aura. The oven-baked Moki, a local variety of fish, with wine-and-caper velouté sauce, baby potatoes, and wilted spinach is a good choice. Follow that with a delightful mochachino mousse and shortbread biscuit. If you prefer casual outdoor dining try the

7

patio with a view of the vineyards there are tasting platters, salads, pizzas, and desserts It all comes with impeccable and friendly service. ⊠ *42 Puruatanga Rd., Martinborough* ☎ *06/306–9933* ⊕ *www. tirohanaestate.com* ⊟ *AE, MC, V.*

WHERE TO STAY

$$–$$$$ 🏨 **Copthorne Resort Solway Park Wairarapa.** On 23 acres of landscaped grounds and gardens in the southern outskirts of Masterton, this is a large resort for a small town. The helpful staff and spacious rooms make this especially good if you're traveling with children. The restaurant ($$$–$$$$) has polished floors, an interesting, exposed timber ceiling and leather furniture; folding doors along the front open to a sunny deck. All-day dining and dinner is served every day. Local produce is popular: the grilled flat point fish served on polenta with sautéed spring onion, bacon, and a lemon-chive beurre blanc is a good choice. **Pros:** all single-story accommodations; plenty of in-house activities; good off-road parking. **Cons:** weekdays popular for corporate conferences; can get crowded on weekends with special family rates. ⊠ *High St. S, Masterton* ☎ *06/370–0500* ⊕ *www.solway.co.nz* ↝ *94 rooms, 8 apartments* ⚉ *In-room: No a/c, kitchen (some). In-hotel: 2 restaurants, bar, tennis court, 2 pools, gym, spa* ⊟ *AE, DC, MC, V* ⎮⊚⎮ *BP.*

$$$$ 🏨 **Parehua Country Estate.** This luxury accommodation is in a parklike country scene next to a vineyard. All suites have rural views, some taking in a man-made lake or extending to the Tararuas. Rooms are modern, spacious, and airy. Their lovely colors and textures emphasize the area's natural beauty. ⊠ *New York St., Martinborough* ☎ *06/306–8405* ⊕ *www.parehua.co.nz* ↝ *28 suites* ⚉ *In-room: Kitchen, DVD. In-hotel: Tennis court, pool, bicycles, no-smoking rooms* ⊟ *AE, DC, MC, V* ⎮⊚⎮ *BP.*

OUTDOOR ACTIVITIES

Get a bird's-eye view of the area with **Ballooning New Zealand Ltd.**; a one-hour trip followed by a champagne breakfast costs $330: allow two to three hours for the whole experience. ⊠ *54b Kent St., next to Paua World, Carterton* ☎ *06/379–8223 or 027/2248–696* ✎ *ballooningnz@ infogen.net.nz.*

SHOPPING

For a unique souvenir, visit **Paua World** (⊠ *54 Kent St., Carterton* ☎ *06/379–4222* ⊕ *www.pauaworld.com*). Just off the main highway in Carterton, Paua World is an interesting and informative diversion. Paua (akin to abalone) has been collected by the Māori since ancient times. The rainbow-color shell interiors are highly prized (used by the Māori to represent eyes in their statues) and are polished and processed, then turned into jewelry and other gifts. Open daily 9–5.

Upper South Island and the West Coast

WORD OF MOUTH

"The next day we headed to Picton, but not before spending the morning touring the enlightening Lavendyl lavender farm . . . Crayfish is a specialty of the area but can be expensive. The roadside caravans . . . on the road just outside of Kaikouria (on route to Blenheim) are the best places to try crayfish without the cost."

—Kasyorks

WELCOME TO UPPER SOUTH ISLAND AND THE WEST COAST

TOP REASONS TO GO

★ **Mountains and Glaciers:** The South Island is piled high with mountains that divide the island lengthwise. You can walk or ski them, or catch a helicopter to a glacier.

★ **Wildlife:** The upper South Island is home to the tuatara, which lives on several protected islands in the Marlborough Sounds. South by Lake Moeraki, you may see Fiordland crested penguins and New Zealand fur seals; At Kaikoura the whales come inshore to feed.

★ **Wine:** In Marlborough the sunny-day–cool-night climate means grapes come off the vines plump with flavor, giving wines with aromas that burst out of the glass. At any of the smaller wineries, you'll likely share your first taste with the winemakers themselves.

1 Marlborough and Kaikoura. Marlborough is all about vineyards, wide shingle riverbeds, and the sheltered waterways of the Marlborough Sounds. Kaikoura, meanwhile, is a rocky strip of boisterous Pacific coastline where sperm whales breach just off shore and snowy mountains drop almost to the sea.

2 Nelson and the Northwest. To the north the curving sheltered bays of the Abel Tasman coast open to the wide expanse of Tasman Bay. A little inland, the economic heart of the region beats with rich farming and forestry. But from this mellow center the countryside rises into layer after dramatic layer of wild mountains in the Kahurangi Park.

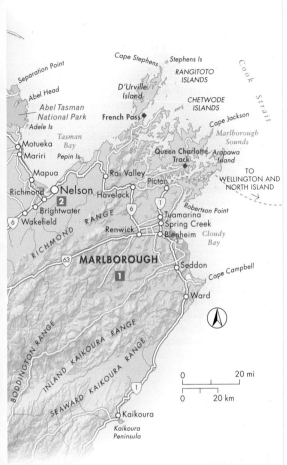

GETTING ORIENTED

A long narrow plain, broken by several mountainous areas, stretches from the Marlborough Sounds down the eastern coast of the upper South Island; State Highway 1 runs along this plain, going through Blenheim and Kaikoura on its way south to Canterbury. To the west, a series of high ranges separates Blenheim and Nelson. The side roads up into the Marlborough Sounds are slow and winding and often unpaved, so the best way to explore is often by boat from either Picton or Havelock. South and west of Nelson, and along the West Coast, the country becomes extremely mountainous. The series of high passes and long river gorges is broken only by small settlements. Much of this area is scenic parkland, a great buildup to the glaciers and mountains in Westland National Park.

8

3 The West Coast. The Coast is a long narrow of strip of land backed by high mountains, ranging from almost subtropical warmth in the north to icy glaciers in the south. Down south the soaring peaks of the Southern Alps run almost to the sea as the countryside becomes the wilderness of Westland National Park.

UPPER SOUTH ISLAND AND THE WEST COAST PLANNER

Planning Your Time

Anything less than three or four days through Nelson and Marlborough and an additional two to three days on the West Coast will be too few. Don't be deceived by the maps; steep, winding roads slow down the drive times. A driving route, the **Treasured Pathway,** runs across the top of the South Island. A guide to the route is available in local bookshops. It's an easy four-day tour from Christchurch, including Kaikoura, Blenheim, Nelson, south over the Lewis Pass to Hanmer Springs, then back to Christchurch.

When to Go

Nelson and Marlborough are pleasant year-round, but beach activities are best from December to mid-March if you plan to be *in* the water. But December to February is busy with New Zealanders on their own vacations so book ahead. Snow covers the mountains from June through October. The best time to go whale-watching off Kaikoura is between October and August. The pleasures of winter weather around the West Coast glaciers—clear skies and no snow at sea level—are a well-kept local secret. Look into local festival schedules; they occur year-round.

Getting Here and Around

Air Travel

Nelson has the major airport in the top of the South Island with flights in from Auckland, Wellington and Christchurch a number of times a day. Blenheim has a lesser number of daily flights in from Auckland, Wellington, and Christchurch; Kaikoura, Picton, Westport, Hokitika, and Golden Bay are serviced by smaller commuter aircraft.

Contacts Air New Zealand (☎ 0800/737–000 ⊕ www.airnewzealand.co.nz).

Car Travel

Roads through the countryside's mountain ranges and deep river gorges can be narrow and winding, and a 160-km (100-mi) drive might take over three hours. However, the roads are generally good and there's always something to look at. There are a number of one-way bridges along the way and several on the West Coast shared with trains. Watch the signposts and road markings for "give way" rules. It can be a long way between gas stations so fill up when you can.

Ferry Travel

Visitors traveling from the North Island can take the Interislander ferry from Wellington to Picton, the northern entrance to the South Island. The trip is spectacular in good weather, but Cook Strait can be rough in bad weather. The one-way adult fare ranges from $53 to $90. Ferries dock in Picton wharf.

Contacts Interislander (☎ 0800/802–802 ⊕ www.interislander.co.nz).

Train Travel

The West Coast is poorly served by rail, but the exception is the **TranzAlpine Express,** which ranks as one of the world's great rail journeys. The train crosses the Southern Alps between Christchurch and Greymouth, winding through beech forests and snow-covered mountains. The train is modern and comfortable, with panoramic windows and a no-frills dining and bar service.

Contacts TranzAlpine Express (☎ 0800/872–467 ⊕ www.tranzscenic.co.nz).

Restaurants

In Marlborough visit a winery restaurant—there's no better way to ensure that your meal suits what you're drinking. Salmon and Greenshell mussels are farmed in the pristine Marlborough Sounds, and local crops—besides grapes—include cherries, wasabi, and garlic. In Kaikoura try crayfish (lobster). The region is named after this delicacy (*kai* means "food" in Māori; *koura* means "lobster"). Nelson is famous for its scallops and seafood. On the West Coast, try whitebait fritters—a sort of omelet starring masses of baby fish.

Some restaurants close in winter (June through August); others may open only on weekends, or curtail their weekday hours. In summer, all doors are open and it's best to make reservations. If a restaurant is open on a major holiday, it may add a surcharge to your bill.

Year-round, the restaurants and cafés around the glaciers and other remote spots can be quick to close their doors at night. Arrive by 8:30 (it's sometimes even earlier in winter), or you might go hungry. Some of the smallest towns, including Punakaiki, settlements in the Marlborough Sounds, and parts of Golden Bay, have few cafés and no general stores, so bring your own supplies.

Hotels

Bed-and-breakfasts, farm stays, and homestays, all a variation on the same theme, abound in the South Island in some spectacular coastal and mountain environments. Your hosts will feed you great breakfasts and advise on where to eat and what to do locally. Other choices include luxury lodges and hotels, or inexpensive motel rooms and backpacker lodges. Accommodations often provide your morning coffee in a plunger (French press).

WHAT IT COSTS IN NEW ZEALAND DOLLARS

	¢	$	$$	$$$	$$$$
Restaurants	under $10	$10–$15	$15–$20	$20–$30	over $30
Hotels	under $75	$75–$125	$125–$200	$200–$300	over $300

Meal prices are per person for a main course at dinner, or the equivalent. Hotel prices are for a standard double room in high season including 12.5% tax.

Visitor Information

Every large, and most small, towns have an information center or i-SITE office; watch for the blue and white "i" sign showing their location. **The Treasured Pathway** (⊕ www.treasuredpathway.co.nz) is an excellent, joint regional endeavor through the Nelson and Marlborough areas outlining the best of the sights in the "Top of the South."

Several regional tourism organizations maintain helpful Web sites: Destination Marlborough (⊕ www.destinationmarlborough.com), Nelson Tasman Tourism (www.nelsonnz.com), **Tourism West Coast** (⊕ www.west-coast.co.nz) and **Glacier Country Tourism Group** (⊕ www.glaciercountry.co.nz). **The Department of Conservation** (⊕ www.doc.govt.nz) is always a good source for the various national parks.

Auto Transfers

Most car rental agencies have North Island–South Island transfer programs for their vehicles: leave one car in Wellington and pick another one up in Picton on the same contract. Some car rental companies are reluctant for their vehicles to leave the sealed roads but Apex Rentals in particular is more lenient about that.

8

ABEL TASMAN NATIONAL PARK

Golden sand, sheltered bays, and granite headlands are washed by clear blue water and fast-moving tides; rocky inshore islands provide habitats for shy native birds, and migrating wading birds crowd the sand flats. It's a vibrant place of sun, sand, and sea.

Abel Tasman is New Zealand's smallest and most accessible national park. The terrain varies from exposed mountaintops swathed in native beech forest to easy walking tracks through low coastal *manuka* bush, to a coastline bejeweled by a long string of sheltered bays. It's small enough that you can spend just a day here walking, kayaking, or simply cruising; or you can get serious and head off on a multiday trip combining all of the above, in quantity. If you're new to outdoor experiences this is the perfect place to start. The park has a number of walking and water-based options, and good road access from the north and south. Shuttles and water taxis can take you to the trailheads or pick you up afterward.

BEST TIME TO GO

October through April is best, but avoid the six-week Christmas rush from late December until early February when the locals invade. If you prefer your solitude, there are far fewer people around in winter, but the weather can be unpredictable.

FUN FACT

Dutch explorer Abel Tasman, for whom the park is named, was the first known European to visit the area, although he never made landfall. His murderous encounter with local Māori is thought to have occurred near Whariwharangi, on the western side of the park.

PARK HIGHLIGHTS

ADELE ISLAND
This pert little island just north of Marahau is completely uninhabited, and its peak is covered in low native forest. Rats and stoats have been eradicated, and native birds like the South Island robin (*kakaruai*) are being reintroduced. There is also a great-spotted kiwi (*roroa*) nursery.

GRANITE HEADLANDS
The prevalent granite headlands in the park drop off dramatically into the sea. This is most obvious around Separation Point, Arch Point, Tonga Quarry and the coastline south of Awaroa Bay. Tonga and Adele islands are also good examples.

HARWOODS HOLE
High in the interior of the park and reached by rough road from the top of the Takaka Hill, Harwoods Hole is a 180-meter-deep, 60-meter-wide karst sinkhole. It drops deeper into the country's largest underground cave system, which runs between Abel Tasman and Kahurangi national parks. The entry rappel drop of 160 meters is only for experienced cavers, but it's worth a look from the top.

TONGA ISLAND
Sitting between Bark Bay and Awaroa, the tiny island looks like a pile of granite blocks covered with a blanket of bush. The fully protected marine reserve is a breeding ground for seals and blue penguins; no fishing is allowed. If you're lucky you'll spot fur seals playing around the coastline.

WEKA (BUSH HEN)
These cheeky flightless birds have disappeared from many parts of the country, but they're still common here. They resemble heavy brown hens. They'll try to help themselves to your lunch (not encouraged, for their sake), and if you leave your tent open they might just run off with a shoe.

TOUR OPERATORS

Abel Tasman is a great place for a leg-stretch. Here are some tour operators that will help you with a short or multiday hiking trip.

Abel Tasman Wilson's Experiences guides day trips and three- and five-day treks in the marvelous coastal park. Spend nights in comfortable lodges and eat well, without having to carry a big pack. Overnight in one of the beachfront lodges; the three-day two-night kayaking and hiking trip or three-day guided walk each start at $1,050.

Bush & Beyond provide an excellent guided walk and hiking service throughout the Abel Tasman and Kahurangi parks. Trips are tailor-made to your level of fitness and interests. There are fully guided and self-catering options available.

8

(above left) Abel Tasman Coastal Track, (bottom) Bark Bay, (above) Tonga Arches at Arch Point

BEST WAYS TO EXPLORE

CRUISE OR WATER TAXI

In mid-summer the coastline buzzes with water taxis and slower catamarans delivering people, supplies, and kayaks to and from various parts of the park. If you just want to sit back and enjoy the idyllic scenery then join a cruise up the coast and back.

KAYAK

Several companies offer sea-kayaking packages. These can be from half-day to multiday trips, freedom or fully guided and catered. It's a pleasant, invigorating trip, especially if the wind is going your way.

SAIL

Almost without fail a healthy sea breeze comes up along the coast every summer afternoon. With this in mind catch a sailboat cruise out of Kaiteriteri in the morning. It's a slow, gentle way to interact with the park.

WALK

The entire 52 km **Abel Tasman Coastal Track**, from Wai-nui Bay in the north to Marahau in the south, can be walked in three to five days. This Great Walk is well formed and easy to follow. You can walk short sections by arranging a drop-off and pickup by water taxi. Bark Bay to Torrent Bay and Awaroa to Torrent Bay are ideal for this. Several short sections of the track are covered at high tide. The tracks inland to the mountain areas are quite rugged, at times unmarked, and best done by experienced trampers.

ECO-STAYS

High up under the Takaka Hill, between the Abel Tasman and Kahurangi parks, **The Resurgence** is a purpose-built lodge with a commanding view. It was constructed with local timbers, using sustainable principles, and the 50-acre grounds are being let go to allow the native bush to regenerate. Although areas look a little unkempt as this process unfolds the owners have chosen to only mow walking tracks through the rough growth. They also promise to plant a tree for every guest who stays; trees are irrigated by grey water and treated black water from the lodge. Hot water for the kitchen is heated by solar energy, and the buildings use passive solar heating.

ONE-DAY ITINERARY

Take a day to cruise and walk the park. Some operators will pick you up from accommodations as far away as Nelson. If you are driving there is parking available at Kaiteriteri and Marahau Beach, depending on where you are catching the boat.

MORNING

Slow catamarans or faster water taxis carry you up the coast to Bark Bay. On the way you may pass Split Apple Rock, an appropriately named giant granite marble in the sea. Farther up the coast you'll pass sandy beaches like Apple Tree Bay and Coquille Bay before cruising past Adele Island. Then, the boat hits open water for a short stretch before rounding Pitt Head and calling in to Torrent Bay and The Anchorage to drop off and pick up walkers, kayakers, and supplies. Stay on the boat to Bark Bay, a little farther up the coast, where you'll be dropped on the beach and shown where to join the Abel Tasman Coastal Track back past Torrent Bay.

AFTERNOON

The track climbs quite steeply from Bark Bay for a time, before ambling around several hillsides. In summer you'll meet plenty of other walkers on the track. Follow the track to Torrent Bay, where it drops sharply to the coast again. Depending on the tide you can either cross the estuary or walk round the all-tide track to The Anchorage. Pass through the DOC campground and wait for your boat back to Kaiteriteri or Marahau down on beach.

STAY THE NIGHT

Plan ahead to stay in the park at the Department of Conservation's hut at **The Anchorage**, a 4-hour, 12-km walk from the start of the track at Marahau. You must buy a $30 per night tickets beforehand in Nelson or Motueka or through the DOC Web site. Huts are basic, with cooking, shower, and toilet facilities. There are 50 campsites if you'd rather sleep under the stars. You will need to bring your food and water, or carry water purification tablets; park water is not potable. Pack out all your rubbish. There's a lovely short walk from the bridge over the Torrent River inland to Cleopatra's Pool, which sits between huge granite boulders. It's a frosty swim, even in summer.

8

(left) Sea kayaking in Torrent Bay, (right) Mother and child on hanging bridge

KAHURANGI NATIONAL PARK

Kahurangi is a vast wilderness area of deep river valleys, thick beech forest, and high marble mountains. Helicopters are dwarfed by house-sized rocks perched on the sides of high precipices. Wild white-water rivers tumble through gorges and calm alpine tarns sit high on the ranges.

The wild **Kahurangi National Park** spans 1.1 million acres of untamed wilderness and is laced with 570 km (353 mi) of hiking tracks of various levels of difficulty; there are also several rafting and kayaking rivers and some serious caving areas. Of the various entry points to the park, one of the most well used is the northern head of the Heaphy Track near Kaituna, 35 km (21 mi) west of Takaka and south of the town of Collingwood. There is also good access from the Flora Carpark on Mt. Arthur, the Wanga-peka River further south near Tapawera, from the Matiri Valley near Murchison, the Cobb Valley near Takaka, and at Karamea on the West Coast, which is also the southern entry to the Heaphy Track.

BEST TIME TO GO

Kahurangi can be visited any time of the year, although snow in winter may inhibit access to the higher areas like Mt. Arthur and the Mt. Owen massif. The Heaphy Track is passable all year unless the weather is unusually bad, when flooding may prevent stream crossings.

FUN FACT

Asbestos Cottage, near the Mt. Arthur Tablelands, was once home to a reclusive couple who lived there for 40 years. They backpacked everything they needed into the remote site and would often go months without seeing another person.

BEST WAY TO EXPLORE

CAVING AND CAVE DIVING

There is a spectacular network of caves beneath the park, and under Mt Arthur in particular. New passages are still being discovered and the cave systems at the northern end of Kahurangi join up with those under Abel Tasman. The Pearce and Riwaka rivers, on the western side of Mt Arthur, are both well-known cave-diving spots with well-defined resurgence caves. The Riwaka resurgence is popular with scuba enthusiasts; again, a local guide is essential.

HELICOPTER OR FIXED WING PLANE

Because of the vastness of Kahurangi, helicopters are used extensively to ferry trampers and rafters to remote rivers and tracks, to get trout fishermen to their favored spots, and for general sight-seeing. A helicopter flight up the winding Karamea River gorge is a particularly good option, and if the pilot throws in a circuit round the Garibaldi Ridge, so much the better. Some operators also fly fixed wing planes.

TRAMPING

The five-day Heaphy Track is one of the country's Great Walks, running down the western side of the park, between Collingwood and Karamea. Other challenging walks are available, but shorter easier tracks are available from the Flora Carpark to the bush line, and to the Cobb Valley north of Takaka.

WHITE-WATER RAFTING AND KAYAKING

The Grade V Karamea River offers some of the country's best white-water rafting and river kayaking. Access is often by helicopter and rafting trips can last up to a week and include camping. The best white-water action is found on the West Coast near Karamea, but there is also good white water on the Buller River near Murchison, which forms part of the southern boundary of the park. Local knowledge is essential on these trips so use a local guiding company of good repute.

ECO-STAYS

Twin Waters Lodge, to the west of Collingwood in Golden Bay, is often a first-night stop for trampers off the northern end of the Heaphy Track. Built on a finger of land jutting out into the Pakawau Inlet, it is a favored stopover for bird-watchers, who come to view the wading and migratory birdlife on the sand flats off Farewell Spit. Only 10 years old, the lodge features local timbers and uses a sound approach to ecological waste disposal, respecting its fragile coastal and estuarine setting. It is self-sufficient in water and uses solar heating for hot water throughout. It is an easy kickoff point for the western Kahurangi Park, Farewell Spit and the wild unspoiled waters of the Westhaven Inlet.

8

(top left) Eroded limestone formations, (bottom) A tramper relaxes at the top of Mt. Owen, (top) Trampers on the Heaphy Track

NELSON LAKES NATIONAL PARK

Snow-covered peaks and high alpine passes loom over two deep brooding lakes. Dense native forest, swampy wetlands, and tumbling rivers line the valleys, and the haunting calls of native birds stir the bush at night. It's an exhilarating environment.

Spread around two stunningly scenic glacial lakes, Rotoroa and Rotoiti, the **Nelson Lakes National Park** is an alpine zone of soaring mountains, rocky rivers, and bush-lined trails. Native beech forest pours down to the lakeshore. On cloudy days, mist swirls through the trees, wetting the draping mosses and silencing the birds. On sunny days the intense greens shine through and the birds' chorus resumes.

Of the two lakes, Lake Rotoroa is the most pristine, with just a few fishing cottages, a campsite, and a lodge on its shore. The village of St. Arnaud sits at the northern end of Lake Rotoiti; it's the gateway to the park, with a small service center, accommodations, and the Department of Conservation (DOC) center.

BEST TIME TO GO

Summer is the most pleasant time of year to visit as the weather is warm (for an alpine region), the lake is swimmable, and, for climbers, the high alpine passes are usually free of snow. Voracious sand flies, however, are a problem at any time so bring your repellent.

FUN FACT

Much of the park was formed by glacial action, hence its deep lakes and huge u-shaped valleys. The last glacial action was between 12,000 and 20,000 years ago.

BEST WAY TO EXPLORE

CLIMBING

Experienced alpine enthusiasts will love the challenges of the tracks and passes that lead high into the mountains. Experience is vital in these remote areas as severe weather can appear without warning. Always carry a mountain radio and inform the DOC center in St. Arnaud of your plans.

KAYAKING

Both Rotoroa and Rotoiti are excellent places to kayak. Although both can attract high winds, summer conditions are usually favorable. Pack a lunch and leave from the jetty at St Arnaud. Pull up to a quiet stretch of pebble beach, where all you will hear are the birds and breeze singing through the trees. But remember sand-fly repellent, too.

SKIING

In winter two small ski areas provide the locals with acres of fun. The public Rainbow Ski Area is an hour's drive from St. Arnaud and has good facilities and excellent access (open June to October). The smaller, club-run ski area on Mt. Robert requires a grueling two-hour climb, while carrying your gear. There is ski hire in St. Arnaud village and up at Rainbow.

WALKING

The park is laced with walking tracks, which center on the two lakes and range from easy 30-minute wanders to serious multiday treks deep into the mountains. In summer they are usually passable, although a cold snap can bring snow. Day walks include the Mt. Robert Pinchgut Track, the climb to Parachute Rocks, and the lakeside walk around Rotoiti.

WATER TAXI

During summer water taxis work on both lakes. They save a half-day walk at the start of a long trail and give nonwalkers access to pristine country. Remember to take everything you need with you as there are no shops, cafés, or amenities away from the two settlements.

ECO-TIPS

Lake Rotoiti is the site of a highly successful kiwi-recovery program; in 2004 several kiwi were released back into the forest after an intense pest-eradication program effectively made the area a predator-free mainland island. This has encouraged reintroduction and return of native birds that were long lost to the area. This program has recently been acknowledged internationally as one of Australasia's top 25 ecological restoration sites.

While you're here, respect nature and monitor your litter. As in all New Zealand's national parks, visitors are asked to pack out all their waste. There are no garbage facilities in the park. Also be mindful of the birdlife, and don't feed them. The cheeky kea, or mountain parrot, loves to steal unwatched lunches and gloves so don't leave anything lying around to encourage them.

8

(top left) View of the Parachute Rocks, (bottom) Looking into a basin at Robert Ridge, (top) A pier on Lake Rotoiti

PAPAROA NATIONAL PARK

Towering granite cliffs and stacks of pancake rocks, dark tannin-stained rivers edged by virgin kahikatea forest, karst landscapes riddled with sinkholes, and surf crashing on to the western shore beaches give Paparoa a look that is almost subtropical with towering nikau palms and strappy flax bushes bending in the breeze.

The **Paparoa National Park,** which runs loosely along the Paparoa Range, is a long rugged chain of mountains running parallel to the coast. With craggy summits, serrated ridges, and cirques carved out of ancient granite and gneiss, it's a formidable environment. But its sheer cliffs, flood-prone rivers, dense temperate rain forest, and extensive cave systems spell out paradise for hikers. The major track entry points—Bullock Creek, Fox River, and Pororari River—open onto an otherworldly zone of jungle green, striking *nikau* palms, rushing streams, and sweeping coastal views. There are several day hikes, canoeing and horse treks, and entry-level caving experiences.

BEST TIME TO GO

Any time of year is good here as the park is far enough north to be free of snow, except at the highest points in mid-winter. Summer is much warmer, although there are more people around, but in winter the weather can be clear and crisp, with less rainfall.

FUN FACT

The two- to three-day Inland Pack Track was built back in 1867 for gold miners as a safer alternative to hazarding the walk down the coast with its dangerous river mouth crossings, steep cliffs, and crashing surf.

BEST WAY TO EXPLORE

CAVING

Caving and cave-rafting in the Nile River valley is splendid. Join a caving trip at Charleston, on the northern end of the park. This suits able-bodied walkers and is a great trip to take older children on, so long as they can walk at least two hours unassisted. The trip also takes you by a glowworm cave and if you're brave you can join a cave-rafting trip back down the river.

HORSE TREKKING

Down the southern end of Punakaiki village you can join a horse trek. Ride up the bed of the Punakaiki River with towering cliffs on either side, or ride along the surf beach to view the pancake rocks from below.

KAYAKING

Take a kayak trip up the Pororari River on the northern side of Punakaiki village. Kayaks can be hired just by the road bridge. This is a beautiful way to see the more gentle aspects of the bush and the canyon walls, without getting muddy boots.

WALKING

You only need 20 minutes to follow the Pancake Rocks walk. You'll see mighty stacks of limestone (yes, shaped like pancakes), the surge pool, and the far-reaching coastal views. If it's a really clear day you can see Mt. Cook, and if the tide and wind are right you'll see the blowholes blowing spray like a breaching whale. The Truman Track and the Punakaiki Cavern walk can also be done in less than an hour; you'll need a torch for the cavern. Tramping tracks here are mostly serious backcountry hikes that require previous experience or a guide. Make your intentions known at the DOC Centre before leaving and carry good survival gear. The area can be lashed by heavy rain at any time of year, so if rivers rise during your trip don't try and cross them.

ECO-STAYS

Birds Ferry Lodge, north of Punakaiki, about 30 minutes toward Westport, is a newly built lodge. It sits atop the *pakihi* (poorly drained mineral soil) country, with distant views of the coast and more intimate views of native forest in the valley below. The lodge and its accompanying cottage have been built to maximize the thermal mass of the flooring, which is heated by solar gain. Native birds are encouraged to visit and the native bush in the valley below acts as a wildlife corridor, allowing birds to move between the mountains and the coast. The lodge has substantial vegetable gardens and all food waste is composted on-site. Other waste is sorted for recycling wherever possible.

8

(top left) Pancake Rocks, (bottom) Kayaking the Pororari River, (top) Tui bird sitting on a flax bush

WESTLAND NATIONAL PARK

Gigantic blocks of ice tumbling off the glacier face; ice fields higher up the glacier, their blue ice sparkling in the sunlight; rugged peaks (the highest in the country) soaring to the skyline; dense, virgin rain forest clawed by rock-strewn river beds.

Westland National Park is a place of extremes, including the extreme precipitation at the top of Westland. Up to 300 inches of snow per annum falls here, feeding Westland's glacier field. Franz Josef Glacier and Fox Glacier are the two most visited.

The park is backed by the main divide of the Southern Alps to the east. High up there are thousands of acres of alpine ski slopes and rugged rocky peaks. Below the bush line, the slopes are clad in thick temperate rain forest, and in places the park runs right to the rugged coastline, home to seals, penguins, and lonely beaches.

BEST TIME TO GO

This part of the country is subject to a very high rainfall, measured in meters rather than inches. This, and its associated cloud, will play havoc with your plans if they involve climbing, flying, or ice-walking. Winter weather is often clearer than summer, although much colder, and there are less people around.

FUN FACT

Westland National Park joins the Fiordland and Mt. Aspiring national parks to form a sweeping World Heritage Area of more than 5 million acres.

BEST WAY TO EXPLORE

FLIGHTSEEING

Whether you choose to fly by helicopter or small fixed-wing plane, a flight to the glacier will be a highlight. Helicopters do flights as short as 10 minutes for a quick aerial tour, or up to three-hour trips where you will get two hours on an upper ice field. Fixed-wing planes can also give you a circuit trip of Mt. Cook. These flights are all weather dependent, with cloud, rain or high winds affecting availability.

HIKING

With its abundance of beautiful rain forest and rugged braided rivers this is a great area to go hiking. There are a number of walks out of Franz Josef and Fox areas and Okarito, but also further south around Lake Moeraki. These vary from hour-long bushwalks to multiday hikes in the high country. Experience is essential in outback areas, and it's important to leave intentions at the local DOC office before heading off. Appropriate gear and safety equipment is also essential.

ICE-WALKING

Most visitors to the park come to see and experience the glaciers. But they are not as accessible as you might imagine. The terminal face of both glaciers is constantly breaking up, with large house-sized chunks of ice falling without warning. There is walking access to within a few hundred meters of each, although this access may be closed at any time due to flooding, rockfalls or other hazards. To experience the glacier fully you need to join a guided ice-walk or heli-hike.

INDOOR FUN

In a high rainfall area like this there are days when you will not be able to see the glaciers or the bush, despite your best intentions. Back in Franz Josef village you can visit the DOC Centre, the Hukawai Glacier Centre or watch the Flowing West movie to see what you are missing. Then head to the hot pools where you relax no matter how hard it is raining.

ECO-STAYS

Lake Moeraki Wilderness Lodge is set at the outlet end of Lake Moeraki, 90 km (56 mi) south of Fox Glacier. This long-standing eco-lodge comes with a good pedigree, as the owners also own the Arthur's Pass Wilderness Lodge on the eastern side of the main divide at Arthur's Pass. Built into the remains of the old road-building camp built for workers pushing the road through to Haast in the 1960s, it offers guests a true eco-stay. Lodge power is generated by their own hydro-station built on the outlet from the lake. It's a 20-minute walk to Monro Beach (there's no road) where fur seals and little Fiordland crested penguins are the only residents. There are many other walks, kayaking, bird-watching, and photography opportunities here so book a few nights so you're not short-changed for time.

(top left) Skier on Franz Josef Glacier, (bottom) Walking on Fox Glacier, (top) Lake Moeraki Wilderness Lodge

Updated by
Sue Farley

Surreal is the immediate impression upon reaching the South Island: the mellow green beauty of the North Island has been replaced by jagged snowcapped mountains and rivers that sprawl across vast, rocky shingle beds. The South Island has been carved by ice and water, a process still rapidly occurring. Minor earthquakes rattle a number of places on the island every month—and residents are so used to them they often barely notice.

The Marlborough province occupies the northeast corner, where the inlets of the Marlborough Sounds flow around verdant peninsulas and sandy coves. Marlborough is now the largest wine-growing region in New Zealand, with more than 27,000 acres of vineyards. It's a relatively dry and sunny area, and in summer the inland plains look like the American West, with mountains rising out of grassy flats.

The northwest corner of the island, the Nelson region, is a sporting paradise with a relatively mild climate that allows a year-round array of outdoor activities. Sun-drenched Nelson, a lively town with fine restaurants and a vibrant network of artists and craftspeople, is the gateway to an area surrounded by national parks and hiking tracks (trails). Abel Tasman National Park, to the west of the city, is ringed with spectacularly blue waters studded with golden beaches and craggy rocks. To the southwest is Kahurangi National Park, home of the Heaphy Track, one of the world's Great Walks; Nelson Lakes National Park with its alpine lakes and snowcapped peaks lies to the south.

After the gentler climes of Marlborough and Nelson, the wild grandeur of the West Coast comes as a surprise. This is Mother Nature with her hair down, flaying the coastline with huge seas and drenching rains and littering its beaches with acres of bleached driftwood. When it rains, you feel like you're inside a fishbowl; then the sun bursts out, and you swear you're in paradise. (Always check local conditions before heading out for an excursion.) It's a region that has created a special breed of people, and the rough-hewn and powerfully independent locals—known to the rest of the country as Coasters—occupy a special place in New Zealand folklore.

MARLBOROUGH AND KAIKOURA

The Marlborough Sounds were originally settled by seafaring Māori people who named the area Te Tau Ihu O Te Waka a Māui ("the prow of Maui's canoe"). As legend has it, the trickster demigod Maui fished up the North Island from his canoe with the jawbone of a whale. Consequently, the North Island is called Te Ika a Māui—"the fish of Maui."

European settlers arrived in the early 1800s to hunt whales and seals. By the 1830s the whale and seal population had dropped drastically, so the settlers looked inland to the fertile river plains of the Wairau Valley, where Blenheim now stands. Surveyors were pressured to open more territory, but local Māori were reluctant to part with more of their land and sabotaged the surveyors' work and equipment.

Outraged European settlers, led by Captain Arthur Wakefield, arrived from Nelson to "talk some sense" into the Māori chiefs. An angry fracas flared up beside the tiny Tuamarina River (now a marked picnic spot on the road between Picton and Blenheim). Captain Wakefield and 21 other Europeans, plus nine Māori, including chief Te Rauparaha's daughter, were killed in what later became known as the "Wairau Incident." Local government officials declared the attack "despicable," and the Nelson settlers were chastised for their actions. The land was later sold reluctantly by the Māori tribes, and by 1850 the Pākehā (non-Māori) began farming.

Thirty years later, the unwittingly prescient Charles Empson and David Herd began planting red muscatel grapes among local sheep and grain farms. Their modest viticultural torch was rekindled in the next century by the Freeth family, and by the 1940s Marlborough wineries were producing port, sherry, and Madeira most successfully. In 1973 New Zealand's largest wine company, Montana, planted vines in Marlborough to increase the supply of New Zealand grapes. Other vintners followed suit, and within a decade today's major players—such as Hunter's and Cloudy Bay—had established the region's international reputation. Marlborough now glories in being New Zealand's single largest area under vine, and many local growers sell grapes to winemakers outside the area.

Down the coast from Blenheim, Kaikoura is another area that the Māori settled, the predominant *iwi* (tribe) being Ngai Tahu. True to their seafaring heritage, they are active in today's whale-watching interests. Ngai Tahu was one of the first major Māori iwi to receive compensation from the New Zealand government—to the tune of $170 million—along with an apology for unjust confiscation of their lands and fishing areas. The iwi today has extensive interests in tourism, fishing, and horticulture.

8

PICTON

29 km (18 mi) north of Blenheim, 110 km (69 mi) east of Nelson.

The maritime township of Picton (population 4,000) lies at the head of Queen Charlotte Sound and is the arrival point for ferries from the North Island, and a modest number of international cruise ships. It provides services and transport by water taxi to remote communities in the vast area of islands, peninsulas, and waterways that make up the Marlborough Sounds Maritime Park. Picton is a popular yachting spot and has two sizable marinas, the smaller at Picton Harbour and the much larger at nearby Waikawa Bay.

There's plenty to do in town, with crafts markets in summer, historical sights, and walking tracks to scenic lookouts over the sounds. The main foreshore is lined by London Quay, which looks up Queen Charlotte Sound to the bays beyond. High Street runs down to London Quay from the hills, and between them these two streets make up the center of town.

BEST BETS FOR CRUISE PASSENGERS

■ Wine tour and mussel cruise. Take a guided tour through some of Marlborough's iconic wineries before joining a Greenshell mussel cruise.

■ Edwin Fox Museum. Visit one of the country's oldest ships, now preserved, with an informative museum.

■ Queen Charlotte Track. Hike, bike, or kayak a short stretch of this highly scenic coastal track.

■ Eco-cruise. Visit a protected island bird sanctuary, Ship's Cove, where Captain Cook landed and view dolphins.

ESSENTIALS

Car Rental Apex (✉ *Ferry Terminal* ☎ *03/573-7009 or 0800/422-744* ⊕ *www.apexrentals.co.nz*). **Avis** (✉ *Ferry Terminal* ☎ *03/520-3156 or 0800/284-722* ⊕ *www.avis.co.nz*). **Budget** (✉ *Ferry Terminal* ☎ *03/573-6081 or 0800/283-438* ⊕ *www.budget.co.nz*). **Hertz** (✉ *Ferry Terminal* ☎ *03/520-3044 or 0800/654-321* ⊕ *www.hertz.co.nz*).

Visitor Information Department of Conservation-Sounds Area Office (✉ *Picton* ☎ *03/520-3002* ✎ *soundsao@doc.govt.nz* ⊕ *www.doc.govt.nz*). **Picton Visitor Information Centre** (✉ *Picton Foreshore* ☎ *03/520-3113* ⊕ *www.marlboroughisites.com* ✎ *picton@i-site.org*).

EXPLORING

The preserved hulk of the *Edwin Fox*, now the **Edwin Fox Maritime Museum** (✉ *Dunbar Wharf* ☎ *03/573-6868 A $10 per person, $4 per child* ☉ *Nov.–Mar., daily 9–5 and Apr.–Oct., daily 9–3.*), demonstrates just how young New Zealand's European settlement is. The ship was used in the Crimean War, transported convicts to Australia, and brought settlers to New Zealand. Now dry-docked and preserved, it serves as a museum, bringing to life the conditions the early immigrants faced. The interpretative displays upstairs outline the ship's history and service. Walking through the ship, you can imagine how the settlers felt when shut below decks for months at a time, seasick, homesick, and unsure of what awaited them at landfall.

The **Picton Museum** (⊠ *London Quay* ☎ *03/573–8283* 🎫 *$4* ⊘ *Daily 10–4*) details much of Picton's early seafaring history. The area was first a key Māori settlement called Waitohi, then an important whaling and sealing location for European immigrants in the early 19th century. Until 1860 there was no road access to Picton, so all trade and travel was done by sea.

Picton is the base for cruising in the **Marlborough Sounds,** the labyrinth of waterways that formed when the rising sea invaded a series of river valleys at the northern tip of the South Island. Backed by forested hills that rise almost vertically from the water, the sounds are a wild, majestic place edged with tiny beaches and rocky coves and studded with islands where native wildlife remains undisturbed by introduced species. (Operators run tours to several of these special islands.) Māori legend says the sounds were formed when a great warrior and navigator called Kupe fought with a giant octopus. Its thrashings separated the surrounding mountains, and its tentacles became parts of the sunken valleys. These waterways are one of the country's favorite areas for boating.

Much of the area around Picton is untamed, forest-covered country, broken by sheltered bays and deep waterways, and it has changed little since Captain Cook found refuge here in the 1770s. There are rudimentary roads on the long fingers of land jutting into the sounds, but the most convenient access is by water. Many properties only have boat access. Several operators travel the waterways on a daily basis, taking visitors along for the ride as they deliver the mail, groceries, and farming supplies to isolated residents and farms. Both Beachcomber and Cougar Line run from Picton and travel throughout Queen Charlotte Sound; or leave from Havelock aboard the Pelorus mail boat, *Pelorus Express,* which delivers mail and supplies to outlying settlements scattered around Pelorus Sound (⇨ *Havelock Tours, below*). To get your feet on the ground in and around the sounds, you can take any number of hikes on the Queen Charlotte Track (⇨ *Outdoor Activities, below*).

EN ROUTE Heading west out of Picton toward the town of Havelock, **Queen Charlotte Drive** rises spectacularly along the edge of Queen Charlotte Sound. It cuts across the base of the peninsula that separates this waterway from Pelorus Sound, then drops onto a small coastal plain before coming to Havelock. Beyond Havelock the road winds through forested river valleys and over several ranges before it rounds the eastern side of Tasman Bay and reaches Nelson. To start the drive from the Interislander ferry terminal in Picton, turn right after leaving the parking lot and follow the signs.

About a third of the way to Havelock, Governor's, Momorangi, and Ngakuta bays are gorgeous spots for a picnic or a stroll along the forested shore. Cullen Point, at the Havelock end of the drive, is a good vantage point to view the inland end of the Pelorus Sound and across the bay to Havelock. The short walk to the lookout is well worth the effort.

CLOSE UP

A Close Encounter with Dolphins

Near the inner entrance to Tory Channel, Dan, the boatman, skillfully brought the boat around as six of us slid into the water right beside a pod of playful Dusky dolphins. The 15-minute boat ride from Torea Bay had given us time to change, have a quick biology lesson, and learn a bit more about the dolphins. Although not as big as the common bottlenose dolphins, these amazing silvery creatures were still at least 6 feet long and strongly built. As we lay face down in the water, buoyant in our thick wet suits, the dolphins blasted up from the depths to swim right by us, time and again. Fins, masks, and snorkels made it easier to watch them as they swirled and twirled around us. They never touched us, but wheeled and turned just inches away. As they swam by, they turned on their sides and looked at us with their dark little eyes, their strong tails pushing them through the water. At other times they leaped from the water and came back down with a resounding splash. This was better than any wildlife documentary.

OUTDOOR ACTIVITIES

COMBINATION TRIPS ★
One way to get the best of the Queen Charlotte Track is a combo trip, with hiking, some arm-flexing in a kayak, and some legwork on a mountain bike. A three-day trip organized by **Marlborough Sounds Adventure Company** (✉ *The Waterfront, Picton* ☎ *03/573–6078 or 0800/283–283* ⊕ *www.marlboroughsounds.co.nz*) combines these three activities in a fully guided experience with meals and lodging taken care of, and your packs ferried ahead each day. Accommodations are bunk-room standard, and you need to be reasonably fit. The $710 fee includes all water transfers, guide, twin-share accommodations, packed lunches, and equipment. The trip kicks off every Wednesday from November through April. Four- and five-day guided walk options include an eco-tour of nearby Motuara Island, which may include dolphin encounters, and provides resort-style twin-share en suite accommodations. They also have an adventure base at the Portage Resort Hotel, where you can hire bikes, kayaks, and yachts to explore around the Kenepuru Sound area.

DIVING
The Marlborough Sounds have an excellent dive site in the *Mikhail Lermontov*; now recognized as one of the world's great wreck dives. In 1986, this massive Russian cruise ship sank on her side in 30 meters (100 feet) of water in Port Gore. (One life was lost.) The 200-meter-long (600-foot-long) ship is now an exciting dive site for anyone with moderate diving skills. Highlights are the swimming pool in its glass veranda room, the bridge, and the huge funnel; and there's some great penetration tech diving if you're competent. September and October generally have the best visibility but the trips run all year.

Go Dive Marlborough's Brent McFadden takes daily and live-aboard guided trips out to the *Mikhail Lermontov* (as long as at least three people want to go, and the weather cooperates). The $285 day-trip fee includes lunch and all diving gear; it costs a bit less if you have

A speedboat enters Queen Charlotte Sound and heads for Picton Harbour.

your own kit, and a bit more if you want nitrox. Tech dive gear available as well, but check on booking. Live-aboard trips start from $595 per person for a two-day, one-night adventure, and there's also dive training available as well. ⊠ *97 High St., Picton* ☎ *03/573–9181* ⊕ *www.godive.co.nz.*

DOLPHIN
ENCOUNTERS
★

Marine biologists Amy and Dan Engelhaupt, who run **Dolphin Watch,** take you on a 15-minute boat ride out of Picton to where you slide into the water and swim with these magnificent creatures ($150), or just watch them from the boat ($100). Dolphin swims aren't available if they are either migrating or breeding, so call ahead. Dan and Amy also run Marine Wildlife and Motuara Island tours, which visit an island wildlife reserve to spy on seals, dolphins, and seabirds. These tours leave at 1:30 (October to April), and cost $100. From June through August, daily tours do not run and all tours are by private arrangement only. ⊠ *Picton Harbour* ☎ *03/573–8040 or 0800/9453–5433* ⊕ *www.dolphinswimming.co.nz.*

HIKING
Fodor's Choice
★

Starting northwest of Picton, the **Queen Charlotte Track** stretches 67 km (42 mi) south to north, playing hide-and-seek with the Marlborough Sounds along the way. Hike through lush native forests, stopping to swim or to pick up shells on the shore. Unlike other tracks, there are no Department of Conservation huts to stay in, just a few camping areas. Other accommodations are on the walk, however, from backpacking options to lodges, resorts, and homestays. Boats such as the *Cougar Line* can drop you at various places for one- to four-day walks (guided or unguided), or you can kayak or bike parts of it.

■**TIP→** Though it's relatively easy to access, the track shouldn't be taken lightly. It has steep inclines and long drop-offs, and the weather can be unpredictable. In particular, on Day 3, if you're walking north to south, a 22-km (14-mi) stretch can test even a good hiker's endurance in bad weather.

KAYAKING A great way to experience the Marlborough Sounds is by sea kayak—and the mostly sheltered waters of Queen Charlotte Sound are perfect for it. **Marlborough Sounds Adventure Company** runs guided and self-guided kayak trips, from half-day to three-day tours, in either Queen Charlotte or Kenepuru Sound. The bays are ringed by dense native forest, echoing with the trilling calls of native birds. Costs range from $75 for a half-day guided trip to $495 for a three-day guided trip. Kayak rental is available from $50 a day. Reservations are essential. ⊠ *The Waterfront, Picton* ☎ *03/573–6078 or 0800/283–283* ⊕ *www. marlboroughsounds.co.nz.*

You can take a one-day guided kayak trip with **Wilderness Guides** for $100, including a yummy lunch. They also do multiday trips beside the Queen Charlotte Track, and kayak rentals if you want to do it on your own (as long as a minimum of two people are paddling together). And there's a special combo day with a guided kayak trip in the morning followed by an independent hike or mountain bike trail along part of the Queen Charlotte Track in the afternoon. Bookings are recommended. ⊠ *Picton Railway Station, 3 Auckland St.* ☎ *03/573-5432 or 0800/266–266* ⊕ *www.wildernessguidesnz.com.*

WHERE TO EAT

$$$–$$$$ ✕**The Chart Room.** True to its name, this smart, centrally located restaurant is decorated with copies of Captain Cook's nautical charts and maps. It's a cut above the rest in Picton. You can eat out by the pool or on the balcony if the weather is cooperating. The kitchen serves local favorites, such as green-lipped mussels, scallops, and seafood chowder entrées; lamb, salmon, and eye-fillet beef are typically favorite mains. ⊠ *Yacht Club Hotel, Waikawa Rd.* ☎ *03/573–7002 or 0800/991–188* ▭ *AE, DC, MC, V* ⊗ *No lunch Apr.–Dec.*

$$–$$$ ✕**Le Café.** Sitting outside Le Café on the waterfront you can look right
CAFÉ down Queen Charlotte Sound and watch the local boat traffic and the big Interislander ferries coming and going. Staff go out of their way to source organic, local, and free-range foods wherever possible—your fish probably landed on the wharf at the end of the street. Casual meals are available all day and well into the evening; as night moves in, the tempo at the bar picks up and live acts appear on a frequent basis. ⊠ *London Quay* ☎ *03/573–5588* ⊕ *www.lecafepicton.co.nz* ▭ *MC, V.*

$–$$ ✕**Seumuss's Irish Nook.** Step inside this superfriendly little pub and you
IRISH can feel a lilt rise in your throat and your "r"s starting to roll. A main course of curry and gravy starts at $6. The Guinness hot pot and stuffed potatoes is a perennial favorite. Wednesday to Sunday they run a full dinner menu, and there is reduced service on Monday and Tuesday. The pub is a short walk from the waterfront and it's open daily from midday until 1 AM, making Seumuss's a great spot to wait for the late-night ferry. ⊠ *25 Wellington St.* ☎ *03/573–8994* ▭ *MC, V.*

WHERE TO STAY

$$$$ ⊞ **Bay of Many Coves Resort.** Designed by the architect of the national
Fodor's Choice museum Te Papa in Wellington, this contemporary beachfront complex
★ complements its surrounding bush and seascape. In the six years since
being developed the site has matured as the plantings have grown.
The Kumatage lounge and restaurant, and the wonderfully furnished
units with private verandas, overlook the surrounding bays. The restaurant specializes in fresh local foods, and goodies baked on-site.
Bathrooms have open tiled showers and fluffy robes. You get here by
water taxi from Picton. **Pros:** idyllic spot in a sheltered, iconic Marlborough Sounds location; cruising, dolphin, and bird-watching tours;
mountain bikes, bushwalks, kayaking all at your front door; kids'
programs; a Māori-style massage available; great views from every
unit **Cons:** boat or foot access only but there is a helipad if you're
in a hurry; the resort is built on a really steep site so ask for a lower
room if mobility is a problem; TV reception isn't great. ✉ *Bay of Many
Coves, Queen Charlotte Sound* ☎ *03/579–9771 or 0800/579–9771*
⊕ *www.bayofmanycovesresort.co.nz* ⇱ *11 1–3 bedroom apartments*
⚐ *In-room: Kitchen, DVD. In-hotel: 2 restaurants, pool, spa, laundry
facilities, Internet terminal* ▭ *AE, DC, MC, V.*

$$–$$$ ⊞ **Jasmine Court Travellers Inn.** A fresh, well-appointed place to stay,
this stylish Kiwi-style motel looks down over the town to the main
harbor. The guest rooms are well sized and done in soft pastels, with
thoughtful touches such as fans, hypoallergenic pillows, and CD and
DVD players with a library of discs. Several bathrooms have either
a whirlpool tub or a multihead shower. A supermarket just opposite
the motel is handy for stocking up before hitting the remote areas
of the Marlborough Sounds. **Pros:** they provide vehicle, bike, and
luggage storage if you're off to walk the Queen Charlotte Track.
Cons: book ahead in summer as it is often full; kids by arrangement
only. ✉ *78 Wellington St.* ☎ *03/573–7110 or 0800/421–999* ⊕ *www.
jasminecourt.co.nz* ⇱ *13 rooms, 1 apartment* ⚐ *In-room: Kitchen,
Wi-Fi. In-hotel: Laundry service, Internet terminal, no kids under 14,
no-smoking rooms* ▭ *AE, DC, MC, V.*

$$–$$$ ⊞ **Punga Cove Resort.** Small private chalets and larger cottages are
tucked into the bush at this Queen Charlotte Track crossroads, with
accommodations ranging from a backpacker lodge ($) to luxury
suites ($$$$). Several larger, more luxurious studio and one- and two-
bedroom chalets have large private decks with vistas of Camp Bay and
Endeavour Inlet. You can rent kayaks, dinghies, and mountain bikes
on-site, and fishing trips can be arranged. Access is quickest by the
water taxi, 60 minutes from Picton. Otherwise, a two-hour-plus drive
winds along Queen Charlotte Sound Drive to the turnoff at Linkwater
and then along the spectacular scenery of the Kenepuru Sound. The
last 5 km (3 mi) is gravel. **Pros:** sitting on the sunny side of Endeavour Inlet, this idyllic place is quite isolated; a favorite overnight stop
on the Queen Charlotte Track; at the right end of the sounds if you
want to join a dive trip to the Mikhail Lermontov. **Cons:** this is not
a luxury stay but more of a family or budget option; to get the best
out of a spot like this plan to stay two nights; set over a steep site.

8

⊠ *Punga Cove, Endeavour Inlet, Queen Charlotte Sound, Picton* ☎ *03/579–8561* ⊕ *www.pungacove.co.nz* ⤳ *3 suites, 14 chalets, 4 lodge rooms, 8 backpacker cabins* ⚇ *In-room: No a/c (some), no phones, kitchen (some), no TV (some). In-hotel: 2 restaurants, bars, pool, spa, water sports, Internet terminal* ⊟ *AE, MC, V.*

$$$–$$$$ ⌂ **Sennen House.** Just a 1-km (½-mi) stroll from downtown Picton is this
★ white, peak-roofed 1886 villa. The verandas overlook 5 acres of lush landscaping and bush, and the harbor hints beyond. The suites and apartments are furnished with carved wooden bedsteads and fireplace mantels, stained glass, rich upholstery, and brass fixtures. The spotless bathrooms have heated towel bars and hair dryers, and there's a common high-speed Internet connection for guests. Owners Richard and Imogen Fawcett bring a yummy continental breakfast hamper to your door each morning, or the preceding evening. Follow the western part of Oxford Street from Nelson Square, crossing two roads, to reach the property. **Pros:** two apartments have full kitchens and three have kitchenettes. **Cons:** ask for the downstairs rooms if you have limited mobility; tricky to find; short winter close-down that varies year to year. ⊠ *9 Oxford St.* ☎ *03/573–5216* ⊕ *www.sennenhouse.co.nz* ⤳ *3 suites, 2 apartments* ⚇ *In-room: No a/c, kitchen, DVD, Internet. In-hotel: Laundry service, Internet terminal, Wi-Fi, no-smoking rooms* ⊟ *AE, MC, V* ⦿⃝ *CP.*

¢ ⌂ **The Villa Backpackers and Lodge.** Like a big, happy tribe, Villa guests fill a small, lovely colonial house. The hostel's central courtyard hums day and night with people relaxing after a day on the water, mountain biking, or walking the Queen Charlotte Track. On rainy days you can lie in front of the fire with a book, play guitar, or curl up in a quiet corner to write letters. Pickups and drop-offs, a hot tub, use of the gym, and bike usage are included in the price. New kitchens have space for cooking your own meals. **Pros:** in winter, apple crumble and ice cream for dessert and a ontinental breakfast are included; doubles and en suite rooms have their own TVs; just 400 meters (¼-mi) from the Ferry terminal. **Cons:** the cheaper double rooms use shared facilities and are smaller. ⊠ *34 Auckland St.* ☎ *03/573–6598* ⊕ *www.thevilla.co.nz* ✐ *stay@thevilla.co.nz* ⤳ *7 double rooms, 2 with en suite, 44 dorm beds* ⚇ *In-room: No a/c, no phone, no TV (some). In-hotel: Gym, spa, bicycles, laundry facilities, Internet terminal, Wi-Fi* ⊟ *MC, V.*

$$ ⌂ **Whatamonga Homestay.** From the lounge you can watch the ferries and hear fish splash in the water below. Whatamonga is a sheltered bay just a short drive from Picton. Each unit has a kitchenette and balcony overlooking the sea. The water taxi can pick you up from the jetty if you want to do a cruise around the Sounds or get transport to the Queen Charlotte Track. A private jetty, kayaks, a dinghy, and golf clubs are on hand for your use. Kids are welcome by prior arrangement. **Pros:** option of a guest room in the main house or a private unit; all have balconies to the sea; magnificent Marlborough Sounds environment with great views. **Cons:** minimum two-night stay in midsummer; particularly steep driveway with concealed exit. ⊠ *425 Port Underwood Rd., Waikawa Bay* ☎ *03/573–7192* ⊕ *www.whsl.co.nz* ✐ *info@whsl.co.nz* ⤳ *2 rooms, 2 units* ⚇ *In-room: No a/c, no phone, no TV. In-hotel: No-smoking rooms* ⊟ *MC, V.*

TOURS

BOAT TOURS **Beachcomber Cruises** runs scenic and eco-cruises throughout Queen Charlotte Sound, including their well-known Mail Run cruise. Similar to the mail run on the *Pelorus Express*, but on a completely different waterway, this trip explores the outer reaches of Queen Charlotte Sound. They can also take you to and from any point on the Queen Charlotte Walkway for one-day or longer unguided walks. Boats depart from the Picton waterfront throughout the morning (times vary according to the time of year; check the Web site for options) and cost from $51 to $95. Kayaks available. ⊠ *Beachcomber Pier, Town Wharf, Picton* ☎ *03/573–6175 or 0800/624–526* ⊕ *www.mailboat.co.nz* ⊘ *office@mailboat.co.nz.*

Cougar Line runs scheduled trips from Picton through the Queen Charlotte Sounds three to four times daily, depending on the time of year, dropping passengers (sightseers included) at accommodations, private homes, or other points. A Queen Charlotte drop-off and pickup service costs $95 for multiday hikes, $68 for day hikes that end at Furneaux Lodge. The twilight Salmon and Sauvignon evening cruise runs through December to February and they have several other scenic cruises varying from their popular three-hour morning and afternoon cruises to shorter ones suitable for passengers waiting for the InterIsland ferry. Water-taxi service to area lodges costs from $35 to $50, depending on distances and number of people; reservations for all trips are essential at peak times and recommended at others. ⊠ *Picton Wharf* ☎ *03/573–7925 or 0800/504–090* ⊕ *www.cougarline.co.nz or www.queencharlottetrack.co.nz.*

Marlborough Sounds Adventure Company has half- to four-day guided kayak tours of the sounds, leaving from Picton, as well as kayak rentals for experienced paddlers. The cost is $75 for a half-day guided tour and $495 for a three-day guided tour, including water transportation, food, and camping equipment. A kayak rental costs $50 per person per day. ⊠ *The Waterfront, London Quay, Picton* ☎ *03/573–6078 or 0800/283–283* ⊕ *www.marlboroughsounds.co.nz* ⊘ *walk@marlboroughsounds.co.nz.*

★ **Marlborough Travel's.** Greenshell Mussel Cruises will take you into the largely untouched Kenepuru and Pelorus sounds, which are part of the labyrinth of waterways that make up the Marlborough Sounds. The world's largest production of Greenshell mussels is done in the Sounds, and the boat explores the intricate system of waterways of these farms. Try the mussels on board, steamed, with a glass of local sauvignon blanc, while hearing the history of the area. The tour costs $110 per person, and the season runs November through March; you can get more information from Marlborough Travel. They also run winery tours and a combo trip combining a winery tour in the morning and mussel cruise in the afternoon (for $195). ☎ *03/577–9997* ⊕ *www. marlboroughtravel.co.nz* ⊘ *info@marlboroughtravel.co.nz.*

FISHING **The Sounds Connection,** a family-run tour company, provides regular half-
TOURS day fishing trips and full-day trips by request. They leave from Picton; a half day runs at $79. They'll supply all the necessary gear and fillet your catch. ⊠ *16 Wellington St., Picton* ☎ *03/573–8843 or 0800/742–866* ⊕ *www.soundsconnection.co.nz* ⊘ *tours@soundsconnection.co.nz.*

WALKING AND
HIKING TOURS

To see the glorious Marlborough Sounds, try a four- or five-day fully catered and guided inn-to-inn walk on the Queen Charlotte Track with **Wilderness Guides** (⊠ *Railway Station, Picton* ☎ *03/520–3095 or 0800/266–266* ⊕ *www.wildernessguidesnz.com* ✉ *info@ wildernessguidesnz.com*). The four-day luxe guided walk includes all land and water transport, as well as overnight stays in three Sounds resorts: Punga Cove Resort, Furneaux Lodge, and Lochmara Lodge. Experienced guides give talks on the area's natural and human history. Advance bookings are essential; trips cost $1,250 (four-day boutique option available as well for $1,995).

WINERY
TOURS

The **Sounds Connection** (⊠ *16 Wellington St., Picton* ☎ *03/573-8843 or 0800/742–866* ⊕ *www.soundsconnection.co.nz* ✉ *tours@sounds-connection.co.nz*) runs full- and half-day tours to a handful of Marlborough's main wineries. Their Gourmet Experience tour (November through April) combines a wine-and-food appreciation tour with a four-course, wine-matched lunch for $199.

HAVELOCK

35 km (22 mi) west of Picton.

Known as the Greenshell mussel capital of the world (Greenshells are a variety of green-lipped mussels), Havelock is at the head of Pelorus Sound, and trips around the sounds on the Pelorus Sound mail boat, *Pelorus Express,* depart here. Locals will forgive you for thinking you've seen what the Marlborough Sounds are all about after crossing from the North Island to the South Island on the ferry—in reality, it's just a foretaste of better things to come. Small seaside Havelock (population 400) is a good place to stroll; check out the busy little marina, poke into a few arts and crafts shops, and enjoy those mussels.

WHERE TO EAT

$$–$$$
SEAFOOD

✕ **The Mussel Pot.** Outside, a giant, fiberglass mussel pot and some keen little mussels play on the roof. Inside, the real things are steamed for three minutes in the whole shell or grilled on the half shell. Choose a light sauce for both steaming and topping: white wine, garlic, and fresh herbs or coconut, chili, and coriander. There are also smoked and marinated mussel salads, platters, and their tasty mussel chowder. Sauvignon blanc from nearby Marlborough perfectly pairs with almost any dish on the menu. There's a courtyard for those sunny days and vegetarian, pasta, and meat choices for those who don't like mussels. Their smoked chicken pasta is quite popular. ⊠ *73 Main Rd.* ☎ *03/574-2824* ▭ *AE, MC, V.*

¢–$
CAFÉ

✕ **Pelorus Bridge Café.** Fancy a wild-pork-and-kūmara (native sweet potato) pie, some mussel fritters, or just a nice cup of coffee? One of the better on-the-road cafés in the area, it even has some kid-friendly options like peanut butter sammies and hot chips. The backdrop beside the rocky, tree-lined Pelorus River is lovely, especially in summer when you can eat under the trees. ⊠ *State Hwy. 6, by Pelorus Bridge* ☎ *03/571–6019* ▭ *MC, V* ⊗ *Closes 5* PM.

$$–$$$
CAFÉ

✕ **Slip Inn.** Down at the marina, the Slip Inn overlooks the main boat ramp and working port area—it's a sunny spot to stop for a light lunch or dinner. After renovations, the café has a smart, contemporary quality;

Greenshell mussels are Havelock's specialty.

it's a little removed from its previous canvas and plastic walls but is still decidedly intimate with its waterfront locale. The chef favors local mussels; one favorite dish is the Kilpatrick, mussels grilled with bacon and cheese. Or try them steamed and served with a creamy coriander sauce. If you're not a mussel fan, other options include the panfried fish with a warm zucchini-and-leek salad and gourmet pizzas. ✉ *Havelock Marina* ☎ *03/574–2345* ▭ *MC, V.*

WHERE TO STAY

$$$ ⊞ **Mudbrick Lodge.** The winding road that leads to Mudbrick Lodge sets the mood for this adorable, welcoming spot. Log fires, soft linens and good country food all feed the senses while just out the window the rugged Marlborough landscape seems like the edge of the world. Experienced hunting and fishing guides can take you to quiet trout pools, deserted islands, and sunny fishing spots and there's horseback riding and kayaking nearby. The suites are self-catering; breakfast ingredients are delivered for the first morning, and dinner materials are available for you to cook your own. **Pros:** a real rural NZ experience; just over the hill from the magical Marlborough Sounds, take a boat cruise from Tennyson Inlet while you're there; pantries are stocked with basic kitchen items. **Cons:** a bit off the beaten-track, but that's also part of its charm. ✉ *Carluke, near Rai Valley* ☎ *03/571–6147* ⊕ *www.mudbricklodge.co.nz* ✍ *tania@ mudbricklodge.co.nz* ⇥ *2 self-contained suites* ⌂ *In-room: No a/c, kitchen, no TV. In-hotel: Bar, pool, spa, Internet terminal* ▭ *MC, V.*

$$$–$$$$ ⊞ **The Portage Resort Hotel.** The remote location doesn't prevent the staff
★ from offering high-quality, well-appointed accommodations. Lodgings range from backpacker beds ($) for hikers straight off the Queen

Charlotte Track to extremely comfortable hotel rooms with private decks and fabulous views across Kenepuru Sound. Dining at the Te Weka restaurant ($$$$) features local seafood and mussels, along with excellent local wines. You can access the Portage by boat (15 minutes on a water taxi) or car from Havelock; the drive takes about 1½ hours on a paved but winding road. Portage is best visited if you want boating, a remote spot to unwind, or are doing the Queen Charlotte Track. **Pros:** on-site Portage Adventure Centre rents kayaks, mountain bikes, scooters, yachts, and other toys to explore the area; try the Waterside Bar and Café overlooking the bay. **Cons:** arrive by boat from Picton if you can, as the road is quite demanding; well off-the-beaten-track for sightseeing. ⊠ *Portage Bay, Kenepuru Sound, 19 km (12 mi) off Queen Charlotte Dr.* ☎ *03/573–4309* ⊕ *www.portage.co.nz* ↰ *41 rooms, 8 dorm beds* ♿ *In-room: refrigerator, Internet. In-hotel: 2 restaurants, bar, pool, spa, laundry facilities, Wi-Fi* ▭ *AE, DC, MC, V.*

TOURS

BOAT TOURS

★

Pelorus Express, the Pelorus Sound Mail Boat, is a sturdy launch that makes a daylong trip around Pelorus Sound, and is one of the best ways to discover the waterway and meet its residents. Join the mailman as he delivers mail and supplies and checks in with the locals, as it's been done for generations. The boat leaves from Havelock, west of Picton, Tuesday, Thursday, and Friday at 9:30 AM and returns in the late afternoon. The fare is $12, children under 15 free, and reservations are advised January through March. It leaves from the northern end of the Havelock Marina. Bring your lunch; there is tea and coffee on board. ☎ *03/574–1088* ⊕ *www.mail-boat.co.nz* ✉ *mail-boat@xtra.co.nz.*

EN
ROUTE

The **Pelorus Bridge Scenic Reserve** is about halfway between both Picton and Nelson, and Blenheim and Nelson, on State Highway 6. It's a good example of the native lowland forest—with beech, *podocarp* (a species of evergreen tree), and broadleaf trees—that once covered this whole region. There's a network of easy walking trails through the reserve, and in summer the river is warm enough for swimming (watch out for the sand flies after the sun goes down). **Kahikatea Flat** (☎ *03/571–6019*), a hidden campground, is part of the reserve; it's in a quiet spot where, most of the year, the loudest noises are made by the bellbirds and the nearby river. A $20 fee ($22 with power) gets you a campsite with access to showers. There are basic cabins across the river as well. Book ahead over mid-summer.

BLENHEIM

29 km (18 mi) south of Picton, 120 km (73 mi) southeast of Nelson, 129 km (80 mi) north of Kaikoura.

People mostly come to Blenheim (pronounced *bleh*-num by the locals) for the wine. There are dozens of wineries in the area, and Blenheim is developing fast, though it still has a small-town veneer, with narrow streets, paved crossings, and low-slung buildings.

In 1973 the Montana (pronounced Mon-*taa*-na here) company paid two Californian wine authorities to investigate local grape-growing potential on a commercial scale. Both were impressed with what they found. It was the locals who were skeptical—until they tasted the first wines produced. After that, Montana opened the first modern winery in Marlborough in 1977, although there had been fledgling efforts over the past 100 years by pioneering wine growers. The region now has more than 100 vineyards and wineries.

Marlborough has lots of sunshine, and this daytime warmth combines with crisp, cool nights to give local grapes a long, slow ripening period. The smooth river pebbles that cover the best vineyards reflect heat onto the ripening bunches; one producer goes so far as to name these "sunstones" in its marketing. All these factors create grapes with audacious flavors. Although Marlborough made its name initially on sauvignon blanc, it's now also known for its excellent riesling, pinot noir, chardonnay, gewürztraminer, and pinot gris wines. The Marlborough Wine and Food Festival held in mid-February each year celebrates the region's success in suitable style.

Don't bury your nose in a tasting glass entirely, though; the landscape shouldn't be overlooked. The vineyards sprawl across the large alluvial plains around the Wairau River, ringed by high mountains. On clear days you can see Mt. Tapuaenuku, which, at 3,000 meters (10,000 feet), is the tallest South Island mountain outside the Southern Alps. Blenheim is also just a 30-minute drive from the Marlborough Sounds to the north and 90 minutes from the Nelson Lakes National Park to the west.

GETTING HERE AND AROUND

Blenheim Airport (BHE) and Picton's Koromiko Airport (PCN) are small regional airports—Picton's Koromiko is little more than a paved runway in farmland. Air New Zealand Link has at least 10 return flights from Wellington daily. Soundsair flies into Picton from Wellington at least six times a day.

InterCity runs between Christchurch, Picton, Blenheim and Nelson a couple of times a day. The ride between Christchurch and Blenheim takes about five hours, from Christchurch to Picton closer to six hours, and from Picton to Nelson, about two-and-a-half hours. At Blenheim, buses stop at the train station; at Picton, they use the ferry terminal.

Aside from tour buses, the only reliable local alternatives are **Atomic Shuttles** and **Southern Link K Bus**. Southern Link K Bus also connects from Picton to the West Coast via Nelson Lakes. The roads to most wineries are arranged more or less in a grid, which makes getting around relatively straightforward. Rapaura Road is the central artery for vineyard visits; wineries also cluster around Jeffries and Jacksons roads, Fairhall, the area around Renwick village, the lower Wairau Valley, and State Highway 1 south of Blenheim. The roads to both Nelson and Picton give access to the Marlborough Sounds, and the road inland towards the West Coast accesses the Nelson Lakes National Park.

■**TIP**➔ Pick up a map of the Marlborough wine region at the Marlborough Visitor Information Centre.

ESSENTIALS

Bus Information Atomic Shuttles (☎ *03/349–0697* ⊕ *www.atomictravel. co.nz*). **InterCity** (☎ *03/365–1113* ⊕ *www.intercity.co.nz*). **Southern Link K Bus** (☎ *0508/458–835* ⊕ *www.southernlinkcoaches.co.nz*).

Hospital **Wairau Hospital** (✉ *Hospital Rd.* ☎ *03/578-4099*).

Visitor Information **Marlborough Visitor Information Centre** (✉ *The Old Railway Station, Sinclair St., along State Hwy. 1* ☎ *03/577–8080* ⊕ *www.marlboroughisites.com* ✉ *blenheim@i-site.org*).

EXPLORING

The **Cape Campbell Walkway** is a 54-km (35-mi), four-day hike wanders through two high country sheep stations on the wild exposed Marlborough coastline, climaxing at the Cape Campbell lighthouse. Accommodations are in homesteads and farm cottages along the way. It's basically a self-catering trip but supplies are available the last two nights to save packing too much food. But rest assured, your packs are transported ahead each day anyway. A highlight is on night three when accommodations are in cottages just below the lighthouse and a few steps from the beach. There's a shorter two-day trip as well, and a good level of fitness is required. Not suitable for children under eight. ✉ *Seddon7285* ☎ *03/575–6876* ⊕ *www.capecampbellwalkway. co.nz* ⊙ *Closed May–Sept.* 🔄 *4-day trip $240, 2-day trip $160, plus extras.*

Garden Marlborough is one of the most popular garden festivals in the country. For five days in November keen gardeners wander through other keen gardeners' gardens and partake in workshops. Marlborough's climatic and soil conditions encourage great gardens so watch the Web site for bookings; tickets go on sale the preceding August. ⊕ *www.garden-marlborough.com.*

☺ The **Omaka Aviation Heritage Centre** showcases a huge display of World War I–era planes and memorabilia in the Knights of the Sky exhibition. Highlights include the world's only Caproni Ca22, an Etrich Taube, and a Morane-Saulinier Type BB. New Zealand's movie-making talents have been drawn into constructing the super-realistic displays. The center is backed by the Classic Fighters Charitable Trust, which runs a three-day international air show in odd-numbered years when vintage and classic aircraft will be on display on the ground and in the sky. ✉ *Omaka Aerodrome, 79 Aerodrome Rd., off New Renwick Rd.* ☎ *03/579–1305* ⊕ *www.omaka.org.nz and www.classicfighters.co.nz* 🔄 *$20* ⊙ *Daily 10–4.*

Blenheim was established by early settlers at the most inland, navigable point on the tiny Opawa River. The **River Queen**, a replica of one of the handsome old boats working this idyllic waterway, ambles sedately along the river every day in true country fashion. Unlike the mountainous majesty of the area's braided stone rivers, the narrow Opawa River twists and turns around historic bends and past sun-drenched homes and gardens bordered by weeping willows and lofty poplars. A tasty platter lunch or dinner is available on board; the lunch cruise takes two hours and the dinner cruise is three hours. ✉ *Riverside Park, under bridge on State Hwy. 1* ☎ *03/577–5510* ⊕ *www.theriverqueen.co.nz* 🔄 *Midday cruise $42, with lunch $62* ⊙ *Noon and evening cruises.*

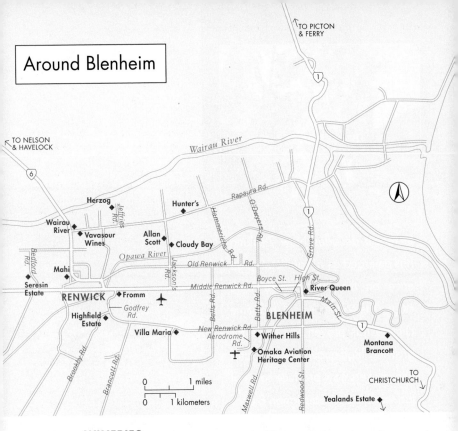

Around Blenheim

TO PICTON & FERRY

TO NELSON & HAVELOCK

Wairau River

Herzog
Hunter's
Wairau River
Vavasour Wines
Allan Scott
Cloudy Bay
Mahi
Seresin Estate
RENWICK
Fromm
Highfield Estate
Godfrey Rd.
Villa Maria
Opawa River
Old Renwick Rd.
Middle Renwick Rd.
New Renwick Rd.
Aerodrome Rd.
Boyce St.
High St.
River Queen
BLENHEIM
Wither Hills
Omaka Aviation Heritage Center
Montana Brancott
Yealands Estate

TO CHRISTCHURCH

Rapaura Rd.

0   1 miles
0   1 kilometers

WINERIES

The wineries described below are among the country's notables, but you won't go wrong at any of the vineyards around Blenheim. Tastings are generally free, although more and more wineries charge a tasting fee, typically around 50¢ per tasting.

★ **Allan Scott Wines.** Allan Scott planted the first grapes in Marlborough in 1973 before planting the family's own vineyard two years later. He helped establish the big-selling Stoneleigh label for Corbans, then the country's second-biggest wine company, before launching his own company in 1990. Now he makes well-respected sauvignon blanc, chardonnay, pinot gris, pinot noir, *methode traditionelle*, gewürztraminer, and riesling (the last two are particularly good). The whole family is involved: Allan's son Joshua is now winemaker, his younger daughter Sara is viticulturist, and elder daughter Victoria looks after marketing. Josh also makes NZ's first methode traditionelle beer—a tasty, rather manly brew called Moa. The tasting room is next to the pleasant indoor-outdoor Twelve Trees restaurant (open for lunch only, $$–$$$). ✉ *Jackson's Rd., Blenheim* ☎ *03/572–9054* ⊕ *www.allanscott.com* ☉ *Daily 9–4:30.*

★ **Cloudy Bay Vineyards.** From its first vintage in 1985, Cloudy Bay has produced first-class sauvignon blanc along with a range that includes an equally impressive chardonnay, pinot noir, riesling, pinot grigio,

Continued on page 428

In recent decades New Zealand has emerged as a significant presence on the international wine stage. The country's cool, maritime climate has proven favorable for growing high-quality grapes, and winemakers now produce some of the world's best Sauvignon Blancs and Pinot Noirs, as well as excellent Chardonnays and Merlots.

Touring wineries in New Zealand is easy, as vineyards stretch virtually the entire length of the country, and most properties have tasting rooms with regular hours. Even if you just sample wines at a shop in Auckland, here's how to get the most out of your sipping experience.

(top) Pinot Noir grapes on a vine
(right) Rippon Vineyard, Lake Wanaka, Otago

Wines of
New Zealand

By Sue Courtney

NEW ZEALAND WINES: THEN AND NOW

(top left) Nikola Nobilo was a New Zealand wine pioneer (right) Central Otago vineyard
(bottom left) Ripe Cabernet Sauvignon grapes

A BRIEF HISTORY

The first grapes were planted by missionaries on the North Island of New Zealand in 1819, and a British official (and hobbyist viticulturist) **James Busby** was the first to make wine almost 20 years later. For the next 150 years, the country's vineyards faced the significant challenges of powdery mildew and phylloxera, a root-killing louse.

New Zealand's modern-day wine production started in the 1970s, as European varietals were planted and started to show promise. Pioneers like Lebanese immigrant **Assid Corban** of Corbans Wines, and Croatian immigrants **Nikola Nobilo** of Nobilo and **Josip Babich** of Babich Wines settled in Henderson Valley, near Auckland, and helped shape the future of New Zealand wine production, innovating with cultured yeast, stainless steel tanks, and temperature-controlled fermentation, which have become widespread practices in many of the world's wine regions.

TODAY'S WINE SCENE

Ever since the country's Sauvignon Blancs captured the imagination of British wine critics at a major international tasting in 1985, wine drinkers worldwide have clamored for this crisp, fruity wine. New Zealand wines are now exported to 80 countries, with Australia biting a 20 percent chunk out of the export share, followed by the U.K. and the United States.

New Zealand is a long, narrow country of 1,000 miles between the north and south islands, with numerous microclimates and soil types, each suited to different varietals. Sauvignon Blanc is eminently well matched to the South Island, particularly Marlborough, while Chardonnay and Pinot Gris conveniently grow in most areas. Pinot Noir—NZ's most-planted red grape—and Riesling do best in Martinborough and on the South Island, with high-quality bottles coming from Marlborough, Nelson, Waipara, and Central

Grapevines at Fairmont Estate, a winery and vineyard in Gladstone, Wairarapa

Otago, the country's southernmost winegrowing area. Heavy-bodied red grapes like Cabernet Sauvignon, Merlot, Malbec, and Syrah excel in warmer Hawke's Bay and Auckland on the North Island.

As for the future, many winegrowers are playing around with new varieties, hoping to find the "next big thing." Gewürztraminer and Viognier are already well established, while varieties like Arneis and Grüner Veltliner are still rare. For red grapes, Sangiovese and Montepulciano show great promise, while Zinfandel and Tempranillo are making inroads.

WHY DID NZ SWITCH FROM CORK?

The New Zealand Screwcap Initiative was formed in 2001 by the country's top producers who were concerned that their wines were being compromised by cork taint and premature oxidation. Even though the public eschewed the screwcap 10 years previously, the winemakers regarded the closure as an evolution in quality packaging. Now, more than 90 percent of New Zealand wines sport screwcaps, and customers worldwide are becoming accustomed to this type of bottle closure.

Sauvignon Blanc grapes

NZ SAUVIGNON BLANC

New Zealand is best known for its celebrated Sauvignon Blanc wines, but the varietal wasn't planted in the country until the 1970s.

In recent years, Sauvignon Blancs from Marlborough have become the worldwide benchmark for the varietal, with concentrated grassy, herbal, and floral notes. Compared to the Sauvignon Blancs of France, New Zealand's wines are more intensely perfumed, with fruitier flavors.

Neudorf Vineyards, Nelson, produces several well-regarded wines

NEW ZEALAND'S WINE REGIONS

AUCKLAND One of the country's original wine regions, this warm area produces high-quality reds, especially from Waiheke Island and Matakana.

GISBORNE Distinctive Chardonnays with peach and melon flavors are the specialty here. The region is also known for its spicy Gewürztraminer wines.

NORTHLAND

AUCKLAND
Auckland ○

Tasman Sea

NORTH ISLAND

BAY OF PLENTY

GISBORNE

HAWKE'S BAY

WAIKATO

○ Napier
○ Hastings

Classic Wine Trail

PACIFIC OCEAN

MARTINBOROUGH The area, which houses the Wairarapa subregion, is known for its rich Pinot Noirs and luscious Cabernet Sauvignons.

MARTINBOROUGH
○ Wellington
Blenheim ○

SOUTH ISLAND

CLASSIC WINE TRAIL

For the ultimate touring experience, take a weeklong excursion down the Classic Wine Trail. The well-marked, 240-mile touring route passes through towns and rural routes full of attractions, like farmer's markets and restaurants, artist's studios and museums, and outdoor activities, including hiking trails, horse riding, and fishing rivers. Download the trail guide at ⊕ www.classicwinetrail.co.nz.

HAWKES BAY A geographically and climatically diverse wine region that produces many wines, such as Chardonnay, Merlot, and Cabernet Sauvignon.

NELSON A small wine region about two hours from Marlborough wineries. The region produces Chardonnay as its primary wine, followed by Riesling.

MARLBOROUGH The country's most important wine region, and the home of its world-class Sauvignon Blancs. Also common are Chardonnay and Riesling.

CANTERBURY This region is cool and dry, making it well-suited to Chardonnay and Pinot Noir. Riesling and Sauvignon Blanc are also produced here.

Wellington

NELSON

Tasman Mountains

Blenheim

MARLBOROUGH

Tasman Sea

Southern Alps

Christchurch

CANTERBURY

SOUTH ISLAND

PACIFIC OCEAN

Queenstown

OTAGO

Dunedin

OTAGO This region is known for growing the world's southernmost grape vines. Its intensely concentrated Pinot Noirs have received great critical acclaim.

WINE-TASTING PRIMER

Ordering and tasting wine—whether at a winery, bar, or restaurant—is easy once you master a few simple steps.

LOOK AND NOTE

Hold your glass by the stem and look at the wine in the glass. Note its color, depth, and clarity.

For whites, is it greenish, yellow, or gold? For reds, is it purplish, ruby, or garnet? Is the wine's color pale or deep? Is the liquid clear or cloudy?

SWIRL AND SNIFF

Swirl the wine gently in the glass to intensify the scents, then sniff over the rim of the glass. What do you smell? Try to identify aromas like:

- **Fruits**—citrus, peaches, berries, figs, melon

- **Minerals**—earth, steely notes, wet stones

- **Flowers**—orange blossoms, honey, perfume

- **Dairy**—butter, cream, cheese, yogurt

- **Spices**—baking spices, pungent, herbal notes

- **Oak**—toast, vanilla, coconut, tobacco

- **Vegetables**—fresh or cooked, herbal notes

- **Animal**—leathery, meaty notes

Are there any unpleasant notes, like mildew or wet dog, that might indicate that the wine is "off"?

SIP AND SAVOR

Prime your palate with a sip, swishing the wine in your mouth. Then spit in a bucket or swallow.

Take another sip and think about the wine's attributes. Sweetness is detected on the tip of the tongue, acidity on the sides of the tongue, and tannins (a mouth-drying sensation) on the gums. Consider the body—does the wine feel light in the mouth, or is there a rich sensation? Are the flavors consistent with the aromas? If you like the wine, try to pinpoint what you like about it, and vice versa if you don't like it.

Take time to savor the wine as you're sipping it—the tasting experience may seem a bit scientific, but the end goal is your enjoyment.

WINE & FOOD PAIRING

Hospitality is a core value in Maori society, something you'll encounter in wineries and eateries

New Zealand cuisine is influenced by Pacific Rim, Asian, and European flavors and traditions. The diversity of the cuisine and its wide variety of ingredients—beef, lamb, venison, pork, poultry, and seafood—makes for a number of interesting food and wine pairings.

Sauvignon Blanc is delicious with shellfish and seafood, summer herbs, feta cheese, and salad greens.

Pinot Noir complements mushroom-based dishes. Lighter wines are best paired with tuna and salmon, while heavier wines suit lamb, duck, venison, and game.

Cabernet Sauvignon and **Merlot** work well with steaks and minted lamb.

Chardonnay goes well with rock lobster.

Pinot Gris matches beautifully with fresh salmon.

Riesling suits South Pacific-influenced dishes, such as seafood with coconut and lime.

Gewürztraminer is especially suited to lightly spiced Asian cuisine.

THE VISITING EXPERIENCE

Many wineries have tasting rooms where wines can be sampled for free or for a nominal fee. Facilities vary from grandiose buildings to rustic barns. Most larger wineries are open daily, all year round, while boutique vintners may close from Easter until Labour Weekend (end of October). If a winery is closed, you may still be able to make an appointment. Regional winegrower associations publish wine trail guides detailing opening hours and other attractions, such as tours, dining options, and vineyard accommodations. Pick up a guide at a visitors center or local wine shop.

(Left) A tour of Marlborough vineyards could last for three hours to three days, depending on your stamina

gewürztraminer, and its unique barrel-aged sauvignon Te Koko. From mid-December to March they do a Marlborough Taste Plate, matched with in-house wines. This is weather-dependent as there is outdoor seating only. With Marlborough's increasing reputation for pinot noir, Cloudy Bay holds an annual international pinot noir tasting each June to highlight this variety. ✉ *Jackson's Rd., Blenheim* ☎ *03/520-9047* ⊕ *www.cloudybay.co.nz* ⊗ *Daily 10–5.*

Fromm Winery. Although Marlborough is best known for its white wines, Fromm pioneered the local use of pinot noir. Rieslings and chardonnays are also Fromm strengths, and they have become well-known for their syrah, malbec, and merlot reserves. All of their wines are produced from organically grown, handpicked grapes; the intense handcrafted vintages are made to cellar. Being one of the region's smallest wineries, their tasting room is compact; visitors can look through the glass wall to the winery while tasting, and watch the winemaker at work. Tastings are free. ✉ *Godfrey Rd., Renwick* ☎ *03/572-9355* ⊕ *www.frommwinery. co.nz* ⊗ *Oct.–Apr., daily 11–5; May–Sept., Fri.–Sun. 11–4.*

Fodor's Choice ★ **Herzog.** Therese and Hans Herzog produce a superb range of wines off their organically managed estate vineyard. Pinot grigio, pinot noir, and *montepulciano* are standouts, along with their wonderful merlot-cabernet, aptly named "The Spirit of Marlborough." The tasting area invites you to spend a long sunny afternoon exploring the delights of the cellar. You can enjoy an elegant bistro lunch in the tasting room, or, if you've made reservations, you can have a full meal at the adjoining restaurant—widely considered one of the best in the country. ✉ *81 Jeffries Rd., off Rapaura Rd.* ☎ *03/572-8770* ⊕ *www.herzog.co.nz* ⊗ *Weekdays 9–5, weekends 11–4, mid-Oct. to mid-May, by appointment rest of yr.*

★ **Highfield Estate.** This magnificent place sits high on the Brookby Ridge, with spectacular views over the Wairau plains all the way to the North Island. The winery building is signposted by an iconic Tuscan-inspired tower that visitors are welcome to climb. Highfield specializes in sauvignon blanc, with interesting pinot noir, chardonnay, and rieslings; their best, however, is a sparkling Elstree Cuvée Brut. Their indoor–outdoor lunch restaurant is popular and bookings are recommended in summer, when they also have a brunch menu. Cuisine is a blend of Mediterranean and New Zealand methods and ingredients; try their juniper-marinated rack of lamb with treacle-sauteed sweetbreads. Grab a table outside on the terrace and enjoy your lunch in the Marlborough sun. ✉ *Brookby Rd., R.D. 2, Blenheim* ☎ *03/572-9244* ⊕ *www.highfield. co.nz* ⊗ *Daily 10–5.*

★ **Hunter's Wines.** Jane Hunter has been described by the London *Sunday Times* as the "star of New Zealand wine," with a string of successes as long as a row of vines. Building on the success of her late husband and now employing a top-notch winemaker, her wines are impressive; the *fume blanc* (oak-aged sauvignon blanc) and pinot noir are legendary. The riesling, gewürztraminer and *mirumiru* (Māori for bubbles) are also big sellers; mirumiru is a sparkling blend of pinot noir, chardonnay, and pinot meunier grapes. There's also an on-site café, an artist-in-residence and an interesting walk-through sculpture and native garden.

✉ *Rapaura Rd., Blenheim* ☎ *03/572–8489 or 0800/486-837* ⊕ *www. hunters.co.nz* ⊗ *Daily 9:30–4:30.*

Mahi. As the saying goes, "what goes around comes around" and Marlborough's wine industry is no exception. Here, ex-Seresin winemaker, Brian Bicknell, produces excellent wines out of the old Cellier Le Brun winery, which has been revamped and extended to accommodate burgeoning demand. Concentrating on texture and feel of the wine, rather than the primary fruit flavors, Brian employs wild fermentation techniques, producing quality pinot noir and sauvignon blanc. He focuses on single vineyard wines, and tastings are free. The tasting room is a long, open, welcoming space with an open fire in winter and cool shade in summer. ✉ *9 Terrace Rd. , Renwick* ☎ *03/572–8859* ⊕ *www.mahiwines.co.nz* ⊗ *Daily 10–4:30.*

Montana Brancott Winery. This imposing brick structure is not really typical of Marlborough; but it's one of the biggest complexes around. It's worth a visit to sample not only their own wines but also many smaller local labels they stock. The visitor center includes a tasting area, a restaurant, a theater, and a shop. Winery tours are given daily from 10 to 3. Their star vintage is sauvignon blanc; their pinot noir is on the rise as well. Tastings cost a few dollars, and if you plan to come in summer, you may need to reserve in advance. ✉ *State Hwy. 1, 4 km (2½ mi) south of Blenheim* ☎ *03/577–5775* ⊕ *www.montanawines.co.nz* ⊗ *Cellar door daily 10–4:30, restaurant daily 10:30–3, tours daily 10:30–3.*

Seresin Estate. Named for owner Michael Seresin, a New Zealand filmmaker, this estate stands out by virtue of its meticulous viticulture and subtle wine-making techniques, producing hand-grown, handpicked, and handmade wine. They pursue high standards of environmentally friendly cultivation while using both biodynamic and organic methods to produce the wines. Seresin also produces a Tuscan-style, extra-virgin olive oil and three citrus oils—lemon, lime, and orange. The cellar door is attached to the winery. During vintage time guests to the cellar door can taste the handpicked grapes and fresh grape juice, and see the wine-making process firsthand. There's a $5 charge to taste the wines and oils. ✉ *Bedford Rd., Blenheim* ☎ *03/572–9408* ⊕ *www.seresin.co.nz* ⊗ *Summer daily 10–4:30.*

Vavasour Wines. This winery pioneered grape growing in the Awatere Valley region. As a result a viticultural subregion of Marlborough was discovered, one that produces wines with distinctive, and much-sought-after characteristics. Based on the quality of a given year's harvest, grapes are used either for Reserve vintages in limited quantities or the medium-price-range Dashwood label. Their premium labels include Vavasour, Goldwater, Clifford Bay, Redwood Pass, and Boatshed Bay. The awards list here is growing annually with a recent triple at the International Wine Challenge in London. Their cellar door is now on Rapaura Road. ✉ *26 Rapaura Rd., Blenheim* ☎ *03/575–7481* ⊕ *www.vavasour.com* ⊗ *Weekdays 10:30–4:30.*

Villa Maria. This producer has several wineries nationally and this one, close to Blenheim, benefits from good design and a central position. The building has strong architectural presence with a soothing tussock-lined

8

water feature out front. Their major grape variety in Marlborough is sauvignon blanc but they also grow pinot noir, chardonnay, and Riesling. Wine tastings cost $5, as do winery tours, which are by appointment only. ✉ *Corner Paynters and New Renwick Rds., Blenheim* ☎ *03/520–8470* ⊕ *www.villamaria.co.nz* ⊙ *Daily 10–5.*

Wairau River Wines. Phil and Chris Rose were the first contract grape growers in Marlborough. Now they produce a notably good range of classic Marlborough-grown wines under their own label. The tasting room is made from mud bricks; it also serves as a restaurant concentrating on local produce, which is open noon–3. Try the multi-award-winning sauvignon blanc and other varietals, all from the Wairau River estate vineyards. ✉ *Rapaura Rd. and State Hwy. 6, Blenheim* ☎ *03/572–9800* ⊕ *www.wairauriverwines.com* ⊙ *Daily 10–5.*

Wither Hills. Their impressive complex is an architectural delight of river rock, tile, concrete, and wood, fronted by a dramatic tussock planting. The three-story tower gives a commanding view across the middle Wairau Valley and the Wither Hills to the south. Winemaker Ben Glover works with sauvignon blanc, chardonnay, and pinot noir, preferring to specialize with these rather than broaden his focus; there are also limited quantities of pinot gris and noble Riesling at the cellar door. Wither Hills is a quick drive from the Aviation Heritage Centre. ✉ *211 New Renwick Rd.* ☎ *03/578–4036* ⊕ *www.witherhills.co.nz* ⊙ *Daily 10–4:30.*

Yealands Estate Winery. Peter Yealand has a vision as big as his vineyards, and neither are small. With over 2,500 acres of vines planted and a new-build state-of-the-art winery, it's an impressive vision. Sauvignon blanc is the star wine but the winery also does great things with the pinot grigio, gewürztraminer, riesling, *viognier,* and pinot noir grapes. They have free tastings of all their wines, including their Estate range, and there are audiovisual displays and interactive monitors to enhance your experience. ✉ *Corner of Seaview and Reserve Rds., Seddon* ☎ *03/575–7618* ⊕ *www.yealands.co.nz* ⊙ *Weekdays 10–4:30.*

WHERE TO EAT

$$$
ECLECTIC
★

✕ **Bellafico Restaurant & Wine Bar.** The number of full-house nights testifies to the high standards here. The kitchen serves wild pork and venison whenever it can get it, and if you're a meat lover, you can try the aged rib eye served with potato-and-bacon rosti and red wine jus. The fillet of salmon and the prawn-and-scallop duo add a maritime touch, and they have a blackboard dessert menu that changes regularly. The wine list is impressive and unashamedly local. ✉ *17 Maxwell Rd.* ☎ *03/577–6072* ▭ *AE, DC, MC, V* ⊙ *Closed Sun. No lunch.*

$$$$
MEDITERRANEAN
★

✕ **Gibbs Vineyard Restaurant.** Currently enjoying the reputation of being one of *the* places to eat around Blenheim, this rustic indoor-outdoor restaurant is edged by potted herbs and vineyards, and is shaded by silk trees. Their rack of lamb is always sought after, led by an entrée of delicate homemade ravioli. The dessert cheese platter has an excellent array of local cheeses. ✉ *258 Jacksons Rd., Rapaura* ☎ *03/572–8048* ⊕ *www.gibbs-restaurant.co.nz* ▭ *MC, V* ⊙ *Closed July and Sun. and Mon. May–Oct. No lunch.*

Herzog offers outstanding food along with its own wines.

$$$$
NEW ZEALAND
Fodor's Choice
★

✕**Herzog.** Marlborough's finest dining experience is tucked away along a short side road leading down to the Wairau River. Superb three- and five-course dinner menus pair Herzog wines with innovative dishes; the set and à la carte menus might include silky yellowfin tuna carpaccio, seared Nelson scallops with asparagus-ricotta ravioli, or a whole red snapper in a salt crust. The legendary degustation dinners ($191 per person, including wines) start from 6:30 and are booked well in advance, but you can often chance a dinner booking a day or so ahead of your visit. In addition to the wine pairings, you can study the wine list of 500 vintages. Retire to the lounge after dinner for a coffee or a digestif. They also run a bistro menu from 12 to 3 (around $24) if you don't want dinner. Herzog runs really popular cooking classes from October to May and has a boutique vineyard cottage accommodation for those planning to stay in the area. ⊠ *Jeffries Rd. off Rapaura Rd.* ☎ *03/572–8770* ⊟ *AE, DC, MC, V* ⊘ *Closed mid-May–mid-Oct.*

¢–$
NEW ZEALAND

✕ **Living Room Café and Lounge Bar.** The sunny corner location in the heart of Blenheim's shopping area means this café never lacks for action. Surrounded by glass on two sides, the triangular Living Room serves excellent breakfasts, with choices such as French toast, bagels, eggs Benedict, and fruit and muesli. Their breakfast loaf is freshly baked each day. They also do a nice lunch ranging from a lamb and kūmara (sweet potato) pie or a classic Caesar salad, and have a daily blackboard menu for dinner. The walls are lined with warm timber and deep colors, a hearty fire burns in winter, and they have a wireless hot spot. ⊠ *Scott St. at Maxwell Rd.* ☎ *03/579–4777* ⊟ *AE, MC, V.*

$$ ✕**Paddy Barry's Bar and Restaurant.** Locals come for a chat and a beer,
NEW ZEALAND and the menu is straightforward and well priced. It's a good place to
come down from over-enthusiastic gourmandizing—a local peril. Pair
a plate of battered-and-fried seafood with a well-poured Guinness.
You'll find Guinness *in* the food, too, in the form of a beef 'n' Guinness
hot pot; but try the bangers and mash or the crumbed fish. If they're
not busy, the kitchen closes by 8:30. ⊠ *51 Scott St.* ☎ *03/578–7470*
⊟ *AE, DC, MC, V.*

$$$ ✕**Raupo.** This impressive new building right on the riverfront has been
NEW ZEALAND opened by top local restaurateurs Marcel and Helen Rood. An imposing
structure of glass, wood, and river stone, it sits beautifully on a small
bend in the Opawa River, and is named for the nearby bulrushes, or
raupo, along the river. Their meals are light and healthy, with a selection of local favorites like mussels, beef, caesar salad, or lamb. But they
are also a favored coffee and cake stop with locals with a considerably
indulgent selection of afternoon tea morsels. ⊠ *2 Symons St., Blenheim*
☎ *03/577–8822* ⊟ *AE, MC, V.*

$$$–$$$$ ✕**The Vintners Room.** Toward the inland end of the Rapaura Road winery
ECLECTIC strip, this bar and elegant dining restaurant enjoys a well-designed Sante
Fe–style setting. Stars on the menu include their baked saddle of lamb
and an herb-crusted salmon. Their beef fillet is also worth stopping for.
Pricing here is quite reasonable for the standard of food and service.
The courtyard is shaded by spreading cherry trees through summer and
there's a small on-site art gallery. ⊠ *190 Rapaura Rd.* ☎ *03/572–5094*
⊟ *AE, MC, V* ☺ *No lunch.*

WHERE TO STAY

$$$$ ▦ **BEC Spa Resort.** This modern purpose-built lodge is perched strategi-
cally on the lower slopes of the Wither Hills, with wide-ranging views
across Cloudy Bay, Blenheim and the vineyards of the lower Wairau
Plains. It's low-aspect, minimal design suits the windswept tussock hill-
side site. The lodge has been built with pampering and wellness in
mind, with a lap pool, steam room, hot tub and massage room, and
the exotic themes reflect hostess Aloka's Sri Lankan roots. There's an
extensive string of walkways in the hills out the back door, while sunny,
sheltered deck areas create a feeling of sanctuary from the Marlborough
winds. **Pros:** four-course dinner available ($95 per person) or with wine
matching ($125) (book ahead); spa treatments include massage, facials,
and body wraps; yoga classes **Cons:** not suitable for children; the only
TV is in the main reception room; steep, narrow, winding drive to the
lodge (but good parking once you get there). ⊠ *81 Cob Cottage Rd.*
☎ *03/579–4446* ⊕ *www.becspa.co.nz* ⬎ *6 suites* ⚲ *In-room: No phone,
no TV, Wi-Fi. In-hotel: Pool, gym, spa, laundry service, Internet termi-
nal, no kids under 18* ⊟ *AE, MC, V* ☺ *June–Aug.* ⦿ *CP, BP.*

$$$ ▦ **Chateau Marlborough.** Behind its Camelot-esque turret and peaked
gables, this quiet hotel in central Blenheim is a relaxing and convenient
place to crash. The good-size rooms have separate kitchen areas; some
have whirlpool baths. Ask for one of the rooms overlooking Seymour
Square, with its stone clock tower and memorial gardens. An expan-
sion in 2009 added 15 rooms, a café and wine bar, and a fitness center.
Pros: super-king beds with quality linens; comfy leather armchairs

in the rooms; good off-street parking. **Cons:** standard hotel without a boutique experience. ✉ *High St. at Henry St.* ☎ *03/578–0064* ⊕ *www.marlboroughnz.co.nz* ⚲ *40 suites, 4 1-bedroom apartments, 1 2-bedroom apartment* ☐ *In-room: No a/c (some), kitchen, refrigerator, DVD (some), Wi-Fi. In-hotel: Restaurant, bar, pool, gym, laundry facilities, no-smoking rooms* ⊟ *AE, DC, MC, V.*

$$–$$$
★
🛏 **Hotel d'Urville.** Every room is unique in this boutique hotel in the well-preserved, art deco style Old Public Trust Building. You could choose the Raja Room, with its Eastern-inspired decorations and carved Javanese daybed; the romantic Angel Room; or the sensory trip of the Colours Room. One room is based on the exploits of Dumont d'Urville, who made voyages to the Pacific and the Antarctic in the 1820s and '30s. The excellent restaurant ($$$$) serves everything from a cup of coffee to tasty breakfasts and delightful dinners, based on local produce. Try the lamb, perhaps matched with an offering from Clayridge or Cloudy Bay vineyards. **Pros:** fabulous old building right on the main street; the downstairs bar is a welcoming spot for an evening cocktail; affordable boutique stay. **Cons:** it's a bit removed from Marlborough's vineyard-winery scene; off-street parking can be a bit tight; only one downstairs accommodation. ✉ *52 Queen St., Blenheim* ☎ *03/577–9945* ⊕ *www.durville.com* ✉ *hotel@durville.com* ⚲ *11 rooms* ☐ *In-room: Refrigerator, DVD. In-hotel: Restaurant, 2 bars, laundry service, Wi-Fi, parking (free), no-smoking rooms* ⊟ *AE, DC, MC, V* ⃝*CP.*

$$$$
Fodor's Choice
★
🛏 **Old St. Mary's Convent.** This striking turn-of-the-20th-century building was once a convent, beloved by a small group of local nuns who still visit for Christmas cheer. The relocated-and-refurbished structure hardly evokes a nunnery now with its luxuriously decorated rooms, rambling lawns and gardens, and evening glasses of Marlborough wine. Pétanque, billiards, croquet, and tennis are available to occupy idle moments. The Chapel honeymoon suite is the pick of the rooms, but each has a lovely view. This place books fast every year, and if you're planning to get married then the chapel in the garden will be perfect for that, too. **Pros:** in 60 acres of vineyard and rambling gardens; in the heart of Rapaura wine country; self-contained vineyard cottage available as well. **Cons:** the upper floor is accessed by a two-tier staircase so book the downstairs room if you have limited mobility. ✉ *Rapaura Rd.* ☎ *03/570–5700* ✉ *retreat@convent.co.nz* ⊕ *www. convent.co.nz* ⚲ *5 rooms, 1 cottage* ☐ *In-room: Refrigerator (some), DVD, Wi-Fi. In-hotel: Bar, pool, no-smoking rooms* ⊟ *AE, MC, V* ⃝ *Closed June–Aug.* ⃝*BP.*

$
⃝
🛏 **St. Leonards Vineyard Cottages.** With five different levels of accommodations dotted around a leafy garden and surrounded by vineyard this rural retreat has something for everyone. Set around an old farm homestead, each accommodation occupies an old farm building, hence names like the Dairy, the Stable, and the Woolshed. Each is furnished in extremely comfortable rural style with private outdoor spaces and verdant views. This is a great place for kids. **Pros:** the Woolshed has an outdoor bath on a private balcony; lots of sheep, deer, and chickens to amuse the kids; the owners love vintage cars and have a 1930 Chrysler available for transfers and wine tours; children under 16 stay free.

8

Cons: kitchens in the cheaper units are fairly basic. ⊠ *St Leonards Rd., just off State Hwy. 6, 3 km (2 mi) from Blenheim* ☎ *03/577–8328* ⊕ *www.stleonards.co.nz* ⇨ *5 self-contained cottages* ♿ *In-room: No a/c, no phone, kitchen, Wi-Fi. In-hotel: Tennis court, pool, bicycles, Wi-Fi, laundry facilities* ☐ *MC, V* ⑂ *CP.*

$$$$ ⚏ **Straw Lodge.** Down a quiet lane near the Wairau River, Straw Lodge
★ is about as peaceful as it gets, with the choice of self-catering or B&B accommodation. The buildings are of solid straw-bale construction, making them extra quiet, warm in winter, and cool in summer. Start your day with breakfast under the grape-covered pergola overlooking the lodge's working vineyard, and end it with a hot tub soak under the stars, sipping the lodge's own excellent vintage. Self-catering facilities are available if you prefer to do it yourself. There is a complimentary platter and wine tasting on arrival, and the property is working toward organic certification. **Pros:** genuine vineyard setting with vines running to the house; free use of bikes with lots of river trails nearby; the owners also have a house in the Marlborough Sounds if you want a base to explore that area from. **Cons:** a 15-minute drive from town; limited availability in June, July, and August. ⊠ *17 Fareham La. off Wairau Valley Rd., Renwick* ☎ *03/572–9767* ⊕ *www.strawlodge.co.nz* ✍ *strawlodge@xtra.co.nz* ⇨ *3 suites, cottage* ♿ *In-room: No a/c (some), no phone, refrigerator, DVD. In-hotel: Spa, water sports, bicycles, laundry facilities, Wi-Fi, no-smoking rooms* ☐ *MC, V* ⑂ *BP.*

$$$$ ⚏ **Timara Lodge.** This 1923 house is one of Marlborough's original home-
Fodor's Choice steads; its craftsmanship, skilled use of native timber, and luxurious inte-
★ rior evoke an elegant past. The gardens extend over 25 acres and include a pool, a tennis court, a private lake, and masses of clipped hedging. Chef Louis Schindler prepares sumptuous four-course table d'hôte dinners based on local ingredients. Wine tours, trout fishing, sea kayaking, golf, skiing, even whale-watching (an hour and a half away in Kaikoura) can be arranged. The owners have their own vineyard and winery, producing the extremely successful Spy Valley label. **Pros:** their extensive and lovely garden is a highlight; the chef is ex-Herzog's and is one of the best around; transfers available from Blenheim airport. **Cons:** down a narrow country lane; 15-minute drive from Blenheim. ⊠ *301 Dog Point Rd., R.D. 2* ☎ *03/572–8276* ⊕ *www.timara.co.nz* ✍ *timaralodge@xtra. co.nz* ⇨ *2 rooms, 2 suites* ♿ *In-room: Wi-Fi.In-hotel: Tennis court, pool, laundry service, Wi-Fi, no kids under 15, no-smoking rooms,* ☐ *AE, DC, MC, V* ⊗ *Closed Dec. 22–27, and July and Aug.* ⑂ *MAP.*

$$$$ ⚏ **Vintners Retreat.** At the heart of Marlborough's wine district, this all-
villas resort has balconies that overlook six vineyards. As the varieties ripen and are harvested and their leaves turn red, the view changes like a Technicolor quilt. Each villa is a fully equipped home-away-from-home and is well suited for families. **Pros:** all units are magnificently presented; easy access and parking; pricing is for up to four adults. **Cons:** its size means it loses some intimacy with its environment; busy main road backdrop. ⊠ *55 Rapaura Rd.* ☎ *03/572–7420 or 0800/484–686* ⊕ *www.vintnersretreat.co.nz* ⇨ *14 1- to 3-bedroom villas* ♿ *In-room: Wi-Fi. In-hotel: Tennis court, pool, bikes, Wi-Fi* ☐ *AE, DC, MC, V.*

EN
ROUTE

The drive from Blenheim to Kaikoura crosses the dry parched Wither Hills and the rolling farmlands and vineyards of the Awatere Valley. A short distance after the small town of Ward the road drops down to a dramatic coastline, which it follows right through to Kaikoura. This coastal section takes an hour with a few scenery stops. The TranzCoastal train also travels this same route. Don't miss the seals at **Ohau Point, south of Kekerengu**, where they can be viewed from the roadside. Don't approach them closely and always maintain at least a 10-meter (30-foot) distance from them— their pungent smell will make that easy. In early summer walk the short track to the nearby waterfall where you may be lucky to see seal pups which have swum up the creek from the sea to play at the base of the falls.

$–$$

SEAFOOD

★

✕ **The Store.** This one-stop store and café is by the rolling surf beach on State Highway 1 heading south, halfway between Blenheim and Kaikoura. On this dramatic perch at the edge of the Pacific, the waves almost reach the open deck. You can choose lunch from either the cabinet or a blackboard menu; try the seafood chowder or a Thai beef salad with a glass of local wine. Dinner bookings are essential in summer (last order taken at 7:30); in winter The Store closes at 7, with the last order taken around 6:30. ⊠ *State Hwy. 1, Kekerengu* ✛ *64 km (40 mi) south of Blenheim* ☎ *03/575–8600* ✍ *the_store@xtra.co.nz* ☐ *MC, V.*

KAIKOURA

129 km (81 mi) south of Blenheim, 182 km (114 mi) north of Christchurch.

8

The town of Kaikoura sits on a rocky protrusion on the east coast, backed by an impressive mountainous upthrust. View it from the expansive **lookout** up on Scarborough Street. Sperm whales frequent this coast in greater numbers than anywhere else on Earth. The sperm whale, the largest toothed mammal, can reach a length of 60 feet and a weight of 70 tons. The whales concentrate in this area because of the abundance of squid—particularly the giant squid of seafaring lore, which is their main food source. Scientists speculate that the whales use a form of sonar to find the squid, which they then bombard with deep, powerful sound waves generated in the massive cavities in the fronts of their heads. Their hunting is all the more remarkable considering that much of it is done at great depths, in darkness. The whales' food source swims in the trench just off the continental shelf, just kilometers off the Kaikoura Coast. You are most likely to see the whales between October and August, but they are generally there year-round.

Kaikoura's main street straggles along the beach behind a high stony bank, which lends some protection from rough weather. Farther south curves South Bay, the docking point for the whale-watching operators. Kaikoura has undergone a transformation over the past decade as its whale-watching has brought thousands of people to its doorstep.

GETTING HERE AND AROUND

State Highway 1 runs right through Kaikoura, so the town is on the main road between Picton and Christchurch and the coastal route between Nelson and Christchurch. It's an easy 2½-hour drive south from Kaikoura to Christchurch and 1¾ hours north to Blenheim.

InterCity runs buses between Christchurch, Kaikoura and Nelson a couple of times a day. In Kaikoura, southbound buses stop at the parking lot by the Craypot restaurant, northbound buses at the Sleepy Whale. Aside from tour buses, the only reliable local alternatives are **Atomic Shuttles** and **Southern Link K Bus**.

The TranzCoastal train follows the coast from Christchurch to Picton, meeting with the Interislander ferry at midday. It stops at Kaikoura both ways.

ESSENTIALS

Bus Information Atomic Shuttle (☎ 03/349–0697 ⊕ www.atomictravel.co.nz). **InterCity** (☎ 03/365–1113 ⊕ www.intercitycoach.co.nz). **Southern Link K Bus** (☎ 03/358–8355 or 0508/458–835 ⊕ www.southernlinkcoaches.co.nz).

Hospital Kaikoura Hospital (✉ 7 Deal St. ☎ 03/319–7760).

Train Information TranzCoastal (⊕ www.tranzscenic.co.nz).

Visitor Information Kaikoura Information and Tourism Centre (✉ West End ☎ 03/319–5641 ⊕ www.kaikoura.co.nz ✍ info@kaikoura.co.nz).

EXPLORING

Fyffe House is Kaikoura's oldest building, erected soon after Robert Fyffe's whaling station was established in 1842. Partly built on whale-bone piles on a low-rise overlooking the sea, the house provides a look at what life was like when people aimed at whales with harpoons rather than cameras. You can stop here on the way to the Point Kean seal colony. ✉ 62 Avoca St. ☎ 03/319–5835 ⊕ www.fyffehouse.co.nz ⊡ $7, family $15 ⊗ Oct.–Apr., daily 10–6; May–Sept., Thurs.–Mon. 10–4.

At **Lavendyl Lavender Farm,** just off the main highway a few minutes' drive north of the town center, rows of lavender stretch out against the stunning backdrop of Mt. Fyffe and the Seaward Kaikouras. Jan and Corry Zeestraten run this working 5-acre farm; the blooms are harvested from December to February, but they're gorgeous anytime. Walk through the heaven-scented gardens, and then head for the shop, where bunches of lavender hang from the ceiling and lavender marmalade, mustards, chutneys, and soap line the shelves. ✉ 268 Postmans Rd. ☎ 03/319–5473 ⊕ www.lavenderfarm.co.nz ⊡ $2 ⊗ Daily 10–4. Closed June–Sept.

On the first Saturday of October Kaikoura celebrates its annual **Seafest,** during which the best of this coastal area's food, wine, and beer is served while top New Zealand entertainers perform on an outdoor stage. Tickets are available from the town's information center but they do sell out so book ahead ⊕ www.seafest.co.nz.

OUTDOOR ACTIVITIES

December and January are the peak months for whale-watching and swimming with dolphins or seals so book well in advance.

BIRD-WATCHING

Albatross Encounter (✉ *96 The Esplanade* ☎ *03/319–6777 or 0800/733–365* ⊕ *www.encounterkaikoura.co.nz* ✍ *info@oceanwings.co.nz*) operates tours by boat to view and feed the large varieties of seabirds off the Kaikoura Coast, including the mighty albatross. Tours operate three times daily in summer and twice daily in winter, and cost $110 for adults and $55 for children. It's an intimate encounter with some of the planet's most spectacular birds.

HIKING

The three-day **Kaikoura Coast Track** walk provides uncrowded, unguided hiking and three nights accommodation along spectacular coastal farmland south of Kaikoura for 10 people at a time maximum. Take binoculars to search out seals, sea birds, and dolphins. The first night is at Hawkswood in the historic sheep station of the **Staging Post**. A moderate four- to six-hour walk through native bush and down to the coast the next day will take you to **Ngaroma,** a 3,000-acre sheep-and-cattle farm. The following day's hike is along the beach, passing an ancient buried forest before heading across farmland to an area of regenerating bush to **Medina,** where you'll spend the third night. On the final day, a moderate four- to six-hour walk takes you over the 2,000-foot-plus Mt. Wilson. The total track length is 40 km (25 mi), suitable for average fitness. Bags are transferred to the next night's accommodations daily, so you only need to carry a daypack. Lunch shelters along the way provide comfort and tea-making stops.

The fee is $185 per person, including bag transfer. If you opt to have all meals included and need bedding, the total cost is available on request. Reservations are essential. The start point is a ¾-hour drive south of Kaikoura on State Highway 1. Public transport can drop you at the gate. ✉ *201 Conway Flat Rd., Cheviot* ☎ *03/319–2715* ✍ *sally@kaikouratrack.co.nz* ⊕ *www.kaikouratrack.co.nz* ☺ *Daily Oct.–Apr.*

With the proximity of extremely high mountains the **Kaikoura Wilderness Walkway** offers an excellent opportunity to get right up in them. There are two- and three-day guided walks, with overnight accommodations in the really comfy **Shearwater Lodge,** high above the Puhi Puhi Valley in the Seaward Kaikoura Ranges. The walkway crosses through rugged inspiring terrain where clouds swirl across the tops and giant scree slopes slither down the valleys. Door-to-door pickup can be arranged from Kaikoura, luggage is transferred to the lodge, all meals are provided, and you need to be moderately fit and agile. ✉ *Puhi Puhi Valley* ☎ *03/319–6966 or 0800/945–337* ⊕ *www.kaikourawilderness.co.nz* ✍ *Reservations essential* 🎫 *Tours from $795 per person (4-person minimum)* ☺ *Oct.–Mar., Wed., and Fri. departures.*

The peninsula near town has a much shorter **walking track** that shows off the spectacular coastal scenery and the seal colonies. Consult the town's information center for maps and track information. The walk starts either at the end of Fyffe Quay or round at South Bay. The entry point at South Bay recognizes the importance of the area to local Māori, whose ancestors lived on this stretch of coast for many generations

8

before Europeans arrived. The first part of the track from South Bay leading to Limestone Bay is wheelchair accessible.

SWIMMING WITH DOLPHINS AND SEALS The dolphin- and seal-spotting opportunities are fantastic. Although operators have led visitors to view and swim with dolphins and seals off the Kaikoura Coast for years, and the animals may be familiar with boats, they are not tame. New Zealand fur seals are common, and you might spot an octopus or crayfish. Pods of dusky dolphins stay in the area year-round; you may even see them doing aerial jumps and flips.

The offerings vary and operators will explain their expectations before you book. Some boat operators go farther offshore, whereas others hug the coast. If you have any questions about the suitability of a trip, pipe up; these guys are happy to help. Guides can prime you with information on the local species and will be in the water with you. Wet suits and other gear are provided.

But you don't have to join an organized tour to get close to seals. At the **Point Kean** sea colony out on the Kaikoura Peninsula you can see seals in their natural habitat, lying in the sun or playing in the kelp-filled shallows. These are wild animals so don't approach closer than 10 meters (30 feet). With seabirds wheeling above and waves breaking along the shore it's a powerful place just minutes from the main street. Follow Fyffe Quay to the colony at the end of the road.

Dolphin Encounter (⊠ *96 The Esplanade* ☎ *03/319–6777 or 0800/733–365* ⊕ *www.encounterkaikoura.co.nz* ✉ *info@dolphin.co.nz*) arranges dolphin watching and swimming. Tours operate three times a day through summer and twice a day in winter, for $165 per person. (It's just $95 to watch the dolphins from the boat.) Because they operate in the open ocean, you need to be confident in the water, and it is an advantage to have some snorkeling experience. They also offer "Albatross Encounter" tours that take you out to view the seabirds off the Kaikoura Coast. **Seal Swim Kaikoura** (☎ *03/319–6182 or 0800/732–579* ⊕ *www.sealswimkaikoura.co.nz* ✉ *info@sealswimkaikoura.co.nz*) is New Zealand's original seal-swimming experience and has boat- and shore-based tours running daily from October to May for $70–$80 per person. The swims are easy because they're behind the shelter of the Kaikoura Peninsula, and you're virtually guaranteed to see fur seals.

WHALE-WATCHING
Fodor's Choice
★ **Whale Watch Kaikoura.** Whale Watch is owned by the Ngai Tahu iwi (tribe). Since arriving in the Kaikoura area in AD 850, Ngai Tahu, the predominant South Island Māori iwi, claims to have lived and worked based on a philosophy of sustainable management and sensible use of natural resources. Having worked these waters since 1987, Whale Watch skippers can recognize individual whales and adjust operations, such as the boat's proximity to the whale, accordingly. Allow 3½ hours for the whole experience, 2¼ hours on the water. Various dolphins and seals and other species of whales may also be seen on any day.

Book in advance: 7 to 10 days November–April, three to four days at other times. Their sturdy catamarans are fully enclosed for sea travel, but once the whales are spotted you can go out on the deck for a closer view. Trips depend on the weather, and should your tour miss seeing a whale, which is rare, you will get an 80% refund. Take motion-sickness

Whale-watchers delight in spotting a whale in the waters near Kaikoura.

pills if you suspect you'll need them: even in calm weather, the sea around Kaikoura often has a sizable swell. They can't accept children under three on the trip. ⊡ *Whaleway Station, Whaleway Station Rd., Kaikoura7300* ☎ *03/319–6767 or 0800/655–121* ✍ *res@whalewatch. co.nz* ⊕ *www.whalewatch.co.nz* ✉ *$145* ▭ *AE, MC, V.*

Wings over Whales. To get above the action, take a half-hour whale-viewing flight. A seven-seater Airvan or three-seater Cessna aircraft gives you a bird's-eye view of the giant sperm whales. While searching for other whales' telltale water spouts, the pilot and co-pilot provide informative commentary on the creatures' habits. You'll also get a stunningly scenic flight over the famous Kaikoura coastline at the same time. Children's under 14 fly for only $75. ⊠ *Kaikoura Airfield, State Hwy. 1, Kaikoura* ☎ *03/319–6580 or 0800/226–629* ✍ *fly@whales. co.nz* ⊕ *www.whales.co.nz* ✉ *$165* ▭ *AE, DC, MC, V.*

WHERE TO EAT

For a small place Kaikoura has an excellent choice of restaurants. But for a taste of the local product visit one of the roadside caravans; on the coast north of town Nin's Bin at Rakautara has a strong fan base. Crays come cooked or uncooked, or you may prefer to get your crayfish fix at a local café. They are expensive; even a casual place can have main courses over $30. Also try the whitefishlike *groper* (grouper) and *terakihi*, or the shellfish and crabs.

$$–$$$ ✗ **Café Encounter.** Here's a bright eatery along the Esplanade, sharing
CAFÉ space with the Dolphin and Albatross Encounter operations. The partially glassed-in courtyard is sheltered in most winds, and there's plenty of indoor seating. Food is available off the menu or from the cabinet;

their range of cakes and slices is quite appealing. But like any outdoor café in Kaikoura, don't leave your food unattended because the birds will snatch it quicker than you can say "seagull!" ⊠ *96 The Esplanade* ☎ *03/319–6777* ▭ *AE, DC, MC, V* ☽ *No dinner.*

$$$–$$$$ ✕ **The Craypot.** This casual café relies strongly on the local delicacy. Cray-
SEAFOOD fish isn't cheap (up to $85 for a whole one), but this kitchen knows how to prepare it. Other seafood also figures large on the menu, and you can choose from several variations on the steak, chicken, and lamb themes. Homemade desserts are worth leaving room for. In summer you can get a table outdoors; in winter an open fire roars at night. ⊠ *70 West End Rd.* ☎ *03/319–6027* ▭ *AE, DC, MC, V.*

$$$ ✕ **Hislops Café.** Wholesome Hislops is a few minutes' walk north of town
CAFÉ and worth the trip. In the morning you'll find tasty eggs and bacon, plus freshly baked, genuinely stone-ground whole-grain bread served with marmalade or their own honey. The lunch and dinner menus use organic ingredients, and there are wheat- and gluten-free options. You might choose between a *kūmara* (native sweet potato), bacon, and avo-cado salad or marinated tofu and falafel. On sunny days, score a table on the veranda. Evening dining includes seafood, lamb, and some veg-etarian and vegan options. ⊠ *33 Beach Rd.* ☎ *03/319–6971* ▭ *AE, DC, MC, V* ☽ *Closed Tues.–Wed. May–Aug.*

$$$–$$$$ ✕ **White Morph Restaurant.** Crayfish is always on the menu at this elegant
SEAFOOD eatery, and options include roasted, in antipasto, or even as a brûlée.
★ Prices vary with availability. Other treats include venison, lamb loin, wild hare, and at least one vegetarian dish. Fish of the Bay is usually a divinely roasted groper (grouper) fillet, served with walnut-and-parsley pesto and lemon-baked risotto. The desserts are fabulous, too. The best decora-tions are the seaside views from the front windows; fishing boats, sturdy launches, and the occasional yacht bob at anchor in the rock-strewn bay. ⊠ *94 The Esplanade* ☎ *03/319–5676* ⊕ *www.whitemorphrestaurant. co.nz* ✍ *camber@ts.co.nz* ▭ *MC, V* ☽ *No lunch.*

WHERE TO STAY

Accommodations are a mix of lodges and pubs out in the country and motels and apartments in town. Another option is seaside camping along the coast. Available from Paia Point, south of town, along to Oaro, it's administered by the Kaikoura Coastal Camp at **Goose Bay** (☎ *03/319–5348* ⊕ *www.happycamping.co.nz/goosebay* ✍ *goosebay@ihug.co.nz*), so call before grabbing a site. Powered and tent sites are available.

$–$$ ⌂ **Alpine-Pacific Holiday Park.** A moderate walk from town, this nicely laid-out site has spotless facilities. There are cabins, en suite, studios, and full motel units available; there are also powered camper-van sites and campsites. The view of the Seaward Kaikoura Mountains is breath-taking. There are two holiday parks on Beach Road—this one is on the inland side of the road. Bookings are essential in summer and there are also standard cabins available from $65 a night. **Pros:** incredibly clean, tidy outfit layered down a terraced slope; trampoline for the kids; bikes for rent. **Cons:** campsites a little cramped if full. ⊠ *69 Beach Rd.* ☎ *03/319–6275* ⊕ *www.alpine-pacific.co.nz* ⇱ *8 cabins, 4 studio units, 8 en suite studio units, 2 2-bedroom units, 50 campsites* ♿ *In-room: No a/c, no phone, kitchen (some), DVD (some), no TV (some).*

CLOSE UP

French Pass and D'Urville Island

They're not easy to get to, but if you have an adventurous spirit and don't mind a rough road, French Pass and D'Urville Island are two of the best-kept secrets in the whole top of the South Island.

The **road to French Pass** splits off State Highway 6 at Rai Valley, halfway between Havelock and Nelson. It's winding, rough, and steep in places, but quite passable in a regular vehicle if you're a competent driver (check that your rental car can go off the sealed road). The sign at the start says FRENCH PASS 2 HRS, and although it's only 64 km (40 mi) to the pass, this estimate is basically true. The road first climbs over the Rongo Saddle and down to Okiwi Bay through native bush; from here, you'll have spectacular views of D'Urville Island in the distance. Then the road crosses to the Pelorus Sound catchment and climbs along the ridge separating the waters of that sound from Tasman Bay to the west. Small side roads drop precariously to hidden bays such as Te Towaka, Elaine Bay, and Deep Bay.

The last 12 km (7 mi) is a dramatic drop down to sea level, skirting Current Basin before arriving at French Pass, the narrow stretch of water separating Tasman Bay from Cook Strait, which moves at up to 9 knots during the tidal run. Both the waterway and the island were named for French explorer Dumont D'Urville, who crossed through the pass in the 1820s when it was uncharted by European navigators. **D'Urville Island** is on the far side of this stretch of water, and it's a fabulous destination to feel what isolated coastal New Zealand is all about. Plan to stay two nights as it's a long drive either way.

Between Okiwi Bay and French Pass there are no facilities—no gas stations, bathrooms, or cafés—so come prepared. Only limited public facilities are at French Pass: a basic toilet, gas pump, and essential supplies during limited hours.

If you want to stay overnight at French Pass, **French Pass Sea Safaris & Beachfront Villas** (☎ *03/576–5204* ⊕ *www.seasafaris.co.nz*) is on the shores of Admiralty Bay. The property has two comfortable, fully self-contained two-bedroom apartments, and one studio unit, and has seal and dolphin swims in season, island walks, kayaking, and wildlife and bird-watching tours. If you're lucky you'll see dolphins from your balcony. Diving and fishing charters can also be arranged. Home-cooked meals, including breakfast, can be arranged but cost extra. It's usually closed June to September, but check the Web site for updates. And if you really want a remote experience, carry on to D'Urville Island, where the best lodging option is the **D'Urville Island Wilderness Resort** (☎ *03/576–5268* ⊕ *www.durvilleisland.co.nz*). The resort is a 30-minute boat ride across French Pass (a water-taxi service picks you up from the French Pass wharf), and overlooks the sheltered waters of Catherine Cove. You can go hiking, mountain biking, and snorkeling here, or just watch the rosy sunrises and the orca whales passing the end of the bay. The resort has a fully licensed bar and restaurant on-site and accommodation reservations are essential.

8

In-hotel: Pool, spa, bicycles, laundry facilities, Internet terminal, Wi-Fi, no-smoking rooms ▭ *MC, V.*

$$$$

★

⊡ **Hapuku Lodge and Tree Houses.** This complex was built by the local Wilson family who have a strong pedigree in New Zealand architecture. Featuring imaginative use of timbers and finishings, the lodge rooms are quietly tasteful. But out in the trees, all that changes in the extremely luxurious but equally funky tree houses. Each stands several stories high up into the surrounding cover of native *manuka* and *kowhai* trees and was built with a combination of rough-sawn timber, copper, glass, and steel. Inside, no luxury is spared, with freestanding fireplaces, whirlpool baths, and elegant handmade furniture. Each unit has a wide-reaching view across the coast to the east and the Seaward Kaikoura Ranges to the west, both just a few kilometers away. Dinner is available by arrangement. **Pros:** specialty breakfasts available on request; surf out the back window and the snow out the front; walking track down to the sea through the olive grove. **Cons:** stay in the main lodge if you're not good with heights. ⊠ *State Hwy. 1 at Station Rd., 12 km (8 mi) north of Kaikoura* ☎ *03/319–6559 or 0800/524–56872* ⊕ *www.hapukulodge. com* ⇴ *6 lodge rooms, 5 1- and 2-bedroom tree houses, 1 apartment* ⌂ *In-room: Refrigerator. In-hotel: Restaurant, Internet terminal* ▭ *AE, DC, MC, V* ⊙⍁ *CP in most rooms.*

$$–$$$

⊡ **Surfwatch B&B.** Perched high on the cliffs overlooking Mangamaunu Beach and just 10 minutes north of town, this extraordinarily pleasant property stands true to its name. Sea views run endlessly to the horizon, north and south; closer in you can watch wetsuit-clad surfers and NZ fur seals shooting the waves on one of the country's well-known surf breaks. Accommodations are in a private en suite B&B room attached to the main house and a character-filled self-contained cottage, a bit back from the view, out in the garden. The hosts are expat Americans with a good local knowledge from many years in New Zealand. **Pros:** views from the B&B suite are exceptional; 5-acre property is a small farm; lots of handcrafted furniture and wood detail **Cons:** really steep access road; opens off a fast stretch of twisting coastal highway so take care crossing the road. ⊠ *State Hwy. 1, Mangamaunu* ☎ *03/319–6611* ⊕ *www.surfwatchbnb.com* ⇴ *1 room, 1 cottage* ⌂ *In-room: No a/c (some), no phone, kitchen. In-hotel: Laundry facilities, Internet terminal, no-smoking rooms* ▭ *MC, V* ⊙⍁ *CP.*

$$–$$$

★

⊡ **White Morph Motor Inn.** A waterfront view is hard to ignore—even more so on the rugged Kaikoura Coast. This hotel is just opposite the beach, a few minutes' walk from the town center. The suites have double whirlpool baths, as do a few of the other rooms; three units are two stories, well suited for families or larger parties. **Pros:** eminently comfortable units in a great esplanade location; breakfast served in the neighboring Encounter Café; the on-site White Morph restaurant is worth a visit. **Cons:** on the tourist strip; motel-style property rather than a hotel. ⊠ *92 The Esplanade* ☎ *03/319–5014* ✎ *info@whitemorph. co.nz* ⊕ *www.whitemorph.co.nz* ⇴ *31 units (12 with whirlpool baths), 16 studios, 3 self-catering family units* ⌂ *In-room: No a/c (some), kitchen, DVD, Wi-Fi. In-hotel: Restaurant, bar, laundry facilities, no-smoking rooms* ▭ *AE, DC, MC, V.*

EN ROUTE

When traveling between Christchurch and Kaikoura the **Mainline Station Cafe** at Domett stands out among the slim eating options along the way. Built in the 100-year-old ex-Domett railway station it is a sunny spot with a sheltered area of tables out the back in the middle of rural North Canterbury. There's a good selection of cakes, slices, and cabinet food and a small blackboard menu of tasty homemade brunch and lunch dishes. Sunday in summer is market day with local foods, arts, and crafts available. ⊠ *Corner State Hwy. 1 and Hurunui Mouth Rd., 106 km (71 mi) north of Christchurch, 7 km (5 mi) south of Cheviot* ☎ *03/319–8776* ☐ *MC, V* ⊙ *Aug.–Apr., daily 9–4; May and June closed Mon.; closed July and Aug.*

NELSON AND THE NORTHWEST

On the broad curve of Tasman Bay with views of the Kahurangi mountains on the far side, Nelson is one of the top areas for year-round adventure. To the west beckon the sandy crescents of Abel Tasman National Park and Golden Bay. To the south, mellow river valleys and the peaks and glacial lakes of Nelson Lakes National Park draw hikers, mountaineers, and sightseers. There's a climatic allure as well; Nelson usually has more hours of sunlight than any other city in the country. New Zealanders are well aware of these attractions, and in December and January the city is swamped with vacationers. Apart from this brief burst of activity, you can expect the roads and beaches to be relatively quiet.

Settled by Māori hundreds of years ago, the site, then called Whakatu, was chosen for its extremely sheltered harbor and good climate. These enticements later caught the eye of the London-based New Zealand Company, and Nelson became the second town developed by that organization, with British immigrants arriving in the 1840s. These days Nelson is the country's chief fishing port and a key forestry area, with vineyards and olive groves developing into another major industry. The quiet magnificent setting has attracted creatively minded people, and there's a significant community of artists, craftspeople, and writers in the countryside around Nelson.

8

NELSON

116 km (73 mi) west of Blenheim.

Relaxed, hospitable, and easy to explore on foot, Nelson has a way of always making you feel as though you should stay longer. You can make your way around the mostly two-story town in a day, poking into crafts galleries and stopping at cafés, but two days is a practical minimum. Use Nelson as a base for a variety of activities within an hour's drive of the town itself.

GETTING HERE AND AROUND

Nelson Airport (NSN) is a small regional airport 10 km (6 mi) south of the city center. **Air New Zealand** links Nelson with Christchurch, Auckland, and Wellington a number of times a day. **Soundsair** flies in from Wellington three times a day with a scenic, low-level flight over the Marlborough Sounds.

Geographically Nelson is quite isolated so no matter which way you drive from there'll be a range of hills to climb. It's a three-hour drive from Westport, 6½ hours from Christchurch via the Lewis Pass, and 1¾ hours from Blenheim. From Nelson, head west to Motueka and the Abel Tasman Park, Golden Bay, and the Kahurangi Park. Once again there are some big hills but the roads are good.

InterCity buses run between Christchurch, Blenheim, and Nelson a couple of times a day. There's also a West Coast service running from Nelson to the glaciers. It's a full day trip, but leaves no opportunity to explore all the sights along the way.

Aside from tour buses, the only reliable local alternatives are **Atomic Shuttles** and **Southern Link K Bus**. Atomic operates coaches between the most popular tourist spots and shuttle vans on the lower-profile regional runs. In the December and January holiday season, book at least a couple of days before you plan to travel, but during the rest of the year a day's advance reservation should do the trick. Bus tickets can also be booked at information centers.

Abel Tasman Coachlines and Southern Link K Bus run the smaller routes to Motueka, Takaka, and the Abel Tasman and Kahurangi national parks.

Many of the smaller routes cut their service frequency in winter, some stop altogether, and others reduce their destinations, so double-check the schedules.

Once you arrive in Nelson get your bearings at the visitor center on the corner of Trafalgar and Halifax streets. The heart of town is farther up **Trafalgar Street**, between Bridge Street and the cathedral steps, also home to the region's museum. This area is fringed with shops, and the block between Hardy Street and the cathedral steps is a sunny spot to enjoy a coffee. The Nelson Saturday Market is held at the Montgomery parking lot. There are a few art stores and galleries on Nile Street, too. For a dose of greenery, the **Queens Gardens** are on Bridge Street between Collingwood and Tasman. The Nelson Arts Guide, available at visitor centers and local shops, is a good resource for the area's crafts offerings.

A five-minute drive around the waterfront from town, Tahunanui Beach offers some of the safest swimming in the country. This long open beach is perfect to watch the sunset from and is a favorite spot for kiteboarders with its rollicking summer sea breeze.

ESSENTIALS

Airline Contacts Air New Zealand (☎ 03/547-8721 or 0800/737-000 ⊕ www.airnewzealand.co.nz). **Soundsair** (☎ 03/520-3080 or 0800/505-005 ⊕ www.soundsair.co.nz).

Airport Nelson Airport (✉ Trent Dr. ☎ 03/547-3199).

Airport Transfers Super Shuttle (☎ 03/547-5782 or 0800/748-885).

Bus Depot Nelson (✉ 27 Bridge St. ☎ 03/548-3290).

Bus Contacts Abel Tasman Coachlines (☎ 03/548-0285 ⊕ www.abeltasmantravel.co.nz). **Atomic Shuttles** (☎ 03/349-0697 ⊕ www.atomictravel.

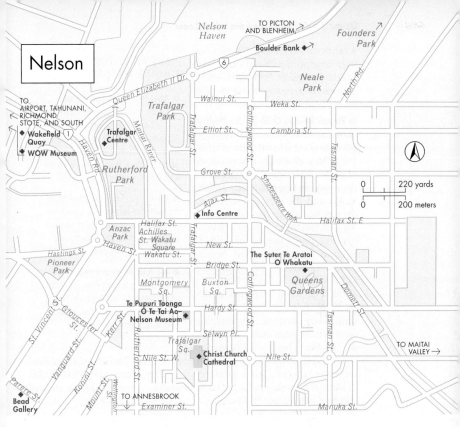

co.nz). **InterCity** (☎ 03/365–1113 ⊕ www.intercitycoach.co.nz). **Southern Link K Bus** (☎ 03/358–8355 or 0508/458–835 ⊕ www.southernlinkcoaches.co.nz).

Emergencies Fire, police, and ambulance (☎ 111).

Hospital Nelson Base Hospital (✉ Waimea Rd. ☎ 03/546–1800).

Rental Cars Apex (✉ Nelson Airport, Tangmere Pl. ☎ 03/546–9028 or 0800/939–777 ⊕ www.apexrentals.co.nz). Avis ✉ Nelson Airport, Trent Dr. ☎ 03/547–2727 or 0800/284–722 ⊕ www.avis.co.nz). Hertz (✉ Nelson Airport, Trent Dr. ☎ 03/547–2299 or 0800/654–321 ⊕ www.hertz.co.nz).

Visitor Information Nelson Visitor Information Centre (✉ 77 Trafalgar St. at Halifax St. ☎ 03/548–2304 ✉ vin@nelsonnz.com ⊕ www.nelsonnz.com).

EXPLORING
TOP ATTRACTIONS
The Suter Te Aratoi o Whakatu. There are exhibits of both historical and contemporary art; it's a good place to see a cross section of work from an area that has long attracted painters, potters, woodworkers, and other artists. Many of them come for the scenery, the lifestyle, and the clay, and as a result, Nelson is considered the ceramics center of New Zealand. In recent years the gallery has increased its emphasis on painting and sculpture. National touring exhibits come through regularly.

A lunch café in the gallery looks out over neighboring Queen's Gardens. ✉ *208 Bridge St.* ☎ *03/548–4699* 🌐 *www.thesuter.org.nz* 💲 *$3, Sat. free* 🕙 *Daily 10:30–4:30.*

Te Pupuri Taonga O Te Tai Ao (Nelson Provincial Museum). Nelson's regional museum occupies part of the original site of New Zealand's first museum. It explores the early settlement of the town, its original Māori inhabitants, and the events that shaped the region. Exhibits include a small-but-outstanding collection of Māori carvings, plus a number of artifacts relating to the so-called Maungatapu murders, grisly goldfields killings committed near Nelson in 1866. The Town Warp is a multimedia wander through the early central-city streets, highlighting local personalities such as Ann Bird the Butcher (a hard-as-nails woman who was one of the town's first European settlers). Their research facility is off-site in nearby Stoke. ✉ *Hardy St. at Trafalgar St.* ☎ *03/548–9588* 🌐 *www.nelsonmuseum.co.nz* 💲 *$5 donation entry and $5 for special seasonal exhibitions* 🕙 *Weekdays 10–5, weekends 10–4:30.*

★ **World of WearableArt & Classic Car Museum (WOW).** Wacky and wonderful, this museum displays garments from the World of WearableArt Awards Show, an event long held in Nelson but now presented in Wellington. The concept of WearableArt is to turn art into garments that adorn the body, something best understood when facing moving mannequins in their inventive ensembles. Imagine brightly colored, hand-painted silks draped into a giant winged headdress. Or papier-mâché fashioned into dramatic body suits, and glittering oceanic creations in the colors of *paua* shells. The elaborate sets, sound, and psychedelic lighting make this gallery a must-see. An adjoining gallery exhibits a superb collection of restored classic cars, ranging from a pink Cadillac to sleek sports tourers. ✉ *95 Quarantine Rd., Annesbrook* ☎ *03/547–4573* 🌐 *www.wowcars.co.nz* 📧 *info@wowcars.co.nz* 💲 *$18* 🕙 *Daily 10–5.*

Christ Church Cathedral. On a hilltop surrounded by gardens is Nelson's boldest architectural "highlight." The site has played an integral part in Nelson's history, first as a Māori *pā* or fortified village, then as the base for the initial city street survey. It housed the immigration barracks when the city was first settled by Europeans. A tent church was erected in 1842, followed by more permanent ones in 1851 and 1887. Work on the current cathedral began in 1925 and dragged on for 40 years, with middling results. But the steps running down to Trafalgar Street have become a destination in their own right, a social hub in the city center. ✉ *Cathedral Sq.* 🌐 *www.nelsoncathedral.org* 💲 *Free.*

BEST BETS FOR CRUISE PASSENGERS

■ Abel Tasman National Park. Bus-ride through to Kaiteriteri to join a boat tour along the Abel Tasman coast. Stop and kayak or walk a stretch, picnic at a secluded bay, then cruise back to Kaiteriteri, and on to Nelson.

■ Wine Tour. Take a guided tour through the hinterland. Check out some of the region's best wineries, enjoy a vineyard lunch, and buy some bottles to take home.

■ Art Tour. There are several tailored arts tours where you can meet some of the region's 300 working artists, visit their studios, and watch them at work.

NEED A BREAK?

Penguino's Cafe (✉ *85 Montgomery Sq.* ☎ *03/545–6450*) is a cool source for delicious gelato—particularly their signature creation, the gelato panini. Like a gussied-up version of an ice-cream sandwich, this treat is heated in a panini press and served warm, but with the ice cream still cold inside. Their white chocolate gelato is hard to go past. Closed July and August.

WORTH NOTING

Boulder Bank. One of the defining features of the landscape is the Boulder Bank, a 13-km (8-mi) natural stone bank, built up by eroding cliff faces farther north along the coast. In creating a sheltered harbor, the bank is essentially the reason Nelson was settled in the first place. You can easily reach it by car, driving 9 km (5½ mi) north of town and turning left into Boulder Bank Drive, then going another mile along a gravel road.

Wakefield Quay. The waterfront area along the quay has been developing steadily for the past few years, and now has several cafés, along with a promenade that incorporates a historic stone seawall built by 19th-century prisoners. A statue commemorates the arrival of the early European pioneers, and Sunderland Quay houses a memorial to local fishermen lost at sea (Nelson is New Zealand's chief fishing port). It's also the site of the annual Blessing of the Fleet in July. ⊕ *www. seafarerstrust.org.nz* for more information.

WHERE TO EAT

$$$
ECLECTIC
★

✕ **Boutereys.** Matt Bouterey brings his reputation with him to this nice spot in central Richmond. The fresh produce is either picked or dug from the Nelson region. Soft jazz playing and fabric panels to soften the open kitchen noise make for an enchanting experience. Locals come for the pan-seared scallops with pork belly and avocado salsa. Others come for the aged sirloin with kūmara and parsley flan with the wild mushroom ravioli. ✉ *251 Queen St., Richmond* ☎ *03/544–1114* ▭ *MC, V* ☺ *Bar opens at 4; dinner begins at 6. No lunch.*

$$$–$$$$
NEW ZEALAND

✕ **Café Affair.** This busy city restaurant is a favorite with both locals and travelers looking for a quick-but-substantial meal. Options range from a quick muffin or big cooked breakfast to full lunch and dinner menus. The locals go for the stone-grill meals, especially the big chunky fillet steaks and the lamb kebabs. The seafood grill is also a nice option. The central bar has been built from local river rock and big bifold doors open out to the street in summer. There are a few outdoor tables and the indoor seating is split over two levels, with several big comfy couches upstairs as well. ✉ *295 Trafalgar St.* ☎ *03/548–8295* ⌂ *Reservations essential* ▭ *AE, DC, MC, V.*

$$–$$$
ASIAN
★

✕ **Harry's Bar.** Although there's no sign of Hemingway here, this intimate bar and café is hidden down at the river end of Hardy Street. Once inside you'll find the vibe upbeat. Asian cuisine is the focus, but the menu also includes dishes like their famous chili salt squid; grilled white fish with green tea noodles; and a not-to-be-missed Kaffir lime tart for dessert. In the interests of quality, dishes are served as soon as they are cooked, not held till the whole table's order is ready. There's a hot selection of cocktails (try Harry's Houdini), and on Friday night the bar fills with locals, often overflowing onto the sidewalk on warm

8

evenings. ✉ *306 Hardy St.* ☎ *03/539–0905* ✉ *harrysbarnelson@xtra. co.nz* ⚓ *Reservations essential in summer* ▭ *AE, DC, MC, V* ⊗ *Closed Sun. and Mon. No lunch.*

$$$–$$$$ ✕**Hopgoods.** Locally recognized chef Kevin Hopgood dishes up
ECLECTIC expertly prepared fresh food at this city restaurant. In the café strip
Fodor'sChoice at the top of Trafalgar Street, you'll have to book ahead here because
★ it's the best spot around. Try the beef, always cooked to trfection with a hint of red, or the fresh fish, battered and served with a crisp green salad. The crispy duck is popular, too. The food is not overdressed contemporary cuisine but instead contains simply cooked fresh, natural (often organic) ingredients, enhanced with tasty dressings and jus. Kevin locally sources lots of goodies like the cheese, oil and saffron, and the drinks menu is unashamedly local. Service is attentive and discreet. ✉ *284 Trafalgar St.* ☎ *03/545–7191* ▭ *AE, DC, MC, V* ⊗ *Closed Sun. No lunch Mon.*

$–$$ ✕**Morrison Street Café.** With its pleasant outdoor terrace and open indoor
ECLECTIC space, this upbeat café has the best coffee in town. Along with a caffeine
★ fix, come for the bacon and eggs served on fresh *ciabatta* bread with pesto and hollandaise. Lunch and Light Bites menus serve tastes like kūmara rosti with salsa, Thai beef salad and the famous BLAT (bacon, lettuce, avocado, and tomato sandwich). Local art is on the walls and the menu changes seasonally, as does the wine list. There's a big selection of low-allergy dishes and a healthy kids' menu. ✉ *244 Hardy St.* ☎ *03/548–8110* ▭ *AE, DC, MC, V* ⊗ *No dinner.*

WHERE TO STAY

¢–$ 🏠 **Accents on the Park.** This guesthouse and backpackers lodge will spoil
★ you for all others. The grand old house in Trafalgar Square, just off the main street of Nelson, feels more like a small hotel than a typical hostel, with its rich brocade fabrics, strong colors, soundproofed rooms, and immaculate bathrooms with high-pressure showers. Rooms vary from en suite doubles with marble bathrooms and kitchenettes to dorm rooms; linen is provided. The balconies overlook the cathedral and its gardens. **Pros:** oh so close to town, a moment's walk to Trafalgar Street; lovely old Victorian building with garden walks just across the road; outdoor bar area and small bistro out the back. **Cons:** on a narrow street so pull around into the parking lot next door to unload; can't use your mobile in upstairs lounges after 9 PM; lots of stairs inside. ✉ *335 Trafalgar Sq.* ☎ *03/548–4335* ⊕ *www.accentsonthepark.com* ✉ *stay@ accentsonthepark.com* ⇲ *18 rooms, some en suites, 2 with bath, tent sites* ⚓ *In-room: No a/c, no phone, no TV (some). In-hotel: Restaurant, bar, laundry facilities, Wi-Fi* ▭ *MC, V.*

$$$–$$$$ 🏠 **Cambria House.** Built for a sea captain, this 1880s house, now a
★ B&B, mixes old and new, from the original fireplaces and matai and rimu paneling to the high-speed Internet access. The design pairs antiques with modern fabrics and conveniences. Each bedroom has an en suite bathroom with shower; the three luxury rooms also have a separate bathtub. You can settle in with coffee or a drink by the wood-burning fireplace or on the garden deck. The house is near the town center. **Pros:** elegant old house in leafy surroundings; close to the Mai-tai River and riverside walkway; easy walk to town and restaurants.

Accent on the Park Hotel, Nelson.

Cons: on an otherwise quiet suburban street; tight off-street parking when at capacity (but plenty of street parking). ✉ *7 Cambria St.* ☎ *03/548–4681* ⊕ *www.cambria.co.nz* ✉ *cambria@cambria.co.nz* ⤴ *6 rooms* △ *In-room: No a/c (some), Wi-Fi. In-hotel: Internet terminal, no-smoking rooms* ▭ *AE, MC, V* ⦿ *BP.*

$$ ⊡ **Delorenzo's Studio Apartments.** These reasonably priced self-contained studio apartments are a short walk from the city center, across the Maitai River Bridge. The decoration is rather neutral, but the spacious rooms have plenty of conveniences, including CD players and washer-dryers. There's also handy off-street parking. **Pros:** literally on the main street, these units are a moment's walk from restaurants, the cinema, and the riverside walk; well maintained and clean; dinner and breakfast are available but not included. **Cons:** a rather busy spot in summer; roadside units have some street noise; it's noisy when, several times a year, Trafalgar Park (across the road) has large events, so check when booking. ✉ *43–55 Trafalgar St.* ☎ *03/548–9774 or 0508/335-673* ⊕ *www.delorenzos.co.nz* ⤴ *25 suites* △ *In-room: Kitchen, DVD, Internet. In-hotel: Pool, laundry* ▭ *AE, DC, MC, V.*

$$ ⊡ **Joya.** This heavenly spot really encapsulates what Nelson is all about, with its focus on low-allergen materials, high eco-values, natural therapies, and wholesome food. Oh, and throw in some lovely hospitality and intelligent conversation and you'll get the idea. There's a B&B room and a studio unit in the main house and a delightful eco-friendly cottage in the garden, complete with its own water garden and turf roof. The cottage also has a wood burner for winter and has been fitted out with low-emission materials and natural fabrics and furnishings. Host Paulina works with Tomatis sound. This is a lovely place to stop a few days and recharge yourself. **Pros:** wide city views from the B&B room and main house; fresh seasonal fruit in the rooms; Paulina speaks English, French, German, and Dutch. **Cons:** extremely steep drive, so park on the street instead; garden pond to be aware of with little children. ⊠ *49 Brougham St. 7010* ☎ *03/539–1350* ⊕ *www.joya.co.nz* ⤴ *1 B&B room, 1 studio, 1 cottage* ♿ *In-room: No a/c, no phone, kitchen (some), DVD (some), Wi-Fi (some). In-hotel: Bicycles, laundry facilities* ⊟ *MC, V* ⏇ *CP.*

$$$ ⛏ **The Little Retreat.** Set above a wellness center in the middle of the city, this stylish retreat is designed to nurture and pamper you. Nelson is known for its holistic health scene and Angela, the owner of this little urban hideaway, is closely involved with this. The apartment is yours for your stay (and some stay for weeks), with a fully equipped kitchen and laundry, two decks (one with a barbecue) and contemporary furnishings and fabrics. It's a two-minute walk to the Trafalgar Street cafés and one minute to the cathedral. Angela's health center downstairs can provide you with various massage techniques, acupuncture, osteopathy, naturopathy, or shiatsu, for an all-round healthy stay. A breakfast hamper is provided. **Pros:** balcony overlooking Nile Street; room rate reduced for multiple nights; Internet by arrangement; tennis rackets and bikes available. **Cons:** busy mid-city location. ⊠ *Level 1, 22 Nile St. W* ☎ *03/545–1411* ⊕ *www.nelsongetaways.co.nz* ✉ *the.little.retreat@ xtra.co.nz* ⤴ *1 apartment* ♿ *In-hotel: Kitchen, DVD, laundry facilities* ⊟ *AE, MC, V* ⏇ *BP.*

$$$ ⛏ **Te Puna Wai Lodge.** The Fifeshire Suite, on the top floor of this 1857 three-story Victorian villa, must have the best view in Nelson, looking out over Tasman Bay, the Kahurangi mountains, Haulashore Island and the harbor. You won't want to drag yourself away for dinner as the sun drops low behind the western ranges and the sea and sky turn a deep red. Downstairs the Wakatu Room and Haulashore Apartment have more intimate views and their own garden and veranda entries. There are luxurious marble bathrooms in all rooms and the Haulashore has a full kitchen, equally well designed. The driveway is steep; it's better to park on the street, though that's just as steep. **Pros:** hosts Richard and James know all the good spots to eat at and visit in Nelson, and have an extensive collection of art and art books. **Cons:** particularly steep driveway; steep staircase to the Fifeshire Suite makes it unsuitable for those with limited mobility. ⊠ *24 Richardson St.,* ☎ *03/548–761* ⊕ *www.tepunawai.co.nz* ⤴ *2 suites, 1 apartment* ♿ *In-room: No a/c, safe, kitchen (some), Wi-Fi (some). In-hotel: Laundry service, Wi-Fi* ⊟ *AE, MC, V* ⏇ *BP.*

$$$$ ⛏ **Wakefield Quay House.** With just the road running between the front
★   door and the sea, Woodi and John Moore's graceful old villa has one of the best waterfront locations in town. Overlooking Haulashore Island and the harbor entrance, the rooms have dark *rimu*-wood floors and luxurious furnishings, and are decorated with local artwork and antique maritime memorabilia. Pure wool rugs and carpets warm the floors while heavy feather duvets warm the beds. A tasty local breakfast (fresh local eggs, juices, salmon, and freshly ground coffee) is served around the dining table; evening drinks and nibbles are served on the veranda,

if the weather is cooperating. Woodi and John's 34-foot yacht is generally on hand for an evening sail. **Pros:** 180-degree views of mountains and sea; watch the shipping through the channel from your room; easy walk to good waterfront restaurants. **Cons:** some road noise; limited off-street parking; two on-site cats (if that's a problem for you); bedrooms are both upstairs. ⊠ *385 Wakefield Quay* ☎ *03/546–7275* ⊕ *www.wakefieldquay.co.nz* ⇨ *2 rooms* ⟂ *In-room: No a/c, no phone, Wi-Fi. In-hotel: Laundry facilities, Internet terminal* ⊘ *Closed June–Aug.* ⊟ *MC, V* ⦿ *BP.*

NIGHTLIFE AND THE ARTS

Seventy years ago the first potters were drawn by the abundant clays in the hills of the hinterlands. Over the decades not only potters, but painters, ceramicists, glass-artists, and mixed-media practitioners have continued to enjoy the climate, colors, and inspiring light of the region. Several hundred artists now work in Nelson and Golden Bay and the locally published *Nelson Arts Guide* is at local visitor centers, bookshops, some hotels and cafés, and online. Check out ⊕ *www. nelsonarts.org.nz.*

The **Nelson School of Music** (⊠ *48 Nile St.* ☎ *03/548–9477* ⊕ *www.nsom. ac.nz*) hosts music performances, mostly local productions (and surprisingly good ones at that). In July, the school is the site of the annual **Winter Festival,** which brings in excellent musicians from elsewhere in New Zealand. A top music and performance event is the **Nelson Arts Festival** in October, likewise a magnet for top-notch Kiwi and international acts. Over the Christmas break, the city rocks to the annual **Jazz Festival,** much of which is held in local cafés and parks and in the streets. For the younger set, several late-night clubs and music spots are along **Bridge Street,** which change as venues and acts come and go. Take a wander along the street after 11 PM to check out the options, or grab a copy of the free *Passport* gig guide—it's available in many cafés. Stingray Bar (⊠ *Church La.,* ☎ *03/545–8957*) is a haunt for the not-quite-so-young set. The Vic's Brewbar (⊠ *281 Trafalgar St.,* ☎ *03/548–7631*) at the top of Trafalgar Street has live jazz on Tuesday nights and is known for a good steak. ⊠ *280 Hardy St.,* ☎ *03/548–1154.*

SHOPPING

More than 300 artists live around Nelson, working full or part-time in various media: ceramics, glassblowing, wood turning, fiber, sculpture, and painting. Not surprisingly there are 16 arts-and-crafts trails to follow, for which there is a brochure at the information center. There is also a colorful Saturday morning crafts market.

Walking through the door of the **Bead Gallery** (⊠ *18 Parere St.* ☎ *03/546– 7807 main store 03/548–4849 Hardy St. 03/541–0036 Richmond Mall* ⊕ *www.beads.co.nz*), you may be overwhelmed by the sheer number and range of beads around you. The owner gets his beads from all around the world, with a good selection of Pacific and New Zealand beads and pendants as well. *Paua* shell is big, and there are local greenstone beads and shells from distant islands, not to mention ceramic, wood, bone, porcelain, Swarovski crystal, semiprecious stone, bone,

An entertainer wows shoppers at the Nelson Saturday Market.

horn, porcelain, and glass beads from far-flung countries. You can put a strand together at a worktable or buy separate beads to take with you. They also have a retail gallery at 157 Hardy Street and another in the Richmond Mall.

The skilled craftspeople of the **Jens Hansen Contemporary Gold & Silver-smith** (⌗ *320 Trafalgar Sq.* ☏ *03/548–0640 or 021/299–3380* ⊕ *www.jenshansen.com*) create lovely gold and silver jewelry. Contemporary pieces are handmade at the workshop–showroom, and many are set with precious stones or *pounamu* (jade) from the West Coast of the South Island. But they may be best known as the jewelers who made the precious "One Ring" used in the *Lord of the Rings* film trilogy. There's an original prototype on display, and you can order a faithful replica. They will open by appointment outside regular work hours (summer, weekdays 9–5:30, Saturday 9–2, Sunday 10–1; winter, week-days 9–5, Saturday 9–2, closed Sunday); you can also preview or order merchandise on their Web site.

★ If you're in Nelson on a Saturday morning, head down to Montgomery Square off Trafalgar Street to the **Nelson Saturday Market**, held from 8 to 1. This market is one of the most successful in the country; it gained its reputation from the wealth of artists and craftspeople who sell their wares here. Now locals and visitors can rely on good bargains while wandering through the maze of stalls, browsing the fresh produce, handmade breads and cheeses, clothing, artwork, flowers, ceramics, and more. The 19th-century, two-story cottage of the **South Street Gallery** (⌗ *10 Nile St.* W ☏ *03/548–8117* ⊕ *www.nelsonpottery.co.nz*) overflows with ceramic art, sculpture, and housewares. The gallery represents 23

Nelson artisans, most with a national, if not international, reputation. Upstairs a number of West Coast artists display their work.

TOURS

ACTIVITY **Bay Tours Nelson** (☎ *03/548–6486* ⊕ *www.baytoursnelson.co.nz*) runs
TOURS daily half- and full-day tours of wine trails, arts-and-crafts tours, and scenic adventure tours by arrangement. Wine tours can include tastings, platters, or full lunches depending on your preference. Trips include the city and its immediate district and also go farther afield to the Marlborough wine region and scenic tours to Motueka and Kaiteriteri Beach and south to Nelson Lakes National Park. Art-and-craft tours of the Nelson areas are a highlight. Prices start at $78 and include all meals and tastings.

AROUND NELSON

Though Nelson's a bustling city, it retains a rural quality. With Tasman Bay before it and the foothills of the Bryant and Richmond ranges behind, open countryside and vineyards are within easy reach. State Highway 6 south from the city winds through the outlying suburb of Stoke and through to Richmond, a good-size neighboring town. The commercial and civic center of the Tasman District, Richmond, has a good library and a modest shopping mall—the only one in the region.

Just south of Richmond, State Highway 60 branches west off State Highway 6, heading toward Mapua, Motueka, and Golden Bay—all friendly rural backwaters. There's a wealth of vineyards along the coastal strip toward Motueka, plus idyllic farms, hop gardens, and craft galleries and serious art studios tucked into the many valleys that run inland. Follow the inland route through **Upper Moutere** on your return. If you carry on south without turning to Motueka look out for the Birth Place of Ernest Rutherford, on the right as you're leaving the small town of Brightwater. Just five minutes south of Richmond the elaborate, atom-shaped monument remembers this local boy's contribution to the world of nuclear science.

8

EXPLORING

Broadgreen is a fine example of a Victorian cob house. Cob houses, made from straw and horsehair bonded together with mud and clay, are common in Devon, the southern English home county of many of Nelson's pioneers. The house is furnished as it might have been in the 1850s, with a fine collection of textiles and quilts, including one of the oldest-known quilts in New Zealand. The backdrop of tall trees and large rose gardens completes the scene. ✉ *276 Nayland Rd., Stoke* ☎ *03/547–0403* 🖃 *$3* ◷ *Daily 10:30–4:30.*

★ One of the best galleries is the **Hoglund Art Glass Studio & Gallery.** From the collectible family of penguins to the bold platters and vases, Hoglund Art Glass is now sold internationally. The glass gallery and museum is open year-round. There are also glass-making classes available. ✉ *Lansdowne Rd., Richmond* ☎ *03/544–6500* ⊕ *www.hoglundartglass.com* 🖃 *No charge* ◷ *Daily 9–5.*

To dip into the local wine scene, drop by the **Grape Escape Complex** for tastings from two top wineries, Te Mania Estate and the organic Richmond Plains. Tastings are free for the wine of the month and 50¢ for all other wines. The complex also has several crafts galleries and an indoor-outdoor café. ⊠ *State Hwy. 60 and McShanes Rd.* ☎ *03/544–4054* ⊘ *Daily 9–5.*

Isel House, in the delightful tree-filled Isel Park in Stoke, was built for Thomas Marsden, one of the region's prosperous pioneers. It was Marsden who laid out the magnificent gardens surrounding the house, which include a towering California redwood and a 140-foot Monterey pine. The well-preserved stone house contains stories of Isel and its surroundings, interpreted in part by local artists; also original anecdotal material, family items, and a herbarium. ⊠ *Isel Park, Stoke* ☎ *03/547–1347* 🖃 *Donation* ⊘ *Sept.–Apr., Tues.–Sun. 11–4; May–Aug., by appointment.*

WINERIES

■**TIP**➔ Grab a wine trail brochure from the Information Centre in Nelson before heading out to find these wineries. Some are quite difficult to find although they are well signposted from the main roads.

Kahurangi Wine Estate, a successful winery that sits beside the main road in the idyllic little village of Upper Moutere, was first developed by Hermann Seifried in the 1970s as one of the area's first commercial vineyards. Now owned by Greg and Amanda Day, they have a good range of Rieslings and chardonnays and also a fine gewürztraminer. The cellar door is open 11 months of the year and has a range of imported wines and cognacs as well as Kahurangi's own wines. They also have a boutique vineyard cottage accommodation on the property ⊠ *Cnr Main and Sunrise Rds., Upper Moutere* ☎ *03/543–2980* ⊕ *www.kahurangiwine. com* ⊘ *Open daily 10:30–4:30, closed July.*

★ Despite its tiny size, **Neudorf Vineyard** has established an international reputation for its pinot noir and chardonnay, but riesling, pinot grigio, and sauvignon blanc are also highly regarded. Owners Tim and Judy Finn will gladly talk at length about local food and wine. The top wines wear the Moutere designation on the label, as the winery is in a valley surrounded by acres of vineyards and hop gardens. Artisan cheeses are served in summer, and they also stock olives, cheese, and oat crackers in their small deli. ⊠ *138 Neudorf Rd., Upper Moutere* ☎ *03/543–2643* ⊕ *www.neudorf.co.nz* ⊘ *Daily 10:30–4:30; closed weekends July and Aug.*

Seifried Estate is a 20-minute drive from Nelson's main center, on the way to Motueka. Hermann Seifried was one of Nelson's modern-day pioneer winemakers and he has gone on to open this busy complex. The large winery produces fresh, zippy sauvignon blanc, a creamy chardonnay, a decidedly tasty riesling, and a lush pinot noir. A restaurant next door to the tasting room is open every day for lunch in summer and Thursday to Sunday in winter; reservations are recommended. ⊠ *Redwood Rd., Appleby* ☎ *03/544–1555* ⊕ *www.seifried. co.nz* ⊘ *Wine shop open daily 10–5.*

Since 1997, **Waimea Estates** has been creating award-winning wines. The range includes sauvignon blanc, chardonnay, pinot grigio, riesling,

Around Nelson

Murchison

Kohatu Junction

Nelson Lakes National Park

Brightwater

Kahurangi National Park

Abel Tasman N.P.
see detail map

ARTHUR RANGE

Upper Moutere

Neudorf Vineyard

Harakeke

Kaiteriteri

Riwaka

Motueka

Port Motueka

JACKETT ISLAND

Tasman

Woollaston Estate

Kahurangi Wine Estate

Grape Escape Complex

Waimea Estates

Hope

Appleby

Seifried Estate

Mapua

Redwood Rd.

Moutere Hwy.

RABBIT ISLAND

Ruby Bay

Richmond

Queen St.

Hoglund Art Glass Studio + Gallery

Stoke

Broadgreen
Isel House

Nelson
see detail map

Boulder Bank

The Glen

Atawhai

Happy Valley Adventures

PEPIN ISLAND

Tasman Bay

Whangamoa Head

Delaware Bay

Cape Soucis

TO FRENCH PASS & D'URVILLE ISLAND

BRYANT RANGE

Rai Valley

TO PICTON & BLENHEIM

Pelorus Bridge Reserve

Pelorus River

Mount Richmond Forest Park

Waimea River

TO MARAHAU, GOLDEN BAY & TAKAKA

Moutea River

5 mi

5 km

rosé, pinot noir, and a cabernet-merlot blend. The well-crafted dessert wines and a funky "strawberries-and-cream" rosé are also worth trying. Their Café in the Vineyard is open for lunch daily, with a roaring fire in winter and outdoor jazz on sunny summer Sunday afternoons. They also run Meet the Winemaker Workshops at selected times where you can do some hands-on wine appreciation and tasting. The cellar door is open in conjunction with the café. ⊠ *22 Appleby Hwy., Appleby* ☎ *03/544–4963* ⊕ *www.waimeaestates.co.nz* ◷ *Wine tours and tastings by appointment. Café Oct.–Mar., daily 11–5; Apr.–Sept.,Thurs.–Sun. 11–4.*

The state-of-the-art, multilevel gravity-fed winery and gallery of **Woollaston Estate** sits on a quiet hillside in Mahana. In an area once known solely for apple production, the wines now being created from this district are maturing superbly. The gallery is beside the cellar door tasting area, and shows internationally acclaimed artists. The work of owner Phillip Woollaston's father, Toss, one of the country's best-known artists, is available to view on request. Woollaston produces pinot rosé (from 100% pinot noir grapes), sauvignon blanc, riesling, and pinot grigio, and their pinot noir has received special accolades. The extensive views over the mountains and Tasman Bay from the lawn suggest bringing a picnic, and tasting platters are available as well. It's also a venue for jazz, literature, and other cultural events on the Nelson festival circuit. ⊠ *School Rd., Mahana* ⊹ *Heading toward Motueka from Nelson, turn off coastal State Hwy. 60 at Dominion Rd., turn left into Old Coach Rd., then right into School Rd. The winery is on right opposite school* ☎ *03/543–2817* ⊕ *www.woollaston.co.nz* ◷ *Late Oct.–Easter, daily 11–4:30 and by arrangement.*

OUTDOOR ACTIVITIES

⟳ **Happy Valley Adventures—4WD Motorbikes and SkyWire.** There's fun at Happy Valley Adventures—4WD Motorbikes and SkyWire, and lots of it. Hop on a four-wheeled motorbike and go headlong up into the bush before breaking out 14 exciting km (8½ mi) later to see a wide-reaching view across Delaware Bay. If you're not happy driving a quad bike, then hop on as a passenger with someone else or take the 4WD van tour. They also do a Tour of Discovery with a local guide who explains the cultural and historical aspects of the land you cross, and who also demonstrates ancient crafts. There's the world's only Skywire, the longest flying fox in the world—a 10-minute, mile-long, high-wire ride that takes you zooming over the surrounding bush and chattering native birds. Or ride an Argo for a thrilling ride through water—and mud! ⊠ *194 Cable Bay Rd. (15-min drive north of Nelson)* ☎ *03/545–0304* ⊕ *www.happyvalleyadventures.co.nz.*

WHERE TO EAT AND STAY

The little town of Mapua has retained one nice area to eat; the area down by the wharf, at the far end of Aranui Street, has several small galleries, cafés, foodie stores, and a fish-and-chips shop. Apart from Mapua and a few outlying wineries, though, there are few restaurants in this area. There are, however, a number of B&Bs and boutique lodges for accommodations.

$$$
SEAFOOD
★

✕ **Smokehouse Café.** Don't try to resist stopping here. The menu is based around delicately hot-smoked products, not just fish but bacon, seafood, veggies, and chicken as well. There's also a "smoke-free" seasonal menu. You won't find a better lunch than their specialty platter piled with smoked whitefish, smoked salmon, mussels, and a sweet chili jam and pesto dipping sauce, all served with fresh, crusty home-baked bread. There are great views up the estuary from the café and across to the Richmond Ranges, often peaked with snow in winter. You can't miss the big, blue, corrugated iron building on the wharf. The café has slightly truncated hours from May through October. Last orders are taken around 8:30 PM. They also have a takeout fish-and-chips shop next door where you can buy their smoked products as well. ⊠ *Mapua Wharf* ☎ *03/540–2280* ⊕ *www.smokehouse.co.nz* ⌲ *Reservations essential in summer* ▭ *MC, V* ☾ *No dinner Mon. June–Sept.*

$$$$
★

🏠 **Bronte Country Estate.** Perched on the edge of the Waimea Estuary, this lodge (which is actually a number of villas and suites) gets you right down to the water. At high tide, the lawn outside the villas is lapped by the sea and at low tide you can walk out onto the sandflats. The villas are decorated with original works by well-known local artists. The 2-acre garden, which slopes down to the sea, is draped with flowering wisteria and shaded by tall trees. Should you be feeling competitive, you can play a game of *pétanque* (bocce) or tennis or take a swim in the heated pool. They also have their own small vineyard and winery next door. Also on-site is a two-bedroom luxury villa ($1,000 for two, fully hosted option). **Pros:** the Fraser family are excellent hosts with wide local knowledge; bird-watching opportunities on the sandflats; right in the heart of wine country. **Cons:** a 10-minute drive to restaurants in Mapua and Richmond; kids not encouraged except in the luxury villa. ⊠ *Bronte Rd. E off State Hwy. 60* ☎ *03/540–2422* ⊕ *www. brontecountryestate.co.nz* ⇆ *2 villas, 2 suites, 1 luxury cottage* ⌂ *Inroom: No a/c, kitchen, DVD. In-hotel: Tennis court, pool, water sports, bicycles, laundry service, Wi-Fi* ☾ *June–Sept.* ▭ *MC, V* ⊧⏐ *BP.*

$$–$$$

🏠 **Matahua Cottages.** Both Miro and Karaka cottages are nestled against the shoreline of the Waimea Estuary, but they are separated by high plantings for privacy. Both began life as apple pickers' cottages and have been refurbished in a pleasing rustic style to suit. Each has a full kitchen, ample decks and a wood fire, and a breakfast hamper is available. Karaka has an outdoor bath on a private deck overlooking the estuary. The area was an important food-gathering place for early Māori, with Matahua meaning "peninsula of abundance." The property represents excellent value for its stunning location, where you can wander the foreshore or do some bird-watching. Take a walk over the 5-acre organic farm and vineyard. **Pros:** intimate waterfront setting and views; fresh farm eggs and fruit when available; filter coffeemaker in the kitchen **Cons:** minimum two-night stay; distant road noise from the nearby highway; there is no curtain on the glass door in the Karaka cottage bathroom, so dare to be bold! ⊠ *Apple Valley Rd. E, Mapua* ☎ *03/540–2214* ⊕ *www.matahuacottages.co.nz* ⇆ *1 1-bedroom cottage, 1 2-bedroom cottage* ⌂ *In-room: No a/c, no phone, kitchen, DVD, Wi-Fi. In-hotel: Water sports, laundry facilities.* ▭ *MC, V.*

8

SHOPPING

Built in an old apple cool store (where apples were stored at cool temperatures after being picked), the funky **Cool Store Gallery** has reasonably priced art and craft work. Much of the work has a vibrant Pacific theme, produced by artists from the Nelson and West Coast regions; paintings, sculpture, textiles, *paua*-shell items, ceramics, glasswork, and jewelry line the walls. They have an arrangement with a local shipping company to get hard-to-travel-with purchases home for you in one piece. ⊠ *7 Aranui Rd., Mapua* ☎ *03/540-3778* ⊕ *www.coolstoregallery.co.nz* ⊗ *Daily 10–5 in summer, Thurs.–Sun. 11–4 in winter.*

MOTUEKA

50 km (31 mi) west of Nelson.

Motueka (mo-too-*eh*-ka) is an agricultural center—hops, kiwifruit, and apples are among its staples. The town sits at the seaward end of the Motueka Valley, under the ranges of the Kahurangi National Park. Like Golden Bay, Motueka is a stronghold for the "alternative" communities around Nelson, and every byway seems to have a few artisans and erstwhile hippies living side by side with the traditional farming families. The hinterland is now also laced with small, well-to-do farms often owned by absentee overseas owners. Most of the good cafés and places to stay are outside the town center, either in the sheltered inland valleys or out along the Abel Tasman coast and nearby bays. South of town, for instance, the Motueka River valley is internationally known for its trout fishing. Motueka's also a good jumping-off point for Abel Tasman National Park, just north of town.

GETTING HERE AND AROUND

Motueka is a 50-minute drive west of Nelson, on State Highway 60. You can also arrive from the south along the Motueka Valley Highway, which leaves State Highway 6 at Kohatu, 50 minutes south of Nelson. From Motueka it's a one-hour drive over the Takaka Hill to Golden Bay.

Abel Tasman Coachlines and Southern Link K Bus run the smaller routes from Nelson to Motueka, Takaka, and the Abel Tasman and Kahurangi national parks. These cut their service frequency in winter, or stop altogether.

ESSENTIALS

Bus Contacts **Abel Tasman Coachlines** (☎ *03/548-0285* ⊕ *www. abeltasmantravel.co.nz*) **Southern Link K Bus** (☎ *03/358-8355 or 0508/ 458-835* ⊕ *www.southernlinkcoaches.co.nz*).

Visitor Information **Motueka Visitor Information Centre** (⊠ *Wallace St.* ☎ *03/528-6543* ⊕ *www.abeltasmangreenrush.co.nz* ⊗ *info@motuekaisite.co.nz*).

OUTDOOR ACTIVITIES

You won't lack for places to land some whopping brown trout. Fishing season here runs from October to April. Fly-fishing excursions to local rivers and remote backcountry areas, involving hiking or helicopter trips, give plenty of excitement to visiting anglers. Daily guiding rates are generally around $780 per day and include lunches, drinks, and

4WD transportation. Best areas to base yourself for trout fishing around Nelson Lakes are: St. Arnaud, Motueka, Murchison, and Nelson city itself. Tony Entwistle and Zane Mirfin run **Strike Adventure** (☎ *03/541–0020* ✉ *fish@strikeadventure.com* ⊕ *www.strikeadventure.com*), the only guiding company in the northern South Island to hold all commercial access permits to crown lands, offering plenty of opportunities in some amazing locations.

WHERE TO EAT AND STAY

$–$$

CAFÉ

✕ **Jester House.** This funky place is as much fun as the name suggests, and is a great spot to bring the kids. The café was rebuilt in 2006 in an eco-friendly style, echoing the owners' feelings about a sustainable environment. The food is all made on the premises and ranges from hearty country fare like soups and quiche to more substantial meals like garlic mussels and panfried fish (their signature dish). In addition to cozy indoor seating, tables are dotted through the garden and on a sunny veranda. For the kids there's a small playground, an enchanted forest, an outdoor chess set, and some extremely tame eels that can be hand-fed (September–May). When the Ruby Bay bypass opens you will have to reach this café by leaving the highway and following the Ruby Bay Scenic Drive. ■TIP➔ Down in the back garden, the Boot B&B has comfy accommodations for couples. ⊠ *Coastal Hwy., Tasman* ☎ *03/526–6742* ⊕ *www.jesterhouse.co.nz* ▭ *MC, V* ☉ *Closed July, Aug. and Mon.–Thurs. May–Sept. No dinner.*

$$–$$$

ECLECTIC

✕ **Riverside Café.** Riverside was initially established as a community for conscientious objectors during the 1940s. Its café is now the hot place to eat around Motueka. In an old cottage, the café is decorated with hand-worked wood, copper and fabric art, and enclosed with a grape-shaded veranda. The menu is built around organic foods from the community's own gardens and nearby suppliers. Choices range from stylish restaurant fare to pizza and fries; desserts often include delights like chocolate and chili ice cream and spicy apple pie. ⊠ *Inland Moutere Hwy., 5 min south of Motueka toward Upper Moutere* ☎ *03/526–7447* ▭ *MC, V* ☉ *Closed Mon. Nov.–Apr.; closed May–Oct.*

$$$

CAFÉ

✕ **Up the Garden Path.** This pleasant lunch spot is right on the main road into Motueka. Surrounded by a leafy garden and lots of local art it's a bright vibrant place, and exudes a really restful feeling. This good spot for a quick-stop lunch has a robust range of pizzas, pasta, and salads off the menu and some tasty cabinet food as well. Try the Nelson scallops in a tempura batter or the tasty souvlaki made with premium lamb fillet. There's a gallery of local art inside and space for the kids to run off a bit of steam outside. ⊠ *473 High St.* ☎ *03/528–9588* ⊕ *www.upthegardenpath.co.nz* ▭ *MC, V.*

$$–$$$

🏠 **Coastal Palms Apartments.** Just a few minutes' drive from the center of town, two of these three lovely apartments overlook the sea off Port Motueka. They're a perfect spot to base yourself while exploring the region, especially if you're not necessarily concentrating on the Abel Tasman Park area. The third apartment is suitable for families and has a private courtyard. **Pros:** book the appropriately named Seaview studio (or the Bayview if it is taken); kayaks, bikes, and a dinghy are available for use; sunrise over the sea is memorable. **Cons:** the seafront is tidal sandflats rather than ocean front; the family unit has smaller rooms and no view; only Seaview apartment has easy stairway access. ✉ *95 Trewavas St., Motueka* ☎ *03/528–0166* ⊕ *www.coastalpalms. co.nz* ⤵ *2 apartments, 1 studio* ♿ *In-room: No a/c, no phone, kitchen, DVD (some), Wi-Fi* ⊟ *MC, V* ⊘ *Closed May–Oct.* ⦿*BP*

$$ 🏨 **Kairuru Farmstay Cottages.** Halfway up the Takaka Hill from Motueka, ♻ with distant views to the Abel Tasman coast, these homey cottages have all you need for a comfy stay in the country. The timber interiors and wooden verandas have a rustic appeal while the dishwasher and modern kitchen take the hard work out of your day. There's room here for the kids to run wild, with sheep, goats, and cattle to pet. Your stay can be either fully self-catered, or with breakfast or dinner provided. It's within easy reach of Golden Bay, Motueka, and the Abel Tasman area, and there are opportunities to go out on the farm with Dave—just ask when you arrive. The Canaan Cottage, farther up the hill, is a remote colonial cottage. **Pros:** Wi-fi available. **Cons:** a steep 15-minute drive up the Takaka Hill from Riwaka; long, narrow driveway onto the farm, but quite suitable for rental cars. ✉ *1014 State Hwy. 60, Takaka Hill* ☎ *03/528–8091* ⊕ *www.kairurufarmstay. co.nz* ⤵ *3 cottages* ♿ *In-room: No a/c, kitchen, DVD In-hotel: Laundry facilities* ⊟ *MC, V.*

$$$$ 🏨 **Motueka River Lodge.** Tranquillity, marvelous scenery, and a superb ★ standard of comfort are the hallmarks here. The lodge is on 35 acres overlooking the Motueka River, with magnificent mountain views. Its sunny deck, vine-covered archways, and fragrant lavender hedges give the place a Mediterranean quality. The interior of the rustic house is accented with antiques from around the world. You can hike the national parks nearby, but the lodge's specialty is fishing, especially dry fly-fishing for brown trout in the wild river country. Great cuisine is prepared by resident chef Angela Bone. Bookings are essential during the October to April fishing season. **Pros:** all meals included in the rate including a four-course dinner; fully stocked wine cellar. **Cons:** 25% surcharge on NZ public holidays; 50-minute drive from Nelson airport. ✉ *Motueka Valley Hwy. (State Hwy. 61), Motueka* ☎ *03/526–8668* ⊕ *www.motuekalodge.com* ✍ *enquiries@motuekalodge.com* ⤵ *5 rooms* ♿ *In-room: No a/c, no phone, Internet. In-hotel: Restaurant, bar, tennis court, spa* ⊟ *AE, DC, MC, V* ⦿*MAP.*

EN ROUTE
If you are headed for the West Coast from Motueka, turn south onto Highway 61 at the Rothmans Clock Tower in Motueka, following the sign to Murchison. The road snakes through the **Motueka Valley** alongside the Motueka River, with the green valley walls pressing close alongside. If this river could talk, it would probably scream, "Trout!" After the town of Tapawera, turn south on State Highway 6 at Kohatu and continue to the West Coast.

ABEL TASMAN NATIONAL PARK

77 km (48 mi) northwest of Motueka, 110 km (69 mi) northwest of Nelson.

GETTING HERE AND AROUND

The drive to the Abel Tasman area from Motueka is just 15 minutes. Tour boats leave from Kaiteriteri and Marahau—turn hard right off State Highway 60 just after Riwaka, at the base of the Takaka Hill, to reach Kaiteriteri. Turn left at the same intersection to reach Marahau, but then take an immediate right over the Marahau Hill to Marahau. Walking access to the park is from Marahau. Take care driving on frosty winter mornings, as some corners stay frozen into the day.

Abel Tasman Coachlines service the Abel Tasman Park from Nelson and Motueka. Many tour operators provide transfers as well.

Abel Tasman Information is in the Abel Tasman Centre on the Marahau waterfront.

ESSENTIALS

Bus Contacts Abel Tasman Coachline (☎ 03/548–0285 ⊕ www. abeltasmantravel.co.nz).

Tour Information Abel Tasman Wilson's Experiences (✉ 265 High St., Motueka ☎ 03/528–2027 or 0800/223–582 ✐ info@AbelTasman.co.nz ⊕ www.abeltasman.co.nz).

Bush & Beyond (☎ 03/528–9058 ⊕ www.bushandbeyond.co.nz).

Visitor Information Abel Tasman Centre (☎ 03/527–8176 ⊕ www. abeltasmancentre.co.nz). **Department of Conservation Motueka** (✉ Corner King Edward and High Sts., Motueka ☎ 03/528–1811 ⊕ www.doc.govt.nz/explore).

EXPLORING

Abel Tasman National Park is a stunning-yet-accessible swath of idyllic beaches backed by a rugged hinterland of native beech forests, granite gorges, and waterfalls. Unlike many of New Zealand's national parks, Abel Tasman has few serious challenges in its climate or terrain, making it a perfect place for an outdoor day trip.

Remember this area is one of the most highly visited spots in the country and you will rarely find yourselves on that dream (read: deserted) beach with nobody else in sight. If you're a die-hard outdoor enthusiast craving peace and quiet and isolation you may want to explore a less busy spot like the Kahurangi or Nelson Lakes national parks. Having said that, Abel Tasman is still an easy, accessible place to wander the coast and paddle through clear green water for hours at a stretch.

★ The approach to **Kaiteriteri Beach** is notably lovely, and the beach is one of New Zealand's prettier ones, with its curve of golden sand, rocky islets offshore, and deep clear water. This place is packed in mid-summer, but once the six-week Christmas rush is over, the area returns to its usual quiet. Farther on, the small town of **Marahau** is the gateway to the national park. There's an interpretation board posted near the park café, but you may want to stop by the Department of

8

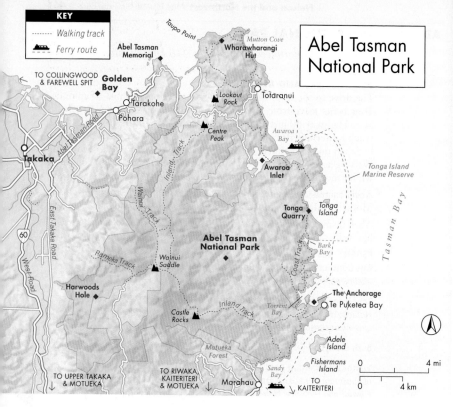

KEY
········· Walking track
▲▬▬ Ferry route

Abel Tasman National Park

Taupo Point

Mutton Cove

Wharawharangi Hut

Abel Tasman Memorial

TO COLLINGWOOD & FAREWELL SPIT

Golden Bay

Tarakohe

Pohara

Lookout Rock

Totaranui

Centre Peak

Awaroa Bay

Tonga Island Marine Reserve

Takaka

60

Inland Track

Wainui Track

Awaroa Inlet

Tonga Quarry

Tonga Island

East Takaka Road

West Road

Rameka Track

Abel Tasman National Park

Wainui Saddle

Coast Track

Bark Bay

Harwoods Hole

Castle Rocks

Inland Track

Torrent Bay

The Anchorage
Te Puketea Bay

Adele Island

Motueka Forest

Sandy Bay

Fishermans Island

0   4 mi

TO UPPER TAKAKA & MOTUEKA

TO RIWAKA, KAITERITERI & MOTUEKA

Marahau

TO KAITERITERI

0   4 km

Conservation (DOC) office in Motueka to get maps. If you're planning to use the DOC huts, you'll need to pick up hut tickets, if you haven't already booked online. Bookings are essential most of the year. The park has excellent hiking, sailing, and sea-kayaking opportunities— and water taxis service the coves (⇨ *Outdoor Activities, below*). Mid-summer, from December to February, is the peak tourist season here, so plan ahead if you'll be visiting then. If you only have a short time, wander along Marahau Beach at low tide; it's a quiet gentle place but stay below the high-tide line so as not to disturb nesting seabirds. Or walk just the first hour or so of the Abel Tasman Track, to Apple Tree Bay or Coquille Bay.

OUTDOOR ACTIVITIES

HIKING Abel Tasman has a number of walking trails, with road access from both Totaranui and Wainui at its north end and Marahau in the south. Shuttles and water taxis can take you to the trailheads or pick you up afterward. The tracks and conditions aren't too grueling, but conditions can change quickly, especially in winter. Carry bottled water, as only some sites have treated water available, and bring warm clothing, food, and sun and insect protection. The sand flies can be voracious. The **Department of Conservation offices** provide trail maps.

The most popular hike is the three- to five-day **Abel Tasman Coast Track**, open year-round. Much of the track's popularity is because of its relatively easy terrain and short distances. Launches and water taxis will drop off and pick up hikers from several points along the track, allowing walks from 2½ hours to five days. There are four huts and 21 campsites along the Coast Track, and spaces in both must be booked year-round. Bookings can be made online or through selected DOC offices or agents. The Nelson Visitors Centre also has more information (⇨ *See Nelson essentials*). For help with bookings contact **Great Walks Helpdesk** (☏ *03/546–8210* ⊕ *www.doc.govt.nz* ✍ *greatwalksbooking@ doc.govt.nz*).

Abel Tasman Wilson's Experiences are the original operators of day excursions to this park. They run day trips from three to eight hours, including bushwalks, trips to beaches, launch cruises, and sea kayaking. They also run one- to five-day hiking or hiking-kayaking treks around the park with overnight accommodations provided in lodges. ✉ *265 High St., Motueka* ☏ *03/528–2027 or 0800/223–582* ⊕ *www. abeltasman.co.nz*.

If you'd like a day in the park without breaking a sweat, call up **Abel Tasman Sailing**. Their three large catamarans sail daily into the heart of the park from Kaiteriteri Beach. On the way you stop at Split Apple Rock before heading off to swim at a gorgeous beach such as the Anchorage, where the water is a translucent green. You can also view a colony of fur seals up close. A day trip costs $160, including lunch, hot and cold drinks, and pickup. A range of sailing and walking options are available from $80. Advance reservations are not always necessary. It's closed June–August. ☏ *03/527–8375 or 0800/467–245* ✍ *info@sailingadventures.co.nz* ⊕ *www.sailingadventures.co.nz*.

The **Sea Kayak Company** leads a range of guided kayaking options through the pristine waters of the national park to beaches and campsites often inaccessible to hikers. These include the "Ab-Fab" one-day kayak and walk trip ($185), a two-day "More than Beaches" tour ($350), and three- and five-day tours ($530 and $950, respectively). All tours are fully catered and all equipment is supplied. Reservations are recommended at least three weeks in advance. Closed June to September. ✉ *506 High St., Motueka* ☏ *03/528–7251 or 0508/252–925* ✍ *info@seakayaknz.co.nz* ⊕ *www.seakayaknz.co.nz*.

WHERE TO STAY

$$–$$$ ⊡ **Abel Tasman Marahau Lodge.** With Abel Tasman National Park 200 yards in one direction and the Marahau beach 200 yards in the other, this location is hard to resist. The boutique lodge has spacious self-contained chalets, clustered in groups of two or four with native gardens between them. Units are finished in natural wood and have high cathedral ceilings opening to the view, New Zealand wool carpets, queen- or king-size beds, and balconies. Room-service breakfasts, prepared packed lunches, and a communal kitchen are available. Staff can help make reservations for sea kayaking, water taxis, seal swims, and hiking. The lodge has a good eco-rating, and fresh vegetables from the garden available when in season. **Pros:** close to everything in Marahau; travelers share tales in

8

DID YOU KNOW?

Abel Tasman National Park is New Zealand's smallest, but that doesn't stop people from coming. The golden sand beaches, estuaries, and fascinating rock formations (mainly granite) dazzle visitors to the area.

CLOSE UP

Farewell Spit

A 35-km (22-mi) protected sand-bar with a 19th-century lighthouse, Farewell Spit is renowned for its tremendous seabird population. A trip with **Farewell Spit Eco Tours** (⊠ *8 Tasman St., Collingwood* ☎ *03/524–8257 or 0800/808–257* ⊕ *www.farewellspit.com*) is a must if you are in Golden Bay. Each of the three tour itineraries takes you out along the Farewell Spit; one tour will take you to a gannet colony. The company is the only one with a DOC license to visit the gannets. Another takes you out to the lighthouse and windswept dunes

on the seaward end of the spit and the third visits the lighthouse, Fossil Point and Cape Farewell. Costs run between $110 and $135; reservations are essential. You could also saddle up with **Cape Farewell Horse Treks** (⊠ *Wharariki Beach Rd., Puponga* ☎ *03/524–8031* ⊕ *www.horsetreksnz.com*) ; this outfit provides some of the best horse trekking in the country, with spectacular beaches and wild views. For the best views, ride the Old Man Range trek ($120) or try the Puponga Beach ride ($60) for something more sedate.

the communal kitchen; nice, not-too-flashy accommodations overlooking the bush-covered hills of the Abel Tasman Park. **Cons:** no breakfast in the room rate; studios don't have kitchen facilities. ⊠ *Marahau Beach Rd Motueka* ☎ *03/527–8250* ✎ *robyn@abeltasmanmarahaulodge.co.nz* ⊕ *www.abeltasmanmarahaulodge.co.nz* ↰ *12 rooms* ♿ *In-room: No a/c, kitchen (some), Wi-Fi. In-hotel: Spa, laundry facilities* ☽ *Closed June and July* ▤ *MC, V.*

$$–$$$ ⊡ **Kimi Ora Spa Resort.** Kimi Ora means "seek health" in Māori. The developer was set on creating an environmentally friendly resort, including a restaurant (not always open so call first) serving as much organic food as possible, and various activities and therapies relating to holistic health. For all the pampering, the overall vibe is low-key. The guest rooms have cozy wood walls and simple furnishings. **Pros:** bordered by a mix of exotic forest and regenerating native bush; all the rooms have a distant sea view; as much a health resort as a holiday spot so come for a few days and recharge your batteries; some rooms have a whirlpool bath on the deck. **Cons:** 10-minute walk to Kaiteriteri beach. ⊠ *Martins Farm Rd., Kaiteriteri* ☎ *03/527–8027 or 0508/5464–672* ⊕ *www.kimiora.com* ↰ *22 units* ♿ *In-room: No a/c (some), kitchen (some), DVD. In-hotel: Pool, gym, spa, bicycles, no-smoking rooms* ▤ *MC, V* ⊠⊡ *BP.*

$$$$ ⊡ **The Resurgence.** Named for the resurgence of the nearby Riwaka River this superb eco-lodge sits snugly under the Takaka Hill seemingly as far from civilization as possible. Yet you're only 20 minutes from Kaiteriteri and 30 minutes from Motueka. Surrounded by regenerating native forest and stunning views the lodge is built of local timbers, using sustainable methods, and has every luxury. Accommodations are in free-standing bush chalets and villas, with four lodge rooms in the main house. Hosts Clare and Peter have a great love of the natural environment and there are some fabulous conversations at predinner drinks or the delicious table d'hôte dinner to follow. Babies under 12 months

8

are welcomed, but children ages 1–18 are not allowed. **Pros:** accommodations are either B&B or with dinner ($75 per person); massage and therapeutic treatments available; bring home a steak and cook on the barbecue out on your deck. **Cons:** long, winding, sealed driveway which is quite narrow and steep in places; villas and chalets are away from the main house, with gravel walks between; parking and turning at the main house is quite tight; generally a two-night minimum stay required. ⊠ *Riwaka Valley Rd., Riwaka* ☎ *03/528–4664* ⊕ *www.resurgence. co.nz* ⤴ *4 lodge rooms, 3 chalets, 3 villas* △ *In-room: No a/c, kitchen (some), no TV, Internet. In-hotel: Pool, spa, bicycles, laundry service, Wi-Fi, no kids under 18, no-smoking rooms* ⊟ *MC, V* ⊗ *Closed May to Sept.* ⦿ *CP, MAP.*

GOLDEN BAY AND TAKAKA

55 km (35 mi) northwest of Motueka, 110 km (70 mi) west of Nelson.

The gorgeous stretch of coastline that begins at Separation Point and runs westward past Takaka is known as **Golden Bay**, named for the gold discovered there in the 1850s. Alternating sandy and rocky shores curve up to the sands of Farewell Spit, the arcing prong that encloses the bay. Other than a 19th-century lighthouse, the spit is pure raw nature. Fault lines slash the cliffs, and the area is a favorite for all kinds of birds. Dutch navigator Abel Tasman anchored here briefly a few days before Christmas 1642. His visit ended abruptly when four of his crew were killed by the then-resident Māori iwi (tribe), Ngāti Tumata Kokiri. Bitterly disappointed, Tasman named the place Moordenaers, or Murderers' Bay, and sailed away without ever setting foot on New Zealand soil. Golden Bay is a delight—a sunny, 40-km (25-mi) crescent with a relaxed crew of locals who firmly believe they live in paradise.

The lifestyle here has always been considered "alternative"—a hideout for hippies, musicians, and artists. But it's also the center of a rich dairy farming area, and its warm, sheltered climate nurtures crops such as citrus, avocados, and kiwifruit that struggle on the colder, Nelson side of "the hill." Overseas buyers have been snapping up Golden Bay properties to get their own little part-time spot of paradise, but local bylaws are changing to encourage full-time residents back to the bay.

GETTING HERE AND AROUND

Capital Air flies scheduled flights from Wellington to Takaka, September–April, and will fly charter on demand all year. It also flies on demand to the southern end of the Heaphy Track and the Abel Tasman Park.

There's only one road into Golden Bay, over the Takaka Hill on State Highway 60—a spectacular hill road, which rises up 2,500 feet before plunging again to sea level to the tiny township of Takaka, a jumping-off point for Farewell Spit, Kahurangi National Park, and the Heaphy Track. This road is a 40-minute climb of twisting corners, steep drop-offs, and occasional passing bays, but don't be tempted to check the views while you're driving. Wait until you reach Bob's Lookout, on the

Nelson side of the hill, and Harwood Lookout, on the Takaka side, for safe viewings.

Golden Bay begs to be explored, so if you take the trouble to cross the Takaka hill into this spectacular area, plan to stay at least two nights or you'll spend your whole time driving and none enjoying the rewards of your travels. Abel Tasman Coachlines run daily services to Takaka, the Heaphy Track and Totaranui.

ESSENTIALS

Airline Contacts Capital Air (☎ *03/525-8725* ⊕ *www.capitalair.co.nz*).

Bus Contacts Abel Tasman Coachlines (☎ *03/548-0285* ⊕ *www. abeltasmantravel.co.nz*).

Visitor Information Golden Bay Visitor Information Centre (✉ *Willow St., Takaka* ☎ *03/525-9136* ✉ *gb.vin@nelsonnz.com* ⊕ *www.nelsonnz.com*). **Department of Conservation** (✉ *62 Commercial S., Takaka* ☎ *03/525-8444* ✉ *goldenbayao@doc.govt.nz* ⊕ *www.doc.govt.nz*).

EXPLORING

Eight kilometers (5 mi) west of Takaka is Te **Waikoropupu Springs,** known locally as Pupu Springs. This is the largest spring system in the Southern Hemisphere, and clear cold water bubbles into the Wai-koropupu Valley after traveling underground from its source at the nearby Takaka Hill. The clarity of this water is second only to the Weddell Sea in Antarctica. Swimming is not allowed because of the effect swimmers have on the delicate flora within the springs. In 2006 scuba diving was prohibited due to the risk of spreading didymo, an invasive exotic algae, so leave your swimsuits and dive gear in the car. Instead, grab your shoes and take a leisurely stroll around the valley on the 90-minute Pupu Walkway. Go quietly—the better to spot *tūī,* bellbirds, wood pigeons, and other birdlife. The turnoff from State Highway 60 at the Waitapu River is signposted.

After winding past several small farming districts and beach communities such as Paton's Rock, Onekaka, and Tukurua, State Highway 60 arrives at **Collingwood,** a small seaside village at the mouth of the giant Aorere River, 26 km (16 mi) west of Takaka. The earliest European settlers came here in the 1840s to build small ships from the timber lining the beaches and to farm the fertile river plains that spill out of the surrounding mountains. In the 1850s, gold was discovered nearby and Collingwood became a thriving port-of-entry town; at one time it was even under consideration to be the country's capital.

Collingwood is the northern access point for the Heaphy Track and a good base for trips to Farewell Spit and the West Coast beaches. The old 1910 council office building houses the small **Collingwood Museum,** which has a good photographic record of the area's past; next door the Aorere Centre also has some interesting history displays. You can make a sweet stop by **Rosy Glow Chocolates** on Beach Road or buy a gift at **Living Light Candles** (closed Monday) on Tukurua Road, back toward Takaka a short way.

OUTDOOR ACTIVITIES

BEACHES   Golden Bay has miles of swimming beaches. **Ligar Bay and Tata Beach** are two of the best near Takaka.

★   Out near Farewell Spit and less suitable for swimming, but with spectacular coastal landscapes, is **Wharariki Beach.** Among the massive sand dunes you're likely to come across sunbathing fur seals. If you get too close to them, they might charge or even bite, so keep a 30-foot distance, and never get between a seal and the sea. To get here, drive past Collingwood to Pakawau and follow the signs. Go as far as the road will take you, and then walk over farmland on a well-defined track for 20 minutes. The beaches along this coast are quite remote and have no lifeguards. Allow at least an hour for the return trip.

> ### ENCHANTED FOREST
>
> The Grove is a small patch of native forest at Rocklands, on the road from Takaka to Pohara, that escaped development when the area was cleared for farming. It is an enchanting collection of giant *rata*, elegant *nikau* palms, and trailing vines. Adding to the magic is the fact they are all growing between and over gnarly limestone outcrops and gulches. In early summer the *rata* wear a cloak of bright scarlet flowers. It's a 10-minute walk each way from the parking lot. Heading towards Pohara from Takaka, turn right off Abel Tasman Drive at Clifton. Follow the signs to The Grove; its not far.

If spending the day on a boat feeling wretched and seasick has no appeal, then try the fishing at **Anatoki Salmon,** a working salmon farm next to the river of the same name. This excellent spot is just 10 minutes out of Takaka, on the edge of the Kahurangi Park. You can fish for salmon then have it cooked and prepared while you wait. Entry is free; just pay for what you catch. Fishing gear is provided, and no experience necessary. Bring a picnic and the kids, and call it a day. ⊠ *McCallums Rd., Anatoki Valley* ☎ *03/525–7241* ⊕ *www.anatokisalmon.co.nz* ✉ *Free* ☾ *Daily 9–4:30.*

WHERE TO EAT

$$$ ✕ **The Brigand.** This day-night bar and café is in a lovely old house on the
NEW ZEALAND   main street and has a sunny courtyard, handmade furniture, and plenty of indoor seating. The menu provides NZ faves like the sticky pork spare ribs and a seafood medley of calamari, white fish, and steamed mussels in a cream sauce; the lamb and steak dishes are always changing and there are some vegetarian options. The restaurant roasts and serves its own Tuatara Coffee. There's live music several nights a week including an Open Mic Night every Thursday. ⊠ *90 Commercial St., Takaka* ☎ *03/525–9636* ⊕ *www.brigand.co.nz* ▭ *MC, V.*

$$–$$$ ✕ **Courthouse Cafe.** In the old Collingwood Courthouse on the main
NEW ZEALAND   crossroads into town, this laid-back café makes good use of local foods like smoked Anatoki salmon, organic sausage, and free-range eggs and local wines. The Spanish-style cockle soup infused with saffron and lime is worth stopping for, and the coffee is better than average. There are indoor and outdoor tables, but it gets packed in the summer. ⊠ *Corner Gibbs Rd. and Elizabeth St., Collingwood* ☎ *03/524–8025 Reservations essential in summer* ▭ *MC, V* ☾ *Days vary so call ahead.*

$$$
NEW ZEALAND

✕ **Mussel Inn.** If you want to experience a quintessential slice of Golden Bay life, swing by this place. Locals come for the live music (usually several evenings a week and more in summer, starting around 8:30 PM), a bowl of mussel chowder, or some fresh, steamed mussels, and some house-brewed beer. A favorite is the famous Captain Cooker manuka beer. There's plenty of other, nonseafood options, too. The design is woolshed chic, self-described as "Kiwi woolshed meets Aussie farmhouse," which seems an apt description. Rough sawn timbers, corrugated iron, an outdoor fire pit, and leafy trees complete the rustic look. ⊠ *State Hwy. 60, Onekaka* ☎ *03/525–9241* ⚏ *Reservations not accepted* ▭ *MC, V* ☺ *Closed late July–early Sept.*

$$$
NEW ZEALAND

✕ **The Naked Possum.** If you don't feel like you've quite hit the heart of backcountry Golden Bay then this place might just do it. Here you can sit on the veranda and look across forest-clad hills, or down by the huge outdoor fire if there's a chill about. The well-presented food is excellent, with a definite wild edge to it—try the rabbit-and-potato or venison-and-mushroom pies, the paua patties or the goat burger. There's also a pleasant bushwalk (the start of the Kaituna Track), and an on-site tannery and possum product retail shop. Service isn't quick here so take your time; enjoy the bush. ⊠ *Carter Rd., Kaituna River* ☎ *03/524–8433* ⊕ *www.thenakedpossum.co.nz* ▭ *DC, MC, V.*

WHERE TO STAY

$$$–$$$$
★

⛾ **Adrift In Golden Bay.** A short walk across soft green grass from your unit gets you to the sea. Sometimes in the evenings sunsets are enhanced with the arrival of little blue penguins, which nest up the creek. Daytimes you can swim, kayak, or wander along the incredibly private beach. Each of the five eco-friendly luxury cottages is self-contained, and there's a studio unit attached to the house; the doors and windows can be left open for the sound of the sea. To get there drive down the signposted driveway and out to the coast. A breakfast hamper is delivered to the units each morning. **Pros:** just a strip of green grass between your unit and the sea; modern-style units; each unit has a Jacuzzi-style hot tub; sun decks out front and private rear courtyards. **Cons:** a long driveway in through farmland off Tukurua Road. ⊠ *52 Tukurua Rd, 18 km (11 mi) north of Takaka* ☎ *03/525–8353* ⊕ *www.adrift.co.nz* ✎ *escape@adrift.co.nz* ⌁ *5 cottages, 1 studio unit* ⌂ *In -room: No a/c, kitchen (some), DVD (some). In-hotel: Laundry, Internet terminal* ☺ *Closed July* ▭ *MC, V* ⧖ *BP.*

$$

⛾ **Anatoki Lodge Motel.** This spacious motel is close to Takaka village center. Owners Gaye and Garth Prince can help point out the main attractions and best places to eat in the area. The lodge has spacious studios and one- and two-bedroom units; each opens out to a private patio and grass courtyard. You can order room-service breakfast. **Pros:** cook up a barbecue in the garden; indoor and solar-heated pool in summer; the two-bedroom family units are excellent value. **Cons:** although handy to town, the motel's semi-urban backdrop is not typical of Golden Bay. ⊠ *87 Commercial St., Takaka* ☎ *03/525–8047* ⊕ *www.anatokimotels. co.nz* ✎ *anatoki@xtra.co.nz* ⌁ *5 studios, 6 units* ⌂ *In-room: No a/c, kitchen, DVD, Internet. In-hotel: Pool, laundry service, no-smoking rooms* ▭ *AE, DC, MC, V.*

8

¢ ⛺ **Golden Bay Holiday Park.** Golden Bay has a number of highly scenic camp areas. This is one of the best; it is located at Tukurua Beach which also has good facilities. Tents, powered sites, and cabins are available and you'll sleep to the sound of the sea. ☎ *03/525–9742 or 0800/525–972* ✉ *goldenbay.holiday@xtra.co.nz.*

$–$$ 🏨 **Sans Souci Inn.** Sans Souci is a mellow, eco-friendly spot with lots of allure a two-minute walk from Pohara Beach. There's a small restaurant, and you can arrange to take breakfast and dinner here, but book this by 4 PM. This hand-built lodge has striking adobe and tile construction and a turf roof; the big communal bathroom is adorned with subtropical plants, and the garden abounds with grape and kiwifruit vines and big leafy shade trees. The rooms are truly comfy and all but one (which is self-contained) share a large bathroom complex. **Pros:** self-contained family unit sleeps up to four; eat in the restaurant or you can cook in the restaurant kitchen for yourself. **Cons:** restaurant is only open late October to Easter, and is fairly simple. ✉ *11 Richmond Rd., Pohara Beach* ☎ *03/525–8663* ⊕ *www.sanssouciinn.co.nz* ➘ *6 rooms, 1 self-contained unit* ⌂ *In-room: No a/c, no phone, kitchen (some), no TV. In-hotel: Restaurant, laundry facilities* ⊗ *Closed July, Aug., and 1st 2 wks of Sept.*

$$$ 🏨 **Twin Waters Lodge.** Built on the edge of the Pakawau Estuary, this small comfy lodge overlooks the surrounding hills and wetlands, and is just a two-minute walk from the sea on the other side of the peninsula. Rooms and shared spaces have sheltered decks, and the simple room decoration is enhanced by the leafy views out the windows. The lodge is extremely close to all the natural wonders of Farewell Spit and its vast coastal wetlands and exceptional birdlife. The hosts give lots of advice about the area. It's just a short drive to Wharariki and the wild beaches on the West Coast. **Pros:** interesting wetland location on the coast; a three-course dinner is available at $65 per person but book ahead; a strong eco-policy is in place with good waste disposal, use of solar energy, and use of rainwater **Cons:** minimum two-night stay over mid-summer. ✉ *Totara Ave., Pakawau, 9 km (5½ mi) past Collingwood on road to Farewell Spit* ☎ *03/524–8014* ⊕ *www.twinwaters.co.nz* ➘ *4 rooms* ⌂ *In-room: No a/c, no phone, refrigerator, no TV. In-hotel: Laundry service, Wi-Fi* ⊟ *MC, V* ⊗ *Closed June–Sept.* ❙⊘❙ *BP.*

KAHURANGI NATIONAL PARK

35 km (21 mi) west of Takaka.

GETTING HERE AND AROUND

The most popular entry to the Park from Takaka is at the northern end of the Heaphy Track, south of Collingwood. However, most people walk the Heaphy one-way so you'll need to arrange a bus drop-off. A less known entry is up the Cobb Valley: turn left at East Takaka, at the base of the Takaka Hill on its western side. The Cobb Valley road ends approximately 22 km (15 mi) further in. Abel Tasman Coachlines run daily connections to the northern end of the Heaphy Track.

ESSENTIALS

Bus Contacts Abel Tasman Coachlines (☎ *03/548-0285* ⊕ *www. abeltasmantravel.co.nz).*

Visitor Information Department of Conservation Golden Bay Area Office ✉ *62 Commercial St., Takaka* ☎ *03/525–8026* ✎ *GoldenBayAO@doc.govt.nz* ⊕ *www.doc.govt.nz).*

EXPLORING

The wild **Kahurangi National Park** spans 1.1 million acres of untamed wilderness, and includes fern-clad forests, rocky rivers, rolling tussock-covered hills, rugged snowcapped mountains, and wind-blown beaches pounded by West Coast surf. The park is laced with 570 km (353 mi) of hiking tracks of various levels of difficulty; there are also several rafting and kayaking rivers and some serious caving areas, especially toward the West Coast. Of the various entry points to the park, one of the most convenient is 35 km (21 mi) west of Takaka, south of the town of Collingwood. This is also the northern head of the Heaphy Track *(see Outdoor Activities, below)*. The Department of Conservation Golden Bay Area Office provides local trail maps.

OFF THE BEATEN PATH

Totaranui. From Takaka the coast road heading east leads around to the northern entry to the Abel Tasman National Park at Totaranui. This scenic road passes through Pohara Beach, which has several cafés and a campground, before winding around to Wainui Bay with its alternative Tui community (a onetime commune that welcomes visitors) and cascading waterfall (a slightly rough 75-minute return walk from the road). From Wainui Bay, the road over the Totaranui Hill is a gravel surface and can be treacherous in wet weather. But in good weather, it's a gorgeous drive through dense native bush to the coast. Totaranui Beach is a long golden-sand beach that is safe for swimming. This area can also be reached by boat from Kaiteriteri and Marahau, on the Motueka side of the Takaka hill. It's a slice of pure beach bliss, and there's an unpowered campground with basic facilities.

OUTDOOR ACTIVITIES

The most famous walk in Kahurangi National Park is the one-way, 82-km (51-mi), five-day **Heaphy Track**. The track is one of the Great Walks trails, so you need to buy a Great Walks Pass for hut stays and campsites—failure to do so incurs a penalty fee. Passes range from $10 to $20 per night, depending on the time of year. It's best to purchase tickets in advance from information centers at Nelson, Motueka, or Takaka or book online through the Department of Conservation Web site. Bookings are essential much of the year to avoid having nowhere to sleep. Track-user numbers are limited by the number of beds available on any one night. Tickets in hand, all you really need to do is get to the track and start walking toward Karamea on the West Coast. You need a reasonable level of fitness; conditions can be challenging in poor weather. Huts along the way have water and toilets and some have gas cooking and heating—check before leaving. You need to carry your own food and bedding and may need a small gas stove and canister as well. Be prepared for weather of all kinds all year-round;

8

bring rain gear and warm clothing even in summer and insect repellent for the sand flies. You can get trail maps from the Department of Conservation Golden Bay Area Office.

If you'd like some expert company on hikes around the national park, **Kahurangi Guided Walks** (☎ 03/525–7177 ✍ john@kahurangiwalks. co.nz ⊕ www.kahurangiwalks.co.nz) runs easy half and one-day treks on routes known to locals but virtually untouched by visitors. A more strenuous, three-day walk goes to the rarely visited Boulder Lake, and there are also the five-day hike on the Heaphy Track and other hikes as well. Prices vary for each customized trip.

NELSON LAKES NATIONAL PARK

100 km (62 mi) south of Nelson.

GETTING HERE AND AROUND

It's a 100-km (65-mi) drive south from Nelson to St. Arnaud, the hub of the park. Head south on State Highway 6; at Wai-iti, just south of Wakefield, veer left off the highway and follow the Golden Downs Road through to St. Arnaud. From the south, head 35 km (21 mi) north from Murchison, and turn left at the Kawatiri Junction. It's a further 30 minutes to St. Arnaud.

Shuttle transport to the park is available through Nelson Lakes Shuttles; they will deliver to most track terminus points and the main stops as well.

ESSENTIALS

Bus Contacts Nelson Lakes Shuttles (☎ 03/521–1900 ⊕ www. nelsonlakesshuttles.co.nz).

Visitor Information Department of Conservation(✉ View Rd., St. Arnaud ☎ 03/521–1806 ⊕ www.doc.govt.nz/explore ⊙ Daily 8–4:30; Christmas–end Jan., daily 8–6).

EXPLORING

Spread around two stunningly scenic glacial lakes, Rotoroa and Rotoiti, the **Nelson Lakes National Park** is an alpine zone of soaring mountains, rocky rivers, and bush-lined trails. The native beech forests pour down to the lakeshore. On cloudy days, mist swirls through the trees, wetting the draping mosses and silencing the birds. On sunny days the intense green comes through and the birds' chorus resumes. Lake Rotoiti is also the site of a kiwi-recovery program; in 2004 several kiwi were released back into the forest after an intense pest-eradication program.

Of the two lakes, Lake Rotoroa is the most pristine, with just a few fishing cottages, a campsite, and a lodge on its shore. The village of St. Arnaud sits at the northern end of Lake Rotoiti; it's the gateway to the park, with a lodge, a handful of B&Bs, a general store, and the Department of Conservation bureau. The **DOC Headquarters** here is particularly good, with information on the area's geology and ecology. Maps and details on the hiking trails are available, and a mountain weather forecast is issued daily. The DOC office administers two excellent campgrounds around the lake frontage.

There are numerous hiking tracks through the untamed forests of Kahurangi National Park.

Call them for details on campsites. Bookings can be heavy through mid-summer. Each year in early March the **Antique and Classic Boat Show** is held at the lake with close to 200 antique boats congregating for several days of boat racing and boat talk. ⊕ *www.nzclassicboats. com or* ✉ *pbrain@xtra.co.nz* for details.

OUTDOOR ACTIVITIES

Nelson Lakes has a number of half-, full-, and multiday trails that can be "freedom walked" (walked without a guide). The **Lake Rotoiti Circuit** gets you around the lake in an easy daylong walk. The rather steep **Mt. Robert Track** zigzags up the face of Mt. Robert, giving you a superb view back across the lake toward St. Arnaud village. The return walk can be done by looping down the face of the mountain to meet up with the Lake Rotoiti Circuit track. Other tracks lead off these into the higher mountain areas. Hut accommodations are available on a "first-in, first-served" basis. Alpine experience and equipment are necessary on the longer tracks.

Nelson Wilderness Guides can take the work out of finding tracks, gear, and accommodations. They have one-, three-, and four-day tours through the park, based at their Golden Downs Lodge, and lead multiday wilderness expeditions into the backcountry. ✉ *Kohatu, Golden Downs* ☎ *03/522–4175* ⊕ *www.goldendowns.co.nz.*

WHERE TO STAY

$–$$ 🏨 **Alpine Lodge and Alpine Chalets.** Accommodations run from full suites ($$) to backpacker dorms (¢). With the wood paneling and dormer windows, the building may feel somewhat European-alpine, but the view out the window is all Kiwi. Although in the center of the village, the lodge is at the national park boundary, a short bushwalk away from Lake Rotoiti. A few two-bedroom apartments are good for families. The lodge has a licensed restaurant and a bar for casual meals. Good meals are also available at Elaine's Café downstairs next door in the Chalets. **Pros:** if you haven't the time or budget for a backcountry lodge then this is a nice substitute; put aside a couple of hours to do a bushwalk. **Cons:** bring repellent for the sand flies; watch for wasps in mid-summer; crowded mid-summer. ⊠ *Main Rd., St. Arnaud* ☎ *03/521–1869* ⊕ *www. alpinelodge.co.nz* ⤴ *24 rooms, 4 suites, 4 apartments, 1 dorm* ⌂ *In-room: No a/c. In-hotel: Restaurant, bar, spa, laundry facilities, no-smoking rooms* ▤ *AE, DC, MC, V.*

$$$$
Fodor's Choice
★

▨ **Lake Rotoroa Lodge.** Now recognized as one of the best fly-fishing lodges in the world, this truly private haven sheltered beneath tall trees beside Lake Rotoroa was built for "gentlemen travelers" in the days when horse and buggy was the local transport. Now it lures anglers with a combination of old-fashioned personality and new-fangled luxury, from the brass beds and hunting trophies to the expert fishing guides and outstanding wine list. **Pros:** old, heritage-style building looks across the lake; some of the best brown trout fishing in the world; lovely walking tracks through native bush. **Cons:** a wonderfully scenic but 90-minute drive from Nelson; use repellent religiously as the sand flies here are legendary; lunch not included in the rate. ⊠ *Lake Rotoroa* ☎ *03/523–9121* ⊕ *www.lakerotoroalodge.com* ⤴ *10 rooms* ⌂ *In-room: No TV, Wi-Fi. In-hotel: Bar, laundry facilities, laundry service, Internet terminal, Wi-Fi* ▤ *AE, MC, V* ⊙ *Closed May–Sept.* ⊠*MAP.*

$$
▨ **Tophouse.** This 120-year-old farm–guesthouse just a few kilometers from Rotoiti gives you a chance to kick back and do absolutely nothing. The house has a historic rating so the B&B rooms in the main house are authentic but basic, complete with their original cob walls. The shared bathrooms are just down the hallway. Four self-contained cottages are behind the house. If you just want to stop for lunch ($12) or afternoon tea ($6), there is café service during the day. Dinner is available on request for $40 per person. Tophouse is close to fishing, skiing (in winter), and hiking trails. **Pros:** a hotbed of local history, check out the bullet holes in the veranda wall, choice of modern cottages and old-fashioned rooms in the main house; a short drive from St. Arnaud. **Cons:** no en suites in the B&B rooms; no-frills accommodations. ⊠ *Tophouse Rd., 9 km (5½ mi) from St. Arnaud toward Nelson* ☎ *03/521–1848 or 0800/544–545* ⊕ *www.tophouse.co.nz* ⤴ *5 rooms, 4 cottages* ⌂ *In-room: No a/c, no phone, no TV. In-hotel: Laundry facilities* ▤ *AE, MC, V* ⊠*CP, MAP (B&B only).*

MURCHISON

125 km (78 mi) south of Nelson, 63 km (40 mi) west of Lake Rotoiti.

Surrounded by high mountains and roaring rivers, this small town is in some big country. With the Nelson Lakes National Park to the west, the Kahurangi National Park to the north, and the Mataki-taki, Buller, Matiri, and Mangles rivers all converging on its doorstep,

Murchison has gained the reputation as New Zealand's "white-water capital," and it boasts the most kayaked stretch of white water in the Southern Hemisphere. There are 13 rivers within 20 km (12½ mi) of town. Fly-fishers, kayakers, hikers, and rafting junkies turn up every year to enjoy the sport. Although most operators now accept credit cards, the only ATM is inside one of the cafes; so make sure you have some cash on you.

Murchison residents still consider their landmark event "the earthquake," a major quake that hit in June 1929. The epicenter was nearby in the Buller Gorge, and the quake drastically altered the landscape. A second in 1968 (centered in nearby Inangahua) also rearranged the landscape considerably but was much less destructive in human terms.

GETTING HERE AND AROUND

Although it's 100 km (62 mi) from the nearest town Murchison is easy to access by road, sitting right on State Highway 6. It's a 1¾-hour drive south of Nelson, 4¼ hours north of Christchurch, and 1½ hours east of Westport (without scenic stops). It is one of only a couple of comfort and fuel stops on these long stretches so take advantage of its conveniences.

InterCity buses and Atomic Shuttles pass through daily. InterCity runs services between Nelson and Christchurch and Nelson and the glaciers. Atomic Shuttles also run Nelson to the glaciers through Murchison as well.

ESSENTIALS

Bus Contacts Atomic Shuttles (☎ 03/349–0697 ⊕ www.atomictravel.co.nz). **InterCity** (☎ 03/365–1113 ⊕ www.intercitycoach.co.nz).

Visitor Information Murchison Information Centre (✉ 47 Waller St. ☎ 03/523–9350 ✉ murchison@nelsonnz.com).

EXPLORING

The local, extremely rustic **Murchison District Museum** (✉ 60 Fairfax St. ☎ 03/523–9392) has an excellent exhibit on the 1929 earthquake. There's also a good collection of farming and agricultural machinery from the town's colonial era, plus displays on a local gold rush.

OUTDOOR ACTIVITIES

Murchison's claim as a white-water destination is not to be ignored. They have some of the best white water anywhere.

RAFTING **Ultimate Descents New Zealand,** with highly experienced guides, runs rafting trips on the Maruia (Grade III), Clarence (Grade II), Buller (Grade III–IV), Mokihinui (Grade IV) and Karamea (Grade V) rivers. It also runs inflatable kayaking on the easier rivers, half-day kayaking trips suitable for kids ($95), and half-day ($125), full-day ($195), and multiday wilderness trips ($450–$1,500)—minimum of four people. All half-day and day trips include a meal, and the multiday trips are fully catered. ✉ 51 Fairfax St., Murchison ☎ 03/523–9899 or 0800/748–377 ⊕ www.rivers.co.nz ✉ ultimate@rivers.co.nz.

8

The cheeky kea parrot delights trampers at Nelson Lakes National Park.

White Water Action, which operates in the Buller Gorge from both Murchison and Westport, also runs rafting trips. ☎ *0800/100–582* ⊕ *www.whitewateraction.com* The **New Zealand Kayak School,** known to be one of the country's best, offers tuition and training camps based at its Murchison facility. ☎ *03/523–9611* ⊕ *www.nzkayakschool. com.*

WHERE TO EAT

Murchison is not a destination for foodies, but if you want a decent meal at a good price, there are several options.

$–$$
CAFÉ
✕ **Beechwoods Café.** Out on the main road heading south of town is a typical roadhouse-style café that is open all day. ⊠ *Waller St.* ☎ *03/523–9571.*

$–$$
CAFÉ
✕ **Rivers Café.** During the summer, this café is open all day every day, serving good food in a funky place. Hours vary in winter. ⊠ *Fairfax St.* ☎ *03/523–9009.*

$$–$$$
CAFÉ
☕
✕ **Riverview Café.** For the best environment, try this little spot on the northern edge of town. It fronts the river below the Riverview Motor Camp and is a nice spot to stop if you're traveling with kids. If it's summer they can jump in the river for a swim. The food is simple but tasty; service can be slow, but what's the hurry—this is Murchison after all. It is closed May through September. ⊠ *State Hwy. 6* ☎ *03/523–9591.*

$$–$$$
CAFÉ
✕ **Stables Café.** In the Commercial Hotel, you'll find tasty café food during the day and good pub-style food in the evening. It's open year-round. ⊠ *Waller and Fairfax Sts.* ☎ *03/523–9696.*

WHERE TO STAY

$$ ⌂ **Murchison Lodge.** Tucked in a tiny back street of Murchison, this rural retreat is within easy walking distance of the mighty Buller River. The guest rooms are comfortably countrified, with strong colors and lots of wood. Breakfast is a big affair with freshly squeezed juices and bread made by Shirley each morning while Merve cooks up bacon and eggs on the barbecue. They can put you in touch with a good local guide for trout fishing. **Pros:** private access to the Buller River through a grassy field. **Cons:** hard to find down a long driveway; friendly on-site dog. ⌂ *15 Grey St.* ☎ *03/523–9196 or 0800/523–9196* ⊕ *www.murchisonlodge. co.nz* ✉ *info@murchisonlodge.co.nz* ⤳ *4 rooms (3 with en suite)* ⌂ *In-room: No a/c, no phone, no TV. In-hotel: Bicycles, Wi-Fi, no-smoking rooms* ⊟ *MC, V* ⊗ *Closed May–Sept.* ⧉ *BP.*

$$$$ ⌂ **Owen River Lodge.** From the dining room you can look across the
★   willow-lined river valley to a large granite escarpment with native forest. Outside, the rush of the river is outdone only by the sometimes-overwhelming chorus of native birds. Host Felix Borenstein is a die-hard fly fisherman who has a strong passion for throwing furry little feathered flies into the sublime reaches of the area's many trout rivers. He delights in the fact that much of the fishing here is sighted fishing and stalking, but also catch-and-release to preserve the stock. **Pros:** nicely appointed cottages overlooking the valley and fronted by sheltered verandas; large garden; the fully equipped tackle room has waders, jackets, boots, rods, reels, and everything else a keen angler should desire. **Cons:** the last mile or two to the lodge is gravel but easy to drive; bring repellent for sand flies. ⌂ *Owen Valley East Rd., 15 min north of Murchison* ☎ *03/523–9075* ⊕ *www.owenriverlodge. co.nz* ⤳ *6 cottage suites* ⌂ *In-room: No phone, refrigerator, no TV. In-hotel: Restaurant, bar, laundry facilities, Internet terminal, Wi-Fi* ⊟ *D, MC, V* ⊗ *Closed May–Sept.*

LEWIS PASS

About 12 km (7½ mi) south of Murchison, State Highway 6 takes a sharp turn to the right over O'Sullivans Bridge towards the West Coast. If you've decided to skip the coast and head back to Christchurch from here, follow State Highway 65 straight through towards the Lewis Pass. The first part of this road is a Heritage Highway, "The Shenandoah," which follows the Maruia River valley as it climbs towards the main divide. This is prime farming country bounded by high mountains clothed in thick bush. Just 15 km (9 mi) before Springs Junction Reids Store provides a welcome coffee and lunch stop, far superior to the offerings farther on at Springs Junction. There's no fuel here, though, so you will have to get that at Springs Junction. From Springs Junction the road starts to climb to the Lewis Pass, one of the lowest crossing points over the Southern Alps. The Maruia Springs Thermal Resort, on the northern side of the pass, has traditional Japanese bathhouses and hot, outdoor rock pools, a restaurant, and accommodations. Cross the Lewis Pass and you're back in Canterbury, where the countryside changes to high arid hills. Hanmer Springs is an hour south of the pass.

8

THE WEST COAST

Southwest of Nelson, the wild West Coast region is a land unto itself. The mystical Pancake Rocks and blowholes around Punakaiki (poon-ah-*kye*-kee) set the scene for the gigantic, rugged, sometimes forlorn landscape. Early *Pākehā* (European) settlers carved out a hardscrabble life during the 1860s, digging for gold and farming where they could, constantly washed by the West Coast rains. After the gold rushes, waves of settlers arrived to mine the vast coal reserves in the surrounding hills. Farmers and loggers followed; although the gold has gone, the coal mining and farming remain. The towns along this stretch of coastline are generally no-frills rural service centers, but they make good bases for exploring the primeval landscape.

The original Māori inhabitants knew this area to be rich in *kai moana* (seafood), *weka* (bush hens), and most important, *pounamu* (greenstone or jade). The Māori name for the South Island, Te Wai Pounamu, reflects this treasure. The riverbeds, beaches, and mountains were threaded with walking trails to transport pounamu for intertribal trade, and you'll still hear references to "greenstone trails" throughout the area.

At the glacier towns of Franz Josef and Fox, the unique combination of soaring mountains and voluminous precipitation means that the massive valleys of ice descend straight into rain forests (a combination also present on the southwest coast of South America). South of the glaciers, the road follows the seacoast, where fur seals and Fiordland crested penguins inhabit fantastical beaches and forests. On sunny days the Tasman Sea along the stretch between Lake Moeraki and Haast takes on a transcendent shade of blue.

Legal changes in 2000 brought an end to commercial logging of the West Coast's native forests; since then the local communities have been in flux, as residents turn to other jobs and property prices climb surprisingly quickly. But it's the environment that continues to determine the lifestyle here. Locals pride themselves on their ability to coexist with the wild landscape and weather. As a visitor, you may need a sense of adventure—be prepared for rain, swirling mist, and cold winter winds alternating with warm, clear days. "The Barber," Greymouth's infamous winter wind, blasts down the Grey River valley to the sea. The meteorological mix can mean that the glacier flight you planned at Franz Josef or Fox won't fly that day. Although the coast is well-known for its rain, it also has clear, bright days when the mountains shine above the green coastal plains and the surf pounds onto sunny, sandy beaches; often the best weather is in winter.

EN ROUTE

If you're driving to the West Coast from Nelson or Motueka, State Highway 6 passes through Murchison before turning right at O'Sullivans Bridge 12 km (7 mi) farther south and heads down through the Buller Gorge toward the West Coast. This twisting, narrow road parallels the tortuous **Buller River** as it carves a deep gorge below the jagged, earthquake-rocked mountain peaks. The upper gorge is tight and hilly but once past Inangahua the lower gorge is easier to negotiate. The Buller once carried a fabulous cargo of gold, but you'll have to use your imagination to reconstruct the days when places such as Lyell, 34 km (21 mi)

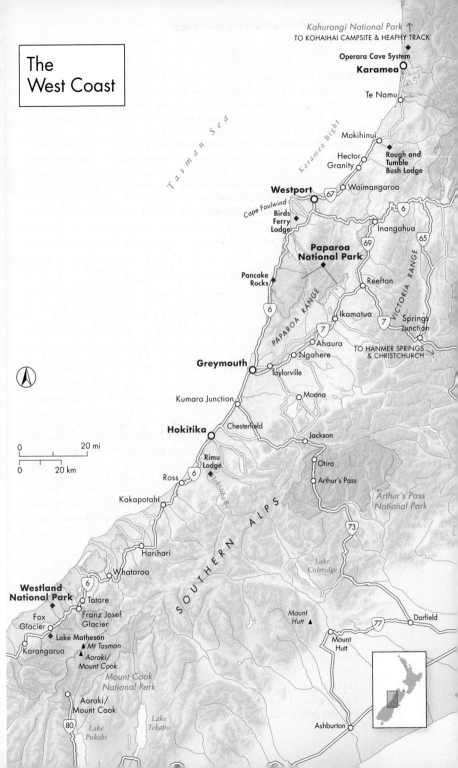

The West Coast

Kahurangi National Park ↑
TO KOHAIHAI CAMPSITE & HEAPHY TRACK

Operara Cave System
Karamea

Te Namu

Tasman Sea

Mokihinui

Karamea Bight

Hector
Granity

Rough and
Tumble
Bush Lodge

Westport 67 Waimangaroa

6

Cape Foulwind
Birds
Ferry
Lodge

Inangahua

69

**Paparoa
National Park**

Reefton

65

Pancake
Rocks

Ikamatua

7

Springs
Junction

6

PAPAROA RANGE

VICTORIA RANGE

7

Ahaura

Ngahere

TO HANMER SPRINGS
& CHRISTCHURCH

Greymouth

Taylorville

Kumara Junction

Moana

Hokitika

Chesterfield

Jackson

Rimu
Lodge

Otira

Ross 6

Hokitika R.

Arthur's Pass

*Arthur's Pass
National Park*

Kakapotahi

73

Harihari

*Lake
Coleridge*

Whataroa

**Westland
National Park**

6 Tatare

Franz Josef
Glacier

*Mount
Hutt* ▲

Darfield

Fox
Glacier

Lake Matheson
▲ Mt Tasman

77

Mount
Hutt

Karangarua

▲ *Aoraki/
Mount Cook*

*Mount Cook
National Park*

Aoraki/
Mount Cook

80

*Lake
Pukaki*

*Lake
Tekapo*

Ashburton

SOUTHERN ALPS

0 ____ 20 mi
0 ____ 20 km

west of Murchison, were bustling mining towns. Not far from here are New Zealand's longest swaying footbridge, the **Buller Gorge Swing Bridge,** and the departure point for the **Buller Experience Jet,** should you want to ride a few rapids. You'll pass high forest-clad mountains, narrow single-lane bridges, and the sleepy little village of Inangahua along the way. **Hawk's Crag and Fern Arch,** where the highway passes beneath rock overhangs with the river wheeling alongside, is another highlight and a low-key café at Berlins offers a pit stop. At the end of the gorge, turn left to continue along State Highway 6 toward Punakaiki, or carry on straight ahead to Westport and Karamea. Although on a map the distances along the West Coast appear small, allow plenty of time to negotiate the hills and to explore the sights. When traveling in mid-summer, watch for the giant, spectacular crimson-flowering *rata* trees lighting the forest with their blooms.

WESTPORT

230 km (144 mi) southeast of Nelson.

One of New Zealand's oldest ports, Westport sits at the mouth of the mighty Buller River. Once a boomtown for two separate gold rushes, it's now a quiet little hub (population 3,100) for the local farming and coal industries, plus the rapidly expanding adventure-tourism niche. It's a quiet place to stop over before heading south toward Punakaiki and the glaciers or north to Karamea and the Heaphy Track; the best of Westport is out of town, either on the coast or up the rivers. The iconic Westport look is breaking white-capped waves, blue sea, seals, rocky outcrops, and acres of flax and wetlands, although there are several striking art deco buildings along the main street. Stop by the little **Coaltown Museum** on Queen Street to learn about the port's history and check out an extensive mineral collection. Another museum at **Denniston,** 18 km (11 mi) north of town up a steep mountain range, details life in this lonely outpost from the late 1800s through the early 1900s. Carving a living from the rich seams of coal in the surrounding tussock-covered hills, the settlers had to struggle with wild weather, isolation, and primitive conditions. An old underground mine is being reopened for visitors and the living history aspect of the settlement is being revitalized. A popular historical novel about these pioneers, *The Denniston Rose,* by New Zealand writer Jenny Pattrick, details the area and the harsh colonial lifestyle.

The **Westport Visitor Centre** can provide information on Karamea and Kahurangi National Park.

GETTING HERE AND AROUND
There are daily flights in from Wellington and Christchurch by small commuter plane. It's a 3¼-hour drive to Westport from Nelson to the north, or a 1½-hour drive from Greymouth to the south. Either way you'll pass along incredibly scenic coastline or river gorge surrounded by thick native bush and high ranges. InterCity buses and Atomic Shuttles travel to Westport daily, en route between Nelson and the glaciers.

ESSENTIALS
Airline Information Air New Zealand (☎ 0800/737–000 ⊕ www.airnewzealand.co.nz.)

Hospital **Buller Hospital** (✉ *Derby St., Westport* ☎ *03/789–7399*).

Visitor Information **Westport Visitor Centre** (✉ *1 Brougham St.* ☎ *03/789–6658* ⊕ *www.westport.org.nz*).

OUTDOOR ACTIVITIES

★ You might actually pray for rain during a tour with **Underworld Adventures**. This popular adventure tour group takes you into the rain forest off the main highway at Charleston. You can sign up for an open-sided bush-train ride through the dense temperate lowland forest, or take a cave walk into one of the giant limestone mountains up the Nile River valley (a glowworm grotto is a highlight). Their most popular trip is a stunning slow drift in a raft through the glowworm caves before breaking out onto the river (four-hour trip costs $145). For something more challenging, go for the day-long "Full On" caving adventure with a 47-meter (154-foot) abseil (rappel) down into the mountain, before crawling, swimming, and climbing your way back to the surface. Prices range from $20 for the train ride to $295 for the "Full On" adventure; reservations are essential. ✉ *Charleston Tavern, Main Rd., Charleston* ☎ *03/788–8168 or 0800/116–686* ⊕ *www.caverafting.com*.

Buller Adventure Tours at the lower end of the Buller Gorge, before you reach Westport, runs jet-boating and rafting on various parts of the river and horse treks and quad-bike tours in the surrounding bush. Try the Earthquake Slip Rapids section, which includes some Grade IV water, a Grade II swim rapid, and a 9-meter (27-foot) cliff jump. They also run the Earthquake Rapids trip from Murchison (☎ *03/523–9581*). Trips start from $75. ✉ *State Hwy. 6, Lower Buller Gorge* ☎ *03/789–7286 or 0800/697–286* ⊕ *www.adventuretours.co.nz*.

OutWest Tours run several interesting tours into the back country, making good use of their off-road and 4WD vehicles. Micky will get you up to Denniston in style, or give you a local's tour of some of the mining sites, which are such a key part of the area's economy and some of its most dramatic locations. ■ **TIP→** Give him a call and remind him the day before your trip is planned. ☎ *0800/688–9378* ⊕ *www.outwest.co.nz*.

WHERE TO EAT

There are several good daytime cafés in Westport. The Bay House, far and away the best, is out of town, but definitely worth the drive. Denniston Dog is a local stalwart for a good down-home West Coast experience.

$$$–$$$$
NEW ZEALAND
Fodor's Choice
★

✕ **The Bay House.** Tucked among flax bushes beside the wild, foaming surf beach at Tauranga Bay, this busy little restaurant serves as fine a menu as you'll get anywhere in the South Island. The chef prepares top-quality local beef, lamb, and seafood dishes, and there are specialties like the whitebait (a local fish delicacy). Or try the West Coast beef fillet with chorizo and mustard-and-cream-cheese ravioli. There's lots of fish; the chowder is recommended, and the kitchen use local touches like *harakeke* seed, *paua*, and *kūmara* (native sweet potato). You'll find an extensive, mainly South Island wine list. It's worth the extra driving and, if you're heading south afterwards, you can follow the signposted shortcut toward Charleston to save going back into

8

Westport. ⊠ *Tauranga Bay, Cape Foulwind, 16 km (10 mi) west of Westport* ☎ *03/789–7133* ▤ *AE, MC, V.*

\$\$–\$\$\$
CAFÉ

✕ **Denniston Dog.** This old bank building, complete with a vault, is loaded with local character in its new guise as a cheerful pub and dinner spot. They serve good Kiwi tucker here, so order up a fritter with feta cheese and whitebait (tiny fish eaten whole). The meals are big, and it's a remarkably kid-friendly spot. The kitchen is closed mid-afternoon but reopens for dinner. There's a big covered courtyard for summer dining. ⊠ *18 Wakefield St.* ☎ *03/789–5030.*

\$\$–\$\$\$
CAFÉ

✕ **Dirty Mary's Café and Bar.** Right in the main street, this café has a daytime and dinner café and late-night bar. The adjoining pub gives it an upbeat environment. ⊠ *198 Palmerston St.* ☎ *03/789–6648.*

\$\$\$
CAFÉ

✕ **Yellow House Café.** Driving into town from the Buller River, you'll see this restaurant, which has an enclosed sunny back lawn and a bright dining area. It serves brunch through dinner every day, has a natural foods menu, and a kid's play area. They close in mid-winter for a time. ⊠ *243 Palmerston St.* ☎ *03/789–8765.*

WHERE TO STAY

\$\$\$–\$\$\$\$

🏠 **Birds Ferry Lodge.** Named for the old river ferry that crossed the nearby Totara River during the gold rush, this purpose-built lodge and self-contained cottage bring the place to life once more. There are three snug rooms in the main lodge, two with commanding views across the surrounding bush lands and the nearby Paparoa National Park. A large guest lounge and dining area provides plenty of space to relax in the evening. The Ferryman's Cottage (sleeps four, \$\$\$\$) is a really private spot and has all the conveniences of home, a cozy wood fire, and an outside bath. Listen to the roar of distant surf at night; and if you're really lucky you may hear kiwi calling in the bush nearby. **Pros:** lots of good walks on the property or at nearby Charleston; a three-course dinner is available on request; both the lodge and the cottage are comfortable **Cons:** hard to find in the dark so watch closely for signs off the highway; the 1.7 km (1 mi) entry road is rough gravel; two small on-site dogs. ⊠ *Birds Ferry Rd., Charleston* ☎ *0800/212–207 or 021/337–217* ⊕ *www.birdsferrylodge.co.nz* ↝ *3 rooms, 1 cottage* ⚙ *In-room: No a/c (some), no phone (some), kitchen, refrigerator (some), DVD, no TV (some), Wi-Fi. In-hotel: Bar, spa, bicycles, laundry facilities, Internet terminal, Wi-Fi, no kids under 12, no-smoking rooms* ▤ *MC, V* ⦾ *BP.*

\$

🏠 **The Steeples Cottage & B&B.** Perched on the cliff top overlooking Three Steeples rocks offshore, this B&B and self-contained cottage is a great value. Hosts Pauline and Bruce have a strong local knowledge and give you the opportunity to be as pampered or as independent as you want. The fully equipped cottage has a separate entrance and its own sea view. It works for a couple or, with a couple of beds added, can do for a family as well. Pauline has a lovely garden to wander or sit at the table on the cliff top and enjoy a wine while watching the sunset. There's an extra studio B&B room for a larger group stay in the cottage. **Pros:** just a 40 minute walk to the seal colony and an hour's walk to Tauranga Bay; there's a private, safe swimming beach at the base of the cliffs. **Cons:** parking can be a bit tight; Lighthouse Road is tricky to find so get instructions first; small, friendly on-site dog. ⊠ *48 Light-house Rd., Cape Foulwind* ☎ *03/789–7876 or 0800/670–708* ⊕ *www.steeplescottage.co.nz* ↩ *1 cottage, 1 studio, 2 rooms* ⚲ *In-room: No a/c (some), no phone, kitchen (some). In-hotel: Spa, beachfront, laundry facilities, Wi-Fi* ⊟ *No credit cards.* ⦿❘*CP*

¢ ⛤ **Trip Inn Hostel.** Backpackers now fill the beds in one of Westport's grandest old 19th-century homes, built as a gentleman's residence in 1863. It's geared for all ages, not just students, and the owners have arranged the rooms for various kinds of travelers, from solos to families. There's a fireplace lounge where people swap stories about their hikes on the Heaphy Track. Lockers and linens are provided. Check out the tall tree ferns on the front lawn. **Pros:** decidedly relaxed place within walking of the town center; family-style units removed from the main house. **Cons:** lounge areas are dated but comfy. ⊠ *72 Queen St.* ☎ *03/789–7367* ⊕ *www.tripinn.co.nz* ✉ *tripinn@clear.net.nz* ↩ *16 rooms with changeable single, double, and family room, dorm beds, tent sites* ⚲ *In-room: No a/c, kitchen, no TV. In-hotel: Internet terminal, no-smoking rooms* ⊟ *MC, V.*

KARAMEA

98 km (61 mi) north of Westport.

North of Westport, the coastline is squeezed between high mountain ranges and pounding surf. The highlight of the tiny settlements along this stretch is Karamea, known to most people as the southern entry to (or exit from) the renowned Heaphy Track, which starts in Golden Bay. But Karamea is also a fine trout-fishing destination, the western entry point to the wild ranges of the Kahurangi National Park with its wild rivers and network of hikes, and is home to the Oparara cave system.

GETTING HERE AND AROUND

You can fly in direct from various places by either small fixed-wing plane or helicopter, although both are extremely weather dependent. **HeliCharter Karamea** specializes in scenic flights but also operates helicopter transfers and day trips to and from Karamea. They provide a shuttle service to the Wangapeka and Heaphy Tracks, hunting and fishing, kayaking, and heli-rafting. **Remote Adventures** runs Heaphy Track trampers between the Brown Hut, Karamea, Nelson, Motueka, and Takaka with a fixed-wing small plane service. They also run scenic flights except in winter.

Karamea is a 100-km (62-mi) drive north of Westport on State Highway 67. Fill up with fuel before leaving Westport as there are no fuel stops between there and Karamea. It's a 16-km (10-mi) drive north from Karamea to Kohaihai, the southern end and entrance to the Heaphy Track.

Hikers arrive at Karamea by the 78-km (48-mi), five-day hike over the Heaphy Track from Golden Bay.

It's a 45-minute drive from Karamea to the Oparara caves system. Follow the road north to Kohaihai for 10 km (6 mi) then turn right into McCallums Mill Road. Follow the signs along this gravel road. Note that the access road to the Oparara area is not suitable for large camper

8

vans. Walks range from 10 minutes to 10 hours; the Oparara Arch is a 25-minute walk each way from the parking lot. Contact the **Karamea Information & Resource Centre** for information on cave tours.

ESSENTIALS

Tour Information HeliCharter Karamea (☎ *03/782-6111* ⊕ *www. adventuresnz.co.nzwww.karameahelicharter.co.nz*). **Remote Adventures** (☎ *0800/150-338 or 03/525-6167* ⊕ *www.remoteadventures.co.nz*).

Visitor Information Karamea Information & Resource Centre ⊠ *Market Cross intersection* ☎ *03/782-6652* ⊕ *www.karameainfo.co.nz*).

EXPLORING

Oparara cave system. These caves are a series of huge limestone arches (including the largest in the Southern Hemisphere at 143 meters [470 feet]), passages, and caverns, surrounded by lush forests. One of the best is the excellent Honeycomb Cave, an underground system of roughly 13 km (8 mi) of passages. Bones from the extinct moa bird have been found here, and you'll likely see glowworms. Karamea is also the start for the five- to six-day hikes through the Wangapeka and Karamea-Leslie river systems. These are serious hiking areas through some stunning wilderness area, but the facilities are of a lower standard than the Heaphy Track (which is a Great Walk).

Visit the Karamea Information Centre (⇨ *above*) for details on the Oparara caves area and the local walking tracks.

EN ROUTE

On the drive up to Karamea from Westport you'll first pass through a series of sleepy coastal villages at Granity, Hector, and Ngakawau. If you want to stay over stop at the really laid-back **Gentle Annie Coastal Enclave** (⊠ *De Malmanche Rd* ⊹ *Turn left directly after crossing Mokihinui River bridge* ☎ *03/782–1826* ⊕ *www.gentleannie. co.nz*) on the coastline north of the Mokihinui River. Accommodations range from tasteful holiday homes to campsites and they run a morning-only café in summer, all overlooking the coast or the bush. Kayaks and bikes are available.

The final hour of the drive from Westport crosses the incredibly scenic **Karamea Bluff.** In the goldrush era of the 1800s and the farming days of the early 1900s this road didn't exist; road access to Karamea was by a more inland route up the Mokihinui Gorge and the Rough and Tumble Creek. But following the 1929 Murchison earthquake, which caused huge land upheaval over a vast area, the road was destroyed. The new road over the bluff, which slowly pushed through, is sealed. It climbs steeply from the Mokihinui River through virgin *podocarp* forest before breaking out on to a plateau of fertile farmland. It then drops away to Little Wanganui, some 15 km (9 mi) from Karamea before winding gently through coastal bush and farms for the last few kilometers.

Rough and Tumble Bush Lodge. Just a few kilometers inland up the Mokihinui River from the highway, this wooden lodge ($) occupies a stunning spot on a bend in the river, surrounded by virgin forest and towering gorge walls. Sit outside on the deck and listen to the rumble of the water as it slices over the rocky riverbed. Walk across the wooden plank bridge to the river and take a cool dip in the deep pool on the far side; or take the kayaks across and paddle in the still backflows and eddies. You'd be hard-pressed to find a more marvelous spot anywhere, with the mountainous Glasgow Range behind and the deep green of the Mokihinui Gorge before you. The rooms all sleep four, with a studio bedroom downstairs and a loft room upstairs. **Pros:** great spot for families, and children are welcomed; the nearby 10 km (6 mi) Charming Creek walkway is well worth doing; hosts Marion and Susan are both keen outdoor enthusiasts, and play the fiddle; outdoor bath overlooking the river. **Cons:** the entry road is rough gravel, with a fjord crossing (OK for small rental vehicles); the ford may flood (but there is a dry access footbridge); watch those sand flies in summer. ✉ *Mokihinui Rd., Seddonville* ☎ *03/782–1337 or 0800/333–746* ⊕ *www.roughandtumble.co.nz* ↘ *5 rooms* ⚴ *In-room: No a/c, no phone, no TV, Wi-Fi (some). In-hotel: Restaurant, laundry facilities, Wi-Fi* ⊟ *AE, MC, V* ⦿ *MAP.*

WHERE TO EAT AND STAY

\$\$ **Saracens Café and Bush Lounge.** In addition to the local pub and the café-
CAFE bar and restaurant at the Last Resort, Saracens Café at Market Cross is a nice daytime café, open for breakfast and lunch. After 4:30 they open their **Bush Lounge**, which serves tasty, good-size meals. Check out the boiler-fireplace and the hand-built furniture, and stick around after if it's a live music night. Call for winter hours. ✉ *99 Bridge St.* ☎ *03/ 782–6600* ⊟ *MC, V.*

\$\$ 🏨 **Karamea Lodge.** Overlooking the huge Otumahana Lagoon, this modern, well-priced, eco-friendly lodge is the perfect place to watch magnificent sunsets and be soothed to sleep with the ocean's distant roar. They have purposefully not installed TV or air-conditioning so you get to enjoy the quiet. Kayaks are for guests' use and rain forest bushwalks are just out the door. The rooms are spacious and private balconies overlook the lagoon. A full kitchen and a large dining–lounge area are available if you want to cook. No kids under 12 are allowed. **Pros:** rooms overlook the lagoon and towards the coast; lodge incorporates lots of natural materials; breakfast is local fruit and homemade muesli, croissants, and bread. **Cons:** bring repellent for the outdoor evening biters. ✉ *4589 Karamea Hwy.* ☎ *03/782–6033* ⊕ *www.karamealodge.co.nz* ✍ *info@karamealodge.co.nz* ↘ *3 rooms* ⚴ *In-room: No a/c, kitchen, DVD. In-hotel: Laundry facilities, no kids under 12.* ⊟ *MC, V* ⦿ *CP.*

¢–\$ 🏨 **The Last Resort.** Karamea is one of those deliciously remote places. The Last Resort was largely hand built; its glowing hardwood beams, stylish local artwork, and unusual turf roof make it look very much at one with its surroundings. They can arrange tours, helicopter rides, and shuttles to and from the Heaphy Track, providing a one-stop booking service for the whole experience. Check out the solid 24-meter-long (80-foot-long) hardwood roof beam in the bar area. **Pros:** there are a bar–bistro and a restaurant; helicopters land nearby to whisk you off into the national park; three two-bedroom cottages are \$150 a night. **Cons:** on the main street of Karamea village. ✉ *71 Waverley St.* ☎ *03/782–6617 or 0800/505–042* ⊕ *www.lastresort.co.nz* ✍ *enquiries@lastresort.co.nz*

8

↩ *18 en suite studios (3 self-contained, 13 with kitchenette), 6 lodge rooms (shared bath), 3 cottages, 3 dorm rooms* ♿ *In-room: No a/c, no phone (some), no TV (some), Wi-Fi. In-hotel: Restaurant, bar, spa, bicycles, Wi-Fi* ⊟ *V, MC.*

¢ ⛺ **Kohaihai Campsite.** At the southern end of the Heaphy Track is a stunning spot to camp if you want to experience the pristine setting of this remote spot. It's just a 16-km (10-mi) drive north of Karamea, the last 5 km (3 mi) are gravel, and there are basic facilities only. Inquire at the Karamea Information Centre. As with most of the West Coast, don't swim in the sea here as there are strong rips and undertows. Jump in the river instead. **Pros:** right at the start of the Heaphy Track and short walks; camp in sight and sound of the sea. **Cons:** basic campsite with toilets and barbecues, fresh water, no showers. ⊠ *End of Council Rd., Kohaihai* ⊕ *www.doc.govt.nz*

PAPAROA NATIONAL PARK

269 km (168 mi) southeast of Nelson.

GETTING HERE AND AROUND

At first glance, Punakaiki looks like nothing more than a small cluster of beach houses and shops—a blip on the radar without even a gas station or ATM. It's worth stopping, though, for its famous Pancake Rocks—a maze of limestone stacked high above the sea, and an easy walk from the road. It is also the main entry point to the Paparoa National Park tracks and river activities. Punakaiki is roughly halfway along the coast between Greymouth and Westport on State Highway 6; 40 minutes north of Greymouth; and one hour south of Westport. The road is winding and steep in places, with high drop-offs to the coast on the stretch north of Punakaiki. InterCity buses and Atomic Shuttles pass through daily. Accommodations range from a DOC campground to holiday homes, B&Bs, and a hotel.

The **Paparoa National Park Visitors Centre**, across the road from the main gate, is a handy place to learn more about the formations.

ESSENTIALS

Visitor Information Paparoa National Park Visitors Centre (⊠ *Main Rd.* ☎ *03/731–1895* ⊕ *www.doc.govt.nz*).

EXPLORING

Paparoa National Park, which is based loosely along the Paparoa Range, is a long rugged chain of mountains running parallel to the coast. With craggy summits, serrated ridges, and cirques carved out of ancient granite and gneiss, it's a formidable environment. But its sheer cliffs, flood-prone rivers, dense rain forest, and extensive cave systems spell out paradise for hikers. The major entry points—Bullock Creek, Fox River, and Pororari River—open onto an otherworldly zone of jungly green, striking *nikau* palms, rushing streams, and sweeping coastal views. Much of this area is serious outback country, requiring either a guide or considerable bush experience. There are several short day hikes, canoeing, and horse treks, though; drop by the **Paparoa National Park Visitors Centre** for maps and information.

Paparoa National Park's eroded coastline leads to the fantastic Pancake Rocks.

★ The star of the park is the **Pancake Rocks.** The huge swells that batter this coast have eroded the limestone cliffs, carving them into fantastical shapes. A paved walkway leads you through the windswept cover of tenacious New Zealand flax and *nikau* palms to see the most dramatic points, including the boiling cauldron called the Surge Pool and the pumping fissure of the Chimney Pot. In the right conditions, at high tide three blowholes spout a thundering geyser of spray. Aoraki (Mt. Cook) is sometimes visible across the sea to the south. To reach the rocks from the highway, take the easy 10-minute walk from the visitor center. Keep turning left along the path so you don't miss the best bits out around the Surge Pool. High tide on a southwest swell under a full moon at midnight is an outstanding time to visit, if you dare. Otherwise, try for high tide or a big westerly swell.

OUTDOOR ACTIVITIES

℃ For many, the essence of this gorgeous region can be understood by a paddle up the Pororari River, just to the north of the village. Glide silently through the dark, brooding waters between huge limestone cliffs studded with *nikau* and giant *rata* trees with **Punakaiki Canoes.** Or head down the estuary toward the coast, where the waterway opens out into a more playful area. These trips are suitable for all abilities and ages, but dependent on the state of the weather and the river. ✉ *State Hwy. 6* ☎ *03/731–1870* ⊕ *www.riverkayaking.co.nz* 💵 *$35 per person for up to 2 hrs, $55 all day. Guided tours from $70. Family rates available.*

WHERE TO STAY

The eating options often fall short in Punakaiki, although the Punakaiki Rocks Hotel with its large oceanfront restaurants and bar has helped that somewhat. Because there are only a couple of places to eat in town, it's best to reserve an evening table in mid-summer. There are two small lunch cafés opposite the entry to the Pancake Rocks. If you decide to stay in a self-catering unit, you'll need to bring in all your food, as there are no general stores in town.

$$–$$$ **Hydrangea Cottages.** You'll be lulled by the constant roar of the ocean here, ½ km (¼ mi) south of the Pancake Rocks. Three of the apartments—Rata, Mamaku, and Nikau—are brightly colored with recycled native timbers and contemporary furniture. The smaller studio cottage, Rimu, goes rustic with a cute indoor shower built of river rock and corrugated iron. The two-bedroom Kiwi House is available mid-May to mid-October, with a minimum stay of three nights, and the Miro cottage has lovely sea views. All are self-catering. **Pros:** horse treks available into the national park or along the beach. **Cons:** entry is a bit hard to find; 600 meters (0.4 mi) south of Pancake Rocks; reception is not always manned but instructions are left at the door. ✉ *Main Rd.* ☎ *03/731–1839* ⊕ *www.pancake-rocks.co.nz* ✉ *info@pancake-rocks.co.nz* ⮑ *3 suites, 3 cottage* ⌂ *In-room: No a/c, no phone, kitchen (some), DVD, Wi-Fi (some). In-hotel: No-smoking rooms* ▭ *MC, V.*

$$$ **Punakaiki Resort.** The modern beach-house design blends well with the dynamic coastal site; the front steps of the hotel reach almost onto the beach, and driftwood, flax, sand, and surf are all part of the deal. There's a mix of hotel rooms on the seaward side of the road and eco-rooms and villas just across the road; the villas have a small kitchenette area. The restaurant and bar have floor-to-ceiling windows and big, comfy leather chairs so you can enjoy the place no matter what the weather. **Pros:** ask for a hotel room on the seaward side for a really salty taste in your mouth; walk the beach on a windy day with the surf crashing in beside you; oceanfront restaurant and bar. **Cons:** eco-suites are across the road from the beach but still have great coastal views. ✉ *State Hwy. 6, 2,200 yards south of Pancake Rocks* ☎ *03/731–1168 or 0800/786–2524* ⊕ *www.punakaiki-resort.co.nz* ⮑ *27 rooms, 12 eco-rooms, 22 villas* ⌂ *In-room: No a/c, kitchen (some), Internet. In-hotel: Restaurant, bar, bicycles, laundry facilities, Internet terminal* ▭ *AE, DC, MC, V.*

GREYMOUTH

44 km (28 mi) south of Punakaiki, 258 km (160 mi) west of Christchurch.

The town of Greymouth is aptly named—at first take, it's a rather dispirited strip of motels and industrial buildings stretched along a wild beach. It sits, as the name suggests, at the mouth of the Grey River and is thus exposed to a bone-chilling wind in winter. But in warmer weather, its good points come to the fore. Many travelers arrive here on the TranzAlpine train from Christchurch and are plopped into the middle of the West Coast without the stunning drives along either the north or the south coasts to set the scene. If you're arriving and returning by train, take a day or two for a trip up to Punakaiki or down to the glaciers, to grasp the scope of the landscape.

GETTING HERE AND AROUND

Drive in from Nelson or Westport to the north, or from the glaciers or Christchurch to the south (although Christchurch is effectively east of Greymouth; the road over Arthur's Pass comes in to Greymouth from the south). InterCity buses and Atomic Shuttles arrive in Greymouth daily.

The TranzAlpine train departs Christchurch daily at 8:15 AM and arrives in Greymouth at 12:45 PM; the return train departs Greymouth at 1:45 PM and arrives at Christchurch at 6:05 PM. The one-way fare is $110–$124, round-trip $182–$235 if returning on the same day.

ESSENTIALS

Bus Depot Greymouth (⊠ *Railway Station, Mackay St.*). **Atomic Shuttles** (☎ *03/349–0697* ⊕ *www.atomictravel.co.nz*). **InterCity** (☎ *03/365–1113* ⊕ *www.intercitycoach.co.nz*).

Hospital Greymouth Base Hospital (⊠ *High St.* ☎ *03/768–0499*).

Train Contacts TranzAlpine Express (☎ *0800/872–467* ⊕ *www.tranzscenic.co.nz*).

Visitor Information Greymouth Visitor Centre (⊠ *Herbert and Mackay, Greymouth* ☎ *03/768–5101* ⊕ *www.greydistrict.co.nz*).

EXPLORING

The land around Greymouth is particularly rich in pounamu, the greenstone highly prized by the Māori. You're in a Ngai Tahu iwi (tribe) area, and as part of the tribe's 1997 Treaty of Waitangi settlement, the government recognized Ngai Tahu as having sole rights to collect and sell the precious jade in its natural form.

The **Left Bank Art Gallery** on the corner of Tainui Street and Mawhera Quay is a good place to see some contemporary pounamu (greenstone or jade) carvings. Built in the old Greymouth branch of the Bank of New Zealand, this progressive little gallery is the best in town. The main chamber of the bank now forms a large open gallery exhibiting a feature artist. The old vault may have a display by the local photography club, the manager's office has more craft-oriented exhibits and retail items, and the contemporary pounamu collection is in a back room. ⊠ *1 Tainui St.,* ☎ *03/768–0038* ⊕ *www.leftbankart. co.nz* ⊙ *Summer, weekdays 10–5; winter, weekends 10–3, Tues.–Fri. 10–4, Sat. 10–3.*

The **Jade Boulder Gallery** exhibits the work of Ian Boustridge, one of the country's best sculptors of greenstone. The gallery is a great place to pick up a distinctive souvenir; earrings start at about $10, pendants generally cost a couple of hundred, and a sculpture can cost thousands. The gallery's latest addition, the Jade Boulder Trail, is an interpretative walk-through detailing the legends and forms of New Zealand greenstone, with displays of carved and raw jade. They also

8

have an on-site café. ⊠ *1 Guinness St.* ☎ *03/768–0700* ⏱ *Nov.–Apr., daily 8:30 AM–9 PM; May–Oct., daily 8:30–5.*

☾ On the southern outskirts of Greymouth **Shantytown** is a lively reenactment of a gold-mining town of the 1880s. This is how the settlers who stayed on after that gold rush would have lived—but without the electricity, running water, and paved entry road. Except for the church and the town hall, most of the buildings are reproductions, including a jail, a blacksmith shop, a railway station, and a barbershop. The gold-digging displays include a water jet for blasting the gold-bearing quartz from the hillside, water sluices, and a stamper—battery-powered by a 30-foot waterwheel—for crushing the ore. You can pan for gold with a good chance of striking "color," as this was the site of the world's last major gold rush, or catch a steam train ride. The train ride is included in the entry price. ⊠ *Rutherglen* ☎ *03/762–6634* ✉ *shantytown@xtra.co.nz* ⊕ *www.shantytown.co.nz* ⊡ *$25* ⏱ *Daily 8:30–5; last train leaves at 4 PM.*

A few miles south of Greymouth is Kūmara's **Carey Dillon Woodworker.** The namesake artisan's workshop and gallery is devoted to wood-turning and landscape photography, and Dillon's work is superb. He turns chunks of aged *rimu*, a native hardwood gathered from fallen logs, into magnificent bowls that glow like amber; each one takes at least a year to create. His large photographs are highly scenic. ⊠ *State Hwy. 73, Main Rd., Kūmara* ☎ *03/736–9741* ⊕ *www.careydillon.com* ⏱ *Apr.–Oct.*

WHERE TO EAT

Quality eating options in Greymouth are hard to find, although there are several spots that have reasonable lunch fare.

$$–$$$ ✕ **124 on Mackay.** There's a light bistro menu as well as cabinet food like
CAFÉ panini, quiche, and café-style baked goods; it's open most days. ⊠ *124 Mackay St.* ☎ *03/768–4929.*

$$$ ✕ **Bridge Bar & Cafe.** Perched high on the edge of the rugged, wild Tara-
NEW ZEALAND makau River, this restaurant and bar has blown into the area like a fresh blast off the Southern Ocean, with crisp clean flavors and good service. The menu, like most places on the coast, is based on local foods, but here they spin a contemporary twist. Whitebait is the signature dish but the rack of lamb with seasonal vegetables and the beef fillet are also treats. The coffee is still the best in town. ⊠ *Main Rd. S, 10 km (6 mi) south of Greymouth* ☎ *03/762–6830* ⊟ *MC, V.*

$$–$$$ ✕ **Speight's Ale House.** Just a few minutes walk from the railway station,
NEW ZEALAND this restaurant has a bistro-style menu and bar service. It is open every day from 11 AM and makes for a good lunch spot. ⊠ *130 Mawhera Quay* ☎ *03/768–0667.*

$$$ ✕ **Station House Café.** You can come to Lake Brunner on a day drive from
ECLECTIC Greymouth, as part of a round-the-lake trip, or stop off the TranzAlpine train for lunch while it hops out to the coast and back—about a three hour stop. The café is an old railway house, perched on a terrace above the railway station and with a superb view across Lake Brunner and the *kahikatea* forests and wetlands beyond. The menu plays up venison, lamb, rib-eye steak, and turbot; there's also a small range of salad meals. Main dishes are served with a healthy side of either cooked greens or

root veggies. ⊠ *Koe St., Moana* ☎ *03/738–0158* ☝ *Reservations essential* ⊟ *AE, DC, MC, V* ☾ *Winter hrs can vary. Call ahead for dinner.*

WHERE TO STAY

$$$$

Fodor's Choice

★

⌂ **Lake Brunner Lodge.** On the southern shore of Lake Brunner, a 40-minute drive southeast of Greymouth, this lodge, first established in 1868, is an enticing retreat at a price that is not as high as most of New Zealand's elite lodges. Rooms are large and well equipped, with the emphasis on comfort rather than opulence. The best rooms are at the front of the villa, overlooking the lake. Brown trout fill the clear waters of the surrounding rivers; fly-fishing is the main sport, but good spin fishing is also available at certain times of the year. (There's a catch-and-release policy.) The lodge is surrounded by forest, which you can explore on a guided environmental tour, and is part of a large working farm, which you can also explore. The kitchen turns out seasonal dishes with a local bent, such as roast lamb with ratatouille. Children are welcome only by advance arrangement. Because of its remote location, the lodge generates power with a hydro plant running off a spectacular waterfall behind the main building. **Pros:** join a farm tour; go fishing or kayaking; put on your walking shoes and climb to the waterfall behind the lodge (you'll need to be moderately agile); nicely decorated. **Cons:** the road to the lodge is narrow, winding, and gravel for the last few kilometers; two-night minimum stay over Christmas–New Year's week. ⊠ *Mitchells, R.D. 1, Kūmara* ☎ *03/738–0163* ✉ *lodge@brunner. co.nz* ⊕ *www.lakebrunner.co.nz* ⇨ *11 rooms* ⌂ *In-room: No a/c, no TV, Internet. In-hotel: Restaurant, bicycles, no-smoking rooms* ⊟ *AE, DC, MC, V* ⨯⃝*MAP.*

$$

⌂ **New River Bluegums B&B.** Looking a bit like the little house on the prairie, this river rock and timber homestay is a delight. There's a B&B room in the main house and two well-appointed, self-contained cottages out past the barn. With particularly rural surroundings and a slightly unkempt acreage this place is full of rustic appeal. It's only a 10-minute walk down to the coast and there's a flood-lighted tennis court for an evening game (racquets provided). **Pros:** kids will love the sheep and pigs and the open spaces; a traditional home-cooked dinner is available on request, with pavlova for dessert; barbecue hampers are also available. **Cons:** big friendly Labrador on-site; wake to the early-morning sounds of roosters and native birds. ⊠ *985 Main Rd. S, 9 km (5½ mi) south of Greymouth* ☎ *03/762–6678* ⊕ *www. bluegumsnz.com* ⇨ *1 room, 2 cottages* ⌂ *In-room: No phone (some), kitchen, DVD (some), Internet. In-hotel: Tennis court, laundry facilities* ⊟ *MC, V* ⨯⃝*BP.*

$$$

⌂ **Rosewood.** Rhonda and Stephan Palten run this B&B in a restored 1920s home close to the town center. Original oak paneling and stained-glass windows remain, and there are cozy seats in the bay windows. Some rooms are done in a contemporary look; others have period furniture. Stephan's a chef, so expect an excellent breakfast of fresh rolls, bacon, pancakes, French toast, or eggs any way you want them. Two rooms share a bathroom. You can get a courtesy pickup at the train station. **Pros:** good off-street parking and disabled access, you can arrange rooms so as not to share a bathroom. **Cons:** busy street. ⊠ *20 High St.*

8

☎ *03/768–4674* ✆ *stay@rosewoodnz.co.nz* ⊕ *www.rosewoodnz.co.nz* ☞ *5 rooms, 3 with bath* �& *In-room: No a/c. In-hotel: Bar, Internet terminal, no-smoking rooms* ⊟ *AE, DC, MC, V* ❍❙ *BP.*

HOKITIKA

41 km (26 mi) south of Greymouth.

Hokitika is the pick of the towns running down the West Coast, with the pounding ocean before it and the bush-covered hills behind. It's a place of simple pleasures: scouting the crafts boutiques, taking a bush-walk, enjoying the seafood, and looking for evocatively shaped driftwood on the beach. Hokitika is central enough to catch a scenic flight to the glaciers, or take a day trip to Punakaiki or Arthur's Pass.

GETTING HERE AND AROUND

There are daily flights to Hokitika from Christchurch by small commuter plane.

Arrive by road from Christchurch or Greymouth to the north, or from the glaciers to the south (via State Highway 6). Either way you will enjoy a spectacular drive through World Heritage country, national park or scenic reserve. InterCity buses and Atomic Shuttles arrive in Hokitika daily.

ESSENTIALS

Bus Depot Hokitika (⊠ *Hokitika Travel Centre, 64 Tancred St.*).

Visitor Information Hokitika Visitor Centre (⊠ *Hamilton and Tancred, Hokitika* ☎ *03/755–6166* ⊕ *www.hokitika.org*).

EXPLORING

In several places along and just off **Tancred Street,** you can check out the work of local artisans, particularly the pounamu carvings the area's known for. For instance, **Westland Greenstone** (⊠ *34 Tancred St.* ☎ *03/755–8713*) has an interesting walk-through workshop where you can watch greenstone being cut, shaped, and polished. At the **Hokitika Craft Gallery Co-operative** (⊠ *25 Tancred St.* ☎ *03/755–8802*) greenstone carvings are joined by pottery, woodwork, and textiles. **Ocean Paua** (⊠ *25 Weld St.* ☎ *03/755–6128*) has a varied range of *paua* shell, greenstone, and bone artworks, jewelry and a workshop. The larger **Jade Factory** (⊠ *41 Weld St.* ☎ *03/755–8007*) also has a greenstone cutting area, stone painting, and a café.

In the colonial days Hokitika was a busy port. The remains of this are still evident today on a walk along the **Quayside Heritage Area** at the southern end of Tancred and Revell Streets, along to Sunset Point Lookout. See the old Custom House and river mouth; on a clear day you'll see Mt. Cook across the sea.

For many Kiwis, Hokitika is on the map purely for its annual **Wildfoods Festival,** which celebrates bush tucker (food from the bush) from the West Coast's natural food sources. Bite into such delectables as *huhu* grubs (they look like large maggots), worm sushi, whitebait patties (far more mainstream), and snail caviar, and follow it all with gorse wine, moonshine, or Monteith's bitter beer. The mid-March fest (book well

Okarito Town

Back in 1866 Okarito was a thriving town of more than 1,200 people, with three theaters and 25 hotels. People came for the gold and for many years there was a working port inside the bar at the entrance to the lagoon. Things have changed dramatically and Okarito is now a nature sanctuary, drawing visitors keen to see kiwi, seabirds, and white herons, and to paddle on the silent lagoon. Its wild black sand surf beach is home to nesting birds and sleeping seals, so watch where you walk. **Okarito Nature Tours** (☎ 03/753–4014 ⊕ www.okarito.co.nz) sticks to the lagoon, which is a good spot to see white herons away from their nesting grounds. Rates start at $45 unguided and $75 for a guided trip (minimum of two people). Ian Cooper's **Okarito Kiwi Tours** (✉ The Strand, Okarito ☎ 03/753–4330 ⊕ www.okaritokiwitours.co.nz ✉ Prices start from $65 ⊙ Evenings only) holds the only concession on the South Island mainland to take visitors to see kiwi in their natural habitat. He'll have you walking softly through the bush, listening for their scuffles and calls, before catching a glimpse of these elusive flightless birds. It's an incredibly rare experience and he gives an 85% chance of seeing one on a night tour; last season had a 96% success rate.

ahead) attracts crowds of up to 20,000, six times the local population. Go down to the beach later and watch as the bonfires light up and people dig in for the night. A good dump of West Coast rain quiets things down—until the next year. Take your gum boots and an open mind. ⊕ *www.wildfoods.co.nz.*

WHERE TO EAT

$$$–$$$$
NEW ZEALAND
✕ **Café de Paris.** Pronounced *"parr*-iss" in these parts, this spot serves French cuisine with a New Zealand accent. The simple interior is in keeping with owner Pierre Esquilat's straightforward approach: unfussy French cooking with fresh local ingredients. The pork fillet wrapped in pancetta and served on mashed *kūmara* and pumpkin is a delicious example, as is local venison seared and finished with a blueberry-and-port wine glaze. There's a liquor license, but you're welcome to BYOB. It's open breakfast through dinner, and there are a few outdoor tables for warm summer evenings. ✉ *19 Tancred St.* ☎ *03/755–8933* ⌸ *Reservations essential* ⊟ *AE, DC, MC, V.*

$–$$
CAFÉ
✕ **Hokitika Cheese and Deli.** As the name suggests this is a cheese shop and a deli, but it's also the nicest daytime café in Hokitika. The coffee is good (comes as a standard double shot) and the small range of cabinet food and all-day breakfast menu make it an easy choice for a whistle-stop lunch. There are the usual eggs done every which way, panini, wraps, and sweet cakes. The cheese room has cheeses from some of the best boutique cheesemakers around, and you might pick up something easy to cook up for dinner while you're there. ✉ *84 Revell St.* ☎ *03/755–5432* ⊟ *MC, V* ⊙ *Daily 10–4.*

WHERE TO STAY

$$$–$$$$ 🖼 **Rimu Lodge.** Just 10 minutes from Hokitika, this modern two-story lodge sits high above the Hokitika River valley, and has extensive views across to the Southern Alps. Closer in the view is leafy and green, framed by native bush and garden. The four guest rooms, named for local native birds, are well sized, as are the en suite bathrooms. The two ground-floor guest rooms open out onto the large breakfast deck area and all four are bathed in natural light. The social hub of the lodge is a large Great Room which also opens to the outdoors, with a big open fire in winter. Beneath the lodge and its neighboring properties lies a long tunnel running deep into the hill, a relic from the district's active gold-mining days. **Pros:** all the surrounding native bush makes this place a bird-watchers delight; good walks (Lakes Mahinapua and Kaniere) and local heritage walks nearby; catch a dramatic sunrise over the Alps on summer mornings; dinner platter available on request. **Cons:** really friendly on-site springer spaniel; bit hard to find at night, watch for the sign for Seddon Terrace Road. ⊠ *33 Seddon Terrace Rd., Rimu* ☎ *03/755–5255* ⊕ *www.rimulodge. co.nz* ⤳ *4 rooms* ⚴ *In-room: No a/c, safe, refrigerator, Wi-Fi. In-hotel: Laundry service, Internet terminal, Wi-Fi, no kids under 13, no-smoking rooms.* ⊟ *AE, MC, V* ⊙ *BP.*

$–$$ 🖼 **Shining Star.** These oceanfront chalets are about as close to the beach ⚘ as you'll get; the surf rolls in, the air has a salty tang, and the sky is filled with wheeling seabirds. The various units range from basic cabins to chalets with full kitchens and big fluffy duvets; a few have whirlpool baths. There's a menagerie of sorts, too, including sheep, goats, alpaca, and pigs. A continental breakfast is available on request, and there are powered sites for camper vans. **Pros:** walk out onto the wild surf beach and build a driftwood fire. **Cons:** driveways and park spots are gravel. ⊠ *11 Richards Dr.* ☎ *03/755–8921* ⊕ *www.accommodationwestcoast. co.nz* ✍ *shining@xtra.co.nz* ⤳ *12 chalets, 8 cabins, 3 1-bedroom apartments* ⚴ *In-room: No a/c (some), safe (some), Wi-Fi (some). In-hotel: Spa, no-smoking rooms* ⊟ *AE, DC, MC, V.*

$$–$$$ 🖼 **Teichelmann's Bed & Breakfast.** Named for Dr. Ebenezer Teichelmann, the surgeon-mountaineer-conservationist who built the original part of the house, this is the most comfortable place in the center of town. Its friendly vibe has a lot to do with hosts Frances Flanagan and Brian Ward, who are happy to make suggestions for local activities. Furnishings are a combination of antique and country-cottage style, using plenty of native wood. The *rimu*-wood bookcase is full of literature about the area. **Pros:** one of the West Coast's accommodations icons; for those who enjoy the quieter side of life. **Cons:** opens onto one of Hokitika's main streets. ⊠ *20 Hamilton St.* ☎ *03/755–8232* ✍ *teichel@ xtra.co.nz* ⊕ *www.teichelmanns.co.nz* ⤳ *5 rooms, 1 cottage* ⚴ *In-room: No a/c, no phone. In-hotel: Internet terminal, no kids under 10, no-smoking rooms* ⊟ *MC, V* ⊙ *BP.*

WESTLAND NATIONAL PARK

Fodor's Choice *North end 146 km (91 mi) south of Hokitika.*

★
GETTING HERE AND AROUND

State Highway 6 passes through this region and is the only major road. Drive in from Hokitika in the north or Wanaka and Haast from the south. There are only a few fuel stops between Hokitika and Haast so watch your fuel gauge. InterCity buses and Atomic Shuttles come through daily from the north and the south, stopping at both glacier villages.

ESSENTIALS

Bus Depot Franz Josef (⊠ *Franz Josef Hotel, Main Rd.; Franz Josef YHA, 2–4 Cron St.; Main Rd., opposite Cheeky Kea Bldg.*). **Fox Glacier** (⊠ *Northbound: Alpine Guides, Main Rd.; Southbound: Fox General Store*).

Hospital Franz Josef Rural Clinic (⊠ *Main Hwy.* ☎ *03/752–0700*).

Visitor Information Fox Glacier Visitor Centre (⊠ *State Hwy. 6, Fox Glacier* ☎ *03/751–0807* ⊕ *www.glaciercountry.co.nz*). **Franz Josef Glacier Visitor Information Centre** (⊠ *State Hwy. 6, Franz Josef* ☎ *03/752–0796* ⊕ *www. glaciercountry.co.nz*).

EXPLORING

Westland National Park joins the Fiordland and Mt. Aspiring national parks to form a sweeping World Heritage Area of more than 5 million acres, including some of the best examples of the plants and animals once found on the ancient Gondwanaland supercontinent. It's a place of extremes, including the extreme precipitation at the top of Westland. Up to 300 inches of snow per annum falls here, feeding Westland's glacier field. The snow is compressed into ice on the névé, or head, of the glaciers (New Zealanders say "glassy-urs"), then flows downhill under its own weight. There are more than 60 glaciers in the park; the most famous and accessible are at Franz Josef and Fox. If you're driving through on a cloudy or wet day you will get no idea of the size of the mountain ranges just a few miles off the road. On a clear day take a moment to stop and admire them disappearing inland, layer after mighty layer. The Harihari, Whataroa, and Fox Glacier valleys are good for this.

The **Fox Glacier** is slightly larger than Franz Josef, but you'll miss nothing important if you see only one.Both glaciers have separate villages, and if you are spending the night, **Franz Josef Glacier** is marginally preferable (Fox is much more seasonal; many places have restricted hours or close completely in winter). Both towns have solid tourist infrastructures, but the summer tourist rush means you should make reservations in advance for lodgings and restaurants. Drive to parking areas outside both towns from which you can walk 20–40 minutes to reach viewing points of the glaciers (access to either glacier may be closed if conditions are not good). Both parking lots are visited by mischievous *kea* (*kee*-ah)—mountain parrots—that may delight in destroying the rubber molding around car windows and eating left-open lunches. Their beaks are like can openers. *Kea* are harmless to humans, but don't encourage them by feeding them. Drive to the south side of the Cook River and up the gravel side road for around 4 km (2 ½ mi) if you want a view

8

of the glacier without the walk—the road is not suitable for campers. Trails from the parking lots wind across the rocky valley floor to the glacier faces, where a tormented chorus of squeaks, creaks, groans, and gurgles can be heard as the glacier creeps down the mountainside at an average rate of up to 3 feet per day. Care must be taken because rocks and chunks of ice frequently drop from the melting face. These faces are dangerous places and, unless you are with a guided group, you won't be allowed to get too close to them

These being New Zealand glaciers, there is much to do besides admire them. You can fly over them in helicopters or planes and land on the stable névé, or hike on them with guides. Remember that these structures are always in motion—an ice cave that was visible yesterday might today be smashed under tons of ice that used to be just uphill of it. Likewise, some of the fascinating formations that you see on the surface of the glacier were fairly recently at the very bottom of it higher up in the valley. Danger comes with this unstable territory; guides know the hazardous areas to avoid.

For the most part, flights are best early in the morning, when visibility tends to be clearest. Seasonal variables around the glaciers are a surprising thing. Summer may be warmer and by far the busiest season, but there is a great deal more rain and fog that can scuttle flightseeing and hiking plans. There's a lot to be said for winter visits. In winter, snow doesn't fall at sea level in Franz Josef or Fox; in fact, in winter this area is a lot warmer than the snow towns farther south. Skies are clearer, which means fewer canceled flights and glacier hikes and more spectacular mountains views. Warm clothing is always essential on the glaciers, and evenings can be cold any time of year. Watch for ice on the roads at any time of day during winter.

Outside the town of Fox Glacier, **Lake Matheson** has one of the country's most famous views. A walking trail winds along the lakeshore, and the snowcapped peaks of Aoraki/Mt. Cook and Mt. Tasman are reflected in the water. Allow at least three hours for the complete walk from town to the "view of views" and back. The best times are sunrise and sunset, when the mirror-like reflections are less likely to be fractured by the wind. From town, walk down Cook Flat Road (it's 5 km [3 mi] each way) toward the sea where a sign points to Gillespies Beach; turn right to reach the lake; the round-the-lake walk on its own is 1½ hours.

Lake Moeraki is in the midst of Westland National Park, 90 km (56 mi) south of Fox Glacier. There isn't a town here; it's the site of a thoughtfully designed wilderness lodge (sister lodge to the Arthur's Pass Wilderness Lodge. Access to the coast is easiest at **Monro Beach.** The 45-minute walk to the beach takes you through spectacular, fern-filled native forest to a truly remarkable beach: rock clusters jut out of incredibly blue waters, and rivers and streams flow over the sand into the Tasman Sea. You might arrive at a time when spunky little Fiordland crested penguins are in transit from the sea to their stream or hillside nests. Early morning and late afternoon provide the best chance of seeing them.

Two kilometers (1 mi) south of the trail entrance on the beach is a seal colony, which you will smell before you see it. If you venture that way, be sure to keep about 30 feet away from the seals, and don't block their path to the sea. A spooked seal will bowl you over on its lurch for the water. Sculpted dark gray rocks also litter the beach to the south, and seals like to lie behind and among them, so look carefully before you cross in front of these rocks.

Monro Beach is an utter dream, not least if you collect driftwood or rocks. On the road 2 km (1 mi) or so south of it, there is a lookout over the rock stacks at **Knights Point.** Farther south still, between Moeraki and Haast, the walkways and beach at **Ship Creek** are another stop for ferny forests and rugged coastline. Sand flies here can be voracious, so bring insect repellent and hope for a windy day. (There are far fewer sand flies in winter.) For weather conditions and other current information visit the **Fox Glacier Visitor Centre** and the **Franz Josef Glacier Visitor Information Centre, both** on State Highway 6.

Visit **Hukawai Glacier Centre** (✉ *Corner Cron and Cowan Sts., Franz Josef* ☎ *03/752–0600 or 0800/485–2921* ⊕ *www.hukawai. co.nz* ✉ *$25*) before you go up on the ice, or if the cloud is down and you're not going to get there anyway. Watch the Māori Creation story, learn how the glaciers are formed, and about the local geology and flora and fauna. If you've got time, and a bit of money, you can have a go on their indoor ice-climbing wall (the only one in the Southern Hemisphere).

OUTDOOR ACTIVITIES

Even though the white heron (known to the Māori as *kotuku*) nests only from October to March, a trip with **White Heron Sanctuary Tours** is worth doing at any time of the year. A rollicking jet-boat ride takes you down the gorgeous Waitangita-ona River to the sea, passing white-bait fishermen and solitary birds on the swampy banks before winding along a short coastal inlet and then drifting into a nature reserve. In season the elegant *kotuku* nest at their only site in the country, and a bird-watching hide has been set up directly opposite. Trip prices are $110 and reservations are essential. ☎ *03/753–4120 or 0800/523–456* ⊕ *www.whiteherontours.co.nz.*

> ### RELAXATION, GLACIER STYLE
>
> At Franz Josef is the Glacier Hot Pools complex, which sits deep in a rain forest. The three public pools range from family-friendly to a completely relaxing. There is also a massage room, providing a range of five different therapies (from $80), and three private hot tubs with their own shower and change areas. This is a great stop if the weather is just not cooperating, but the compact complex may fill up on these days. ⊠ *Cron St.7856* ☎ *03/752–0161 or 0800/044–044* ⊕ *www.glacierhotpools.co.nz* 🛁 *Public pool $22.50, private pools $40* ☻ *Daily noon–late.*

GLACIER TOURS The walks to the glacier heads mentioned above are the easiest way of seeing the glaciers from a distance. But joining a guided walk and getting up close to the glaciers' ice formations is unforgettable. Flying over the glaciers is quite thrilling, but expensive. The ultimate combination is to fly by fixed-wing plane or helicopter to the top or middle of the glacier and get out and walk on it. Heli-hikes give you the most time on the ice, two to three hours of snaking up and down the middle of the glacier.

Fox Glacier Guiding has are trips to suit all fitness levels, budgets, and time frames, and even ones that are good for kids (over the age of seven). The four-hour walk travels about 2 km (1 mi) up the glacier. The climb requires some fitness. Arguably the best option is to heli-hike, combining a helicopter flight onto and off Fox Glacier and walking for 2½ hours on the ice with a guide ($399). Reservations are recommended. ⊠ *Fox Glacier Guiding Bldg., Main St., Fox Glacier* ☎ *03/751–0825 or 0800/111–600* ✐ *info@foxguides.co.nz* ⊕ *www. foxguides.co.nz.*

Franz Josef Glacier Guides provides a comprehensive guide service with a popular half-day walk ($105) for those short on time, a full day trip ($160) or a heli-hike tour ($390) where you'll get flown up onto the ice field, dropped for a two-hour hike, then picked up again. Bookings are essential. ⊠ *Main Rd., Franz Josef* ☎ *03/752–0763 or 0800/484–337* ⊕ *www.franzjosefglacier.com.*

If you want a more personalized helicopter experience then try **Mountain Helicopters** They fly out of both Franz Josef and Fox with flights starting at 10 minutes for $95 (out of Fox). The smaller choppers mean that everyone gets a window seat, and the experience is more intimate than with the bigger operators, often suiting the more mature market. ✉ *Main St., Franz Josef* ☎ *03/751–0045 or 0800/369-423* ⊕ *www.mountainhelicopters.co.nz.*

Mt. Cook Ski Planes has fixed-wing ski planes that fly over the glaciers, landing amid craggy peaks in the high-altitude ski slopes at the head of the glaciers. They provide a less edgy experience than a helicopter, if flying in small craft isn't really your thing, and the company has over 50 years experience flying through these mountains. The planes have a retractable ski, which allows them to do airfield take-offs and on-the-ice landings, or vice versa, on the same trip. Departures are from Franz Josef and Fox Glacier villages. ✉ *Main Rd., Franz Josef* ☎ *03/752–0714 or 0800/368-000* ⊕ *www.mtcookskiplanes.com.*

WHERE TO EAT

Both Fox and Franz Josefs are on the backpacker circuit and are well serviced with hostel accommodations, but there is also a good range of hotel lodgings.

$$$

NEW ZEALAND

✗ **The Alice May.** This café and bar is one of those cozy, buzzing places so prevalent on the West Coast. The food is good, plentiful country fare. Favorites are the roast of the day, the deep-sea cod with chips, apple crumble, and ice cream sundaes. The wine and beer lists are stacked with NZ favorites. ✉ *Cowan and Cron Sts., Franz Josef* ☎ *03/752–0740* ▭ *AE, MC, V.*

$$$–$$$$

NEW ZEALAND

✗ **Beeches.** This place filled a gap in the glaciers' evening dining scene with its strong emphasis on local foods. The stag heads on the wall are courtesy of the chef and the good range of whiskeys and cocktails should provide something for everyone. The whitebait fritters are a mainstay, and the venison is always an attraction. The lighter main dishes on the menu will appeal to those who don't have a downhill ski-er's appetite. ✉ *Main Rd.7856* ☎ *03/752–0721* ✍ *Reservations essential* ▭ *AE, D, MC, V* ⊘ *No breakfast.*

$$–$$$

NEW ZEALAND

✗ **Café Neve.** A standout along Fox Glacier's main street, the Neve sparks up no-nonsense options with fresh local flavors, such as the pizza topped with locally made Blackball salami, field mushrooms, spinach, rosemary, and tomato. For a tiny place, the wine list of 150 vintages is impressive. The lunch menu is more varied, and they're even open for breakfast. ✉ *Main Rd., Fox Glacier* ☎ *03/751–0110* ✍ *Reservations not accepted* ▭ *DC, MC, V.*

$–$$

CAFÉ

✗ **Matheson Cafe.** After an early start, stop at the café for a really good coffee and breakfast. The view from the café is stunning in its own way, surrounded by an amphitheater of distant mountains and *kahikatea* forest. The food is as good as the views, and the sunny terrace is pleasant on a still day. Try the blue cod open sandwich for a tasty lunch. ✉ *Lake Matheson parking lot, Fox Glacier* ☎ *03/751–0878* ▭ *MC, V.*

WHERE TO STAY

$$–$$$

⊡ **58 On Cron Motel.** This modern motel-style accommodation offers great value at the cheaper end of the market, with its well-appointed suites and sunny environment. In bush surroundings and just over the road from the Glacier Hot Pools, it's an easy walk to restaurants as well. Some units have a whirlpool bath and all have kitchen facilities; light breakfasts are available ($). **Pros:** a good budget option;

parking is right outside the door; good winter rates. **Cons:** central courtyard means there is little privacy; on a back street. ✉ *58 Cron St.* ☎ *03/752–0627* ⊕ *www.58oncron.co.nz* ⤶ *10 studios, 6 1- and 2-bedroom units* ♨ *In-room: No a/c, kitchen, Wi-Fi. In-hotel: Laundry facilities, parking (free).* ☐ *MC, V.*

$$$$ 🏠 **Franz Josef Glacier Country Retreat.** Although this grand home was only built in 2006, it evokes a feeling of the past that climbs right out of the landscape. The lodge is surrounded by a 200-acre working farm and backed by tall snowcapped peaks often shrouded in mist. It's only a five-minute drive into Franz Josef village. **Pros:** farm walks; salmon in the creek; a pet sheep; transfers to Franz Josef village are available on request. **Cons:** well back from road; some of the downstairs rooms are rather small. ✉ *State Hwy. 6, Lake Mapourika* ☎ *03/752–0021* ⊕ *www.glacier-retreat.co.nz* ⤶ *10 rooms, 2 suites* ♨ *In-room: No a/c, refrigerator, Wi-Fi. In-hotel: Restaurant, laundry facilities, Internet terminal* ☐ *MC, V* ⦿ *BP.*

$$$ 🏠 **Glenfern Villas.** A short drive north of the village these tidy self-contained villas are in a quiet rural environment away from the tourist bustle and helicopters around the village. Eight villas each have two bedrooms and each villa has a private park. Kids can run off some energy in the playground. **Pros:** villas are a real home-away-from-home in size and feel. **Cons:** some road noise from the highway. ✉ *State Hwy. 6, 3.5 km (2 mi) north of Franz Josef village, Franz Josef* ☎ *03/752–0054* ⊕ *www.glenfern.co.nz* ⤶ *10 1-bedroom units, 8 2-bedroom units* ♨ *In-room: No a/c, kitchen, DVD, Wi-Fi. In-hotel: Laundry facilities, Internet terminal* ☐ *AE, DC, MC, V.*

$$$$ 🏠 **Westwood Lodge.** For unpretentious luxury among the glaciers, turn
★   to this spacious, modern B&B with exceptional alpine views. Rooms are big, with timber surroundings and a neutral color palette. A huge open fire warms the guest lounge and has exceptional alpine and bush outlook. **Pros:** light dinner platter available; billiard table; alpine gardens; some private decks with views of the mountains. **Cons:** busy road position. ✉ *Main Rd., Franz Josef* ☎ *03/752–0112* ⊕ *www.westwood-lodge.co.nz* ⤶ *8 rooms, 1 suite* ♨ *In-room: No a/c, refrigerator, DVD, Wi-Fi. In-hotel: Bar, Internet terminal, no kids under 12, no-smoking rooms* ☐ *AE, DC, MC, V* ⦿ *BP.*

$$$$ 🏠 **Wilderness Lodge Lake Moeraki.** In a World Heritage–listed rain
Fodor'sChoice   forest on the banks of the Moeraki River and an easy 20-minute
★   bushwalk from the Tasman Sea—the superb surroundings and team of eco-guides make this lodge an ideal place to get absorbed in the environment. On-site naturalists introduce you to native plants and animals. Rates include a full breakfast, four-course dinner, use of canoes and kayaks, and two short, guided activities daily. **Pros:** an intense eco-experience; generates own hydropower; rate includes two walks. **Cons:** a long way from anywhere. ✉ *State Hwy. 6, 90 km (56 mi) south of Fox Glacier* ☎ *03/750–0881* ✉ *lakemoeraki@ wildernesslodge.co.nz* ⊕ *www.wildernesslodge.co.nz* ⤶ *24 rooms, 4 suites* ♨ *In-room: No TV. In-hotel: Water sports, laundry facilities, Internet terminal, Wi-Fi, no-smoking rooms* ☐ *MC, V* ☻ *Closed June and July* ⦿ *MAP.*

Christchurch and Canterbury

WORD OF MOUTH

"Just north of Christchurch, don't overlook Waipara. Pegasus Bay is the most well known, but if you're interested in smaller wineries and meeting the winemakers, you can do that here. Some of the small places are appointment only. Don't miss a chance to try NZ's Pinot Gris."

—mlgb

WELCOME TO CHRISTCHURCH AND CANTERBURY

TOP REASONS TO GO

★ **The Arts:** Christchurch has a solid collection of galleries, museums, heritage buildings, and cultural activities, often housed in original 19th-century buildings.

★ **Fantastic Festivals:** Hardly a month goes by in Christchurch without a festival staged by one organization or another. Festivals honor various professions, gardens, seasons, and heritage days.

★ **Hiking and Trekking:** Arthur's Pass and the Rakaia and Rangitata river gorges have walking and hiking trails and boating and picnicking areas.

★ **Parks and Gardens:** The city on the swamp, as it might have been called 150 years ago, blossomed into the Garden City thanks to the foresight of Christchurch's city fathers.

★ **Superb Skiing:** There are eight major ski slopes and a number of club runs within two hours' drive of Christchurch. Season runs from June until September.

1 Christchurch. From the Port Hills the city spreads out below, radiating from the central greenery of Hagley Park. A civic green thumb earned Christchurch the moniker "the Garden City," which it still displays; each spring numerous public and private gardens are open for viewing. But the genteel city is being infused with energy from the arts, technology, and a growing immigrant population.

2 Arthur's Pass and Canterbury. Arthur's Pass and Hanmer Springs are alpine regions; Akaroa is a seaside village tucked under high hills; and the southern areas around Geraldine and Timaru are the center of large, fertile farming areas. The Waipara Valley, just to the north of the city, is known for its excellent pinot noir, chardonnay, sauvignon blanc, and rieslings.

GETTING ORIENTED

Canterbury is a roughly rectangular province, with a natural boundary formed by the Main Divide (the peaks of the Southern Alps) in the west and stretching from near Kaikoura in the north down to the Waitaki River in the south. This chapter focuses on the section of Canterbury near the main city of Christchurch, including Banks Peninsula, the Waipara wine country, the ski town of Methven, and the alpine resort town of Hanmer Springs, north and west of the city, plus the towns sprinkled on the plains to the south. The chapter also includes Arthur's Pass National Park, a few hours northwest of Christchurch by car or train and a great mountain day trip from the city.

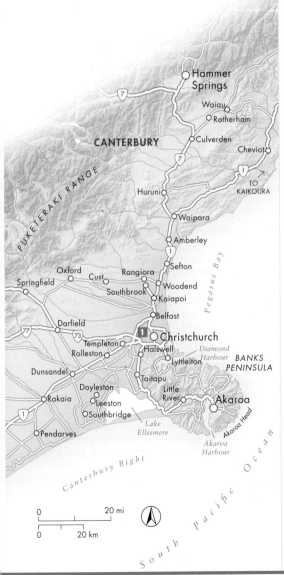

Hammer Springs

Waiau

Rotherham

CANTERBURY

Culverden

Cheviot

TO
KAIKOURA

Huruni

Waipara

Amberley

Oxford

Cust

Rangiora

Sefton

Springfield

Southbrook

Woodend

Kaiapoi

Darfield

Belfast

Templeton

Christchurch

Rolleston

Halswell

Diamond
Harbour

BANKS
PENINSULA

Lyttelton

Dunsandel

Taitapu

Doyleston

Little
River

Akaroa

Rakaia

Leeston

Southbridge

Lake
Ellesmere

Akaroa Head

Pendarves

Akaroa
Harbour

Canterbury Bight

South Pacific Ocean

PUKETERAKI RANGE

Pegasus Bay

0   20 mi

0   20 km

9

CHRISTCHURCH AND CANTERBURY PLANNER

Planning Your Time

Take at least three days to explore the Canterbury region. A full day in the city only skims the surface. An overnight trip to Hanmer, Arthur's Pass, or to Akaroagives you a taste of the hinterland. Waipara and Hanmer Springs can be visited when heading north to Kaikoura and Nelson. Arthur's Pass is on the main road to the West Coast, and Timaru and Geraldine are on the main routes south to Dunedin and Queenstown.

When to Go

In summer, Christchurch is especially busy. The Garden City SummerTimes festival runs from New Year's until late February, while mid-January brings the World Buskers Festival; the Festival of Flowers is in February; and the International Jazz & Blues Festival is in late March. The Antarctic Festival is in September or October.

Summer days can be amazingly changeable, while winter's weather is more settled but colder. For skiing and snowboarding, this is the time to come. From the first weekend in June through October you can be assured of snow at Mt. Hutt Snow on the ground in Christchurch is a rarity.

Getting Here and Around

Air Travel

Direct flights arrive into Christchurch from the major New Zealand cities, the larger Australian cities, some parts of Asia, and the Pacific Islands. There are no direct flights from North America. **Air New Zealand Link** and the smaller regional airlines connect Christchurch to Auckland and Wellington, many South Island centers, and the Chatham Islands. Charter helicopters connect to high country and remote lodges.

Contacts Air Chathams (📞 03/305–0209 or 0508/247–248 ⊕ www.airchathams.co.nz). **Air New Zealand Link** (📞 03/374–7100 or 0800/737–000 ⊕ www.airnewzealand.co.nz) **Pacific Blue** (📞 0800/670–000 ⊕ www.pacificblue.co.nz).

Bus Travel

InterCity bus service connects Christchurch with major towns and cities in the South IslandThe **TranzCoastal** train runs from Picton and Blenheim to the north and, connects with the **InterIslander Ferry** from the North Island. The **TranzAlpine** train is one of the Great Train Journeys of the World. Christchurch has a good metropolitan bus service. A free shuttle bus service connects points of interest in central Christchurch, and a good network of suburban bus routes links the outer areas of the city.

Contacts InterCity Buses (📞 03/365–1113 ⊕ www.intercity.co.nz). **InterIslander Ferry** (📞 0800/802–802 ⊕ www.interislander.co.nz). **TranzScenic** (📞 04/495–0775 or 0800/872–467 ⊕ www.tranzscenic.co.nz).

Car Travel

Outside the city the best way to explore the region is by car. Roads across the Canterbury Plains tend to be straight and flat with good signage and low traffic volume. State Highway 1 runs the length of the region's coast, linking all the major towns. State Highway 72 follows the contours of the hills, farther inland, beneath the Alps. State Highway 7 leaves the main road at Waipara and heads inland to Hanmer Springs before heading north to Nelson, and State Highway 73 heads west across the plains before leaping into the Southern Alps on its way to the West Coast.

Restaurants

Christchurch's restaurants are sophisticated and diverse. There's an established Asian influence and you can find everything from Cajun to Indian. New Zealand cuisine is a serious contender in its own right, blending the best fresh-and-local ingredients with Asian-Pacific tastes. Restaurants in the city are usually open every day; if they do close it is either Sunday or Monday. Outside Christchurch, restaurants are more likely to close on Monday and Tuesday and during the winter.

The Waipara Valley is seeing a surge in exotic food production. North Canterbury is now a key producer in the country's fledgling black truffle industry. Locally sourced saffron, hazelnuts, *manuka* (an indigenous kind of tea tree) honey, olive oil, and ostrich meat are making their way onto area menus.

Hotels

No matter where you stay in Christchurch, you'll find some of the best lodging in New Zealand. The two main motel strips are along Papanui Road and Riccarton Road, both outside the city center. Most of the bigger hotels are in the central city; although the more substantial lodges tend to be out in the hinterland. Many accommodations do not include breakfast in their room rates. Reservations are most necessary in summer, on public holidays, and during rugby game finals.

Outside Christchurch, it can be hard to find a place to stay in summer, especially over the holidays. If you're planning on going to Akaroa, Hanmer Springs, or Waipara during peak season, be sure to reserve well in advance. Bookings can also be heavy in winter around the ski areas and during school holidays.

WHAT IT COSTS IN NEW ZEALAND DOLLARS

	¢	$	$$	$$$	$$$$
Restaurants	under $10	$10–$15	$15–$20	$20–$30	over $30
Hotels	under $75	$75–$125	$125–$200	$200–$300	over $300

Meal prices are per person for a main course at dinner, or the equivalent. Hotel prices are for a standard double room in high season, including 12.5% tax.

Visitor Information

The **Christchurch–Canterbury i-SITE Visitor Information Centre** is open daily from 8:30 to 6. Its Web site is a great resource where you can find out about everything from lodging to bike rentals. Another good local Web site is LocalEye. *Avenues*, a local magazine with events listings and reviews, is also worth a browse. For a list of events and festivals go to the Be There Web site.

Contacts Be There (⊕ www.bethere.co.nz). **Christchurch–Canterbury i-SITE Visitor Information Centre** (✉ *Old Post Office Bldg., Cathedral Sq.* ☎ *03/379-9629* ⊕ *www. christchurchnz.com*). **LocalEye** (⊕ *www.localeye.info*).

Flower Power

Until 2008 the **Ellerslie Flower Show** (⊕ *www.ellerslieflower. co.nz*) was held in Auckland. From 2009 it is being held in Christchurch, recognizing the city's contribution to the gardening world since 1916, when it was named "The Garden City." It's a five-day extravaganza held in March each year in Hagley Park. There's plenty of information on the Web site to help plan your visit. Bear in mind that thousands of New Zealanders will also be visiting at that time so book everything before arriving. You'll also see lots of wine and food as well as some great gardening ideas.

9

ARTHUR'S PASS NATIONAL PARK

The journey is the thing. Nowhere in New Zealand does this Homeric phrase resound more than at Arthur's Pass, where the way itself is the marvel. Highway 73 is one of the park's prized features. Humble bipeds need only point a car west from Christchurch to enjoy heady mountain vistas.

You don't need to be a mountain goat or a kea to get properly alpine. Arthur's Pass offers richly diverse landscapes: the beech forests and tussock grasslands of the eastern slopes give way to snowcapped mountains and wildflower fields; dense rainy forests dominate the west. Established in 1929, Arthur's Pass is the South Island's first national park and the home to the kea, a mountain parrot, and the rare great-spotted kiwi. Follow in the footsteps of ancient Māori hunters, 1860s gold rushers, and 1990s road workers who constructed the 440-meters (1,444-foot) Otira Viaduct. Each of the many twists and turns reveals another photo op: waterfalls, fields of wildflowers, dizzying drops. And it's all easily accessible from Christchurch.

BEST TIME TO GO

November through March bring gorgeous wildflowers to the park. Ski at Temple Basin from late June to early October. Remember: with 2000-meter (6,562-foot) peaks, the weather in the park can change for the worse *anytime* at this altitude.

FUN FACT

The enormous moa, a native New Zealand bird, has long been extinct. But according to Paddy Freaney, the former owner of the Arthur's Pass Bealey Hotel, a moa popped up in a nearby valley! Despite Paddy's photographic evidence (a blurry image of a large running bird), many scientists remain dubious of his claims.

BEST WAYS TO EXPLORE

THE JOURNEY IS THE TAR-SEALED THING

Driving offers the flexibility to stop for hikes and sightseeing when you please. The road, extensively revamped in the 1990s, is a feat of engineering, particularly the Otira Viaduct. Five thousand cubic meters of concrete were used to create the viaduct on a steep unstable foundation in an area prone to flash floods. As you navigate the turns, spare some thoughts for the men who spent backbreaking years creating it.

STRETCH YOUR LEGS

Everything from 10-minute strolls to multiday hikes are available in the park. We recommend the Devil's Punchbowl Waterfall (one hour return from Arthur's Pass Village) and Dobson Nature Walk (30 minutes return), which follows a lovely loop at the summit of Arthur's Pass. Marvel at brilliantly colored alpine lichen splashed across boulders and cliff faces. Kea, wrybill (with bent beaks), and green bellbirds populate the park. Lucky visitors will spot the roroa—or great-spotted kiwi—that roam the steep terrain.

CHOOCHOO FROM "CHCH"

Take to the tracks and relax onboard the TranzAlpine Scenic Journey. It takes you from Christchurch ("ChCh" to locals) to Greymouth in 4½ hours, through 16 tunnels and over 5 viaducts. The train has an open-air carriage which provides breathtaking views of the plains, gorges, valleys, and beech forests.

UP YOU GO

There are plenty of ways up the peaks of Arthur's Pass. Mountain climbing in the area is prone to changeable weather and many routes involve river crossings, so check in with the Department of Conservation before any endeavor and make sure you are up to the challenge.

ECO-STAYS

As a guest at the luxurious **Arthur's Pass Wilderness Lodge**, you're invited to "walk the walk" and help remove invasive plants on nature hikes, and you're also welcome to do your own thing and take advantage of the extensive trails throughout the property. The owners are passionate about the conservation of this alpine environment and eager to share their knowledge with you. The lodge itself is built of local stone and wood. There's no need to worry about your cuisine's "food miles"—the delectable slow-cooked lamb on your plate was raised on the farm out the window. A more wallet-friendly but equally environment-conscious accommodation is the **Mountain House Backpackers**. The operators practice "responsible tourism" down to the last detail, using compact fluorescent lighting, organically based cleansers, recycled paper products and non-native firewood. They also initiated and run the recycling effort for the entire town.

9

Updated by
Sue Farley

John Robert Godley, whose bronze memorial statue stands in Christchurch's Cathedral Square, would have seen the spectacular views of the Southern Alps when he paused for breath at the top of the Port Hills in 1850. The Canterbury Association, a British organization, had sent him to New Zealand to prepare for the arrival of settlers for a planned Church of England community. That year, four settler ships arrived bearing roughly 800 pioneers, and their new town was named for Godley's college at Oxford.

Built in a Gothic Revival style of dark gray stone, civic buildings such as the Arts Centre (originally Canterbury University) and Canterbury Museum give the city an English quality. This style, plus elements such as punting and cricket, often pegs Christchurch as a little slice of England. Though the city may have a conservative exterior, it has been a nursery for social change. It was here that Kate Sheppard began organizing a campaign that led to New Zealand being the first country in the world to grant women the vote. It has become known as the southern gateway to Antarctica and is developing a keen arts community and a vibrant cuisine scene.

Beyond Christchurch the wide-open Canterbury Plains sweep to the north, west, and south of the city. This is some of New Zealand's finest pastureland, and the higher reaches are sheep-station territory, where life and lore mingle in South Island's cowboy country. This is where young Samuel Butler dreamed up the satirical *Erewhon*—the word is an anagram of *nowhere*. But the towns here are no longer considered the back of beyond; communities such as Hanmer Springs, Akaroa, Timaru, and Geraldine are now favorite day-trip destinations. Arthur's Pass is probably the best place for a one-day–wonder experience of the Southern Alps while the Waipara Valley is one of the country's developing vineyard areas.

CHRISTCHURCH

Your initial impression of Christchurch will likely be one of a genteel, green city. But the face of Christchurch is changing, fueled by both internal and international immigration. The Māori community, although still below the national average in size, is growing. Ngai Tahu, the main South Island Māori tribe, settled Treaty of Waitangi claims in 1997 and has been investing in tourism ventures. There is a growing Asian population, reflected in the number of restaurants and stores catering to their preferences. Old wooden bungalows are making way for town houses, the arts scene is flourishing, and the city's university attracts cutting-edge technology companies.

With a population approaching 350,000, Christchurch is the largest South Island city, and the second largest in the country. It is also the forward supply depot for the main U.S. Antarctic base at McMurdo Sound, and if you come in by plane in summer, you are likely to see the giant U.S. Air Force transport planes of Operation Deep Freeze parked on the tarmac at Christchurch International Airport.

GETTING HERE AND AROUND

The inner city is compact and easy to explore by foot; the central sights can be reached during an afternoon's walk. Four avenues (Bealey, Fitzgerald, Moorhouse, and Rolleston) define the city center. Beyond this core are a number of special-interest museums and activities, about 20 minutes away by car.

Outside the Four Avenues, the best way to get around the city is to use the network of buses that radiates from the center, or the tram within the city's inner loop. The easiest place to catch a bus is the Bus Exchange, as most buses go through it. Yellow buses and some specially signed red buses are free shuttles that run through the city center, linking the Casino with Moorhouse Avenue. The Red Bus line offers Metro-cards, or prepaid travel cards; it also runs the Midnight Express, four routes that run from midnight to 4 AM on Friday and Saturday night.

The Christchurch Best Attractions bus service provides transport (combinable with the entry fees) for several attractions: Willowbank, the Gondola, and the Antarctic Centre at $6.50 per attraction. Tickets can be booked at the Information Centre or you can pay when you hop on; the bus stop is opposite the main entrance to the visitor bureau.

ESSENTIALS

Airport Christchurch International Airport (✉ *Memorial Ave., Harewood* ☎ *03/358–5029* ⊕ *www.christchurch-airport.co.nz*).

Bus Depot Bus Exchange (✉ *237–239 Lichfield St.*).

Bus Companies Best Attractions (⊕ *www.chchattractions.co.nz*).

Medical Assistance Christchurch Hospital (✉ *2 Riccarton Ave.* ☎ *03/364–0640*). **Fire, police, and ambulance** (☎ *111*). **24 Hour Surgery** (✉ *Bealey Ave. and Colombo St.* ☎ *03/365–7777*). **Urgent Pharmacy** (✉ *Bealey Ave. and Colombo St.* ☎ *03/366–4439*). **Moorhouse Medical Centre** (✉ *3 Pilgrim Pl.* ☎ *03/365–7900*).

The Christchurch tramway stops at the Christchurch Art Gallery and the city center's other main attractions.

Rental Cars Apex (✉ *Christchurch International Airport* ☎ *03/357–4536 or 0800/400–121, 800/7001–8001 from North America* ⊕ *www.apexrentals.co.nz*). **Avis** (✉ *Christchurch International Airport* ☎ *03/358–9661 or 0800/284–722* ⊕ *www.avis.co.nz*). **Budget** (✉ *15 Lichfield St.* ☎ *03/366–0072 or 0800/283–438* ⊕ *www.budget.co.nz*). **Hertz** (✉ *46 Lichfield St.* ☎ *03/366–0549 or 0800/654–321* ⊕ *www.hertz.co.nz*). **Maui Motorhomes** (✉ *530 Memorial Ave.* ☎ *03/357–5610 or 0800/651–080* ⊕ *www.maui.co.nz*).

Train Information TranzAlpine and TranzCoastal (☎ *0800/872–467* ⊕ *www.tranzscenic.co.nz*).

Train Station Christchurch Railway Station (✉ *Troup Dr.* ☎ *03/341–2588*).

EXPLORING

CENTRAL CHRISTCHURCH
TOP ATTRACTIONS

Arts Centre. By moving to the suburbs in the 1970s, Canterbury University left vacant a fine collection of Gothic Revival stone buildings, which were then transformed into this terrific arts, shopping, and dining complex. Beside the center's information desk in the clock tower you'll find **Rutherford's Den,** where physicist Ernest Rutherford (1871–1937), the university's most illustrious student, conducted early experiments in radioactivity. It was Rutherford who first succeeded in splitting the atom, a crucial step in the harnessing of atomic power. In 1908 Rutherford's work earned him the Nobel Prize—not for physics but for chemistry. Now a dynamic multimedia presentation depicts Rutherford and daily life in the 1890s at Canterbury College, as the campus was known

Fodor's Choice
★

then. The Arts Centre houses more than 40 specialty shops and studios, as well as art galleries, theaters, and art-house cinemas. It's an excellent stop for food, coffee, or a glass of wine—there are several cafés and a wine bar. At the **Saturday and Sunday Market** you'll find jewelry, prints, and handmade clothing and crafts, as well as food stalls. Free live entertainment kicks off at noon on weekends and goes until 3 PM. They also run a produce market on Fridays, starting at noon, highlighting local, organic, sustainable, and ethical foods. Stop by the information desk to join one of the free guided tours, offered daily from 11 to 3:30. ⊠ *Worcester Blvd. between Montreal St. and Rolleston Ave.* 🕾 *03/363–2836 tours, 03/366–0980* ⊕ *www.artscentre.org.nz* 🕙 *Shops and galleries daily 10–5; Rutherford's Den daily 10–5.*

❼ **Canterbury Museum.** When this museum was founded in 1867, its trad-
★ ing power with national and international museums was in moa bones.
☾ These Jurassic birds roamed the plains of Canterbury and are believed to have been hunted to extinction by early Māori. The museum still houses one of the largest collections of artifacts from the moa hunting period. You'll also find a natural-history center, called Discovery, where kids can handle bones and fossils. The Hall of Antarctic Discovery charts the links between the city and Antarctica, from the days when Captain Cook's ship skirted the continent in a small wooden ship. Among the 20th-century explorers celebrated here are the Norwegian Roald Amundsen, who was first to visit the South Pole, and Captain Robert Falcon Scott, who died returning from the continent. *Fred & Myrtle's Paua Shell House* tells the story of an iconic Kiwi couple and recreates their *paua* (abalone) shell-covered living room. The café looks out over the Botanic Gardens. ⊠ *Rolleston Ave.* 🕾 *03/366–5000* ⊕ *www.canterburymuseum.com* 🗐 *Free admission, donations appreciated; Discovery exhibition $2* 🕙 *Oct.–Mar., daily 9–5:30; Apr.–Sept., daily 9–5.*

❿ **Christchurch Art Gallery—Te Puna O Waiwhetu.** The city's stunning art gal-
★ lery wows visitors as much for its architecture as for its artwork. Its tall, wavy glass facade was inspired by Christchurch's Avon River and the shape of the native *koru* fern. Outside the building is a growing collection of sculpture, and the downstairs galleries hold special national and international exhibitions. Free guided tours, entertaining events, family activities, and iPod audio tours make the gallery a must-see. Shop for a great selection of gifts, or relax at Alchemy Café and Wine Bar. The museum's Māori name refers to an artesian spring on the site and means "the wellspring of star-reflecting waters." ⊠ *Worcester Blvd. and Montreal St.* 🕾 *03/941–7300* ⊕ *www.christchurchartgallery.org.nz* 🗐 *Free* 🕙 *Daily 10–5, Wed. to 9.*

❻ **Christchurch Botanic Gardens.** One of the largest city parks in the world,
☾ these superb gardens are known for the magnificent trees planted here
★ in the 19th century. Pick up the Historic Tree Walk brochure from the information center for a self-guided Who's Who tour of the tree world. Spend time in the conservatories to discover tropical plants, cacti, and ferns on days when you'd rather not be outside. Go to the New Zealand plants area at any time of the year. ⊠ *Rolleston Ave.* 🕾 *03/366–1701* 🗐 *Free* 🕙 *Daily 7 AM–dusk, conservatories daily 10:15–4.*

9

DID YOU KNOW?

Hagley Park includes, among other things, a botanic gardens, a hospital, 11 rugby fields, 13 soccer fields, polo ground, tennis courts, croquet lawns, a golf course, and a small lake— and there's room for more.

1 **ChristChurch Cathedral.** The city's dominating landmark was begun in 1864, 14 years after the arrival of the Canterbury Pilgrims, dedicated in 1881 and completed in 1904. Carvings inside commemorate the work of the Anglican missionaries, including Tamihana Te Rauparaha, the son of a fierce and, for the settlers, troublesome Māori chief. Free guided tours begin daily at 11 and 2, Monday to Friday, Saturday at 11 and Sunday at 11.30, and there's a $10 self-guided audio tour available. For a view across the city to the Southern Alps, climb the 133 steps to the top of the bell tower. The cathedral is known for its boys' choir, which sings evensong at 4:30 on Friday; the full choir sings evensong on Tuesday and Wednesday, and the men's evensong is every Thursday at 5:30. **Cathedral Square,** the city's focal point, buzzes with an arts-and-crafts market on Thursday and Friday, complete with food stalls and street musicians. ⊠ *Cathedral Sq.* ☎ *03/366–0046* ⊕ *www. christchurchcathedral.co.nz* ⊠ *Tower $5* ⊙ *Oct.–Mar. 8:30–7; Apr.– Sept. 8:30–5.*

WORTH NOTING

5 **Antigua Boat Hire & Cafe.** Built for the Christchurch Boating Club in 1882, this green-and-white wooden structure is the last shed standing of a half dozen that once lined the Avon. On sunny days, punts and canoes ply the river paddled by visitors and families alike. Join them by renting a boat and taking a champagne picnic into the Botanic Gardens or farther up into the woodlands of Hagley Park, spectacular in autumn and spring. Even winter has its own beauty. The boat shed has a licensed café (open for breakfast and lunch) with a deck overlooking the Avon. ⊠ *2 Cambridge Terr.* ☎ *03/366–5885 boat shed, 03/366–6768 café* ⊕ *www.boatsheds.co.nz* ⊠ *Single canoe $10 per hr, double canoe $20 per hr, rowboat $20 per hr (3–4 people), paddle boat $20 per ½ hr (minimum 2 people)* ⊙ *Dec.–Apr., daily 9–4:30; May–Nov., daily 9–4.*

NEED A BREAK?

The Arts Centre has several eateries in its stone buildings and quadrangles. Annies Wine Bar (⊠ *41 Hereford St.* ☎ *03/365-0566*) is the most refined option, a pleasant place to taste New Zealand wine alongside bistro fare. The Backstage Bakery (☎ *03/377-7948*) turns out specialty breads daily—try their delicious sourdough or ciabatta. It's in the center of the complex. Dux de Lux (☎ *03/366-6919*) is a sprawling, upbeat, cafeteria-style restaurant in a mock-Tudor building on the Montreal Street side of the campus. The huge courtyard is a great spot to enjoy a beer from the on-site boutique brewery. The Nor-wester is their most popular brew.

3 **Bridge of Remembrance.** Arching over Cashel Street, this Oamaru, limestone, memorial arch was built in memory of the soldiers who crossed the river here from King Edward Barracks on their way to the battlefields of Europe during World War I. ⊠ *Avon River at Cashel St.*

11 **Captain Robert Falcon Scott statue.** Scott of the Antarctic (1868–1912), who stayed in Christchurch while preparing for his two Antarctic expeditions, is memorialized by this unfinished white marble statue sculpted by his widow, Kathleen. It's inscribed DO NOT REGRET THIS

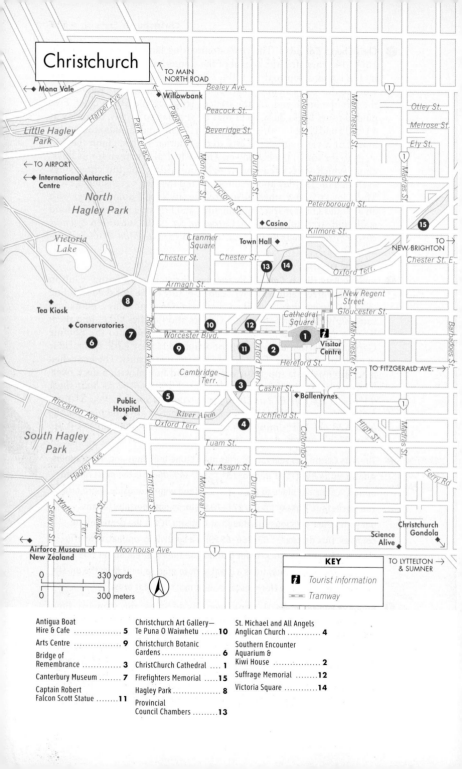

Christchurch

TO MAIN
NORTH ROAD

← Mona Vale
♦ Willowbank

Bealey Ave.
Peacock St.
Beveridge St.

Otley St.
Metrose St.
Ely St.

Little Hagley
Park

← TO AIRPORT

← ♦ International Antarctic
Centre

North
Hagley Park

Victoria
Lake

♦ Tea Kiosk

♦ Conservatories

Harper Ave.
Park Terrace
Papanui Rd.
Montreal St.
Victoria St.
Durham St.
Colombo St.
Manchester St.

Salisbury St.
Peterborough St.
Kilmore St.

Madras St.

♦ Casino

Cranmer
Square

Town Hall ♦

Chester St.   Chester St.

Armagh St.

8

6 **7**

Rolleston Ave.

Worcester Blvd.
10
9

13 **14**

Oxford Terr.

New Regent
Street
Gloucester St.

Cathedral
Square

12
11 **2** **1** *i*

Hereford St.

Cambridge
Terr.
3

5

Public
Hospital

Oxford Terr.

River Avon

Visitor
Centre

Cashel St.
♦ Ballentynes

Lichfield St.

4

Colombo St.

Chester St. E.

TO →
NEW BRIGHTON

15

Manchester St.

Barbadoes St.

TO FITZGERALD AVE. →

High St.

Madras St.

Riccarton Ave.

South Hagley
Park

Hagley Ave.
Antigua St.
Montreal St.
Durham St.

Tuam St.
St. Asaph St.

Ferry Rd.

Waller Ter.
Selwyn St.
Stewart St.

Airforce Museum of
New Zealand

Moorhouse Ave.

Science
Alive

Christchurch
Gondola

KEY
i Tourist information
Tramway

TO LYTTELTON →
& SUMNER

| 0 | 330 yards |
| 0 | 300 meters |

TRAM AROUND TOWN

★ Jump on the Christchurch Tramway for a quick whiz round the central city sights. A ticket gives you 48 hours to hop on and off and visit many of the choice spots—the Arts Centre in Worcester Boulevard with its cafés, working artists, and craft markets on weekends; the Canterbury Museum, where you can check out the historical development of the region; Christchurch Cathedral and Cathedral Square, the hub of the city center and where all roads lead. The Christchurch Art Gallery–Te Puna Wai O Waiwhetu has some exciting architecture and sculpture on the outside and interesting collections inside; New Regent Street is a tiny art deco shopping street; and Hagley Park and Victoria Square combine leafy green walks with some history along the way. The circuit, without any stops, will only take 20 minutes. ⊠ *Worcester Blvd, outside the Arts Centre* ☎ *03/366-7830* ⊕ *www. tram.co.nz* ✉ *$15.*

JOURNEY, WHICH SHOWS THAT ENGLISHMEN CAN ENDURE HARDSHIPS, HELP ONE ANOTHER AND MEET DEATH WITH AS GREAT FORTITUDE AS EVER IN THE PAST. Scott wrote these words in his diary as he and his party lay dying in a blizzard on their return journey from the South Pole—a story of endurance taught to all New Zealand schoolkids. ⊠ *Worcester Blvd. and Oxford Terr.*

🟢 **Firefighters Memorial.** Local artist Graham Bennett used crooked girders from the collapsed World Trade Center in this memorial sculpture. The work is dedicated not only to the firefighters who died in New York on September 11, 2001, but also to other firefighters who have died in the course of duty. You can reach the memorial along the riverside path; sit awhile in the small park beside the Avon, not far from the central fire station. ⊠ *Kilmore and Madras Sts.*

🟢 **Hagley Park.** Once cultivated Māori land, Hagley Park was developed by Pākehā settlers in the mid-1800s with imported plants given trial runs in what would become the Botanic Gardens. Now the park is divided into four sections, which include walking and jogging tracks, cycling paths, and self-guided historic tours. Hagley Park North has sports fields and also draws people to its tennis and *pétanque* (boccie) courts; Little Hagley Park, which runs beside Harper Ave., is classified as a Heritage area. South Hagley Park has more sports facilities. The Botanic Gardens makes up the fourth quadrant and is closest to the city center (⇨ *Christchurch Botanic Gardens, above*). ⊠ *Main entrance at Armagh St. and Rolleston Ave.*

🟢 **Provincial Council Chambers.** This complex of Gothic Revival stone buildings beside the Avon River was once the seat of Canterbury's government, which ran from 1853 to 1876. The elaborate decorations include a painted ceiling, stone carvings, and stained-glass windows. It now houses a small museum devoted to the building's history. A large clock intended for the tower proved too big and stands a few blocks away, at the intersection of Victoria, Salisbury, and Montreal streets.

9

⊠ *Durham St. at Gloucester St.* ☎ *03/941–7680* ⌲ *Free* ⊗ *Mon.–Sat. 10:30–3.*

2 ☺ **Southern Encounter Aquarium & Kiwi House.** The giant aquarium has an enormous variety of New Zealand fish species—from rocky tidal-pool creatures to those from lakes, rivers, and the briny deep. You can touch some of these critters in the Touch Tank. Watch divers feed giant eels, carpet sharks, cod, and skate. ■TIP➔ Try to be there for the afternoon salmon-and-trout feeding at 1. The entrance is through the visitor center or Pathway Shop. ⊠ *Cathedral Sq.* ☎ *03/359–7109* ⊕ *www.southernencounter.co.nz* ⌲ *Adults $16, children $6* ⊗ *Daily 9–4.30, kiwis on display 10:30–4.45; last entry at 4:30.*

12 **Suffrage Memorial.** Unveiled in 1993, this bronze memorial wall commemorates 100 years of votes for women. New Zealand was the first country in the world to grant women the vote, and Christchurch resident Kate Sheppard played a key role in petitioning Parliament for this essential right. The vote for all women over 21, including Māori women, was granted on September 19, 1893; the work of Sheppard and other activists is celebrated each year on that date at the memorial. ⊠ *Oxford Terr.*

4 **St. Michael and All Angels Anglican Church.** One of the bells in this church's belfry came out with the Canterbury Pilgrims on one of the first Four Ships and was rung hourly to indicate time for early settlers; it is still rung every day. The current white-timber church was built in 1872, entirely of *matai*, a native black pine, and was one of the largest neo-Gothic churches in Australasia. It sat on rubble stone foundations, but recent renovations have seen some of these replaced, and there are 26 English-made stained-glass windows, dating back as far as 1858. The original building, built in 1851, was the first church to be built in Christchurch. ⊠ *Oxford Terr. at Durham St.* ☎ *03/379–5236* ⊗ *Mon.–Thurs. 8.30–5, Fri. 10–4.*

14 ☺ **Victoria Square.** This square was named for Queen Victoria in her jubilee year. On its north side sits the striking Town Hall, with its auditorium, theater, and conference spaces. Nearby stands a *poupou*, a tall, carved, wood column, acknowledging the site's history as a trading point between Māori and the European settlers. You'll also see Christchurch's oldest iron bridge, a floral clock, two fountains, including one that's illuminated with colored lights at night, and statues of Queen Victoria and Captain Cook. ⊠ *Armagh and Colombo Sts.*

BOAT TOUR

Punting on the Avon. Sit back and enjoy the diverse architecture of the central city from water level, framed by weeping willows and ornate bridges. The boat tours leave from the Worcester Street Bridge, near the corner of Oxford Terrace, daily from 9 to 8 in summer and from 10 to 4 the rest of the year. A 30-minute trip costs $20. Call ahead or just stop at the landing. The company also runs tours from the historic Antigua Boat Sheds at 2 Cambridge Terrace, where you can punt up through the leafy glades of Hagley Park (⇨ Hagley Park listing). ⊠ *Worcester Blvd. bridge landing* ☎ *03/353–5994.*

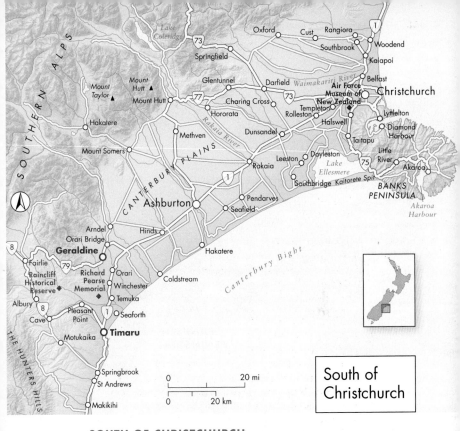

Map labels:
Lake Coleridge · Oxford · Cust · Rangiora · 73 · Southbrook · Woodend · 1 · Springfield · Kaiapoi · Glentunnel · Darfield · Waimakariri River · Belfast · Air Force Museum of · Christchurch · Mount Taylor · Mount Hutt · 77 · Charing Cross · 73 · Templeton · New Zealand · Mount Hutt · Hororata · Rolleston · Lyttelton · Hakatere · Rakaia River · Halswell · Diamond Harbour · Methven · Dunsandel · Taitapu · Mount Somers · Leeston · Doyleston · Little River · 75 · CANTERBURY PLAINS · Rakaia · Lake Ellesmere · Akaroa · Ashburton · Pendarves · Southbridge · Kaitorete Spit · BANKS PENINSULA · Seafield · Akaroa Harbour · Arndel · Hinds · Hakatere · Canterbury Bight · Orari Bridge · 8 · Geraldine · Fairlie · 79 · Orari · Coldstream · Raincliff Historical Reserve · Richard Pearse Memorial · Winchester · Albury · 8 · Temuka · Cave · Pleasant Point · 1 · Seaforth · Motukaika · Timaru · Springbrook · 0 20 mi · St Andrews · 0 20 km · Makikihi · THE HUNTERS HILLS · SOUTHERN ALPS

South of Christchurch

SOUTH OF CHRISTCHURCH

Air Force Museum of New Zealand. Starting in 1916, New Zealand pilots learned how to fly at Wigram Airport. The airport's old hangars now hold exhibits on aviation history, including the Royal New Zealand Air Force, flight simulators, and 28 classic aircraft, with more being restored behind-the-scenes in other hangars. To get here by bus, take the number 5 and walk from the Main South Road, just south of the Sockburn Overbridge. ✉ *45 Harvard Ave., Wigram* ☎ *03/343–9532* 🌐 *www.airforcemuseum.co.nz* ✈ *Free* ⊙ *Daily 10–5.*

EAST OF CHRISTCHURCH

Christchurch Gondola. From high on the Port Hills east of the city, the gondola is the best vantage point to view Christchurch, the Canterbury Plains, and Lyttelton Harbour. At the top, you can journey through the **Time Tunnel** to experience the history and geological evolution of the Canterbury region, and there's a one-hour guided walk that leaves from the Summit Station at 11 AM and 1 PM ($20). Afterward, sit with a glass of local wine at the Summit Café or Pinnacle Restaurant. Ride the gondola with your back to the Port Hills for the best views of the Southern Alps. The adventurous can walk or mountain-bike back down (⇨ *Sports and the Outdoors, below*); it's steep in parts so watch your footing. If you don't have a car, you

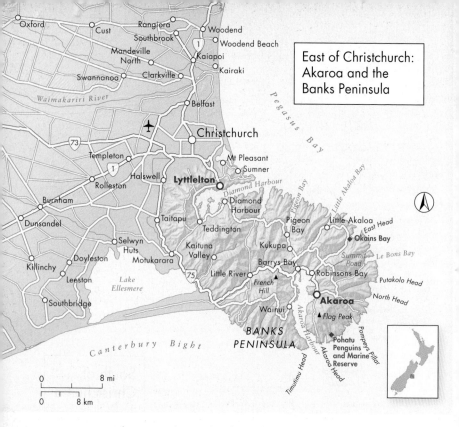

can hop a number 28 bus from the city center; the Best Attractions Direct bus also includes the gondola. ✉ *10 Bridle Path Rd., Heathcote* ☎ *03/384–0700* ⊕ *www.gondola.co.nz* 🎟 *$22* ⊙ *Thurs.–Sat. 10–9, Sun.–Wed. 10–6.*

🄲 **Science Alive.** Kids (and mom and dad) wind through a maze of challenging science mysteries and activities. It's a highly interactive space where kids can learn while they play, extending their travel-tired minds at the same time. They get a notebook on entry to tally their results and ultimately solve the puzzle at the end. And after that they can kick back at a movie in the multiplex center in the same building. It's a great spot for a rainy day. ✉ *392 Moorhouse Ave.* ☎ *03/365–5199* ⊕ *www. sciencealive.co.nz* 🎟 *Adults $14, kids $10, family pass (2 adults, 3 children) $45* ⊙ *Daily 10–5.*

WEST OF CHRISTCHURCH

🄲 **International Antarctic Centre.** Ever since Scott wintered his dogs at nearby
★ Quail Island in preparation for his ill-fated South Pole expedition of 1912, Christchurch has maintained a close connection with the frozen continent. You can experience a small taste of the modern polar experience here. For instance, bundle up in extra clothing (provided) and brave a simulated storm in which a bitingly cold wind chills the room to 25 degrees below for a few minutes. Or you could take a ride on the

Youngsters press in close to see penguins at the International Antarctic Centre.

Hägglund vehicle used to get around the ice. The audiovisual show of life at New Zealand's Scott Base is superb, and the Penguin Encounter lets you get up close with some blue penguins, the smallest penguin species. It's roughly 20 minutes from central Christchurch by car or on the Penguin Express shuttle. A ticket gives you an all-day pass, and there's even a free shuttle directly from the airport. ✉ *38 Orchard Rd., Harewood* ☎ *03/353–7798* ⊕ *www.iceberg.co.nz* 🖃 *$50;* ⊘ *Oct.–Apr., daily 9–7; May–Sept., daily 9–5:30.*

Mona Vale. One of Christchurch's great historic homesteads, the riverside Mona Vale was built in 1899. The house and 13½-acre garden have been part of the city since 1967—when the estate was "sold" to individual Christchurch residents for $10 per square foot. Come for lunch, high tea, or Devonshire tea, and you can make believe that you're strolling through your own grounds along the Avon River as you wander under the trees and through the well-tended perennial gardens. The Fernery sits in the building used in the 1907 International Exhibition, and the Blue and White Border garden is worth a look. Pick up their handy map so you don't miss anything. If the mood really takes you, go for a punt ride (October–March). Catch a number 9 bus from the city; there's a stop outside the front gate near the gingerbread gatehouse (which is not open to the public). ✉ *63 Fendalton Rd., Fendalton* ⊹ *2 km (1 mi) from city center* ☎ *03/348–9660* ⊕ *www.monavale.co.nz* 🖃 *Free* ⊘ *Grounds: daily 7 AM to 1 hr after dusk; gates open 24 hrs to pedestrians, only vehicle access closes. Restaurant: Oct.–Apr., daily 9:30–5; May–Sept., daily 9:30–4.*

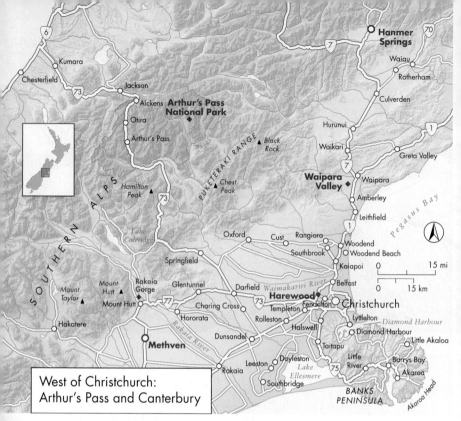

West of Christchurch:
Arthur's Pass and Canterbury

    🐚 **Willowbank.** In addition to familiar farm animals and other zoo regulars, Willowbank has a section devoted to New Zealand wildlife. It is also the most accessible Māori cultural experience. Here you can have a close encounter with the cheeky mountain parrot, the *kea*. Kiwi can be viewed in an artificially darkened area from 10:30 AM to 10 PM. You can get a special viewing of the native animals on the Māori cultural tour given from **Ko Tane,** a reproduction Māori village. You'll be greeted with a *powhiri*, a traditional welcome, and you can try your hand at swinging *poi*, flaxen balls on long strings used in traditional Māori dances (it's not as easy as it looks). The Ko Tane tour starts at $45; with a Guided Kiwi Tour Experience it is $59, and $99 if you include a Taste NZ Buffet Dinner (reservations advised for the dinner). There are guided tours through the "New Zealand Natural Area"—where the native animals are—at 11:30 and 2:30 on request and scheduled tours hourly between 6:30 PM and 9:30 PM in summer. To get here without a car, use the Best Attractions bus. Ko Tane Māori Cultural Performance provides complimentary return transport from the city center. ✉ *60 Hussey Rd., Harewood* ☎ *03/359–6226* ⊕ *www.willowbank.co.nz* 🖃 *$25* ☉ *Daily 9:30–dusk.*

SPORTS AND THE OUTDOORS

BEACHES

The three main beaches around Christchurch are New Brighton Beach, Sumner Beach, and Taylor's Mistake. **New Brighton Beach,** about 8 km (5 mi) from the city center, is popular with surfers and fishers. The long pier that goes well out into the surf is a great place to stroll when the sea is calm, but even better when it's rough. Buses 5, 40 and 60 go here. **Sumner Beach** is pleasant for the long relaxing walk between Shag Rock and Scarborough Hill. Walk the first section along the sand to Cave Rock, which you can climb or walk through at low tide; it has wonderful acoustics. Walk the rest of the way along the esplanade, as the beach is fairly rocky. Sumner Village is based around the Cave Rock area, and there are a number of restaurants, including one right on the beach. You can catch a number 30 bus if you don't have a car. Experienced surfers prefer **Taylor's Mistake, near Sumner,** because the waves are higher. You can drive there over the Scarborough Hill or walk over a track, but there is no public transport. If you're lucky, you'll see tiny, rare, Hector's dolphins playing off Sumner Head on your way out.

NEED A BREAK?

Petrini (✉ *9 Humphreys Dr, Ferrymead* ☎ *03/943-8888* ⊕ *www.petrini.co.nz* ⊗ *Closed Mon. and public holidays*) has a strong following and is a perfect place to stop on your way to Sumner Beach for some snacks. In deference to the founder of the slow food movement, Carlo Petrini, this place packages up take-out with class. Try the braised lamb shanks or the beef cheeks in a red wine jus. There's a Cheese Room, on-site bakery, and a substantial wine list so you can take a BYO back to the hotel as well. They also have a stylish restaurant serving modern European lunch and dinner.

BICYCLING

Christchurch's relative flatness makes for easy biking, and the city has cultivated good resources for cyclists. White lines, and sometimes red-color tarmac, denote cycling lanes on city streets, and holding bays are at the ready near intersections. You can pick up a route map from the city council; a particularly nice paved pedestrian and cycling path is along the Avon running from the Bridge of Remembrance. Other popular cycle trails include the Rail Trail at Little River and the spectacular trails around the Port Hills.

City Cycle Hire (✉ *68 Waltham Rd., Sydenham* ☎ *03/377–5952 or 0800/424–534* ⊕ *www.cyclehire-tours.co.nz*) has mountain, touring, and tandem bikes. Rentals include helmets, locks, and cycle map and costs about $25 for a half day and $35 for a full day; they'll deliver your bike to your hotel. he **Mountain Bike Adventure Company** (✉ *68 Waltham Rd., Sydenham* ☎ *03/377–5952 or 0800/424–534*) offers a $60 package including a ride up on the Christchurch Gondola to the summit station. Then there's the choice of either an off-road mountain-bike trail or a scenic-road route down to the beach and back to the Gondola base—cycle distance is approximately 16 km (10 mi).

9

★ **Little River Rail Trail Day Cycle Tour** (☎ *03/377–5952* ✉ *$100 per person* ⊗ *Sept.–May)* follows the new Little River Rail Trail with all off-road flat cycling around Lake Ellesmere. It's ideal for a family group with a cycling distance of 19 km (12 mi). Bookings are essential for this full-day trip, and return transfers to Little River are included. Bring insect repellent to stave off the sand flies.

GOLF

The 18-hole championship golf course at the **Clearwater Golf Club** (✉ *Clearwater Ave. Harewood* ☎ *03/360-2146* ⊕ *www.clearwaternz.com)* was built on the old Waimakariri riverbed near Christchurch Airport. Home to the NZPGA Championship, it is playable year-round and offers a choice of five tee positions. The green fee is $130; rental equipment is on hand. With extensive views of Mt. Hutt and Rakaia Gorge, the 18-hole championship course at **Terrace Downs** (✉ *Coleridge Rd.* ☎ *03/318–6943* ⊕ *www. terracedowns.co.nz)* has to be one of the most scenic courses in the South Island. You can rent equipment, and you can even book a villa for the night. The luxurious suites and chalets overlook the golf course and the mighty Southern Alps. Green fees start at $125 per person for 18 holes.

HIKING

If you're driving from Christchurch to Lyttelton via the coast road through Sumner take a left turn at the summit intersection leading to **Godley Head Farm Park**. The road climbs and winds for several kilometers before breaking out above Lyttelton Harbour with startling views to the hills of Banks Peninsula. Take a walk out to the World War II coastal defense battery built in 1939 and now rated as one of the country's significant defense-heritage sites. There's also a 3½-hour walking track from here back to Taylors Mistake near Sumner (although you'll need to arrange a pickup at the other end, or do the seven-hour return trip). The Godley Head lookout is particularly exciting in a strong southerly wind!

HORSE TREKKING

Horse whisperer Kate Tapley and her team guide gentle rides with **Otahuna Horse Riding** (✉ *Rhodes Rd., Tai Tapu* ☎ *03/329–0160* ⊕ *www. otahunariding.co.nz)*, around the Port Hills. To aid the horse–rider connection, each ride begins with a partnering session. You'll have stunning views of the Canterbury Plains and the encircling mountain ranges from your saddle. Guided rides start at $100 for 2½ hours; $220 for a full day. Overnight rides to Governors Bay are available for $320. All gear is provided.

RUGBY

Canterbury fans are as rugby-mad as the rest of the country. In fact the first match ever played in New Zealand took place in 1862 in Cranmer Square, in central Christchurch. Every Saturday in winter you can catch little All-Blacks-in-the-making playing games in Hagley Park and suburban parks. Then cheer the Crusaders, the Canterbury rugby team, on their home turf at **AMI Stadium**, which began life in 1880 as Lancaster Park. In summer it's the city's premier cricket ground. (✉ *30 Stevens St., Phillipstown* ☎ *03/379–1765* ⊕ *www.amistadium.co.nz).* The season runs from February through September. The stadium also hosts All Blacks games and international cricket matches.

50 on Park in the George Hotel serves elegant meals in an elegant setting.

WHERE TO EAT

Use the coordinate (✛ B2) at the end of each listing to locate a site on the corresponding map.

For bargain eats around Christchurch, look to the simpler restaurants such as Winnie Bagoes on Gloucester Street, a good steak meal from Bealey's Speights Ale House on Bealey Avenue, or pizza or pasta from the Spagalimis chain. For a really cheap take-out meal, you can't beat the price of fish-and-chips or a burger bought at the local take-out store and eaten from the paper wrapping.

CENTRAL CHRISTCHURCH

$$$$
NEW ZEALAND
★
✕ **Canterbury Tales.** This elegant spot is one of three restaurants in the Crowne Plaza Hotel. Service shines, while the lights are low and the music subdued. The menu has local fish, meats, veggies, and seasonal treats like asparagus and truffles. The monkfish wrapped in prosciutto and spinach, with truffle croquettes and a saffron mussel fumet, is delicious. The desserts are excellent, and a glossary in the menu helps with the exotic culinary terms. ⊠ *Kilmore and Durham Sts.* ☎ *03/365–7799 Ext. 360* ▤ *AE, DC, MC, V* ⊗ *Closed Sun. and Mon. mid-Sept.–mid-Apr.; closed Sun.–Wed. mid-Apr.–mid-Sept; closed 1st 2 wks of Jan. No lunch* ✛ *C3.*

$$$
CONTEMPO-
RARY THAI
★
✕ **Chinwag Eathai.** This funky upbeat restaurant oozes character and personality from the first freshly pressed juice or cocktail to the last mouthful of caramel custard with crunchy banana dessert. Lighting is low and the intimate dining areas are spread over two stories. The wok-fried duck with cashews, bean sprouts, and chili is a favorite meal, as is the caramelized pork hock with chili vinegar. It's a

10-minute walk from Cathedral Square. ⊠ *161 High St.* ☎ *03/365–7363* ⊕ *www.chinwageathai.co.nz* ⊟ *AE, MC, V* ☾ *No lunch* ✛ *D5.*

$$$$ ✕ **Curator's House.** Here you can dine in a 1920s Tudor-style Arts and
SPANISH   Crafts house, looking out on the Botanic Gardens and the Peacock
Fountain, or take a garden table and be part of it. The menu has tapas
selections and a good variety of seafood, and chef Javier adds Spanish
flair with a grand paella (serves 2). Try the slow-roasted spring lamb
or something a bit lighter like the West Coast whitebait. The kitchen
garden supplies herbs, berries, and vegetables to the restaurant, and
they have a strong environmental policy to keep things green. ⊠ *7
Rolleston Ave.* ☎ *03/379–2252* ⊟ *AE, DC, MC, V* ✛ *B4.*

$$–$$$ ✕ **Dux de Lux.** This Arts Centre vegetarian-and-seafood restaurant inhab-
ECLECTIC   its a mock Tudor-style building that was once the university's student
center. You'll usually find Akaroa salmon on the menu, along with
vegetarian picks such as pasta, pizzas, or enchiladas. The courtyard
is popular for dining in summer, particularly on weekends during the
market and live music performances. The Dux complex also has a boutique brewery, cocktail lounge, and live bands four nights a week, and
was voted Pub of the Year 2006 and 2008 by the national Bartender
Magazine. The restaurant has counter service only and can be busy at
times, especially Friday evenings. Occasionally reviews are mixed, but
the standard is usually quite good, and it's a reliable, year-round eating
spot. ⊠ *Hereford and Montreal Sts.* ☎ *03/366–6919* ⊕ *www.thedux.
co.nz* ⊟ *AE, MC, V* ✛ *B4.*

$$$ ✕ **50 on Park.** Don't miss the breakfasts at this restaurant in the George
Fodor's Choice   Hotel, where you can look out at early-morning joggers in Hagley Park.
★   Start with the likes of homemade baked beans on ciabatta or a smoked
grouper hash with poached eggs and spinach. Or for something really
different try the chive-scented waffle with roasted tomatoes, eggs, and
bacon. Unusual for New Zealand, there's no eggs Benedict in sight! In
the evenings, favorites include seared scallops with broccoli puree, pork
crackling, and porcini risotto with duck confit; they have a good range
of grilled meats and sides to match. ⊠ *50 Park Terr.* ☎ *03/379–4560*
⊟ *AE, DC, MC, V* ✛ *B3.*

$–$$ ✕ **The Globe.** This will take you back to the 1990s with its cosmopolitan
CAFÉ   mix of customers and its café-style food. It's one of those places where
people keep coming back, year after year, for its predictably good food
and coffee and its buzzing friendly vibe. There's nothing modern or
minimalist here; just a huge funky globe strung from the ceiling high
above your head and lots of posters on the walls. There's a good mix
of breakfast and lunch fare with cabinet food like panini, quiche, and
baked goods, and an all-day menu including muesli, eggs benedict,
French toast, and pancakes. Or try their homemade fruit toast with
lashings of real butter and berry jam. ⊠ *171 High St.,* ☎ *03/366–4704*
⊟ *AE, MC, V* ✛ *D5.*

$$$–$$$$ ✕ **Indochine.** The space is an intriguing mix of Christchurch and Asia—
ASIAN   clearly the interior designer had fun creating various intimate corners,
Fodor's Choice   large group spaces, and a leafy courtyard. The menu also bridges the
★   two cultures; light options include pan-seared scallops with green tea
noodles or Peking duck with mandarin sauce. Dinner may be grilled,

teriyaki fillet steak, fried tofu and butternut curry, or glazed pork belly with prawn-and-crab pastries. It's also becoming known as a cool spot to head to late in the evening. ✉ *209 Cambridge Terr.* ☎ *03/365–7323* ▭ *AE, MC, V* ⊘ *No lunch* ✛ *C3.*

$$$$
NEW ZEALAND
★
✕**Pescatore.** This second-floor restaurant looking out to Hagley Park is known for creative, conceptual New Zealand cuisine, and the über-cool space is designed to enhance all the senses. Presentation is thoughtful and sometimes spectacular. Local foods dominate the menu, with New Zealand specialties such as Smoked Scallops with black fennel puree, chorizo, confit orange, or the Canterbury Lamb trio of poached loin, braised lamb neck, and lamb bacon. For dessert, go for the Valrhona chocolate fondant with saltwater caramel, yogurt sorbet and milk powder. There's an extensive wine list. ✉ *50 Park Terr.* ☎ *03/371–0257* ▭ *AE, DC, MC, V* ⊘ *Closed Sun. and Mon. No lunch* ✛ *B3.*

$$$$
ECLECTIC
★
✕**Saggio di vino.** Wine is the raison d'être for this long-established Christchurch vinotheque on a prominent corner on Victoria Street, but it's also sought out for its slow food ethos. The lighting is low here and the walls are dark, creating a lovely cocoonlike aura. Mix that with one of the 400 wines on the wine list and a long slow meal and you're in for a nice relaxing evening. Try the pan-fried hapuka (grouper) with lemon saffron and a tomato butter sauce. Some parking out back in the evenings. ✉ *185 Victoria St.* ☎ *03/379–4006* ▭ *AE, DC, MC, V* ⊘ *No lunch* ✛ *A1.*

$$$–$$$$
ECLECTIC
✕**Sticky Fingers.** The Oxford Terrace strip isn't just for evenings. This place is a nice breakfast spot overlooking the Avon River. It was apparently named for its previous life as a pizzeria. Breakfast has standards like eggs a dozen different ways and a big fry-up. But they also have less common breakfasts like sirloin steak with all the trimmings or roasted chorizo sausage with French toast and a mushroom potato cake. Both the food and the coffee are good, and the big-screen TVs are usually muted. Later in the evening the bar crowd raises the tempo. ✉ *Oxford Terr.* ☎ *03/366–6452* ▭ *AE, DC, MC, V* ✛ *C4.*

NORTH OF CENTRAL CHRISTCHURCH

$$$$
NEW ZEALAND
✕**The Cornershop Bistro.** Just a block back from Sumner Beach this urban-style establishment has drummed up an extremely loyal, local clientele. It's a busy café during the day before morphing in to something a little more serious at night. The organic chicken is always popular, either as coq au vin or roasted and served with pancetta, seasonal vegetables, and a lemon butter sauce. Dinner gets exciting with tasty options like a pork-and-pistachio terrine and a blue-cheese soufflé. ✉ *32 Nayland St., Sumner* ☎ *03/326–6720* ⊕ *www.cornershopbistro. co.nz* ▭ *AE, MC, V* ⊘ *Closed Mon. and Tues.* ✛ *C6.*

9

WHERE TO STAY

Use the coordinate (✛ B2) at the end of each listing to locate a site on the corresponding map.

CENTRAL CHRISTCHURCH

$$ ⌃ **The Chateau on the Park.** Surrounded by 5 acres of landscaped gardens, this Kiwi take on a French château even has its own boutique vineyard that will soon produce wine. The main building, with its glass walls and heavy, dark wooden beams, has an indoor water garden that wraps around the main entrance and foyer. Rooms are spacious, well-appointed, and all have a view of part of the greenery. **Pros:** opposite Hagley Park and a pleasant walk to town; long glass-walled corridors with lovely garden views; free golf rounds at the Hagley Park golf course. **Cons:** in a high-traffic area, so watch when arriving or leaving by car; parking spaces can be tight, especially for campers. ⊠ *189 Deans Ave.* ☎ *03/348–8999 or 0800/808–999* ⊕ *www.chateau-park. co.nz* ⤳ *190 rooms, 6 suites* ⌃ *In-room: Internet. In-hotel: Restaurant, bar, pool, laundry service* ▭ *AE, DC, MC, V* ✛ *A2.*

$$$–$$$$ ⌃ **The Classic Villa.** This bright-pink, Italian-style villa, directly opposite
★   the Arts Centre, is one of Christchurch's cooler spots to stay. Rooms are stylishly decorated and the amenities and services are tops. Breakfast is Mediterranean style with lots of fruit, cheeses, and cold meats, and is served at the big kitchen table downstairs. The sheltered courtyard is a wonderfully private spot for an evening drink. Children under 12 are not allowed, but exceptions are made for babies under six months. **Pros:** a moment's walk from the city center; fabulous linen and duvets; freshly made pizza and espresso for breakfast. **Cons:** small off-street parking; accessed off one-way street. ⊠ *17 Worcester Blvd.* ☎ *03/377–7905* ⊕ *www.theclassicvilla.co.nz* ⤳ *11 rooms, 1 suite* ⌃ *In-room: No a/c, Wi-Fi. In-hotel: Laundry service, no kids under 12 (babies under 6 mos allowed)* ▭ *AE, DC, MC, V* ⎟◉⎟ *BP, CP* ✛ *B4.*

$$$$ ⌃ **The George.** In the spacious, modern guest rooms, a crisp, mono-
★   chromatic color scheme weaves through everything, from the bedside notepads to the luxe bathroom products. Lovely details continually crop up, such as the magnificent brass handles on the entrance door and the verdigris brass banister. It's just a short walk from the Arts Centre and downtown shopping, and the two on-site restaurants, Pescatore and 50 On Park, are top-notch. **Pros:** consistently voted one of the country's best small hotels; right next to the Avon River and Hagley Park; easy walk to the city center. **Cons:** can be really busy in the public areas with local functions and casual visitors. ⊠ *50 Park Terr.* ☎ *03/379–4560* ⊕ *www.thegeorge.com* ⤳ *41 rooms, 12 suites* ⌃ *In-room: Refrigerator, Wi-Fi. In-hotel: 2 restaurants, bar, gym, bicycles, laundry facilities, laundry service, parking (free)* ▭ *AE, DC, MC, V* ✛ *B3*

$$–$$$ ⌃ **Orari B&B.** There's a good selection of modern rooms in this historic
☾   villa environment. Rooms are well sized with lots of interesting angles as they follow the intriguing rooflines and spaces. The interior is decidedly welcoming, bathrooms are generous, and there is good off-street parking. **Pros:** many rooms have skylights for extra natural light; there are also five modern three-bedroom apartments on site for $330; sunny

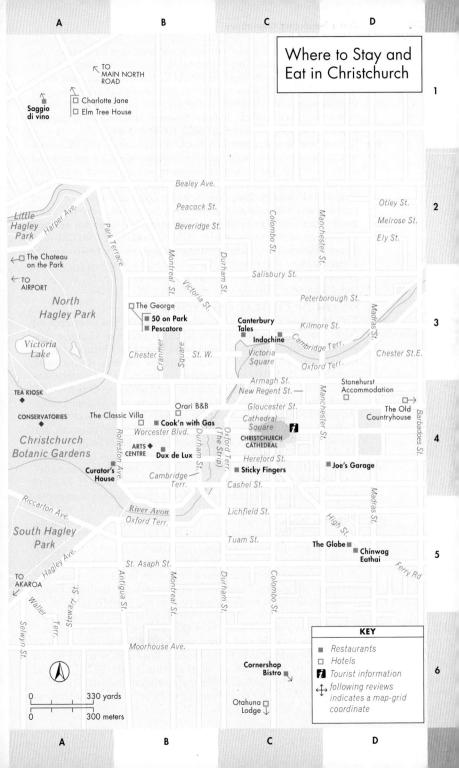

Where to Stay and Eat in Christchurch

A   **B**   **C**   **D**

1

↖ TO MAIN NORTH ROAD

↖ Saggio di vino

□ Charlotte Jane
□ Elm Tree House

2

Little Hagley Park

Harper Ave.

Park Terrace

Bealey Ave.

Peacock St.

Beveridge St.

Montreal St.

Durham St.

Colombo St.

Manchester St.

Otley St.

Melrose St.

Ely St.

← The Chateau on the Park

← TO AIRPORT

North Hagley Park

Victoria Lake

Salisbury St.

Victoria St.

Peterborough St.

Madras St.

3

□ The George

■ 50 on Park

■ Pescatore

Chester St. W.

Cranmer Square

Canterbury Tales

Indochine

Victoria Square

Armagh St.

New Regent St. —

Kilmore St.

Cambridge Terr.

Oxford Terr.

Chester St. E.

TEA KIOSK ◆

CONSERVATORIES ◆

The Classic Villa □

Christchurch Botanic Gardens

Orari B&B □

■ Cook'n with Gas

Worcester Blvd.

Rolleston Ave.

ARTS CENTRE ◆

■ Dux de Lux

Curator's House

Cambridge Terr.

Durham St.

Oxford Terr. (The Strip)

Gloucester St.

Cathedral Square

CHRISTCHURCH CATHEDRAL

Hereford St.

■ Sticky Fingers

Cashel St.

Manchester St.

Stonehurst Accommodation □

The Old Countryhouse □ →

Barbadoes St.

4

■ Joe's Garage

Riccarton Ave.

South Hagley Park

Hagley Ave.

River Avon

Oxford Terr.

Lichfield St.

Tuam St.

High St.

Madras St.

The Globe ■

■ Chinwag Eathai

Ferry Rd

5

TO AKAROA ←

Waller Terr.

Selwyn St.

Stewart St.

Antigua St.

Montreal St.

Durham St.

St. Asaph St.

Colombo St.

Moorhouse Ave.

Cornershop Bistro ■

Otahuna Lodge □ ↓

6

| 0 | | 330 yards |
| 0 | | 300 meters |

KEY

■ Restaurants
□ Hotels
🛈 Tourist information
↔ following reviews indicates a map-grid coordinate

A   **B**   **C**   **D**

courtyard areas and garden corners to sit; good spot for families who need adjoining rooms **Cons:** Montreal St. is on the one-way system so plan your arrival on the map; the central location makes for some week-end night noise; only basic toiletries in bathrooms. ⊠ *Corner Montreal and Gloucester Sts.,* ☎ *03/365–6569* ⊕ *www.orari.co.nz* ➦ *10 rooms* ⚘ *In-room: No a/c, Wi-Fi. In-hotel: Laundry facilities, Wi-Fi, parking (free), no-smoking rooms* ▤ *AE, MC, V* ⦿⍾ *BP* ✛ *B4.*

¢–$ 🛏 **Stonehurst Accommodation.** Two blocks from the city center, this cluster
★   of eight bright-yellow buildings offers various options, from powered camper-van sites and backpacker rooms to well-appointed apartments that can sleep up to six, with two bathrooms, dishwasher, private bal-cony, and full laundry. **Pros:** close to the city center and nightspots; good public spaces with nice aura. **Cons:** a big complex that can feel like a small village of its own; some minimum-stay requirements on their apartments. ⊠ *241 Gloucester St.* ☎ *03/379–4620 or 0508/786–633* ✎ *accom@stonehurst.co.nz* ⊕ *www.stonehurst.co.nz* ➦ *46 rooms, 20 motel rooms, 14 apartments, 78 dorm beds* ⚘ *In-room: No a/c, no phone (some), safe (some), refrigerator, Internet. In-hotel: Bar, pool, laundry facilities, parking (free)* ▤ *AE, DC, MC, V* ✛ *D4.*

NORTH OF CENTRAL CHRISTCHURCH

$$$$ 🛏 **Charlotte Jane.** Once a girls' school, this 1891 villa now sees pampered
Fodor'sChoice   guests instead of disciplined students, and its luxurious Victorian style
★   introduces visitors to the uniquely English heritage of Christchurch. The centrally located house brims with gorgeous elements: the Victorian veranda, a stained-glass window above the entrance depicting the *Charlotte Jane* (one of the first four ships to bring settlers to Christchurch), a native kauri- and rimu-wood staircase, a rimu-paneled dining room, and period furniture throughout the 12 magnificent guest rooms. **Pros:** B&B and full lodge options available; small luxury-hotel character; pri-vate two-bedroom cottage in the garden; on-site Michelin chefs. **Cons:** busy main road location; no children under 12 (except in 2 bedroom suites). ⊠ *110 Papanui Rd., Merivale* ☎ *03/355–1028* ⊕ *www.charlotte-jane.co.nz* ➦ *12 rooms, 1 cottage* ⚘ *In-room: No a/c, Wi-Fi. In-hotel: Restaurant, bar, laundry service, Internet terminal, no-smoking rooms* ▤ *AE, MC, V* ⦿⍾ *BP, MAP* ✛ *A1.*

$$$$ 🛏 **Elm Tree House.** If you'd prefer a friendly experience away from the city center, this B&B should fit the bill. The 1920s Arts and Crafts–style house takes its name from the large tree in the front garden. Most of the rooms are upstairs, and each has a distinctive look, from the wood-pan-eled honeymoon suite to the ground-floor room with French doors that open onto the garden. Papanui sun streams into the enormous lounge through leaded-glass windows, and you can pop an old favorite on the Wurlitzer jukebox. Windows are triple-glazed to quiet the road noise. **Pros:** on the main road north from the city; comfy colonial elegance; two luggage racks in each room; wonderful hosts Karen and Allan are really knowledgeable. **Cons:** Papanui Road can be noisy; several bathrooms are quite small; off-street parking is tight. ⊠ *236 Papanui Rd., Merivale* ☎ *03/355–9731* ⊕ *www.elmtreehouse.co.nz* ➦ *6 rooms* ⚘ *In-room: No a/c, Wi-Fi. In-hotel: Laundry service, Internet terminal* ▤ *AE, MC, V* ⦿⍾ *BP, CP* ✛ *A1.*

EAST OF THE CENTRAL CHRISTCHURCH

¢–$ 🏠 **The Old Countryhouse.** This old country house is actually three color-
★ ful, restored villas with polished wooden floors and handmade, native-
wood furniture. You can whip up breakfast in one of the two large,
cheery communal kitchens. The dorm rooms have three to seven beds
apiece. Colors are bright, there's lots of natural light and wood trim, and
some good scenic photos of New Zealand on the walls. It's a 15-minute
walk from town but you can take the bus (routes 21 and 83); shops are
close by. **Pros:** pleasant garden to relax in; well heated in winter; free
tea, coffee and home-baked bread for hot toast in the morning; good
kitchens and bathrooms. **Cons:** check-in only between 8 AM and 8 PM;
no kids under 14; minimum stay requirements over Christmas–New
Year (about 8 days, but it varies); on a busy road. ✉ *437 Gloucester St.*
☎ *03/381–5504* ⊕ *www.oldcountryhousenz.com* ➶ *13 private rooms
(some en suite), 6 dorm rooms* 🛏 *In-room: No a/c, no phone, kitchen,
no TV, Wi-Fi. In-hotel: Bar, laundry facilities, Internet terminal, parking (free), no kids under 14* ▤ *MC, V* ✛ *D4.*

SOUTH OF THE CENTRAL CHRISTCHURCH

$$$$ 🏠 **Otahuna Lodge.** Just 20 minutes from Christchurch and almost hidden
by glorious century-old gardens is one of New Zealand's most important historic homes. Built in 1895 in Queen Anne style for Sir Heaton
Rhodes, a high profile Member of Parliament of the time, the three-
story homestead has been lovingly restored to its former grandeur, yet
has all the modern amenities you would expect in an exclusive luxury
lodge. Each of Otahuna's seven suites has a distinctive character and
reveals a different element of the Otahuna story. Original fireplaces
complement the rooms and the wisteria-blue drawing room is divine.
Be sure to wander the 30 acres of gardens (guided tours available), and
take a dip in the heated pool (summer only). **Pros:** unlike most luxury
lodges this one is just out of town; memorable five-course degustation
dinner included, with wine matching; lots of fresh homegrown fruits
and vegetables and cooking classes are available. **Cons:** not for the
budget-minded; TV only available by request. ✉ *224 Rhodes Rd., 17
km (10 mi) from Christchurch, Tai Tapu* ☎ *03/329–6333* ⊕ *www.ota-
huna.co.nz* ➶ *7 suites* 🛏 *In-room: No a/c. In-hotel: Restaurant, tennis
court, pool, gym, spa, bicycles, laundry service, Wi-Fi, no kids under
13* ▤ *AE, MC, V* 🍴 *MAP* ✛ *C6.*

9

NIGHTLIFE AND THE ARTS

The *Christchurch Press* is a reliable source on the city's arts and entertainment scenes. The Wednesday edition's special arts section lists events
and venues, and Thursday's edition has a gig guide on shows and more.
You could also check out the Web sites Be There (⊕ *www.bethere.co.nz*)
for arts and entertainment listings and Jagg (⊕ *www.jagg.co.nz*) for
information on live music, though it can be a little slow to be updated.
If you're out late on a weekend and looking for a cheap way back to
your room, try the $6 After Midnight Express bus, which runs on the
hour from 1am to 4 AM, Saturday and Sunday nights from Oxford Terrace (between Hereford and Worcester streets).

Tickets for many performance venues and concerts are sold through **Ticketek** (☎ 03/377–8899 ⊕ premier.ticketek.co.nz). You can find Ticketek outlets in shopping malls or online.

THE ARTS

Christchurch has a strong arts scene, with choirs, orchestras, and theater, not to mention dozens of art galleries. In odd-numbered years (e.g., 2011) the city hosts a mid-winter **Arts Festival** (⊕ www.artsfestival. co.nz). In even-numbered years, between September and November the biennial arts festival called **SCAPE** (⊕ www.artandindustry.org.nz) focuses on urban and alternative arts.

ART GALLERIES Although the Christchurch Art Gallery Te Puna O Waiwhetu is the city's visual arts mother ship, there are many smaller galleries to check out. For more information, pick up the annually published *Canterbury Arts Trail* booklet at the visitor bureau.

Centre of Contemporary Art (COCA). This gallery actually has a long history of showing contemporary works by Canterbury artists—it was founded as the Canterbury Society of Arts back in 1880. Now their shows mix established names with up-and-coming, mainly Kiwi, artists. One gallery, the Top Floor, exhibits work by children and runs art classes. ✉ *66 Gloucester St.* ☎ *03/366–7261* ⊕ *www.coca.org.nz* ✉ *Donation requested* ☉ *Tues.–Fri. 10–5, weekends noon–4, closed Mon.*

Te Toi Mana. Māori artist Riki Manuel often carves in this Arts Centre space. The gallery focuses on traditional and contemporary Māori art and is a good place to find creative souvenirs and travel mementos. ✉ *Arts Centre, Hereford St.* ☎ *03/366–4943* ☉ *Daily 10–5.*

FILMS Short film festivals have become popular, particularly in the Christchurch Art Gallery auditorium. Each year in late July or early August there is an international film festival with showings at the Rialto cinema, and it often includes a homegrown section. The independent **Academy Theatre** and **Cloisters Film House** (✉ *25 Hereford St.* ☎ *03/366–0167* ⊕ *www. artfilms.co.nz*) are both in the Arts Centre and are the places to hit for indie, art-house and foreign flicks.

MUSIC If you're here in summer, be sure to check out the **SummerTimes Festival** (⊕ *www.summertimes.org.nz*), which includes several free concerts in Hagley Park. The festival kicks off with a New Year's Eve party in Cathedral Square and includes "Classical Sparks," music punctuated with fireworks, usually held in late February or early March. **Town Hall** (✉ *86 Kilmore St.*) is host to many performances of the classical persuasion, including those by the **Southern Opera** (☎ *03/363–3131* ⊕ *www. southernopera.co.nz*), the **Christchurch City Choir** (☎ *03/366–6927* ⊕ *www.christchurchcitychoir.co.nz*) whose Christmas "Hallelujah!" always packs the house, and the **Christchurch Symphony Orchestra** (☎ *03/379–3886* ⊕ *www.chsymph.co.nz*).

THEATER The **Court Theatre** (✉ *Arts Centre, 20 Worcester Blvd.* ☎ *03/963–0870, 0800/333–100 bookings* ⊕ *www.courttheatre.org.nz*) is New Zealand's leading theater company. In its two auditoriums the company performs everything from Shakespeare to contemporary plays by New Zealand playwrights. The Court also offers children's plays during the holidays; the Court Jesters run the ever-popular Scared Scriptless improv-comedy sessions on Friday night (10 to 11:30 PM, $15) with a second performance on Saturday nights. It is now Australasia's longest-running comedy show.

NIGHTLIFE

For concentrated action, one good option is to head to the bars and cafés along the area known as **the Strip.** This is a small section of Oxford Terrace, one of the streets that follow the curves of the Avon River, between Cashel Street and Worcester Boulevard. The end of the Strip near the Bridge of Remembrance has the younger rowdier crowds. People often spill out onto the footpath, but do all of your drinking in the bars; drinking in public places is banned in parts of the city. The other is the club scene along the area known as South of Lichfield (SOL), with some of the city's most popular dance clubs and late night bars.

The **Coyote** (✉ *126 Oxford Terr.* ☎ *03/366–6055*) serves good food during the day and then transforms into a popular bar, with live music on Wednesday evenings. The **Viaduct** (✉ *136 Oxford Terr.* ☎ *03/377–9968*), with its ancient Greek columns and mosaic-tiled counter front, alludes to a more hedonistic time. But it's an easy place to kick back if you like the music a bit quieter or if you want to enjoy good food with your drinks.Head to **Minx Dining Room & Bar** (✉ *96 Lichfield St.* ☎ *03/374–9944* for cocktails or an excellent meal. The vibe is elegant and exciting and there's a flamboyant, pink, retro cocktail lounge connected.

For some natural suds in the city center try the **Loaded Hog Bar & Restaurant** (✉ *178 Cashel St.* ☎ *03/366–6674*). This brewery produces excellent beers such as Hog Dark and Hog Gold and the food's pretty good, too. The **Victoria Street Cafe** (✉ *Kilmore and Durham Sts.* ☎ *03/365–7799 Ext. 363*) in the imposing atrium of the Crowne Plaza Hotel is a good spot to unwind with a wine or coffee.

Blue Note Piano Bar & Restaurant (✉ *20 Regent St.* ☎ *03/379–9674*) has live music on Wednesday and Thursday evenings 7:30–9:30, and on Friday and Saturday 8–11. Their food is excellent. When all else has closed, make your way to the 24-hour **Christchurch Casino** (✉ *30 Victoria St.* ☎ *03/365–9999*) for blackjack, American roulette, baccarat, and gaming machines. Dress is smart-casual or better; you will be turned away if you arrive in jeans. Free shuttles go to and from local hotels and motels.

9

SHOPPING

Central Christchurch lost its shopping heart to the suburbs a number of years ago, but the last few years have seen a shift back. This is most evident in the High Street area, where many of the city's design stores line the otherwise nondescript street. If your tastes are a little more conservative then the stores around Cashel Street may suit your taste. If you're after travel souvenirs there are any number of stores in and around Cathedral Square selling everything from little woolly novelty sheep to All Black jerseys and shearling-lined boots.

SHOPPING STREETS

Parts of the **City Mall** area around Cashel and High streets are out of bounds to cars. Major branches of music and clothing chains make up most of the frontage, but there are some one-offs worth stopping at, like the Vault craft and design boutique and Wild Places for souvenirs, both in the Cashel Mall. Ballantynes, on the corner of Cashel and Colombo streets, is one of the country's better-known department stores.

Graduates from the polytechnic fashion school only have to cross the road to show their wares on **High Street**, where places such as d'Orsay, Plush, Storm, and Victoria Black display cutting-edge clothes. More daring shoppers seeking amazing jewelry should visit Mask in **Tuam Street.** Secondhand booksellers, antiques and housewares stores, and the overflowing Globe café keep things busy.

Victoria Street, which cuts diagonally across the city center's grid pattern out from Bealey Avenue, has a good mix of clothing and housewares shops interspersed with cafés. If you need a hat for a wedding or the horse races in November, the Hat Shop has a good range, even for men. **Merivale Mall,** north of the city center in Papanui, has a range of classier boutiques and stores—try Quinns for clothing and Bella Silver for jewelry. Outside on Papanui Rd the design stores continue.

SPECIALTY SHOPS

de Spa Chocolatier's (✉ *663 Colombo St.* ☎ *03/379–2203*) delicious sweets pair Belgian chocolate with Kiwi ingredients (fruit fillings, for instance). For a behind-the-scenes look, visit the factory at Ferrymead Heritage Park. **Kathmandu** (✉ *40 Lichfield St.* ☎ *03/366–7148*)sells a colorful range of well-priced outdoor clothing, backpacks, accessories, and tents. Base camp for the whole global operation is in Christchurch. There's another branch at 124 Riccarton Road and a clearance store at the Tower Junction Mega Centre in Blenheim Road.

Untouched World. All things hip and natural in New Zealand meet up here. While some labels appeal to the backpacker end of the market, Untouched World has much more of a designer edge. Apart from the store's own line of stylish lifestyle clothing made from Merinomink (a mixture of possum fur and merino wool), organic cotton, and a silky-fine machine-washable organic merino, you'll find New Zealand handcrafted jewelry, natural skin-care products, and great gift ideas. The attached licensed café serves fresh food in its native garden environment. There's also a branch in the Arts Centre (301 Montreal Street) in the central city. Both are open daily. ✉ *155 Roydvale Ave., Burnside* ☎ *03/357–9399.*

TOURS

BICYCLE TOURS
Christchurch Bike Tours (☎ *0800/733–257* ⊕ *www.chchbiketours.co.nz*) organizes city bicycle tours ($35 per person, limit of 10 people so book ahead), offered daily from November to March. The two-hour route follows the Avon River through the city's parks and gardens before heading back into the city center. Bikes are retro style with a basket for your goodies, and helmets are provided. Meet at the bike sign outside the visitor center for a 2 PM start.

Continued on page 540

TAKING NEW ZEALAND HOME

By Debra A. Klein and Sue Courtney

You can't pack New Zealand's ocean breezes, pristine alpine pastures, rare birds, ubiquitous sheep, or quirky sense of humor, but you can take a bit of Kiwiana home in the form of colorful, practical, and often eco-friendly souvenirs.

"Kiwiana" refers to quirky items that celebrate New Zealand's identity: nature- and Māori-inspired prints on clothing; wood, shell, and stone products; and the cutest soft toys. The kiwi-bird appears on shirts and keychains and as plush toys. New Zealand's famous wool products are widely available, as are travel-friendly food items.

Major travel and tramping hubs like Christchurch, Auckland, Wellington, and Queenstown are retail havens with everything from boutiques to large souvenir shops. Outside the cities, look for roadside signs pointing to workshops and markets for local goods. Remember that U.S. Customs and Border Patrol will confiscate plants, meats, fruits, and vegetables.

LAST-STOP SHOPPING

If you were too busy hiking to pick up souvenirs, never fear. Auckland International Airport's clothing, craft, and food shops (located both before and after security) are as good as those in town. Duty-free outlets have great selections of Kiwi-made lotions, soaps, and sweets all at prices that are comparable to those elsewhere in New Zealand.

Top: Paua, a native abalone with unique iridescent shell

NEW ZEALAND WOOL

New Zealand is the world's second-largest wool producer (after Australia). Fine pure-breed wool accounts for 5% of the market; high-country merino wool is the most sought after for fashion garments. Kiwi innovation has produced blended wool products that are usually practical, sometimes fashionable, and often eco-friendly.

Brush-tail possums, a non-native pest, threaten New Zealand's native flora and fauna. In 1991, the company Possumdown pioneered a method of weaving possum fur fibers with superfine merino wool. This resulted in a lighter, more durable yarn with a very soft, luxurious feel that provides more insulation and warmth. It also provided an economically advantageous method of pest control that has helped rejuvenate

Shearing at sheep show. Rotorua, North Island

the biological balance throughout the country. (Note that the WWF, Greenpeace New Zealand, and the New Zealand Forest and Bird organization support the culling of the possum and the sale of possum products.)

WOOL AND NATURAL PRODUCTS FOR . . .

. . . THE OUTDOORS PERSON

Swanndri (⊕ *www.swanndri.co.nz*) developed the now-iconic 100% wool, waterproof bush shirt in 1913, as well as the shearer's black, knee-length singlet made from coarse wool. Today Swanndri offers a range of clothing, footwear, and accessories. You'll still find the singlets, but they're more for fashion than function these days.

Hats, scarves, gloves, mittens, socks, and thermal underwear from natural wool and sheepskin products, as well as from merino-possum blends, are plentiful in sports shops throughout the country. The "baacode" that comes with **Icebreaker**'s (⊕ *www.icebreaker. com*) merino clothing allows customers to trace the wool in their outerwear back to the farm where it originated.

Hikers may be able to source their own wool too; just pick it off the fence lines in sheep farm country. Lanolin from natural wool soothes blistered toes and adds comfort while tramping.

Icebreaker wool wares

...THE FASHIONISTA

Some of the finest merino from the South Island high country becomes men's Italian designer suits. Wool and merino-possum blends can be found in boutiques and upmarket stores. Some jackets, sweaters, and cardigans even have luxurious possum fur trim. Away from the cities you'll find outlets where creative wool artists spin wool straight from the fleece for knitting, weaving, and making hand-felted products. Hand-knitted sweaters, cardigans, and beanies can provide an individual look, while a woven bag or a lacy merino shawl makes for an affordable fashion accessory. Beautiful gossamer-like scarves, made with felted merino wool and often embellished with silk, can be exquisite.

...THE COMFORT MAVEN

Wool and sheepskin products, such as sheepskin slippers, fleece-lined Ugg-style boots, 100% New Zealand wool leisure wear, wool underlays, and cozy wool blankets, sheepskin rugs, and fleece car seat covers have been comforting New Zealanders for generations.

Wool and sheep products are sold throughout New Zealand, particularly in tourist destinations, airports, and main city centers. The best stores will have a range of brands and will also

Newly shorn fleece

stock alpaca and other natural animal wool, fur, and skin products.

For babies you'll find hand-knitted lambswool hats, jackets, and booties. The well-known lightweight aircell baby blankets made from first-shear wool have an open weave that ensures circulation while retaining warmth and dissipating moisture. **Thermacell** is one of several brands; studies have shown that these types of blankets help the little ones get to sleep.

For extra-cuddly warmth on a chilly night, warm up with a possum fur hot water bottle cover. Lanolin creams extracted from merino wool will calm dry skin (⊕ *www. lanolin.co.nz*).

9

TIPS FOR BUYING NEW ZEALAND WOOL PRODUCTS

Ensure that manufacturing was carried out in New Zealand. Look for labels that read "100% Pure New Zealand Merino," "Buy New Zealand," and "New Zealand Made."

You can spend as little as $NZ20 on lambswool gloves or socks, up to $500 for a lambskin trimmed jacket, or more than $1,000 for a full sheepskin jacket. Sheepskin rugs range from $99 for a single fleece to $2500 for a designer rug.

Merino Wool

KIWIANA

Carry home a reminder of New Zealand's natural wonders, tastes, and culture with these great products.

FOR THE CRAFTY ONES

PUKEKO

The pukeko, or swamp hen, is a ubiquitous native bird, but it took artist Kevin Kilsby to turn the bright blue and red creature into an icon. His whimsical, decorative clay creations—with big red beaks, impossibly long, skinny legs, and gumboot-clad feet—come in several sizes and designs. The lovable design has inspired similar products from other artists, and there's even a plush version for the kids. Find the statuettes in souvenir shops all over, or go to the source: Kilsby has a shop in Auckland (⊕ www.kilsby.co.nz).

OTHER FEATHERED FRIENDS

During your travels you'll fall in love with other native birds such as the cheeky kea, the nectar-loving tui, the flitty piwakawaka (fantail), and the berry-loving kereru (wood pigeon). Bring home your favorite without causing an international incident at the airport by purchasing one of the soft toy versions sold at Department of Conservation and regional park information centers. If space is at a premium, look for Wild-Cards; when opened they play the distinctive song of the bird depicted on the card's front (⊕ www.wild-card.org/NZ-product.html).

Paua

PAUA

Find the iridescent blue-gray abalone shell inlaid on wooden home wares or silver jewelry. You can even beach comb to find slivers in the sand that wash ashore all over the country.

GREENSTONE

Local legend says that it's bad luck to buy jade (greenstone or *pounamu*) for yourself, so have a travel companion officially purchase greenstone for you. Māori tradition states you should wear jade for 24 hours before gifting it to infuse your spirit into the object. If you're lucky, you'll find your own piece of pounamu on a South Island beach.

CHILD'S PLAY

The brightly colored, wood-crafted **Buzzy Bee** toy has been delighting Kiwi toddlers since the 1940s. Check that you're buying an NZ-made one. Sports fans will delight in **All Blacks** uniforms, hats, and scarves from **Rebel Sport** stores throughout New Zealand. Buy online at the All Blacks Web site (⊕ www.allblackshop.com).

Pukeko

FOR SOME LOCAL FLAVOR

OLIVE OIL

More than 20 varieties of olive trees are available in New Zealand and olives are grown from Northland to Central Otago, but New Zealand's nascent olive oil industry varies widely in quality. The best olive oils have smooth, non-cloying texture and nutty, piquant, peppery flavors. Simunovich Olive Estate (south of Auckland), and Frog's End Estate (outside Nelson), have earned accolades for their extra, extra virgin presses.

CULINARY TREATS

Kinaki Wild Herbs (⊕ *www. Maorifood.com*) packages traditional Māori spices. Find *The Māori Cookbook*, written by Kinaki Wild Herbs founder and chef Charles Royal, at gourmet food stores and better supermarkets.

Seriously Good Chocolate Company (⊕ *www.seriouslygoodchocolate.com*) makes chocolates infused with New Zealand wine. At Mangawhai, on the North Island, you'll find **Bennetts of Mangawhai** (⊕ *www.bennettsofmangawhai.com*), which makes drool-inducing chocolate in traditional blocks.

You'll have to leave the great fruits behind, but consider taking home some feijoa or kiwi candy from **Remarkable Sweets** in Queenstown and Arrowtown or **Candyland** (⊕ *www.candyland.co.nz*) at Taupiri, just north of Hamilton.

Chocolate making at Bennetts

HONEY

New Zealand honey is usually creamed, so it's thick, spreadable, and has a pearl-like sheen. You'll note subtle differences in taste but obvious differences in color of honey types. The lighter the color, the milder the taste. The rare, delicate Pohutukawa honey is sometimes white. Dark honeys, like manuka (prized for its medicinal qualities), are the most caramel-like. There are honey producers everywhere, but just north of Auckland you'll find **Bees Online** (⊕ *www.beesonline.co.nz*), where an extensive range of organic, genetic-engineering free, New Zealand native flora honeys and honey culinary products are available to taste.

Native flora honeys

FOR SOME PERSONAL PAMPERING

SKINCARE

Pacifica Skincare (⊕ *www.pacificaskincare.co.nz*) has a dazzling array of products made from native flowers, leaves, manuka honey, and flaxseed oil. Kowhai tree and pohutukawa essence products are popular. Wine fans will love the soaps made from the pulp of Chardonnay, Pinot Gris, or Pinot Noir. **Living Nature** in Kerikeri uses harakeke's (flax) natural gels in ointments, and Kumerahou plant in shampoos, soaps, and make-up remover.

9

PRIVATE
GUIDES

Descendant of a pre-Adamite (pre-1850) settler, **Jack Tregear** (☎ *03/344–5588 or 0800/344–5588* ⊕ *www.jtnztours.co.nz*) provides a personal historic tour of Christchurch, covering Lyttelton, Sumner, and the Canterbury Provincial Council buildings. The tour takes just over three hours and includes an elegant morning tea. Jack also takes trips to Akaroa, the West Coast, and around the South Island and is happy to put a trip together at your request.

SIGHTSEEING
TOURS

Christchurch Sightseeing Tours (☎ *03/366–9660 or 0508/669–660* ⊕ *www.christchurchtours.co.nz*) has three routes: major town sights plus the beaches at Sumner and the Lyttelton Harbour, Heritage homes, and private gardens (not in winter). Each costs $46; book the City tour with one of the others for $75 or all three for $110.

WALKING
TOURS

Two-hour guided daily walking tours ($15) of the city led by members of the **Christchurch Personal Guiding Service** (☎ *03/353–5990* ✉ *chchpgs@xtra.co.nz*) depart daily at 10 and 1 from the red-and-black kiosk in Cathedral Square. There is no morning walk from May to September.

Taking the **TranzAlpine & High Country Explorer** (☎ *03/377–1391 or 0800/863–975* ⊕ *www.high-country.co.nz* ✉ *info@high-country.co.nz*) is definitely one of the best and most action-packed ways of getting into the Canterbury Plains and the Southern Alps, and experiencing the world-famous TranzAlpine train journey. The full-day trip starts with a hotel pickup for a two-hour trip on the TranzAlpine train, then a 65-km (40-mi) four-wheel-drive safari through the vast 35,000-acre Flock Hill sheep station (filming location for *The Lion, The Witch and the Wardrobe*), a 15-km (9-mi) jet-boat cruise, and a one-hour bus trip back to your Christchurch hotel. The scenery is spectacular, the boat ride a thrill, and your safari guide will discuss the region's human and natural history. A full-day trip is $375 per person, bookings recommended and three-course lunch included.

Using four-wheel-drive minicoaches, **Canterbury Trails, Ltd.** (☎ *03/337–1185* ⊕ *www.canterburytrails.co.nz*) gets in to the backcountry on its personally guided group or exclusive tours. Among its itineraries is a full-day tour to Akaroa and the Banks Peninsula, which includes a dolphin-sighting cruise. Other day trips visit Arthur's Pass, Kaikoura, and Hanmer and reservations are essential. Prices start at $300 per person per day.

Discovery Travel (☎ *03/357–8262* ⊕ *www.discoverytravel.co.nz*) runs day tours to the Waipara wine district, Akaroa, Hanmer and Arthur's Pass; it also organizes tours of some of the area's exceptional private gardens; a favorite is Ohinetahi.

EN
ROUTE

If you've left Christchurch a bit late for breakfast, about 30 minutes south, stop at the **Dunsandel Store** (✉ *Main South Rd., Dunsandel* ☎ *03/325–4037* ⊙ *Mon.–Thurs.* 7 AM–5 PM, *Fri.–Sun.* 7AM–6 PM). It's a fascinating mix of local store, deli, and café, where they sell their own juices, local wines, and excellent food. The cabinets are stuffed with tasty quiches, panini, and baked goods. They have a good range of breakfasts, and for an afternoon treat try the old-fashioned, Victorian sponge cake served with an abundance of cream and strawberries. There are tables indoors and out, surrounded by a courtyard full of fruit trees and vegetables.

ARTHUR'S PASS AND CANTERBURY

East of the city, you can explore the wonderful coastline of Banks Peninsula. The peninsula's two harbors, Lyttelton and Akaroa, were formed from the remnants of two ancient volcanoes; their steep grassy walls drop dramatically to the sea. Looking north, consider stopping in Waipara and its wineries if you're en route to or from Kaikoura or Hanmer Springs. Hanmer Springs' thermal baths are good for a relaxing soak, or you can ride the white water on the river, ski, or mountain bike. Head south or west of town into the Canterbury Plains countryside, and you can ski at Mt. Hutt (in winter) or drive the scenic inland highway to Geraldine and Timaru. Where once only sheep and cattle grazed, you're now just as likely to spot deer and ostriches. If you're heading to the West Coast by road or rail, then Arthur's Pass is worth investigating. You should set an entire day aside for any of these side trips, or, better still, stay overnight.

ARTHUR'S PASS NATIONAL PARK

153 km (96 mi) northwest of Christchurch.

GETTING HERE AND AROUND

For any confident driver the road through Arthur's Pass is a glorious drive—sealed all the way, but with a few steep, gnarly sections in the middle. The train and bus tours are good options, but you lose the flexibility to stop and do a walk or follow a waterfall track, or just admire the breathtaking scenery if you're stuck on a tour.

To drive there from Christchurch head out on the West Coast Road—it is particularly well signposted from town. The turnoff is near the airport. There is only one road over the Alps within 100 km (62 mi) either way so you can't go wrong. The road heads out through the small town of Springfield then heads up towards Porter's Pass and Cass before hitting the real stuff at Arthur's Pass.

Information on the park is available on the **Department of Conservation's** Web site and at the DoC run **Arthur's Pass Visitor Centre**. The **Arthur's Pass Mountaineering** site is another good source for information on local mountaineering conditions.

ESSENTIALS

Visitor Information Arthur's Pass Mountaineering (⊕ www.softrock.co.nz). **Department of Conservation Arthur's Pass Visitor Centre** (✉ State Hwy. 73, Arthur's Pass ☎ 03/318–9211 ⊕ www.doc.govt.nz).

EXPLORING

Arthur's Pass National Park, a spectacular alpine region, is a favorite hiking destination. Initially hacked through as a direct route to the West Coast gold fields in 1865, the road over Arthur's Pass was a tortuous dangerous track. It was frequently shut due to bad weather and slips. When the railway arrived, in 1923, the pass's skiing and hiking opportunities came to the fore, and the TranzAlpine train service now offers a supreme way to see this rugged area without getting your shoes dirty.

9

CLOSE UP

Thematic Trails

Enterprising local tourist offices have sketched out thematically linked, self-guided sightseeing routes throughout the region. You can pick up pamphlets at the pertinent visitor bureaus. The following are the best of the bunch:

Alpine Pacific Triangle. This links three of the most popular getaways in Canterbury: Waipara, Hanmer Springs, and Kaikoura.

The Peninsula Pioneers. Pick up a brochure from the Akaroa visitor center for information on five different routes through the Banks Peninsula bays. Keep in mind that some of the bay roads are unpaved and steep.

Pioneer Trail. Connecting several historic sights between Timaru and Geraldine, this route includes the Richard Pearse Memorial, dedicated to a local aviation innovator.

Scenic Highway 72. Scenic Highway 72 runs from Amberley, north of Christchurch, along the foothills of the Southern Alps through two spectacular gorges, past Geraldine to Winchester. You can join up with it at various points along the way.

On the way to the pass, along State Highway 73 from Christchurch, you'll pass the **Castle Hill Conservation Area,** which is filled with interesting rock formations. The gray limestone rocks range in height from 3 to 164 feet and in spring and fall they're tackled by climbers keen to go bouldering. Nearby **Craigieburn Conservation Park** has wonderful beech and fern forests and some great mountain biking trails. Sheltered as they are by the Southern Alps, these parklands get far less precipitation than the western side of the mountains, which gets five times more rain than the eastern side. Still, the area is subject to heavy snowfalls in winter.

Above the tree line you'll find ski slopes and, between November and March, masses of wildflowers, including giant buttercups. Around the summit you'll also have a good chance of seeing *kea*, the South Island's particularly intelligent and curious mountain parrots.

The west side of the pass has had a bad reputation for its steep, winding, narrow road. The good news is that the highway has been upgraded and a viaduct now eliminates the need to drive through the main slip-prone area. **Arthur's Pass Village,** at 737 meters (2,395 feet), isn't much to speak of, and in bad weather it looks rather forlorn. A couple of restaurants and a store provide basic food supplies, and there are several places to stay, including an excellent wilderness lodge at nearby Cass. There's also a Department of Conservation visitor center to help with enjoying the vast selection of mountains and rivers in the area. Both the Devil's Punchbowl and Bridal Veil Falls are worth the short walk. The tracks are in good condition and, although they're a bit steep and rocky in places, no serious hiking experience is required.

SPORTS AND THE OUTDOORS

HIKING AND WALKING   Arthur's Pass National Park has plenty of half- and full-day **hikes** and 11 backcountry trails with overnight huts for backpacking. A popular walk near Arthur's Pass Village is the short Dobson Walk, which crosses the summit. It's a good introduction to subalpine and alpine plants; the alpine flowers are in bloom from November to February. It takes roughly 1½ hours to do the circuit. For a full-day hike, trails leading to the summits of various mountains are all along State Highway 73. Be prepared for variable weather conditions. Two of the most popular and challenging overnight treks are the Cass Saddle trip and the Minga–Deception route over Goat Pass. For these, you'll need an experienced leader and full gear. The Department of Conservation Visitor Centre has up-to-date information on weather and trail conditions. Fill out an intention form, and remember to let them know when you have completed your trip.

WHERE TO EAT AND STAY

\$\$–\$\$\$ ✕ **The Wobbly Kea Café and Bar.** This surprisingly pleasant place is named
CAFÉ for the cheeky mountain parrots that circle above it day after day. It's open from early in the morning until well into the evening—presuming people are around. The two most popular dishes are their lamb rump salad and the fresh beer-battered fish; both have people asking for more. They also have full breakfast and lunch menus and do pizza all day as well. ⊠ *Main Rd.* ☎ *03/318–9101* ▭ *AE, DC, MC, V.*

\$ 🏠 **Mountain House Backpackers and Cottages.** Having bought out the neighboring hostels this is now the biggest spot in town. The main lodge has private and shared rooms; the cottages are up on School Terrace, just behind the main lodge, and there are backpacker dorms across the road from the main lodge, in the old YHA lodge which is now also part of Mountain House. You can sign up for one of the bedrooms in the cottages, reserve an entire cottage, or choose a bed in the private rooms or dorm rooms in the main lodge. The interior design may be homely, but you can't argue with the impressive peaks right outside your window. **Pros:** a wing of new facilities and private rooms is the pick for clean and tidy; two buildings have Internet kiosks, memory card readers, CD burners, Wi-Fi, and Skype; one women-only bunk room. **Cons:** the whole complex is spread out over about a kilometer; no en suite bathrooms. ⊠ *State Hwy. 73* ☎ *03/318–9258* ⊕ *www.trampers.co.nz* ⤴ *12 double rooms* ⤴ *4 cottages (3–4 bedrooms), 11 share rooms* ⌂ *In-room: Kitchen (some). In-hotel: Laundry facilities, Internet terminal* ▭ *MC, V.*

\$\$\$\$ 🏠 **Wilderness Lodge Arthur's Pass.** Surrounded by spectacular peaks, beech
Fodor's Choice forests, and serene lakes, this sophisticated (and pricey) back-to-nature
★ lodge shares 6,000 acres with its own working 5,000-sheep farm and nature reserve in a valley called Te Ko Awa a Aniwaniwa (Valley of the Mother of Rainbows) by its first Māori visitors. From a hillside perch it overlooks the Waimakariri River, which has carved a gaping swath through the pass. Rooms have balcony views of this incredible area. By taking advantage of the walks and guided, nature day trips with resident biologists (several included in the rate), you also get an education in rare high-country ecology. Full-day guided trips in the region can take you to limestone caves, a tranquil lake, a glacier basin, or to spots where you can glimpse rare alpine plants and cheeky kea (the native mountain parrot). There is a sister lodge at Lake Moeraki on the West Coast. **Pros:** on alternate days, you can muster sheep with border collies and help blade-shear sheep the old-fashioned way; the owners are

9

committed to preserving the alpine environment. **Cons:** a long way from Christchurch unless you're planning to cross Arthur's Pass to the West Coast anyway; a one-night stop is not enough to experience the activities and environment here. ✉ *130 km (81 mi) west of Christchurch on State Hwy. 73, Arthur's Pass* ☎ *03/318–9246* ⊕ *www.wilderness-lodge.co.nz* ↝ *20 rooms, 4 suites* ⚲ *In-room: No a/c, refrigerator, no TV, Internet. In-hotel: Restaurant, bar, water sports, laundry facilities, Wi-Fi* ▭ *MC, V* ☺ *Closed June and July* ⍐ *MAP.*

LYTTELTON

12 km (7½ mi) east of Christchurch.

Lyttelton, a sleepy port town, was the arrival point for many of the early Canterbury settlers. The Canterbury Pilgrims' landing place is marked by a rock near the road entrance to the port. A mix of renovated wooden villas and contemporary homes now rises halfway up what was once a volcanic crater. Today, because of its relative isolation from Christchurch, Lyttelton has developed its own distinctive quality, attracting creative types who like the small-town character.

GETTING HERE AND AROUND

Lyttelton can be reached by driving down Ferry Road from Christchurch, heading toward Sumner and then taking the road tunnel. Although the tunnel road is convenient, the best way to explore the area is to head over Evans Pass from Sumner—stopping to walk on the beach there—and down into Lyttelton. Another scenic route is to follow the main street, Colombo, east out of the city, up the Port Hills, and over Dyers Pass to Governors Bay. Then turn left and head back along the harbor edge to Lyttelton. If you don't have a car you can catch buses 35 or 28 from Christchurch.

Lyttelton stretches along a terrace above the port. Norwich Quay runs along the waterfront, but the main street, London Street, runs parallel a block higher up the hill. London Street joins the road back over to Sumner, and in the other direction back past the tunnel entrance along Simeon Quay toward Governors Bay.

ESSENTIALS

Visitor Information Lyttelton i-SITE Information Centre (✉ *20 Oxford St.* ☎ *03/328-9093* ⊕ *www.lytteltonharbour.co.nz*)

BEST BETS FOR CRUISE PASSENGERS

■ **A Day in the City.** Explore Christchurch city, ride the tram and stop off at the art gallery, the museum, the Arts Centre, and Cathedral Square.

■ **Arthur's Pass.** Take a day trip into the Southern Alps by TranzAlpine train. Walk to a waterfall, follow a bush trail, and see some bold kea birds.

■ **Banks Peninsula and Akaroa.** Take a bus tour over the hills to Akaroa, hop on a harbor cruise to see the dolphins, and enjoy a winery lunch at French Farm.

9

EXPLORING

There's a small maritime museum on Gladstone Quay, but the main local nautical sight is the castlelike **Timeball Station.** In the days before GPS and atomic clocks, ships would make sure their chronometers were accurate by checking them when the large ball at the Timeball Station was lowered. Clocks were used to calculate longitude while ships were at sea. Though it's no longer needed, the Historic Places Trust maintains the station and keeps the ball dropping. The ball is raised above the tower five minutes before 1 and then dropped exactly on the hour. ✉ *2 Reserve Terr.* ☎ *03/328–7311* 🖃 *$7* ⊙ *Oct.–Apr., daily 10–5:30; May–Sept., Wed.–Sun. 10–5:30.*

Fodor's Choice ★   Sir Miles Warren is one of New Zealand's foremost architects with a pedigree as large as his garden. **Ohinetahi,** which is also the Māori name for the area, features not only his large, stone, colonial villa, but also his immaculate garden—considered one of the best formal gardens in the country. Blending Sir Miles's eye for detail and design with a stunning situation this garden maximizes the use of "garden rooms"—the red room being particularly memorable—hedging, and color. ✉ *Governors Bay–Teddington Rd.* ☎ *03/329–9852* 🖃 *$10* ⊙ *Mid-Sept.–Dec. 23, weekdays 10–4; Jan. 7–end of Mar., weekends by appointment; closed Apr.–mid-Sept.*

Quail Island, in Lyttelton Harbour, was used by the early European settlers as a quarantine zone and leper colony and was named after the now-extinct native quail. It was once a significant area for collecting birds' eggs by local Māori. These days Quail Island, also known as Otamahua, is being restored as an ecological reserve, and is home to many native birds including kingfisher, fantail, *silvereye* (a small bird common in New Zealand), and various sea birds. The *Black Cat* ferry from Lyttelton can zip you out here for a hike or a picnic. Allow for at least three hours on the island. Reservations are recommended. ✉ *Jetty B, 17 Norwich Quay* ☎ *03/328–9078 or 0800/436–574* 🖃 *$20* ⊙ *Sept.–Apr., daily 12:20; Dec.–Mar., extra sailing daily at 10:20; May–Aug., by charter only.*

SPORTS AND THE OUTDOORS

Diamond Harbour is the largest township on the far side of Lyttelton Harbour. Its main feature is Godley House (✉ *2 Waipapa Ave.* ☎ *03/329–4880* ⊕ *www.godleyhouse.co.nz*), a large colonial house with a restaurant, bar, and accommodations. You can drive to Diamond Harbour or take a 10-minute journey on the Black Diamond ferry from Jetty B at Norwich Quay ($10 return). Sailings are frequent.

DOLPHIN-WATCHING ℃   To see some of the small, endangered Hector's dolphins, do the **Christchurch Wildlife Cruise** on the *Canterbury Cat.* During a tour of the outer harbor you'll likely see these playful dolphins; the staff will also point out old shipwrecks, defensive fortifications, and the seabirds that nest in the cliffs. The boat leaves at 1:30 daily and there's a free shuttle from Cathedral Square in Christchurch. ✉ *Jetty B, 17 Norwich Quay* ☎ *03/328–9078 or 0800/436–574* ⊕ *www.blackcat.co.nz* 🖃 *$60.*

HIKING   Quail Island is a good option, but if you'd rather stay on the mainland, you could instead follow in the trail of the early settlers by taking the **Bridle Path.** The steep zigzag track goes from Cunningham Street up to the crater rim. You can walk to the Gondola Summit Station, a few minutes' farther, to see the Canterbury Plains from the site of the memorial to the pioneer women, or walk down the rest of the trail to finish near the Christchurch Gondola base station. A number 28 bus will take you to Lyttelton, and the same bus will pick you up on the other side. Allow an hour and a half for the walk—some of which is quite steep.

WHERE TO EAT

$$–$$$

NEW ZEALAND

✕ **Governors Bay Hotel.** First granted a license in 1870, this historic old pub makes a great, casual lunch stop if you're doing a round trip from Christchurch through Lyttelton and back. Perched on a hill overlooking Lyttelton Harbour, it offers good Kiwi hospitality in an unembellished place, with an open fire in winter and a sunny veranda in summer. Their Kiwi Burger is a substantial pub lunch with all the usuals and a big beef patty. ✉ *52 Main Rd., Governors Bay* ☎ *03/329–9433* ⊕ *www. governorsbayhotel.co.nz* ▭ *AE, MC, V* ⊘ *No breakfast.*

$$$–$$$$

NEW ZEALAND

✕ **London Street Restaurant.** Started by the guys who run the local farmers' market, this place features what the owners call "Local Ingredients, Global Flavours." Try their Farmers Market Brunch on Saturday. The central bar, brick walls, polished wood floors, and cool-color interior project a degree of urban chic, which is rather out of character for Lyttelton, although not unwelcome. There's a huge wine list and dinner includes a *manuka*-grilled, rib-eye steak, pan-seared tarakihi, and a grilled pork cutlet on Parmesan polenta. The Small Plates menu (tapas style), where you can choose five plates for $50, is delicious—choices include tasty treats like eggplant tortellini, grilled sardines with smoked tomato sauce, and smoked duck breast with fig puree. Dessert may be an apple crumble with pouring custard. There's a Saturday brunch 10–4. ✉ *2 London St.* ☎ *03/328–7171* ▭ *AE, MC, V.*

AKAROA AND THE BANKS PENINSULA

9

82 km (50 mi) east of Christchurch.

Sheep graze almost to the water's edge in the many small bays indenting the coastline of Banks Peninsula, the nub that juts into the Pacific east of Christchurch. On the southern side of the peninsula, in a harbor created when the crater wall of an extinct volcano collapsed into the sea, nestles the fishing village of Akaroa (Māori for "long harbor"). The port is a favorite day trip for Christchurch residents on Sunday drives, and on weekends and over the summer holidays (December to February) it can be extremely busy. If you're planning to stay the night during the busy times (summer and weekends), book a room and dinner before you leave Christchurch.

Although **Akaroa** was chosen as the site for a French colony in 1838, the first French settlers arrived in 1840 only to find that the British had already established sovereignty over New Zealand by the Treaty of Waitangi. Less than 10 years later, the French abandoned their attempt at colonization, but the settlers remained and gradually intermarried with the local English community. Apart from the *rue* (street) names, a few family surnames, and architectural touches, there is little sign of a French connection anymore, but the village has splendid surroundings. A day trip from Christchurch will get you to and from Akaroa, including a drive along the Summit Road on the edge of the former volcanic dome, but take an overnight trip if you want to explore the peninsula bays as well as the town. It's an easy drive most of the way but the last hill over to Akaroa is narrow and winding with few passing areas. By the time you've checked out a winery, taken a harbor cruise, driven around a few bays, and stopped for a meal, you'll be right in the mood to kick back overnight in this quiet spot.

GETTING HERE AND AROUND

The main route to Akaroa is State Highway 75, which leaves the southwest corner of Christchurch as Lincoln Road. The 82-km (50-mi) drive takes about 90 minutes. You can also head out through Lyttelton and Teddington, then over the hill to Little River for a really-scenic-but-slightly longer trip.

> ### BEST BETS FOR CRUISE PASSENGERS
>
> ■ **Walking Tours of Akaroa.** Try the "Village Walk," or the "Country Ramble" or climb the 800-meter (2,400-foot) Stony Bay Peak behind town for a stunning view from the sea to the Southern Alps.
>
> ■ **Mail Runs.** Join one of the local mail runs for a guided tour around the peninsula, stopping in to deliver mail at isolated farms and bays, and maybe a winery or a cheese factory, along the way.
>
> ■ **A Day in the City.** Take a scenic tour over the hill to Christchurch; explore the city, ride the tram and stop off at the museum, the art gallery, the Arts Centre, and Cathedral Square.

If you'd rather not drive, the Akaroa Shuttle has daily service between Christchurch and Akaroa in summer and four days a week in winter: up to three trips a day in high season (December–April) ranging from a direct shuttle to a scenic tour. Direct shuttles run twice a day in summer from Christchurch, with an extra run on Friday night, and there are three runs a day from Akaroa. They also run a Banks Peninsula Lunch Tour, with a minimum of three passengers.

ESSENTIALS

Bus Companies Akaroa Shuttle (☎ 0800/500–929 ⊕ www.akaroashuttle.co.nz).

Medical Assistance Akaroa Hospital (✉ Onuku Rd. ☎ 03/304–7023). **Akaroa Health Centre** (✉ Aylmers Valley Rd. ☎ 03/304–7004).

Visitor Information Akaroa Information Centre (✉ 80 Rue Lavaud ☎ 03/304–8600).

EXPLORING
TOP ATTRACTIONS

EN ROUTE

State Highway 75 leads from Christchurch out onto the peninsula, curving along the southern portion past Lake Ellesmere. There are interesting stops on your way out to Akaroa. The small town of **Little River** used to be the end of the line for a now-defunct railway line from Christchurch; the route is now a walkway and bicycle trail. The old, wooden train station houses a crafts gallery and information office, and a café is next door in the grocery store. Pick up the *Peninsula Pioneers* brochure of the area, which details the Heritage drive from Little River to Akaroa. When you reach **Hilltop,** pause for your first glimpse of Akaroa Harbour; on a sunny day it's magnificent. (At Hilltop the highway crosses the Summit Road, the other major route through the peninsula.) And if you're hungry after the drive over the hill, swing by **Barry's Bay Cheese Factory** (☎ 03/304–5809) and taste the local product, one of Akaroa's earliest exports; they've been making cheese since 1895. It's only made every second day and if you're there before about 2, you can watch the day's cheese being manufactured.

> **BASTILLE DAY IN AKAROA**
>
> In recognition of how close this tiny town came to being the seat of a French government in New Zealand, a French Festival is held in early October with films, music, local food, wine, and family entertainment—all themed "le Français."

★ **French Farm Winery.** The only winery on Banks Peninsula occupies a stunning site overlooking Akaroa Harbour. The 20-acre vineyard produces pinot gris, chardonnay, and pinot noir. The cellar door also has Akaroa Harbour merlot, riesling, and rosé, so there's something for everyone. The on-site restaurant is hailed for its rack of lamb and Akaroa salmon—main courses cost $18 to $32—and the massive indoor fireplace makes it a cozy spot in winter. There's an alfresco Pizza Bar out back through the summer. ⊠ *Just off Wainui Bay Rd., turn off toward the coast at Barry's Bay Cheeses* ☎ *03/304–5784* ⊕ *www.frenchfarm.co.nz.*

WORTH NOTING

Akaroa Historic Area Walk. Amble along the narrow streets past old-fashioned little cottages and historic buildings which reflect the area's multicultural background. A free map that outlines the walk and points of interest is available from the information center. You can start this easy two-hour walk at the Akaroa Information Centre.

Akaroa Museum. Along the waterfront from the Garden of Tane to Jubilee Park, the focus of historic interest is the Akaroa Museum, which has a display of Māori *pounamu* (greenstone) as well as alternating exhibits on the area's multicultural past. The Peninsula supported a significant Māori population and the collections and displays tell some of the exciting stories of Kai Tahu, the people of the land. The museum complex includes the Old Courthouse and Langlois-Eteveneaux House, the two-room cottage of an early French settler. ⊠ *Rue Lavaud at Rue Balguerie* ☎ *03/304–1013* 🏷 *$3.50* ☉ *Daily 10:30–4:30; closes at 4 in winter.*

Okains Bay. The contrast of the rim of the old volcanic cone and the coves below is striking—and when you drop into one of the coves, you'll probably feel like you've found your own little corner of the world. One of the easiest bays to access is Okains Bay. Take the Summit Road at Hilltop if approaching from Christchurch, or Ngaio Point Road behind Duvauchelle if approaching from Akaroa. It's about 24 km (15 mi) from Akaroa and takes about a half hour to drive. The small settlement lies at the bottom of Okains Bay Road, which ends at a beach sheltered by tall headlands.

9

Okains Bay Māori and Colonial Museum. This collection of buildings contains 20,000 Māori and 19th-century colonial artifacts, including *waka* (canoes) used in Waitangi Day celebrations and displays such as a smithy and print shop. There are also a *wharenui* (Māori meetinghouse), colonial homes, including a *totara* slab cottage, and a saddlery and harness shop. ✉ *Main Rd.* ☎ *03/304–8611* 🎟 *$6* ⊙ *Daily 10–5.*

SPORTS AND THE OUTDOORS

The *Black Cat* catamaran runs two **Akaroa Harbour Nature Cruises.** You'll pull in beside huge volcanic cliffs and caves and bob around in the harbor entrance while tiny Hector's dolphins—an endangered and adorable species of dolphin with rounded dorsal fins that look like Mickey Mouse ears stuck on their backs—play in the wake of the boat. On some cruises you can swim with them, the only place in the world you can do so. Trips leave daily at 1:30 PM all year-round, plus 11 AM and 3:40 PM December to March, and cost $65. Dolphin swim trips leave daily at 11:30 AM, and cost $130. Advance reservations are essential; bring your swimsuit. Wet suits are provided in summer and dry suits in winter. ✉ *Main Wharf* ☎ *03/304–7641 or 0800/436–574* ⊕ *www.blackcat.co.nz.*

The 35-km (22-mi) **Banks Peninsula Track** crosses lovely coastal terrain. From Akaroa you hike over headlands and past several bays, waterfalls, and seal and penguin colonies, and you might even see Hector's dolphins at sea. Two-day ($150) and four-day ($230) self-guided hikes are available from October to April. The tracks follow the same route, so if you're a novice hiker or have plenty of time, take the four-day option. You will stay overnight in cabins with fully equipped kitchens, which you might share with other hikers. Rates include lodging, transport from Akaroa to the first hut, landowners' fees, and a booklet describing the features of the trail. No fear of overcrowding here—the track is limited to 16 people at a time. ☎ *03/304–7612* ⊕ *www.bankstrack. co.nz* ⊙ *Closed May–Sept.*

★ **Pohatu Penguins and Marine Reserve.** Pohatu Marine Reserve is a key breeding area for the white-flippered penguin (*korora*), which are endemic to the Canterbury region. The best time for viewing is during the breeding season, September to January. You may also see the yellow-eyed penguin (*hoiho*). Options range from day and evening penguin or nature tours (from $55 per person) and sea-kayaking trips (from $70 from Akaroa). Price includes a scenic drive to Pohatu with photo stops along the way and there are several tour options available. ✉ *Akaroa Info Centre* ☎ *03/304–8600* ⊕ *www.pohatu.co.nz* ⊙ *Subject to penguin breeding season.*

WHERE TO EAT

¢–$ ✕ **Akaroa Fish and Chips.** Acclaimed around the country as having some
CAFÉ of the best fish-and-chips available, this take-out–style eatery often has queues out the door. Buy deep-fried fish, fresh off the boat, served with a big side of perfectly cooked chips and a big chunk of lemon, and eat them out of the paper at one of the outdoor tables. You'll never want to eat fish-and-chips with a knife and fork again. ✉ *59 Beach Rd.* ☎ *03/304–7464* ▬ *DC, MC, V.*

$$$–$$$$
NEW ZEALAND
★

✕ **Bully Hayes Restaurant & Bar.** Named after a famous American pirate, this modern restaurant occupies a great site. If you don't feel like elegant dining or sharing a table, then sit outside on the deck, overlooking the sea, and enjoy a laid-back meal in the evening sun watching the yachts moored in the harbor. Seafood is a highlight, and why not in a place like Akaroa? There are light and full-size main courses, and other options include lamb, venison, and beef fillet. ✉ *57 Beach Rd.* ☎ *03/304–7533* ⊕ *www.bullyhayes.co.nz* ▭ *AE, DC, MC, V.*

$$$$
ECLECTIC
★

✕ **Harbour Seventy One.** Eclectic spins on New Zealand produce, meat, and seafood, along with a seaside location, make for sought-after reservations here. Dark wooden floors, provincial-style drapes, and leather chairs lend a country chic quality. Seafood is the highlight, and the grouper comes straight from the fishing boat. Their set $65 menu is great value for a three-course offering. The New Zealand wines on the list include Canterbury labels such as Akaroa Harbour and Pegasus Bay. ✉ *71 Beach Rd.* ☎ *03/304–7659* ▭ *AE, MC, V* ⊘ *Closed Tues. and Wed. and July and Aug. No lunch Mon.–Sat.*

WHERE TO STAY

¢–$
★

🛏 **Chez la Mer Backpackers.** This comfortable hostel fills an old but adorable 1871 building. There's no TV; the preferred form of entertainment is sharing travelers' tales in the kitchen or over the barbecue in the sunny courtyard garden. The hosts share travel advice and free bicycles for exploring Akaroa. **Pros:** on the main street; feels just like home, only older; fishing rods available if you're keen; outdoor kitchen and barbecue area. **Cons:** no credit or debit cards accepted; no breakfast. ✉ *50 Rue Lavaud, Akaroa* ☎ *03/304–7024* ⊕ *www.chezlamer.co.nz* ⤳ *5 rooms, 2 with en suite, 3 dorm rooms* ⌂ *In-room: No TV In-hotel: Bicycles, laundry facilities, Internet terminal, Wi-Fi, laundry facilities* ▭ *No credit cards.*

$$$–$$$$
★

🛏 **Linton.** Nicknamed the Giant's House, because it looked like one to a visiting child, Linton is full of art in unexpected places. Up the steep driveway hides a large garden crisscrossed by paths, fantastic larger-than-life mosaics, and colorful, welded sculptures. One of the guest rooms has a boat-shaped bed, another opens to a mosaic rose garden and conservatory. The 1880 house and garden are open for tours from 2 to 4 daily, April to Christmas and noon to 4, Christmas to the end of Easter ($15). The garden is now a Garden of National Significance. **Pros:** fabulous, crazy mosaic artwork; pleasant garden and leafy outlook; contemporary art gallery. **Cons:** very steep driveway; garden tour visitors wander through in the afternoon. ✉ *68 Rue Balguerie, Akaroa* ☎ *03/304–7501* ⊕ *www.linton.co.nz* ⤳ *3 rooms* ⌂ *In-room: No TV. In-hotel: Bar* ▭ *MC, V* ⏐⚬⏐ *CP.*

$$$
★

🛏 **Oinako Lodge.** Surrounded by a tranquil garden, just a two-minute walk from town and a few steps from Akaroa Harbour, this old-fashioned Victorian manor house has its original, ornate plaster ceilings and marble fireplaces. You'll also find fresh flowers in the spacious and pleasantly decorated rooms; four have whirlpool baths. Drive to the far end of Beach Road where the road runs on to what looks like a private driveway shared by a number of properties. Just follow that road a little farther to Oinako, which is marked. **Pros:** old-fashioned

9

Wine tastings are available at the Pegasus Bay cellar door.

leafy garden overlooking the harbor; chocolates, feather pillows, and duvets add a luxurious touch. **Cons:** a bit hard to find so follow directions; there is no broadband in the rooms, but a Wi-Fi hotspot in the lobby; no children 10 years or under. ⊠ *99 Beach Rd.* ☎ *03/304–8787* ⊕ *www.oinako.co.nz* ↝ *6 rooms* ⚬ *In-room: No a/c, no phone, no TV, spa baths (some). In-hotel: Wi-Fi, laundry service* ⊟ *AE, DC, MC, V* ☽ *Closed June–Aug.* ⦿ *BP.*

WAIPARA VALLEY

65 km (40 mi) north of Christchurch.

Once known for its hot, dry summers and sheep farms, the Waipara Valley is now an established vineyard area. The local riesling, chardonnay, and sauvignon blanc are particularly good. Sheltered from the cool easterly wind by the Teviotdale hills, the valley records hotter temperatures than the rest of Canterbury, and warm dry autumns ensure a longer time for the grapes to mature. Winemakers are also exploiting the area's limestone soil to grow pinots—pinot noir, pinot gris, and *pinotage.* Two dozen labels have sprouted up, with more to come, and the area produces more than 200,000 cases of wine a year.

GETTING HERE AND AROUND

To reach Waipara from Christchurch, take State Highway 1 north. Waipara's about 45 minutes away, where State Highway 7 turns left off the main road. You can head from here to Hanmer Springs and Nelson on State Highway 7 and other northern towns along State Highway 1. The Hanmer Connection runs a daily service between Hanmer Springs and Christchurch, stopping in Waipara and elsewhere en route in the Waipara Valley.

ESSENTIALS

Bus Company Hanmer Connection (☎ *0800/242–663 or 03/382–2952,* ⊕ *www.hanmerconnection.co.nz*).

WINERIES

Waipara's wines are celebrated each year at the Waipara Wine and Food Celebration. Held in late March, it fills (ironically enough) the grounds of the local Glenmark Church. The major wineries in the region are listed here. Athena Olives are also big locally.

There is no specified wine trail or information center in the valley, but a good place to start your visit is the **Pukeko Junction Regional Wine Centre** at Leithfield, 10 km (6 mi) south of Waipara. Rather than a cellar door the center is a café, wine shop, information bureau, and gallery rolled into one. There's a solid range of local wines, often at particularly good prices, many from smaller wineries not open to the public. The café has an excellent range of light food and is famous for its caramel oat slice—a sweet biscuit base, a creamy caramel center, and topping of toasted oats . ⊠ *458 Ashworths Rd., (part of State Hwy. 1), Leithfield* ☎ *03/314–8834* ⊗ *Daily 10:30–5:30.*

Although Waipara's vineyards are reasonably close together, they can be hard to find. **Waipara Wine Tours** offers a four-hour tour for $75 to visit three of the area's excellent options or a full-day tour of five wineries for $125 (includes lunch). There are transfers from your Christchurch accommodations. ☎ *0800/081–155 or 03/315–7522* ⊕ *www.waiparavalley.co.nz.*

Daniel Schuster is one of Canterbury's pioneering winemakers. His vines are grown in a traditional manner, without irrigation, and his wines are crafted by hand—a little from this barrel and a little from that. He is a master at work, and his wines are some of the best coming out of Canterbury. Tastings cost $3 (refunded on a wine purchase) and the tasting room is open from 10 to 5 every day. Tea and coffee are served out on the deck, and cellar tours are by appointment. Parking is limited; if they're busy there's a short walk up the hill from the lower parking lot. ⊠ *192 Reeces Rd., Omihi, Waipara* ☎ *03/314–5901* ⊕ *www.danielschusterwines.com.*

Muddy Water Fine Wines is the English translation of Waipara, but the name has no reflection on the wines. The varieties are unusual in this region, with pinotage and syrah on offer as well as the standard chardonnay, riesling, and pinot noir. Tasting are mostly by appointment only, so call ahead to arrange a time to drop in. ⊠ *414 Omihi Rd, (part of State Hwy. 1), Waipara* ☎ *03/314–6944* ⊕ *www.muddywater.co.nz* ⊗ *By appointment only.*

★ Family-run **Pegasus Bay** has one of the region's best reputations for wine and food in Canterbury, and the helicopters lined up on the lawn at lunchtime will confirm that. Taste the award-winning Rieslings, chardonnay, and pinot noir while you look through a window at floor-to-ceiling stacks of oak aging casks. It has been ranked among the top five wine producers nationally by Robert Parker's buyer's guide, and the restaurant was named Best Winery Restaurant in NZ by Cuisine magazine for the second consecutive year in 2009. In good weather, dine outdoors in the garden or picnic in a natural auditorium by a small man-made lake. It's best to book if visiting for a meal or large group tastings. There's a helipad if you're in a hurry. ⊠ *Stockgrove Rd., Waipara* ☎ *03/314–6869* ⊕ *www.pegasusbay.com* ⊙ *Tasting room 10–5, restaurant noon–4.*

Kym Rayner is a consummate winemaker, and one of the modern-day pioneers of Waipara winemaking. At **Torlesse Wines** he uses grapes from several vineyards around Waipara and further afield, and riesling is their biggest seller. Sauvignon blanc, gewürztraminer, chardonnay, pinot grigio, and pinot noir are also produced. They also do a couple of fun offerings—a pinot pop and a savvy pop—high quality takes on the wine spritzer, using local pinot noir and sauvignon blanc. While you're there you can also check out the gallery selling clothing and local art. ⊠ *off State Hwy. 1, Waipara* ☎ *03/314–6929* ⊕ *www.torlesse. co.nz* ⊙ *Daily 11–5.*

Waipara Springs Winery is one of the valley's oldest wineries; you can stop for lunch along with a wine tasting ($4). The café, in converted farm buildings, serves tasty dishes made with local foods such as olives, goat cheese, asparagus, and bacon. Try their antipasto platter for some of each. These match well with the vineyard's sauvignon blanc (their biggest seller), pinot noir, botrytized Riesling, gewürztraminer, and *barrique* chardonnay (the signature wine). The wine bar and cellar door are open every day from 11 to 5. The café is open for lunch every day, August to May, but only open on the weekend through June and July. ⊠ *State Hwy. 1* ☎ *03/314–6777* ⊕ *www.waiparasprings.co.nz* ⊟ *AE, DC, MC, V.*

HIKING

Mt. Cass Walkway. Here's a moderately strenuous way to wear off some of those wine- and lunch-induced calories. This two- to three-hour climb up Mt. Cass ends with a spectacular view over the surrounding countryside of the Waipara Valley. As it crosses through working farmland on the Tiromoana Station, be careful to leave gates and marker posts as you find them. Use the stiles provided for crossing fence lines and wear strong walking shoes. The track is closed each year in spring while the sheep are lambing. ⊠ *Mt. Cass Rd.* ⊙ *Closed approx. Aug.–Sept.*

WHERE TO EAT AND STAY

$$$–$$$$
NEW ZEALAND
★

✕ **Nor'Wester Café & Bar.** Sophisticated dining in rural places is one of life's great pleasures. Here you can enjoy a meal inside the mellow 1928 bungalow with its fireplace or outside on the palm-shaded veranda. While their most popular dish is the peppered lambs fry and bacon, there is also a good selection of tapas, like oysters, smoked salmon, Parmesan dumplings, and veggie spring rolls. There are locally made breads and a good range of gluten-free dishes. The espresso is superb, and you can complement your meal with a fabulous local wine. ⊠ *95 Main North Rd., Amberley* ✛ *7 km (4½ mi)* *south of Waipara* ☎ *03/314–9411* ▭ *AE, DC, MC, V* ⊘ *May close some weeknights in winter.*

$$$$
Fodor'sChoice
★

🛏 **Claremont Country Estate.** Watch where you walk—that white stone you see might turn out to be a marine dinosaur fossil. This spectacular deer and sheep station is up the Waipara Gorge, a 10-minute drive inland from Amberley; its luxurious homestead was built from limestone quarried on the property in the late 1860s. The three lodge suites are elegantly furnished with antiques, so families with children under 14 are encouraged to stay in the on-site, self-contained, three-bedroom cottage. There is also a private two-bedroom villa, which is suited to two couples traveling together. An interesting self-drive, four-wheel-drive tour is thrown in if you stay three or more nights. You can wander about the 2,400-acre farm, extensive gardens, and private nature reserve as well. **Pros:** superb colonial homestead reminiscent of earlier days; options include a full lodge stay, including four-course dinner, or cheaper B&B accommodations; a winner in Andrew Harper's Hideaway report. **Cons:** last part of the drive in is narrow and winding; can be a chilly spot in spring and autumn, but the accommodations are well heated. ⊠ *828 Ram Paddock Rd., Amberley* ☎ *03/314–7559* ⊕ *www.claremont-estate.com* ⌂ *3 suites, 3-bedroom cottage, 2-bedroom villa* ⚷ *In-room: No a/c (some). In-hotel: Restaurant, bar, tennis court, pool, spa* ▭ *AE, MC, V* ⊘ *Lodge closed May–Sept. but villa and cottage remain open* ⑂ *MAP, BP.*

¢

🛏 **Waipara Sleepers.** Wake up to fresh-baked bread and newly laid eggs every morning at this really-basic-but-rather-quirky backpackers lodge housed in old railway carriages and huts. It's first-come, first-served for breakfast in the station waiting room (now a basic, communal kitchen). Some of the carriages retain old leather seating and travel posters. There are also powered camper-van sites and a number of tent sites. **Pros:** very rustic and rural; complete with all the sounds and smells of the country; a good stop for anyone cycle-touring. **Cons:** some of the accommodations and services are quite basic, but so is the price (where else in NZ advertises *color* TV!). ⊠ *10–12 Glenmark Dr.* ☎ *03/314–6003* ⊕ *www.waiparasleepers.co.nz* ⌂ *4 rooms, 2 dorms* ⚷ *In-room: No TV (some). In-hotel: Bar, laundry facilities* ▭ *MC, V.*

EN ROUTE

Built from limestone blocks, the **Hurunui Hotel**, New Zealand's oldest, continually licensed hotel (since 1860), refreshed weary drovers bringing sheep down from Marlborough. A bed for the night is relatively cheap ($45 per person, including a cooked breakfast), and the restaurant with its old-fashioned pub serves à la carte dinners from $17 and an all-day menu from $15. Repeat visitors come for the tasty game pies— wild pork or wild goat, local rabbit with lemon and bacon, ostrich with blue cheese, or venison and red currant. ⊠ *State Hwy. 7, about 20-min. drive from Waipara turnoff* ☎ *03/314–4207* ⊕ *www.hurunuihotel.co.nz.*

9

HANMER SPRINGS

120 km (75 mi) northwest of Christchurch.

People used to come to Hanmer Springs to chill out with quiet soaks in the hot pools and to take gentle forest walks; but things have been changing fast. The number of boutique stores and restaurants has doubled, and an increasing number of off-road and backcountry activities are turning Hanmer Springs into Canterbury's adventure-sports hub. On holidays and weekends the springs can be busy. The Amuri Ski Field, a small ski area in the mountains behind town, attracts a dedicated following of local skiers in winter. Mountain biking is especially big, and Hanmer Springs is now the end point for several long-distance mountain-bike and endurance races through the backcountry. During the summer months Hanmer Springs is also the southern terminus of the drive along the Acheron road through the Molesworth Station, which runs through from the Awatere Valley in Marlborough and is the country's highest public road. This backcountry trail is open for only a few months a year and is a solid six-hour drive on an unpaved road through some spectacular country. Go to the **Department of Conservation** Web site and search for Molesworth for more information.

For additional information, maps, and as a meeting point, go to the **Hurunui Visitor Information Centre.**

GETTING HERE AND AROUND

The Hanmer Connection runs a daily service between Hanmer Springs and Christchurch. Service goes through Waipara on the way. By car, take State Highway 1 north out of Christchurch. About 45 minutes north, State Highway 7 turns left off the main road toward Nelson. From here drive through the small town of Culverden and the foothills for another 45 minutes on State Highway 7, before turning onto Highway 7A toward Hanmer Springs (this is well signposted).

Navigation around Hanmer Springs is easy as it's a really small place. The main road into town, Amuri Drive, is a wide, dual-carriageway, tree-lined road, with the thermal resort and visitors center opening off it. Conical Hill Road carries on up the hill and has most of the stores and cafés along its lower portion. Jacks Pass Road to the left and Jollies Pass Road to the right lead to the great outdoors and many of the adventure activities.

ESSENTIALS

Bus Company Hanmer Connection (☎ *0800/242–663 or 03/382–2952,* ⊕ *www.hanmerconnection.co.nz*).

Medical Assistance Hanmer Health Centre (✉ *Amuri Ave.* ☎ *03/315–7503*).

Visitor Information Department of Conservation (⊕ *www.doc.govt.nz*). **Hurunui Visitor Information Centre** (✉ *42 Amuri Ave., Hanmer Springs* ☎ *03/315–7128 or 0800/442–663* ⊕ *www.hurunui.com*).

EXPLORING

The scenic gravel drive along **Jacks Pass,** to the north of the village, crosses the lower slopes of Mt. Isobel before dropping into the upper Clarence River valley, an alpine area 10 minutes from Hanmer Springs. This is the beginning of some serious backcountry. The tiny stream trickling past the road at the end of the pass eventually reaches the coast north of Kaikoura as the rough and rumbling Clarence River—a favorite for rafters and kayakers. This is also the southern end of the Acheron Road through the Molesworth Station and the 4WD Rainbow Road through to St. Arnaud and the Nelson Lakes (access key required) (⇨ *above*).

The **Hanmer Springs Thermal Reserve** consists of nine outdoor thermal pools and three sulfur pools of varying temperatures, one freshwater pool, a family activity pool, and two waterslides. There are also four private thermal pools, as well as private sauna and steam rooms. Massage and beauty treatments are available at the on-site spa. ⊠ *Amuri Ave.* ☎ *03/315–7511 or 0800/442–663* ⊕ *www.hanmersprings.co.nz* 🖃 *$14; private pool, steam, or sauna $24 per ½ hr (minimum 2 people), waterslide $6* ⊗ *Daily 10–9.*

The **Wisteria Cottage Day Spa** caters to those who don't want or need to soak in a hot pool for their entire stay or want to avoid the business of the thermal resort. Specialty treatments are available, including hot-stone massage, Vichy showers, holistic facials, steam capsule, and massage. ⊠ *34 Conical Hill Rd.* ☎ *03/315–7026* ⊕ *www.nzhotsprings. com/dayspa* ⊗ *Open by appointment daily 10 to 7:30.*

SPORTS AND THE OUTDOORS

ADVENTURE SPORTS

Hanmer Springs Adventure Centre runs quad-bike tours, clay-bird shooting, mountain biking, and archery in the backcountry behind Hanmer Springs. Quad-bike tours leave at 10, 1:30, and 4 each day, bouncing through some spectacular hill country, native bush, river crossings, hill climbs, and stunning scenery over their 24,000-acre Woodbank Station. The two-hour trip costs $129; the one-hour trip costs $89, and $75 per pillion (secondary seat) passenger. Mountain-bike tours also head into the Hanmer Forest Park. ⊠ *20 Conical Hill Rd.* ☎ *03/315–7233 or 0800/368–7386* ⊕ *www.hanmeradventure.co.nz.*

Thrillseekers Canyon Adventure Centre organizes 35-meter (115-foot) bungy jumps off the 19th-century Ferry Bridge ($145). You can also choose to raft or ride on a jet-boat through the scenic Gorge or let the kids do a quad-bike safari. Try clay-bird shooting or paintball, or just peer off the 30-meter-high (100-foot-high) balcony and watch the bungy jumpers and jet-boats in the canyon below. ⊠ *Main Rd.* ☎ *03/315–7046 or 0800/661–538* ⊕ *www.thrillseekerscanyon.co.nz.*

HORSE TREKKING

Hanmer Horse Trekking takes beginner and advanced riders on guided rides through forest, farmland, and native bush. Be prepared for river crossings and spectacular views. Rides last from 1 to 2½ hours, prices range from $50 to $95. The 1-hour ride is suitable for kids over five and the 2½-hour ride for kids 12 years and over. There are also ½-hour pony rides for the kids for $20. ⊠ *187 Rogerson Track* ☎ *03/315–7444 or 0800/873–546* ⊕ *www.hanmerhorses.co.nz* ⊗ *Sept.–Apr., rides leave at 10, noon, 2, and 4; May–Aug., rides leave at 11, 1, and 3.*

9

WHERE TO EAT

$$$–$$$$ ✕ **The Laurels.** In a renovated villa on the main road into Hanmer, The
ECLECTIC   Laurels maintains high standards of cuisine and service. Their focus has
★   changed from a strong Latin American flavor to a more eclectic style.
The chili salt–rubbed beef fillet is a top seller as are the king prawns
in a rich red tomato sauce. Venison and pork belly arrangements also
have a strong following. It's recommended by locals as the best in town.
✉ *31 Amuri Ave.* ☎ *03/315–7788* ⊙ *Limited hrs in winter. No dinner
Tues.; no lunch some days.*

$$$–$$$$ ✕ **Malabar Restaurant.** Looking out toward Conical Hill, this restaurant
ASIAN FUSION   has a fine reputation for its Indian and Asian-fusion food presented with
a Kiwi flair. The "Four Curries" meal on a traditional thali (a medley
of dishes) is a favorite, as is the grilled rack of New Zealand lamb on
cumin-crusted potatoes and the barbecued belly of pork with roasted
ginger kūmara (native sweet potatoes). Their lemongrass-and-coconut
ice cream is a treat. They provide take-out service. ✉ *Alpine Pacific
Centre, 5 Conical Hill Rd.* ☎ *03/315–7745* ◠ *Reservations essential*
▭ *AE, DC, MC, V.*

$–$$ ✕ **Springs Deli Cafe.** For either breakfast or lunch this place has all the
CAFÉ   comforts of home—tasty café-style food, good coffee, and either a roar-
ing log fire when it's cold, or balmy outdoor eating when it's not. There's
a solid breakfast menu with all the usuals and a cabinet stuffed full of
tasty lunch or coffee treats like generously filled panini, quiches, bagels,
croissants, and pastries. They also have a retail shelf with local wines,
honey, oils, and preserves. There are occasional mixed reviews. ✉ *Amuri
Ave, opposite Thermal Springs* ☎ *03/315–7430* ▭ *DC, MC, V.*

WHERE TO STAY

$$–$$$ ⊡ **Albergo Hanmer Lodge and Alpine Villas.** Experience mountain views—
★   even from the showers. The arty-chic interior design has handcrafted
touches like textured fabrics, unusual artworks, quirky colors, and many
seahorses dotted throughout. Stay in the alpine villa with its private spa
pool or in the lodge. The three-course breakfast is delicious, with 10
meal choices, homemade Swiss miniloaves, and fresh Italian coffee, and
is served at your convenience, any time of the day. They can arrange spa
treatment and cuisine packages, reiki healing treatments, and spirit read-
ings; Swiss-Kiwi cuisine is a specialty, including warming winter fondues
and the Albergo Egg Nests (it's a secret recipe so don't ask what they
are!), which keep people coming back for more. Coming into town take
the center branch of Argelins Rd 300 meters (328 yards) past the Caltex
garage, then second road on your left. **Pros:** funky but tasteful interior
high on visual stimulation; outdoor courtyard overlooked by surrounding mountains. **Cons:** slightly out of town and hard to find. ✉ *88 Rip-
pingale Rd.* ☎ *03/315–7428 or 0800/342–313* ⊕ *www.albergohanmer.
com* ⇱ *3 suites, 2 villas* ♨ *In-room: No phone, kitchen (some), DVD.
In-hotel: Bar, Wi-Fi, laundry facilities* ▭ *AE, DC, MC, V* ⦿ *BP.*

$$$$ ⊡ **Braemar Lodge & Spa.** Part lodge, part boutique hotel, these brand-
new accommodations were built around all that remains of the original
Braemar Lodge—an impressive two-story-high river stone fireplace.
Rooms are big and all have expansive views across the river plain to
Hanmer and its snowy backdrop (in winter). The warm sunny aspect is

sheltered from the cold southerly winds that sweep through this area so you'll get real value from your own deck. Interior is neutrally contemporary in red, gray, and ocher; the rooms all have gas fires, swiveling TVs and marble bathrooms. **Pros:** spa units have a hot tub on the deck; all units have a whirlpool bath in the bathroom; on-site day spa and hydrotherapy suite; lots of packages available with outdoor activities included. **Cons:** a 10-minute drive from Hanmer and its restaurants; access is by several kms of gravel road, with a steep but sealed driveway. ⊠ *283 Medway Rd.* ☎ *03/315–7555* ⊕ *www.selectbraemarlodge.com* ⤷ *24 suites* ⚐ *In-room: Refrigerator, Wi-Fi. In-hotel: Restaurant, bar, gym, spa, Wi-Fi, no-smoking rooms* ⊟ *AE, MC, V.*

$$–$$$
★
🏨 **Heritage Hanmer Springs.** First built in 1897, this getaway reopened in 1932 after a devastating fire, as the Hanmer Lodge; it was the largest hotel in Australasia at the time. Stay in rooms inside the hotel or take a garden suite in among the pine trees on Jollies Pass Road; there are also villas on the rise above the hotel, around a man-made pond. Hotel decoration reflects its country heritage, with the public spaces retaining their colonial sparseness, much as they have for years. The rooms, however, are comfortable and more contemporary in finish. The thermal springs are a short walk away. Breakfast is served in the front courtyard. **Pros:** lovely old Spanish Mission–style building; in the middle of town within easy walk of most things. **Cons:** public areas have not really been modernized. ⊠ *1 Conical Hill Rd.* ☎ *03/315–7021* ⊕ *www. heritagehotels.co.nz/hanmer-springs* ⤷ *38 rooms, 11 villas, 16 singles* ⚐ *In-room facilities: Internet (some), no a/c. In-hotel: Restaurant, bar, tennis court, pool, Wi-Fi* ⊟ *AE, DC, MC, V.*

¢–$
🏨 **Kakapo Lodge.** You reach this lodge where State Highway 7 ends and the tree-divided Amuri Avenue begins. A short walk from the hot pools, this large two-story building has under-floor heating and comfy wooden-slat beds, and offers various options to the budget conscious, from dorm rooms and double rooms to motel accommodations. The sunny hostel is kept quite clean and tidy, with views over the mountains and surrounding park. It also doubles as the Hanmer YHA. **Pros:** nice public areas with plenty of seating and relaxing spaces; right at the end of the main street and close to everything. **Cons:** only a few en suite rooms. ⊠ *14 Amuri Ave.* ☎ *03/315–7472* ⊕ *www.kakapolodge.co.nz* ⤷ *10 rooms (2 with en suite), 1 motel unit, 3 family rooms, 5 dorm rooms* ⚐ *In-room: Kitchen (some). In-hotel: Laundry facilities, Wi-Fi* ⊟ *MC, V.*

NIGHTLIFE

Saints Pizzeria and Bar can claim to be Hanmer Spring's first nightclub. It's open until 1 AM Friday and Saturday, but closes around 11 on other nights. It has a dance floor and pool table and features a DJ most Saturday nights. There's no lunch during the week. Service can be a bit slow if they're really busy. ⊠ *6 Jacks Pass Rd.* ☎ *03/315–5262.*

EN ROUTE The northern section of State Highway 72, also known as the Inland Scenic Route, starts at Amberley, eventually joining the southern section near Sheffield on the West Coast Road through to Arthurs Pass. Oxford is a small rural town on this northern section which has undergone a transformation of late, largely due to the arrival of nationally renowned TV chef, Jo Seagar, who opened her café and cooking school here a few

9

The central Canterbury Plains area is the premier hot air ballooning spot.

years back. It is now a favorite lunch stop for Christchurch folk out for a drive in the country.

$$-$$$ ✕ **Seagars at Oxford.** Good things don't usually happen by accident, and
CAFÉ this place is no exception. This bustling daytime café features all the good home cooking that TV chef and celebrity, Jo Seagar, is famous for, and a few other treats as well. Try the Belgian Buttermilk pancakes with bacon and banana or the chicken, tarragon and cider pie. Jo's Mud Fudge Cake is legendary. Rural art features on the walls and there's a gift shop, cooking school, and small B&B attached. ✉ *78 Main St., Oxford* ☎ *03/312–1439* ⊕ *www.joseagar.com* ⊟ *AE, DC, MC, V* ☾ *No dinner, closed public holidays.*

METHVEN

95 km (59 mi) southwest of Christchurch.

Methven's main claim to fame is as a ski town—it's the closest town to Mt. Hutt, which does not allow accommodations on its slopes. If you happen to be here in summer, don't be put off by the empty streets. There are some bargains to be had, and you can take advantage of walking, salmon fishing, jet-boating, and hot-air ballooning.

GETTING HERE AND AROUND

The best way to get to Methven by car is the underused Scenic Highway 72, which you can join near Darfield, or via Hororata (but be wary of icy spots in the shade and hidden speed cameras on these straight roads). You could also travel down the busy State Highway 1 to Rakaia and take Thompson's Track (clearly signposted and paved) to Methven.

Or join it from the north at Amberley, passing through Oxford and Sheffield. This stretch of highway, known as the Inland Scenic Route, makes a nice day drive from Christchurch, taking in the upper Rakaia and Rangitata River gorges, the small towns of Darfield, Methven, and Geraldine, scenic views of the Southern Alps, and the wide open farmlands of the plains.

There are plenty of buses from Christchurch to Methven and Mt. Hutt in ski season, but the options drop off in summer. InterCity also run through Methven daily on their way north and south. Mt. Hutt SNOW-BUS runs daily in winter and Methven Travel run a daily bus in winter and four times a week in summer.

ESSENTIALS

Bus Company InterCity (☎ *03/365–1113* ⊕ *www.intercity.co.nz*). **Mt. Hutt SNOWBUS** (☎ *03/383–5512 or 0800/766–928* ⊕ *www.mtthuttsnowbus.com*). **Methven Travel** (☎ *03/382–8106 or 0800/684–888* ⊕ *www.methventravel.co.nz*).

Medical Assistance Methven Medical Centre (✉ *The Square* ☎ *03/302–8105*).

Visitor Information Methven Visitor Centre (✉ *93 Main St.* ☎ *03/302–8955* ⊕ *www.methveninfo.co.nz*).

SPORTS AND THE OUTDOORS

BALLOONING On a clear morning you might catch a glimpse of a rainbow-striped balloon floating high above Methven—chances are it's **Aoraki Balloon Safaris.** From their balloons, you get an incredible view of the patchwork pattern of farm paddocks, the braided systems of the Rakaia and Ashburton rivers, and a full 300-km (190-mi) panorama of the Canterbury Plains and Aoraki/Mt. Cook, the "Cloud Piercer." On landing, you'll be served a buffet breakfast. Flights start at daybreak, and you'll be pitching in to help with the launch. The actual time in the air is about one hour, but the whole experience takes at least four hours, starting at daybreak. Rates for Premier flights (which include breakfast in a meadow after landing) go up to $365 per adult. ☎ *03/302–8172 or 0800/256–837* ✉ *aoraki@ nzballooning.com* ⊕ *www.nzballooning.com.*

HIKING One of New Zealand's top 10 walkways, the **Mt. Somers Track** is a great way to get a taste of the subalpine New Zealand bush. Start at the Mt. Somers–Woolshed Creek end and hike downhill to the Staveley end and Sharplin Falls. The walk will take one to two days, and there are two huts to stay in along the way—or do it in reverse. Call the Staveley Village Store (☎ *03/303–0859*) for information on transport to the end of the trail; there are a number of small guiding companies. Leaving from just below the Rakaia River Gorge bridge, the **Rakaia Gorge Walkway** provides upstream access to the northern bank of the river and offers easy walking. You can also take a jet-boat upriver and walk back—just name your distance. Rakaia Gorge Scenic Jet also does a guided trip on the trail.

JET-BOATING Zoom along the glacier-fed Rakaia River with **Rakaia Gorge Scenic Jet;** the walkway trip costs $25 and the 40-minute jet-boat ride costs $75. Salmon fishing is available and rafting–jet or heli-jet combos are an excellent option, subject to minimum numbers. The Rakaia's jewel-like aqua water contrasts wonderfully with the white limestone cliffs. You'll

9

CLOSE UP

The Chatham Islands

Although officially part of New Zealand, the Chatham Islands, 800 km (500 mi) east of the South Island, are a land apart. Bearing the full force of the open Southern Ocean, the islands are wild and weather-beaten. The air has a salty taste to it, the colors of the landscapes are more muted, and the vegetation is stunted and gnarly. Many unusual plants and birds are about—including the extremely rare black robin—and the empty beaches invite fishing and diving (although the presence of sharks makes the latter unadvised).

Locals here refer to the mainland as New Zealand, as though it were an entirely separate country. Just two of the 10 islands are inhabited—the main island and tiny, neighboring Pitt Island. Most residents are either farmers or fishermen, but tourism is increasing. The Chathams were first settled by the Moriori, a race of Polynesian descent, about 800–1,000 years ago, although there are now no full-blooded Moriori left. Māori and Europeans followed,

and conflicts broke out between the separate populations throughout the 1800s. By the end of the 19th century, however, tensions had died down after the Native Land Court intervened in key disputes, and the new settlers established the strong maritime culture that still prevails on the islands.

When booking to fly to the Chathams it's imperative that you make lodging reservations in advance. There is only one round-trip flight a week from Christchurch but you can return earlier through Auckland or Wellington, and Air Chathams (☎ *03/305-0209 or 0508/247-248* ⊕ *www.airchathams. co.nz*) is the only carrier. The islands are 45 minutes ahead of NZ time and therefore the first place on Earth to see the sun each day. Check out ⊕ *www.newzealandnz.co.nz/chatham-islands* for more details. Allow at least four days—you'll rarely get the chance to visit anywhere this remote. And don't forget to try the crayfish (lobsters).

usually find the jet-boat down at the river's edge, just below the Rakaia Gorge bridge on State Highway 72. But call first in case the river is in flood or the boat is busy. ☎ *03/318–6515 or 0800/435–453.*

SKIING   Methven is the gateway to a number of ski slopes (Kiwis say ski fields). Thanks to its altitude (6,780 feet) and snowmaking machines, **Mt. Hutt's** access begins in early June. Its wide basin and a vertical drop of 655 meters (2,148 feet) ensure a 2-km (1-mi) run, with some of the best powder in Australasia. From the chairlifts you'll have terrific views of the mountains and the Canterbury Plains below. Shuttles to the slopes run from Methven and Christchurch, often as part of a package offer including lift fees and equipment rental. You can drive if you've got tire chains, but the road isn't paved and it has a number of hairpin turns. Lift tickets start at $87 for a full day. Rental equipment is available, and the area is family- and beginner-friendly. There's a ski school and crèche (kids under seven ski for free). Mt. Hutt is occasionally closed by high winds; beginning daily at 7 AM, up-to-date ski conditions are available by phone or on the Web site (☎ *03/302–8811* ⊕ *www.nzski.com*). Intermediate and advanced skiers can sign up for **heli-skiing** on Mt. Hutt, flying into slopes where no one else may have skied that day. North Peak Run, the most popular, offers an 800-vertical-meter run (2,600 vertical feet). Costs start at roughly $175 for one run; other options include a full day to the Arrowsmiths Range for $795, with elegant lunch provided. Heli-skiing is a winter-only option, but spectacular scenic and adventure flights are available in summer. ☎ 03/302–8401 ✍ info@mthuthelicopters.co.nz ⊕ www.mthuthelicopters.co.nz.

WHERE TO EAT AND STAY

Methven isn't a culinary hotbed, but it has several good casual places. The Blue Pub ($$–$$$) on Main Street in the middle of town does have reasonably priced bistro-style meals and a courtyard where you can sit and have a beer. For a more café-style experience head to Arabica ($$–$$$) on the corner of MacMillan Street and the Mall for good food and excellent coffee any time of the day. Lisah's ($$$–$$$$), also on Main Street, is the best place for an evening meal or quiet cocktail.

Accommodations vary between larger resort- and hotel-style venues and backpacker lodges. Until lately many of these accommodations were rather tired, but several properties have been refurbished and several new ones have opened. Apart from a few isolated farm stays and the large Terrace Downs resort, all the accommodations are in Methven township. There is no accommodation at Mt. Hutt.

¢–$ 🏠 **Alpenhorn Chalet.** This wonderfully pleasant backpacker lodge is in
★ an old wooden villa built in the early 1900s, very typical of small-town Victorian architecture in New Zealand at the time. A log fire in the huge kitchen helps keep the place warm; the bedrooms are centrally heated. At the end of the day, relax in the hot tub or simply sit in the sun—even in winter it can be intense—to bask and read. It's popular with skiers, fishers, and "flashpackers" (well-off travelers who choose backpacker hostels). **Pros:** homey aura is far removed from the usual backpackers-hostel vibe; conservatory garden; free Internet; superb espresso coffee. **Cons:** a short walk from the center of Methven. ✉ 44 Allen St. ☎ 03/302–8779 ✍ 1 room with en suite, 2 dorm rooms and 2 double rooms share a double bathroom ⚹ In–room: no a/c, no phone, no TV. In-hotel: Spa, laundry facilities, Internet terminal 🚫 No credit cards.

$$–$$$ 🏠 **Central Luxury Apartments.** These new-build apartments just off the main street of Methven offer all the amenities. All six apartments have two bedrooms, a full kitchen, and laundry facilities. And they are built to catch the best of the Southern Alps' views. There are three apartments upstairs, and three on the ground floor, each with either a sunny terrace or deck. High season here is winter, so the summer rates are good value. **Pros:** drying room downstairs for the skis and ski gear; good parking **Cons:** style is neutral with minimal decoration. ✉ 6 Chertsey Rd., ☎ 03/302-8829 ⊕ www.centralapartmentsmethven.co.nz ✍ 6 apartments ⚹ In-room: Kitchen, Internet. In-hotel: Laundry facilities, parking (free) 🚫 AE, DC, MC, V.

$$$$ 🏠 **Terrace Downs.** Although not strictly in Methven, Terrace Downs is a 20-minute drive away, with spectacular views of the Rakaia Gorge and the looming presence of Mt. Hutt. Set on one of the country's better golf courses, this resort is a good place to base yourself for a vacation away from the crowds. Accommodations are in a series of

9

contemporary timber-and-stone villas perched on a ridge above the clubhouse and restaurant, with views from their balconies over the golf course and of the mountains. **Pros:** impressive use of river stone on the exterior and in the public areas, 18-hole championship golf course on-site; newly opened day spa and extended list of on and off-site activities; kids club underway. **Cons:** you'll need two nights if you want to really appreciate the surroundings and venue. ✉ *Coleridge Rd., Rakaia Gorge* ☎ *03/318–6943* ⊕ *www.terracedowns.co.nz* ↘ *19 1-and 2-bedroom suites, 16 3-bedroom villas, 5 4-bedroom chalets* ⌂ *In-room: Kitchen, DVD, Internet. In-hotel: 3 restaurants, golf course, tennis courts, spa, bicycles, laundry facilities* ▭ *AE, DC, MC, V* ⊙ *CP.*

GERALDINE

138 km (85½ mi) southwest of Christchurch.

For years, this lovely town has been a favorite stop on the road to Aoraki/Mt. Cook; these days, it's becoming a magnet in southern Canterbury for art mavens and foodies.

GETTING HERE AND AROUND

State Highway 1 is the fastest route there from Christchurch; just after crossing the Rangitata River, turn inland for about 10 minutes on State Highway 79. State Highway 72—known as the Inland Scenic Route—gives you closer views of the mountains and river gorges but takes a bit longer. The rolling downs around Geraldine are especially breathtaking in the late afternoon, when the sun turns them golden.

Because Geraldine is between Christchurch and the popular draws of Aoraki/Mt. Cook and Queenstown, it's served by several bus companies, including InterCity and Newmans.

ESSENTIALS

Bus Companies InterCity Coachlines (☎ *03/365–1113* ⊕ *www.intercitycoach. co.nz*). **Newmans Coachlines** (☎ *03/365–1114* ⊕ *www.newmanscoach.co.nz*).

EXPLORING

You know you're in small-town New Zealand when the biggest store on the main street is the rural merchandiser. Luckily, along Geraldine's main drag, **Talbot Street**, you'll find other stores and galleries to browse as well. Check out Māori portraits and carvings in the **Peter Caley Art Gallery** (✉ *3 Talbot St.* ☎ *03/693–7278*). **Plums Cafe** (✉ *44 Talbot St.* ☎ *03/693–9770*) is probably the nicest café in town with a good range of cabinet food and coffee and a growing selection of chocolate treats. For foodie treats, stop by **Barker's** in the Berry Barn Complex (✉ *76 Talbot St.* ☎ *0800/227–537*) to try fruit chutneys, juices and cordials, sauces, and Glory (an intense spread, better than jam, and often made with black currants). Or stop in at **Talbot Forest Cheese**, in the same complex. At the **Geraldine Vintage Car and Machinery Museum** (✉ *178 Talbot St.* ☎ *03/693–8756*), there's some good rural stuff with more than 100 tractors (some dating back to 1912) and other farm machinery sharing space with vintage cars. Admission is $7 and the museum is open daily 10–4 between early October and late May, weekends only in winter.

★ Looking more like a shearing shed than a store, the **Tin Shed** is exactly that. Surrounded by farmland and animals it is an authentic piece of rural New Zealand architecture being put to good use. Inside is one of the country's largest selections of lifestyle and handmade clothing. There's a good range of merino and possum fur knits and shawls, knitwear, and thermals, oilskins, sheepskin footwear, and locally produced skin-care items. This is a great spot to stock up with gifts before leaving the country, and they can arrange postage. Watch the turn-in off the main road as traffic moves fast here. ⊠ *State Hwy. 79, just off State Hwy. 1 at Rangitata* ☎ *03/693–9416* ⊕ *www.thetinshed.co.nz* ⊙ *Sept.– May, daily 8–5; June–Aug. 8:30–5*

SPORTS AND THE OUTDOORS

Rangitata Rafts runs white-water rafting trips on the Grade V Rangitata River from September through May. If you can't face the Grade V section (the last part of the trip), you can walk around with the photographer. The $210 price includes pickup from Geraldine or Christchurch and lunch, hot showers, spectacular scenery, and an evening barbecue. Reservations are essential. If a great deal of white water is a worry for you they also do a more gentile Grade II trip that's suitable for anyone eight or older; it doesn't provide quite the same adrenaline rush, but it's good fun all the same and a nice introduction to white-water rafting. ☎ *03/696–3534 or 0800/251–251* ⊕ *www.rafts.co.nz.*

The Unimog vehicles used by **Wilderness Adventures 4x4 New Zealand** go just about anywhere, including riverbeds, through the backcountry of South Canterbury. You can get to the upper reaches of the Rangitata River, seen in the *Lord of the Rings* films; sites in the area portrayed the Misty Mountains, Helms Deep, Edoras and its city, Rohan. This is also Samuel Butler country; his story *Erewhon* was set nearby. Trips range from half a day to more than a week long; rates start at $135 for the half-day trip. Reservations are essential. ☎ *03/693–7254* ⊕ *www.4x4newzealand.co.nz.*

WHERE TO STAY

$$–$$$ 🛏 **The Downs B&B.** Spread across a large hilltop section in the outskirts of Geraldine this tidy place offers a homey place to stay, with lots of room to spread out and enjoy the rural and garden views. The Geraldine room is the one to book with its huge corner window and giant dressing room. If that's full, ask for the Fitzgerald room as it's not much smaller. The third room also has a smaller room for children if you're traveling as a family. **Pros:** quiet rural backdrop close to town; nice family spot with loads of room and a big garden; free bar open 24/7; quite clean and tidy. **Cons:** quite conservatively decorated; slightly out of the way if traveling without a vehicle. ⊠ *5 Ribbonwood Rd.* ☎ *03/693–7388* ⊕ *www.thedowns.co.nz* 🛏 *3 rooms* �) *In room: No a/c, no phone, DVD (some), Wi-Fi. In-hotel: Bar, gym, bicycles, laundry facilities* ▭ *AE, DC, MC, V* ⫶◯⫶ *BP.*

9

TIMARU

162 km (101 mi) south of Christchurch.

Timaru, whose name comes from the Māori Te Maru (shelter), began life as two towns, one called Government Town and the other Rhodestown. The two towns met at George Street and merged in 1868. As Timaru's harbor was developed and its foreshore reclaimed, the Caroline Bay beach took shape and became a popular summer venue for its concerts and sideshows. Take a walk around the waterfront area at Caroline Bay where various festivals and events are held throughout the year. There's a rose garden, semi-enclosed soundshell for outdoor performances, paddling pool and play area; the boardwalk and sand dune area down at the beach are a great spot to unwind after a day in the car.

These days, Timaru is the urban hub for South Canterbury and is a two-hour drive south of Christchurch—close enough for a weekend trip but far enough away to have its own strong identity. Mountain biking is a growing sport here with some good trails through Centennial Park Reserve in the city, and a number further out in the hinterlands.

GETTING HERE AND AROUND

State Highway 1 will take you to points south from Christchurch, including Timaru. The town is about a half hour south and east from Geraldine on the coast. If you take State Highway 1, be prepared to share the lanes with long-haul trucks, sheep trucks, and logging vehicles. Buses to Dunedin and Invercargill pass through Timaru on the coast. Just north of the city, the turn inland at Washdyke (up State Highway 8) to Pleasant Point heads on to Mt. Cook and Queenstown.

Timaru's main shopping street, Stafford Street, was, until a few years ago, also the main road south. State Highway 1 now bypasses the main street so to get into the center of town take a left turn off Theodesia Street at the top of the Bay Hill (it's signposted). This will also get you to the port area and Caroline Bay. To head south continue along the Theodesia Street section of State Highway 1.

ESSENTIALS

Bus Company InterCity Coachlines (☎ *03/365–1113* ⊕ *www.intercity.co.nz*).

Medical Assistance Timaru Hospital (✉ *Queen St.* ☎ *03/684–4000*). **Timaru Medical Centre** (✉ *46a Harper St.* ☎ *03/684–7533*).

Visitor Information Timaru Visitor Centre (✉ *2 George St.* ☎ *03/688–6163* ⊕ *www.southisland.org.nz*).

EXPLORING

TOP ATTRACTIONS

Aigantighe Art Gallery. Pronounced "egg and tie," this is one of the largest, most intriguing art museums in the South Island. It has special regional, New Zealand, and international exhibitions and rotates the extensive permanent collection, including works by painter Colin McCahon (a Timaru native). In the gardens of the historic mansion are sculptures carved by African, Japanese, and New Zealand artists. ✉ *49 Wai-iti Rd.*

🖷 *03/688–4424* ✉ *gallery@timdc. govt.nz* ⊕ *www.timaru.govt.nz/art-gallery.html* 🖷 *Free* ⏱ *Tues.–Fri. 10–4, weekends noon–4.*

Landing Service Building. Once a harborside office, the Landing Service Building is now set back from the port because of the foreshore's land reclamation. The restored bluestone building houses the information center, a restaurant, and a small maritime display. A significant Māori rock art exhibition is currently under construction. Just outside the building sits *Captain Cain*, cast in bronze. This harbormaster was at the center of a 19th-century scandal when it was revealed that he had been poisoned by his son-in-law. ⊠ *2 George St.* 🖷 *03/688–6163* ✉ *timaru@i-site.org.*

WORTH NOTING

Pleasant Point. A 20-minute drive northwest from Timaru is Pleasant Point, an area known for its role in aviation history. Some months before the Wright brothers took flight in America, a local farmer nicknamed "Bamboo Dick" took bicycle wheels somewhere they'd never been before, launching New Zealand's first powered flight out in the fields a few miles outside town. The **Richard Pearse Memorial**, a reproduction of his plane, marks the spot where Pearse crashed into a hedge on March 31, 1903. To get here, take the Waitohi–Pleasant Point Road, then take a left on Opihi Terrace Road, and another left onto Main Waitohi Road. ⊠ *Main Waitohi Rd.*

Raincliff Historical Reserve. Although it's a bit of a mission to get there you can see Māori rock art in its original form on this rural site. South Canterbury has one of the country's highest concentrations of Māori rock art paintings, which are documented by the Ngai Tahu Māori Rock Art Trust. Six hundred years ago or more, Māori moa hunters made drawings of animals, birds, and people in black charcoal or red ocher on stone walls created by limestone overhangs. Although many works are on private land, the Raincliff reserve is open to the public. Faint drawings are visible here, particularly on the small overhang. To reach the reserve, follow the signpost in Pleasant Point that points to Raincliff Bridge. Allow at least two hours for the return trip from Timaru. ⊠ *Middle Valley Rd. off State Hwy. 79* 🖷 *Free.*

South Canterbury Museum. Anything to do with South Canterbury's past gets covered here, from fossils to fashions, Māori artifacts to 19th-century shipwrecks, and Richard Pearse's aviation antics, which predate the Wright Brothers. ⊠ *Perth St.* 🖷 *03/687–7212* ⊕ *www.timaru.govt. nz/museum* 🖷 *Free* ⏱ *Tues.–Fri. 10–4:30, weekends 1:30–4:30.*

BEST BETS FOR CRUISE PASSENGERS

■ **Day Trip to Mt. Cook (Aoraki).** Head inland before climbing Burkes Pass up to the Mackenzie Country. Skirt Lakes Tekapo and Pukaki before arriving at the base of Mt. Cook, the country's highest peak at 3,754 meters (12,315 feet).

■ **High Country Tour.** Explore a huge sheep station, see locations from *The Lord of the Rings* movies or scream down a Grade V river in a raft.

■ **Timaru Tour** Visit the Aigantighe Art Gallery, see some Māori rock art, check out the museum, then lunch in a café overlooking Caroline Bay.

9

WHERE TO EAT AND STAY

$$–$$$ ✕**Blue Bay Cafe.** Perched above Caroline Bay, along Timaru's tiny café
CAFÉ   strip, this fresh clean place has indoor and outdoor tables. There's an
all-day breakfast, a full cabinet, and a large blackboard menu, and they
have a solid range of espresso options. ⊠ *68 The Bay Hill* 🕾 *03/688–
0561* ▤ *AE, DC, MC, V* ☻ *No dinner.*

$$$–$$$$ ✕**Ginger & Garlic Café.** In winter, a big fire warms you up, and, in sum-
NEW ZEALAND mer, fabulous sunsets can be seen from a window table. In a bold three-
★   sided building at the top of the main street, the restaurant, one of
Timaru's best eateries, overlooks Caroline Bay and the port—where
the head chef, Kerina, gets her seafood fresh each day. ⊠ *335 Stafford
St.* 🕾 *03/688–3981* ▤ *AE, DC, MC, V* ☻ *Closed Sun. and 1st 2 wks of
Jan. No lunch weekends.*

$$$–$$$$ ✕**Le Monde.** With its modern red, white, and black interior, this well-
ECLECTIC   loved establishment features dishes from around the world, highlighting
local ingredients at the same time. Try the Canterbury lamb in a rogan
josh curry with pakoras of local vegetables. Or the Italian-style chicken
with a sweet corn risotto cake, bacon, and balsamic-roasted tomatoes.
The chef is a previous NZ Chef of the Year and they are well known
for their market fish dishes. Le Monde sits along the hill above Caroline
Bay and enjoys far-reaching sea and port views with indoor and outdoor
dining. ⊠ *64 The Bay Hill* 🕾 *03/688–8550* ⊕ *www.restaurantlemonde.
co.nz* ▤ *AE, DC, MC, V* ☻ *No breakfast.*

$–$$ 🏠**Panorama Motor Lodge.** Sitting back a bit on the Bay Hill, the Panorama has views of the Pacific Ocean from the front units on the Bay
Wing, and smaller views of Mt. Cook from the Alpine Wing units. It's
a family-style accommodation ranging from studios to two-bedroom
units—ideal if you're traveling with a few others. Each modestly furnished self-contained unit has a kitchen or kitchenette. **Pros:** walk to
anywhere in town from here; spa and sauna available; breakfast service is available. **Cons:** off-street parking is a bit cramped, especially if
you're driving a camper; basic motel with good value but no frills. ⊠ *52
The Bay Hill* 🕾 *03/688–0097* ✎ *lets-stay@panorama.net.nz* ⊕ *www.
panorama.net.nz* ➫ *20 units* ⌂ *In-room: No a/c, kitchen, Internet. In-
hotel: Spa, laundry facilities* ▤ *AE, MC, V.*

$–$$ 🏠**Sefton Homestay B&B.** Set on a wide leafy street in suburban Timaru
this really comfortable B&B inhabits a brick and rough-cast 1919 Arts
and Crafts house. Lots of stained glass and mullioned windows, period
furnishings and a lovely cottage garden complete the look. All rooms
are upstairs; the Tartan Suite has an additional sunroom to catch that
late afternoon sun but uses a private bathroom along the hall. The Blue
Room room is smaller, with its own en suite bathroom. There's also
an upstairs guest lounge with TV, computer, and tea and coffee. **Pros:**
the owners are full of information on the local mountain biking scene;
this place is an extremely good value for money; kids are welcome
Cons: upstairs floors are a bit creaky; restricted off-street parks. ⊠ *32
Sefton St.,* 🕾 *03/688–0017* ⊕ *www.seftonhomestay.co.nz* ➫ *3 rooms*
⌂ *In-room: No a/c, no phone, no TV, Wi-Fi. In-hotel: Bicycles, laundry
service, Internet terminal, Wi-Fi, parking (free), no-smoking rooms*
▤ *MC, V* ⦿*BP.*

The Southern Alps and Fiordland

WORD OF MOUTH

"Te Anau strikes me as somewhat overlooked . . . We were overwhelmed with the walking options . . . For those who love the outdoors, walking/hiking and related activities, Te Anau, Milford Sound, and Manapouri offer countless options; we could have easily stayed much longer."

—Melnq8

WELCOME TO THE SOUTHERN ALPS AND FIORDLAND

TOP REASONS TO GO

★ **Bungy Jumping:** Don't worry, there is no pressure to jump off a bridge with an elastic cord tied to your ankles. But if you have a desire to bungy (Kiwi for "bungee"), this is where to do it.

★ **Fly-Fishing:** The lakes and rivers of the Southern Alps are some of the world's best fly-fishing spots. The waters are so clear half the challenge is hiding from your target.

★ **Hiking:** Tramping doesn't get any better than the Milford Track, the Kepler, the Routeburn, and the Hollyford. You'll see mountains, fjords, waterfalls, and rain forests, and because the Department of Conservation (DOC) keeps a close eye on trail traffic, you'll have the sense of being alone in the wilderness.

★ **Scenic Flights:** With high mountain peaks, deep fjords, thick forest, and open tussock lands all in close proximity, a scenic flight is money well spent.

1 The Southern Alps.
In Mt. Cook National Park, activities naturally revolve around the mountain—climbing, hiking, skiing, and scenic flights. But as you travel down into the foothills and valleys, the choices for adventure multiply. Stargaze at Lake Tekapo, or go gliding at Omarama, "the place of light." Enjoy the miles of hills and farmland as you travel through Lindis Pass; soon the uninhabited country will give way to Wanaka and the bustle of Queenstown.

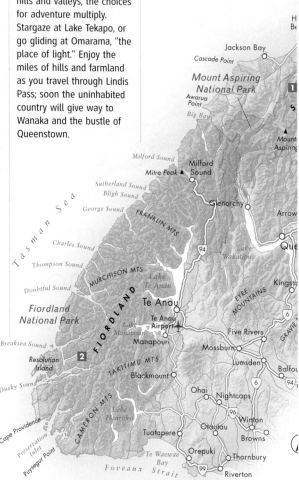

GETTING ORIENTED

The Southern Alps start in the northern end of the South Island around Kaikoura and stretch through the provinces of Canterbury, inland Otago, Westland, and Southland. These are serious mountains, with jagged 9,000-feet-plus peaks. The Mt. Cook area is the center of Kiwi mountaineering. These majestic formations take center stage, and amazing landscape unfurls at their feet—green rivers braided with white stone banks, acres of lupines, and lakes hued with indescribable blues. From Lake Tekapo, you finally come to "rest" at the adventure-friendly cities of Queenstown and Wanaka, historic Arrowtown, and the truly restful aura of the Otago vineyards. To the west, magnificent Milford Sound dominates Fiordland.

10

2 **Fiordland.** Te Anau is often referred to as a "jumping-off point" to explore Milford Sound. But the town, on the country's second-largest lake, is worth a stay to see the glowworms in Te Anau Caves. Milford has two strikes against it: lots of sand flies and bus-loads of tourists. However, it's a truly wondrous place, and the enormous beauty makes mere humans and insects—even busloads of them—seem insignificant.

THE SOUTHERN ALPS AND FIORDLAND PLANNER

Planning Your Time

Give yourself two–three days to explore the Mt Cook area: two days is a good idea at Mt. Cook in case the namesake peak is hiding behind clouds, and you'll want to allow for an evening at the space observatory in Tekapo. Once you head south you can use Queenstown or Wanaka as a base from which you can visit Mt. Aspiring National Park, wine country, and take on some exciting adrenaline-fueled activities around Queenstown—three days should be sufficient to pack it all in. Then head to Te Anau, which is a perfect base for seeing Fiordland National Park. An overnight on Milford or Doubtful Sound is recommended for unwinding and reflecting after the road-tripping, bungy-jumping excitement of the past week.

When to Go

Although the Southern Alps and Fiordland have four distinct seasons, it's not unusual for the mountains to get snow even in summer. If you're traveling in winter, check the weather forecasts and road conditions regularly. The road into Milford Sound can close for days at a time because of snow or avalanche risk.

Getting Here and Around

Air Travel

Qantas and Air New Zealand fly from Auckland and Christchurch into Queenstown, the main hub. Air New Zealand also serves Wanaka Airport. Tourist enterprises operate helicopters and fixed-wing planes which buzz between Queenstown, Wanaka, Milford Sound, Franz Josef, and Mt. Cook. You can do fly-cruise-fly packages from Queenstown to Milford, although the flight from Wanaka to Milford is the most spectacular.

Bus Travel

It may take a full day, but you can take buses to and from the major towns in the Southern Alps and Fiordland area. InterCity operates a daily bus service between Christchurch and Queenstown via Mt. Cook Village, with a one-hour stop at the Hermitage Hotel for lunch. Their coaches also make daily trips from the Franz Josef and Fox glaciers through Wanaka to Queenstown. InterCity also goes down the South Island's eastern flank from Christchurch to Queenstown via Dunedin. Newmans, meanwhile, runs a daily bus service from Christchurch through Mt. Cook to Queenstown and a daily bus round-trip route from Queenstown to Milford Sound and Te Anau to Milford Sound. Wanaka Connexions sends buses between Wanaka and Queenstown several times a day. They also run to Christchurch, Te Anau, Dunedin, and Invercargill.

Contacts InterCity Coachlines ☎ 03/365–1113 ⊕ intercity.co.nz). **Newmans Coach** ☎ 649/623–1504 ⊕ www.newmanscoach.co.nz). **Wanaka Connexions** ⊕ www.time2.co.nz).

Car Travel

Exploring is best done by car on the state highways that weave through the vast mountain ranges, skirting several major lakes and rivers. Be prepared for rugged, quickly changing terrain, ice in winter, and frequent downpours, particularly around Milford Sound. Rental-car companies may discourage driving on some of the smaller, unpaved roads, so it is best to avoid them. That said, an ideal way to see the Alps is to "tiki-tour" (wander around) by car, as the main network of roads is paved and easy to negotiate.

Restaurants

Queenstown, as the main regional resort, has the widest range of restaurants. Throughout the area, menus focus on local produce, seafood, lamb, and venison. Wine lists often highlight South Island wines, especially those from central Otago and Gibbston Valley. Cafés and restaurants driven by the summer tourist trade shorten their hours in winter. Dress standards are generally relaxed, with jeans or khakis acceptable almost everywhere. At high-end places, particularly in Queenstown, you'll need to reserve a table at least a day in advance.

Outside of Queenstown and Wanaka dining options can be limited. In summer, meals of some sort are available almost everywhere, but outside the high season, options in the smaller settlements can be minimal.

Hotels

Lodgings in the Southern Alps and Fiordland milk the fantastic views for all they're worth. You can almost always find a room that looks out on a lake, river, or rugged mountain range. Queenstown and Wanaka are busy in the summer (January through March) and winter (July through September), so you should reserve in advance. Luxury options are plentiful in Queenstown, and costs are correspondingly high. Other towns, such as Aoraki/Mt. Cook Village, have extremely limited options, so you should plan ahead there, too. Air-conditioning is rare since it's rarely needed. Heating, though, is standard, and essential in winter.

WHAT IT COSTS IN NEW ZEALAND DOLLARS

	¢	$	$$	$$$	$$$$
Restaurants	under $10	$10–$15	$15–$20	$20–$30	over $30
Hotels	under $75	$75–$125	$125–$200	$200–$300	over $300

Meal prices are per person for a main course at dinner, or the equivalent. Hotel prices are for a standard double room in high season, including 12.5% tax.

Visitor Information

The regional visitor bureaus are open daily year-round, with slightly longer hours in summer. These local tourism organizations have helpful Web sites, including Destination Fiordland and Mackenzie Winter.

Contacts Destination Fiordland (⊕ www.fiordland.org.nz). Mackenzie Winter (⊕ www.mackenziewinter.co.nz).

Cloud Cover

If you're locked into a mindset that seeing and photographing Aoraki/Mt. Cook is your goal, then you could well be disappointed. There have been plenty of visitors to the park that never got to glimpse the mountain due to cloud shroud. Focus on experiencing the park and environs as a whole—hike through wildflowers, laugh at keas, walk on a glacier and kayak through icebergs.

And if you get to see the ice-capped beauty, well, that's just the icing on your cake.

10

AORAKI/MT. COOK NATIONAL PARK

Endless rolling hills, bungy jumps off high bridges, the glittering Skytower of Auckland . . . so you think you've experienced the grandeur of New Zealand. HA! Aoraki glowers severely at these puny sideshows as if to say *try and bungy jump this, wee clown.*

A couple things about Aoraki/Mt. Cook: Yes, it's dually named with Māori and Anglo titles, but no one's going to spit in your eye if you just run with one or alternate for fun. Second, you may never see New Zealand's tallest mountain, as weather can shroud the peaks for days. Plan to stay in the park overnight in case your arrival coincides with curtains of clouds. The ice cornices and granite faces are the realm of serious mountain climbers. Nonclimbers can still get a strong sense of the place with hikes, scenic flights, glacier ski trips, and a visit to the excellent Sir Edmund Hillary Alpine Centre at the Hermitage Hotel. And finally, be prepared to be awed by these majestic peaks.

BEST TIME TO GO

For driving to and hiking in the park unhampered by bad weather, visit in the summer. Book accommodations and activities in advance between November and March. If your trip revolves around skiing or snowboarding, then winter is a wonderland here, albeit a somewhat inaccessible one during snow storms.

FUN FACT

In December 1991, Aoraki shrunk 10 meters when 10 million cubic meters of rock and ice tumbled off its peak, but it remains New Zealand's highest mountain (3754 meters [12,316 feet]).

BEST WAY TO EXPLORE

BIKE MOUNTAINING

Mountain biking is a great way to feel the bumps and dips of this dramatic landscape. Rent a bike and follow the Tasman Glacier Road from Mt. Cook Village. If you want something more adrenaline surging, sign up for a heli-bike trip and get dropped into the foothills of the Southern Alps.

PAT ICEBERGS WITH YOUR PADDLE

Some activities are cool because they're genuinely enjoyable thrills; some activities are cool because they're unique and rare life experiences; and some things are literally *cool*. Glacial kayaking amongst icebergs falls into all of these categories, and this triumvirate of coolness is an intimate and beautiful way to see a glacial environment. It's available October through April.

TAKE TO THE AIR

Spectacular as the mountains are, focusing on them means missing out on the enormity of the whole park. Touring the peaks in a fixed-wing airplane or helicopter is an excellent way to experience it. We highly recommend taking a ski-plane to one or all of the park's glaciers. In winter you can ski the Tasman Glacier, but just standing on this 27-km (17-mi) tongue of dazzling ice is exhilarating. Many visitors consider flightseeing here to be their best New Zealand adventure.

WALK, DON'T CLIMB

Sir Edmund Hillary used Mt. Cook as practicing grounds for his famous ascent of Mt. Everest; for some serious climbers Aoraki is their Everest. But there's no shame in just ambling along one of the park's 10 walks, all of which offer stunning panoramic views. Keep an eye out for alpine sundew, a glistening insect-eating plant, and the lovely Mt. Cook lily, which is the world's biggest type of buttercup. If you are climbing-curious there are plenty of courses available for every skill level.

ECO-STAYS

The Hermitage is committed to conservation initiatives when it comes to many aspects of the facility: they recycle and compost everything when possible, use recycled paper products, biodegradable bins and bag liners, and low-energy lighting. Exotic plant species are removed from the property, and they are nearing the completion of a 20-year, native gene-stock planting program. Many items on the Hermitage restaurant menus such as cheese, wine, salmon, and venison are sourced locally.

If you want to travel responsibly in the park adhere to the alpine code: *Pack it Out.* Don't leave *any* of your waste in the backcountry. Poo Pots are available at the visitor center, and using them will keep this pristine country *giardia* free. Do your part before doing your business and put a poo pot in your pack.

10

(top left) Braving the swing bridge on Hooker Valley Track, (bottom) Lake Matheson on a calm morning, (top) Mt. Cook's snowy peaks

MT. ASPIRING NATIONAL PARK

Roads only skirt the edge of this huge park, which compels you to hike, boat, and fly to see it. Only a winged, hoofed super-creature could possibly see the majority of Aspiring's wilderness. Daunting yet tantalizing: that's the magic draw of this unspoiled landscape.

At 355,000 hectares (877,224 acres), Mt. Aspiring is the country's third-largest national park. The park's namesake mountain is only one of numerous geological wonders. The area has yielded much *pounamu* or greenstone, and the famous Otago schist featured in the architecture of the gateway communities. One unusual stretch of peaks is known as the Red Hills, where the toxic minerals in the soil rendered the landscape barren (and a deep rusty red). Most of the park is marked by cool green beech forests and wildflowered valleys. The park is home to the famous Routeburn Track, a three-day Great Walk, and dozens of shorter hikes. Gateway communities include lively Wanaka which offers a multitude of choices for lodging, dining, shopping, and those rewarding post-hike pints.

BEST TIME TO GO

Late spring and summer (November through April) mean great walking weather and plenty of birds and flowers to see. Autumn in this part of the country is glorious for fall foliage. Weather is changeable in the park so check with the DOC before hitting the trail, or planning a long hike.

FUN FACT

In 1994, a once-in-250-year storm bamboozled the park with insane amounts of rain. The resulting floods and landslide wiped out a dozen bridges on the Routeburn Track and it was closed for two months for repairs.

BEST WAY TO EXPLORE

FLY

There are several flightseeing options for the park. One superb adventure combines a flight with hiking and jet-boating: fly from Makarora to the Siberia Valley, hike to a hut for an overnight stay, and then jet-boat the Wilkins River back to Makarora.

HELI-FUN

If you visit the park in the winter, consider heli-skiing or heli-boarding, where you can avoid the crowds of the ski resorts and explore fresh powder in premiere locations with views of Lake Wanaka and Lake Hawea.

RIVER TRIPPING

Fly fishermen, picnickers, and kayakers might be enjoying the blissful serenity of the park's crystal rivers, until a roar fills the air and a jet-boat full of squealing humans hurtles past, sending waves of water and noise in every direction. Hey, if you can't beat'em, join'em, and you will surely have fun. Jet-boating is a hallucinogen-free way of watching a scenic postcard expand and morph into vibrant 3-D as you travel at top speed. Yeah. It's fun.

TRAMPING

This park is a paradise for walkers. Many avid hikers and naturalists in New Zealand have settled in Aspiring's gateway communities to have access to its backcountry routes. While the Routeburn is the park's most well-known track, there are countless missions waiting for anyone with good soles and a pack. ⚠ Please be careful crossing rivers. If you have any doubts stay on shore; visitors have perished crossing swollen rivers here.

ECO-STAYS

Eco-friendly and *luxury* don't always go hand in hand, but beautiful Wanaka Homestead has made an excellent effort. The lodge's hot water, which supplies the taps, hot tub and cozy under-floor heating, is solar heated. This lodge has been highly commended with a New Zealand Ener-gyWise award recognizing efforts that have reduced "brought-in" power needs by half. The lodge uses low-energy appliances and controllers, and it was designed and built with energy efficiency and environmental sensitiv-ity in mind. Wanaka's Minaret Lodge is another luxurious facility which practices eco-sensitivity in its daily routines, using biodegradable cleansers, organic produce and fair trade coffee, energy-efficient light bulbs, and the great Kiwi answer to energy-efficient insulation: sheep's wool in the walls.

10

(top left) Tramper following the Routeburn Track, (bottom) Routeburn Falls hut on the track, (top) Warming up by the campfire

FIORDLAND NATIONAL PARK

There is a reason Fiordland is considered a must-see destination. Prose, pixels, and paint all fail to describe Milford Sound and its surrounding beauty. You simply have to experience the place yourself.

Encompassing over a million hectares (almost 2.5 million acres) of wilderness, Fiordland is the country's biggest national park. About half a million people visit each year to see playful dolphins and rainforest-cloaked mountains, but most converge on Milford and Doubtful sounds, the park's stars. Don't worry—the park is massive enough to easily absorb the crowds. The scenery actually shuts them up too: entire boatloads of visitors have been known to just *hush* out on the water. Sandflies and rain (along with your job, breaking news, and the rest of the world) will seem like mere details when you behold Milford Sound, with Mitre Peak rising along the coast and waterfalls tumbling into the sea. *I see the falls,* said one returning visitor, *and everything just falls away.*

BEST TIME TO GO

Spring and summer (October through April) are the best, but busiest, times to go. Still there are many opportunities to commune quietly with the park, including kayaking, scuba diving, or hiking. If you only have time for a cruise, it is still well worth the trip.

FUN FACT

The sounds of Fiordland see 7200 mm of rain a year. There is so much rain there that the sea is topped by a 20-foot deep layer of fresh water.

PARK HIGHLIGHTS

MILFORD'S WATERFALLS

Milford Sound mass-produces waterfalls. Silver threads of spontaneous waterfalls join Bowen Falls' 520-foot drop. Torrents of rain cause lush green walls to spring leaks. Occasionally, fierce winds stop the flow and appear push water back *up* the cliff faces. That's Milford's drama: lovely on nice days and spectacular on nasty days. A scenic flight will take you over Sutherland Falls, the tallest in New Zealand at 580 m.

DOUBTFUL SOUND

Doubtful Sound has all of the beauty of Milford, but it's less accessible and therefore less crowded and more serene. So if Milford's too hustle-bustle for you, arrange a trip to Doubtful, which will doubtless include a stop at its gateway, Lake Manapouri, and the enormous hydroelectric power station situated there.

TE ANAU

This little town's restaurants, shops, and lodgings make it a perfect base for your Fiordland adventures. Situated on its picturesque namesake lake, it also has an excellent cinema/wine bar, which features the locally filmed *Ata Whenua: Shadowland*, well worth the ticket price. A short boat ride across the lake will take you to glowworm caves; it's a two-hour drive to Milford Sound and a 20-minute bus ride to Lake Manapouri.

BE PREPARED

Sandflies may be a useful cog in the great big eco-machine, but when you (inevitably) encounter them you'll just want them—and their irritating, itchy bites—to go away. They are drawn to warmth (your body heat), dark colors (your navy or black clothing), anyone standing still or moving slowly (you trying to relax) and, well, *you*, no matter what you do. Arm yourself with sandfly repellant before hitting the park.

TOUR OPERATORS

BY WATER: Fiordland Expeditions tours Doubtful Sound on its little boat, *Tutuko*. **Milford Sound Red Boat Cruises** offers daily scenic cruises on catamarans to Milford Sound. **Real Journeys** runs bus-and-boat trips and overnight cruises in Milford and Doubtful sounds. **Fiordland Wilderness Experiences** has day- and multiday kayaking trips on sounds and lakes.

BY LAND: Guided multiday treks with **Ultimate Hikes** require deep pockets but include comfy beds and meals. Day hikes on Milford or Routeburn tracks are available.

BY AIR: **Air Fiordland** has scenic flights on fixed-wing aircraft to the sounds. **Wings and Water Te Anau Ltd.** flies floatplanes over Doubtful, Dusky, and Milford sounds. **Glacier Southern Lakes Helicopters Ltd.'s** Milford Sound Fantastic trip includes at least two landings.

10

(left above) Mitre Peak and Milford Sound, (bottom) Hiker and kea bird on Kepler Track, (above) Hollyford Track.

BEST WAY TO EXPLORE

CRUISE THE SOUND

Milford and Doubtful sound cruises run all day and include scenic, nature, and overnight trips. Most of Milford's daytrips get you close to a waterfall. View New Zealand fur seals, penguins, and dolphins from kayaks or charter a fishing trips in the Tasman Sea.

WALK THE FINEST WALK

The Milford Track, the "Finest Walk in the World," requires a bit of gumption and organization—and boat transport from either end—to complete. The four days of rainforests, glacial lakes, mountains, and massive waterfalls is worth the effort. There are other wonderful walks, like the 60-km, 4-day Kepler Track, which includes the Luxmore Cave and beech forests.

DIP IN

Scuba divers come here for uncommonly accessible glimpses of spiny sea dragons, sea pens, and black coral. If you don't want to suit up, visit the Milford Deep Underwater Observatory.

DRIVE MILFORD ROAD

Most visitors drive scenic Milford Road to access the park. There are places to stop and enjoy short walks: Mirror Lake and the Avenue of the Disappearing Mountain live up to their names. The Chasm Walk (20 minute return) includes a river crossing and waterfall views. Traffic in the Homer Tunnel may cause delays, but just think: it took 20 years to build!

ECO-STAYS

Misty Mountain Eco-Retreat is a self-contained cabin constructed with native silver beech from Doubtful Sound's sea-washed logs; wool has been used for insulation, and naturally, the owners recycle.

Another eco-friendly self-accommodation cottage is **Mararoa Cottage**. The free range hens provide lovely eggs. Owners Paul and Catherine use green cleaning products at the cottage and compost and recycle all rubbish. They are involved in conservation projects, and they are happy to point you in the right direction of a hands-on conservation experience. If you arrive in the spring you can bottle-feed the lambs.

ONE-DAY ITINERARY

Te Anau is a 2 ½ hour drive from Queenstown, so rise early and spend a full day in the park.

MORNING

8–10: Have breakfast in **Te Anau** and stop in one of the stores or cafés to pick up a picnic lunch, snacks, and drinks. Then hit the **Milford Road.**

10–1:30: Give yourself three hours to drive to **Milford Sound.** Take time for plenty of scenic stops, leg stretches, the **Chasm Walk**, and a picnic lunch along the way.

AFTERNOON

1:30–4: Take one of the two-hour Milford Sound cruises that leave hourly. Choose one that stops at the **Milford Deep Underwater Observatory.** In peak season book at least two weeks in advance.

4–6:30: Drive back to Te Anau.

EVENING

7–7:30: See *Ata Whenua: Shadowland* at the Fiordland Cinema. The 30-minute movie takes you through parts of the park you'd never get to see.

8: Grab a very quick dinner and catch the last boat across the lake to the glowworm cave. Or save this for tomorrow and enjoy dinner in town.

10:30: You're a champ! Find a tavern and reward yourself with a pint. If you're too tired, head to bed. As they say in these parts, good on ya mate and sweet dreams.

STAY THE NIGHT

Overnight cruises are a leisurely, thorough way to experience the sounds. If you choose Doubtful Sound the tour company will provide transport from Lake Manapouri to the vessel. Sleeping quarters range from four-person bunks to private, ensuite cabins. Dinner and breakfast are included; picnic lunches are by arrangement. Lucky cruisers will see Fiordland crested penguins or bottle-nose dolphins. You can explore by kayak once you anchor for the evening, or you can take in the sights from the viewing deck. Milford cruises depart around 4:30 PM and return around 9 AM; Doubtful cruises leave around noon and return around noon the next day.

10

(left) Milford Sound and Mitre Peak, (right) Mackinnon Pass, Milford Track.

Updated by
Jessica Kany

As many as 60 glaciers are locked in the Southern Alps, slowly grinding their way down to lower altitudes, where they melt into running rivers of uncanny blue-green hues.

Aoraki, or Mt. Cook, at 12,283 feet, is New Zealand's highest mountain, and 27 other peaks in this alpine chain are higher than 9,750 feet. Aoraki/Mt. Cook National Park is a UNESCO World Heritage Area, and the alpine region around it contains the Tasman Glacier, at 27 km (17 mi), New Zealand's longest.

The Southern Alps region is great for hiking. Terrain varies from high alpine tundra to snow-covered peaks, heavily forested mountains, and wide, braided river valleys. A good network of trails and marked routes are throughout the mountains, but be well informed before venturing into them. Always make your intentions known to the local DOC sign-in office before leaving, and check in with them after returning.

There are many easier options for exploring the foothills and less arduous parts of the Southern Alps. On the southwest corner of the island, glaciers over millennia have cut the Alps into stone walls dropping into fjords, and walking trails take you into the heart of wild Fiordland National Park. The Milford Track is the best known—it has been called the finest walk in the world since a headline to that effect appeared in the London *Spectator* in 1908. If you're not keen on walking to Milford Sound, hop on a boat and take in the sights from on deck. Most river valleys with road access have well-marked walking trails leading to scenic waterfalls, gorges, and lookout points.

THE SOUTHERN ALPS

The Canterbury Plains ring Christchurch and act as a brief transition between the South Pacific and the soaring New Zealand Alps. The drive south along the plain is mundane by New Zealand standards until you leave State Highway 1 and head toward the Southern Alps.

The route south, along the eastern flank of the Alps, can leave you breathless. Head through Lindis Pass by traveling inland to Fairlie and Tekapo, then south to Omarama; you'll be entering the country's

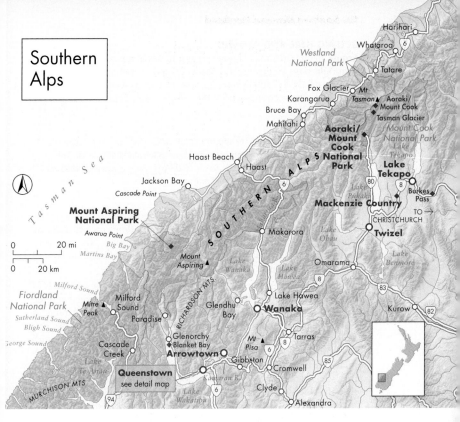

Southern
Alps

Harihari

Whataroa 6

Westland
National Park

Tatare

Fox Glacier Mt

Karangarua **Tasman▲** Aoraki/
Mount Cook

Bruce Bay

Tasman Glacier

Mahitahi

Aoraki/ *Mount Cook*
Mount *National Park*
Cook *Lake*
National *Tekapo*
Park

Haast Beach **Lake**
Tekapo

Haast 6 80 8 Burkes
Pass

Jackson Bay *Lake*
Pukaki

Cascade Point **Mackenzie Country** TO →
CHRISTCHURCH

Mount Aspiring
National Park

Twizel

Awarua Point Makarora *Lake*
Ohau

Big Bay *Lake*
Benmore

0   20 mi *Martins Bay* Mount
Aspiring ▲ *Lake*
Wanaka *Lake*
Hawea Omarama

0   20 km 8

Milford Sound 83

Fiordland Milford *Lake Hawea*
National Park Mitre ▲ Sound
Sutherland Sound Peak Glendhu Kurow 82
Bligh Sound Paradise Bay **Wanaka**

George Sound Glenorchy Tarras

Cascade ● Blanket Bay Mt 8
Creek **Arrowtown** Pisa 6
Gibbston
Lake **Queenstown** Cromwell 85
Te Anau see detail map *Kawarau R.*

MURCHISON MTS 94 Clyde

Lake Alexandra
Wakatipu

Tasman Sea

S O U T H E R N   A L P S

RICHARDSON MTS

adventure-sports playground, where Wanaka and Queenstown provide
at least a dozen ways to get your adrenaline pumping. A handful of
notable vineyards calm the nerves post-extreme-sport experience.

MACKENZIE COUNTRY AND LAKE TEKAPO

227 km (141 mi) west of Christchurch.

You will know you have reached the **Mackenzie Country** after you cross
Burkes Pass and the woodland is suddenly replaced by high-country
tussock grassland, which is full of lupines in the summer months.
The area is named for James ("Jock") McKenzie, one of the most
intriguing and enigmatic figures in New Zealand history. McKenzie
was a Scot who may or may not have stolen the thousand sheep
found with him in these secluded upland pastures in 1855. Arrested,
tried, and convicted, he made several escapes from jail before he was
granted a pardon nine months after his trial—and disappeared from
the pages of history. Regardless of his innocence or guilt, McKenzie
was a master bushman and herdsman. A commemorative obelisk
marks Mackenzie Pass, 30 km (18 mi) off the main highway if you
turn off at Burkes Pass.

GETTING HERE AND AROUND

From Christchurch take Highway 1 south. At the tiny town of Rangitata turn right onto Highway 79 to Lake Tekapo. A half dozen bus companies serve Lake Tekapo including InterCity Coach, Wanaka Connexions, and Cook Connections—check the Lake Tekapo Tourism Web site for a complete list.

ESSENTIALS

Visitor Information Lake Tekapo Information (⌧ *Main Rd., Lake Tekapo* ☎ *03/680–6686*). **Lake Tekapo Tourism** (⊕ *www.tekapotourism.co.nz*). **The Resource Centre** (⌧ *64 Main St., Fairlie* ☎ *03/685–8496* ⊕ *www.southisland. org.nz/heritagetrails/bullockwagon.html*).

EXPLORING

The long, narrow expanse of **Lake Tekapo** anchors the area. Its extraordinary milky-turquoise color comes from rock flour, rock ground by glacial action and held in a soupy suspension. Tekapo, the country's highest large lake, has good fly-fishing in the lake and in the surrounding rivers and canals.

On the east side of the lakeside power station is the tiny **Church of the Good Shepherd.** The simple stone structure doesn't need stained glass; the view through the window is the lake's brilliant blue. A nearby memorial commemorates the sheepdogs of the area. As you drive into the small town, you'll notice a knot of restaurants with tour buses parked outside. It's a rather off-putting image, but it's relatively easy to keep the township at your back and your eyes on the lake and mountains. If you're not planning to stay at Mt. Cook, then Tekapo is the best place in the Mackenzie Basin to stop for the night. And once the buses have passed through for the day, it's a quiet spot—at least until the hordes of Cantabrians arrive for the summer break. A pleasant lakefront recreation area separates the town retail area from the lakeshore.

OFF THE BEATEN PATH

Bullock Wagon Trail. This 268-km (167-mi) heritage highway, which stretches from Timaru to Twizel via Mt. Cook, recognizes the long, arduous journeys early settlers in the region made by bullock wagon. Leaving the Canterbury Plains at Geraldine or Pleasant Point (depending on whether you are coming directly from Christchurch or through from Timaru), the highways join at Fairlie and quickly climb toward the first of the alpine passes—Burkes Pass—along the Bullock Wagon Trail. The Burkes Pass monument marks the division between the high and low country, and from there the country immediately dries out and takes on the look of high-country tussock lands. To learn more about the trail and the history of the region, stop in at one of two information centers along the way: **Lake Tekapo Information** (⌧ *Main Rd., Lake Tekapo* ☎ *03/680–6686*). **The Resource Centre** (⌧ *64 Main St., Fairlie* ☎ *03/685–8496* ⊕ *www.southisland.org.nz/heritagetrails/ bullockwagon.html*).

SPORTS AND THE OUTDOORS

FISHING **Barry Clark Fly-Fishing & Small Game Hunting Guide** (⌧ *1 Esther-Hope St., Lake Tekapo* ☎ *03/680–6513* ⊕ *www.fredadufaur.co.nz*) will take you fly-fishing or spinning, whatever your preference, to the most suitable lake or river spot of the day. Barry's knowledge of the local spots is exhaustive. He and his wife Dawn run a luxury B&B so you can arrange to stay with them as well.

HIKING   At the Tekapo Information Centre you can pick up a walking-trail map and then take off to hike the **Domain to Mt. John Lookout track.** In a couple of hours you can be well above the township, enjoying extensive views of the Mackenzie Basin, Southern Alps, and Lake Tekapo.

STARGAZING   If you're extremely lucky, you'll see the southern lights! **Earth and Sky** (⊠ *Main St., State Hwy. 8, Lake Tekapo* ☎ *03/680–6960* ⊕ *www. earthandsky.co.nz*) operates from the Mt. John Observatory and studies the skies above Lake Tekapo. A sign asks you to dim your headlights on approach; the galaxy is considered part of the park and nobody wants you to outshine the stars. The Astro Café has ham-off-the-bone sandwiches, telescopes, and dizzying views. Stargazing trips leave from the town office at 8 PM in the winter and 10 PM in the summer; they cost $75 per adult ($30 per child), and reservations are essential. Daytime tours of the facility cost $25 ($10 per child) and can be booked at the café.

WHERE TO EAT

¢–$ ✕ **Doughboys.** In a town where most of the dining options are along the
CAFÉ   main drag of souvenir shops and cafés, it's nice to escape with a sandwich, a pastry, or a pie and eat down at the lakefront. Doughboys bakes several different breads, croissants, and 10 different pies. Sandwiches have yummy fillings such as seafood, chicken, or bacon and eggs, and the scones are legendary. In case that's not enough, you can grab a sit-down breakfast (bacon, two eggs, tomato), for about $12. ⊠ *State Hwy. 8* ☎ *03/680–6655* ⊟ *No credit cards* ⊗ *No dinner.*

$$$ ✕ **The Garden Courtyard.** An impressive buffet appears three times a
NEW ZEALAND   day in this pleasant dining room. Lunch and dinner selections always include six entrées and another half dozen vegetable dishes, as well as soups, salads, and several desserts. The salmon is reliably good, and if you've caught your own, the restaurant kitchen will cook it for you. Between lunch and dinner, a snack menu serves panini, soup, mussels, warm chicken salad, and the like, all for less than $12. ⊠ *The Godley Hotel, State Hwy. 8* ☎ *03/680–6848* ⊟ *AE, MC, V.*

$ ✕ **Jade Palace.** You might pat the big Buddha's tummy on the way into
CHINESE   this restaurant, but you will soon be patting your own as it is hard to give the chopsticks a rest here. There is nothing fancy on this menu, just straightforward, really good Chinese food in a spacious dining room. At busy times service can be brusque. ⊠ *State Hwy. 8* ☎ *03/680–6828* ⊟ *AE, MC, V.*

$$$$ ✕ **Kohan Japanese Restaurant.** Masato Itoh runs the only Japanese res-
JAPANESE   taurant in town, which gives him guaranteed access to busloads of tourists from his home country. Sushi, sashimi, and tempura are all on the menu. The restaurant has some of the best views over Lake Tekapo, but it lacks personality. The food, however, is a refreshing change from the more traditional lunch options in town. ⊠ *State Hwy. 8* ☎ *03/680–6688* ⊟ *AE, DC, MC, V* ⊗ *Lunch 11–2, dinner 6 PM on. No dinner Sun.*

10

$$$–$$$$ ✕**Reflections Café.** Great views of the lake are seen from almost every
ECLECTIC   table at this rustically decorated restaurant. Reflections consistently
wins awards for its beef and lamb dishes, and salmon from a nearby
hatchery is also delicious. As many ingredients as possible are obtained
locally to maintain freshness in the meals. ⊠ *Lake Tekapo Scenic Resort,
State Hwy. 8* ☎ *03/680–6234* ▭ *MC, V.*

WHERE TO STAY

$$$ 🏠**Aldourie Lodge.** With a fireplace, clawfoot bathtub, lake views, and
★   library, this enchanting house is the perfect place to unwind. The own-
ers Graeme and Carolyn Murray saved Lake Tekapo's oldest cottage
from being torn down and renovated it, retaining the character while
adding modern luxuries. The view is superb. The price is for two people; each additional guest is $35. Inquire about the Murrays' other
properties, which are just as delightful and cozy. (The Garden Cottage,
across the street, has the Prime Minister and a member of royalty in its
guest book!) **Pros:** all properties are cozy and thoughtfully decorated.
Cons: it books quickly, so try to reserve well in advance. ⊠ *3 Sealy St.*
☎ *03/680–6709* ⊕ *www.parkbrae.co.nz* ⇆ *3 rooms* ⌂ *In-room: DVD.
In-hotel: Laundry facilities* ▭ *AE, DC, MC, V.*

$$–$$$ 🏠**The Chalet.** The Chalet's six fully, self-contained apartments stretch
beside the turquoise waters of Lake Tekapo. Units range from studio
size to a two-bedroom cottage apartment. The best have spacious living rooms and lake views; two of the rooms open onto a small patio
area and lovely alpine gardens. You can arrange a customized local
expedition with the host, an experienced hunting, fishing, and nature
guide. Tekapo Township is a scenic five-minute walk away. **Pros:** superb
views. **Cons:** hard to pick which room has the best view. ⊠ *14 Pioneer
Dr.* ☎ *03/680–6774* ⊕ *www.thechalet.co.nz* ⇆ *6 units* ⌂ *In-room: No
a/c. In-hotel: Laundry service* ▭ *AE, MC, V.*

$$–$$$ 🏠**Lake Tekapo Scenic Resort.** A nice mid-range alternative with good
family-style facilities, this resort is in the center of town. It opens out
to the lakefront area, and many units have lake views. A big three-
bedroom apartment is available if you're traveling with family. Meals
at Reflections restaurant next door are on a charge-back basis. **Pros:**
good value; friendly management; minigolf with lake view. **Cons:** truly
basic rooms; no frills. ⊠ *State Hwy. 8* ☎ *03/680–6808 or 0800/118–666*
⊕ *www.laketekapo.com* ⇆ *6 family units, 12 studios, 1 3-bedroom
apartment* ⌂ *In-hotel: Laundry facilities* ▭ *DC, MC, V.*

¢   🏠**Tailor-Made-Tekapo Backpackers.** The gorgeous garden is made for
sunbathing in warm weather. In winter, there's a cozy lounge with a
fireplace to curl up in front of. There are various room arrangements,
from singles to four- and six-bed dorm rooms; all, including the dorms,
have regular beds (no bunks). It's a decidedly kid-friendly spot. Bring
your Budget Backpackers Hostel (BBH) card if you have one. **Pros:** as
nice as backpackers can be. **Cons:** in residential neighborhood back
from the lake. ⊠ *9–11 Aorangi Crescent* ☎ *03/680–6700* ⊕ *www.tailor-
made-backpackers.co.nz* ⇆ *13 rooms, 10 with shared bath, 3 dorms*
⌂ *In-room: No TV. In-hotel: Tennis court* ▭ *MC, V.*

AORAKI/MT. COOK NATIONAL PARK

99 km (62 mi) from Lake Tekapo.

GETTING HERE AND AROUND

The 330-km (205-mi) drive from Christchurch straight through to Aoraki/Mt. Cook Village takes four hours. Take Highway 1 south out of Christchurch. At the tiny town of Rangitata turn right onto Highway 79 to Lake Tekapo. Pass through Lake Tekapo and look on the right for Highway 80 to Aoraki/Mt. Cook Village. InterCity buses make daily stops at Mt. Cook Village. The village itself is small and manageable on foot.

ESSENTIALS

Bus Company InterCity (☎ 03/443–7885 in Wanaka, 03/249–7559 in Te Anau, 03/442–8238 in ⊕ www.intercitycoach.co.nz).

Visitor Information Aoraki/Mt. Cook National Park Visitor Centre (✉ Aoraki/Mt. Cook Village ☎ 03/435–1186 ⊕ www.doc.govt.nz 📠 03/435–1186). **Weather Phone** (☎ 03/435–1171).

EXPLORING

Fodor's Choice Above the grassy Mackenzie Basin towers the South Island's highest
★ peak **Mt. Cook,** at approximately 12,283 feet. There are 22 peaks over 10,000 feet in **Aoraki/Mt. Cook National Park.** The mountain's Māori name is Aoraki (Aorangi to North Island Māori), and the Māori and Anglo-names are often used interchangeably or together. According to Māori legend, Aoraki was one of three sons of Rakinui, the sky father. Their canoe was caught on a reef and frozen, forming the South Island. In these parts, South Island's oldest Māori name is Te Waka O Aoraki (Aoraki's canoe) and the highest peak is Aoraki, frozen by the south wind, and turned to stone. Māori see these mountains as their ancestors. The officially recognized names of this mountain, the national park, and many other South Island places have been changed to their original Māori names as part of a 1998 settlement between the government and the major South Island Māori tribe, Ngai Tahu.

At 439 square km (270 square mi), the park is a formidable area of ice and rock, with glaciers covering 40% of the land and little forest cover. The high altitude attracts its share of bad weather. Visitors can often stand at the end of Lake Tekapo or Lake Pukaki, looking westward, and not know that the country's highest mountain is just a few miles away. But that shouldn't prevent you from taking the 40-km (25-mi) paved road up to Mt. Cook village. Stay the night while you're there—nowhere else in the region compares for a true alpine experience. If the clouds lift, you'll be glad you stayed: the vistas are beyond spectacular.

The national park surrounds **Aoraki/Mt. Cook Village** (population 300), which consists of a visitor center, a grocery store, an airfield, a pub, a little school, a hotel-motel complex, and several hostels. Walking is always an option, and in winter there's heli-skiing. If the weather is clear, a scenic flight around the Mt. Cook area and across to the West Coast can be the highlight of your stay in New Zealand. Contact the **Aoraki/Mt. Cook National Park Visitor Centre** or the **weather phone** to check

10

DID YOU KNOW?

Practice makes perfect at Aoraki/Mt. Cook. Sir Edmund Hillary would never have had his Step without New Zealand's highest peak. Hillary honed his climbing skills here before taking on Mt. Everest.

conditions before setting out on an unguided excursion. A network of hiking trails radiates from the Aoraki/Mt. Cook National Park Visitor Centre, providing everything from easy walking paths to full-day challenges. A cairn just a few minutes along the track up the Hooker Valley remembers 40 of the more than 180 people who have died in the park since climbing began there. Be sure to fill your car's gas tank before leaving Twizel or Tekapo; although fuel is available at the Hermitage hotel, there are no credit card facilities at the pumps and the hours are limited.

For a unique hands-on educational experience take a half-hour hike to the fast-growing 2-square-km (1-square-mi) **Terminus Lake of the Tasman Glacier.** Fed by the glacier and the Murchison River, the lake was formed only in the past couple of decades, because of the glacier's retreat. From Terminus Lake, which is officially growing by a foot a week, you can examine up close the terminal face of the glacier, which is 3 km (2 mi) wide. A trip with Glacier Explorers (⇨ *Tours at the end of this chapter)* can take you by boat to explore some of the large floating icebergs that have calved (fallen away) from the Tasman Glacier. It's an eerie experience skimming across the milky-white water and closing in on icebergs—even riding *through* where they have melted—to touch rocks caught in the ice.

SPORTS AND THE OUTDOORS

CLIMBING AND MOUNTAINEERING Summer is the best climbing season in the Aoraki/Mt. Cook National Park area. **Adventure Consultants** (☎ *03/443–8711* ⊕ *www.adventure. co.nz*), a group specializing in the world's top peaks, guides ascents of Aoraki and Mt. Tasman. They also give multiday mountaineering, alpine-climbing, and ice-climbing courses. Because the company is based in Wanaka, they work Mt. Cook only in good weather, so call and reserve ahead. Experienced climbers or beginners can sign up for the appropriate level of **Alpine Guides'** (✉ *Bowen Dr., Mt. Cook Village* ☎ *03/435–1834* ⊕ *www.alpineguides.co.nz*) 6- to 10-day mountaineering courses, which begin around $2,350. They offer half-day rock-climbing trips costing $150, including equipment. From July to September they also run heli-ski trips, ski tours, ice climbing, and ski mountaineering.

FLIGHTSEEING Flightseeing gives you an unparalleled view of the mountains, with the added thrill of landing on a glacier for a short walk. The light can be intensely bright in such dazzlingly white surroundings, so be sure to bring sunglasses. Generally, the best time for flights is early morning. **Mount Cook Ski Planes** (☎ *03/430–8034 or 0800/800–702* ⊕ *www.mtcookskiplanes.com*) has four flightseeing options, including a 25-minute flight over two glaciers ($220) or a 55-minute flight with a glacier landing ($430). Or take a breathtaking 50-minute scenic flight to see Aoraki, the Tasman, Murchison, Fox, and Franz Josef glaciers, and the rain forests on the west side of the Main Divide with **Air Safaris** (☎ *03/680–6545* ⊕ *www.airsafaris.co.nz*). Flights start at $260 per adult. The **Helicopter Line** (✉ *Glentanner Station, State Hwy. 80* ☎ *03/435–1801 or 0800/650–651* ⊕ *www.helicopter.co.nz)* runs 20-minute and 45-minute flights from Glentanner Station, about 20

10

km (12 mi) toward Pukaki from the Hermitage. You can land on the glaciers or high ski slopes, depending on the weather.

HIKING The hiking trails spooling out from the visitor center range in difficulty and length, from the 10-minute Bowen Track to the 5½-hour climb to the 4,818-foot summit of Mt. Sebastopol. Seven tracks can be done in running shoes and don't require hiking experience; the rest of the park's trails require some hiking experience, and the higher routes require serious mountaineering experience. The Mueller Hut route is a popular climb, taking about three hours; a new 30-bed hut provides overnight accommodation. The rewarding Hooker Valley walk, a four-hour round-trip, will take you across a couple of swingbridges to the Hooker Glacier terminus lake, and the Tasman Glacier Lake walk gives an intimate view of New Zealand's longest glacier.

WHERE TO STAY

$$ 🏨 **Aoraki/Mt. Cook Alpine Lodge.** This lodge, run by a young local family, has dorm rooms, twin, triple, and family rooms, many with private bathrooms. All rooms have mountain views (some are greater than others). The alpine-style decoration uses lots of native timber and glass, and a huge stone fireplace is in the lobby. **Pros:** great guest lounge. **Cons:** not many meal options, so be prepared to buy groceries and cook. ✉ *Bowen Dr., Mt. Cook Village* ☎ *03/435–1860 or 0800/680–680* ⊕ *www.aorakialpinelodge.co.nz* ⤳ *16 rooms* ⌂ *In-hotel: Kitchen, laundry facilities, Wi-Fi* ▭ *MC, V.*

$$$–$$$$ 🏨 **The Hermitage Hotel.** Famed for its stupendous mountain vistas, this rambling hotel has been substantially revamped over the past few years. The improved layout now gives most of the rooms, as well as the lobby, terrific views over Aoraki and Mt. Sefton. Some accommodations, such as the motel rooms and self-contained chalets, are separate from the main lodge, and the views aren't as spectacular, but the prices and space are good for families. Room rates include breakfast. The Hermitage Hotel houses two excellent restaurants. As the name suggests, the Panorama Room ($$$–$$$$) restaurant takes in the scenery, too. Its menu leans toward both the Pacific Rim and Europe; you could try panfried monkfish or a char-grilled beef tenderloin. The Alpine Restaurant ($$$–$$$$) serves a huge buffet-style meal for lunch and dinner. **Pros:** brand-new, multimillion-dollar Sir Edmund Hillary Alpine Center including planetarium; efficiently run establishment. **Cons:** rooms with views are quite pricey. ✉ *Aoraki/Mt. Cook Village* ☎ *03/435–1809 or 0800/686–800* ⊕ *www.mount-cook.com* ⤳ *212 rooms, 18 chalets, 32 motel units* ⌂ *In-room: No a/c (some). In-hotel: 2 restaurants, bar, tennis courts, spa, laundry facilities, Internet terminal* ▭ *AE, DC, MC, V* ⌾ *BP, CP.*

$$$ 🏨 **Lake View Homestay.** In addition to views of Lake Pukaki, you'll spy Aoraki/Mt. Cook and the Ben Ohau mountains through the floor-to-ceiling windows or from the porch. The peaks of the roofline mirror the toothy ranges beyond; timber walls inside are comforting. If you'd like to go fishing or take a helicopter trip, just say the word to your hosts. Breakfast is included. **Pros:** breathtaking location and views. **Cons:** half-hour drive to Mt. Cook. ✉ *Lake View, Private Bag 66010, Fairlie* ☎ *03/435–0567* ⊕ *www.lakeviewhomestay.co.nz* ⤳ *4 rooms, 3*

CLOSE UP

Safety in the High Country

The Fiordland region's remoteness and changeable weather make it necessary to take some sensible precautions. So, before you head out on that trek or boat trip, keep the following in mind:

Be sure to wear the right protective clothing: sturdy hiking boots, a waterproof jacket, and a warm layer such as a fleece or wool pullover. Weather in this region, especially at high altitude, can change dramatically in a short time.

Watch out for sunburn—take sunscreen and a hat with you. Also bring bug repellent for sand flies, which are impossible to avoid in this region unless you're traveling offshore by boat.

If you're heading off without a guide for more than an hour or two, let someone know where and when you're going and when you've returned. DOC visitor centers have sign-in books and issue regular weather and trail updates.

Use extreme caution when crossing rivers. Especially after rain, mountain runoff can quickly turn a gentle stream into an angry torrent, and drowning is a major hazard. If you do get trapped on one side of a quickly rising river, wait for the water to recede rather than risk crossing.

For longer treks into serious country always carry a map and compass, first-aid gear, bottled water, high-energy foods, warm clothes and tent, and a mountain radio or EPIRB (locator beacon—these can be rented locally). Cell phones don't work in the mountains.

with bath △ *In-room: No a/c, no TV. In-hotel: No kids under 12* ═ *No credit cards* ¦○¦ *BP, CP.*

¢ ⚠ **White Horse Hill Campground.** Although this DOC-managed campsite is really just a grassy basin surrounded by massive mountains and a rumbling glacier, its basic facilities and closeness to trails make it ideal to park a camper or pitch a tent in. Make sure those keas don't steal your lunch or rip the rubber parts off your cars! You can pay at the DOC Visitors Centre before setting up camp or in the honesty box down at the campsite. The running water needs to be boiled for three minutes before you drink it; you can grab a shower back at the Day Shelter in the village for $1. No reservations are taken; it's first-come, first-served. **Pros:** keas are amusing **Cons:** keas are destructive. ⊠ *Hooker Valley Rd., end of road* ☎ *03/435–1186* ⊕ *www.doc.govt.nz.*

TOURS

BOAT TOURS **Glacier Explorers** (⊠ *Aoraki/Mt. Cook Village* ☎ *03/435–1077* ⊕ *www. glacierexplorers.com*) leave from the Hermitage Hotel, the visitor center, or the Mt. Cook Youth Hostel Association (YHA) for guided boat trips on the Tasman Glacier Lake ($105). Tours run at 10 and 2, October–April, and last three hours.

10

TWIZEL

65 km (40 mi) from Lake Tekapo, 40 km (25 mi) from Aoraki/Mt. Cook.

A service town to its core, Twizel was built in 1968 as a base for workers constructing a major hydroelectric power plant. When the hydroelectric scheme wrapped up, the residents fought to keep their town intact. Now it's a handy place for tourist overflow in the Aoraki/Mt. Cook area. Birders should check with the visitor center about tours to the *kakī* aviary to see these striking, endangered, red-legged birds.

Twizel is close to five good-size boating and leisure lakes and has a great place to eat called Poppies. Having already passed Tekapo and Pukaki, you'll find Lake Ruataniwha a little tame. Lake Ohau is a little off the main road, but is another high-country fishing gem. A ski slope, Ohau Snow Fields, opens in July each winter, and a number of walks are in the nearby Ohau Forest Range.

GETTING HERE AND AROUND

Twizel is on State Highway 8. If you're driving south from Christchurch on Highway 1, turn onto Highway 8 at Fairlie. If you're coming north from Queenstown, follow Highway 6 to Cromwell, then turn onto Highway 8 and continue over the Lindis Pass to Twizel. InterCity Bus serves Twizel.

For area information stop by the **Twizel Information Centre** and the **Lake Pukaki Visitor Information Centre.**

ESSENTIALS

Bus Information InterCity Bus (☎ 3/443–7885 in Wanaka, 03/249–7559 in Te Anau, 03/442–8238 in Queenstown ⊕ www.intercitycoach.co.nz).

Visitor Information Twizel Information Centre (✉ 61 Mackenzie Dr. ☎ 03/435–3124 ⊕ www.twizel.com). **Lake Pukaki Visitor Information Centre** (✉ State Hwy. 8, Twizel ☎ 03/435–3280 ⊕ www.mtcook.org.nz).

WHERE TO EAT AND STAY

$$$ ✕ **Poppies Cafe.** This is the best place to eat in town. Meat, seafood, pizza, and pasta are complimented by organic produce from the garden, fresh-baked bread and pizza bases, homemade sausage, and a terrific wine list. On hot days Poppies opens up into a garden with long tables: it's a great place to eat, drink, socialize, and bask in the sun. Poppies serves breakfast, lunch, and dinner daily. ✉ *Benmore Pl.* ☎ *03/435–0848* ⊕ *www.poppiescafe.com* ▭ *AE, MC, V* ☺ *Open from 9* AM *weekdays and 8* AM *weekends.*

$$ ⌂ **MacKenzie Country Inn.** Its imposing stone-and-timber buildings make an impression in this otherwise nondescript town. Filled mainly by busloads of package tourists, its comfortable rooms and large lounges, complete with welcoming fires, are often full to capacity. All linens and beds are new as of 2009. Rooms range from deluxe to superior. **Pros:** reasonably priced. **Cons:** food isn't great—check out Poppies across the street. ✉ *Corner Ostler Rd. and Wairepo Rd.* ☎ *03/435–0869 or*

0800/500–869 ⊕ www.mackenzie.co.nz ⤴ 28 deluxe and 80 superior rooms � In-hotel: Restaurant, bar ▤ AE, DC, MC, V.

$$$$ ⊡ **Matuka Lodge.** This lodge is ideal for anyone wanting to enjoy the hikes and activities of the Mt. Cook area, and is particularly nice for fly fishermen. You can arrange for a guide to the nearby rivers to go after rainbow and brown trout. Each room has a veranda with mountain views. The less expensive rate is a room with a shower and no bathtub. Your room rate includes breakfast and predinner drink. **Pros:** endearing hosts. **Cons:** 40-minute drive to Mt. Cook. ✉ *395 Glen Lyon Rd.* ☎ *03/435–0144* ⊕ *www.matukalodge.co.nz* ⤴ *4 suites* ᗢ *In-room: No TV. In-hotel: Internet terminal, no kids under 12* ▤ *AE, DC, MC, V* ⦿ *MAP.*

MT. ASPIRING NATIONAL PARK

GETTING HERE AND AROUND

Gateway communities to the park are Wanaka, Glenorchy, Queenstown and Te Anau. These towns are all served by bus companies, and you can fly into Wanaka, Queenstown, and Te Anau. Major thoroughfares lead to them and driving to any of these locations is a treat—the scenery in this part of the country is dramatic and roadside attractions include gorgeous vineyards, fresh fruit stands, mountain passes, white-water rivers, and if you're en route to Wanaka from Queenstown you can stop and bungy jump!

For maps, information on local walks, and information on the three campgrounds and 20 backcountry huts in the park, contact the DOC. Many tours to the park leave from Waneka. ⇨ *See Tours in Waneka, below, for more details.*

ESSENTIALS

Hospital Contact Lakes District Hospital (✉ *20 Douglas St., Frankton* ☎ *03/441–0015 or 111*).

Visitor Information Department of Conservation (✉ *Ardmore St.* ☎ *03/477–0677*).

SPORTS AND THE OUTDOORS

★ **Siberia Experience** (☎ *0800/345–666* ⊕ *www.siberiaexperience.co.nz*) has one of the best adventure packages. For $280, the journey begins with a funky little yellow plane in a paddock-cum-airstrip. After a breathtaking 25-minute journey from Makarora, the pilot drops you off in the pristine wilderness of Mt. Aspiring National Park's Siberia Valley, and points you to a trailhead. From there, embark on a magnificent three-hour hike on a well-marked, relatively easy trail. Finally, a jet-boat meets you at the Wilkin River and returns you to Makarora. There is a hut out there if you'd like to arrange overnight stays. **Wild Walks** (☎ *03/443–4476* ⊕ *www.wildwalks.co.nz*) also leads treks through Mt. Aspiring National Park, including Rabbit Pass, considered one of the most strenuous trails in the country.

10

WANAKA

70 km (44 mi) northeast of Queenstown, 140 km (87 mi) southwest of Twizel.

On the southern shore of Lake Wanaka, with some of New Zealand's most striking mountains behind it, Wanaka is the welcome mat for Mt. Aspiring National Park. It's a favorite of Kiwis on vacation, an alternative of sorts to Queenstown. The region has numerous trekking and river-sports opportunities, and if you arrive on a rainy day, you can hit a couple of unusual cultural attractions. These good points have not gone unnoticed, and Wanaka is one of the fastest-growing towns in New Zealand, with new housing popping up in record time.

Up in the Crown Range, the Snow Park in the Cardrona Valley is the country's only dedicated snowboard park. The 60-acre property has more than 30 rails and kickers, a super-pipe, a half-pipe, and a quarter-pipe as well as a bar and restaurant. In summer it becomes the Dirt Park and is a hot spot for mountain bike enthusiasts.

GETTING HERE AND AROUND

If you're coming from Queenstown you have two choices for getting to Wanaka: go over the Crown Range for stunning views (not recommended in snow) or take the winding road along the Kawarau River through wine and fruit country. From Christchurch, drive south through Geraldine and Twizel. Once in Wanaka it's easy to park and walk around town, and a taxi service can get you back to your accommodations if you take advantage of the nightlife. A short but pleasant drive to the western side of the lake brings you to Glendhu Bay. With nothing here but a campground and fabulous mountain and lake views, the real beauty in this drive lies in the unspoiled calm and surreal quiet (except in mid-summer, when it is packed full of vacationing locals). This road also leads to the Aspiring region and the Treble Cone ski area. Several bus companies serve Wanaka, and Air New Zealand flies into Wanaka Airport.

ESSENTIALS

Bus Companies InterCity (☎ 03/443–7885 in Wanaka, 03/249–7559 in Te Anau, 03/442–8238 in Queenstown ⊕ www.intercitycoach.co.nz). **Wanaka Connexions** (☎ 03/443–9122 ⊕ www.time2.co.nz/transport/wanaka_connexions).

Bus Depot Wanaka (✉ Edgewater Adventures, 59a Brownston St.).

Internet Café Bits N Bytes (✉ 46 Helwick St., Wanaka ☎ 03/443–7078).

Mail Wanaka (✉ 39 Ardmore St. ☎ 03/443–8211).

Visitor Information Wanaka Visitor Information Centre (✉ The Log Cabin, Ardmore St. ☎ 03/443–1233).

EXPLORING

Lying spectacularly by the shores of Lake Wanaka, **Rippon Vineyard** is one of the most photographed in the country. The vineyard's portfolio includes sparkling wine, riesling, gewürztraminer, chardonnay, sauvignon blanc, and fine (but expensive) pinot noir. There is a nine-hole

10

golfcross (goals rather than holes and an oval ball) course here, and you're welcome to rent clubs and play while sipping wine with your friends. Every other year, it's the venue for the Rippon Open Air Festival, one of the country's most popular music festivals. Head west from Wanaka along the lake on Mt. Aspiring Road for 4 km (2½ mi). ⊠ *246 Mt. Aspiring Rd.* ☎ *03/443–8084* ⊕ *www.rippon.co.nz* ⊘ *Dec.–Apr., daily 11–5; July–Nov., daily 1:30–4:30.*

On your way into town on State Highway 6, you'll pass the **New Zealand Fighter Pilots Museum**. The museum is a tribute to New Zealand fighter pilots. The collection of planes includes aircraft used during the two world wars, such as the British Spitfire and rarities like the Russian Polikarpov I–16. Check out the biennial international air show Warbirds over Wanaka, where you can see some of these magnificent aircraft in flight. ⊠ *State Hwy. 6* ☎ *03/443–7010* ⊕ *www. nzfpm.co.nz* ⊠ *$8* ⊘ *Daily 9–4.*

Ⓒ **Stuart Landsborough's Puzzling World** showcases a number of puzzling life-size brainteasers, including the amazing Tumbling Towers and the Tilted House, which is on a 15-degree angle (is the water really running uphill?), as well as the Leaning Tower of Wanaka. But the place to really take your time is the popular Puzzle Centre. Just take on the puzzle of your choice, order a cup of coffee, and work yourself into a puzzled frenzy. The place is 2 km (1 mi) east of town—just look for the cartoonlike houses built at funny angles. ⊠ *Hwy. 84* ☎ *03/443–7489* ⊕ *www.puzzlingworld.co.nz* ⊠ *$12.50* ⊘ *Nov.–Apr., daily 8:30–5:30; May–Oct., daily 8:30–5.*

Ⓒ Pretend you're Tiger Woods or Robin Hood at **Have a Shot**. At this excellent rainy-day facility you can have a hand at clay bird shooting, archery, or rifle shooting, or get a basket of golf balls and chip away. Prices start at $4 and there's an activity for everyone. ⊠ *Mt. Barker Rd. opposite Wanaka Airport* ☎ *03/443–6656* ⊕ *www.haveashot.co.nz* ⊘ *Daily 9–5:30.*

SPORTS AND THE OUTDOORS

BICYCLING   Rent a bicycle and explore along the shores of Lake Wanaka, and out along the Clutha River toward Albert Town. There are many places to rent bikes including Good Sports or Thunderbikes, for hard-core mountain bikes. For three weeks in January, Treble Cone (⊕ *www.treblecone. co.nz*) opens intermediate and expert trails to mountain bikers. The Sticky Forest and Dirt Park NZ (the Snow Park in winter) both have a network of trails for mountain biking. Treble Cone and Dirt Park provide a joint 10-day pass.

CANYONING   With the steep rugged waterways of the Matukituki and Wilkin valleys within easy reach, Wanaka is a key spot in the country for canyoning. **Deep Canyon** leads expeditions down the Niger Stream, Wai Rata Canyon, and the Leaping Burn; trips start at $215 for a full day. ☎ *03/443–7922* ⊕ *www.deepcanyon.co.nz* ⊘ *Nov.–Mar. or Apr.*

FISHING   Locals will tell you that fishing on Lake Wanaka and nearby Lake Hawea is better than at the more famed Taupo area. You won't want to enter that argument, but chances are good you'll catch fish if you have the right guide. Fishing is year-round. **Gerald Telford**

(☎ 03/443–9257 ⊕ www.flyfishhunt.co.nz) will take you fly-fishing, including night-fishing and multiday Otago–Southland fishing expeditions. **Harry Urquhart** (☎ 03/443–1535) has trolling excursions for rainbow trout, brown trout, and quinnat salmon on Lake Hawea. Craig Smith at **Hatch Fishing** (☎ 03/443–8446 ⊕ www.hatchfishing. co.nz) is a superb guide and a really nice bloke who runs several fishing packages. **Wanaka Fly Fishing** (☎ 03/443–9072 ⊕ www.fly-fishing-guide-wanaka-new-zealand.co.nz) provides instruction, guided trips, and wilderness fishing safaris, including a heli-fishing option. If you're not keen on hiring a guide, you can rent fly fishing gear at **Wanaka Sports** at 8 Helwick Street or **Lakeland Adventures** in the Log Cabin on Ardmore Street.

RAFTING AND KAYAKING

Exploring this stunning region's rivers with **Alpine Kayak Guides'** (✉ 70 Main Rd., Luggate ☎ 03/443–9023 ⊕ www.alpinekayaks.co.nz) Geoff Deacon is a must while in Wanaka. This company caters to smaller groups, which means a lot of attention for beginners. You'll learn how to glide into a calm eddy, to wave surf, and to safely charge down the center of the white water. You *will* spill, and for this reason all your gear, right down to the polypropylene underwear, is provided. The full-day trip costs $200 per person and a half day is $125. If you're looking for something mellower, sign up for the half-day "relaxed" float, which is rapids-free ($75).

At **Pioneer Rafting** (☎ 03/443–1246 or 027/295–0418) you can finally do some white-water rafting at a calm pace. Lewis Verduyn is New Zealand's leading eco-rafting specialist. His highly informative eco-rafting adventure, suitable for most ages, retraces a historic pioneer log-raft route. Both full-day ($165) and half-day ($115) trips are available, and leave from the Visitor Information Centre in Wanaka.

SCENIC FLIGHTS

The weather around Wanaka is clear much of the time, which has allowed it to become a scenic-flight base for fixed-wing planes and helicopters. Flights take in Mt. Cook and the West Coast glaciers, the Mt. Aspiring area, Queenstown, and Fiordland. **Alpine Helicopters** (☎ 03/443–4000 ⊕ www.alpineheli.co.nz) has heli-skiing options in season, as well as heli-fishing excursions in Fiordland. **Aspiring Helicopters** (☎ 03/443–1454 or 027/432–3121 ⊕ www.aspiringhelicopters.co.nz) does trips ranging from a 25-minute local flight for $155 to a half-day trip to Milford Sound, where you join a boat cruise on the fjord before heading back to Wanaka (from $770). A Mt. Aspiring trip lands on the ski slopes (for $375 per person). **Wanaka Flightseeing** (✉ Wanaka Airport ☎ 03/443–8787 or 0800/105–105 ⊕ www.flightseeing.co.nz) runs small Cessna aircraft to all the hot spots.

SKIING

With reliable snow and dry powder, Wanaka has some of the best skiing and snowboarding in New Zealand. Cardrona and Treble Cone are the two biggest winter-sports resorts. For more information about skiing and snowboarding in the area, check out ⊕ www.skilakewanaka. com. **Cardrona** (☎ 03/443–7341 ⊕ www.cardrona.com), 34 km (21 mi) southwest of Wanaka, has a kids' ski school and activity center, plus three kid- and beginner-friendly "Magic Carpet" lifts, and five food outlets. A special "heavy metal" trail pours on the rails and jumps.

10

Two quad chairlifts and a detachable high-speed lift are available. The season is roughly June–October, and a day's lift pass costs $85. A bonus at Cardrona is the 12 apartments up on the mountain (rates range from $180 to $475 a night).

Treble Cone (☎ *03/443–7443* ⊕ *www.treblecone.com*), 19 km (11½ mi) west of Wanaka, is the South Island's largest ski area, with lots of advanced trails and off-piste skiing. A quad lift and expanded trails have just been completed. A day's lift pass costs $99. For snowboarders, the **Snow Park** (⊠ *Cardrona Valley, 20 km [12 mi] southwest of Wanaka* ☎ *03/443–9991* ⊕ *www.snowparknz.com*) supplies a huge selection of rails, jumps, pipes, and terrain features.

WALKING AND TREKKING
The Mt. Aspiring National Park provides serious hiking and mountaineering opportunities, including Wilkins Valley, Makarora River, and Mt. Aspiring tracks and trails. The complete **Diamond Lake Track** takes three hours and starts 25 km (15½ mi) west of Wanaka, also on the Glendhu Bay–Mt. Aspiring road. The track rises to 2,518 feet at Rocky Peak, passing Diamond Lake along the way. If you've got time for only a short walk, take the one that heads to the lake; it takes only 20 minutes. The Diamond Lake area is also popular with mountain bikers and rock climbers. You get maximum views for minimal challenge on one of the prettiest local trails, which meanders along the Clutha River from the **Lake Wanaka Outlet** to Albert Town. This is a kid-friendly route, and also fly-fisherman-, bicyclist-, and picnicker-friendly. If you have time for only one walk, **Mt. Iron**, rising 780 feet above the lake, is relatively short and rewarding. The access track begins 2 km (1 mi) from Wanaka, and the walk to the top takes 45 minutes. You can descend on the alternative route down the steep eastern face.

WHERE TO EAT

$–$$
NEW ZEALAND
✕ **Ardmore Street Food Company.** The owners of this fully licensed café have a breakfast menu as sophisticated and extensive as their dinner menu: try the salmon-and-kūmara cakes with wasabi hollandaise, or the Green Eggs and Ham (with pesto). Plenty of Kiwi flavors infuse selections like green-lipped mussels with manuka honey, and duck confit with roasted tamarillo, and not many places serve *rewana* (Māori bread) filled with chicken livers! This place is busy, lively, and warm. Visit the on-site deli and bakery, which have perfect ski-day take-out like breakfast wraps and spiced omelet sandwiches. ⊠ *155 Ardmore St., beneath Speight's Ale House, on lakefront* ☎ *03/443–2230* ▭ *MC, V.*

¢–$
CAFÉ
✕ **Hammer & Nail.** "Someone must have been in a really good mood when they made this." So a consumer once described a generously cream-filled donut from this popular bakery. Regardless the mood of the kitchen staff, customers are happy enough to regularly flock to Hammer & Nail for breakfast goodies, coffee, and lunch. There's indoor and patio seating, but if you prefer Lake Wanaka to Mitre 10 for views, take your sandwich or square of perfect bacon-egg pie down the hill. ⊠ *3 Cliff Wilson St., opposite Mitre 10 Garden Centre* ☎ *03/443–8500* ▭ *AE, DC, MC, V* ☺ *Closed Sun. No dinner.*

$$–$$$ ✕ **Kai Whaka Pai.** There's no better place to stop for breakfast on a crisp
ECLECTIC sunny morning than this café, which has more tables outside than in.
It's just across the road from the lake, so the views range from pretty
nice on a cloudy day to fantastic on a fine one. Meanwhile, the menu
ranges from simple breakfast and lunch choices (coffee and croissants,
salads, nachos, and kebabs), to beef ribs or rump roast for dinner.
In addition to consistently good meals, "The Kai" has local beers on
tap, fresh bread, and banana cream pies. ⊠ *Helwick and Ardmore Sts.*
☎ *03/443–7795* ⊟ *AE, DC, MC, V.*

$$$–$$$$ ✕ **Missy's Kitchen.** A local favorite, Missy's pulls in a ski crowd to its
NEW ZEALAND bar and its dining room. They've got a fun cocktail list including a
Kiwi Lush, and dozens of beers and wines. In summer the balcony is a
favored spot for dinner or for a glass of wine, and a fireplace warms din-
ers in winter. If the Lake Wanaka view has you thinking of shellfish, lap
up some Marlborough mussels flavored with lemongrass, lime, and chili
jam. You can also try the rib-eye steak or the escalope of salmon and
choose from a list of yummy desserts. The venison is excellent. ⊠ *Ard-
more St. and Lakefront Dr.* ☎ *03/443–5099* ⊕ *www.missyskitchen.com*
⊟ *AE, DC, MC, V* ⊗ *No lunch.*

$–$$ ✕ **Relishes Cafe.** You could hit this lakeside spot for every meal of the
NEW ZEALAND day, starting with breakfast—perhaps some homemade muesli with a
side of toast and jam (or Vegemite for homesick Aussies), or the bacon
or salmon eggs Benedict. At lunch and dinner, you'll find ever-changing
blackboard specials and good service. ⊠ *99 Ardmore St.* ☎ *03/443–
9018* ⊟ *AE, DC, MC, V* ⊗ *Closed 1 wk in June.*

$$ ✕ **Thai Siam.** Directly under Missy's Kitchen, this Thai restaurant has
THAI interesting alternatives if you prefer a vegetarian cuisine—although they
also run the full range of local salmon, steak, and Nelson Bay scallops.
Using Thai methods, they incorporate South Island vegetables into their
dishes. ⊠ *Ardmore St. and Lakefront Dr.* ☎ *03/443–5010* ⊟ *AE, DC,
MC, V* ⊗ *No lunch.*

WHERE TO STAY

$$ 🏨 **Cardrona Hotel.** The recipe for their famous mulled wine is a secret,
★ but the ingredients that make this place so special are evident. This clas-
sic old country hotel and pub, 20 minutes from Wanaka on the Crown
Range Road, is the Cardrona après-ski spot for mulled wine in front
of the outdoor fireplace. Another fireplace roars inside the spacious bar
and restaurant. In the summertime, the outdoor beer garden is a great
place to relax after a day spent in Wanaka. The hotel was pictured in
a well-known Speight's ad depicting hundreds of sheep "parked" outside the pub. **Pros:** stay in a genuinely historic property. **Cons:** historic
properties mean squeaky floorboards and hinges. ⊠ *9 Lakeside Rd.*
☎ *03/443–8153* ⊕ *www.cardronahotel.co.nz* ⤶ *16 rooms* ⌂ *In-hotel:
Pool, spa* ⊟ *AE, MC, V.*

$$ 🏨 **Lake Hawea Station.** Since 1912, the Rowley family has run this vast
working sheep station which comprises 28,000 acres from lake level to
5,000 feet and has more than 10,000 merino sheep! Choose between
two historic musterer cottages: the Packhorse Cottage or the Homespur
Cottage. The cottages have modern amenities (kitchen facilities) and
rustic character (patchwork quilts). The Homespur is heated with a

10

cozy woodstove, and the Packhorse has a gas heater. Both have decks with views of the mountains and lake. Go fishing in the lake, or explore the splendid homestead garden. **Pros:** uncommonly friendly hosts; outstanding location. **Cons:** real working farm means barking dogs real early. ⊠ *20 min north of Wanaka, 22 Timaru River Rd., Lake Hawea* 🕾 *03/443–1744* ⊕ *www.lakehaweastation.co.nz* ⤳ *2 units* ⚃ *In-room: Kitchen* ▭ *No credit cards* ❍| *CP.*

$$$$ 🏠 **Minaret Lodge.** A 10-minute walk from town, this five-star luxury retreat has eco-friendly accommodations, from the natural materials used in the rooms to organic coffee and cuisine. It's also hobbit-friendly: they have a themed *Lord of the Rings* room. The rooms have mountain views and are surrounded by trees and gardens, and facilities include tennis court, pétanque, mountain bikes, spa, and sauna. Rates include elegant breakfast, regional wine tastings and hors d'oeuvres; you can also arrange for dinner. **Pros:** stay in a hobbit room and dine from a hobbit menu. **Cons:** you'll gain weight from your hosts' delicious cooking. ⊠ *34 Eely Point Rd.* 🕾 *03/443–1856* ⊕ *www. minaretlodge.co.nz* ⤳ *5 rooms* ⚃ *In-room: Refrigerator, Internet. In-hotel: Bar, tennis court, bicycles, no kids under 10, no-smoking rooms* ▭ *AE, MC, V* ❍| *BP.*

$$$–$$$$ 🏠 **Mountain Range Lodge.** Travelers hell-bent on a lake view in Wanaka might stay at a property half as luxurious as this and for twice the coin. Hosts Erica and Chris have thought of everything here to make their guests feel pampered, relaxed, and happy. Amenities include ski storage, a library, complimentary predinner drinks and fresh baked goodies, hammock, hot tub, DVDs, a computer and free Wi-Fi, and more. The luxurious rooms open out onto a native garden and mountain views easily make up for the lack of lake views. **Pros:** one of the nicest B&Bs in the area; reasonable rate. **Cons:** you'll need a vehicle to get to town. ⊠ *Heritage Park, Cardrona Valley Rd. (2 km [1 mi] from Wanaka)* 🕾 *03/443–7400* ⊕ *www.mountainrange.co.nz* ⤳ *7 rooms* ⚃ *In-room: DVD, Wi-Fi In-hotel: Restaurant, bar* ▭ *MC, V* ❍| *CP, BP*

$$–$$$ 🏠 **Oakridge Pool & Spa Resort.** With its refreshing contemporary design, this rather expansive resort is a departure from the usual alpine stone-and-timber lodgings in the region. Oakridge looks across an open valley to the peaks of Aspiring National Park. Four heated swimming pools and a series of warm spas are in a rock-lined amphitheater, overlooked by the resort restaurant. Enjoy a glass of local wine while soaking in the spa after a day on the road. **Pros:** the warm outdoor spas and pools. **Cons:** in the busy season the pools are sometimes swamped with kids. ⊠ *Cardrona Valley Rd. at Studholme Rd.* 🕾 *03/443–7707 or 0800/869–262* ⊕ *www.oakridge.co.nz* ⤳ *46 rooms, 19 studios, 27 1- and 2-bedroom apartments* ⚃ *In-room: DVD In-hotel: Restaurant, bar, 4 pools, spa, laundry facilities* ▭ *AE, DC, MC, V.*

¢–$ 🏠 **Purple Cow Backpackers.** Shoot pool with a view of the mountains and lake. This is the best-known and most well-liked backpackers in town. The Purple Cow, not to be mistaken with the Cow, a pizza joint on Post Office Lane, is within walking distance of shops and stumbling distance from the bars. While the cost of a bed is relatively cheap, frills are extra: towels, duvets, and bicycles are for rent. And be sure you have an extra pocketful of "shrapnel" as the laundry, Internet, and barbecue are all coin-operated. **Pros:** best location; well run. **Cons:** you'll get nickel-and-dimed for extras. ✉ *94 Brownston St.* ☎ *03/443–8153* ⊕ *www.purplecow.co.nz* ⌂ *In-hotel: Laundry facilities* ☐ *AE, DC, MC, V.*

$$$ 🏠 **Renmore House.** This cheerful B&B has trellises of flowers at its entrance and the spring-fed Bullock Creek burbling by the back door. Hosts Rosie and Blair understand the traveler's desire to eat in sometimes, so they have provided a kitchenette and a barbecue area in the garden. Afternoon tea and predinner drinks are complimentary; ditto your hosts' extensive knowledge of the area. Bicycles, maps, and a "wee library" are on hand. **Pros:** hosts are quite friendly; the place is clean and cheerful. **Cons:** located on a nondescript residential street. ✉ *44 Upton St.* ☎ *03/443–6566* ⊕ *www.renmore-house.co.nz* ⇗ *3 rooms* ⌂ *In-room: Wi-Fi In-hotel: bicycles, laundry facilities* ☐ *MC, V* ⦿ *BP.*

NIGHTLIFE

Woodys Pool Bar (✉ *Post Office La.* ☎ *03/443–5551*) sees a local crowd shooting pool and watching rugby. **Barluga** (✉ *Post Office La.* ☎ *03/443–5400*) is a bit sophisticated with leather sofas and a fine wine list.

Red Rock (✉ *68 Ardmore St.* ☎ *03/443–5545*), crosses the line from cozy to crowded some nights. Serious Guinness drinkers lurk at **Scruffy Murphy's** (✉ *21 Dunmore St., across from New World* ☎ *03/443–7645*), and a plaque on the wall lists drinkers in the hundred-pints club.

Speight's Ale House (✉ *155 Ardmore St.* ☎ *03/443–2920*) is always buzzing; head upstairs to the **Bar** for a game of pool. The **Pa Runga Wine Bar** (✉ *Ardmore St. at Helwick St.* ☎ *03/443–7795*) comes alive at sunset. Bar meals are available, and there's a lounge bar, a nice cozy fire, and a balcony overlooking the lake.

If you've worked up an appetite dancing with twentysomething backpackers at **Shooters** (✉ *145 Ardmore St.* ☎ *03/443–4345*), stop by the Doughbin, open until all hours, for a tasty meat pie. ■ TIP→ Bar staff will call a cab for you, but if it's a hopping night in town, it can be a drama getting a taxi to pick you up along the main drag, so ask the cab to meet you a block inland from the busy lakefront area.

10

★ The local institution **Cinema Paradiso** (✉ *1 Ardmore St.* ☎ *03/443–1505* ⊕ *www.paradiso.net.nz*) is not your usual movie house—its seating includes couches, recliners, pillows, and even a yellow Morris Minor car. During intermission you can snack on homemade ice cream and warm cookies or have dinner with a glass of wine.

QUEENSTOWN

Fodor's Choice ★ *103 km (64 mi) southeast of Wanaka, 480 km (300 mi) southwest of Christchurch.*

Set on the edge of the glacial Lake Wakatipu, with stunning views of the sawtooth peaks of the Remarkables mountain range, Queenstown is the most popular tourist stop in the South Island. Once prized by the Māori as a source of greenstone, the town boomed when gold was discovered in the Shotover River during the 1860s; the Shotover quickly became famous as "the richest river in the world." By the 1950s

Queenstown had become the center of a substantial farming area, and with ready access to mountains, lakes, and rivers, the town has since become the adventure capital of New Zealand. Today, New Zealanders' penchant for bizarre adventure sports culminates in Queenstown; it was here that the sport of leaping off a bridge with a giant rubber band wrapped around the ankles—bungy jumping—took root as a commercial enterprise.

If you're not an extreme adventure enthusiast, you might recoil a bit and view the city with a cynical eye. Luckily there's a side to Queenstown that doesn't run on pure adrenaline: find a nice café, have wine by the lake, and sample the cuisine.

GETTING HERE AND AROUND

Highway 6 enters Queenstown from the West Coast; driving time for the 400-km (250-mi) journey from Franz Josef is eight hours. It takes approximately an hour and a half to drive between Queenstown and Wanaka; the drive between Queenstown and Te Anau generally lasts a little over two hours. Bus and airplane service are also available between Christchurch and Queenstown. The city is small and fun for seeing on foot. If you're out and about at night there are several taxi services available.

ESSENTIALS

Airport Queenstown Airport (✉ *Frankton Rd., Queenstown* ☎ *03/442–2670* ⊕ *www.queenstownairport.co.nz*).

Airport Transfers Super Shuttle Queenstown (☎ *03/442–3639 or 0800/748–8853*).

Bus Companies InterCity (☎ *03/443–7885 in Wanaka, 03/249–7559 in Te Anau, 03/442–8238 in Queenstown* ⊕ *www.intercitycoach.co.nz*). **Newmans** (☎ *09/913–6188 or 0508/353–947* ⊕ *www.newmanscoach.co.nz*).

Bus Depot Queenstown (✉ *Athol St.*).

Medical Assistance Queenstown Medical Centre (✉ *9 Isle St.* ☎ *03/441–0500*). **Wilkinson's Pharmacy** (✉ *The Mall at Rees St., Queenstown* ☎ *03/442–7313*).

Rental Cars Apex (✉ *Terminal Bldg., Queenstown Airport* ☎ *03/442–8040 or 0800/531–111*). **Avis** (✉ *Terminal Bldg., Queenstown Airport* ☎ *03/442–7280*).

Visitor Information Queenstown Visitor Information Centre (✉ *Clocktower Centre, Shotover St. at Camp St.* ☎ *03/442–4100 or 0800/668–888* ⊕ *www.queenstown-nz.co.nz* ☉ *Daily 7–7*).

EXPLORING

Get the lay of the land by taking the **Skyline Gondola** up to the heights of Bob's Peak, 1,425 feet above the lake, for a smashing panoramic view of the town and the Remarkables. You can also walk to the top on the **One Mile Creek Trail** and watch the paragliders jump off the summit for their slow cruise back down to lake level. There are restaurants at the summit, plus a *haka, or* Māori song and dance, show in the evening. For something a little faster, there's a luge ride, weather permitting. If even that isn't exciting enough, you can bungy

Outdoor diners along Queenstown's main drag enjoy views of Lake Wakatipu and the Remarkable mountains.

jump from the summit terminal (⇨ *AJ Hackett Bungy in Sports and the Outdoors, below*). ⊠ *Brecon St.* ☎ *03/441–0101* ⊕ *www.skyline. co.nz* 🚡 *Gondola $19, $26 for gondola and basic luge package* ⏱ *Daily 9* AM–*9:30* PM.

⏱ The steamship T.S.S. *Earnslaw* runs across Lake Wakatipu to Walter Peak Station on a 1½-hour cruise. Additional options allow a stopover for several hours at **Walter Peak High Country Farm** to see how a high-country sheep station works, and to enjoy a good farmhouse morning or afternoon tea. The steamship boilers are still stoked by hand, and the steam engines chuff noisily away just as they did 90 years ago. On the ride back to Queenstown, folks gather around the piano and sing old standards. ⊠ *Steamer Wharf* ☎ *03/442–7500 or 0800/656–503* ⊕ *www. realjourneys.co.nz* 🚢 *$40 cruise, $60 with farm visit.*

One of the enduring attractions in the area is the drive up **Skippers Canyon.** Harking back to the days when the hills were filled with gold diggers, the Skippers Road was hand carved out of rock, and it reaches into the deep recesses of the Shotover Valley. It's breathtakingly gorgeous but you could also be breathtakingly scared: if you're not confident about navigating a twisty, narrow, unsealed road fraught with slips and vertical drops, we suggest you take a tour. **Nomad Safaris** (☎ *03/442–6699 or 0800/688–222* ⊕ *www.queenstown4wd. com*) runs two trips a day up the Skippers Canyon in specialized 4WD vehicles. **Queenstown Heritage Tours** (☎ *03/442–5949* ⊕ *www. queenstown-holiday.co.nz*) gives historical tours with the comforts of air-conditioned vehicles, delicious snacks, and local wines.

☼ Some of the best views of the town, lake, and mountains are from the **Deer Park**. Not only will you have outstanding views, some of which you may recognize from the *Lord of the Rings* films, but you'll also find yourself an object of attention from the resident creatures, which include thars (goatlike animals), goats, bison, and llamas. The animals are used to being fed by people, so they're not skittish. Keep your car window rolled down if you want to find out what bison breath is like. Bring some $1 coins for the food dispensers and wear something you won't mind getting nuzzled. ⊠ *Peninsula Rd.* ☎ *0800/843-333* ⊕ *www.thedeerpark.co.nz* ⊠ *$20 self-drive tour, $59 guided tour* ☉ *Daily 9–dark.*

WINERIES

The vineyards across Central Otago and into the Queenstown and Wanaka areas constitute the world's southernmost wine region. Specifically, Bannockburn, Gibbston Valley, and Lowburn are home to big plantings. More than 75 wineries are in the region. The 177 local vineyards have 2,250 acres in production, producing more than 3,500 tons of grapes each year. The predominant variety is pinot noir. Each year, in February, the region showcases its prowess at the **Central Otago Wine & Food Festival** (⊕ *www.winetastes.com*) held in the Queenstown Gardens down by the lake. Check the Web site for details and ticket sales.

Wine Tastes provides a winery tour with no driving! Purchase a wine card, peruse 84 tasting machines featuring New Zealand wines, insert the card into your chosen machine, and voilà, the machine debits your card and squirts a taste into your glass. You can buy any value card you like; $10 buys 6–10 tastes. If Woody Allen had imagined the future of wine tasting, this might be it. ⊠ *14 Beach St.* ☎ *03/409–2226* ⊕ *www. winetastes.com* ☉ *Daily 10–10.*

Amisfield Winery & Bistro is the latest hot-shot winery to join the Queenstown scene. Both the wines and the restaurant, which serves French Basque cuisine, have earned a strong reputation. The restaurant, in a huge stone-and-timber building with a sunny courtyard and reflection pool, opens for early dinners as well as lunch, although it closes around 8 PM. Pinot noir, aromatic whites such as riesling and pinot grigio, and the methode traditionelle are all worth sampling. ⊠ *10 Lake Hayes Rd.* ☎ *03/442–0556* ⊕ *www.amisfield.co.nz* ☉ *Bistro closed Mon.*

Aurum Wines Pinot Noir won the gold last year in the New Zealand International Wine Show, and was a finalist in the Winestate Magazine Wine of the Year Awards. Aurum's wine labels feature the paintings of Central Otago artist Neil Driver, and the tasting room serves as a gallery for his work. Stop in the shop and buy some Aurum cold-pressed olives while you're there. ⊠ *Rapid 140 State Hwy. 6, Cromwell* ☎ *03/445–3620* ⊕ *www.aurumwines.co.nz* ☉ *Open daily 10–5 (less in winter).*

Spoil yourself and have lunch at **Carrick Wines** where the views of the mountains and Lake Dunstan are as satisfying as the cuisine. The pinot noir has been described as "archetypal Central Otago Pinot," which is a high compliment considering the caliber of the region's reds. ⊠ *247*

Cairnmuir Rd., Bannockburn ☎ *03/445–3480* ⊕ *www.carrick.co.nz* ⊙ *Daily 11–5, from noon for lunch.*

At **Gibbston Valley Wines,** the best-known vineyard in central Otago, you can taste wines in a cool, barrel-lined cave. The showcase wine is pinot noir, but you can sip rieslings and a pinot grigio as well. At the cheesery, you can watch sheep's-milk and goat's-milk cheeses being made. ⊠ *State Hwy. 6, Gibbston* ✛ *20-min drive east of Queenstown on State Hwy. 6* ☎ *03/442–6910* ⊕ *www.gvwines.co.nz* 🍷 *Wine-cave tour and tasting $9.50, less for larger groups* ⊙ *Tasting room daily 10–5, cave tours on the hr daily 10–4, restaurant daily noon–3.*

An architectural standout in the Gibbston Valley, **Peregrine** winery has been designed to look like a falcon's wing. Uplifting musical shows have paired their award-winning pinots with musicians such as Jose Gonzalez and Kiwi greats Dave Dobbyn and Hollie Smith. Call or check the Web site for upcoming events. ⊠ *Kawarau Gorge Rd.* ☎ *03/442–4000* ⊕ *www.peregrinewines.co.nz.*

SPORTS AND THE OUTDOORS

BUNGY JUMPING **AJ Hackett Bungy,** the pioneer in the sport, runs a variety of jumps in the area. Kawarau Bridge is the original jump site, 23 km (14 mi) from Queenstown on State Highway 6 and leads a "Secrets of Bungy" tour in the Kawarau Bungy Centre, an interactive guided tour designed for those who are fascinated by bungy but just can't face the leap. Daredevils who graduate from the 142-foot plunge might like to test themselves on the 230-foot Skippers Canyon Bridge. Top that with the Nevis Highwire Bungy, suspended 440 feet above the Nevis River. If you're short on time, head to the Ledge Urban Bungy and Ledge Urban Sky Swing, the jumping point by the Skyline Gondola; from April through September you can jump or swing by moonlight. Prices start at $165 for the Kawarau or Ledge jump, $240 for Nevis Highwire Bungy (all three include a T-shirt), and $120 for the Ledge Sky Swing. Extra fees apply for DVDs of your exploits. Be sure to check the age, height, and weight requirements. Hours vary seasonally. ⊠ *The Station, Camp and Shotover Sts.* ☎ *03/442–4007 or 0800/286–495* ⊕ *www.ajhackett.com.*

For those who think bungy jumping doesn't keep the adrenaline pumping long enough, the **Shotover Canyon Swing** gives a terrifying jump with an added scenic boost. Choose your jump style—go forwards, backwards, or tied to a chair—and leave the edge of a cliff 109 meters (358 feet) above the Shotover Canyon. It's $179 for your first jump and $39 for an additional one; DVDs and photos are available. Age, height, and weight requirements apply. ☎ *03/441–3579, 03/442–6990 bookings* ⊕ *www.canyonswing.co.nz.*

Jumping off a mountain isn't everyone's idea of fun, but paragliding is a fantastic way to see Queenstown. These huge sails swoop down over the town like pterodactyls, whirling out over the lake and back in to a gentle landing in a nearby park. **Paraglide** leads jumps from the peak above the top of the gondola every day that weather permits. ☎ *03/441–8581 or 0800/759–688* ⊕ *www.paraglide.co.nz.*

10

HIKING   Several scenic walks branch out from town. For a history lesson with your ramble, head to the **Time Walk**, entering through an iron gateway on the Queenstown Hill trail. Narrative panels line the route; it takes about two hours. The **Ben Lomond Track** takes you to one of the highest peaks in the basin. Take the gondola to the summit, then follow signs to the saddle and the steep climb to the peak (5,730 feet). This can be a full-day walk, so make sure you bring all the necessary supplies.

HORSE TREKKING   **Moonlight Stables** has a choice of full- or half-day rides with spectacular views of the mountains and rivers around the Wakatipu–Arrow Basin. Ride across its 800-acre deer farm. Novice and experienced riders are welcome. Transportation from Queenstown is provided. The company operates a clay-bird shooting range, and you can shoot in combination with the ride. ⌂ *Morven Ferry Rd., Arrow Junction, Queenstown9371* ☎ *03/442–1229* ⊕ *www.moonlightcountry.co.nz* ✉ *½-day trip $95 per person.*

JET-BOAT RIDES   With **Dart River Safaris** you can get a nonpareil look at rugged Mt. Aspiring National Park, one of the most spectacular parts of South Island. The Safari route includes jet-boating on the upper and lower Dart River, along with a bit of walking. The longer Heritage Trail takes private charters on a jet-boat and walking trip with a historic focus. The Funyak option takes you upstream by jet-boat, then you paddle gently downstream, exploring the Rockburn Chasm on the way. Shuttle buses depart daily from Queenstown for the 45-minute ride to the boats. Costs range from $179 plus transfer to $255 plus transfer. ■**TIP→** Even though the company provides you with rain gear, wear another raincoat under it. You're going to get extremely wet. ✉ *27 Shotover St., Queenstown* ☎ *03/442–9992* ⊕ *www.dartriver.co.nz.*

Shotover Jet leads high-speed, heart-stopping rides in the Shotover River canyons; it's got exclusive rights to operate in these waters. The boat pirouettes within inches of canyon walls. The boats are based at the Shotover Jet Beach beneath the historic Edith Cavell Bridge, a 10-minute drive from Queenstown. If you don't have transport, a free shuttle makes frequent daily runs. Reservations are essential. Costs start at $99. ✉ *Box 189, Queenstown* ☎ *03/442–8570* ⊕ *www.shotoverjet.co.nz.*

RAFTING   Rafting is an adult thrill; children must be at least 13 to participate. You'll need your swimsuit and a towel, but all other gear, including wet suit, life jacket, helmet, and wet-suit booties, are provided by the rafting companies. Instructors spend quite a bit of time on safety issues and paddling techniques before you launch.

Mad Dog River Boarding proves that looks can be deceiving. The Kawerau seems calmer than the Shotover; but that's debatable. In addition to riding down the Kawerau River on a bodyboard, there's a giant waterslide, big rope swing, and good old rock jumping (beat your chest and holler). ✉ *37 Shotover St., Queenstown* ☎ *03/442–7797* ⊕ *www.riverboarding.co.nz.*

Queenstown Rafting runs various half-, full-, and three-day white-water rafting trips in the Queenstown area year-round, advertising trips on the Shotover and Kawerau rivers. The Kawerau is pitched as a more scenic first-timer river. Or go all out with the Nevis Triple Challenge, which

Jetboats offer a thrillingly wet way to enjoy the Queenstown area's natural beauty.

includes a jet-boat ride, a helicopter trip, rafting on the Shotover, and a bungy jump, all in one day. Rates start at $145 and go above $1,000 for the multi-activity trips. ⊠ *35 Shotover St., Queenstown* ☎ *03/442–9792 or 0800/442–9792* ⊕ *www.rafting.co.nz.*

SAILING Lake Wakatipu gets extremely windy, and sailing is a popular pastime. **Sail Queenstown** (☎ *03/442–7517* ⊕ *www.sailqueenstown.co.nz*) runs a two-hour lake cruise on *NZL 14,* an America's Cup–class boat that was built for the 1992 challenge in San Diego and sailed by Russell Coutts. The boat is fitted with full safety gear and gives a really comfortable ride on these almost-waveless waters. Trips leave from the Convelle Wharf in central Queenstown every day at 2—more often in summer, if necessary.

SCENIC **Over the Top Helicopters** (☎ *03/442–2233 or 0800/123–359* ⊕ *www.flynz.*
FLIGHTS *co.nz*) runs a diverse selection of flights, including glacier and alpine ski slope landings, and scenic tours above Queenstown, the Remarkables, Fiordland, and Milford and Doubtful sounds. They'll also deliver you to fly-fishing spots absolutely miles from anywhere, or take you heli-skiing or on eco-tours as far away as Stewart Island.

SKIING **Coronet Peak** (☎ *03/442–4620* ⊕ *www.nzski.com*), 10 minutes from Queenstown along Gorge Road, rocks day and night to a ski and snowboard crowd that returns year after year. Queenstown's original ski resort now has a skiable area of 700 acres, a vertical drop of 1,360 feet, and six tows and chairlifts, including a quad lift. The season usually runs June to October, and night skiing is available from mid-July to mid-September. Adult day passes cost $93. Just across the valley, **the Remarkables** (☎ *03/442–615* ⊕ *www.nzski.com*) is a newer ski area that is good for beginner and intermediate skiing and hard-core off-piste runs. The vertical drop here is 1,160 feet, there are five tows and chairlifts, and 30% of the terrain is classified advanced. It's a 45-minute drive from Queenstown to the ski area parking lot on State Highway 6. Adult day passes cost $87.

WHERE TO EAT

Use the coordinate (✛ B2) at the end of each listing to locate a site on the corresponding map.

At first glance Queenstown's little side streets seem full of party bars and pizza joints, but that's because all the really great spots are hidden away or down at Steamer Wharf, which juts out into Lake Wakatipu. Some places aren't easy to find, so ask if you can't find what you're looking for.

$$$$ ✕ **The Bunker.** Log fires, leather armchairs, and a clubby vibe make the
ECLECTIC Bunker especially cozy. Whet your appetite with an aperitif at the bar
★ before heading downstairs for some of the finest lamb, venison, scampi, duck, and quail you'll find in Queenstown. The wine list is equally impressive. The Bunker stays open really late and is often booked days in advance for dinner. ⊠ *Cow La.* ☎ *03/441–8030* ⊕ *www.thebunker. co.nz* ⚱ *Reservations essential*▭ *AE, DC, MC, V* ✛ *B2.*

$$$–$$$$ ✕ **Coronation Café & Bathhouse.** Originally, it was exactly that—a 1911
ECLECTIC Victorian bathhouse, right on the beach, built to commemorate the coronation of Britain's King George V. Now it's a casual café in the mornings and afternoons, and a full restaurant for dinner. The surroundings remain Victorian, but the kitchen is up-to-date, specializing in starters such as a mille-feuille of wild rabbit ragout and main courses such as the sea-run salmon and the wild Blenheim hare. ⊠ *28 Marine Parade* ☎ *03/442–5625* ▭ *AE, DC, MC, V* ◷ *Closed Mon. in winter, 6 wks in May and June* ✛ *B2.*

$–$$ ✕ **Golden Elephant.** There are several Thai places in Queenstown, but
THAI the Golden Elephant is the best. Overlooking the lake, this BYO eatery has authentic Thai and good service. ⊠ *69 Beach St.* ☎ *03/441–8380* ▭ *MC, V* ◷ *Daily noon–11 PM* ✛ *B2.*

$ ✕ **Joe's Garage.** Don't be fooled by the name; this place is one of the
CAFÉ country's best cafés. The all-day menu includes simple pleasures such as bacon and eggs, pancakes, and paninis. But it's the trifecta of a laid-back aura, quick and friendly service, and outstanding coffee that really puts Joe's on the map. The place is popular with locals, but it's worth the wait for a table. ⊠ *Searle La.* ☎ *03/442–5282* ▭ *AE, MC, V* ◷ *No dinner* ✛ *B2.*

$$$–$$$$ ✕ **Pier 19 Restaurant.** This bright and breezy eatery sits at the town end of
NEW ZEALAND Steamer Wharf. The regularly changing and ambitious menu might include river-run salmon with colcannon (a traditional Irish mash made with leek, potato, and kale) or char-grilled Denver leg of venison. ⊠ *Steamer Wharf* ☎ *03/442–4006* ⊕ *www.pier19.co.nz* ▭ *AE, DC, MC, V* ✛ *B2.*

$–$$ ✕ **Vudu Café.** One of the best spots for breakfast in Queenstown, the
CAFÉ petite Vudu is up and running when everyone is still sleeping off last night's party. The specially roasted coffee is a treat, and the breakfast choices include lots of home-baked goodies. Later in the day they

The historic Eichardt's Hotel.

transform into a dinner restaurant and carry on until late. Reservations aren't accepted, so come early to snag a table. ✉ *23 Beach St.* ☎ *03/442–5357* ♨ *Reservations not accepted* 🖃 *DC, MC, V* ✛ *B2.*

$$$–$$$$
NEW ZEALAND

✕ **Wai.** Occupying a corner spot on Steamer Wharf, Wai has one of the best views, and reputations, in town. The fillet of grouper, oven roasted and wrapped in prosciutto, is a standout. You also might enjoy the rack of lamb, venison, salmon, or veal. The degustation menu and the fabulous oyster menu are worth a second visit. ✉ *Steamer Wharf* ☎ *03/442–5969* ⊕ *www.wai.net.nz* 🖃 *AE, DC, MC, V* ✛ *B2.*

WHERE TO STAY

Use the coordinate (✛ B2) at the end of each listing to locate a site on the corresponding map.

10

$$$–$$$$

🖼 **Aurum Hotel and Suites.** Wide, floor-to-ceiling windows with views over the town, lake, and across to the mountains are the best part of these modern, spacious rooms. It's a short walk downhill to the town center (though a rather steep one on the way back). The neighboring A-Line, a more modestly priced sister hotel, shares the reception area, restaurant, and bar. **Pros:** nice big rooms. **Cons:** steep (but short) walk from town. ✉ *27 Stanley St.* ☎ *03/442–4718* ⊕ *www.scenic-circle. co.nz* ✉ *aurum@scenic-circle.co.nz* ⤵ *42 rooms, 42 suites* ♨ *In-room: Kitchen (some). In-hotel: Restaurant, bar* 🖃 *AE, MC, V* ✛ *C2.*

$$$$
Fodor's Choice
★

🖼 **Eichardt's Private Hotel.** Once patronized by miners during the 1860s gold rush, the pricey Eichardt's now welcomes flush travelers drawn by the rush of adventure sports. Guest rooms are done in rich cocoa brown and cream; all have sitting areas with fireplaces, dressing rooms, and bathrooms with heated floors and double vanities. You can request a lake or mountain view. The staff is exceptionally helpful and can arrange anything from a massage to a helicopter ride. The House Bar ($$$) has delicious takes on lamb and salmon, along with an impressive selection of Otago and other New Zealand wines. Eichardt's now has cottages with full kitchens, two bedrooms, and a common area in a nearby building. **Pros:** centrally located; great service. **Cons:** a bit pricey; breakfast service can be slow. ⊠ *Marine Parade* ☎ *03/441–0450* ⊕ *www.eichardtshotel.co.nz* ⤶ *5 rooms* ⌂ *In-room: Internet. In-hotel: Bar* ⊟ *AE, DC, MC, V* ⃝⌽ *BP* ⊹ *B2.*

$$ 🏨 **Heritage Queenstown.** On Fernhill, just a few minutes from the town center, the Heritage is quieter than other local hotels and has great views of the Remarkables and Lake Wakatipu. The hotel was built almost entirely out of South Island materials, including central Otago schist and wooden beams from old, local railway bridges. Rooms are notably spacious and are fitted with writing tables and comfortable sitting areas. **Pros:** great service; nice rooms. **Cons:** 10-plus minute walk to downtown. ⊠ *91 Fernhill Rd.* ☎ *03/442–4988* ⊕ *www. heritagehotels.co.nz* ⤶ *136 rooms, 39 suites, 36 3-bedroom villas* ⌂ *In-room: Safe, Internet. In-hotel: Restaurant, bar, pool, gym, spa* ⊟ *AE, DC, MC, V* ⊹ *A2.*

$$ 🏨 **Lakeside Motel.** At the economy end of the spectrum this homey motel has a premium lakefront location. The interior is plain, but there are some nice amenities for the price. Two two-bedroom family units come with full cooking and laundry facilities, but book well in advance for these. **Pros:** great value. **Cons:** on the edge of town. ⊠ *18 Lake Esplanade* ☎ *03/442–8976* ⊕ *www.queenstownaccommodation.co.nz* ⤶ *13 studios, 2 family units* ⌂ *In-room: Kitchen (some). In-hotel: Laundry facilities* ⊟ *AE, DC, MC, V* ⊹ *A2.*

$$$$ 🏨 **Nugget Point Boutique Hotel.** Check out the open-air whirlpool here,
★   perched on the south side of Shotover Valley; it's perfect with a glass of champagne. Large rooms have balconies and separate seating areas. The lodge is a 10-minute drive from Queenstown on the road to Coronet Peak, one of the top ski areas in the country. The bright glassed-in public rooms give it an especially cheerful quality, even if the weather outside is less than gorgeous. The views up and down the Shotover River are to die for. **Pros:** excellent restaurant. **Cons:** you'll need a car as this is outside town. ⊠ *146 Arthur's Point Rd.* ☎ *03/441–0288* ⊕ *www. nuggetpoint.co.nz* ⤶ *35 rooms* ⌂ *In-room: Kitchen. In-hotel: Restaurant, bar, tennis court, pool, spa* ⊟ *AE, DC, MC, V* ⊹ *D2.*

$$$$ 🏨 **Pencarrow.** It's not just the hillside backdrop by Lake Wakatipu, or
★   the gardens, or the spacious guest rooms—the friendliness and service of the hosts, Bill and Kari Moers, sets this place apart. Less expensive than many lodges in this neck of the woods, Pencarrow has all kinds of thoughtful details, from a special "concierge" room, stocked with information on local attractions, to the welcoming teddy bears on the beds. You can have breakfast in the dining room or on a tray in your room. You can also arrange to go gold panning in a local river, if you're feeling lucky. **Pros:** first-rate hospitality. **Cons:** it's outside town, so you'll need a car. ⊠ *678 Frankton Rd.* ☎ *03/442–8938* ⊕ *www.pencarrow.net* ⤶ *4*

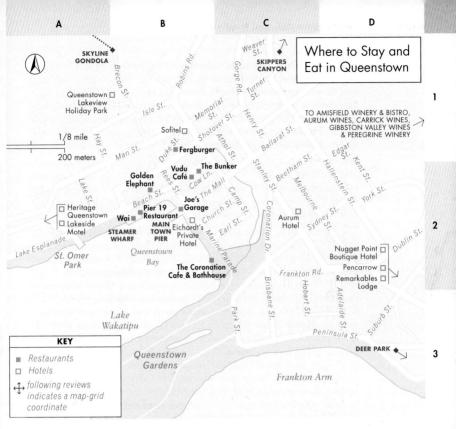

KEY

- ■ Restaurants
- □ Hotels
- ✛ following reviews indicates a map-grid coordinate

suites ⟨ In-room: DVD, Wi-Fi. In-hotel: Bar, laundry service, Internet terminal ▭ AE, DC, MC, V ⦿ BP ✛ D2.

$ ▦ **Queenstown Lakeview Holiday Park.** With everything from spic-and-span, fully equipped apartments to studios, cabins, and campsites, this park is a varied budget pick. It's right near the Skyline Gondola terminal, with good views of the Remarkables. The staff can help you get good deals on tours and activities. **Pros:** centrally located. **Cons:** can get a bit crowded. ✉ *Brecon St.* ☎ *03/442-7252* ⊕ *www.holidaypark. net.nz* ⤺ *16 rooms, 22 lodges, 8 cabins* ⟨ *In-room: Kitchen (some). In-hotel: Internet terminal* ▭ *AE, MC, V* ✛ *B1.*

$$$$ ▦ **Remarkables Lodge.** Sitting almost right under the mountains, Remarkables Lodge has extensive views of the jagged grandeur of the Remarkables Range. Breakfast and a splendid dinner are included in the rate, and may include prawn ravioli for a starter, Moroccan rack of lamb, and poached pears for dessert. The Remarkables ski area is nearby, and if you can drag yourself away from the outdoor fireplace in the garden, Queenstown activities are a 10-minute drive away. **Pros:** unbeatable views. **Cons:** you'll want a vehicle as it's outside of town. ✉ *595 Kingston Rd., about 6 km (3½ mi) south of Queenstown toward Invercargill* ☎ *03/442-2720* ⊕ *www.remarkables.co.nz* ⤺ *3 rooms, 4 suites* ⟨ *In-room: Refrigerator In-hotel: Bar, pool, spa* ▭ *AE, MC, V* ⦿ *MAP* ✛ *D2.*

10

NIGHTLIFE

After days spent testing limits, visitors cram Queenstown's clubs and bars. Don't be surprised to encounter more than one "hens' party" or "stag do" on any given weekend night. Kiwi guys are notoriously vile to their groom-to-be mates, so steer clear if you see a pack of rowdy bachelors as things often get messy in their midst. All the popular venues are in the center of town, within easy walking distance of one another. Grab a copy of *The Source* weekly gig guide, available in most cafés and bars.

While you're out remember that prostitution is legal in New Zealand, and Queenstown has its share of brothels. Mind you, these are not establishments with blinking neon BROTHEL signs in the window; so be aware if you're seeking a massage that some parlors might not provide exactly what you had in mind.

The "after-work" scene takes place at **Pig & Whistle** (✉ *19 Camp St.* ☎ *03/442–9055*), which also attracts lots of backpackers. **Dux de Luxe** (✉ *14–16 Church St.* ☎ *03/442–9688*) is a popular brewery-restaurant and hosts local bands and DJs. The upstairs **Winnies** (✉ *The Mall* ☎ *03/442–8635*) slings pizza before transforming into a happening nightspot, extremely popular with backpackers. **Bardeux** (✉ *The Mall* ☎ *03/442–8284*) is a wine bar that's good for an intimate subdued evening. **Skybar** (✉ *26 Camp St.* ☎ *03/442–4283*) is a quiet sophisticated place where you can munch on whitebait fritters in front of the fireplace. The touristy **Minus 5°** (✉ *Steamer Wharf* ☎ *03/442–6050*) is literally a place for chilling out—with ice chairs, an ice bar, and ice glasses. However, warm gear—boots, big Eskimo-style jackets, and gloves—is supplied for you. End your night on the town (or kick it off) in classic Queenstown style with a famous **Fergburger** (✉ *42 Shotover St.* ☎ *03/441–1232*). If they're closed you know you've had a big night— this institution is open until 5 AM!

TOURS

BUS TOURS The **Double Decker** (☎ *0800/668–888)* is an original London bus that makes a three-hour circuit from Queenstown to Arrowtown and the bungy-jumping platform on the Karawau River. Leaving Queenstown, it goes via Frankton, Lake Hayes, and Gibbston Valley Wines before heading for a break at Arrowtown. The return trip to Queenstown goes by the Shotover River valley. Tours (about $38) depart Queenstown daily at 9:30 and 1:30 from the Mall outside McDonald's.

COMBINA-TION TRIPS **Nomad Safaris** (✉ *19 Shotover St., Queenstown* ☎ *03/442–6699 or 0800/688–222* ⊕ *www.queenstown4wd.com*) runs 4WD "safari" trips to old gold-rush settlements (or their remains), such as Skippers Canyon and Macetown. Another off-roading trip takes you to see some of the areas filmed for the *Lord of the Rings* trilogy. Costs start at $110. For a wide choice of fly-drive-cruise tour options to Milford and Doubtful sounds from Queenstown, Te Anau, and Milford, check out **Real Journeys** (✉ *Lakefront Dr., Te Anau* ☎ *03/249–7416 or 0800/656–501* ✉ *Steamer Wharf, Queenstown* ☎ *03/442–4846 or 0800/656–503* ⊕ *www.realjourneys.co.nz*).

A former gold-rush town, Arrowtown now only sees gold in the autumn leaves.

ARROWTOWN

22 km (14 mi) northeast of Queenstown, 105 km (66 mi) south of Wanaka.

Arrowtown lies northeast of Queenstown. Jack Tewa, or Māori Jack, as he was known, found gold along the Arrow River in 1861, and when William Fox, an American, was seen selling large quantities of the precious metal in nearby Clyde shortly afterward, the hunt was on. Eventually a large party of prospectors stumbled on Fox and his team of 40 miners. The secret was out, miners rushed to stake their claims, and Arrowtown was born. At the height of the rush there were more than 30,000 hardy souls in this tiny settlement.

After the gold rush ended in 1865, the place became another sleepy rural town until tourism created a boom. This village at the foot of the steep Crown Range, with weathered-timber shop fronts and white stone churches shaded by ancient sycamores, was simply too gorgeous to escape the attention of tour buses. It has become a tourist trap, but a highly photogenic one, especially when autumn gilds the hillsides. Each April, Arrowtown celebrates the Autumn Festival when the trees are at their most spectacular. On a stroll along **Buckingham Street**, you can stop in the old post and telegraph office, still open for business. Take time to explore some of the lanes and arcades, filled with cafés and boutique shops.

GETTING HERE AND AROUND

Arrowtown is a 20-minute drive from Queenstown, and you can take a bus there. Exploring the town is easily and enjoyably done on foot. If you'd like to venture out toward the old gold-mining settlement Macetown you can walk or bike if you're a hearty sort (it's 16 km [10 mi] and entails 22 river crossings). If you drive, a 4WD is required—you can rent one from Nomad Safaris or do a guided tour.

ESSENTIALS

Bus Contacts Arrowtown Scenic Bus (☎ 03/442–1900 ⊕ www. arrowtownbus.co.nz).

Car Rental Nomad Safaris (☎ 03/442–6699 ⊕ www.nomadsafaris.co.nz).

Visitor Information Arrowtown Visitor Information Centre (✉ 49 Buckingham St. ☎ 03/442–1824 ⊕ www.arrowtown.org.nz).

EXPLORING

To get the full story, stop by the **Lakes District Museum,** which has artifacts of the gold-rush days, an information center, and a small bookstore and gallery. You can even rent pans and get gold-panning tips to try your luck in the Arrow River. When your patience frays and your hands go icy, keep in mind that a hobby prospector found a 275g nugget in this very river in 2006! (He sold it on eBay for US$15,000.) ✉ Buckingham St. ☎ 03/442–1824 ⊕ www.museumqueenstown.com 🗔 $5 ☉ Daily 8:30–5.

OUTDOOR ACTIVITIES

There are several walks—**Tobin's Track, the Loop, Sawpit Gully,** and the **Lake Hayes Walk**—to raise the fitness levels and give you a feeling for where you are. Some investigate the old gold history, but others give nice views. You can get details on all of them from the Lakes District Museum Information Centre. For easier ambles take the Arrow River Trail or the Bush Creek Trail. And if you want a real challenge tackle the hike out to the old gold settlement Macetown. Although you might hear the Macetown Bakery mentioned, be aware the place is a ghost town now and all that remains are remnants of the settlement.

WHERE TO EAT

$$$ ✕ **Cafe Mondo.** Tucked into a sheltered courtyard off the main street, this
CAFÉ   is the place for refreshing, slightly quirky cold drinks like the Mondo Combo, a blend of orange, carrot, and apple juices with a hint of ginger. You could also dig into a substantial lunch or dinner of salmon or chicken with couscous. There's a kids' menu as well. ✉ 4 Ballarat Arcade ☎ 03/442–0227 ▭ AE, DC, MC, V.

¢–$ ✕ **Joe's Garage.** Sitting above Blue Moon in the Mall, this branch of the
CAFÉ   Queenstown's café provides a sunny, quiet spot away from the tour-bus crowd. The menu of casual sandwiches and great coffee is the same as in the main branch. ✉ Arrow La. ☎ 03/442–1116 ▭ AE, MC, V ☉ No dinner.

$$$ ✕ **Pesto.** This casual eatery makes great pizza and pasta. If you want a
PIZZA   drink in a really nice, comfortable bar, duck across the alley and poke your nose into the affiliated **Blue Door.** Enjoy the cozy quality of the bar. If you get hungry, don't worry; you can order from Pesto and enjoy your meal without losing your seat next to the bar's roaring fire. ✉ 18 Buckingham St. ☎ 03/442–0885 ▭ AE, DC, MC, V.

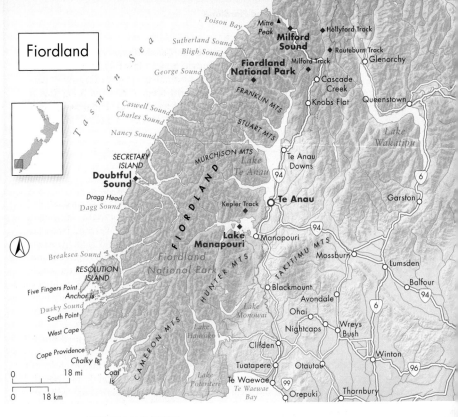

WHERE TO STAY

$$–$$$ 📷 **Arrowtown Lodge.** Designed to blend in with Arrowtown's historic buildings, these four cottage-style suites are just a two-minute walk from the center of town. All have views toward the Arrow River gorge, which ideally will inspire you to go on a day hike, the hosts' expertise. **Pros:** delicious breakfast. **Cons:** a block from the fire station so the siren might wake you. ⊠ *7 Anglesea St.* ☎ *03/442–1101 or 0800/258–802* ⊕ *www.arrowtownlodge.co.nz* ⤴ *4 rooms* ⌂ *In-room: Internet. In-hotel: Laundry facilities, Internet terminal* ▭ *AE, MC, V* ⓧⓘ *BP.*

$$$$ 📷 **Millbrook Resort.** A 20-minute drive from Queenstown, this glamorous resort has a special appeal for golfers: an 18-hole championship golf course that was designed by New Zealand professional Bob Charles. A luxurious spa pampers you whether or not you've taken advantage of the extensive exercise options. Accommodations range from rooms in the resort's main hotel to villas and multibedroom cottages. Standard rooms have private balconies and fireplaces. The villas have kitchens, laundry facilities, and large lounge–dining rooms. **Pros:** the golf course; the location. **Cons:** big, sprawling, and impersonal. ⊠ *Malaghans Rd.* ☎ *03/441–7000 or 0800/800–604* ⊕ *www.millbrook.co.nz* ⤴ *13 villas, 70 villa suites, 51 rooms, 24 cottage apartments* ⌂ *In-room: No a/c, kitchen (some). In-hotel: 2 restaurants, bar, golf course, tennis court, pool, gym, spa, bicycles* ▭ *AE, DC, MC, V* ⓧⓘ *BP, CP.*

10

NIGHTLIFE

★ It may not have a flashy marquee, but **Dorothy Brown's Boutique Cinema and Bar** is a truly memorable movie house. The theater doesn't seat many people, but the chairs are cushy and have plenty of legroom. Better yet, you can get a glass of wine at the fireplace bar and bring it with you. The schedule mixes Hollywood releases with art and international films. ⊠ *Off Buckingham St., upstairs* ☎ *03/442–1968 or 03/442–1964* ⊕ *www.dorothybrowns.com.*

FIORDLAND

Fiordland, the name generally given to the southwest coast, is a majestic wilderness of rocks, ice, and beech forest, where glaciers have carved mile-deep notches into the coast. Most of this terrain is officially designated **Fiordland National Park**, and in conjunction with South Westland National Park, is a designated UNESCO Te Wahipounamu World Heritage Area. Parts of the park are so remote that they have never been explored, and visitor activities are mostly confined to a few of the sounds and the walking trails. Te Anau serves as the base, with lodgings and sports outfitters. The most accessible scenic highlight of this area—and perhaps of the whole country—is Milford Sound, where tremendous green slopes plunge into the sea, and rare species of coral wait just below the water's surface.

The extreme landscape and the soggy climate have prevented much development; neither the first Māori, the early European explorers, sealers, whalers, nor modern arrivals have made many inroads here. If you really want to take in the raw grandeur of Fiordland, hike one of the many trails in the area, among them the famous four-day Milford Track, long considered one of the finest walks in the world.

GETTING HERE AND AROUND

There are regular bus services to Te Anau and Milford Sound from Queenstown, Christchurch, and Invercargill. The town of Te Anau is small enough to explore on foot. You will need to take a bus and a boat if you want to see Doubtful Sound. The drive to Milford Sound is one of the most magnificent in the country. Once there, one of the best ways to experience the park is by boat. Te Anau has a small airport, but many people fly into the more regularly serviced Queenstown or Invercargill airports and then drive.

ESSENTIALS

Fiordland National Park Visitor Centre (⊠ *Lakefront Dr., Te Anau* ☎ *03/249–7924*) hours vary a bit seasonally; summer hours are 8:30–6 and winter hours are 8:30–4:30.

TE ANAU

175 km (109 mi) southwest of Queenstown.

Lake Te Anau (tay-*ah*-no), which is 53 km (33 mi) long and up to 10 km (6 mi) wide, is the largest lake in New Zealand after Lake Taupo. The town of Te Anau, on the southern shores, serves as a base for Fiordland National Park. From Te Anau, you can set out on sightseeing trips by bus, boat, or plane to Milford and Doubtful sounds, or take off on one of the park's superb hiking trails. Of these, the most accessible to town is the Kepler Track. The town itself is not much to write home about, but it does have a few attractions. It's busiest in summer; in winter, some cafés and shops close or reduce their hours.

ESSENTIALS

Bus Companies InterCity (☎ *03/443–7885 in Wanaka, 03/249–7559 in Te Anau, 03/442–8238 in Queenstown* ⊕ *www.intercitycoach.co.nz*). **Newmans** (☎ *09/913–6188 or 0508/353–947* ⊕ *www.newmanscoach.co.nz*). **Wanaka Connexions** (☎ *03/443–9122* ⊕ *www.time2.co.nz/transport/wanaka_connexions*).

Bus Depot Te Anau (✉ *Miro St.*).

Internet Café e-Stop Internet (✉ *Jailhouse Mall, Town Centre, Te Anau* ☎ *03/249–9461*).

Mail Te Anau (✉ *102–104 Town Centre* ☎ *03/249–7348*).

EXPLORING

At **Te Anau Caves,** boats and walkways take you through a maze of caves containing underground whirlpools, waterfalls, and gushing streams. On the cave walls, glowworms shine like constellations in a clear night sky. The caves can be reached only by water, and the entire trip takes 2½ hours. There are three trips per day during summer and two per day the rest of the year. ✉ *Real Journeys, Lakefront Dr.* ☎ *03/249–7416 or 0800/656–502* ⊕ *www.realjourneys.co.nz* 🎟 *$50.*

The lakeshore **Te Anau Wildlife Centre** gives you the chance to preview some of the wildlife you're likely to encounter when hiking in Fiordland. The center houses one of New Zealand's rare flightless birds, the takahē, which was once thought to be extinct. The lakeside walk to the center makes for a pleasant one-hour stroll. ✉ *Manapouri Rd., 1 km (½ mi) west of Te Anau* ☎ *03/249–7921* 🎟 *Donation requested* ⊗ *Daily dawn–dusk.*

SPORTS AND THE OUTDOORS

HIKING   Information, transport options, and maps for the plethora of hikes near Te Anau, including the Kepler Track, can be obtained from the **Fiordland National Park Visitor Centre** ✉ *Lakefront Dr.* ☎ *03/249–7924* ⊕ *www.doc.govt.nz).*

★   The 60-km (37-mi) **Kepler Track** loops from the south end of Lake Te Anau, starting just 4 km (2½ mi) from Te Anau township. It skirts the lakeshore, climbs up to the bush line, passing limestone bluffs and going through extensive beech forest, and has incredible views of the South Fiord and Te Anau Basin. An alpine crossing takes you to the high point near the peak of Mt. Luxmore. It's a moderate walking trail that takes three to four days to complete. If you're on a tight schedule, it's possible to take day hikes to the Luxmore and Moturau huts.

KAYAKING   **Fiordland Wilderness Experiences** ✉ *66 Quintin Dr.* ☎ *03/249–7700* ⊕ *www.fiordlandseakayak.co.nz)* runs kayaking day trips and multiday tours on Milford and Doubtful sounds and on Lakes Te Anau and Manapouri. Beginners are welcome. They operate from September to May, with some differences according to location, so call ahead; costs start around $135.

10

SCENIC **Air Fiordland** (✉ *Te Anau Airport* ☎ *03/249–6720 or 0800/107–505*
FLIGHTS ⊕ *www.airfiordland.co.nz*) provides a range of scenic flights on its
fixed-wing aircraft to Milford Sound and Doubtful Sound, with prices
hovering around $390. It also has combined packages providing the
option of flying to Milford Sound and then taking a cruise boat or kayaking before returning to either Te Anau or Queenstown ($425). **Wings
and Water Te Anau Ltd.** (✉ *Lakefront Dr.9600* ☎ *03/249–7405* ⊕ *www.
wingsandwater.co.nz*) operates scenic flights with a floatplane that takes
travelers to some of the region's most inaccessible areas, including a
10-minute trip over Lake Te Anau, Lake Manapouri, and the Kepler
Track and longer flights over Doubtful, Dusky, and Milford sounds.
Costs range from $95 for a 10-minute flight to $295 for 40 minutes.

WHERE TO EAT

$$$–$$$$ ✗ **Fat Duck Cafe.** This relatively new restaurant has been receiving rave
NEW ZEALAND   reviews from satisfied visitors and locals. The personality, service, and
cuisine are excellent. Try the venison. ✉ *164 Milford Rd.* ☎ *03/249–
8480* ▭ *MC, V.*

$–$$$ ✗ **La Toscana.** The wine-color walls in this café put you in the mood for
ITALIAN   the well-priced selection of Tuscan soups, pastas, and pizzas. Starters
are typically Italian breads or antipasti. Sensibly, both pastas and pizzas
are available in medium or large sizes, but keep dessert in mind—the
torta di cioccolata (chocolate cake smothered in hot fudge sauce) is a
local legend. Take-out is also available. ✉ *Uptown arcade, 108 Town
Centre* ☎ *03/249–7756* ▭ *AE, MC, V* ⊗ *No lunch.*

$$$–$$$$ ✗ **Redcliff Café & Bar.** Te Anau might not strike you as a crème brûlée
NEW ZEALAND   kind of place, but Redcliff pulls it off. Among the dishes served in this
cottage environment, the Fiordland crayfish and the wild venison on
the Fiordland platter are excellent. Reservations aren't accepted—so
try to arrive by 6 if you don't want to join the wait list. ✉ *12 Mokonui
St.* ☎ *03/249–7431* ⌲ *Reservations not accepted* ▭ *MC, V* ⊗ *Closed
July and Aug. No lunch.*

$$$ ✗ **Settlers Steakhouse.** A carnivore's friend, Settlers revolves around red
NEW ZEALAND   meat; but it's not all beef—you can also choose from grilled lamb,
venison, local salmon, or blue cod. The all-you-can-eat salad bar is the
counterpoint. ✉ *Town Centre* ☎ *03/249–8454* ▭ *AE, DC, MC, V* ⊗ *No
lunch. Reduced hrs June and July.*

WHERE TO STAY

$$ ▥ **Cats Whiskers.** Hosts Anne Marie and Lindsay Bernstone keep things
homey at their modern lakefront B&B, complete with, you guessed it,
a resident cat (there's also a small dog). Each room has pluses such as
tea-making facilities and hair dryers; ask for the one with a lake view.
The house is a 10-minute walk from the town center and is opposite
the National Park Visitor Centre. A courtesy car can take you to any of
the local restaurants. **Pros:** friendly hosts; cheerful place. **Cons:** fills up
quickly, so try to book in advance. ✉ *2 Lakefront Dr.* ☎ *03/249–8112*
⊕ *www.catswhiskers.co.nz* ⌁4 *rooms* ⌂ *In-room: Refrigerator In-
hotel: Laundry facilities, Internet terminal* ▭ *MC, V* ⏷*BP.*

$$$$ ▥ **Murrell's Grand View House.** Twenty minutes south of Te Anau, this
B&B sits on one of New Zealand's prettiest and most pristine lakes—
Lake Manapouri. The fourth generation of the Murrell family runs this

historic property built in 1889. Take in the views from the veranda, walk over to the wharf for a boat tour of Doubtful Sound, or curl up in the library by the fire with a drink. Dinner can be arranged. **Pros:** a perfect launching point to explore crystal clear Lake Manapouri or incredible Doubtful Sound. **Cons:** it's a bit of a detour from the usual tourist circuit. ⊠ *Murrell Ave., Manapouri* ☎ *03/249–6642* ⊕ *www. murrells.co.nz* ⌑ *4 rooms* ⊟ *AE, MC, V* ⏏ *BP.*

$$$ ⬚ **Radfords Lakeview Motel.** This reasonably priced lakefront motel has clean spacious rooms and is located a few minutes' walk from town. Five units have whirlpool baths. **Pros:** great location; good value. **Cons:** forgettable vibe. ⊠ *56 Lakefront Dr.* ☎ *03/249–9186* ⊕ *www. radfordslakeviewmotel.co.nz* ⌑ *4 studios, 10 rooms* ⌂ *In-room: Kitchen, Wi-Fi. In-hotel: Laundry service, parking (free)* ⊟ *AE, DC, MC, V.*

$ ⬚ **Te Anau Top 10 Holiday Park Mountain View.** Ideally set across from the lakefront and just a couple of blocks from the town's commercial strip, this well-serviced park provides motel rooms, cabins, and campervan and camping sites. For the cabins, you'll need to rent linens for a small extra cost. The Matai Lodge also has basic rooms with private baths. Their architecture is reminiscent of upmarket tramping huts, with exposed ceiling beams. **Pros:** popular, well-run facility with options for everyone. **Cons:** terribly busy during high season, so book ahead. ⊠ *Te Anau Terr.* ☎ *03/249–7462 or 0800/249–746* ⊕ *www.teanautop10. co.nz* ⌂ *In-room: Kitchen (some), refrigerator. In-hotel: Bicycles, laundry facilities, spa, Internet terminal* ⊟ *MC, V.*

EN ROUTE The **Milford Road,** from Te Anau to Milford Sound, winds through deep valleys where waterfalls cascade into mossy beech forests. It's a spectacular route, but if you're making the trip between May and November, check local information for avalanche warnings and come equipped with tire chains, which you can rent in any Te Anau service station. The road is narrow and winding at times, so allow at least 2½ hours.

MILFORD SOUND

120 km (75 mi) northwest of Te Anau, 290 km (180 mi) west of Queenstown.

EXPLORING

Fodor's Choice ★ Fiordland National Park's most accessible and busiest attraction is **Milford Sound,** the sort of overpowering place where poets run out of words. Hemmed in by walls of rock that rise from the waterline sheer up to 4,000 feet, the 13-km-long (18-mi-long) fjord was carved by a succession of glaciers as they gouged a track to the sea. Its dominant feature is the 5,560-foot pinnacle of **Mitre Peak,** which is capped with snow for all but the warmest months of the year. Opposite the peak, Bowen Falls tumbles 520 feet before exploding into the sea. You'll often see seals on rocks soaking up the sun; dolphins sometimes flirt with the boats. Milford Sound is also spectacularly wet: the average annual rainfall is around 20 feet, and it rains an average of 183 days a year. In addition to a raincoat you'll need insect repellent—the sound has voracious sand flies.

Even in heavy rain and storms Milford Sound is magical. Rainfall is so excessive that a coat of up to 20 feet of fresh water floats on the surface

10

of the saltwater fjord. This creates a unique underwater environment similar to that found at a much greater depth in the open ocean. You can observe this at the **Milford Deep Underwater Observatory,** a 15-minute boat ride from the wharf in Milford at Harrison Cove. Several boating companies, such as Real Journeys and Mitre Peak Cruises, make regular trips to the observatory. ⊠ *Milford Sound* ☎ *03/249–9442 or 0800/329–969* ⊕ *www.milforddeep.co.nz* ⊘ *Daily 8:30–5.*

SPORTS AND THE OUTDOORS

CRUISING   The gorgeous views from the water account for the popularity of cruising here. It's essential to book ahead between mid-December and March. Some include a visit to the Milford Sound Underwater Observatory *(⇨ above)*. All boats leave from the Milford wharf area. Avoid the midday sailings, as they link with tour buses and are most crowded. Milford Sound Red Boat Cruises and Real Journeys run more than a dozen cruises a day between them, with extra options in summer.

⟶▷ **Milford Sound Red Boat Cruises** (⊠ *Milford Sound Wharf* ☎ *03/441–1137* ⊕ *www.redboats.co.nz*) provides frequent, daily scenic cruises on its catamarans to Milford Sound or to the Milford Deep Underwater Observatory. The basic tour, which lasts less than two hours, loops through the sound to the Tasman Sea; the fare starts at $50 and goes up to $79 if you include a stop at the observatory. **Real Journeys** (⊠ *Lakefront Dr., Te Anau* ☎ *03/249–7416 or 0800/656–501* ⊕ *www.realjourneys.co.nz*) offers daily cruises on the *Milford Monarch* and its companion the *Milford Haven*. These trips cruise the full length of Milford Sound to the Tasman Sea, with views of waterfalls, rain forest, mountains, and wildlife. There's a choice of 1½-hour scenic cruises and 2½-hour nature cruises, at $60 and $80, respectively. To have the most intense experience on the sound, sign up for one of the three overnight cruise options that are available from October to April. The *Milford Mariner* sleeps 60 passengers in private cabins with bathrooms ($350 per person twin share, September–May), the *Milford Wanderer* has bunk-style accommodation for 61 passengers ($210 per person quad share, October–April), and the M.V. *Friendship* has bunks for just 12 passengers ($210 per person; multishare, November–March).

HIKING   If you plan to walk the **Milford Track**—a rewarding four-day bushwalk
Fodor's Choice   through Fiordland National Park—understand that it is one of New
★   Zealand's most popular hikes. The 53½-km (33-mi) track is strictly one-way, and because park authorities control access, you can feel as though you have the wilderness more or less to yourself. Independent and guided groups stay in different overnight huts. The trailheads for the track are remote. Guided and unguided walks begin with a two-hour ferry ride to Glade Wharf on Lake Te Anau and end with a ferry taking you from Sandfly Point over to the Milford Sound wharf. Because of the good condition of the track, the walk is rarely demanding. But because the trail is often blocked by snow in winter, there is a restricted hiking season from late April until late October. Reservations are essential through the season, and there are no camping sites winter or summer. You can make a reservation with the **Great Walks Booking Office** (☎ *03/249–8514* ⊕ *www.doc.govt.nz*). If you don't have enough time for the whole Milford Track, try a day trip with **Real Journeys** (☎ *03/219–7416 or*

0800/656–501 ⊕ *www.realjourneys.co.nz*), which includes a Lake Te Anau cruise and a guided day walk. The 33-km (20½-mi) **Routeburn Track,** like the Milford Track, is designated one of the country's Great Walks. Routeburn goes between Lake Wakatipu, near Glenorchy, and the road between Milford and Te Anau; it takes about three days to hike. The alpine landscape is stunning, and once you're above the treeline, the sand flies back off. As on the Milford, be prepared for rain and mud.

If you're itching to see some coastline during your hike, consider the **Hollyford Track** (⊠ *Lakefront Dr., Te Anau* ☎ *03/249–8514* ⊕ *www.doc. govt.nz*). At 56 km (35 mi), it's a four-day endeavor, taking you from the Hollyford Road down to Martins Bay by roughly following the Hollyford River. You'll pass a couple of lakes and waterfalls on your way; at the coastline you'll likely spy seals and penguins. Be particularly careful of flooded creek crossings. For DOC huts on the track, book in advance through the **Fiordland National Park Visitor Centre.** Going with a guide from **Ultimate Hikes** (⊠ *1st fl., AJ Hackett Station Bldg., Camp St. at Duke St., Queenstown* ☎ *03/441–1138 or 0800/659–255* ⊕ *www.ultimatehikes.co.nz*) requires deep pockets but provides comfortable beds and a cook. For the Milford Track, it'll cost $1,750 in high season (in multishare accommodation), $1,590 in low season, including a cruise on Milford Sound and transport to and from Queenstown; the Routeburn is a bit cheaper at $1,090 in the high season, $950 in low. If you're not up for a multiday trek, you can take a single-day "encounter" hike on either the Milford or Routeburn Track for $135.

KAYAKING **Milford Sound Sea Kayaks** (⊠ *Milford Sound* ☎ *03/249–8500, 0800/476– 726 in New Zealand* ⊕ *www.kayakmilford.co.nz*) leads guided kayaking on the sound that includes a hike along part of the Milford track. Prices range from $69 to $169 per person.

SCENIC "Flightseeing" combines a round-trip flight from Queenstown to Milford
FLIGHTS with a scenic cruise. Flights are weather-dependent. **Milford Sound Scenic Flights** (☎ *03/442–3065 or 0800/207–206* ⊕ *www.milfordflights. co.nz*) start with one-hour flights for $275. The **Glacier Southern Lakes Helicopters Ltd.** (☎ *03/442–3016* ⊕ *www.heli-flights.co.nz*) will get you buzzing over Milford Sound; the Milford Sound Fantastic trip has at least two landings and costs $610.

WHERE TO EAT AND STAY

Accommodations are scant at Milford Sound, and it's best to stay in Te Anau and make your visit a long day trip.

$$–$$$ ✕ **Blue Duck Café & Bar.** The view out the front window, across Milford
CAFÉ Sound to Mitre Peak and the mountains beyond, is amazing—and the food's not bad, either. Lunch choices include wraps, rolls, and sandwiches, as well as a full buffet; there are even options for vegetarians. Dinner goes à la carte, and the restaurant and bar stay open until late. And if you're brave and don't mind a few sand flies, you can even eat outside. ⊠ *Milford Sound* ☎ *03/249–7982* ▭ *MC, V.*

$–$$ ▦ **Milford Sound Lodge.** Just 1 km (½ mi) out of the Milford settlement, on the banks of the Cleddau River, this hostel has basic but fresh accommodations. A few years ago the guest rooms were completely revamped. The range of rooms includes twin and double rooms with linen for $80 per

10

person, four-person bunk rooms at $30 per bed, and dormitories for six people or more at $30 a bed. All rooms have shared facilities. The lodge now also provides Riverside Chalets ($185–$225 per night, $30 per extra person) with either one super-king or twin bed, kitchenette, and spectacular mountain and river views. The lodge serves inexpensive breakfast, or people can cook for themselves in the on-site kitchen. Powered and non-powered campsites are also available. **Pros:** clean bathrooms; good value. **Cons:** no power 11 PM–6 AM. ⊠ *Milford Sound* ☎ *03/249–8071* ⊕ *www. milfordlodge.com* ↰ *24 rooms with shared bath, 4 riverside chalets (en suite)* ♿ *In-room: (chalet only) Refrigerator, DVD. In-hotel: Restaurant, bar, laundry facilities, Internet terminal* ☐ *MC, V.*

LAKE MANAPOURI AND DOUBTFUL SOUND

Just 20 minutes south of Te Anau, Lake Manapouri has long had the reputation as one of New Zealand's prettiest lakes. The lake is unspoiled, hemmed by high mountains and studded by many bush-covered islands. Cruises run several times a day to the head of the lake, where you can join a tour of the West Arm hydro-station, deep underground. West Arm is also the departure point for those traveling on to Doubtful Sound, a stunning stretch of water, largely untouched by visitors. A connecting bus crosses you over the 2,177-foot Wilmot Pass before dropping steeply down to sea level at Deep Arm, the head of Doubtful Sound.

TOURS

CRUISING   Doubtful Sound is three times as long as Milford Sound and sees far fewer visitors. **Real Journeys** (⊠ *Lakefront Dr.* ☎ *03/249–7416 or 0800/656–502* ⊕ *www.realjourneys.co.nz*) runs a range of combined bus and boat trips there. Tours include a 2-km (1-mi) bus trip down a spiral tunnel to the Lake Manapouri Power Station machine hall, an extraordinary engineering feat built deep beneath the mountain. On the sound itself, you may see bottlenose dolphins or fur seals. Most people take an eight-hour day trip from Lake Manapouri; there are bus connections from Te Anau and Queenstown. Between October and May you can overnight on the sound, aboard the *Fiordland Navigator*. Rates for the day excursion are $275 per person, and for the overnight cruise, $365 (for a quad share) to $675 (twin share).

Fiordland Expeditions (⊠ *Deep Cove, Doubtful Sound* ☎ *03/442–2996* ⊕ *www.fiordlandexpeditions.co.nz*) provides a truly New Zealand experience on their great little boat, *Tutuko*. Skipper Richard Abernethy is totally at home on these waters and will take you to the most inaccessible reaches of Doubtful Sound, or out and around the coast, weather permitting (which doesn't happen often). This is the tour to do if you want to do a bit of fishing, dive some of the excellent water beneath the boat, or just soak up the scenery, of which there is plenty. Tours are run by arrangement, rather than on a set schedule, so you'll need to make a group, or join one.

Otago, Invercargill, and Stewart Island

WORD OF MOUTH

"As far as seeing rare birds on Stewart Island, as with any wild-life viewing, there's no guarantee you'll see any. Silly wildlife just won't keep to any schedule! So, you have to weigh the costs with the possibility that you might end up just seeing some nice scenery. Obviously, odds decrease with a day trip vs. a 3-day stay."

—wlzmatilda

WELCOME TO OTAGO, INVERCARGILL, AND STEWART ISLAND

TOP REASONS TO GO

★ **Bird-Watching:** See yellow-eyed penguin or an albatross on the peninsula or a kiwi on Stewart Island. Predator-free Ulva Island is often called the jewel in the crown of New Zealand's national parks.

★ **Kiwi Sports:** Dunedin's Highlanders play at Carisbrook Rugby Stadium, and Invercargill has the netball team—women's-only outdoor basketball— the Southern Sting.

★ **Pubs and Clubs:** Thanks to the presence of 20,000 university students Dunedin is full of funky bars, late-night pubs, value-for-the-money cafés, and rocking music venues.

★ **The Southern Sea:** The lower coast of the South Island is wild and woolly, bordering the great Southern Ocean that swirls around the base of the globe. Head south along the Catlins section of the Southern Scenic Route for ocean views, diving seabirds, and sandy beaches.

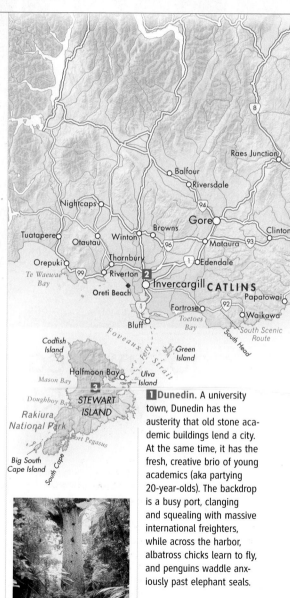

1 Dunedin. A university town, Dunedin has the austerity that old stone academic buildings lend a city. At the same time, it has the fresh, creative brio of young academics (aka partying 20-year-olds). The backdrop is a busy port, clanging and squealing with massive international freighters, while across the harbor, albatross chicks learn to fly, and penguins waddle anxiously past elephant seals.

| 0 | 20 mi |
| 0 | 20 km |

GETTING ORIENTED

The region is bordered by the snowcapped Southern Alps to the west and a string of golden, albeit chilly, beaches to the east. The north is met by the wide Canterbury Plains and the south by the timeless Catlins region. The two major hubs of civilization in the "deep south" are both coastal cities: Dunedin to the east and Invercargill to the south. The Otago Peninsula stretches east from "Dunners" into the Pacific and is home to the Royal Albatross and yellow-eyed penguins. Take the rugged coastal route west of Dunedin to explore the Catlins, where farms and forest meet the sea. Invercargill is flat and doesn't feel particularly coastal, as you can't see the sea from within the city. To avoid any "civilization hub," continue south, across Foveaux Strait, to Stewart Island.

2 Invercargill. Cast your gaze upward! The architecture of Invercargill is a treat to behold. Due to its proximity to the sea, "Invers" has been called the "City of Water and Light." The wide flat roads of downtown and the enormous sweep of Oreti Beach were perfect training grounds for home-grown hero Burt Munro (motorcycle land speed record holder).

3 Stewart Island. If your hand represents the island, your pinky fingernail would be the amount that is actually inhabited. Roads link the main township, Halfmoon Bay, to the other "neighborhoods"—a few homes nestled around one bay or another. Beaches are pristine; the sea is crystal green and bountiful. Flowers spill from grounded dories. Beyond town is wilderness teeming with wonderful birds.

OTAGO, INVERCARGILL, AND STEWART ISLAND PLANNER

Planning Your Time

Most people spend a few days in Dunedin and migrate south via State Highway 1. Once you reach Balclutha, you can continue south either by staying on the highway and heading straight for Invercargill or by going via the Catlins on the Southern Scenic Route. The Catlins route is more demanding, but also more scenic. Whichever route you take, by the time you hit the Southland border all roads are wide, flat, and point to Invercargill.

When to Go

Dunedin gets more visitors in summer, but during the university vacations it's quieter. Inland Otago remains dry year-round, and you can expect crisp, sunny days in winter, but the coast gets more rain, and Dunedin can have day after day of clouds and showers. Southland in winter isn't any colder, but it is wetter.

It's often said of New Zealand that you experience all four seasons in one day; on Stewart Island you may experience them all in an hour. In winter, there's a better chance of seeing the aurora australis, but some of the island's walking trails may be closed.

Getting Here and Around

Air Travel

Most flights to Dunedin and Invercargill go via Christchurch. Fog occasionally causes delays; luckily Christchurch Airport has a decent food court, a pool table, and an air hockey table to amuse you. Stewart Island Flights operates from Invercargill, or you can take a boat to the island. One local described the choices as "either 60 minutes of fear or 20 minutes of terror," but that's true only on a bad day—both journeys afford breathtaking views.

Bus Travel

InterCity's two daily runs between Christchurch and Dunedin take about five to six hours. The company makes an extra run on Friday and Sunday. One daily InterCity bus continues on from Dunedin to Invercargill; this takes another four hours. Other bus companies operating in the region include Atomic Shuttles, Citibus, and Bottom Bus.

Car Travel

The best way to explore is by car, particularly if you want to take your time seeing the Catlins. You cannot ferry your rental car to Stewart Island; there is secure parking in Invercargill and Bluff. Buses serve most places of interest, including daily routes between South Island cities. They go the direct route between Dunedin and Invercargill on State Highway 1. If you are driving and want to see the Catlins, leave State Highway 1 at Balclutha and take the well-marked Southern Scenic Route.

Restaurants

Dunedin has the area's highest concentration of good restaurants. Seafood is a big player, in part because of Dunedin's coastal location but also because of its proximity to Bluff, the home of New Zealand's great delicacy, the Bluff oyster. Many of the least-expensive options are café-like Asian restaurants; these tend to close early, around 9 PM. Locals don't usually dress up or make reservations for anything other than the most exclusive establishments.

Invercargill has a more limited selection of mostly moderately priced restaurants. Stewart Island has a reasonable selection considering its location, but in winter some places limit their hours or close.

Hotels

Dunedin has a full range of accommodations, from modest hostels to luxury hotels, whereas Invercargill has more motels than anything else. Local motels generally provide clean rooms with kitchens and TVs. Stewart Island's lodging options tend to be smaller boutique establishments, and usually on the expensive side. Throughout the region, air-conditioning is a rarity, but given the cool climate, this isn't a problem. Heating, on the other hand, is standard in most places.

It's a good idea to make reservations, especially in summer. In Dunedin, rooms can be scarce around special events, such as graduation ceremonies and high-profile rugby games.

WHAT IT COSTS IN NEW ZEALAND DOLLARS

	¢	$	$$	$$$	$$$$
Restaurants	under $10	$10–$15	$15–$20	$20–$30	over $30
Hotels	under $75	$75–$125	$125–$200	$200–$300	over $300

Meal prices are per person for a main course at dinner, or the equivalent. Hotel prices are for a standard double room in high season, including 12.5% tax.

Visitor Information

11

Both Dunedin and Invercargill have centrally located i-SITE visitor centers: you can find Dunedin's at the Octagon in city center and a branch at the wharf to greet cruise ships; the Invercargill i-SITE is in the Southland Museum. At the time of this writing the Stewart Island i-SITE had just closed, so check www.stewartisland.co.nz before your visit. Or on-island go to the Department of Conservation office or the Stewart Island Experience office (in the red building at the wharf).

Inside and Out

This region has plenty of indoor and outdoor options. If your temperament or the weather (which can sometimes be rather frightful in this neck of the country) are telling you to stay inside, stick around Dunedin for museums, galleries, cafés, and all the amenities that a city furnishes. But if you're game for exploring the natural world, venture onto the Otago Peninsula or further to the Catlins; these can be a day trip from Dunedin. If you're truly feeling adventurous and ready to leave all urban comforts behind, take a few days and head down to Stewart Island.

RAKIURA NATIONAL PARK

Between rocky beach and primitive forest, a plaque at the park's entrance quotes a Stewart Islander: "I must go over to New Zealand some day." More than 200 km of trail unfurls at your feet into pure wilderness: the rest of the world is indeed far removed.

Somewhere in the stands of ancient rimu trees and the thick tangle of supplejack vines and ferns are remnants of steam engines, trypots, and wagon tracks—vestiges of human attempts over the centuries to live and work in these parts. Ancient Maori muttonbirders, Southern Ocean whalers, millers, and miners have all come and gone. A few commercial fishing boats still operate from Halfmoon Bay, the last of an industry has dwindled over the years. While the rest of the planet succumbs to pavement and steel, Rakiura has become less developed, and the decision to make 85% of it a national park will preserve it so. As you adjust your pack, you may ponder what the island's industry is now. It's tourism (aka you)!

BEST TIME TO GO

The summer (November through March) is the best time to visit. Weather is unpredictable this far south, and Christmas BBQs have been known to see a sudden hailstorm. But generally this is the best bet for lovely long days (and the local businesses are all open as opposed to the off-season).

FUN FACT

The sculpture of an anchor chain (representing Maui's anchor) marks the entrance to Rakiura National Park. If you look closely you can see a bullet hole made when a drunk local used his rifle to express his opinion about art (or DOC).

BEST WAYS TO EXPLORE

MUD WALK

Eight-five percent of the island is national park, and it's thrilling to think that much of that is impenetrable wilderness, never seen or trodden upon by people. Over 200 km (124 mi) of walking trails create some of New Zealand's greatest hikes, including the three-day Rakiura Track and the challenging 11-day Northern Circuit. A popular adventure is taking a water taxi to the trailhead at Freshwater on the East side of the island, and walking across to the west coast's amazing Mason Bay beach, where you can arrange to have a plane pick you up. It takes close to three hours to walk to the end of the beach, which is home to most of the island's 20,000 kiwis. Unless you happen upon the island after a rare dry spell, you are sure to encounter copious quantities of mud on these trails so come prepared.

SEA-SIGHTING

Local companies offer a variety of boat tours: go fishing for Stewart Island blue cod, do a pelagic bird tour, or take a semi-submersible and view the gorgeous kelp gardens beneath the surface. Water taxi companies can drop you at bird sanctuary Ulva Island or at destinations along the Rakiura coast, or show you the aquaculture (muscle, salmon and oyster farms) of Big Glory Bay. If the weather is right, nothing beats a kayak trip in Paterson Inlet, where you can visit Ulva, circumnavigate half a dozen tiny islands, and observe penguins (little blue and yellow-eyed).

FROM THE AIR

Seeing the island by helicopter is an unforgettable experience. If you don't have a week or more to properly tackle the trails, then heli-hiking makes a lot of sense—get dropped at Mason Bay and walk back, or spend a day visiting various far-flung bays and beaches and be back in Halfmoon Bay in time for dinner. Tours can show you the magnificent southern coast, and you will be privy to views of Stewart Island that many life-long locals have never seen.

ECO-STAYS

Green comes naturally on Stewart Island. Reduce your carbon footprint by walking instead of driving; order the muttonbird, blue cod, groper, salmon, muscles, or oysters, and you'll be eating locally. Drinking water here is collected rainwater. Power costs four times as much for island residents than for mainlanders so most accommodations are quite green: eco-friendly bulbs are used, and wet socks get dried by the fire. Port of Call is run by extremely eco-minded longtime locals Ian and Phillipa Wilson. They keep their seaside property free of introduced weeds and full of native plants which is a rigorous year-round gardening challenge. All of their product choices from cleansers to food are eco-friendly. Ian is a member of the Ulva Island Charitable Trust. They both support of Stewart Island Community and Environment Trust (SIRCET), a project to reintroduce native birds to Halfmoon Bay that is centered on their property.

(top left) Beach on the Rakiura Track, (bottom) Trampers on Stewart Island's Māori Beach, (top) The native Weka bird

Updated by
Jessica Kany

The province of Otago occupies much of the southeast quadrant of the South Island. During the first three decades of the 1800s, European whaling ships cruised its coast and ventured ashore, yielding a mixed response from the Māori, who had been living here for hundreds of years. In 1848 Dunedin was settled, and all the land from the top of the Otago Peninsula south to the Clutha River and sections farther inland were purchased from the Māori. By the mid-1860s Dunedin was the economic hub of the Otago gold rush. Dunedin's historical wealth endures in such institutions as the University of Otago, the oldest in the country.

Invercargill, to the south, was born out of different economic imperatives. After the Dunedin settlers bought swaths of the Southland for their sheep, they needed a local port to bring in more stock from Australia. The town of Bluff, already familiar to sealers, was selected as an ideal location. Invercargill became the administrative center to the port and then the whole region. Until recent years, the town's economic focus remained that of raising sheep and other livestock and crops; it is now becoming a more diverse metropolis.

Hanging off the bottom of South Island, Stewart Island is a study in remoteness. Commercial-fishing settlements give way to bushland that the kiwi bird still haunts. At night, the birds can be seen wandering the beaches. On some nights the aurora australis, the Southern Hemisphere equivalent of the northern lights, light up the sky.

DUNEDIN

11

280 km (175 mi) east of Queenstown, 362 km (226 mi) south of Christchurch.

Clinging to the walls of the natural amphitheater at the west end of Otago Harbour, the South Island's second-largest city is enriched with inspiring nearby seascapes and wildlife. Because Dunedin's a university town, floods of students give the city a vitality far greater than its population of 122,000 might suggest. Its manageable size makes it easy to explore on foot—with the possible exception of Baldwin Street, the world's steepest residential street and home to the annual "gutbuster" race, in which people run up it, and the "Jaffa" race, in which people roll the namesake spherical chocolate candy down it.

Dunedin, the Gaelic name for Edinburgh, was founded in 1848 by settlers of the Free Church of Scotland, a breakaway group from the Presbyterian Church. The city's Scottish roots are still visible; you'll find the only kilt shop in the country, the first and only (legal) whisky distillery, and a statue of Scottish poet Robert Burns. The Scottish settlers and local Māori came together in relative peace, but this wasn't true of the European whalers who were here three decades before, as places with names such as Murdering Beach illustrate.

Dunedin has always had a reputation for the eccentric. Wearing no shoes and a big beard here marks a man as bohemian rather than destitute, and the residents wouldn't have it any other way. The University of Otago was the country's first university and has been drawing writers ever since its founding in 1871, most notably Janet Frame and the poet James K. Baxter. Dunedin also has a musical heritage, which blossomed into the "Dunedin Sound" of the 1970s and '80s. The movement, which included the Chills and the Verlaines, is making a comeback.

GETTING HERE AND AROUND

Dunedin Airport lies 20 km (13 mi) south of the city. Both Qantas and Air New Zealand link Dunedin and Christchurch; the flight takes just under an hour. Air New Zealand also flies regularly from Dunedin to Auckland and Wellington

Confusing, one-way roads and twisting hills in the suburbs make driving in Dunedin a challenge. Street parking is limited. Local buses to the peninsula depart from Stand 5, Cumberland Street.

ESSENTIALS

Airport Dunedin International Airport (⊠ *25 Miller Rd., Momona* ☎ *03/486–2879* ⊕ *www.dnairport.co.nz*).

Bus Depot Dunedin (⊠ *205 St. Andrew St.9016*).

Bus Information Citibus (☎ *03/477–5577* ⊕ *www.citibus.co.nz*). **InterCity** (☎ *03/471–7143* ⊕ *www.intercitycoach.co.nz*).

Medical Assistance Dunedin Hospital (⊠ *201 Great King St., Dunedin* ☎ *03/474–7930*).

BEST BETS FOR CRUISE PASSENGERS

■ Otago Peninsula. Visit the Royal Albatross Centre at Taiaroa Head and the yellow-eyed penguins at Penguin Place.

■ Museum-hopping. Otago Museum and Discovery World, Otago Settlers Museum, and the Dunedin Public Art Gallery.

■ City Sights. Explore the shops and galleries around the Octagon, and tour Cadbury World, the Speights Brewery and the famous "ginger-

bread house"—the Dunedin Railway Station.

■ Taieri Gorge Railway. There's a train scheduled just for cruise passengers. A half-day trip will take you to Pukerangi and back through breathtaking scenery.

Tour Information Double Decker Bus Tour (⊠ *630 Princes St., Dunedin* ☎ *03/477–5577* ⊕ *www.citibus.co.nz*). **Twilight Tours** (⊠ *25 Coolock St., Dunedin* ☎ *03/474–3300* ⊕ *www.wilddunedin.co.nz*).

Visitor Information Dunedin Visitor Information Centre (⊠ *48 The Octagon* ☎ *03/474–3300* 🖶 *03/474–3311* ⊕ www.cityofdunedin.com). **Dunedin NZ's Official Tourist Information Web site** (⊕ www.dunedinnz.com).

EXPLORING

TOP ATTRACTIONS

♺ **Cadbury World.** Which came first, the Cadbury factory or the Cadbury Creme Egg? At Cadbury World you can watch chocolate candy in the making; keep an eye out for the chocolate waterfall. Kiwis from as far away as Stewart Island have memories of school field trips here and ensuing tummy aches (the tour includes free samples of candy). It's best to prebook a tour. ⊠ *280 Cumberland St.* ☎ *03/467–7967 or 0800/223–287* ⊕ *www.cadburyworld.co.nz* 🎫 *$18* ☽ *Daily 9–4, 9–7 in summer.*

★ **Dunedin Railway Station.** The 1906 Dunedin Railway Station, a cathedral to the power of steam, is a massive bluestone structure in Flemish Renaissance style, lavishly decorated with heraldic beasts, nymphs, scrolls, a mosaic floor, and even stained-glass windows of steaming locomotives. This extravagant building earned its architect, George Troup, a knighthood from the king—and the nickname Gingerbread George from the people of Dunedin. The station is also home to the **Sports Hall of Fame** (☎ *03/477–7775* ⊕ *www.nzhalloffame.co.nz* 🎫 *$5* ☽ *Daily 10–4*), the country's only sports museum. ⊠ *Anzac Ave. at Stuart St.* ☎ *03/477–4449* ☽ *Daily 7–6.*

Speight's Brewery Heritage Centre. For more tasty indulgences, head to the Speight's Brewery Heritage Centre for a tour of the South's top brewery, which dates back to 1876. Here you can see the various stages of gravity-driven brewing, learn the trade's lingo such as *wort* and

The extravagant Dunedin Railway Station is fronted by manicured grounds.

grist, and taste the results. Speight's makes several traditional beers, the most common being its Gold Medal Ale. The company claims that this is the drink of choice for every "Southern Man," which isn't far from the truth. Watch a video of various Speight's television ads and learn to say the tough Southern way, *Good on ya, mate.* ✉ *200 Rattray St.* ☎ *03/477–7697* ✉ *tours@speights.co.nz* ⚓ *Reservations essential* 🎫 *$17* ⌚ *Weekend tours at 10, noon, and 2 (sometimes an additional 4 PM tour is added on busy days); weekday tours at 10, noon, 2, and 7.*

WORTH NOTING

Botanic Gardens. Relax and enjoy the birdsong amid 70 acres of international and native flora. In addition to the seasonal gardens with their 6,800 plant species are the year-round attractions: an aviary, a winter garden hothouse, a native plant collection, and a rhododendron garden. Parking at the lower part of the gardens, off Cumberland Street, has easier access than the Opoho end, which is steeper, but both parts are worth visiting. ✉ *Great King St. at Opoho Rd.* ☎ *03/477–4000* 🎫 *Free* ⌚ *Gardens dawn–dusk, buildings 10–4.*

Dunedin Public Art Gallery. The Dunedin Public Art Gallery has lovely exhibit spaces. The shell of an original municipal building has been paired with a sweeping, modern, glass facade. The collection includes European masters Monet, Turner, and Gainsborough, as well as New Zealand and Otago artists. A special gallery highlights Dunedin native Frances Hodgkins, whose work won acclaim in the 1930s and '40s. Hodgkins's style changed through her career, but some of her most distinctive works are postimpressionist watercolors. ✉ *30 The Octagon* ☎ *03/474–3240* 🌐 *www.dunedin.art.museum* 🎫 *Free* ⌚ *Daily 10–5.*

CLOSE UP

The Northern Otago Coast and Oamaru

Driving south from Timaru, **Oamaru** is the first stop of interest. Described as the best example of Victorian architecture in use in New Zealand today, the ornate Oamaru limestone facades of the buildings in the port precinct gleam. During the second week of November the town hosts the **Victorian Heritage Celebrations.** Festivities include the New Zealand Penny Farthing Championships, a Heritage Golf Classic, a Heritage Ball, and a Victorian Garden Party. The town's visitor center has information about the festival and the buildings themselves. ⊠ *Oamaru i-SITE Info Centre, 1´ Thames St., Oamaru* ☎ *03/434–1656* ⊕ *www.tourismwaitaki.co.nz.*

Oamaru's other claim to fame is penguins. Each evening, enthusiastic blue penguins—the world's smallest penguin breed—emerge from the sea and waddle up the beach to their nests. The **Oamaru Blue Penguin Colony** (⊠ *Waterfront Rd.* ☎ *03/433–1195* ⊕ *www.penguins. co.nz* ⌑ *Tour $15*) can be visited any time of the year, and providing penguins are present, tours and viewing opportunities run day and evening. **Pen-y-bryn Lodge** (⊠ *41 Towey St.* ☎ *03/434–7939* ⊕ *www. penybryn.co.nz*) extends entry to the penguin colony as part of the hotel's room rate. Each night, between the appetizer and the main course in the dining room, guests are encouraged to leave the table and head down to the ocean to watch the penguins come in, before returning to their meal and a quiet port afterward.

An even more significant population of **yellow-eyed penguins**, or *hoiho,* come ashore south of Oamaru. The best places to view them are Bushy Beach and Katiki Point, where hides

(camouflaged viewing huts) have been constructed. These penguins are one of the world's rarest breeds, and they are considered an endangered species. Ask at the **local information office** (☎ *03/434–1656* ⊕ *www. tourismwaitaki.co.nz*) for details on viewing them.

Along the coast north of Dunedin, you can stop to see the striking **Moeraki Boulders.** These giant spherical rocks are concretions, formed by a gradual buildup of minerals around a central core. Some boulders have sprung open, revealing—no, not alien life forms, but—interesting calcite crystals. The boulders stud the beach north of the town of Moeraki and south as well at Katiki Beach off Highway 1, about 60 km (37 mi) above Dunedin, or 40 km (25 mi) south of Oamaru. Sadly, the boulders at Moeraki Beach have become a bit of a tourist item, and there are often whole busloads of people wandering the beach. Watch for little dolphins jumping in the surf just offshore; they're as interesting as the boulders. If you're feeling a bit hungry after the sea air, pop into **Fleurs Place** (⊠ *169 Haven St., Moeraki* ☎ *03/439–5980*) out on the old jetty. Here you can enjoy fish straight out of the sea, which is the highlight of the lunch and dinner menus. The mouthwatering menu at **Riverstone Kitchen** (⊠ *1431 State Hwy. 1, North Oamaru* ☎ *03/431–3505* ⊙ *Sun.–Wed. 9–5; Thurs.–Sat. 9–late,* serves organic, locally grown, seasonal produce. The deli and restaurant are open daily for breakfast and lunch, and dinner is served from 6 PM Thursday through Saturday.

OTAGO CENTRAL RAIL TRAIL

From Dunedin Railway Station, take the Taieri Gorge Train to Middle-march (or Pukerangi, 19 km (12 mi) from Middlemarch), one end of the **Otago Central Rail Trail**. This 150 km (93 mi) pleasantly undulating bicycle path follows the old railway line and includes a dizzying wooden viaduct, a 150 meter (500-foot)-long tunnel, and places to eat, sleep and drink along the way. The only traffic you'll encounter is the occasional herd of muddy-bottomed sheep. The ride takes about five days to complete, passing through sheep farms and lovely wee towns such as Ranfurly, an "oasis of art deco"

and Alexander, one of the busier hubs in Central Otago on the banks of the paint green Clutha River. The trail eventually ends in Thyme-scented Clyde. The route can be traversed in either direction; Clyde is approximately 80 km (50 mi) from Queenstown. The Otago Central Rail Trail is a great way to experience the sheep stations, puzzling sheep station gates with puzzling locks (a couple dozen of them), mud, wind, rivers, dags, pubs, and old gold fields of the South Island on a bicycle-friendly path. ⊕ www.otagocentralrailtrail.co.nz.

Octagon. The city's hub is the eight-sided town center. It's lined with several imposing buildings, and a smattering of market stalls, cafés, and bars with tables spilling onto the pavement. In summer it's a meeting place, and it's also the site for the occasional student demonstration. A **statue of Robert Burns** sits in front of **St. Paul's Cathedral,** a part-Victorian Gothic, part-modern building with an imposing marble staircase leading up to a towering facade of Oamaru stone. On Stuart Street at the corner of Dunbar, check out the late-Victorian **Law Courts.** Their figure of Justice stands with scales in hand but without her customary blindfold (she wears a low helmet instead).

☺ **Otago Museum.** The Otago Museum demonstrates what galleries and museums were like in Victorian times. In this museum's 1877 building, you can visit the "Animal Attic," a restored, magnificent skylighted gallery. The museum's first curator was a zoologist, and many of the original animals collected from 1868 are still on display. "Southern Land, Southern People" explores the cultural heritage of this region, and other galleries focus on Māori and Pacific Island artifacts, animal and insect specimens, and nautical items, including ship models and a whale skeleton. ⊠ *419 Great King St.* ☎ *03/474–7474* ⊕ *www.otago-museum.govt.nz* ▣ *Free, Discovery World $6, special galleries and visiting exhibitions $10* ☉ *Daily 10–5.*

Otago Settlers Museum. The Otago Settlers Museum tells the stories of all Otago settlers, from Māori and early European and Chinese to later Pacific Islanders and Asians. On display are documents, works of art, technological items, and forms of transport. The museum has changing exhibits, events, and historical walking tours of the city. ⊠ *31 Queens Gardens* ☎ *03/477–5052* ⊕ *www.otago.settlers.museum* ▣ *$4* ☉ *Daily 10–5.*

🕭 **Taieri Gorge Railway.** The Taieri Gorge Railway tourist train runs from Dunedin through the now-closed Otago Central Railway to Pukerangi and Middlemarch (home of the annual Middlemarch Singles' Ball; each year this very train imports young city gals up to a dance with lonely Otago sheep shearers). Also available is a seasonal *Seasider* route from Dunedin up the coast to Palmerston. The train runs every day; check the timetable for its destination. Reservations are essential. Cyclists can connect at Middlemarch to the wonderful Otago Central Rail Trail. ⇨ *Otago Central Rail Trail box.* ⊠ *Dunedin Railway Station* ☎ *03/477–4449* ⊕ *www.taieri.co.nz* ▭ *$59–$75.*

SPORTS AND THE OUTDOORS

BEACHES To get to **St. Clair Beach** either drive south on State Highway 1 or hop on the Normanby–St. Clair bus from George Street or the Octagon. The sea at Dunedin can be a little wild; in summer an area between flags is patrolled by lifeguards. St. Clair has some good surfing; it hosts some prestigious competitions. Don't be too spooked by the shark bell on the Esplanade: a fatal attack hasn't occurred for 30 years, just the occasional nibble. South of town is the **Tunnel Beach walk,** which heads through a sandstone tunnel to a secluded beach (this walk is closed from August through October for lambing).

HIKING AND **Signal Hill,** to the northeast, with good views of the city below and the WALKING hills surrounding it, is a popular walking destination and an excellent mountain-biking venue. At the opposite end of town, Saddle Hill looks southward to Mosgiel and the Taieri Plain.

RUGBY Rugby is followed with cultish devotion in Dunedin, and **Carisbrook Stadium** (⊠ *Burns St.* ☎ *03/466–4010 or 0800/227–472* ⊕ *www.orfu. co.nz*), also known as the "House of Pain," is where fans go to worship. Fans of the local Super 14 team, the Highlanders, paint themselves blue and yellow on match days. Games are played on weekends. Terrace tickets start at $12, and the main stand is just $27. Walking with the crowds out to the stadium for night games is an event unto itself, and can be a hasty pub crawl out of the city. Make sure to get to the game in time for the opening *haka* (traditional Māori warrior dance)!

WHERE TO EAT

Use the coordinate (⊕ B2) at the end of each listing to locate a site on the corresponding map.

$$–$$$ ✕ **The Ale House Bar & Restaurant.** A rugged interior with heavy wood NEW ZEALAND furniture, old brewing equipment, and a huge schist fireplace makes the ★ Speight's brewery restaurant welcoming. Its hub, naturally, is the bar. The menu includes a "drunken" steak (steak marinated in dark, malty porter) and beer-battered fish. You also get recommendations for the best Speight's ale to match your meal. Several special seasonal beers are released each year; in the past, these have included Harvest (an apricot beer), Chocolate, and Samradh (a ginger-and-pimiento beer). ⊠ *200 Rattray St.* ☎ *03/471–9050* ▭ *AE, DC, MC, V* ⊕ *A2.*

$
INDIAN
✕**Anarkali.** Once named Ananda, Anarkali has retained the same chef and still serves the authentic Indian vegetarian *thalis* (meals made up of several small individual servings) served on traditional metal platters. You can choose from (in order of ascending size) the Prince, Rani, Raja, or Maharaja thali. Anarkali is best suited for lunches and early dinners. Although it has a liquor license, you're welcome to bring your own bottle. ✉ *365 George St.* ☎ *03/477–1120* ▭ *MC, V* ✛ *B1.*

$$$–$$$$
NEW ZEALAND
★
✕**Bell Pepper Blues.** Inside a converted historic hotel, this casual restaurant with its mullioned bay windows and dark-wood interior is where Michael Coughlin, one of the country's most respected chefs, brings an inventive flair to his dishes. His lamb, beef, and *cervena* (farmed venison) dishes are well known; the pan-seared beef sirloin with a spring roll of slow-braised veal shin and aromatic Asian vegetables is a particular standout. Pre- and postdinner drinks can be had next door at the restaurant's Chilé Club Bar. ✉ *474 Princes St.* ☎ *03/474–0973* ⊕ *www.bellpepperblues.co.nz* ▭ *AE, DC, MC, V* ☺ *Closed Sun. No lunch* ✛ *A3.*

$$–$$$
NEW ZEALAND
★
✕**Plato Cafe.** A favorite among locals, this waterfront eatery provides great food and excellent service. Everything from the bread and house-made duck liver–cognac pate, to the perfectly cooked seafood and chicken dishes, is delicious. They do a mean coffee and great desserts, too. ✉ *2 Birch St.* ☎ *03/477–4235* ⊕ *www.platocafe.co.nz* ▭ *AE, DC, MC, V* ☺ *Daily for dinner from 6 on. Lunch and brunch offered Sun. 11* ✛ *C3.*

$$–$$$
NEW ZEALAND
✕**Salt Bar Restaurant.** In an iconic art deco building, this is St. Clair's newest place to dine and take in the salty sea views. Sate yourself with shepherd's pie, pumpkin-sage risotto, or bacon-wrapped scallops, or sip an Oranjeboom on tap. The bar's cool aura of chrome finishing and art deco style is warmed by the dining area which has a brick fireplace. The service is extremely friendly. The Salt Bar serves breakfast, lunch, and dinner. ✉ *240 Forbury Rd., St. Clair's* ☎ *03/455–1077* ▭ *AE, DC, MC, V* ✛ *A3.*

$–$$
THAI
✕**Thai Hanoi.** This popular Thai restaurant has some Vietnamese influence. Try one of the green or red Thai curries, or a yellow or jungle (hot) Vietnamese curry. Because it's opposite the Rialto Cinema, Thai Hanoi makes for a convenient pre- or postmovie dinner spot—but reserving a table is a good idea. ✉ *24 Moray Pl.* ☎ *03/471–9500* ▭ *AE, DC, MC, V* ☺ *No lunch* ✛ *B2.*

WHERE TO STAY

Use the coordinate (✛ B2) at the end of each listing to locate a site on the corresponding map.

$$–$$$
🏨 **Bluestone on George.** This hotel gives its guests all the nice amenities in spanking-clean, brand-new rooms. Rooms include bathrobes, heated bathroom floors, and kitchen facilities, and most rooms have whirlpool baths. **Pros:** centrally located; relatively new. **Cons:** not terribly Dunediny—a bit of an impersonal business-trip vibe. ✉ *571 George St.* ☎ *03/477–9201* ⊕ *www.bluestonedunedin.co.nz* ⇆ *15 rooms* ♨ *In-room: Kitchen. In-hotel: Gym, parking (free)* ▭ *AE, DC, MC, V* ✛ *B1.*

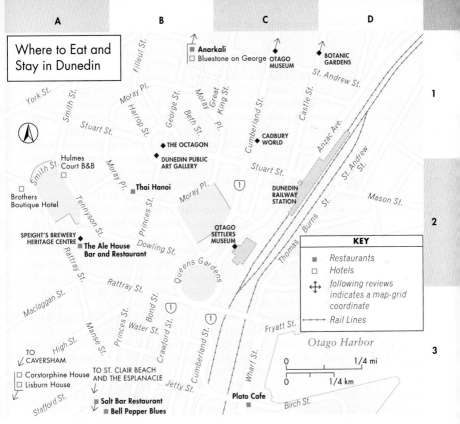

Where to Eat and Stay in Dunedin

A B C D

Anarkali
Bluestone on George
OTAGO MUSEUM
BOTANIC GARDENS
St. Andrew St.

Filleul St.
York St.
Moray Pl.
Smith St.
Harrop St.
George St.
Moray Pl.
Great King St.
Beth St.
Cumberland St.
Castle St.
Stuart St.

1

CADBURY WORLD

THE OCTAGON

Anzac Ave.

Hulmes Court B&B

DUNEDIN PUBLIC ART GALLERY

Stuart St.

St. Andrew St.

Smith St.
Moray Pl.

Thai Hanoi

Princes St.

Moray Pl.

DUNEDIN RAILWAY STATION

Mason St.

Brothers Boutique Hotel

Tennyson St.

OTAGO SETTLERS MUSEUM

Thomas Burns St.

2

SPEIGHT'S BREWERY HERITAGE CENTRE
The Ale House Bar and Restaurant

Rattray St.
Dowling St.

Queens Gardens

KEY

Restaurants
Hotels
following reviews indicates a map-grid coordinate
Rail Lines

Maclaggan St.

Rattray St.

Bond St.

Princes St.
Water St.
Crawford St.

Manse St.

Fryatt St.

Otago Harbor

3

TO CAVERSHAM

High St.

Cumberland St.

Wharf St.

0   1/4 mi
0   1/4 km

Corstorphine House
Lisburn House

TO ST. CLAIR BEACH AND THE ESPLANACLE

Jetty St.

Plato Cafe

Stafford St.

Salt Bar Restaurant
Bell Pepper Blues

Birch St.

$$–$$$ **Brothers Boutique Hotel.** This centrally located historic building once housed members of the Christian Brothers Order. The priciest room is the old chapel with a super-king bed and stained-glass windows. Two rooms have balconies with city and harbor views. All rooms were refurbished in 2005 and have updated bathrooms. The owners are friendly and helpful. Free broadband Internet is offered in the lounge and complimentary breakfast and evening drinks are provided. **Pros:** clean rooms; quirky interior; friendly staff including Baron the Labrador concierge. **Cons:** standard rooms on the small side. ⊠ *295 Rattray St.* ☎ *03/477–0043* ⊕ *www.brothershotel.co.nz* ⇗ *15 rooms. In-hotel: Internet terminal, parking (free)* ⊟ *AE, MC, V* ⊕ *A2.*

$$$$ **Corstorphine House.** This restored Edwardian mansion, surrounded by private gardens, exudes luxurious gentility. The lavish interior extends from the public areas, with carved fireplaces and custom-made furniture, to the themed rooms, which include the Egyptian Room and the Indian Room. Bathrooms have de-misting mirrors and heated floors, and your bed comes with a pillow menu. Organic produce grown on the property appears in the highly acclaimed conservatory restaurant's ($$$) dishes, so your meals include free-range eggs, and fresh vegetables, all seasoned with handpicked herbs. The room rate includes a full breakfast. **Pros:** gorgeous rooms and grounds. **Cons:** on the outskirts of the city, car required to get here. ⊠ *23 Milburn St.* ☎ *03/487–1000*

Fodor's Choice ★

⊕ *www.corstorphine.co.nz* ⤳ *7 rooms* ⚄ *In-room: DVD, Wi-Fi. In-hotel: Restaurant* ▤ *AE, DC, MC, V* ◉ *BP* ⊹ *A3*.

$–$$ ⚇ **Hulmes Court Bed & Breakfast.** In an 1860 house built for one of the founders of the Otago Medical School, this bed-and-breakfast maintains its scholarly ties: the host, Norman Wood, employs University of Otago students and graduates. The complex includes a 1907 house next door. Rooms are characterized by their architectural elements, such as large bay windows. From Hulmes Court it's a short walk to the center of town. Children are welcome. There's a resident cat named Solstice. Some of the rooms have shared bathrooms, so make sure you inquire if you want a private toilet. **Pros:** friendly staff; interesting decoration. **Cons:** not ideal for folks with cat allergies. ✉ *52 Tennyson St.* ☎ *03/477–5319* ⊕ *www.hulmes.co.nz* ⤳ *14 rooms, 8 with bath* ⚄ *In-room: Internet (some). In-hotel: Bar, bicycles, Internet terminal* ▤ *AE, DC, MC, V* ◉ *CP* ⊹ *A2*.

$$–$$$ ⚇ **Lisburn House.** This Victorian-Gothic inn is a romantic retreat amid
★   lovingly tended gardens. Many of its 1865 details are intact, including decorative Irish brickwork and fishtail slate roof tiles. Inside are high, molded plaster ceilings, an impressive turn-of-the-20th-century stained-glass entrance, and a welcoming fireplace. The three sumptuous bedrooms have four-poster queen beds. At the Claddagh Restaurant ($$$), with its extensive wine list and plush interior, the venison and seafood chowder are always delicious. Dining reservations are essential, and Claddagh is open Tuesday–Saturday. **Pros:** cute rooms; fabulous dining. **Cons:** on the outskirts of city center. ✉ *15 Lisburn Ave.* ☎ *03/455–8888* ⊕ *www.lisburnhouse.co.nz* ⤳ *3 rooms* ⚄ *In-room: No phone, no TV. In-hotel: Restaurant, bar* ▤ *AE, DC, MC, V* ◉ *BP* ⊹ *A3*.

NIGHTLIFE AND THE ARTS

Many venues are on or near George and Princes streets, often down dark alleys with no signs, so follow the crowd. Information about what's going on can be found on the Fink Web site (⊕ *www.fink.net. nz*), Radio One (91 FM), and in the student paper, *The Critic*.

THE ARTS

ART GALLERIES   The **Marshall Seifert Gallery** (✉ *1 Dowling St.* ☎ *03/477–5260*) is in a triangular-shape building with a dizzying spiral staircase. It's overflowing with fine art, antiques, prints, and contemporary New Zealand art. It's open weekdays 11–5:30, and Saturday 11–2. **Milford Galleries** (✉ *18 Dowling St.* ☎ *03/477–7727* ⊕ *www.milfordgalleries.co.nz*), a major fine-art dealer, presents solo and group exhibitions of New Zealand paintings, drawings, sculpture, glasswork, ceramic art, and photography. Among the artists are Neil Frazer (who does large-scale abstract expressionist paintings) and Elizabeth Rees (whose oils explore New Zealand machismo).

THEATER   Since 1961, the **Globe Theatre** (✉ *104 London St.* ☎ *03/477–3274*) has produced high-quality plays, beginning with local author James K. Baxter. The **Regent Theatre** (✉ *17 The Octagon* ☎ *03/477–6481, 03/477–8597 ticket reservations* ⊕ *www.regenttheatre.co.nz*), in a historic

CLOSE UP

The Southern Scenic Route—Catlins Sections

11

The Southern Scenic Route, 440 km (273 mi) long, follows the coast south of Dunedin, picks up the highway to Balclutha, and swings around the Catlins coast before pushing through Invercargill to Milford Sound. The Catlins stretch (200 km, or 125 mi) is a treat, although some side roads are rough. Split your journey over two days. The *Southern Scenic Route* brochure, available at the Dunedin visitor center, describes the sights; attractions are signposted. Visit ⊕ *www. southernscenicroute.co.nz.*

When you leave the highway at Balclutha, you'll notice that the native bush is dense and relatively untouched. This, coupled with rich birdsong, gives the countryside a tropical quality.

The first stop is **Nugget Point**. Its Māori name, Tokatā, means "rocks standing up out of water." Wildlife abounds, including yellow-eyed penguins, fur and elephant seals, and sea lions. The town at Nugget Point is **Kaka Point**. There are several places to stay the night, and you should spend time at the "hide" observing the yellow-eyed penguins coming in from the sea. If you want a coffee served with an excellent sea view, stop in the **Point** at Kaka Point. Inland is **Owaka**, the Catlins' only town. With a population of roughly 400, Owaka has a cluster of shops, a Department of Conservation Field Centre, a small museum, and basic services.

At the settlement of **Papatowai**, there's a convenient picnic spot behind a tidal inlet. Here you can enjoy rock pools with bush on one side and coastline on the other. Just south of here, stop at the **Florence Hill Lookout**. The view of Tautuku

Bay is one of the best coastal views in New Zealand. There's a 30-minute loop walk onto the estuary at Tautuku Bay.

Farther on is **Curio Bay**, home to a petrified forest visible at low tide. From Curio Bay a back road runs over to **Slope Point**, mainland New Zealand's southernmost point. Heavy rains or unusually high tides can make the road impassable. Slope Point is a bit of a disappointment—just some farmland sloping to the sea. However, it gets plenty of visitors. There is no access during the lambing season in September and October. If you skip Slope Point and continue on the main road, stop at the general store in Waikawa, where the art of the meat pie has been perfected.

By now the rugged Catlins landscape smoothes out into gentle green hills. From the township of Fortrose the roads are straight once more across the wide flats of Southland; before you know it, you've reached Invercargill. The road continues westward to Tuatapere, the self-proclaimed "sausage capital of New Zealand." Stops along the way include a surf at Colac Bay, a try at the "Bull Ring" in Dusty's Pub, and a tour of Cosy Nook.

On the edge of Balclutha, the **Garvan Hotel** ($$–$$$) looks like a pleasant B&B with pleasant gardens, nothing more. But luxury awaits: perfect hollandaise, crackling fires, accommodating hosts. The menu is divine. (What could be richer than beef fillet with merlot–blue cheese sauce? Answer: their chocolate dessert.) ⊠ *State Hwy. 1, Lovells Flat, Milton* ☎ *03/417–8407* ⊕ *www.garvan.co.nz* ⌐ *4 rooms* ⊟ *MC, V* ⏐○⏐ *BP.*

building, holds large-scale musicals, dance, and theater performances, and hosts the Royal New Zealand Ballet, the New Zealand Film Festival, and the World Cinema Showcase each year. The highly rated **Bean Scené** café ($$), in the same building, is a nice stop for dinner (don't be fooled by the tired interior—the food is excellent).

NIGHTLIFE

You could spend all night bar-hopping and never leave the **Octagon**, with its many drinking establishments, from the swank upstairs wine bar **Bacchus** (⌧ *12 The Octagon* 9016) to the rowdy live music of Irish pub **The Craic** (⌧ *24 The Octagon*).

The **Arc Café** (⌧ *135 High St.* ☎ *03/474–1135*) is a bar, performance venue, café, and gallery all rolled into one. This really informal and affordable joint is probably the only place in town you can ask for a cognac with your morning coffee without raising an eyebrow.

★ Possibly the snuggest bar in Dunedin, **Pequeno** (⌧ *Savoy Bldg., lower ground fl., 50 Princes St.* ☎ *03/477–7830*) came to notoriety as the hangout of choice for Gwyneth Paltrow and Chris Martin, of the band Coldplay, during the Dunedin shoot of the film *Sylvia*. The wine list is good, if pricey, and there's live jazz on Thursday evenings. **Refuel** (⌧ *640 Cumberland St.* ☎ *03/479–5309* ⊕ *www.dunedinmusic.com*), in the heart of the university campus, has a predominantly student clientele, though everyone is welcome. Nights are split between local or national (or even international) live rock acts and DJ-driven nights of '80s hits, hip-hop, house, and drum 'n' bass music.

SHOPPING

Nearly all the good shops are clustered around George Street and Moray Place.

Koru (⌧ *Lower Stuart St., opposite Dunedin Railway Station* ☎ *03/477–2138* ⊕ *www.nzartandjade.co.nz*) is a local artists' co-op gallery and interactive studio, which sells crafts made of *pounamu* (New Zealand greenstone), *paua* (abalone shell), and wood, as well as weaving and pottery. Bargain hunting bibliophiles will be in heaven (or a level closer to it) on the second floor of the **University Bookshop** (⌧ *378 Great King St.* ☎ *03/477–6976* ⊕ *www.unibooks.co.nz*), where there is a constant sale. Kiwi spirit is at **Outré** (⌧ *380 Great King St., opposite University Bookshop* ☎ *03/471–7005*), where New Zealand–made crafts are mixed in with clothing, trinkets, and eco-friendly goods— possibly inspired by the Green Party offices across the street. **Plume** (⌧ *310 George St.* ☎ *03/477–9358*) carries major international and New Zealand designer clothes. Great New Zealand labels abound, such as Nom D, Zambesi, Kate Sylvester, and Workshop. Girls: if you're looking for fun, funky sundresses, **Slick Willy's** (⌧ *323 George St., upstairs* ☎ *03/477–1406*) has a great selection. For sweets, drop by **Guilty by Confection** (⌧ *44–46 Stuart St.* ☎ *03/474–0835*) for a hot chocolate or some homemade fudge.

Otago
Peninsula

TO
CHRISTCHURCH

Middlemarch

Sutton

Palmerston

Waikouaiti
Cornish Head
Puketeraki

Taieri Gorge Railway

Evansdale
Warrington

Clarks Junction

Waitati

Aramoana
Taiaroa Head

Port Chalmers
Sawyers Bay

Otago Harbour

Outram

Portobello
"Disappearing Gun"

Lake
Mahinerangi

Larnach
Castle

Broad
Bay

OTAGO
PENINSULA

Mosgiel

Allanton

Waverley

St Clair

Lawrence

Westwood
Brighton

Dunedin
see detail map

Kuri Bush

South Pacific Ocean

Milton

Toko Mouth

0   15 mi

0   15 km

Balclutha

← Invercargill

Kaitangata

OTAGO PENINSULA

The main items of interest along the claw-shaped peninsula that extends northeast from Dunedin are an albatross colony and Larnach Castle. The road on the west side of the peninsula consists of 15 km (9½ mi) of tight curves along the harbor, so be careful while driving, or you could find yourself having an impromptu marine adventure. Along the road are a handful of settlements; these get progressively more rustic as you near the peninsula's tip. On the east side of the peninsula there's a string of rugged beaches; some are accessible via walking paths. On the journey back to Dunedin, the Highcliff Road, which turns inland at the village of Portobello, is a scenic alternative to the coastal Portobello Road and gives easiest access to Larnach Castle. Allow an hour to drive from the city.

GETTING HERE AND AROUND

Driving to the peninsula gives you freedom to stop when and where you choose, and the route is quite scenic, as much of the road hugs the water. The Dunedin city bus leaves throughout the day from Cumberland Street to the peninsula; check the Otago Regional Council Web site for the schedule. You can also see the peninsula sights via a harbor boat cruise.

Visitor information is available at the Dunedin Visitor Information Centre but for facts specific to the peninsula, check out the Visit Otago Peninsula Web site.

ESSENTIALS

Bus Information Otago Regional Council (⊕ orc.govt.nz/custom/bustime-table/search.html).

Tour Information Catlins Natural Wonders (☎ 0800/353–941 ⊕ www. catlinsnatural.co.nz). **Catlins Wildlife Trackers Ecotours** (⊠ 5 Mirren St., Papatowai ☎ 03/415–8613 ⊕ www.catlins-ecotours.co.nz). **Monarch Wildlife Cruises** (⊠ Wharf St. at Fryatt St., Dunedin ☎ 03/477–4276 ⊕ www.wildlife.co.nz). **Natures Wonders Naturally** (⊠ Harington Point, Portobello ☎ 03/478–1150 ⊕ www.natureswondersnaturally.com).

Visitor Information Dunedin Visitor Information Centre ⊠ 48 The Octagon ☎ 03/474–3300 ⊕ www.cityofdunedin.com). **Visit Otago Peninsula** ⊕ www.otago-peninsula.co.nz).

EXPLORING

★ High on a hilltop with commanding views from its battlements, **Larnach Castle** is the grand baronial fantasy of William Larnach, an Australian-born businessman and politician. The castle, built in the mid-1870s, was a vast extravagance even in the free-spending days of the gold rush. Larnach imported an English craftsman to carve the ceilings, which took 12 years to complete. The solid marble bath, marble fireplaces, tiles, glass, and even much of the wood came from Europe. The mosaic in the foyer depicts Larnach's family crest and the modest name he gave to his stately home: the Camp. Larnach rose to a prominent position in the New Zealand government of the late 1800s, but in 1898, beset by a series of financial disasters and possible marital problems, he committed suicide in Parliament House. According to one version of the story, Larnach's third wife, whom he married at an advanced age, ran off with his youngest son; devastated, Larnach shot himself. The 35 acres of grounds around the castle include lodging, a rhododendron garden, a rain-forest garden with kauri, *rimu*, and *totara* trees, statues of *Alice in Wonderland* characters, a herbaceous walk, and a South Seas Walkway lined with palms and aloe plants. ⊠ *Camp Rd.* ☎ 03/476–1616 ⊕ www.larnachcastle. co.nz ⊠ $20 ☉ Daily 9–5.

Fodor's Choice **Taiaroa Head**, the wild and exposed eastern tip of the Otago Peninsula,
★ is the site of a breeding colony of royal albatrosses. Among the largest birds in the world, with a wingspan of up to 10 feet, they can take off only from steep slopes with the help of a strong breeze. With the exception of this colony and those in the Chatham Islands to the east, the birds are only on windswept islands deep in southern latitudes, far from human habitation. Under the auspices of the **Royal Albatross Centre,** the colony is open for viewing all year, except during a two-month break between mid-September and mid-November when the birds lay their eggs; the visitor center is open year-round. The greatest number of birds are present shortly after the young albatrosses hatch near the

A tramper gets close to a Royal Albatross.

end of January. Between March and September parents leave the fledglings in their nests while they gather food for them. In September, the young birds fly away, returning about eight years later to start their own breeding cycle. Access to the colony is strictly controlled, and you must book in advance. From the visitor center you go in groups up a steep trail to the Albatross Observatory, from which you can see the birds through narrow windows.

Overlooking the albatross colony is the **"Disappearing" Gun at Fort Taiaroa**, a 6-inch artillery piece installed during the Russian Scare of 1886, when Russia was making hostile maneuvers through the Pacific. The gun was shot in anger only once, during World War II, when it was fired across the bow of a fishing boat that failed to observe correct procedures. Tours range from 30 to 90 minutes and can include albatross viewing, Fort Taiaroa, and an Albatross Insight presentation. ⊠ *Taiaroa Head* ☎ *03/478–0499* ⊕ *www.albatross.org.nz* ✉ *Prices range from $8 for Insight presentation to $33 for Unique Taiaroa Tour* ⊗ *Royal Albatross Centre opens at 8:30; tours run 9* AM*–dusk Dec.–mid-Mar. 10* AM*–dusk mid-Mar.– Nov.*

ℭ If you'd like to observe the world's most endangered penguin in its natural habitat, visit the **Yellow-Eyed Penguin Reserve**, also called the **Penguin Place**, where a network of tunnels has been disguised so that you can get close. The penguins, also known as *hoiho*, are characterized by their yellow irises and headbands. ⊠ *Harington Point* ☎ *03/478–0286* ✎ *penguin.place@clear.net.nz* ⊕ *www.penguinplace.co.nz* ⌖ *Reservations essential* ✉ *$33* ⊗ *Daily 9–5.*

OFF THE BEATEN PATH

The Mole, at the end of the Aramoana peninsula, is a 1-km-long (½-mi-long) breakwater protecting the entrance to Otago Harbour. A dozen or so small ships were sunk between 1920 and 1950 to protect the breakwater from the relentless Southern Ocean. You can check these ships out, and the tall kelp forest that protects them, with **Dive Otago** (☒ *2 Wharf St., Dunedin* ☎ *03/466–4370* ⊕ *www.diveotago. co.nz*), which run trips when the weather allows.

WHERE TO EAT AND STAY

$$–$$$
ECLECTIC
✕ **1908 Café & Bar.** There are good views from this converted post office "where the high road meets the low road." The interior still feels Edwardian, and classic seafood dishes and steaks lead the menu. Hours can be changeable in winter, and crowds come in summer. ☒ *7 Harington Point Rd.* ☎ *03/478–0801* ⊟ *AE, DC, MC, V.*

$$$
CAFÉ
✕ **Bay Café and Bar.** In the first settlement you reach on the peninsula, this well-known café has fine views across the harbor. Scallops, prawns, blue cod, and mussels are popular, as are the tasty pizzas with smoked salmon and prawns. The brunch menu is served between 11 and 3, and the dinner menu kicks in at 5. ☒ *494 Portobello Rd.* ☎ *03/476–1357* ⚐ *Reservations essential* ⊟ *MC, V.*

$$$
★
🖼 **Larnach Lodge.** It's hard to beat panoramic sea views, 35 acres of gardens, the Larnach Castle next door, and luxury theme rooms. The Scottish Room has classic tartan bedcovers and curtains, heavy brass bedsteads, and a Robbie Burns rug; the Enchanted Forest Room has 19th-century William Morris wallpaper. Rooms with shared bathrooms in a converted 1870 coach house are about half the regular rate. Entry to the castle and breakfast is included in the room rate. **Pros:** how often do you get to stay at a castle? **Cons:** the food is not consistently good. ☒ *Camp Rd.* ☎ *03/476–1616* ⊕ *www.larnachcastle.co.nz* ⬗ *12 rooms* ♿ *In-room: refrigerator. In-hotel: Restaurant, Wi-Fi* ⊟ *MC, V* ⊙ *BP.*

INVERCARGILL

182 km (113 mi) south of Queenstown, 217 km (135 mi) southwest of Dunedin.

Originally settled by Scottish immigrants, Invercargill has retained much of its turn-of-the-20th-century character, with broad main avenues (Tay Street and Dee Street) and streetscapes with richly embellished buildings. You'll find facades with Italian and English Renaissance styles, Gothic stone tracery, and Romanesque designs on a number of its well-preserved buildings.

Invercargill was featured in the movie *The World's Fastest Indian* (2005) starring Sir Anthony Hopkins as Invercargill-bred Burt Munro, who raced his Indian motorcycle on Oreti Beach in preparation for breaking a world land speed record. Mayor Tim Shadbolt had a cameo in the film, which is worth seeing. Invercargill has a reputation to this day for "boy racers," and you'll notice them roaring up and down the city streets in tricked-out cars. Indignant Invercargillites blame the epidemic on *Gorons,* boy racers from neighboring city Gore. You might have a

CLOSE UP

The Southern Man

The laconic "Southern Man" has a special niche in the Kiwi mind—the typical specimen lives in the country, has a trusty dog by his side, is a rabid rugby fan, and adheres to a rugged lifestyle of farmwork, fixing the ute (pickup truck), and hitting the bars for pool and beer. Speight's beer has gotten a lot of mileage from this icon, using it for a successful Southern Man ad campaign, complete with a Southern Man theme song. ("Cuz here we just know/what makes a Southern boy tick/and it ain't margaritas/with some fruit on a stick…"). But this stereotype is rooted in reality. There are plenty of good, hardy blokes in Otago and Southland who dress in shorts

and Swannies (Swanndri woolen bush shirts), drink Speight's beer, and work on farms. Before long some visitors may develop similar traits. If you find yourself saying things like "She's a hard road" and "She'll be right" when the going gets tough, then the process is well under way. To help the Southern Man find the right lady there is an annual Perfect Woman competition, with challenges such as digging in a fence post, backing a trailer loaded with hay, fitting snow chains, tipping a 242-pound ram, and opening a bottle of Speight's without a bottle opener. As the ad says, "It's a hard road to find the perfect woman."

—Joseph Gelfer and Sue Farley

'50s flashback if you're waiting at a light and a lowrider next to you starts to rumble and rev its engine.

GETTING HERE AND AROUND

Invercargill's airport (IVC) is 3 km (2 mi) from city center. From Invercargill, Air New Zealand runs direct flights to Christchurch, and Stewart Island Flights hops over to Stewart Island. Several rental car companies operate in the terminal. Taxis from Invercargill Airport into town cost $8–$9. A shuttle run by Executive Car Services costs $8–$14 per person, and there's usually a shuttle waiting for each flight. Executive Car Service also rents secure car storage. Invercargill is extremely walkable, and also particularly driver-friendly. One daily InterCity bus continues on from Dunedin to Invercargill; this takes another four hours.

ESSENTIALS

Airport Invercargill Airport (✉ 106 Airport Ave. ☎ 03/218–6920 ⊕ www.invercargillairport.co.nz).

Bus Companies InterCity (☎ 03/471–7143 ⊕ www.intercitycoach.co.nz).

Bus Depot Invercargill (✉ Queens Park, 108 Gala St.).

Medical Assistance Southland Hospital (✉ Kew Rd., Invercargill ☎ 03/218–1949). **Urgent Doctor Service** (✉ 103 Don St., Invercargill ☎ 03/218–8821).

Tour Information Lynette Jack Scenic Sights (✉ 22 Willis St., Invercargill ☎ 025/338–370 or 03/215–7741).

Visitor Information Invercargill Visitor Information Centre (✉ Southland Museum and Art Gallery, Victoria Ave., Queens Park ☎ 03/214–6243 ⊕ www.invercargill.org.nz).

EXPLORING

The **Anderson Park Art Gallery** is in a splendid 1925 Georgian-style house. The 60 acres of surrounding gardens and lawns include a traditionally carved Māori house and short bushwalks. The gallery displays New Zealand art, sculpture, and pottery. ⊠ *McIvor Rd.* ☎ *03/215–7432* ☞ *Donation* ⊙ *Daily 10:30–5.*

☯ The **Southland Museum and Art Gallery** contains the largest public display of live *tuatara*, New Zealand's extremely rare and ancient lizards. The museum has also established a successful captive-breeding program for the creatures. It's usually easy to spot these minidinosaurs, but they do a successful job of hiding themselves if it gets too noisy. Southland also contains fine displays of Māori and settler artifacts. The gallery has both older and modern New Zealand art on permanent display as well as temporary exhibits. It's in Queens Park, with an on-site café and information center. ⊠ *108 Gala St.* ☎ *03/218–9753* ⊕ *www.southlandmuseum.com* ☞ *Donation suggested; Tuatara and Gallery tours $3* ⊙ *Daily 10–5.*

☯ The 200 acres in the center of town that make up **Queens Park** create a
★ fine layout of public gardens. Included are two rose gardens with both modern and "antique" rose varieties; a Japanese garden complete with meditation area; and an impressive hothouse, which acts as a sanctuary on a wet day. The park has miles of gentle walking paths and waterways, an 18-hole golf course, and a decent café. There's also a small zoo area and an aviary with a walk-through section that children love. The main entrance is next to the Southland Museum. ⊠ *Queens Dr. at Gala St.* ☎ *03/217–7368.*

Invercargill's most famous store is a 100-year-old hardware store! **E. Hayes and Sons** (⊠ *168 Dee St.* ☎ *03/218–2059*) has every little thing you can think of. It's totally yin-yang (grandma-grandpa) with one half devoted to little glass lemon juicers and whisks and the other half filled with tools and wheelbarrows. The store alsohas a popular "World's Fastest Indian" exhibit where you can view memorabilia of Invercargill's famous son Burt Munro.

SPORTS AND THE OUTDOORS

It would be a brave person who swims at **Oreti Beach**, 11 km (7 mi) southeast of town, but people do surf and windsurf, taking advantage of the wind and swells that whip the coast almost constantly. Another good walking spot is **Sandy Point**, which can be reached by taking a left after crossing the Oreti River on the way out to Oreti Beach. A 13-km (8-mi) network of easygoing trails covers the riverbanks, estuary, and the bush. A leaflet detailing the paths is available from the visitor information center in town. On the western side of the Southern Scenic Route, the **Tuatapere Hump Ridge Track** (☎ *03/226–6739 or 0800/486–774* ⊕ *www.humpridgetrack.co.nz*) is a challenging circular three-day, two-night walk that combines beach, bush, and subalpine environments in its 53 km (33 mi). The track starts near Tuatapere, about two hours' drive west of Invercargill and right on the edge of the Fiordland National Park (⇨ *Chapter 10*). It's no amble; you'll spend about nine hours walking each day, but two good huts each sleep about 40 people. You will need to buy hut tickets in advance.

WHERE TO EAT

$$$–$$$$
NEW ZEALAND

✕ **Cabbage Tree.** For his ideal restaurant, owner Neville Kidd revamped this old store on the way to Oreti Beach. Resembling a vineyard restaurant, the inside is spacious and lined with wood and brick. Popular dishes are Stewart Island blue cod, lamb shanks, prawns, and pan-seared venison. The wine list includes mostly New Zealand wines, with the occasional European bottle for the stubborn. The outdoor garden bar is a perfect place to enjoy the Southland sun with a glass of wine. ⊠ *379 Dunns Rd., Otatara* ☎ *03/213–1443* ⊕ *www.thecabbagetree. com* ⊟ *AE, DC, MC, V.*

$$$–$$$$
CONTEMPORARY

✕ **The Rocks Café.** An urban-chic-meets-Tuscany personality is achieved here, where the interior showcases terra-cotta, brick, and river stone. The kitchen employs bounty from the nearby bush and sea paired with inventive sauces and sides. Enjoy the venison with sticky red pepper marmalade, Stewart Island salmonn and pickled cucumber, or blue cod with mussel and choritzo gumbo. ⊠ *101 Dee St., at Courtville Arcade* ☎ *03/218–7597* ⊟ *AE, DC, MC, V* ☾ *Closed Sun. No lunch Sat.*

$$–$$$
PIZZA

✕ **Sopranos Wood Fired Pizzeria.** The tasty pizzas here are named after various fictional and nonfictional mobsters and gangsters. It makes sense that "Meadow" is the vegetarian option and that "Dr. Melfi" is the smoked salmon, but how "Tony" became a Thai green curry–chicken topping we'll never know. There's a good local wine list. ⊠ *33 Tay St.* ☎ *03/218–3464* ⊟ *MC, V.*

$$–$$$
CAFÉ

✕ **Ziff's Café and Bar.** This enormously popular restaurant on the way to Oreti Beach (past the airport) is a local favorite. Ziff's does steak, blue cod, chicken, and pasta, and customers love the home-smoked salmon and the venison hot pot. The establishment provides a taxi service for $2 per person, so you can indulge in their excellent wines and cognacs, too. Some nights it can be noisy, so if you want a *sotto* dining experience have lunch here on the way to the "World's Fastest Indian's" training grounds. The house seafood chowder, flavored with capers, lime, and smoky bacon, is quite good. Breakfast is served until 2 PM. ⊠ *143 Dunns Rd.* ☎ *03/213–0501* ⊟ *AE, DC, MC, V.*

FOR THE CAFFEINE FIEND

Invercargill is home to the world's southernmost Starbucks, so you might want to pop in for the mug saying so. As for cafés there are many other, tastier options like **Rain Espresso** (⊠ *35 Kelvin St., corner of Don*), the **Seriously Good Chocolate Company** (⊠ *147 Sprey St.*), and **Three Bean Cafe** (⊠ *73 Dee St., corner of Don*).

WHERE TO STAY

Many of Invercargill's motels are on Tay Street, handy if you're coming from Dunedin and North Road, convenient if you're arriving from Queenstown.

$$ **Ascot Park Hotel.** This rambling complex is a welcome sight if you've just battled the rugged gravel roads of the Catlins. The largest hotel in town is just a five-minute drive from the town center. Spacious, modern rooms come with small balconies. An on-site restaurant serves traditional and contemporary New Zealand fare. **Pros:** big rooms. **Cons:** restaurant pricey; pool tiny. ⊠ *Tay St. at Racecourse Rd.* ☎ *03/217–6195* ↪ *64 rooms, 24 motel rooms, 2 suites, 4 studio rooms* ⚘ *In-room: No a/c. In-hotel: Restaurant, bar, pool, gym* ⊟ *AE, DC, MC, V.*

$$ **Kelvin Hotel.** The big advantage of this modern, rather bland hotel is that it's really central, and just about ideal if you're not driving. The rooms facing the back are quieter. **Pros:** couldn't be more centrally located. **Cons:** rooms a bit shabby. ⊠ *16 Kelvin St.* ☎ *03/218–2829* ↪ *58 rooms, 2 suites* ⚘ *In-room: No a/c. In-hotel: Restaurant, bar, laundry facilities* ⊟ *AE, DC, MC, V.*

$$ **Mohua Park.** If you're traveling to Invercargill via the Southern Scenic Route, this lovely self-service accommodation makes a perfect rest stop before you get to the "big smoke." Located between Papatowai and Owaka in the Catlins River Valley, these four eco-cottages are run by the same couple who do the Catlins Eco-Tours. They built this place with conservation and coziness is mind. **Pros:** situated on 35 acres of native forest; winner of Otago Business Excellence Award 2008. **Cons:** extra $30 fee if you're only staying for one night ⊠ *Mohua* ☎ *03/415–8631* ⊕ *catlinsmohuapark.co.nz* ↪ *4 cottages* ⚘ *In-room: No phone, no TV. In-hotel: Laundry facilities* ⊟ *MC, V.*

¢–$ **Tuatara Backpackers Lodge.** The world's southernmost YHA hostel is in the center of Invercargill, next door to the Speight's Ale House and the main city library. The Tuatara has the usual group of bunks, twins, and double rooms, along with a couple of "executive suites" (with private bathrooms, TVs, and DVD players). It's on the main drag near some popular hangouts for bored teens, so the noise from the street can be high at night. **Pros:** inexpensive; centrally located. **Cons:** can be noisy at night. ⊠ *30–32 Dee St.* ☎ *03/214–0954 or 0800/488–282* ⊕ *tuatarlodge.co.nz* ↪ *23 rooms, 3 suites* ⚘ *In-room: No TV (some). In-hotel: Laundry facilities, Internet terminal* ⊟ *MC, V.*

**EN
ROUTE**   In the tiny township of **Bluff** (*the Bluff* to locals) you can taste its coveted namesake oysters. An annual festival, held in late April at the town's wharf, wallows in seafood delicacies; oyster-opening and oyster-eating competitions and cook-offs are part of the fun. If you miss the festival, the most spectacular place for oysters, in season, is **Lands End Restaurant** (⊠ *10 Ward Parade* ☎ *03/212–7575*) overlooking the sea. The Lands End Inn is also the best place to stay the night. The bakery on Gore Street is open from 5:30 AM and has nice pastries and meals. Don't miss the Maritime Museum on the Foreshore Road (the Oyster boat *Monica* sits beside it). Bluff is also home to the frequently photographed

Stirling Point signpost, at the southern end of State Highway 1, which gives directions to places all over the world, including the South Pole. If it's a nice day follow the signs up to Bluff Lookout: the views encompass the Catlins and Stewart Island, and give you an excellent lay of the land. Good walking tracks are around Bluff; many begin at Stirling Point. The town is also the main jumping-off point for Stewart Island. It's about 30 km (19 mi) from Invercargill to Bluff, an easy ½-hour drive south on State Highway 1. For more on Bluff go to ⊕ *www.bluff.co.nz.*

STEWART ISLAND

Stewart Island is home to New Zealand's newest national park, Rakiura National Park. The third and most southerly of New Zealand's main islands, Stewart Island is separated from the South Island by the 24-km (15-mi) Foveaux Strait. Its original Māori name, Te Punga O Te Waka a Maui, means "the anchor stone of Maui's canoe." Māori mythology says the island's landmass held the god Maui's canoe secure while he and his crew raised the great fish—the North Island. Today the island is more commonly referred to by its other Māori name, Rakiura, which means "the land of the glowing skies." This refers to the spectacular sunrises and sunsets and to the southern lights, or aurora australis. The European name of Stewart Island dates back to 1809. It memorializes an officer on an early sealing vessel, the *Pegasus,* who was the first to chart the island.

The island covers some 1,700 square km (650 square mi). It measures about 75 km (46 mi) from north to south and about the same distance across at its widest point. On the coastline, sharp cliffs rise from a succession of sheltered bays and beaches. In the interior, forested hills rise gradually toward the west side of the island. Seals and penguins frequent the coast, and the island's prolific birdlife includes a number of species rarely seen in any other part of the country. In fact, this is the surest place to see a kiwi. The Stewart Island brown kiwi, or *tokoeka,* is the largest species of this kind of bird. Unlike their mainland cousins, these kiwis can be seen during the day as well as at night. It's a rare and amusing experience to watch these pear-shaped birds scampering on a remote beach as they feed on sand hoppers and grubs.

Māori have visited Stewart Island for centuries. Archaeologists' studies of 13th-century Māori middens (refuse heaps) indicate that the island was once a rich, seasonal resource for hunting, fishing, and gathering seafood. A commonly eaten delicacy at that time, the *titi,* also known as the muttonbird, still occasionally appears on menus.

In the early 19th century, explorers, sealers, missionaries, and miners settled the island. They were followed by fishermen and sawmillers who established settlements around the edges of Paterson Inlet and Halfmoon and Horseshoe Bays. In the 1920s Norwegians set up a whaling enterprise, and many descendants of these seafaring people remain. Fishing, aquaculture, and tourism are now the mainstays of the island's economy.

Even by New Zealand standards, Stewart Island is remote, raw, and untouched. The appeal is its seclusion, its relaxed way of life, and its untouched quality. Stewart Island is not for everyone: if you must have shopping malls, casinos, or umbrella drinks on the beach, don't come here. Visitors should be prepared for the fact that Stewart Island can be chilly, windy, and rainy, even in the middle of summer.

GETTING HERE AND AROUND

Stewart Island Flights has three scheduled flights daily between Invercargill and Halfmoon Bay. The 20-minute flight costs $155 round-trip; for the best views ask to sit up front with the pilot.

Stewart Island Experience runs the ferry between the island and Bluff. There are three departures daily October to April, and two during the low season. The cost is $63 each way. The island's bare-bones-but-paved Ryan's Creek Airstrip is about 2 km (1 mi) from Oban (population 390). The shuttle that meets each flight is included in the airfare.

The best mode of transportation on the island is the 10-toe express. There are cars, mopeds, and bicycles for rent on the island, but there are only 20 km (13 mi) of paved road. Most of the traffic road signs you'll see are big yellow caution ones depicting silhouettes of kiwi and penguins.

Water taxis are an excellent option if you want to "mix it up" a bit when seeing the park. Most one-way fares are about $45, and the Ulva Island return is about $30. Four taxis operate from Golden Bay Wharf, a scenic 15-minute walk from town. The visitor center can make a booking for you.

The **Department of Conservation Rakiura National Park Visitor Centre** is open daily. The **Environment Centre**, located next to the Glowing Sky T-shirt shop, has information about the habitat recovery projects on the Island. The **Library** in the **Community Centre** has a complete collection of books about Stewart Island, and field guides of native flora and fauna.

ESSENTIALS

Air Carrier Rakiura Helicopters (☎ 03/219–1155 or 027/221-9217 ⊕ www.rakiurahelicopters.co.nz). **Stewart Island Flights** (☎ 03/218-9129 ⊕ www.stewartislandflights.com).

Boat Company Stewart Island Experience (✉ Stewart Island Visitor Terminal, Main Wharf, Halfmoon Bay ☎ 03/212–7660 or 0800/000–511 ⊕ www.stewartislandexperience.co.nz).

Medical Assistance Stewart Island Health Centre (✉ Argyle St. ☎ 03/219–1098 or 0800/100–776).

Tour Information Bravo Adventure Cruises (✉ Box 104, Stewart Island ☎ 03/219–1144 ✍ philldismith@xtra.co.nz). **Kiwi Wilderness Walks** (☎ 03/226–6739 ⊕ www.nzwalk.com). **Rakiura Helicopters** (☎ 03/219–1155 or 027/221–9217 ⊕ www.rakiurahelicopters.co.nz). **Seaview Enterprises** (☎ 03/219–1014). **Stewart Island Flights** (☎ 03/218–9129 ⊕ www.stewartislandflights.com). **Ulva's Guided Walks** (✉ Elgin Terr., Oban ☎ 03/219–1216 wwww.ulva.co.nz).

Visitor Information Department of Conservation Rakiura National Park Visitor Centre (✉ *Main Rd., Oban* ☎ *03/219–0002* ⊕ *www.doc.govt.nz*). **Stewart Island Web Site** (⊕ *www.stewartisland.co.nz*).

RAKIURA NATIONAL PARK

In spring 2002, about 85% of Stewart Island was designated as **Rakiura National Park.** The park encompasses areas that were formerly nature reserves and the like. More than 200 walking trails thread through the park, and a dozen huts give shelter for overnight stays.

For information on Rakiura as well as the rest of Stewart Island, contact the **Department of Conservation,** or check out the Stewart Island Web site (⊕ *www.stewartisland.co.nz*).

SPORTS AND THE OUTDOORS
BIRD WATCHING

One of the best places for bird-watching is **Ulva Island** (⊕ *www.stewartisland.co.nz*), 620 acres of thick native bush. The rare birds that live here have no predators, so they have an excellent survival rate. Among the resident species are the *weka,* saddleback, *kaka* (a parrot), and kiwi. The forest, which has walking paths accessible to the public, is made up primarily of *rimu, rata,* and *kamahi* trees. To get here, take a boat or water taxi from Halfmoon or Golden Bay, or paddle a kayak from Thule Bay. You can also join a tour; the best guide is the aptly named Ulva Goodwillie. ⇨ *For more information on Ulva Island, see Birding on Ulva Island.*

HIKING

For information on Rakiura National Park's walks, contact the Department of Conservation Visitor Centre.

Rakiura National Park has outstanding multiday treks. The **Rakiura Track,** one of New Zealand's Great Walks, takes three days. Day 1 goes from Halfmoon Bay to Port William Hut via Horseshoe and Lee bays. Day 2 heads inland through native bush and wood across the ridge, allowing for good views of Paterson Inlet and the Tin Range. Day 3 connects back to Halfmoon Bay via *rimu* and *kamahi* forest. The huts accommodate up to 30 people on a first-come, first-served basis. They come with mattresses, a wood-burning stove, running water, and toilets. (If you're relatively fit and you leave early, you can do this track in one day, but you will be sore.) Another popular trek, a big step up in both distance and difficulty, is the **North West Circuit,** a 9- to 11-day walk from Halfmoon Bay that circles the north coast and then cuts through the interior. If that's not enough for you, five days can be tacked on by including the Southern Circuit. Stewart Island's climate is notoriously changeable, so be prepared for sun, wind, rain, and *lots* of mud. Take the usual safety precautions for these hikes: bring suitable boots, clothing, food, and a portable stove;

TRAIL RUNS

Are you the kind of traveler who packs running shoes? The park is paradise for **trail running.** Try trails leading to Fern Gully, Little River, and beyond.

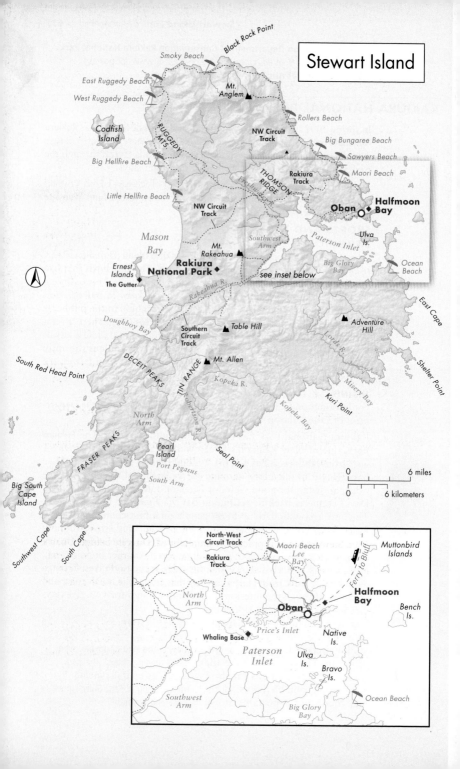

Stewart Island

Smoky Beach

Black Rock Point

East Ruggedy Beach

West Ruggedy Beach

Mt. Anglem ▲

Rollers Beach

Codfish Island

RUGGEDY MTS.

NW Circuit Track

THOMSON RIDGE

Big Bungaree Beach

Sawyers Beach

Maori Beach

Big Hellfire Beach

Rakiura Track

Little Hellfire Beach

NW Circuit Track

Freshwater R.

Oban ○

Halfmoon Bay ◆

Ulva Is.

Mason Bay

Mt. Rakeahua ▲

Southwest Arm

Paterson Inlet

Big Glory Bay

Ocean Beach

Ernest Islands

Rakiura National Park ◆

The Gutter

see inset below

Rakeahua R.

East Cape

Doughboy Bay

Southern Circuit Track

▲ Table Hill

Adventure Hill ▲

Shelter Point

South Red Head Point

DECEIT PEAKS

TIN RANGE

▲ Mt. Allen

Kopeka R.

Lords R.

Misery Bay

Kuri Point

Robertson R.

North Arm

Kopeka Bay

FRASER PEAKS

Pearl Island

Port Pegasus

Seal Point

Kopeka Bay

Big South Cape Island

South Arm

Southwest Cape

South Cape

0   6 miles

0   6 kilometers

Inset

North-West Circuit Track

Maori Beach

Lee Bay

Muttonbird Islands

Rakiura Track

Ferry to Bluff

North Arm

Oban ○

Halfmoon Bay ◆

Bench Is.

Whaling Base ◆

Price's Inlet

Native Is.

Paterson Inlet

Ulva Is.

Bravo Is.

Southwest Arm

Big Glory Bay

Ocean Beach

Marrow grass grows on Smoky Beach's sand dunes near the popular North West Circuit.

complete an intentions form at the Department of Conservation (DOC) office before setting out; and, ideally, bring along with you a locator beacon or a guide who knows the trails.

TREK REHAB

If you're aching after a day (or 10) on the island's muddy trails, take advantage of the island's resident massage therapist. Mitch Murdoch of Clinical Massage Therapy specializes in sports but also does relaxation, pregnancy and deep-tissue massage. Enjoy ocean views from her studio. ⊠ *Main Rd., Oban* ☎ *027/470–9686* ✍ *mitch.massage@yahoo.co.nz.*

OBAN AND HALFMOON BAY

Apart from the tiny township of **Oban** at **Halfmoon Bay** on Paterson Inlet, Stewart Island is practically uninhabited. Directly behind Oban's waterfront is a short main street with a small collection of establishments. A handful of roads head up the surrounding hills. The hills are mostly thick bush, with houses poking their heads out for a view of the bay.

ESSENTIALS
Tour Information Sails Experience (⊠ *11 View St.* ☎ *03/219–1151* ⊕ *www. sailsashore.co.nz*). **Stewart Island Experience** (⊠ *Main Wharf, Halfmoon Bay, Oban* ☎ *03/212–7660* or *0800/000–511* ⊕ *www.stewartisland-experience.co.nz*).

EXPLORING

Birds are plentiful in Halfmoon Bay. Here are some of their hangouts: walk up Argyle Street, which dead-ends into a drive. Continue up (it turns into a path) and you'll be certain to see the noisy parrots (*kaka*) clowning in the trees around you. Ducks loiter at Mill Creek (locals have named many of them) and a little kingfisher often sits on the phone wire above them. Rare albino wood pigeons (*kereru*) reside in the *rimu* tree by the "*rimu* tree phone" on the road leading down into Horseshoe Bay. Little blue penguins are seen in Paterson Inlet, ditto yellow-eyed penguins and Stewart Island shags. Mollymawks soar past Acker's Point. Tūī, bellbirds, fantails, and robins can be seen throughout Halfmoon Bay gardens and on day walks. *Weka* have been recently reintroduced to the area and favor the gardens of Deep Bay Road (they cut through homes if residents leave the door open!). Oystercatchers live on every town beach, and pied oystercatchers like grazing the schoolyard. Kiwis are rarely seen around town but they are there; telltale tracks have been seen at Traill Park and their shrill unmistakable cry is heard some nights.

The **Rakiura Museum** has an eclectic collection of Māori artifacts, ambergris, old schoolhouse memorabilia, tools from gold and tinning prospectors, and a china "moustache cup" (there's a story behind every item). The museum also forgivingly showcases an old-world globe that doesn't include Stewart Island! ⊠ *Ayr St. across from Community Centre* 🖃 *$2* 🕑 *Mon.–Sat. 10–noon, Sun. noon–2.*

SPORTS AND THE OUTDOORS

FISHING

If you go fishing your catch will likely be the succulent Stewart Island blue cod. Go with a guide and he or she will fillet and bag it for you. Some will cook it for your lunch! We recommend going out with one of the real salt dogs who have fished these waters all their lives. **John Leask** (⊠ *Halfmoon Bay Wharf* 🕾 *03/21919–1023*) of the *Rawhiti* is also known as Hurricane Johnny. He's been fishing Foveaux Straight for 60 years and provides a knowledgeable and safe experience for people of all ages and abilities.

Richard Squires (aka Squizzy) (⊠ *Halfmoon Bay Wharf* 🕾 *03/21919–1141* ⊕ *www.loloma.co.nz*) runs an old-school operation with a historic wooden boat and hand lines. The fisherman, of the *Lo Loma*, guides those with limited or extensive fishing experience on safe excursions.

GOLF

Ringaringa Heights Golf Course is Australasia's most southerly course. It overlooks Ringaringa Bay and Paterson Inlet. Play a round at this six-hole course as kakas screech overhead, and then relax at the clubhouse (BYOB). The Flight Centre/Post Office rents clubs; the course is a 20-minute walk by road or bush track from there.

HIKING

Numerous day walks on well-maintained trails are in and around the township. Free maps are available at the Flight Centre–Post Office and Visitor Centre, and detailed maps and information are at the Department of Conservation Office. Some walks, such as the Observation Rock

Continued on page 666

BIRDING ON ULVA ISLAND

Ulva Island is not only a birdwatcher's paradise, but also a living time capsule. Visiting it gives you the chance to experience New Zealand in a time before human contact. Then, as now, birds seen nowhere else in the world find sanctuary and thrive here.

By Kathy Ombler

Isolated as it was for millions of years, New Zealand was the ideal environment for the evolution of unique birds and flora. Indeed, it was one of the last of the Earth's landmasses to be discovered, with only a 1,000-year history of settlement. Without native mammals, only those that could swim (sea lions, seals, and whales) made it to the islands, so flightless birds flourished absent of predators. It took just the last few hundred years of human contact to endanger many indigenous birds—some have become extinct.

In recent years, New Zealand conservationsts have developed ground-breaking techniques for creating predator-free sanctuaries on many islands, where native birds now flourish. Ulva Island's 250 hectares (618 acres) of forested land in a sheltered inlet of Stewart Island form one such sanctuary. Following the eradication of rats here in 1996 several previously endangered species are now flourishing.

The bird sightings begin on the 10-minute water-taxi ride from Golden Bay (Stewart Island), with glimpses of penguins, petrels, and, possibly, albatrosses. Beneath ancient rimu, totara, and miro trees, walk well-warked trails across rocky coasts and sandy beaches, while the forest resounds with bird chatter, song, and wing-flapping.

Above: Tui bird feeding on nectar of native Kakabeak flowers

ULVA ISLAND BIRDS

Early Maori settlers named New Zealand's distinctive birds, many according to the sounds of their calls. For example they gave the name "ruru" to the morepork, for its mournful nighttime cry and "whio" to the blue duck, echoing its high-pitched whistle. Many of these names (noted in parentheses below), some with tribal variations, remain in use along with more recently established English names.

Tui
(A) Possibly New Zealand's best-known native bird, the tui is abundant in both remote forests and private gardens, even in towns and cities. It's distinctive for the white tuft of feathers at its throat (some call it the parson bird) and loved for its melodious songs and mimicry.

Kiwi (Stewart Island tokoeka)
(B) One of New Zealand's five kiwi species, tokoeka live throughout Stewart Island where, unlike their strictly nocturnal mainland cousins, they feed dur-

ing the day and night. The few that live on Ulva Island are rarely seen. However, Stewart Island guided tours—such as the Ocean Beach evening tour with Bravo Adventure Cruises—provide excellent chances to see kiwi. You might also get lucky while taking a solo evening stroll around Oban—kiwis are sometimes spotted in the town's parks and on trails.

Fantail (piwakawaka)
(C) Its eponymous fanlike tail makes this tiny bird easy to spot. The tail isn't just for show, though; the bird catches flies and other insects with it and uses it to navigate. Like robins, fantails are attracted to track walkers.

Northern Royal Albatross (torea)
(D) One of the world's largest albatrosses and the only one to breed on New Zealand's mainland (on Otago Peninsula, just one hour's drive from Dunedin city), the torea is also seen on the boat trip to Ulva. They're more likely seen, however, on a fishing or pelagic bird

watching cruise; ask at the visitor center for operator details. Alternatively, visit the Royal Albatross Centre on the Otago Peninsula, or take an Albatross Encounter cruise from Kaikoura.

Stewart Island Robin (toutouwai)
(E) The island's "friendliest" birds have a habit of following you on treks. They're not just trying to get into photographs (and they do); they nab the insects disturbed by your feet. Ulva's robin population has grown to more than 200 since 2000, when just 20 birds were transferred here following the rat eradication.

Parakeet (kakariki)
(F) Both red- and yellow-crowned parakeets live on Ulva. The bright green, red, and yellow colorings of these small parrots stand out against the darker forest greens. Their high-pitched "ka-ka-ka" chatter is also distinctive.

Saddleback (tieke)
(G) Ulva is the only place to see the South Island saddleback, named for the distinctive saddle-like reddish stripe across its back. The species has recovered from near extinction in the 1960s. The more prolific North Island saddleback lives on several island and mainland reserves.

Kaka
(H) These colorful, boisterous bush parrots screech their greetings, congregate in loud social groups, and commute over long distances between islands and forests. Look for bark torn by the kaka foraging for grubs and for the spectacle of their bright red underwings.

Yellowhead (mohua)
Island sanctuaries such as Ulva have become bastions for yellowhead as mainland populations dwindle. Their presence is signalled by persistent chatter, and they're found mostly in flocks high in the trees, especially in winter.

TIPS AND TOUR OPERATORS

Hiker photographing kea bird near Luxmore Hut, on the Kepler Track, Fiordland National Park

KEEP ULVA PREDATOR FREE. Check your clothes and boots for seeds. Check and re-pack your belongings before getting off the boat. Rats have been known to stow away!

TAKE YOUR TIME. You will see more birds. Most guided tours take an unhurried three to four hours. If walking on your own, purchase the Ulva Island Charitable Trust self-guided brochure ($2) from the i-SITE Visitor Centre or Department of Conservation Visitor Centre.

ENJOY THE ISLAND'S FLORA. With no browsing from introduced animals the plants' abilities to fruit have increased and the forest has flourished. While giant totara, rimu, and miro dominate, there's also old, gnarled red-flowering rata; a tangled understorey of ferns; mosses; orchids; and rare, ancient plants now found in few other places.

COST. Guided Ulva Island trips cost $95, water taxi included. For independent trips, water taxis cost $20 to $35 return (depending on passenger numbers). Several companies operate both scheduled and private charter trips daily.

BEST TIME TO GO. You can go to Ulva any time of the year. Winter will be colder but the weather is more predictable.

TOUR OPERATORS
The DOC has approved the following guided tours: **Ulva's Guided Walks** (⊕ www.ulva. co.nz); **Ruggedy Range™ Wilderness Experience** (⊕ www.ruggedyrange.com); **Stewart Island Water Taxi and Eco Guiding** (⊕ www.portofcall.co.nz); and **Sail Ashore** (⊕ www.sailashore.co.nz)

USEFUL WEB SITES
Stewart Island i-SITE Visitors Centre (⊕ www.stewartisland.co.nz)

Department of Conservation and Ulva Island Charitable Trust (⊕ www.doc.govt.nz)

OTHER SOURCES
Where to Watch Birds in New Zealand, Kathy Ombler, New Holland, 2007. A guidebook to more than 30 of the country's best birding locations.

TOP BIRDING SPOTS IN NEW ZEALAND

Native weka seeking food from a visitor on Ulva Island

There are plenty of exceptional birding areas, and all are simply great places to visit even if birds aren't your main thing.

NORTH ISLAND

Cape Kidnappers Nature Reserve, Hawke's Bay. The world's largest mainland concentration of Australasian gannets congregates on dramatic sea cliffs. Visit November–April.

Kapiti Island Nature Reserve, Kapiti Island. Located 5 km off North Island's west coast, near Wellington, the bird population includes endangered little spotted kiwi and takahe. The Department of Conservation can book day trips; overnight stays are available at Kapiti Island Lodge. Visit anytime.

Kiwi Encounter/Rainbow Springs Nature Park, Rotorua. Visit this kiwi hatchery and nursery to learn about the groundbreaking work raising chicks for release into the wild. Daily tours are conducted all year; chicks hatch September to April.

Tiritiri Matangi Island Scientific Reserve, Hauraki Gulf (Auckland). This is one of the easiest places to see New Zealand's rarest birds, including takahe, kokako, saddleback, and stitchbird. Day trips depart from downtown Auckland. Walking treks range from one to five hours. Visit year-round.

Miranda Ramsar Site, Firth of Thames. From roadside viewings and hides, see some of the tens of thousands of Arctic migratory waders that live in the vast, tidal flats and shellbanks in the Firth of Thames. It's a one-hour drive south of Auckland. Visit September–March.

SOUTH ISLAND

Farewell Spit Nature Reserve, Golden Bay and Takaka. A massive sandspit and tidal flats at South Island's northeastern tip provide a summer home to thousands of Arctic waders and winter breeding grounds for other wetland birds. Guided 4WD tours are available. Visit year round; September–March for Arctic waders.

Kaikoura, between Christchurch and Picton. Feeding grounds, just a 10 minute boat trip from shore, attract some 16 albatross species, as well as prions, petrels, and more. Specialist pelagic tours and whale- and dolphin-watching cruises are available. Visit year round.

Otago Peninsula. A mainland colony of Northern Royal Albatross, several yellow-eyed penguin colonies, and a host of seabirds and shorebirds live on the peninsula's headlands, beaches, and tidal inlets, within one hour's drive of Dunedin city. Several guided tours operate from Dunedin. Visit year-round; summer is best for the Northern Royal Albatross.

and Fuchsia walks, are measured in minutes; others, such as the walks to Fern Gully, Ryan's Creek, and Horseshoe Point, are measured in hours. If you only have a few hours, the walk from town out to the **Acker's Point** lighthouse is marvelous and encompasses town, boat sheds, a historic homestead, lush forest, and ocean views. This is nesting ground for *titi* (sooty shearwaters or muttonbirds), and little blue (fairy) penguins, which can often be seen from the lookout, along with albatross and fishing boats.

SEA KAYAKING

You will share the water with raucous fairy penguins, yellow-eyed penguins, elephant seals, leopard seals, Stewart Island shags, and occasionally dolphins. The mostly uninhabited Paterson Inlet is 100 square km (38 square mi) of bush-clad, sheltered waterways. It has 20 islands, four DOC huts, and two navigable rivers.

Contact **Rakiura Kayaks** (⊠ *Argyle St., Oban* ☎ *03/219–1160* ⊕ *www.rakiura.co.nz*) for kayak rentals and gear (including bathyscopes for underwater viewing). Liz Cave, a lifelong islander and paddler (a circumnavigation of Rakiura is under her belt) runs the operation. Prices start at $45 for a full-day rental to $85 for a full-day guided trip. Guided trips might include hand-lining for cod and trumpeter from a kayak. Liz's family owns one of two homes on a Paterson Inlet island: the old Norwegian whalers' cookhouse makes a perfect base for your adventure. Ask for recommendations on reliable water taxi operators and guides for kayak–hiking combos. Liz knows Paterson Inlet intimately. She can tell you where to spot baby oystercatchers, or where to best find a *paua*.

WHERE TO EAT

There are only a few places to eat on Stewart Island, and the only place open year-round for lunch and dinner is the South Sea Hotel Restaurant.

$$$–$$$$ ✕ **Church Hill Cafe Bar & Restaurant.** You know this is the Islanders' "fancy
NEW ZEALAND   restaurant" when you see the sign on the door: *No gumboots please.* The meat melts off the bone of the lamb shank, and they have a cook-it-yourself hot stone with pork, chicken, venison, and steak options. The seafood salad and the house-smoked salmon are standouts. ⊠ *36 Kamahi Rd., next to red-steepled church on hill, Oban* ☎ *03/219–1323* ⊙ *Daily for lunch and dinner* ▭ *MC, V.*

¢–$ ✕ **Justcafé.** American Britt Moore has set up her cybercafe in this faraway
CAFÉ   outpost. Stop in for great coffee, muffins, waffles, and cold smoked-salmon sandwiches—and surf the Net (broadband) while you nibble and sip. Britt also makes and sells paua jewelry, and runs a day spa (make

Fisherman's Wharf at Halfmoon Bay twinkles at twilight.

a booking at the café). ⊠ *Main Rd., Oban* ☎ *03/219–1422* ▭ *MC, V* ⊙ *Closed June–Sept. No dinner.*

$$–$$$
NEW ZEALAND
✕ **Kai Kart.** Come here for good old-fashioned fish-and-chips wrapped in a newspaper. There isn't an ounce of pretense in this cheerful little place between the museum and the "skateboard park" (a wooden ramp). The owner has a mussel farm in Paterson Inlet, and the cod comes from the Halfmoon Bay fishery. Try the bacon-wrapped mussels or chef Hilli's divine mussel chowder. ⊠ *Ayr St., Oban* ☎ *03/219–1225* ▭ *MC, V.*

$$–$$$
PIZZA
✕ **Lighthouse Wine Bar Pizzeria.** Make sure you have a nice big bottle of cold imported beer on hand if you try the seriously spicy Hellfire pizza. The wood-fired oven pies are all named for island locales, and some come generously topped with Stewart Island seafood. Depending on the crowd this summertime business stays open late. It serves beers from around the world and nice Kiwi wines. ⊠ *10 Main Rd. (across from DOC building), Halfmoon Bay, Oban* ▭ *MC, V.*

$$–$$$
NEW ZEALAND
✕ **Wharfside Café.** Located upstairs in the ferry terminal, this café shudders and squeaks as boats dock. It is a perfect spot for grabbing coffee, breakfast, or a meat pie before setting out to tackle the island. Lunch dishes include seafood, pastas, and salads. ⊠ *Main Wharf, Halfmoon Bay, Oban* ☎ *03/219–1470* ▭ *MC, V.*

WHERE TO STAY

In contrast with the lack of dining options there are scores of accommodations catering to every budget and fancy. All lodging is guaranteed to have a gorgeous view of bush, sea, or both. Look for accommodations on the Stewart Island Web site (⊕ *www.stewartisland.co.nz*). Around

Christmas time and New Year's every available bed is often taken, including the DOC huts, so prebooking is a must.

$$ 🏨 **Bay Motel.** Above town, this place has comfortable rooms, each with a deck. The view takes in Halfmoon Bay so you can observe the comings and goings of the wharf and pub, and the antics of the kakas from this "busybody" perch. For an extra 10 bucks choose the "honeymoon suite," the two-person Jacuzzi bath is nice after a day tramping. **Pros:** relatively new; nice and clean. **Cons:** a wee walk from town. ⌂ *9 Dundee St.* ☎ *03/219–1119* ⊕ *www.baymotel.co.nz* ⤴ *11 rooms* ⌂ *In-room: Kitchen, Wi-Fi. In-hotel: laundry facilities* ▭ *MC, V.*

$ 🏨 **Beach House Holiday Home.** You couldn't be in a more prime location at the old postmaster's house, which sits next door to the Post Office–Flight Centre. Hosts Brenda and Roger Hicks have ties to the island that go back generations, and they will happily help you book your activities. This three-bedroom waterfront home sleeps up to seven; there is a $25 per person charge after two. **Pros:** conveniently situated. **Cons:** the house is a bit dated. ⌂ *44 Elgin Terr., next to Flight Centre/Post Office* ☎ *03/219–1348* ⤴ *1 unit* ⌂ *In-hotel: Laundry facilities, kitchen* ▭ *MC, V.*

$$$ 🏨 **Glendaruel.** At this beautiful B&B a short walk from town, you can have private views over Golden Bay. There are two double rooms and a cozy wee single. Kaka (parrots) are frequent visitors to the deck, and the gorgeous garden is nice for strolling. Continental or cooked breakfasts are available, as is dinner by arrangement. **Pros:** lovely garden, birdlife, and views **Cons:** a bit of a walk uphill from town. ⌂ *38 Golden Bay Rd., Oban* ☎ *03/219–1092* ⊕ *www.glendaruel.co.nz* ⤴ *3 rooms* ⌂ *In-room: kitchen. In-hotel: bar* ▭ *MC, V* ⭗ *BP, CP.*

$$–$$$ 🏨 **Port of Call.** Philippa Fraser-Wilson and sixth-generation islander Ian Wilson opened this modern B&B overlooking Halfmoon Bay and the Foveaux Strait. You can wander the trails through their 20 acres of native bush, which border a lush wilderness teeming with birdlife leading to Acker's Point. Return to drinks by a cozy fire in the guest lounge. This friendly couple owns and operates Stewart Island Water Taxi & Eco-guiding, which leads guided and nonguided trips around the island. They also have two other fully equipped and totally enchanting properties: **the Bach** and **Turner Cottage**, where you can choose to "self-cater," or have Philippa spoil you with baskets of homemade breakfast goodies. **Pros:** lovely, historic properties, courtesy transfers from flight or ferry. **Cons:** PoC and Bach are a 15-minute walk from town. ⌂ *Leask Bay Rd., Halfmoon Bay* ☎ *03/219–1394* ⊕ *www.portofcall.co.nz* ⤴ *1 room* ▭ *MC, V* ⭗ *CP.*

$–$$ 🏨 **South Sea Hotel.** This handsome, historic building dominates the main road in Oban. The hotel rooms are comfortable, and the three at the front of the building have sea views. This is an old-fashioned hotel, which means that you share a bathroom with other guests if you stay upstairs. If you'd like your own bathroom and a more peaceful room, ask for a studio unit behind the hotel. **Pros:** great value for a real island experience. **Cons:** can be noisy some nights; shared bathroom in hotel. ⌂ *Main Rd., Oban* ☎ *03/219–1059* ⊕ *www.stewart-island.co.nz* ⤴ *9 studios, 8 rooms with shared bath* ⌂ *In-room: No phone (some), kitchen (some), no TV (some)* ▭ *MC, V.*

Travel Smart
New Zealand

WORD OF MOUTH

"The weather in NZ is unpredictable year-round. Personally, I prefer the off-season and have visited the SI in April, May, August and September—and I'd definitely visit during those months again . . . plan to dress in layers, pack a fleece and waterproof jacket, and go have yourself a grand old time."

—Melnq8

GETTING HERE & AROUND

■ AIR TRAVEL

The least expensive airfares to New Zealand are priced for round-trip travel and must usually be purchased in advance. Airlines generally allow you to change your return date for a fee; most low-fare tickets, however, are nonrefundable. To expedite an airline fare search on the Web, check travel search engines with meta-search technology, such as ⊕ *www. mobissimo.com*. These search across a broad supplier base so you can compare rates offered by travel agents, consolidators, and airlines in one fell swoop.

Although budget air travel within New Zealand is still expensive compared with the cost of bus or train travel, the one-way fare system does make it easy to get around, especially if you don't want to spend all your time on the road. These days, booking your domestic flights in conjunction with your international flight won't save you any money, but it allows you to travel with the international luggage allowance (2 x 23 kg [50 lbs] bags when flying with Air New Zealand, 2 x 32 kg [70 lbs] bags when flying with Qantas), significantly higher than domestic allowances (2 x 20 kg [44 lbs] bags). Some airlines give great deals if you add stopovers to your flight itinerary. You'll need to stop in at a Pacific destination like Tahiti or Fiji for a limited time before heading to New Zealand. Check with the airline and see what they're offering; make sure that New Zealand is included in Pacific deals since sometimes it's the one exception. Qantas has launched a low-budget airline called Jetstar which serves tran-Tasman and between major New Zealand hubs Aucklna,d Christchurch and Wellington. When booking make sure you read the fine print regarding baggage allowance, as the cheaper fares have zero checked baggage allowance.If you hold an international student identification card, you'll save even more.

From New York to Auckland (via Los Angeles) flights take about 19 hours; from Chicago, about 17 hours; from Los Angeles to Auckland (nonstop), about 12 hours. From the United States and Canada, you will have to connect to a New Zealand–bound flight in L.A. or San Francisco.

When taking your return flight from New Zealand, you will need to pay a departure tax. This tax is already factored into your airfare on your way to New Zealand. When you're leaving New Zealand via Auckland, the tax is also included in your fare but must be paid separately when leaving from other airports. It's NZ$25 and you pay it between checking in and going through the immigration checkpoint.

For domestic flights within New Zealand, check in at least a half hour before departure.

It is not required that you reconfirm outbound flights from or within New Zealand.

All New Zealand domestic flights and flights between New Zealand and Australia are no-smoking. Air New Zealand has banned smoking on all of its flights worldwide.

Airlines and Airports Airline and Airport Links.com (⊕ *www.airlineandairportlinks.com*) has links to many of the world's airlines and airports.

Airline Security Issues Transportation Security Administration (⊕ *www.tsa.gov*) has answers for almost every question that might come up.

AIRPORTS

The major airport is Auckland International Airport (AKL). It is usually a bit cheaper to fly into and out of this airport, but the supplemental fees for flights to Wellington (WLG) or Christchurch (CHC) are reasonable. New Zealand's airports are relatively compact and easy to negotiate. But if you're in Auckland's airport, don't wait to hear your boarding announcement, because it has adopted "the quiet airport" concept. There are usually no flight announcements made over a loudspeaker; instead, information on flight arrivals and departures appears on display boards and TV monitors.

A less quiet feature of Auckland's airport is its children's play areas, including a playground on the top floor of the terminal. Complimentary showers are also available to all passengers on the "Arrivals" side of the international terminal. Towels and toiletries can be rented at the nearby florist on the ground floor.

New Zealand has a dense network of domestic air routes, so hopping from one area to another is fairly easy, if not inexpensive. The regional airlines that service the smaller airports such as Picton and Kaikoura often partner with Air New Zealand or Qantas, so you can make these flight arrangements when booking your international flight. There are also numerous charter companies with planes carrying a dozen passengers or less. *For details on local services, see this guide's destination chapters.*

Airport Information Auckland International Airport (☎ 09/275–0789 ⊕ www.auckland-airport.co.nz). Christchurch International Airport (☎ 03/358–5029 ⊕ www.christchurch-airport.co.nz). Wellington International Airport (☎ 04/385–5100 ⊕ www.wlg-airport.co.nz).

FLIGHTS

Air New Zealand flies two to three times a day from Los Angeles to Auckland and is the only carrier that extends a daily nonstop flight from San Francisco to Auckland. Qantas flies nonstop from Los Angeles to New Zealand. United and Air Canada, affiliates of Air New Zealand, connect from points in North America to Los Angeles.

Within New Zealand, Air New Zealand, Pacific Blue, Jetstar, and Qantas compete on intercity trunk routes. Air New Zealand serves a wide network of provincial and tourist centers. ☞ *For more information about regional travel, see the Essentials sections within regional chapters.*

Pacific Blue provides direct flights between New Zealand, Australia, Vanuatu, the Cook Islands, and Samoa. Freedom Airlines operates low-cost flights between New Zealand and Australia, including direct flights from Dunedin. Jetstar provides service to Australia.

Airline Contacts Air Canada (☎ 888/247–2262 in U.S. and Canada, 09/969–7470 in New Zealand, 0508/747–767 toll-free in New Zealand ⊕ www.aircanada.ca). Air New Zealand (☎ 310/615–1111, 800/262–1234 in U.S., 800/663–5494 in Canada, 0800/737–000 toll-free in New Zealand ⊕ www.airnewzealand.co.nz). British Airways (☎ 800/247–9297 in U.S., 09/966–9777 in New Zealand ⊕ www.britishairways.com). Cathay Pacific (☎ 020/8834–8888 in U.K., 0800/800–454 toll-free in New Zealand ⊕ www.cathaypacific.com). Freedom Air (☎ 0800/600–500 toll-free in New Zealand ⊕ www.freedomair.co.nz). Japan Airlines (☎ 800/525–3663 in U.S., 845/774–7700 in U.K., 09/379–3202 or 0800/525–747 toll-free in New Zealand ⊕ www.jal.com). Jetstar (☎ 0800/800–995 toll-free in New Zealand ⊕ www.jetstar.co.nz). Pacific Blue (☎ 0800/670–000 toll-free in New Zealand ⊕ www.pacificblue.co.nz). Qantas (☎ 800/227–4500 in U.S. and Canada, 0845/774–7767 in U.K., 0800/808–767 toll-free in New Zealand ⊕ www.qantas.com.au). Singapore Airlines (☎ 800/742–3333 in U.S., 0844/800–2380 in U.K., 0800/808–909 toll-free in New Zealand ⊕ www.singaporeair.com). United Airlines (☎ 800/864–8331 for U.S. reservations, 800/538–2929 for international reservations, 0800/747–400 toll-free in New Zealand ⊕ www.united.com).

▌ BOAT TRAVEL

To travel between the North Island and the South Island take Tranz Scenic's Interislander ferry or the Bluebridge ferry between Wellington and Picton. Both ferries carry cars. They also connect with Tranz Scenic's trains, and a free shuttle is available between the railway station and ferry terminal in both Wellington and Picton. The Interislander travels four to five times a day; Bluebridge, twice daily. Standard one-way fare can be as much as $70, but there are off-peak deals to be had for as low as $39. The fare for a medium-size sedan costs around $200. Be sure to ask about specials, including ferry-train package deals through Tranz Scenic, when you book. *For package ideas that include ferry travel, see Discounts and Deals, below.*

Schedules are available at train stations and visitor-information centers around the country. Most will arrange Interislander ferry bookings. You can also check schedules and fares and book online via the Interislander Web site. Some fares allow you to make schedule changes up to the last minute and guarantee a full refund if you cancel prior to check-in. Discount fares can be booked once in New Zealand; these have some restrictions. No matter how you go about it, it's a good idea to reserve in advance, especially during holiday periods.

Information Bluebridge (☎ *0800/844–844 toll-free in New Zealand* ⊕ *www.bluebridge.co.nz*). **Tranz Scenic Interislander** (☎ *04/498–3302, 0800/802–802 toll-free in New Zealand* ⊕ *www.interislander.co.nz*).

▮ BUS TRAVEL

New Zealand is served by an extensive bus network. InterCity and Newmans are the main bus lines. They operate under a collective marketing umbrella and are part of a larger shareholder group. Newmans differentiates itself by having newer spiffier vehicles, which conform to a strict criteria based upon vehicle age and amenities.

Some Newmans and InterCity bus routes overlap, but Newmans tends to have fewer stops and sticks to the key corridors, making travel times shorter. InterCity buses, on the other hand, cover more remote areas. Nevertheless, both services stop at small towns along the way.

Although Newmans and InterCity are the top national carriers, there are also many regional bus services. For instance, Bottom Bus runs around the Catlins and Southland; Atomic Travel also covers the majority of the South Island. *See the Essentials sections in regional chapters for more details on local services.*

Take a hop-on, hop-off bus if you prefer a more flexible itinerary. Although the buses run by companies like Kiwi Experience and Magic Travellers Network may not be as comfortable as Newmans and InterCity, they provide flexible coach passes, typically valid for 12 months. Some passes cover all of New Zealand, whereas others are limited to specific regions. Most of these backpacker buses have affiliations with hostels and hotels, and various combination packages are available. Stray Travel, operated by the people who founded Kiwi Experience, gives you the option of using the service as a tour or having unlimited stopovers for the duration of your chosen pass.

Putting a dent in even the most flexible schedule are unexpected road closings. It's a good idea to call ahead to confirm your itinerary. Otherwise, the buses tend to run on schedule.

Bus fares vary greatly. A standard full fare between Auckland and Wellington is $100 but can be obtained for as low as $48. A certain number of seats are sold at a discounted rate, so book your tickets as early as possible, especially during the holidays. Individual companies' Web sites are the best way to find out about special fares; both Newmans and InterCity have online reservation systems. Look into the various flexible passes that allow coach travel over a set route in a given time frame, usually three or six months. You can travel whenever you like, without paying extra, as long as you stick to the stops covered by your pass. Both Newmans and InterCity give a 20% discount to students and 15%

for Youth Hostel members. Identification cards are required. Discounts are given to senior citizens and children, too.

There is also the New Zealand Travelpass, which allows unlimited travel on buses and trains and on the Interislander ferries that link the North and South islands *See Discounts and Deals, below.*

The Flexi-Pass, ⊕ *www.flexipass.co.nz*, is sold in blocks of time during which you're eligible to travel on regular InterCity bus routes or on any Newmans sightseeing packages, or both. This is such a good deal that locals even use this pass for their daily commute. Typically valid for a year, you can hop on and off, changing your plans without a penalty at least two hours prior to your departure. You must schedule in advance, as independent bus ticketing windows don't track your Flexi-Pass hours.

Kiwi Experience and Magic Travellers Network provide packages that combine one-way domestic flights with bus passes to help you cover a little more ground for a little less money.

Credit cards and traveler's checks are accepted by the major bus companies. Naked Bus offers a backpacker bus pass where you choose how many trips you'd like to take in increments of five trips, or they offer an unlimited trip pass for about $600.

Bus Information Atomic Travel (☎ *03/349–0697* ⊕ *www.atomictravel.co.nz*). **Bottom Bus** (☎ *03/434–7370* ⊕ *www.bottombus. co.nz*). **InterCity** (☎ *09/623–1503* ⊕ *www. intercitycoach.co.nz*). **Kiwi Experience** (☎ *09/366–9830* ⊕ *www.kiwiexperience.com*). **Magic Travellers Network** (☎ *09/358–5600* ⊕ *www.magicbus.co.nz*). **Naked Bus** (☎ *0900–NAKED, per-minute cost per call* ⊕ *www. nakedbus.com*). **Newmans** (☎ *09/623–1504* ⊕ *www.newmanscoach.co.nz*). **Stray Travel** (☎ *09/309–8772 or 03/377–6192* ⊕ *www. straytravel.co.nz*).

▌CAR TRAVEL

Nothing beats the freedom and mobility of a car for exploring. Even if you're nervous about driving on the "wrong" side of the road, driving here is relatively easy. Many rental cars will have a sticker right next to the steering wheel reading STAY TO THE LEFT.

Remember this simple axiom: drive left, look right. That means keep to the left lane, and when turning right or left from a stop sign, the closest lane of traffic will be coming from the right, so look in that direction first. By the same token, pedestrians should look right before crossing the street. Americans and Canadians can blindly step into the path of an oncoming car by looking left as they do when crossing streets at home. You'll find yourself in a constant comedy of errors when you go to use directional signals and windshield wipers—in Kiwi cars it's the reverse of what you're used to.

Japanese brands dominate rental agencies in New Zealand. For some local flavor, rent a Holden Commodore, a popular car in New Zealand. Most major agencies will have this as a luxury option and some even offer Lexus convertibles and other high-end hot rods. Domestic agency Smart Cars specializes in luxury rentals such as Mercedes and Audi convertibles. Stick shifts are the norm, so specify if you prefer an automatic.

Kiwi companies Maui Rentals and Kea Campers are best known for wide selections of campers, motor homes, and 4X4 vehicles. Other reputable domestic agencies are Apex Car Rental and Auto Rentals NZ Wide, which have several branches throughout the country.

Rates in New Zealand begin at $40 a day and $320 a week—although you can sometimes get even cheaper deals on economy cars with unlimited mileage. This does not include tax on car rentals, which is 12.5%. Reserve a vehicle well in advance if renting during holiday seasons, especially Christmas.

Most major international companies (and some local companies) have a convenient service if you are taking the ferry between the North and South islands and want to continue your rental contract. You simply drop off the car in Wellington and on the same contract pick up a car in Picton, or vice versa. It saves you from paying the fare for taking a car across on the ferry. Your rental contract is terminated only at the far end of your trip, wherever you end up. In this system, there is no drop-off charge for one-way rentals, making an Auckland–Queenstown rental as easy as it could be.

Check for rates based on a south-to-north itinerary; it may be less expensive as it's against the normal flow. Special rates should be available whether you book from abroad or within New Zealand.

In New Zealand your own driver's license is acceptable. Still, an International Driver's Permit is a good idea; it's available from the American Automobile Association. These international permits are universally recognized, and having one in your wallet may save you problems with the local authorities.

For most major rental companies in New Zealand, 21 is the minimum age for renting a car. With some local rental companies, however, drivers under 21 years old can rent a car but may be liable for a higher deductible. Children's car seats are mandatory for kids under five years old. Car-rental companies may ask drivers not to take their cars onto certain roads, so ask about such restrictions.

Major Rental Agencies Avis (☎ 09/526–3256, 0800/284–722 toll-free in New Zealand ⊕ www.avis.com). **Budget** (☎ 0800/283–438 toll-free in New Zealand ⊕ www.budget. com). **Hertz** (☎ 0800/654–321 toll-free in New Zealand ⊕ www.budget.com). **National** (☎ 09/275–0066 in New Zealand ⊕ www. nationalcar.com).

Local Rental Agencies Apex Rental Car (☎ 03/379–6897, 0800/93–9597 toll-free in New Zealand ⊕ www.apexrentals.co.nz). **Auto Rentals NZ Wide, Ltd.** (☎ 03/3717–343, 0800/736–893 toll-free in New Zealand ⊕ www.autorentals.co.nz). **Kea Campers** (☎ 09/441–7833, 0800/520–052 toll-free in New Zealand ⊕ www.keacampers.com). **Maui Rentals** (☎ 09/275–3013, 0800/651–080 toll-free in New Zealand ⊕ www.maui-rentals.com). **Smart Cars** (☎ 09/307–3553, 0800/458–987 toll-free in New Zealand ⊕ www.smartcars. co.nz).

GASOLINE

On main routes you'll find stations at regular intervals. However, if you're traveling on back roads where the population is sparse don't let your tank get low—it can be a long walk to the nearest farmer.

The price of gas (Kiwis say "petrol") in New Zealand is more volatile than the fuel itself. At this writing, prices hovering around NZ$1.70 a liter. Credit cards are widely accepted, though not necessarily at small country gas stations, so ask before you fill up.

Unleaded gas is widely available and often referred to as 91. High-octane unleaded gas is called 96. The 91 is usually a couple of cents cheaper than 96; most rental cars run on 91. Virtually all gas stations will have staff on hand to pump gas or assist motorists in other ways; however, they tend to have self-service facilities for anyone in a hurry. These are simply operated by pushing numbers on a console to coincide with the dollar value of the gas required. When you pump the gas, the pump will automatically switch off when you have reached the stated amount. Pay at the counter inside the station after you fill your tank.

ROAD CONDITIONS

Roads are well maintained and generally not crowded. In rural areas, you may find some unpaved roads. On most highways, it's easier to use the signposted names of upcoming towns to navigate rather than route numbers.

Due to the less-than-flat terrain, many New Zealand roads are "wonky," or crooked. So when mapping out your itinerary, don't plan on averaging 100 kph (62 mph) too often. Expect two or three lanes; there are no special multi-occupant lanes on the major highways. In areas where there is only one lane for each direction, cars can pass, with care, while facing oncoming traffic, except where there is a double-yellow center line. Rural areas still have some one-lane roads. One-lane bridges are common and are sometimes used by trains as well as cars. ☞ *Rules of the Road, below.*

New Zealanders are seldom as good at driving as they think they are (they're terrible), so the best policy is just to keep at a safe distance. Dangerous overtaking, speeders, lack of indication, and slow drivers in passing lanes are all afflictions suffered on New Zealand highways. In saying that, driving has improved over recent years due to increased education about speeding, drunk driving, and bad driving in general.

ROADSIDE EMERGENCIES

In the case of a serious accident, immediately pull over to the side of the road and phone ☎ 111. Emergency phone boxes are not common; you may have to rely on a cellular phone. You will find New Zealanders quick to help if they are able to, particularly if you need to use a phone. Minor accidents are normally sorted out in a calm and collected manner at the side of the road. However, "road rage" is not unknown. If the driver of the other vehicle looks particularly angry or aggressive, you are within your rights to take note of the registration number and then report the accident at the local or nearest police station.

The New Zealand Automobile Association (NZAA) provides emergency road service and is associated with the American Automobile Association (AAA). If you are an AAA member, you will be covered by the service as long as you register in person with an NZAA office in New Zealand and present your membership card with an expiration date showing it is still valid. NZAA advises that you register before you begin your trip.

Should you find yourself at a panel beater (repair shop) after a prang (minor car accident), talking about your vehicle might end up sounding like more of an Abbott and Costello routine if you're not prepared with the appropriate vehicle vernacular. For instance, you might hear the mechanic say, "Crickey dick! What are ya?! Doing the ton on loose metal when it was hosing down was two sammies short of a picnic. You have a chip in the windscreen, the fender has to be reattached under the boot, and your axle is puckeroo. Pop the bonnet and let's take a look." Translation: "Wow! Are you nuts?! Driving so fast on a gravel road in the rain was crazy (aka two sandwiches short of a picnic). You chipped the windshield, the bumper needs to be reattached under the trunk, and the axle is broken. Pop the hood."

Emergency Services New Zealand Automobile Association (✉ *99 Albert St., Auckland* ☎ *09/966–8800, 0800/500–222, 0800/500–222 toll-free in New Zealand, *222 toll-free from cell phone* ⊕ *www.aa.co.nz*).

RULES OF THE ROAD

The speed limit is 100 kph (62 mph) on the open road and 50 kph (31 mph) in towns and cities. A circular sign with the letters LSZ (Limited Speed Zone) means speed should be governed by prevailing road conditions but still not exceed 100 kph. Watch out for speed cameras, particularly in city suburbs and on approaches to and exits from small towns. The police force (not to mention the money counters) has taken to them with relish. Fines start at about $60 for speeds 10 kph (6 mph) over the speed limit.

Right turns are not permitted on red lights. New Zealand law states that you must always wear a seat belt, whether you are driving or a passenger. You can be fined for any passenger under the age of 15 not wearing a seat belt or approved child restraint if under the age of 5. If you are caught without a seat belt and you are clearly not a New Zealander, the result is likely to be a friendly-but-firm warning. Drunk drivers are not tolerated in New Zealand. The blood alcohol limit is 0.05 (80 milligrams of alcohol per 100 milliliters of blood for adults), and it's safest to avoid driving altogether if you've had a drink. If you are caught driving over the limit you will be taken to the nearest police station to dry out and required to pay a high fine. Repeat offenses or instances of causing injury or death while under the influence of alcohol are likely to result in jail terms.

When driving in rural New Zealand, cross one-lane bridges with caution—there are plenty of them. A yellow sign on the left will usually warn you that you are approaching a one-lane bridge, and another sign will tell you whether you have the right-of-way. A rectangular blue sign means you have the right-of-way, and a circular sign with a red border means you must pull over to the left and wait to cross until oncoming traffic has passed. Even when you have the right-of-way, slow down and take care. Some one-lane bridges on the South Island are used by trains as well as cars. Trains always have the right-of-way.

Roundabouts can be particularly confusing for newcomers. When entering a roundabout, yield to all vehicles coming from the right. A blue sign with a white arrow indicates that you should keep to the left of the traffic island as you come up to the roundabout. In a multilane roundabout, stay in the lane closest to the island until ready to exit the circle.

You can only pass on the left if there are two or more lanes on your side of the center line, if the vehicle you are passing has stopped, or if the vehicle ahead is signaling a right turn. At all other times, you must pass on the right.

When you encounter fog, remember to drive with low-beamed headlights, as high beams refract light and decrease visibility.

It is illegal to drive with only your parking lights on.

The usual fine for parking over the time limit on meters is $10–$15. In the last few years "pay-and-display" meters have been put up in cities. You'll need to drop a couple of dollars' worth of coins in the meter, take the dispensed ticket, and put it in view on the dashboard of your car. The fine for running over the time for these meters runs about $12, but if you don't display your ticket at all, the fine will be at least $40 and you may risk being towed. So carry a few coins at all times—any denomination will usually do. Make sure to observe all NO PARKING signs. If you don't, your car will almost certainly be towed away. It will cost about $100 to have the car released, and most tow companies won't accept anything but cash.

For more road rules and safety tips, check the Land Transport Safety Authority (LTSA) Web site.

Contacts Land Transport Safety Authority (⊕ *www.ltsa.govt.nz*).

TRAFFIC

The only city with a serious congestion problem during rush hour is Auckland, particularly on inner-city highways and on- and off-ramps. Avoid driving between 7:30 AM and 9 AM, and 5 PM and 6:30 PM. Traffic around other cities, such as Wellington and Christchurch, builds up at these times, too, and it is worth taking this into account if you have important appointments or a plane to catch. Give yourself a spare 30 minutes to be on the safe side.

▌ CRUISE SHIP TRAVEL

Auckland's bright cruise depot, opened in 2001, reflects the upswing in the cruising industry in recent years. Since the 1990s more companies have been drawn to Auckland's superb harbor, as well as to the gorgeous scenery in places such as the Bay of Islands and Marlborough Sounds. World-cruise itineraries with Crystal

Cruises *and* Regent Seven Seas Cruises now include New Zealand. But some of the best cruising programs are those that concentrate entirely on the South Pacific and combine New Zealand with destinations such as Fiji, New Caledonia, Tonga, and Samoa. Generally, such cruises start and finish in Auckland and visit South Pacific islands in between.

P&O Cruises runs a couple cruises out of Auckland to the South Pacific. Another choice is the Holland America Line vessel *Volendam* with its cruises around New Zealand, Australia, and the South Pacific.

Cruise Lines Crystal Cruises (☎ *310/785–9300 or 888/722-0021* ⊕ *www.crystalcruises.com*). **Holland America Line** (☎ *206/281–3535 or 877/724-5425* ⊕ *www.hollandamerica.com*). **P&O Cruises** (☎ *0800/441-766, 0800/951-200 toll-free in New Zealand* ⊕ *www.pocruises.com.au*). **Princess Cruises** (☎ *800/774-6237, 0800/951-200 toll-free in New Zealand* ⊕ *www.princess.com*). **Regent Seven Seas Cruises** (☎ *954/776-6123 or 800/477-7500* ⊕ *www.rssc.com*).

▌ TRAIN TRAVEL

New Zealand's Tranz Scenic trains travel, as a rule, north and south along the main trunk of New Zealand. If you want to crisscross the country, then you'll have to abandon the country's rail network. There are some exceptions, most notably the famous TranzAlpine Express, a spectacular scenic ride across Arthur's Pass and the mountainous spine of the South Island between Greymouth and Christchurch.

Even the most popular services tend to run only once daily. They do leave and arrive on time as a rule. Trains have one class, with standard comfortable seats and a basic food service selling light meals, snacks, beer, wine, and spirits. Special meals (diabetic, wheat free, or vegetarian) can be arranged, but you have to order at least 48 hours before you board the train. Most carriages have large windows from which to view the spectacular passing

scenery, and some routes have a commentary on points of interest. Most trains also have a viewing carriage at the rear.

Travelers can purchase a New Zealand Travelpass for unlimited travel by train, bus, and Interislander ferry for a variety of periods. *See Discounts and Deals, below, for more information.* For Youth Hostel Association members, InterCity provides a 15% discount on most train service, all InterCity coach service, and on Interislander ferries. Students with an International Student Identity Card (ISIC) get a 20% discount. Senior citizens (over 60) get a 20% discount with proof of age.

You can obtain both schedules and tickets at visitor information centers and at train stations. Major credit cards are accepted, as are cash and traveler's checks. Reservations are advised, particularly in the summer months. Book at least 48 hours in advance.

Information InterCity Travel Centres (☎ *09/623-1503 in Auckland, 03/365-1113 in Christchurch, 04/385-0520 in Wellington, 0508/353-947 toll-free in New Zealand*).

Train Information Tranz Scenic (☎ *04/495-0775, 0800/872-467 toll-free in New Zealand for bookings, 0800/277-482 toll-free in New Zealand for train schedule and update information* ⊕ *www.tranzscenic.co.nz*).

▌ DISCOUNTS AND DEALS

Look into the New Zealand Travelpass to save money by combining bus, ferry, and train costs. The Travelpass has no fixed itineraries and gives you 3,000 different stops to choose from. You choose from a certain number of days of travel and kinds of transportation; there's also an option to tack on air travel. Most Travelpasses are valid for one year; the bus-only version is valid for unlimited travel on InterCity and Newmans coaches over a one-, two-, or three-month period, with an incremental-rate structure. You can purchase an open-ended pass from your travel agent prior to leaving and then call the Travelpass reservations center to make reservations.

The Tranz Scenic rail service also has a couple of deals worth checking out, including ThroughFares, which combine Tranz Scenic train trips with SoundsAir flights and the Interislander ferries.

■**TIP**➔ Ask the local tourist board about hotel and local transportation packages that include tickets to major museum exhibits or other special events.

Discount Resources New Zealand Travelpass (☎ *09/638–5788, 0800/339–966 toll-free in New Zealand* ⊕ *www.travelpass.co.nz*). **Tranz Scenic** (☎ *04/495–0775, 0800/872–467 toll-free in New Zealand* ⊕ *www.tranzscenic.com*).

ESSENTIALS

■ ACCOMMODATIONS

Tourism New Zealand (⇨ *Visitor Information, below*) publishes an annual "Where to Stay" directory listing more than 1,000 properties. This directory lists all properties who register for it, but it gives priority to those accredited by Qualmark, the national tourism–quality assurance organization.

The lodgings we list are the cream-of-the-crop in each price category. We always list the facilities but we don't specify whether they cost extra; when pricing accommodations, always ask what's included and what costs extra. Properties are assigned price categories based on the range from their least-expensive standard double room at high season (excluding holidays) to the most expensive. All rooms listed have an en suite or private bath unless otherwise noted. In New Zealand, the phrase "en suite bathroom" means that the bathroom is connected directly with the bedroom, while a "private bath" often is outside the bedroom but is not shared with other guests.

■ **TIP** → Assume that hotels operate on the European Plan (**EP**, no meals) unless we specify that they use the Breakfast Plan (**BP**, with full breakfast), Continental Plan (**CP**, continental breakfast), Full American Plan (**FAP**, all meals), Modified American Plan (**MAP**, breakfast and dinner) or are **all-inclusive** (**AI**, all meals and most activities).

BED AND BREAKFASTS

There are some helpful resources on the Web for researching and booking B&B choices. On Web sites such as those maintained by SelectionsNZ and Jasons Travel Media, you'll find hundreds of listings and advertisements for B&Bs throughout the country. Heritage & Character Inns of New Zealand specializes in higher-end B&Bs.

Once in New Zealand you will find the *New Zealand Bed & Breakfast Book* in most major bookstores, or you can look at their listings online for free. It lists about 1,000 B&Bs, but be aware that property owners, not independent writers, provide the editorial copy.

Reservation Services Heritage & Character Inns of New Zealand (⊕ *www.heritageinns. co.nz*).

Jasons Travel Media (⊕ *www.jasons.com*). **The New Zealand Bed & Breakfast Book** (⊕ *www.bnb.co.nz*). **SelectionsNZ** (⊕ *www. selections.co.nz*).

HOME AND FARM STAYS

If you think green acres is the place to be, New Zealand has plenty of them. Home and farm stays provide not only comfortable accommodations but a chance to experience the countryside and the renowned Kiwi hospitality. Most operate on a B&B basis, though some also serve evening meals. Farm accommodations vary from modest shearers' cabins to elegant homesteads. Some hosts offer day trips, as well as horseback riding, hiking, and fishing. For two people, the average cost ranges from $90 to $200 per night, including meals. Check New Zealand Farm Holidays for options.

Farm Helpers in New Zealand (FHINZ) advertises dozens of positions throughout the country where you can stay for free in exchange for working on a farm. Tasks include fruit picking, gardening, and light carpentry.

Homestays, the urban equivalent of farm stays, are less expensive. Most New Zealanders seem to have vacation homes, called *baches* in the North Island, *cribs* in the South Island; these are frequently available for rent. New Zealand Vacation Homes lists houses and apartments for rent on both the North and South Islands. Baches and Holiday Homes to Rent Ltd. publishes an annual directory of rental homes throughout the country, with color photos for each listing.

Another accommodation option is a home exchange. Intervac, one of the largest international home-exchange services, has a New Zealand representative on hand.

Contacts Baches and Holiday Homes to Rent Ltd. (✉ *Box 3107, Richmond, Nelson* 📞 *03/544–4799* ⊕ *www.holidayhomes. co.nz*). **Farm Helpers in New Zealand** (✉ *31 Moerangi St., Palmerston North* 📞 *06/354–1104* ⊕ *www.fhinz.co.nz*). **Intervac** (✉ *13 Zetland St., Wellington* ⊕ *www.intervac.co.nz*). **New Zealand Farm Holidays Ltd.** (✉ *Box 74, Auckland* 📞 *09/412–9649* ⊕ *www.nzaccom. co.nz*). **New Zealand Vacation Homes Ltd.** (✉ *Box 76112, Auckland* 📞 *09/268–2161* ⊕ *www.nzvacationhomes.co.nz*).

HOME EXCHANGES

With a direct home exchange you stay in someone else's home while they stay in yours. Some outfits also deal with vacation homes.

Exchange Clubs Home Exchange.com (📞 *800/877–8723* ⊕ *www.homeexchange.com* ✉ *$99.95 for a 1-yr online listing*). **HomeLink International** (📞 *800/638–3841* ⊕ *www. homelink.org* ✉ *$110 yearly for online membership; $170 also includes printed directories*). **Intervac U.S.** (📞 *800/756–4663* ⊕ *www.intervacus.com* ✉ *$95 for Web-only membership; $140 includes Web access and catalogs*).

HOSTELS

The Youth Hostels Association of New Zealand (YHA NZ)—there's also an Australian YHA—is similar to Hosteling International (HI). A year's membership costs about $30, which taps you into a network of hostels throughout the country and discounts on various activities, tours, and transportation.

In addition to the YHA NZ, a network of low-cost, independent backpacker hostels operates in New Zealand. They are in nearly every city and tourist spot, and they provide clean, twin- and small dormitory-style accommodations and self-catering kitchens, similar to those of the YHA NZ and HI-affiliated hostels, with no membership required.

Qualmark, New Zealand's official tourism quality-assurance company, rates backpacker hostels on a five-star system.

Information Hostelling International—USA (📞 *301/495–1240* ⊕ *www.hiusa.org*). **Youth Hostels Association of New Zealand** (📞 *800/278–299 toll-free in New Zealand* ⊕ *www. yha.co.nz*). **Qualmark** (⊕ *www.qualmark.co.nz*).

HOTELS

When looking up hotel information, you'll often see a reference to Qualmark, New Zealand's official tourism quality-assurance agency. This nonprofit service grades hotels on a one- to five-star system and participation is voluntary. Each business applies and undergoes a strict assessment and licensing process to win Qualmark accreditation, shelling out some cash in the process. These ratings are generally fair gauges of each property's cleanliness and security. You can check a hotel's Qualmark rating on the Web site.

Information Qualmark (⊕ *www.qualmark. co.nz*).

LUXURY LODGES

At the high end of the price scale, luxury lodges put forth the best of country life, elegant dining, and superb accommodations. Many specialize in fishing, but there is usually a range of outdoor activities for nonanglers. Tariffs run about $400–$2,000 per day for two people; meals are generally included. For information, visit the New Zealand Lodge Association's Web site, where you can download an electronic catalog of New Zealand lodges.

Information **New Zealand Lodge Association** (⊕ *www.lodgesofnz.co.nz*).

MOTELS

Motels are the most common accommodations, and most provide comfortable rooms for $70–$195 per night. They're usually open every day of the year. Unlike in the United States, motels in New Zealand are not always below the standard of hotels. For instance, "motel flats" are set up like apartments, with living areas as well as bedrooms. Accommodations with more basic facilities are called "serviced motels." All motel rooms come with tea- and coffee-making equipment; many have full kitchens. The Motel Association of New Zealand (MANZ) is an independent company with nearly 1,000 members. Its Web site allows you to find properties by region or by motel name.

Information **Motel Association of New Zealand** (⊕ *www.manz.co.nz*).

MOTOR CAMPS

The least expensive accommodations are the tourist cabins and flats in most of the country's 400 motor camps. Tourist cabins provide basic accommodation and shared cooking, laundry, and bathroom facilities. Bedding and towels are not provided. A notch higher up the comfort scale, tourist flats usually provide bedding, fully equipped kitchens, and private bathrooms. Tent sites and caravan sites usually cost less than $10 and overnight rates for cabins range anywhere from $6 to $20. More fully equipped tourist flats will cost $25 to $70.

■ COMMUNICATIONS

INTERNET

Traveling with a laptop does not present any problems in New Zealand, where the electricity supply is reliable. However, you will need a converter and adapter as with other electronic equipment (⇨ *Electricity, below*). It pays to carry a spare battery and adapter, since they're expensive and can be hard to replace.

City hotels, provincial hotels, and motels are well equipped to handle computers and modems. You may get a little stuck in family-run B&Bs and farm stays in remote areas, but even these places can usually sort something out for you.

The Cybercafes Web site lists more than 4,000 Internet cafes worldwide.

Contacts **Cybercafes** (⊕ *www.cybercafes. com*).

PHONES

The country code for New Zealand is 64. When dialing from abroad, drop the initial "0" from the local area code. Main area codes within New Zealand include 09 (Auckland and the North), 04 (Wellington), and 03 (South Island). Dialing from New Zealand to back home, the country code is 1 for the United States and Canada, 61 for Australia, and 44 for the United Kingdom. The prefixes 0800 and 0867 are used for toll-free numbers in New Zealand.

Dial 018 for New Zealand directory assistance. For international numbers, dial 0172. To call the operator, dial 010; for international operator assistance, dial 0170. To find phone numbers within New Zealand go to the White Pages Web site.

White Pages (⊕ *www.whitepages.co.nz*).

CALLING OUTSIDE NEW ZEALAND

To make international calls directly, dial 00, then the international access code, area code, and number required. The country code for the United States is 1.

Access Codes **AT&T Direct** (☎ *000–911*). **MCI WorldPhone** (☎ *000–912*). **Sprint International Access** (☎ *000–999*).

CALLING CARDS

Most pay phones now accept PhoneCards or major credit cards rather than coins. PhoneCards, available in denominations of $5, $10, $20, or $50, are sold at post offices, dairies (convenience stores), tourist centers, and any other shops displaying the green PhoneCard symbol. To use a PhoneCard, lift the receiver, put the card in the slot in the front of the phone, and dial. The cost of the call is automatically deducted from your card; the display on the telephone tells you how much credit you have left at the end of the call. A local call from a public phone costs 70¢. Don't forget to take your PhoneCard with you when you finish your call or those minutes will be lost—or spent by a stranger.

Telecom has a reliable card called Easy Call, which covers minutes to the United States for as low as 3¢ per minute. You can add minutes to the card by using your credit card; unlike a PhoneCard, you don't need to purchase a new one when you're running out of time. Other phone cards include Kia Ora and Talk 'n' Save (both sold by Compass Phone Cards), which operate in the same way; you can call the United States for as low as 3.9¢ per minute. You can buy these phone cards at gas stations, dairies, and most hostels.

The Net2Phone Direct Calling Card provides an affordable solution by utilizing local access numbers to make calls utilizing the Internet. This is used in the same manner as a regular calling card, but depending upon the area from which you are calling there is sometimes a slight voice delay. This type of technology has also made it possible to make phone calls right from your laptop computer. If you are going to have free access to the Internet, this can prove to be the most affordable means of making international calls, with rates from New Zealand to the United States being approximately 4¢ per minute with Net2Phone's PC2Phone plan. It is advisable to use a headset for the best clarity.

Calling Cards Compass Phone Cards (☎ 0800/646–444 toll-free in New Zealand). **Telecom Easy Call** (☎ 0800/922–2248 toll-free in New Zealand).

MOBILE PHONES

There are both analog and digital mobile-communications networks covering most of New Zealand, which operate on both the GSM and CDMA systems. U.S.-based phones should work, but contact your provider about specific requirements for your phone. If you have a tri-band GSM phone you can rent a SIM card for about $10 per week. Keep in mind, however, that the phone must be unlocked, so you should be sure to get that number from your provider prior to leaving.

Cell phones can be rented at Auckland, Wellington, Queenstown, and Christchurch airports, starting at $6 a day. Look for a Vodafone stand in the arrival area of each airport. Prior reservations are a good idea, though not absolutely necessary. Make phone-rental arrangements in advance so you can give family and friends your number before you leave.

Roaming fees can be steep: 99¢ a minute is considered reasonable. And overseas you normally pay the toll charges for incoming calls. It's almost always cheaper to send a text message than to make a call, since text messages have a really low set fee (often less than 5¢).

If you just want to make local calls, consider buying a SIM card (your provider may have to unlock your phone for you to use a different SIM card) and a prepaid service plan in the destination. You'll then have a local number and can make local calls at local rates. If your trip is extensive, you could also simply buy a cell phone in your destination, as the initial cost will be offset over time.

■ **TIP→** If you travel internationally frequently, save one of your old mobile phones or buy a cheap one on the Internet; ask your cell phone company to unlock it for you, and take it with you as a travel phone, buying a new SIM card with pay-as-you-go service in each destination.

Contacts Cellular Abroad (☎ 800/287–5021 ⊕ www.cellularabroad.com) rents and sells GMS phones and sells SIM cards that work

LOCAL DO'S AND TABOOS

CUSTOMS OF THE COUNTRY

In general, Kiwis are accommodating folk who are more likely to good-naturedly tease you about a cultural faux pas than to take offense, but there are a few etiquette points to keep in mind. First, the word "kiwi" refers to either people (New Zealanders) or to the protected kiwi bird, but not the kiwifruit. Also, don't lump New Zealanders in with Australians. A New Zealand accent does not sound just like an Australian one, or a British accent for that matter, and a Kiwi will be the first to point this out.

Be considerate of Māori traditions. For instance, *marae*, the area in front of a meetinghouse, should not be entered unless you are invited or unless it's in use as a cultural center. Also, it's best not to use *hongi* (touching foreheads and noses in greeting) unless someone else initiates it. *For more on Māori traditions, see the Understanding New Zealand Chapter.*

If you're visiting someone's house, take along a small gift. Among gestures, avoid the "V" symbol with the first two fingers with the palm facing in—an offensive vulgarity.

LANGUAGE

Kiwi English can be mystifying. The colloquialisms alone can make things puzzling, not to mention rural slang. Known as "cow cockie" talk, this is what you'll hear when "girls" refers to someone's cows, and "gummies" (galoshes) are the favored footwear.

The Māori language has added many commonly used words to the New Zealand lexicon. For instance, the Māori greeting is *kia ora*, which can also mean "thank you," "good-bye," "good health," or "good luck." You'll hear it from everyone, *Pākehā* (non-Māori) and Māori alike. Many place names are Māori as well and can be so long as to seem unpronounceable. (A Māori word stands as the longest place-name in the world.) *See the Talk Like a Local and Māori Vocabulary pages in the Experience New Zealand chapter for common phrases.*

The biggest communication glitch between New Zealanders and visitors often involves the Kiwis' eloquent use of the understatement. This facet of Kiwi speech is both blessing and curse. Everything sounds relaxed and easygoing...but if you're trying to judge something like distance or difficulty you may run into trouble. No matter how far away something is, people often say it's "just down the road" or "just over the hill." Ask specific questions to avoid a misunderstanding.

SIGHTSEEING

If you are driving a road maggot (camper van), be considerate of the drivers behind you, pull over when safe and possible to let them pass.

There is etiquette when visiting a marae, best illustrated in the book *Te Marae: A Guide to Māori Protocol*, available through Raupo Publishing (⊕ *www.raupopublishing.co.nz*).

New Zealand is big on sheep, and you might lose smarty points if you ask dumb sheep questions. "When do you cut their fur?" or "When do their tails fall off?" will elicit laughter: sheep have wool, and their tails are cut off. And remember, there isn't a sheep joke here that hasn't been heard.

in many countries. **Mobal** (☎ 888/888–9162 ⊕ www.mobalrental.com) rents mobiles and sells GSM phones (starting at $49) that will operate in 140 countries. Per-call rates vary throughout the world. **Planet Fone** (☎ 888/988–4777 ⊕ www.planetfone.com) rents cell phones, but the per-minute rates are expensive. **Vodaphone** (☎ 09/275–8154, 0800/800–021 toll-free in New Zealand ⊕ www.vodarent.co.nz).

As of November 2009, it is illegal to drive and use a handheld mobile phone in New Zealand.

■ CUSTOMS AND DUTIES

New Zealand has stringent regulations governing the import of weapons, food-stuffs, and certain plant and animal material. Anti-drug laws are strict and penalties severe. In addition to personal effects, nonresidents over 17 years of age may bring in, duty-free, 200 cigarettes or 250 grams of tobacco or 50 cigars, 4.5 liters of wine, three bottles of spirits or liqueur containing not more than 1,125 mls, and personal purchases and gifts up to the value of NZ$700.

Equally stringent is the agricultural quarantine. The authorities don't want any non-native seeds (or popcorn kernels or honey) haplessly transported into the country. You must declare even a single piece of fruit, and all camping and hiking gear must be declared and inspected at customs. You'll be hit with an instant $250 fine if you're caught bringing in fruit—those cute beagles at customs will bark if they smell even a banana. And be truthful about your camping gear because they *will* take it into a back room, unravel your tent and sleeping bag and check for grass and muck. Do yourself a favor and make sure any camping gear and hiking boots are reasonably clean when entering the country. Check the following Web sites for a more detailed description and explanations of no-nos. All bags coming into the country are X-rayed.

Information in New Zealand MAF Biosecurity New Zealand (⊕ www.biosecurity.govt.nz). **New Zealand Customs** (⊕ www.customs.govt. nz/travellers).

U.S. Information U.S. Customs and Border Protection (⊕ www.cbp.gov).

■ EATING OUT

Some restaurants serve a fixed-price dinner, but the majority are à la carte. Remember that "entrée" in Kiwi English is the equivalent of an appetizer. It's wise to make a reservation and inquire if the restaurant has a liquor license or is "BYOB" or "BYO" (Bring Your Own Bottle)—many places have both. This only pertains to wine, not bottles of beer or liquor. Be prepared to pay a corkage fee, which is usually a couple of dollars.

Many restaurants add a 15% surcharge on public holidays. Employers are required by law to pay staff a higher wage during these. This amount will be itemized separately on your bill.

New Zealand's *Cuisine* magazine has a special annual issue devoted to restaurants throughout the country; hit their Web site if you'd like to get a copy before your trip. There are also a few helpful New Zealand dining Web sites worth a look. Through some, you can make online reservations. These include Cup, an independent nationwide café guide; Dine Out, a national database with customer reviews; and Menus, which posts photos and menus of restaurants in Auckland and Wellington.

For information on food-related health issues, see Health below.

Information Cuisine Magazine (⊕ www. cuisine.co.nz). **Cup** (⊕ www.cup.co.nz. **Dine Out** (⊕ www.dineout.co.nz). **Menus** (⊕ www. menus.nz).

MEALS AND MEALTIMES

When in New Zealand, have a little lamb. No matter where you go in the country, it's sure to be on the menu. Cervena, or farm-raised venison, is another local delicacy available all over New Zealand, and farmed ostrich is gaining popularity as well.

In New Zealand restaurants, many vegetables have two names, used interchangeably. Eggplants are often called aubergines, zucchini are also known as courgettes. The vegetable North Americans know as a bell pepper is a capsicum here. The tropical fruit papaya is known by its British name, pawpaw.

Don't miss a Māori *hāngi*. This culinary experience can be loosely compared to a family barbecue (hosted by a family that likes to do a lot of dancing and singing). The traditional preparation involves steaming meat, seafood, and vegetables in a large underground pit, and the meal is accompanied by Māori performances. *See the "Dinner on the Rocks" Close-Up box in Chapter 5.* Also be sure to try *kūmara*, an indigenous sweet potato that's sacred to the Māori. Many Kiwis view muttonbird as a special treat, but some outsiders balk at its peculiar smell and unusual flavor. It is an acquired taste, but if you're an adventurous eater it's definitely one to try.

Of course, seafood is a specialty, and much of the fish is not exported so this is your chance to try it! The tastiest fish around is snapper in the North, and blue cod (not a true cod relative) in the South. Grouper (often listed by its Māori name of *hapuku*), flounder, and salmon are also menu toppers, as is whitebait, the juvenile of several fish species, in spring. As for shellfish: try the Bluff oysters (in season March–August), Greenshell mussels (also known as green-lipped or New Zealand green mussels), scallops, crayfish (spiny lobster), and local clamlike shellfish, *pipi* and *tuatua. For more on native foods, see Tastes of New Zealand in Chapter 1.*

Burgers are a staple for a quick bite. However, you'll find there's a whole lot more than two all-beef patties and a bun—two of the most popular toppings are beetroot and a fried egg. Cheese on burgers (and sandwiches) is often grated bits sprinkled atop. Another Kiwi snack staple, meat pies, are sold just about everywhere. The classic steak-and-mince fillings are getting gussied up these days with cheese or oysters. And who could forget good ol' fish-and-chips in this former British colony? Appropriately called "greasies," this mainstay is often made of shark but called lemon fish or flake. You might notice bowls by the cash registers of take-out shops containing packets of tartar sauce or tomato sauce (catsup). These are usually not free for the taking; they cost about 50¢ each.

Be aware that "bacon" might consist of a thick blubbery slice of ham or a processed fatty, pink, spongy substance. If you love your bacon streaky and crisp, politely inquire what kind of bacon they serve before ordering a BLT.

Lemon & Paeroa, otherwise known as L&P, is New Zealand's most famous soft drink. Keep in mind that if you order a lemonade you will be served a carbonated lemon-flavored drink. If you've a sweet tooth, nibble a chocolate fish, a chocolate-covered fish-shaped marshmallow. This treat has become so popular in New Zealand that it's now synonymous with success. You'll often hear someone say, "you deserve a chocolate fish!" in place of "job well done!" Hokey pokey, a lacy honey toffee, is another favorite candy. And if you're traveling in the heat of the summer, don't leave town until you've tried a hokey pokey ice cream, another New Zealand mainstay. If you want to try a truly unique bit of New Zealand grub, and we do mean grub, taste the larvae of the huhu beetle.

Restaurants serve breakfast roughly between 7 and 9:30. Lunch usually starts about noon and is over by 2. Dinners are usually served from 5 PM, but the most popular dining time is around 7. Restaurants in cities and resort areas will serve dinner well into the night, but some places in small towns or rural areas still shut their doors at around 8.

Unless otherwise noted, the restaurants listed in this guide are open daily for lunch and dinner.

PAYING

Credit cards are widely accepted in restaurants and cafés. There are exceptions to this rule, so check first. In some areas, American Express and Diners Club cards are accepted far less frequently than MasterCard and Visa. *For guidelines on tipping see Tipping below.*

RESERVATIONS AND DRESS

We only mention reservations specifically when they're essential or when they are not accepted. For popular restaurants, book as far ahead as you can (often 30 days) and reconfirm as soon as you arrive. Large parties should always call ahead to check the reservations policy. We mention dress only when men are required to wear a jacket or a jacket and tie.

Attire countrywide is pretty casual; unless you're planning to dine at the finest of places, men won't need to bring a jacket and tie. At the same time, the most common dinner attire is usually a notch above jeans and T-shirts.

WINES, BEER, AND SPIRITS

New Zealand is best known for its white wines, particularly sauvignon blanc, riesling, and chardonnay. The country is now gaining a reputation for red wines such as cabernet sauvignon, pinot noir, and merlot. The main wine-producing areas are West Auckland, Hawke's Bay, Martinborough, Marlborough, and Nelson. Emerging regions include Canterbury and Central Otago. Restaurants almost without exception serve New Zealand products on their wine list. *For a rundown on New Zealand's wine industry, see "Wines of New Zealand in Chapter 8.*

When ordering a beer, you'll get either a handle (mug) or a one-liter jug (pitcher). In some Southland country pubs you'll see all the blokes drinking "big botts" of Speight's (500 ml). To get beer served in a glass, you usually have to request it. Monteith's Brewery and Macs are South Island–based breweries that distribute around the country and have a strong local following. Steinlager, probably the most famous (but not the tastiest) of New Zealand beers, is brewed by Lion Breweries and widely available. There are a number of boutique microbreweries in New Zealand, some of which have won international beer awards, such as Tuatara, West Coast Brewing, and Emersons; each brand has its own fan base. Most restaurants and liquor stores sell beers from Australia, the United States, Europe, and other parts of the world. Some of the beer in New Zealand is stronger than the 4% alcohol per volume brew that is the norm in the United States. Many go up to 7% or 8% alcohol per volume, so check that number before downing your usual number of drinks.

New Zealand only has a couple of spirits it can really call its own. One is Wilson's Whisky, distilled in Dunedin—a city with a strong Scottish heritage. Another popular drink is 42 Below. With its claim to fame as "the world's southernmost vodka," 42 Below incorporates local flavors: feijoa, manuka honey, passion fruit, and kiwifruit. Most inner-city bars will have it on the menu if you want to try before you buy a bottle; and having won a slew of gold and silver medals at international wine and spirit competitions around the world, it makes a cool duty-free gift to bring to vodka connoisseurs back home. You'll also sometimes find sticky-sweet kiwifruit or feijoa liqueurs.

Use your judgment about ordering "off the drinks menu." If you're in a South Island country pub, don't try to order an umbrella cocktail. By insisting on a margarita from an establishment that doesn't have the mix, the recipe, or the right glass, you're not gaining anything except a lousy margarita and a reputation as an obnoxious customer.

Since 1999 it has been possible to purchase beer and wine in supermarkets as well as specialized shops and to do so seven days a week. People under 18 are not permitted by law to purchase alcohol, and shops, bars, and restaurants strictly enforce this. If you look younger than you are, carry photo identification to prove your age.

ELECTRICITY

If you forget to pack a converter, you'll find a selection at duty-free shops in Auckland's airport and at electrical shops around the city. The electrical current in New Zealand is 240 volts, 50 cycles alternating current (AC); wall outlets take slanted three-prong plugs (but not the U.K. three-prong) and plugs with two flat prongs set at a "V" angle.

Consider making a small investment in a universal adapter, which has several types of plugs in one lightweight, compact unit. Most laptops and mobile phone chargers are dual voltage (i.e., they operate equally well on 110 and 220 volts), requiring only an adapter. These days the same is true of small appliances such as hair dryers. Always check labels and manufacturer instructions to be sure. Don't use 110-volt outlets marked FOR SHAVERS ONLY for high-wattage appliances such as hair dryers.

Steve Kropla's Help for World Traveler's has information on electrical and telephone plugs around the world. Walkabout Travel Gear has a good coverage of electricity under "adapters."

Contacts Steve Kropla's Help for World Traveler's (⊕ www.kropla.com). **Walkabout Travel Gear** (⊕ www.walkabouttravelgear.com).

EMERGENCIES

For fire, police, or ambulance services, dial ☎ 111.

In Auckland, the U.S. Consulate is open only from 9:30 until around 12:30 on weekdays.

In Wellington, the U.S. Embassy is open weekdays 10–noon and 2–4.

United States U.S. Consulate (✉ Level 3, Citigroup Bldg., 23 Customs St., Auckland ☎ 09/303–2724). **U. S. Embassy** (✉ 29 Fitzherbert Terr., Thorndon, Wellington ☎ 04/462–6000).

HEALTH

The most common types of illnesses are caused by contaminated food and water. Especially in developing countries, drink only bottled, boiled, or purified water and drinks; don't drink from public fountains or use ice. You should even consider using bottled water to brush your teeth. Make sure food has been thoroughly cooked and is served to you fresh and hot; avoid vegetables and fruits that you haven't washed (in bottled or purified water) or peeled yourself. If you have problems, mild cases of traveler's diarrhea may respond to Imodium (known generically as loperamide) or Pepto-Bismol. Be sure to drink plenty of fluids; if you can't keep fluids down, seek medical help immediately.

Infectious diseases can be airborne or passed via mosquitoes and ticks and through direct or indirect physical contact with animals or people. Some, including Norwalk-like viruses that affect your digestive tract, can be passed along through contaminated food. If you are traveling in an area where malaria is prevalent, use a repellent containing DEET and take malaria-prevention medication before, during, and after your trip as directed by your physician. Condoms can help prevent most sexually transmitted diseases, but they aren't absolutely reliable and their quality varies from country to country. Speak with your physician and check the CDC or World Health Organization Web sites for health alerts, particularly if you're pregnant, traveling with children, or have a chronic illness.

Health Warnings National Centers for Disease Control and Prevention (*CDC* ☎ *877/394–8747 international travelers' health line* ⊕ *wwwn.cdc.gov/travel*). **World Health Organization** (*WHO* ⊕ *www.who.int*).

SPECIFIC ISSUES IN NEW ZEALAND

General health standards in New Zealand are high, and it would be hard to find a more pristine natural environment.

The major health hazard in New Zealand is sunburn or sunstroke. Even people who are not normally bothered by strong sun should cover up with a long-sleeve shirt, a hat, and pants or a beach wrap. At higher altitudes you will burn more easily, so apply sunscreen liberally before you go out—even for a half hour—and wear a visor or sunglasses.

Dehydration is another serious danger that can be easily avoided, so be sure to carry water and drink often. Limit the amount of time you spend in the sun for the first few days until you are acclimatized, and avoid sunbathing in the middle of the day.

There are no venomous snakes, and the only native poisonous spider, the *katipo*, is a rarity. The whitetail spider, an unwelcome and accidental import from Australia, packs a nasty bite and can cause discomfort but is also rarely encountered.

One New Zealander you will come to loathe is the tiny black sand fly (some call it the state bird), common to the western half of the South Island, which inflicts a painful bite that can itch for several days. In other parts of the country, especially around rivers and lakes, you may be pestered by mosquitoes. Be sure to use insect repellent.

One of New Zealand's rare health hazards involves its pristine-looking bodies of water; don't drink water from natural outdoor sources. Although the country's alpine lakes might look like backdrops for mineral-water ads, some in the South Island harbor a tiny organism that can cause "duck itch," a temporary but intense skin irritation. The organism is found only on the shallow lake margins, so the chances of infection are greatly reduced if you stick to deeper water. Streams can be infected by giardia, a waterborne protozoal parasite that can cause gastrointestinal disorders, including acute diarrhea. Giardia is most likely contracted when drinking from streams that pass through an area inhabited by mammals (such as cattle or possums). There is no risk of infection if you drink from streams above the tree line.

Less common, but a risk nevertheless, is the possibility of contracting amoebic meningitis from the water in geothermal pools. The illness is caused by an organism that can enter the body when the water is forced up the nose. The organism is quite rare, but you should avoid putting your head underwater in thermal pools or jumping in them. Also remember not to drink geothermic water.

OVER-THE-COUNTER REMEDIES

Popular headache, pain, and flu medicines are Nurofen (contains Ibuprofen), Panadol (contains Paracetamol), and Dispirin (contains Aspirin). Dispirin often comes as large tabs, which you must dissolve in water. Many Kiwi households and wheelhouses have a green tube of Berocca, the soluble vitamin supplement often taken the morning after a big night out.

HOURS OF OPERATION

Banks are open weekdays 9–4:30, but some cease trading in foreign currencies at 4.

Gas stations are usually open, at the least, from 7 to 7 daily. Large stations on main highways are commonly open 24 hours.

Museums around the country do not have standard hours, but many are open daily from 10 to 5. Larger museums and government-run collections are generally open daily, but the hours of small local museums vary, as many are run by volunteers. The New Zealand Museums Web site (⊕ *www.nzmuseums.co.nz*) is a helpful information source; you can search by collection, region, or museum name.

Pharmacies are open from 9 to 5. In larger cities, you will find basic nonprescription drugstore items in supermarkets, many of which are open until 10 PM. During off-hours there will usually be emergency-hour pharmacies in the major cities. Phone the local hospital for details.

Shops are generally open Monday through Thursday 9–5:30, Friday 9–9, and Saturday 9–noon (until 5 in main cities). Sunday trading is becoming more common but still varies greatly from place to place. In many rural areas, stores are closed on Sunday, but most Auckland shopping centers are at least open Sunday morning. Liquor stores are often open daily. In major cities supermarkets and convenience stores, called "dairies," are usually open from 7 AM to 10 PM; a few stay open 24 hours.

HOLIDAYS

On Christmas Day, Good Friday, Easter Sunday, and the morning of ANZAC Day, everything closes down in New Zealand except for a few gas stations, some shops selling essential food items, and emergency facilities. On other public holidays (often referred to as bank holidays) many museums and attractions stay open, as do transportation systems, though on a reduced schedule. Local anniversary days, which vary regionally, pop up as once-a-year three-day weekends in each particular area; some businesses close but hotels and restaurants stay open. Around Christmas and New Year's Kiwis go to the beach, so seaside resorts will be difficult to visit unless you have booked well in advance. You'll get plenty of sunshine and far fewer crowds if you visit from late January through to the colder period of late March. Cities such as Auckland and Wellington are quite pleasant over Christmas and New Year's. Fewer cars are on the road, and you'll get good prices from hotels making up for the lack of corporate guests.

▌ MAIL

Airmail should take around six or seven days to reach the United Kingdom or the United States and two or three days to reach Australia.

Most post offices are open weekdays 8:30–5, and in some areas on Saturday 9–12:30 or 10–1. The cost of mailing a letter within New Zealand is 50¢ standard post, $1 fast post. Sending a standard-size letter by airmail costs $2.30 to North America or Europe and $1.80 to Australia. Aerograms and postcards are $1.80 to any overseas destination.

If you wish to receive correspondence, have mail sent to New Zealand, held for you for up to one month at the central post office in any town or city if it is addressed to you "c/o Poste Restante, CPO," followed by the name of the town. This service is free; you may need to show ID.

Postal Service New Zealand Post (☎ *0800/501–501* toll-free in New Zealand ⊕ *www.nzpost.co.nz*).

SHIPPING PACKAGES

Overnight services are available between New Zealand and Australia but to destinations farther afield "overnight" will in reality be closer to 48 hours. Even to Australia, truly overnight service is only available between major cities and can be subject to conditions, such as the time you call in. A number of major operators are represented in New Zealand and the services are reliable, particularly from cities.

You can use the major international overnight companies listed above or purchase packaging and prepaid mail services from the post office. Major duty-free stores and stores that deal frequently with travelers will be able to help with international shipping, but if you purchase from small shops, particularly in country areas, arrange shipping with a company in the nearest city.

Express Services DHL World Express (☎ 0800/800–020 toll-free in New Zealand ⊕ www.dhl.co.nz). Federal Express (☎ 0800/733–339 toll-free in New Zealand ⊕ www.fedex.com). TNT International Express (☎ 0800/275–868 toll-free in New Zealand ⊕ www.tnt.com).

■ MONEY

For most travelers, New Zealand is not an expensive destination. The cost of meals, accommodations, and travel prove comparable to larger cities within the United States and somewhat less than in Western Europe. At about $1.70 per liter—equal to about US$4.90 per gallon—premium-grade gasoline costs more than it does in North America; prices are much cheaper than in Europe.

Prices throughout this guide are given for adults. Substantially reduced fees are almost always available for children, students, and senior citizens.

■ TIP→ Banks never have every foreign currency on hand, and it may take as long as a week to order. If you're planning to exchange funds before leaving home, don't wait until the last minute.

ATMS AND BANKS

Your own bank will probably charge a fee for using ATMs abroad; the foreign bank you use may also charge a fee. Nevertheless, you'll usually get a better rate of exchange at an ATM than you will at a currency-exchange office or even when changing money in a bank. And extracting

funds as you need them is a safer option than carrying around a large amount of cash.

EFTPOS (Electronic Fund Transfer at Point of Sale) is widely used in New Zealand stores and gas stations. ATMs are easily found in city and town banks and in shopping malls. The number of ATMs in small rural communities continues to grow, but there are still areas where ATMs or banks are few and far between. For example, there are no ATMs on Stewart Island. All the major banks in New Zealand (Bank of New Zealand, Westpac, and Auckland Savings Bank) accept cards in the Cirrus and Plus networks. ■ TIP→ The norm for PINs in New Zealand is four digits. If the PIN for your account has a different number of digits, you must change your PIN number before you leave for New Zealand.

CREDIT CARDS

Throughout this guide, the following abbreviations are used: **AE**, American Express; **DC**, Diners Club; **MC**, Master-Card; and **V**, Visa.

MasterCard and Visa are the most widely accepted cards throughout New Zealand. Discover Cards are not recognized.

Reporting Lost Cards American Express (☎ 800/992–3404 in U.S., 336/393–1111 collect from abroad, for New Zealand offices call 09/583–8300 or 0800/656–660 toll-free ⊕ www.americanexpress.com). Diners Club (☎ 800/234–6377 in U.S., 303/799–1504 collect from abroad, for New Zealand offices call 09/359–7797 or 0800/657–373 toll-free ⊕ www.dinersclub.com). MasterCard (☎ 800/622–7747 in U.S., 636/722–7111 collect from abroad, for New Zealand offices call 0800/449–140 toll-free ⊕ www.master-card.com). Visa (☎ 800/847–2911 in U.S., 410/581–9994 collect from abroad, for New Zealand offices call 0508/600–300 toll-free ⊕ www.visa.com).

CURRENCY AND EXCHANGE

New Zealand's unit of currency is the dollar, divided into 100 cents. Bills are in $100, $50, $10, and $5 denominations.

Coins are $2, $1, 50¢, 20¢, and 10¢. At this writing the rate of exchange was NZ$1.40 to the U.S. dollar, NZ$1.30 to the Canadian dollar, NZ$2.27 to the pound sterling, NZ$2.04 to the Euro, and NZ$1.20 to the Australian dollar. Exchange rates change on a daily basis.

Currency Conversion Google (⊕ www. google.com). **Oanda.com** (⊕ www.oanda.com). **XE.com** (⊕ www.xe.com).

PACKING

In New Zealand, be prepared for weather that can turn suddenly and temperatures that vary greatly from day to night, particularly at the change of seasons. Wear layers. You'll appreciate being able to remove or put on a jacket. Take along a light raincoat and umbrella, but remember that plastic raincoats and nonbreathing polyester are uncomfortable in the humid climates of Auckland and its northern vicinity. Many shops in New Zealand sell lightweight and mid-weight merino wool garments, which are expensive but breathe, keep you warm, and don't trap body odor, making them ideal attire for tramping. Don't wear lotions or perfume in humid places like Southland, either, since they attract mosquitoes and other bugs; carry insect repellent. Sand flies seem drawn to black and dark blue colors. Bring a hat with a brim to provide protection from the strong sunlight (⇨ *Health, above*) and sunglasses for either summer or winter; the glare on snow and glaciers can be intense. There's a good chance you'll need warm clothing in New Zealand no matter what the season; a windbreaker is a good idea wherever you plan to be.

Dress is casual in most cities, though top resorts and restaurants may require a jacket and tie. Some bouncers for big city bars will shine a flashlight on your shoes; if you like these kinds of places bring some spiffy spats. In autumn, a light wool sweater or a jacket will suffice for evenings in coastal cities, but winter demands a heavier coat—a raincoat with a zip-out wool lining is ideal. Comfortable walking shoes are a must. You should have a pair of what Kiwis call "tramping boots," or at least running shoes if you're planning to trek, and rubber-sole sandals or canvas shoes for the beaches.

Weather New Zealand Weather Today (⊕ www.weather.co.nz).

▋RESTROOMS

Shopping malls in cities, major bus and train stations, gas stations, and many rest areas on main highways have public toilets. Look for a blue sign with white figures (ladies and gents) for directions to a public toilet. New Zealanders often use the word "loo," or, better yet, "super loo."

Most New Zealand public restroom facilities are clean and tidy and often have a separate room for mothers with young children.

Some gas stations, shops, and hotels have signs stating that only customers can use the restroom. Kiwis are generally fairminded folk, so if you're genuinely caught short and explain the situation you will probably not be turned away.

Most gas stations in New Zealand have toilet facilities, but their standard is varied. As a rule of thumb, the newer and more impressive the gas station, the cleaner and better the toilet facilities.

Find a Loo The Bathroom Diaries (⊕ www. thebathroomdiaries.com) is flush with unsanitized info on restrooms the world over—each one located, reviewed, and rated.

▋SAFETY

New Zealand is safe for travelers, but international visitors have been known to get into trouble when they take their safety for granted. Use common sense, particularly if walking around cities at night. Stay in populated areas, and avoid deserted alleys. Although New Zealand is an affluent society by world standards, it has its share of poor and homeless (often referred to as "street kids" if they are young), and violent gangs such as the Mongrel Mob have footholds in major cities. Avoid bus and train stations or city squares and parks late at night. The crowds in some pubs can get a bit rough late, so if you sense irritation, leave.

Hotels furnish safes for guests' valuables, and it pays to use them. Don't show off your wealth, and remember to lock doors of hotel rooms and cars. Sadly, opportunist criminals stake out parking lots at some popular tourist attractions. Put valuables out of sight under seats or lock them in your trunk *before* you arrive at the destination.

Most visitors have no trouble and find New Zealanders among the friendliest people in the world. Nine times out of 10, offers of help or other friendly gestures will be genuine.

Women will not attract more unwanted attention than in most other Western societies, nor will they be immune from the usual hassles. In cities at night, stick to well-lighted areas and avoid being totally alone. Hotel staff will be happy to give tips on any areas to avoid, and the times to avoid them. New Zealand is relatively safe for women, but don't be complacent. Female travelers have been victim to sexual assault in New Zealand; hitchhiking is not recommended for solo females.

Some top Kiwi destinations have accommodations especially geared to women. Wellington, for instance, has a women-only guesthouse, and the Base Backpacker hostel chain (⊕ *www.basebackpackers. com*), with locations in major New Zealand cities, created Sanctuary Floors, secure women-only zones with special amenities.

Contact Transportation Security Administration (TSA) (⊕ *www.tsa.gov*).

General Information and Warnings Australian Department of Foreign Affairs and Trade (⊕ *www.smartraveller.gov.au*). Consular Affairs Bureau of Canada (⊕ *www.voyage.*

gc.ca). U.K. Foreign & Commonwealth Office (⊕ *www.fco.gov.uk/travel*). U.S. Department of State (⊕ *www.travel.state.gov*).

▌ TAXES

Many restaurants add a 15% surcharge to your bill on public holidays, reflecting the need to pay staff a higher wage on holidays. This tax will be itemized separately on your bill when applicable.

Visitors exiting New Zealand must pay a departure tax of $25. *(See Air Travel, above.)*

A goods and services tax (GST) of 12.5% is levied throughout New Zealand. It's usually incorporated into the cost of an item, but in some hotels and some restaurants it is added to the bill.

▌ TIME

Trying to figure out just what time it is in New Zealand can get dizzying, especially because of cross-hemisphere daylight-saving times and multi-time-zone countries. Without daylight saving time, Auckland is 17 hours ahead of New York; 18 hours ahead of Chicago and Dallas; 20 hours ahead (or count back 4 hours and add a day) of Los Angeles; 12 hours ahead of London; and 2 hours ahead of Sydney.

From the States, call New Zealand after 5 PM.

Time Zones Timeanddate.com (⊕ *www.time-anddate.com/worldclock*).

▌ TOURS

Among companies that sell tours to New Zealand, the following are nationally known organizations with a proven reputation. The key difference between the categories listed below is usually in the accommodations, which run best to better-yet, and better to budget.

LUXURY

Abercrombie & Kent, otherwise known as A&K, is the benchmark for pairing deluxe accommodations with soft adventure. Its itineraries can be combined with a visit to Australia or focus solely New Zealand. Sometimes better deals can be landed by booking a flight package with their affiliate airlines, Qantas. Tauck World Discovery leads trips with private chartered plane service. Antipodes Tours combed New Zealand for posh accommodations and tailors tours to individual requests. The "Connoisseur Collection" tour series with Luxury Vacations New Zealand takes small groups of just eight people to both the North and South islands.

**Luxury Tour Companies Abercrombie &
Kent** (✉ 1520 Kensington Rd., Oak Brook, IL ☎ 800/554-7016 or 630/954-2944 ⊕ www.abercrombiekent.com). **Antipodes Tours** (✉ 5777 W. Century Blvd., Los Angeles, CA ☎ 800/354-7471 or 310/410-9734 ⊕ www.antipodestours.com). **Luxury Vacations New Zealand** (✉ 121 Elliot St., 1st fl., Howick, Auckland ☎ 09/537-2325 ⊕ www.luxuryvacationsnz.com). **Tauck World Discovery** (✉ 10 Norden Pl., Norwalk, CT ☎ 800/788-7885 or 203/899-6500 ⊕ www.tauck.com).

MODERATE

Grey Line of Auckland and Pacific Travel of Christchurch formed a joint marketing venture to promote North and South Island tours called Scenic Pacific Tours. Their tours depart daily from Auckland, Wellington, Picton, Christchurch, and Queenstown. You can mix and match your tours and choose your level of accommodations to fit your budget. ATS Tours and Australian Pacific Touring (APT) both specialize in South Pacific vacations and can arrange everything from self-drive to fully escorted tours.

Moderate Tour Companies ATS Tours (✉ 300 Continental Blvd., Suite 350, El Segundo, CA ☎ 888/781-5170 or 310/643-0044 ⊕ www.atstours.com). **Australian Pacific Touring (APT)** (✉ 2 Augustus Terr., Parnell, Auckland ☎ 0800/278-687 toll-free in New Zealand, 800/290-8687 in U.S. ⊕ www.aptours.

com). **Scenic Pacific Tours** (✉ Box 14037, Christchurch ☎ 03/359-3999, 0800/500-388 toll-free in New Zealand ⊕ www.scenicpacific.co.nz).

BUDGET

Thrifty Tours New Zealand packaged holidays are flexible, combining regular bus, train, and ferry services with prebooked accommodation. Flying Kiwi Wilderness Expeditions Ltd. helps tie up loose ends for those on a shoestring budget. It's geared to camping rather than hotels and sometimes the major means of transit are your two feet, but this tour company has been a longtime Kiwi favorite.

Budget Tour Companies Flying Kiwi Wilderness Expeditions Ltd. (✉ 4B Forests Rd., Nelson ☎ 03/547-0171, 0800/693-296 toll-free in New Zealand ⊕ www.flyingkiwi.com). **Thrifty Tours New Zealand** (✉ Auckland ☎ 09/359-8380, 0800/803-550 toll-free in New Zealand ⊕ www.thriftytours.co.nz).

SPECIAL-INTEREST TOURS

Golf Wine New Zealand and Grape Escape Food and Wine Tours share astute insights on Hawke's Bay, Martinborough, and Marlborough vintages, the former with some time on the links as well. Homestay NZ Ltd. will arrange theme trips based upon your individual interests, be it wine or whale-watching. One of their more unique options includes having dinner at a local New Zealand family's home.

Lord of the Rings fans will find there are numerous companies giving tours of Middle Earth by helicopter, four-wheel drive, and bus. One of the most stunning trips is a horseback tour around Glenorchy—contact Dart Stables about the "Ride of the Rings."

Serious outdoor enthusiasts can take a walk on the wild side, or bike, kayak, or bungy jump with Active New Zealand. *For more New Zealand–based outfitters who organize multiday sports trips, the Experience New Zealand chapter.*

Theme-Tour Companies Active New Zealand (✉ Box 972, Queenstown

☎ 03/450–0414 or 800/500–3398, 800/661–9073 in U.S., 603/251–1051 in U.S. ⊕ www.activenewzealand.com). **Dart Stables** (✉ Box 47, Glenorchy ☎ 03/442–5688, 0800/474–3464 toll-free in New Zealand ⊕ www.dartstables.com). **Golf Wine New Zealand** (✉ 10869 N. Scottsdale Rd., Suite 103 Scottsdale, AZ ☎ 888/607–1717, 480/607–1717, 09/445–3757 in New Zealand ⊕ www.golfwinenewzealand.com). **Grape Escape** (✉ Box 1058, Napier ☎ 0800//100–489 toll-free in New Zealand ⊕ www.grapeescapenz.co.nz).**Homestay NZ Ltd.** (✉ Box 146, Auckland ☎ 09/411–9166). **New Zealand Wine Tourism Network** (⊕ www.wtn.co.nz).

▌ TIPPING

Tipping is not as widely practiced in New Zealand as in the United States or Europe, but in city restaurants and hotels it's appreciated if you acknowledge good service with a 10% tip.

Taxi drivers will appreciate rounding up the fare to the nearest $5 amount, but don't feel you have to do this. Porters will be happy with a $1 or $2 coin. Most other people, like bartenders, theater attendants, gas-station attendants, or barbers, will probably wonder what you are doing if you try to give them a tip.

▌ VISITOR INFORMATION

Tourism New Zealand is a government agency that serves as a hub for the 28 different Regional Tourism Organizations (RTOs) based throughout the country. These locally funded RTOs run most of the 71 i-SITE visitor centers. Many of these have computerized booking systems in place, so rather than drive from lodge to B&B to hotel, making inquiries, the i-SITE can be a good place to let you know instantly which places are vacant. These centers are marked with blue signs and a lowercase white letter i. *Please see the individual chapter Essentials sections for details on local visitor bureaus.*

Contact Tourism New Zealand (✉ 501 Santa Monica Blvd., Los Angeles, CA ☎ 310/395–7480 or 866/639–9325 ⊕ www.newzealand.com).

ONLINE TRAVEL TOOLS

Tourism New Zealand's site includes city and regional overviews, travel journals, information on major events like the America's Cup, and cultural background. Stuff and NZ Pages are also good catchall sites for Kiwi news, links to local resources, and more.

For the latest on the grape, Wine OnLine and New Zealand Wine, the official site for the country's wine and grape industry, post updates on some of the country's top wineries. NZ Gardens Online cultivates information on New Zealand's public and private gardens. At Maori.org, you can find answers to cultural FAQs.

For detailed information on New Zealand's wilderness areas, visit the Department of Conservation's site, which covers all the national parks, major walking tracks, campgrounds and huts, safety tips, and so forth. Snowco provides countrywide snow reports; the New Zealand Alpine Club focuses on climbing. To get up to speed on rugby, check out the New Zealand Rugby Union's or the comprehensive Planet Rugby.

The New Zealand Historic Places Trust site will give you the latest on heritage sights throughout the country. And at NZMusic.com you can get the scoop on New Zealand bands and shows.

Contacts Tourism New Zealand (www.newzealand.com). **Stuff** (⊕ www.stuff.co.nz). **NZ Pages** (⊕ www.nzpages.co.nz). **Wine OnLine** (⊕ www.wineonline.co.nz). **New Zealand Wine** (⊕ www.nzwine.com). **NZ Gardens Online** (⊕ www.gardens.co.nz). **Maori.org** (⊕ www.maori.org.nz). **Department of Conservation** (⊕ www.doc.govt.nz). **Snowco** (⊕ www.snow.co.nz). **New Zealand Alpine Club** (⊕ www.alpineclub.org.nz). **New Zealand Rugby Union** (⊕ www.allblacks.com). **Planet Rugby** (⊕ www.planet-rugby.com). **New Zealand Historic Places Trust** (⊕ www.historic.org.nz). **NZMusic.com** (⊕ www.nzmusic.com).

INDEX

PHOTO CREDITS

1, Kim Karpeles/age fotostock. 2, Gilbert van Reenen/Tourism New Zealand. 5, Destination Northland/ Tourism New Zealand. **Chapter 1: Experience New Zealand:** 8-9, Fri Gilbert/Tourism New Zealand. 11 (left), Simon Russell. 11 (right), NZONE - The Ultimate Jump)/Tourism New Zealand. 12 (top), James Heremaia/Tourism New Zealand. 12 (center), Legend Photography/Tourism New Zealand. 12 (bottom), David Wall/Tourism New Zealand. 13, Rob Suisted/www.naturespic.com. 14 (left), Ian Trafford/Tourism New Zealand. 14 (top right), David Wall/Tourism New Zealand. 14 (bottom right), Tourism New Zealand. 14 (bottom center), Gilbert van Reenen/Tourism New Zealand. 15, Ian Trafford/ Tourism New Zealand. 18 (left, top right and bottom right), Rob Suisted. 18 (bottom center), Robert Cumming/Shutterstock. 19 (top left), Heliworks Queenstown Helicopters. 19 (bottom left), Rob Suisted. 19 (bottom center), Chris McLennan /Tourism New Zealand. 19 (right), Rob Suisted. 20, Tourism Holdings/Tourism New Zealand. 21 (left), James Heremaia/Tourism New Zealand. 21 (right), Gareth Eyres/Tourism New Zealand. 22, Small World Productions/Tourism New Zealand. 23 (left), Holly Wademan/Tourism New Zealand. 23 (right), Tourism New Zealand. 24, Treble Cone Ski/Tourism New Zealand. 25 (left), Chris McLennan/Tourism New Zealand. 25 (right), Ian Trafford/Tourism New Zealand. 26, Becky Nunes/Tourism New Zealand. 27 (left), Tim Whittaker/Tourism New Zealand. 27 (right), Becky Nunes/Tourism New Zealand. 29 (left), Matt Jones/Shutterstock. 29 (right), Kieran Scott/ Tourism New Zealand. 34, David Wall/Tourism New Zealand. 35, Arno Gasteiger/Tourism New Zealand. 36-39, Rob Suisted. 40, Paul Mercer/age fotostock. 41 (top left and bottom left), Jason Friend/ www.jasonfriend.net. 41 (right) and 42 (left and right), Rob Suisted. 43 (left), Cate Starmer. 43 (right) and 46, Rob Suisted. **Chapter 2: Auckland:** 47, Walter Bibikow/viestiphoto.com. 52, ARCO/G Therin-Weise/age fotostock. 53 (top), Linus Boman/iStockphoto. 53 (bottom), Shades0404/wikipedia.org. 54, Trelise Cooper. 55 (top), Kate Sylvester. 55 (bottom), Wendell Teodoro. 56, Rob Suisted. 62, Mark Carter. 67, Joe Gough/Shutterstock. 74, Chris Gin/Shutterstock. 76, Phil Crawford. 84, David White/ Te Whau. 90 (top), Hilton Hotel/Tourism New Zealand. 90 (bottom left), Cotter House. 90 (bottom right), Stephen Fitzgerald/Mollies Boutique Hotel. 97, Chris Cameron/Tourism New Zealand. 100-01, Simon Russell. 102 (top and center), Rob Suisted, 102 (botom), America's Cup Sailing Experience, Explore New Zealand. 103 (top), Pride of Auckland, Explore New Zealand. 103 (center), Tallship Soren Larsen, Auckland. 103 (bottom), Elaine Macey/kayakwaiheke.co.nz. 104 (top), Jocelyn Carlin/ Tourism New Zealand. 104 (bottom), Holger Leue/Tourism New Zealand. 105, Simon Russell. 106-07, Rob Suisted. 109, Tourism New Zealand. 113, Kieran Scott/Tourism New Zealand. **Chapter 3: Northland and the Bay of Islands:** 115, Julia Thorne/age fotostock. 116, Destination Northland/Tourism New Zealand. 117 (top), Ben Crawford/Tourism New Zealand. 117 (bottom), Rob Suisted. 120, Alistair Trevino/age fotostock. 121 (top), Ben Crawford/Tourism New Zealand. 121 (bottom), Matt Jones/ Shutterstock. 122 and 126-27, Rob Suisted. 130, Kim Westerkov/Tourism New Zealand. 135, Marc von Hacht/Shutterstock. 140, GARDEL Bertrand/age fotostock. 144, Holger Leue/Tourism New Zealand. 145, Destination Northland/Tourism New Zealand. 146 (bottom left), jamie thorpe/Shutterstock. 146 (bottom center), Ruth Black/Shutterstock. 146 (bottom right), Gareth Eyres/Tourism New Zealand. 147 (top left), Small World Productions/Tourism New Zealand. 147 (bottom left), Scott Venning/ Tourism New Zealand. 147 (right), Destination Rotorua. 148 (top), Becky Nunes/Tourism New Zealand. 148 (center), Rob Suisted. 148 (bottom), Scott Venning/Tourism New Zealand. 149 (top left), Fay Looney/Tourism New Zealand. 149 (top right), Scott Venning/Tourism New Zealand. 149 (bottom), Adventure Films/Tourism New Zealand. **Chapter 4: Coromandel Peninsula and the Bay of Plenty:** 159, Colin Monteath/age fotostock. 161 (top), Rob Suisted. 161 (center), David Wall/Tourism New Zealand. 161 (bottom), Peter Morath/Tourism New Zealand. 164, 170-71, and 176-77, Rob Suisted. 185, David Wall/Tourism New Zealand. 199, Stuart Pearce/age fotostock. 203, Simon Russell. 204, Four Peaks Lodge/Tourism New Zealand. 205 (top left), Rob Suisted/www.naturespic.com. 205 (top right), Ben Crawford/Tourism New Zealand. 205 (bottom), 206 (left and right), and 207 (top and bottom), Rob Suisted. 208, Four Peaks Lodge/Tourism New Zealand. **Chapter 5: East Coast and the Volcanic Zone:** 215, Jeremy Bright/age fotostock. 216, Destination Lake Taupo/Tourism New Zealand. 217, Bob McCree/Tourism New Zealand. 220, Pichugin Dmitry/Shutterstock. 221 (top), Destination Lake Taupo/Tourism New Zealand. 221 (bottom), Falk Kienas/Shutterstock. 222, Rob Suisted. 223, Robert Francis/age fotostock. 224, Rob Suisted. 225 (top), Cate Starmer. 225 (bottom), Jason Friend. 226, Wai-o-tapu Thermal Wonderland/Tourism New Zealand. 230, Sircha/wikipedia.org. 232, James Heremaia/Tourism New Zealand. 237, Chris McLennan/Tourism New Zealand. 240, Pichugin Dmitry/Shutterstock. 245, Rob Suisted. 248, Chris McLennan/Tourism New Zealand. 249, FB-Fischer/age fotostock. 250 (left), Stanislas Fautre/viestiphoto.com. 250 (right), Fay Looney/Tourism New Zealand. 251, David Wall/Alamy. 252, Wai-O-Tapu Thermal Wonderland. 255, Rob Suisted. 257 (left), Rob Suisted. 257

(right), Tourism Rotorua/Tourism New Zealand. 258 (top left), Cate Starmer. 258 (top right), Tony Waltham/age fotostock. 258 (bottom), Rob Driessen/age fotostock. 269, Rob Suisted. 275, Chris McLennan/Tourism New Zealand. 281, Paul McCredie (Sybille Hetet, NZ House & Garden/On Holiday Fairfax Media/Tourism New Zealand. **Chapter 6: North Island's West Coast:** 285, Andy Belcher/age fotostock. 286, Chris McLennan/Tourism New Zealand. 290, Colin Monteath/age fotostock. 291 (top), robinvanmourik/Flickr. 291 (bottom), Horizon/age fotostock. 292, Ben Crawford/Tourism New Zealand. 293 (top), Ian Trafford/Tourism New Zealand. 293 (bottom) and 294, Rob Suisted. 297, Colin Monteath/age fotostock. 305, Tourism Holdings/Tourism New Zealand. 307, David Wall/age fotostock. 320-21, Rob Suisted. 324, Don Fuchs/age fotostock. 331, Don Smith/age fotostock. **Chapter 7: Wellington and the Wairarapa:** 341, Hauke Dressler/age fotostock. 342, Scott Venning/Tourism New Zealand. 343 (top and bottom), Ian Trafford/Tourism New Zealand. 346, Rob Suisted. 351, Rob Suisted. 352, stefano brozzi/age fotostock. 359, Nick Servian/Tourism New Zealand. 364-65, Rob Suisted. 375, New Line Cinema/Courtesy Everett Collection. 376 (top), David Wall/Tourism New Zealand. 376 (bottom) and 377 (top), Rob Suisted. 377 (center), Holger Leue/Tourism New Zealand. 377 (bottom), Rob Suisted. 378 (top), Miles Holden/Tourism New Zealand. 378 (bottom), Gilbert van Reenen/Tourism New Zealand. **Chapter 8: Upper South Island and the West Coast:** 387, Ian Trafford/age fotostock. 388, Adventure Films/Tourism New Zealand. 389, Ian Trafford/Tourism New Zealand. 392, Ian Trafford/age fotostock. 393 (top), Rob Suisted. 393 (bottom), Gunar Streu/age fotostock. 394, Rob Suisted. 395, Hauke Dressler/age fotostock. 396, Colin Monteath/age fotostock. 397 (top), Gareth Eyres/Tourism New Zealand. 397 (bottom), Colin Monteath/age fotostock. 398, Ian Trafford/age fotostock. 399 (top), Carsten Lampe/iStockphoto. 399 (bottom), Rob Suisted. 400, Schimmelpfennig/age fotostock. 401 (top), Matt Binns/wikipedia.org. 401 (bottom), Tony Stewart/age fotostock. 402, Colin Monteath/age fotostock. 403 (top), David Wall/Alamy. 403 (bottom), timparkinson/Flickr. 404, Gareth Eyres/Tourism New Zealand. 409, Rob Suisted. 415, foodfolio/age fotostock. 420, Rob Suisted. 421, David Wall/Tourism New Zealand. 422 (top left), Cherryfarm22/wikipedia.org. 422 (bottom left), Rob Suistedm. 422 (right), David Wall/Tourism New Zealand. 423 (top left), Rob Suisted. 423 (bottom), Ian Trafford/Tourism New Zealand. 423 (right), Filipe Raimundo/Shutterstock. 424 (left), Rob Suisted. 424 (right), Chris McLennan/Tourism New Zealand. 425 (top), Ian Trafford/Tourism New Zealand. 425 (bottom), Gilbert van Reenen/Tourism New Zealand. 427 (top left), James Heremaia/Tourism New Zealand. 427 (top right), Kieran Scott/Tourism New Zealand. 427 (bottom), Ian Trafford/Tourism New Zealand. 431, Herzog Winery. 439, Whale Watch Kaikoura. 449, Accents on the Park Hotel. 452, Nita Knight. 464, Rob Suisted. 473, Gunar Streu/age fotostock. 476, Mark Jones/age fotostock. 487 and 496-97, Colin Monteath/age fotostock. 499, Rob Suisted. **Chapter 9: Christchurch and Canterbury:** 503, Rob Suisted. 505 (top), Tourism New Zealand. 505 (bottom), Kieran Scott/Tourism New Zealand. 508, Gavin Hellier/age fotostock. 509 (top), Wilderness Lodge. 509 (bottom), Tourism New Zealand. 510, Pegasus Bay. 512, David Wall/Tourism New Zealand. 514, Christchurch Botanic Gardens. 521, International Antarctic Centre. 525, 50 On Park. 535, Rob Suisted. 536 (top), José Fuste Raga/age fotostock. 536 (bottom), Jono Rotman, Icebreaker. 537 (top), Lloyd Park/age fotostock. 537 (bottom), www.needleworks-pleasure.com. 538 (left), Akaroa artist Jennifer Maxwell. 538 (top right), Rob Suisted. 538 (center right), Simon Russell. 538 (bottom right), Buzzy Bee. 539 (top left), Simunovich Olive Estate. 539 (bottom left), Bennetts of Mangawhali. 537 (top right), Rob Suisted. 539 (bottom right), Pacifica Skincare. 542-43, Colin Monteath/age fotostock. 546, Jason Friend/www.jasonfriend.net. 554, Pegasus Bay/pegasusbay.com. 562, Tourism New Zealand. **Chapter 10: The Southern Alps and Fiordland:** 571, David Wall/Tourism New Zealand. 572, AJ Hackett Bungy New Zealand/Tourism New Zealand. 573, Rob Suisted/www.naturespic.com. 576, Fraser Gunn/Tourism New Zealand. 577 (top), Jason Friend. 577 (bottom), Rob Suisted. 578, Michael Krabs/age fotostock. 579 (top), Jason Friend/www.jasonfriend.net. 579 (bottom), Rob Suisted. 580 and 581 (top), Jason Friend. 581 (bottom), Rob Suisted. 582, Holger Leue/Tourism New Zealand. 583, Rob Suisted. 584, Julian Apse/Tourism New Zealand. 590, Colin Monteath/age fotostock. 596, Rob Suisted. 605, Chris McLennan/Destination Queenstown. 609, Rob Suisted. 611, Eichardts Hotel/Tourism New Zealand. 615, Destination Queenstown/Tourism New Zealand. 622–23, Paul Thuysbaert/age fotostock. **Chapter 11: Otago, Invercargill, and Stewart Island:** 627, Destination Northland/Tourism New Zealand. 628, Tourism New Zealand. 629 (top), Ian Trafford/Tourism New Zealand. 629 (bottom), Jocelyn Carlin/Tourism New Zealand. 632 and 633 (top and bottom), Rob Suisted. 634, Jochen Schlenker/age fotostock. 637, David Wall/age fotostock. 638, Jason Friend. 649, ARCO/Therin-Weise/age fotostock. 659, Jason Friend. 661 and 662 (left), Rob Suisted. 662 (top center), Jochen Tack/age fotostock. 662 (top right), Rob Suisted. 662 (bottom right), Mark Jones/age fotostock. 663 (left), Rob Suisted. 663 (top center), Brent Beaven. 663 (top right), Rob Suisted. 663 (bottom right), Venture Southland/Tourism New Zealand. 664-67, Rob Suisted.

ABOUT OUR WRITERS

A writer by trade and a traveler by compulsion, **Alia Bloom** worked in the publishing industry in New York City before heading back home to Aotearoa, New Zealand, where she now lives on the Kapiti Coast with her partner and two children. For this edition, she updated the Coromandel chapter and wrote *New Zealand Farmstays*.

Sue Courtney is a New Zealand wine writer who also hosts New Zealand's longest-running wine review Web site, www.wineoftheweek.com. Wine and food matching and traveling New Zealand in her convertible yellow sports car, particularly to wine destinations, are her passions. She wrote *New Zealand Wines*.

Sue Farley, a 15-year veteran of travel writing, has been to a diverse spectrum of environments, from deep, dark Fiordland nights to bright, sunny, tropical days on the beach. She combines off-the-beaten track writing in NZ with a selection of quality guidebook work to keep her solvent. She updated the Upper South Island and Christchurch and Canterbury chapters for this edition.

Jessica Kany, who updated the Southern Alps and Fiordland, Otago, and Invercargill chapters and wrote national park spotlights and *City of Sails*, was born in New York City, attended Washington University in St. Louis, and then spent a decade moving around the United States. Now a resident of Stewart Island, New Zealand, Jess is a freelance writer, an avid runner, an unskilled but enthusiastic paua diver, the editor of *S.I.N. (Stewart Island News)*, and field scribe for the Yellow-eyed penguin team.

Debra A. Klein fell in love with New Zealand on her first trip in 2001, and returns to shop, eat, and play annually. Her travel essays and reporting have appeared in *Condé Nast Traveler*, *The New York Times*, and *Newsweek*. She wrote *City of Sails*, *Māori Art*, *Searching for Middle-Earth*, *Taking New Zealand Home*, and the Auckland spotlights.

Bob Marriott was born in Nottingham, England, but has lived in New Zealand for many years. He loves the harbor, the rivers, and the bush-clad hills around Wellington, which he calls home. Bob contributes to several Fodor's guides, and for this edition he wrote the chapters on the East Coast and Volcanic Zone and Wellington and Wairarapa.

Carrie Miller has lived in New Zealand for six years and recently became a New Zealand citizen. She is addicted to travel, rugby, wine, and mountains, and is working on her first book. She wrote the Experience New Zealand chapter.

Kathy Ombler updated the Western North Island chapter and wrote *Ulva Island*. Kathy is a freelance writer focusing on nature tourism. She has written several guide books, including *Where to Watch Birds in New Zealand* and *A Visitor's Guide to New Zealand National Parks*. Kathy grew up on a Waikato farm, has lived in many places throughout New Zealand from big cities to small rural settlements in national parks, and is now based in Wellington.

Richard Pamatatau was born in Auckland and grew up on the relaxed North Shore. As a child he spent some time mucking around in boats on the Waitemata Harbour, and as an enthusiastic surfer and triathlete, he loves playing outdoors. Richard is now Radio New Zealand's Pacific Issues Correspondent, and while he travels a lot, he still enjoys discovering new things in Auckland. For this edition he updated the Auckland and Northland chapters.

An avid traveler and lover of the outdoors, **Oliver Wigmore** has explored most of New Zealand and tramped throughout Patagonia and the Andes. Currently he is a postgraduate student of Geography and lives in Auckland. Oliver has also contributed to Fodor's Peru. He wrote *Tramping New Zealand*.